WAR AND PEACE
VOLUME I

The Public Papers of Woodrow Wilson
Authorized Edition

WAR AND PEACE

Presidential Messages, Addresses, and Public Papers (*1917-1924*)

BY

WOODROW WILSON

EDITED BY

RAY STANNARD BAKER AND WILLIAM E. DODD

IN TWO VOLUMES

VOLUME I

HARPER & BROTHERS PUBLISHERS
NEW YORK AND LONDON

WAR AND PEACE

Copyright, 1927
By Edith Bolling Wilson
Printed in the U. S. A.

A - B

CONTENTS

CONTENTS

CONTENTS

PREFACE

War and Peace make up the final volumes of the authorized collection of the Public Papers of Woodrow Wilson. Beginning with the inaugural address delivered March 5, 1917, they include all of the important messages, addresses, and other documents of Woodrow Wilson's second term in the Presidency, and of the three years of retirement that followed, to the close of his life.

While the method of the editors is still selective, these volumes are more nearly definitive than the earlier ones in the series. It has been difficult in some cases to draw the line between public and private papers, since many of Mr. Wilson's letters, by widespread contemporary publication in the newspapers or in the *Congressional Record,* must be considered as "Public Papers," and are reproduced as such in these pages. It has also been a problem for the editors to draw the line exactly in the case of many diplomatic notes where the authorship was uncertain or coöperative. Routine proclamations signed by the President have been generally excluded except in cases where the President himself made significant changes or additions.

Every effort has been made in these volumes, as in those previously issued, to secure absolute verity in the text by reading each document back to the original copy in Mr. Wilson's own files where such was available. Nevertheless, the editors have been compelled in some instances, where strictly original sources were undiscoverable, to rely upon the publication, usually entirely accurate, in the *Congressional Record,* the *Official Bulletin,* and, rarely, in newspapers.

The editors have omitted here the publication of what may well be regarded in future times as the greatest series of public documents with which Woodrow

Wilson was concerned—the original draft of the Covenant of the League of Nations, with the various revisions of it, made in part by Mr. Wilson, although the Covenant as originally adopted by the League of Nations Commission may be found in Mr. Wilson's address of February 14, 1919. These documents are so voluminous and the alterations and amendments in the various texts so significant, that they require separate and more expansive treatment. They may be found presented *in extenso* with full explanations in *Woodrow Wilson and World Settlement,* by Ray Stannard Baker, Volume I, Part III, and Volume III, pages 67-175.

In the work of collecting the material for these volumes, which has proved far more arduous than we anticipated, the editors acknowledge much valuable assistance from many sources, particularly from Allen R. Boyd of the Library of Congress, James Thayer Gerould of the Library of Princeton University, Dr. James Brown Scott of the Carnegie Endowment for International Peace, and Dr. L. S. Rowe of the Pan-American Union.

Every effort has been made to secure a bibliography at once complete and accurate, and a thorough-going and comprehensive index.

The editors are grateful for suggestions, additions, and corrections from a number of careful readers and reviewers of the earlier volumes, especially Charles S. Hamlin and John Randolph Bolling.

In assembling and editing the material for these volumes and especially in the painstaking labor of proof reading, Mr. Baker acknowledges his special obligation for the assistance of Katharine E. Brand.

INTRODUCTION

WOODROW WILSON's second term in the Presidency, from 1917 to 1921, comprises the most important period of years in recent American history. The inaugural address of March 1917 presaged war; April saw the solemn declaration. The mobilization which followed, guided by the firm hand of the President, was upon a scale as vast and orderly as it was unprecedented. Four million men were called to the colors, munition plants were built to arm, and ships to transport them. Billions of dollars were raised to finance these stupendous operations. Following the vanguard of the American forces which were landed in France in June, 1917, nearly two million men were transported across three thousand miles of submarine-infested ocean. The tide of a deadlocked war was turned, and victory for the Allied arms assured. It was such an exhibition of gigantic power, utilized with coöperative skill and swift effectiveness, as the world had never seen before.

The recession and demobilization which followed the Armistice of November, 1918, was as striking in its way as the creation of the army had been, for it was wholly without disorder, and within four months after the close of hostilities the country had practically returned to normal conditions.

While these vast administrative processes were under way, the President, as the undisputed spokesman of the Allied and Associated Powers, became the dominating force in world diplomacy. He defined the objects for which America was entering the war, lifted the entire struggle to a new plane of moral purpose, and conducted with masterly skill the complicated negotiations with the enemy powers which led up to the Armistice. He laid down the accepted bases of the peace, the corner stone of which was to be a new world organization, a League of Nations. It would be difficult anywhere in history to match this series of notes and addresses for weightiness of subject matter or for elevation of tone.

Woodrow Wilson's preëminence at the apex of his fame—during the year 1918—was quite unexampled. No leader was ever more ardently followed by greater numbers of the people of all nations. No American ever exerted a more powerful impression upon the events of his time. In a real sense Woodrow Wilson's words made history. Scholars of the future can make no adequate study of the epoch of the Great War or the Peace that followed it without minute examination of the papers contained in these volumes; and general readers will nowhere find a more succinct and felicitous presentation of the dominating American principles and ideals of the period, or a more powerful appeal for the realization of one of the exalted visions of mankind.

The months that followed the Armistice of November, 1918, were rich in the essence of great and swift-moving drama. Breaking the century-old precedents of his office, the President set sail for Europe to join in the making of the peace. He was received by the people like some emperor turned savior; he declared again his ideals, again set forth his principles—but with ominous clouds of doubt and opposition beginning to gather. He entered the councils at Paris, bore a vital part in reconstituting the nations of the world, and by the exercise of sheer personal power secured the immediate adoption of the Covenant of a world League of Nations. He returned to his own country to find his policies attacked, his support crumbling away. A nation saved from danger and raised to a new preëminence was turning swiftly from the visions its leader had inspired to the flesh pots of a new prosperity. A bitter struggle with the Senate over the ratification of the treaty continued for months. The tide which had been flowing so long and so powerfully with the Covenanter had now turned against him. He continued to fight the harder. In September, 1919, he made his great final appeal to the people for a renewal of their support. He had never for a moment lost faith in the people. If he could explain his purpose to the people they would compel the Senate to act! He had warnings enough of impaired physical vigor; he had been told that any such campaign would result disastrously. Nevertheless he went forward. He delivered forty addresses in twenty-two days, he traveled six thousand miles; a feat as amazing intellectually as it was physically. A reading of these addresses, included complete in these volumes, is evidence enough of the powers of the aroused President. But the best that he had, all that he had, was not enough. The forces arrayed against him, his own physical limitations among them, were too strong. The worn Covenanter broke down before his appeal was concluded and there followed the sad return to Washington, the grim and tragic later years, and death on the winter day in 1924 with the street outside crowded with people kneeling in prayer.

II

These volumes, the last two of the Public Papers, appropriately called *War and Peace,* include practically all of Woodrow Wilson's important public utterances during the great years of his second administration, and to the end of his life. Both in substance—for they deal with the problems of a world on fire—and in literary form they are the greatest of his life. Some of his earlier writings took too much thought for literary expression, but these addresses, dealing with transcendent issues, are of a more direct eloquence, a superb and moving simplicity.

"Immortality," says Maximilian Harden, "is as certain to Wilson's speeches as to the meditations of the

Roman Emperor Marcus Aurelius, who also dropped halfway up the heights."

The address which opens these volumes, the inaugural of 1917, is couched in the solemn and elevated language of high statesmanship. It is brief indeed for a presidential inaugural, but there is packed into it his entire message to the people regarding the national attitude toward the war in which, he sees clearly, we must soon become involved. It is a message of spiritual preparedness, a counsel of high aims.

"I know now what the task means. I realize to the full the responsibility which it involves. I pray God I may be given the wisdom and the prudence to do my duty in the true spirit of this great people."

He sets forth the essential principles of a disinterested humanity upon which he believes America, when called upon, shall enter the war:

"We desire neither conquest nor advantage. We wish nothing that can be had only at the cost of another people. We have always professed unselfish purpose and we covet the opportunity to prove that our professions are sincere."

A month later comes the address before Congress, one of his noblest, asking for a declaration of war against Germany. It cannot be read today without something of the thrill of that hour. It has an elevation of appeal equal to the occasion.

"The world must be made safe for democracy. Its peace must be planted upon the tested foundations of political liberty. We have no selfish ends to serve. We desire no conquest, no dominion. We seek no indemnities for ourselves, no material compensation for the sacrifices we shall freely make. We are but one of the champions of the rights of mankind."

And it closes with an admonition at once thrilling and solemn:

"There are, it may be, many months of fiery trial and sacrifice ahead of us. It is a fearful thing to lead this great peaceful people into war, into the most terrible and disastrous of all wars, civilization itself seeming to be in the balance. But the right is more precious than peace, and we shall fight for the things which we have always carried nearest our hearts,—for democracy, for the right of those who submit to authority to have a voice in their own Governments, for the rights and liberties of small nations, for a universal dominion of right by such a concert of free peoples as shall bring peace and safety to all nations and make the world itself at last free. To such a task we can dedicate our lives and our fortunes, everything that we are and everything that we have, with the pride of those who know that the day has come when America is privileged to spend her blood and her might for the principles that gave her birth and happiness and the peace which she has treasured. God helping her, she can do no other."

We find in the addresses and papers which follow an extraordinary combination of practicality and idealism. At one moment he is dealing in forthright fashion with the problems of registration for the draft, food administration, the price of wheat, the raising of money, and at the next he is going to the people with powerful statements of the principles underlying American participation in the war, persuasive appeals to all that is highest and best in the American spirit. Great decisions, like the speech asking for a declaration of war in April and the selective draft in May, are inevitably followed by explanatory addresses to the people. He will go no step without making sure of their full support and approval. Following the declaration of war, and feeling that the "supreme test of the nation has come," he addresses the nation:

"There is not a single selfish element, so far as I can see, in the cause we are fighting for. We are fighting for what we believe and wish to be the rights of mankind and for the future peace and security of the world.

To do this great thing worthily and successfully we must devote ourselves to the service without regard to profit or material advantage and with an energy and intelligence that will rise to the level of the enterprise itself. We must realize to the full how great the task is and how many things, how many kinds and elements of capacity and service and self-sacrifice, it involves."

But ideals are not all: he goes on in the next breath to explain the practical necessities of war—food, ships, money, unified effort.

There is something of Cromwell and of John Knox in the man: he can fight, he can also pray. On August 11, 1917, we find him addressing the officers of the Atlantic fleet and telling them stoutly to "leave out of your vocabulary the word 'prudent' "—"throw tradition to the wind"—"fight"; he can say in his response at Baltimore, April 6, 1918, to German ruthlessness:

"Force, Force to the utmost, Force without stint or limit, the righteous and triumphant Force which shall make Right the law of the world. . . ."

And yet he can send this message to the soldiers and sailors:

"The Bible is the word of life. I beg that you will read it and find this out for yourselves. . . ."

In a later message he says:

"My affectionate confidence goes with you in every battle and every test. God keep and guide you!"

Still later (December 28, 1918) he discloses the secure foundation of his faith, where his courage is stayed:

"You are quite right, sir, in saying that I do recognize the sanctions of religion in these times of perplexity with matters so large to settle that no man can feel that his mind can compass them. I think one would go crazy if he did not believe in Providence. It would be a maze without a clue. Unless there were some supreme guidance we would despair of the results of human counsel."

He sought to bring into full coöperation every element of the population. We have a series of addresses to coal-mine operators, July 12, 1917, to the women of the nation, July 28, 1917, to school officers and teachers, August 23, 1917, and many to farmers, workers, members of labor unions; and later when the war grew more intense there is something magnificent in the easy power, reflected in these addresses, with which the President "took over" the entire railroad system of the country, the cables and telegraphs, assumed fuel control, and set prices upon staple commodities, each 'ime going to the people to explain the necessity.

Important as these addresses were, however, they m. t take second place when compared with the President handling of the diplomacy of the peace. Beginning with the reply to the Pope, August 27, 1917, a "masterpiece of diplomacy," these notes and addresses continued throughout the year 1918 until they culminated in the acceptance by Germany of the terms of the Armistice as based upon certain of the President's notes and messages. He maintained throughout the high ground, the elevated tone, of his reply to the Pope:

"They (the American people) believe that peace should rest upon the rights of peoples, not the rights of governments,—the rights of peoples great or small, weak or powerful,—their equal right to freedom and security and self-government and to a participation upon fair terms in the economic opportunities of the world. . . ."

On January 8, 1918, came the Fourteen Points speech, setting forth the essentials of the settlements, in February the notable address to Congress on German war-aims, and on July 4th, at Mount Vernon, the Four Points speech, one of his greatest, in which he compressed into a single sentence what he conceived to be the essential object of the war:

"What we seek is the reign of law, based upon the consent of the governed and sustained by the organized opinion of mankind."

These addresses, translated swiftly into a score of languages, smuggled through close-held military lines, broadcast from radio towers, dropped from aëroplanes, published in thousands of newspapers, worked a strange magic upon the peoples of the world. They were "worth army corps" to the Allied cause; they gave the worn fighters a new draught of courage and hope; they drove a sharp wedge between the "people" of enemy countries and their mistaken rulers.

With the end of the war the President entered upon a new phase of his career—the struggle for a just peace, the creation of a League of Nations. He knew well that victory on the field of battle gave no assurance of the attainment of the high purpose which he was seeking. He had long feared the passions that would arise out of a peace with victory. Shortly before he sailed for Europe he said to a group of Jews who called upon him (November 28, 1919):

". . . I know the great tasks that lie ahead of us. The past is secure, but the future is doubtful, and there are so many questions intimately associated with justice that are to be solved at the peace table and by the commissions which no doubt will be arranged for at the peace table, that I feel in one sense as if our work of justice had just begun."

Nevertheless, his addresses in Europe made before the opening of the peace conference, when he was the most acclaimed of men, were marked by a renewed spirit of determination. He pledged again, in unforgettable words, his allegiance to his ideals. He reached an elevation of mind and of spirit in such addresses as those at Manchester and at Carlisle, England, and later in the memorial address at the Suresnes Cemetery in France, as he had rarely, if ever before, equaled. We hear him setting forth the power of moral force, "It is moral force that is irresistible"; we hear him advancing the idea, strange indeed in international relationships, that the greatest nation is the servant of all; that the material interests of peoples should be a secondary consideration.

"Interest does not bind men together. Interest separates men, for the moment there is the slightest departure from the nice adjustment of interests jealousies begin to spring up. There is only one thing that can bind peoples together and that is a common devotion to right. Ever since the history of liberty began men have talked about their rights, and it has taken several hundred years to make them perceive that the principal part of right is duty, and that unless a man performs his full duty he is entitled to no right."

A number of important addresses were made during the peace conference, almost all of them dealing, not with specific settlements, but with the ideals and principles of a new world organization. In two great addresses, at Boston and New York during the President's visit in America in February and March, 1919, he reported upon the task at Paris and argued powerfully for the Covenant which had been tentatively adopted. Although these addresses were full of courage and determination, there was not wanting the sense that there might be failure—a failure, above all, of his own people:

"I do not mean any disrespect to any other great people when I say that America is the hope of the world. And if she does not justify that hope results are unthinkable. Men will be thrown back upon bitterness of disappointment not only but bitterness of despair. All nations will be set up as hostile camps again; men at the peace conference will go home with their heads upon their breasts, knowing they have failed —for they were bidden not to come home from there until they did something more than sign the treaty of peace."

Almost immediately upon his final return to America in July, 1919, the expected storm broke in all of its fury. On the 10th he laid the peace treaty before the Senate and the struggle began for ratification and the acceptance of the Covenant of the League of Nations. Attack and criticism now took the place of the support and approval which had marked the great months of 1918. The President reasoned with the Senate Foreign Relations Committee—see the speech of August 19, 1919—always sure in his own mind that if everything else failed he had only to go to the people. In September he prepared to fling his last reserves into the battle: he made his desperate and tragic Western tour in the course of which he finally fell, broken but not surrendering. It was not the statesman, as General Smuts well expressed it, who had failed so much as the spirit of the people behind him.

In the overshadowing importance of the struggle over the ratification of the treaty, few people realized at the time the immense vitality which the President was also applying to the problems of national reconstruction which followed the close of the war. A vast army was demobilized, railroads and other utilities were returned to their owners, fixed prices for various commodities were abolished without shaking the economic structure of the nation, and far-reaching and delicate problems of capital and labor were adjusted. All these were matters of executive function. The series of addresses, notes, appeals and proclamations dealing with these diverse subjects are fully gathered together for the first time in these volumes. They give renewed evidence of the extraordinary power and vitality of the President even when he was fighting a losing battle. Many of them were written after the President was stricken and while he lay ill in bed. An examination of them gives no hint that the writer was anything but a man of stout health and undimmed courage.

Whether the world was with him or against him, whether he himself was strong or stricken, he never for a moment lost his faith in his ideals or failed in his courage. Faith was the essence of the man, faith in God, faith in the people, faith in democratic institutions.

" . . . believe me, my fellow countrymen, the only people in the world who are going to reap the harvest of the future are the people who can entertain ideals, who can follow ideals to the death."

In the sad years after his retirement from the White House—years of physical suffering but of undimmed mind and undaunted purpose—he made only three brief public utterances. There is not a word of discouragement or of pessimism in any of them. He closes his very last public expression—a telegram sent to his supporters in Pittsburgh only a month before his death—with an appeal for an "aggressive fight for the establishment of high principles and just action" to "restore the prestige of our nation." He was a fighter to the last breath in his broken body—a fighter for all that was noblest in the American tradition.

WAR AND PEACE

SECOND INAUGURAL ADDRESS

DELIVERED MARCH 5, 1917. FROM OFFICIAL GOVERN-
MENT PUBLICATION IN MR. WILSON'S FILES.

THE four years which have elapsed since last I stood
in this place have been crowded with counsel and
action of the most vital interest and consequence. Perhaps no equal period in our history has been so fruitful
of important reforms in our economic and industrial life
or so full of significant changes in the spirit and purpose
of our political action. We have sought very thoughtfully to set our house in order, correct the grosser errors
and abuses of our industrial life, liberate and quicken
the processes of our national genius and energy, and lift
our politics to a broader view of the people's essential
interests. It is a record of singular variety and singular distinction. But I shall not attempt to review it. It
speaks for itself and will be of increasing influence as
the years go by. This is not the time for retrospect.
It is time, rather, to speak our thoughts and purposes
concerning the present and the immediate future.

Although we have centered counsel and action with
such unusual concentration and success upon the great
problems of domestic legislation to which we addressed
ourselves four years ago, other matters have more
and more forced themselves upon our attention, matters lying outside our own life as a nation and over
which we had no control, but which, despite our wish
to keep free of them, have drawn us more and more
irresistibly into their own current and influence.

It has been impossible to avoid them. They have
affected the life of the whole world. They have shaken
men everywhere with a passion and an apprehension
they never knew before. It has been hard to preserve
calm counsel while the thought of our own people

swayed this way and that under their influence. We are a composite and cosmopolitan people. We are of the blood of all the nations that are at war. The currents of our thoughts as well as the currents of our trade run quick at all seasons back and forth between us and them. The war inevitably set its mark from the first alike upon our minds, our industries, our commerce, our politics, and our social action. To be indifferent to it or independent of it was out of the question.

And yet all the while we have been conscious that we were not part of it. In that consciousness, despite many divisions, we have drawn closer together. We have been deeply wronged upon the seas, but we have not wished to wrong or injure in return; have retained throughout the consciousness of standing in some sort apart, intent upon an interest that transcended the immediate issues of the war itself. As some of the injuries done us have become intolerable we have still been clear that we wished nothing for ourselves that we were not ready to demand for all mankind,—fair dealing, justice, the freedom to live and be at ease against organized wrong.

It is in this spirit and with this thought that we have grown more and more aware, more and more certain that the part we wished to play was the part of those who mean to vindicate and fortify peace. We have been obliged to arm ourselves to make good our claim to a certain minimum of right and of freedom of action. We stand firm in armed neutrality since it seems that in no other way we can demonstrate what it is we insist upon and cannot forego. We may even be drawn on, by circumstances, not by our own purpose or desire, to a more active assertion of our rights as we see them and a more immediate association with the great struggle itself. But nothing will alter our thought or our purpose. They are too clear to be obscured. They are too deeply rooted in the principles of our national life to be altered. We desire neither conquest nor advantage. We wish nothing that can be had only at the cost of another people. We have always professed unselfish purpose and we covet the opportunity to prove that our professions are sincere.

There are many things still to do at home, to clarify our own politics and give new vitality to the industrial processes of our own life, and we shall do them as time and opportunity serve; but we realize that the greatest things that remain to be done must be done with the whole world for stage and in coöperation with the wide and universal forces of mankind, and we are making our spirits ready for those things. They will follow in the immediate wake of the war itself and will set civilization up again. We are provincials no longer. The tragical events of the thirty months of vital turmoil through which we have just passed have made us citizens of the world. There can be no turning back. Our own fortunes as a nation are involved, whether we would have it so or not.

And yet we are not the less Americans on that account. We shall be the more American if we but remain true to the principles in which we have been bred. They are not the principles of a province or of a single continent. We have known and boasted all along that they were the principles of a liberated mankind. These, therefore, are the things we shall stand for, whether in war or in peace:

That all nations are equally interested in the peace of the world and in the political stability of free peoples, and equally responsible for their maintenance;

That the essential principle of peace is the actual equality of nations in all matters of right or privilege;

That peace cannot securely or justly rest upon an armed balance of power;

That governments derive all their just powers from the consent of the governed and that no other powers should be supported by the common thought, purpose, or power of the family of nations.

That the seas should be equally free and safe for the use of all peoples, under rules set up by common agreement and consent, and that, so far as practicable, they should be accessible to all upon equal terms;

That national armaments should be limited to the necessities of national order and domestic safety;

That the community of interest and of power upon which peace must henceforth depend imposes upon each nation the duty of seeing to it that all influences proceeding from its own citizens meant to encourage or assist revolution in other states should be sternly and effectually suppressed and prevented.

I need not argue these principles to you, my fellow countrymen: they are your own, part and parcel of your own thinking and your own motive in affairs. They spring up native amongst us. Upon this as a platform of purpose and of action we can stand together.

And it is imperative that we should stand together. We are being forged into a new unity amidst the fires that now blaze throughout the world. In their ardent heat we shall, in God's providence, let us hope, be purged of faction and division, purified of the errant humors of party and of private interest, and shall stand forth in the days to come with a new dignity of national pride and spirit. Let each man see to it that the dedication is in his own heart, the high purpose of the Nation in his own mind, ruler of his own will and desire.

I stand here and have taken the high and solemn oath to which you have been audience because the people of the United States have chosen me for this august delegation of power and have by their gracious judgment named me their leader in affairs. I know now what the task means. I realize to the full the responsibility which it involves. I pray God I may be given the wisdom and the prudence to do my duty in the true spirit of this great people. I am their servant and can succeed only as they sustain and guide me by their confidence and their counsel. The thing I shall count upon, the thing without which neither counsel nor action will avail, is the unity of America,—an America united in feeling, in purpose, and in its vision of duty, of opportunity, and of service. We are to beware of all men who would turn the tasks and the necessities of the Nation to their own private profit or use them for the building up of private power; beware that no faction or disloyal intrigue break the harmony or embarrass the spirit of our people; beware that our Government be kept pure and incorrupt in all its parts. United alike in the conception of our duty and in the high resolve to perform it in the face of all men, let us dedicate ourselves to the great task to which we must now set our hand. For myself I beg your tolerance, your countenance, and your united aid. The shadows that now lie dark upon our path will soon be dispelled and we shall walk with the light all about us if we be but true to ourselves,—to ourselves as we have wished to be known in the counsels of the world and in the thought of all those who love liberty and justice and the right exalted.

FOR DECLARATION OF WAR AGAINST GERMANY

ADDRESS DELIVERED AT A JOINT SESSION OF THE TWO
HOUSES OF CONGRESS, APRIL 2, 1917. FROM 65TH
CONGRESS, 1ST SESSION, SENATE DOCUMENT NO. 5.

I HAVE called the Congress into extraordinary session because there are serious, very serious, choices of policy to be made, and made immediately, which it was neither right nor constitutionally permissible that I should assume the responsibility of making.

On the third of February last I officially laid before you the extraordinary announcement of the Imperial German Government that on and after the first day of February it was its purpose to put aside all restraints of law or of humanity and use its submarines to sink every vessel that sought to approach either the ports of Great Britain and Ireland or the western coasts of Europe or any of the ports controlled by the enemies of Germany within the Mediterranean. That had seemed to be the object of the German submarine warfare earlier in the war, but since April of last year the Imperial Government had somewhat restrained the commanders of its undersea craft in conformity with its promise then given to us that passenger boats should not be sunk and that due warning would be given to all other vessels which its submarines might seek to destroy, when no resistance was offered or escape attempted, and care taken that their crews were given at least a fair chance to save their lives in their open boats. The precautions taken were meager and haphazard enough, as was proved in distressing instance after instance in the progress of the cruel and unmanly business, but a certain degree of restraint was observed. The new policy has swept every restriction aside. Vessels of every kind,

6

whatever their flag, their character, their cargo, their destination, their errand, have been ruthlessly sent to the bottom without warning and without thought of help or mercy for those on board, the vessels of friendly neutrals along with those of belligerents. Even hospital ships and ships carrying relief to the sorely bereaved and stricken people of Belgium, though the latter were provided with safe conduct through the proscribed areas by the German Government itself and were distinguished by unmistakable marks of identity, have been sunk with the same reckless lack of compassion or of principle.

I was for a little while unable to believe that such things would in fact be done by any government that had hitherto subscribed to the humane practices of civilized nations. International law had its origin in the attempt to set up some law which would be respected and observed upon the seas, where no nation had right of dominion and where lay the free highways of the world. By painful stage after stage has that law been built up, with meager enough results, indeed, after all was accomplished that could be accomplished, but always with a clear view, at least, of what the heart and conscience of mankind demanded. This minimum of right the German Government has swept aside under the plea of retaliation and necessity and because it had no weapons which it could use at sea except these which it is impossible to employ as it is employing them without throwing to the winds all scruples of humanity or of respect for the understandings that were supposed to underlie the intercourse of the world. I am not now thinking of the loss of property involved, immense and serious as that is, but only of the wanton and wholesale destruction of the lives of non-combatants, men, women, and children, engaged in pursuits which have always, even in the darkest periods of modern history, been deemed innocent and legitimate. Property can be paid for; the lives of peaceful and innocent people cannot be.

The present German submarine warfare against commerce is a warfare against mankind.

It is a war against all nations. American ships have been sunk, American lives taken, in ways which it has stirred us very deeply to learn of, but the ships and people of other neutral and friendly nations have been sunk and overwhelmed in the waters in the same way. There has been no discrimination. The challenge is to all mankind. Each nation must decide for itself how it will meet it. The choice we make for ourselves must be made with a moderation of counsel and a temperateness of judgment befitting our character and our motives as a nation. We must put excited feeling away. Our motive will not be revenge or the victorious assertion of the physical might of the nation, but only the vindication of right, of human right, of which we are only a single champion.

When I addressed the Congress on the twenty-sixth of February last I thought that it would suffice to assert our neutral rights with arms, our right to use the seas against unlawful interference, our right to keep our people safe against unlawful violence. But armed neutrality, it now appears, is impracticable. Because submarines are in effect outlaws when used as the German submarines have been used against merchant shipping, it is impossible to defend ships against their attacks as the law of nations has assumed that merchantmen would defend themselves against privateers or cruisers, visible craft giving chase upon the open sea. It is common prudence in such circumstances, grim necessity indeed, to endeavor to destroy them before they have shown their own intention. They must be dealt with upon sight, if dealt with at all. The German Government denies the right of neutrals to use arms at all within the areas of the sea which it has proscribed, even in the defense of rights which no modern publicist has ever before questioned their right to defend. The intimation is conveyed that the armed guards which we have placed on our merchant ships will be treated as beyond the pale of law and subject to be dealt with as pirates would be. Armed neutrality is ineffectual enough at best; in such circumstances and in the face of such pretensions it is worse than ineffectual: it is likely only to produce what it was meant to prevent; it is practically certain to draw us into the war without either the rights or the effectiveness of belligerents. There is one choice we cannot make, we are incapable of making: we will not choose the path of submission and suffer the most sacred rights of our Nation and our people to be ignored or violated. The wrongs against which we now array ourselves are no common wrongs; they cut to the very roots of human life.

With a profound sense of the solemn and even tragical character of the step I am taking and of the grave responsibilities which it involves, but in unhesitating obedience to what I deem my constitutional duty, I advise that the Congress declare the recent course of the Imperial German Government to be in fact nothing less than war against the government and people of the United States; that it formally accept the status of belligerent which has thus been thrust upon it; and that it take immediate steps not only to put the country in a more thorough state of defense but also to exert all its power and employ all its resources to bring the Government of the German Empire to terms and end the war.

What this will involve is clear. It will involve the utmost practicable coöperation in counsel and action with the governments now at war with Germany, and, as incident to that, the extension to those governments of the most liberal financial credits, in order that our resources may so far as possible be added to theirs. It will involve the organization and mobilization of all the material resources of the country to supply the materials of war and serve the incidental needs of the Nation in the most abundant and yet the most economical and efficient way possible. It will involve the immediate full equipment of the navy in all respects but particularly in supplying it with the best means of dealing with the enemy's submarines. It will involve the immediate addition to the armed forces of the United States already provided for by law in case of war at least five hundred thousand men, who should, in my opinion, be chosen upon the principle of universal liability to service, and also the authorization of subsequent additional increments of equal force so soon as they may be needed and can be handled in training. It will involve also, of course, the granting of adequate credits to the Government, sustained, I hope, so far as they can equitably be sustained by the present generation, by well conceived taxation.

I say sustained so far as may be equitable by taxation because it seems to me that it would be most unwise to base the credits which will now be necessary entirely on money borrowed. It is our duty, I most respectfully urge, to protect our people so far as we may against the very serious hardships and evils which would be likely to arise out of the inflation which would be produced by vast loans.

In carrying out the measures by which these things are to be accomplished we should keep constantly in mind the wisdom of interfering as little as possible in our own preparation and in the equipment of our own military forces with the duty,—for it will be a very practical duty,—of supplying the nations already at war with Germany with the materials which they can obtain only from us or by our assistance. They are in the field and we should help them in every way to be effective there.

I shall take the liberty of suggesting, through the several executive departments of the Government, for the consideration of your committees, measures for the accomplishment of the several objects I have mentioned. I hope that it will be your pleasure to deal with them as having been framed after very careful thought by the branch of the Government upon which the responsibility of conducting the war and safeguarding the Nation will most directly fall.

While we do these things, these deeply momentous things, let us be very clear, and make very clear to all the world what our motives and our objects are. My own thought has not been driven from its habitual and normal course by the unhappy events of the last two months, and I do not believe that the thought of the Nation has been altered or clouded by them. I have exactly the same things in mind now that I had in mind when I addressed the Senate on the twenty-second of January last; the same that I had in mind when I addressed the Congress on the third of February and on the twenty-sixth of February. Our object now, as then, is to vindicate the principles of peace and justice in the life of the world as against selfish and autocratic power and to set up amongst the really free and self-governed peoples of the world such a concert of purpose and of action as will henceforth insure the observance of those principles. Neutrality is no longer feasible or desirable where the peace of the world is involved and the freedom of its peoples, and the menace to that peace and freedom lies in the existence of autocratic governments backed by organized force which is controlled wholly by their will, not by the will of their people. We have seen the last of neutrality in such circumstances. We are at the beginning of an age in which it will be insisted that the same standards of conduct and of responsibility for wrong done shall be observed among nations and their governments that are observed among the individual citizens of civilized states.

We have no quarrel with the German people. We have no feeling towards them but one of sympathy and friendship. It was not upon their impulse that their government acted in entering this war. It was not with their previous knowledge or approval. It was a war determined upon as wars used to be determined upon in the old, unhappy days when peoples were nowhere consulted by their rulers and wars were provoked and waged in the interest of dynasties or of little groups of ambitious men who were accustomed to use their fellow men as pawns and tools. Self-governed nations do not fill their neighbor states with spies or set the course of intrigue to bring about some critical posture of affairs which will give them an opportunity to strike and make conquest. Such designs can be successfully worked out only under cover and where no one has the right to ask questions. Cunningly contrived plans of deception or aggression, carried, it may be, from generation to generation, can be worked out and kept from the light only within the privacy of courts or behind the carefully guarded confidences of a narrow and privileged class. They are happily impossible where public opinion commands and insists upon full information concerning all the nation's affairs.

A steadfast concert for peace can never be maintained except by a partnership of democratic nations. No autocratic government could be trusted to keep faith within it or observe its covenants. It must be a league of honor, a partnership of opinion. Intrigue would eat its vitals away; the plottings of inner circles who could plan what they would and render account to no one would be a corruption seated at its very heart. Only free peoples can hold their purpose and their honor steady to a common end and prefer the interests of mankind to any narrow interest of their own.

Does not every American feel that assurance has been added to our hope for the future peace of the world by the wonderful and heartening things that have been happening within the last few weeks in Russia? Russia was known by those who knew it best to have been always in fact democratic at heart, in all the vital habits of her thought, in all the intimate relationships of her people that spoke their natural instinct, their habitual attitude towards life. The autocracy that crowned the summit of her political structure, long as it had stood and terrible as was the reality of its power, was not in fact Russian in origin, character, or purpose; and now it has been shaken off and the great, generous Russian people have been added in all their naïve majesty and might to the forces that are fighting for freedom in the world, for justice, and for peace. Here is a fit partner for a League of Honor.

One of the things that has served to convince us that the Prussian autocracy was not and could never be our friend is that from the very outset of the present war it has filled our unsuspecting communities and even our offices of government with spies and set criminal intrigues everywhere afoot against our national unity of counsel, our peace within and without, our industries and our commerce. Indeed, it is now evident that its spies were here even before the war began; and it is unhappily not a matter of conjecture but a fact proved in our courts of justice that the intrigues which have more than once come perilously near to disturbing the peace and dislocating the industries of the country have been carried on at the instigation, with the support, and even under the personal direction of official agents of the Imperial Government accredited to the Government of the United States. Even in checking these things and trying to extirpate them we have sought to put the most generous interpretation possible upon them because we knew that their source lay not in any hostile feeling or purpose of the German people towards us (who were no doubt as ignorant of them as we ourselves were), but only in the selfish designs of a Government that did what it pleased and told its people nothing. But they have played their part in serving to convince us at last that that Government entertains no real friendship for us and means to act against our peace and security at its convenience. That it means to stir up enemies against us at our very doors the intercepted note to the German Minister at Mexico City is eloquent evidence. We are accepting this challenge of hostile purpose because we know that in such a Government, following such methods, we can never have a friend; and that in the presence of its organized power, always lying in wait to accomplish we know not what purpose, there can be no assured security for the democratic Governments of the world. We are now about to accept gage of battle with this natural foe to liberty and shall, if necessary, spend the whole force of the Nation to check and nullify its pretensions and its power. We are glad, now that we see the facts with no veil of false pretense about them, to fight thus for the ultimate peace of the world and for the liberation of its peoples, the German peoples included: for the rights of nations great and small and the privilege of men everywhere to choose their way of life and of obedience. The world must be made safe for democracy. Its peace must be planted upon the tested foundations of political liberty. We have no selfish ends to serve. We desire no conquest, no dominion. We seek no indemnities for ourselves, no material compensation for the sacrifices we shall freely make. We are but one of the champions of the rights of mankind. We shall be satisfied when those rights have been made as secure as the faith and the freedom of nations can make them.

Just because we fight without rancor and without selfish object, seeking nothing for ourselves but what we shall wish to share with all free peoples, we shall, I feel confident, conduct our operations as belligerents without passion and ourselves observe with proud punctilio the principles of right and of fair play we profess to be fighting for.

I have said nothing of the Governments allied with the Imperial Government of Germany because they have not made war upon us or challenged us to defend our right and our honor. The Austro-Hungarian Government has, indeed, avowed its unqualified indorsement and acceptance of the reckless and lawless submarine warfare adopted now without disguise by the Imperial

German Government, and it has therefore not been possible for this Government to receive Count Tarnowski, the Ambassador recently accredited to this Government by the Imperial and Royal Government of Austria-Hungary; but that Government has not actually engaged in warfare against citizens of the United States on the seas, and I take the liberty, for the present at least, of postponing a discussion of our relations with the authorities at Vienna. We enter this war only where we are clearly forced into it because there are no other means of defending our rights.

It will be all the easier for us to conduct ourselves as belligerents in a high spirit of right and fairness because we act without animus, not in enmity towards a people or with the desire to bring any injury or disadvantage upon them, but only in armed opposition to an irresponsible government which has thrown aside all considerations of humanity and of right and is running amuck. We are, let me say again, the sincere friends of the German people, and shall desire nothing so much as the early reëstablishment of intimate relations of mutual advantage between us,—however hard it may be for them, for the time being, to believe that this is spoken from our hearts. We have borne with their present Government through all these bitter months because of that friendship,—exercising a patience and forbearance which would otherwise have been impossible. We shall, happily, still have an opportunity to prove that friendship in our daily attitude and actions towards the millions of men and women of German birth and native sympathy who live amongst us and share our life, and we shall be proud to prove it towards all who are in fact loyal to their neighbors and to the Government in the hour of test. They are, most of them, as true and loyal Americans as if they had never known any other fealty or allegiance. They will be prompt to stand with us in rebuking and restraining the few who may be of a different mind and purpose. If there should be disloyalty, it will be dealt with with a firm hand of stern repression; but, if it lifts its head at all, it will lift it only here and there and without countenance except from a lawless and malignant few.

It is a distressing and oppressive duty, Gentlemen of the Congress, which I have performed in thus addressing you. There are, it may be, many months of fiery trial and sacrifice ahead of us. It is a fearful thing to lead this great peaceful people into war, into the most terrible and disastrous of all wars, civilization itself seeming to be in the balance. But the right is more precious than peace, and we shall fight for the things which we have always carried nearest our hearts,—for democracy, for the right of those who submit to authority to have a voice in their own Governments, for the rights and liberties of small nations, for a universal dominion of right by such a concert of free peoples as shall bring peace and safety to all nations and make the world itself at last free. To such a task we can dedicate our lives and our fortunes, everything that we are and everything that we have, with the pride of those who know that the day has come when America is privileged to spend her blood and her might for the principles that gave her birth and happiness and the peace which she has treasured. God helping her, she can do no other.

WAR WITH GERMANY

PROCLAMATION OF STATE OF WAR AND OF ALIEN ENEMY REGULATIONS, APRIL 6, 1917. FROM "UNITED STATES STATUTES AT LARGE," VOL. 40, PT. 2, PP. 1650-1652.

WHEREAS the Congress of the United States in the exercise of the constitutional authority vested in them have resolved, by joint resolution of the Senate and House of Representatives bearing date this day "That the state of war between the United States and the Imperial German Government which has . . . been thrust upon the United States is hereby formally declared":

WHEREAS it is provided by Section four thousand and sixty-seven of the Revised Statutes, as follows:

Whenever there is declared a war between the United States and any foreign nation or government, or any invasion or predatory incursion is perpetrated, attempted, or threatened against the territory of the United States, by any foreign nation or government, and the President makes public proclamation of the event, all natives, citizens, denizens, or subjects of the hostile nation or government, being males of the age of fourteen years and upwards, who shall be within the United States, and not actually naturalized, shall be liable to be apprehended, restrained, secured, and removed, as alien enemies. The President is authorized, in any such event, by his proclamation thereof, or other public act, to direct the conduct to be observed, on the part of the United States, toward the aliens who become so liable; the manner and degree of the restraint to which they shall be subject, and in what cases, and upon what security their residence shall be permitted, and to provide for the removal of those who, not being permitted to reside within the United States, refuse or neglect to depart therefrom; and to establish any other regulations which are found necessary in the premises and for the public safety;

WHEREAS, by Sections four thousand and sixty-eight, four thousand and sixty-nine, and four thousand and seventy, of the Revised Statutes, further provision is made relative to alien enemies;

NOW, THEREFORE, I, Woodrow Wilson, President of the United States of America, do hereby proclaim to all whom it may concern that a state of war exists between the United States and the Imperial German Government; and I do specially direct all officers, civil or military, of the United States that they exercise vigilance and zeal in the discharge of the duties incident to such a state of war; and I do, moreover, earnestly appeal to all American citizens that they, in loyal devotion to their country, dedicated from its foundation to the principles of liberty and justice, uphold the laws of the land, and give undivided and willing support to those measures which may be adopted by the constitutional authorities in prosecuting the war to a successful issue and in obtaining a secure and just peace;

And, acting under and by virtue of the authority vested in me by the Constitution of the United States and the said sections of the Revised Statutes, I do hereby further proclaim and direct that the conduct to be observed on the part of the United States towards all natives, citizens, denizens, or subjects of Germany, being males of the age of fourteen years and upwards, who shall be within the United States and not actually naturalized, who for the purpose of this proclamation and under such sections of the Revised Statutes are termed alien enemies, shall be as follows:

All alien enemies are enjoined to preserve the peace towards the United States and to refrain from crime against the public safety, and from violating the laws of the United States and of the States and Territories thereof, and to refrain from actual hostility or giving information, aid, or comfort to the enemies of the United States, and to comply strictly with the regulations which are hereby or which may be from time to time promulgated by the President; and so long as they shall conduct themselves in accordance with law, they shall be undisturbed in the peaceful pursuit of their lives and occupations and be accorded the consideration due to all peaceful and law-abiding persons, except so far as restrictions may be necessary for their own protection and for the safety of the United States; and towards such alien enemies as conduct themselves in accordance with law, all citizens of the United States are enjoined to preserve the peace and to treat them with all such friendliness as may be compatible with loyalty and allegiance to the United States.

And all alien enemies who fail to conduct themselves as so enjoined, in addition to all other penalties prescribed by law, shall be liable to restraint, or to give security, or to remove and depart from the United States in the manner prescribed by Sections four thousand and sixty-nine and four thousand and seventy of the Revised Statutes, and as prescribed in the regulations duly promulgated by the President:

And pursuant to the authority vested in me, I hereby declare and establish the following regulations, which I find necessary in the premises and for the public safety:

(1) An alien enemy shall not have in his possession, at any time or place, any firearm, weapon, or implement of war, or component part thereof, ammunition, maxim or other silencer, bomb or explosive or material used in the manufacture of explosives;

(2) An alien enemy shall not have in his possession at any time or place, or use or operate any aircraft or wireless apparatus, or any form of signaling device, or any form of cipher code, or any paper, document or book written or printed in cipher or in which there may be invisible writing.

(3) All property found in the possession of an alien enemy in violation of the foregoing regulations shall be subject to seizure by the United States;

(4) An alien enemy shall not approach or be found within one-half of a mile of any Federal or State fort, camp, arsenal, aircraft station, Government or naval vessel, navy yard, factory, or workshop for the manufacture of munitions of war or of any products for the use of the Army or Navy;

(5) An alien enemy shall not write, print, or publish any attack or threats against the Government or Congress of the United States, or either branch thereof, or against the measures or policy of the United States, or against the person or property of any person in the military, naval, or civil service of the United States, or of the States or Territories, or of the District of Columbia, or of the municipal governments therein;

(6) An alien enemy shall not commit or abet any hostile act against the United States, or give information, aid, or comfort to its enemies;

(7) An alien enemy shall not reside in or continue to reside in, to remain in, or enter any locality which the President may from time to time designate by Executive Order as a prohibited area in which residence by an alien enemy shall be found by him to constitute a danger to the public peace and safety of the United States, except by permit from the President and except under such limitations or restrictions as the President may prescribe;

(8) An alien enemy whom the President shall have reasonable cause to believe to be aiding or about to aid the enemy, or to be at large to the danger of the public peace or safety of the United States, or to have violated or to be about to violate any of these regulations, shall remove to any location designated by the President by Executive Order, and shall not remove therefrom without a permit, or shall depart from the United States if so required by the President;

(9) No alien enemy shall depart from the United States until he shall have received such permit as the President shall prescribe, or except under order of a court, judge, or justice, under Sections 4069 and 4070 of the Revised Statutes;

(10) No alien enemy shall land in or enter the United States, except under such restrictions and at such places as the President may prescribe;

(11) If necessary to prevent violations of these regulations, all alien enemies will be obliged to register;

(12) An alien enemy whom there may be reasonable cause to believe to be aiding or about to aid the enemy, or who may be at large to the danger of the public peace or safety, or who violates or attempts to violate, or of whom there is reasonable ground to believe that he is about to violate, any regulation duly promulgated by the President, or any criminal law of the United States, or of the States or Territories thereof, will be subject to summary arrest by the United States Marshal, or his deputy, or such other officer as the President shall designate, and to confinement in such penitentiary, prison, jail, military camp, or other place of detention as may be directed by the President.

This proclamation and the regulations herein contained shall extend and apply to all land and water, continental or insular, in any way within the jurisdiction of the United States.

"THE SUPREME TEST OF THE NATION HAS COME"

AN APPEAL TO THE PEOPLE, APRIL 16, 1917. FROM OFFICIAL GOVERNMENT PUBLICATION IN MR. WILSON'S FILES.

MY FELLOW COUNTRYMEN:

The entrance of our own beloved country into the grim and terrible war for democracy and human rights which has shaken the world creates so many problems of national life and action which call for immediate consideration and settlement that I hope you will permit me to address to you a few words of earnest counsel and appeal with regard to them.

We are rapidly putting our navy upon an effective war footing and are about to create and equip a great army, but these are the simplest parts of the great task to which we have addressed ourselves. There is not a single selfish element, so far as I can see, in the cause we are fighting for. We are fighting for what we believe and wish to be the rights of mankind and for the future peace and security of the world. To do this great thing worthily and successfully we must devote ourselves to the service without regard to profit or material advantage and with an energy and intelligence that will rise to the level of the enterprise itself. We must realize to the full how great the task is and how many things, how many kinds and elements of capacity and service and self-sacrifice, it involves.

These, then, are the things we must do, and do well, besides fighting,—the things without which mere fighting would be fruitless:

We must supply abundant food for ourselves and for our armies and our seamen not only, but also for a large part of the nations with whom we have now made common cause, in whose support and by whose sides we shall be fighting;

We must supply ships by the hundreds out of our shipyards to carry to the other side of the sea, submarines or no submarines, what will every day be needed there, and abundant materials out of our fields and our mines and our factories with which not only to clothe and equip our own forces on land and sea, but also to clothe and support our people for whom the gallant fellows under arms can no longer work, to help clothe and equip the armies with which we are coöperating in Europe, and to keep the looms and manufactories there in raw material; coal to keep the fires going in ships at sea and in the furnaces of hundreds of factories across the sea; steel out of which to make arms and ammunition both here and there; rails for worn-out railways back of the fighting fronts; locomotives and rolling stock to take the place of those every day going to pieces; mules, horses, cattle for labor and for military service; everything with which the people of England and France and Italy and Russia have usually supplied themselves but cannot now afford the men, the materials, or the machinery to make.

It is evident to every thinking man that our industries, on the farms, in the shipyards, in the mines, in the factories, must be made more prolific and more efficient than ever, and that they must be more economically managed and better adapted to the particular requirements of our task than they have been; and what I want to say is that the men and the women who devote their thought and their energy to these things will be serving the country and conducting the fight for peace and freedom just as truly and just as effectively as the men on the battlefield or in the trenches. The industrial forces of the country, men and women alike, will be a great national, a great international, Service Army,—a notable and honored host engaged in the service of the Nation and the world, the efficient friends and saviors of free men everywhere. Thousands, nay hundreds of thousands, of men otherwise liable to military service will of right and of necessity be excused from that service and assigned to the fundamental, sustaining work of the fields and factories and mines, and they will be as much part of the great patriotic forces of the Nation as the men under fire.

I take the liberty, therefore, of addressing this word to the farmers of the country and to all who work on the farms: The supreme need of our own Nation and of the nations with which we are coöperating is an abundance of supplies, and especially of foodstuffs. The importance of an adequate food supply, especially for the present year, is superlative. Without abundant food, alike for the armies and the peoples now at war, the whole great enterprise upon which we have embarked will break down and fail. The world's food reserves are low. Not only during the present emergency but for some time after peace shall have come both our own people and a large proportion of the people of Europe must rely upon the harvests in America.

Upon the farmers of this country, therefore, in large measure rests the fate of the war and the fate of the nations. May the Nation not count upon them to omit no step that will increase the production of their land or that will bring about the most effectual coöperation in the sale and distribution of their products? The time is short. It is of the most imperative importance that everything possible be done and done immediately to make sure of large harvests. I call upon young men and old alike and upon the able-bodied boys of the land to accept and act upon this duty—to turn in hosts to the farms and make certain that no pains and no labor is lacking in this great matter.

I particularly appeal to the farmers of the South to plant abundant foodstuffs as well as cotton. They can show their patriotism in no better or more convincing way than by resisting the great temptation of the present price of cotton and helping, helping upon a great scale, to feed the Nation and the peoples everywhere who are fighting for their liberties and for our own. The variety of their crops will be the visible measure of their comprehension of their national duty.

The Government of the United States and the Governments of the several States stand ready to coöperate. They will do everything possible to assist farmers in securing an adequate supply of seed, an adequate force of laborers when they are most needed, at harvest time, and the means of expediting shipments of fertilizers and farm machinery, as well as of the crops themselves when harvested. The course of trade shall be as unhampered as it is possible to make it and there shall be no unwarranted manipulation of the Nation's food supply by those who handle it on its way to the consumer. This is our opportunity to demonstrate the efficiency of a great Democracy and we shall not fall short of it!

This let me say to the middlemen of every sort, whether they are handling our foodstuffs or our raw materials of manufacture or the products of our mills and factories: The eyes of the country will be especially upon you. This is your opportunity for signal service, efficient and disinterested. The country expects you, as it expects all others, to forego unusual profits, to organize and expedite shipments of supplies of every kind, but especially of food, with an eye to the service you are rendering and in the spirit of those who enlist in the ranks, for their people, not for themselves. I shall confidently expect you to deserve and win the confidence of people of every sort and station.

To the men who run the railways of the country, whether they be managers or operative employees, let me say that the railways are the arteries of the Nation's life and that upon them rests the immense responsibility of seeing to it that those arteries suffer no obstruction of any kind, no inefficiency or slackened power. To the merchant let me suggest the motto, "Small profits and quick service"; and to the shipbuilder the thought that the life of the war depends upon him. The food and the war supplies must be carried across the seas no matter how many ships are sent to the bottom. The places of those that go down must be supplied and supplied at once. To the miner let me say that he stands where the farmer does: the work of the world waits on him. If he slackens or fails, armies and statesmen are helpless. He also is enlisted in the great Service Army. The manufacturer does not need to be told, I hope, that the Nation looks to him to speed and perfect every process; and I want only to remind his employees that their service is absolutely indispensable and is counted on by every man who loves the country and its liberties.

Let me suggest, also, that every one who creates or cultivates a garden helps, and helps greatly, to solve the problem of the feeding of the nations; and that every housewife who practices strict economy puts herself in the ranks of those who serve the Nation. This is the time for America to correct her unpardonable fault of wastefulness and extravagance. Let every man and every woman assume the duty of careful, provident use and expenditure as a public duty, as a dictate of patriotism which no one can now expect ever to be excused or forgiven for ignoring.

In the hope that this statement of the needs of the Nation and of the world in this hour of supreme crisis may stimulate those to whom it comes and remind all who need reminder of the solemn duties of a time such as the world has never seen before, I beg that all editors and publishers everywhere will give as prominent publication and as wide circulation as possible to this appeal. I venture to suggest, also, to all advertising agencies that they would perhaps render a very substantial and timely service to the country if they would give it widespread repetition. And I hope that clergymen will not think the theme of it an unworthy or inappropriate subject of comment and homily from their pulpits.

The supreme test of the Nation has come. We must all speak, act, and serve together!

WELCOME TO REPRESENTATIVES OF STATE COUNCILS OF NATIONAL DEFENSE

ADDRESS AT THE WHITE HOUSE, MAY 2, 1917. FROM "OFFICIAL BULLETIN," NO. 1.

MR. SECRETARY (SECRETARY OF WAR) AND GENTLEMEN:

It goes without saying that I am very glad to see you and very glad to see you on such an errand. I have no homily to deliver to you, because I know you are as intensely interested as I am in drawing all of our efforts and energies together in a common action. My function has not of recent days been to give advice but to get things coördinated so that there will not be any, or at any rate too much, lost motion, and in order that things should not be done twice by different bodies or done in conflict.

It is for that reason that I particularly welcome a conference such as this you are holding to-day and to-morrow—the conference which will acquaint you with exactly the task as it is conceived here in Washington and with the ways in which coöperation can be best organized. For, after all, the task is comparatively simple. The means of accomplishing the task are very complicated, because we must draw many pieces of machinery together and we must see that they act not only to a common object but at the same time and in a common spirit. My function, therefore, to-day is the very pleasant function of saying how much obliged to you I am for having come here and associated yourself with us in the great task of making good what the Nation has promised to do—go to the defense and vindication of the rights of people everywhere to live as they have a right to live under the very principles of our Nation.

It is a thing one does not dare to talk about because a certain passion comes into one's thought and one's feeling as one thinks of the nature of the task, the ideal nature of it, of the opportunity that America has now to show to all the world what it means to have been a democracy for 145 years and to mean every bit of the creed which we have so long professed. And in this thing it ought to be easy to act and delightful to coöperate.

I thank you very much indeed for your courtesy in coming here.

CREATING A RED CROSS WAR COUNCIL

LETTER TO MR. ELIOT WADSWORTH, VICE-CHAIRMAN OF
THE RED CROSS EXECUTIVE COMMITTEE, MAY 10,
1917. FROM ORIGINAL COPY IN MR. WILSON'S
FILES.

MY DEAR MR. WADSWORTH:
The American National Red Cross must now carry on the purposes of its organization under the stress of the great war in which our Nation is now involved, with the fullest recognition of its obligations under its federal charter and the Treaty of Geneva. To do this it is necessary that an immediate development and reinforcement of Red Cross organization should be effected in order to enable it to respond adequately to the great needs which will arise in our own country and those which already exist abroad.

After consideration of the situation with the active officers of the American Red Cross and with the members of its Executive Committee I, therefore, hereby create a Red Cross War Council of seven members, two of whom shall be the Chairman and Vice-Chairman of the Executive Committee, to serve for the period of the war. The War Council thus created is to deal with especial emergencies arising from the present war crisis in this country and abroad.

Sincerely yours,

WOODROW WILSON.

HENRY P. DAVISON APPOINTED TO RED CROSS WAR COUNCIL

LETTER TO MR. HENRY P. DAVISON, MAY 10, 1917. FROM ORIGINAL COPY IN MR. WILSON'S FILES.

MY DEAR MR. DAVISON:

After consultation with my active associates in the American Red Cross, it has been thought wise to create a Red Cross War Council of seven members, including the chairman and the vice-chairman of the executive committee. I have to-day created the council. This letter is to ask you to accept the chairmanship, a patriotic service which I trust it will be possible for you to perform.

The close coöperation between the American National Red Cross and the military branch of the Government has already suggested new avenues of helpfulness in the immediate business of our organization for war, but the present crisis is larger than that and there are unlimited opportunities of broad humanitarian service in view for the American National Red Cross. Battlefield relief will be affected through Red Cross agencies operating under the supervision of the War Department, but civilian relief will present a field of increasing opportunity in which the Red Cross organization is especially adapted to serve, and I am hopeful that our people will realize that there is probably no other agency with which they can associate themselves which can respond so effectively and universally to allay suffering and relieve distress.

Cordially yours,

WOODROW WILSON.

NEEDS OF THE RED CROSS

ADDRESS AT THE DEDICATION OF THE RED CROSS BUILD-
ING, MAY 12, 1917. FROM "OFFICIAL BULLETIN,"
NO. 4.

IT GIVES me a very deep gratification as the titular
head of the American Red Cross to accept in the
name of that association this significant and beautiful
gift, the gift of the Government and of private individuals who have conceived their duty in a noble spirit
and upon a great scale. It seems to me that the archi-
tecture of the building to which the Secretary[1] alluded
suggests something very significant.

There are few buildings in Washington more simple
in their lines and in their ornamentation than the beautiful building we are dedicating this evening. It breathes
a spirit of modesty and seems to adorn duty with its
proper garment of beauty. It is significant that it should
be dedicated to women who served to alleviate suffering
and comfort those who were in need during our Civil
War, because their thoughtful, disinterested, self-sacri-
ficing devotion is the spirit which should always illustrate the services of the Red Cross.

The Red Cross needs at this time more than ever it
needed before the comprehending support of the American people and all the facilities which could be placed
at its disposal to perform its duties adequately and
efficiently. I believe that the American people perhaps
hardly yet realize the sacrifices and sufferings that are
before them. We thought the scale of our Civil War
was unprecedented, but in comparison with the struggle
into which we have now entered the Civil War seems
almost insignificant in its proportions and in its expenditure of treasure and of blood. And, therefore, it is a

[1] Secretary of War, Mr. Baker.

matter of the greatest importance that we should at the outset see to it that the American Red Cross is equipped and prepared for the things that lie before it.

It will be our instrument to do the works of alleviation and mercy which will attend this struggle. Of course, the scale upon which it shall act will be greater than the scale of any other duty that it has ever attempted to perform. It is in recognition of that fact that the American Red Cross has just added to its organization a small body of men whom it has chosen to call its war council—not because they are to counsel war, but because they are to serve in this special war those purposes of counsel which have become so imperatively necessary.

Their first duty will be to raise a great fund out of which to draw the resources for the performance of their duty, and I do not believe that it will be necessary to appeal to the American people to respond to their call for funds, because the heart of this country is in this war, and if the heart of the country is in the war, its heart will express itself in the gifts that will be poured out for these humane purposes. I say the heart of the country is in this war because it would not have gone into it if its heart had not been prepared for it. It would not have gone into it if it had not first believed that here was an opportunity to express the character of the United States. We have gone in with no special grievance of our own, because we have always said that we were the friends and servants of mankind.

We look for no profit. We look for no advantage. We will accept no advantage out of this war. We go because we believe that the very principles upon which the American Republic was founded are now at stake and must be vindicated.

In such a contest, therefore, we shall not fail to respond to the call for service that comes through the instrumentality of this particular organization. And I think it not inappropriate to say this: There will be many expressions of the spirit of sympathy and mercy and philanthropy, and I think that it is very necessary that we should not disperse our activities in those lines too much; that we should keep constantly in view the desire to have the utmost concentration and efficiency of effort, and I hope that most, if not all, of the philanthropic activities of this war may be exercised if not through the Red Cross, then through some already-constituted and experienced organization.

This is no war for amateurs. This is no war for mere spontaneous impulse. It means grim business on every side of it, and it is the mere counsel of prudence that in our philanthropy as well as in our fighting we should act through the instrumentalities already prepared to our hand and already experienced in the tasks which are going to be assigned to them. This should be merely the expression of the practical genius of America itself, and I believe that the practical genius of America will dictate that the efforts in this war in this particular field should be concentrated in experienced hands as our efforts in other fields will be.

There is another thing that is significant and delightful to my thought about the fact that this building should be dedicated to the memory of the women both of the North and of the South. It is a sort of landmark of the unity to which the people have been brought so far as any old question which tore our hearts in days gone by is concerned; and I pray God that the outcome of this struggle may be that every other element of difference amongst us will be obliterated and that some day historians will remember these momentous years as the years which made a single people out of the great body of those who call themselves Americans. The evidences are already many that this is happening. The divisions which were predicted have not occurred and will not occur. The spirit of this people is already united, and when effort and suffering and sacrifice have completed the union, men will no longer speak of any lines either of race or association cutting athwart the great body of this Nation. So that I feel that we are now beginning the processes which will some day require another beautiful memorial erected to those whose hearts uniting united America.

"SPONTANEOUS COÖPERATION OF MEN FROM ALL WALKS OF LIFE"

ADDRESS TO THE LABOR COMMITTEE OF THE COUNCIL OF NATIONAL DEFENSE, MAY 15, 1917. FROM "OFFICIAL BULLETIN," NO. 5.

MR. GOMPERS AND LADIES AND GENTLE-MEN:

This is a most welcome visit because it makes a most welcome thing, the spontaneous coöperation of men from all walks of life interested to see that we do not forget any of the principles of our lives in meeting the great emergency that has come upon us.

Mr. Gompers has expressed already one of the things that have been very much in my mind of late. I have been very much alarmed at one or two things that have happened: at the apparent inclination of the legislatures of one or two of our States to set aside even temporarily the laws which have safeguarded the standards of labor and of life. I think nothing would be more deplorable than that. We are trying to fight in a cause which means the lifting of the standards of life, and we can fight in that cause best by voluntary coöperation. I do not doubt that any body of men representing labor in this country, speaking for their fellows, will be willing to make any sacrifice that is necessary in order to carry this contest to a successful issue, and in that confidence I feel that it would be inexcusable if we deprived men and women of such a spirit of any of the existing safeguards of law. Therefore, I shall exercise my influence as far as it goes to see that that does not happen and that the sacrifices we make shall be made voluntarily and not under the compulsion which mistakenly is interpreted to mean a lowering of the standards which we have sought through so many generations to bring to their present level.

Mr. Gompers has not overstated the case in saying that we are fighting for democracy in a larger sense than can be expressed in any political terms. There are many forms of democratic government, and we are not fighting for any particular form; but we are fighting for the essential part of it all, namely, that we are all equally interested in our social and political life and all have a right to a voice in the Government under which we live; and that when men and women are equally admitted to those rights we have the best safeguard of justice and of peace that the world affords. There is no other safeguard. Let any group of men, whatever their original intentions, attempt to dictate to their fellow men what their political fortunes shall be, and the result is injustice, and hardship, and wrong of the deepest sort. Therefore, we are just now feeling as we have never felt before our sense of comradeship. We shall feel it even more, because we have not yet made the sacrifices that we are going to make, we have not yet felt the terrible pressure of suffering and pain of war, and we are going presently to feel it, and I have every confidence that as its pressure comes upon us our spirits will not falter, but rise and be strengthened, and that in the last we shall have a national feeling and a national unity such as never gladdened our hearts before.

I want to thank you for the compliment of this visit and say if there is any way in which I can coöperate with the purposes of this committee or with those with whom you are laboring, it will afford me a sense of privilege and of pleasure.

REGISTRATION FOR THE DRAFT

STATEMENT ACCOMPANYING PROCLAMATION CALLING
FOR THE REGISTRATION FOR THE DRAFT OF "ALL
MALE PERSONS BETWEEN THE AGES OF 21 AND 30,"
MAY 18, 1917. FROM "UNITED STATES STATUTES
AT LARGE," VOL. 40, PT. 2, P. 1666.

THE power against which we are arrayed has sought to impose its will upon the world by force. To this end it has increased armament until it has changed the face of war. In the sense in which we have been wont to think of armies there are no armies in this struggle. There are entire nations armed. Thus, the men who remain to till the soil and man the factories are no less a part of the army that is in France than the men beneath the battle flags. It must be so with us. It is not an army that we must shape and train for war; it is a nation. To this end our people must draw close in one compact front against a common foe. But this cannot be if each man pursues a private purpose. All must pursue one purpose. The Nation needs all men; but it needs each man, not in the field that will most pleasure him, but in the endeavor that will best serve the common good. Thus, though a sharpshooter pleases to operate a trip-hammer for the forging of great guns, and an expert machinist desires to march with the flag, the Nation is being served only when the sharpshooter marches and the machinist remains at his levers.

The whole Nation must be a team in which each man shall play the part for which he is best fitted. To this end, Congress has provided that the Nation shall be organized for war by selection and that each man shall be classified for service in the place to which it shall best serve the general good to call him.

The significance of this cannot be overstated. It is

a new thing in our history and a landmark in our progress. It is a new manner of accepting and vitalizing our duty to give ourselves with thoughtful devotion to the common purpose of us all. It is in no sense a conscription of the unwilling; it is, rather, selection from a nation which has volunteered in mass. It is no more a choosing of those who shall march with the colors than it is a selection of those who shall serve an equally necessary and devoted purpose in the industries that lie behind the battle line.

The day here named is the time upon which all shall present themselves for assignment to their tasks. It is for that reason destined to be remembered as one of the most conspicuous moments in our history. It is nothing less than the day upon which the manhood of the country shall step forward in one solid rank in defense of the ideals to which this Nation is consecrated. It is important to those ideals no less than to the pride of this generation in manifesting its devotion to them, that there be no gaps in the ranks.

It is essential that the day be approached in thoughtful apprehension of its significance and that we accord to it the honor and the meaning that it deserves. Our industrial need prescribes that it be not made a technical holiday, but the stern sacrifice that is before us, urges that it be carried in all our hearts as a great day of patriotic devotion and obligation when the duty shall lie upon every man, whether he is himself to be registered or not, to see to it that the name of every male person of the designated ages is written on these lists of honor.

DECLINING ROOSEVELT'S OFFER
OF SERVICE IN FRANCE

STATEMENT, MAY 18, 1917. FROM "OFFICIAL BULLE-TIN," NO. 9.

I SHALL not avail myself, at any rate at the present stage of the war, of the authorization conferred by the act to organize volunteer divisions. To do so would seriously interfere with the carrying out of the chief and most immediately important purpose contemplated by this legislation, the prompt creation and early use of an effective army, and would contribute practically nothing to the effective strength of the armies now engaged against Germany.

I understand that the section of this act which authorizes the creation of volunteer divisions in addition to the draft was added with a view to providing an independent command for Mr. Roosevelt and giving the military authorities an opportunity to use his fine vigor and enthusiasm in recruiting the forces now at the western front. It would be very agreeable to me to pay Mr. Roosevelt this compliment and the Allies the compliment of sending to their aid one of our most distinguished public men, an ex-President who has rendered many conspicuous public services and proved his gallantry in many striking ways. Politically, too, it would no doubt have a very fine effect and make a profound impression. But this is not the time or the occasion for compliment or for any action not calculated to contribute to the immediate success of the war. The business now in hand is undramatic, practical, and of scientific definiteness and precision. I shall act with regard to it at every step and in every particular under expert and professional advice, from both sides of the water.

That advice is that the men most needed are men of

the ages contemplated in the draft provisions of the present bill, not men of the age and sort contemplated in the section which authorizes the formation of volunteer units, and that for the preliminary training of the men who are to be drafted we shall need all of our experienced officers. Mr. Roosevelt told me, when I had the pleasure of seeing him a few weeks ago, that he would wish to have associated with him some of the most effective officers of the Regular Army. He named many of those whom he would desire to have designated for the service, and they were men who cannot possibly be spared from the too small force of officers at our command for the much more pressing and necessary duty of training Regular troops to be put into the field in France and Belgium as fast as they can be got ready. The first troops sent to France will be taken from the present forces of the Regular Army and will be under the command of trained soldiers only.

The responsibility for the successful conduct of our own part in this great war rests upon me. I could not escape it if I would. I am too much interested in the cause we are fighting for to be interested in anything but success. The issues involved are too immense for me to take into consideration anything whatever except the best, most effective, most immediate means of military action. What these means are I know from the mouths of men who have seen war as it is now conducted, who have no illusions, and to whom the whole grim matter is a matter of business. I shall center my attention upon those means and let everything else wait. I should be deeply to blame should I do otherwise, whatever the argument of policy or of personal gratification or advantage.

WARTIME FOOD ADMINISTRATION

STATEMENT ON THE FOOD LAW, MAY 19, 1917. FROM "OFFICIAL BULLETIN," NO. 10.

IT IS very desirable, in order to prevent misunderstandings or alarms and to assure coöperation in a vital matter, that the country should understand exactly the scope and purpose of the very great powers which I have thought it necessary in the circumstances to ask the Congress to put in my hands with regard to our food supplies. Those powers are very great indeed, but they are no greater than it has proved necessary to lodge in the other Governments which are conducting this momentous war, and their object is stimulation and conservation, not arbitrary restraint or injurious interference with the normal processes of production. They are intended to benefit and assist the farmer and all those who play a legitimate part in the preparation, distribution, and marketing of foodstuffs.

It is proposed to draw a sharp line of distinction between the normal activities of the Government represented in the Department of Agriculture in reference to food production, conservation, and marketing on the one hand and the emergency activities necessitated by the war in reference to the regulation of food distribution and consumption on the other.

All measures intended directly to extend the normal activities of the Department of Agriculture in reference to the production, conservation, and the marketing of farm crops will be administered as in normal times through that department, and the powers asked for over distribution and consumption, over exports, imports, prices, purchase, and requisition of commodities, storing, and the like which may require regulation during the war will be placed in the hands of a commis-

42

sioner of food administration appointed by the President and directly responsible to him.

The objects sought to be served by the legislation asked for are: Full inquiry into the existing available stocks of foodstuffs and into the costs and practices of the various food-producing and distributing trades; the prevention of all unwarranted hoarding of every kind and of the control of foodstuffs by persons who are not in any legitimate sense producers, dealers, or traders; the requisitioning when necessary for the public use of food supplies and of the equipment necessary for handling them properly; the licensing of wholesome and legitimate mixtures and milling percentages; and the prohibition of the unnecessary or wasteful use of foods. Authority is asked also to establish prices, but not in order to limit the profits of the farmers, but only to guarantee to them when necessary a minimum price which will insure them a profit where they are asked to attempt new crops and to secure the consumer against extortion by breaking up corners and attempts at speculation when they occur by fixing temporarily a reasonable price at which middlemen must sell.

I have asked Mr. Herbert Hoover to undertake this all-important task of food administration. He has expressed his willingness to do so on condition that he is to receive no payment for his services and that the whole of the force under him, exclusive of clerical assistance, shall be employed so far as possible upon the same volunteer basis. He has expressed his confidence that this difficult matter of food administration can be successfully accomplished through the voluntary coöperation and direction of legitimate distributors of foodstuffs and with the help of the women of the country.

Although it is absolutely necessary that unquestionable powers shall be placed in my hands in order to insure the success of this administration of the food supplies of the country, I am confident that the exercise of those powers will be necessary only in the few cases where some small and selfish minority proves unwilling to put the Nation's interests above personal advantage and that the whole country will heartily support Mr. Hoover's efforts by supplying the necessary volunteer agencies throughout the country for the intelligent control of food consumption and securing the coöperation of the most capable leaders of the very interests most directly affected, that the exercise of the powers deputed to him will rest very successfully upon the good will and coöperation of the people themselves, and that the ordinary economic machinery of the country will be left substantially undisturbed.

The proposed Food Administration is intended, of course, only to meet a manifest emergency and to continue only while the war lasts. Since it will be composed for the most part of volunteers, there need be no fear of the possibility of a permanent bureaucracy arising out of it. All control of consumption will disappear when the emergency has passed. It is with that object in view that the administration considers it to be of preëminent importance that the existing associations of producers and distributors of foodstuffs should be mobilized and made use of on a volunteer basis. The successful conduct of the projected food administration by such means will be the finest possible demonstration of the willingness, the ability, and the efficiency of democracy, and of its justified reliance upon the freedom of individual initiative. The last thing that any American could contemplate with equanimity would be the introduction of anything resembling Prussian autocracy into the food control in this country.

It is of vital interest and importance to every man who produces food and to every man who takes part in its distribution that these policies thus liberally administered should succeed and succeed altogether. It is only in that way that we can prove it to be absolutely unnecessary to resort to the rigorous and drastic measures which have proved to be necessary in some of the European countries.

COLLEGE SPORTS A REAL CONTRIBUTION TO NATIONAL DEFENSE

LETTER TO MR. LAWRENCE PERRY, MAY 21, 1917. FROM ORIGINAL COPY IN MR. WILSON'S FILES.

MY DEAR MR. PERRY:
I entirely agree with the conclusions contained in your letter of May 15. I would be sincerely sorry to see the men and boys in our colleges and schools give up their athletic sports and I hope most sincerely that the normal course of college sports will be continued so far as possible, not to afford a diversion to the American people in the days to come when we shall no doubt have our share of mental depression, but as a real contribution to the national defense, for our young men must be made physically fit in order that later they may take the place of those who are now of military age and exhibit the vigor and alertness which we are proud to believe to be characteristic of our young men.

Cordially and sincerely yours,

WOODROW WILSON.

NECESSITY FOR CENSORSHIP

LETTER TO HON. EDWIN Y. WEBB, CONGRESSMAN FROM NORTH CAROLINA, MAY 22, 1917. FROM ORIGINAL COPY IN MR. WILSON'S FILES.

MY DEAR MR. WEBB:

I have been very much surprised to find several of the public prints stating that the administration had abandoned the position which it so distinctly took, and still holds, that authority to exercise censorship over the press to the extent that that censorship is embodied in the recent action of the House of Representatives is absolutely necessary to the public safety. It, of course, has not been abandoned, because the reasons still exist why such authority is necessary for the protection of the Nation.

I have every confidence that the great majority of the newspapers of the country will observe a patriotic reticence about everything whose publication could be of injury, but in every country there are some persons in a position to do mischief in this field who cannot be relied upon and whose interests or desires will lead to actions on their part highly dangerous to the Nation in the midst of a war. I want to say again that it seems to me imperative that powers of this sort should be granted.

Cordially and sincerely yours,
WOODROW WILSON.

"OUR OBJECTS IN GOING INTO THE WAR"

LETTER TO CONGRESSMAN J. THOMAS HEFLIN OF ALA-
BAMA, MAY 22, 1917. FROM ORIGINAL COPY IN
MR. WILSON'S FILES.

MY DEAR MR. HEFLIN:
It is incomprehensible to me how any frank or
honest person could doubt or question my position with
regard to the war and its objects. I have again and
again stated the very serious and long-continued wrongs
which the Imperial German Government has perpetrated against the rights, the commerce, and the citizens
of the United States. The list is long and overwhelming. No nation that respected itself or the rights of
humanity could have borne those wrongs any longer.

Our objects in going into the war have been stated
with equal clearness. The whole of the conception
which I take to be the conception of our fellow countrymen with regard to the outcome of the war and the
terms of its settlement I set forth with the utmost ex-
plicitness in an address to the Senate of the United
States on the 22d of January last. Again, in my message to Congress on the 2d of April last those objects
were stated in unmistakable terms. I can conceive no
purpose in seeking to becloud this matter except the
purpose of weakening the hands of the Government and
making the part which the United States is to play in
this great struggle for human liberty an inefficient and
hesitating part. We have entered the war for our own
reasons and with our own objects clearly stated, and
shall forget neither the reasons nor the objects. There
is no hate in our hearts for the German people, but
there is a resolve which cannot be shaken even by mis-

representation to overcome the pretensions of the autocratic Government which acts upon purposes to which the German people have never consented.

　　　　　Cordially and sincerely yours,

　　　　　　　　　　　WOODROW WILSON.

"FRIENDSHIP OF THE AMERICAN PEOPLE FOR THE PEOPLE OF RUSSIA"

MESSAGE TO RUSSIA ON THE OCCASION OF THE VISIT OF THE AMERICAN MISSION, MAY 26, 1917.[1] FROM "OFFICIAL BULLETIN," NO. 26.

IN VIEW of the approaching visit of the American delegation to Russia to express the deep friendship of the American people for the people of Russia and to discuss the best and most practical means of coöperation between the two peoples in carrying the present struggle for the freedom of all peoples to a successful consummation, it seems opportune and appropriate that I should state again, in the light of this new partnership, the objects the United States has had in mind in entering the war. Those objects have been very much beclouded during the past few weeks by mistaken and misleading statements, and the issues at stake are too momentous, too tremendous, too significant, for the whole human race to permit any misinterpretations or misunderstandings, however slight, to remain uncorrected for a moment.

The war has begun to go against Germany, and in their desperate desire to escape the inevitable ultimate defeat, those who are in authority in Germany are using every possible instrumentality, are making use even of the influence of groups and parties among their own subjects to whom they have never been just or fair, or even tolerant, to promote a propaganda on both sides of the sea which will preserve for them their influence

---

[1] On March 15, 1917, Tsar Nicholas II of Russia abdicated and a provisional government was formed. In May, 1917, Mr. Wilson sent a special commission to Russia, headed by Elihu Root. The President's message was delivered to the provisional government upon the arrival of the commission in Russia, on May 26, 1917, but was not made public in Washington until June 9, 1917.

at home and their power abroad, to the undoing of the very men they are using.

The position of America in this war is so clearly avowed that no man can be excused for mistaking it. She seeks no material profit or aggrandizement of any kind. She is fighting for no advantage or selfish object of her own, but for the liberation of peoples everywhere from the aggressions of autocratic force.

The ruling classes in Germany have begun of late to profess a like liberality and justice of purpose, but only to preserve the power they have set up in Germany and the selfish advantages which they have wrongly gained for themselves and their private projects of power all the way from Berlin to Bagdad and beyond. Government after Government has by their influence, without open conquest of its territory, been linked together in a net of intrigue directed against nothing less than the peace and liberty of the world. The meshes of that intrigue must be broken, but cannot be broken unless wrongs already done are undone, and adequate measures must be taken to prevent it from ever again being rewoven or repaired.

Of course, the Imperial German Government and those whom it is using for their own undoing are seeking to obtain pledges that the war will end in the restoration of the *status quo ante*. It was the *status quo ante* out of which this iniquitous war issued forth, the power of the Imperial German Government within the Empire and its widespread domination and influence outside of that Empire. That status must be altered in such fashion as to prevent any such hideous thing from ever happening again.

We are fighting for the liberty, the self-government, and the undictated development of all peoples, and every feature of the settlement that concludes this war must be conceived and executed for that purpose. Wrongs must first be righted and then adequate safeguards must be created to prevent their being committed again. We ought not to consider remedies merely because they have a pleasing and sonorous sound. Practical questions can be settled only by practical means. Phrases will not accomplish the result. Effective readjustments will, and whatever readjustments are necessary must be made.

But they must follow a principle and that principle is plain. No people must be forced under sovereignty under which it does not wish to live. No territory must change hands except for the purpose of securing those who inhabit it a fair chance of life and liberty. No indemnities must be insisted on except those that constitute payment for manifest wrongs done. No readjustments of power must be made except such as will tend to secure the future peace of the world and the future welfare and happiness of its peoples.

And then the free peoples of the world must draw together in some common covenant, some genuine and practical coöperation that will in effect combine their force to secure peace and justice in the dealings of nations with one another.

The brotherhood of mankind must no longer be a fair but empty phrase; it must be given a structure of force and reality. The nations must realize their common life and effect a workable partnership to secure that life against the aggressions of autocratic and self-pleasing power.

For these things we can afford to pour out blood and treasure. For these are the things we have always professed to desire, and unless we pour out blood and treasure now and succeed we may never be able to unite or show conquering force again in the great cause of human liberty. The day has come to conquer or submit. If the forces of autocracy can divide us they will overcome us; if we stand together victory is certain and the liberty which victory will secure. We can afford then to be generous, but we cannot afford then or now to be weak or omit any single guarantee of justice and security.

"AMERICA WAS BORN TO SERVE MANKIND"

MEMORIAL DAY ADDRESS AT ARLINGTON NATIONAL CEM-
ETERY, MAY 30, 1917. FROM "OFFICIAL BULLE-
TIN," NO. 18.

THE program has conferred an unmerited dignity
upon the remarks I am going to make by calling
them an address, because I am not here to deliver an
address. I am here merely to show in my official capacity the sympathy of this great Government with the
objects of this occasion, and also to speak just a word of
the sentiment that is in my own heart.

Any Memorial Day of this sort is, of course, a day
touched with sorrowful memory, and yet I for one do
not see how we can have any thought of pity for the
men whose memory we honor to-day. I do not pity
them. I envy them, rather; because theirs is a great
work for liberty accomplished and we are in the midst
of a work unfinished, testing our strength where their
strength has already been tested.

There is a touch of sorrow, but there is a touch of
reassurance also in a day like this, because we know
how the men of America have responded to the call of
the cause of liberty and it fills our minds with a perfect
assurance that that response will come again in equal
measure, with equal majesty, and with a result which
will hold the attention of all mankind.

When you reflect upon it, these men who died to preserve the Union died to preserve the instrument which
we are now using to serve the world—a free Nation
espousing the cause of human liberty. In one sense the
great struggle into which we have now entered is an
American struggle, because it is in defense of American
honor and American rights, but it is something even
greater than that; it is a world struggle. It is a strug-

gle of men who love liberty everywhere, and in this cause America will show herself greater than ever because she will rise to a greater thing.

We have said in the beginning that we planned this great Government that men who wished freedom might have a place of refuge and a place where their hope could be realized, and now, having established such a Government, having preserved such a Government, having vindicated the power of such a Government, we are saying to all mankind, "We did not set this Government up in order that we might have a selfish and separate liberty, for we are now ready to come to your assistance and fight out upon the field of the world the cause of human liberty."

In this thing America attains her full dignity and the full fruition of her great purpose.

No man can be glad that such things have happened as we have witnessed in these last fateful years, but perhaps it may be permitted to us to be glad that we have an opportunity to show the principles that we profess to be living, principles that live in our hearts, and to have a chance by the pouring out of our blood and treasure to vindicate the thing which we have professed. For, my friends, the real fruition of life is to do the thing we have said we wished to do. There are times when words seem empty and only action seems great. Such a time has come, and in the providence of God America will once more have an opportunity to show to the world that she was born to serve mankind.

"A DAY OF NOBLE MEMORIES, A DAY OF DEDICATION"

ADDRESS TO CONFEDERATE VETERANS AT WASHINGTON, JUNE 5, 1917. FROM "OFFICIAL BULLETIN," NO. 22.

MR. COMMANDER, LADIES AND GENTLE-
MEN:

I esteem it a very great pleasure and a real privilege to extend to the men who are attending this reunion the very cordial greetings of the Government of the United States.

I suppose that as you mix with one another you chiefly find these to be days of memory, when your thoughts go back and recall those days of struggle in which your hearts were strained, in which the whole Nation seemed in grapple, and I dare say that you are thrilled as you remember the heroic things that were then done. You are glad to remember that heroic things were done on both sides, and that men in those days fought in something like the old spirit of chivalric gallantry.

There are many memories of the Civil War that thrill along the blood and make one proud to have been sprung of a race that could produce such bravery and constancy; and yet the world does not live on memories. The world is constantly making its toilsome way forward into new and different days, and I believe that one of the things that contributes satisfaction to a reunion like this and a welcome like this is that this is also a day of oblivion. There are some things that we have thankfully buried, and among them are the great passions of division which once threatened to rend this Nation in twain. The passion of admiration we still entertain for the heroic figures of those old days, but the passion of separation, the passion of difference of principle, is gone—gone out of our minds, gone out of our hearts; and one of the things that will thrill this country as it reads of this reunion is that it will read also of a rededication on the part of all of us to the great Nation which we serve in common.

These are days of oblivion as well as of memory, for we are forgetting the things that once held us asunder. Not only that, but they are days of rejoicing, because we now at last see why this great Nation was kept united, for we are beginning to see the great world purpose which it was meant to serve. Many men I know, particularly of your own generation, have wondered at some of the dealings of Providence, but the wise heart never questions the dealings of Providence, because the great long plan as it unfolds has a majesty about it and a definiteness of purpose, an elevation of ideal, which we were incapable of conceiving as we tried to work things out with our short sight and weak strength. And now that we see ourselves part of a Nation united, powerful, great in spirit and in purpose, we know the great ends which God in His mysterious Providence wrought through our instrumentality, because at the heart of the men of the North and of the South there was the same love of self-government and of liberty, and now we are to be an instrument in the hands of God to see that liberty is made secure for mankind.

At the day of our greatest division there was one common passion amongst us, and that was the passion for human freedom. We did not know that God was working out in His own way the method by which we should best serve human freedom—by making this Nation a great united, indivisible, indestructible instrument in His hands for the accomplishment of these great things.

As I came along the streets a few minutes ago, my heart was full of the thought that this is registration day. Will you not support me in feeling that there is some significance in this coincidence that this day, when I come to welcome you to the national capital, is a day

when men, young as you were in those old days when
you gathered together to fight, are now registering their
names as evidence of this great idea that in a democracy
the duty to serve and the privilege to serve falls upon
all alike? There is something very fine, my fellow citizens, in the spirit of the volunteer, but deeper than the
volunteer spirit is the spirit of obligation. There is not
a man of us who must not hold himself ready to be summoned to the duty of supporting the great Government
under which we live. No really thoughtful and patriotic man is jealous of that obligation. No man who
really understands the privilege and the dignity of being
an American citizen quarrels for a moment with the idea
that the Congress of the United States has the right
to call upon whom it will to serve the Nation. These
solemn lines of young men going to-day all over the
Union to the places of registration ought to be a signal
to the world, to those who dare flout the dignity and
honor and rights of the United States, that all her manhood will flock to that standard under which we all
delight to serve, and that he who challenges the rights
and principles of the United States challenges the united
strength and devotion of a nation.

There are not many things that one desires about
war, my fellow citizens, but you have come through
war, you know how you have been chastened by it, and
there comes a time when it is good for a Nation to know
that it must sacrifice if need be everything that it has to
vindicate the principles which it professes. We have
prospered with a sort of heedless and irresponsible prosperity. Now we are going to lay all our wealth, if necessary, and spend all our blood, if need be, to show that
we were not accumulating that wealth selfishly, but were
accumulating it for the service of mankind. Men all
over the world have thought of the United States as a
trading and money-getting people, whereas we who have
lived at home know the ideals with which the hearts of
this people have thrilled; we know the sober convictions

which have lain at the basis of our life all the time; and we know the power and devotion which can be spent in heroic wise for the service of those ideals that we have treasured. We have been allowed to become strong in the Providence of God that our strength might be used to prove, not our selfishness, but our greatness, and if there is any ground for thankfulness in a day like this, I am thankful for the privilege of self-sacrifice, which is the only privilege that lends dignity to the human spirit.

And so it seems to me that we may regard this as a very happy day, because a day of reunion, a day of noble memories, a day of dedication, a day of the renewal of the spirit which has made America great among the peoples of the world.

MOBILIZATION OF FORCES FOR FOOD ECONOMY

LETTER TO MR. HERBERT HOOVER, JUNE 12, 1917.
FROM ORIGINAL COPY IN MR. WILSON'S FILES.

MY DEAR MR. HOOVER:
It seems to me that the inauguration of that portion of the plan for Food Administration which contemplates a national mobilization of the great voluntary forces of the country which are ready to work towards saving food and eliminating waste admits of no further delay.

The approaching harvest, the immediate necessity for wise use and saving, not only in food but in all other expenditures, the many undirected and overlapping efforts being made towards this end, all press for national direction and inspiration. While it would in many ways be desirable to await complete legislation establishing the Food Administration, it appears to me that so far as voluntary effort can be assembled we should not wait any longer, and therefore I would be very glad if you would proceed in these directions at once.

The women of the Nation are already earnestly seeking to do their part in this our greatest struggle for the maintenance of our national ideals, and in no direction can they so greatly assist as by enlisting in the service of the Food Administration and cheerfully accepting its direction and advice. By so doing they will increase the surplus of food available for our own Army and for export to the Allies. To provide adequate supplies for the coming year is of absolutely vital importance to the conduct of the war, and without a very conscientious elimination of waste and very strict economy in our food consumption we cannot hope to fulfill this primary duty.

I trust, therefore, that the women of the country will not only respond to your appeal and accept the pledge to the Food Administration which you are proposing, but that all men also who are engaged in the personal distribution of foods will coöperate with the same earnestness and in the same spirit. I give you full authority to undertake any steps necessary for the proper organization and stimulation of their efforts.

Cordially and sincerely, yours,

WOODROW WILSON.

"THIS IS A PEOPLE'S WAR"

FLAG DAY ADDRESS DELIVERED AT WASHINGTON, JUNE 14, 1917. FROM OFFICIAL GOVERNMENT PUBLICATION IN MR. WILSON'S FILES.

WE MEET to celebrate Flag Day because this flag which we honor and under which we serve is the emblem of our unity, our power, our thought and purpose as a Nation. It has no other character than that which we give it from generation to generation. The choices are ours. It floats in majestic silence above the hosts that execute those choices, whether in peace or in war. And yet, though silent, it speaks to us,— speaks to us of the past, of the men and women who went before us and of the records they wrote upon it. We celebrate the day of its birth; and from its birth until now it has witnessed a great history, has floated on high the symbol of great events, of a great plan of life worked out by a great people. We are about to carry it into battle, to lift it where it will draw the fire of our enemies. We are about to bid thousands, hundreds of thousands, it may be millions, of our men, the young, the strong, the capable men of the Nation, to go forth and die beneath it on fields of blood far away, —for what? For some unaccustomed thing? For something for which it has never sought the fire before? American armies were never before sent across the seas. Why are they sent now? For some new purpose, for which this great flag has never been carried before, or for some old, familiar, heroic purpose for which it has seen men, its own men, die on every battlefield upon which Americans have borne arms since the Revolution?

These are questions which must be answered. We are Americans. We in our turn serve America, and can serve her with no private purpose. We must use her

flag as she has always used it. We are accountable at
the bar of history and must plead in utter frankness
what purpose it is we seek to serve.

It is plain enough how we were forced into the war.
The extraordinary insults and aggressions of the Imperial German Government left us no self-respecting
choice but to take up arms in defense of our rights as
a free people and of our honor as a sovereign government. The military masters of Germany denied us the
right to be neutral. They filled our unsuspecting communities with vicious spies and conspirators and sought
to corrupt the opinion of our people in their own behalf.
When they found that they could not do that, their
agents diligently spread sedition amongst us and sought
to draw our own citizens from their allegiance,—and
some of those agents were men connected with the
official Embassy of the German Government itself here
in our own capital. They sought by violence to destroy
our industries and arrest our commerce. They tried to
incite Mexico to take up arms against us and to draw
Japan into a hostile alliance with her,—and that, not by
indirection, but by direct suggestion from the Foreign
Office in Berlin. They impudently denied us the use of
the high seas and repeatedly executed their threat that
they would send to their death any of our people who
ventured to approach the coasts of Europe. And many
of our own people were corrupted. Men began to look
upon their own neighbors with suspicion and to wonder
in their hot resentment and surprise whether there was
any community in which hostile intrigue did not lurk.
What great nation in such circumstances would not have
taken up arms? Much as we had desired peace, it was
denied us, and not of our own choice. This flag under
which we serve would have been dishonored had we
withheld our hand.

But that is only part of the story. We know now as
clearly as we knew before we were ourselves engaged
that we are not the enemies of the German people and

that they are not our enemies. They did not originate
or desire this hideous war or wish that we should be
drawn into it; and we are vaguely conscious that we are
fighting their cause, as they will some day see it, as well
as our own. They are themselves in the grip of the
same sinister power that has now at last stretched its
ugly talons out and drawn blood from us. The whole
world is at war because the whole world is in the grip
of that power and is trying out the great battle which
shall determine whether it is to be brought under its
mastery or fling itself free.

The war was begun by the military masters of Germany, who proved to be also the masters of Austria-
Hungary. These men have never regarded nations as
peoples, men, women, and children of like blood and
frame as themselves, for whom governments existed
and in whom governments had their life. They have
regarded them merely as serviceable organizations
which they could by force or intrigue bend or corrupt
to their own purpose. They have regarded the smaller
states, in particular, and the peoples who could be overwhelmed by force, as their natural tools and instruments
of domination. Their purpose has long been avowed.
The statesmen of other nations, to whom that purpose
was incredible, paid little attention; regarded what
German professors expounded in their classrooms and
German writers set forth to the world as the goal of
German policy as rather the dream of minds detached
from practical affairs, as preposterous private conceptions of German destiny, than as the actual plans of
responsible rulers; but the rulers of Germany themselves
knew all the while what concrete plans, what well-
advanced intrigues lay back of what the professors and
the writers were saying, and were glad to go forward
unmolested, filling the thrones of Balkan states with
German princes, putting German officers at the service
of Turkey to drill her armies and make interest with
her government, developing plans of sedition and re-

bellion in India and Egypt, setting their fires in Persia. The demands made by Austria upon Serbia were a mere single step in a plan which compassed Europe and Asia, from Berlin to Bagdad. They hoped those demands might not arouse Europe, but they meant to press them whether they did or not, for they thought themselves ready for the final issue of arms.

Their plan was to throw a broad belt of German military power and political control across the very center of Europe and beyond the Mediterranean into the heart of Asia; and Austria-Hungary was to be as much their tool and pawn as Serbia or Bulgaria or Turkey or the ponderous states of the East. Austria-Hungary, indeed, was to become part of the central German Empire, absorbed and dominated by the same forces and influences that had originally cemented the German states themselves. The dream had its heart at Berlin. It could have had a heart nowhere else! It rejected the idea of solidarity of race entirely. The choice of peoples played no part in it at all. It contemplated binding together racial and political units which could be kept together only by force,—Czechs, Magyars, Croats, Serbs, Rumanians, Turks, Armenians,—the proud states of Bohemia and Hungary, the stout little commonwealths of the Balkans, the indomitable Turks, the subtile peoples of the East. These peoples did not wish to be united. They ardently desired to direct their own affairs, would be satisfied only by undisputed independence. They could be kept quiet only by the presence or the constant threat of armed men. They would live under a common power only by sheer compulsion and await the day of revolution. But the German military statesmen had reckoned with all that and were ready to deal with it in their own way.

And they have actually carried the greater part of that amazing plan into execution! Look how things stand. Austria is at their mercy. It has acted, not upon its own initiative or upon the choice of its own people, but at Berlin's dictation ever since the war began. Its people now desire peace, but cannot have it until leave is granted from Berlin. The so-called Central Powers are in fact but a single Power. Serbia is at its mercy, should its hands be but for a moment freed. Bulgaria has consented to its will, and Rumania is overrun. The Turkish armies, which Germans trained, are serving Germany, certainly not themselves, and the guns of German warships lying in the harbor at Constantinople remind Turkish statesmen every day that they have no choice but to take their orders from Berlin. From Hamburg to the Persian Gulf the net is spread.

Is it not easy to understand the eagerness for peace that has been manifested from Berlin ever since the snare was set and sprung? Peace, peace, peace has been the talk of her Foreign Office for now a year and more; not peace upon her own initiative, but upon the initiative of the nations over which she now deems herself to hold the advantage. A little of the talk has been public, but most of it has been private. Through all sorts of channels it has come to me, and in all sorts of guises, but never with the terms disclosed which the German Government would be willing to accept. That government has other valuable pawns in its hands besides those I have mentioned. It still holds a valuable part of France, though with slowly relaxing grasp, and practically the whole of Belgium. Its armies press close upon Russia and overrun Poland at their will. It cannot go further; it dare not go back. It wishes to close its bargain before it is too late and it has little left to offer for the pound of flesh it will demand.

The military masters under whom Germany is bleeding see very clearly to what point Fate has brought them. If they fall back or are forced back an inch, their power both abroad and at home will fall to pieces like a house of cards. It is their power at home they are thinking about now more than their power abroad. It is that power which is trembling under their very feet; and deep fear has entered their hearts. They have but one chance to perpetuate their military power or even their controlling political influence. If they can secure peace now with the immense advantages still in their hands which they have up to this point apparently gained, they will have justified themselves before the German people: they will have gained by force what they promised to gain by it: an immense expansion of German power, an immense enlargement of German industrial and commercial opportunities. Their prestige will be secure, and with their prestige their political power. If they fail, their people will thrust them aside; a government accountable to the people themselves will be set up in Germany as it has been in England, in the United States, in France, and in all the great countries of the modern time except Germany. If they succeed they are safe and Germany and the world are undone; if they fail Germany is saved and the world will be at peace. If they succeed, America will fall within the menace. We and all the rest of the world must remain armed, as they will remain, and must make ready for the next step in their aggression; if they fail, the world may unite for peace and Germany may be of the union.

Do you not now understand the new intrigue, the intrigue for peace, and why the masters of Germany do not hesitate to use any agency that promises to effect their purpose, the deceit of the nations? Their present particular aim is to deceive all those who throughout the world stand for the rights of peoples and the self-government of nations; for they see what immense strength the forces of justice and of liberalism are gathering out of this war. They are employing liberals in their enterprise. They are using men, in Germany and without, as their spokesmen whom they have hitherto despised and oppressed, using them for their own destruction,—socialists, the leaders of labor, the thinkers they have hitherto sought to silence. Let them once succeed and these men, now their tools, will be ground to powder beneath the weight of the great military empire they will have set up; the revolutionists in Russia will be cut off from all succor or coöperation in western Europe and a counter revolution fostered and supported; Germany herself will lose her chance of freedom; and all Europe will arm for the next, the final struggle.

The sinister intrigue is being no less actively conducted in this country than in Russia and in every country in Europe to which the agents and dupes of the Imperial German Government can get access. That Government has many spokesmen here, in places high and low. They have learned discretion. They keep within the law. It is opinion they utter now, not sedition. They proclaim the liberal purposes of their masters; declare this a foreign war which can touch America with no danger to either her lands or her institutions; set England at the center of the stage and talk of her ambition to assert economic dominion throughout the world; appeal to our ancient tradition of isolation in the politics of the nations; and seek to undermine the Government with false professions of loyalty to its principles.

But they will make no headway. The false betray themselves always in every accent. It is only friends and partisans of the German Government whom we have already identified who utter these thinly disguised disloyalties. The facts are patent to all the world, and nowhere are they more plainly seen than in the United States, where we are accustomed to deal with facts and not with sophistries; and the great fact that stands out above all the rest is that this is a Peoples' War, a war for freedom and justice and self-government amongst all the nations of the world, a war to make the world safe for the peoples who live upon it and have made it their own, the German people themselves included; and that with us rests the choice to break through all these hypocrisies and patent cheats and masks of brute force and help set the world free, or else stand aside and let it be dominated a long age through by sheer weight of arms, and the arbitrary choices of self-constituted masters, by the nation which can maintain the biggest armies and the most irresistible armaments,—a power to which the world has afforded no parallel and in the face of which political freedom must wither and perish.

For us there is but one choice. We have made it. Woe be to the man or group of men that seeks to stand in our way in this day of high resolution when every principle we hold dearest is to be vindicated and made secure for the salvation of the nations. We are ready to plead at the bar of history, and our flag shall wear a new luster. Once more we shall make good with our lives and fortunes the great faith to which we were born, and a new glory shall shine in the face of our people.

SYMPATHY AND FRIENDSHIP TOWARD BELGIUM

REPLY TO THE ADDRESS OF BARON MONCHEUR DELIVER-
ING THE MESSAGE OF KING ALBERT OF BELGIUM,
JUNE 18, 1917, FROM "OFFICIAL BULLETIN," NO.
34.

IT IS with peculiar satisfaction that I receive from Your Excellency's hands the letter in which His Majesty the King of the Belgians is pleased to express his sentiments of friendship towards this country. May I not ask that Your Excellency be good enough to convey to His Majesty the assurances that his message has been received by the Government and people of the United States with deep appreciation and pleasure?

Your Excellency is good enough to express the thanks of the Belgian people for the participation of America in feeding the people of your stricken country. This work in which so many Americans have been enthusiastically engaged since the beginning of the war is one which has brought as much of benefit to them as to the innocent civilian population whom it was intended to aid. America engaged upon this work as being the only means, however inadequate, of expressing our deep and sincere admiration for the valiant nation that had gone forth unhesitatingly to meet the onslaughts of a ruthless enemy rather than sacrifice her honor and her self-respect. The American people have been able to understand and glory in the unflinching heroism of the Belgian people and their Sovereign, and there is not one among us who does not to-day welcome the opportunity of expressing to you our heartfelt sympathy and friendship, and our solemn determination that on the inevitable day of victory Belgium shall be restored to the place she has so richly won among the self-respecting and respected nations of the earth.

EXPLANATION OF THE POLICY OF EXPORT CONTROL

STATEMENT ISSUED JUNE 26, 1917. FROM "OFFICIAL BULLETIN," NO. 40.

IT IS important that the country should understand just what is intended in the control of exports which is about to be undertaken, and since the power is vested by the Congress in the President I can speak with authority concerning it. The Exports Council will be merely advisory to the President.

There will, of course, be no prohibition of exports. The normal course of trade will be interfered with as little as possible, and, so far as possible, only its abnormal course directed. The whole object will be to direct exports in such a way that they will go first and by preference where they are most needed and most immediately needed, and temporarily to withhold them, if necessary, where they can best be spared.

Our primary duty in the matter of foodstuffs and like necessaries is to see to it that the peoples associated with us in the war get as generous a proportion as possible of our surplus; but it will also be our wish and purpose to supply the neutral nations whose peoples depend upon us for such supplies as nearly in proportion to their need as the amount to be divided permits.

There will thus be little check put upon the volume of exports, and the prices obtained for them will not be affected by this regulation.

This policy will be carried out, not by prohibitive regulations, therefore, but by a system of licensing exports which will be as simply organized and administered as possible, so as to constitute no impediment to the normal flow of commerce. In brief, the free play of trade will not be arbitrarily interfered with; it will only be intelligently and systematically directed in the light of full information with regard to needs and market conditions throughout the world and the necessities of our people at home and our armies and the armies of our associates abroad.

The Government is taking, or has taken, steps to ascertain, for example, just what the available present supply of wheat and corn is remaining from the crops of last year; to learn from each of the countries exporting these foodstuffs from the United States what their purchases in this country now are, where they are stored, and what their needs are, in order that we may adjust things so far as possible to our own needs and free stocks; and this information is in course of being rapidly supplied.

The case of wheat and corn will serve as an illustration of all the rest of supplies of all kinds. Our trade can be successfully and profitably conducted now, the war pushed to a victorious issue, and the needs of our own people and of the other people with whom we are still free to trade efficiently met only by systematic direction; and that is what will be attempted.

WELCOME TO THE FIRST AMBASSADOR OF FREE RUSSIA

REPLY TO THE RUSSIAN AMBASSADOR, MR. BORIS BAKHMETEFF, UPON HIS PRESENTATION OF CREDENTIALS, JULY 5, 1917. FROM "OFFICIAL BULLETIN," NO. 48.

MR. AMBASSADOR, to the keen satisfaction which I derived from the fact that the Government of the United States was the first to welcome, by its official recognition, the new democracy of Russia to the family of free States is added the exceptional pleasure which I experience in now receiving from your hand the letters whereby the provisional Government of Russia accredits you as its ambassador extraordinary and plenipotentiary to the United States and in according to you formal recognition as the first ambassador of free Russia to this country.

For the people of Russia the people of the United States have ever entertained friendly feelings, which have now been greatly deepened by the knowledge that, actuated by the same lofty motives, the two Governments and peoples are coöperating to bring to a successful termination the conflict now raging for human liberty and a universal acknowledgment of those principles of right and justice which should direct all Governments. I feel convinced that when this happy day shall come no small share of the credit will be due to the devoted people of Russia, who, overcoming disloyalty from within and intrigue from without, remain steadfast to the cause.

The mission which it was my pleasure to send to Russia has already assured the provisional Government that in this momentous struggle and in the problems that confront and will confront the free Government of Russia that Government may count on the steadfast friendship of the Government of the United States and its constant coöperation in all desired appropriate directions.

It only remains for me to give expression to my admiration of the way in which the provisional Government of Russia is meeting all requirements, to my entire sympathy with them in their noble object to insure to the people of Russia the blessings of freedom and of equal rights and opportunity, and to my faith that through their efforts Russia will assume her rightful place among the great free nations of the world.

"AMELIORATION OF FOOD CONDITIONS"

STATEMENT ACCOMPANYING THE FIRST EMBARGO PROC-
LAMATION, JULY 9. 1917.   FROM ORIGINAL COPY
IN MR. WILSON'S FILES.

IN CONTROLLING by license the export of certain
indispensable commodities from the United States,
the Government has first and chiefly in view the amelioration of the food conditions which have arisen or are
likely to arise in our own country before new crops are
harvested.   Not only is the conservation of our prime
food and fodder supplies a matter which vitally concerns our own people, but the retention of an adequate
supply of raw materials is essential to our program· of
military and naval construction and the continuance of
our necessary domestic activities.   We shall, therefore,
similarly safeguard all our fundamental supplies.

It is obviously the duty of the United States, in liberating any surplus products over and above our own
domestic needs, to consider first the necessities of all the
nations engaged in war against the Central Empires.
As to neutral nations, however, we also recognize our
duty.   The Government does not wish to hamper them.
On the contrary, it wishes and intends, by all fair and
equitable means, to coöperate with them in their difficult
task of adding from our available surpluses to their
own domestic supply and of meeting their pressing
necessities or deficits.   In considering the deficits of food
supplies the Government means only to fulfill its obvious
obligation to assure itself that neutrals are husbanding
their own resources and that our supplies will not become available, either directly or indirectly, to feed the
enemy.

"PATRIOTISM LEAVES PROFITS OUT OF THE QUESTION"

ADDRESS TO MINE OPERATORS AND MANUFACTURERS, JULY 12, 1917. FROM THE "CONGRESSIONAL RECORD," VOL. 55, PP. 4995-4996.

M Y FELLOW COUNTRYMEN:

The Government is about to attempt to determine the prices at which it will ask you henceforth to furnish various supplies which are necessary for the prosecution of the war and various materials which will be needed in the industries by which the war must be sustained.

We shall, of course, try to determine them justly and to the best advantage of the Nation as a whole; but justice is easier to speak of than to arrive at, and there are some considerations which I hope we shall all keep steadily in mind while this particular problem of justice is being worked out. I therefore take the liberty of stating very candidly my own view of the situation and of the principles which should guide both the Government and mine-owners and manufacturers of the country in this difficult matter.

A just price must, of course, be paid for everything the Government buys. By a just price I mean a price which will sustain the industries concerned in a high state of efficiency, provide a living for those who conduct them, enable them to pay good wages, and make possible expansions of their enterprises which will from time to time become necessary as the stupendous undertakings of this great war develop.

We could not wisely or reasonably do less than pay such prices. They are necessary for the maintenance and development of industry; and the maintenance and development of industry are necessary for the great task we have in hand. But I trust that we shall not surround the matter with a mist of sentiment. Facts are our masters now. We ought not to put the acceptance of such prices on the ground of patriotism.

Patriotism has nothing to do with profits in a case like this. Patriotism and profits ought never in the present circumstances to be mentioned together.

It is perfectly proper to discuss profits as a matter of business, with a view to maintaining the integrity of capital and the efficiency of labor in these tragical months when the liberty of free men everywhere and of industry itself trembles in the balance; but it would be absurd to discuss them as a motive for helping to serve and save our country. Patriotism leaves profits out of the question.

In these days of our supreme trial, when we are sending hundreds of thousands of our young men across the seas to serve a great cause, no true man who stays behind to work for them and sustain them by his labor will ask himself what he is personally going to make out of that labor.

No true patriot will permit himself to take toll of their heroism in money or seek to grow rich by the shedding of their blood. He will give as freely and with as unstinted self-sacrifice as they. When they are giving their lives will he not give at least his money?

I hear it insisted that more than a just price, more than a price that will sustain our industries, must be paid; that it is necessary to pay very liberal and unusual profits in order to "stimulate production"; that nothing but pecuniary rewards will do it—rewards paid in money, not in the mere liberation of the world.

I take it for granted that those who argue thus do not stop to think what that means. Do they mean that you must be paid, must be bribed, to make your contribution, a contribution that costs you neither a drop of blood nor a tear, when the whole world is in travail and men everywhere depend upon and call to you to bring them out of bondage and make the world a fit place to live in again, amidst peace and justice?

Do they mean that you will exact a price, drive a bargain, with the men who are enduring the agony of this war on the battlefield, in the trenches, amidst the lurking dangers of the sea, or with the bereaved women and the pitiful children, before you will come forward to do your duty and give some part of your life, in easy, peaceful fashion, for the things we are fighting for, the things we have pledged our fortunes, our lives, our sacred honor to vindicate and defend—liberty and justice and fair dealing and the peace of nations? Of course you will not.

It is inconceivable. Your patriotism is of the same self-denying stuff as the patriotism of the men dead or maimed on the fields of France, or else it is no patriotism at all.

Let us never speak, then, of profits and of patriotism in the same sentence, but face facts and meet them.

Let us do sound business, but not in the midst of a mist. Many a grievous burden of taxation will be laid on this Nation, in this generation and in the next, to pay for this war. Let us see to it that for every dollar that is taken from the people's pockets it shall be possible to obtain a dollar's worth of the sound stuffs they need.

Let us turn for a moment to the ship-owners of the United States, and the other ocean carriers whose example they have followed, and ask them if they realize what obstacles, what almost insuperable obstacles, they have been putting in the way of the successful prosecution of this war by the ocean freight rates they have been exacting.

They are doing everything that high freight charges can do to make the war a failure, to make it impossible. I do not say that they realize this or intend it.

The thing has happened naturally enough, because the commercial processes which we are content to see operate in ordinary times have without sufficient thought been continued into a period where they have no proper place.

I am not questioning motives. I am merely stating a fact and stating it in order that attention may be fixed upon it. The fact is that those who have fixed war freight rates have taken the most effective means in their power to defeat the armies engaged against Germany.

When they realize this we may, I take it for granted, count upon them to reconsider the whole matter. It is high time. Their extra hazards are covered by war-risk insurance.

I know and you know what response to this great challenge of duty and of opportunity the Nation will expect of you; and I know what response you will make.

Those who do not respond, who do not respond in the spirit of those who have gone to give their lives for us on bloody fields far away, may safely be left to be dealt with by opinion and the law, for the law must, of course, command these things.

I am dealing with the matter thus publicly and frankly, not because I have any doubt or fear as to the result, but only in order that in all our thinking and in all our dealings with one another we may move in a perfectly clear air of mutual understanding.

And there is something more that we must add to our thinking. The public is now as much part of the Government as are the Army and Navy themselves; the whole people in all their activities are now mobilized and in service for the accomplishment of the Nation's task in this war; it is in such circumstances impossible justly to distinguish between industrial purchases made by the Government and industrial purchases made by the managers of individual industries; and it is just as much our duty to sustain the industries of the country, all the industries that contribute to its life, as it is to sustain our forces in the field and on sea.

We must make the prices to the public the same as the prices to the Government. Prices mean the same thing everywhere now; they mean the efficiency or the inefficiency of the Nation, whether it is the Government that pays them or not. They mean victory or defeat.

They mean that America will win her place once for all among the foremost free nations of the world or that she will sink to defeat and become a second-rate power alike in thought and in action. This is a day of her reckoning, and every man among us must personally face that reckoning along with her.

The case needs no arguing. I assume that I am only expressing your own thoughts—what must be in the mind of every true man when he faces the tragedy and the solemn glory of the present war for the emancipation of mankind.

I summon you to a great duty, a great privilege, a shining dignity and distinction.

I shall expect every man who is not a slacker to be at my side throughout this great enterprise. In it no man can win honor who thinks of himself.

GREETING TO FRANCE ON BASTILE DAY

MESSAGE TO FRANCE THROUGH PRESIDENT POINCARÉ, ON JULY 16, 1917. FROM "OFFICIAL·BULLETIN," NO. 56

ON THIS anniversary of the birth of democracy in France I offer on behalf of my countrymen and on my own behalf fraternal greeting as befits the strong ties that unite our peoples, who to-day stand shoulder to shoulder in defense of liberty in testimony of the steadfast purpose of our two countries to achieve victory for the sublime cause of the rights of the people against oppression. The lesson of the Bastile is not lost to the world of free peoples. May the day be near when on the ruins of the dark stronghold of unbridled power and conscienceless autocracy a nobler structure, upbuilt, like your own great republic, on the eternal foundations of peace and right, shall arise to gladden an enfranchised world.

AN APPEAL TO THE WOMEN OF THE NATION

LETTER TO SECRETARY OF AGRICULTURE D. F. HOUSTON
AND THE NATIONAL VOLUNTEER COMMITTEE ON
THE PRESERVING OF FRUIT AND GARDEN PROD-
UCTS, JULY 28, 1917. FROM "OFFICIAL BULLE-
TIN," NO. 68.

M R. SECRETARY AND GENTLEMEN OF THE COMMITTEE:

I very earnestly desire to commend your plans and to second your efforts to secure the conservation of surpluses of perishable food products. Out of the depths of their patriotism the farmers of the Nation gave an immediate and effective response to my appeal to increase production. Providence favored them, and we have not only the prospect of increased crops of a number of staples, but also the certainty of a large production of fruits and vegetables.

But increased production, important as it is, is only a part of the solution of the food problem. It is of the first importance that we take care of what has been raised and make it available for consumption. This task is of peculiar urgency with reference to our perishable farm products. It is essential not only that adequate measures be taken to secure their conservation, but also that the Department of Agriculture redouble its efforts to assist producers in the matter of marketing.

I am informed that in many sections in which fruits and vegetables have been produced in abundance the people already are canning and drying them in large quantities. But we should be content with nothing short of the perfection of organization and should be unwilling that anything should be lost. In this hour of peril

I am concerned, as I know you are, with the necessity of avoiding waste. Every bushel of potatoes properly stored, every pound of vegetables properly put by for future use, every jar of fruit preserved, add that much to our insurance of victory, add that much to hasten the end of this conflict. To win we must have maximum efficiency in all directions. We cannot win without complete and effective concentration of all our efforts.

We can all aid by increasing our consumption of perishable products. Such of them as we can efficiently utilize we must utilize, and by so doing relieve the strain on our store of staples. We must aim to consume these things locally so far as possible and thus relieve the pressure on transportation agencies, freeing them for the more efficient handling of products required for military purposes. What we cannot presently consume we must conserve.

The service we are asking the people to render in this matter is a public service. It is one primarily for the household. Upon the housewife much of the burden of the task will fall. I join you in your appeal to the women of the Nation, whether living in a city, town, or country, to devote their time, so far as it may be feasible and necessary, to the performance of this very essential work. Among them some will be found who are fitted by experience to teach others, and they will put their knowledge whole-heartedly at the service of their neighbors.

I am sure that we may confidently count upon the coöperation of the editors of the Nation in disseminating the necessary information. I am equally certain that the Governors and the food committees appointed by them in the States in which this problem is urgent will leave nothing undone to attack it promptly and to assist in solving it.

Faithfully yours,
WOODROW WILSON.

"LEAVE OUT OF YOUR VOCABULARY THE WORD 'PRUDENT'"

ADDRESS TO THE OFFICERS OF THE ATLANTIC FLEET
AUGUST 11, 1917.[1] FROM OFFICIAL GOVERNMENT
PUBLICATION IN MR. WILSON'S FILES

I HAVE not come here with malice prepense to make a speech, but I have come here to have a look at you and to say some things that perhaps may be intimately said and, even though the company is large, said in confidence. Of course, the whole circumstance of the modern time is extraordinary and I feel that just because the circumstances are extraordinary there is an opportunity to see to it that the action is extraordinary. One of the deprivations which any man in authority experiences is that he cannot come into constant and intimate touch with the men with whom he is associated and necessarily associated in action.

Most of my life has been spent in contact with young men and, though I would not admit it to them at the time, I have learned a great deal more from them than they ever learned from me. I have had most of my thinking stimulated by questions being put to me which I could not answer, and I have had a great many of my preconceived conceptions absolutely destroyed by men who had not given half the study to the subject that I myself had given. The fact of the matter is that almost every profession is pushed forward by the men who do not belong to it and know nothing about it, because they ask the ignorant questions which it would not occur to the professional man to ask at all; he supposes that they have been answered, whereas it may be that most

---

[1] The President went to sea in the *Mayflower*, boarded an American dreadnaught, and talked to the officers like "a football coach to his team between the halves."

82

of them had not been answered at all. The naïveté of the point of view, the whole approach of the mind that has had nothing to do with the question, creates an entirely different atmosphere. There is many a question asked you about the Navy which seems to you so simple-minded when you hear it that you laugh, and then you find you cannot answer it. It never occurred to you that anybody could ask that question before, it is so simple.

Now, the point that is constantly in my mind, gentlemen, is this: This is an unprecedented war and, therefore, it is a war in one sense for amateurs. Nobody ever before conducted a war like this and therefore nobody can pretend to be a professional in a war like this. Here are two great navies, not to speak of the others associated with us, our own and the British, outnumbering by a very great margin the navy to which we are opposed, and yet casting about for a way in which to use our superiority and our strength, because of the novelty of the instruments used, because of the unprecedented character of the war, because, as I said just now, nobody ever before fought a war like this, in the way that this is being fought at sea—or on land either for that matter. The experienced soldier,—experienced in previous wars,—is a back number so far as his experience is concerned; not so far as his intelligence is concerned. His experience does not count, because he never fought a war as this is being fought, and therefore he is an amateur along with the rest of us. Now, somebody has got to think this war out. Somebody has got to think out the way not only to fight the submarine, but to do something different from what we are doing.

We are hunting hornets all over the farm and letting the nest alone. None of us knows how to go to the nest and crush it, and yet I despair of hunting for hornets all over the sea when I know where the nest is and know that the nest is breeding hornets as fast as I can find them. I am willing for my part, and I know you

are willing because I know the stuff you are made of,—
I am willing to sacrifice half the navy Great Britain and
we together have to crush that nest, because if we crush
it, the war is won. I have come here to say that I do
not care where it comes from, I do not care whether
it comes from the youngest officer or the oldest, but I
want the officers of this Navy to have the distinction
of saying how this war is going to be won. The Secretary of the Navy and I have just been talking over plans
for putting the planning machinery of the Navy at the
disposal of the brains of the Navy and not stopping to
ask what rank that brains has, because, as I have said
before and want to repeat, so far as experience in this
kind of war is concerned we are all of the same rank.
I am not saying that I do not expect the Admirals to
tell us what to do, but I am saying that I want the
youngest and most modest youngster in the service to
tell us what we ought to do if he knows what it is. I
am willing to make any sacrifice for that. I mean any
sacrifice of time or anything else. I am ready to put
myself at the disposal of any officer in the Navy who
thinks he knows how to run this war. I will not undertake to tell you whether he does or not, because I know
I cannot, but I will undertake to put him in communication with those who can find out whether his idea will
work or not. I have the authority to do that and I will
do it with the greatest pleasure.

The idea that is in my mind all the time is that we
are comrades in this thing. I was talking the other
day with some commercial men about certain questions
which seemed to affect their material interest in this
war, and I said, "I can't imagine a man thinking about
those things. If we don't win this war, your material
interest won't make any difference. The prices you are
charging are a matter of indifference with regard to the
results of this war because if we don't win it, you will
not have the chance to charge any prices, and I can't
imagine a man in the present circumstances of the world

sitting down and thinking about his own interest or the interest of anybody personally associated with him as compared with the interest of the world." I cannot say it too often to any audience, we are fighting a thing, not a people. The most extraordinary circumstance of modern history is the way in which the German people have been subordinated to the German system of authority, and how they have accepted their thinking from authority as well as their action from authority. Now, we do not intend to let that method of action and of thinking be imposed upon the rest of the world. Knowing as some of us do the fine quality of the German people, we are sorry that it was ever imposed upon them and we are anxious to see that they have their glad emancipation, but we intend to see to it that no other people suffers a like limitation and subordination. We went into this war because this system touched us. These people that stopped at nothing paid no attention to our rights, destroyed the lives of our people, invaded the dignity of our sovereignty, tried to make interest against us in the minds of our own people, and the thing was intolerable. We had to strike, but thank God we were striking not only for ourselves but for everybody else that loves liberty under God's heaven, and therefore we are in some peculiar sense the trustees of liberty.

I wish that I could think and had the brains to think in the terms of marine warfare, because I would feel then that I was figuring out the future history of the political freedom of mankind. I do not see how any man can look at the flag of the United States and fail having his mind crowded with reminiscences of the number of unselfish men, seeking no object of their own, the advantage of no dynasty, the advantage of no group of privileged people, but the advantage of his fellow men, who have died under the folds of that beautiful emblem. I wonder if men who do die under it realize the distinction they have. There is no comparison between dying in your bed in quiet times for nothing in particular and dying under that emblem of the might and destiny and pride of a great free people. There is distinction in the privilege and I for my part am sorry to play so peaceful a part in the business as I myself am obliged to play, and I conceive it a privilege to come and look at you men who have the other thing to do and ask you to come and tell me or tell anybody you want to tell how this thing can be better done; and we will thank God that we have got men of originative brains among us.

We have got to throw tradition to the wind. As I have said, gentlemen, I take it for granted that nothing that I say here will be repeated and therefore I am going to say this: Every time we have suggested anything to the British Admiralty the reply has come back that virtually amounted to this, that it had never been done that way, and I felt like saying, "Well, nothing was ever done so systematically as nothing is being done now. Therefore, I should like to see something unusual happen, something that was never done before; and inasmuch as the things that are being done to you were never done before, don't you think it is worth while to try something that was never done before against those who are doing them to you." There is no other way to win, and the whole principle of this war is the kind of thing that ought to hearten and stimulate America. America has always boasted that she could find men to do anything. She is the prize amateur nation of the world. Germany is the prize professional nation of the world. Now, when it comes to doing new things and doing them well, I will back the amateur against the professional every time, because the professional does it out of the book and the amateur does it with his eyes open upon a new world and with a new set of circumstances. He knows so little about it that he is fool enough to try the right thing. The men that do not know the danger are the rashest men, and I have several times ventured to make this suggestion to the men about me in both arms of the service: Please leave out of your vocabulary altogether the word "prudent." Do not stop to think about what is prudent for a moment. Do the thing that is audacious to the utmost point of risk and daring, because that is exactly the thing that the other side does not understand, and you will win by the audacity of method when you cannot win by circumspection and prudence. I think that there are willing ears to hear this in the American Navy and the American Army because that is the kind of folks we are. We get tired of the old ways and covet the new ones.

So, gentlemen, besides coming down here to give you my personal greeting and to say how absolutely I rely on you and believe in you, I have come down here to say also that I depend on you, depend on you for brains as well as training and courage and discipline. You are doing your job admirably, the job that you have been taught to do; now let us do something that we were never taught to do and do it just as well as we are doing the older and more habitual things, and do not let anybody ever put one thought of discouragement into your minds. I do not know what is the matter with the newspapers of the United States! I suppose they have to vary the tune from time to time just to relieve their minds, but every now and then a wave of the most absurd discouragement and pessimism goes through the country and we hear nothing except of the unusual advantages and equipment and sagacity and preparation and all the other wonderful things of the German Army and Navy. My comment is always the very familiar comment, "Rats!" They are working under infinite disadvantages. They not only have no more brains than we have, but they have a different and less serviceable kind of brains than we have, if we will use the brains we have got. I am not discouraged for a moment, particularly because we have not even begun and, without saying anything in disparagement of those with whom we are associated in the war, I do expect things to begin when we begin. If they do not, American history will have changed its course; the American Army and Navy will have changed their character. There will have to come a new tradition into a service which does not do new and audacious and successful things.

I am very much obliged to you for having given me this opportunity to see you and I hope you will also give me the pleasure of shaking hands with each one of you. If you ever want me again for anything in particular—because I am a busy man and cannot come for anything that is not particular—send for me and I will come.

THE BIBLE

LETTER TO THE SOLDIERS AND SAILORS OF THE UNITED
STATES, AUGUST, 1917. FROM THE "CONGRES-
SIONAL RECORD," VOL. 55, P. 6041.

THE Bible is the word of life. I beg that you will read it and find this out for yourselves—read, not little snatches here and there, but long passages that will really be the road to the heart of it. You will find it full of real men and women not only, but also of things you have wondered about and been troubled about all your life, as men have been always; and the more you read the more it will become plain to you what things are worth while and what are not, what things make men happy—loyalty, right dealings, speaking the truth, readiness to give everything for what they think their duty, and, most of all, the wish that they may have the real approval of the Christ, who gave everything for them—and the things that are guaranteed to make men unhappy—selfishness, cowardice, greed, and everything that is low and mean. When you have read the Bible you will know that it is the Word of God, because you will have found it the key to your own heart, your own happiness, and your own duty.

WOODROW WILSON.

MOBILIZING THE SCHOOLS

LETTER TO SCHOOL OFFICERS OF THE UNITED STATES, AUGUST 23, 1917. FROM "OFFICIAL BULLETIN" NO. 121.

TO SCHOOL OFFICERS:

The war is bringing to the minds of our people a new appreciation of the problems of national life and a deeper understanding of the meaning and aims of democracy. Matters which heretofore have seemed commonplace and trivial are seen in a truer light. The urgent demand for the production and proper distribution of food and other national resources has made us aware of the close dependence of individual on individual and nation on nation. The effort to keep up social and industrial organizations in spite of the withdrawal of men for the Army has revealed the extent to which modern life has become complex and specialized.

These and other lessons of the war must be learned quickly if we are intelligently and successfully to defend our institutions. When the war is over we must apply the wisdom which we have acquired in purging and ennobling the life of the world.

In these vital tasks of acquiring a broader view of human possibilities the common school must have a large part. I urge that teachers and other school officers increase materially the time and attention devoted to instruction bearing directly on the problems of community and national life.

Such a plea is in no way foreign to the spirit of American public education or of existing practices. Nor is it a plea for a temporary enlargement of the school program appropriate merely to the period of the war. It is a plea for a realization in public education of the new emphasis which the war has given to the ideals of democracy and to the broader conceptions of national life.

In order that there may be definite material at hand with which the schools may at once expand their teaching, I have asked Mr. Hoover and Commissioner Claxton to organize the proper agencies for the preparation and distribution of suitable lessons for the elementary grades and for the high-school classes. Lessons thus suggested will serve the double purpose of illustrating in a concrete way what can be undertaken in the schools and of stimulating teachers in all parts of the country to formulate new and appropriate materials drawn directly from the communities in which they live.

Sincerely yours,

WOODROW WILSON.

WELCOME TO THE AMBASSADOR FROM JAPAN

REPLY TO THE REMARKS OF VISCOUNT ISHII UPON HIS PRESENTATION OF CREDENTIALS, AUGUST 23, 1917. FROM "OFFICIAL BULLETIN," NO. 90.

M R. AMBASSADOR:
It is with a sense of deep satisfaction that I receive from your hands the letters whereby you are accredited as the ambassador extraordinary and plenipotentiary of Japan on special mission to the United States. It is a pleasure to accept through you from your Imperial Sovereign congratulations on the entrance of the United States into the great conflict which is now raging.

The present struggle is especially characterized by the development of the spirit of coöperation throughout the greater part of the world for the maintenance of the rights of nations and the liberties of individuals. I assure Your Excellency that, standing as our countries now do, associated in this great struggle for the vindication of justice, there will be developed those closer ties of fellowship which must come from the mutual sacrifice of life and property. May the efforts now being exerted by an indignant humanity lead, at the proper time, to the complete establishment of justice and to a peace which will be both permanent and serene.

I trust that Your Excellency will find your sojourn among us most agreeable and I should be gratified if you would be so good as to make known to His Imperial Majesty my best wishes for his welfare, for that of your wonderful country, and for the happiness of its people.

I am most happy to accord you recognition in your high capacity.

REPLY TO THE POPE'S PEACE PROPOSAL

REPLY TO THE COMMUNICATION OF THE POPE TO THE
BELLIGERENT GOVERNMENTS, AUGUST 27, 1917.
FROM ORIGINAL COPY IN MR. WILSON'S FILES.

TO HIS HOLINESS BENEDICTUS XV, POPE.
In acknowledgment of the communication of
Your Holiness to the belligerent peoples, dated August
1, 1917, the President of the United States requests me
to transmit the following reply:

Every heart that has not been blinded and hardened
by this terrible war must be touched by this moving appeal of His Holiness the Pope, must feel the dignity and
force of the humane and generous motives which
prompted it, and must fervently wish that we might take
the path of peace he so persuasively points out. But it
would be folly to take it if it does not in fact lead to
the goal he proposes. Our response must be based upon
the stern facts and upon nothing else. It is not a mere
cessation of arms he desires; it is a stable and enduring
peace. This agony must not be gone through with
again, and it must be a matter of very sober judgment
what will insure us against it.

His Holiness in substance proposes that we return to
the *status quo ante bellum,* and that then there be a general condonation, disarmament, and a concert of
nations based upon an acceptance of the principle of
arbitration; that by a similar concert freedom of the
seas be established; and that the territorial claims of
France and Italy, the perplexing problems of the Balkan states, and the restitution of Poland be left to such
conciliatory adjustments as may be possible in the new
temper of such a peace, due regard being paid to the
aspirations of the peoples whose political fortunes and
affiliations will be involved.

It is manifest that no part of this program can be successfully carried out unless the restitution of the *status quo ante* furnishes a firm and satisfactory basis for it. The object of this war is to deliver the free peoples of the world from the menace and the actual power of a vast military establishment controlled by an irresponsible government which, having secretly planned to dominate the world, proceeded to carry the plan out without regard either to the sacred obligations of treaty or the long-established practices and long-cherished principles of international action and honor; which chose its own time for the war; delivered its blow fiercely and suddenly; stopped at no barrier either of law or of mercy; swept a whole continent within the tide of blood, —not the blood of soldiers only, but the blood of innocent women and children also and of the helpless poor; and now stands balked but not defeated, the enemy of four-fifths of the world. This power is not the German people. It is the ruthless master of the German people. It is no business of ours how that great people came under its control or submitted with temporary zest to the domination of its purpose; but it is our business to see to it that the history of the rest of the world is no longer left to its handling.

To deal with such a power by way of peace upon the plan proposed by His Holiness the Pope would, so far as we can see, involve a recuperation of its strength and a renewal of its policy; would make it necessary to create a permanent hostile combination of nations against the German people, who are its instruments; and would result in abandoning the new-born Russia to the intrigue, the manifold subtle interference, and the certain counter-revolution which would be attempted by all the malign influences to which the German Government has of late accustomed the world. Can peace be based upon a restitution of its power or upon any word of honor it could pledge in a treaty of settlement and accommodation?

Responsible statesmen must now everywhere see, if they never saw before, that no peace can rest securely upon political or economic restrictions meant to benefit some nations and cripple or embarrass others, upon vindictive action of any sort, or any kind of revenge or deliberate injury. The American people have suffered intolerable wrongs at the hands of the Imperial German Government, but they desire no reprisal upon the German people, who have themselves suffered all things in this war, which they did not choose. They believe that peace should rest upon the rights of peoples, not the rights of governments,—the rights of peoples great or small, weak or powerful,—their equal right to freedom and security and self-government and to a participation upon fair terms in the economic opportunities of the world,—the German people of course included, if they will accept equality and not seek domination.

The test, therefore, of every plan of peace is this: Is it based upon the faith of all the peoples involved or merely upon the word of an ambitious and intriguing government, on the one hand, and of a group of free peoples, on the other? This is a test which goes to the root of the matter; and it is the test which must be applied.

The purposes of the United States in this war are known to the whole world,—to every people to whom the truth has been permitted to come. They do not need to be stated again. We seek no material advantage of any kind. We believe that the intolerable wrongs done in this war by the furious and brutal power of the Imperial German Government ought to be repaired, but not at the expense of the sovereignty of any people, —rather in vindication of the sovereignty both of those that are weak and those that are strong. Punitive damages, the dismemberment of empires, the establishment of selfish and exclusive economic leagues, we deem inexpedient and in the end worse than futile, no proper basis for a peace of any kind, least of all for an enduring peace.   That must be based upon justice and fairness and the common rights of mankind.

We cannot take the word of the present rulers of Germany as a guarantee of anything that is to endure, unless explicitly supported by such conclusive evidences of the will and purpose of the German people themselves as the other peoples of the world would be justified in accepting.   Without such guarantees treaties of settlement, agreements for disarmament, covenants to set up arbitration in the place of force, territorial adjustments, reconstitutions of small nations, if made with the German Government, no man, no nation could now depend on.   We must await some new evidence of the purposes of the great peoples of the Central Empires.   God grant it may be given soon and in a way to restore the confidence of all peoples everywhere in the faith of nations and the possibility of a covenanted peace.

EXPORT CONTROL

STATEMENT ACCOMPANYING EXPORT CONTROL PROCLA-
MATION, AUGUST 27, 1917. FROM "OFFICIAL BUL-
LETIN," NO. 93.

THE purpose and effect of this proclamation is not export prohibition, but merely export control. It is not the intention to interfere unnecessarily with our foreign trade; but our own domestic needs must be adequately safeguarded and there is the added duty of meeting the necessities of all the nations at war with the Imperial German Government. After these needs are met it is our wish and intention to minister to the needs of the neutral nations as far as our resources permit. This task will be discharged without other than the very proper qualification that the liberation of our surplus products shall not be made the occasion of benefit to the enemy, either directly or indirectly.

The two lists have been prepared in the interests of facility and expediency. The first list, applicable to the enemy and his allies and to the neutral countries of Europe, brings under control practically all articles of commerce, while the second list, applicable to all the other countries of the world makes only a few additions to the list of commodities controlled by the proclamation of July 9, 1917. It is obvious that a closer supervision and control of exports is necessary with respect to those European neutrals within the sphere of hostilities than is required for those countries farther removed.

The establishment of these distinctions will simplify the administrative processes and enable us to continue our policy of minimizing the interruption of trade.

No licenses will be necessary for the exportation of coin, bullion, currency, and evidences of indebtedness until required by regulations to be promulgated by the Secretary of the Treasury in his discretion.

ASSURANCE OF ASSISTANCE TO RUSSIA

CABLEGRAM TO THE PRESIDENT OF THE NATIONAL
COUNCIL ASSEMBLY AT MOSCOW, AUGUST 27, 1917
FROM "OFFICIAL BULLETIN," NO. 92.

I TAKE the liberty to send to the members of the great council now meeting in Moscow the cordial greetings of their friends, the people of the United States, to express their confidence in the ultimate triumph of ideals of democracy and self-government against all enemies within and without, and to give their renewed assurance of every material and moral assistance they can extend to the Government of Russia in the promotion of the common cause in which the two nations are unselfishly united.

WOODROW WILSON.

A FAIR PRICE FOR WHEAT

STATEMENT ANNOUNCING THE PRICE OF WHEAT "FOR ALL TRANSACTIONS THROUGHOUT THE PRESENT CROP YEAR," AUGUST 30, 1917. FROM "OFFICIAL BULLETIN," NO. 96.

SECTION 11 of the food act provides, among other things, for the purchase and sale of wheat and flour by the Government, and appropriates money for the purpose. The purchase of wheat and flour for our allies, and to a considerable degree for neutral countries also, has been placed under the control of the Food Administration. I have appointed a committee to determine a fair price to be paid in Government purchases. The price now recommended by that committee—$2.20 per bushel at Chicago for the basic grade—will be rigidly adhered to by the Food Administration.

It is the hope and expectation of the Food Administration, and my own also, that this step will at once stabilize and keep within moderate bounds the price of wheat for all transactions throughout the present crop year, and in consequence the prices of flour and bread also. The food act has given large powers for the control of storage and exchange operations, and these powers will be fully exercised. An inevitable consequence will be that financial dealings cannot follow their usual course. Whatever the advantages and disadvantages of the ordinary machinery of trade, it cannot function well under such disturbed and abnormal conditions as now exist. In its place the Food Administration now fixes for its purchases a fair price, as recommended unanimously by a committee representative of all interests and all sections, and believes that thereby it will eliminate speculation, make possible the conduct of every operation in the full light of day, maintain the publicly stated price for all, and, through economies made possible by stabilization and control, better the position of consumers also.

Mr. Hoover, at his express wish, has taken no part in the deliberations of the committee on whose recommendation I determine the Government's fair price, nor has he in any way intimated an opinion regarding that price.

"GOD KEEP AND GUIDE YOU"

MESSAGE TO THE SOLDIERS OF THE NATIONAL ARMY, SEPTEMBER 4, 1917. FROM COPY IN MR. WILSON'S FILES.

YOU are undertaking a great duty. The heart of the whole country is with you. Everything that you do will be watched with the deepest interest and with the deepest solicitude not only by those who are near and dear to you, but by the whole Nation besides. For this great war draws us all closer together, makes us all comrades and brothers, as all true Americans felt themselves to be when we first made good our national independence. The eyes of all the world will be upon you, because you are in some special sense the soldiers of freedom.

Let it be your pride, therefore, to show all men everywhere not only what good soldiers you are, but also what good men you are, keeping yourselves fit and straight in everything, and pure and clean through and through. Let us set for ourselves a standard so high that it will be a glory to live up to it, and then let us live up to it and add a new laurel to the crown of America. My affectionate confidence goes with you in every battle and every test. God keep and guide you!

APPEAL FOR THE JUNIOR RED CROSS

PROCLAMATION TO THE SCHOOL CHILDREN OF THE
    UNITED STATES, DATED SEPTEMBER 5, 1917, IS-
... SUED SEPTEMBER 15, 1917. FROM ORIGINAL COPY
    IN MR. WILSON'S FILES.

THE President of the United States is also President of the American Red Cross. It is from these offices joined in one that I write you a word of greeting at this time when so many of you are beginning the school year.

The American Red Cross has just prepared a Junior Membership with School Activities in which every pupil in the United States can find a chance to serve our country. The school is the natural center of your life. Through it you can best work in the great cause of freedom to which we have all pledged ourselves.

Our Junior Red Cross will bring to you opportunities of service to your community and to other communities all over the world and guide your service with high and religious ideals. It will teach you how to save in order that suffering children elsewhere may have the chance to live. It will teach you how to prepare some of the supplies which wounded soldiers and homeless families lack. It will send to you through the Red Cross Bulletins the thrilling stories of relief and rescue. And best of all, more perfectly than through any of your other school lessons, you will learn by doing these kind things under your teacher's direction to be the future good citizens of this great country which we all love.

And I commend to all school teachers in the country the simple plan which the American Red Cross has worked out to provide for your coöperation, knowing as I do that school children will give their best service under the direct guidance and instruction of their teachers. Is not this perhaps the chance for which you have been looking to give your time and efforts in some measure to meet our national needs?

COMMENDATION OF THE WORK OF CONGRESS

STATEMENT REGARDING THE PROMPT PASSAGE OF EFFICIENT WAR MEASURES BY THE 65TH CONGRESS, OCTOBER 6, 1917. FROM "OFFICIAL BULLETIN," NO. 126.

THE Sixty-fifth Congress, now adjourning, deserves the gratitude and appreciation of a people whose will and purpose I believe it has faithfully expressed. One cannot examine the record of its action without being impressed by its completeness, its courage, and its full comprehension of a great task. The needs of the Army and the Navy have been met in a way that assures the effectiveness of American arms and the war-making branch of the Government has been abundantly equipped with the powers that were necessary to make the action of the Nation effective.

I believe that it has also in equal degree, and as far as possible in the face of war, safeguarded the rights of the people and kept in mind the considerations of social justice so often obscured in the hasty readjustment of such a crisis.

It seems to me that the work of this remarkable session has not only been done thoroughly, but that it has also been done with the utmost dispatch possible in the circumstances or consistent with a full consideration of the exceedingly critical matters dealt with. Best of all, it has left no doubt as to the spirit and determination of the country, but has affirmed them as loyally and as emphatically as our fine soldiers will affirm them on the firing line.

APPEAL FOR THE SECOND LIBERTY LOAN

PROCLAMATION DECLARING OCTOBER 24TH TO BE
LIBERTY DAY, ISSUED OCTOBER 12, 1917. FROM
"UNITED STATES STATUTES AT LARGE," VOL. 40,
PT. 2, P. 1706.

THE Second Liberty Loan gives the people of the
United States another opportunity to lend their
funds to their Government to sustain their country at
war. The might of the United States is being mobilized
and organized to strike a mortal blow at autocracy in
defense of outraged American rights and of the cause
of liberty. Billions of dollars are required to arm, feed,
and clothe the brave men who are going forth to fight
our country's battles and to assist the nations with
whom we are making common cause against a common
foe. To subscribe to the Liberty Loan is to perform a
service of patriotism.

Now, therefore, I, Woodrow Wilson, President of
the United States of America, do appoint Wednesday,
the twenty-fourth of October, as Liberty Day, and urge
and advise the people to assemble in their respective
communities and pledge to one another and to the Government that represents them the fullest measure of
financial support. On the afternoon of that day I request that patriotic meetings be held in every city, town,
and hamlet throughout the land under the general direction of the Secretary of the Treasury and the immediate direction of the Liberty Loan Committees which
have been organized by the Federal Reserve Banks.
The people responded nobly to the call of the First
Liberty Loan with an over subscription of more than
50 per cent. Let the response to the Second Loan be
even greater and let the amount be so large that it will
serve as an assurance of unequaled support to hearten

the men who are to face the fire of battle for us. Let the result be so impressive and emphatic that it will echo throughout the Empire of our enemy as an index of what America intends to do to bring this war to a victorious conclusion.

For the purpose of participating in Liberty Day celebrations, all employees of the Federal Government throughout the country whose services can be spared, may be excused at twelve o'clock noon, Wednesday, the twenty-fourth of October.

"MAY AWAKENED RUSSIA AND ENFRAN-CHISED AMERICA ADVANCE SIDE BY SIDE"

TELEGRAM TO MADAME BRESSOVSKY, CHAIRMAN OF THE RUSSIAN COMMITTEE ON CIVIC EDUCATION, DRAFTED BY SECRETARY LANSING, PUBLISHED OCTOBER 18, 1917, FROM ORIGINAL COPY IN MR. WILSON'S FILES.

IT HAS afforded me genuine pleasure to receive your eloquent message of September twenty-fifth. At this hour, when the historic events of the past few months have brought Russia into such close touch with America, it is most enheartening to witness the courage with which the new Russia faces the problems of the future, especially when the high mission of national enlightenment and preparedness for the great duties which fall upon a civic democracy is advanced and promoted by such an educational organization as yours. We of America long since learned that intellectual development and moral fitness are the most powerful elements of national advancement. As the individual is the type of the nation, so the nation should embody the highest individual ideals of civil perfection, in order to assert and maintain its honorable position in the world-family of commonwealths, fulfilling its material and moral duties toward its neighbors, strong in the might of right and fearless in the cause of truth and justice. In the effort to attain this goal, may awakened Russia and enfranchised America advance side by side with mutual affection and confident trust.

WOODROW WILSON.

WOMAN SUFFRAGE A FUNDAMENTAL QUESTION

REPLY TO A DELEGATION FROM THE NEW YORK STATE
WOMAN SUFFRAGE PARTY AT THE WHITE HOUSE,
OCTOBER 25, 1917. FROM ORIGINAL COPY IN MR.
WILSON'S FILES.

M RS. WHITEHOUSE AND LADIES:
It is with great pleasure that I receive you. I
esteem it a privilege to do so. I know the difficulties
which you have been laboring under in New York State
so clearly set forth by Mrs. Whitehouse, but in my judgment those difficulties cannot be used as an excuse by
the leaders of any party or by the voters of any party
for neglecting the question which you are pressing upon
them. Because, after all, the whole world now is witnessing a struggle between two ideals of government.
It is a struggle which goes deeper and touches more of
the foundations of the organized life of men than any
struggle that has ever taken place before, and no settlement of the questions that lie on the surface can satisfy
a situation which requires that the questions which lie
underneath and at the foundation should also be settled
and settled right. I am free to say that I think the
question of woman suffrage is one of those questions
which lie at the foundation.

The world has witnessed a slow political reconstruction, and men have generally been obliged to be satisfied
with the slowness of the process. In a sense it is wholesome that it should be slow, because then it is solid and
sure; but I believe that this war is going so to quicken
the convictions and the consciousness of mankind with
regard to political questions that the speed of reconstruction will be greatly increased. And I believe that
just because we are quickened by the questions of this

war we ought to be quickened to give this question of woman suffrage our immediate consideration.

As one of the spokesmen of a great party, I would be doing nothing less than obeying the mandates of that party if I gave my hearty support to the question of woman suffrage which you represent, but I do not want to speak merely as one of the spokesmen of a party. I want to speak for myself and say that it seems to me that this is the time for the states of this Union to take this action. I perhaps may be touched a little too much by the traditions of our politics, traditions which lay such questions almost entirely upon the states, but I want to see communities declare themselves quickened at this time and show the consequence of the quickening. I think the whole country has appreciated the way in which the women have risen to this great occasion. They not only have done what they have been asked to do and done it with ardor and efficiency, but they have shown a power to organize for doing things of their own initiative which is quite a different thing and a very much more difficult thing, and I think the whole country has admired the spirit and the capacity and the vision of the women of the United States.

It is almost absurd to say that the country depends upon the women for a large part of the inspiration of its life. That is too obvious to say; but it is now depending upon the women also for suggestions of service, which have been rendered in abundance and with the distinction of originality. I, therefore, am very glad to add my voice to those which are urging the people of the great State of New York to set a great example by voting for woman suffrage. It would be a pleasure if I might utter that advice in their presence. Inasmuch as I am bound too close to my duties here to make that possible, I am glad to have the privilege to ask you to convey that message to them.

It seems to me that this is a time of privilege. All our principles, all our hearts, all our purposes, are being searched; searched not only by our own consciences, but searched by the world, and it is time for the people of the states of this country to show the world in what practical sense they have learned the lessons of democracy, that they are fighting for democracy because they believe it, and that there is no application of democracy which they do not believe in. I feel, therefore, that I am standing upon the firmest foundations of the age in bidding godspeed to the cause which you represent and in expressing the ardent hope that the people of New York may realize the great occasion which faces them on election day and may respond to it in noble fashion.

THANKSGIVING DAY

PROCLAMATION ISSUED NOVEMBER 7, 1917. FROM
"UNITED STATES STATUTES AT LARGE," VOL. 40,
PT. 2, PP. 1712-1713.

IT HAS long been the honored custom of our people
to turn in the fruitful autumn of the year in praise
and thanksgiving to Almighty God for His many blessings and mercies to us as a nation. That custom we can
follow now even in the midst of the tragedy of a world
shaken by war and immeasurable disaster, in the midst
of sorrow and great peril, because even amidst the darkness that has gathered about us we can see the great
blessings God has bestowed upon us, blessings that are
better than mere peace of mind and prosperity of enterprise.

We have been given the opportunity to serve mankind
as we once served ourselves in the great day of our Declaration of Independence, by taking up arms against a
tyranny that threatened to master and debase men
everywhere and joining with other free peoples in demanding for all the nations of the world what we then
demanded and obtained for ourselves. In this day of
the revelation of our duty not only to defend our own
rights as a nation, but to defend also the rights of free
men throughout the world, there has been vouchsafed
us in full and inspiring measure the resolution and spirit
of united action. We have been brought to one mind
and purpose. A new vigor of common counsel and common action has been revealed in us. We should especially thank God that in such circumstances, in the midst
of the greatest enterprise the spirits of men have ever
entered upon, we have, if we but observe a reasonable
and practicable economy, abundance with which to
supply the needs of those associated with us as well as

our own. A new light shines about us. The great duties of a new day awaken a new and greater national spirit in us. We shall never again be divided or wonder what stuff we are made of.

And while we render thanks for these things let us pray Almighty God that in all humbleness of spirit we may look always to Him for guidance; that we may be kept constant in the spirit and purpose of service; that by His grace our minds may be directed and our hands strengthened; and that in His good time liberty and security and peace and the comradeship of a common justice may be vouchsafed all the nations of the earth.

Wherefore, I, Woodrow Wilson, President of the United States of America, do hereby designate Thursday, the twenty-ninth day of November next, as a day of thanksgiving and prayer, and invite the people throughout the land to cease upon that day from their ordinary occupations and in their several homes and places of worship to render thanks to God, the great ruler of nations.

"MORE PERFECT ORGANIZATION OF OUR MAN POWER"

FOREWORD TO THE SELECTIVE SERVICE REGULATIONS, NOVEMBER 8, 1917. FROM ORIGINAL COPY IN MR. WILSON'S FILES, CORRECTED IN HIS OWN HAND.

THE task of selecting and mobilizing the first contingent of the National Army is nearing completion. The expedition and accuracy of its accomplishment were a most gratifying demonstration of the efficiency of our democratic institutions. The swiftness with which the machinery for its execution had to be assembled, however, left room for adjustment and improvement. New Regulations putting these improvements into effect are, therefore, being published to-day. There is no change in the essential obligation of men subject to selection. The first draft must stand unaffected by the provisions of the new Regulations. They can be given no retroactive effect.

The time has come for a more perfect organization of our man-power. The selective principle must be carried to its logical conclusion. We must make a complete inventory of the qualifications of all registrants in order to determine, as to each man not already selected for duty with the colors, the place in the military, industrial, or agricultural ranks of the Nation in which his experience and training can best be made to serve the common good. This project involves an inquiry by the Selection Boards into the domestic, industrial, and educational qualifications of nearly ten million men.

Members of these Boards have rendered a conspicuous service. The work was done without regard to personal convenience and under a pressure of immediate necessity which imposed great sacrifices. Yet the services of men trained by the experience of the first draft must of necessity be retained and the Selection Boards must provide the directing mechanism for the new classification. The thing they have done is of scarcely one-tenth the magnitude of the thing that remains to be done. It is of great importance both to our military and to our economic interests that the classification be carried swiftly and accurately to a conclusion. An estimate of the time necessary for the work leads to the conclusion that it can be accomplished in sixty days; but only if this great marshaling of our resources of men is regarded by all as a national war undertaking of such significance as to challenge the attention and compel the assistance of every American.

I call upon all citizens, therefore, to assist Local and District Boards by proffering such service and such material conveniences as they can offer and by appearing before the boards, either upon summons or upon their own initiative, to give such information as will be useful in classifying registrants. I urge men of the legal profession to offer themselves as associate members of the Legal Advisory Boards to be provided in each community for the purpose of advising registrants of their rights and obligations and of assisting them in the preparation of their answers to the questions which all men subject to draft are required to submit. I ask the doctors of the country to identify themselves with the Medical Advisory Boards which are to be constituted in the various districts throughout the United States for the purpose of making a systematic physical examination of the registrants. It is important also that police officials of every grade and class should be informed of their duty under the Selective Service Law and Regulations, to search for persons who do not respond promptly and to serve the summons of Local and District Boards. Newspapers can be of very great assistance in giving wide publicity to the requirements of the Law and Regulations and to the numbers and names of those who are called to present themselves to their Local

Boards from day to day. Finally, I ask that during the time hereafter to be specified as marking the sixty-day period of the classification all citizens give attention to the task in hand in order that the process may proceed to a conclusion with swiftness and yet with even and considerate justice to all.

TO ORGANIZED LABOR

ADDRESS TO THE AMERICAN FEDERATION OF LABOR CON-
VENTION AT BUFFALO, N. Y., NOVEMBER 12, 1917.
FROM OFFICIAL GOVERNMENT PUBLICATION IN MR.
WILSON'S FILES.

I ESTEEM it a great privilege and a real honor to
be thus admitted to your public counsels. When
your executive committee paid me the compliment of
inviting me here I gladly accepted the invitation because
it seems to me that this, above all other times in our
history, is the time for common counsel, for the drawing together not only of the energies but of the minds
of the Nation. I thought that it was a welcome opportunity for disclosing to you some of the thoughts
that have been gathering in my mind during these last
momentous months.

I am introduced to you as the President of the United
States, and yet I would be pleased if you would put
the thought of the office into the background and regard
me as one of your fellow citizens who has come here to
speak, not the words of authority, but the words of
counsel; the words which men should speak to one another who wish to be frank in a moment more critical
perhaps than the history of the world has ever yet
known; a moment when it is every man's duty to forget himself, to forget his own interests, to fill himself
with the nobility of a great national and world conception, and act upon a new platform elevated above
the ordinary affairs of life and lifted to where men have
views of the long destiny of mankind.

I think that in order to realize just what this moment
of counsel is it is very desirable that we should remind
ourselves just how this war came about and just what
it is for. You can explain most wars very simply, but

the explanation of this is not so simple. Its roots run
deep into all the obscure soils of history, and in my
view this is the last decisive issue between the old principle of power and the new principle of freedom.

The war was started by Germany. Her authorities
deny that they started it, but I am willing to let the
statement I have just made await the verdict of history.
And the thing that needs to be explained is why Germany started the war. Remember what the position
of Germany in the world was—as enviable a position
as any nation has ever occupied. The whole world
stood at admiration of her wonderful intellectual and
material achievements. All the intellectual men of the
world went to school to her. As a university man I
have been surrounded by men trained in Germany, men
who had resorted to Germany because nowhere else
could they get such thorough and searching training,
particularly in the principles of science and the principles that underlie modern material achievement. Her
men of science had made her industries perhaps the
most competent industries of the world, and the label
"Made in Germany" was a guarantee of good work-
manship and of sound material. She had access to all
the markets of the world, and every other nation who
traded in those markets feared Germany because of her
effective and almost irresistible competition. She had
a "place in the sun."

Why was she not satisfied? What more did she
want? There was nothing in the world of peace that
she did not already have and have in abundance. We
boast of the extraordinary pace of American advancement. We show with pride the statistics of the increase
of our industries and of the population of our cities.
Well, those statistics did not match the recent statistics
of Germany. Her old cities took on youth and grew
faster than any American cities ever grew. Her old
industries opened their eyes and saw a new world and

went out for its conquest. And yet the authorities of Germany were not satisfied.

You have one part of the answer to the question why she was not satisfied in her methods of competition. There is no important industry in Germany upon which the Government has not laid its hands, to direct it and, when necessity arose, control it; and you have only to ask any man whom you meet who is familiar with the conditions that prevailed before the war in the matter of national competition to find out the methods of competition which the German manufacturers and exporters used under the patronage and support of the Government of Germany. You will find that they were the same sorts of competition that we have tried to prevent by law within our own borders. If they could not sell their goods cheaper than we could sell ours at a profit to themselves they could get a subsidy from the Government which made it possible to sell them cheaper anyhow, and the conditions of competition were thus controlled in large measure by the German Government itself.

But that did not satisfy the German Government. All the while there was lying behind its thought and in its dreams of the future a political control which would enable it in the long run to dominate the labor and the industry of the world. They were not content with success by superior achievement; they wanted success by authority. I suppose very few of you have thought much about the Berlin-to-Bagdad Railway. The Berlin-Bagdad Railway was constructed in order to run the threat of force down the flank of the industrial undertakings of half a dozen other countries; so that when German competition came in it would not be resisted too far, because there was always the possibility of getting German armies into the heart of that country quicker than any other armies could be got there.

Look at the map of Europe now! Germany is thrusting upon us again and again the discussion of peace talks,—about what? Talks about Belgium; talks about northern France; talks about Alsace-Lorraine. Well those are deeply interesting subjects to us and to them, but they are not the heart of the matter. Take the map and look at it. Germany has absolute control of Austria-Hungary, practical control of the Balkan States, control of Turkey, control of Asia Minor. I saw a map in which the whole thing was printed in appropriate black the other day, and the black stretched all the way from Hamburg to Bagdad—the bulk of German power inserted into the heart of the world. If she can keep that, she has kept all that her dreams contemplated when the war began. If she can keep that, her power can disturb the world as long as she keeps it, always provided, for I feel bound to put this proviso in—always provided the present influences that control the German Government continue to control it. I believe that the spirit of freedom can get into the hearts of Germans and find as fine a welcome there as it can find in any other hearts, but the spirit of freedom does not suit the plans of the Pan-Germans. Power cannot be used with concentrated force against free peoples if it is used by free people.

You know how many intimations come to us from one of the Central Powers that it is more anxious for peace than the chief Central Power, and you know that it means that the people in that Central Power know that if the war ends as it stands they will in effect themselves be vassals of Germany, notwithstanding that their populations are compounded of all the peoples of that part of the world, and notwithstanding the fact that they do not wish in their pride and proper spirit of nationality to be so absorbed and dominated. Germany is determined that the political power of the world shall belong to her. There have been such ambitions before. They have been in part realized, but never before have those ambitions been based upon so exact and precise and scientific a plan of domination.

May I not say that it is amazing to me that any group of persons should be so ill-informed as to suppose, as some groups in Russia apparently suppose, that any reforms planned in the interest of the people can live in the presence of a Germany powerful enough to undermine or overthrow them by intrigue or force? Any body of free men that compounds with the present German Government is compounding for its own destruction. But that is not the whole of the story. Any man in America or anywhere else that supposes that the free industry and enterprise of the world can continue if the Pan-German plan is achieved and German power fastened upon the world is as fatuous as the dreamers in Russia. What I am opposed to is not the feeling of the pacifists, but their stupidity. My heart is with them, but my mind has a contempt for them. I want peace, but I know how to get it, and they do not.

You will notice that I sent a friend of mine, Colonel House, to Europe, who is as great a lover of peace as any man in the world; but I didn't send him on a peace mission yet. I sent him to take part in a conference as to how the war was to be won, and he knows, as I know, that that is the way to get peace, if you want it for more than a few minutes.

All of this is a preface to the conference that I have referred to with regard to what we are going to do. If we are true friends of freedom, our own or anybody else's, we will see that the power of this country and the productivity of this country are raised to their absolute maximum, and that absolutely nobody is allowed to stand in the way of it. When I say that nobody is allowed to stand in the way I do not mean that he shall be prevented by the power of the Government, but by the power of the American spirit. Our duty, if we are to do this great thing and show America to be what we believe her to be—the greatest hope and energy of the world—is to stand together night and day until the job is finished.

While we are fighting for freedom we must see, among other things, that labor is free; and that means a number of interesting things. It means not only that we must do what we have declared our purpose to do, see that the conditions of labor are not rendered more onerous by the war, but also that we shall see to it that the instrumentalities by which the conditions of labor are improved are not blocked or checked. That we must do. That has been the matter about which I have taken pleasure in conferring from time to time with your president, Mr. Gompers; and if I may be permitted to do so, I want to express my admiration of his patriotic courage, his large vision, and his statesman-like sense of what has to be done. I like to lay my mind alongside of a mind that knows how to pull in harness. The horses that kick over the traces will have to be put in corral.

Now, to stand together means that nobody must interrupt the processes of our energy if the interruption can possibly be avoided without the absolute invasion of freedom. To put it concretely, that means this: Nobody has a right to stop the processes of labor until all the methods of conciliation and settlement have been exhausted. And I might as well say right here that I am not talking to you alone. You sometimes stop the courses of labor, but there are others who do the same, and I believe I am speaking from my own experience not only, but from the experience of others when I say that you are reasonable in a larger number of cases than the capitalists. I am not saying these things to them personally yet, because I have not had a chance, but they have to be said, not in any spirit of criticism, but in order to clear the atmosphere and come down to business. Everybody on both sides has now got to transact business, and a settlement is never impossible when both sides want to do the square and right thing.

Moreover, a settlement is always hard to avoid when the parties can be brought face to face. I can differ from a man much more radically when he is not in the room than I can when he is in the room, because then the awkward thing is he can come back at me and answer what I say. It is always dangerous for a man to have the floor entirely to himself. Therefore, we must insist in every instance that the parties come into each other's presence and there discuss the issues between them, and not separately in places which have no communication with each other. I always like to remind myself of a delightful saying of an Englishman of the past generation, Charles Lamb. He stuttered a little bit, and once when he was with a group of friends he spoke very harshly of some man who was not present. One of his friends said: "Why, Charles, I didn't know that you knew So-and-so." "O-o-oh," he said, "I-I d-d-don't; I-I can't h-h-hate a m-m-man I-I know." There is a great deal of human nature, of very pleasant human nature, in the saying. It is hard to hate a man you know. I may admit, parenthetically, that there are some politicians whose methods I do not at all believe in, but they are jolly good fellows, and if they only would not talk the wrong kind of politics to me, I would love to be with them.

So it is all along the line, in serious matters and things less serious. We are all of the same clay and spirit, and we can get together if we desire to get together. Therefore, my counsel to you is this: Let us show ourselves Americans by showing that we do not want to go off in separate camps or groups by ourselves, but that we want to coöperate with all other classes and all other groups in the common enterprise which is to release the spirits of the world from bondage. I would be willing to set that up as the final test of an American. That is the meaning of democracy. I have been very much distressed, my fellow citizens, by some of the things that have happened recently. The mob spirit is displaying itself here and there in this country. I have no sympathy with what some men are saying, but I have no sympathy with the men who take their punishment into their own hands; and I want to say to every man who does join such a mob that I do not recognize him as worthy of the free institutions of the United States. There are some organizations in this country whose object is anarchy and the destruction of law, but I would not meet their efforts by making myself partner in destroying the law. I despise and hate their purposes as much as any man, but I respect the ancient processes of justice; and I would be too proud not to see them done justice, however wrong they are.

So I want to utter my earnest protest against any manifestation of the spirit of lawlessness anywhere or in any cause. Why, gentlemen, look what it means. We claim to be the greatest democratic people in the world, and democracy means first of all that we can govern ourselves. If our men have not self-control, then they are not capable of that great thing which we call democratic government. A man who takes the law into his own hands is not the right man to coöperate in any formation or development of law and institutions, and some of the processes by which the struggle between capital and labor is carried on are processes that come very near to taking the law into your own hands. I do not mean for a moment to compare them with what I have just been speaking of, but I want you to see that they are mere gradations in this manifestation of the unwillingness to coöperate, and that the fundamental lesson of the whole situation is that we must not only take common counsel, but that we must yield to and obey common counsel. Not all of the instrumentalities for this are at hand. I am hopeful that in the very near future new instrumentalities may be organized by which we can see to it that various things that are now going on ought not to go on. There are various processes of the dilution of labor and the unnecessary substitution of labor and the bidding in distant markets and unfairly upsetting the whole competition of labor which ought not to go on. I mean now on the part of employers, and we must interject some instrumentality of coöperation by which the fair thing will be done all around. I am hopeful that some such instrumentalities may be devised, but whether they are or not, we must use those that we have and upon every occasion where it is necessary have such an instrumentality originated upon that occasion.

So, my fellow citizens, the reason I came away from Washington is that I sometimes get lonely down there. So many people come to Washington who know things that are not so, and so few people who know anything about what the people of the United States are thinking about. I have to come away and get reminded of the rest of the country. I have to come away and talk to men who are up against the real thing, and say to them, "I am with you if you are with me." And the only test of being with me is not to think about me personally at all, but merely to think of me as the expression for the time being of the power and dignity and hope of the United States.

GREETING TO BRAZIL

CABLEGRAM TO THE PRESIDENT OF BRAZIL ON THE AN-
NIVERSARY OF THE INDEPENDENCE OF HIS COUN-
TRY, NOVEMBER 15, 1917. FROM "OFFICIAL
BULLETIN," NO. 162.

ON THIS anniversary of the independence of Brazil
I extend to Your Excellency and the people of your
great Republic cordial greetings. The United States
has welcomed with applause and admiration the entry
of Brazil in the great struggle which confronts us. The
day you now celebrate marks your country's achievement of independence. To-day our two countries are
engaged in a war for the maintenance of world independence and for the rights of humanity and the life
of democracy. We are both making sacrifices for
this common cause. United to Brazil by this strong
bond of democracy and still more by antagonism
against a mutual foe, I hope and feel assured that the
United States and our sister Republic of South America will at the close of the present conflict stand even
closer together in victory.

WOODROW WILSON.

GREETING AND SYMPATHY TO BELGIUM

CABLEGRAM TO KING ALBERT OF BELGIUM ON HIS BIRTHDAY, NOVEMBER 16, 1917. FROM ORIGINAL COPY IN MR. WILSON'S FILES.

I TAKE pleasure in extending to Your Majesty greetings of friendship and good will on this your fête day.

For the people of the United States, I take this occasion to renew expressions of deep sympathy for the sufferings which Belgium has endured under the willful, cruel, and barbaric force of a disappointed Prussian autocracy.

The people of the United States were never more in earnest than in their determination to prosecute to a successful conclusion this war against that power and to secure for the future, obedience to the laws of nations and respect for the rights of humanity.

WOODROW WILSON.

"A WAR FOR EVERY STRAIGHT-OUT AMERICAN"

TELEGRAM TO THE NORTHWEST LOYALTY MEETINGS AT ST. PAUL, MINNESOTA, NOVEMBER 16, 1917. FROM "OFFICIAL BULLETIN," NO. 162.

NOTHING could be more significant than your gathering to express the loyalty of the Great Northwest. If it were possible, I should gladly be with you. You have come together as the representative of that Western Empire in which the sons of all sections of America and the stocks of all the nations of Europe have made the prairie and the forest the home of a new race and the temple of a new faith.

The time has come when that home must be protected and that faith affirmed in deeds. Sacrifice and service must come from every class, every profession, every party, every race, every creed, every section. This is not a banker's war or a farmer's war or a manufacturer's war or a laboring-man's war—it is a war for every straight-out American whether our flag be his by birth or by adoption.

We are to-day a Nation in arms and we must fight and farm, mine and manufacture, conserve food and fuel, save and spend to the one common purpose. It is to the Great Northwest that the Nation looks, as once before in critical days, for that steadiness of purpose and firmness of determination which shall see this struggle through to a decision that shall make the masters of Germany rue the day they unmasked their purpose and challenged our Republic.

WOODROW WILSON.

RECOMMENDING WAR WITH AUSTRIA-HUNGARY

ADDRESS DELIVERED AT A JOINT SESSION OF THE TWO HOUSES OF CONGRESS, DECEMBER 4, 1917. FROM OFFICIAL GOVERNMENT PUBLICATION IN MR. WILSON'S FILES.

EIGHT months have elapsed since I last had the honor of addressing you. They have been months crowded with events of immense and grave significance for us. I shall not undertake to retail or even to summarize those events. The practical particulars of the part we have played in them will be laid before you in the reports of the Executive Departments. I shall discuss only our present outlook upon these vast affairs, our present duties, and the immediate means of accomplishing the objects we shall hold always in view.

I shall not go back to debate the causes of the war. The intolerable wrongs done and planned against us by the sinister masters of Germany have long since become too grossly obvious and odious to every true American to need to be rehearsed. But I shall ask you to consider again and with a very grave scrutiny our objectives and the measures by which we mean to attain them; for the purpose of discussion here in this place is action, and our action must move straight towards definite ends. Our object is, of course, to win the war; and we shall not slacken or suffer ourselves to be diverted until it is won. But it is worth while asking and answering the question, When shall we consider the war won?

From one point of view it is not necessary to broach this fundamental matter. I do not doubt that the American people know what the war is about and what sort of an outcome they will regard as a realization of their purpose in it. As a nation we are united in spirit and intention. I pay little heed to those who tell me otherwise. I hear the voices of dissent,—who does not? I hear the criticism and the clamor of the noisily thoughtless and troublesome. I also see men here and there fling themselves in impotent disloyalty against the calm, indomitable power of the Nation. I hear men debate peace who understand neither its nature nor the way in which we may attain it with uplifted eyes and unbroken spirits. But I know that none of these speaks for the Nation. They do not touch the heart of anything. They may safely be left to strut their uneasy hour and be forgotten.

But from another point of view I believe that it is necessary to say plainly what we here at the seat of action consider the war to be for and what part we mean to play in the settlement of its searching issues. We are the spokesmen of the American people and they have a right to know whether their purpose is ours. They desire peace by the overcoming of evil, by the defeat once for all of the sinister forces that interrupt peace and render it impossible, and they wish to know how closely our thought runs with theirs and what action we propose. They are impatient with those who desire peace by any sort of compromise,—deeply and indignantly impatient,—but they will be equally impatient with us if we do not make it plain to them what our objectives are and what we are planning for in seeking to make conquest of peace by arms.

I believe that I speak for them when I say two things: First, that this intolerable Thing of which the masters of Germany have shown us the ugly face, this menace of combined intrigue and force which we now see so clearly as the German power, a Thing without conscience or honor or capacity for covenanted peace, must be crushed and, if it be not utterly brought to an end, at least shut out from the friendly intercourse of the nations; and, second, that when this Thing and its power are indeed defeated and the time comes that we can discuss peace,—when the German people have spokesmen whose word we can believe and when those spokesmen are ready in the name of their people to accept the common judgment of the nations as to what shall henceforth be the bases of law and of covenant for the life of the world,—we shall be willing and glad to pay the full price for peace, and pay it ungrudgingly. We know what that price will be. It will be full, impartial justice,—justice done at every point and to every nation that the final settlement must affect, our enemies as well as our friends.

You catch, with me, the voices of humanity that are in the air. They grow daily more audible, more articulate, more persuasive, and they come from the hearts of men everywhere. They insist that the war shall not end in vindictive action of any kind; that no nation or people shall be robbed or punished because the irresponsible rulers of a single country have themselves done deep and abominable wrong. It is this thought that has been expressed in the formula 'No annexations, no contributions, no punitive indemnities.' Just because this crude formula expresses the instinctive judgment as to right of plain men everywhere it has been made diligent use of by the masters of German intrigue to lead the people of Russia astray—and the people of every other country their agents could reach, in order that a premature peace might be brought about before autocracy has been taught its final and convincing lesson, and the people of the world put in control of their own destinies.

But the fact that a wrong use has been made of a just idea is no reason why a right use should not be made of it. It ought to be brought under the patronage of its real friends. Let it be said again that autocracy must first be shown the utter futility of its claims to power or leadership in the modern world. It is impossible to apply any standard of justice so long as such forces are unchecked and undefeated as the present masters of Germany command. Not until that has been done can Right be set up as arbiter and peace-maker among the nations. But when that has been done,—as, God willing, it assuredly will be,—we shall at last be free to do an unprecedented thing, and this is the time to avow our purpose to do it. We shall be free to base peace on generosity and justice, to the exclusion of all selfish claims to advantage even on the part of the victors.

Let there be no misunderstanding. Our present and immediate task is to win the war, and nothing shall turn us aside from it until it is accomplished. Every power and resource we possess, whether of men, of money, or of materials, is being devoted and will continue to be devoted to that purpose until it is achieved. Those who desire to bring peace about before that purpose is achieved I counsel to carry their advice elsewhere. We will not entertain it. We shall regard the war as won only when the German people say to us, through properly accredited representatives, that they are ready to agree to a settlement based upon justice and the reparation of the wrongs their rulers have done. They have done a wrong to Belgium which must be repaired. They have established a power over other lands and peoples than their own,—over the great Empire of Austria-Hungary, over hitherto free Balkan states, over Turkey, and within Asia,—which must be relinquished.

Germany's success by skill, by industry, by knowledge, by enterprise we did not grudge or oppose, but admired, rather. She had built up for herself a real empire of trade and influence, secured by the peace of the world. We were content to abide the rivalries of manufacture, science, and commerce that were involved for us in her success and stand or fall as we had or did not have the brains and the initiative to surpass her. But at the moment when she had conspicuously won her triumphs of peace she threw them away, to establish in their stead what the world will no longer permit to be established, military and political domination by arms, by which to oust where she could not excel the rivals she most feared and hated. The peace we make must remedy that wrong. It must deliver the once fair lands and happy peoples of Belgium and northern France from the Prussian conquest and the Prussian menace, but it must also deliver the peoples of Austria-Hungary, the peoples of the Balkans, and the peoples of Turkey, alike in Europe and in Asia, from the impudent and alien dominion of the Prussian military and commercial autocracy.

We owe it, however, to ourselves to say that we do not wish in any way to impair or to re-arrange the Austro-Hungarian Empire. It is no affair of ours what they do with their own life, either industrially or politically. We do not purpose or desire to dictate to them in any way. We only desire to see that their affairs are left in their own hands, in all matters, great or small. We shall hope to secure for the peoples of the Balkan peninsula and for the people of the Turkish Empire the right and opportunity to make their own lives safe, their own fortunes secure against oppression or injustice and from the dictation of foreign courts or parties.

And our attitude and purpose with regard to Germany herself are of a like kind. We intend no wrong against the German Empire, no interference with her internal affairs. We should deem either the one or the other absolutely unjustifiable, absolutely contrary to the principles we have professed to live by and to hold most sacred throughout our life as a nation.

The people of Germany are being told by the men whom they now permit to deceive them and to act as their masters that they are fighting for the very life and existence of their Empire, a war of desperate self-defense against deliberate aggression. Nothing could be more grossly or wantonly false, and we must seek by the utmost openness and candor as to our real aims to convince them of its falseness. We are in fact fighting for their emancipation from fear, along with our own, —from the fear as well as from the fact of unjust attack by neighbors or rivals or schemers after world empire. No one is threatening the existence or the independence or the peaceful enterprise of the German Empire.

The worst that can happen to the detriment of the German people is this, that if they should still, after the war is over, continue to be obliged to live under ambitious and intriguing masters interested to disturb the peace of the world, men or classes of men whom the other peoples of the world could not trust, it might be impossible to admit them to the partnership of nations which must henceforth guarantee the world's peace. That partnership must be a partnership of peoples, not a mere partnership of governments. It might be impossible, also, in such untoward circumstances to admit Germany to the free economic intercourse which must inevitably spring out of the other partnerships of a real peace. But there would be no aggression in that; and such a situation, inevitable because of distrust, would in the very nature of things sooner or later cure itself, by processes which would assuredly set in.

The wrongs, the very deep wrongs, committed in this war will have to be righted. That of course. But they cannot and must not be righted by the commission of similar wrongs against Germany and her allies. The world will not permit the commission of similar wrongs as a means of reparation and settlement. Statesmen must by this time have learned that the opinion of the world is everywhere wide awake and fully comprehends the issues involved. No representative of any self-governed nation will dare disregard it by attempting any such covenants of selfishness and compromise as were entered into at the Congress of Vienna. The thought of the plain people here and everywhere throughout the world, the people who enjoy no privilege and have very simple and unsophisticated standards of right and wrong, is the air all governments must henceforth breathe if they would live. It is in the full disclosing light of that thought that all policies must be conceived and executed in this midday hour of the world's life. German rulers have been able to upset the peace of the world only because the German people were not suffered under their tutelage to share the comradeship of the other peoples of the world either in thought or in purpose. They were allowed to have no opinion of their own which might be set up as a rule of conduct for those who exercised authority over them. But the congress that concludes this war will feel the full strength of the tides than run now in the hearts and conscience of free men everywhere. Its conclusions will run with those tides.

All these things have been true from the very beginning of this stupendous war; and I cannot help thinking that if they had been made plain at the very outset the sympathy and enthusiasm of the Russian people might have been once for all enlisted on the side of the Allies, suspicion and distrust swept away, and a real and lasting union of purpose effected. Had they believed these things at the very moment of their revolution and had they been confirmed in that belief since, the sad reverses which have recently marked the progress of their affairs toward an ordered and stable government of free men might have been avoided. The Russian people have been poisoned by the very same falsehoods that have kept the German people in the dark, and the poison has been administered by the very same hands. The only possible antidote is the truth. It cannot be uttered too plainly or too often.

From every point of view, therefore, it has seemed to be my duty to speak these declarations of purpose, to add these specific interpretations to what I took the liberty of saying to the Senate in January. Our entrance into the war has not altered our attitude towards the settlement that must come when it is over. When I said in January that the nations of the world were entitled not only to free pathways upon the sea but also to assured and unmolested access to those pathways I was thinking, and I am thinking now, not of the smaller and weaker nations alone, which need our countenance and support, but also of the great and powerful nations, and of our present enemies as well as our present associates in the war. I was thinking, and am thinking now, of Austria herself, among the rest, as well as of Serbia and of Poland. Justice and equality of rights can be had only at a great price. We are seeking permanent, not temporary, foundations for the peace of the world and must seek them candidly and fearlessly. As always, the right will prove to be the expedient.

What shall we do, then, to push this great war of freedom and justice to its righteous conclusion? We must clear away with a thorough hand all impediments to success and we must make every adjustment of law that will facilitate the full and free use of our whole capacity and force as a fighting unit.

One very embarrassing obstacle that stands in our way is that we are at war with Germany but not with her allies. I therefore very earnestly recommend that the Congress immediately declare the United States in a state of war with Austria-Hungary. Does it seem strange to you that this should be the conclusion of the argument I have just addressed to you? It is not. It is in fact the inevitable logic of what I have said. Austria-Hungary is for the time being not her own mistress but simply the vassal of the German Government. We must face the facts as they are and act upon them without sentiment in this stern business. The government of Austria-Hungary is not acting upon its own initiative or in response to the wishes and feelings of its own peoples but as the instrument of another nation. We must meet its force with our own and regard the Central Powers as but one. The war can be successfully conducted in no other way. The same logic would lead also to a declaration of war against Turkey and Bulgaria. They also are the tools of Germany. But they are mere tools and do not yet stand in the direct path of our necessary action. We shall go wherever the necessities of this war carry us, but it seems to me that we should go only where immediate and practical considerations lead us and not heed any others.

The financial and military measures which must be adopted will suggest themselves as the war and its undertakings develop, but I will take the liberty of proposing to you certain other acts of legislation which seem to me to be needed for the support of the war and for the release of our whole force and energy.

It will be necessary to extend in certain particulars the legislation of the last session with regard to alien enemies; and also necessary, I believe, to create a very definite and particular control over the entrance and departure of all persons into and from the United States.

Legislation should be enacted defining as a criminal offense every willful violation of the presidential proclamations relating to alien enemies promulgated under section 4067 of the Revised Statutes and providing appropriate punishments; and women as well as men should be included under the terms of the acts placing restraints upon alien enemies. It is likely that as time goes on many alien enemies will be willing to be fed and housed at the expense of the Government in the detention camps and it would be the purpose of the legislation I have suggested to confine offenders among them in penitentiaries and other similar institutions where they could be made to work as other criminals do.

Recent experience has convinced me that the Congress must go further in authorizing the Government to set limits to prices. The law of supply and demand, I am sorry to say, has been replaced by the law of unrestricted selfishness. While we have eliminated profiteering in several branches of industry it still runs impudently rampant in others. The farmers, for example, complain with a great deal of justice that, while the regulation of food prices restricts their incomes, no restraints are placed upon the prices of most of the things they must themselves purchase; and similar inequities obtain on all sides.

It is imperatively necessary that the consideration of the full use of the water power of the country and also the consideration of the systematic and yet economical development of such of the natural resources of the country as are still under the control of the federal government should be immediately resumed and affirmatively and constructively dealt with at the earliest possible moment. The pressing need of such legislation is daily becoming more obvious.

The legislation proposed at the last session with regard to regulated combinations among our exporters, in order to provide for our foreign trade a more effective organization and method of coöperation, ought by all means to be completed at this session.

And I beg that the members of the House of Representatives will permit me to express the opinion that it will be impossible to deal in any but a very wasteful and extravagant fashion with the enormous appropriations of the public moneys which must continue to be made, if the war is to be properly sustained, unless the House will consent to return to its former practice of initiating and preparing all appropriation bills through a single committee, in order that responsibility may be centered, expenditures standardized and made uniform, and waste and duplication as much as possible avoided.

Additional legislation may also become necessary before the present Congress again adjourns in order to effect the most efficient coördination and operation of the railway and other transportation systems of the country; but to that I shall, if circumstances should demand, call the attention of the Congress upon another occasion.

If I have overlooked anything that ought to be done

for the more effective conduct of the war, your own counsels will supply the omission. What I am perfectly clear about is that in the present session of the Congress our whole attention and energy should be concentrated on the vigorous, rapid, and successful prosecution of the great task of winning the war.

We can do this with all the greater zeal and enthusiasm because we know that for us this is a war of high principle, debased by no selfish ambition of conquest or spoliation; because we know, and all the world knows, that we have been forced into it to save the very institutions we live under from corruption and destruction. The purposes of the Central Powers strike straight at the very heart of everything we believe in; their methods of warfare outrage every principle of humanity and of knightly honor; their intrigue has corrupted the very thought and spirit of many of our people; their sinister and secret diplomacy has sought to take our very territory away from us and disrupt the Union of the States. Our safety would be at an end, our honor forever sullied and brought into contempt were we to permit their triumph. They are striking at the very existence of democracy and liberty.

It is because it is for us a war of high, disinterested purpose, in which all the free peoples of the world are banded together for the vindication of right, a war for the preservation of our Nation and of all that it has held dear of principle and of purpose, that we feel ourselves doubly constrained to propose for its outcome only that which is righteous and of irreproachable intention, for our foes as well as for our friends. The cause being just and holy, the settlement must be of like motive and quality. For this we can fight, but for nothing less noble or less worthy of our traditions. For this cause we entered the war and for this cause will we battle until the last gun is fired.

I have spoken plainly because this seems to me the time when it is most necessary to speak plainly, in order that all the world may know that even in the heat and ardor of the struggle and when our whole thought is of carrying the war through to its end we have not forgotten any ideal or principle for which the name of America has been held in honor among the nations and for which it has been our glory to contend in the great generations that went before us. A supreme moment of history has come. The eyes of the people have been opened and they see. The hand of God is laid upon the nations. He will show them favor, I devoutly believe, only if they rise to the clear heights of His own justice and mercy.

PROCLAMATION OF WAR WITH AUSTRIA-HUNGARY

PROCLAMATION [1] ISSUED DECEMBER 11, 1917. FROM "UNITED STATES STATUTES AT LARGE," VOL. 40, PT. 2, PP. 1729-1731.

* * * Now, therefore, I, Woodrow Wilson, President of the United States of America, do hereby proclaim to all whom it may concern that a state of war exists between the United States and the Imperial and Royal Austro-Hungarian Government; and I do specially direct all officers, civil or military, of the United States that they exercise vigilance and zeal in the discharge of the duties incident to such a state of war; and I do, moreover, earnestly appeal to all American citizens that they, in loyal devotion to their country, dedicated from its foundation to the principles of liberty and justice, uphold the laws of the land, and give undivided and willing support to those measures which may be adopted by the constitutional authorities in prosecuting the war to a successful issue and in obtaining a secure and just peace;

And, acting under and by virtue of the authority vested in me by the Constitution of the United States and the aforesaid sections of the Revised Statutes, I do hereby further proclaim and direct that the conduct to be observed on the part of the United States toward all natives, citizens, denizens, or subjects of Austria-Hungary, being males of the age of fourteen years and upward, who shall be within the United States and not actually naturalized, shall be as follows:

[1] In the first part of this Proclamation the President cites the resolution of Congress, December 7, 1917, declaring war with Austria-Hungary.

All natives, citizens, denizens, or subjects of Austria-Hungary, being males of fourteen years and upwards who shall be within the United States and not actually naturalized, are enjoined to preserve the peace towards the United States and to refrain from crime against the public safety, and from violating the laws of the United States and of the States and Territories thereof, and to refrain from actual hostility or giving information, aid or comfort to the enemies of the United States, and to comply strictly with the regulations which are hereby or which may be from time to time promulgated by the President; and so long as they shall conduct themselves in accordance with law, they shall be undisturbed in the peaceful pursuit of their lives and occupations and be accorded the consideration due to all peaceful and law-abiding persons, except so far as restrictions may be necessary for their own protection and for the safety of the United States; and toward such of said persons as conduct themselves in accordance with law, all citizens of the United States are enjoined to preserve the peace and to treat them with all such friendliness as may be compatible with loyalty and allegiance to the United States.

And all natives, citizens, denizens or subjects of Austria-Hungary, being males of the age of fourteen years and upwards, who shall be within the United States and not actually naturalized, who fail to conduct themselves as so enjoined, in addition to all other penalties prescribed by law, shall be liable to restraint, or to give security, or to remove and depart from the United States in the manner prescribed by Sections 4069 and 4070 of the Revised Statutes, and as prescribed in regulations duly promulgated by the President;

And pursuant to the authority vested in me, I hereby declare and establish the following regulations, which I find necessary in the premises and for the public safety:

1. No native, citizen, denizen or subject of Austria-Hungary, being a male of the age of fourteen years and upwards, and not actually naturalized, shall depart from the United States until he shall have received such permit as the President shall prescribe, or except under order of a court, judge, or justice, under Sections 4069 and 4070 of the Revised Statutes;

2. No such person shall land in or enter the United States, except under such restrictions and at such places as the President may prescribe;

3. Every such person of whom there may be reasonable cause to believe that he is aiding or about to aid the enemy, or who may be at large to the danger of the public peace or safety, or who violates or attempts to violate, or of whom there is reasonable ground to

believe that he is about to violate any regulation duly promulgated by the President, or any criminal law of the United States, or of the States or Territories thereof, will be subject to summary arrest by the United States Marshal, or his deputy, or such other officer as the President shall designate, and to confinement in such penitentiary, prison, jail, military camp, or other place of detention as may be directed by the President.

This proclamation and the regulations herein contained shall extend and apply to all land and water, continental or insular, in any way within the jurisdiction of the United States.

PLACING RAILROADS UNDER GOVERN-MENT CONTROL

PROCLAMATION [1] ISSUED DECEMBER 26, 1917. FROM SIGNED COPY, IN MR. WILSON'S FILES, CORRECTED IN HIS OWN HAND.

* * * Now, therefore, I, Woodrow Wilson, President of the United States, under and by virtue of the powers vested in me by the foregoing resolutions and statute, and by virtue of all other powers thereto me enabling, do hereby, through Newton D. Baker, Secretary of War, take possession and assume control at 12 o'clock noon on the twenty-eighth day of December, 1917, of each and every system of transportation and the appurtenances thereof located wholly or in part within the boundaries of the continental United States and consisting of railroads, and owned or controlled systems of coastwise and inland transportation, engaged in general transportation, whether operated by steam or by electric power, including also terminals, terminal companies and terminal associations, sleeping and parlor cars, private cars and private car lines, elevators, warehouses, telegraph and telephone lines and all other equipment and appurtenances commonly used upon or operated as a part of such rail or combined rail and water systems of transportation;—to the end that such systems of transportation be utilized for the transfer and transportation of troops, war material and equipment, to the exclusion so far as may be necessary of all other traffic thereon; and that so far as such exclusive use be not necessary or desirable, such systems of transportation be

[1] In the first part of this proclamation, the President cites the joint resolutions of Congress on April 6, 1917, declaring war with Germany, and on December 7, 1917, declaring war with Austria-Hungary, and gives the statutory authorization for his action in taking over the railroads.

operated and utilized in the performance of such other services as the national interest may require and of the usual and ordinary business and duties of common carriers.

It is hereby directed that the possession, control, operation and utilization of such transportation systems hereby by me undertaken shall be exercised by and through William G. McAdoo, who is hereby appointed and designated Director General of Railroads. Said Director may perform the duties imposed upon him, so long and to such extent, as he shall determine, through the Boards of Directors, Receivers, officers and employees of said systems of transportation. Until and except so far as said Director shall from time to time by general or special orders otherwise provide, the Boards of Directors, Receivers, officers and employees of the various transportation systems shall continue the operation thereof in the usual and ordinary course of the business of common carriers, in the names of their respective companies.

Until and except so far as said Director shall from time to time otherwise by general or special orders determine, such systems of transportation shall remain subject to all existing statutes and orders of the Interstate Commerce Commission, and to all statutes and orders of regulating commissions of the various states in which said systems or any part thereof may be situated. But any orders, general or special, hereafter made by said Director, shall have paramount authority and be obeyed as such.

Nothing herein shall be construed as now affecting the possession, operation and control of street electric passenger railways, including railways commonly called interurbans, whether such railways be or be not owned or controlled by such railroad companies or systems. By subsequent order and proclamation, if and when it shall be found necessary or desirable, possession, control or operation may be taken of all or any part of such street railway systems, including subways and tunnels; and by subsequent order and proclamation possession, control and operation in whole or in part may also be relinquished to the owners thereof of any part of the railroad systems or rail and water systems, possession and control of which are hereby assumed.

The Director shall as soon as may be after having assumed such possession and control enter upon negotiations with the several companies looking to agreements for just and reasonable compensation for the possession, use and control of their respective properties on the basis of an annual guaranteed compensation, above accruing depreciation and the maintenance of their properties, equivalent, as nearly as may be, to the average of the net operating income thereof for the three-year period ending June 30, 1917,—the results of such negotiations to be reported to me for such action as may be appropriate and lawful.

But nothing herein contained, expressed or implied, or hereafter done or suffered hereunder, shall be deemed in any way to impair the rights of the stockholders, bondholders, creditors and other persons having interests in said systems of transportation or in the profits thereof, to receive just and adequate compensation for the use and control and operation of their property hereby assumed.

Regular dividends hitherto declared, and maturing interest upon bonds, debentures and other obligations, may be paid in due course; and such regular dividends and interest may continue to be paid until and unless the said Director shall from time to time otherwise by general or special orders determine; and, subject to the approval of the Director, the various carriers may agree upon and arrange for the renewal and extension of maturing obligations.

Except with the prior written assent of said Director, no attachment by mesne process or on execution shall be levied on or against any of the property used by any of said transportation systems in the conduct of their business as common carriers; but suits may be brought by and against said carriers and judgments rendered as hitherto until and except so far as said Director may, by general or special orders, otherwise determine.

From and after 12 o'clock on said twenty-eighth day of December, 1917, all transportation systems included in this order and proclamation shall conclusively be deemed within the possession and control of said Director without further act or notice. But for the purpose of accounting said possession and control shall date from 12 o'clock midnight on Dec. 31, 1917.

GOVERNMENT CONTROL OF RAILWAYS

STATEMENT TO CONGRESS, DECEMBER 26, 1917. FROM
COPY IN MR. WILSON'S FILES.

I HAVE exercised the powers over the transportation systems of the country which were granted me
by the Act of Congress of last August because it has become imperatively necessary for me to do so. This is
a war of resources no less than of men, perhaps even
more than of men, and it is necessary for the complete
mobilization of our resources that the transportation
systems of the country should be organized and employed under a single authority and a simplified method
of coördination which have not proved possible under
private management and control. The committee of
railway executives who have been coöperating with
the Government in this all-important matter have done
the utmost that it was possible for them to do; have
done it with patriotic zeal and with great ability; but
there were difficulties that they could neither escape
nor neutralize. Complete unity of administration in
the present circumstances involves upon occasion and at
many points a serious dislocation of earnings, and the
committee was, of course, without power or authority
to re-arrange charges or effect proper compensations
and adjustments of earnings. Several roads which were
willingly and with admirable public spirit accepting the
orders of the committee have already suffered from
these circumstances and should not be required to suffer
further. In mere fairness to them the full authority
of the Government must be substituted. The Government itself will thereby gain an immense increase of
efficiency in the conduct of the war and of the innumerable activities upon which its successful conduct
depends.

The public interest must be first served and, in addition, the financial interests of the Government and the financial interests of the railways must be brought under a common direction. The financial operations of the railways need not then interfere with the borrowings of the Government, and they themselves can be conducted at a greater advantage. Investors in railway securities may rest assured that their rights and interests will be as scrupulously looked after by the Government as they could be by the directors of the several railway systems. Immediately upon the reassembling of Congress I shall recommend that these definite guarantees be given: first, of course, that the railway properties will be maintained during the period of federal control in as good repair and as complete equipment as when taken over by the Government, and, second, that the roads shall receive a net operating income equal in each case to the average net income of the three years preceding June 30, 1917; and I am entirely confident that the Congress will be disposed in this case, as in others, to see that justice is done and full security assured to the owners and creditors of the great systems which the Government must now use under its own direction or else suffer serious embarrassment.

The Secretary of War and I are agreed that, all the circumstances being taken into consideration, the best results can be obtained under the immediate executive direction of the Hon. William G. McAdoo, whose practical experience peculiarly fits him for the service and whose authority as Secretary of the Treasury will enable him to coördinate as no other man could the many financial interests which will be involved and which might, unless systematically directed, suffer very embarrassing entanglements.

The Government of the United States is the only great Government now engaged in the war which has not already assumed control of this sort. It was thought to be in the spirit of American institutions to attempt to do everything that was necessary through private management, and if zeal and ability and patriotic motive could have accomplished the necessary unification of administration, it would certainly have been accomplished; but no zeal or ability could overcome insuperable obstacles, and I have deemed it my duty to recognize that fact in all candor now that it is demonstrated and to use without reserve the great authority reposed in me. A great national necessity dictated the action and I was therefore not at liberty to abstain from it.

METHODS OF RAILWAY CONTROL

ADDRESS DELIVERED AT A JOINT SESSION OF THE TWO HOUSES OF CONGRESS, JANUARY 4, 1918. FROM OFFICIAL GOVERNMENT PUBLICATION IN MR. WILSON'S FILES.

I HAVE asked the privilege of addressing you in order to report to you that on the twenty-eighth of December last, during the recess of the Congress, acting through the Secretary of War and under the authority conferred upon me by the Act of Congress approved August 29, 1916, I took possession and assumed control of the railway lines of the country and the systems of water transportation under their control. This step seemed to be imperatively necessary in the interest of the public welfare, in the presence of the great tasks of war with which we are now dealing. As our own experience develops difficulties and makes it clear what they are, I have deemed it my duty to remove those difficulties wherever I have the legal power to do so. To assume control of the vast railway systems of the country is, I realize, a very great responsibility, but to fail to do so in the existing circumstances would have been a much greater. I assumed the less responsibility rather than the weightier.

I am sure that I am speaking the mind of all thoughtful Americans when I say that it is our duty as the representatives of the Nation to do everything that it is necessary to do to secure the complete mobilization of the whole resources of America by as rapid and effective means as can be found. Transportation supplies all the arteries of mobilization. Unless it be under a single and unified direction, the whole process of the Nation's action is embarrassed.

It was in the true spirit of America, and it was right,

that we should first try to effect the necessary unification under the voluntary action of those who were in charge of the great railway properties; and we did try it. The directors of the railways responded to the need promptly and generously. The group of railway executives who were charged with the task of actual coördination and general direction performed their difficult duties with patriotic zeal and marked ability, as was to have been expected, and did, I believe, everything that it was possible for them to do in the circumstances. If I have taken the task out of their hands, it has not been because of any dereliction or failure on their part but only because there were some things which the Government can do and private management cannot. We shall continue to value most highly the advice and assistance of these gentlemen and I am sure we shall not find them withholding it.

It had become unmistakably plain that only under Government administration can the entire equipment of the several systems of transportation be fully and unreservedly thrown into a common service without injurious discrimination against particular properties. Only under Government administration can an absolutely unrestricted and unembarrassed common use be made of all tracks, terminals, terminal facilities and equipment of every kind. Only under that authority can new terminals be constructed and developed without regard to the requirements or limitations of particular roads. But under Government administration all these things will be possible,—not instantly, but as fast as practical difficulties, which cannot be merely conjured away, give way before the new management.

The common administration will be carried out with as little disturbance of the present operating organizations and personnel of the railways as possible. Nothing will be altered or disturbed which it is not necessary to disturb. We are serving the public interest and safeguarding the public safety, but we are also regardful of the interest of those by whom these great properties are owned and glad to avail ourselves of the experience and trained ability of those who have been managing them. It is necessary that the transportation of troops and of war materials, of food and of fuel, and of everything that is necessary for the full mobilization of the energies and resources of the country, should be first considered, but it is clearly in the public interest also that the ordinary activities and the normal industrial and commercial life of the country should be interfered with and dislocated as little as possible, and the public may rest assured that the interest and convenience of the private shipper will be as carefully served and safeguarded as it is possible to serve and safeguard it in the present extraordinary circumstances.

While the present authority of the Executive suffices for all purposes of administration, and while of course all private interests must for the present give way to the public necessity, it is, I am sure you will agree with me, right and necessary that the owners and creditors of the railways, the holders of their stocks and bonds, should receive from the Government an unqualified guarantee that their properties will be maintained throughout the period of federal control in as good repair and as complete equipment as at present, and that the several roads will receive under federal management such compensation as is equitable and just alike to their owners and to the general public. I would suggest the average net railway operating income of the three years ending June 30, 1917. I earnestly recommend that these guarantees be given by appropriate legislation, and given as promptly as circumstances permit.

I need not point out the essential justice of such guarantees and their great influence and significance as elements in the present financial and industrial situation of the country. Indeed, one of the strong arguments for assuming control of the railroads at this time is the financial argument. It is necessary that the values of railway securities should be justly and fairly protected and that the large financial operations every year necessary in connection with the maintenance, operation and development of the roads should, during the period of the war, be wisely related to the financial operations of the Government. Our first duty is, of course, to conserve the common interest and the common safety and to make certain that nothing stands in the way of the successful prosecution of the great war for liberty and justice, but it is also an obligation of public conscience and of public honor that the private interests we disturb should be kept safe from unjust injury, and it is of the utmost consequence to the Government itself that all great financial operations should be stabilized and coördinated with the financial operations of the Government. No borrowing should run athwart the borrowings of the federal treasury, and no fundamental industrial values should anywhere be unnecessarily impaired. In the hands of many thousands of small investors in the country, as well as in national banks, in insurance companies, in savings banks, in trust companies, in financial agencies of every kind, railway securities, the sum total of which runs up to some ten or eleven thousand millions, constitute a vital part of the structure of credit, and the unquestioned solidity of that structure must be maintained.

The Secretary of War and I easily agreed that, in view of the many complex interests which must be safeguarded and harmonized, as well as because of his exceptional experience and ability in this new field of governmental action, the Honorable William G. McAdoo was the right man to assume direct administrative control of this new executive task. At our request, he consented to assume the authority and duties of organizer and Director General of the new Railway Administration. He has assumed those duties and his work is in active progress.

It is probably too much to expect that even under the unified railway administration which will now be possible sufficient economies can be effected in the operation of the railways to make it possible to add to their equipment and extend their operative facilities as much as the present extraordinary demands upon their use will render desirable without resorting to the national treasury for the funds. If it is not possible, it will, of course, be necessary to resort to the Congress for grants of money for that purpose. The Secretary of the Treasury will advise with your committees with regard to this very practical aspect of the matter. For the present, I suggest only the guarantees I have indicated and such appropriations as are necessary at the outset of this task. I take the liberty of expressing the hope that the Congress may grant these promptly and ungrudgingly. We are dealing with great matters and will, I am sure, deal with them greatly.

THE FOURTEEN POINTS SPEECH

ADDRESS DELIVERED AT A JOINT SESSION OF THE TWO HOUSES OF CONGRESS, JANUARY 8, 1918. FROM OFFICIAL GOVERNMENT PUBLICATION IN MR. WILSON'S FILES.

ONCE more, as repeatedly before, the spokesmen of the Central Empires have indicated their desire to discuss the objects of the war and the possible bases of a general peace. Parleys have been in progress at Brest-Litovsk between representatives of the Central Powers to which the attention of all the belligerents has been invited for the purpose of ascertaining whether it may be possible to extend these parleys into a general conference with regard to terms of peace and settlement. The Russian representatives presented not only a perfectly definite statement of the principles upon which they would be willing to conclude peace but also an equally definite program of the concrete application of those principles. The representatives of the Central Powers, on their part, presented an outline of settlement which, if much less definite, seemed susceptible of liberal interpretation until their specific program of practical terms was added. That program proposed no concessions at all either to the sovereignty of Russia or to the preferences of the populations with whose fortunes it dealt, but meant, in a word, that the Central Empires were to keep every foot of territory their armed forces had occupied,—every province, every city, every point of vantage,—as a permanent addition to their territories and their power. It is a reasonable conjecture that the general principles of settlement which they at first suggested originated with the more liberal statesmen of Germany and Austria, the men who have begun to feel the force of their own peoples' thought and purpose,

while the concrete terms of actual settlement came from
the military leaders who have no thought but to keep
what they have got. The negotiations have been broken
off. The Russian representatives were sincere and in
earnest. They cannot entertain such proposals of conquest and domination.

The whole incident is full of significance. It is also
full of perplexity. With whom are the Russian representatives dealing? For whom are the representatives
of the Central Empires speaking? Are they speaking
for the majorities of their respective parliaments or for
the minority parties, that military and imperialistic
minority which has so far dominated their whole policy
and controlled the affairs of Turkey and of the Balkan
states which have felt obliged to become their associates
in this war? The Russian representatives have insisted,
very justly, very wisely, and in the true spirit of modern
democracy, that the conferences they have been holding
with the Teutonic and Turkish statesmen should be held
within open, not closed, doors, and all the world has
been audience, as was desired. To whom have we been
listening, then? To those who speak the spirit and intention of the Resolutions of the German Reichstag of the
ninth of July last, the spirit and intention of the liberal
leaders and parties of Germany, or to those who resist
and defy that spirit and intention and insist upon conquest and subjugation? Or are we listening, in fact,
to both, unreconciled and in open and hopeless contradiction? These are very serious and pregnant questions.
Upon the answer to them depends the peace of the
world.

But, whatever the results of the parleys at Brest-
Litovsk, whatever the confusions of counsel and of purpose in the utterances of the spokesmen of the Central
Empires, they have again attempted to acquaint the
world with their objects in the war and have again challenged their adversaries to say what their objects are
and what sort of settlement they would deem just and

satisfactory. There is no good reason why that challenge should not be responded to, and responded to with the utmost candor. We did not wait for it. Not once, but again and again, we have laid our whole thought and purpose before the world, not in general terms only, but each time with sufficient definition to make it clear what sort of definitive terms of settlement must necessarily spring out of them. Within the last week Mr. Lloyd George has spoken with admirable candor and in admirable spirit for the people and Government of Great Britain. There is no confusion of counsel among the adversaries of the Central Powers, no uncertainty of principle, no vagueness of detail. The only secrecy of counsel, the only lack of fearless frankness, the only failure to make definite statement of the objects of the war, lies with Germany and her Allies. The issues of life and death hang upon these definitions. No statesman who has the least conception of his responsibility ought for a moment to permit himself to continue this tragical and appalling outpouring of blood and treasure unless he is sure beyond a peradventure that the objects of the vital sacrifice are part and parcel of the very life of Society and that the people for whom he speaks think them right and imperative as he does.

There is, moreover, a voice calling for these definitions of principle and of purpose which is, it seems to me, more thrilling and more compelling than any of the many moving voices with which the troubled air of the world is filled. It is the voice of the Russian people. They are prostrate and all but helpless, it would seem, before the grim power of Germany, which has hitherto known no relenting and no pity. Their power, apparently, is shattered. And yet their soul is not subservient. They will not yield either in principle or in action. Their conception of what is right, of what it is humane and honorable for them to accept, has been stated with a frankness, a largeness of view, a generosity of spirit, and a universal human sympathy which must challenge the admiration of every friend of mankind; and they have refused to compound their ideals or desert others that they themselves may be safe. They call to us to say what it is that we desire, in what, if in anything, our purpose and our spirit differ from theirs; and I believe that the people of the United States would wish me to respond, with utter simplicity and frankness. Whether their present leaders believe it or not, it is our heartfelt desire and hope that some way may be opened whereby we may be privileged to assist the people of Russia to attain their utmost hope of liberty and ordered peace.

It will be our wish and purpose that the processes of peace, when they are begun, shall be absolutely open and that they shall involve and permit henceforth no secret understandings of any kind. The day of conquest and aggrandizement is gone by; so is also the day of secret covenants entered into in the interest of particular governments and likely at some unlooked-for moment to upset the peace of the world. It is this happy fact, now clear to the view of every public man whose thoughts do not still linger in an age that is dead and gone, which makes it possible for every nation whose purposes are consistent with justice and the peace of the world to avow now or at any other time the objects it has in view.

We entered this war because violations of right had occurred which touched us to the quick and made the life of our own people impossible unless they were corrected and the world secured once for all against their recurrence. What we demand in this war, therefore, is nothing peculiar to ourselves. It is that the world be made fit and safe to live in; and particularly that it be made safe for every peace-loving nation which, like our own, wishes to live its own life, determine its own institutions, be assured of justice and fair dealing by the other peoples of the world as against force and selfish aggression. All the peoples of the world are in effect partners in this interest, and for our own part we see very clearly that unless justice be done to others it will not be done to us. The program of the world's peace, therefore, is our program; and that program, the only possible program, as we see it, is this:

I. Open covenants of peace, openly arrived at, after which there shall be no private international understandings of any kind but diplomacy shall proceed always frankly and in the public view.

II. Absolute freedom of navigation upon the seas, outside territorial waters, alike in peace and in war, except as the seas may be closed in whole or in part by international action for the enforcement of international covenants.

III. The removal, so far as possible, of all economic barriers and the establishment of an equality of trade conditions among all the nations consenting to the peace and associating themselves for its maintenance.

IV. Adequate guarantees given and taken that national armaments will be reduced to the lowest point consistent with domestic safety.

V. A free, open-minded, and absolutely impartial adjustment of all colonial claims, based upon a strict observance of the principle that in determining all such questions of sovereignty the interests of the populations concerned must have equal weight with the equitable claims of the government whose title is to be determined.

VI. The evacuation of all Russian territory and such a settlement of all questions affecting Russia as will secure the best and freest coöperation of the other nations of the world in obtaining for her an unhampered and unembarrassed opportunity for the independent determination of her own political development and national policy and assure her of a sincere welcome into the society of free nations under institutions of her own choosing; and, more than a welcome, assistance also of every kind that she may need and may herself desire. The treatment accorded Russia by her sister nations in the months to come will be the acid test of their good will, of their comprehension of her needs as distinguished from their own interests, and of their intelligent and unselfish sympathy.

VII. Belgium, the whole world will agree, must be evacuated and restored, without any attempt to limit the sovereignty which she enjoys in common with all other free nations. No other single act will serve as this will serve to restore confidence among the nations in the laws which they have themselves set and determined for the government of their relations with one another. Without this healing act the whole structure and validity of international law is forever impaired.

VIII. All French territory should be freed and the invaded portions restored, and the wrong done to France by Prussia in 1871 in the matter of Alsace-Lorraine, which has unsettled the peace of the world for nearly fifty years, should be righted, in order that peace may once more be made secure in the interest of all.

IX. A readjustment of the frontiers of Italy should be effected along clearly recognizable lines of nationality.

X. The peoples of Austria-Hungary, whose place among the nations we wish to see safeguarded and assured, should be accorded the freest opportunity of autonomous development.

XI. Rumania, Serbia, and Montenegro should be evacuated; occupied territories restored; Serbia accorded free and secure access to the sea; and the relations of the several Balkan states to one another determined by friendly counsel along historically established lines of allegiance and nationality; and international guarantees of the political and economic independence and territorial integrity of the several Balkan states should be entered into.

XII. The Turkish portions of the present Ottoman Empire should be assured a secure sovereignty, but the other nationalities which are now under Turkish rule should be assured an undoubted security of life and an absolutely unmolested opportunity of autonomous development, and the Dardanelles should be permanently opened as a free passage to the ships and commerce of all nations under international guarantees.

XIII. An independent Polish state should be erected which should include the territories inhabited by indisputably Polish populations, which should be assured a free and secure access to the sea, and whose political and economic independence and territorial integrity should be guaranteed by international covenant.

XIV. A general association of nations must be formed under specific covenants for the purpose of affording mutual guarantees of political independence and territorial integrity to great and small states alike.

In regard to these essential rectifications of wrong and assertions of right we feel ourselves to be intimate partners of all the governments and peoples associated together against the Imperialists. We cannot be separated in interest or divided in purpose. We stand together until the end.

For such arrangements and covenants we are willing to fight and to continue to fight until they are achieved; but only because we wish the right to prevail and desire a just and stable peace such as can be secured only by removing the chief provocations to war, which this program does remove. We have no jealousy of German greatness, and there is nothing in this program that impairs it. We grudge her no achievement or distinction of learning or of pacific enterprise such as have made her record very bright and very enviable. We do not wish to injure her or to block in any way her legitimate influence or power. We do not wish to fight her either with arms or with hostile arrangements of trade if she is willing to associate herself with us and the other peace-loving nations of the world in covenants of justice and law and fair dealing. We wish her only to accept a place of equality among the peoples of the world,—the new world in which we now live,—instead of a place of mastery.

Neither do we presume to suggest to her any alteration or modification of her institutions. But it is necessary, we must frankly say, and necessary as a preliminary to any intelligent dealings with her on our part, that we should know whom her spokesmen speak for when they speak to us, whether for the Reichstag majority or for the military party and the men whose creed is imperial domination.

We have spoken now, surely, in terms too concrete to admit of any further doubt or question. An evident principle runs through the whole program I have outlined. It is the principle of justice to all peoples and nationalities, and their right to live on equal terms of liberty and safety with one another, whether they be strong or weak. Unless this principle be made its foundation no part of the structure of international justice can stand. The people of the United States could act upon no other principle; and to the vindication of this principle they are ready to devote their lives, their honor, and everything that they possess. The moral climax of this the culminating and final war for human liberty has come, and they are ready to put their own strength, their own highest purpose, their own integrity and devotion to the test.

WELCOME TO THE FIRST RUMANIAN MINISTER AT WASHINGTON

REPLY TO THE RUMANIAN MINISTER, DR. CONSTANTIN ANGELESCO, UPON HIS PRESENTATION OF CREDENTIALS, JANUARY 15, 1918. FROM "OFFICIAL BULLETIN," NO. 211.

I AM happy to accept the letters by which His Majesty, the King of Rumania, accredits you as envoy extraordinary and minister plenipotentiary to the Government of the United States, and to accord you formal recognition in that capacity.

I appreciate and thank you for the views you express with regard to the present effect of the entrance of the Government of the United States of America into the fearful war now raging in Europe and your hopeful prediction that through this a new order of things built upon the freedom of nations and international equity will result.

The United States has been forced into this great conflict much against its will, and yet there is a great underlying satisfaction in the thought that no longer must the United States stand off, a mute spectator, in the presence of the cruel and barbaric acts which have been heaped upon your people. Your nation has endured with extraordinary patience and self-possession a long series of tyrannies at the hands of a relentless oppressor, and the United States, in fighting to protect her own liberty and integrity as a nation, is glad to have freed its arm for the like protection of your country and your country's allies. I am glad to express the confidence that our combined efforts will issue in a final triumph of right and liberty.

The intercourse between our two countries in the past, while always animated by trust and confidence, has not been extensive, but Rumania and the United States are now drawn closer together as common sufferers in a common cause, and the action of the Government of Rumania in sending a diplomatic representative to this country is accepted as an added evidence of fraternal good will and a welcome recognition of the importance of unity and good understanding.

I welcome you to our country as the first Rumanian Minister at Washington, and I am sure that your efforts in that high capacity to promote the common interest of both Rumania and the United States will be successful. In these efforts I shall be most happy to give you my hearty coöperation.

I trust that you will find your residence at this capital most agreeable.

FUEL CONTROL

STATEMENT UPHOLDING THE FUEL CURTAILMENT
ORDER, JANUARY 19, 1918. FROM ORIGINAL COPY
IN MR. WILSON'S FILES.

I WAS, of course, consulted by Mr. Garfield before
the fuel order of yesterday was issued, and fully
agreed with him that it was necessary, much as I regretted the necessity. This war calls for many sacrifices, and sacrifices of the sort called for by this order
are infinitely less than sacrifices of life which might
otherwise be involved. It is absolutely necessary to
get the ships away, it is absolutely necessary to relieve
the congestion at the ports and upon the railways, it
is absolutely necessary to move great quantities of food,
and it is absolutely necessary that our people should
be warmed in their homes if nowhere else, and halfway measures would not have accomplished the desired
ends. If action such as this had not been taken, we
should have limped along from day to day with a
slowly improving condition of affairs with regard to
the shipment of food and of coal, but without such
immediate relief as had become absolutely necessary
because of the congestions of traffic which have been
piling up for the last few months.

I have every confidence that the result of action of
this sort will justify it and that the people of the
country will loyally and patriotically respond to necessities of this kind as they have to every other sacrifice
involved in the war. We are upon a war footing, and
I am confident that the people of the United States are
willing to observe the same sort of discipline that
might be involved in the actual conflict itself.

"ORDERLY OBSERVANCE OF THE SABBATH"

MESSAGE TO THE ARMY AND NAVY OF THE UNITED STATES, JANUARY 20, 1918. FROM COPY IN MR. WILSON'S FILES.

THE President, commander in chief of the Army and Navy, following the reverent example of his predecessors, desires and enjoins the orderly observance of the Sabbath by the officers and men in the military and naval service of the United States. The importance for man and beast of the prescribed weekly rest, the sacred rights of Christian soldiers and sailors, a becoming deference to the best sentiment of a Christian people, and a due regard for the Divine Will demand that Sunday labor in the Army and Navy be reduced to the measure of strict necessity. Such an observance of Sunday is dictated by the best traditions of our people and by the convictions of all who look to Divine Providence for guidance and protection, and, in repeating in this order the language of President Lincoln, the President is confident that he is speaking alike to the hearts and to the consciences of those under his authority.

EFFICIENCY OF WAR DEPARTMENT

STATEMENT ANSWERING SENATOR CHAMBERLAIN'S
CHARGE OF GOVERNMENT INEFFICIENCY, JANU-
ARY 21, 1918. FROM "OFFICIAL BULLETIN,"
NO. 214.

SENATOR CHAMBERLAIN'S statement as to the
present inaction and ineffectiveness of the Government is an astonishing and absolutely unjustifiable dis-
tortion of the truth. As a matter of fact, the War
Department has performed a task of unparalleled magnitude and difficulty with extraordinary promptness and
efficiency. There have been delays and disappointments
and partial miscarriages of plans, all of which have
been drawn into the foreground and exaggerated by
the investigations which have been in progress since
the Congress assembled—investigations which drew
indispensable officials of the department constantly
away from their work and officers from their commands and contributed a great deal to such delay and
confusion as had inevitably arisen. But, by comparison with what has been accomplished, these things,
much as they were to be regretted, were insignificant,
and no mistake has been made which has been repeated.

Nothing helpful or likely to speed or facilitate the
war tasks of the Government has come out of such
criticism and investigation. I understand that reorgani-
zations by legislation are to be proposed—I have not
been consulted about them and have learned of them
only at second hand—but their proposal came after
effective measures of reorganization had been thoughtfully and maturely perfected, and inasmuch as these
measures have been the result of experience, they are
much more likely than any others to be effective, if the
Congress will but remove the few statutory obstacles of

rigid departmental organization which stand in their way. The legislative proposals I have heard of would involve long additional delays and turn our experience into mere lost motion. My association and constant conference with the Secretary of War have taught me to regard him as one of the ablest public officials I have ever known. The country will soon learn whether he or his critics understand the business in hand.

To add, as Senator Chamberlain did, that there is inefficiency in every department and bureau of the Government is to show such ignorance of actual conditions as to make it impossible to attach any importance to his statement. I am bound to infer that that statement sprang out of opposition to the administration's whole policy rather than out of any serious intention to reform its practice.

APPEAL TO THE FARMERS TO "STAND BY"

MESSAGE TO THE FARMERS' CONFERENCE AT URBANA, ILLINOIS, JANUARY 31, 1918. FROM "OFFICIAL BULLETIN," NO. 222.

I AM very sorry indeed that I cannot be present in person at the Urbana conference.[1] I should like to enjoy the benefit of the inspiration and exchange of counsel which I know I should obtain, but in the circumstances it has seemed impossible for me to be present, and therefore I can only send you a very earnest message expressing my interest and the thoughts which such a conference must bring prominently into every mind.

I need not tell you, for I am sure you realize as keenly as I do, that we are as a Nation in the presence of a great task which demands supreme sacrifice and endeavor of every one of us. We can give everything that is needed with the greater willingness, and even satisfaction, because the object of the war in which we are engaged is the greatest that free men have ever undertaken. It is to prevent the life of the world from being determined and the fortunes of men everywhere affected by small groups of military masters, who seek their own interest and the selfish dominion throughout the world of the Governments they unhappily for the moment control. You will not need to be convinced that it was necessary for us as a free people to take part in this war. It had raised its evil hand against us. The rulers of Germany had sought to exercise their power in such a way as to shut off our economic

[1] Mr. Wilson was prevented by illness from being present at the Conference. Since Secretary Houston, who was to have represented the President, was also unable to attend the Conference, owing to a tie-up in transportation facilities, the message was presented by President James of the University of Illinois.

life so far as our intercourse with Europe was concerned, and to confine our people within the Western Hemisphere while they accomplished purposes which would have permanently impaired and impeded every process of our national life and have put the fortunes of America at the mercy of the Imperial Government of Germany.

This was no threat. It had become a reality. Their hand of violence had been laid upon our own people and our own property in flagrant violation not only of justice but of the well-recognized and long-standing covenants of international law and treaty. We are fighting, therefore, as truly for the liberty and self-government of the United States as if the war of our own Revolution had to be fought over again; and every man in every business in the United States must know by this time that his whole future fortune lies in the balance. Our national life and our whole economic development will pass under the sinister influences of foreign control if we do not win. We must win, therefore, and we shall win. I need not ask you to pledge your lives and fortunes with those of the rest of the Nation to the accomplishment of that great end.

You will realize, as I think statesmen on both sides of the water realize, that the culminating crisis of the struggle has come and that the achievements of this year on the one side or the other must determine the issue. It has turned out that the forces that fight for freedom, the freedom of men all over the world as well as our own, depend upon us in an extraordinary and unexpected degree for sustenance, for the supply of the materials by which men are to live and to fight, and it will be our glory when the war is over that we have supplied those materials and supplied them abundantly, and it will be all the more glory because in supplying them we have made our supreme effort and sacrifice.

In the field of agriculture we have agencies and instrumentalities, fortunately, such as no other government in the world can show. The Department of Agriculture is undoubtedly the greatest practical and scientific agricultural organization in the world. Its total annual budget of $46,000,000 has been increased during the last four years more than 72 per cent. It has a staff of 18,000, including a large number of highly trained experts, and alongside of it stand the unique land-grant colleges, which are without example elsewhere, and the 69 state and federal experiment stations. These colleges and experiment stations have a total endowment of plant and equipment of $172,000,000 and an income of more than $35,000,000, with 10,271 teachers, a resident student body of 125,000, and a vast additional number receiving instruction at their homes. County agents, joint officers of the Department of Agriculture and of the colleges, are everywhere coöperating with the farmers and assisting them. The number of extension workers under the Smith-Lever Act and under the recent emergency legislation has grown to 5,500 men and women working regularly in the various communities and taking to the farmer the latest scientific and practical information.

Alongside these great public agencies stand the very effective voluntary organizations among the farmers themselves which are more and more learning the best methods of coöperation and the best methods of putting to practical use the assistance derived from governmental sources. The banking legislation of the last two or three years has given the farmers access to the great lendable capital of the country, and it has become the duty both of the men in charge of the Federal Reserve Banking System and of the Farm Loan Banking System to see to it that the farmers obtain the credit, both short term and long term, to which they are not only entitled, but which it is imperatively necessary should be extended to them if the present tasks of the country are to be adequately performed. Both by direct purchase of nitrates and by the establishment of plants to produce nitrates the Government is doing its utmost to assist in the problem of fertilization. The Department of Agriculture and other agencies are actively assisting the farmers to locate, safeguard, and secure at cost an adequate supply of sound seed. The Department has $2,500,000 available for this purpose now and has asked the Congress for $6,000,000 more.

The labor problem is one of great difficulty and some of the best agencies of the Nation are addressing themselves to the task of solving it, so far as it is possible to solve it. Farmers have not been exempted from the draft. I know that they would not wish to be. I take it for granted they would not wish to be put in a class by themselves in this respect. But the attention of the War Department has been very seriously centered upon the task of interfering with the labor of the farms as little as possible, and under the new draft regulations I believe that the farmers of the country will find that their supply of labor is very much less seriously drawn upon than it was under the first and initial draft, made before we had had our present full experience in these perplexing matters. The supply of labor in all industries is a matter we must look to and are looking to with diligent care.

And let me say that the stimulation of the agencies I have enumerated has been responded to by the farmers in splendid fashion. I dare say that you are aware that the farmers of this country are as efficient as any other farmers in the world. They do not produce more per acre than the farmers in Europe. It is not necessary that they should do so. It would perhaps be bad economy for them to attempt it. But they do produce by two to three or four times more per man, per unit of labor and capital, than the farmers of any European country. They are more alert and use more labor-saving devices than any other farmers in the world. And their response to the demands of the present emergency has been in every way remarkable. Last spring their

planting exceeded by 12,000,000 acres the largest planting of any previous year, and the yields from the crops
were record-breaking yields. In the fall of 1917 a
wheat acreage of 42,170,000 was planted, which was
one million larger than for any preceding year, three
millions greater than the next largest, and seven millions
greater than the preceding five-year average.

But I ought to say to you that it is not only necessary
that these achievements should be repeated, but that
they should be exceeded. I know what this advice involves. It involves not only labor but sacrifice, the
painstaking application of every bit of scientific knowledge and every tested practice that is available. It
means the utmost economy, even to the point where the
pinch comes. It means the kind of concentration and
self-sacrifice which is involved in the field of battle
itself, where the object always looms greater than the
individual. And yet the Government will help and
help in every way that is possible. The impression
which prevails in some quarters, that while the Government has sought to fix the prices of foodstuffs, it has
not sought to fix other prices which determine the expenses of the farmer is a mistaken one. As a matter of
fact, the Government has actively and successfully regulated the prices of many fundamental materials underlying all the industries of the country, and has regulated
them, not only for the purchases of the Government,
but also for the purchases of the general public, and I
have every reason to believe that the Congress will
extend the powers of the Government in this important
and even essential matter, so that the tendency to
profiteering which is showing itself in too many quarters, may be effectively checked. In fixing the prices of
foodstuffs the Government has sincerely tried to keep
the interests of the farmer as much in mind as the interests of the communities which are to be served, but it
is serving mankind as well as the farmer, and every-

thing in these times of war takes on the rigid aspect of duty.

I will not appeal to you to continue and renew and increase your efforts. I do not believe that it is necessary to do so. I believe that you will do it without any word or appeal from me, because you understand as well as I do the needs and opportunities of this great hour when the fortunes of mankind everywhere seem about to be determined and when America has the greatest opportunity she has ever had to make good her own freedom and in making it good to lend a helping hand to men struggling for their freedom everywhere. You remember that it was farmers from whom came the first shots at Lexington, that set aflame the revolution that made America free. I hope and believe that the farmers of America will willingly and conspicuously stand by to win this war also.

The toil, the intelligence, the energy, the foresight, the self-sacrifice, and devotion of the farmers of America will, I believe, bring to a triumphant conclusion this great last war for the emancipation of men from the control of arbitrary government and the selfishness of class legislation and control, and then, when the end has come, we may look each other in the face and be glad that we are Americans and have had the privilege to play such a part.

CONFIDENCE IN THE FARMERS

REPLY TO A DELEGATION FROM THE FARMERS' COÖP-
ERATIVE AND EDUCATIONAL UNION, FEBRUARY 8,
1918. FROM "OFFICIAL BULLETIN," NO. 230.

I CANNOT, of course, offhand answer so important a
memorial as this, and I need not tell you that it will
receive my most careful and respectful attention. Many
of the questions that are raised here have been matters
of very deep and constant concern with us for months
past, and I believe that many of them are approaching
as successful a solution as we can work out for them,
but just what those steps are I cannot now detail to
you. You are probably familiar with some of them.

I want to say that I fully recognize, as Mr. Davis
has said, that you gentlemen do not mean that your
utmost efforts will be dependent upon the acceptance
of these suggestions. I know you are going to do your
level best in any circumstances, and I count on you with
the utmost confidence in that. There has never been a
time, gentlemen, which tested the real quality of folks
as this time is going to test it; because we are fighting
for something bigger than any man's imagination can
grasp. This is the final tackle between the things that
America has always been opposed to and was organized
to fight and the things that she stands for. It is the
final contest, and to lose it would set the world back,
not a hundred—perhaps several—years in the development of human rights. The thing cannot be exaggerated
in its importance, and I know that you men are ready,
as I am, to spend every ounce of energy we have got
in solving this thing. If we cannot solve it in the best
way, we will solve it in the next best way, and if the
next best way is not available, we will solve it in the way

next best to that, but we will tackle it in some way and do it as well as we can.

I am complimented by a visit of so large a representation, and thank you for the candid presentation of this interesting memorial.

WAR AIMS OF GERMANY AND AUSTRIA

ADDRESS DELIVERED AT A JOINT SESSION OF THE TWO
HOUSES OF CONGRESS, DISCUSSING THE GERMAN
AND AUSTRIAN REPLIES TO THE STATEMENT OF
ALLIED WAR AIMS. FEBRUARY 11, 1918. FROM
OFFICIAL GOVERNMENT PUBLICATION IN MR. WIL-
SON'S FILES.

ON THE eighth of January I had the honor of
addressing you on the objects of the war as our
people conceive them. The Prime Minister of Great
Britain had spoken in similar terms on the fifth of January. To these addresses the German Chancellor replied
on the twenty-fourth and Count Czernin, for Austria,
on the same day. It is gratifying to have our desire so
promptly realized that all exchanges of view on this
great matter should be made in the hearing of all the
world.

Count Czernin's reply, which is directed chiefly to my
own address of the eighth of January, is uttered in a
very friendly tone. He finds in my statement a sufficiently encouraging approach to the views of his own
Government to justify him in believing that it furnishes
a basis for a more detailed discussion of purposes by
the two Governments. He is represented to have intimated that the views he was expressing had been communicated to me beforehand and that I was aware of
them at the time he was uttering them; but in this I am
sure he was misunderstood. I had received no intimation of what he intended to say. There was, of course,
no reason why he should communicate privately with
me. I am quite content to be one of his public audience.

Count von Hertling's reply is, I must say, very vague
and very confusing. It is full of equivocal phrases and
leads it is not clear where. But it is certainly in a very

different tone from that of Count Czernin, and apparently of an opposite purpose. It confirms, I am sorry to say, rather than removes, the unfortunate impression made by what we had learned of the conferences at Brest-Litovsk. His discussion and acceptance of our general principles lead him to no practical conclusions. He refuses to apply them to the substantive items which must constitute the body of any final settlement. He is jealous of international action and of international counsel. He accepts, he says, the principle of public diplomacy, but he appears to insist that it be confined, at any rate in this case, to generalities and that the several particular questions of territory and sovereignty, the several questions upon whose settlement must depend the acceptance of peace by the twenty-three states now engaged in the war, must be discussed and settled, not in general council, but severally by the nations most immediately concerned by interest or neighborhood. He agrees that the seas should be free, but looks askance at any limitation to that freedom by international action in the interest of the common order. He would without reserve be glad to see economic barriers removed between nation and nation, for that could in no way impede the ambitions of the military party with whom he seems constrained to keep on terms. Neither does he raise objection to a limitation of armaments. That matter will be settled of itself, he thinks, by the economic conditions which must follow the war. But the German colonies, he demands, must be returned without debate. He will discuss with no one but the representatives of Russia what disposition shall be made of the peoples and the lands of the Baltic provinces; with no one but the Government of France the "conditions" under which French territory shall be evacuated; and only with Austria what shall be done with Poland. In the determination of all questions affecting the Balkan states he defers, as I understand him, to Austria and Turkey; and with regard to the agreements to be entered into concerning the non-Turkish peoples of the present Ottoman Empire, to the Turkish authorities themselves. After a settlement all around, effected in this fashion, by individual barter and concession, he would have no objection, if I correctly interpret his statement, to a league of nations which would undertake to hold the new balance of power steady against external disturbance.

It must be evident to everyone who understands what this war has wrought in the opinion and temper of the world that no general peace, no peace worth the infinite sacrifices of these years of tragical suffering, can possibly be arrived at in any such fashion. The method the German Chancellor proposes is the method of the Congress of Vienna. We cannot and will not return to that. What is at stake now is the peace of the world. What we are striving for is a new international order based upon broad and universal principles of right and justice,—no mere peace of shreds and patches. Is it possible that Count von Hertling does not see that, does not grasp it, is in fact living in his thought in a world dead and gone? Has he utterly forgotten the Reichstag Resolutions of the nineteenth of July, or does he deliberately ignore them? They spoke of the conditions of a general peace, not of national aggrandizement or of arrangements between state and state. The peace of the world depends upon the just settlement of each of the several problems to which I adverted in my recent address to the Congress. I, of course, do not mean that the peace of the world depends upon the acceptance of any particular set of suggestions as to the way in which those problems are to be dealt with. I mean only that those problems each and all affect the whole world; that unless they are dealt with in a spirit of unselfish and unbiased justice, with a view to the wishes, the natural connections, the racial aspirations, the security, and the peace of mind of the peoples involved, no permanent peace will have been attained.

They cannot be discussed separately or in corners. None of them constitutes a private or separate interest from which the opinion of the world may be shut out. Whatever affects the peace affects mankind, and nothing settled by military force, if settled wrong, is settled at all. It will presently have to be reopened.

Is Count von Hertling not aware that he is speaking in the court of mankind, that all the awakened nations of the world now sit in judgment on what every public man, of whatever nation, may say on the issues of a conflict which has spread to every region of the world? The Reichstag Resolutions of July themselves frankly accepted the decisions of that court. There shall be no annexations, no contributions, no punitive damages. Peoples are not to be handed about from one sovereignty to another by an international conference or an understanding between rivals and antagonists. National aspirations must be respected; peoples may now be dominated and governed only by their own consent. "Self-determination" is not a mere phrase. It is an imperative principle of action, which statesmen will henceforth ignore at their peril. We cannot have general peace for the asking, or by the mere arrangements of a peace conference. It cannot be pieced together out of individual understandings between powerful states. All the parties to this war must join in the settlement of every issue anywhere involved in it; because what we are seeking is a peace that we can all unite to guarantee and maintain and every item of it must be submitted to the common judgment whether it be right and fair, an act of justice, rather than a bargain between sovereigns.

The United States has no desire to interfere in European affairs or to act as arbiter in European territorial disputes. She would disdain to take advantage of any internal weakness or disorder to impose her own will upon another people. She is quite ready to be shown that the settlements she has suggested are not the best or the most enduring. They are only her own provisional sketch of principles and of the way in which they should be applied. But she entered this war because she was made a partner, whether she would or not, in the sufferings and indignities inflicted by the military masters of Germany, against the peace and security of mankind; and the conditions of peace will touch her as nearly as they will touch any other nation to which is entrusted a leading part in the maintenance of civilization. She cannot see her way to peace until the causes of this war are removed, its renewal rendered as nearly as may be impossible.

This war had its roots in the disregard of the rights of small nations and of nationalities which lacked the union and the force to make good their claim to determine their own allegiances and their own forms of political life. Covenants must now be entered into which will render such things impossible for the future; and those covenants must be backed by the united force of all the nations that love justice and are willing to maintain it at any cost. If territorial settlements and the political relations of great populations which have not the organized power to resist are to be determined by the contracts of the powerful governments which consider themselves most directly affected, as Count von Hertling proposes, why may not economic questions also? It has come about in the altered world in which we now find ourselves that justice and the rights of peoples affect the whole field of international dealing as much as access to raw materials and fair and equal conditions of trade. Count von Hertling wants the essential bases of comercial and industrial life to be safeguarded by common agreement and guarantee, but he cannot expect that to be conceded him if the other matters to be determined by the articles of peace are not handled in the same way as items in the final accounting. He cannot ask the benefit of common agreement in the one field without according it in the other. I take it for granted that he sees that separate and selfish compacts with regard to trade and the essential materials of manufacture would afford no foundation for peace. Neither, he may rest assured, will separate and selfish compacts with regard to provinces and peoples.

Count Czernin seems to see the fundamental elements of peace with clear eyes and does not seek to obscure them. He sees that an independent Poland, made up of all the indisputably Polish peoples who lie contiguous to one another, is a matter of European concern and must of course be conceded; that Belgium must be evacuated and restored, no matter what sacrifices and concessions that may involve; and that national aspirations must be satisfied, even within his own Empire, in the common interest of Europe and mankind. If he is silent about questions which touch the interest and purpose of his allies more nearly than they touch those of Austria only, it must of course be because he feels constrained, I suppose, to defer to Germany and Turkey in the circumstances. Seeing and conceding, as he does, the essential principles involved and the necessity of candidly applying them, he naturally feels that Austria can respond to the purpose of peace as expressed by the United States with less embarrassment than could Germany. He would probably have gone much farther had it not been for the embarrassments of Austria's alliances and of her dependence upon Germany.

After all, the test of whether it is possible for either government to go any further in this comparison of views is simple and obvious. The principles to be applied are these:

First, that each part of the final settlement must be based upon the essential justice of that particular case and upon such adjustments as are most likely to bring a peace that will be permanent;

Second, that peoples and provinces are not to be bartered about from sovereignty to sovereignty as if they were mere chattels and pawns in a game, even the great

game, now forever discredited, of the balance of power;
but that

Third, every territorial settlement involved in this
war must be made in the interest and for the benefit of
the populations concerned, and not as a part of any mere
adjustment or compromise of claims amongst rival
states; and

Fourth, that all well-defined national aspiration shall
be accorded the utmost satisfaction that can be accorded
them without introducing new or perpetuating old elements of discord and antagonism that would be likely
in time to break the peace of Europe and consequently
of the world.

A general peace erected upon such foundations can
be discussed. Until such a peace can be secured we have
no choice but to go on. So far as we can judge, these
principles that we regard as fundamental are already
everywhere accepted as imperative except among the
spokesmen of the military and annexationist party in
Germany. If they have anywhere else been rejected,
the objectors have not been sufficiently numerous or influential to make their voices audible. The tragical circumstance is that this one party in Germany is apparently willing and able to send millions of men to their
death to prevent what all the world now sees to be just.

I would not be a true spokesman of the people of
the United States if I did not say once more that we
entered this war upon no small occasion, and that we can
never turn back from a course chosen upon principle.
Our resources are in part mobilized now, and we shall
not pause until they are mobilized in their entirety. Our
armies are rapidly going to the fighting front, and will
go more and more rapidly. Our whole strength will be
put into this war of emancipation,—emancipation from
the threat and attempted mastery of selfish groups of
autocratic rulers,—whatever the difficulties and present
partial delays. We are indomitable in our power of
independent action and can in no circumstances consent

to live in a world governed by intrigue and force. We believe that our own desire for a new international order under which reason and justice and the common interests of mankind shall prevail is the desire of enlightened men everywhere. Without that new order the world will be without peace and human life will lack tolerable conditions of existence and development. Having set our hand to the task of achieving it, we shall not turn back.

I hope that it is not necessary for me to add that no word of what I have said is intended as a threat. That is not the temper of our people. I have spoken thus only that the whole world may know the true spirit of America,—that men everywhere may know that our passion for justice and for self-government is no mere passion of words but a passion which, once set in action, must be satisfied. The power of the United States is a menace to no nation or people. It will never be used in aggression or for the aggrandizement of any selfish interest of our own. It springs out of freedom and is for the service of freedom.

MESSAGE TO STRIKING SHIP CARPENTERS

TELEGRAM TO MR. WILLIAM L. HUTCHESON, GENERAL
PRESIDENT OF THE UNITED BROTHERHOOD OF CAR-
PENTERS AND JOINERS OF AMERICA, NEW YORK,
FEBRUARY 17, 1918. FROM ORIGINAL COPY IN
MR. WILSON'S FILES.

I HAVE received your telegram of yesterday and am very glad to note the expression of your desire as a patriotic citizen to assist in carrying on the work by which we are trying to save America and men everywhere who work and are free. Taking advantage of that assurance, I feel it to be my duty to call your attention to the fact that the strike of the carpenters in the shipyards is in marked and painful contrast to the action of labor in other trades and places. Ships are absolutely necessary for the winning of this war. No one can strike a deadlier blow at the safety of the Nation and of its forces on the other side than by interfering with or obstructing the shipbuilding program.

All the other unions engaged in this indispensable work have agreed to abide by the decisions of the Shipbuilding Wage Adjustment Board. That Board has dealt fairly and liberally with all who have resorted to it.

I must say to you very frankly that it is your duty to leave to it the solution of your present difficulties with your employers and to advise the men whom you represent to return at once to work pending the decision. No body of men have the moral right in the present circumstances of the Nation to strike until every method of adjustment has been tried to the limit. If you do not act upon this principle you are undoubtedly giving aid and comfort to the enemy, whatever may be your own conscious purpose.

I do not see that anything will be gained by my seeing you personally until you have accepted and acted
upon that principle. It is the duty of the Government
to see that the best possible conditions of labor are
maintained, as it is also its duty to see to it that there
is no lawless and conscienceless profiteering and that
duty the Government has accepted and will perform.
Will you coöperate or will you obstruct?

                            WOODROW WILSON.

FIXING THE PRICE OF WHEAT

STATEMENT ISSUED IN EXPLANATION OF THE PROCLA-
MATION OF FEBRUARY 21ST, WHICH ANNOUNCED
THE PRICE OF WHEAT, FEBRUARY 25, 1918. FROM
"OFFICIAL BULLETIN," NO. 242.

UNDER the food control act of August 10, 1917, it is my duty to announce a guaranteed price for wheat of the 1918 harvest. I am, therefore, issuing a proclamation setting the price at the principal interior primary markets. It makes no essential alteration in the present guarantee. It is a continuation of the present prices of wheat, with some adjustments arising from the designation of additional terminal marketing points.

This guaranteed price assures the farmer of a reasonable profit even if the war should end within the year and the large stores of grain in those sections of the world that are now cut off from transportation should again come into competition with his products. To increase the price of wheat above the present figure, or to agitate any increase of price, would have the effect of very seriously hampering the large operations of the Nation and of the Allies by causing the wheat of last year's crop to be withheld from the market. It would, moreover, dislocate all the present wage levels that have been established after much anxious discussion, and would, therefore, create an industrial unrest which would be harmful to every industry in the country.

I know the spirit of our farmers and have not the least doubt as to the loyalty with which they will accept the present decision. The fall wheat planting, which furnishes two-thirds of our wheat production, took place with no other assurance than this, and the farmers' confidence was demonstrated by the fact that they planted an acreage larger than the record of any preceding year, larger by 2,000,000 acres than the second largest record year, and 7,000,000 acres more than the average for the five years before the outbreak of the European war.

It seems not to be generally understood why wheat is picked out for price determination, and only wheat, among the cereals. The answer is that, while normal distribution of all our farm products has been subject to great disturbances during the last three years because of war conditions, only two important commodities, namely, wheat and sugar, have been so seriously affected as to require governmental intervention. The disturbances which affect these products (and others in less degree) arise from the fact that all of the over-seas shipping in the world is now under Government control and that the Government is obliged to assign tonnage to each commodity that enters into commercial over-seas traffic. It has, consequently, been necessary to establish single agencies for the purchase of the food supplies which must go abroad. The purchase of wheat in the United States for foreign use is of so great volume in comparison with the available domestic supply that the price of wheat has been materially disturbed, and it became necessary, in order to protect both the producer and the consumer, to prevent speculation. It was necessary, therefore, for the Government to exercise a measure of direct supervision and as far as possible to control purchases of wheat and the processes of its exportation. This supervision necessarily amounted to price fixing, and I, therefore, thought it fair and wise that there should be a price stated that should be at once liberal and equitable.

Those peculiar circumstances governing the handling and consumption of wheat put the farmer at the very center of war service. Next to the soldier himself, he is serving the country and the world and serving it in a way which is absolutely fundamental to his own future safety and prosperity. He sees this and can be relied upon as the soldier can.

The farmer is also contributing men to the Army, and I am keenly alive to the sacrifices involved. Out of 13,800,000 men engaged in farm industries, 205,000 have been drafted, or about 1.48 per cent of the whole number. In addition to these there have been volunteers, and the farmers have lost a considerable number of laborers because the wages paid in industrial pursuits drew them away. In order to relieve the farming industry as far as possible from further drains of labor the new draft regulations have been drawn with a view to taking from the farms an even smaller proportion of men, and it is my hope that the local exemption boards will make the new classifications with a view of lightening the load upon the farmers to the utmost extent. The Secretary of War has asked for authority to furlough soldiers of the National Army if conditions permit it, so that they may return to their farms when assistance is necessary in the planting and harvesting of the crops. National and local agencies are actively at work, besides, in organizing community help for the more efficient distribution of available labor and in drawing upon new sources of labor. While there will be difficulties, and very serious ones, they will be difficulties which are among the stern necessities of war.

The Federal Railway Administration is coöperating in the most active, intelligent, and efficient way with the Food Administration to remove the difficulties of transportation and of the active movement of the crops. Their marketing is to be facilitated and the farmers given the opportunity to realize promptly upon their stocks.

The Department of Agriculture and the Food Administration will continue to coöperate as heretofore to assist the farmers in every way possible. All questions of production, of the marketing of farm products, of conservation in the course of production, and of agricultural labor and farm problems generally will be handled by the Department of Agriculture, while all questions of distribution of food supplies to the Allies and of conservation in consumption will be handled by the Food Administration; but the chief reliance is upon the farmer himself, and I am sure that that reliance will be justified by the results. The chief thing to be kept clearly in mind is that regulations of this sort are only a part of the great general plan of mobilization into which every element in the Nation enters in this war as in no other. The business of war touches everybody. It is a stern business, a coöperative business, a business of energy and sacrifice, a business of service in the largest and best and most stirring sense of that great word.

SYMPATHY FOR THE RUSSIAN PEOPLE

MESSAGE TO THE PEOPLE OF RUSSIA THROUGH THE SOVIET CONGRESS, MARCH 11, 1918. FROM "OFFICIAL BULLETIN," NO. 255.

MAY I not take advantage of the meeting of the Congress of the Soviets to express the sincere sympathy which the people of the United States feel for the Russian people at this moment when the German power has been thrust in to interrupt and turn back the whole struggle for freedom and substitute the wishes of Germany for the purposes of the people of Russia?

Although the Government of the United States is unhappily not now in a position to render the direct and effective aid it would wish to render, I beg to assure the people of Russia through the Congress that it will avail itself of every opportunity to secure for Russia once more complete sovereignty and independence in her own affairs and full restoration to her great rôle in the life of Europe and the modern world.

The whole heart of the people of the United States is with the people of Russia in the attempt to free themselves forever from autocratic government and become the masters of their own life.

OPEN DIPLOMACY

LETTER TO SECRETARY ROBERT LANSING, MARCH 12, 1918. FROM THE "CONGRESSIONAL RECORD," VOL. 56, P. 7653.

MY DEAR MR. SECRETARY:
I wish you would be kind enough to formulate a careful and conclusive memorandum for the use of the committee of the Senate with regard to the inclosed resolution. I take it for granted that you feel as I do, that this is no time to act as the resolution prescribes, and certainly when I pronounced for open diplomacy I meant not that there should be no private discussions of delicate matters, but that no secret agreement of any sort should be entered into and that all international relations, when fixed, should be open, aboveboard, and explicit.

Cordially and sincerely yours,
WOODROW WILSON.

"EVERY PARTY MUST TRY TO SERVE HUMANITY"

LETTER TO THE DEMOCRATS OF NEW JERSEY, MARCH 20, 1918. FROM THE "CONGRESSIONAL RECORD," VOL. 56, PP. 5491–5492.

MY DEAR MR. TOASTMASTER:
I sincerely regret that matters of pressing importance will prevent my taking part in the reorganization banquet to which you have generously invited me. It is my feeling, as I am sure it will be the feeling of those present, that my clear duty is to stay here on the job. My work can be properly done only if I devote my whole thought and attention to it and think of nothing but the immediate task in hand.

At the time it is clear that in the present posture of affairs in New Jersey I cannot overlook my responsibility as leader of a great party, and that it is my privilege to point out what I believe to be the duty of the Democrats in New Jersey, now and in the months to come, in order that the exigency of a great hour of crisis may properly be met.

During the months that I had the privilege of serving the people of New Jersey in the office of governor we sought to accomplish this definite purpose, namely, to open the processes of government to the access and inspection of every citizen in order that the people might feel that the government of New Jersey represented their hopes, their impulses, and their sympathies.

It was with this great purpose in mind that we succeeded in establishing electoral machinery which took away from selfish political leaders the power to hold the mass of the party voters of the State in subjection to themselves.

In the matter of employers' liability, we substituted

193

for the cold letter of the old law the warm and wholesome tonic of a humane statute.

In every act of legislation we cut a clear pathway
of public service and achieved a record remarkable for
its variety and humanity, in every way comprehensive in
character and touching no vital interest in the State
with a spirit of injustice or demagogy.

We gave the people, after many tedious and discouraging years of waiting, a government which they could
feel was their own, free and unhampered by special
privilege.

A time of grave crisis has come in the life of the
Democratic party in New Jersey, a time when its
friends and supporters must face the facts of the situation if they would serve the cause of free government
in New Jersey. Every sign of these terrible days of
war and revolutionary change, when economic and social
forces are being released upon the world whose effect
no political seer dare venture to conjecture, bids us
search our hearts through and through and make them
ready for the birth of a new day, a day we hope and
believe of greater opportunity and greater prosperity
for the average mass of struggling men and women,
and of greater safety and opportunity for children.

The old party slogans have lost their significance and
will mean nothing to the voter of the future, for the
war is certain to change the mind of Europe as well as
the mind of America. Men everywhere are searching
democratic principles to their hearts in order to determine their soundness, their sincerity, their adaptability
to the real needs of their life, and every man with any
vision must see that the real test of justice and right
action is presently to come as it never came before.
The men in the trenches, who have been freed from the
economic serfdom to which some of them had been accustomed, will, it is likely, return to their homes with
a new view and a new impatience of all mere political

phrases, and will demand real thinking and sincere action.

Let the Democratic party in New Jersey therefore forget everything but the new service which it is to be called upon to render. The days of political and economic reconstruction which are ahead of us no man can now definitely assess, but we know this: That every program must be shot through and through with utter disinterestedness; that no party must try to serve itself, but every party must try to serve humanity, and that the task is a very practical one, meaning that every program, every measure in every program, must be tested by this question and this question only:

Is it just; is it for the benefit of the average man, without influence or privilege; does it embody in real fact the highest conception of social justice and of right dealing without respect of person or class or particular interest? This is a high test. It can be met only by those who have genuine sympathy with the mass of men and real insight into their needs and opportunities and a purpose which is purged alike of selfish and of partisan intention. The party which rises to this test will receive the support of the people, because it deserves it.

Very sincerely yours,
WOODROW WILSON.

MESSAGE OF CONFIDENCE TO
FIELD-MARSHAL HAIG

CABLEGRAM TO FIELD-MARSHAL HAIG, IN COMMAND OF
THE BRITISH FORCES, MARCH 25, 1918. FROM
"OFFICIAL BULLETIN," NO. 266.

MAY I not express to you my warm admiration of the splendid steadfastness and valor with which your troops have withstood the German onset, and the perfect confidence all Americans feel that you will win a secure and final victory?

WOODROW WILSON.

MESSAGE OF CONGRATULATION TO
GENERAL FOCH

CABLEGRAM TO GENERAL FOCH ON HIS ASSUMPTION OF COMMAND OF THE ALLIED ARMIES, MARCH 29, 1918. FROM "OFFICIAL BULLETIN," NO. 271.

MAY I not convey to you my sincere congratulations on your new authority? Such unity of command is a most hopeful augury of ultimate success. We are following with profound interest the bold and brilliant action of your forces.

WOODROW WILSON.

OPENING THE THIRD LIBERTY LOAN
CAMPAIGN

ADDRESS AT BALTIMORE, MARYLAND, APRIL 6, 1918.
FROM OFFICIAL GOVERNMENT PUBLICATION IN MR.
WILSON'S FILES.

THIS is the anniversary of our acceptance of Germany's challenge to fight for our right to live and be free, and for the sacred rights of free men everywhere. The Nation is awake. There is no need to call to it. We know what the war must cost, our utmost sacrifice, the lives of our fittest men and, if need be, all that we possess. The loan we are met to discuss is one of the least parts of what we are called upon to give and to do, though in itself imperative. The people of the whole country are alive to the necessity of it, and are ready to lend to the utmost, even where it involves a sharp skimping and daily sacrifice to lend out of meager earnings. They will look with reprobation and contempt upon those who can and will not, upon those who demand a higher rate of interest, upon those who think of it as a mere commercial transaction. I have not come, therefore, to urge the loan. I have come only to give you, if I can, a more vivid conception of what it is for.

The reasons for this great war, the reason why it had to come, the need to fight it through, and the issues that hang upon its outcome, are more clearly disclosed now than ever before. It is easy to see just what this particular loan means because the Cause we are fighting for stands more sharply revealed than at any previous crisis of the momentous struggle. The man who knows least can now see plainly how the cause of Justice stands and what the imperishable thing is he is asked to invest in. Men in America may be more sure than they ever were before that the cause is their own, and that, if it should be lost, their own great Nation's place and mission in the world would be lost with it.

I call you to witness, my fellow countrymen, that at no stage of this terrible business have I judged the purposes of Germany intemperately. I should be ashamed in the presence of affairs so grave, so fraught with the destinies of mankind throughout all the world, to speak with truculence, to use the weak language of hatred or vindictive purpose. We must judge as we would be judged. I have sought to learn the objects Germany has in this war from the mouths of her own spokesmen, and to deal as frankly with them as I wished them to deal with me. I have laid bare our own ideals, our own purposes, without reserve or doubtful phrase, and have asked them to say as plainly what it is that they seek.

We have ourselves proposed no injustice, no aggression. We are ready, whenever the final reckoning is made, to be just to the German people, deal fairly with the German power, as with all others. There can be no difference between peoples in the final judgment, if it is indeed to be a righteous judgment. To propose anything but justice, even-handed and dispassionate justice, to Germany at any time, whatever the outcome of the war, would be to renounce and dishonor our own cause. For we ask nothing that we are not willing to accord.

It has been with this thought that I have sought to learn from those who spoke for Germany whether it was justice or dominion and the execution of their own will upon the other nations of the world that the German leaders were seeking. They have answered, answered in unmistakable terms. They have avowed that it was not justice but dominion and the unhindered execution of their own will.

The avowal has not come from Germany's statesmen. It has come from her military leaders, who are her real rulers. Her statesmen have said that they wished peace, and were ready to discuss its terms whenever their opponents were willing to sit down at the conference table with them. Her present Chancellor has said,—in indefinite and uncertain terms, indeed, and in phrases that often seem to deny their own meaning, but with as much plainness as he thought prudent,— that he believed that peace should be based upon the principles which we had declared would be our own in the final settlement. At Brest-Litovsk her civilian delegates spoke in similar terms; professed their desire to conclude a fair peace and accord to the peoples with whose fortunes they were dealing the right to choose their own allegiances. But action accompanied and followed the profession. Their military masters, the men who act for Germany and exhibit her purpose in execution, proclaimed a very different conclusion. We cannot mistake what they have done,—in Russia, in Finland, in the Ukraine, in Rumania. The real test of their justice and fair play has come. From this we may judge the rest. They are enjoying in Russia a cheap triumph in which no brave or gallant nation can long take pride. A great people, helpless by their own act, lies for the time at their mercy. Their fair professions are forgotten. They nowhere set up justice, but everywhere impose their power and exploit everything for their own use and aggrandizement; and the peoples of conquered provinces are invited to be free under their dominion!

Are we not justified in believing that they would do the same things at their western front if they were not there face to face with armies whom even their countless divisions cannot overcome? If, when they have felt their check to be final, they should propose favorable and equitable terms with regard to Belgium and France and Italy, could they blame us if we concluded that they did so only to assure themselves of a free hand in Russia and the East?

Their purpose is undoubtedly to make all the Slavic

peoples, all the free and ambitious nations of the Baltic peninsula, all the lands that Turkey has dominated and misruled, subject to their will and ambition and build upon that dominion an empire of force upon which they fancy that they can then erect an empire of gain and commercial supremacy,—an empire as hostile to the Americas as to the Europe which it will overawe,— an empire which will ultimately master Persia, India, and the peoples of the Far East. In such a program our ideals, the ideals of justice and humanity and liberty, the principle of the free self-determination of nations upon which all the modern world insists, can play no part. They are rejected for the ideals of power, for the principle that the strong must rule the weak, that trade must follow the flag, whether those to whom it is taken welcome it or not, that the peoples of the world are to be made subject to the patronage and overlordship of those who have the power to enforce it.

That program once carried out, America and all who care or dare to stand with her must arm and prepare themselves to contest the mastery of the world, a mastery in which the rights of common men, the rights of women and of all who are weak, must for the time being be trodden under foot and disregarded, and the old, age-long struggle for freedom and right begin again at its beginning. Everything that America has lived for and loved and grown great to vindicate and bring to a glorious realization will have fallen in utter ruin and the gates of mercy once more pitilessly shut upon mankind!

The thing is preposterous and impossible; and yet is not that what the whole course and action of the German armies has meant wherever they have moved? I do not wish, even in this moment of utter disillusionment, to judge harshly or unrighteously. I judge only what the German arms have accomplished with unpitying thoroughness throughout every fair region they have touched.

What, then, are we to do? For myself, I am ready, ready still, ready even now, to discuss a fair and just and honest peace at any time that it is sincerely purposed,—a peace in which the strong and the weak shall fare alike. But the answer, when I proposed such a peace, came from the German commanders in Russia, and I cannot mistake the meaning of the answer.

I accept the challenge. I know that you accept it. All the world shall know that you accept it. It shall appear in the utter sacrifice and self-forgetfulness with which we shall give all that we love and all that we have to redeem the world and make it fit for free men like ourselves to live in. This now is the meaning of all that we do. Let everything that we say, my fellow countrymen, everything that we henceforth plan and accomplish, ring true to this response till the majesty and might of our concerted power shall fill the thought and utterly defeat the force of those who flout and misprize what we honor and hold dear. Germany has once more said that force, and force alone, shall decide whether Justice and peace shall reign in the affairs of men, whether Right as America conceives it or Dominion as she conceives it shall determine the destinies of mankind. There is, therefore, but one response possible from us: Force, Force to the utmost, Force without stint or limit, the righteous and triumphant Force which shall make Right the law of the world, and cast every selfish dominion down in the dust.

APPEAL FOR THE THIRD LIBERTY LOAN

PROCLAMATION SETTING APRIL 26 AS LIBERTY DAY, ISSUED APRIL 18, 1918. FROM "UNITED STATES STATUTES AT LARGE," VOL. 40, PT. 2, PP. 1771–1772.

AN ENEMY who has grossly abused the power of organized government and who seeks to dominate the world by the might of the sword, challenges the rights of America and the liberty and life of all the free nations of the earth. Our brave sons are facing the fire of battle in defense of the honor and rights of America and the liberty of nations. To sustain them and to assist our gallant associates in the war, a generous and patriotic people have been called upon to subscribe to the Third Liberty Loan.

NOW, THEREFORE, I, WOODROW WILSON, PRESIDENT OF THE UNITED STATES OF AMERICA, do appoint Friday, the twenty-sixth day of April, One Thousand Nine Hundred and Eighteen, as Liberty Day. On the afternoon of that day I request the people of the United States to assemble in their respective communities and liberally pledge anew their financial support to sustain the Nation's cause. Patriotic demonstrations should be held in every city, town and hamlet throughout the land under the general direction of the Secretary of the Treasury and the immediate direction of the Liberty Loan Committees organized by the Federal Reserve Banks. Let the Nation's response to the Third Liberty Loan express in unmistakable terms the determination of America to fight for peace, the permanent peace of justice.

For the purpose of participating in Liberty Day celebrations, all employees of the Federal Government throughout the country whose services can be spared, may be excused at twelve o'clock noon, Friday, the twenty-sixth of April.

FOR THE AMERICAN RED CROSS

ADDRESS OPENING THE CAMPAIGN IN NEW YORK FOR
THE SECOND RED CROSS FUND, MAY 18, 1918,
FROM OFFICIAL GOVERNMENT PUBLICATION IN MR.
WILSON'S FILES.

I SHOULD be very sorry to think that Mr. Davison in any degree curtailed his exceedingly interesting speech for fear that he was postponing mine, because I am sure you listened with the same intent and intimate interest with which I listened to the extraordinarily vivid account he gave of the things which he had realized because he had come in contact with them on the other side of the water. We compassed them with our imagination. He compassed them in his personal experience.

I am not come here to-night to review for you the work of the Red Cross. I am not competent to do so, because I have not had the time or the opportunity to follow it in detail. I have come here simply to say a few words to you as to what it all seems to me to mean.

It means a great deal. There are two duties with which we are face to face. The first duty is to win the war. The second duty, that goes hand in hand with it, is to win it greatly and worthily, showing the real quality of our power not only, but the real quality of our purpose and of ourselves. Of course, the first duty, the duty that we must keep in the foreground of our thought until it is accomplished, is to win the war. I have heard gentlemen recently say that we must get five million men ready. Why limit it to five million? I have asked the Congress of the United States to name no limit, because the Congress intends, I am sure, as we all intend, that every ship that can carry men or supplies

205

shall go laden upon every voyage with every man and every supply she can carry.

And we are not to be diverted from the grim purpose of winning the war by any insincere approaches upon the subject of peace. I can say with a clear conscience that I have tested those intimations and have found them insincere. I now recognize them for what they are, an opportunity to have a free hand, particularly in the East, to carry out purposes of conquest and exploitation. Every proposal with regard to accommodation in the West involves a reservation with regard to the East. Now, so far as I am concerned, I intend to stand by Russia as well as France. The helpless and the friendless are the very ones that need friends and succor, and if any man in Germany thinks we are going to sacrifice anybody for our own sake, I tell them now they are mistaken. For the glory of this war, my fellow citizens, so far as we are concerned, is that it is, perhaps for the first time in history, an unselfish war. I could not be proud to fight for a selfish purpose, but I can be proud to fight for mankind. If they wish peace, let them come forward through accredited representatives and lay their terms on the table. We have laid ours, and they know what they are.

But behind all this grim purpose, my friends, lies the opportunity to demonstrate not only force, which will be demonstrated to the utmost, but the opportunity to demonstrate character, and it is that opportunity that we have most conspicuously in the work of the Red Cross. Not that our men in arms do not represent our character, for they do, and it is a character which those who see and realize appreciate and admire, but their duty is the duty of force. The duty of the Red Cross is the duty of mercy and succor and friendship.

Have you formed a picture in your imagination of what this war is doing for us and for the world? In my own mind I am convinced that not a hundred years of peace could have knitted this Nation together as this single year of war has knitted it together; and better even than that, if possible, it is knitting the world together. Look at the picture! In the center of the scene, four nations engaged against the world, and at every point of vantage, showing that they are seeking selfish aggrandizement; and against them, twenty-three governments, representing the greater part of the population of the world, drawn together into a new sense of community of interest, a new sense of community of purpose, a new sense of unity of life. The Secretary of War told me an interesting incident the other day. He said when he was in Italy a member of the Italian Government was explaining to him the many reasons why Italy felt near to the United States. He said, "If you want to try an interesting experiment, go up to any one of these troop trains and ask in English how many of them have been in America, and see what happens." He tried the experiment. He went up to a troop train and he asked, "How many of you boys have been in America," and he said it seemed to him as if half of them sprang up: "Me from San Francisco," "Me from New York,"—all over. There was part of the heart of America in the Italian Army,—people that had been knitted to us by association, who knew us, who had lived amongst us, who had worked shoulder to shoulder with us, and now, friends of America, were fighting for their native Italy.

Friendship is the only cement that will ever hold the world together. And this intimate contact of the great Red Cross with the peoples who are suffering the terrors and deprivations of this war is going to be one of the greatest instrumentalities of friendship that the world ever knew; and the center of the heart of it all, if we sustain it properly, will be this land that we so dearly love.

My friends, a great day of duty has come, and duty finds a man's soul as no kind of work can ever find it. May I say this: The duty that faces us all now is to serve one another. No man can afford to make a fortune out of this war. There are men amongst us who have forgotten that, if they ever saw it. Some of you are old enough—I am old enough—to remember men who made fortunes out of the Civil War, and you know how they were regarded by their fellow citizens. That was a war to save one country. This is a war to save the world. And your relation to the Red Cross is one of the relations which will relieve you of the stigma. You cannot give anything to the Government of the United States. It will not accept it. There is a law of Congress against accepting even services without pay. The only thing that the Government will accept is a loan and duties performed, but it is a great deal better to give than to lend or to pay, and your great channel for giving is the American Red Cross. Down in your hearts you cannot take very much satisfaction in the last analysis in lending money to the Government of the United States, because the interest which you draw will burn your pockets. It is a commercial transaction; and some men have even dared to cavil at the rate of interest, not knowing the incidental commentary that that constitutes upon their attitude.

But when you give, something of your heart, something of your soul, something of yourself goes with the gift, particularly when it is given in such form that it never can come back by way of direct benefit to yourself. You know there is the old cynical definition of gratitude, as "the lively expectation of favors to come." Well, there is no expectation of favors to come in this kind of giving. These things are bestowed in order that the world may be a fitter place to live in, that men may be succored, that homes may be restored, that suffering may be relieved, that the face of the earth may have the blight of destruction removed from it, and that wherever force goes, there shall go mercy and helpfulness.

And when you give, give absolutely all that you can

spare, and do not consider yourself liberal in the giving. If you give with self-adulation, you are not giving at all, you are giving to your own vanity, but if you give until it hurts, then your heart-blood goes into it.

Think what we have here! We call it the American Red Cross, but it is merely a branch of a great international organization which is not only recognized by the statutes of each of the civilized governments of the world, but is recognized by international agreement and treaty, as the recognized and accepted instrumentality of mercy and succor. And one of the deepest stains that rest upon the reputation of the German Army is that they have not respected the Red Cross. That goes to the root of the matter. They have not respected the instrumentality they themselves participated in setting up as the thing which no man was to touch because it was the expression of common humanity. By being members of the American Red Cross, we are members of a great fraternity and comradeship which extends all over the world. This cross which these ladies bore to-day is an emblem of Christianity itself.

It fills my imagination, ladies and gentlemen, to think of the women all over this country who are busy to-night, and are busy every night and every day, doing the work of the Red Cross, busy with a great eagerness to find out the most serviceable thing to do, busy with a forgetfulness of all the old frivolities of their social relationships, ready to curtail the duties of the house-hold in order that they may contribute to this common work that all their hearts are engaged in and in doing which their hearts become acquainted with each other. When you think of this, you realize how the people of the United States are being drawn together into a great intimate family whose heart is being used for the serv-ice of the soldiers not only, but for the service of civilians where they suffer and are lost in a maze of distresses and distractions.

You have, then, this noble picture of justice and

mercy as the two servants of liberty. For only where men are free do they think the thoughts of comradeship, only where they are free do they think the thoughts of sympathy, only where they are free are they mutually helpful, only where they are free do they realize their dependence upon one another and their comradeship in a common interest and common necessity. If you ladies and gentlemen could read some of the touching dispatches which come through official channels, for even through those channels there come voices of humanity that are infinitely pathetic; if you could catch some of those voices that speak the utter longing of oppressed and helpless peoples all over the world to hear something like the Battle Hymn of the Republic, to hear the feet of the great hosts of Liberty coming to set them free, to set their minds free, set their lives free, set their children free; you would know what comes into the heart of those who are trying to contribute all the brains and power they have to this great enterprise of Liberty. I summon you to the comradeship. I summon you in this next week to say how much and how sincerely and how unanimously you sustain the heart of the world.

GODSPEED TO ITALY

MESSAGE TO THE ITALIAN PEOPLE ON THE THIRD ANNI-
VERSARY OF THEIR ENTRANCE INTO THE WAR,
MAY 23, 1918. FROM "OFFICIAL U. S. BULLETIN,"
NO. 318.

I AM sure that I am speaking for the people of the United States in sending to the Italian people warm fraternal greetings upon this the anniversary of the entrance of Italy into this great war in which there is being fought out once for all the irrepressible conflict between free self-government and the dictation of force.

The people of the United States have looked with profound interest and sympathy upon the efforts and sacrifices of the Italian people, are deeply and sincerely interested in the present and future security of Italy, and are glad to find themselves associated with a people to whom they are bound by so many personal and intimate ties in a struggle whose object is liberation, freedom, the rights of men and nations to live their own lives and determine their own fortunes, the rights of the weak as well as of the strong, and the maintenance of justice by the irresistible force of free nations leagued together in the defense of mankind.

With ever increasing resolution and force we shall continue to stand together in this sacred common cause. America salutes the gallant Kingdom of Italy and bids her Godspeed.

OUTLINE OF EXPENDITURES FROM FUND FOR NATIONAL SECURITY AND DEFENSE

LETTER TO CONGRESSMAN SWAGAR SHERLEY OF KEN-
TUCKY, MAY 24, 1918. FROM ORIGINAL COPY IN
MR. WILSON'S FILES.

M Y DEAR MR. SHERLEY:
I take the liberty of writing to call your attention to an appropriation which seems to me of capital
importance in connection with the effective conduct of
the war. I refer to the sum for National Security and
Defense which has been placed at my disposal during
the past fiscal year. I think that it is of the utmost
importance that a similar fund should be put at my
disposal for the next fiscal year, though in my judgment
it need not be so large as the last appropriation for
that purpose. I think that a sum of half the amount,
namely, $50,000,000, would be abundant.

I believe that you and your colleagues on the Committee on Appropriations are familiar with the objects
for which I have used the appropriation, but perhaps
you will permit me to summarize them and to append
an outline of the actual expenditures.

I have used considerable sums for the maintenance
of the Food Administration, the Fuel Administration,
and the War Trade Board, and for the maintenance of
the proper agencies for the allocation of labor, a matter
of very great consequence and of no little difficulty just
now when there is so general a dislocation of labor
throughout the country. For these objects it seems
probable that the fund is no longer necessary, inasmuch
as their administration has now been quite thoroughly
organized and is susceptible of being maintained by

definite appropriations assigned to their use in the usual
manner.   Of course, this method of appropriation is
preferable to any other.

Besides these objects I have spent very large sums
for the repair of ships owned by alien enemies which
we took possession of immediately after our entrance
into the war and which, as you know, had been deliberately damaged in the most serious way by their own
crews; for the providing of temporary accommodations
for the newly-created services connected with the war;
for advances to the regular departments for services
appropriated for in the usual way when it seemed unwise
in the circumstances to wait until appropriations, which
could certainly be counted upon, could be acted upon by
the Congress; to provide additional facilities for the
Civil Service Commission in order that it might more
nearly meet the exceptional demands of the time for
clerical aid; for miscellaneous expenses connected with
the very serviceable action of the Council of National
Defense; and for labor matters of many sorts, investigation, mediation, the settlement of strikes, and many
objects arising from time to time and impossible to
foresee or calculate for beforehand.   Most of these
matters may also now, fortunately, be taken care of
in the regular way, though similar occasions for the
immediate expenditure of money may no doubt arise on
a smaller scale than before.   Some of these objects,
as for example, the repair of ships, have now been, I
assume, entirely covered.

There remain the uses for such a fund which I may
perhaps characterize as continuing but incalculable.   I
refer to the conduct of many necessary investigations,
for example in connection with the determination of the
prices which the Government is to pay and which the
governments associated with us in the war are to pay:

To indispensable secret service and to confidential
uses abroad:

To the very large necessities of record and information:

To the maintenance of the instrumentalities, both on this side of the water and on the other, which are doing admirable work in informing public opinion both here and there of the real aims of America, of the progress she is making in the conduct of the war, and of the real facts with regard to all the larger aspects of our policy:

And to the service and guidance to all sorts of patriotic movements in the United States which appeal to the Government for its assistance and for materials wherewith to conduct their work.

Besides these things which can now be stated, the experience of the past year convinces me that there are many occasions which will arise which I cannot now even conjecture, but which will make it necessary that I should have a free fund at my disposal.

May I not take the liberty of saying a word of special emphasis with regard to the work which the Committee on Public Information has been doing? I have had very close personal connections with the work of that committee and have watched its development and its activities with particular care and interest, feeling a special responsibility. The work of the Committee has, on the whole, been admirably done, and I think it very likely that nobody, not even those intimately connected with the Government, is aware of the extent, the variety and the usefulness of that work or of the really unusually economical manner in which it has been accomplished, so far as the expenditure of money is concerned. I should feel personally crippled if any obstacle of any kind were put in the way of that work.

It is probable that it will now be possible to a considerable extent to submit estimates of the usual sort to take care of the work of the committee, and I hope that in connection with those estimates at least some of the members of the Committee on Appropriations may have an opportunity to know more particularly what it has been doing.

Cordially and sincerely yours,

WOODROW WILSON.

MONEY FOR THE WAR

ADDRESS DELIVERED AT A JOINT SESSION OF THE TWO
HOUSES OF CONGRESS, MAY 27, 1918. FROM OFFI-
CIAL GOVERNMENT PUBLICATION IN MR. WILSON'S
FILES.

I T IS with unaffected reluctance that I come to ask you
to prolong your session long enough to provide more
adequate resources for the Treasury for the conduct of
the war. I have reason to appreciate as fully as you do
how arduous the session has been. Your labors have
been severe and protracted. You have passed a long
series of measures which required the debate of many
doubtful questions of judgment and many exceedingly
difficult questions of principle as well as of practice. The
summer is upon us in which labor and counsel are twice
as arduous and are constantly apt to be impaired by lassi-
tude and fatigue. The elections are at hand and we
ought as soon as possible to go and render an intimate
account of our trusteeship to the people who delegated
us to act for them in the weighty and anxious matters
that crowd upon us in these days of critical choice and
action. But we dare not go to the elections until we
have done our duty to the full. These are days when
duty stands stark and naked and even with closed eyes
we know it is there. Excuses are unavailing. We have
either done our duty or we have not. The fact will be as
gross and plain as the duty itself. In such a case lassi-
tude and fatigue seem negligible enough. The facts
are tonic and suffice to freshen the labor.

And the facts are these: Additional revenues must
manifestly be provided for. It would be a most un-
sound policy to raise too large a proportion of them
by loan, and it is evident that the four billions now provided for by taxation will not of themselves sustain the

greatly enlarged budget to which we must immediately look forward. We cannot in fairness wait until the end of the fiscal year is at hand to apprise our people of the taxes they must pay on their earnings of the present calendar year, whose accountings and expenditures will then be closed. We cannot get increased taxes unless the country knows what they are to be and practices the necessary economy to make them available. Definiteness, early definiteness, as to what its tasks are to be is absolutely necessary for the successful administration of the Treasury: it cannot frame fair and workable regulations in haste; and it must frame its regulations in haste if it is not to know its exact task until the very eve of its performance. The present tax laws are marred, moreover, by inequities which ought to be remedied. Indisputable facts, every one; and we cannot alter or blink them. To state them is argument enough.

And yet perhaps you will permit me to dwell for a moment upon the situation they disclose. Enormous loans freely spent in the stimulation of industry of almost every sort produce inflations and extravagances which presently make the whole economic structure questionable and insecure and the very basis of credit is cut away. Only fair, equitably distributed taxation, of the widest incidence and drawing chiefly from the sources which would be likely to demoralize credit by their very abundance, can prevent inflation and keep our industrial system free of speculation and waste. We shall naturally turn, therefore, I suppose, to war profits and incomes and luxuries for the additional taxes. But the war profits and incomes upon which the increased taxes will be levied will be the profits and incomes of the calendar year 1918. It would be manifestly unfair to wait until the early months of 1919 to say what they are to be. It might be difficult, I should imagine, to run the mill with water that had already gone over the wheel.

Moreover, taxes of that sort will not be paid until

the June of next year, and the Treasury must anticipate
them. It must use the money they are to produce
before it is due. It must sell short-time certificates of
indebtedness. In the autumn a much larger sale of long-
time bonds must be effected than has yet been attempted.
What are the bankers to think of the certificates if they
do not certainly know where the money is to come from
which is to take them up? And how are investors to
approach the purchase of bonds with any sort of confidence or knowledge of their own affairs if they do not
know what taxes they are to pay and what economies
and adjustments of their business they must effect? I
cannot assure the country of a successful administration
of the Treasury in 1918 if the question of further taxation is to be left undecided until 1919.

The consideration that dominates every other now,
and makes every other seem trivial and negligible, is
the winning of the war. We are not only in the midst
of the war, we are at the very peak and crisis of it.
Hundreds of thousands of our men, carrying our hearts
with them and our fortunes, are in the field, and ships
are crowding faster and faster to the ports of France
and England with regiment after regiment, thousand
after thousand, to join them until the enemy shall be
beaten and brought to a reckoning with mankind. There
can be no pause or intermission. The great enterprise
must, on the contrary, be pushed with greater and
greater energy. The volume of our might must steadily and rapidly be augmented until there can be no question of resisting it. If that is to be accomplished, gentlemen, money must sustain it to the utmost. Our financial program must no more be left in doubt or suffered
to lag than our ordnance program or our ship program
or our munitions program or our program for making
millions of men ready. These others are not programs,
indeed, but mere plans upon paper, unless there is to be
an unquestionable supply of money.

That is the situation, and it is the situation which

creates the duty, no choice or preference of ours. There is only one way to meet that duty. We must meet it without selfishness or fear of consequences. Politics is adjourned. The elections will go to those who think least of it; to those who go to the constituencies without explanations or excuses, with a plain record of duty faithfully and disinterestedly performed. I, for one, am always confident that the people of this country will give a just verdict upon the service of the men who act for them when the facts are such that no man can disguise or conceal them. There is no danger of deceit now. An intense and pitiless light beats upon every man and every action in this tragic plot of war that is now upon the stage. If lobbyists hurry to Washington to attempt to turn what you do in the matter of taxation to their protection or advantage, the light will beat also upon them. There is abundant fuel for the light in the records of the Treasury with regard to profits of every sort. The profiteering that cannot be got at by the restraints of conscience and love of country can be got at by taxation. There is such profiteering now and the information with regard to it is available and indisputable.

I am advising you to act upon this matter of taxation now, gentlemen, not because I do not know that you can see and interpret the facts and the duty they impose just as well and with as clear a perception of the obligations involved as I can, but because there is a certain solemn satisfaction in sharing with you the responsibilities of such a time. The world never stood in such case before. Men never before had so clear or so moving a vision of duty. I know that you will begrudge the work to be done here by us no more than the men begrudge us theirs who lie in the trenches and sally forth to their death. There is a stimulating comradeship knitting us all together. And this task to which I invite your immediate consideration will be performed under favorable influences if we will look to what the country is thinking and expecting and care nothing at all for what is being said and believed in the lobbies of Washington hotels, where the atmosphere seems to make it possible to believe what is believed nowhere else.

Have you not felt the spirit of the Nation rise and its thought become a single and common thought since these eventful days came in which we have been sending our boys to the other side? I think you must read that thought, as I do, to mean this, that the people of this country are not only united in the resolute purpose to win this war but are ready and willing to bear any burden and undergo any sacrifice that it may be necessary for them to bear in order to win it. We need not be afraid to tax them, if we lay taxes justly. They know that the war must be paid for and that it is they who must pay for it, and if the burden is justly distributed and the sacrifice made a common sacrifice from which none escapes who can bear it at all, they will carry it cheerfully and with a sort of solemn pride. I have always been proud to be an American, and was never more proud than now, when all that we have said and all that we have foreseen about our people is coming true. The great days have come when the only thing that they ask for or admire is duty greatly and adequately done; when their only wish for America is that she may share the freedom she enjoys; when a great, compelling sympathy wells up in their hearts for men everywhere who suffer and are oppressed; and when they see at last the high uses for which their wealth has been piled up and their mighty power accumulated and, counting neither blood nor treasure now that their final day of opportunity has come, rejoice to spend and to be spent through a long night of suffering and terror in order that they and men everywhere may see the dawn of a day of righteousness and justice and peace. Shall we grow weary when they bid us act?

"A NATIONAL CONCERTED THRIFT MOVEMENT"

STATEMENT URGING THE BUYING OF GOVERNMENT SECURITIES AND WAR SAVINGS STAMPS, MAY 31, 1918. FROM "OFFICIAL U. S. BULLETIN," NO. 323.

THIS war is one of nations—not of armies—and all of our one hundred million people must be economically and industrially adjusted to war conditions if this Nation is to play its full part in the conflict. The problem before us is not, primarily, a financial problem, but rather a problem of increased production of war essentials and the saving of the materials and the labor necessary for the support and equipment of our Army and Navy. Thoughtless expenditure of money for non-essentials uses up the labor of men, the products of the farm, mines and factories, and overburdens transportation, all of which must be used to the utmost and at their best for war purposes.

The great results which we seek can be obtained only by the participation of every member of the Nation, young and old, in a national concerted thrift movement. I therefore urge that our people everywhere pledge themselves, as suggested by the Secretary of the Treasury, to the practice of thrift; to serve the Government to their utmost in increasing production in all fields necessary to the winning of the war; to conserve food and fuel and useful materials of every kind; to devote their labor only to the most necessary tasks; and to buy only those things which are essential to individual health and efficiency; and that the people, as evidence of their loyalty, invest all that they can save in Liberty bonds and war-savings stamps. The securities issued by the Treasury Department are so many of them within the reach of every one that the door of opportunity in this matter is wide open to all of us. To practice thrift in peace times is a virtue and brings great benefit to the individual at all times; with the desperate need of the civilized world to-day for materials and labor with which to end the war, the practice of individual thrift is a patriotic duty and a necessity.

I appeal to all who now own either Liberty bonds or war-savings stamps to continue to practice economy and thrift and to appeal to all who do not own Government securities to do likewise and purchase them to the extent of their means. The man who buys Government securities transfers the purchasing power of his money to the United States Government until after this war, and to that same degree does not buy in competition with the Government.

I earnestly appeal to every man, woman, and child to pledge themselves on or before the 28th of June to save constantly and to buy as regularly as possible the securities of the Government; and to do this as far as possible through membership in war-savings societies. The 28th of June ends this special period of enlistment in the great volunteer army of production and saving here at home. May there be none unenlisted on that day!

SINCERE FRIENDSHIP FOR MEXICO

ADDRESS TO A PARTY OF MEXICAN EDITORS, AT THE WHITE HOUSE, JUNE 7, 1918. FROM "OFFICIAL U. S. BULLETIN," NO. 332.

I HAVE never received a group of men who were more welcome than you are, because it has been one of my distresses during the period of my Presidency that the Mexican people did not more thoroughly understand the attitude of the United States towards Mexico. I think I can assure you, and I hope you have had every evidence of the truth of my assurance, that that attitude is one of sincere friendship. And not merely the sort of friendship which prompts one not to do his neighbor any harm, but the sort of friendship which earnestly desires to do his neighbor service.

My own policy, the policy of my own administration, towards Mexico was at every point based upon this principle, that the internal settlement of the affairs of Mexico was none of our business; that we had no right to interfere with or to dictate to Mexico in any particular with regard to her own affairs. Take one aspect of our relations which at one time may have been difficult for you to understand: When we sent troops into Mexico, our sincere desire was nothing else than to assist you to get rid of a man who was making the settlement of your affairs for the time being impossible. We had no desire to use our troops for any other purpose, and I was in hopes that by assisting in that way and then immediately withdrawing I might give substantial proof of the truth of the assurances that I had given your Government through President Carranza.

And at the present time it distresses me to learn that certain influences which I assume to be German in their origin are trying to make a wrong impression through-

223

out Mexico as to the purposes of the United States, and not only a wrong impression, but to give an absolutely untrue account of things that happen. You know the distressing things that have been happening just off our coasts. You know of the vessels that have been sunk. I yesterday received a quotation from a paper in Guadalajara which stated that thirteen of our battleships had been sunk off the capes of the Chesapeake. You see how dreadful it is to have people so radically misinformed. It was added that our Navy Department was withholding the truth with regard to these sinkings. I have no doubt that the publisher of the paper published that in perfect innocence without intending to convey wrong impressions, but it is evident that allegations of that sort proceed from those who wish to make trouble between Mexico and the United States.

Now, gentlemen, for the time being at any rate—and I hope it will not be a short time—the influence of the United States is somewhat pervasive in the affairs of the world, and I believe that it is pervasive because the nations of the world which are less powerful than some of the greatest nations are coming to believe that our sincere desire is to do disinterested service. We are the champions of those nations which have not had a military standing which would enable them to compete with the strongest nations in the world, and I look forward with pride to the time, which I hope will soon come, when we can give substantial evidence, not only that we do not want anything out of this war, but that we would not accept anything out of it, that it is absolutely a case of disinterested action. And if you will watch the attitude of our people, you will see that nothing stirs them so deeply as assurances that this war, so far as we are concerned, is for idealistic objects. One of the difficulties that I experienced during the first three years of the war—the years when the United States was not in the war—was in getting the foreign offices of European nations to believe that the United States was seeking nothing for herself, that her neutrality was not selfish, and that if she came in, she would not come in to get anything substantial out of the war, any material object, any territory, or trade, or anything else of that sort. In some of the foreign offices there were men who personally knew me and they believed, I hope, that I was sincere in assuring them that our purposes were disinterested, but they thought that these assurances came from an academic gentleman removed from the ordinary sources of information and speaking the idealistic purposes of the cloister. They did not believe that I was speaking the real heart of the American people, and I knew all along that I was. Now I believe that everybody who comes into contact with the American people knows that I am speaking their purposes.

The other night in New York, at the opening of the campaign for funds for our Red Cross, I made an address. I had not intended to refer to Russia, but I was speaking without notes and in the course of what I said my thought was led to Russia, and I said that we meant to stand by Russia just as firmly as we would stand by France or England or any other of the Allies. The audience to which I was speaking was not an audience from which I would have expected an enthusiastic response to that. It was rather too well dressed. It was not an audience, in other words, made of the class of people whom you would suppose to have the most intimate feeling for the sufferings of the ordinary man in Russia, but that audience jumped into the aisles, the whole audience rose to its feet, and nothing that I had said on that occasion aroused anything like the enthusiasm that that single sentence aroused. Now, there is a sample, gentlemen. We cannot make anything out of Russia. We cannot make anything out of standing by Russia at this time—the most remote of the European nations, so far as we are concerned, the one with which we have had the least connections in trade and advantage—and yet the people of the United States rose to that suggestion as to no other that I made in that address. That is the heart of America, and we are ready to show you by any act of friendship that you may propose our real feelings toward Mexico.

Some of us, if I may say so privately, look back with regret upon some of the more ancient relations that we have had with Mexico long before our generation; and America, if I may so express it, would now feel ashamed to take advantage of a neighbor. So I hope that you can carry back to your homes something better than the assurances of words. You have had contact with our people. You know your own personal reception. You know how gladly we have opened to you the doors of every establishment that you wanted to see and have shown you just what we were doing, and I hope you have gained the right impression as to why we were doing it. We are doing it, gentlemen, so that the world may never hereafter have to fear the only thing that any nation has to dread, the unjust and selfish aggression of another nation. Some time ago, as you probably all know, I proposed a sort of Pan-American agreement. I had perceived that one of the difficulties of our relationship with Latin America was this: The famous Monroe Doctrine was adopted without your consent, without the consent of any of the Central or South American States.

If I may express it in the terms that we so often use in this country, we said, "We are going to be your big brother, whether you want us to be or not." We did not ask whether it was agreeable to you that we should be your big brother. We said we were going to be. Now, that was all very well so far as protecting you from aggression from the other side of the water was concerned, but there was nothing in it that protected you from aggression from us, and I have repeatedly seen the uneasy feeling on the part of representatives of the states of Central and South America that our self-appointed protection might be for our own benefit and our own interests and not for the interest of our neighbors. So I said, "Very well, let us make an arrangement by which we will give bond. Let us have a common guarantee, that all of us will sign, of political independence and territorial integrity. Let us agree that if any one of us, the United States included, violates the political independence or the territorial integrity of any of the others, all the others will jump on her." I pointed out to some of the gentlemen who were less inclined to enter into this arrangement than others that that was in effect giving bonds on the part of the United States, that we would enter into an arrangement by which you would be protected from us.

Now, that is the kind of agreement that will have to be the foundation of the future life of the nations of the world, gentlemen. The whole family of nations will have to guarantee to each nation that no nation shall violate its political independence or its territorial integrity. That is the basis, the only conceivable basis, for the future peace of the world, and I must admit that I was ambitious to have the states of the two continents of America show the way to the rest of the world as to how to make a basis of peace. Peace can come only by trust. As long as there is suspicion there is going to be misunderstanding, and as long as there is misunderstanding there is going to be trouble. If you can once get a situation of trust then you have got a situation of permanent peace. Therefore, everyone of us, it seems to me, owes it as a patriotic duty to his own country to plant the seeds of trust and of confidence instead of the seeds of suspicion and variety of interest. That is the reason that I began by saying to you that I have not had the pleasure of meeting a group of men who were more welcome than you are, because you are our near neighbors. Suspicion on your part or misunderstanding on your part distresses us more than we would be distressed by similar feelings on the part of those less nearby.

When you reflect how wonderful a storehouse of treasure Mexico is, you can see how her future must depend upon peace and honor, so that nobody shall exploit her. It must depend upon every nation that has any relations with her, and the citizens of any nation that has relations with her, keeping within the bounds of honor and fair dealing and justice, because so soon as you can admit your own capital and the capital of the world to the free use of the resources of Mexico, it will be one of the most wonderfully rich and prosperous countries in the world. And when you have the foundations of established order, and the world has come to its senses again, we shall, I hope, have the very best connections that will assure us all a permanent cordiality and friendship.

REPLY TO THE FRENCH UNION FOR WOMAN SUFFRAGE

LETTER TO MRS. CARRIE CHAPMAN CATT, PRESIDENT OF THE INTERNATIONAL WOMAN SUFFRAGE ALLIANCE, JUNE 13, 1918. FROM ORIGINAL COPY IN MR. WILSON'S FILES.

MY DEAR MRS. CATT:

May I not thank you for transmitting to me the very interesting memorial of the French Union for Woman Suffrage addressed to me under the date of February first, last? Since you have been kind enough to transmit this interesting and impressive message to me, will you not be good enough to convey to the subscribers this answer:

"I have read your message with the deepest interest and I welcome the opportunity to say that I agree without reservation that the full and sincere democratic reconstruction of the world for which we are striving, and which we are determined to bring about at any cost, will not have been completely or adequately attained until women are admitted to the suffrage, and that only by that action can the nations of the world realize for the benefit of future generations the full ideal force of opinion or the full humane forces of action. The services of women during this supreme crisis of the world's history have been of the most signal usefulness and distinction. The war could not have been fought without them, or its sacrifices endured. It is high time that some part of our debt of gratitude to them should be acknowledged and paid, and the only acknowledgment they ask is their admission to the suffrage. Can we justly refuse it? As for America, it is my earnest hope that the Senate of the United

States will give an unmistakable answer to this question by passing the suffrage amendment to our federal Constitution before the end of this session."

Cordially and sincerely yours,

WOODROW WILSON.

THE FOUR-POINT SPEECH

ADDRESS DELIVERED AT MOUNT VERNON, JULY 4, 1918.
FROM OFFICIAL GOVERNMENT PUBLICATION IN MR.
WILSON'S FILES.

GENTLEMEN OF THE DIPLOMATIC CORPS
AND MY FELLOW CITIZENS:

I am happy to draw apart with you to this quiet place
of old counsel in order to speak a little of the meaning
of this day of our Nation's independence. The place
seems very still and remote. It is as serene and untouched by the hurry of the world as it was in those
great days long ago when General Washington was here
and held leisurely conference with the men who were to
be associated with him in the creation of a nation.
From these gentle slopes they looked out upon the
world and saw it whole, saw it with the light of the
future upon it, saw it with modern eyes that turned
away from a past which men of liberated spirits could
no longer endure. It is for that reason that we cannot
feel, even here, in the immediate presence of this sacred
tomb, that this is a place of death. It was a place of
achievement. A great promise that was meant for all
mankind was here given plan and reality. The associations by which we are here surrounded are the inspiriting associations of that noble death which is only a
glorious consummation. From this green hillside we
also ought to be able to see with comprehending eyes
the world that lies about us and should conceive anew
the purposes that must set men free.

It is significant,—significant of their own character
and purpose and of the influences they were setting
afoot,—that Washington and his associates, like the
barons at Runnymede, spoke and acted, not for a class,
but for a people. It has been left for us to see to it

that it shall be understood that they spoke and acted, not for a single people only, but for all mankind. They were thinking, not of themselves and of the material interests which centered in the little groups of landholders and merchants and men of affairs with whom they were accustomed to act, in Virginia and the colonies to the north and south of her, but of a people which wished to be done with classes and special interests and the authority of men whom they had not themselves chosen to rule over them. They entertained no private purpose, desired no peculiar privilege. They were consciously planning that men of every class should be free and America a place to which men out of every nation might resort who wished to share with them the rights and privileges of free men. And we take our cue from them,—do we not? We intend what they intended. We here in America believe our participation in this present war to be only the fruitage of what they planted. Our case differs from theirs only in this, that it is our inestimable privilege to concert with men out of every nation what shall make not only the liberties of America secure but the liberties of every other people as well. We are happy in the thought that we are permitted to do what they would have done had they been in our place. There must now be settled once for all what was settled for America in the great age upon whose inspiration we draw to-day. This is surely a fitting place from which calmly to look out upon our task, that we may fortify our spirits for its accomplishment. And this is the appropriate place from which to avow, alike to the friends who look on and to the friends with whom we have the happiness to be associated in action, the faith and purpose with which we act.

This, then, is our conception of the great struggle in which we are engaged. The plot is written plain upon every scene and every act of the supreme tragedy. On the one hand stand the peoples of the world,—not only the peoples actually engaged, but many others also who suffer under mastery but cannot act; peoples of many races and in every part of the world,—the people of stricken Russia still, among the rest, though they are for the moment unorganized and helpless. Opposed to them, masters of many armies, stand an isolated, friendless group of governments who speak no common purpose but only selfish ambitions of their own by which none can profit but themselves, and whose peoples are fuel in their hands; governments which fear their people and yet are for the time their sovereign lords, making every choice for them and disposing of their lives and fortunes as they will, as well as of the lives and fortunes of every people who fall under their power,— governments clothed with the strange trappings and the primitive authority of an age that is altogether alien and hostile to our own. The Past and the Present are in deadly grapple and the peoples of the world are being done to death between them.

There can be but one issue. The settlement must be final. There can be no compromise. No halfway decision would be tolerable. No halfway decision is conceivable. These are the ends for which the associated peoples of the world are fighting and which must be conceded them before there can be peace:

I. The destruction of every arbitrary power anywhere that can separately, secretly, and of its single choice disturb the peace of the world; or, if it cannot be presently destroyed, at the least its reduction to virtual impotence.

II. The settlement of every question, whether of territory, of sovereignty, of economic arrangement, or of political relationship, upon the basis of the free acceptance of that settlement by the people immediately concerned, and not upon the basis of the material interest or advantage of any other nation or people which may desire a different settlement for the sake of its own exterior influence or mastery.

III. The consent of all nations to be governed in their conduct towards each other by the same principles of honor and of respect for the common law of civilized society that govern the individual citizens of all modern states in their relations with one another; to the end that all promises and covenants may be sacredly observed, no private plots or conspiracies hatched, no selfish injuries wrought with impunity, and a mutual trust established upon the handsome foundation of a mutual respect for right.

IV. The establishment of an organization of peace which shall make it certain that the combined power of free nations will check every invasion of right and serve to make peace and justice the more secure by affording a definite tribunal of opinion to which all must submit and by which every international readjustment that cannot be amicably agreed upon by the peoples directly concerned shall be sanctioned.

These great objects can be put into a single sentence. What we seek is the reign of law, based upon the consent of the governed and sustained by the organized opinion of mankind.

These great ends cannot be achieved by debating and seeking to reconcile and accommodate what statesmen may wish, with their projects for balances of power and of national opportunity. They can be realized only by the determination of what the thinking peoples of the world desire, with their longing hope for justice and for social freedom and opportunity.

I can fancy that the air of this place carries the accents of such principles with a peculiar kindness. Here were started forces which the great nation against which they were primarily directed at first regarded as a revolt against its rightful authority but which it has long since seen to have been a step in the liberation of its own people as well as of the people of the United States; and I stand here now to speak,—speak proudly and with confident hope,—of the spread of this revolt,

this liberation, to the great stage of the world itself!
The blinded rulers of Prussia have roused forces they
knew little of,—forces which, once roused, can never be
crushed to earth again; for they have at their heart an
inspiration and a purpose which are deathless and of
the very stuff of triumph!

FOUR-MINUTE MEN

FOUR-MINUTE ADDRESS BY THE PRESIDENT, READ BY
FOUR-MINUTE MEN IN 5,300 COMMUNITY MEET-
INGS IN THE UNITED STATES, JULY 4, 1918. FROM
"OFFICIAL U. S. BULLETIN," NO. 352.

YOU are met, my fellow citizens, to commemorate
the signing of that Declaration of Independence
which marked the awakening of a new spirit in the lives
of nations. Since the birth of our Republic, we have
seen this spirit grow. We have heard the demand and
watched the struggle for self-government spread and
triumph among many peoples. We have come to regard the right to political liberty as the common right
of humankind. Year after year, within the security
of our borders, we have continued to rejoice in the
peaceful increase of freedom and democracy throughout
the world. And yet now, suddenly, we are confronted
with a menace which endangers everything that we have
won and everything that the world has won.

In all its old insolence, with all its ancient cruelty and
injustice, military autocracy has again armed itself
against the pacific hopes of men. Having suppressed
self-government among its own people by an organization maintained in part by falsehood and treachery, it
has set out to impose its will upon its neighbors and
upon us. One by one, it has compelled every civilized
nation in the world either to forego its aspirations or to
declare war in their defense. We find ourselves fighting again for our national existence. We are face to
face with the necessity of asserting anew the fundamental right of free men to make their own laws and
choose their own allegiance, or else permit humanity to
become the victim of a ruthless ambition that is determined to destroy what it cannot master.

Against its threat the liberty-loving people of the world have risen and allied themselves. No fear has deterred them, and no bribe of material well-being has held them back. They have made sacrifices such as the world has never known before, and their resistance in the face of death and suffering has proved that the aim which animates the German effort can never hope to rule the spirit of mankind. Against the horror of military conquest, against the emptiness of living in mere bodily contentment, against the desolation of becoming part of a State that knows neither truth nor honor, the world has so revolted that even people long dominated and suppressed by force have now begun to stir and arm themselves.

Centuries of subjugation have not destroyed the racial aspirations of the many distinct peoples of eastern Europe, nor have they accepted the sordid ideals of their political and military masters. They have survived the slow persecutions of peace as well as the agonies of war and now demand recognition for their just claims to autonomy and self-government. Representatives of these races are with you to-day, voicing their loyalty to our ideals and offering their services in the common cause. I ask you, fellow citizens, to unite with them in making this our Independence Day the first that shall be consecrated to a declaration of independence for all the peoples of the world.

"EVERY MOB CONTRIBUTES TO GERMAN LIES"

STATEMENT DENOUNCING MOB ACTION, JULY 26, 1918.
FROM "OFFICIAL U. S. BULLETIN," NO. 370.

I TAKE the liberty of addressing you upon a subject which so vitally affects the honor of the Nation and the very character and integrity of our institutions that I trust you will think me justified in speaking very plainly about it.

I allude to the mob spirit which has recently here and there very frequently shown its head amongst us, not in any single region, but in many and widely separated parts of the country. There have been many lynchings, and every one of them has been a blow at the heart of ordered law and humane justice. No man who loves America, no man who really cares for her fame and honor and character, or who is truly loyal to her institutions, can justify mob action while the courts of justice are open and the governments of the States and the Nation are ready and able to do their duty. We are at this very moment fighting lawless passion. Germany has outlawed herself among the nations because she has disregarded the sacred obligations of law and has made lynchers of her armies. Lynchers emulate her disgraceful example. I, for my part, am anxious to see every community in America rise above that level with pride and a fixed resolution which no man or set of men can afford to despise.

We proudly claim to be the champions of democracy. If we really are, in deed and in truth, let us see to it that we do not discredit our own. I say plainly that every American who takes part in the action of a mob or gives it any sort of countenance is no true son of this great democracy, but its betrayer, and does more to discredit her by that single disloyalty to her standards of law and of right than the words of her statesmen or the sacrifices of her heroic boys in the trenches can do to make suffering peoples believe her to be their savior. How shall we commend democracy to the acceptance of other peoples, if we disgrace our own by proving that it is, after all, no protection to the weak? Every mob contributes to German lies about the United States what her most gifted liars cannot improve upon by the way of calumny. They can at least say that such things cannot happen in Germany except in times of revolution, when law is swept away!

I therefore very earnestly and solemnly beg that the governors of all the States, the law officers of every community, and, above all, the men and women of every community in the United States, all who revere America and wish to keep her name without stain or reproach, will coöperate—not passively merely, but actively and watchfully—to make an end of this disgraceful evil. It cannot live where the community does not countenance it.

I have called upon the Nation to put its great energy into this war and it has responded—responded with a spirit and a genius for action that has thrilled the world. I now call upon it, upon its men and women everywhere, to see to it that its laws are kept inviolate, its fame untarnished. Let us show our utter contempt for the things that have made this war hideous among the wars of history by showing how those who love liberty and right and justice and are willing to lay down their lives for them upon foreign fields stand ready also to illustrate to all mankind their loyalty to the things at home which they wish to see established everywhere as a blessing and protection to the peoples who have never known the privileges of liberty and self-government. I can never accept any man as a champion of liberty either for ourselves or for the world who does not reverence and obey the laws of our own beloved land, whose laws we ourselves have made. He has adopted the standards of the enemies of his country, whom he affects to despise.

"INCREASE THE COAL OUTPUT"

AN APPEAL TO THOSE ENGAGED IN COAL MINING, AU-
GUST 11, 1918. FROM ORIGINAL COPY IN MR. WIL-
SON'S FILES, CORRECTED IN HIS OWN HAND.

TO ALL THOSE ENGAGED IN COAL MINING:

The existing scarcity of coal is creating a grave danger—in fact the most serious which confronts us—and
calls for prompt and vigorous action·on the part of both
operators and miners. Without an adequate supply our
war program will be retarded; the effectiveness of our
fighting forces in France will be lessened; the lives of
our soldiers will be unnecessarily endangered and their
hardships increased, and there will be much suffering
in many homes throughout the country during the coming winter.

I am well aware that your ranks have been seriously
depleted by the draft, by voluntary enlistment, and by
the demands of other essential industries. This handi-
cap can be overcome however and sufficient coal can be
mined in spite of it, if every one connected with the
industry, from the highest official to the youngest boy,
will give his best work each day for the full number of
work hours. The operators must be zealous as never
before to bring about the highest efficiency of management, to establish the best possible working conditions,
and to accord fair treatment to everybody, so that the
opportunity to work at his best may be accorded every
workman. The miners should report for work every
day, unless prevented by unavoidable causes, and should
not only stay in the mines the full time, but also see to
it that they get out more coal than ever before. The
other workers in and about the mines should work
as regularly and faithfully so that the work of the

miner may not be retarded in any way. This will be especially necessary from this time forward for your numbers may be further lessened by the draft, which will induct into the Army your fair share of those not essential to industry. Those who are drafted but who are essential will be given deferred classification and it is their patriotic duty to accept it. And it is the patriotic duty of their friends and neighbors to hold them in high regard for doing so. The only worker who deserves the condemnation of his community is the one who fails to give his best in this crisis; not the one who accepts deferred classification and works regularly and diligently to increase the coal output. A great task is to be performed. The operators and their staffs alone cannot do it, nor can the mine workers alone do it; but both parties working hand in hand with a grim determination to rid the country of its greatest obstacle to winning the war, can do it. It is with full confidence that I call upon you to assume the burden of producing an ample supply of coal. You will, I am sure, accept this burden and will successfully carry it through and in so doing you will be performing a service just as worthy as service in the trenches, and will win the applause and gratitude of the whole Nation.

ENDORSEMENT OF THE ZIONIST MOVEMENT

LETTER TO RABBI STEPHEN S. WISE, FORMER PRESIDENT OF THE PROVISIONAL ZIONIST COMMITTEE, AUGUST 31, 1918. FROM ORIGINAL COPY IN MR. WILSON'S FILES.

M Y DEAR RABBI WISE:
I have watched with deep and sincere interest the reconstructive work which the Weitzman Commission has done in Palestine at the instance of the British Government, and I welcome an opportunity to express the satisfaction I have felt in the progress of the Zionist movement in the United States and in the Allied countries since the declaration by Mr. Balfour, on behalf of the British Government, of Great Britain's approval of the establishment in Palestine of a national home for the Jewish people, and his promise that the British Government would use its best endeavors to facilitate the achievement of that object, with the understanding that nothing would be done to prejudice the civil and religious rights of non-Jewish people in Palestine or the rights and political status enjoyed by Jews in other countries.

I think that all Americans will be deeply moved by the report that even in this time of stress the Weitzman Commission has been able to lay the foundation of the Hebrew University at Jerusalem, with the promise that that bears of spiritual rebirth.

Cordially and sincerely yours,

WOODROW WILSON.

SECOND CONSCRIPTION PROCLAMATION

STATEMENT INCLUDED IN SECOND CONSCRIPTION PROC-
LAMATION,[1] AUGUST 31, 1918. FROM "UNITED
STATES STATUTES AT LARGE," VOL. 40, PT. 2, PP.
1840-1844.

. . . Fifteen months ago the men of the country from
twenty-one to thirty years of age were registered.
Three months ago, and again this month, those who
had just reached the age of twenty-one were added. It
now remains to include all men between the ages of
eighteen and forty-five.

This is not a new policy. A century and a quarter
ago it was deliberately ordained by those who were then
responsible for the safety and defense of the Nation
that the duty of military service should rest upon all
able-bodied men between the ages of eighteen and forty-
five. We now accept and fulfill the obligation which
they established, an obligation expressed in our national
statutes from that time until now. We solemnly purpose a decisive victory of arms and deliberately to devote the larger part of the military man-power of the
Nation to the accomplishment of that purpose.

The younger men have from the first been ready to
go. They have furnished voluntary enlistments out of
all proportion to their numbers. Our military authorities regard them as having the highest combatant
qualities. Their youthful enthusiasm, their virile eagerness, their gallant spirit of daring, make them the admiration of all who see them in action. They covet not
only the distinction of serving in this great war but also
the inspiring memories which hundreds of thousands of
them will cherish through the years to come, of a great

[1] In the first part of this Proclamation the President cited the provisions of the new Man-power Act, stated the regulations for registration, and named September 12, 1918, as registration day.

day and a great service for their country and for mankind.

By the men of the older group now called upon, the
opportunity now opened to them will be accepted with
the calm resolution of those who realize to the full the
deep and solemn significance of what they do. Having
made a place for themselves in their respective communities, having assumed at home the graver responsibilities of life in many spheres, looking back upon
honorable records in civil and industrial life, they will
realize as perhaps no others could, how entirely their
own fortunes and the fortunes of all whom they love
are put at stake in this war for right, and will know
that the very records they have made render this new
duty the commanding duty of their lives. They know
how surely this is the Nation's war, how imperatively
it demands the mobilization and massing of all our resources of every kind. They will regard this call as
the supreme call of their day and will answer it accordingly.

Only a portion of those who register will be called
upon to bear arms. Those who are not physically fit
will be excused; those exempted by alien allegiance;
those who should not be relieved of their present responsibilities; above all, those who cannot be spared
from the civil and industrial tasks at home upon which
the success of our armies depends as much as upon the
fighting at the front. But all must be registered in
order that the selection for military service may be
made intelligently and with full information.

This will be our final demonstration of loyalty, democracy, and the will to win, our solemn notice to all the
world that we stand absolutely together in a common
resolution and purpose. It is the call to duty to which
every true man in the country will respond with pride
and with the consciousness that in doing so he plays
his part in vindication of a great cause at whose summons every true heart offers its supreme service.

"A WAR WHICH INDUSTRY MUST SUSTAIN"

LABOR DAY MESSAGE TO THE AMERICAN PEOPLE, SEP-
TEMBER 2, 1918. FROM "OFFICIAL U. S. BULLE-
TIN," NO. 402.

LABOR DAY, 1918, is not like any Labor Day that
we have known. Labor Day was always deeply
significant with us. Now it is supremely significant.
Keenly as we were aware a year ago of the enterprise
of life and death upon which the Nation had embarked,
we did not perceive its meaning as clearly as we do
now. We knew that we were all partners and must
stand and strive together, but we did not realize as we
do now that we are all enlisted men, members of a single
army, of many parts and many tasks but commanded by
a single obligation, our faces set toward a single object.
We now know that every tool in every essential industry
is a weapon, and a weapon wielded for the same purpose that an Army rifle is wielded—a weapon which if
we were to lay down no rifle would be of any use.

And a weapon for what? What is the war for?
Why are we enlisted? Why should we be ashamed if
we were not enlisted? At first it seemed hardly more
than a war of defense against the military aggression
of Germany. Belgium had been violated, France invaded, and Germany was afield again, as in 1870 and
1866, to work out her ambitions in Europe; and it was
necessary to meet her force with force. But it is clear
now that it is much more than a war to alter the balance
of power in Europe. Germany, it is now plain, was
striking at what free men everywhere desire and must
have—the right to determine their own fortunes, to
insist upon justice, and to oblige governments to act
for them and not for the private and selfish interest of
a governing class. It is a war to make the nations and

peoples of the world secure against every such power as the German autocracy represents. It is a war of emancipation. Not until it is won can men anywhere live free from constant fear or breathe freely while they go about their daily tasks and know that governments are their servants, not their masters.

This is, therefore, the war of all wars which labor should support and support with all its concentrated power. The world cannot be safe, men's lives cannot be secure, no man's rights can be confidently and successfully asserted against the rule and mastery of arbitrary groups and special interests, so long as governments like that which, after long premeditation, drew Austria and Germany into this war are permitted to control the destinies and the daily fortunes of men and nations, plotting while honest men work, laying the fires of which innocent men, women, and children are to be the fuel.

You know the nature of this war. It is a war which industry must sustain. The army of laborers at home is as important, as essential, as the army of fighting men in the far fields of actual battle. And the laborer is not only needed as much as the soldier. It is his war. The soldier is his champion and representative. To fail to win would be to imperil everything that the laborer has striven for and held dear since freedom first had its dawn and his struggle for justice began. The soldiers at the front know this. It steels their muscles to think of it. They are crusaders. They are fighting for no selfish advantage for their own Nation. They would despise anyone who fought for the selfish advantage of any nation. They are giving their lives that homes everywhere, as well as the homes they love in America, may be kept sacred and safe, and men everywhere be free as they insist upon being free. They are fighting for the ideals of their own land—great ideals, immortal ideals, ideals which shall light the way for all men to the places where justice is done and men live with lifted heads and emancipated spirits. That is the reason they fight with solemn joy and are invincible.

Let us make this, therefore, a day of fresh comprehension not only of what we are about, and of renewed and clear-eyed resolution, but a day of consecration also, in which we devote ourselves without pause or limit to the great task of setting our own country and the whole world free to render justice to all and of making it impossible for small groups of political rulers anywhere to disturb our peace or the peace of the world or in any way to make tools and puppets of those upon whose consent and upon whose power their own authority and their own very existence depend.

We may count upon each other. The Nation is of a single mind. It is taking counsel with no special class. It is serving no private or single interest. Its own mind has been cleared and fortified by these days which burn the dross away. The light of a new conviction has penetrated to every class amongst us. We realize as we never realized before that we are comrades, dependent on one another, irresistible when united, powerless when divided. And so we join hands to lead the world to a new and better day.

FORBIDDING USE OF FOODSTUFFS FOR MALT LIQUORS

PROCLAMATION ISSUED SEPTEMBER 16, 1918.[1] FROM "UNITED STATES STATUTES AT LARGE," VOL. 40, PT. 2, PP. 1848-1849.

WHEREAS, Under and by virtue of an act of Congress entitled "An Act to provide further for the national security and defense by encouraging the production, conserving the supply, and controlling the distribution of food products and fuel," approved by the President on August 10, 1917, it is provided in section 15, among other things, as follows:

"Whenever the President shall find that limitation, regulation, or prohibition of the use of foods, fruits, food materials, or feeds in the production of malt or vinous liquors for beverage purposes, or that reduction of the alcoholic content of any such malt or vinous liquor, is essential, in order to assure an adequate and continuous supply of food, or that the national security and defense will be subserved thereby, he is authorized, from time to time, to prescribe and give public notice of the extent of the limitation, regulation, prohibition, or reduction so necessitated. Whenever such notice shall have been given and shall remain unrevoked, no person shall, after a reasonable time prescribed in such notice, use any foods, fruits, food materials, or feeds in the production of malt or vinous liquors, or import any such liquors except under license issued by the President and in compliance with rules and regulations determined by him governing the production and importation of such liquors and the alcoholic content thereof."

Now, therefore, I, Woodrow Wilson, President of the United States of America, by virtue of the powers conferred on me by said act of Congress, do hereby

---

[1] At the time of this Proclamation, half the states of the Union had been voted "dry," the prohibition amendment to the Constitution had been ratified by fourteen states, and the manufacture of whiskey as well as the sale of liquor after June 30, 1919, had been prohibited by Congress.

find and determine that it is essential, in order to assure
an adequate and continuous supply of food, in order to
subserve the national security and defense, and because
of the increasing requirements of war industries for
the fuel productive capacity of the country, the strain
upon transportation to serve such industries, and the
shortage of labor caused by the necessity of increasing
the armed forces of the United States, that the use of
sugar, glucose, corn, rice or any other foods, fruits, food
materials and feeds in the production of malt liquors
including near beer, for beverage purposes be prohibited.
And by this proclamation I prescribe and give public
notice that on and after October 1, 1918, no person
shall use any sugar, glucose, corn, rice or any other
foods, fruits, food materials or feeds, except malt now
already made, and hops, in the production of malt
liquors, including near beer, for beverage purposes,
whether or not such malt liquors contain alcohol, and
on and after December 1, 1918, no person shall use
any sugar, glucose, corn, rice or any other foods, fruits,
food materials or feeds, including malt, in the production of malt liquors, including near beer, for beverage
purposes, whether or not such malt liquors contain
alcohol.

REPLY TO THE AUSTRIAN PEACE PROPOSAL

DISPATCH TO THE AUSTRO-HUNGARIAN GOVERNMENT
THROUGH MR. W. A. F. EKENGREN, MINISTER OF
SWEDEN, IN CHARGE OF AUSTRO-HUNGARIAN IN-
TERESTS, SIGNED BY SECRETARY LANSING, SEPTEM-
BER 17, 1918. FROM "OFFICIAL STATEMENTS OF
WAR AIMS AND PEACE PROPOSALS." CARNEGIE EN-
DOWMENT FOR INTERNATIONAL PEACE, DIVISION
OF INTERNATIONAL LAW, PAMPHLET NO. 31.

I HAVE the honor to acknowledge the receipt of your note dated September 16th, communicating to me a note from the Imperial Government of Austria-Hungary, containing a proposal to the Governments of all the belligerent States to send delegates to a confidential and unbinding discussion on the basic principles for the conclusion of peace. Furthermore it is proposed that the delegates would be charged to make known to one another the conception of their Governments regarding these principles and to receive analogous communications, as well as to request and give frank and candid explanations on all those points which need to be precisely defined.

In reply I beg to say that the substance of your communication has been submitted to the President who now directs me to inform you that the Government of the United States feels that there is only one reply which it can make to the suggestion of the Imperial Austro-Hungarian Government. It has repeatedly and with entire candor stated the terms upon which the United States would consider peace and can and will entertain no proposal for a conference upon a matter concerning which it has made its position and purpose so plain.

REINSTATEMENT OF STRIKING WORKMEN

LETTER TO MUNITIONS PLANTS AT BRIDGEPORT, CONN.,
    SEPTEMBER 17, 1918. FROM ORIGINAL COPY IN MR.
    WILSON'S FILES.

REMINGTON ARMS,
U. M. C. PLANT,
LIBERTY ORDNANCE COMPANY (AND OTHERS), BRIDGE-
    PORT, CONN.

MY ATTENTION has been called to the fact that several thousand machinists and others employed in connection with war industries in Bridgeport, Connecticut, engaged in a strike to obtain further concessions because they were not satisfied with the decision rendered by the umpire appointed under the authority conferred upon the National War Labor Board. On the 13th instant, I communicated with the workmen engaged in the strike, demanding that they accept the decision of the arbitrator and return to work, and stated the penalties which would be imposed if they refused to do so. The men at a meeting voted to return to work this morning, but I am informed by their representative that the manufacturers refuse to reinstate their former employees. In view of the fact that the workmen have so promptly complied with my directions, I must insist upon the reinstatement of all these men.

WOODROW WILSON.

FOURTH LIBERTY LOAN

ADDRESS OPENING THE CAMPAIGN FOR THE FOURTH LIBERTY LOAN DELIVERED IN NEW YORK CITY, SEPTEMBER 27, 1918. FROM OFFICIAL GOVERNMENT PUBLICATION IN MR. WILSON'S FILES.

I AM not here to promote the loan. That will be done,—ably and enthusiastically done,—by the hundreds of thousands of loyal and tireless men and women who have undertaken to present it to you and to our fellow citizens throughout the country; and I have not the least doubt of their complete success; for I know their spirit and the spirit of the country. My confidence is confirmed, too, by the thoughtful and experienced coöperation of the bankers here and everywhere, who are lending their invaluable aid and guidance. I have come, rather, to seek an opportunity to present to you some thoughts which I trust will serve to give you, in perhaps fuller measure than before, a vivid sense of the great issues involved, in order that you may appreciate and accept with added enthusiasm the grave significance of the duty of supporting the Government by your men and your means to the utmost point of sacrifice and self-denial. No man or woman who has really taken in what this war means can hesitate to give to the very limit of what he or she has; and it is my mission here to-night to try to make it clear once more what the war really means. You will need no other stimulation or reminder of your duty.

At every turn of the war we gain a fresh consciousness of what we mean to accomplish by it. When our hope and expectation are most excited we think more definitely than before of the issues that hang upon it and of the purposes which must be realized by means of it. For it has positive and well-defined purposes

which we did not determine and which we cannot alter.
No statesman or assembly created them; no statesman
or assembly can alter them. They have arisen out of
the very nature and circumstances of the war. The
most that statesmen or assemblies can do is to carry
them out or be false to them. They were perhaps not
clear at the outset; but they are clear now. The war
has lasted more than four years and the whole world
has been drawn into it. The common will of mankind
has been substituted for the particular purposes of individual states. Individual statesmen may have started
the conflict, but neither they nor their opponents can
stop it as they please. It has become a peoples' war,
and peoples of all sorts and races, of every degree of
power and variety of fortune, are involved in its sweeping processes of change and settlement. We came into
it when its character had become fully defined and it
was plain that no nation could stand apart or be indifferent to its outcome. Its challenge drove to the heart
of everything we cared for and lived for. The voice
of the war had become clear and gripped our hearts.
Our brothers from many lands, as well as our own
murdered dead under the sea, were calling to us, and
we responded, fiercely and of course.

The air was clear about us. We saw things in their
full, convincing proportions as they were; and we have
seen them with steady eyes and unchanging comprehension ever since. We accepted the issues of the war as
facts, not as any group of men either here or elsewhere
had defined them, and we can accept no outcome which
does not squarely meet and settle them. Those issues
are these:

Shall the military power of any nation or group of
nations be suffered to determine the fortunes of peoples over whom they have no right to rule except the
right of force?

Shall strong nations be free to wrong weak nations
and make them subject to their purpose and interest?

Shall peoples be ruled and dominated, even in their own internal affairs, by arbitrary and irresponsible force or by their own will and choice?

Shall there be a common standard of right and privilege for all peoples and nations or shall the strong do as they will and the weak suffer without redress?

Shall the assertion of right be haphazard and by casual alliance or shall there be a common concert to oblige the observance of common rights?

No man, no group of men, chose these to be the issues of the struggle. They *are* the issues of it; and they must be settled,—by no arrangement or compromise or adjustment of interests, but definitely and once for all and with a full and unequivocal acceptance of the principle that the interest of the weakest is as sacred as the interest of the strongest.

This is what we mean when we speak of a permanent peace, if we speak sincerely, intelligently, and with a real knowledge and comprehension of the matter we deal with.

We are all agreed that there can be no peace obtained by any kind of bargain or compromise with the governments of the Central Empires, because we have dealt with them already and have seen them deal with other governments that were parties to this struggle, at Brest-Litovsk and Bucharest. They have convinced us that they are without honor and do not intend justice. They observe no covenants, accept no principle but force and their own interest. We cannot "come to terms" with them. They have made it impossible. The German people must by this time be fully aware that we cannot accept the word of those who forced this war upon us. We do not think the same thoughts or speak the same language of agreement.

It is of capital importance that we should also be explicitly agreed that no peace shall be obtained by any kind of compromise or abatement of the principles we have avowed as the principles for which we are fighting. There should exist no doubt about that. I am, therefore, going to take the liberty of speaking with the utmost frankness about the practical implications that are involved in it.

If it be in deed and in truth the common object of the Governments associated against Germany and of the nations whom they govern, as I believe it to be, to achieve by the coming settlements a secure and lasting peace, it will be necessary that all who sit down at the peace table shall come ready and willing to pay the price, the only price, that will procure it; and ready and willing, also, to create in some virile fashion the only instrumentality by which it can be made certain that the agreements of the peace will be honored and fulfilled.

That price is impartial justice in every item of the settlement, no matter whose interest is crossed; and not only impartial justice, but also the satisfaction of the several peoples whose fortunes are dealt with. That indispensable instrumentality is a League of Nations formed under covenants that will be efficacious. Without such an instrumentality, by which the peace of the world can be guaranteed, peace will rest in part upon the word of outlaws and only upon that word. For Germany will have to redeem her character, not by what happens at the peace table, but by what follows.

And, as I see it, the constitution of that League of Nations and the clear definition of its objects must be a part, is in a sense the most essential part, of the peace settlement itself. It cannot be formed now. If formed now, it would be merely a new alliance confined to the nations associated against a common enemy. It is not likely that it could be formed after the settlement. It is necessary to guarantee the peace; and the peace cannot be guaranteed as an afterthought. The reason, to speak in plain terms again, why it must be guaranteed is that there will be parties to the peace whose promises have proved untrustworthy, and means must be found in connection with the peace settlement itself to remove that source of insecurity. It would be folly to leave the guarantee to the subsequent voluntary action of the Governments we have seen destroy Russia and deceive Rumania.

But these general terms do not disclose the whole matter. Some details are needed to make them sound less like a thesis and more like a practical program. These, then, are some of the particulars, and I state them with the greater confidence because I can state them authoritatively as representing this Government's interpretation of its own duty with regard to peace:

First, the impartial justice meted out must involve no discrimination between those to whom we wish to be just and those to whom we do not wish to be just. It must be a justice that plays no favorites and knows no standard but the equal rights of the several peoples concerned;

Second, no special or separate interest of any single nation or any group of nations can be made the basis of any part of the settlement which is not consistent with the common interest of all;

Third, there can be no leagues or alliances or special covenants and understandings within the general and common family of the League of Nations.

Fourth, and more specifically, there can be no special, selfish economic combinations within the League and no employment of any form of economic boycott or exclusion except as the power of economic penalty by exclusion from the markets of the world may be vested in the League of Nations itself as a means of discipline and control.

Fifth, all international agreements and treaties of every kind must be made known in their entirety to the rest of the world.

Special alliances and economic rivalries and hostilities have been the prolific source in the modern world of the plans and passions that produce war. It would be an insincere as well as insecure peace that did not exclude them in definite and binding terms.

The confidence with which I venture to speak for our people in these matters does not spring from our traditions merely and the well-known principles of international action which we have always professed and followed. In the same sentence in which I say that the United States will enter into no special arrangements or understandings with particular nations let me say also that the United States is prepared to assume its full share of responsibility for the maintenance of the common covenants and understandings upon which peace must henceforth rest. We still read Washington's immortal warning against "entangling alliances" with full comprehension and an answering purpose. But only special and limited alliances entangle; and we recognize and accept the duty of a new day in which we are permitted to hope for a general alliance which will avoid entanglements and clear the air of the world for common understandings and the maintenance of common rights.

I have made this analysis of the international situation which the war has created, not, of course, because I doubted whether the leaders of the great nations and peoples with whom we are associated were of the same mind and entertained a like purpose, but because the air every now and again gets darkened by mists and groundless doubtings and mischievous perversions of counsel and it is necessary once and again to sweep all the irresponsible talk about peace intrigues and weakening morale and doubtful purpose on the part of those in authority utterly, and if need be unceremoniously, aside and say things in the plainest words that can be found, even when it is only to say over again what has been said before, quite as plainly if in less unvarnished terms.

As I have said, neither I nor any other man in governmental authority created or gave form to the issues of this war. I have simply responded to them with such

vision as I could command. But I have responded
gladly and with a resolution that has grown warmer
and more confident as the issues have grown clearer and
clearer. It is now plain that they are issues which no
man can pervert unless it be willfully. I am bound to
fight for them, and happy to fight for them as time and
circumstance have revealed them to me as to all the
world. Our enthusiasm for them grows more and more
irresistible as they stand out in more and more vivid
and unmistakable outline.

And the forces that fight for them draw into closer
and closer array, organize their millions into more and
more unconquerable might, as they become more and
more distinct to the thought and purpose of the peoples
engaged. It is the peculiarity of this great war that
while statesmen have seemed to cast about for definitions of their purpose and have sometimes seemed to
shift their ground and their point of view, the thought
of the mass of men, whom statesmen are supposed to
instruct and lead, has grown more and more unclouded;
more and more certain of what it is that they are fighting for. National purposes have fallen more and more
into the background and the common purpose of enlightened mankind has taken their place. The counsels
of plain men have become on all hands more simple and
straightforward and more unified than the counsels of
sophisticated men of affairs, who still retain the impression that they are playing a game of power and playing
for high stakes. That is why I have said that this is a
peoples' war, not a statesmen's. Statesmen must follow the clarified common thought or be broken.

I take that to be the significance of the fact that assemblies and associations of many kinds made up of
plain workaday people have demanded, almost every
time they came together, and are still demanding, that
the leaders of their Governments declare to them plainly
what it is, exactly what it is, that they were seeking in
this war, and what they think the items of the final

settlement should be. They are not yet satisfied with what they have been told. They still seem to fear that they are getting what they ask for only in statesmen's terms,—only in the terms of territorial arrangements and divisions of power, and not in terms of broad-visioned justice and mercy and peace and the satisfaction of those deep-seated longings of oppressed and distracted men and women and enslaved peoples that seem to them the only things worth fighting a war for that engulfs the world. Perhaps statesmen have not always recognized this changed aspect of the whole world of policy and action. Perhaps they have not always spoken in direct reply to the questions asked because they did not know how searching those questions were and what sort of answers they demanded.

But I, for one, am glad to attempt the answer again and again, in the hope that I may make it clearer and clearer that my one thought is to satisfy those who struggle in the ranks and are, perhaps above all others, entitled to a reply whose meaning no one can have any excuse for misunderstanding, if he understands the language in which it is spoken or can get some one to translate it correctly into his own. And I believe that the leaders of the governments with which we are associated will speak, as they have occasion, as plainly as I have tried to speak. I hope that they will feel free to say whether they think that I am in any degree mistaken in my interpretation of the issues involved or in my purpose with regard to the means by which a satisfactory settlement of those issues may be obtained. Unity of purpose and of counsel are as imperatively necessary in this war as was unity of command in the battlefield; and with perfect unity of purpose and counsel will come assurance of complete victory. It can be had in no other way. "Peace drives" can be effectively neutralized and silenced only by showing that every victory of the nations associated against Germany brings the nations nearer the sort of peace which will bring security and reassurance to all peoples and make the recurrence of another such struggle of pitiless force and bloodshed forever impossible, and that nothing else can. Germany is constantly intimating the "terms" she will accept; and always finds that the world does not want terms. It wishes the final triumph of justice and fair dealing.

ENDORSEMENT OF THE FOURTH LIBERTY LOAN

ADVERTISEMENT ISSUED SEPTEMBER 28, 1918. FROM ORIGINAL COPY IN MR. WILSON'S FILES.

A GAIN the Government comes to the people of the country with the request that they lend their money, and lend it upon a more liberal scale than ever before, in order that the great war for the rights of America and the liberation of the world may be carried on with ever-increasing vigor to a victorious conclusion. And it makes the appeal with the greatest confidence because it knows that every day it is becoming clearer to thinking men everywhere that the winning of the war is an essential investment.

The money that is held back now will be of little use or value if the war is not won and the selfish masters of Germany dictate what America may and may not do. Men in America, besides, have from the first until now dedicated both their lives and their fortunes to the maintenance and vindication of the great principles and objects for which our Government was set up. They will not fail now to show the world for what their wealth was intended.

APPEAL FOR WOMAN SUFFRAGE

ADDRESS DELIVERED IN THE SENATE OF THE UNITED
STATES, SEPTEMBER 30, 1918.   FROM OFFICIAL
GOVERNMENT PUBLICATION IN MR. WILSON'S
FILES.

THE unusual circumstances of a world war in which
we stand and are judged in the view not only of
our own people and our own consciences but also in
the view of all nations and peoples will, I hope, justify
in your thought, as it does in mine, the message I have
come to bring you.   I regard the concurrence of the
Senate in the constitutional amendment proposing the
extension of the suffrage to women as vitally essential
to the successful prosecution of the great war of humanity in which we are engaged.   I have come to urge upon
you the considerations which have led me to that conclusion.   It is not only my privilege, it is also my duty to
apprise you of every circumstance and element involved
in this momentous struggle which seems to me to affect
its very processes and its outcome.   It is my duty to
win the war and to ask you to remove every obstacle
that stands in the way of winning it.

I had assumed that the Senate would concur in the
amendment because no disputable principle is involved,
but only a question of the method by which the suffrage
is to be extended to women.   There is and can be no
party issue involved in it.   Both of our great national
parties are pledged, explicitly pledged, to equality of
suffrage for the women of the country.   Neither party,
therefore, it seems to me, can justify hesitation as to
the method of obtaining it, can rightfully hesitate to
substitute federal initiative for state initiative, if the
early adoption of this measure is necessary to the successful prosecution of the war and if the method of

state action proposed in the party platforms of 1916 is impracticable within any reasonable length of time, if practicable at all. And its adoption is, in my judgment, clearly necessary to the successful prosecution of the war and the successful realization of the objects for which the war is being fought.

That judgment I take the liberty of urging upon you with solemn earnestness for reasons which I shall state very frankly and which I shall hope will seem as conclusive to you as they seem to me.

This is a peoples' war and the peoples' thinking constitutes its atmosphere and morale, not the predilections of the drawing room or the political considerations of the caucus. If we be indeed democrats and wish to lead the world to democracy, we can ask other peoples to accept in proof of our sincerity and our ability to lead them whither they wish to be led nothing less persuasive and convincing than our actions. Our professions will not suffice. Verification must be forthcoming when verification is asked for. And in this case verification is asked for,—asked for in this particular matter. You ask by whom? Not through diplomatic channels; not by Foreign Ministers. Not by the intimations of parliaments. It is asked for by the anxious, expectant, suffering peoples with whom we are dealing and who are willing to put their destinies in some measure in our hands, if they are sure that we wish the same things that they do. I do not speak by conjecture. It is not alone the voices of statesmen and of newspapers that reach me, and the voices of foolish and intemperate agitators do not reach me at all. Through many, many channels I have been made aware what the plain, struggling, workaday folk are thinking upon whom the chief terror and suffering of this tragic war falls. They are looking to the great, powerful, famous Democracy of the West to lead them to the new day for which they have so long waited; and they think, in their logical simplicity, that democracy means that women shall play their part in

affairs alongside men and upon an equal footing with
them. If we reject measures like this, in ignorance or
defiance of what a new age has brought forth, of what
they have seen but we have not, they will cease to believe in us; they will cease to follow or to trust us. They
have seen their own Governments accept this interpretation of democracy,—seen old Governments like that
of Great Britain, which did not profess to be democratic,
promise readily and as of course this justice to
women, though they had before refused it, the strange
revelations of this war having made many things new
and plain, to governments as well as to peoples.

Are we alone to refuse to learn the lesson? Are we
alone to ask and take the utmost that our women can
give,—service and sacrifice of every kind,—and still say
we do not see what title that gives them to stand by
our sides in the guidance of the affairs of their Nation
and ours? We have made partners of the women in this
war; shall we admit them only to a partnership of suffering and sacrifice and toil and not to a partnership of
privilege and right? This war could not have been
fought, either by the other nations engaged or by America, if it had not been for the services of the women,—
services rendered in every sphere,—not merely in the
fields of effort in which we have been accustomed to see
them work, but wherever men have worked and upon the
very skirts and edges of the battle itself. We shall not
only be distrusted but shall deserve to be distrusted if
we do not enfranchise them with the fullest possible en-
franchisement, as it is now certain that the other great
free nations will enfranchise them. We cannot isolate
our thought and action in such a matter from the
thought of the rest of the world. We must either conform or deliberately reject what they propose and re-
sign the leadership of liberal minds to others.

The women of America are too noble and too intelligent and too devoted to be slackers whether you give
or withhold this thing that is mere justice; but I know

the magic it will work in their thoughts and spirits if you give it them. I propose it as I would propose to admit soldiers to the suffrage, the men fighting in the field for our liberties and the liberties of the world, were they excluded. The tasks of the women lie at the very heart of the war, and I know how much stronger that heart will beat if you do this just thing and show our women that you trust them as much as you in fact and of necessity depend upon them.

Have I said that the passage of this amendment is a vitally necessary war measure, and do you need further proof? Do you stand in need of the trust of other peoples and of the trust of our own women? Is that trust an asset or is it not? I tell you plainly, as the commander-in-chief of our armies and of the gallant men in our fleets, as the present spokesman of this people in our dealings with the men and women throughout the world who are now our partners, as the responsible head of a great Government which stands and is questioned day by day as to its purposes, its principles, its hopes, whether they be serviceable to men everywhere or only to itself, and who must himself answer these questionings or be ashamed, as the guide and director of forces caught in the grip of war and by the same token in need of every material and spiritual resource this great Nation possesses,—I tell you plainly that this measure which I urge upon you is vital to the winning of the war and to the energies alike of preparation and of battle.

And not to the winning of the war only. It is vital to the right solution of the great problems which we must settle, and settle immediately, when the war is over. We shall need then in our vision of affairs, as we have never needed them before, the sympathy and insight and clear moral instinct of the women of the world. The problems of that time will strike to the roots of many things that we have not hitherto questioned, and I for one believe that our safety in those questioning days, as well as our comprehension of matters that touch society to the quick, will depend upon the direct and authoritative participation of women in our counsels. We shall need their moral sense to preserve what is right and fine and worthy in our system of life as well as to discover just what it is that ought to be purified and reformed. Without their counselings we shall be only half wise.

That is my case. This is my appeal. Many may deny its validity, if they choose, but no one can brush aside or answer the arguments upon which it is based. The executive tasks of this war rest upon me. I ask that you lighten them and place in my hands instruments, spiritual instruments, which I do not now possess, which I sorely need, and which I have daily to apologize for not being able to employ.

"COMRADES IN THE COMMON CAUSE"

MESSAGE READ AT VARIOUS ASSEMBLIES OF THE STU-
DENTS' ARMY TRAINING CORPS, OCTOBER 1, 1918.
FROM "OFFICIAL U. S. BULLETIN," NO. 426.

THE step you have taken is a most significant one. By it you have ceased to be merely individuals, each seeking to perfect himself to win his own place in the world, and have become comrades in the common cause of making the world a better place to live in. You have joined yourselves with the entire manhood of the country and pledged, as did your forefathers, "your lives, your fortunes and your sacred honor" to the freedom of humanity.

The enterprise upon which you have embarked is a hazardous and difficult one. This is not a war of words; this is not a scholastic struggle. It is a war of ideals, yet fought with all the devices of science and with the power of machines. To succeed you must not only be inspired by the ideals for which this country stands, but you must also be masters of the technique with which the battle is fought. You must not only be thrilled with zeal for the common welfare, but you must also be masters of the weapons of to-day.

There can be no doubt of the issue. The spirit that is revealed and the manner in which America has responded to the call is indomitable. I have no doubt that you, too, will use your utmost strength to maintain that spirit, and to carry it forward to the final victory that will certainly be ours.

APPEAL IN BEHALF OF MERCHANT MARINE

MESSAGE "TO ALL THOSE ON LAND OR SEA WHO HAVE FOLLOWED A SEAFARING LIFE," OCTOBER 1, 1918. FROM "OFFICIAL U. S. BULLETIN," NO. 426.

THE men who go down to the sea in ships have become an important factor in our national life. Their services are extremely essential in handling the ships to carry our soldiers in safety to Europe, in transporting the munitions and food supplies for their maintenance and the material for the sustenance of the armies and peoples of the countries with which we are associated.

Safety in handling transports and merchant vessels requires not only a knowledge of navigation and the details of management, maintenance and control, but also that long experience with the various conditions at sea which gives confidence, quick judgment and steady action in an emergency. There are many men with this kind of experience employed on our merchant marine and many others who have left the sea and are now following other occupations. The vigorous prosecution of the war has impelled us to build vessels in larger numbers than ever before. We are launching a continuously increasing tonnage. These vessels will need skilled seamen to man them. No more honorable or serviceable task can come to any of our people than that of manning our merchant marine. With an increasing tonnage being put into service we must know where skilled men can be obtained to furnish at least the basis of the crews that are to man them. With such information available there will be no doubt about the efficient manning of our vessels for the entire period of the war.

The history of American seamanship is a glowing record of patriotism, courage and achievement unsurpassed by any people anywhere. I therefore confidently call upon all seamen and all men engaged in other occupations who have heretofore been seamen to give, in connection with the questionnaires they submit to the local draft boards, full information about their rating and experience at sea to enable the boards to place them in their proper classification and give to the Government a knowledge of where experienced seamen may be secured when their services are required. The kind of skill that makes an efficient seaman can only be obtained at sea. It is the product of experience, and must include, among other things, that subconscious swaying of the body to the motion of the vessel known as "sea legs." There can be no safe, efficient management of vessels that does not include a large proportion of officers and crew having skill and experience. It is indispensable in emergencies, such as we must be prepared to meet in times of war.

It is the patriotic duty of young men who join the merchant service to make every effort to learn their work in the shortest possible time and of the skilled men to assist these young men in their efforts. It is the duty of owners and managers of vessels to coöperate in this work, and to give to the young men such shipmates and such treatment as will cause them to respect the service and build up within them a desire to make it their life work. The work of a seaman is so vitally important to the conduct of the war that it has become necessary for the Government to provide deferred classification for them in its efforts to secure a sufficient supply of skilled men for the maintenance of speed and safety. Having in mind the brilliant record of the American merchant marine, the honorable position it occupies in economic affairs, and the important part it plays in winning the war, every seaman should give to the service the best that is in him and should not hesitate to accept deferred classification when the Government has decided that such deferred classification is necessary, no matter how eager he may be to join the fighting forces of the Army or the Navy.

ON WOMAN SUFFRAGE

ADDRESS TO THE LADIES REPRESENTING WOMAN SUF-
FRAGE, AT THE WHITE HOUSE, OCTOBER 3, 1918.
FROM COPY IN MR. WILSON'S FILES.

I JUST wanted to say, Mrs. Catt and ladies, and I can say most unaffectedly, that I do not deserve your gratitude. You know, some of you have regretted the fact that I was slow of conversion to this cause, but I do not see how any man's processes of conviction can be slow in the presence of the influences now abroad in the world. So that when my conversion to this idea came, it came with an overwhelming command that made it necessary that I should omit nothing and use the position I occupied to enforce it, if I could possibly do so. I pride myself on only one feature of it, that I did understand when circumstances instructed me. There are some men who, I am sorry to say, have recently illustrated the fact that they would not learn. Their minds are provincial. They do not know a great influence when it is abroad. They have given themselves a life-long task. They will have to explain for the rest of their lives. And I should like to tell some of them that, having been a historian myself, I can assure them that historians are very dull persons and do not accept ingenious explanations, and that therefore history will deal very candidly with the circumstances in which the head of a Government asked the kind of support that I asked the other day, and did not get it. It is one of the serious circumstances in the history of the United States. I have to restrain myself sometimes from intellectual contempt. That is a sin, I am afraid, and being a good Presbyterian, I am trying to refrain from it.

But I had not meant to dwell on that side of it. I

want to say that it has been a matter of deep gratification to me to have the opportunity to render service,
such as it was, and I want you to know that my heart
not only, but my conviction and my purpose were with
you, and I was speaking from knowledge.   The other
day, when I told the Senate that I had not been listening to the public men, I had not been listening to editors,
but I had been listening to the heart of the world, which
comes to me with very authentic throb, through many
instrumentalities which it has set up.   There are all
sorts of under-currents which are growing more and
more powerful and are perceptible in the official dispatches, and come to me in all sorts of letters and communications.   There seems to be growing a great voice
in the world which it will be very dangerous for any
statesman not to pay attention to.   It was to that voice
that I thought, and still think, that I had been listening,
and that voice speaks with very authentic tones.   So that
I want to repeat again that I do not deserve your gratitude.   I am only proud to coöperate with you.

REPLY TO THE GERMAN PEACE PROPOSAL OF OCTOBER 6

MESSAGE TO THE GERMAN GOVERNMENT THROUGH MR. FREDERICK OEDERLIN, SWISS CHARGÉ D'AFFAIRES, SIGNED BY SECRETARY LANSING, OCTOBER 8, 1918. FROM "OFFICIAL U. S. BULLETIN," NO. 433.

I HAVE the honor to acknowledge on behalf of the President, your note of October 6, inclosing a communication from the German Government to the President; and I am instructed by the President to request you to make the following communication to the Imperial German Chancellor:

"Before making reply to the request of the Imperial German Government, and in order that that reply shall be as candid and straightforward as the momentous interests involved require, the President of the United States deems it necessary to assure himself of the exact meaning of the note of the Imperial Chancellor. Does the Imperial Chancellor mean that the Imperial German Government accepts the terms laid down by the President in his address to the Congress of the United States on the eighth of January last and in subsequent addresses and that its object in entering into discussions would be only to agree upon the practical details of their application?

"The President feels bound to say with regard to the suggestion of an armistice that he would not feel at liberty to propose a cessation of arms to the Governments with which the Government of the United States is associated against the Central Powers so long as the armies of those powers are upon their soil. The good faith of any discussion would manifestly depend upon the consent of the Central Powers immediately to withdraw their forces everywhere from invaded territory.

"The President also feels that he is justified in asking whether the Imperial Chancellor is speaking merely for the constituted authorities of the Empire who have so far conducted the war. He deems the answers to these questions vital from every point of view."

APPEAL FOR THE FOURTH LIBERTY LOAN

STATEMENT ISSUED OCTOBER 11, 1918. FROM ORIGINAL COPY IN MR. WILSON'S FILES.

RECENT events have enhanced, not lessened, the importance of this loan, and I hope that my fellow countrymen will let me say this to them very frankly. The best thing that could happen would be that the loan should not only be fully subscribed, but very greatly over-subscribed. We are in the midst of the greatest exercise of the power of this country that has ever been witnessed or forecast, and a single day of relaxation in that effort would be of tragical damage alike to ourselves and to the rest of the world. Nothing has happened which makes it safe or possible to do anything but push our effort to the utmost. The time is critical, and the response must be complete.

CONDITIONS OF PEACE

DISPATCH TO THE GERMAN GOVERNMENT THROUGH MR. FREDERICK OEDERLIN, SWISS CHARGÉ D'AFFAIRES, SIGNED BY SECRETARY LANSING, OCTOBER 14, 1918. FROM "OFFICIAL U. S. BULLETIN," NO. 437.

IN reply to the communication of the German Government, dated the twelfth instant, which you handed me to-day, I have the honor to request you to transmit the following answer:

"The unqualified acceptance by the present German Government and by a large majority of the German Reichstag of the terms laid down by the President of the United States of America in his address to the Congress of the United States on the eighth of January, 1918, and in his subsequent addresses justifies the President in making a frank and direct statement of his decision with regard to the communications of the German Government of the eighth and twelfth of October, 1918.

"It must be clearly understood that the process of evacuation and the conditions of an armistice are matters which must be left to the judgment and advice of the military advisers of the Government of the United States and the Allied Governments, and the President feels it his duty to say that no arrangement can be accepted by the Government of the United States which does not provide absolutely satisfactory safeguards and guarantees of the maintenance of the present military supremacy of the armies of the United States and of the Allies in the field. He feels confident that he can safely assume that this will also be the judgment and decision of the Allied Governments.

"The President feels that it is also his duty to add that neither the Government of the United States nor, he is quite sure, the Governments with which the Government of the United States is associated as a belligerent will consent to consider an armistice so long as the armed forces of Germany continue the illegal and inhumane practices which they still persist in. At the very time that the German Government approaches the Government of the United States with proposals of peace its submarines are engaged in sinking passenger ships at sea, and not the ships alone, but the very boats in which their passengers and crews seek to make their way to safety; and in their present inforced withdrawal from Flanders and France the German armies are pursuing a course of wanton destruction which has always been regarded as in direct violation of the rules and practices of civilized warfare. Cities and villages, if not destroyed, are being stripped of all they contain not only, but often of their very inhabitants. The nations associated against Germany cannot be expected to agree to a cessation of arms while acts of inhumanity, spoliation, and desolation are being continued which they justly look upon with horror and with burning hearts.

"It is necessary also in order that there may be no possibility of misunderstanding, that the President should very solemnly call the attention of the Government of Germany to the language and plain intent of one of the terms of peace which the German Government has now accepted. It is contained in the address of the President delivered at Mount Vernon on the fourth of July last. It is as follows: 'The destruction of every arbitrary power anywhere that can separately, secretly, and of its single choice disturb the peace of the world; or, if it cannot be presently destroyed, at least its reduction to virtual impotency.' The power which has hitherto controlled the German Nation is of the sort here described. It is within the choice of the German Nation to alter it. The President's words just quoted naturally constitute a condition precedent to peace, if peace is to come by the action of the German people themselves. The President feels bound to say that the whole process of peace will, in his judgment, depend upon the definiteness and the satisfactory character of the guarantees which can be given in this fundamental matter. It is indispensable that the Governments associated against Germany should know beyond a peradventure with whom they are dealing.

"The President will make a separate reply to the Royal and Imperial Government of Austria-Hungary."

URGING SUBSCRIPTION TO THE FOURTH LIBERTY LOAN

STATEMENT ISSUED OCTOBER 14, 1918. FROM "OFFI-CIAL U. S. BULLETIN," NO. 437.

THE reply of the German Government to my note of inquiry dated October 8 gives occasion for me to say to my fellow countrymen that neither that reply nor any other recent events have in any way diminished the vital importance of the Liberty Loan. Relaxation now, hesitation now, would mean defeat when victory seems to be in sight; would mean years of war instead of peace upon our own terms.

I earnestly request every patriotic American to leave to the Governments of the United States and of the Allies the momentous discussions initiated by Germany and to remember that for each man his duty is to strengthen the hands of these Governments and to do it in the most important way now immediately presented—by subscribing to the utmost of his ability for bonds of the Fourth Liberty Loan. That loan must be successful. I am sure that the American people will not fail to see their duty and make it successful.

ASPIRATIONS OF THE CZECHO-SLOVAKS AND JUGO-SLAVS

MESSAGE TO THE GOVERNMENT OF AUSTRIA-HUNGARY THROUGH MR. W. A. F. EKENGREN, MINISTER OF SWEDEN, SIGNED BY SECRETARY LANSING, OCTOBER 18, 1918. FROM "OFFICIAL U. S. BULLETIN," NO. 441.

I HAVE the honor to acknowledge the receipt of your note of the seventh instant in which you transmit a communication of the Imperial and Royal Government of Austria-Hungary to the President. I am now instructed by the President to request you to be good enough, through your Government, to convey to the Imperial and Royal Government the following reply:

"The President deems it his duty to say to the Austro-Hungarian Government that he cannot entertain the present suggestions of that Government because of certain events of utmost importance which, occurring since the delivery of his address of the eighth of January last, have necessarily altered the attitude and responsibility of the Government of the United States. Among the fourteen terms of peace which the President formulated at that time occurred the following:

"X. The peoples of Austria-Hungary, whose place among the nations we wish to see safeguarded and assured, should be accorded the freest opportunity of autonomous development.

"Since that sentence was written and uttered to the Congress of the United States the Government of the United States has recognized that a state of belligerency exists between the Czecho-Slovaks and the German and Austro-Hungarian Empires and that the Czecho-Slovak National Council is a *de facto* belligerent government clothed with proper authority to direct the military and political affairs of the Czecho-Slovaks. It has also recognized in the fullest manner the justice of the nationalistic aspirations of the Jugo-Slavs for freedom.

"The President is, therefore, no longer at liberty to accept the mere 'autonomy' of these peoples as a basis of peace, but is obliged to insist that they, and not he, shall be the judges of what action on the part of the Austro-Hungarian Government will satisfy their aspirations and their conception of their rights and destiny as members of the family of nations."

ARMISTICE TERMS

MESSAGE TO THE GERMAN GOVERNMENT THROUGH
MR. FREDERICK OEDERLIN, CHARGÉ D'AFFAIRES OF
SWITZERLAND, SIGNED BY SECRETARY LANSING, OC-
TOBER 23, 1918. FROM "OFFICIAL U. S. BULLE-
TIN," NO. 445.

I HAVE the honor to acknowledge the receipt of your note of the twenty-second transmitting a communication under date of the twentieth from the German Government and to advise you that the President has instructed me to reply thereto as follows:

"Having received the solemn and explicit assurance of the German Government that it unreservedly accepts the terms of peace laid down in his address to the Congress of the United States on the eighth of January, 1918, and the principles of settlement enunciated in his subsequent addresses, particularly the address of the twenty-seventh of September, and that it desires to discuss the details of their application, and that this wish and purpose emanate, not from those who have hitherto dictated German policy and conducted the present war on Germany's behalf, but from ministers who speak for the majority of the Reichstag and for an overwhelming majority of the German people; and having received also the explicit promise of the present German Government that the humane rules of civilized warfare will be observed both on land and sea by the German armed forces, the President of the United States feels that he cannot decline to take up with the Governments with which the Government of the United States is associated the question of an armistice.

"He deems it his duty to say again, however, that the only armistice he would feel justified in submitting for consideration would be one which should leave the

283

United States and the powers associated with her in a position to enforce any arrangements that may be entered into and to make a renewal of hostilities on the part of Germany impossible. The President has, therefore, transmitted his correspondence with the present German authorities to the Governments with which the Government of the United States is associated as a belligerent, with the suggestion that, if those Governments are disposed to effect peace upon the terms and principles indicated, their military advisers and the military advisers of the United States be asked to submit to the Governments associated against Germany the necessary terms of such an armistice as will fully protect the interests of the peoples involved and insure to the associated Governments the unrestricted power to safeguard and enforce the details of the peace to which the German Government has agreed, provided they deem such an armistice possible from the military point of view. Should such terms of armistice be suggested, their acceptance by Germany will afford the best concrete evidence of her unequivocal acceptance of the terms and principles of peace from which the whole action proceeds.

"The President would deem himself lacking in candor did he not point out in the frankest possible terms the reason why extraordinary safeguards must be demanded. Significant and important as the constitutional changes seem to be which are spoken of by the German Foreign Secretary in his note of the twentieth of October, it does not appear that the principle of a government responsible to the German people has yet been fully worked out or that any guarantees either exist or are in contemplation that the alterations of principle and of practice now partially agreed upon will be permanent. Moreover, it does not appear that the heart of the present difficulty has been reached. It may be that future wars have been brought under the control of the German people, but the present war has not been;

and it is with the present war that we are dealing. It is evident that the German people have no means of commanding the acquiescence of the military authorities of the Empire in the popular will; that the power of the King of Prussia to control the policy of the Empire is unimpaired; that the determining initiative still remains with those who have hitherto been the masters of Germany.

"Feeling that the whole peace of the world depends now on plain speaking and straightforward action, the President deems it his duty to say, without any attempt to soften what may seem harsh words, that the nations of the world do not and cannot trust the word of those who have hitherto been the masters of German policy, and to point out once more that in concluding peace and attempting to undo the infinite injuries and injustices of this war the Government of the United States cannot deal with any but veritable representatives of the German people who have been assured of a genuine constitutional standing as the real rulers of Germany. If it must deal with the military masters and the monarchical autocrats of Germany now, or if it is likely to have to deal with them later in regard to the international obligations of the German Empire, it must demand, not peace negotiations, but surrender. Nothing can be gained by leaving this essential thing unsaid."

APPEAL FOR A DEMOCRATIC CONGRESS

STATEMENT ISSUED OCTOBER 25, 1918. FROM THE "CONGRESSIONAL RECORD," VOL. 56, P. 11494.

MY FELLOW COUNTRYMEN,—The Congressional elections are at hand. They occur in the most critical period our country has ever faced or is likely to face in our time. If you have approved of my leadership and wish me to continue to be your unembarrassed spokesman in affairs at home and abroad, I earnestly beg that you will express yourselves unmistakably to that effect by returning a Democratic majority to both the Senate and the House of Representatives. I am your servant and will accept your judgment without cavil, but my power to administer the great trust assigned me by the Constitution would be seriously impaired should your judgment be adverse, and I must frankly tell you so because so many critical issues depend upon your verdict. No scruple of taste must in grim times like these be allowed to stand in the way of speaking the plain truth.

I have no thought of suggesting that any political party is paramount in matters of patriotism. I feel too keenly the sacrifices which have been made in this war by all our citizens, irrespective of party affiliations, to harbor such an idea. I mean only that the difficulties and delicacies of our present task are of a sort that makes it imperatively necessary that the Nation should give its undivided support to the Government under a unified leadership, and that a Republican Congress would divide the leadership.

The leaders of the minority in the present Congress have unquestionably been pro war, but they have been anti-administration. At almost every turn, since we entered the war they have sought to take the choice of policy and the conduct of the war out of my hands and put it under the control of instrumentalities of their own choosing. This is no time either for divided counsel or for divided leadership. Unity of command is as necessary now in civil action as it is upon the field of battle. If the control of the House and Senate should be taken away from the party now in power an opposing majority could assume control of legislation and oblige all action to be taken amidst contest and obstruction.

The return of a Republican majority to either House of the Congress would, moreover, certainly be interpreted on the other side of the water as a repudiation of my leadership. Spokesmen of the Republican Party are urging you to elect a Republican Congress in order to back up and support the President, but even if they should in this way impose upon some credulous voters on this side of the water, they would impose on no one on the other side. It is well understood there as well as here that the Republican leaders desire not so much to support the President as to control him. The peoples of the allied countries with whom we are associated against Germany are quite familiar with the significance of elections. They would find it very difficult to believe that the voters of the United States had chosen to support their President by electing to the Congress a majority controlled by those who are not in fact in sympathy with the attitude and action of the administration.

I need not tell you, my fellow countrymen, that I am asking your support not for my own sake or for the sake of a political party, but for the sake of the Nation itself, in order that its inward unity of purpose may be evident to all the world. In ordinary times I would not feel at liberty to make such an appeal to you. In ordinary times divided counsels can be endured without permanent hurt to the country. But these are not ordinary times. If in these critical days it is your wish to sustain me with undivided minds, I beg that you will say so in a way which it will not be possible to misunderstand either here at home or among our associates on the other side of the sea. I submit my difficulties and my hopes to you.

NO ECONOMIC DISCRIMINATION BETWEEN NATIONS

LETTER TO SENATOR F. M. SIMMONS OF NORTH CARO-
LINA, OCTOBER 28, 1918. FROM ORIGINAL COPY
IN MR. WILSON'S FILES.

DEAR SENATOR:
I am glad to respond to the question addressed to
me by your letter of October 26. The words I used in
my address to the Congress of January 8, 1918, were:

"The removal, so far as possible, of all economic
barriers and the establishment of an equality of trade
conditions among all the nations consenting to the peace
and associating themselves for its maintenance."

I of course meant to suggest no restriction upon the
free determination by any nation of its own economic
policy, but only that, whatever tariff any nation might
deem necessary for its own economic service, be that
tariff high or low, it should apply equally to all foreign
nations; in other words, that there should be no discriminations against some nations that did not apply to
others. This leaves every nation free to determine for
itself its own internal policies and limits only its right
to compound those policies of hostile discriminations
between one nation and another. Weapons of economic
discipline and punishment should be left to the joint
action of all nations for the purpose of punishing those
who will not submit to a general program of justice and
equality.

The experiences of the past among nations have
taught us that the attempt by one nation to punish another by exclusive and discriminatory trade agreements
has been a prolific breeder of that kind of antagonism
which oftentimes results in war, and that if a permanent
peace is to be established among nations every obstacle

that has stood in the way of international friendship should be cast aside. It was with that fundamental purpose in mind that I announced this principle in my address of January eighth. To pervert this great principle for partisan purposes, and to inject the bogey of free trade, which is not involved at all, is to attempt to divert the mind of the Nation from the broad and humane principle of a durable peace by introducing an internal question of quite another kind. American business has in the past been unaffected by a policy of the kind suggested, and it has nothing to fear now from a policy of simple international justice. It is indeed lamentable that the momentous issues of this solemn hour should be seized upon in an effort to bend them to partisan service. To the initiated and discerning, the motive is transparent and the attempt fails.

FURTHER ARMISTICE TERMS

MESSAGE TO THE GERMAN GOVERNMENT THROUGH MR. HANS SULZER, MINISTER OF SWITZERLAND, IN CHARGE OF GERMAN INTERESTS IN THE UNITED STATES, SIGNED BY SECRETARY LANSING, NOVEMBER 5, 1918. FROM "OFFICIAL U. S. BULLETIN," NO. 456.

I HAVE the honor to request you to transmit the following communication to the German Government:

"In my note of October 23, 1918, I advised you that the President had transmitted his correspondence with the German authorities to the Governments with which the Government of the United States is associated as a belligerent, with the suggestion that, if those Governments were disposed to accept peace upon the terms and principles indicated, their military advisers and the military advisers of the United States be asked to submit to the Governments associated against Germany the necessary terms of such an armistice as would fully protect the interests of the peoples involved and insure to the associated Governments the unrestricted power to safeguard and enforce the details of the peace to which the German Government had agreed, provided they deemed such an armistice possible from the military point of view.

"The President is now in receipt of a memorandum of observations by the Allied Governments on this correspondence, which is as follows:

" ' The Allied Governments have given careful consideration to the correspondence which has passed between the President of the United States and the German Government. Subject to the qualifications which follow they declare their willingness to make peace with the Government of Germany on the terms of peace laid down in the President's address to Congress of January, 1918, and the principles of settlement enunciated in his subsequent addresses. They must point out, however, that clause 2 relating to what is usually described as the freedom of the seas, is open to various interpretations, some of which they could not accept. They must, therefore, reserve to themselves complete freedom on this subject when they enter the peace conference.

" 'Further, in the conditions of peace laid down in his address to Congress of January 8, 1918, the President declared that invaded territories must be restored as well as evacuated and freed, the Allied Governments feel that no doubt ought to be allowed to exist as to what this provision implies. By it they understand that compensation will be made by Germany for all damage done to the civilian population of the Allies and their property by the aggression of Germany by land, by sea, and from the air.' "

I am instructed by the President to say that he is in agreement with the interpretation set forth in the last paragraph of the memorandum above quoted. I am further instructed by the President to request you to notify the German Government that Marshal Foch has been authorized by the Government of the United States and the Allied Governments to receive properly accredited representatives of the German Government, and to communicate to them the terms of an armistice.

ARMISTICE

ANNOUNCEMENT OF THE SIGNING OF THE ARMISTICE
NOVEMBER 11, 1918. FROM "OFFICIAL U. S. BUL-
LETIN," NO. 460.

MY FELLOW COUNTRYMEN:
The armistice was signed this morning. Everything for which America fought has been accomplished.
It will now be our fortunate duty to assist by example,
by sober, friendly counsel and by material aid in the
establishment of just democracy throughout the world.

WOODROW WILSON.

END OF THE WAR

ADDRESS DELIVERED AT A JOINT SESSION OF THE TWO
HOUSES OF CONGRESS NOVEMBER 11, 1918. FROM
OFFICIAL GOVERNMENT PUBLICATION IN MR. WIL-
SON'S FILES.

I N these anxious times of rapid and stupendous change
it will in some degree lighten my sense of responsibility to perform in person the duty of communicating
to you some of the larger circumstances of the situation
with which it is necessary to deal.

The German authorities who have, at the invitation
of the Supreme War Council, been in communication
with Marshal Foch have accepted and signed the terms
of armistice which he was authorized and instructed
to communicate to them. Those terms are as follows:

I. MILITARY CLAUSES ON WESTERN FRONT.

One. Cessation of operations by land and in the air six hours after
the signature of the armistice.

Two. Immediate evacuation of invaded countries: Belgium,
France, Alsace-Lorraine, Luxembourg, so ordered as to be completed
within fourteen days from the signature of the armistice. German
troops which have not left the above mentioned territories within the
period fixed will become prisoners of war. Occupation by the Allied
and United States forces jointly will keep pace with evacuation in
these areas. All movements of evacuation and occupation will be
regulated in accordance with a note annexed to the stated terms.

Three. Repatriation beginning at once and to be completed within
fourteen days of all inhabitants of the countries above mentioned,
including hostages and persons under trial or convicted.

Four. Surrender in good condition by the German armies of the
following equipment: five thousand guns (two thousand five hundred
heavy, two thousand five hundred field), thirty thousand machine
guns. Three thousand minenwerfer. Two thousand aeroplanes
(fighters, bombers—firstly D. Seventy three's and night bombing
machines). The above to be delivered in Simmstu to the Allies

and United States troops in accordance with the detailed conditions laid down in the annexed note.

Five. Evacuation by the German armies of the countries on the left bank of the Rhine. These countries on the left bank of the Rhine shall be administered by the local authorities under the control of the Allied and United States armies of occupation. The occupation of these territories will be determined by Allied and United States garrisons holding the principal crossings of the Rhine, Mayence, Coblenz, Cologne, together with bridgeheads at these points in thirty kilometer radius on the right bank and by garrisons similarly holding the strategetic points of the regions. A neutral zone shall be reserved on the right of the Rhine between the stream and a line drawn parallel to it forty kilometers to the east from the frontier of Holland to the parallel of Gernsheim and as far as practicable a distance of thirty kilometers from the east of stream from this parallel upon Swiss frontier. Evacuation by the enemy of the Rhine lands shall be so ordered as to be completed within a further period of eleven days, in all nineteen days after the signature of the armistice. All movements of evacuation and occupation will be regulated according to the note annexed.

Six. In all territory evacuated by the enemy there shall be no evacuation of inhabitants; no damage or harm shall be done to the persons or property of the inhabitants. No destruction of any kind to be committed. Military establishments of all kinds shall be delivered intact as well as military stores of food, munitions, equipment not removed during the periods fixed for evacuation. Stores of food of all kinds for the civil population, cattle, etc., shall be left *in situ*. Industrial establishments shall not be impaired in any way and their personnel shall not be moved. Roads and means of communication of every kind, railroad, waterways, main roads, bridges, telegraphs, telephones, shall be in no manner impaired.

Seven. All civil and military personnel at present employed on them shall remain. Five thousand locomotives, fifty thousand wagons and ten thousand motor lorries in good working order with all necessary spare parts and fittings shall be delivered to the Associated Powers within the period fixed for the evacuation of Belgium and Luxembourg. The railways of Alsace-Lorraine shall be handed over within the same period, together with all pre-war personnel and material. Further material necessary for the working of railways in the country on the left bank of the Rhine shall be left *in situ*. All stores of coal and material for the up-keep of permanent ways, signals and repair shops left entire *in situ* and kept in an efficient state by Germany during the whole period of armistice. All barges taken from the Allies shall be restored to them. A note appended regulates the details of these measures.

Eight. The German command shall be responsible for revealing all mines or delay acting fuses disposed on territory evacuated by the German troops and shall assist in their discovery and destruction. The German command shall also reveal all destructive measures that may have been taken (such as poisoning or polluting of springs, wells, etc.) under penalty of reprisals.

Nine. The right of requisition shall be exercised by the Allied and the United States armies in all occupied territory. The up-keep of the troops of occupation in the Rhine land (excluding Alsace-Lorraine) shall be charged to the German Government.

Ten. An immediate repatriation without reciprocity according to detailed conditions which shall be fixed, of all Allied and United States prisoners of war. The Allied Powers and the United States shall be able to dispose of these prisoners as they wish.

Eleven. Sick and wounded who cannot be removed from evacuated territory will be cared for by German personnel who will be left on the spot with the medical material required.

II. Disposition Relative to the Eastern Frontiers of Germany.

Twelve. All German troops at present in any territory which before the war belonged to Russia, Rumania or Turkey shall withdraw within the frontiers of Germany as they existed on August 1, 1914.

Thirteen. Evacuation by German troops to begin at once and all German instructors, prisoners, and civilian as well as military agents, now on the territory of Russia (as defined before 1914) to be recalled.

Fourteen. German troops to cease at once all requisitions and seizures and any other undertaking with a view to obtaining supplies intended for Germany in Rumania and Russia (as defined on August 1, 1914).

Fifteen. Abandonment of the treaties of Bucharest and Brest-Litovsk and of the supplementary treaties.

Sixteen. The Allies shall have free access to the territories evacuated by the Germans on their eastern frontier either through Danzig or by the Vistula in order to convey supplies to the populations of those territories or for any other purpose.

III. Clause Concerning East Africa.

Seventeen. Unconditional capitulation of all German forces operating in East Africa within one month.

IV. General Clauses.

Eighteen. Repatriation, without reciprocity, within a maximum period of one month, in accordance with detailed conditions hereafter to be fixed, of all civilians interned or deported who may be citizens of other Allied or Associated States than those mentioned in clause three, paragraph nineteen, with the reservation that any future claims and demands of the Allies and the United States of America remain unaffected.

Nineteen. The following financial conditions are required: Reparation for damage done. While such armistice lasts no public securities shall be removed by the enemy which can serve as a pledge to the Allies for the recovery or reparation for war losses. Immediate restitution of the cash deposit, in the National Bank of Belgium, and in general immediate return of all documents, specie, stocks, shares, paper money together with plant for the issue thereof, touching public or private interests in the invaded countries. Restitution of the Russian and Rumanian gold yielded to Germany or taken by that power. This gold to be delivered in trust to the Allies until the signature of peace.

V. Naval Conditions.

Twenty. Immediate cessation of all hostilities at sea and definite information to be given as to the location and movements of all German ships. Notification to be given to neutrals that freedom of navigation in all territorial waters is given to the naval and mercantile marines of the Allied and Associated Powers, all questions of neutrality being waived.

Twenty-one. All naval and mercantile marine prisoners of war of the Allied and Associated Powers in German hands to be returned without reciprocity.

Twenty-two. Surrender to the Allies and the United States of America of one hundred and sixty German submarines (including all submarine cruisers and mine laying submarines) with their complete armament and equipment in ports which will be specified by the Allies and the United States of America. All other submarines to be paid off and completely disarmed and placed under the supervision of the Allied Powers and the United States of America.

Twenty-three. The following German surface warships which shall be designated by the Allies and the United States of America shall forthwith be disarmed and thereafter interned in neutral ports, or, for the want of them, in Allied ports, to be designated by the Allies and the United States of America and placed under the surveillance of the Allies and the United States of America, only caretakers being left on board, namely: Six battle cruisers, ten battleships, eight light cruisers, including two mine layers, fifty destroyers of the most modern type. All other surface warships (including river craft) are to be concentrated in German naval bases to be designated by the Allies and the United States of America, and are to be paid off and completely disarmed and placed under the supervision of the Allies and the United States of America. All vessels of the auxiliary fleet (trawlers, motor vessels, etc.) are to be disarmed.

Twenty-four. The Allies and the United States of America shall have the right to sweep up all mine fields and obstructions laid by Germany outside German territorial waters, and the positions of these are to be indicated.

Twenty-five. Freedom of access to and from the Baltic to be given to the naval and mercantile marines of the Allied and Associated Powers. To secure this the Allies and the United States of America shall be empowered to occupy all German forts, fortifications, batteries and defense works of all kinds in all the entrances from the Cattegat into the Baltic, and to sweep up all mines and obstructions within and without German territorial waters without any question of neutrality being raised, and the positions of all such mines and obstructions are to be indicated.

Twenty-six. The existing blockade conditions set up by the Allies and Associated Powers are to remain unchanged and all German merchant ships found at sea are to remain liable to capture.

Twenty-seven. All naval aircraft are to be concentrated and immobilized in German bases to be specified by the Allies and the United States of America.

Twenty-eight. In evacuating the Belgian coasts and ports, Germany shall abandon all merchant ships, tugs, lighters, cranes and all other harbor materials, all materials for inland navigation, all aircraft and all materials and stores, all arms and armaments, and all stores and apparatus of all kinds.

Twenty-nine. All Black Sea ports are to be evacuated by Germany; all Russian war vessels of all descriptions seized by Germany in the Black Sea are to be handed over to the Allies and the United States of America; all neutral merchant vessels seized are to be released; all warlike and other materials of all kinds seized in those ports are to be returned and German materials as specified in clause twenty-eight are to be abandoned.

Thirty. All merchant vessels in German hands belonging to the Allied and Associated Powers are to be restored in ports to be specified by the Allies and the United States of America without reciprocity.

Thirty-one. No destruction of ships or of materials to be permitted before evacuation, surrender or restoration.

Thirty-two. The German Government shall formally notify the neutral Governments of the world, and particularly the Governments of Norway, Sweden, Denmark and Holland, that all restrictions placed on the trading of their vessels with the Allied and Associated Countries, whether by the German Government or by private German interests, and whether in return for specific concessions such as the export of shipbuilding materials or not, are immediately canceled.

Thirty-three. No transfers of German merchant shipping of any description to any neutral flag are to take place after signature of the armistice.

VI. Duration of Armistice.

Thirty-four. The duration of the armistice is to be thirty days, with option to extend. During this period, on failure of execution of any of the above clauses, the armistice may be denounced by one of the contracting parties, on forty eight hours previous notice.

VII. Time Limit for Reply.

Thirty-five. This armistice to be accepted or refused by Germany within seventy-two hours of notification.

The war thus comes to an end; for, having accepted these terms of armistice, it will be impossible for the German command to renew it.

It is not now possible to assess the consequences of this great consummation. We know only that this tragical war, whose consuming flames swept from one nation to another until all the world was on fire, is at an end and that it was the privilege of our own people to enter it at its most critical juncture in such fashion and in such force as to contribute in a way of which we are all deeply proud to the great result. We know, too, that the object of the war is attained; the object upon which all free men had set their hearts; and attained with a sweeping completeness which even now we do not realize. Armed imperialism such as the men conceived who were but yesterday the masters of Germany is at an end, its illicit ambitions engulfed in black disaster. Who will now seek to revive it? The arbitrary power of the military caste of Germany which once could secretly and of its own single choice disturb the peace of the world is discredited and destroyed. And more than that,—much more than that,—has been accomplished. The great nations which associated themselves to destroy it have now definitely united in the common purpose to set up such a peace as will satisfy the longing of the whole world for disinterested justice, embodied in settlements which are based upon something much better and much more lasting than the selfish competitive interests of powerful states. There is no longer conjecture as to the objects the victors have in mind. They have a mind in the matter, not only, but a heart also. Their avowed and concerted purpose is to satisfy and protect the weak as well as to accord their just rights to the strong.

The humane temper and intention of the victorious Governments has already been manifested in a very practical way. Their representatives in the Supreme War Council at Versailles have by unanimous resolution assured the peoples of the Central Empires that everything that is possible in the circumstances will be done to supply them with food and relieve the distressing want that is in so many places threatening their very lives; and steps are to be taken immediately to organize these efforts at relief in the same systematic manner that they were organized in the case of Belgium. By the use of the idle tonnage of the Central Empires it ought presently to be possible to lift the fear of utter misery from their oppressed populations and set their minds and energies free for the great and hazardous tasks of political reconstruction which now face them on every hand. Hunger does not breed reform; it breeds madness and all the ugly distempers that make an ordered life impossible.

For with the fall of the ancient governments which rested like an incubus upon the peoples of the Central Empires has come political change not merely, but revolution; and revolution which seems as yet to assume no final and ordered form but to run from one fluid change to another, until thoughtful men are forced to ask themselves, With what Governments, and of what sort, are we about to deal in the making of the covenants of peace? With what authority will they meet us, and with what assurance that their authority will abide and sustain securely the international arrangements into which we are about to enter? There is here matter for no small anxiety and misgiving. When peace is made, upon whose promises and engagements besides our own is it to rest?

Let us be perfectly frank with ourselves and admit that these questions cannot be satisfactorily answered now or at once. But the moral is not that there is little hope of an early answer that will suffice. It is only that we must be patient and helpful and mindful above all of the great hope and confidence that lie at the heart of what is taking place. Excesses accomplish nothing. Unhappy Russia has furnished abundant recent proof of that. Disorder immediately defeats itself. If excesses should occur, if disorder should for a time raise its head, a sober second thought will follow and a day of constructive action, if we help and do not hinder.

The present and all that it holds belongs to the nations and the peoples who preserve their self-control and the orderly processes of their governments; the future to those who prove themselves the true friends of mankind. To conquer with arms is to make only a temporary conquest; to conquer the world by earning its esteem is to make permanent conquest. I am confident that the nations that have learned the discipline of freedom and that have settled with self-possession to its ordered practice are now about to make conquest of the world by the sheer power of example and of friendly helpfulness.

The peoples who have but just come out from under the yoke of arbitrary government and who are now coming at last into their freedom will never find the treasures of liberty they are in search of if they look for them by the light of the torch. They will find that every pathway that is stained with the blood of their own brothers leads to the wilderness, not to the seat of their hope. They are now face to face with their initial test. We must hold the light steady until they find themselves. And in the meantime, if it be possible, we must establish a peace that will justly define their place among the nations, remove all fear of their neighbors and of their former masters, and enable them to live in security and contentment when they have set their own affairs in order. I, for one, do not doubt their purpose or their capacity. There are some happy signs that they know and will choose the way of self-control and peaceful accommodation. If they do, we shall put our aid at their disposal in every way that we can. If they do not, we must await with patience and sympathy the awakening and recovery that will assuredly come at last.

THANKSGIVING FOR VICTORY

THANKSGIVING PROCLAMATION, ISSUED NOVEMBER 16, 1918. FROM "UNITED STATES STATUTES AT LARGE," VOL. 40, PT. 2, PP. 1888-1889.

IT has long been our custom to turn in the autumn of the year in praise and thanksgiving to Almighty God for His many blessings and mercies to us as a nation. This year we have special and moving cause to be grateful and to rejoice. God has in His good pleasure given us peace. It has not come as a mere cessation of arms, a mere relief from the strain and tragedy of war. It has come as a great triumph of right. Complete victory has brought us, not peace alone, but the confident promise of a new day as well in which justice shall replace force and jealous intrigue among the nations. Our gallant armies have participated in a triumph which is not marred or stained by any purpose of selfish aggression. In a righteous cause they have won immortal glory and have nobly served their nation in serving mankind. God has indeed been gracious. We have cause for such rejoicing as revives and strengthens in us all the best traditions of our national history. A new day shines about us, in which our hearts take new courage and look forward with open hope to new and greater duties.

While we render thanks for these things, let us not forget to seek the Divine guidance in the performance of those duties, and Divine mercy and forgiveness for all errors of act or purpose, and pray that in all that we do we shall strengthen the ties of friendship and mutual respect upon which we must assist to build the new structure of peace and good will among the nations.

Wherefore, I, Woodrow Wilson, President of the United States of America, do hereby designate Thursday, the twenty-eighth day of November next as a day of thanksgiving and prayer and invite the people throughout the land to cease upon that day from their ordinary occupations and in their several homes and places of worship to render thanks to God, the ruler of nations.

"EXPECTS TO SAIL FOR FRANCE"

STATEMENT ANNOUNCING INTENTION TO VISIT EUROPE, NOVEMBER 18, 1918. FROM ORIGINAL IN MR. WILSON'S FILES.

THE President expects to sail for France immediately after the opening of the regular session of Congress, for the purpose of taking part in the discussion and settlement of the main features of the treaty of peace. It is not likely that it will be possible for him to remain throughout the sessions of the formal Peace Conference, but his presence at the outset is necessary, in order to obviate the manifest disadvantages of discussion by cable in determining the greater outlines of the final treaty, about which he must necessarily be consulted. He will, of course, be accompanied by delegates who will sit as the representatives of the United States throughout the conference. The names of the delegates will be presently announced.

"THE GREAT TASKS THAT LIE AHEAD OF US"

ADDRESS TO THE REPRESENTATIVES OF THE B'NAI B'RITH, WASHINGTON, NOVEMBER 28, 1918. FROM ORIGINAL COPY IN MR. WILSON'S FILES.

I CANNOT, extemporaneously, reply adequately to the very beautiful address you have just read, sir, but I can reply with great feeling, and with the most genuine gratitude to the order for the distinguished honor they have paid me.

I am sometimes embarrassed by occasions of this sort, because I know the great tasks that lie ahead of us. The past is secure, but the future is doubtful, and there are so many questions intimately associated with justice that are to be solved at the peace table and by the commissions which no doubt will be arranged for at the peace table, that I feel in one sense as if our work of justice had just begun. I realize that, for one thing, one of the most difficult problems will be to secure the proper guarantees for the just treatment of the Jewish peoples in the countries where they have not been justly dealt with, and unhappily there are several countries of which that may be said.

And the embarrassment in that connection is this. It is one thing to give a people its right of self-determination, but it is another to enter into its internal affairs and get satisfactory guarantees of the use it will make of its independence and its power, because that, in a way, involves a kind of supervision which is hateful to the people concerned and difficult to those who undertake it.

But I do not care to dwell on the difficulties. I would rather dwell upon the purpose that we all have at heart to see that the nearest possible approach is made to a proper solution of questions of this sort, and I think that this will be evident to everybody who is dealing with the affairs of the world at this time, that if we truly intend peace we must truly intend contentment, because there cannot be any peace with disturbed spirits. There cannot be any peace with a constantly recurring sense of injustice. And therefore we have this challenge to put to the peoples who will be concerned with the settlement. Do you, or do you not, truly desire permanent peace, and are you ready to pay the price—the only price—which will secure it? It will be awkward for them to answer that question except in the affirmative, and impossible for them to answer it genuinely in the affirmative unless they intend that every race shall have justice. So that I think the probability is that the more plainly we speak—I do not mean the more harshly —but the more plainly and candidly we speak, the more probable it will be that we shall arrive at a just settlement. And in the attempt that I shall personally make, I shall be very much encouraged by kindly acts such as your order, as represented by you, performed to-day, and I hope that you will convey to your associates my very deep sense of the honor and distinction they have conferred upon me. Thank you very much indeed.

ANNUAL MESSAGE

ADDRESS DELIVERED AT A JOINT SESSION OF THE TWO HOUSES OF CONGRESS, DECEMBER 2, 1918. FROM OFFICIAL GOVERNMENT PUBLICATION IN MR. WILSON'S FILES.

THE year that has elapsed since I last stood before you to fulfill my constitutional duty to give to the Congress from time to time information on the state of the Union has been so crowded with great events, great processes and great results that I cannot hope to give you an adequate picture of its transactions or of the far-reaching changes which have been wrought in the life of our nation and of the world. You have yourselves witnessed these things, as I have. It is too soon to assess them; and we who stand in the midst of them and are part of them are less qualified than men of another generation will be to say what they mean, or even what they have been. But some great outstanding facts are unmistakable and constitute, in a sense, part of the public business with which it is our duty to deal. To state them is to set the stage for the legislative and executive action which must grow out of them and which we have yet to shape and determine.

A year ago we had sent 145,918 men overseas. Since then we have sent 1,950,513, an average of 162,542 each month, the number in fact rising, in May last to 245,951, in June to 278,760, in July to 307,182, and continuing to reach similar figures in August and September,—in August 289,570 and in September 257,438. No such movement of troops ever took place before, across three thousand miles of sea, followed by adequate equipment and supplies, and carried safely through extraordinary dangers of attack,—dangers which were alike strange and infinitely difficult to guard against. In all this movement only seven hundred and fifty-eight men were lost by enemy attack,—six hundred and thirty of whom were upon a single English transport which was sunk near the Orkney Islands.

I need not tell you what lay back of this great movement of men and material. It is not invidious to say that back of it lay a supporting organization of the industries of the country and of all its productive activities more complete, more thorough in method and effective in result, more spirited and unanimous in purpose and effort than any other great belligerent had been able to effect. We profited greatly by the experience of the nations which had already been engaged for nearly three years in the exigent and exacting business, their every resource and every executive proficiency taxed to the utmost. We were their pupils. But we learned quickly and acted with a promptness and a readiness of coöperation that justify our great pride that we were able to serve the world with unparalleled energy and quick accomplishment.

But it is not the physical scale and executive efficiency of preparation, supply, equipment and dispatch that I would dwell upon, but the mettle and quality of the officers and men we sent over and of the sailors who kept the seas, and the spirit of the nation that stood behind them. No soldiers or sailors ever proved themselves more quickly ready for the test of battle or acquitted themselves with more splendid courage and achievement when put to the test. Those of us who played some part in directing the great processes by which the war was pushed irresistibly forward to the final triumph may now forget all that and delight our thoughts with the story of what our men did. Their officers understood the grim and exacting task they had undertaken and performed it with an audacity, efficiency and unhesitating courage that touch the story of convoy and battle with imperishable distinction at every turn, whether the enterprise were great or small,—from their great chiefs, Pershing and Sims, down to the youngest lieutenant; and their men were worthy of them,—such men as hardly need to be commanded, and go to their terrible adventure blithely and with the quick intelligence of those who know just what it is they would accomplish. I am proud to be the fellow countryman of men of such stuff and valor. Those of us who stayed at home did our duty; the war could not have been won or the gallant men who fought it given their opportunity to win it otherwise; but for many a long day we shall think ourselves "accurs'd we were not there, and hold our manhoods cheap while any speaks that fought" with these at St. Mihiel or Thierry. The memory of those days of triumphant battle will go with these fortunate men to their graves; and each will have his favorite memory. "Old men forget; yet all shall be forgot, but he'll remember with advantages what feats he did that day!"

What we all thank God for with deepest gratitude is that our men went in force into the line of battle just at the critical moment when the whole fate of the world seemed to hang in the balance and threw their fresh strength into the ranks of freedom in time to turn the whole tide and sweep of the fateful struggle,—turn it once for all, so that thenceforth it was back, back, back for their enemies, always back, never again forward! After that it was only a scant four months before the commanders of the Central Empires knew themselves beaten; and now their very empires are in liquidation!

And throughout it all how fine the spirit of the Nation was: what unity of purpose, what untiring zeal! What elevation of purpose ran through all its splendid display of strength, its untiring accomplishment. I have said that those of us who stayed at home to do the work of organization and supply will always wish that we had been with the men whom we sustained by our labor; but we can never be ashamed. It has been an inspiring thing to be here in the midst of fine men who had turned aside from every private interest of their own and devoted the whole of their trained capacity to the tasks that supplied the sinews of the whole great undertaking! The patriotism, the unselfishness, the thoroughgoing devotion and distinguished capacity that marked their toilsome labors, day after day, month after month, have made them fit mates and comrades of the men in the trenches and on the sea. And not the men here in Washington only. They have but directed the vast achievement. Throughout innumerable factories, upon innumerable farms, in the depths of coal mines and iron mines and copper mines, wherever the stuffs of industry were to be obtained and prepared, in the shipyards, on the railways, at the docks, on the sea, in every labor that was needed to sustain the battle lines, men have vied with each other to do their part and do it well. They can look any man-at-arms in the face, and say, We also strove to win and gave the best that was in us to make our fleets and armies sure of their triumph!

And what shall we say of the women,—of their instant intelligence, quickening every task that they touched; their capacity for organization and coöperation, which gave their action discipline and enhanced the effectiveness of everything they attempted; their aptitude at tasks to which they had never before set their hands; their utter self-sacrifice alike in what they did and in what they gave? Their contribution to the great result is beyond appraisal. They have added a new luster to the annals of American womanhood.

The least tribute we can pay them is to make them the equals of men in political rights as they have proved themselves their equals in every field of practical work they have entered, whether for themselves or for their country. These great days of completed achievement would be sadly marred were we to omit that act of justice. Besides the immense practical services they have rendered, the women of the country have been the moving spirits in the systematic economies by which our people have voluntarily assisted to supply the suffering peoples of the world and the armies upon every front with food and everything else that we had that might serve the common cause. The details of such a story can never be fully written, but we carry them at our hearts and thank God that we can say that we are the kinsmen of such.

And now we are sure of the great triumph for which every sacrifice was made. It has come, come in its completeness, and with the pride and inspiration of these days of achievement quick within us we turn to the tasks of peace again,—a peace secure against the violence of irresponsible monarchs and ambitious military coteries and made ready for a new order, for new foundations of justice and fair dealing.

We are about to give order and organization to this peace not only for ourselves but for the other peoples of the world as well, so far as they will suffer us to serve them. It is international justice that we seek, not domestic safety merely. Our thoughts have dwelt of late upon Europe, upon Asia, upon the near and the far East, very little upon the acts of peace and accommodation that wait to be performed at our own doors. While we are adjusting our relations with the rest of the world is it not of capital importance that we should clear away all grounds of misunderstanding with our immediate neighbors and give proof of the friendship we really feel? I hope that the members of the Senate will permit me to speak once more of the unratified treaty of friendship and adjustment with the Republic of Colombia. I very earnestly urge upon them an early and favorable action upon that vital matter. I believe that they will feel, with me, that the stage of affairs is now set for such action as will be not only just but generous and in the spirit of the new age upon which we have so happily entered.

So far as our domestic affairs are concerned the problem of our return to peace is a problem of economic and industrial readjustment. That problem is less serious for us than it may turn out to be for the nations which have suffered the disarrangements and the losses of war longer than we. Our people, moreover, do not wait to be coached and led. They know their own business, are quick and resourceful at every readjustment, definite in purpose, and self-reliant in action. Any leading strings we might seek to put them in would speedily become hopelessly tangled because they would pay no attention to them and go their own way. All that we can do as their legislative and executive servants is to mediate the process of change here, there, and elsewhere as we may. I have heard much counsel as to the plans that should be formed and personally conducted to a happy consummation, but from no quarter have I seen any general scheme of "reconstruction" emerge which I thought it likely we could force our spirited business men and self-reliant laborers to accept with due pliancy and obedience.

While the war lasted we set up many agencies by which to direct the industries of the country in the services it was necessary for them to render, by which to make sure of an abundant supply of the materials needed, by which to check undertakings that could for the time be dispensed with and stimulate those that were most serviceable in war, by which to gain for the purchasing departments of the Government a certain control over the prices of essential articles and materials, by which to restrain trade with alien enemies, make the most of the available shipping, and systematize financial transactions, both public and private, so that there would be no unnecessary conflict or confusion,—by which, in short, to put every material energy of the country in harness to draw the common load and make of us one team in the accomplishment of a great task. But the moment we knew the armistice to have been signed we took the harness off. Raw materials upon which the Government had kept its hand for fear there should not be enough for the industries that supplied the armies have been released and put into the general market again. Great industrial plants whose whole output and machinery had been taken over for the uses of the Government have been set free to return to the uses to which they were put before the war. It has not been possible to remove so readily or so quickly the control of foodstuffs and of shipping, because the world has still to be fed from our granaries and the ships are still needed to send supplies to our men overseas and to bring the men back as fast as the disturbed conditions on the other side of the water permit; but even there restraints are being relaxed as much as possible and more and more as the weeks go by.

Never before have there been agencies in existence in this country which knew so much of the field of supply, of labor, and of industry as the War Industries Board, the War Trade Board, the Labor Department, the Food Administration, and the Fuel Administration have known since their labors became thoroughly systematized; and they have not been isolated agencies; they have been directed by men who represented the permanent Departments of the Government and so have been the centers of unified and coöperative action. It has been the policy of the Executive, therefore, since the armistice was assured (which is in effect a complete submission of the enemy) to put the knowledge of these bodies at the disposal of the business men of the country and to offer their intelligent mediation at every point and in every matter where it was desired. It is surprising how fast the process of return to a peace footing has moved in the three weeks since the fighting stopped. It promises to outrun any inquiry that may be instituted and any aid that may be offered. It will not be easy to direct it any better than it will direct itself. The American business man is of quick initiative.

The ordinary and normal processes of private initiative will not, however, provide immediate employment for all of the men of our returning armies. Those who are of trained capacity, those who are skilled workmen, those who have acquired familiarity with established businesses, those who are ready and willing to go to the farms, all those whose aptitudes are known or will be sought out by employers will find no difficulty, it is safe to say, in finding place and employment. But there will be others who will be at a loss where to gain a livelihood unless pains are taken to guide them and put them in the way of work. There will be a large floating residuum of labor which should not be left wholly to shift for itself. It seems to me important, therefore, that the development of public works of every sort should be promptly resumed, in order that opportunities should be created for unskilled labor in particular, and that plans should be made for such development of our unused lands and our natural resources as we have hitherto lacked stimulation to undertake.

I particularly direct your attention to the very practical plans which the Secretary of the Interior has developed in his annual report and before your Committees for the reclamation of arid, swamp, and cut-over lands which might, if the States were willing and able to coöperate, redeem some three hundred million acres of land for cultivation. There are said to be fifteen or twenty million acres of land in the West, at present arid, for whose reclamation water is available, if properly conserved. There are about two hundred and thirty million acres from which the forests have been cut but which have never yet been cleared for the plow and which lie waste and desolate. These lie scattered all over the Union. And there are nearly eighty million acres of land that lie under swamps or subject to periodical overflow or too wet for anything but grazing which it is perfectly feasible to drain and protect and redeem. The Congress can at once direct thousands of the returning soldiers to the reclamation of the arid lands which it has already undertaken, if it will but enlarge the plans and the appropriations which it has intrusted to the Department of the Interior. It is possible in dealing with our unused land to effect a great rural and agricultural development which will afford the best sort of opportunity to men who want to help themselves; and the Secretary of the Interior has thought the possible methods out in a way which is worthy of your most friendly attention.

I have spoken of the control which must yet for a while, perhaps for a long while, be exercised over shipping because of the priority of service to which our forces overseas are entitled and which should also be accorded the shipments which are to save recently liberated peoples from starvation and many devasted regions from permanent ruin. May I not say a special word about the needs of Belgium and northern France? No sums of money paid by way of indemnity will serve of themselves to save them from hopeless disadvantage for years to come. Something more must be done than merely find the money. If they had money and raw materials in abundance to-morrow they could not resume their place in the industry of the world to-morrow, —the very important place they held before the flame of war swept across them. Many of their factories are razed to the ground. Much of their machinery is destroyed or has been taken away. Their people are scattered and many of their best workmen are dead. Their markets will be taken by others, if they are not in some special way assisted to rebuild their factories and replace their lost instruments of manufacture. They should not be left to the vicissitudes of the sharp competition for materials and for industrial facilities which is now to set in. I hope, therefore, that the Congress will not be unwilling, if it should become necessary, to grant to some such agency as the War Trade Board the right to establish priorities of export and supply for the benefit of these people whom we have been so happy to assist in saving from the German terror and whom we must not now thoughtlessly leave to shift for themselves in a pitiless competitive market.

For the steadying and facilitation of our own domestic business readjustiments nothing is more important than the immediate determination of the taxes that are to be levied for 1918, 1919 and 1920. As much of the burden of taxation must be lifted from business as sound methods of financing the Government will permit, and those who conduct the great essential industries of the country must be told as exactly as possible what obligations to the Government they will be expected to meet in the years immediately ahead of them. It will be of serious consequence to the country to delay removing all uncertainties in this matter a single day longer than the right processes of debate justify. It is idle to talk of successful and confident business reconstruction before those uncertainties are resolved.

If the war had continued it would have been necessary to raise at least eight billion dollars by taxation payable in the year 1919; but the war has ended and I agree with the Secretary of the Treasury that it will be safe to reduce the amount to six billions. An immediate rapid decline in the expenses of the Government is not to be looked for. Contracts made for war supplies will, indeed, be rapidly canceled and liquidated, but their immediate liquidation will make heavy drains on the Treasury for the months just ahead of us. The maintenance of our forces on the other side of the sea is still necessary. A considerable proportion of those forces must remain in Europe during the period of occupation, and those which are brought home will be transported and demobilized at heavy expense for months to come. The interest on our war debt must of course be paid and provision made for the retirement of the obligations of the Government which represent it. But these demands will of course fall much below what a continuation of military operations would have entailed and six billions should suffice to supply a sound foundation for the financial operations of the year.

I entirely concur with the Secretary of the Treasury in recommending that the two billions needed in addition to the four billions provided by existing law be obtained from the profits which have accrued and shall accrue from war contracts and distinctively war business, but that these taxes be confined to the war profits accruing in 1918, or in 1919 from business originating in war contracts. I urge your acceptance of his recommendation that provision be made now, not subsequently, that the taxes to be paid in 1920 should be reduced from six to four billions. Any arrangements less definite than these would add elements of doubt and confusion to the critical period of industrial readjustment through which the country must now immediately pass, and which no true friend of the Nation's essential business interests can afford to be responsible for creating or prolonging. Clearly determined conditions, clearly and simply charted, are indispensable to the economic revival and rapid industrial development which may confidently be expected if we act now and sweep all interrogation points away.

I take it for granted that the Congress will carry out the naval program which was undertaken before we entered the war. The Secretary of the Navy has submitted to your Committees for authorization that part of the program which covers the building plans of the next three years. These plans have been prepared along the lines and in accordance with the policy which the Congress established, not under the exceptional conditions of the war, but with the intention of adhering to a definite method of development for the navy. I earnestly recommend the uninterrupted pursuit of that policy. It would clearly be unwise for us to attempt to adjust our programs to a future world policy as yet undetermined.

The question which causes me the greatest concern

is the question of the policy to be adopted towards the
railroads. I frankly turn to you for counsel upon it.
I have no confident judgment of my own. I do not
see how any thoughtful man can have who knows anything of the complexity of the problem. It is a problem which must be studied, studied immediately, and
studied without bias or prejudice. Nothing can be
gained by becoming partisans of any particular plan of
settlement.

It was necessary that the administration of the railways should be taken over by the Government so long
as the war lasted. It would have been impossible otherwise to establish and carry through under a single direction the necessary priorities of shipment. It would
have been impossible otherwise to combine maximum
production at the factories and mines and farms with
the maximum possible car supply to take the products
to the ports and markets; impossible to route troop
shipments and freight shipments without regard to the
advantage or disadvantage of the roads employed;
impossible to subordinate, when necessary, all questions of convenience to the public necessity; impossible
to give the necessary financial support to the roads from
the public treasury. But all these necessities have now
been served, and the question is, what is best for the
railroads and for the public in the future.

Exceptional circumstances and exceptional methods
of administration were not needed to convince us that
the railroads were not equal to the immense tasks of
transportation imposed upon them by the rapid and
continuous development of the industries of the country.
We knew that already. And we knew that they were
unequal to it partly because their full coöperation was
rendered impossible by law and their competition made
obligatory, so that it has been impossible to assign to
them severally the traffic which could best be carried
by their respective lines in the interests of expedition
and national economy.

We may hope, I believe, for the formal conclusion of the war by treaty by the time spring has come. The twenty-one months to which the present control of the railways is limited after formal proclamation of peace shall have been made will run at the farthest, I take it for granted, only to the January of 1921. The full equipment of the railways which the federal administration had planned could not be completed within any such period. The present law does not permit the use of the revenues of the several roads for the execution of such plans except by formal contract with their directors, some of whom will consent while some will not, and therefore does not afford sufficient authority to undertake improvements upon the scale upon which it would be necessary to undertake them. Every approach to this difficult subject-matter of decision brings us face to face, therefore, with this unanswered question: What is it right that we should do with the railroads, in the interest of the public and in fairness to their owners?

Let me say at once that I have no answer ready. The only thing that is perfectly clear to me is that it is not fair either to the public or to the owners of the railroads to leave the question unanswered and that it will presently become my duty to relinquish control of the roads, even before the expiration of the statutory period, unless there should appear some clear prospect in the mean time of a legislative solution. Their release would at least produce one element of a solution, namely certainty and a quick stimulation of private initiative.

I believe that it will be serviceable for me to set forth as explicitly as possible the alternative courses that lie open to our choice. We can simply release the roads and go back to the old conditions of private management, unrestricted competition, and multiform regulation by both state and federal authorities; or we can go to the opposite extreme and establish complete Government control, accompanied, if necessary, by

actual Government ownership; or we can adopt an inter-
mediate course of modified private control, under a
more unified and affirmative public regulation and under
such alterations of the law as will permit wasteful competition to be avoided and a considerable degree of
unification of administration to be effected, as, for example, by regional corporations under which the railways of definable areas would be in effect combined in
single systems.

The one conclusion that I am ready to state with
confidence is that it would be a disservice alike to the
country and to the owners of the railroads to return to
the old conditions unmodified.   Those are conditions
of restraint without development.   There is nothing
affirmative or helpful about them.   What the country
chiefly needs is that all its means of transportation
should be developed, its railways, its waterways, its
highways, and its countryside roads.   Some new element
of policy, therefore, is absolutely necessary,—necessary
for the service of the public, necessary for the release
of credit to those who are administering the railways,
necessary for the protection of their security holders.
The old policy may be changed much or little, but surely
it cannot wisely be left as it was.   I hope that the
Congress will have a complete and impartial study of
the whole problem instituted at once and prosecuted
as rapidly as possible.   I stand ready and anxious to
release the roads from the present control and I must
do so at a very early date if by waiting until the statutory limit of time is reached I shall be merely prolonging the period of doubt and uncertainty which is hurtful
to every interest concerned.

I welcome this occasion to announce to the Congress
my purpose to join in Paris the representatives of the
governments with which we have been associated in
the war against the Central Empires for the purpose
of discussing with them the main features of the treaty
of peace.   I realize the great inconveniences that will

attend my leaving the country, particularly at this time, but the conclusion that it was my paramount duty to go has been forced upon me by considerations which I hope will seem as conclusive to you as they have seemed to me.

The allied Governments have accepted the bases of peace which I outlined to the Congress on the eighth of January last, as the Central Empires also have, and very reasonably desire my personal counsel in their interpretation and application, and it is highly desirable that I should give it in order that the sincere desire of our Government to contribute without selfish purpose of any kind to settlements that will be of common benefit to all the nations concerned may be made fully manifest. The peace settlements which are now to be agreed upon are of transcendent importance both to us and to the rest of the world, and I know of no business or interest which should take precedence of them. The gallant men of our armed forces on land and sea have consciously fought for the ideals which they knew to be the ideals of their country; I have sought to express those ideals; they have accepted my statements of them as the substance of their own thought and purpose, as the associated Governments have accepted them; I owe it to them to see to it, so far as in me lies, that no false or mistaken interpretation is put upon them, and no possible effort omitted to realize them. It is now my duty to play my full part in making good what they offered their life's blood to obtain. I can think of no call to service which could transcend this.

I shall be in close touch with you and with affairs on this side the water, and you will know all that I do. At my request, the French and English Governments have absolutely removed the censorship of cable news which until within a fortnight they had maintained and there is now no censorship whatever exercised at this end except upon attempted trade communications with enemy countries. It has been necessary to keep an open wire constantly available between Paris and the Department of State and another between France and the Department of War. In order that this might be done with the least possible interference with the other uses of the cables, I have temporarily taken over the control of both cables in order that they may be used as a single system. I did so at the advice of the most experienced cable officials, and I hope that the results will justify my hope that the news of the next few months may pass with the utmost freedom and with the least possible delay from each side of the sea to the other.

May I not hope, Gentlemen of the Congress, that in the delicate tasks I shall have to perform on the other side of the sea, in my efforts truly and faithfully to interpret the principles and purposes of the country we love, I may have the encouragement and the added strength of your united support? I realize the magnitude and difficulty of the duty I am undertaking; I am poignantly aware of its grave responsibilities. I am the servant of the Nation. I can have no private thought or purpose of my own in performing such an errand. I go to give the best that is in me to the common settlements which I must now assist in arriving at in conference with the other working heads of the associated Governments. I shall count upon your friendly countenance and encouragement. I shall not be inaccessible. The cables and the wireless will render me available for any counsel or service you may desire of me, and I shall be happy in the thought that I am constantly in touch with the weighty matters of domestic policy with which we shall have to deal. I shall make my absence as brief as possible and shall hope to return with the happy assurance that it has been possible to translate into action the great ideals for which America has striven.

FIRST ADDRESS IN FRANCE

RESPONSE TO THE WELCOMING ADDRESS OF PRESIDENT POINCARÉ OF FRANCE, AT A LUNCHEON IN HONOR OF PRESIDENT WILSON, DECEMBER 14, 1918. FROM ORIGINAL IN MR. WILSON'S FILES.

MR. PRESIDENT:
I am deeply indebted to you for your gracious greeting. It is very delightful to find myself in France and to feel the quick contact of sympathy and unaffected friendship between the representatives of the United States and the representatives of France. You have been very generous in what you were pleased to say about myself, but I feel that what I have said and what I have tried to do has been said and done only in an attempt to speak the thought of the people of the United States truly and to carry that thought out in action. From the first the thought of the people of the United States turned toward something more than the mere winning of this war. It turned to the establishment of eternal principles of right and justice. It realized that merely to win the war was not enough; that it must be won in such a way and the questions raised by it settled in such a way as to insure the future peace of the world and lay the foundation for the freedom and happiness of its many peoples and nations.

Never before has war worn so terrible a visage or exhibited more grossly the debasing influence of illicit ambitions. I am sure that I shall look upon the ruin wrought by the armies of the Central Empires with the same repulsion and deep indignation that it stirs in the hearts of the men of France and Belgium, and I appreciate, as you do, sir, the necessity of such action in the final settlement of the issues of the war as will not only rebuke such acts of terror and spoliation, but make men everywhere aware that they cannot be ventured upon without the certainty of just punishment.

I know with what ardor and enthusiasm the soldiers and sailors of the United States have given the best that was in them to this war of redemption. They have expressed the true spirit of America. They believe their ideals to be acceptable to free peoples everywhere and are rejoiced to have played the part they have played in giving reality to those ideals in coöperation with the armies of the Allies. We are proud of the part they have played and we are happy that they should have been associated with such comrades in a common cause.

It is with peculiar feelings, Mr. President, that I find myself in France joining with you in rejoicing over the victory that has been won. The ties that bind France and the United States are peculiarly close. I do not know in what other comradeship we could have fought with more zest or enthusiasm. It will daily be a matter of pleasure with me to be brought into consultation with the statesmen of France and her Allies in concerting the measures by which we may secure permanence for these happy relations of friendship and coöperation, and secure for the world at large such safety and freedom in its life as can be secured only by the constant association and coöperation of friends.

I greet you, sir, not only with deep personal respect but as the representative of the great people of France, and beg to bring you the greetings of another great people to whom the fortunes of France are of profound and lasting interest.

I raise my glass to the health of the President of the French Republic and to Madame Poincaré, and to the prosperity of France.

TO A SOCIALIST DELEGATION

REPLY TO THE ADDRESS OF A SOCIALIST DELEGATION AT PARIS, DECEMBER 16, 1918.

I RECEIVED with great interest the address which you have just read to me. The war through which we have just passed has illustrated in a way which never can be forgotten the extraordinary wrongs which can be perpetrated by arbitrary and irresponsible power.

It is not possible to secure the happiness and prosperity of the world, to establish an enduring peace, unless the repetition of such wrongs is rendered impossible. This has indeed been a people's war. It has been waged against absolutism and militarism, and these enemies of liberty must from this time forth be shut out from the possibility of working their cruel will upon mankind.

In my judgment, it is not sufficient to establish this principle. It is necessary that it should be supported by a coöperation of the nations which shall be based upon fixed and definite covenants, and which shall be made certain of effective action through the instrumentality of a League of Nations. I believe this to be the conviction of all thoughtful and liberal men.

I am confident that this is the thought of those who lead your own great nation, and I am looking forward with peculiar pleasure to coöperating with them in securing guarantees of a lasting peace of justice and right dealing which shall justify the sacrifices of this war and cause men to look back upon those sacrifices as the dramatic and final processes of their emancipation.

AT THE HÔTEL DE VILLE

REPLY TO THE GREETINGS OF THE PREFECT OF THE
SEINE AND OF THE PRESIDENT OF THE MUNICIPAL
COUNCIL AT THE HÔTEL DE VILLE, PARIS, DECEM-
BER 16, 1918. FROM ORIGINAL IN MR. WILSON'S
FILES.

YOUR greeting has raised many emotions within
me. It is with no ordinary sympathy that the
people of the United States, for whom I have the
privilege of speaking, have viewed the sufferings of the
people of France. Many of our own people have been
themselves witnesses of those sufferings. We were the
more deeply moved by the wrongs of the war because we
knew the manner in which they were perpetrated. I
beg that you will not suppose that because a wide ocean
separated us in space, we were not in effect eye-witnesses
of the shameful ruin that was wrought and the cruel and
unnecessary sufferings that were brought upon you.
Those sufferings have filled our hearts with indignation.
We knew what they were not only, but we knew what
they signified, and our hearts were touched to the quick
by them, our imaginations filled with the whole picture of
what France and Belgium in particular had experienced.
When the United States entered the war, therefore,
they entered it not only because they were moved by a
conviction that the purposes of the Central Empires
were wrong and must be resisted by men everywhere who
loved liberty and the right, but also because the illicit
ambitions which they were entertaining and attempting
to realize had led to practices which shocked our hearts
as much as they offended our principles. Our resolution was formed because we knew how profoundly
great principles of right were affected, but our hearts
moved also with our resolution.

You have been exceedingly generous in what you have been gracious enough to say about me, generous far beyond my personal deserts, but you have interpreted with real insight the motives and resolution of the people of the United States. Whatever influence I exercise, whatever authority I speak with, I derive from them. I know what they have thought, I know what they have desired, and when I have spoken what I knew was in their minds, it has been delightful to see how the consciences and purposes of freemen everywhere responded. We have merely established our right to the full fellowship of those peoples here and throughout the world who reverence the right and whose purpose is inflexibly fixed upon the establishment of genuine liberty and justice.

You have made me feel very much at home here, not merely by the delightful warmth of your welcome but also by the manner in which you have made me realize to the utmost the intimate community of thought and ideal which characterizes your people and the great Nation which I have the honor for the time to represent. Your welcome to Paris I shall always remember as one of the unique and inspiring experiences of my life, and while I feel that you are honoring the people of the United States in my person, I shall nevertheless carry away with me a very keen personal gratification in looking back upon these memorable days. Permit me to thank you from a full heart.

AT THE UNIVERSITY OF PARIS

ADDRESS AT THE UNIVERSITY OF PARIS UPON RECEIVING
AN HONORARY DEGREE, DECEMBER 21, 1918.
FROM OFFICIAL GOVERNMENT PUBLICATION IN MR.
WILSON'S FILES.

MR. PRESIDENT, MR. RECTEUR:
I feel very keenly the distinguished honor
which has been conferred upon me by the great University of Paris, and it is very delightful to me also to
have the honor of being inducted into the great company of scholars whose life and fame have made the
history of the University of Paris a thing admired
among men of cultivation in all parts of the world.

By what you have said, sir, of the theory of education
which has been followed in France, and which I have
tried to promote in the United States, I am tempted
to venture upon a favorite theme. I have always
thought, sir, that the chief object of education was to
awaken the spirit, and that inasmuch as literature whenever it touched its great and higher notes was an expression of the spirit of mankind, the best induction
into education was to feel the pulses of humanity which
had beaten from age to age through the utterances of
men who had penetrated to the secrets of the human
spirit. And I agree with the intimation which has been
conveyed to-day that the terrible war through which we
have just passed has not been only a war between nations, but that it has been also a war between systems
of culture—the one system, the aggressive system, using
science without conscience, stripping learning of its
moral restraints, and using every faculty of the human
mind to do wrong to the whole race; the other system
reminiscent of the high traditions of men, reminiscent
of all those struggles, some of them obscure but others

clearly revealed to the historian, of men of indomitable spirit everywhere struggling toward the right and seeking above all things else to be free. The triumph of freedom in this war means that spirits of that sort now dominate the world. There is a great wind of moral force moving through the world, and every man who opposes himself to that wind will go down in disgrace. The task of those who are gathered here, or will presently be gathered here, to make the settlements of this peace is greatly simplified by the fact that they are masters of no one; they are the servants of mankind, and if we do not heed the mandates of mankind we shall make ourselves the most conspicuous and deserved failures in the history of the world.

My conception of the League of Nations is just this, that it shall operate as the organized moral force of men throughout the world, and that whenever or wherever wrong and aggression are planned or contemplated, this searching light of conscience will be turned upon them and men everywhere will ask, "What are the purposes that you hold in your heart against the fortunes of the world?" Just a little exposure will settle most questions. If the Central powers had dared to discuss the purposes of this war for a single fortnight, it never would have happened, and if, as should be, they were forced to discuss it for a year, war would have been inconceivable.

So I feel that this war is, as has been said more than once to-day, intimately related with the university spirit. The university spirit is intolerant of all the things that put the human mind under restraint. It is intolerant of everything that seeks to retard the advancement of ideals, the acceptance of the truth, the purification of life; and every university man can ally himself with the forces of the present time with the feeling that now at last the spirit of truth, the spirit to which universities have devoted themselves, has prevailed and is triumphant. If there is one point of pride that I venture to entertain, it is that it has been my privilege in some measure to interpret the university spirit in the public life of a great nation, and I feel that in honoring me to-day in this unusual and conspicuous manner you have first of all honored the people whom I represent. The spirit that I try to express I know to be their spirit, and in proportion as I serve them I believe that I advance the cause of freedom.

I, therefore, wish to thank you, sir, from the bottom of my heart for a distinction which has in a singular way crowned my academic career.

CHRISTMAS GREETING TO THE SOLDIERS OF THE UNITED STATES

ADDRESS TO AMERICAN TROOPS AT HUMES, FRANCE, DE-CEMBER 25, 1918. FROM OFFICIAL GOVERNMENT PUBLICATION IN MR. WILSON'S FILES.

I WISH that I could give to each one of you the message that I know you are longing to receive from those at home who love you. I cannot do that, but I can tell you how everybody at home is proud of you; how everybody at home has followed every movement of this great Army with confidence and affection; and how the whole people of the United States are now waiting to welcome you home with an acclaim which probably has never greeted any other army. Because this is a war into which our country, like these countries we have been so proud to stand by, has put its whole heart, and the reason that we are proud of you is that you have put your heart into it; you have done your duty, and something more, you have done your duty and done it with a spirit which gave it distinction and glory.

And now we are to have the fruits of victory. You knew when you came over what you came over for, and you have done what it was appointed you to do. I know what you expect of me. Some time ago a gentleman from one of the countries with which we are associated was discussing with me the moral aspects of this war, and I said that if we did not insist upon the high purposes for which this war was entered by the United States I could never look those gallant fellows across the seas in the face again. You knew what we expected of you and you did it. I know what you and the people at home expect of me; and I am happy to say, my fellow countrymen, that I do not find in the hearts of the great leaders with whom it is my privilege now to coöperate any difference of principle or of fundamental purpose. It happened that it was the privilege of America to present the chart for peace, and now the process of settlement has been rendered comparatively simple by the fact that all the nations concerned have accepted that chart and that the application of those principles laid down there will be their explication. The world will now know that the nations that fought this war, as well as the soldiers who represented them, are ready to make good—make good not merely in the assertion of their own interests, but make good in the establishment of peace upon the permanent foundations of right and of justice. Because this is not a war in which the soldiers of the free nations have obeyed masters. You have commanders, but you have no masters. Your very commanders represent you in representing the Nation of which you constitute so distinguished a part, and this being a people's war, everybody concerned in the settlement knows that it must be a people's peace, that nothing must be done in the settlement of the issues of the war which is not as handsome as the great achievements of the armies of the United States and the Allies.

It is difficult, very difficult, men, in a formal speech like this to show you my real heart. You men probably do not realize with what anxious attention and care we have followed every step you have advanced, and how proud we are that every step was in advance and not in retreat; that every time you set your faces in any direction, you kept your faces in that direction. A thrill has gone through my heart, as it has gone through the heart of every American, with almost every gun that was fired and every stroke that was struck in the gallant fighting that you have done; and there has been only one regret in America, and that was the regret that every man there felt that he was not here in France, too. It has been a hard thing to perform civil tasks in the United States. It has been a hard thing to take part in directing what you did without coming over and helping you do it. It has taken a lot of moral courage to stay at home, but we were proud to back you up in every way that was possible to back you up, and now I am happy to find what splendid names you have made for yourselves among the civilian population of France as well as among your comrades in arms of the French Army. It is a fine testimony to you men that these people like you and love you and trust you, and the finest part of it all is that you deserve their trust.

I feel a comradeship with you to-day which is delightful as I look about upon these undisturbed fields and think of the terrible scenes through which you have gone and realize now that the quiet peace, the tranquillity of settled hope, has descended upon us all; and while it is hard so far away from home confidently to bid you a Merry Christmas, I can, I think, confidently promise you a Happy New Year, and I can from the bottom of my heart say, God bless you.

AT CHAUMONT, FRANCE

RESPONSE TO AN ADDRESS OF WELCOME BY THE MAYOR
OF CHAUMONT, DECEMBER 25, 1918. FROM OF-
FICIAL GOVERNMENT PUBLICATION IN MR. WIL-
SON'S FILES.

I FEEL that I have been peculiarly honored in the
generous reception you have given me, and it is the
more delightful because it so obviously comes from the
heart; and I cannot but believe that it is an instinctive
response to the feeling that is in my own breast. Because I think that even you, after contact with our
soldiers, cannot realize the depth and sincerity of the
feeling of the United States for France. It is an ancient
friendship, but it has been renewed and has taken on
a new youth. It is a friendship which is not only one
of sentiment, but one based upon a communion of principle.

You have spoken very generously and very beautifully
of the relations which have sprung up between yourselves and our soldiers. That is because they came not
only to associate themselves with you as the champions
of liberty, but they came with personal affection in their
hearts for the people of France, and it must have been
that which you realized. They did not come as strangers
in their thoughts. They brought with them something
that made them feel at home the moment they were at
Havre or Brest in France.

So I am very much moved by being thus drawn, as
they have been, into your midst and into your confidence,
and wish to thank you very warmly for them and for
the people of the United States. I, like them, shall
carry away with me the most delightful recollections,
and my heart will always say, as I now say, "Vive la
France."

AT DOVER, ENGLAND

RESPONSE TO AN ADDRESS OF WELCOME BY THE MAYOR
OF DOVER, DECEMBER 26, 1918. FROM OFFICIAL
GOVERNMENT PUBLICATION IN MR. WILSON'S FILES.

MR. MAYOR:
You have certainly extended to me and to those who are accompanying me a very cordial and gracious hand of welcome. Even the sea was kind to us this morning and gave us a very pleasant passage, so that it tallied perfectly with our expectations of the pleasure we should have in landing in England.

We have gone through many serious times together, and therefore we can regard each other in a new light as comrades and associates, because nothing brings men together like a common understanding and a common purpose. I think that in spite of all the terrible sufferings and sacrifices of this war we shall some day in looking back upon them realize that they were worth while, not only because of the security they gave the world against unjust aggression, but also because of the understanding they established between great nations which ought to act with each other in the permanent maintenance of justice and of right. It is, therefore, with emotions of peculiar gratification that I find myself here. It affords the opportunity to match my mind with the minds of those who with a like intention are purposing to do the best that can be done in the great settlements of the struggle.

I thank you very warmly, gentlemen, for your greeting and beg to extend to you in the name of my own countrymen the most cordial greetings.

RESPONSE TO KING GEORGE

ADDRESS AT BUCKINGHAM PALACE, DECEMBER 27, 1918. FROM OFFICIAL GOVERNMENT PUBLICATION IN MR. WILSON'S FILES.

Y OUR MAJESTY:
    I am deeply complimented by the gracious words which you have uttered. The welcome which you have given me and Mrs. Wilson has been so warm, so natural, so evidently from the heart that we have been more than pleased; we have been touched by it, and I believe that I correctly interpret that welcome as embodying not only your own generous spirit towards us personally, but also as expressing for yourself and the great nation over which you preside that same feeling for my people, for the people of the United States. For you and I, sir—I temporarily—embody the spirit of two great nations; and whatever strength I have, and whatever authority, I possess only so long and so far as I express the spirit and purpose of the American people.

Any influence that the American people have over the affairs of the world is measured by their sympathy with the aspirations of free men everywhere. America does love freedom, and I believe that she loves freedom unselfishly. But if she does not, she will not and cannot help the influence to which she justly aspires. I have had the privilege, sir, of conferring with the leaders of your own Government and with the spokesmen of the Governments of France and of Italy, and I am glad to say that I have the same conceptions that they have of the significance and scope of the duty upon which we have met. We have used great words, all of us, we have used the great words "right" and "justice," and now we are to prove whether or not we understand those words and how they are to be applied to the particular

337

settlements which must conclude this war. And we must not only understand them, but we must have the courage to act upon our understanding.

Yet, after I have uttered the word "courage," it comes into my mind that it would take more courage to resist the great moral tide now running in the world than to yield to it, than to obey it. There is a great tide running in the hearts of men. The hearts of men have never beaten so singularly in unison before. Men have never before been so conscious of their brotherhood. Men have never before realized how little difference there was between right and justice in one latitude and in another, under one sovereignty and under another; and it will be our high privilege, I believe, sir, not only to apply the moral judgments of the world to the particular settlements which we shall attempt, but also to organize the moral force of the world to preserve those settlements, to steady the forces of mankind and to make the right and the justice to which great nations like our own have devoted themselves the predominant and controlling force of the world.

There is something inspiring in knowing that this is the errand that we have come on. Nothing less than this would have justified me in leaving the important tasks which fall upon me upon the other side of the sea, nothing but the consciousness that nothing else compares with this in dignity and importance. Therefore it is the more delightful to find myself in the company of a body of men united in ideal and in purpose, to feel that I am privileged to unite my thought with yours in carrying forward those standards which we are so proud to hold high and to defend.

May I not, sir, with a feeling of profound sincerity and friendship and sympathy propose your own health and the health of the Queen, and the prosperity of Great Britain?

"THE SANCTIONS OF RELIGION"

REPLY TO A COMMITTEE OF THE NATIONAL COUNCIL OF
EVANGELICAL FREE CHURCHES, LONDON, DECEM-
BER 28, 1918. FROM OFFICIAL GOVERNMENT PUB-
LICATION IN MR. WILSON'S FILES.

GENTLEMEN:

I am very much honored, and might say, touched, by this beautiful address that you have just read, and it is very delightful to feel the comradeship of spirit which is indicated by a gathering like this.

You are quite right, sir, in saying that I do recognize the sanctions of religion in these times of perplexity with matters so large to settle that no man can feel that his mind can compass them. I think one would go crazy if he did not believe in Providence. It would be a maze without a clue. Unless there were some supreme guidance we would despair of the results of human counsel. So that it is with genuine sympathy that I acknowledge the spirit and thank you for the generosity of your address.

A GROWING INTEREST IN THE LEAGUE OF NATIONS

REPLY TO THE LEAGUE OF NATIONS UNION AT THE
AMERICAN EMBASSY, LONDON, DECEMBER 28, 1918.
FROM OFFICIAL GOVERNMENT PUBLICATION IN MR.
WILSON'S FILES.

G ENTLEMEN:
I am very much complimented that you should
come in person to present this address, and I have been
delighted and stimulated to find the growing and prevailing interest in the subject of the League of Nations,
not only a growing interest merely, but a growing purpose which I am sure will prevail. And it is very delightful that members of the Government which brought
this Nation into the war because of the moral obligations based upon treaty should be among those who
have brought me this paper, because on the other side
of the water we have greatly admired the motives and
subscribed to the principles which actuated the Government of Great Britain. In obeying that moral dictate
you have shown what we must organize, namely, that
same force and sense of obligation, and unless we organize it the thing that we do now will not stand. I feel
that so strongly that it is particularly cheering to know
just how strong and imperative the idea has become.

I thank you very much indeed. It has been a privilege
to see you personally.

I was just saying to Lord Grey that we had indirect
knowledge of each other and that I am glad to identify
him. I feel as if I met him long ago; and I had the
pleasure of matching minds with Mr. Asquith yesterday.

AT THE GUILDHALL, LONDON

RESPONSE TO AN ADDRESS OF WELCOME BY THE LORD
MAYOR AT THE GUILDHALL, LONDON, DECEMBER
28, 1918. FROM OFFICIAL GOVERNMENT PUBLICA-
TION IN MR. WILSON'S FILES.

M R. LORD MAYOR:
We have come upon times when ceremonies like
this have a new significance, and it is that significance
which most impresses me as I stand here. The address
which I have just heard is most generously and
graciously conceived and the delightful accent of sincerity in it seems like a part of that voice of counsel
which is now everywhere to be heard.

I feel that a distinguished honor has been conferred
upon me by this reception, and I beg to assure you, sir,
and your associates of my very profound appreciation,
but I know that I am only part of what I may call a
great body of circumstances. I do not believe that it
was fancy on my part that I heard in the voice of welcome uttered in the streets of this great city and in the
streets of Paris something more than a personal welcome. It seemed to me that I heard the voice of one
people speaking to another people, and it was a voice
in which one could distinguish a singular combination
of emotions. There was surely there the deep grate-
fulness that the fighting was over. There was the pride
that the fighting had had such a culmination. There
was that sort of gratitude that the nations engaged
had produced such men as the soldiers of Great Britain
and of the United States and of France and of Italy—
men whose prowess and achievements they had witnessed with rising admiration as they moved from culmination to culmination. But there was something
more in it, the consciousness that the business is not

yet done, the consciousness that it now rests upon others to see that those lives were not lost in vain.

I have not yet been to the actual battlefields, but I have been with many of the men who have fought the battles, and the other day I had the pleasure of being present at a session of the French Academy when they admitted Marshal Joffre to their membership. The sturdy, serene soldier stood and uttered, not the words of triumph, but the simple words of affection for his soldiers, and the conviction which he summed up, in a sentence which I will not try accurately to quote but reproduce in its spirit, was that France must always remember that the small and the weak could never live free in the world unless the strong and the great always put their power and strength in the service of right. That is the afterthought—the thought that something must be done now not only to make the just settlements, that of course, but to see that the settlements remained and were observed and that honor and justice prevailed in the world. And as I have conversed with the soldiers, I have been more and more aware that they fought for something that not all of them had defined, but which all of them recognized the moment you stated it to them. They fought to do away with an old order and to establish a new one, and the center and characteristic of the old order was that unstable thing which we used to call the "balance of power"—a thing in which the balance was determined by the sword which was thrown in the one side or the other; a balance which was determined by the unstable equilibrium of competitive interests; a balance which was maintained by jealous watchfulness and an antagonism of interests which, though it was generally latent, was always deep-seated. The men who have fought in this war have been the men from free nations who were determined that that sort of thing should end now and forever.

It is very interesting to me to observe how from every quarter, from every sort of mind, from every concert of

counsel, there comes the suggestion that there must now
be, not a balance of power, not one powerful group of
nations set off against another, but a single overwhelming, powerful group of nations who shall be the trustee
of the peace of the world. It has been delightful in
my conferences with the leaders of your Government to
find how our minds moved along exactly the same line,
and how our thought was always that the key to the
peace was the guarantee of the peace, not the items of
it; that the items would be worthless unless there stood
back of them a permanent concert of power for their
maintenance. That is the most reassuring thing that
has ever happened in the world. When this war began
the thought of a League of Nations was indulgently considered as the interesting thought of closeted students.
It was thought of as one of those things that it was
right to characterize by a name which as a university
man I have always resented; it was said to be academic,
as if that in itself were a condemnation, something that
men could think about but never get. Now we find the
practical leading minds of the world determined to get
it. No such sudden and potent union of purpose has
ever been witnessed in the world before. Do you wonder, therefore, gentlemen, that in common with those
who represent you I am eager to get at the business and
write the sentences down; and that I am particularly
happy that the ground is cleared and the foundations
laid—for we have already accepted the same body of
principles? Those principles are clearly and definitely
enough stated to make their application a matter which
should afford no fundamental difficulty. And back of
us is that imperative yearning of the world to have all
disturbing questions quieted, to have all threats against
peace silenced, to have just men everywhere come together for a common object. The peoples of the world
want peace and they want it now, not merely by conquest of arms, but by agreement of mind.

It was this incomparably great object that brought me

overseas. It has never before been deemed excusable for a President of the United States to leave the territory of the United States; but I know that I have the support of the judgment of my colleagues in the Government of the United States in saying that it was my paramount duty to turn away even from the imperative tasks at home to lend such counsel and aid as I could to this great, may I not say, final enterprise of humanity.

AT THE LORD MAYOR'S LUNCHEON

ADDRESS AT A LUNCHEON GIVEN AT THE MANSION HOUSE, LONDON, DECEMBER 28, 1918. FROM OFFICIAL GOVERNMENT PUBLICATION IN MR. WILSON'S FILES.

MR. LORD MAYOR, YOUR ROYAL HIGHNESS, YOUR GRACE, LADIES AND GENTLEMEN:

You have again made me feel, sir, the very wonderful and generous welcome of this great city, and you have reminded me of what has perhaps become one of the habits of my life. You have said that I have broken all precedents in coming across the ocean to join in the counsels of the peace conference, but I think those who have been associated with me in Washington will testify that that is nothing surprising. I said to members of the press in Washington one evening that one of the things that had interested me most since I lived in Washington was that every time I did anything perfectly natural it was said to be unprecedented. It was perfectly natural to break this precedent, natural because the demand for intimate conference took precedence over every other duty. And, after all, breaking of precedents, though this may sound strange doctrine in England, is the most sensible thing to do. The harness of precedent is sometimes a very sad and harassing trammel. In this case the breaking of precedent is sensible for a reason that is very prettily illustrated in a remark attributed to Charles Lamb. One evening in a company of his friends they were discussing a person who was not present, and Lamb said, in his hesitating manner, "I h-hate that fellow." "Why, Charles," one of his friends said, "I didn't know that you knew him." "Oh," he said, "I-I-I d-don't; I c-can't h-hate a man I-I-I know." And perhaps that simple and attractive remark may furnish a secret for cordial international relationship. When we know one another we cannot hate one another.

I have been very much interested before coming here to see what sort of person I was expected to be. So far as I can make it out, I was expected to be a perfectly bloodless thinking machine; whereas, I am perfectly aware that I have in me all the insurgent elements of the human race. I am sometimes by reason of long Scotch tradition able to keep those instincts in restraint. The stern Covenanter tradition that is behind me sends many an echo down the years.

It is not only diligently to pursue business but also to seek this sort of comradeship that I feel it a privilege to have come across the seas, and in the welcome that you have accorded Mrs. Wilson and me you have made us feel that that companionship was accessible to us in the most delightful and enjoyable form. I thank you sincerely for this welcome, sir, and am very happy to join in a love feast which is all the more enjoyable because there is behind it a background of tragical suffering. Our spirits are released from the darkness of clouds that at one time seemed to have settled upon the world in a way that could not be dispersed; the suffering of your own people, the suffering of the people of France, the infinite suffering of the people of Belgium. The whisper of grief that has blown all through the world is now silent, and the sun of hope seems to spread its rays and to change the earth with a new prospect of happiness. So our joy is all the more elevated because we know that our spirits are lifted out of that valley.

AT HIS GRANDFATHER'S CHURCH
AT CARLISLE

ADDRESS AT THE LOWTHER STREET CONGREGATIONAL CHURCH, CARLISLE, ENGLAND,[1] DECEMBER 29, 1918. FROM ORIGINAL COPY IN MR. WILSON'S FILES.

IT IS with unaffected reluctance that I project myself into this solemn service. I remember my grandfather very well, and, remembering him as I do, I am confident that he would not approve of it. I remember how much he required. I remember the stern lessons of duty he spoke to me. I remember also painfully the things which he expected me to know which I did not know. I know there has come a change of times when a layman like myself is permitted to speak in a congregation. But I was reluctant because the feelings that have been excited in me are too intimate and too deep to permit of public expression. The memories that have come to me to-day of the mother who was born here are very affecting, and her quiet character, her sense of duty and dislike of ostentation, have come back to me with increasing force as those years of duty have accumulated. Yet perhaps it is appropriate that in a place of worship I should acknowledge my indebtedness to her and to her remarkable father, because, after all, what the world is now seeking to do is to return to the paths of duty, to turn away from the savagery of interest to the dignity of the performance of right. And I believe that as this war has drawn the nations temporarily together in a combination of

---

[1] Woodrow Wilson's mother was born at Carlisle, England, December 20, 1826. His grandfather, Thomas Woodrow, was minister of the church, then located in Annetwell Street. The President attended service and was called upon to speak.

physical force we shall now be drawn together in a combination of moral force that will be irresistible.

It is moral force that is irresistible. It is moral force as much as physical that has defeated the effort to subdue the world. Words have cut as deep as the sword. The knowledge that wrong was being attempted has aroused the nations. They have gone out like men upon a crusade. No other cause could have drawn so many nations together. They knew that an outlaw was abroad who purposed unspeakable things. It is from quiet places like this all over the world that the forces accumulate which presently will overbear any attempt to accomplish evil on a large scale. Like the rivulets gathering into the river and the river into the seas, there come from communities like this streams that fertilize the consciences of men, and it is the conscience of the world that we are trying to place upon the throne which others would usurp.

AT LORD MAYOR'S LUNCHEON, MANCHESTER

ADDRESS AT A LUNCHEON IN THE MIDLAND HOTEL, MANCHESTER, ENGLAND, DECEMBER 30, 1918. FROM OFFICIAL GOVERNMENT PUBLICATION IN MR. WILSON'S FILES.

MY LORD MAYOR, LADIES AND GENTLE-MEN:

You have again made me feel the cordiality of your friendship, and I want to tell you how much I appreciate it, not only on my own behalf but on behalf of my partner.

It is very interesting that the Lord Mayor should have referred in his address to a vital circumstance in our friendship. He referred to the fact that our men and your men had fought side by side in the great battles in France, but there was more than that in it. For the first time, upon such a scale at any rate, they fought under a common commander. That is the advance which we have made over previous times, and what I have been particularly interested in has been the generosity of spirit with which that unity of command has been assented to. I not only had the pleasure of meeting Marshal Foch, who confirmed my admiration of him by the direct and simple manner in which he dealt with every subject that we talked about, but I have also had the pleasure of meeting your own commanders, and I understand how they coöperated, because I saw that they were real men. It takes a real man to subordinate himself. It takes a real soldier to know that unity of command is the secret of success, and that unity of command did swing the power of the nations into a mighty force. I think we all must have felt the new momentum which got into all the armies so soon as they became a single army, and we felt that we had overcome one of the most serious obstacles in the strength of the enemy, that he had unity of command and could strike where he would with a common plan and we could not.

And with that unity of command there rose the unity of spirit. The minute we consented to coöperate our hearts were drawn together in the coöperation. So, from the military side we have given ourselves an example for the years to come; not that in the years to come we must submit to a unity of command, but it does seem to me that in the years to come we must plan a unity of purpose, and in that unity of purpose we shall find that great recompense, the strengthening of our spirits in everything that we do. There is nothing so hampering and nothing so demeaning as jealousy. It is a canker. It is a canker in the heart not only, but it is a canker in the counting-room; it is a canker throughout all the processes of civilization. Having now seen that we can fight shoulder to shoulder, we will continue to advance shoulder to shoulder, and I think that you will find that the people of the United States are not the least eager of the parties.

I remember hearing a story of a warning which one of your Australian soldiers gave to one of ours. Our soldiers were considered by the older men a bit rash when they went in. I understand that even the Australians said that our men were a "bit rough," and on one occasion a friendly Australian said to one of our men, "Man, a barrage is not a thing meant to lean up against." They were a little bit inclined to lean up against the barrage, and yet I must confide to you that I was a bit proud of them for it. They had come over to get at the enemy, and they did not know why they should delay.

And now that there is no common enemy except distrust and marring of plans, we can all feel the same eagerness in the new comradeship, and can feel that there is a common enterprise for it. For, after all, though we boast of the material sides of our civilization, they are merely meant to support the spiritual side. We are not men because we have skill of hand, but we are men because we have elevation of spirit. It is in the spirit that we live and not in the task of the day. If it is not, why is it that you hang the lad's musket or his sword up above the mantelpiece and never hang his yardstick up? There is nothing discreditable in the yardstick. It is altogether honorable, but he is using it for his own sake. When he takes the musket or the sword, he is giving everything he has and getting nothing. It is honorable, not as an instrument of force, but as a symbol of self-sacrifice. A friend of mine said very truly that when peace is conducted in the spirit of war, there will be no war; when business is done with the point of view of the soldier, that he is serving his country, then business will be as histrionic as war. And I believe that from generation to generation conceptions of that sort are getting more and more currency and that men are beginning to see, not perhaps a golden age, but at any rate an age which is brightening from decade to decade and may lead us some time to an elevation from which we can see the things for which the heart of mankind has longed.

IN FREE TRADE HALL, MANCHESTER

ADDRESS AT A LUNCHEON GIVEN DECEMBER 30, 1918.
FROM OFFICIAL GOVERNMENT PUBLICATION IN
MR. WILSON'S FILES.

MY LORD MAYOR, LADIES, AND GENTLE-
MEN—PERHAPS I MAY BE PERMITTED
TO ADD FELLOW CITIZENS:
You have made me feel in a way that is deeply delightful the generous welcome which you have accorded
me. Back of it I know there lies the same sort of feeling for the great people whom I have the privilege of
representing. There is a feeling of cordial fraternity
and friendship between these two great nations, and
as I have gone from place to place and been made
everywhere to feel the pulse of sympathy that is now
beating between us, I have been led to some very serious thoughts as to what the basis of it all is. For I
think you will agree with me that friendship is not a
mere sentiment. Patriotism is not a mere sentiment. It
is based upon a principle—upon a principle that leads
a man to give more than he demands. And, similarly,
friendship is based not merely upon affection, but upon
common service. A man is not your friend who is not
willing to serve you, and you are not his friend unless
you are willing to serve him, and out of that impulse
of common interest and a desire of common service
rises that noble feeling which we have consecrated as
friendship.

So it has seemed to me that the theme that we must
have in our minds now in this great day of settlement
is the theme of common interest and the determination
of what it is that is our common interest. You know
that heretofore the world has been governed, or at
any rate an attempt has been made to govern it, by part-

nerships of interest, and they have broken down.
Interest does not bind men together. Interest separates men, for the moment there is the slightest departure from the nice adjustment of interests jealousies
begin to spring up. There is only one thing that can
bind peoples together and that is a common devotion to
right. Ever since the history of liberty began men have
talked about their rights, and it has taken several hundred years to make them perceive that the principal
part of right is duty, and that unless a man performs
his full duty he is entitled to no right. This fine correla-
tion of the two things of duty and of right is the
equipoise and balance of society. So when we analyze
the present situation and the future that we now have
to mold and control, it seems to me that there is no
other thought than that that can guide us.

You know that the United States has always felt
from the very beginning of her history that she must
keep herself separate from any kind of connection with
European politics, and I want to say very frankly to
you that she is not now interested in European politics.
But she is interested in the partnership of right between
America and Europe. If the future had nothing for
us but a new attempt to keep the world at a right poise
by a balance of power, the United States would take
no interest, because she will join no combination of
power which is not the combination of all of us. She
is not interested merely in the peace of Europe, but in
the peace of the world. Therefore it seems to me that
in the settlement that is just ahead of us something
more delicate and difficult than was ever attempted before is to be accomplished, a genuine concert of mind
and of purpose. But while it is difficult there is an
element present that makes it easy. Never before in
the history of the world, I believe, has there been such a
keen international consciousness as there is now. Men
all over the world know that they have been embarrassed by national antagonisms and that the interest of

each is the interest of all, and that men as men are the objects of government and international arrangements. There is a great voice of humanity abroad in the world just now which he who cannot hear is deaf. There is a great compulsion of the common conscience now in existence which if any statesman resist he has gained the most unenviable eminence in history. We are not obeying the mandates of parties or of politics. We are obeying the mandates of humanity. That is the reason why it seems to me that the things that are most often in our minds are the least significant. I am not hopeful that the individual items of the settlements which we are about to attempt will be altogether satisfactory. One has but to apply his mind to any one of the questions of boundary and of altered sovereignty and of racial aspiration to do something more than conjecture that there is no man and no body of men who know just how it ought to be settled. Yet if we are to make unsatisfactory settlements, we must see to it that they are rendered more and more satisfactory by the subsequent adjustments which are made possible.

So that we must provide a machinery of readjustment in order that we may have a machinery of good will and of friendship. Friendship must have a machinery. If I cannot correspond with you, if I cannot learn your mind, if I cannot coöperate with you, I cannot be your friend, and if the world is to remain a body of friends it must have the means of friendship, the means of constant friendly intercourse, the means of constant watchfulness over the common interest— not making it necessary to make a great effort upon some great occasion and confer with one another, but have an easy and constant method of conference, so that troubles may be taken when they are little and not allowed to grow until they are big. I never thought that I had a big difference with a man that I did not find when I came into conference with him that, after all, it was rather a little difference and that if we were frank with one another, and did not too much stand upon that great enemy of mankind which is called pride, we could come together. It is the wish to come together that is more than half of the process. This is a doctrine which ought to be easy of comprehension in a great commercial center like this. You cannot trade with men who suspect you. You cannot establish commercial and industrial relations with those who do not trust you. Good will is the forerunner of trade, and trade is the great amicable instrument of the world on that account.

I feel—I felt before I came here—at home in Manchester, because Manchester has so many of the characteristics of our great American cities. I was reminded of the anecdote of a humorous fellow countryman who was sitting at lunch in his club one day and a man whom he did not like particularly came by and slapped him on the shoulder. "Hello, Ollie, old fellow, how are you?" he said. Ollie looked at him coldly and said, "I don't know your face; I don't know your name; but your manners are very familiar." I don't know your names, but your manners are very familiar. They are very delightfully familiar. So that I feel that in the community of interest and of understanding which is established in great currents of trade, we are enabled to see international processes perhaps better than they can be seen by others. I take it that I am not far from right in supposing that that is the reason why Manchester has been a center of the great forward-looking sentiments of men who had the instinct of large planning, not merely for the city itself, but for the Kingdom and the Empire and the world, and with that outlook we can be sure that we can go shoulder and shoulder together.

I wish that it were possible for us to do something like some of my very stern ancestors did, for among my ancestors are those very determined persons who were known as the Covenanters. I wish we could, not only for Great Britain and the United States, but for France and Italy and the world, enter into a great league and covenant, declaring ourselves, first of all, friends of mankind and uniting ourselves together for the maintenance and the triumph of right.

TRIBUTE TO THE ITALIAN PEOPLE

ADDRESS AT THE QUIRINAL, ROME, JANUARY 3, 1919. FROM OFFICIAL GOVERNMENT PUBLICATION IN MR. WILSON'S FILES.

YOUR MAJESTY:
I have been very much touched by the generous terms of the address which you have just read. I feel it would be difficult for me to make a worthy reply, and yet if I could speak simply the things that are in my heart I am sure they would constitute an adequate reply.

I had occasion at the Parliament this afternoon to speak of the strong sympathy that had sprung up between the United States and Italy during the terrible years of the war, but perhaps here I could speak more intimately and say how sincerely the people of the United States have admired your own course and your own constant association with the armies of Italy, and the gracious and generous and serving association of Her Majesty the Queen.

It has been a matter of pride with us that so many men of Italian origin were in our own armies and associated with their brethren of Italy itself in the great enterprise of freedom. These are no small matters, and they complete that process of welding together of the sympathies of nations which has been going on so long between our peoples. The Italians in the United States have excited a particular degree of admiration. They, I believe, are the only people of a given nationality who have been careful to organize themselves to see that their compatriots coming to America were from month to month and year to year guided to the places of the industries most suitable to their previous habits. No other nationality has taken such pains as that, and in serving their fellow countrymen they have served the United States, because these people have found places where they would be most useful and would most immediately earn their own living, and they have thereby added to the prosperity of the country itself. In every way we have been happy in our association at home and abroad with the people of this great State.

I was saying playfully to Mr. Orlando and Baron Sonnino this afternoon that in trying to put the peoples of the world under their proper sovereignties we would not be willing to part with the Italians in the United States. We would not be willing, unless they desired it, that you should resume possession of them, because we too much value the contribution that they have made, not only to the industry of the United States but to its thought and to many elements of its life. This is, therefore, a very welcome occasion upon which to express a feeling that goes very deep. I was touched the other day to have an Italian, a very plain man, say to me that we had helped to feed Italy during the war, and it went to my heart, because we had been able to do so little. It was necessary for us to use our tonnage so exclusively for the handling of troops and of the supplies that had to follow them from the United States that we could not do half as much as it was our desire to do, to supply grain to this country, or coal, or any of the supplies which it so much needed during the progress of the war. And knowing as we did in this indirect way the needs of the country, you will not wonder that we were moved by its steadfastness. My heart goes out to the little poor families all over this great kingdom who stood the brunt and the strain of the war and gave their men gladly to make other men free and other women and children free. Those are the people, and many like them, to whom after all we owe the glory of this great achievement, and I want to join with you, for I am sure I am joining with you, in expressing my profound sympathy not only, but my very profound admiration as well.

It is my privilege and honor to propose the health of His Majesty the King and of Her Majesty the Queen, and long prosperity to Italy.

AT THE CAPITOL

ADDRESS AT ROME, JANUARY 3, 1919. FROM OFFICIAL
GOVERNMENT PUBLICATION IN MR. WILSON'S
FILES.

YOU have done me a very great honor. Perhaps you
can imagine what a feeling it is for a citizen of one
of the newest of the great nations to be made a citizen
of this ancient city. It is a distinction which I am sure
you are conferring upon me as the representative of
the great people for whom I speak. One who has been
a student of history cannot accept an honor of this sort
without having his memory run back to the extraordinary series of events which have centered in this place.
But as I have thought to-day, I have been impressed
by the contrast between the temporary and the permanent things. Many political changes have centered
about Rome, from the time when from a little city she
grew to be the mistress of an empire, and change after
change has swept away many things, altering the very
form of her affairs, but the thing that has remained
permanent has been the spirit of Rome and of the
Italian people. That spirit seems to have caught with
each age the characteristic purpose of the age. This
imperial people now gladly represents the freedom of
nations. This people which at one time seemed to conceive the purpose of governing the world now takes part
in the liberal enterprise of offering the world its own
government. Can there be a finer or more impressive
illustration of the indestructible human spirit, and of
the unconquerable spirit of liberty?

I have been reflecting in these recent days about a
colossal blunder that has just been made—the blunder
of force by the Central Empires. If Germany had
waited a single generation, she would have had a com-

mercial empire of the world. She was not willing to conquer by skill, by enterprise, by commercial success. She must needs attempt to conquer by arms, and the world will always acclaim the fact that it is impossible to conquer it by arms; that the only thing that conquers it is the sort of service which can be rendered in trade, in intercourse, in friendship, and that there is no conquering power which can suppress the freedom of the human spirit.

I have rejoiced personally in the partnership of the Italian and the American people, because it was a new partnership in an old enterprise, an enterprise predestined to succeed wherever it is undertaken—the enterprise that has always borne that handsome name which we call "Liberty." Men have pursued it sometimes like a mirage that seemed to elude them, that seemed to run before them as they advanced, but never have they flagged in their purpose to achieve it, and I believe that I am not deceived in supposing that in this age of ours they are nearer to it than they ever were before. The light that shined upon the summit now seems almost to shine at our feet, and if we lose it, it will be only because we have lost faith and courage, for we have the power to attain it.

So it seems to me that there never was a time when a greater breath of hope and of confidence had come into the minds and the hearts of men like the present. I would not have felt at liberty to come away from America if I had not felt that the time had arrived when, forgetting local interests and local ties and local purposes, men should unite in this great enterprise which will ever tie free men together as a body of brethren and a body of free spirits.

I am honored, sir, to be taken into this ancient comradeship of the citizenship of Rome.

BEFORE THE ITALIAN PARLIAMENT

ADDRESS ON BEING MADE A CITIZEN OF ROME, JANUARY 3, 1919. FROM OFFICIAL GOVERNMENT PUBLICATION IN MR. WILSON'S FILES.

YOUR MAJESTY, MR. PRESIDENT, MR. PRESIDENT OF THE CHAMBER:

You are bestowing upon me an unprecedented honor, which I accept because I believe that it is extended to me as the representative of the great people for whom I speak, and I am going to take this opportunity to say how entirely the heart of the American people has been with the great people of Italy. We have seemed no doubt indifferent at times, to look on from a great distance, but our hearts have never been far away. All sorts of ties have long bound the people of America to the people of Italy, and when the people of the United States, knowing this people, have witnessed its sufferings, its sacrifices, its heroic action upon the battlefield and its heroic endurance at home—its steadfast endurance at home touching us more nearly to the quick even than its heroic action on the battlefield—we have been bound by a new tie of profound admiration. Then, back of it all and through it all, running like the golden thread that wove it together, was our knowledge that the people of Italy had gone into this war for the same exalted principles of right and justice that moved our own people. And so I welcome this opportunity of conveying to you the heartfelt greetings of the people of the United States.

But we cannot stand in the shadow of this war without knowing that there are things awaiting us which are in some senses more difficult than those we have undertaken. While it is easy to speak of right and justice, it is sometimes difficult to work them out in practice, and there will require a purity of motive and disinterestedness of object which the world has never witnessed before in the councils of nations. It is for that reason that it seems to me that you will forgive me if I lay some of the elements of the new situation before you for a moment. The distinguishing fact of this war is that great empires have gone to pieces, and the characteristic of those empires was that they held different peoples reluctantly together under the coercion of force and the guidance of intrigue. The great difficulty among such States as those of the Balkans has been that they were always accessible to secret influence; that they were always being penetrated by intrigue of one sort and another; and that north of them lay disturbed populations which were held together, not by sympathy and friendship, but by the coercive force of a military power. Now the intrigue is checked and the bands are broken, and what are we going to do to provide a new cement to hold these people together? They have not been accustomed to being independent. They must now be independent. I am sure that you recognize the principle as I do that it is not our privilege to say what sort of government they shall set up, but we are friends of these people and it is our duty as their friends to see to it that some kind of protection is thrown around them, something supplied which will hold them together. There is only one thing that holds nations together, if you exclude force, and that is friendship and good will. The only thing that binds men together is friendship and by the same token the only thing that binds nations together is friendship.

Therefore, our task at Paris is to organize the friendship of the world, to see to it that all the moral forces that make for right and justice and liberty are united and are given a vital organization to which the peoples of the world will readily and gladly respond. In other words, our task is no less colossal than this, to set up a new international psychology, to have a new atmosphere. I am happy to say that in my dealings with the distinguished gentlemen who lead your nation and those who lead France and England, I feel that atmosphere gathering, that desire to do justice, that desire to establish friendliness, that desire to make peace rest upon right; and with this common purpose no obstacle need be formidable. The only use of an obstacle is to be overcome. All that an obstacle does with brave men is, not to frighten them, but to challenge them. So that it ought to be our pride to overcome everything that stands in the way.

We know that there cannot be another balance of power. That has been tried and found wanting, for the best of all reasons that it does not stay balanced inside itself, and a weight which does not hold together cannot constitute a makeweight in the affairs of men. Therefore, there must be something substituted for the balance of power, and I am happy to find everywhere in the air of these great nations the conception that that thing must be a thoroughly united league of nations. What men once considered theoretical and idealistic turns out to be practical and necessary. We stand at the opening of a new age in which a new statesmanship will, I am confident, lift mankind to new levels of endeavor and achievement.

RELIEF FOR STARVING PEOPLES IN EUROPE

CABLEGRAM TO THE SECRETARY OF THE TREASURY,[1] REQUESTING THE APPROPRIATION BY CONGRESS OF A SUM FOR THE RELIEF OF NEEDY EUROPEAN PEOPLES OUTSIDE OF GERMANY, JANUARY 4, 1919. FROM "OFFICIAL U. S. BULLETIN," NO. 504.

EXTENDED investigation and consideration of the food situation in certain parts of Europe disclose that especially the urban populations in certain areas are not only facing absolute starvation during the coming winter, but that many of these populations are unable to find immediate resources with which to purchase their food. These regions have been so subjected to destruction by war, not only of their foodstuffs but of their financial resources and their power of production and export, that they are utterly incapable of finding any resources that can be converted into international exchange for food purchases. While the Secretary of the Treasury can accept obligations of certain governments and through these measures their situations can be cared for temporarily, there are still other areas through eastern and southern Europe where such arrangements cannot be made. This applies more particularly to the liberated peoples of Austria, Turkey, Poland, and western Russia. In these countries freedom and government will slowly emerge from the chaos and require our every assistance.

The total shipments of foodstuffs from the United States to all parts of Europe during the next seven months will be likely to exceed one and one-half billion

---

[1] This cablegram was transmitted to Secretary McAdoo through the Secretary of State. It was then sent to the House of Representatives.

dollars, and from our abundance we can surely afford to offer succor to those countries destitute of resources or credit. The minimum sums upon which this work can be carried on for the next six months in the countries above mentioned will amount to at least $100,000,000 for such services and supplies as we can render, and even this sum contemplates the finding of resources by so much of the population as can do so and as much assistance as can be given by the allied Governments. The high mission of the American people to find a remedy for starvation and absolute anarchy renders it necessary that we should undertake the most liberal assistance to these destitute regions.

The situation is one of extreme urgency, for foodstuffs must be placed in certain localities within the next fifteen to thirty days if human life and order are to be preserved. I, therefore, request that you ask Congress to make available to me an immediate appropriation of $100,000,000 for the broad purpose of providing foodstuffs and other urgent supplies, for the transportation, distribution and administration thereof to such populations in Europe, outside of Germany, as may be determined upon by me from time to time as necessary. I wish to appeal to the great sense of charity and good will of the American people towards the suffering, and to place this act upon a primarily humanitarian basis of the first magnitude. While the sum of money is in itself large, it is so small compared with the expenditures we have undertaken in the hope of bettering the world, that it becomes a mere pittance compared to the results that will be obtained from it, and the lasting effect that will remain in the United States through an act of such broad humanity and statesmanlike influence.

AT THE ACADEMY OF THE LENCEI, ROME

ADDRESS UPON BEING MADE A MEMBER, JANUARY 4, 1919. FROM OFFICIAL GOVERNMENT PUBLICATION IN MR. WILSON'S FILES.

YOUR MAJESTY, MR. PRESIDENT, AND GENTLEMEN OF THE ACADEMY:

I have listened, sir, with the profoundest appreciation to the beautiful address which you have been kind enough to deliver, and I want to say how deeply I appreciate the honor you conferred upon me in permitting me to become a member of this great Academy, because there is a sense in which the continuity of human thought is in the care of bodies like this. There is a serenity, a long view on the part of science which seems to be of no age, but to carry human thought along from generation to generation, freed from the elements of passion. Therefore, it is, I dare say, with all men of science a matter of profound regret and shame that science should in a nation which had made science its boast have been put to such dishonorable uses in the recent war. Every just mind must condemn those who so debased the studies of men of science as to use them against humanity, and therefore, it is part of your task and of ours to reclaim science from this disgrace, to show that she is devoted to the advancement and interest of humanity and not to its embarrassment and destruction.

I wish very much, sir, that I could believe that I was in some sense a worthy representative of the men of science of the United States. I cannot claim to be in any proper sense a man of science. My studies have been in the field of politics all my life and, while politics may by courtesy be called a science, it is a science which is often practiced without rule and is very hard to set up standards for, so that one can be sure that one is steering the right course. At the same time, while perhaps there is no science of government, there ought to be I dare say in government itself the spirit of science, that is to say, the spirit of disinterestedness, the spirit of seeking after the truth so far as the truth is ready to be applied to human circumstances. Because, after all, the problem of politics is to satisfy men in the arrangements of their lives, is to realize for them so far as possible the objects which they have entertained generation after generation and have seen so often postponed. Therefore, I have often thought that the university and the academy of science have their part in simplifying the problems of politics and therefore assisting to advance human life along the lines of political structure and political action.

It is very delightful to draw apart for a little while into this quiet place and feel again that familiar touch of thought and of knowledge which it has been my privilege to know familiarly through so great a part of my life. If I have come out upon a more adventurous and disordered stage, I hope that I have not lost the recollection and may in some sense be assisted by counsels such as yours.

TO PRESS REPRESENTATIVES AT ROME

ADDRESS, JANUARY 4, 1919. FROM OFFICIAL GOVERN-
MENT PUBLICATION IN MR. WILSON'S FILES.

LET me thank you, gentlemen, very warmly, for this stirring address, because it goes straight to my heart as well as to my understanding. If I had known that this important delegation was coming to see me, I would have tried to say something worthy of the occasion. As it is, speaking without preparation, I can only say that my purpose is certainly expressed in that paper, and I believe that the purpose of those associated at Paris is a common purpose. Justice and right are big things, and in these circumstances they are big with difficulty. I am not foolish enough to suppose that our decisions will be easy to arrive at, but the principles upon which they are to be arrived at ought to be indisputable, and I have the conviction that if we do not rise to the expectation of the world and satisfy the souls of great peoples like the people of Italy, we shall have the most unenviable distinction in history. Because what is happening now is that the soul of one people is crying to the soul of another, and no people in the world with whose sentiments I am acquainted wishes a bargaining settlement. They all want settlements based upon what is right, or as nearly right as human judgment can arrive at, and with this atmosphere of the opinion of mankind to work in, it ought to be impossible to go very far astray. So that so long as the thought of the people keeps clear, the conclusions of their representatives ought to keep clear. We need the guidance of the people; we need the constant expression of the purposes and ideals of the people.

I have been associated with so many of your fellow countrymen in America, and I am proud to call so many of them my own fellow countrymen, that I would be ashamed if I did not feel the pulse of this great people beating in these affairs. I believe there are almost as many Italians in New York City as in almost any city in Italy, and I was saying to-day that in redistributing sovereignty we could hardly let Italy have these valued fellow citizens. They are men who have done some things that the men of no other nationality have done. They have looked after the people coming from Italy to the United States in a systematic way, to see that they were guided to the places and occupations for which they were best prepared, and they have won our admiration by this thoughtfulness for us. It is with a feeling of being half at home that I find myself in this capital of Italy.

SPEECHES AT GENOA, JANUARY 5, 1919

FROM OFFICIAL GOVERNMENT PUBLICATION IN
MR. WILSON'S FILES.

AT THE MONUMENT OF MAZZINI

I AM very much moved, sir, to be in the presence of this monument. On the other side of the water we have studied the life of Mazzini with almost as much pride as if we shared in the glory of his history, and I am very glad to acknowledge that his spirit has been handed down to us of a later generation on both sides of the water. It is delightful to me to feel that I am taking some small part in accomplishing the realization of the ideals to which his life and thought were devoted. It is with a spirit of veneration, sir, and with a spirit I hope of emulation, that I stand in the presence of this monument and bring my greetings and the greetings of America with our homage to the great Mazzini.

AT THE MUNICIPALITÉ, UPON BEING MADE A CITIZEN OF GENOA

MR. MAYOR:

It is with many feelings of a very deep sort, perhaps too deep for adequate expression, that I find myself in Genoa. Genoa is a natural shrine for Americans. The connections of America with Genoa are so many and so significant that there are some senses in which it may be said that we drew our life and beginnings from this city. You can realize, therefore, sir, with what emotion I receive the honor which you have so generously conferred upon me of the citizenship of this great city. In a way it seems natural for an American to be a citizen of Genoa, and I shall always count it among the most delightful associations of my life that you should have conferred this honor upon me, and in taking away this beautiful edition of the works of Mazzini I hope that I shall derive inspiration from these volumes, as I have already derived guidance from the principles which Mazzini so eloquently expressed. It is very inspiring, sir, to feel how the human spirit is refreshed again and again from its original sources. It is delightful to feel how the voice of one people speaks to another through the mouth of men who have by some gift of God been lifted above the common level and seen the light of humanity, and therefore these words of your prophet and leader will, I hope, be deeply planted in the hearts of my fellow countrymen. There is already planted in those hearts, sir, a very deep and genuine affection for the great Italian people, and the thoughts of my own Nation turn constantly as we read our own history to this beautiful and distinguished city.

May I not thank you, sir, for myself and for Mrs. Wilson and for my daughter, for the very gracious welcome you have accorded us and again express my pride and pleasure?

AT THE MONUMENT OF COLUMBUS

In standing in front of this monument, sir, I fully recognize the significance of what you have said. Columbus did do a service to mankind in discovering America, and it is America's pleasure and America's pride that she has been able to show that it was a service to mankind to open that great continent to settlement, the settlement of a free people, of a people, because free, desiring to see other peoples free and to share their liberty with the people of the world. It is for this reason, no doubt, besides his fine spirit of adventure, that Columbus will always be remembered and honored not only here in the land of his birth, but throughout the world as the man who led the way to those fields of freedom which, planted with a great seed, have now sprung up to the fructification of the world.

FROM OFFICIAL GOVERNMENT PUBLICATION IN
MR. WILSON'S FILES

AT THE STATION

LADIES AND GENTLEMEN:
You make my heart very warm indeed by a welcome like this, and I know the significance of this sort of welcome in Milan, because I know how the heart of Italy and of the Italian people beats strong here. It is delightful to feel how your thoughts have turned towards us, because our thoughts first turned towards you, and they turn towards you from not a new but an ancient friendship, because the American people have long felt the pulse of Italy beat with their pulse in the desire for freedom. We have been students of your history, sir. We know the vicissitudes and struggles through which you have passed. We know that no nation has more steadfastly held to a single course of freedom in its desires and its efforts than have the people of Italy, and therefore I come to this place, where the life of Italy seems to beat so strong, with a peculiar gratification. I feel that I am privileged to come into contact with you, and I want you to know how the words that I am uttering of sympathy and of friendship are not my own alone, but they are the words of the great people whom I represent. I was saying a little while ago at the monument to Columbus that he did a great thing, greater even than was realized at the time it was done. He discovered a new continent not only, but he opened it to children of freedom, and those children are now privileged to come back to their mother and to assist her in the high enterprise upon which her heart had always been set.

It is therefore with the deepest gratification that I find myself here and thank you for your generous welcome.

At the Palazzio

I cannot tell you how much complimented I am by your coming in person to give me this greeting. I have never known such a greeting as the people of Milan have given me on the streets. It has brought tears to my eyes, because I know that it comes from their hearts. I can see in their faces the same things that I feel towards them, and I know that it is an impulse of their friendship towards the Nation that I represent as well as a gracious welcome to myself. I want to reëcho the hope that we may all work together for a great peace as distinguished from a mean peace. And may I suggest this, that is a great deal in my thoughts: The world is not going to consist now of great empires. It is going to consist for the most part of small nations apparently, and the only thing that can bind small nations together is the knowledge that each wants to treat the others fairly. That is the only thing. The world has already shown that its progress is industrial. You cannot trade with people whom you do not trust, and who do not trust you. Confidence is the basis of everything that we must do, and it is a delightful feeling that those ideals are sustained by the people of Italy and by a wonderful body of people such as you have in this great city of Milan. It is with a sense of added encouragement and strength that I return to Paris to take part in the counsels that will determine the items of the peace. I thank you with all my heart.

To the League of Mothers and Widows

I am very much touched by this evidence of your confidence, and I would like to express to you if I could the very deep sympathy I have for those who have suffered irreparable losses in Italy. Our hearts have been touched. And you have used the right word. Our men have come with the spirit of the crusades against that which was wrong and in order to see to it, if it is possible, that such terrible things never happen again. I am very grateful to you for your kindness.

AT THE MUNICIPALITÉ

MR. MAYOR:

May I not say to you as the representative of this great city that it is impossible for me to put into words the impressions I have received to-day? The overwhelming welcome, the spontaneous welcome, the welcome that so evidently came from the heart, has been profoundly moving to me, sir, and I have not failed to see the significance of that welcome. You have yourself referred to it. I am as keenly aware, I believe, sir, as anybody can be that the social structure rests upon the great working classes of the world, and that those working classes in the several countries of the world have by their consciousness of community of interest, by their consciousness of community of spirit, done perhaps more than any other influence has to establish a world opinion, an opinion which is not of a nation, which is not of a continent, but is the opinion, one might say, of mankind. And I am aware, sir, that those of us who are now charged with the very great and serious responsibility of concluding the peace must think and act and confer in the presence of this opinion; that we are not masters of the fortunes of any nation, but that we are the servants of mankind; that it is not our privilege to follow special interests, but that it is our manifest duty to study only the general interest.

This is a solemn thing, sir, and here in Milan, where I know so much of the pulse of international sympathy beats, I am glad to stand up and say that I believe that

that pulse beats also in my own veins, and that I am
not thinking of particular settlements so much as I am
of the general settlement. I was very much touched
to-day, sir, to receive at the hands of wounded soldiers
a memorial in favor of a league of nations, and to be
told by them that that was what they had fought for;
not merely to win this war, but to secure something
beyond, some guarantee of justice, some equilibrium for
the world as a whole which would make it certain that
they would never have to fight a war like this again.
This is the added obligation that is upon us who make
peace. We cannot merely sign a treaty of peace and
go home with clear consciences. We must do something
more. We must add, so far as we can, the securities
which suffering men everywhere demand; and when I
speak of suffering men I think also of suffering women.
I know that splendid as have been the achievements of
your armies, and tremendous as have been the sacrifices
which they have made, and great the glory which they
have achieved, the real, hard pressure of the burden
came upon the women at home, whose men had gone to
the front and who were willing to have them stay there
until the battle was fought out; and as I have heard
from your Minister of Food the story how for days
together there would be no bread, and then know that
when there was no bread the spirit of the people did not
flag, I take off my hat to the great people of Italy and
tell them that my admiration is merged into friendship
and affection. It is in this spirit that I receive your
courtesy, sir, and thank you from the bottom of my
heart for this unprecedented reception which I have
received at the hands of your generous people.

At La Scala

Mr. Chairman:
Again you have been very gracious, and again you
have filled my heart with gratitude because of your

references to my own country, which is so dear to me. I have been very much interested to be told, sir, that you are the chairman of a committee of entertainment which includes all parties, without distinction. I am glad to interpret that to mean that there is no division recognized in the friendship which is entertained for America, and I am sure, sir, that I can assure you that in America there would be a similar union of all parties to express friendship and sympathy with Italy. Because, after all, parties are founded upon differences of program and not often upon differences of national sympathy. The thing that makes parties workable and tolerable is that all parties love their own country and therefore participate in the general sentiments of that country.

And so it is with us, sir. We have many parties, but we have a single sentiment in this war and a single sentiment in the peace; and at the heart of that sentiment lies our feeling towards those with whom we have been associated in the great struggle. At first the struggle seemed the mere natural resistance to aggressive force, but as the consciousness of the nations grew it became more and more evident to them that they were fighting something that was more than the aggression of the Central Empires. It was the spirit of militarism, the spirit of autocracy, the spirit of force; and against that spirit rose, as always in the past, the spirit of liberty and of justice. Force can always be conquered, but the spirit of liberty never can be, and the beautiful circumstance about the history of liberty is that its champions have always shown the power of self-sacrifice, have always been willing to subordinate their personal interests to the common good, have not wished to dominate their fellow men, but have wished to serve them. This is what gives dignity; this is what gives imperishable victory. And with that victory has come about things that are exemplified by a scene like this—the coming together of the hearts of nations, the sympathy of great bodies of people who do not speak the same vocabulary but do speak the same ideas. I am heartened by this delightful experience and hope that you will accept, not only my thanks for myself and for those who are with me, but also my thanks on behalf of the American people.

On the Balcony of La Scala

I wish I could take you all to some place where a similar body of my fellow countrymen could show you their heart towards you as you have shown me your heart towards them, because the heart of America has gone out to the heart of Italy. We have been watchful of your heroic struggle and of your heroic suffering. And it has been our joy in these recent days to be associated with you in the victory which has liberated Italy and liberated the world. Viva l'Italia!

SPEECHES AT TURIN, JANUARY 6, 1919

FROM OFFICIAL GOVERNMENT PUBLICATION IN
MR. WILSON'S FILES

AT THE MUNICIPALITÉ

MR. MAYOR:
Both on the streets of this interesting city and here you have made me feel at home. I feel almost as if it were the greeting of a people of whom I was indeed a fellow citizen. I am very much honored that this great city, playing so important a rôle in the life and in the industrial endeavor of Italy, should have conferred this high distinction upon me, and I take the liberty of interpreting your action, sir, not merely as a personal compliment to myself, to whom you ascribe virtues and powers which I feel I do not possess, but as a tribute to the people whom I represent.

The people of the United States were reluctant to take part in the war, not because they doubted the justice of the cause, but because it was the tradition of the American Republic to play no part in the politics of other continents; but as the struggle grew from stage to stage they were more and more moved by the conviction that it was not a European struggle; that it was a struggle for the freedom of the world and the liberation of humanity, and with that conviction it was impossible that they should withhold their hand. Their hearts had been with you from the first, and then when the time of their conviction came they threw every resource of men and money and enthusiasm into the struggle. It has been a very happy circumstance that America should be thus associated with Italy. Our ties had been many and intimate before the war, and now they constitute a pledge of friendship and of permanent association of purpose which must delight both people.

May I not, therefore, again thank you for the honor you have conferred upon me, and take the privilege of greeting you affectionately as my fellow citizens?

On the Balcony of the Municipalité

My friends of Turin, I now have the privilege of addressing you as my fellow citizens. It is impossible at this distance that my voice should reach all of you, but I want you to know that I bring the greetings, and affectionate greetings, of the people of the United States to the people of Italy and the people of the great city of Turin. My sentiment, coming from the heart, is the sentiment of the American people. Viva, l'Italia!

At the Philharmonic Club

MR. MAYOR, YOUR EXCELLENCY, FELLOW CITIZENS:

You show your welcome in many delightful ways and in no more delightful way than that in which you have shown it in this room. The words which the mayor has uttered have touched me very much and I have been most touched and stimulated by the words which Senor Postorelli has so kindly uttered in behalf of the Government of this great kingdom. It is very delightful to feel my association with that government and with this city. I know how much of the vitality of Italian effort comes out of this great center of industry and of thought. As I passed through your streets I had this sensation, a sensation which I have often had in my own dear country at home—a sensation of friendship and close sympathetic contact. I could have believed myself in an American city. And I felt more than that. I felt, as I have also felt at home, that the real blood of the country flowed there in the street, in the veins of those plain people who more than some of the rest of us have borne the stress and burden of the war.

Because think of the price at which you and at which we have purchased the victory which we have won. Think of the price of blood and treasure not only, but the price of tears, the price of hunger on the part of little children, the hopes delayed, the dismay of the prospects, that bore heavy upon the homes of simple people everywhere. That is the price of liberty. Those of us who plan battles, those of us who conceive policies, do not bear the burden of it. We direct and others execute. We plan and others suffer, and the conquest of spirit is greater than the conquest of arms. These are the people that hold tight. These are the people that never let go and say nothing. They merely live from day to day, determined that the glory of Italy or the glory of the United States shall not depart from her. I have been thinking as I have passed through your streets and sat here that this was the place of the labors of the great Cavour, and I have thought how impossible many of the things that have happened in Italy since, how impossible the great achievements of Italy in the last three years, would have been without the work of Cavour. Ever since I was a boy one of my treasured portraits has been a portrait of Cavour; because I had read about him, of the way in which his mind took in the nation, the national scope of it, of the strong determined patriotic endeavor that never allowed obstacles to dismay him, and of the way he always stood at the side of the King and planned the great things which the King was enabled to accomplish.

And I have another thought. This is a great industrial center. Perhaps you gentlemen think of the members of your Government and the members of the other Governments who are going to confer now at Paris as the real makers of war and of peace. We are not. You are the makers of war and of peace. The pulse of the modern world beats on the farm and in the mine and in the factory. The plans of the modern world are made in the counting-house. The men who do the business of the world now shape the destinies of the world, and peace or war is in large measure in the hands of those who conduct the commerce of the world. That is one reason why unless we establish friendships, unless we establish sympathies, we clog all the processes of modern life. As I have several times said, you cannot trade with a man who does not trust you, and you will not trade with a man whom you do not trust. Trust is the very life and breath of business; and suspicion, unjust national rivalry, stands in the way of trade, stands in the way of industry. A country is owned and dominated by the capital that is invested in it. I do not need to instruct you gentlemen in that fundamental idea. In proportion as foreign capital comes in amongst you and takes its hold, in that proportion does foreign influence come in and take its hold. And therefore the processes of capital are in a certain sense the processes of conquest.

I have only this to suggest, therefore. We go to Paris to conclude a peace. You stay here to continue it. We start the peace. It is your duty to continue it. We can only make the large conclusions. You constantly transact the details which constitute the processes of the life of nations.

And so it is very delightful to me to stand in this company and feel that we are not foreigners to each other. We think the same thoughts. We entertain the same purposes. We have the same ideals; and this war has done this inestimable service: It has brought nations into close vital contact, so that they feel the pulses that are in each other, so that they know the purposes by which each is animated. We know in America a great deal about Italy, because we have so many Italian fellow citizens. When Baron Soninno was arguing the other day for the extension of the sovereignty of Italy over Italian populations, I said, "I am sorry we cannot

let you have New York, which, I understand, is the
greatest Italian city in the world." I am told that there
are more Italians in New York City than in any city in
Italy, and I am proud to be President of a Nation
which contains so large an element of the Italian race,
because, as a student of literature, I know the genius
that has originated in this great nation, the genius of
thought and of poetry and of philosophy and of music,
and I am happy to be a part of a Nation which is en-
riched and made better by the introduction of such elements of genius and of inspiration.

May I not again thank the representative of this
great city and the representative of the Government for
the welcome they have given me, and say again, for I
cannot say it too often, Viva l'Italia?

On the Balcony of the Philharmonic Club

It is very delightful to feel your friendship given so
cordially and so graciously, and I hope with all my
heart that in the peace that is now about to be concluded Italy may find her happiness and her prosperity.
I am sure that I am only speaking the sentiments that
come from the heart of the American people when I
say, Viva l'Italia.

At the University

Mr. Rector, Gentlemen of the Faculties of the
University, Ladies and Gentlemen:

It is with a feeling of being in very familiar scenes
that I come here to-day. So soon as I entered the quad-
rangle and heard the voices of the students it seemed to
me as if the greater part of my life had come back to
me, and I am particularly honored that this distinguished university should have received me among its
sons. It will always be a matter of pride with me to

remember this association and the very generous words in which these honors have been conferred upon me.

When I think seriously of the significance of a cere: mony like this, some very interesting reflections come to my mind, because, after all, the comradeships of letters, the intercommunications of thought, are among the permanent things of the world. There was a time when scholars, speaking in the beautiful language in which the last address was made, were the only international characters of the world; when there was only one international community; the community of scholars. As ability to read and write has extended, international intercommunication has extended. But one permanent common possession has remained, and that is the validity of sound thinking. When men have thought along the lines of philosophy, have had revealed to them the visions of poetry, have worked out in their studies the permanent lines of law, have realized the great impulses of humanity, and then begun to advance human life materially by the instrumentalities of science, they have been weaving a human web which no power can permanently tear and destroy. And so in being taken into the comradeship of this university I feel that I am being taken into one of those things which will always bind the nations together. After all, when we are seeking peace, we are seeking nothing else than this, that men shall think the same thoughts, govern their conduct by the same ideals, entertain the same purposes, love their own people, but also love humanity, and above all else, love that great and indestructible thing which we call justice and right.

These things are greater than we are. These are our real masters, for they dominate our spirits, and the universities will have forgotten their duty when they cease to weave this immortal web. It is one of the chief griefs of this great war that the universities of the Central Empires used the thoughts of science to destroy mankind. It is the duty of the great universities of

Italy and of the rest of the world to redeem science from this disgrace, to show that the pulse of humanity beats in the classroom, that the pulse of humanity also beats in the laboratory, and that there are sought out, not the secrets of death but the secrets of life.

DEATH OF THEODORE ROOSEVELT

PROCLAMATION CABLED FROM PARIS, JANUARY 7, 1919. FROM "UNITED STATES STATUTES AT LARGE," VOL. 40, PT. 2, PP. 1921-1922.

IT BECOMES my sad duty to announce officially the death of Theodore Roosevelt, President of the United States from September 14, 1901, to March 4, 1909, which occurred at his home at Sagamore Hill, Oyster Bay, New York, at 4.15 o'clock in the morning of January 6, 1919. In his death the United States has lost one of its most distinguished and patriotic citizens, who had endeared himself to the people by his strenuous devotion to their interests and to the public interests of his country.

As president of the Police Board of his native city, as member of the Legislature and Governor of his State, as Civil Service Commissioner, as Assistant Secretary of the Navy, as Vice-President, and as President of the United States, he displayed administrative powers of a signal order and conducted the affairs of these various offices with a concentration of effort and a watchful care which permitted no divergence from the line of duty he had definitely set for himself.

In the War with Spain he displayed singular initiative and energy and distinguished himself among the commanders of the army in the field. As President he awoke the Nation to the dangers of private control which lurked in our financial and industrial systems. It was by thus arresting the attention and stimulating the purpose of the country that he opened the way for subsequent necessary and beneficent reforms.

His private life was characterized by a simplicity, a virtue and an affection worthy of all admiration and emulation by the people of America.

In testimony of the respect in which his memory is held by the Government and people of the United States, I do hereby direct that the flags of the White House and the several Departmental Buildings be displayed at half-staff for a period of thirty days, and that suitable military and naval honors under orders óf the Secretaries of War and of the Navy may be rendered on the day of the funeral.

APPEAL FOR FOOD RELIEF IN EUROPE

CABLEGRAM TO THE HON. SWAGAR SHERLEY, OF KENTUCKY, CHAIRMAN OF THE APPROPRIATIONS COMMITTEE OF THE HOUSE OF REPRESENTATIVES, JANUARY 13, 1919. FROM "OFFICIAL U. S. BULLETIN," NO. 511.

I CANNOT too earnestly or solemnly urge upon the Congress the appropriation for which Mr. Hoover has asked for the administration of food relief. Food relief is now the key to the whole European situation and to the solutions of peace. Bolshevism is steadily advancing westward, is poisoning Germany. It cannot be stopped by force, but it can be stopped by food; and all the leaders with whom I am in conference agree that concerted action in this matter is of immediate and vital importance. The money will not be spent for food for Germany itself, because Germany can buy its food; but it will be spent for financing the movement of food to our real friends in Poland and to the people of the liberated units of the Austro-Hungarian Empire and to our associates in the Balkans. I beg that you will present this matter with all possible urgency and force to the Congress. I do not see how we can find definite powers with whom to conclude peace unless this means of stemming the tide of anarchism be employed.

WOODROW WILSON.

OPENING THE PEACE CONFERENCE

ADDRESS AT THE FIRST PLENARY SESSION, PARIS, JANU-
ARY 18, 1919. FROM OFFICIAL GOVERNMENT PUB-
LICATION IN MR. WILSON'S FILES.

M R. CHAIRMAN:

It gives me great pleasure to propose as permanent chairman of the conference M. Clemenceau, the
president of the council. I would do this as a matter
of custom. I would do it as a tribute to the French
Republic. But I wish to do it as something more than
that. I wish to do it as a tribute to the man. France
deserves the precedence not only because we are meeting
in her capital and because she has undergone some of
the most tragical sufferings of the war, but also because
her capital, her ancient and beautiful capital, has so
often been the center of conferences of this sort upon
which the fortunes of large parts of the world turned.
It is a very delightful thought that the history of the
world, which has so often centered here, will now be
crowned by the achievements of this conference. Because there is a sense in which this is the supreme conference of the history of mankind. More nations are
represented here than were ever represented in such a
conference before. The fortunes of all peoples are
involved. A great war is ended which seemed about to
bring a universal cataclysm. The danger is passed. A
victory has been won for mankind, and it is delightful
that we should be able to record these great results in
this place.

But it is the more delightful to honor France because
we can honor her in the person of so distinguished a
servant. We have all felt in our participation in the
struggles of this war the fine steadfastness which characterized the leadership of the French people in the

hands of M. Clemenceau. We have learned to admire him, and those of us who have been associated with him have acquired a genuine affection for him. Moreover, those of us who have been in these recent days in constant consultation with him know how warmly his purpose is set toward the goal of achievement to which all our faces are turned. He feels as we feel, as I have no doubt everybody in this room feels, that we are trusted to do a great thing, to do it in the highest spirit of friendship and accommodation, and to do it as promptly as possible, in order that the hearts of men may have fear lifted from them and that they may return to those pursuits of life which will bring them happiness and contentment and prosperity. Knowing his brotherhood of heart in these great matters, it affords me a personal pleasure to propose not only that the president of the council of ministers, but M. Clemenceau, shall be the permanent chairman of this conference.

TO THE FRENCH SENATE

ADDRESS IN THE LUXEMBOURG PALACE, JANUARY 20, 1919. FROM OFFICIAL GOVERNMENT PUBLICATION IN MR. WILSON'S FILES.

MR. PRESIDENT OF THE SENATE, MR. PRESIDENT OF THE REPUBLIC:

You have made me feel your welcome in words as generous as they are delightful, and I feel that you have paid me to-day a very unusual and distinguished honor. You have graciously called me your friend. May not I in turn call this company a company of my friends? For everything that you have so finely said to-day, sir, has been corroborated in every circumstance of our visit to this country. Everywhere we have been welcomed not only, but welcomed in the same spirit and with the same thought, until it has seemed as if the spirits of the two countries came together in an unusual and beautiful accord.

We know the long breeding of peril through which France has gone. France thought us remote in comprehension and sympathy, and I dare say there were times when we did not comprehend as you comprehended the danger in the presence of which the world stood. There was no time when we did not know of its existence, but there were times when we did not know how near it was. And I fully understand sir, that throughout these trying years, when mankind has waited for the catastrophe, the anxiety of France must have been the deepest and most constant of all. For she did stand at the frontier of freedom. She had carved out her own fortunes through a long period of eager struggle. She had done great things in building up a great new France; and just across the border, separated from her only by a few fortifications and a little country whose neutrality it has turned out the enemy did not respect, lay the shadow cast by the cloud which enveloped Germany, the cloud of intrigue, the cloud of dark purpose, the cloud of sinister design. This shadow lay at the very borders of France. And yet it is fine to remember, sir, that for France this was not only a peril but a challenge. France did not tremble. France waited and got ready, and it is a fine thing that though France quietly and in her own way prepared her sons for the struggle that was coming, she never took the initiative or did a single thing that was aggressive. She had prepared herself for defense, not in order to impose her will upon other peoples. She had prepared herself that no other people might impose its will upon her.

As I stand with you and as I mix with the delightful people of this country I see this in their thoughts: "America always was our friend. Now she understands. Now she comprehends; and now she has come to bring us this message, that understanding she will always be ready to help." And, while, as you say, sir, this danger may prove to be a continuing danger, while it is true that France will always be nearest this threat, if we cannot turn it from a threat into a promise, there are many elements that ought to reassure France. There is a new world, not ahead of us, but around us. The whole world is awake, and it is awake to its community of interest. It knows that its dearest interests are involved in its standing together for a common purpose. It knows that the peril of France, if it continues, will be the peril of the world. It knows that not only France must organize against this peril, but that the world must organize against it.

So I see in these welcomes not only hospitality, not only kindness, not only hope, but purpose, a definite, clearly defined purpose that men, understanding one another, must now support one another, and that all the sons of freedom are under a common oath to see that freedom never suffers this danger again. That to my mind is the impressive element of this welcome. I know how much of it, sir, and I know how little of it, to appropriate to myself. I know that I have the very distinguished honor to represent a Nation whose heart is in this business, and I am proud to speak for the people whom I represent. But I know that you honor me in a representative capacity, and that my words have validity only in proportion as they are the words of the people of the United States. I delight in this welcome, therefore, as if I had brought the people of the United States with me and they could see in your faces what I see—the tokens of welcome and affection.

The sum of the whole matter is that France has earned and has won the brotherhood of the world. She has stood at the chief post of danger, and the thoughts of mankind and her brothers everywhere, her brothers in freedom, turn to her and center upon her. If this be true, as I believe it to be, France is fortunate to have suffered. She is fortunate to have proved her mettle as one of the champions of liberty, and she has tied to herself once and for all all those who love freedom and truly believe in the progress and rights of man.

"MAKE THIS LEAGUE OF NATIONS A VITAL THING"

ADDRESS BEFORE THE SECOND PLENARY SESSION OF THE PEACE CONFERENCE; PARIS, JANUARY 25, 1919. FROM OFFICIAL GOVERNMENT PUBLICATION IN MR. WILSON'S FILES.

MR. CHAIRMAN:

I consider it a distinguished privilege to be permitted to open the discussion in this conference on the League of Nations. We have assembled for two purposes, to make the present settlements which have been rendered necessary by this war, and also to secure the peace of the world, not only by the present settlements, but by the arrangements we shall make at this conference for its maintenance. The League of Nations seems to me to be necessary for both of these purposes. There are many complicated questions connected with the present settlements which perhaps cannot be successfully worked out to an ultimate issue by the decisions we shall arrive at here. I can easily conceive that many of these settlements will need subsequent reconsideration, that many of the decisions we make shall need subsequent alteration in some degree; for, if I may judge by my own study of some of these questions, they are not susceptible of confident judgments at present.

It is, therefore, necessary that we should set up some machinery by which the work of this conference should be rendered complete. We have assembled here for the purpose of doing very much more than making the present settlements. We are assembled under very peculiar conditions of world opinion. I may say without straining the point that we are not representatives of Governments, but representatives of peoples. It will not suffice to satisfy governmental circles anywhere. It is necessary that we should satisfy the opinion of mankind. The burdens of this war have fallen in an unusual degree upon the whole population of the countries involved. I do not need to draw for you the picture of how the burden has been thrown back from the front upon the older men, upon the women, upon the children, upon the homes of the civilized world, and how the real strain of the war has come where the eye of government could not reach, but where the heart of humanity beats. We are bidden by these people to make a peace which will make them secure. We are bidden by these people to see to it that this strain does not come upon them again, and I venture to say that it has been possible for them to bear this strain because they hoped that those who represented them could get together after this war and make such another sacrifice unnecessary.

It is a solemn obligation on our part, therefore, to make permanent arrangements that justice shall be rendered and peace maintained. This is the central object of our meeting. Settlements may be temporary, but the action of the nations in the interest of peace and justice must be permanent. We can set up permanent processes. We may not be able to set up permanent decisions. Therefore, it seems to me that we must take, so far as we can, a picture of the world into our minds. Is it not a startling circumstance, for one thing, that the great discoveries of science, that the quiet studies of men in laboratories, that the thoughtful developments which have taken place in quiet lecture rooms, have now been turned to the destruction of civilization? The powers of destruction have not so much multiplied as gained facility. The enemy whom we have just overcome had at his seats of learning some of the principal centers of scientific study and discovery, and he used them in order to make destruction sudden and complete; and only the watchful, continuous coöperation of men can see to it that science as well as armed men is kept within the harness of civilization.

In a sense the United States is less interested in this subject than the other nations here assembled. With her great territory and her extensive sea borders, it is less likely that the United States should suffer from the attack of enemies than that many of the other nations here should suffer; and the ardor of the United States—for it is a very deep and genuine ardor—for the society of nations is not an ardor springing out of fear or apprehension, but an ardor springing out of the ideals which have come to consciousness in this war. In coming into this war the United States never for a moment thought that she was intervening in the politics of Europe or the politics of Asia or the politics of any part of the world. Her thought was that all the world had now become conscious that there was a single cause which turned upon the issues of this war. That was the cause of justice and of liberty for men of every kind and place. Therefore, the United States should feel that its part in this war had been played in vain if there ensued upon it merely a body of European settlements. It would feel that it could not take part in guaranteeing those European settlements unless that guarantee involved the continuous superintendence of the peace of the world by the associated nations of the world.

Therefore, it seems to me that we must concert our best judgment in order to make this League of Nations a vital thing—not merely a formal thing, not an occasional thing, not a thing sometimes called into life to meet an exigency, but always functioning in watchful attendance upon the interests of the nations—and that its continuity should be a vital continuity; that it should have functions that are continuing functions and that do not permit an intermission of its watchfulness and of its labor; that it should be the eye of the nations to keep watch upon the common interest, an eye that does not slumber, an eye that is everywhere watchful and attentive.

And if we do not make it vital, what shall we do?

We shall disappoint the expectations of the peoples. This is what their thought centers upon. I have had the very delightful experience of visiting several nations since I came to this side of the water, and every time the voice of the body of the people reached me through any representative, at the front of its plea stood the hope for the League of Nations. Gentlemen, the select classes of mankind are no longer the governors of mankind. The fortunes of mankind are now in the hands of the plain people of the whole world. Satisfy them, and you have justified their confidence not only, but established peace. Fail to satisfy them, and no arrangement that you can make will either set up or steady the peace of the world.

You can imagine, gentlemen, I dare say, the sentiments and the purpose with which representatives of the United States support this great project for a League of Nations. We regard it as the keystone of the whole program which expressed our purposes and ideals in this war and which the associated nations have accepted as the basis of the settlement. If we returned to the United States without having made every effort in our power to realize this program, we should return to meet the merited scorn of our fellow citizens. For they are a body that constitutes a great democracy. They expect their leaders to speak their thoughts and no private purpose of their own. They expect their representatives to be their servants. We have no choice but to obey their mandate. But it is with the greatest enthusiasm and pleasure that we accept that mandate; and because this is the keystone of the whole fabric, we have pledged our every purpose to it, as we have to every item of the fabric. We would not dare abate a single part of the program which constitutes our instruction. We would not dare compromise upon any matter as the champion of this thing—this peace of the world, this attitude of justice, this principle that we are the masters of no people but are here to see that every people in the world

shall choose its own masters and govern its own destinies, not as we wish, but as it wishes. We are here to
see, in short, that the very foundations of this war are
swept away. Those foundations were the private choice
of small coteries of civil rulers and military staffs.
Those foundations were the aggression of great powers
upon the small. Those foundations were the holding
together of empires of unwilling subjects by the duress
of arms. Those foundations were the power of small
bodies of men to work their will upon mankind and use
them as pawns in a game. And nothing less than the
emancipation of the world from these things will accomplish peace. You can see that the representatives of the
United States are, therefore, never put to the embarrassment of choosing a way of expediency, because they
have laid down for them the unalterable lines of principle. And, thank God, those lines have been accepted
as the lines of settlement by all the high-minded men
who have had to do with the beginnings of this great
business.

I hope, Mr. Chairman, that when it is known, as I
feel confident it will be known, that we have adopted the
principle of the League of Nations and mean to work
out that principle in effective action, we shall by that
single thing have lifted a great part of the load of anxiety from the hearts of men everywhere. We stand in a
peculiar case. As I go about the streets here I see
everywhere the American uniform. Those men came into
the war after we had uttered our purposes. They came
as crusaders, not merely to win a war, but to win a
cause; and I am responsible to them, for it fell to me
to formulate the purposes for which I asked them to
fight, and I, like them, must be a crusader for these
things, whatever it costs and whatever it may be necessary to do, in honor, to accomplish the object for which
they fought. I have been glad to find from day to day
that there is no question of our standing alone in this
matter, for there are champions of this cause upon every

hand. I am merely avowing this in order that you may understand why, perhaps, it fell to us, who are disengaged from the politics of this great continent and of the Orient, to suggest that this was the keystone of the arch and why it occurred to the generous mind of our president to call upon me to open this debate. It is not because we alone represent this idea, but because it is our privilege to associate ourselves with you in representing it.

I have only tried in what I have said to give you the fountains of the enthusiasm which is within us for this thing, for those fountains spring, it seems to me, from all the ancient wrongs and sympathies of mankind, and the very pulse of the world seems to beat to the surface in this enterprise.

TO THE WORKING-WOMEN OF FRANCE

ADDRESS AT PARIS, JANUARY 25, 1919. FROM OFFICIAL
GOVERNMENT PUBLICATION IN MR. WILSON'S FILES.

MLLE. THOMPSON AND LADIES:

You have not only done me a great honor, but you have touched me very much by this unexpected tribute; and may I add that you have frightened me? Because, realizing the great confidence you place in me, I am led to question my own ability to justify that confidence. You have not placed your confidence wrongly in my hopes and purposes, but perhaps not all of those hopes and purposes can be realized in the great matter that you have so much at heart, the right of women to take their full share in the political life of the nations to which they belong. That is necessarily a domestic question for the several nations. A conference of peace, settling the relations of nations with each other, would be regarded as going very much outside its province if it undertook to dictate to the several States what their internal policy should be.

At the same time, those considerations apply also to conditions of labor, and it does seem to be likely that the conference will take some action by way of expressing its sentiments at any rate with regard to the international aspects at least of labor, and I should hope that some occasion might be offered for the case not only of the women of France, but of their sisters all over the world, to be presented to the consideration of the conference. The conference is turning out to be a rather unwieldy body, a very large body, representing a great many nations, large and small, old and new, and the method of organizing its work successfully, I am afraid, will have to be worked out stage by stage. Therefore,

I have no confident prediction to make as to the way in which it can take up questions of this sort.

But what I have most at heart to-day is to avail myself of this opportunity to express my admiration for the women of France, and my admiration for the women of all the nations that have been engaged in the war. By the fortunes of this war the chief burden has fallen upon the women of France, and they have borne it with a spirit and a devotion which have commanded the admiration of the world. I do not think that the people of France fully realize, perhaps, the intensity of sympathy that other nations have felt for them. They think of us in America, for example, as a long way off, and we are in space, but we are not in thought. You must remember that the United States is made up of the nations of Europe; that French sympathies run straight across the seas, not merely by historic association, but by blood connection; and that these nerves of sympathy are quick to transmit the impulses of the one nation to the other. We have followed your sufferings with a feeling that we were witnessing one of the most heroic and, may I add at the same time, satisfactory things in the world—satisfactory because it showed the strength of the human spirit, the indomitable power of women and men alike to sustain any burden if the cause was great enough. In an ordinary war there might have been some shrinking, some sinking of effort, but this was not an ordinary war. This was a war not only to redeem France from an enemy, but to redeem the world from an enemy, and France, therefore, and the women of France, strained their heart to sustain the world.

I hope that the strain has not been in vain. I know that it has not been in vain. This war has been peculiar and unlike other wars, in that it seemed sometimes as if the chief strain was behind the lines and not at the lines. It took so many men to conduct the war that the older men and the women at home had to carry the nation. Not only so, but the industries of the nation were almost as much part of the fighting as what actually took place at the fronts. So it is for that reason that I have said to those with whom I am at present associated that this must be a people's peace, because this was a people's war. The people won this war, not the Governments, and the people must reap the benefits of the war. At every turn we must see to it that it is not an adjustment between Governments merely, but an arrangement for the peace and security of men and women everywhere. The little, obscure sufferings and the daily unknown privations, the unspoken sufferings of the heart, are the tragical things of this war. They have been borne at home, and the center of the home is the woman. My heart goes out to you, therefore, ladies, in a very unusual degree, and I welcome this opportunity to bring you this message, not from myself merely, but from the great people whom I represent.

"THE RIGHTS OF MAN"

REPLY TO THE LEAGUE FOR THE RIGHTS OF MAN, PARIS, JANUARY 28, 1919. FROM OFFICIAL GOVERNMENT PUBLICATION IN MR. WILSON'S FILES.

I PARTICULARLY appreciate your courtesy in coming in person to convey these admirable sentiments to me. The phrase "the rights of man" is somehow associated more intimately with the history of France than with the history of any other country, and I think that the whole world has regarded France as a sort of pioneer in the ideal interpretation of that phrase. It was not an accident which drew France and the United States into close association. The Marquis Lafayette did not come to the United States because he alone entertained the sentiment of sympathy. He came, and we recognized that he came as a representative—shall I say, knight errant?—of the sympathy of France; and when this opportunity came, not to repay our debt to France, for such debts are not repaid, but to show the similar sentiment that moved us and the equal willingness on our part to help France in her time of need, it was with genuine satisfaction that we came to help. It is true, sir, I believe, that our coming prevented a catastrophe that might have overwhelmed the world. That adds to our delight; that adds to our gratification that we could have served France in so exigent an hour.

Therefore, when you, who have through many difficulties represented an ideal principle, bring me these assurances of your friendship, it causes me an unusual emotion. I am grateful to you. I appreciate your homage and feel that it brings a message not only of friendly feeling but a message of comprehension and sympathy which is peculiarly delightful and acceptable.

AT THE FRENCH CHAMBER OF DEPUTIES

ADDRESS AT PARIS, FEBRUARY 3, 1919. FROM ORIGINAL
COPY IN MR. WILSON'S FILES.

I AM keenly aware of the unusual and distinguished honor you are paying me by permitting me to meet you in this place and address you from this historic platform. Indeed, sir, as day follows day, and week has followed week, in this hospitable land of France, I have felt the sense of comradeship every day become more and more vivid; the thrill of sympathy every day become more and more intimate, and it has seemed to me that the meaning of history was being singularly made clear. We knew before this war began that France and America were united in affection. We knew the occasion which drew the two nations together in those years, which now seem so far away, when the world was first beginning to thrill with the impulse of human liberty, when soldiers of France came to help the struggling little Republic of America to get to its feet and proclaim one of the first victories of freedom.

We have never forgotten that, but we did not see the full meaning of it. A hundred years and more went by and the spindles were slowly weaving the web of history. We did not see the pattern until the threads began to come together; we did not see it to be complete, the whole art of the designer to be made plain. For look what has happened. In that far-off day when France came to the assistance of America, America was fighting Great Britain, and now she is linked as closely to Great Britain as she is to France. We see now how these apparently diverging lines of history are coming together. The nations which once stood in battle array against one another are now shoulder and shoulder facing a common enemy. It was a long time before we saw that, and in the last four years something has happened that is unprecedented in the history of mankind. It is nothing less than this, that bodies of men on both sides of the sea and in all parts of the world have come to realize their comradeship in freedom.

France, in the meantime, as we have so often said, stood at the frontier of freedom. Her lines ran along the very lines that divided the home of freedom from the home of military despotism. Hers was the immediate peril. Hers was the constant dread. Hers was the most pressing necessity of preparation; and she had constantly to ask herself this question, "If the blow falls, who will come to our assistance?" And the question was answered in the most unexpected way. Her allies came to her assistance, but many more than her allies. The free peoples of the world came to her assistance. And then America paid her debt of gratitude to France by sending her sons to fight upon the soil of France. She did more. She assisted in drawing the forces of the world together in order that France might never again feel her isolation, in order that France might never again feel that hers was a lonely peril, would never again have to ask the question who would come to her assistance.

For the alternative is a terrible alternative for France. I do not need to point out to you that east of you in Europe the future is full of questions. Beyond the Rhine, across Germany, across Poland, across Russia, across Asia, there are questions unanswered, and they may be for the present unanswerable. France still stands at a frontier. France still stands in the presence of those threatening and unanswered questions,—threatening because unanswered,—stands waiting for the solution of matters which touch her directly and intimately and constantly. And if she must stand alone, what must she do? She must be constantly armed. She must put upon her people a constant burden of taxation. She must undergo a sacrifice that may become intolerable.

And not only she, but the other nations of the world, must do the like. They must stand armed *cap-à-pie*. They must be ready for any terrible incident of injustice. The thing is not conceivable. I visited the other day a portion of the devastated regions of France. I saw the noble city of Rheims in ruin, and I could not help saying to myself, "Here is where the blow fell, because the rulers of the world did not sooner see how to prevent it." The rulers of the world have been thinking of the relations of governments and forgetting the relations of peoples. They have been thinking of the maneuvers of international dealings, when what they ought to have been thinking of was the fortunes of men and women and the safety of homes, and the care that they should take that their people should be happy because they were safe. They now know that the only way to do it is to make it certain that the same thing will happen always that happened this time, that there shall never be any doubt or waiting or surmise, but that whenever France or any other free people is threatened the whole world will be ready to vindicate its liberty.

It is for that reason, I take it, that I find such a warm and intelligent enthusiasm in France for the society of nations. The society of nations, France with her keen vision, France with her prophetic vision, sees to be not only the need of France, but the need of mankind. And she sees that the sacrifices which are necessary for the establishment of the society of nations are not to be compared with the sacrifices that will be necessary if she does not have the society. A little abatement of independence of action is not to be compared with the constant dread of another catastrophe.

The whole world's heart has bled that the catastrophe should have fallen on the fair cities and areas of France. There was no more beautiful country. There was no more prosperous country. There was no more free-spirited people in it. All the world admired France, and none of the world grudged France her greatness and her prosperity, except those who grudged her her liberty. And it profited us, terrible as the cost has been, to witness what has happened, to see with the physical eye what has happened because injustice was wrought. The President of the Chamber has pictured as I cannot picture the appalling sufferings, the terrible tragedy of France, but it is a tragedy which need not be repeated. As the pattern of history has disclosed itself, it has disclosed the hearts of men drawing towards one another. Comradeships have become vivid. The purpose of association has become evident. The nations of the world are about to consummate a brotherhood which will make it unnecessary in the future to maintain those crushing armaments which make the peoples suffer almost as much in peace as they suffer in war.

When the soldiers of America crossed the ocean, they did not bring with them merely their arms. They brought with them a very vivid conception of France. They landed upon the soil of France with quickened pulses. They knew that they had come to do a thing which the heart of America had long wished to do. When General Pershing stood at the tomb of Lafayette and said, "Lafayette, we are here," it was as if he had said, "Lafayette, here is the completion of the great story whose first chapter you assisted to write." The world has seen the great plot worked out, and now the people of France may rest assured that their prosperity is secure, because their homes are secure; and men everywhere not only wish her safety and prosperity, but are ready to assure her that with all the force and wealth at their command they will guarantee her security and safety. So, as we sit from day to day at the Quai d'Orsay, I think to myself, "We might, if we could gain audience of the free peoples of the world, adopt the language of General Pershing and say, 'Friends, men, humble women, little children, we are here; we are here as your friends, as your champions, as your representatives. We have come to work out for you a world which is fit to live in and in which all countries can enjoy the heritage of liberty for which France and America and England and Italy have paid so dear.' "

TO A DELEGATION FROM FRENCH
SOCIETY OF NATIONS

ADDRESS AT PARIS, FEBRUARY 12, 1919. FROM OFFI-
CIAL GOVERNMENT PUBLICATION IN MR. WILSON'S
FILES.

I APPRECIATE very deeply what Mr. M —— has said, and I take it that his kind suggestion is that some time after my return we should arrange a public meeting at which I am quite confident, as I think he is, we may celebrate the completion of the work, at any rate up to a certain very far advanced stage, the consummation of which we have been hoping for and working for for a long time. It would be a very happy thing if that could be arranged. I can only say for myself that I sincerely hope it can be. I should wish to lend any assistance possible to so happy a consummation.

I cannot help thinking of how many miracles this war has already wrought—miracles of comprehension as to our interdependence as nations and as human beings; miracles as to the removal of the obstacles which seemed big and now have grown small, in the way of the active and organized coöperation of nations in regard to the establishment and maintenance of justice. And the thoughts of the people having been drawn together, there has already been created a force which is not only very great, but very formidable, a force which can be rapidly mobilized, a force which is very effective when mobilized, namely, the moral force of the world. One advantage in seeing one another and talking with one another is to find that, after all, we all think the same way. We may try to put the result of the thing into different forms, but we start with the same principles.

I have often been thought of as a man more interested in principles than in practice, whereas, as a matter of fact, I can say that in one sense principles have never interested me. Because principles prove themselves when stated. They do not need any debate. The thing that is difficult and interesting is how to put them into practice. Large discourse is not possible on the principles, but large discourse is necessary on the matter of realizing them. So that, after all, principles until translated into practice are very thin and abstract and, I may add, uninteresting things. It is not interesting to have far-away visions, but it is interesting to have near-by visions, of what it is possible to accomplish; and in a meeting such as you are projecting perhaps we can record the success that we shall then have achieved, of putting a great principle into practice and demonstrated that it can be put into practice, though only, let us say five years ago, it was considered an impracticable dream.

I will coöperate with great happiness in the plans that you may form after my return, and I thank you very warmly for the compliment of this personal visit.

CABLEGRAM TO THE UNITED STATES SENATE

CABLEGRAM THROUGH JOSEPH P. TUMULTY, SECRE-
TARY TO THE PRESIDENT, TO THE MEMBERS OF
THE FOREIGN RELATIONS COMMITTEE OF THE SEN-
ATE AND THE FOREIGN AFFAIRS COMMITTEE OF
THE HOUSE, FEBRUARY 14, 1919. FROM "OFFI-
CIAL U. S. BULLETIN," NO. 540.

LAST night the committee of the conference charged with the duty of drafting a constitution for a League of Nations concluded its work and this afternoon before leaving for the United States it is to be my privilege and duty to read to a plenary session of the conference the text of the 26 articles agreed upon by the committee.

The committee which drafted these articles was fairly representative of the world. Besides the representatives of the United States, Great Britain, France, Italy, and Japan, representatives of Belgium, Serbia, China, Greece, Rumania, Czecho-Slovakia, Poland, Brazil, Portugal, actively participated in the debates and assisted materially in the drafting of this constitution. Each article was passed only after the most careful examination by each member of the committee. There is a good and sufficient reason for the phraseology and substance of each article. I request that I be permitted to go over with you article by article the constitution before this part of the work of the conference is made the subject of debate of Congress. With this in view I request that you dine with me at the White House as soon after I arrive in the United States as my engagements permit.

PRESENTATION OF THE COVENANT OF THE LEAGUE OF NATIONS

ADDRESS BEFORE THE THIRD PLENARY SESSION OF THE PEACE CONFERENCE, FEBRUARY 14, 1919. FROM OFFICIAL GOVERNMENT PUBLICATION IN MR. WILSON'S FILES.

I HAVE the honor and as I esteem it the very great privilege of reporting in the name of the commission constituted by this conference on the formulation of a plan for the league of nations. I am happy to say that it is a unanimous report, a unanimous report from the representatives of fourteen nations—the United States, Great Britain, France, Italy, Japan, Belgium, Brazil, China, Czecho-Slovakia, Greece, Poland, Portugal, Rumania, and Serbia. I think it will be serviceable and interesting if I, with your permission, read the document as the only report we have to make.

COVENANT

PREAMBLE

In order to promote international coöperation and to secure international peace and security by the acceptance of obligations not to resort to war, by the prescription of open, just and honorable relations between nations, by the firm establishment of the understandings of international law as the actual rule of conduct among governments, and by the maintenance of justice and a scrupulous respect for all treaty obligations in the dealings of organized peoples with one another, the Powers signatory to this Covenant adopt this constitution of the League of Nations.

ARTICLE I

The action of the High Contracting Parties under the terms of this Covenant shall be effected through the instrumentality of meetings of a Body of Delegates representing the High Contracting

Parties, of meetings at more frequent intervals of an Executive Council, and of a permanent international Secretariat to be established at the Seat of the League.

Article II

Meetings of the Body of Delegates shall be held at stated intervals and from time to time as occasion may require for the purpose of dealing with matters within the sphere of action of the League. Meetings of the Body of Delegates shall be held at the Seat of the League or at such other place as may be found convenient and shall consist of representatives of the High Contracting Parties. Each of the High Contracting Parties shall have one vote but may have not more than three representatives.

Article III

The Executive Council shall consist of representatives of the United States of America, the British Empire, France, Italy and Japan, together with representatives of four other States, members of the League. The selection of these four States shall be made by the Body of Delegates on such principles and in such manner as they think fit. Pending the appointment of these representatives of the other States, representatives of   shall be members of the Executive Council.

Meetings of the Council shall be held from time to time as occasion may require and at least once a year at whatever place may be decided on, or failing any such decision, at the Seat of the League, and any matter within the sphere of action of the League or affecting the peace of the world may be dealt with at such meetings.

Invitations shall be sent to any Power to attend a meeting of the Council at which matters directly affecting its interests are to be discussed and no decision taken at any meeting will be binding on such Power unless so invited.

Article IV

All matters of procedure at meetings of the Body of Delegates or the Executive Council including the appointment of Committees to investigate particular matters shall be regulated by the Body of Delegates or the Executive Council and may be decided by a majority of the States represented at the meeting.

The first meeting of the Body of Delegates and of the Executive Council shall be summoned by the President of the United States of America.

ARTICLE V

The permanent Secretariat of the League shall be established at which shall constitute the Seat of the League. The Secretariat shall comprise such secretaries and staff as may be required, under the general direction and control of a Secretary-General of the League, who shall be chosen by the Executive Council; the Secretariat shall be appointed by the Secretary-General subject to confirmation by the Executive Council.

The Secretary-General shall act in that capacity at all meetings of the Body of Delegates or of the Executive Council.

The expenses of the Secretariat shall be borne by the States members of the League in accordance with the apportionment of the expenses of the International Bureau of the Universal Postal Union.

ARTICLE VI

Representatives of the High Contracting Parties and officials of the League when engaged on the business of the League shall enjoy diplomatic privileges and immunities, and the buildings occupied by the League or its officials or by representatives attending its meetings shall enjoy the benefits of extraterritoriality.

ARTICLE VII

Admission to the League of States not signatories to the Covenant and not named in the Protocol hereto as States to be invited to adhere to the Covenant requires the assent of not less than two-thirds of the States represented in the Body of Delegates, and shall be limited to fully self-governing countries including Dominions and Colonies.

No State shall be admitted to the League unless it is able to give effective guarantees of its sincere intention to observe its international obligations, and unless it shall conform to such principles as may be prescribed by the League in regard to its naval and military forces and armaments.

ARTICLE VIII

The High Contracting Parties recognize the principle that the maintenance of peace will require the reduction of national armaments to the lowest point consistent with national safety and the enforcement by common action of international obligations, having special regard to the geographical situation and circumstances of each State; and the Executive Council shall formulate plans for effecting such reduction. The Executive Council shall also determine for the consideration and action of the several governments what military equipment and armament is fair and reasonable in proportion to the scale of forces laid down in the program of disarmament; and these limits, when adopted, shall not be exceeded without the permission of the Executive Council.

The High Contracting Parties agree that the manufacture by private enterprise of munitions and implements of war lends itself to grave objections, and direct the Executive Council to advise how the evil effects attendant upon such manufacture can be prevented, due regard being had to the necessities of those countries which are not able to manufacture for themselves the munitions and implements of war necessary for their safety.

The High Contracting Parties undertake in no way to conceal from each other the condition of such of their industries as are capable of being adapted to war-like purposes or the scale of their armaments, and agree that there shall be full and frank interchange of information as to their military and naval programs.

Article IX

A permanent Commission shall be constituted to advise the League on the execution of the provisions of Article VIII and on military and naval questions generally.

Article X

The High Contracting Parties undertake to respect and preserve as against external aggression the territorial integrity and existing political independence of all States members of the League. In case of any such aggression or in case of any threat or danger of such aggression the Executive Council shall advise upon the means by which this obligation shall be fulfilled.

Article XI

Any war or threat of war, whether immediately affecting any of the High Contracting Parties or not, is hereby declared a matter of concern to the League, and the High Contracting Parties reserve the right to take any action that may be deemed wise and effectual to safeguard the peace of nations.

It is hereby also declared and agreed to be the friendly right of each of the High Contracting Parties to draw the attention of the Body of Delegates or of the Executive Council to any circumstances affecting international intercourse which threaten to disturb international peace or the good understanding between nations upon which peace depends.

Article XII

The High Contracting Parties agree that should disputes arise between them which cannot be adjusted by the ordinary processes of diplomacy, they will in no case resort to war without previously submitting the questions and matters involved either to arbitration or to inquiry by the Executive Council and until three months after the award by the arbitrators or a recommendation by the Executive Council; and that they will not even then resort to war as against a member of the League which complies with the award of the arbitrators or the recommendations of the Executive Council.

In any case under this Article, the award of the arbitrators shall be made within a reasonable time, and the recommendation of the Executive Council shall be made within six months after the submission of the dispute.

Article XIII

The High Contracting Parties agree that whenever any dispute or difficulty shall arise between them which they recognize to be suitable for submission to arbitration and which cannot be satisfactorily settled by diplomacy, they will submit the whole subject matter to arbitration. For this purpose the Court of arbitration to which the case is referred shall be the court agreed on by the parties or stipulated in any Convention existing between them. The High Contracting Parties agree that they will carry out in full good faith any award that may be rendered. In the event of any failure to carry out the award, the Executive Council shall propose what steps can best be taken to give effect thereto.

Article XIV

The Executive Council shall formulate plans for the establishment of a Permanent Court of International Justice and this Court shall, when established, be competent to hear and determine any matter which the parties recognize as suitable for submission to it for arbitration under the foregoing Article.

Article XV

If there should arise between States members of the League any dispute likely to lead to a rupture, which is not submitted to arbitration as above, the High Contracting Parties agree that they will refer the matter to the Executive Council; either party to the dispute may give notice of the existence of the dispute to the Secretary-General, who will make all necessary arrangements for a full investigation and consideration thereof. For this purpose the parties agree to communicate to the Secretary-General, as promptly as possible, statements of their case with all the relevant facts and papers, and the Executive Council may forthwith direct the publication thereof.

Where the efforts of the Council lead to the settlement of the dispute, a statement shall be published indicating the nature of the dispute and the terms of settlement, together with such explanations as may be appropriate. If the dispute has not been settled, a report by the Council shall be published, setting forth with all necessary facts and explanations the recommendation which the Council think just and proper for the settlement of the dispute. If the report is unanimously agreed to by the members of the Council other than the parties to the dispute, the High Contracting Parties agree that they will not go to war with any party which complies with the recommendation and that, if any party shall refuse so to comply, the Council shall propose the measures necessary to give effect to the recommendation. If no such unanimous report can be made, it shall be the duty of the majority and the privilege of the minority to issue statements indicating what they believe to be the facts and containing the recommendations which they consider to be just and proper.

I pause to point out that a misconception might arise in connection with one of the sentences I have just read —"If any party shall refuse so to comply, the council shall propose the measures necessary to give effect to the recommendation." A case in point, a purely hypothetical case, is this: Suppose that there is in the possession of a particular power a piece of territory or some other substantial thing in dispute to which it is claimed that it is not entitled. Suppose that the matter is submitted to the executive council for a recommendation as to the settlement of the dispute, diplomacy having failed; and suppose that the decision is in favor of the party which claims the subject matter of dispute as against the party which has the subject matter in dispute. Then, if the party in possession of the subject matter in dispute merely sits still and does nothing, it has accepted the decision of the council, in the sense that it makes no resistance; but something must be done to see that it surrenders the subject matter in dispute. In such a case, the only case contemplated, it is provided that the executive council may then consider what steps may be necessary to oblige the party against whom judgment has gone to comply with the decisions of the council.

The Executive Council may in any case under this Article refer the dispute to the Body of Delegates. The dispute shall be so referred at the request of either party to the dispute, provided that such request must be made within fourteen days after the submission of the dispute. In any case referred to the Body of Delegates all the provisions of this Article and of Article XII relating to the action and powers of the Executive Council shall apply to the action and powers of the Body of Delegates.

Article XVI

Should any of the High Contracting Parties break or disregard its covenants under Article XII, it shall thereby *ipso facto* be deemed to have committed an act of war against all the other members of the League, which hereby undertake immediately to subject it to the severance of all trade or financial relations, the prohibition of all intercourse between their nationals and the nationals of the covenant-breaking State, and the prevention of all financial, commercial, or personal intercourse between the nationals of the covenant-breaking State and the nationals of any other State, whether a member of the League or not.

It shall be the duty of the Executive Council in such case to recommend what effective military or naval force the members of the League shall severally contribute to the armed forces to be used to protect the covenants of the League.

The High Contracting Parties agree, further, that they will mutually support one another in the financial and economic measures which are taken under this Article, in order to minimize the loss and inconvenience resulting from the above measures, and that they will mutually support one another in resisting any special measures aimed at one of their number by the covenant-breaking State, and that they will afford passage through their territory to the forces of any of the High Contracting Parties who are coöperating to protect the covenants of the League.

Article XVII

In the event of disputes between one State member of the League and another State which is not a member of the League, or between States not members of the League, the High Contracting Parties agree that the State or States not members of the League shall be invited to accept the obligations of membership in the League for the purposes of such dispute, upon such conditions as the Executive Council may deem just, and upon acceptance of any such invitation, the above provisions shall be applied with such modifications as may be deemed necessary by the League.

Upon such invitation being given the Executive Council shall immediately institute an inquiry into the circumstances and merits of the dispute and recommend such action as may seem best and most effectual in the circumstances.

In the event of a Power so invited refusing to accept the obligations of membership in the League for the purposes of such dispute, and taking any action against a State member of the League which in the case of a State member of the League would constitute a breach of Article XII, the provisions of Article XVI shall be applicable as against the State taking such action.

If both parties to the dispute when so invited refuse to accept the obligations of membership in the League for the purposes of such dispute, the Executive Council may take such action and make such recommendations as will prevent hostilities and will result in the settlement of the dispute.

Article XVIII

The High Contracting Parties agree that the League shall be entrusted with the general supervision of the trade in arms and ammunition with the countries in which the control of this traffic is necessary in the common interest.

Let me say before reading Article XIX, that before being embodied in this document it was the subject matter of a very careful discussion by representatives of the five greater parties, and that their unanimous conclusion in the matter is embodied in this article.

Article XIX

To those colonies and territories which as a consequence of the late war have ceased to be under the sovereignty of the States which formerly governed them and which are inhabited by peoples not yet able to stand by themselves under the strenuous conditions of the modern world, there should be applied the principle that the well-being and development of such peoples form a sacred trust of civilization and that securities for the performance of this trust should be embodied in the constitution of the League.

The best method of giving practical effect to this principle is that the tutelage of such peoples should be entrusted to advanced nations who by reason of their resources, their experience or their geographical position, can best undertake this responsibility, and that this tutelage should be exercised by them as mandatories on behalf of the League.

The character of the mandate must differ according to the stage of the development of the people, the geographical situation of the territory, its economic conditions and other similar circumstances.

Certain communities formerly belonging to the Turkish Empire have reached a stage of development where their existence as independent nations can be provisionally recognized subject to the rendering of administrative advice and assistance by a mandatory power until such time as they are able to stand alone. The wishes of these communities must be a principal consideration in the selection of the mandatory power.

Other peoples, especially those of Central Africa, are at such a stage that the mandatary must be responsible for the administration of the territory subject to conditions which will guarantee freedom of conscience or religion, subject only to the maintenance of public order and morals, the prohibition of abuses such as the slave trade, the arms traffic and the liquor traffic, and the prevention of the establishment of fortifications or military and naval bases and of military training of the natives for other than police purposes and the defense of territory, and will also secure equal opportunities for the trade and commerce of other members of the League.

There are territories, such as South-west Africa and certain of the South Pacific Islands, which, owing to the sparseness of their population, or their small size, or their remoteness from the centers of civilization, or their geographical contiguity to the mandatory state, and other circumstances, can be best administered under the laws of the mandatory state as integral portions thereof, subject to the safeguards above-mentioned in the interests of the indigenous population.

In every case of mandate, the mandatory state shall render to the League an annual report in reference to the territory committed to its charge.

The degree of authority, control, or administration to be exercised by the mandatory State shall if not previously agreed upon by the High Contracting Parties in each case be explicitly defined by the Executive Council in a special Act or Charter.

The High Contracting Parties further agree to establish at the seat of the League a Mandatory Commission to receive and examine the annual reports of the Mandatory Powers, and to assist the League in ensuring the observance of the terms of all Mandates.

Article XX

The High Contracting Parties will endeavor to secure and maintain fair and humane conditions of labor for men, women and children both in their own countries and in all countries to which their commercial and industrial relations extend; and to that end agree to establish as part of the organization of the League a permanent Bureau of Labor.

Article XXI

The High Contracting Parties agree that provision shall be made through the instrumentality of the League to secure and maintain freedom of transit and equitable treatment for the commerce of all States members of the League, having in mind, among other things, special arrangements with regard to the necessities of the regions devastated during the war of 1914-1918.

Article XXII

The High Contracting Parties agree to place under the control of the League all international bureaux already established by general treaties if the parties to such treaties consent. Furthermore, they agree that all such international bureaux to be constituted in future shall be placed under the control of the League.

Article XXIII

The High Contracting Parties agree that every treaty or international engagement entered into hereafter by any State member of the League, shall be forthwith registered with the Secretary-General and as soon as possible published by him, and that no such treaty or international engagement shall be binding until so registered.

Article XXIV

It shall be the right of the Body of Delegates from time to time to advise the reconsideration by States members of the League, of treaties which have become inapplicable, and of international conditions, of which the continuance may endanger the peace of the world.

Article XXV

The High Contracting Parties severally agree that the present Covenant is accepted as abrogating all obligations *inter se* which are inconsistent with the terms thereof, and solemnly engage that they will not hereafter enter into any engagements inconsistent with the terms thereof.

In case any of the Powers signatory hereto or subsequently admitted to the League shall, before becoming a party to this Covenant, have undertaken any obligations which are inconsistent with the terms of this Covenant, it shall be the duty of such Power to take immediate steps to procure its release from such obligations.

ARTICLE XXVI

Amendments to this Covenant will take effect when ratified by the States whose representatives compose the Executive Council and by three-fourths of the States whose representatives compose the Body of Delegates.

It gives me pleasure to add to this formal reading of the result of our labors that the character of the discussion which occurred at the sittings of the commission was not only of the most constructive but of the most encouraging sort. It was obvious throughout our discussions that, although there were subjects upon which there were individual differences of judgment, with regard to the method by which our objects should be obtained, there was practically at no point any serious difference of opinion or motive as to the objects which we were seeking. Indeed, while these debates were not made the opportunity for the expression of enthusiasms and sentiments, I think the other members of the commission will agree with me that there was an undertone of high resolve and of enthusiasm for the thing we were trying to do, which was heartening throughout every meeting; because we felt that in a way this conference had intrusted to us the expression of one of its highest and most important purposes, to see to it that the concord of the world in the future with regard to the objects of justice should not be subject to doubt or uncertainty; that the coöperation of the great body of nations should be assured from the first in the maintenance of peace upon the terms of honor and of the strict regard for international obligation. The compulsion of that task was constantly upon us, and at no point was there shown the slightest desire to do anything but suggest the best means to accomplish that great object. There is very great significance, therefore, in the fact that the result was reached unanimously. Fourteen nations were represented, among them all of those powers which for convenience we have called the great powers, and among the rest a representation of the greatest variety of circumstance and interest. So that I think we are justified in saying that it was a representative group of the members of this great conference. The significance of the result, therefore, has that deepest of all meanings, the union of wills in a common purpose, a union of wills, which cannot be resisted, and which I dare say no nation will run the risk of attempting to resist.

Now, as to the character of the document. While it has consumed some time to read this document, I think you will see at once that it is, after all, very simple, and in nothing so simple as in the structure which it suggests for the League of Nations—a body of delegates, an executive council, and a permanent secretariat. When it came to the question of determining the character of the representation in the body of delegates, we were all aware of a feeling which is current throughout the world. Inasmuch as I am stating it in the presence of official representatives of the various Governments here present, including myself, I may say that there is a universal feeling that the world cannot rest satisfied with merely official guidance. There reached us through many channels the feeling that if the deliberative body of the League was merely to be a body of officials representing the various Governments, the peoples of the world would not be sure that some of the mistakes which preoccupied officials had admittedly made might not be repeated. It was impossible to conceive a method or an assembly so large and various as to be really representative of the great body of the peoples of the

world, because, as I roughly reckon it, we represent as
we sit around this table more than twelve hundred million people. You cannot have a representative assembly
of twelve hundred million people, but if you leave it
to each Government to have, if it pleases, one or two or
three representatives, though only a single vote, it may
vary its representation from time to time, not only but
it may originate the choice of its several representatives,
if it should have several in different ways. Therefore,
we thought that this was a proper and a very prudent
concession to the practically universal opinion of plain
men everywhere that they wanted the door left open to
a variety of representation instead of being confined to
a single official body with which they might or might
not find themselves in sympathy.

And you will notice that this body has unlimited
rights of discussion—I mean of discussion of anything
that falls within the field of international relationship—
and that it is specially agreed that war or international
misunderstandings or anything that may lead to friction
and trouble is everybody's business, because it may affect
the peace of the world. And in order to safeguard the
popular power so far as we could of this representative
body it is provided, you will notice, that when a subject
is submitted, not to arbitration, but to discussion by the
executive council, it can upon the initiative of either one
of the parties to the dispute be drawn out of the executive council onto the larger forum of the general body
of delegates, because throughout this instrument we are
depending primarily and chiefly upon one great force,
and that is the moral force of the public opinion of the
world—the cleansing and clarifying and compelling influences of publicity—so that intrigues can no longer
have their coverts, so that designs that are sinister can
at any time be drawn into the open, so that those things
that are destroyed by the light may be properly destroyed by the overwhelming light of the universal expression of the condemnation of the world.

Armed force is in the background in this program, but it *is* in the background, and if the moral force of the world will not suffice, the physical force of the world·shall. But that is the last resort, because this is intended as a constitution of peace, not as a league of war.

The simplicity of the document seems to me to be one of its chief virtues, because, speaking for myself, I was unable to foresee the variety of circumstances with which this League would have to deal. I was unable, therefore, to plan all the machinery that might be necessary to meet differing and unexpected contingencies. Therefore, I should say of this document that it is not a straitjacket, but a vehicle of life. A living thing is born, and we must see to it that the clothes we put upon it do not hamper it—a vehicle of power, but a vehicle in which power may be varied at the discretion of those who exercise it and in accordance with the changing circumstances of the time. And yet, while it is elastic, while it is general in its terms, it is definite in the one thing that we were called upon to make definite. It is a definite guarantee of peace. It is a definite guarantee by word against aggression. It is a definite guarantee against the things which have just come near bringing the whole structure of civilization into ruin. Its purposes do not for a moment lie vague. Its purposes are declared and its powers made unmistakable.

It is not in contemplation that this should be merely a League to secure the peace of the world. It is a League which can be used for coöperation in any international matter. That is the significance of the provision introduced concerning labor. There are many ameliorations of labor conditions which can be effected by conference and discussion. I anticipate that there will be a very great usefulness in the bureau of labor which it is contemplated shall be set up by the League. While men and women and children who work have been in the background through long ages, and sometimes seemed to be forgotten, while Governments have had their watchful and suspicious eyes upon the maneuvers of one another, while the thought of statesmen has been about structural action and the large transactions of commerce and of finance, now, if I may believe the picture which I see, there comes into the foreground the great body of the laboring people of the world, the men and women and children upon whom the great burden of sustaining the world must from day to day fall, whether we wish it to do so or not; people who go to bed tired and wake up without the stimulation of lively hope. These people will be drawn into the field of international consultation and help, and will be among the wards of the combined Governments of the world. There is, I take leave to say, a very great step in advance in the mere conception of that.

Then, as you will notice, there is an imperative article concerning the publicity of all international agreements. Henceforth no member of the League can claim any agreement valid which it has not registered with the secretary general, in whose office, of course, it will be subject to the examination of anybody representing a member of the League. And the duty is laid upon the secretary general to publish every document of that sort at the earliest possible time. I suppose most persons who have not been conversant with the business of foreign offices do not realize how many hundreds of these agreements are made in a single year, and how difficult it might be to publish the more unimportant of them immediately—how uninteresting it would be to most of the world to publish them immediately—but even they must be published just so soon as it is possible for the secretary general to publish them.

Then there is a feature about this covenant which to my mind is one of the greatest and most satisfactory advances that has been made. We are done with annexations of helpless people, meant in some instances by some powers to be used merely for exploitation. We recognize in the most solemn manner that the helpless and undeveloped peoples of the world, being in that condition, put an obligation upon us to look after their interests primarily before we use them for our interest; and that in all cases of this sort hereafter it shall be the duty of the League to see that the nations who are assigned as the tutors and advisers and directors of those peoples shall look to their interest and to their development before they look to the interests and material desires of the mandatory nation itself. There has been no greater advance than this, gentlemen. If you look back upon the history of the world you will see how helpless peoples have too often been a prey to powers that had no conscience in the matter. It has been one of the many distressing revelations of recent years that the great power which has just been happily defeated put intolerable burdens and injustices upon the helpless people of some of the colonies which it annexed to itself; that its interest was rather their extermination than their development; that the desire was to possess their land for European purposes, and not to enjoy their confidence in order than mankind might be lifted in those places to the next higher level. Now, the world, expressing its conscience in law, says there is an .end of that. Our consciences shall be applied to this thing. States will be picked out which have already shown that they can exercise a conscience in this matter, and under their tutelage the helpless peoples of the world will come into a new light and into a new hope.

So I think I can say of this document that it is at one and the same time a practical document and a humane document. There is a pulse of sympathy in it. There is a compulsion of conscience throughout it. It is practical, and yet it is intended to purify, to rectify, to elevate. And I want to say that, so far as my observation instructs me, this is in one sense a belated document. I believe that the conscience of the world has long been prepared to express itself in some such way. We are not just now discovering our sympathy for these people and our interest in them. We are simply expressing it, for it has long been felt, and in the administration of the affairs of more than one of the great States represented here—so far as I know, of all the great States that are represented here—that humane impulse has already expressed itself in their dealings with their colonies whose peoples were yet at a low stage of civilization. We have had many instances of colonies lifted into the sphere of complete self-government. This is not the discovery of a principle. It is the universal application of a principle. It is the agreement of the great nations which have tried to live by these standards in their separate administrations to unite in seeing that their common force and their common thought and intelligence are lent to this great and humane enterprise. I think it is an occasion, therefore, for the most profound satisfaction that this humane decision should have been reached in a matter for which the world has long been waiting and until a very recent period thought that it was still too early to hope.

Many terrible things have come out of this war, gentlemen, but some very beautiful things have come out of it. Wrong has been defeated, but the rest of the world has been more conscious than it ever was before of the majesty of right. People that were suspicious of one another can now live as friends and comrades in a single family, and desire to do so. The miasma of distrust, of intrigue, is cleared away. Men are looking eye to eye and saying, "We are brothers and have a common purpose. We did not realize it before, but now we do realize it, and this is our covenant of fraternity and of friendship."

FIRST FAREWELL MESSAGE TO FRANCE

STATEMENT UPON THE OCCASION OF THE PRESIDENT'S
FIRST RETURN FROM FRANCE, FEBRUARY 14, 1919.
FROM THE NEW YORK "TIMES," FEBRUARY 16,
1919.

I CANNOT leave France without expressing my profound sense of the great hospitality of the French people and the French Government. They have received and treated me as I most desired to be treated, as a friend, a friend alike in spirit and in purpose.

I am happy to say that I am to return to assist with all my heart in completing the just settlements which the Peace Conference is seeking and I shall carry with me during my absence very happy memories of the two months I have spent here.

I have been privileged to see here at first hand what my sympathies had already conceived—the sufferings and problems of France—and every day has deepened my interest in the solution of the grave questions upon whose proper solution the future prosperity of France and her associates and the whole world depends. May I not leave my warm and affectionate farewell greetings?

SYMPATHY TO M. CLEMENCEAU

MESSAGE OF CONDOLENCE SENT FROM THE U. S. STEAM-
SHIP "GEORGE WASHINGTON" TO SECRETARY LAN-
SING, AT THE AMERICAN MISSION, PARIS, ON
LEARNING OF THE ATTACK UPON PREMIER CLEM-
ENCEAU. FEBRUARY 20, 1919. FROM THE NEW
YORK "TIMES," FEBRUARY 21, 1919.

PLEASE convey to M. Clemenceau my heartfelt sympathy and my joy at his escape.

I sincerely hope that the report that he was only slightly injured is altogether true. I was deeply shocked by the news of the attack.

WOODROW WILSON.

AT BOSTON

ADDRESS ON RETURN TO AMERICA, FEBRUARY 24, 1919.
FROM OFFICIAL GOVERNMENT PUBLICATION IN MR.
WILSON'S FILES.

GOVERNOR COOLIDGE, MR. MAYOR, FEL-
LOW CITIZENS:

I wonder if you are half as glad to see me as I am
to see you. It warms my heart to see a great body of
my fellow citizens again because in some respects during
recent months I have been very lonely, indeed, without
your comradeship and counsel, and I tried at every step
of the work which fell to me to recall what I was sure
would be your counsel with regard to the great matters
which were under consideration.

I do not want you to think that I have not been appreciative of the extraordinarily generous reception which
was given me on the other side, in saying it makes me
very happy to get home again. I do not mean to say I
was not very deeply touched by the cries that came from
greater crowds on the other side. But I want to say to
you in all honesty, I felt them to be the call of greeting
to you rather than to me. I did not feel that the greeting was personal. I had in my heart the overcrowning
pride of being your representative and of receiving the
plaudits of men everywhere who felt that your hearts
beat with theirs in the cause of liberty. There was no
mistaking the tone in the voices of these great crowds.
It was not the tone of mere greeting, it was not the tone
of mere generous welcome, it was the calling of comrade to comrade, the cry that comes from men who say
we have waited for this day when the friends of liberty
should come across the sea and shake hands with us to
see that the new world was constructed upon a new
basis and foundation of justice and right.

I cannot tell you the inspiration that came from the sentiments that came out of these simple voices of the crowd. And the proudest thing I have to report to you is that this great country of ours is trusted throughout the world. I have not come to report the proceedings or results of the proceedings of the peace conference— that would be premature. I can say that I have received very happy impressions from this conference, impressions that while there are many differences of judgment, while there are some divergencies of object, there is nevertheless a common spirit and a common realization of the necessity of setting up a new standard of right in the world. Because the men who are in conference in Paris realize as keenly as any American can realize that they are not masters of their people, that they are servants of their people, and that the spirit of their people has awakened to a new purpose and a new conception of their power to realize that purpose, and that no man dare go home from that conference and report anything less noble than was expected of it.

The conference seems to you to go slowly; from day to day in Paris it seems to go slowly, but I wonder if you realize the complexity of the task which is undertaken. It seems as if the settlements of this war affect, and affect directly, every great, and I sometimes think every small, nation in the world. And no one decision can prudently be made which is not properly linked in with the great series of other decisions which must accompany it, and it must be reckoned in with the final result if the real quality and character of that result is to be properly judged.

What we are doing is to hear the whole case, hear it from the mouths of the men most interested, hear it from those who are officially commissioned to state it, hear the rival claims, hear the claims that affect new nationalities, that affect new areas of the world, that affect new commercial and economic connections that have been established by the great world war through which we have gone. And I have been struck by the moderateness of those who have represented national claims. I can testify that I have nowhere seen the gleam of passion. I have seen earnestness, I have seen tears come to the eyes of men who plead for downtrodden people whom they were privileged to speak for, but they were not tears of anger, they were tears of ardent hope; and I do not see how any man can fail to have been subdued by these pleas, subdued to this feeling that he was not there to assert an individual judgment of his own but to try to assist the cause of humanity.

And in the midst of it all every interest seeks out first of all when it reaches Paris the representatives of the United States. Why? Because—and I think I am stating the most wonderful fact in history—because there is no nation in Europe that suspects the motives of the United States. Was there ever so wonderful a thing seen before? Was there ever so moving a thing? Was there ever any fact that so bound the Nation that had won that esteem forever to deserve it? I would not have you understand that the great men who represent the other nations there in conference are disesteemed by those who know them. Quite the contrary. But you understand that the nations of Europe have again and again clashed with one another in competitive interest. It is impossible for men to forget these sharp issues that were drawn between them in times past. It is impossible for men to believe that all ambitions have all of a sudden been foregone. They remember territory that was coveted, they remember rights it was attempted to extort, remember political ambitions which it was attempted to realize, and while they believe men have come into different temper they cannot forget these things, and so they do not resort to one another for dispassionate view of matters in controversy.

They resort to that Nation which has won enviable distinction, being regarded as the friend of mankind. Whenever it is desired to send a small force of soldiers to occupy a piece of territory where it is thought nobody else will be welcome, they ask for American soldiers. And where other soldiers would be looked upon with suspicion and perhaps met with resistance, the American soldier is welcomed with acclaim. I have had so many grounds for pride on the other side of the water that I am very thankful that they are not grounds for personal pride, but for national pride.

If they were grounds for personal pride, I would be the most stuck-up man in the world. And it has been an infinite pleasure to me to see these gallant soldiers of ours, of whom the Constitution of the United States made me the proud commander. Everybody praises the American soldier with the feeling that in praising him he is subtracting from the credit of no one else. I have been searching for the fundamental fact that converted Europe to believe in us. Before this war Europe did not believe in us as she does now. She did not believe in us throughout the first three years of the war. She seems really to have believed that we were holding off because we thought we could make more by staying out than by going in. And all of a sudden, in short eighteen months, the whole verdict is reversed. There can be but one explanation for it. They saw what we did, that without making a single claim we put all our men and all our means at the disposal of those who were fighting for their homes in the first instance, but for the cause—the cause of human right and justice—and that we went in, not to support their national claims, but to support the great cause which they held in common. And when they saw that America not only held the ideals but acted the ideals, they were converted to America and became firm partisans of those ideals.

I met a group of scholars when I was in Paris. Some gentlemen from one of the Greek universities who had come to see me and in whose presence, or rather in the presence of the traditions of learning, I felt very young, indeed. And I told them that I had had one of the delightful revenges that sometimes come to men. **All** my life I have heard men speak with a sort of condescension of ideals and of idealists, and particularly of those separated, encloistered persons whom they choose to term academic, who were in the habit of uttering ideals in a free atmosphere when they clash with nobody in particular. And I said I have had this sweet revenge. Speaking with perfect frankness in the name of the people of the United States I have uttered as the objects of this great war ideals, and nothing but ideals, and the war has been won by that inspiration.

Men were fighting with tense muscle and lowered head until they came to realize those things, feeling they were fighting for their lives and their country, and when these accents of what it was all about reached them from America they lifted their heads, they raised their eyes to heaven, then they saw men in khaki coming across the sea in the spirit of crusaders, and they found these were strange men, reckless of danger not only, but reckless because they seemed to see something that made that danger worth while. Men have testified to me in Europe that our men were possessed by something that they could only call religious fervor. They were not like any of the other soldiers. They had vision; they had dream, and they were fighting in dream; and fighting in dream they turned the whole tide of battle, and it never came back. And now do you realize that this confidence we have established throughout the world imposes a burden upon us—if you choose to call it a burden. It is one of those burdens which any nation ought to be proud to carry. Any man who resists the present tides that run in the world will find himself thrown upon a shore so high and barren that it will seem as if he had been separated from his human kind forever.

Europe that I left the other day was full of something that it had never felt fill its heart so full before. It was full of hope. The Europe of the second year of the war—the Europe of the third year of the war—was sinking to a sort of stubborn desperation. They did not see any great thing to be achieved even when the war should be won. They hoped there would be some salvage; they hoped they could clear their territories of invading armies; they hoped they could set up their homes and start their industries afresh. But they thought it would simply be a resumption of the old life that Europe had led—led in fear; led in anxiety; led in constant suspicion and watchfulness. They never dreamed that it would be a Europe of settled peace and justified hope. And now these ideals have wrought this new magic that all the peoples of Europe are buoyed up and confident in the spirit of hope, because they believe that we are at the eve of a new age in the world, when nations will understand one another; when nations will support one another in every just cause; when nations will unite every moral and every physical strength to see that right shall prevail. If America were at this juncture to fail the world, what would come of it?

I do not mean any disrespect to any other great people when I say that America is the hope of the world. And if she does not justify that hope results are unthinkable. Men will be thrown back upon bitterness of disappointment not only but bitterness of despair. All nations will be set up as hostile camps again; men at the peace conference will go home with their heads upon their breasts, knowing they have failed—for they were bidden not to come home from there until they did something more than sign the treaty of peace. Suppose we sign the treaty of peace and that it is the most satisfactory treaty of peace that the confusing elements of the modern world will afford and go home and think about our labors we will know that we have left written upon the historic table at Versailles, upon which Vergennes and Benjamin Franklin wrote their names, nothing but a modern scrap of paper, no nations united to defend it, no great forces combined to make it good, no assurance given to the downtrodden and fearful people of the world that they shall be safe. Any man who thinks that America will take part in giving the world any such rebuff and disappointment as that does not know America. I invite him to test the sentiments of the Nation.

We set this Nation up to make men free and we did not confine our conception and purpose to America, and now we will make men free. If we did not do that all the fame of America would be gone and all her power would be dissipated. She would then have to keep her power for those narrow, selfish, provincial purposes which seem so dear to some minds that have no sweep beyond the nearest horizon. I should welcome no sweeter challenge than that. I have fighting blood in me and it is sometimes a delight to let it have scope, but if it is challenged on this occasion it will be an indulgence. Think of the picture, think of the utter blackness that would fall on the world. America has failed. America made a little essay at generosity and then withdrew. America said, "We are your friends," but it was only for to-day, not for to-morrow. America said, "Here is our power to vindicate right," and then next day said, "Let right take care of itself and we will take care of ourselves." America said, "We set up light to lead men along the paths of liberty, but we have lowered it—it is intended only to light our own path."

We set up a great ideal of liberty, and then we said, "Liberty is a thing that you must win for yourself." Do not call upon us and think of the world that we would leave. Do you realize how many new nations are going to be set up in the presence of old and powerful nations in Europe and left there, if left by us, without a disinterested friend? Do you believe in the Polish cause as I do? Are you going to set up Poland, immature, inexperienced, as yet unorganized, and leave her with a circle of armies around her? Do you believe in the aspirations of the Czecho-Slovaks and

Jugo-Slavs as I do? Do you know how many powers would be quick to pounce upon them if there were not guarantees of the world behind their liberty? Have you thought of the sufferings of Armenia? You poured out your money to help succor Armenians after they suffered. Now set up your strength so that they shall never suffer again.

Arrangements of the present peace cannot stand a generation unless they are guaranteed by the united forces of the civilized world. And if we do not guarantee them can you not see the picture? Your hearts have instructed you where the burden of this war fell. It did not fall upon national treasuries; it did not fall upon the instruments of administration; it did not fall upon the resources of nations. It fell upon the voiceless homes everywhere, where women were toiling in hope that their men would come back. When I think of the homes upon which dull despair would settle if this great hope is disappointed, I should wish for my part never to have had America play any part whatever in this attempt to emancipate the world.

But I talk as if there were any question. I have no more doubt of the verdict of America in this matter than I have doubt of the blood that is in me. And so, my fellow citizens, I have come back to report progress, and I do not believe that progress is going to stop short of the goal. The nations of the world have set their heads now to do a great thing, and they are not going to slacken their purpose. And when I speak of the nations of the world I do not speak of the governments of the world. I speak of peoples who constitute the nations of the world. They are in the saddle, and they are going to see to it that if their present governments do not do their will some other governments shall. The secret is out, and present governments know it. There is a great deal of harmony to be got out of common knowledge.

There is a great deal of sympathy to be got of living

in the same atmosphere, and except for the differences of languages, which puzzled my American ear very sadly, I could have believed I was at home in France or Italy or in England when I was on the streets, when I was in the presence of crowds, when I was in great halls where men were gathered irrespective of class. I did not feel quite as much at home there as I do here, but I felt that now, at any rate after this storm of war had cleared the air men were seeing eye to eye everywhere and that these were the kind of folks who would understand what the kind of folks at home would understand; that they were thinking the same things.

It is a great comfort, for one thing, to realize that you all understand the language I am speaking. A friend of mine said that to talk through an interpreter was like witnessing the compound fracture of an idea. But the beauty of it is that whatever the impediments of the channel of communication the idea is the same, that it gets registered, and it gets registered in responsive hearts and receptive purposes. I have come back for a strenuous attempt to transact business for a little while in America, but I have really come back to say to you, in all soberness and honesty, that I have been trying my best to speak your thoughts. When I sample myself I think I find that I am a typical American, and if I sample deep enough and get down to what probably is the true stuff of the man, then I have hope that it is part of the stuff that is like the other fellow's at home. And, therefore, probing deep in my heart and trying to see things that are right without regard to the things that may be debated as expedient, I feel that I am intepreting the purpose and the thought of America; and in loving America I find I have joined the great majority of my fellow men throughout the world.

PROBLEMS OF RECONSTRUCTION

ADDRESS OF WELCOME TO A CONFERENCE OF GOVERNORS AND MAYORS, CALLED TO CONSIDER RECONSTRUCTION PROBLEMS, MARCH 3, 1919. FROM "OFFICIAL U. S. BULLETIN," NO. 551.

I WISH that I could promise myself the pleasure and the profit of taking part in your deliberations. I find that nothing deliberate is permitted me since my return. I have been trying, under the guidance of my secretary, Mr. Tumulty, to do a month's work in a week, and I am hoping that not all of it has been done badly, but inasmuch as there is a necessary pressure upon my time I know that you will excuse me from taking a part in your conference, much as I should be profited by doing so.

My pleasant duty is to bid you a very hearty welcome and to express my gratification that so many executives of cities and of States have found the time and the inclination to come together on the very important matter we have to discuss. The primary duty of caring for our people in the intimate matters that we want to discuss here, of course, falls upon the States and upon the municipalities, and the function of the Federal Government is to do what it is trying to do in a conference of this sort—draw the executive minds of the country together so that they may profit by each other's suggestions and plans, and so that we may offer our services to coördinate their efforts in any way that they may deem it wise to coördinate. In other words, it is the privilege of the Federal Government in matters of this sort to be the servants of the executives of the States and municipalities and counties, and we shall perform that duty with the greatest pleasure if you will guide us with your suggestions.

I hope that the discussions of this conference will take as wide a scope as you think necessary. We are not met to discuss any single or narrow subject. We are met to discuss the proper method of restoring all the labor conditions of the country to a normal basis as soon as possible, and to effecting such fresh allocations of labor and industry as the circumstances may make necessary. I think I can testify from what I have seen on the other side of the water that we are more fortunate than other nations in respect to these great problems. Our industries have been disturbed and disorganized—disorganized as compared with a peace basis, very seriously, indeed, by the war, but not so seriously as the industries of other countries; and it seems to me, therefore, that we should approach these problems that we are about to discuss with a good deal of confidence—with a good deal of confidence that if we have a common purpose we can realize that common purpose without serious or insurmountable difficulties.

The thing that has impressed me most, gentlemen, not only in the recent weeks when I have been in conference on the other side of the water, but for many months before I went across the water, was this: We are at last learning that the business of government is to take counsel for the average man. We are at last learning that the whole matter of the prosperity of peoples runs down into the great body of the men and women who do the work of the world, and that the process of guidance is not completed by the mere success of great enterprises—it is completed only by the standard of the benefit that it confers upon those who in the obscure ranks of life contribute to the success of those enterprises. The hearts of the men and women and children of the world are stirred now in a way that has never been known before. They are not only stirred by their individual circumstances, but they are beginning to get a vision of what the general circumstances of the world are, and there is for the first time in history an international sympathy which is quick and vital—a sympathy which does not display itself merely in the contact of Governments, but displays itself in the silent intercourse of sympathy between great bodies that constitute great nations, and the significance of a conference like this is that we are expressing in it, and will, I believe, express in the results of this conference, our consciousness that we are servants of this great silent mass of people who constitute the United States, and that as their servants it is our business, as it is our privilege, to find out how we can best assist in making their lives what they wish them to be, giving them the opportunities that they ought to have, assisting by public counsel in the private affairs upon which the happiness of men depends.

And so I am the more distressed that I cannot take part in these councils because my present business is to understand what plain men everywhere want. It is perfectly understood in Paris that we are not meeting there as the masters of anybody—that we are meeting there as the servants of, I believe it is, about 700,000,000 people, and that unless we show that we understand the business of servants we will not satisfy them and we will not accomplish the peace of the world, and that if we show that we want to serve any interest but theirs we will have become candidates for the most lasting discredit that will ever attach to men in history. And so it is with this profound feeling of the significance of the things you are undertaking that I bid you welcome, because I believe you have come together in the spirit which I have tried to indicate, and that we will together concert methods of coöperation and individual action which will really accomplish what we wish to see accomplished in steadying and easing and facilitating the whole labor processes of the United States.

METROPOLITAN OPERA HOUSE SPEECH

ADDRESS AT A PUBLIC MEETING IN NEW YORK CITY, ON
THE EVE OF HIS DEPARTURE FOR EUROPE, MARCH
4, 1919. FROM OFFICIAL GOVERNMENT PUBLICA-
TION IN MR. WILSON'S FILES.

I ACCEPT the intimation of the air just played.[1] I
will not come back "'til it's over, over there." And
yet I pray God in the interests of peace of the world
that that may be soon.

The first thing that I am going to tell the people on
the other side of the water is that an overwhelming
majority of the American people is in favor of the
League of Nations. I know that that is true. I have
had unmistakable intimations of it from all parts of
the country, and the voice rings true in every case. I
account myself fortunate to speak here under the unusual circumstances of this evening. I am happy to
associate myself with Mr. Taft in this great cause. He
has displayed an elevation of view and devotion to public duty which is beyond praise.

And I am the more happy because this means that this
is not a party issue. No party has a right to appropriate this issue and no party will in the long run dare
oppose it.

We have listened to so clear and admirable an exposition [2] of many of the main features of the proposed covenant of the League of Nations that it is perhaps not
necessary for me to discuss in any particular way the
contents of the document. I will seek rather to give you
its setting. I do not know when I have been more impressed than by the conferences of the commission set up
by the conference of peace to draw up the covenant for

[1] "Over There."
[2] Mr. Taft's address preceding that of the President.

444

a League of Nations. The representatives of fourteen
nations sat around that board—not young men, not men
inexperienced in the affairs of their own countries, not
men inexperienced in the politics of the world—and the
inspiring influence of every meeting was the concurrence
of purpose on the part of all those men to come to an
agreement and an effective working agreement with regard to this league of the civilized world.

There was a conviction in the whole impulse; there
was conviction of more than one sort; there was the
conviction that this thing ought to be done; and there
was also the conviction that not a man there would venture to go home and say that he had not tried to do it.

Mr. Taft has set a picture for you of what failure of
this great purpose would mean. We have been hearing
for all these weary months that this agony of war has
lasted of the sinister purpose of the Central Empires
and we have made maps of the course that they meant
their conquests to take. Where did the lines of that map
lie, of that central line that we used to call from Bremen
to Bagdad? They lay through these very regions to
which Mr. Taft has called your attention, but they lay
then through a united empire. The Austro-Hungarian
Empire, whose integrity Germany was bound to respect
as her ally, lay in the path of that line of conquest; the
Turkish Empire, whose interests she professed to make
her own, lay in the direct path that she intended to
tread. And now what has happened? The Austro-
Hungarian Empire has gone to pieces and the Turkish
Empire has disappeared, and the nations that effected
that great result—for it was the result of liberation—
are now responsible as the trustees of the assets of those
great nations. You not only would have weak nations
lying in this path, but you would have nations in which
that old poisonous seed of intrigue could be planted with
the certainty that the crop would be abundant, and one
of the things that the League of Nations is intended to
watch is the course of intrigue. Intrigue cannot stand

publicity, and if the League of Nations were nothing but a great debating society it would kill intrigue.

It is one of the agreements of this covenant that it is the friendly right of every nation a member of the League to call attention to anything that it thinks will disturb the peace of the world, no matter where that thing is occurring. There is no subject that may touch the peace of the world which is exempt from inquiry and discussion, and I think everybody here present will agree with me that Germany would never have gone to war if she had permitted the world to discuss the aggression upon Serbia for a single week. The British Foreign Office pleaded that there might be a day or two delay so that representatives of the nations of Europe could get together and discuss the possibilities of a settlement. Germany did not dare permit a day's discussion. You know what happened. So soon as the world realized that an outlaw was at large the nations began, one by one, to draw together against her. We know for certainty that if Germany had thought for a moment that Great Britain would go in with France and Russia she never would have undertaken the enterprise, and the League of Nations is meant as notice to all outlaw nations that not only Great Britain but the United States and the rest of the world will go in to check enterprises of that sort. And so the League of Nations is nothing more nor less than the covenant that the world will always maintain the standards which it has now vindicated by some of the most precious blood ever spilt.

The liberated peoples of the Austro-Hungarian Empire and of the Turkish Empire call out to us for this thing. It has not arisen in the councils of statesmen. Europe is a bit sick at heart at this very moment because it sees that the statesmen have had no vision and that the only vision has been the vision of the people. Those who suffer see. Those 'against whom wrong is wrought know how desirable is the right of the righteous. Nations that have long been under the heel of Austria, that have long cowered before the German, that have long suffered the indescribable agonies of being governed by the Turk, have called out to the world generation after generation for justice, liberation, and succor, and no cabinet in the world has heard them. Private organizations, pitying hearts, philanthropic men and women, have poured out their treasure in order to relieve these sufferings, but no nation has said to the nations responsible, "You must stop; this thing is intolerable and we will not permit it." And the vision has been with the people. My friends, I wish you would reflect upon this proposition; the vision as to what is necessary for great reforms has seldom come from the top in the nations of the world. It has come from the need and aspiration and self-assertion of great bodies of men who meant to be free. And I can explain some of the criticisms which have been leveled against this great enterprise only by the supposition that men who utter the criticisms have never felt the great pulse of the heart of the world.

And I am amazed—not alarmed but amazed—that there should be in some quarters such a comprehensive ignorance of the state of the world. These gentlemen do not know what the mind of men is just now. Everybody else does. I do not know where they have been closeted, I do not know by what influences they have been blinded, but I do know they have been separated from the general currents of the thought of mankind.

And I want to utter this solemn warning, not in the way of a threat; the forces of the world do not threaten, they operate. The great tides of the world do not give notice that they are going to rise and run; they rise in their majesty and overwhelming might, and those who stand in the way are overwhelmed. Now the heart of the world is awake and the heart of the world must be satisfied. Do not let yourselves suppose for a moment that uneasiness in the populations of Europe is due entirely to economic causes or economic motives; something very much deeper underlies it all than that. They see that their Governments have never been able to defend them against intrigue or aggression, and that there is no force of foresight or of prudence in any modern cabinet to stop war. And therefore they say, "There must be some fundamental cause for this," and the fundamental cause they are beginning to perceive to be that nations have stood singly or in little jealous groups against each other, fostering prejudice, increasing the danger of war rather than concerting measures to prevent it; and that if there is right in the world, if there is justice in the world, there is no reason why nations should be divided in support of justice.

They are, therefore, saying if you really believe that there is a right, if you really believe that wars ought to be stopped, stop thinking about the rival interests of nations and think about men and women and children throughout the world. Nations are not made to afford distinction to their rulers by way of success in the maneuvers of politics; nations are meant, if they are meant for anything, to make the men, women, and children in them secure and happy and prosperous, and no nation has the right to set up its special interests against the interests and benefits of mankind, least of all this great Nation which we love. It was set up for the benefit of mankind; it was set up to illustrate the highest ideals and to achieve the highest aspirations of men who wanted to be free; and the world—the world of to-day—believes that and counts on us, and would be thrown back into the blackness of despair if we deserted it.

I have tried once and again, my fellow citizens, to say to little circles of friends or to larger bodies what seems to be the real hope of the peoples of Europe, and I tell you frankly I have not been able to do so, because when the thought tries to crowd itself into speech the profound emotion of the thing is too much; speech will not carry. I have felt the tragedy of the hope of those suffering peoples.

It is a tragedy because it is a hope which cannot be realized in its perfection; and yet I have felt besides its tragedy its compulsion, its compulsion upon every living man to exercise every influence that he has to the utmost to see that as little as possible of that hope is disappointed, because if men cannot now, after this agony of bloody sweat, come to their self-possession and see how to regulate the affairs of the world we will sink back into a period of struggle in which there will be no hope and therefore no mercy. There can be no mercy where there is no hope, for why should you spare another if you yourself expect to perish? Why should you be pitiful if you can get no pity? Why should you be just if, upon every hand, you are put upon?

There is another thing which I think the critics of this covenant have not observed. They not only have not observed the temper of the world but they have not even observed the temper of those splendid boys in khaki that they sent across the seas. I have had the proud consciousness of the reflected glory of those boys because the Constitution made me their commander-in-chief, and they have taught me some lessons. When we went into the war we went into it on the basis of declarations which it was my privilege to utter because I believed them to be an interpretation of the purpose and thought of the people of the United States.

And those boys went over there with the feeling that they were sacredly bound to the realization of those ideals; that they were not only going over there to beat Germany; they were not going over there merely with resentment in their hearts against a particular outlaw nation; but that they were crossing those 3,000 miles of sea in order to show to Europe that the United States, when it became necessary, would go anywhere where the rights of mankind were threatened. They would not sit still in the trenches. They would not be restrained by the prudence of experienced continental commanders. They thought they had come over there to do a particular thing, and they were going to do it and do it at once. And just as soon as that rush of spirit as well as the rush of body came in contact with the lines of the enemy they began to break, and they continued to break until the end. They continued to break, my fellow citizens, not merely because of the physical force of those lusty youngsters but because of the irresistible spiritual force of the armies of the United States. It was that that they felt. It was that that awed them. It was that that made them feel if these youngsters ever got a foothold they could never be dislodged, and that therefore every foot of ground that they won was permanently won for the liberty of mankind.

And do you suppose that, having felt that crusading spirit of these youngsters who went over there not to glorify America but to serve their fellow men, I am going to permit myself for one moment to slacken in my effort to be worthy of them and of their cause? What I said at the opening I said with a deeper meaning than perhaps you have caught; I do not mean to come back until it's over over there, and it must not be over until the nations of the world are assured of the permanency of peace.

Gentlemen on this side of the water would be very much profited by getting into communication with some gentlemen on the other side of the water. We sometimes think, my fellow citizens, that the experienced statesmen of European nations are an unusually hardheaded set of men, by which we generally mean, although we do not admit it, they are a bit cynical; they say "This is a practical world," by which you always mean that it is not an ideal world; that they do not believe things can be settled upon an ideal basis. Well, I never came into intimate contact with them before, but if they used to be that way they are not that way now. They have been subdued, if that was once their temper, by the awful significance of recent events and the awful importance of what is to ensue, and there is not one of them with whom I have come in contact who does not feel he cannot in conscience return to his people from Paris unless he has done his utmost to do something more than attach his name to a treaty of peace. Every man in that conference knows the treaty of peace in itself will be inoperative, as Mr. Taft has said, without this constant support and energy of a great organization such as is supplied by the League of Nations.

And men who, when I first went over there, were skeptical of the possibility of forming a league of nations, admitted that if we could but form it it would be an invaluable instrumentality through which to secure the operation of the various parts of the treaty; and when that treaty comes back gentlemen on this side will find the Covenant not only in it, but so many threads of the treaty tied to the covenant that you cannot dissect the covenant from the treaty without destroying the whole vital structure. The structure of peace will not be vital without the League of Nations, and no man is going to bring back a cadaver with him.

I must say that I have been puzzled by some of the criticisms—not by the criticisms themselves—I can understand them perfectly even when there was no foundation for them—but by the fact of the criticism. I cannot imagine how these gentlemen can live and not live in the atmosphere of the world. I cannot imagine how they can live and not be in contact with the events of their times, and I particularly cannot imagine how they can be Americans and set up a doctrine of careful selfishness thought out to the last detail. I have heard no counsel of generosity in their criticism. I have heard no constructive suggestion. I have heard nothing except, "Will it not be dangerous to us to help the world?" It would be fatal to us not to help it.

From being what I will venture to call the most famous and the most powerful nation in the world, we would of a sudden have become the most contemptible. So I did not need to be told, as I have been told, that the people of the United States would support this Covenant. I am an American and I knew they would. What a sweet revenge it is upon the world. They laughed at us once; they thought we did not mean our professions of principle. They thought so until April of 1917. It was hardly credible to them that we would do more than send a few men over and go through the forms of helping, and when they saw multitudes hastening across the sea, and saw what those multitudes were eager to do when they got to the other side, they stood at amaze and said, "The thing is real; this nation is the friend of mankind as it said it was." The enthusiasm, the hope, the trust, the confidence in the future bred by that change of view are indescribable. Take an individual American and you may often find him selfish and confined to his special interests; but take the American in the mass and he is willing to die for an ideal. The sweet revenge therefore is this, that we believed in righteousness and now we are ready to make the supreme sacrifice for it, the supreme sacrifice of throwing in our fortunes with the fortunes of men everywhere.

Mr. Taft was speaking of Washington's utterance about entangling alliances, and if he will permit me to say so, he put the exactly right interpretation upon what Washington said, the interpretation that is inevitable if you read what he said, as most of these gentlemen do not. And the thing that he longed for was just what we are now about to supply; an arrangement which will disentangle all the alliances in the world.

Nothing entangles, nothing enmeshes a man except a selfish combination with somebody else. Nothing entangles a nation, hampers it, binds it, except to enter into a combination with some other nation against the other nations of the world. And this great disentanglement of all alliances is now to be accomplished by this

Covenant, because one of the Covenants is that no nation shall enter into any relationship with another nation inconsistent with the covenants of the League Nations. Nations promise not to have alliances. Nation promise not to make combinations against each other. Nations agree there shall be but one combination, and that is the combination of all against the wrongdoer.

And so I am going back to my task on the other side with renewed vigor. I had not forgotten what the spirit of the American people is. But I have been immensely refreshed by coming in contact with it again. I did not know how good home felt until I got here.

The only place a man can feel at home is where nothing has to be explained to him. Nothing has to be explained to me in America, least of all the sentiment of the American people. I mean, about great fundamental things like this. There are many differences of judgment as to policy—and perfectly legitimate. Sometimes profound differences of judgment, but those are not differences of sentiment, those are not differences of purpose, those are not differences of ideals. And the advantage of not having to have anything explained to you is that you recognize a wrong explanation when you hear it.

In a certain rather abandoned part of the frontier at one time it was said they found a man who told the truth; he was not found telling it, but he could tell it when he heard it. And I think I am in that situation with regard to some of the criticisms I have heard. They do not make any impression on me because I know there is no medium that will transmit them, that the sentiment of the country is proof against such narrowness and such selfishness as that. I commend these gentlemen to communion with their fellow citizens.

What are we to say, then, as to the future? I think, my fellow citizens, that we can look forward to it with great confidence. I have heard cheering news since I came to this side of the water about the progress that is being made in Paris towards the discussion and clarification of a great many difficult matters; and I believe settlements will begin to be made rather rapidly from this time on at those conferences. But what I believe—what I know as well as believe—is this: that the men engaged in those conferences are gathering heart as they go, not losing it; that they are finding community of purpose, community of ideal to an extent that perhaps they did not expect; and that amidst all the interplay of influence—because it is infinitely complicated—amidst all the interplay of influence, there is a forward movement which is running towards the right. Men have at last perceived that the only permanent thing in the world is the right, and that a wrong settlement is bound to be a temporary settlement for the very best reason of all, that it ought to be a temporary settlement, and the spirits of men will rebel against it, and the spirits of men are now in the saddle.

When I was in Italy, a little limping group of wounded Italian soldiers sought an interview with me. I could not conjecture what it was they were going to say to me, and with the greatest simplicity, with touching simplicity, they presented me with a petition in favor of the League of Nations.

Their wounded limbs, their impaired vitality, were the only argument they brought with them. It was a simple request that I lend all the influence that I might happen to have to relieve future generations of the sacrifices that they had been obliged to make. That appeal has remained in my mind as I have ridden along the streets in European capitals and heard cries of the crowd, cries for the League of Nations from lips of people who, I venture to say, had no particular notion of how it was to be done, who were not ready to propose a plan for a League of Nations, but whose hearts said that something by way of a combination of all men everywhere must come out of this. As we drove along country roads weak old women would come out and hold flowers to us. Why should they hold flowers up to strangers from across the Atlantic? Only because they believed that we were the messengers of friendship and of hope, and these flowers were their humble offerings of gratitude that friends from so great a distance should have brought them so great a hope.

It is inconceivable that we should disappoint them, and we shall not. The day will come when men in America will look back with swelling hearts and rising pride that they should have been privileged to make the sacrifice which it was necessary to make in order to combine their might and their moral power with the cause of justice for men of every kind everywhere.

God give us the strength and vision to do it wisely. God give us the privilege of knowing that we did it without counting the cost, and because we were true Americans, lovers of liberty and of right.

DELIBERATE OBSTRUCTION IN THE SENATE

STATEMENT ISSUED UPON THE ADJOURNMENT OF CON-
GRESS, MARCH 4, 1919. FROM "OFFICIAL U. S.
BULLETIN," NO. 552.

A GROUP of men in the Senate have deliberately chosen to embarrass the administration of the Government, to imperil the financial interests of the railway systems of the country, and to make arbitrary use of powers intended to be employed in the interests of the people.

It is plainly my present duty to attend the Peace Conference in Paris. It is also my duty to be in close contact with the public business during a session of the Congress. I must make my choice between these two duties, and I confidently hope that the people of the country will think that I am making the right choice. It is not in the interest of the right conduct of public affairs that I should call the Congress in special session while it is impossible for me to be in Washington, because of a more pressing duty elsewhere, to coöperate with the Houses.

I take it for granted that the men who have obstructed and prevented the passage of necessary legislation have taken all of this into consideration and are willing to assume the responsibility of the impaired efficiency of the government and the embarrassed finances of the country during the time of my enforced absence.

LEAGUE AN INTEGRAL PART OF
TREATY OF PEACE

STATEMENT ISSUED IN PARIS,[1] MARCH 15, 1919. FROM
ORIGINAL IN MR. WILSON'S FILES.

THE President said to-day that the decision made
at the Peace Conference at its plenary session,
January 25, 1919, to the effect that the establishment
of a League of Nations should be made an integral
part of the Treaty of Peace, is of final force and that
there is no basis whatever for the reports that a change
in this decision was contemplated.

The resolution on the League of Nations, adopted
January 25, 1919, at the plenary session of the Peace
Conference, was as follows:

1. It is essential to the maintenance of the world settlement, which
the associated nations are now met to establish, that a League of
Nations be created to promote international coöperation, to insure
the fulfillment of accepted international obligations, and to provide
safeguards against war.

2. This League should be treated as an integral part of the
general Treaty of Peace, and should be open to every civilized
nation which can be relied upon to promote its objects.

3. The members of the League should periodically meet in international conference, and should have a permanent organization and
secretariat to carry on the business of the League in the intervals
between the conferences.

[1] For full account of the origin of this statement, see *Woodrow Wilson and World Settlement*, vol I, chap. xvii, by Ray Stannard Baker.

URGING MR. LLOYD GEORGE TO REMAIN IN PARIS

JOINT LETTER TO THE ENGLISH PRIME MINISTER, MARCH 17, 1919. FROM "OFFICIAL U. S. BULLETIN," NO. 566.

DEAR MR. PRIME MINISTER:
It seems to us imperative, in order that the world may wait no longer for peace than is actually unavoidable, that you should remain in Paris until the chief questions connected with the peace are settled, and we earnestly beg that you will do so. If you can arrange to remain for another two weeks we hope and believe that this all-important result can be attained.

We write this with a full comprehension of the very urgent matters that are calling you to England, and with a vivid consciousness of the sacrifices we are asking you to make.

Sincerely yours,
WOODROW WILSON,
G. O. CLEMENCEAU,
L. ORLANDO.

DEFENSE OF THE LEAGUE OF NATIONS COMMISSION

STATEMENT ISSUED IN PARIS, MARCH 27, 1919. FROM ORIGINAL IN MR. WILSON'S FILES.

IN VIEW of the very surprising impression which seems to exist in some quarters that it is the discussions of the Commission on the League of Nations that are delaying the final formulation of peace, I am very glad to take the opportunity of reporting that the conclusions of this commission were the first to be laid before the Plenary Conference. They were reported on February 14, and the world has had a full month in which to discuss every feature of the draft Covenant then submitted. During the last few days the commission has been engaged in an effort to take advantage of the criticisms which the publication of the Covenant has fortunately drawn out. A committee of the commission has also had the advantage of a conference with representatives of the neutral nations, who are evidencing a very deep interest and a practically unanimous desire to allign themselves with the League. The revised Covenant is now practically finished. It is in the hands of a committee for the final process of drafting and will almost immediately be presented a second time to the public.

The conferences of the commission have invariably been held at times when they could not interfere with the consultation of those who have undertaken to formulate the general conclusions of the Conference with regard to the many other complicated problems of peace, so that the members of the commission congratulate themselves on the fact that no part of their conferences has ever interposed any form of delay.

ITALIAN CLAIMS ON THE ADRIATIC

MEMORANDUM SENT TO THE ITALIAN DELEGATION TO
THE PEACE CONFERENCE, APRIL 14, 1919, MADE
PUBLIC APRIL 30, 1919. FROM ORIGINAL IN MR.
WILSON'S FILES.

THERE is no question to which I have given more
careful or anxious thought than I have given to
this, because in common with all my colleagues it is my
earnest desire to see the utmost justice done to Italy.
Throughout my consideration of it, however, I have felt
that there was one matter in which I had no choice and
could wish to have none.

I felt bound to square every conclusion that I should
reach as accurately as possible with the fourteen principles of peace which I set forth in my address to the
Congress of the United States on the eighth of January,
1918, and in subsequent addresses.

These fourteen points and the principles laid down
in the subsequent addresses were formally adopted, with
only a single reservation, by the Powers associated
against Germany, and will constitute the basis of peace
with Germany. I do not feel at liberty to suggest one
basis for peace with Germany and another for peace
with Austria.

It will be remembered that in reply to a communication from the Austrian Government offering to enter
into negotiations for an armistice and peace on the basis
of the fourteen points to which I have alluded, I said
that there was one matter to which those points no
longer applied.

They had demanded autonomy for the several States
which had constituted parts of the Austro-Hungarian
Empire, and I pointed out that it must now be left to

460

the choice of the people of those several countries what their destiny and political relations should be.

They have chosen, with the sympathy of the whole world, to be set up as independent States. Their complete separation from Austria and the consequent complete dissolution of the Austro-Hungarian Empire has given a new aspect and significance to the settlements which must be effected with regard at any rate to the eastern boundaries of Italy.

Personally, I am quite willing that Italy should be accorded along the whole length of her northern frontier and wherever she comes into contact with Austrian territory all that was accorded her in the so-called Pact of London, but I am of the clear opinion that the Pact of London can no longer apply to the settlement of her eastern boundaries.

The line drawn in the Pact of London was conceived for the purpose of establishing an absolutely adequate frontier of safety for Italy against any possible hostility or aggression on the part of Austria-Hungary. But Austria-Hungary no longer exists.

These eastern frontiers will touch countries stripped of the military and naval power of Austria, set up in entire independence of Austria, and organized for the purpose of satisfying legitimate national aspirations, and created States not hostile to the new European order, but arising out of it, interested in its maintenance, dependent upon the cultivation of friendships, and bound to a common policy of peace and accommodation by the covenants of the League of Nations.

It is with these facts in mind that I have approached the Adriatic question. It is commonly agreed, and I very heartily adhere to the agreement, that the ports of Trieste and Pola, and with them the greater part of the Istrian Peninsula, should be ceded to Italy, her eastern frontier running along the natural strategic line established by the physical conformation of the country, a line which it has been attempted to draw with some degree of accuracy on the attached map.

Within this line on the Italian side will lie considerable bodies of non-Italian population, but their fortunes are so naturally linked by the nature of the country itself with the fortunes of the Italian people that I think their inclusion is fully justified.

There would be no such justification, in my judgment, in including Fiume or any part of the coast lying to the south of Fiume within the boundaries of the Italian kingdom.

Fiume is by situation and by all the circumstances of its development not an Italian but an international port, serving the countries to the east and north of the Gulf of Fiume. Just because it is an international port and cannot with justice be subordinated to any one sovereignty it is my clear judgment that it should enjoy a very considerable degree of genuine autonomy and that, while it should be included no doubt within the customs system of the new Jugo-Slav State, it should nevertheless be left free in its own interest and in the interest of the States lying about it to devote itself to the service of the commerce which naturally and inevitably seeks an outlet or inlet at its port.

The States which it serves will be new States. They will need to have complete confidence in their access to an outlet on the sea. The friendships and the connections of the future will largely depend upon such an arrangement as I have suggested; and friendship, coöperation, freedom of action, must underlie every arrangement of peace if peace is to be lasting.

I believe that there will be common agreement that the Island of Lissa should be ceded to Italy and that she should retain the port of Volna. I believe that it will be generally agreed that the fortifications which the Austrian Government established upon the islands near the eastern coast of the Adriatic should be permanently dismantled under international guarantees, and that the disarmament which is to be arranged under the League of Nations should limit the States on the eastern coast of the Adriatic to only such minor naval forces as are necessary for policing the waters of the islands and the coast.

These are the conclusions to which I am forced by the compulsion of the understandings which underlay the whole initiation of the present peace. No other conclusions seem to me susceptible of being rendered consistent with these understandings. They were understandings accepted by the whole world, and bear with peculiar compulsion upon the United States because the privilege was accorded her of taking the initiative in bringing about the negotiations for peace and her pledges underlie the whole difficult business.

And certainly Italy obtains under such a settlement the great historic objects which her people have so long had in mind. The historical wrongs inflicted upon her by Austria-Hungary and by a long series of unjust transactions which I hope will before long sink out of the memory of man are completely redressed. Nothing is denied her which will complete her national unity.

Here and there upon the islands of the Adriatic and upon the eastern coast of that sea there are settlements containing large Italian elements of population, but the pledges under which the new States enter the family of nations will abundantly safeguard the liberty, the development, and all the just rights of national or racial minorities, and back of these safeguards will always lie the watchful and sufficient authority of the League of Nations.

And at the very outset we shall have avoided the fatal error of making Italy's nearest neighbors on the east her enemies and nursing just such a sense of injustice as has disturbed the peace of Europe for generations together and played no small part in bringing on the terrible conflict through which we have just passed.

INVITING THE GERMANS TO VERSAILLES

FIRST OFFICIAL ANNOUNCEMENT OF THE COUNCIL OF
FOUR MADE BY THE PRESIDENT OF THE UNITED
STATES, APRIL 14, 1919. FROM ORIGINAL IN MR.
WILSON'S FILES, CORRECTED BY HIM IN HIS OWN
HAND.

IN VIEW of the fact that the questions which must
be settled in the peace with Germany have been
brought so near complete solution that they can now
quickly be put through the final process of drafting,
those who have been most constantly in conference
about them have decided to advise that the German
plenipotentiaries be invited to meet representatives of
the associated belligerent nations at Versailles on the
twenty-fifth of April.

This does not mean that the many other questions
connected with the general peace settlement will be interrupted or that their consideration, which has long
been under way, will be retarded. On the contrary,
it is expected that rapid progress will now be made with
those questions, so that they may also presently be
expected to be ready for final settlement. It is hoped
that the questions most directly affecting Italy, especially the Adriatic question, can now be brought to a
speedy agreement. The Adriatic question will be given
for the time precedence over other questions and
pressed by continual study to its final stage.

The settlements that belong especially to the treaty
with Germany will in this way be got out of the way at
the same time that all other settlements are being
brought to a complete formulation. It is realized that
though this process must be followed, all the questions
of the present great settlement are parts of a single
whole.

ON THE ITALIAN SETTLEMENT

STATEMENT ISSUED AT PARIS,[1] APRIL 23, 1919. FROM
ORIGINAL IN MR. WILSON'S FILES.

IN VIEW of the capital importance of the questions
affected, and in order to throw all possible light
upon what is involved in their settlement I hope that
the following statement will contribute to the final
formation of opinion and to a satisfactory solution.

When Italy entered the war she entered upon the
basis of a definite, but private, understanding with Great
Britain and France, now known as the Pact of London.
Since that time the whole face of circumstance has been
altered. Many other powers, great and small, have
entered the struggle, with no knowledge of that private
understanding. The Austro-Hungarian Empire, then
the enemy of Europe, and at whose expense the Pact of
London was to be kept in the event of victory, has gone
to pieces and no longer exists. Not only that. The
several parts of that Empire, it is now agreed by Italy
and all her associates, are to be erected into independent states and associated in a League of Nations, not
with those who were recently our enemies, but with Italy
herself and the powers that stood with Italy in the great
war for liberty. We are to establish their liberty as
well as our own. They are to be among the smaller
states whose interests are henceforth to be as scrupulously safeguarded as the interests of the most powerful states.

The war was ended, moreover, by proposing to Germany an armistice and peace which should be founded
on certain clearly defined principles which should set up
a new order of right and justice. Upon those principles

[1] For full account of the origin and results of this statement, see
Woodrow Wilson and World Settlement, vol. ii, chap. xxxii, by Ray
Stannard Baker.

the peace with Germany has been conceived, not only, but formulated. Upon those principles it will be executed. We cannot ask the great body of powers to propose and effect peace with Austria and establish a new basis of independence and right in the states which originally constituted the Austro-Hungarian Empire and in the states of the Balkan group on principles of another kind. We must apply the same principles to the settlement of Europe in those quarters that we have applied in the peace with Germany. It was upon the explicit avowal of those principles that the initiative for peace was taken. It is upon them that the whole structure of peace must rest.

If those principles are to be adhered to, Fiume must serve as the outlet and inlet of the commerce, not of Italy, but of the lands to the north and northeast of that port: Hungary, Bohemia, Rumania, and the states of the new Jugoslavic group. To assign Fiume to Italy would be to create the feeling that we had deliberately put the port upon which all these countries chiefly depend for their access to the Mediterranean in the hands of a power of which it did not form an integral part and whose sovereignty, if set up there, must inevitably seem foreign, not domestic or identified with the commercial and industrial life of the regions which the port must serve. It is for that reason, no doubt, that Fiume was not included in the Pact of London but there definitely assigned to the Croatians.

And the reason why the line of the Pact of London swept about many of the islands of the eastern coast of the Adriatic and around the portion of the Dalmatian coast which lies most open to that sea was not only that here and there on those islands and here and there on that coast there are bodies of people of Italian blood and connection, but also, and no doubt chiefly, because it was felt that it was necessary for Italy to have a foothold amidst the channels of the eastern Adriatic in order that she might make her own coasts safe against the naval aggression of Austria-Hungary. But Austria-Hungary no longer exists. It is proposed that the fortifications which the Austrian government constructed there shall be razed and permanently destroyed. It is part, also, of the new plan of European order which centers in the League of Nations that the new states erected there shall accept a limitation of armaments which puts aggression out of the question. There can be no fear of the unfair treatment of groups of Italian people there because adequate guarantees will be given, under international sanction, of equal and equitable treatment of all racial or national minorities.

In brief, every question associated with this settlement wears a new aspect,—a new aspect given it by the very victory for right for which Italy has made the supreme sacrifice of blood and treasure. Italy, along with the four other great powers, has become one of the chief trustees of the new order which she has played so honorable a part in establishing.

And on the north and northeast her natural frontiers are completely restored, along the whole sweep of the Alps from northwest to southeast to the very end of the Istrian Peninsula, including all the great watershed within which Trieste and Pola lie, and all the fair regions whose face nature has turned towards the great peninsula upon which the historic life of the Latin people has been worked out through centuries of famous story ever since Rome was first set upon her seven hills. Her ancient unity is restored. Her lines are extended to the great walls which are her natural defense. It is within her choice to be surrounded by friends; to exhibit to the newly liberated peoples across the Adriatic that noblest quality of greatness, magnanimity, friendly generosity, the preference of justice over interest.

The nations associated with her, the nations that know nothing of the Pact of London or of any other special understanding that lies at the beginning of this great struggle, and who have made their supreme sacrifice also in the interest, not of national advantage or defense, but of the settled peace of the world, now unite with her older associates in urging her to assume a leadership which cannot be mistaken in the new order of Europe. America is Italy's friend. Her people are drawn, millions strong, from Italy's own fair countrysides. She is linked in blood as well as in affection with the Italian people. Such ties can never be broken. And America was privileged, by the generous commission of her associates in the war, to initiate the peace we are about to consummate,—to initiate it upon terms she had herself formulated and in which I was her spokesman. The compulsion is upon her to square every decision she takes a part in with those principles. She can do nothing else. She trusts Italy, and in her trust believes that Italy will ask nothing of her that cannot be made unmistakably consistent with these sacred obligations. Interest is not now in question, but the rights of peoples, of states new and old, of liberated peoples and peoples whose rulers have never accounted them worthy of right; above all, the right of the world to peace and to such settlements of interest as shall make peace secure.

These, and these only, are the principles for which America has fought. These, and these only, are the principles upon which she can consent to make peace. Only upon these principles, she hopes and believes, will the people of Italy ask her to make peace.

REVISED COVENANT OF THE LEAGUE

ADDRESS BEFORE THE FIFTH PLENARY SESSION OF THE
PEACE CONFERENCE, UPON PRESENTING THE RE-
VISED COVENANT OF THE LEAGUE OF NATIONS,
PARIS, APRIL 28, 1919.

MR. PRESIDENT:
When the text of the Covenant of the League
of Nations was last laid before you I had the honor of
reading the Covenant *in extenso*. I will not detain you
to-day to read the Covenant as it has now been altered,
but will merely take the liberty of explaining to you
some of the alterations that have been made.

The report of the commission has been circulated.
You yourselves have in hand the text of the Covenant,
and will no doubt have noticed that most of the changes
that have been made are mere changes of phraseology,
not changes of substance, and that, besides that, most
of the changes are intended to clarify the document, or,
rather, to make explicit what we all have assumed was
implicit in the document as it was originally presented
to you. But I shall take the liberty of calling your
attention to the new features such as they are. Some
of them are considerable, the rest trivial.

The first paragraph of Article I is new. In view of
the insertion of the Covenant in the Peace Treaty, specific provision as to the signatories of the treaty, who
would become members of the League, and also as to
neutral States to be invited to accede to the Covenant,
were obviously necessary. The paragraph also provides for the method by which a neutral State may accede to the Covenant.

The third paragraph of Article I is new, providing
for the withdrawal of any member of the League on a
notice given of two years.

The second paragraph of Article IV is new, providing for a possible increase in the Council, should other powers be added to the League of Nations whose present accession is not anticipated. The two last paragraphs of Article IV are new, providing specifically for one vote for each member of the League in the Council which was understood before, and providing also for one representative of each member of the League.

The first paragraph of Article V is new, expressly incorporating the provision as to the unanimity of voting, which was at first taken for granted.

The second paragraph of Article VI has had added to it that a majority of the Assembly must approve the appointment of the Secretary General.

The first paragraph of Article VII names Geneva as the seat of the League and is followed by a second paragraph, which gives the Council power to establish the seat of the League elsewhere should it subsequently deem it necessary.

The third paragraph of Article VII is new, establishing equality of employment of men and women—that is to say, by the League.

The second paragraph of Article XIII is new, inasmuch as it undertakes to give instances of disputes which are generally suitable for submission to arbitration, instances of what have latterly been called "justiciable" questions.

The eighth paragraph of Article XV is new. This is the amendment regarding domestic jurisdiction, that where the Council finds that a question arising out of an international dispute affects matters which are clearly under the domestic jurisdiction of one or other of the parties, it report to that effect and make no recommendation.

The last paragraph of Article XV is new, providing for an expulsion from the League in certain extraordinary circumstances.

Article XXI is new. The second paragraph of Article XXII inserts the words with regard to mandatories "and who are willing to accept it," thus explicitly introducing the principle that a mandate cannot be forced upon a nation unwilling to accept it.

Article XXIII is a combination of several former articles and also contains the following: A clause providing for the just treatment of aborigines, a clause looking toward a prevention of the white slave traffic and the traffic in opium, and a clause looking toward progress in international prevention and control of disease.

Article XXV specifically mentions the Red Cross as one of the international organizations which are to connect their work with the work of the League.

Article XXVI permits the amendment of the Covenant by a majority of the States composing the Assembly, instead of three-fourths of the States, though it does not change the requirement in that matter with regard to the vote in the Council.

The second paragraph of Article XXVI is also new and was added at the request of the Brazilian delegation, in order to avoid certain constitutional difficulties. It permits any member of the League to dissent from an amendment, the effect of such dissent being withdrawal from the League.

And the annex is added giving the names of the signatories of the treaty, who become members, and the names of the States invited to accede to the Covenant. These are all the changes, I believe, which are of moment.

Mr. President, I take the opportunity to move the following resolutions in order to carry out the provisions of the Covenant. You will notice that the Covenant provides that the first Secretary General shall be chosen by this conference. It also provides that the first choice of the four member States who are to be added to the five great powers on the Council is left to this conference.

I move, therefore, that the first Secretary General of the Council shall be the Honorable Sir James Eric Drummond, and, second, that until such time as the Assembly shall have selected the first four members of the League to be represented on the Council in accordance with Article IV of the Covenant, representatives of Belgium, Brazil, Greece and Spain shall be members; and, third, that the powers to be represented on the Council of the League of Nations are requested to name representatives who shall form a Committee of Nine to prepare plans for the organization of the League and for the establishment of the seat of the League and to make arrangements and to prepare the agenda for the first meeting of the Assembly, this committee to report both to the Council and to the Assembly of the League.

I think it not necessary to call your attention to other matters we have previously discussed—the capital significance of this Covenant, the hopes which are entertained as to the effect it will have upon steadying the affairs of the world, and the obvious necessity that there should be a concert of the free nations of the world to maintain justice in international relations, the relations between people and between the nations of the world.

If Baron Makino will pardon me for introducing a matter which I absent-mindedly overlooked, it is necessary for me to propose the alteration of several words in the first line of Article V. Let me say that in several parts of the treaty, of which this Covenant will form a part, certain duties are assigned to the Council of the League of Nations. In some instances it is provided that the action they shall take shall be by a majority vote. It is therefore necessary to make the Covenant conform with the other portions of the treaty by adding these words. I will read the first line and add the words:

Except where otherwise expressly provided in this Covenant, or by the terms of this Treaty, decisions at any meeting of the Assembly or of the Council shall require the agreement of all the members of the League represented at the meeting.

"Except where otherwise expressly provided in this covenant" is the present reading, and I move the addition of "or by the terms of this treaty." With that addition, I move the adoption of the Covenant.

THE SHANTUNG SETTLEMENT

STATEMENT CABLED TO MR. TUMULTY, APRIL 30, 1919.
FROM ORIGINAL IN MR. WILSON'S FILES.

THE Japanese-Chinese matter has been settled in a way which seems to me as satisfactory as could be got out of the tangle of treaties in which China herself was involved, and it is important that the exact facts should be known. I therefore send you the following for public use at such time as the matter may come under public discussion. In the treaty all the rights at Kiauchau and in Shantung Province belonging to Germany are to be transferred without reservation to Japan, but Japan voluntarily engages, in answer to questions put in conference, that it will be her immediate policy "to hand back the Shantung Peninsula in full sovereignty to China, retaining only the economic privileges granted to Germany and the right to establish a settlement under the usual conditions at Tsingtao. Owners of the railway will use special police only to insure security for traffic. They will be used for no other purpose. The police force will be composed of Chinese, and such Japanese instructors as the directors of the railway may select will be appointed by the Chinese Government." It was understood in addition that inasmuch as the sovereign rights receded to China were to be unqualified, all Japanese troops remaining on the peninsula should be withdrawn at the earliest possible time. Japan thus gets only such rights as an economic concessionaire as are possessed by one or two other great powers and are only too common in China, and the whole future relationship between the two countries falls at once under the guarantee of the League of Nations of territorial integrity and political independence. I find a general disposition to look with favor upon the proposal that at an early date through the mediation of the League of Nations all extraordinary foreign rights in China and all spheres of influence should be abrogated by the common consent of all the nations concerned. I regard the assurances given by Japan as very satisfactory in view of the complicated circumstances. Please do not give out any of the above as a quotation from me, but use it in some other form for public information at the right time.

WOODROW WILSON.

APPEAL FOR BOY SCOUTS

PROCLAMATION ISSUED MAY 1, 1919, DECLARING JUNE
8 TO JUNE 14 BOY SCOUT WEEK. FROM "UNITED
STATES STATUTES AT LARGE," VOL. 41, PT. 2, PP.
1747-1748.

THE Boy Scouts of America have rendered notable service to the Nation during the World War. They have done effective work in the Liberty Loan and War Savings campaigns, in discovering and reporting upon the black walnut supply, in coöperating with the Red Cross and other war-work agencies, in acting as dispatch bearers for the Committee on Public Information, and in other important fields. The Boy Scouts have not only demonstrated their worth to the Nation, but have also materially contributed to a deeper appreciation by the American people of the higher conceptions of patriotism and good citizenship.

The Boy Scout movement should not only be preserved, but strengthened. It deserves the support of all public-spirited citizens. The available means for the Boy Scout movement have thus far sufficed for the organization and training of only a small proportion of the boys of the country. There are approximately 10,-000,000 boys in the United States, between the ages of twelve and twenty-one. Of these only 375,000 are enrolled as members of the Boy Scouts of America.

America cannot acquit herself commensurately with her power and influence in the great period now facing her and the world unless the boys of America are given better opportunities than heretofore to prepare themselves for the responsibilities of citizenship.

Every nation depends for its future upon the proper training and development of its youth. The American boy must have the best training and discipline our great

476

democracy can provide if America is to maintain her ideals, her standards, and her influence in the world.

The plan, therefore, for a Boy Scout week during which a universal appeal will be made to all Americans to supply the means to put the Boy Scouts of America in a position to carry forward effectively and continuously the splendid work they are doing for the youth of America, should have the unreserved support of the Nation.

Therefore, I, Woodrow Wilson, President of the United States of America, do hereby recommend that the period beginning Sunday, June 8, to Flag Day, June 14, be observed as Boy Scout Week through the United States for the purpose of strengthening the work of the Boy Scouts of America.

I earnestly recommend that, in every community, a Citizens' Committee, under the leadership of a National Citizens' Committee, be organized to coöperate in carrying out a program for a definite recognition of the effective services rendered by the Boy Scouts of America; for a survey of the facts relating to the boyhood of each community, in order that with the coöperation of churches, schools and other organizations definitely engaged in work for boys, adequate provision may be made for extending the Boy Scout program to a larger proportion of American boyhood.

The Boy Scout movement offers unusual opportunity for volunteer service. It needs men to act as committeemen and as leaders of groups of boys. I hope that all who can will enlist for such personal service, enroll as associate members and give all possible financial assistance to this worthy organization of American boyhood. Anything that is done to increase the effectiveness of the Boy Scouts of America will be a genuine contribution to the welfare of the Nation.

BEFORE THE INTERNATIONAL LAW SOCIETY

ADDRESS AT PARIS, MAY 9, 1919.   FROM THE NEW YORK "TIMES," MAY 11, 1919.

I ESTEEM it a very great pleasure to find myself in this distinguished company and in this companionship of letters. Sir Thomas [1] has been peculiarly generous, as have the gentlemen at the other end of the table, in what they have said of me, but they have given me too high a rôle to play up to. It is particularly difficult to believe oneself to be what has been described in so intimate a company as this. When a great body of people is present, one can assume a pose which is impossible when there is so small a number of critical eyes looking directly at you.

And yet there was one part of Sir Thomas's generous interpretation which was true. What I have tried to do, and what I have said in speaking for America, was to speak the mind of America, to speak the impulse and the principles of America. And the only proof I have of my success is that the spirit of America responded—responded without stint or limit—and proved that it was ready to do that thing which I was privileged to call upon it to do.

And we have illustrated in this spirit of America something which perhaps may serve as a partial guide for the future. May I say that one of the things that has disturbed me in recent months is the unqualified hope that men have entertained everywhere of immediate emancipation from the things that have hampered and oppressed them. You cannot in human experience rush into the light. You have to go through the twilight into the broadening day before the noon comes and the

[1] Sir Thomas Barclay, President of the International Law Society.

478

full sun is on the landscape; and we must see to it that those who hope are not disappointed, by showing them the processes by which that hope must be realized— processes of law, processes of slow disentanglement from the many things that have bound us in the past.

You cannot throw off the habits of society immediately any more than you can throw off the habits of the individual immediately. They must be slowly got rid of, or, rather, they must be slowly altered. They must be slowly adapted, they must be slowly shapen to the new ends for which we would use them. That is the process of law, if law is intelligently conceived.

I thought it a privilege to come here to-night, because your studies were devoted to one of the things which will be of most consequence to men in the future, the intelligent development of international law. In one sense, this great, unprecedented war was fought to give validity to international law, to prove that it has a reality which no nation could afford to disregard; that, while it did not have the ordinary sanctions, while there was no international authority as yet to enforce it, it nevertheless had something behind it which was greater than that, the moral rectitude of mankind.

If we can now give to international law the kind of vitality which it can have only if it is a real expression of our moral judgment, we shall have completed in some sense the work which this war was intended to emphasize.

International law has perhaps sometimes been a little too much thought out in the closet. International law has—may I say it without offense?—been handled too exclusively by lawyers. Lawyers like definite lines. They like systematic arrangements. They are uneasy if they depart from what was done yesterday. They dread experiments. They like charted seas and, if they have no charts, hardly venture to undertake the voyage.

Now we must venture upon uncharted seas, to some extent, in the future. In the new League of Nations we are starting out on uncharted seas, and therefore we must have, I will not say the audacity, but the steadiness of purpose which is necessary in such novel circumstances. And we must not be afraid of new things, at the same time that we must not be intolerant of old things. We must weave out of the old materials the new garments which it is necessary that men should wear.

It is a great privilege if we can do that kind of thinking for mankind—human thinking, thinking that is made up of comprehension of the needs of mankind. And when I think of mankind, I must say I do not always think of well-dressed persons. Most persons are not well dressed. The heart of the world is under very plain jackets, the heart of the world is at very simple firesides, the heart of the world is in very humble circumstances; and, unless you know the pressure of life of the humbler classes, you know nothing of life whatever. Unless you know where the pinch comes you do not know what the pulse has to stand, you do not know what strain the muscles have to bear, you do not know what trial the nerves have to go through to hold on.

To hold on where there is no glee in life is the hard thing. Those of us who can sit sometimes at leisure and read pleasant books and think of the past, the long past, that we have no part in, and project the long future— we are not specimens of mankind. The specimens of mankind have not time to do that, and we must use our leisure when we have it to feel with them and think for them, so that we can translate their desire into a fact, so far as that is possible, and see that that most complicated and elusive of all things which we call justice is accomplished. An easy word to say, and a noble word upon the tongue, but one of the most difficult enterprises of the human spirit!

It is hard to be just to those with whom you are intimate; how much harder it is to conceive the problems of those with whom you are not intimate, and be just to them. To live and let live, to work for people and with people, is at the bottom of the kind of experience which must underlie justice.

The sympathy that has the slightest touch of condescension in it has no touch of helpfulness about it. If you are aware of stooping to help a man, you cannot help him. You must realize that he stands on the same earth with yourself and has a heart like your own, and that you are helping him, standing on that common level and using that common impulse of humanity.

In a sense the old enterprise of national law is played out. I mean that the future of mankind depends more upon the relations of nations to one another, more upon the realization of the common brotherhood of mankind, than upon the separate and selfish development of national systems of law; so that the men who can, if I may express it so, think without language, think the common thoughts of humanity, are the men who will be most serviceable in the immediate future.

God grant that there may be many of them, that many men may see this hope and wish to advance it, and that the plain men everywhere may know that there is no language of society in which he has no brothers or co-laborers, in order to reach the great ends of equity and of high justice.

"THAT QUICK COMRADESHIP OF LETTERS"

ADDRESS AT THE INSTITUTE OF FRANCE, PARIS, MAY 10, 1919. FROM ORIGINAL IN MR. WILSON'S FILES.

IT IS with the keenest sense of gratification and pleasure that I find myself in this company. You have not only said that I was at home here, but you have made me feel at home, sir, by the whole tone and tenor of your cordial welcome. I should in one sense in any case have felt at home, because I am more or less familiar with the works of the members of this Institute. I have worked in the same field. I have felt that quick comradeship of letters which is a very real comradeship, because it is a comradeship of thought and of principle. Therefore, I was prepared to feel at home in the company of men who have worked as I have in a common field.

Fortunately, sir, there is one thing which does not excite the jealousy of nations against one another. That is the distinction of thought, the distinction of literature, the achievement of the mind. Nations have always cheered one another in these accomplishments rather than envied one another. Their rivalry has been a generous rivalry, and never an antagonistic rivalry. They have coöperated in the fields of thought as they have not coöperated in other fields. Therefore, this is an old association of sentiment and of principle into which you have permitted me to enter. I would have liked very much sooner to take my actual seat in this company, except that I wanted to deserve your confidence by preferring my duty to my privilege. I wanted to be certain that I was not neglecting the things that you as well as my fellow countrymen would wish me to do in order to have the pleasure of being here in your presence and receiving a greeting, as well as giving to you my own very cordial greeting and adherence.

I have had in recent months one very deep sense of privilege. I have been keenly aware that there have been times when the peoples of Europe have not understood the people of the United States. We have been too often supposed to be a people devoted chiefly, if not entirely, to material enterprises. We have been supposed, in the common phrase, to worship the almighty dollar. We have accumulated wealth, sir, we have devoted ourselves to material enterprises, with extraordinary success, but there has underlain all of that all the time a common sense of humanity and a common sympathy with the high principles of justice, which have never grown dim in the field even of enterprise; and it has been my very great joy in these recent months to interpret the people of the United States to the people of the world. I have not done more, sir. I have not uttered in my public capacity my own private thoughts. I have uttered what I knew to be the thoughts of the great people whom I represent. I have uttered the things that have been stored up in their heart and purpose from the time of our birth as a nation. We came into the world consecrated to liberty, and whenever we see the cause of liberty imperilled we are ready to cast in our lot in common with the lot of those whose liberty is threatened. This is the spirit of the people of the United States, and they have been privileged to send two million men over here to tell you so. It has been their great privilege not merely to tell you so in words, but to tell you so in men and material,—the pouring out of their wealth and the offering of their blood.

So may I not take to myself the pleasant thought that in joining this company I am joining it in some sense as a representative of the people of the United States? Because my studies in the field of political science, sir, have been hardly more than my efforts as a public man. They have constituted an attempt to put into the words of learning the thoughts of a nation, the attitude of a people towards public affairs. A great many of my colleagues in American university life got their training even in political science, as so many men in the civil sciences did, in German universities. I have been obliged at various times to read a great deal of bad German, difficult German, awkward German, and I have been aware that the thought was as awkward as the phrase, that the thought was rooted in a fundamental misconception of the state and of the political life of people. And it has been a portion of my effort to disengage the thought of American university teachers from this misguided instruction which they have received on this side of the sea. Their American spirit emancipated most of them as a matter of course, but the form of the thought sometimes misled them. They spoke too often of the State as a thing which could ignore the individual, as a thing which was privileged to dominate the fortune of men by a sort of inherent and sacred authority. Now, as an utter democrat I have never been able to accept that view of the State. My view of the State is that it must stoop and listen to what I have to say, no matter how humble I am, and that each man has the right to have his voice heard and his counsel heeded, in so far as it is worthy of heed.

I have always been among those who believed that the greatest freedom of speech was the greatest safety, because if a man is a fool, the best thing to do is to encourage him to advertise the fact by speaking. It cannot be so easily discovered if you allow him to remain silent and look wise, but if you let him speak, the secret is out and the world knows that he is a fool. So it is by the exposure of folly that it is defeated; not by the seclusion of folly, and in this free air of free speech men get into that sort of communication with one another which constitutes the basis of all common achievement. France through many vicissitudes and through many bitter experiences found the way to this sort of freedom, and now she stands at the front of the world as the representative of constitutional liberty.

DOMESTIC PROBLEMS AFTER THE WAR

MESSAGE COMMUNICATED BY CABLE TO THE TWO HOUSES
OF CONGRESS AT THE BEGINNING OF THE FIRST SES-
SION OF THE SIXTY-SIXTH CONGRESS, MAY 20, 1919.
FROM OFFICIAL GOVERNMENT PUBLICATION IN MR.
WILSON'S FILES.

I DEEPLY regret my inability to be present at the opening of the extraordinary session of the Congress. It still seems to be my duty to take part in the counsels of the Peace Conference and contribute what I can to the solution of the innumerable questions to whose settlement it has had to address itself: for they are questions which affect the peace of the whole world and from them, therefore, the United States cannot stand apart. I deemed it my duty to call the Congress together at this time because it was not wise to postpone longer the provisions which must be made for the support of the government. Many of the appropriations which are absolutely necessary for the maintenance of the government and the fulfillment of its varied obligations for the fiscal year 1919-1920 have not yet been made; the end of the present fiscal year is at hand; and action upon these appropriations can no longer be prudently delayed. It is necessary, therefore, that I should immediately call your attention to this critical need. It is hardly necessary for me to urge that it may receive your prompt attention.

I shall take the liberty of addressing you on my return on the subjects which have most engrossed our attention and the attention of the world during these last anxious months, since the armistice of last November was signed, the international settlements which must form the subject matter of the present treaties of peace and of our national action in the immediate future. It would be premature to discuss them or to express a judgment about them before they are brought to their complete formulation by the agreements which are now being sought at the table of the Conference. I shall hope to lay them before you in their many aspects so soon as arrangements have been reached.

I hesitate to venture any opinion or press any recommendation with regard to domestic legislation while absent from the United States and out of daily touch with intimate sources of information and counsel. I am conscious that I need, after so long an absence from Washington, to seek the advice of those who have remained in constant contact with domestic problems and who have known them close at hand from day to day; and I trust that it will very soon be possible for me to do so. But there are several questions pressing for consideration to which I feel that I may, and indeed must, even now direct your attention, if only in general terms. In speaking of them I shall, I dare say, be doing little more than speak your own thoughts. I hope that I shall speak your own judgment also.

The question which stands at the front of all others in every country amidst the present great awakening is the question of labor; and perhaps I can speak of it with as great advantage while engrossed in the consideration of interests which affect all countries alike as I could at home and amidst the interests which naturally most affect my thought, because they are the interests of our own people.

By the question of labor I do not mean the question of efficient industrial production, the question of how labor is to be obtained and made effective in the great process of sustaining populations and winning success amidst commercial and industrial rivalries. I mean that much greater and more vital question, how are the men and women who do the daily labor of the world to obtain progressive improvement in the conditions of their labor, to be made happier, and to be served better

by the communities and the industries which their labor
sustains and advances? How are they to be given their
right advantage as citizens and human beings?

We cannot go any further in our present direction.
We have already gone too far. We cannot live our
right life as a nation or achieve our proper success as an
industrial community if capital and labor are to continue
to be antagonistic instead of being partners. If they
are to continue to distrust one another and contrive how
they can get the better of one another. Or, what perhaps amounts to the same thing, calculate by what form
and degree of coercion they can manage to extort on the
one hand work enough to make enterprise profitable, on
the other justice and fair treatment enough to make life
tolerable. That bad road has turned out a blind alley.
It is no thoroughfare to real prosperity. We must find
another, leading in another direction and to a very different destination. It must lead not merely to accommodation but also to a genuine coöperation and partnership based upon a real community of interest and
participation in control.

There is now in fact a real community of interest
between capital and labor, but it has never been made
evident in action. It can be made operative and manifest only in a new organization of industry. The genius
of our business men and the sound practical sense of
our workers can certainly work such a partnership out
when once they realize exactly what it is that they seek
and sincerely adopt a common purpose with regard to it.

Labor legislation lies, of course, chiefly with the
states; but the new spirit and method of organization
which must be effected are not to be brought about by
legislation so much as by the common counsel and voluntary coöperation of capitalist, manager, and workman.
Legislation can go only a very little way in commanding
what shall be done. The organization of industry is a
matter of corporate and individual initiative and of
practical business arrangement. Those who really desire

a new relationship between capital and labor can readily find a way to bring it about; and perhaps Federal legislation can help more than state legislation could.

The object of all reform in this essential matter must be the genuine democratization of industry, based upon a full recognition of the right of those who work, in whatever rank, to participate in some organic way in every decision which directly affects their welfare or the part they are to play in industry. Some positive legislation is practicable. The Congress has already shown the way to one reform which should be worldwide, by establishing the eight-hour day as the standard day in every field of labor over which it can exercise control. It has sought to find the way to prevent child labor, and will, I hope and believe, presently find it. It has served the whole country by leading the way in developing the means of preserving and safeguarding life.and health in dangerous industries. It can now help in the difficult task of giving a new form and spirit to industrial organization by coördinating the several agencies of conciliation and adjustment which have been brought into existence by the difficulties and mistaken policies of the present management of industry, and by setting up and developing new Federal agencies of advice and information which may serve as a clearing-house for the best experiments and the best thought on this great matter, upon which every thinking man must be aware that the future development of society directly depends. Agencies of international counsel and suggestion are presently to be created in connection with the League of Nations in this very field; but it is national action and the enlightened policy of individuals, corporations, and societies within each nation that must bring about the actual reforms. The members of the committees on labor in the two houses will hardly need suggestions from me as to what means they shall seek to make the Federal Government the agent of the whole

Nation in pointing out and, if need be, guiding the process of reorganization and reform.

I am sure that it is not necessary for me to remind you that there is one immediate and very practical question of labor that we should meet in the most liberal spirit. We must see to it that our returning soldiers are assisted in every practicable way to find the places for which they are fitted in the daily work of the country. This can be done by developing and maintaining upon an adequate scale the admirable organization created by the Department of Labor for placing men seeking work; and it can also be done, in at least one very great field, by creating new opportunities for individual enterprise. The Secretary of the Interior has pointed out the way by which returning soldiers may be helped to find and take up land in the hitherto undeveloped regions of the country which the Federal Government has already prepared or can readily prepare for cultivation and also on many of the cutover or neglected areas which lie within the limits of the older states; and I once more take the liberty of recommending very urgently that his plans shall receive the immediate and substantial support of the Congress.

Peculiar and very stimulating conditions await our commerce and industrial enterprise in the immediate future. Unusual opportunities will presently present themselves to our merchants and producers in foreign markets, and large fields for profitable investment will be opened to our free capital. But it is not only of that that I am thinking; it is not chiefly of that that I am thinking. Many great industries prostrated by the war wait to be rehabilitated, in many parts of the world where what will be lacking is not brains or willing hands or organizing capacity or experienced skill, but machinery and raw materials and capital. I believe that our business men, our merchants, our manufacturers and our capitalists will have the vision to see that prosperity in one part of the world ministers to prosperity every-

where: that there is in a very true sense a solidarity of
interest throughout the world of enterprise, and that
our dealings with the countries that have need of our
products and our money will teach them to deem us
more than ever friends whose necessities we seek in the
right way to serve.

Our new merchant ships, which have in some quarters
been feared as destructive rivals, may prove helpful
rivals, rather, and common servants, very much needed
and very welcome. Our great shipyards, new and old,
will be so opened to the use of the world that they will
prove immensely serviceable to every maritime people
in restoring, much more rapidly than would otherwise
have been possible, the tonnage wantonly destroyed in
the war. I have only to suggest that there are many
points at which we can facilitate American enterprise
in foreign trade by opportune legislation and make it
easy for American merchants to go where they will be
welcomed as friends rather than as dreaded antagonists.
America has a great and honorable service to perform in
bringing the commercial and industrial undertakings of
the world back to their old scope and swing again, and
putting a solid structure of credit under them. All
our legislation should be friendly to such plans and
purposes.

And credit and enterprise alike will be quickened by
timely and helpful legislation with regard to taxation.
I hope that the Congress will find it possible to undertake an early reconsideration of Federal taxes, in order
to make our system of taxation more simple and easy
of administration and the taxes themselves as little burdensome as they can be made and yet suffice to support
the Government and meet all its obligations. The figures to which those obligations have arisen are very
great indeed, but they are not so great as to make it
difficult for the Nation to meet them, and meet them,
perhaps, in a single generation, by taxes which will
neither crush nor discourage. These are not so great

as they seem, not so great as the immense sums we have had to borrow, added to the immense sums we have had to raise by taxation, would seem to indicate; for a very large proportion of those sums were raised in order that they might be loaned to the governments with which we were associated in the war, and those loans will, of course, constitute assets, not liabilities, and will not have to be taken care of by our taxpayers.

The main thing we shall have to care for is that our taxation shall rest as lightly as possible on the productive resources of the country, that its rates shall be stable, and that it shall be constant in its revenue-yielding power. We have found the main sources from which it must be drawn. I take it for granted that its mainstays will henceforth be the income tax, the excess profits tax, and the estate tax. All these can so be adjusted to yield constant and adequate returns and yet not constitute a too grievous burden on the taxpayer. A revision of the income tax has already been provided for by the act of 1918, but I think you will find that further changes can be made to advantage both in the rates of the tax and in the method of its collection. The excess profits tax need not long be maintained at the rates which were necessary while the enormous expenses of the war had to be borne; but it should be made the basis of a permanent system which will reach undue profits without discouraging the enterprise and activity of our business men. The tax on inheritances ought, no doubt, to be reconsidered in its relation to the fiscal systems of the several states, but it certainly ought to remain a permanent part of the fiscal system of the Federal Government also.

Many of the minor taxes provided for in the revenue legislation of 1917 and 1918, though no doubt made necessary by the pressing necessities of the war time, can hardly find sufficient justification under the easier circumstances of peace, and can now happily be got rid of. Among these, I hope you will agree, are the excises upon various manufacturers and the taxes upon retail sales. They are unequal in the incidence on different industries and on different individuals. Their collection is difficult and expensive. Those which are levied upon articles sold at retail are largely evaded by the readjustment of retail prices. On the other hand, I should assume that it is expedient to maintain a considerable range of indirect taxes; and the fact that alcoholic liquors will presently no longer afford a source of revenue by taxation makes it the more necessary that the field should be carefully restudied in order that equivalent sources of revenue may be found which it will be legitimate, and not burdensome, to draw upon. But you have at hand in the Treasury Department many experts who can advise you upon the matters much better than I can. I can only suggest the lines of a permanent and workable system, and the placing of the taxes where they will least hamper the life of the people.

There is, fortunately, no occasion for undertaking in the immediate future any general revision of our system of import duties. No serious danger of foreign competition now threatens American industries. Our country has emerged from the war less disturbed and less weakened than any of the European countries which are our competitors in manufacture. Their industrial establishments have been subjected to greater strain than ours, their labor force to a more serious disorganization, and this is clearly not the time to seek an organized advantage. The work of mere reconstruction will, I am afraid, tax the capacity and the resources of their people for years to come. So far from there being any danger or need of accentuated foreign competition, it is likely that the conditions of the next few years will greatly facilitate the marketing of American manufactures abroad. Least of all should we depart from the policy adopted in the Tariff Act of 1913, of permitting the free entry into the United States of the raw materials needed to supplement and enrich our own abundant supplies.

Nevertheless, there are parts of our tariff system which need prompt attention. The experiences of the war have made it plain that in some cases too great reliance on foreign supply is dangerous, and that in determining certain parts of our tariff policy domestic considerations must be borne in mind which are political as well as economic. Among the industries to which special consideration should be given is that of the manufacture of dyestuffs and related chemicals. Our complete dependence upon German supplies before the war made the interruption of trade a cause of exceptional economic disturbance. The close relation between the manufacturer of dyestuffs, on the one hand, and of explosives and poisonous gases, on the other, moreover, has given the industry an exceptional significance and value. Although the United States will gladly and unhesitatingly join in the program of international disarmament, it will, nevertheless, be a policy of obvious prudence to make certain of the successful maintenance of many strong and well-equipped chemical plants. The German chemical industry, with which we will be brought into competition, was and may well be again, a thoroughly knit monopoly capable of exercising a competition of a peculiarly insidious and dangerous kind.

The United States should, moreover, have the means of properly protecting itself whenever our trade is discriminated against by foreign nations, in order that we may be assured of that equality of treatment which we hope to accord and to promote the world over. Our tariff laws as they now stand provide no weapon of retaliation in case other governments should enact legislation unequal in its bearing on our products as compared with the products of other countries. Though we are as far as possible from desiring to enter upon any course of retaliation, we must frankly face the fact that hostile legislation by other nations is not beyond the range of possibility, and that it may have to be met by counter legislation. This subject, has, fortunately, been exhaustively investigated by the United States Tariff Commission. A recent report of that Commission has shown very clearly that we lack and that we ought to have the instruments necessary for the assurance of equal and equitable treatment. The attention of the Congress has been called to this matter on past occasions, and the past measures which are now recommended by the Tariff Commission are substantially the same that have been suggested by previous administrations. I recommend that this phase of the tariff question receive the early attention of the Congress.

Will you not permit me, turning from these matters, to speak once more and very earnestly of the proposed amendment to the Constitution which would extend the suffrage to women and which passed the House of Representatives at the last session of the Congress? It seems to me that every consideration of justice and of public advantage calls for the immediate adoption of that amendment and its submission forthwith to the legislatures of the several states. Throughout all the world this long-delayed extension of the suffrage is looked for; in the United States, longer, I believe, than anywhere else, the necessity for it, and the immense advantage of it to the national life, has been urged and debated, by women and men who saw the need for it and urged the policy of it when it required steadfast courage to be so much beforehand with the common conviction; and I, for one, covet for our country the distinction of being among the first to act in a great reform.

The telegraph and telephone lines will of course be returned to their owners so soon as the retransfer can be effected without administrative confusion, so soon, that is, as the change can be made with least possible inconvenience to the public and to the owners themselves. The railroads will be handed over to their owners at the end of the calendar year; if I were in immediate contact with the administrative questions which must govern the retransfer of the telegraph and telephone lines, I could name the exact date for their return also. Until I am in direct contact with the practical questions involved I can only suggest that in the case of the telegraphs and telephones, as in the case of the railways, it is clearly desirable in the public interest that some legislation should be considered which may tend to make of these indispensable instrumentalities of our modern life a uniform and coördinated system which will afford those who use them as complete and certain means of communication with all parts of the country as has so long been afforded by the postal system of the Government, and at rates as uniform and intelligible. Expert advice is, of course, available in this very practical matter, and the public interest is manifest. Neither the telegraph nor the telephone service of the country can be said to be in any sense a national system. There are many confusions and inconsistencies of rates. The scientific means by which communication by such instrumentalities could be rendered more thorough and satisfactory has not been made full use of. An exhaustive study of the whole question of electrical communication and of the means by which the central authority of the Nation can be used to unify and improve it, if undertaken, by the appropriate committees of the Congress, would certainly result, indirectly even if not directly, in a great public benefit.

The demobilization of the military forces of the country has progressed to such a point that it seems to me entirely safe now to remove the ban upon the manufacture and sale of wines and beers, but I am advised that without further legislation I have not the legal authority to remove the present restrictions. I therefore recommend that the Act approved November 21, 1918, entitled, "An Act to enable the Secretary of Agriculture to carry out, during the fiscal year ending June 30, 1919, the purposes of the Act entitled 'An Act to provide fur-

ther for the national security and defense by stimulating
agriculture and facilitating the distribution of agricultural products,' and for other purposes," be amended
or repealed in so far as it applies to wines and beers.

I sincerely trust that I shall very soon be at my post
in Washington again to report upon the matters which
made my presence at the peace table apparently imperative, and to put myself at the service of the Congress in
every matter of administration or counsel that may
seem to demand executive action or advice.

TRIBUTE TO PRESIDENT-ELECT OF BRAZIL

SPEECH AT DINNER GIVEN BY THE PAN-AMERICAN PEACE DELEGATION IN HONOR O.F DR. EPITACIO PESSOA, PRESIDENT-ELECT OF BRAZIL. PARIS, MAY 27, 1919. FROM THE NEW YORK "TIMES," MAY 28, 1919.

THE honor has been accorded me of making the first speech to-night, and I am very glad to avail myself of that privilege. I want to say that I feel very much at home in this company, though, after all I suppose no one of us feels thoroughly at home except on the other side of the water. We all feel in a very real sense that we have a common home, because we live in the atmosphere of the same conceptions and, I think, with the same political ambitions and principles.

I am particularly glad to have the opportunity of paying my respects to Mr. Pessoa. It is very delightful, for one thing, if I may say so, to know that my presidency is not ahead of me and that his presidency is ahead of him. I wish him every happiness and every success with the greatest earnestness, and yet I cannot, if I may judge by my own experience, expect for him a very great exhilaration in the performance of the duties of his office, because, after all, to be the head of an American State is a task of unrelieved responsibility. American constitutions as a rule put so many duties of the highest sort upon the President, and so much of the responsibility of affairs of state is centered upon him, that his years of office are apt to be years a little weighted with anxiety, a little burdened with the sense of the obligation of speaking for his people, speaking what they really think and endeavoring to accomplish what they really desire.

I suppose no more delicate task is given any man than

to interpret the feelings and the purposes of a great people. I know that, if I may speak for myself, the chief anxiety I have had has been to be the true interpreter of a national spirit, expressing no private and peculiar views, but trying to express the general spirit of a nation. And a nation looks to its President to do that; and the comradeship of an evening like this does not consist merely of the sense of neighborhood. We are neighbors. We have always been friends. But that is all old. Something new has happened. I am not sure that I can put it into words, but there has been added to the common principles which have united the Americas time out of mind a feeling that the world at large has accepted those principles, that there has gone a thrill of hope and of expectation throughout the nations of the world which somehow seems to have its source and fountain in the things we always believed in. It is as if the pure waters of the fountains we had always drunk from had now been put to the lips of all peoples, and they had drunk and were refreshed.

And it is a delightful thought to believe that these are fountains which sprang up out of the soil of the Americas. I am not, of course, suggesting or believing that political liberty had its birth in the American hemisphere, because of course it had not, but the peculiar expression of it characteristic of the modern time, that broad republicanism, that genuine feeling and practice of democracy, that is becoming characteristic of the modern world, did have its origin in America, and the response of the peoples of the world to this new expression is, we may perhaps pride ourselves, a response to an American suggestion.

If that is true, we owe the world a peculiar service. If we originated great practices, we must ourselves be worthy of them. I remember not long ago attending a very interesting meeting which was held in the interest of combining Christian missionary effort throughout the world. I mean eliminating the rivalry between churches and agreeing that Christian missionaries should not represent this, that or the other church, but represent the general Christian impulse and principle of the world. I said I was thoroughly in sympathy with the principle, but that I hoped, if it was adopted, the inhabitants of the heathen countries would not come to look at us, because we were not ourselves united, but divided; that while we were asking them to unite, we ourselves did not set the example.

My moral from that recollection is this: We, among other friends of liberty, are asking the world to unite in the interest of brotherhood and mutual service and the genuine advancement of individual and corporate liberty throughout the world; therefore we must set the example.

I will recall here to some of you an effort that I myself made some years ago, soon after I assumed the Presidency of the United States, to do that very thing. I was urging the other States of America to unite with the United States in doing something which very closely resembled the formation of the present League of Nations. I was ambitious to have the Americas do the thing first and set the example to the world of what we are now about to realize. I had a double object in it, not only my pride that the Americas should set the example and show the genuineness of their principles, but that the United States should have a new relation to the other Americas. The United States upon a famous occasion warned the governments of Europe that it would regard it as an unfriendly act if they tried to overturn free institutions in the Western Hemisphere and to substitute their own systems of government, which at that time were inimical to those free institutions; but, while the United States thus undertook of its own motion to be the champion of America against such aggressions from Europe, it did not give any conclusive assurance that it would never itself be the aggressor. What I wanted to do in the proposals to which I have just referred was to offer to the other American States our own bond that they were safe against us, and any illicit ambitions we might entertain, as well as safe, so far as the power of the United States could make them safe, against foreign nations.

Of course, I am sorry that happy consummation did not come, but, after all, no doubt the impulse was contributed to by us which has now led to a sort of mutual pledge on the part of all the self-governing nations of the world that they will be friends to each other, not only, but that they will take pains to secure each other's safety and independence and territorial integrity.

No greater thing has ever happened in the political world than that, and I am particularly gratified to-night to think of the hours I have had the pleasure of spending with Mr. Pessoa as a member, along with him, of the Commission on the League of Nations, which prepared the Covenant which was submitted to the Conference. I have felt, as I looked down the table and caught his eye, that we had the same American mind in regard to the business, and when I made suggestions or used arguments that I felt were characteristically American, I would always catch sympathy in his eyes. When others perhaps did not catch the point at once, he always caught it, because, though we were not bred to the same language literally, we were bred to the same political language and the same political thought, and our ideas were the same.

It is, therefore, with a real sense of communication and of fellowship and of something more than neighborly familiarity that I find myself in this congenial company and that I take my part with you in paying my tribute and extending my warmest, best wishes to the great country of Brazil and to the gentleman who will worthily represent her in her Presidential chair.

I ask you to join with me in drinking the health of the President-elect of Brazil.

MEMORIAL DAY MESSAGE

CABLEGRAM TO THE AMERICAN PEOPLE, MAY 30, 1919.
FROM THE "CONGRESSIONAL RECORD," VOL. 58,
P. 446.

MY FELLOW COUNTRYMEN:
Memorial Day this year wears an added significance, and I wish, if only by a message, to take part with you in its observation and in expressing the sentiments which it inevitably suggests. In observing the day we commemorate not only the reunion of our own country, but also the liberation of the world from one of the most serious dangers to which free government and the free life of men were ever exposed.

We have buried the gallant and now immortal men who died in this great war of liberation with a new sense of consecration. Our thoughts and purposes now are consecrated to the maintenance of the liberty of the world and of the union of its people in a single comradeship of liberty and of right. It was for this that our men conscientiously offered their lives. They came to the field of battle with the high spirit and pure heart of crusaders. We must never forget the duty that their sacrifice has laid upon us of fulfilling their hopes and their purposes to the utmost. This, it seems to me, is the impressive lesson and inspiring mandate of the day.

SURESNES CEMETERY SPEECH

MEMORIAL DAY ADDRESS AT SURESNES CEMETERY, NEAR
PARIS, MAY 30, 1919.   FROM ORIGINAL IN MR.
WILSON'S FILES.

NO ONE with a heart in his breast, no American, no lover of humanity, can stand in the presence of these graves without the most profound emotion. These men who lie here are men of a unique breed. Their like has not been seen since the far days of the Crusades. Never before have men crossed the seas to a foreign land to fight for a cause which they did not pretend was peculiarly their own, but knew was the cause of humanity and of mankind. And when they came, they found fit comrades for their courage and their devotion. They found armies of liberty already in the field—men who, though they had gone through three years of fiery trial, seemed only to be just discovering, not for a moment losing, the high temper of the great affair, men seasoned in the bloody service of liberty. Joining hands with these, the men of America gave that greatest of all gifts, the gift of life and the gift of spirit.

It will always be a treasured memory on the part of those who knew and loved these men that the testimony of everybody who saw them in the field of action was of their unflinching courage, their ardor to the point of audacity, their full consciousness of the high cause they had come to serve, and their constant vision of the issue. It is delightful to learn from those who saw these men fight and saw them waiting in the trenches for the summons to the fight that they had a touch of the high spirit of religion, that they knew they were exhibiting a spirit as well as a physical might, and those of us who know and love America know that they were discovering to the whole world the true spirit and devotion of their motherland. It was America who came in the person of these men and who will forever be grateful that she was so represented.

And it is the more delightful to entertain these thoughts because we know that these men, though buried in a foreign, are not buried in an alien soil. They are at home, sleeping with the spirits of those who thought the same thoughts and entertained the same aspirations. The noble women of Suresnes have given evidence of the loving sense with which they received these dead as their own, for they have cared for their graves, they have made it their interest, their loving interest, to see that there was no hour of neglect, and that constantly through all the months that have gone by, the mothers at home should know that there were mothers here who remembered and honored their dead.

You have just heard in the beautiful letter from Monsieur Clemenceau what I believe to be the real message of France to us on a day like this, a message of genuine comradeship, a message of genuine sympathy, and I have no doubt that if our British comrades were here, they would speak in the same spirit and in the same language. For the beauty of this war is that it has brought a new partnership and a new comradeship and a new understanding into the field of the effort of the nations.

But it would be no profit to us to eulogize these illustrious dead if we did not take to heart the lesson which they have taught us. They are dead; they have done their utmost to show their devotion to a great cause, and they have left us to see to it that that cause shall not be betrayed, whether in war or in peace. It is our privilege and our high duty to consecrate ourselves afresh on a day like this to the objects for which they fought. It is not necessary that I should rehearse to you what those objects were. These men did not come across the sea merely to defeat Germany and her associated powers in the war. They came to defeat forever the things for which the Central powers stood, the sort of power they meant to assert in the world, the arrogant, selfish dominance which they meant to establish; and they came, moreover, to see to it that there should never be a war like this again. It is for us, particularly for us who are civilians, to use our proper weapons of counsel and agreement to see to it that there never is such a war again. The nation that should now fling out of this common concord of counsel would betray the human race.

So it is our duty to take and maintain the safeguards which will see to it that the mothers of America and the mothers of France and England and Italy and Belgium and all the other suffering nations should never be called upon for this sacrifice again. This can be done. It must be done. And it will be done. The thing that these men left us, though they did not in their counsels conceive it, is the great instrument which we have just erected in the League of Nations. The League of Nations is the covenant of governments that these men shall not have died in vain. I like to think that the dust of those sons of America who were privileged to be buried in their mother country will mingle with the dust of the men who fought for the preservation of the Union, and that as those men gave their lives in order that America might be united, these men have given their lives in order that the world might be united. Those men gave their lives in order to secure the freedom of a nation. These men have given theirs in order to secure the freedom of mankind; and I look forward to an age when it will be just as impossible to regret the results of their labor as it is now impossible to regret the result of the labor of those who fought for the Union of the States. I look for the time when every man who now puts his counsel against the united service of mankind under the League of Nations will be just as ashamed of it as if he now regretted the Union of the States.

You are aware, as I am aware, that the airs of an older day are beginning to stir again, that the standards of an old order are trying to assert themselves again. There is here and there an attempt to insert into the counsel of statesmen the old reckonings of selfishness and bargaining and national advantage which were the roots of this war, and any man who counsels these things advocates the renewal of the sacrifice which these men have made; for if this is not the final battle for right, there will be another that will be final. Let these gentlemen not suppose that it is possible for them to accomplish this return to an order of which we are ashamed and that we are ready to forget. They cannot accomplish it. The peoples of the world are awake and the peoples of the world are in the saddle. Private counsels of statesmen cannot now and cannot hereafter determine the destinies of nations. If we are not the servants of the opinion of mankind, we are of all men the littlest, the most contemptible, the least gifted with vision. If we do not know our age, we cannot accomplish our purpose, and this age is an age which looks forward, not backward; which rejects the standards of national selfishness that once governed the counsels of nations and demands that they shall give way to a new order of things in which the only questions will be, "Is it right?" "Is it just?" "Is it in the interest of mankind?"

This is a challenge that no previous generation ever dared to give ear to. So many things have happened, and they have happened so fast, in the last four years, that I do not think many of us realize what it is that has happened. Think how impossible it would have been to get a body of responsible statesmen seriously to entertain the idea of the organization of a League of Nations four years ago! And think of the change that has taken place! I was told before I came to

France that there would be confusion of counsel about this thing, and I found unity of counsel. I was told that there would be opposition, and I found union of action. I found the statesmen with whom I was about to deal united in the idea that we must have a League of Nations, that we could not merely make a peace settlement and then leave it to make itself effectual, but that we must conceive some common organization by which we should give our common faith that this peace would be maintained and the conclusions at which we had arrived should be made as secure as the united counsels of all the great nations that fought against Germany could make them. We have listened to the challenge, and that is the proof that there shall never be a war like this again.

Ladies and gentlemen, we all believe, I hope, that the spirits of these men are not buried with their bodies. Their spirits live. I hope—I believe—that their spirits are present with us at this hour. I hope that I feel the compulsion of their presence. I hope that I realize the significance of their presence. Think, soldiers, of those comrades of yours who are gone. If they were here, what would they say? They would not remember what you are talking about to-day. They would remember America which they left with their high hope and purpose. They would remember the terrible field of battle. They would remember what they constantly recalled in times of danger, what they had come for and how worth while it was to give their lives for it. And they would say, "Forget all the little circumstances of the day. Be ashamed of the jealousies that divide you. We command you in the name of those who, like ourselves, have died to bring the counsels of men together, and we remind you what America said she was born for. She was born, she said, to show mankind the way to liberty. She was born to make this great gift a common gift. She was born to show men the way of experience by which they might realize this gift and maintain it, and we adjure you in the name of all the great traditions of America to make yourselves soldiers now once for all in this common cause, where we need wear no uniform except the uniform of the heart, clothing ourselves with the principles of right and saying to men everywhere, 'You are our brothers and we invite you into the comradeship of liberty and of peace.'"

Let us go away hearing these unspoken mandates of our dead comrades.

If I may speak a personal word, I beg you to realize the compulsion that I myself feel that I am under. By the Constitution of our great country I was the commander-in-chief of these men. I advised the Congress to declare that a state of war existed. I sent these lads over here to die. Shall I—can I—ever speak a word of counsel which is inconsistent with the assurances I gave them when they came over? It is inconceivable. There is something better, if possible, that a man can give than his life, and that is his living spirit to a service that is not easy, to resist counsels that are hard to resist, to stand against purposes that are difficult to stand against, and to say, "Here stand I, consecrated in spirit to the men who were once my comrades and who are now gone, and who have left me under eternal bonds of fidelity."

INVESTIGATION OF UNAUTHORIZED POSSESSION OF THE TREATY

CABLEGRAM, THROUGH MR. TUMULTY, TO SENATOR G. M. HITCHCOCK OF NEBRASKA, JUNE 7, 1919. FROM THE "CONGRESSIONAL RECORD," VOL. 58, P. 781.

I AM heartily glad that you have demanded an investigation with regard to the possession of text of the treaty by unauthorized persons. I have felt that it was highly undesirable officially to communicate the text of a document which is still in negotiation and subject to change. Anyone who has possession of the official English text has what he is clearly not entitled to have or to communicate. I have felt in honor bound to act in the same spirit and in the same way as the representatives of the other great powers in this matter, and am confident that my fellow countrymen will not expect me to break faith with them. I hope the investigation will be most thoroughly prosecuted.

WOODROW WILSON.

ADDRESSES AT BRUSSELS, JUNE 19, 1919

FROM ORIGINALS IN MR. WILSON'S FILES.

AT LUNCHEON GIVEN BY BRAND WHITLOCK AT THE AMERICAN LEGATION

I WANT to express my pleasure, not only to be in Belgium, but to be personally associated with the King and Queen. We have found them what all the world had told us they were, perfectly genuine, perfectly delightful and perfectly devoted to the interests of their people; and not only so but, what is very rare just now, very just in their judgments of the events of the past and of the events that are now taking place.

I could not help expressing the opinion which I did yesterday that that must arise from the fact that they had intimately associated themselves in life with their people. If you live with the talkers, you get one impression; if you live with the liver, you get another impression. You come into contact with the realities, and only realities make you wise and just. I want, with this very brief preface, in which I am speaking from my heart, to propose the health and long life of His Majesty the King and Her Majesty the Queen.

BEFORE THE BELGIAN CHAMBER OF DEPUTIES

YOUR MAJESTY, AND GENTLEMEN OF THE CHAMBER:
It is with such profound emotion that I express my deep appreciation of the generous welcome you have given me that I am not at all sure that I can find the words to say what it is in my heart to say. Monsieur Hymans has recited to you some of the things which America tried to do to show her profound friendship and sympathy with Belgium, but M. Hymans was not

able to testify as I am to the heart of America that was back of her efforts; for America did not do these things merely because she conceived it her duty to do them, but because she rejoiced in this way to show her real humanity and her real knowledge of the needs of an old and faithful friend, and these things, I hope will be the dearer in your memory because of the spirit which was behind them. They were small in themselves. We often had the feeling that we were not doing as much as we could do. We knew all the time that we were not doing as much as we wanted to do, and it is this spirit, and not what was done, which deserves, I hope, to be remembered.

It is very delightful to find myself at last in Belgium. I have come at the first moment that I was relieved from imperative duty. I could not come for my own pleasure and in neglect of duty to a country where I knew that I should meet men who had done their duty; where I knew I should meet a Sovereign who had constantly identified himself with the interests and the life of his people at every necessary sacrifice to himself; where I should be greeted by a Burgomaster who never allowed the enemy to thrust him aside and always asserted the majesty and authority of the municipality which he represented; where I should have the privilege of meeting a Cardinal who was the true shepherd of his flock, the majesty of whose spiritual authority awed even the unscrupulous enemy himself, who knew that they did not dare lay a hand upon this servant of God; and where I should have the privilege of grasping the hand of a General who never surrendered, and on every hand should meet men who had known their duty and done it. I could not come to Belgium until I felt that I was released from my duty. I sought in this way to honor you by recognizing the spirit which I knew I should meet with here.

When I realize that at my back are the fighting standards of Belgium, it pleases me to think that I am in the presence of those who knew how to shed their blood as well as do their duty for their country. They need no encomium from me. I would rather turn for a moment with you to the significance of the place which Belgium bears in this contest which now, thank God, is ended. I came here because I wished to associate myself in council with the men who I know had felt so deeply the pulse of this terrible struggle, and I wanted to come also because I realized,—I believed,—that Belgium and her part in the war is in one sense the key of the whole struggle, because the violation of Belgium was the call to duty which aroused the nations. The enemy committed many outrages in this war, gentlemen, but the initial outrage was the fundamental outrage of all. They, with an insolent indifference, violated the sacredness of treaties. They showed that they did not care for the honor of any pledge. They showed that they did not care for the independence of any nation, whether it had raised its hand against them or not, that they were ruthless in their determination to have their whim at their pleasure. Therefore, it was the violation of Belgium that wakened the world to the realization of the character of the struggle.

A very interesting thing came out of that struggle which seems almost like an illogical consequence. One of the first things that the representatives of Belgium said to me after the war began was that they did not want their neutrality guaranteed. They did not want any neutrality. They wanted equality. Not because, as I understood them, their neutrality was insecure, but because their neutrality put them upon a different basis of action from other peoples. In their natural and proper pride, they desired to occupy a place that was not exceptional, but in the ranks of free peoples under all governments. I honored this instinct in them, and it was for that reason that the first time I had occasion to speak of what the war might accomplish for Belgium I spoke of her winning a place of equality among the nations.

So Belgium has, so to say, once more come into her own through this deep valley of suffering through which she has gone. Not only that, but her cause has linked the governments of the civilized world together. They have realized their common duty. They have drawn together as if instinctively into a league of right. They have put the whole power of organized mankind behind the conception of justice, which is common to mankind. That is the significance, gentlemen, of the League of Nations.

The League of Nations was an inevitable consequence of this war. It was a league of right, and no thoughtful statesman who let his thought run into the future could wish for a moment to slacken those bonds. His first thought would be to strengthen them and to perpetuate this combination of the great governments of the world for the maintenance of justice. The League of Nations is the child of this great war for right. It is the expression of those permanent resolutions which grew out of the temporary necessities of this great struggle, and any nation which declines to adhere to this Covenant deliberately turns away from the most telling appeal that has ever been made to its conscience and to its manhood. The nation that wishes to use the League of Nations for its convenience, and not for the service of the rest of the world, deliberately chooses to turn back to those bad days of selfish contest, when every nation thought first and always of itself and not of its neighbor, thought of its rights and forgot its duties, thought of its power and overlooked its re sponsibility. Those bad days, I hope, are gone, and the great moral power, backed if need be, by the great physical power of the civilized nations of the world will now stand firm for the maintenance of the fine partnership which we have thus inaugurated.

It cannot be otherwise. Perhaps the conscience of some chancellories was asleep and the outrage of Germany awakened it. You cannot see one great nation

violate every principle of right without beginning to
know what the principles of right are and to love them,
to despise those who violate them, and to form the firm
resolve that such a violation shall now be punished and
in the future be prevented.

These are the feelings with which I have come to
Belgium, and it has been my thought to propose to the
Congress of the United States as a recognition, as a
welcome of Belgium into her new status of complete
independence, to raise the mission of the United States
of America to Belgium to the rank of an Embassy and
send an Ambassador. This is the rank which Belgium
enjoys in our esteem. Why should she not enjoy it in
form and in fact?

So, gentlemen, we turn to the future. M. Hymans
has spoken in true terms of the necessities that lie
ahead of Belgium, and of many another nation that has
come through this great war with suffering and with
loss. We have shown Belgium, in the forms which he
has been generous enough to recite, our friendship in
the past. It is now our duty to organize our friendship
along new lines. The Belgian people and the Belgian
leaders need only the tools to restore their life. Their
thoughts are not crushed. Their purposes are not obscured. Their plans are complete, and their knowledge
of what is involved in industrial revival is complete.
What their friends must do is to see to it that Belgium
gets the necessary priority with regard to obtaining raw
materials, the necessary priority in obtaining the means
to restore the machinery by which she can use these raw
materials, and the credit by which she can bridge over
the years during which it will be necessary for her to
wait to begin again. These are not so much tasks for
governments as they are tasks for thoughtful business
men and financiers and those who are producers in other
countries. It is a question of shipping also, but the
shipping of the world will be relieved of its burdens of
troops in a comparatively near future, and there will be

new bottoms in which to carry the cargoes, and the cargoes ought readily to impel the master of the ship to steer for Belgian ports. I believe, after having consulted many times with my very competent advisers in these matters that an organized method of accomplishing these things can be found. It is a matter of almost daily discussion in Paris, and I believe that as we discuss it from day to day we come nearer and nearer to a workable solution and a practicable plan. I hope, not only, but I believe that such a plan will be found, and you may be sure that America will be pleased,—I will not say more than any other friend of Belgium, but as much as any other friend of Belgium, if these plans are perfected and carried out.

Friendship, gentlemen, is a very practical matter. One thing that I think I have grown weary of is sentiment that does not express itself in action. How real the world has been made by this war: How actual all its facts seem: How terrible the circumstances of its life. And if we be friends, we must think of each other not only, but we must act for each other. We must not only have a sentimental regard, but we must put that regard into actual deeds. There is an old proverb which has no literary beauty but it has a great deal of significance, "The proof of the pudding is the eating thereof." It is by that maxim that all friendships are to be judged. It is when a friendship is put to the proof that its quality is found. So our business now is not to talk but to act; is not so much to debate as to resolve; is not so much to hesitate upon the plan as to perfect the details of the plan, and at every turn to be sure that we think not only of ourselves but of humanity. For, gentlemen, the realities of this world are not discussed around dinner tables. Do you realize for how small a percentage of mankind it is possible to get anything to eat to-morrow if you do not work to-day; how small a percentage of mankind can slacken their physical and thoughtful effort for a moment and not find the means of subsistence fail them? Some men can take holidays. Some men can relieve themselves from the burden of work, but most men cannot, most women cannot, and the children wait upon the men and women who work,—work every day, work from the dawn until the evening. These are the people we must think about. They constitute the rank and file of mankind. They are the constituents of statesmen, and statesmen must see to it that policies are not now run along the lines of national pride, but along the lines of humanity, along the lines of service, along those lines which we have been taught are the real lines by the deep sufferings of this war. This is the healing peace of which M. Hymans eloquently spoke. You heal the nations by serving the nations, and you serve them by thinking of mankind.

AT THE HÔTEL DE VILLE

MR. BURGOMASTER:

I feel highly honored to be received with such words from you, sir, speaking as the representative of this ancient municipality, with so many distinguished events associated with its sturdy independence and self-government; and I feel the more honored, sir, because the whole world recognizes in you a worthy representative of this great municipality.

I think the reflection which comes uppermost in one's mind in thinking about this war is that no nation is conquered that is not conquered in its spirit; that an unconquerable spirit is the last word in politics, and that the unconquerable spirit lives particularly in those nations which are self-governed. The one thing that is indestructible in our time is the spirit of self-governed people. Therefore, it is inspiriting to me and I think to all believers in self-government to be welcomed by an ancient municipality like this, which represents in so distinguished a way the spirit and practice of self-government. I know something, sir, of the history,—

the independence, the self-confidence, the proper self-confidence,—of the municipalities of Belgium. I know how there has persisted into modern times something of that solidarity of the commune, something of that individuality of the municipality, which was characteristic of the Middle Ages and which brought the spirit of self-government through that dark period when nations had ceased to govern themselves, but when localities continued to assert their right of self-government. So that I feel welcomed to-day by those whom I would fain believe to be my friends and the friends of the American people, as the American people are certainly your friends.

They are your friends in a very deep and true sense. They understand what Belgian liberty signifies. They understand what Belgian suffering signifies; and it is, I believe, one of their deepest ambitions to satisfy the duty of friendship as towards the Belgian people. They have tried to do so in the past. It has been one of my pleasures on this trip to be accompanied by my distinguished fellow countryman, Mr. Herbert Hoover, who I know has had Belgium written on his heart throughout this war, and whose pleasure it has been touching to see as in going about the country we have seen healthy children and robust men and women, whom he could properly believe were served by the food which came from America. I believe that I have the privilege of speaking his thoughts. One of the peculiarities of Mr. Hoover is that he is too modest to speak for himself, and therefore I am proud to share with him some of your welcome. I am accompanied by other colleagues with whom I have been in counsel throughout the war and whose thought, I can tell you, has been constantly upon the methods by which Belgium could be helped, whose thought is now upon that subject, whose hope is that some method will be worked out, as I had the privilege of saying to your Parliament today, by which systematic help can be rendered to Belgium.

So I feel peculiarly honored, in this ancient building of this ancient city, to be received at your hands, sir, and I bring you the warm greeting of the people of America. I am sure I express their wish when I say, Long live the prosperity of Brussels and of Belgium, and of her King and Queen.

At a Dinner Given in the President's Honor By the King of Belgium

Let me express, sir, the very deep appreciation with which I have heard your remarks. You truly say that I have come to Belgium to express my own deep personal interest and sympathy,—sympathy with her sufferings and interest in her prosperity. But I would have no personal consequence if it were not my privilege for the time being to represent the people of the United States. What gives me confidence in expressing this sympathy and this interest is that I know in expressing those sentiments that I am expressing the feelings of the people of the United States. There has never been in the United States a more general and universal comprehension of sympathy with the affairs of another Nation than that which the people of the United States have had for the affairs and the people of Belgium.

I have had the very great advantage of seeing the little that I have had time to see of the experiences of Belgium under your guidance, and I know how true it is, sir, that you speak for your people. One of the delightful experiences of these last days has been to hear the acclaim from the heart which everywhere greeted *le roi*. Their first cry was for their king, their second thought was the welcome of the stranger, and I was glad in my heart that it should be so, because I know that I was with a real statesman and a real ruler. No man has any power, sir, except that which is given him by the things and the people he represents.

I have felt many points of sympathy between the

people whom I have the pleasure of representing and the people whom you represent. They are a very democratic people, and it has been very delightful to find, sir, that you are a true democrat. All real masters of the sentiments of the people are parts of the people, and one of the things that gives confidence in the future of Belgium is the consciousness that one has of the self-reliance and the indomitable spirit of her people. They need to have a friendly hand extended to them, but they do not need to have anybody take care of them. A people that is taken care of by its government is a people that its government will always have to take care of, but the people of Belgium, if I have caught any glimpse of their spirit and character, do not need to have anybody take care of them. They need, because of the catastrophes of this war, temporary assistance, to get the means to take care of themselves, but the moment they have these means, then the rest of us will have to take care to see that they do not do the work they are addicted to do better than we do. The minute we cease to offer this assistance, they will become our generous and dangerous rivals, and for my part I believe I can say truthfully that the people of the United States want the people of Belgium to recover their power to be rivals, to be rivals in those fields in which they have for so long a time proved themselves masters.

It is, therefore, with a peculiar feeling of being among the people that I understand that I have found myself under your guidance, sir, touching shoulders with the people of Belgium. To-day when I went to the great destroyed plant of Charleroi, though most of the chimneys were smokeless, the whole region seemed like so many regions I am familiar with in my own country, and if the air had only been full of smoke, I should have felt entirely at home. The air was too clear to be natural in such a region; and yet I had the feeling that smoke was going to come in its old abundance from those chimneys, and the world of industry was once more going to feel the pulse of Belgium, that vital pulse which no discouragement can restrain.

So it is with a heart full of genuine sympathy, of comradeship and of friendship that I beg to drink to your health, sir, and the Queen's and to the long and abounding prosperity of the kingdom over which you preside.

AT A DINNER GIVEN BY M. POINCARÉ

SPEECH AT A DINNER IN HIS HONOR IN PARIS, GIVEN BY
PRESIDENT POINCARÉ OF FRANCE, JUNE 26, 1919.

I THANK you most sincerely for the words that you
have uttered. I cannot pretend, sir, that the prospect of going home is not very delightful to me, but I
can say with the greatest sincerity that the prospect of
leaving France is very painful to me.

I have received a peculiarly generous welcome here,
and it has been pleasing for me to feel that that welcome was intended not so much for myself as for the
people whom I represented.

Sometimes the work of the conference has seemed to
go very slowly indeed. Sometimes it has seemed as if
there were unnecessary obstacles to agreement, but as the
weeks have lengthened I have seemed to see the profit
that came out of that. Quick conclusions would not
have produced that intimate knowledge of each other's
mind which I think has come out of these daily conferences.

These six months have been six months which have
woven new fibers of connections between the hearts of
our people. And something more than friendship and
intimate sympathy has come out of this intercourse.

A new thing that has happened is that we have translated our common principles and our common purposes
into a common plan.

When we part, we are not going to part with a finished work, but with a work one portion of which is
finished and the other portion of which is only begun.

We have finished the formulation of the peace, but
we have begun a plan of coöperation which I believe will
broaden and strengthen as the years go by.

We shall continue to be co-workers in tasks which, because they are common, will weave out of our sentiments a common conception of duty and a common conception of the rights of men of every race and of every clime. If it be true that that has been accomplished, it is a very great thing.

As I go away from these scenes, I think I shall realize that I have been present at one of the most vital things that has happened in the history of nations. Nations have formed contracts with each other before, but they never have formed partnerships. They have associated themselves temporarily, but they have never before associated themselves permanently.

The wrong that was done in the waging of this war was a great wrong, but it wakened the world to a great moral necessity of seeing that it was necessary that men should band themselves together in order that such a wrong should never be perpetrated again.

Merely to beat a nation that was wrong once is not enough. There must follow the warning to all other nations that would do like things that they in turn will be vanquished and shamed if they attempt a dishonorable purpose.

ON DEPARTURE FROM FRANCE

STATEMENT ON THE EVE OF FINAL DEPARTURE FROM FRANCE, JUNE 28, 1919. FROM THE NEW YORK "TIMES," JUNE 29, 1919.

AS I LOOK back over the eventful months I have spent in France, my memory is not of conferences and hard work alone, but also of innumerable acts of generosity and friendship which have made me feel how genuine the sentiments of France are towards the people of America and how fortunate I have been to be the representative of our people in the midst of a nation which knows how to show us kindness with so much charm and so much open manifestation of what is in its heart.

Deeply happy as I am at the prospect of joining my own countrymen again, I leave France with genuine regret, my deep sympathy for her people and belief in her future confirmed, my thought enlarged by the privilege of association with her public men, conscious of more than one affectionate friendship formed, and profoundly grateful for unstinted hospitality and for countless kindnesses which have made me feel welcome and at home.

I take the liberty of bidding France godspeed as well as good-by, and of expressing once more my abiding interest and entire confidence in her future.

"THE TREATY HAS BEEN SIGNED"

CABLEGRAM, THROUGH MR. TUMULTY, TO THE AMER-
ICAN PEOPLE, JUNE 28, 1919. FROM THE "CON-
GRESSIONAL RECORD," VOL. 58, PP. 1952-1953.

THE treaty of peace has been signed. If it is ratified and acted upon in full and sincere execution of its terms it will furnish the charter for a new order of affairs in the world. It is a severe treaty in the duties and penalties it imposes upon Germany, but it is severe only because great wrongs done by Germany are to be righted and repaired; it imposes nothing that Germany cannot do; and she can regain her rightful standing in the world by the prompt and honorable fulfillment of its terms. And it is much more than a treaty of peace with Germany. It liberates great peoples who have never before been able to find the way to liberty. It ends once for all, an old and intolerable order under which small groups of selfish men could use the peoples of great empires to serve their own ambition for power and dominion. It associates the free Governments of the world in a permanent league in which they are pledged to use their united power to maintain peace by maintaining right and justice. It makes international law a reality supported by imperative sanctions. It does away with the right of conquest and rejects the policy of annexation and substitutes a new order under which backward nations—populations which have not yet come to political consciousness and peoples who are ready for independence but not yet quite prepared to dispense with protection and guidance—shall no more be subjected to the domination and exploitation of a stronger nation, but shall be put under the friendly direction and afforded the helpful assistance of governments which undertake to be responsible to the opinion

of mankind in the execution of their task by accepting
the direction of the League of Nations. It recognizes
the inalienable rights of nationality; the rights of minorities and the sanctity of religious belief and practice. It
lays the basis for conventions which shall free the commercial intercourse of the world from unjust and vexa-
tious restrictions and for every sort of international
coöperation that will serve to cleanse the life of the
world and facilitate its common action in beneficent service of every kind. It furnishes guarantees such as
were never given or even contemplated before for the
fair treatment of all who labor at the daily tasks of
the world. It is for this reason that I have spoken of
it as a great charter for a new order of affairs. There
is ground here for deep satisfaction, universal reassurance, and confident hope.

TO GREAT BRITAIN, ON COMPLETION OF THE TREATY

MESSAGE TO THE ENGLISH PEOPLE THROUGH THE "DAILY MAIL" AND THE "WEEKLY DISPATCH," JUNE 30, 1919. FROM THE NEW YORK "TIMES," JUNE 30, 1919.

MANY things crowd into the mind to be said about the Peace Treaty, but the thought that stands out in front of all others is that by the terms of the treaty the greatest possible measure of compensation has been provided for peoples whose homes and lives were wrecked by the storm of war, and security has been given them that the storm shall not arise again.

In so far as we came together to insure these things, the work of the Conference is finished, but in a larger sense its work begins to-day. In answer to an unmistakable appeal, the League of Nations has been constituted and a covenant has been drawn which shows the way to international understanding and peace.

We stand at the crossroads, however, and the way is only pointed out. Those who saw through the travail of war the vision of a world made secure for mankind must now consecrate their lives to its realization.

TO SOLDIERS AND SAILORS ON THE "GEORGE WASHINGTON"

ADDRESS TO THE SOLDIERS AND SAILORS ON THE AFTER
HATCH OF THE U. S. S. "GEORGE WASHINGTON,"
JULY 4, 1919. FROM "THE HATCHET," A PAPER
PUBLISHED ON BOARD THE U. S. S. "GEORGE WASH-
INGTON."

IT IS very delightful to find myself here and in this
company. I know a great many of you have been
homesick on the other side of the water, but I do not
believe a man among you has been as homesick as I
have. It is with profound delight that I find myself
bound westward again for the country we all love and
are trying to serve, and when I was asked to make a
speech and sat down and tried to think out what I should
say, I found that the suggestions of this Fourth of July
crowded into my mind in such a way that they could
not be set in order, and I doubt if I can find expression
to them. Because this Fourth of July has a significance
that no preceding Fourth of July ever had in it, not
even the first. I think that we can look back upon the
history of the years that separated us from the first
Fourth of July with very great satisfaction, because we
have kept the vision in America, we have kept the promise to ourselves that we would maintain a régime of
liberty and of constitutional government.

We have made errors of judgment, we have committed errors of action, but we have always tried to
correct the errors when we have made them. We have
always tried to get straight in the road again for that
goal for which we set out in those famous days when
America was made as a Government. So there has always been abundant justification for what was not self-
glorification, but self-gratulation in our Fourth of July
celebrations. We have successfully maintained the lib-

erties of a great Nation. The past is secure and the past is glorious; and in the present the Fourth of July has taken on a new significance.

We told our fellow men throughout the world when we set up the free state of America that we wanted to serve liberty everywhere and be the friends of men in every part of the world who wanted to throw off the unjust shackles of arbitrary government. Now we have kept our pledge to humanity as well as our pledge to ourselves, for we have thrown everything that we possessed,—all the gifts that nature had showered upon us and our own lives,—into the scales to show that we meant to be the servants of humanity and of free men everywhere.

America did not at first see the full meaning of the war that has just ended. At first it looked like a natural raking out of the pent-up jealousies and rivalries of the complicated politics of Europe. Nobody who really knew anything about history supposed that Germany could build up a great military machine like she did and not refrain from using it. They were constantly talking about it as a guarantee of peace, but every man in his senses knew that it was a threat of war, and the threat was finally fulfilled and the war began. We at the distance of America looked on at first without a full comprehension of what the plot was getting into, and then at last we realized that there was here nothing less than a threat against the freedom of free men everywhere.

Then America went in, and if it had not been for America the war would not have been won. My heart swells with a pride that I cannot express when I think of the men who crossed the seas from America to fight on those battlefields. I was proud of them when I could not see them, and now that I have mixed with them and seen them, I am prouder of them still. For they are men to the core, and I am glad to have had Europe see this specimen of our manhood.

I am proud to know how the men who performed the least conspicuous services and the humblest services performed them just as well as the men who performed the conspicuous services and the most complicated and difficult. I will not say that the men were worthy of their officers. I will say that the officers were worthy of their men. They sprang out of the ranks, they were like the ranks, and all,—rank and file,—were specimens of America.

And you know what has happened. Having sampled America that way, Europe believes in and trusts America. Is not that your own personal experience and observation? In all the counsels at Paris, whenever they wanted to send soldiers anywhere and not have the people jealous of their presence or fear the consequences of their presence, they suggested that we should send Americans there, because they knew that everywhere in Europe we were believed to be the friends of the countries where we sent garrisons and where we sent forces of supervision. We were welcome. Am I not, therefore, justified in saying that we have fulfilled our pledge to humanity? We have proved that we were the champions of liberty throughout the world, that we did not wish to keep it as a selfish and private possession of our own but wanted to share it with men everywhere and of every kind.

When you look forward to the future, do you not see what a compulsion that puts upon us? You cannot earn a reputation like that and then not live up to it. You cannot reach a standard like that and then let it down by never so little. Every man of us has to live up to it. The welcome that was given to our arms and the cheers that received us are the compulsion that is now put upon us to continue to be worthy of that welcome and of those cheers. We must continue to put America at the service of mankind. Not for any profit we shall get out of it, not for any private benefit we shall reap from it, but because we believe in the right and mean to serve it wherever we have a chance to serve it.

I was thinking to-day that a new freedom has come to the peoples of the world out of this war. It has no date. It has no Fourth of July. There has nowhere been written a Declaration of Independence. The only date I can think of for it is the eleventh of last November, when the Central Powers admitted they were beaten and accepted an armistice. From that time they knew they had to submit to the terms of liberty, and perhaps some of these days we shall date the freedom of the peoples from the eleventh of November, 1918.

And yet if that be not the date of it, it interests my thought to think that as it had no date for beginning, we should see to it that it had no date for ending: that as it began without term, it should end without term, and that in every counsel we enter into, in every force we contribute to, we shall make it a condition that the liberty of men throughout the world shall be served and that America shall continue to redeem her pledge to humanity and to mankind.

Why, America is made up of mankind. We do not come from any common stock. We do not come from any single nation. The characteristic of America is that it is made up of the best contributed out of all nations. Sometimes when I am in the presence of an American citizen who was an immigrant to America, I think that he has a certain advantage over me. I did not choose to be an American, but he did. I was born to it. I hope if I had not been, I would have had sense enough to choose it. But the men who came afterwards deliberately chose to be Americans.

They came out of other countries, and said, "We cast in our lot with you, we believe in you, and will live with you." A country made up like that ought to understand other nations. It ought to know how to fraternize with and assist them. It is already the friend of mankind, because it is made up out of all people, and it ought to redeem its lineage. It ought to show that it is playing for no private hand. It ought to show that it is trying to serve all the stocks of mankind from which it itself is bred. And more than that, my fellow coun-try-men, we ought to continue to prove that we know what freedom is.

Freedom is not a mere sentiment. We all feel the weakness of mere sentiment. If a man professes to be fine, we always wait for him to show it. We do not take his word for it. If he professes fine motives, we expect him thereafter to show that he is acting upon fine motives. And the kind of freedom that America has always represented is a freedom expressing itself in fact. It is not the profession of principles, merely, but the redemption of those principles, making good on those principles and knowing how to make good on those principles.

When I have thought of liberty, I have sometimes thought how we deceived ourselves in the way we talked about it. Some people talk as if liberty meant the right to do anything you please. Well, in some sense you have that right. You have the right to jump overboard, but if you do, this is what will happen: Nature will say: "You fool, didn't you know the consequences? Didn't you know that water will drown you?" You can jump off the top of the mast, but when you get down your liberty will be lost, and you will have lost it because if it was not an accident you made a fool of yourself. The sailor, when he is sailing a ship, talks about her running free in the wind. Does he mean that she is resisting the wind? Throw her up into the wind and see the canvas shake, see her stand still, "caught in irons," as the sailor says. But let her fall off: she is free. Free, why? Because she is obeying the laws of nature, and she is a slave until she does. And no man is free who does not obey the laws of freedom.

The laws of freedom are these: Accommodate your interests to other people's interests, that you shall not insist on standing in the light of other people, but that you shall make a member of a team of yourself and nothing more or less, and that the interests of the team shall take precedence in everything that you do to your interest as an individual.

That is freedom, and men who live under autocratic governments are not free because the autocrat arranges the government to suit himself. The minute he arranges it to suit his subjects, then his subjects are free.

But if I disobey the laws of freedom, if I infringe on the rights of others, then I presently find myself deprived of my freedom. I am clapped in jail, it may be, and if the jailer is a philosopher, he will say: "You brought it upon yourself, my dear fellow. You were free to do right, but you were not free to do wrong. Now, what I blame you for is not so much for your malice as for your ignorance." One reason why America has been free, I take leave to say, is that America has been intelligent enough to be free. It takes a lot of intelligence to be free. Stupid people do not know how, and we all go to the school of intelligence that comes out of the discipline of our own self-chosen institutions.

That is what makes you free, and my confident ambition for the United States is that she will know in the future how to make each Fourth of July as it comes grow more distinguished and more glorious than its predecessor, by showing that she, at any rate, understands the laws of freedom by understanding the laws of service, and that mankind may always confidently look to her as a friend, as a coöperator, as one who will stand shoulder to shoulder with free men everywhere to assert the right. That is what I meant at the outset of these few remarks by saying that the suggestions of this Fourth of July crowd too thick and fast to be set in order. This is the most tremendous Fourth of July that men ever imagined, for we have opened its franchises to all the world.

RESPONSE TO WELCOME HOME

ADDRESS IN CARNEGIE HALL, NEW YORK, JULY 8, 1919.
FROM THE NEW YORK "TIMES," JULY 9, 1919.

I AM not going to try this afternoon to make you a real speech. I am a bit alarmed to find how many speeches I have in my system undelivered, but they are all speeches that come from the mind, and I want to say to you this afternoon only a few words from the heart.

You have made me deeply happy by the generous welcome you have extended to me. But I do not believe that the welcome you extend to me is half as great as that which I extend to you. Why, Jerseyman though I am, this is the first time I ever thought Hoboken beautiful. I really have, though I have tried on the other side of the water to conceal it, been the most homesick man in the American Expeditionary Force, and it is with feelings that it would be vain for me to try to express that I find myself in this beloved country again.

I do not say that because I lack in admiration of other countries. There have been many things that softened my homesickness. One of the chief things that softened it was the very generous welcome that they extended to me as your representative on the other side of the water, and it was still more softened by the pride that I had in discovering that America had at last convinced the world of her true character. I was welcome because they had seen with their own eyes what America had done for the world. They had deemed her selfish; they had deemed her devoted to material interests, and they had seen her boys come across the water with a vision even more beautiful than that which they conceived when they had entertained dreams of liberty and of peace. And when I had the added pride of finding out

532

by personal observation the kind of men we had sent over—I had crossed the seas with the kind of men who had taken them over; without whom they could not have got to Europe—and then when I got there I saw that army of men, that army of clean men, that army of men devoted to the highest interests of humanity, that army that one was glad to point out and say, "These are my fellow countrymen"—it softens the homesickness a good deal to have so much of home along with you.

And these boys were constantly reminding me of home. They did not walk the streets like anybody else. I do not mean that they walked the streets self-assertively; they did not. They walked the streets as if they knew that they belonged wherever free men lived, that they were welcome in the great Republic of France and were comrades with the other armies that had helped to win the great battle and to show the great sacrifice. It is a wonderful thing for this Nation, hitherto isolated from the large affairs of the world, to win not only the universal confidence of the people of the world, but their universal affection. And that, and nothing less than that, is what has happened. Wherever it was suggested that troops should be sent and it was desired that troops of occupation should excite no prejudice, no uneasiness on the part of those to whom they were sent, the men who represented the other nations came to me and asked me to send American soldiers. They not only implied but they said that the presence of American soldiers would be known not to mean anything except friendly protection and assistance. Do you wonder that it made our hearts swell with pride to realize these things?

But while these things in some degree softened my homesickness they made me all the more eager to get home where the rest of the folks live; to get home where the great dynamo of national energy was situated; to get home where the great purposes of national action were formed, and to be allowed to take part in the

counsels and in the actions which were formed and to
be taken by this great Nation, which from first to last
has followed the vision of the men who set it up and
created it.

We have had our eyes very close upon our tasks at
times, but whenever we lifted them we were accustomed
to lift them to a distant horizon. We were aware that
all the peoples of the earth had turned their faces
toward us as those who were the friends of freedom and
of right, and whenever we thought of national policy
and of its reaction upon the affairs of the world we
knew we were under bonds to do the large thing and the
right thing. It is a privilege, therefore, beyond all com-
putation for a man, whether in a great capacity or a
small, to take part in the counsels and in the resolutions
of a people like this.

I am afraid some people, some persons, do not understand that vision. They do not see it. They have
looked too much upon the ground. They have thought
too much of the interests that were near them and they
have not listened to the voices of their neighbors. I
have never had a moment's doubt as to where the heart
and purpose of this people lay. When any one on the
other side of the water has raised the question, "Will
America come in and help?" I have said, "Of course
America will come in and help." She cannot do anything else. She will not disappoint any high hope that
has been formed of her. Least of all will she in this day
of new-born liberty all over the world fail to extend
her hand of support and assistance to those who have
been made free.

I wonder if at this distance, you can have got any
conception of the tragic intensity of the feeling of those
peoples in Europe who have just had yokes thrown off
them. Have you reckoned up in your mind how many
peoples, how many nations, were held unwillingly under
the yoke of the Austro-Hungarian Empire, under the
yoke of Turkey, under the yoke of Germany? These

yokes have been thrown off. These peoples breathe the air and look around to see a new day dawn about them, and whenever they think of what is going to fill that day with action they think first of us. They think first of the friends who through the long years have spoken for them, who were privileged to declare that they came into the war to release them, who said that they would not make peace upon any other terms than their liberty, and they have known that America's presence in the war and in the conference was the guarantee of the result.

The Governor has spoken of a great task ended. Yes, the formulation of the peace is ended, but it creates only a new task just begun. I believe that if you will study the peace you will see that it is a just peace and a peace which, if it can be preserved, will save the world from unnecessary bloodshed. And now the great task is to preserve it. I have come back with my heart full of enthusiasm for throwing everything that I can, by way of influence or action, in with you to see that the peace is preserved—that when the long reckoning comes men may look back upon this generation of America and say, "They were true to the vision which they saw at their birth."

TO THE CITIZENS OF WASHINGTON

REPLY TO GREETINGS AT WASHINGTON, JULY 8, 1919. FROM THE "CHICAGO DAILY NEWS ALMANAC," 1920, P. 302.

I CAME home confident that the people of the United States were for the League of Nations, but to receive this immediate assurance of it in to-night's reception is particularly pleasing to me. It makes my homecoming just that much more delightful. I never have been quite so eager to get home as I was this time, and everything I have seen since I sighted land until now has made me gladder and gladder that I am home. No country can possibly look so good as this country looks to me.

PRESENTING THE TREATY FOR RATIFI-CATION

ADDRESS TO THE SENATE OF THE UNITED STATES, JULY 10, 1919. FROM OFFICIAL GOVERNMENT PUBLICATION IN MR. WILSON'S FILES.

G ENTLEMEN OF THE SENATE:
The treaty of peace with Germany was signed at Versailles on the twenty-eighth of June. I avail myself of the earliest opportunity to lay the treaty before you for ratification and to inform you with regard to the work of the Conference by which that treaty was formulated.

The treaty constitutes nothing less than a world settlement. It would not be possible for me either to summarize or to construe its manifold provisions in an address which must of necessity be something less than a treatise. My services and all the information I possess will be at your disposal and at the disposal of your Committee on Foreign Relations at any time, either informally or in session, as you may prefer; and I hope that you will not hesitate to make use of them. I shall at this time, prior to your own study of the document, attempt only a general characterization of its scope and purpose.

In one sense, no doubt, there is no need that I should report to you what was attempted and done at Paris. You have been daily cognizant of what was going on there,—of the problems with which the Peace Conference had to deal and of the difficulty of laying down straight lines of settlement anywhere on a field on which the old lines of international relationship, and the new alike, followed so intricate a pattern and were for the most part cut so deep by historical circumstances which dominated action even where it would have been best to ignore or reverse them. The cross currents of politics and of interest must have been evident to you. It would be presuming in me to attempt to explain the questions which arose or the many diverse elements that entered into them. I shall attempt something less ambitious than that and more clearly suggested by my duty to report to the Congress the part it seemed necessary for my colleagues and me to play as the representatives of the Government of the United States.

That part was dictated by the rôle America had played in the war and by the expectations that had been created in the minds of the peoples with whom we had associated ourselves in that great struggle.

The United States entered the war upon a different footing from every other nation except our associates on this side the sea. We entered it, not because our material interests were directly threatened or because any special treaty obligations to which we were parties had been violated, but only because we saw the supremacy, and even the validity, of right everywhere put in jeopardy and free government likely to be everywhere imperiled by the intolerable aggression of a power which respected neither right nor obligation and whose very system of government flouted the rights of the citizen as against the autocratic authority of his governors. And in the settlements of the peace we have sought no special reparation for ourselves, but only the restoration of right and the assurance of liberty everywhere that the effects of the settlement were to be felt. We entered the war as the disinterested champions of right and we interested ourselves in the terms of the peace in no other capacity.

The hopes of the nations allied against the Central Powers were at a very low ebb when our soldiers began to pour across the sea. There was everywhere amongst them, except in their stoutest spirits, a somber foreboding of disaster. The war ended in November, eight months ago, but you have only to recall what was feared in midsummer last, four short months before the armistice, to realize what it was that our timely aid accomplished alike for their morale and their physical safety. That first, never-to-be-forgotten action at Chateau-Thierry had already taken place. Our redoubtable soldiers and marines had already closed the gap the enemy had succeeded in opening for their advance upon Paris,—had already turned the tide of battle back towards the frontiers of France and begun the rout that was to save Europe and the world. Thereafter the Germans were to be always forced back, back, were never to thrust successfully forward again. And yet there was no confident hope. Anxious men and women, leading spirits of France, attended the celebration of the Fourth of July last year in Paris out of generous courtesy,—with no heart for festivity, little zest for hope. But they came away with something new at their hearts; they have themselves told us so. The mere sight of our men,—of their vigor, of the confidence that showed itself in every movement of their stalwart figures and every turn of their swinging march, in their steady comprehending eyes and easy discipline, in the indomitable air that added spirit to everything they did, —made everyone who saw them that memorable day realize that something had happened that was much more than a mere incident in the fighting, something very different from the mere arrival of fresh troops. A great moral force had flung itself into the struggle. The fine physical force of those spirited men spoke of something more than bodily vigor. They carried the great ideals of a free people at their hearts and with that vision were unconquerable. Their very presence brought reassurance; their fighting made victory certain.

They were recognized as crusaders, and as their thousands swelled to millions their strength was seen to mean salvation. And they were fit men to carry such a hope and make good the assurance it forecast. Finer men never went into battle; and their officers were worthy of them. This is not the occasion upon which to utter a eulogy of the armies America sent to France, but perhaps, since I am speaking of their mission, 1 may speak also of the pride I shared with every American who saw or dealt with them there. They were the sort of men America would wish to be represented by, the sort of men every American would wish to claim as fellow countrymen and comrades in a great cause. They were terrible in battle, and gentle and helpful out of it, remembering the mothers and the sisters, the wives and the little children at home. They were free men under arms, not forgetting their ideals of duty in the midst of tasks of violence. I am proud to have had the privilege of being associated with them and of calling myself their leader.

But I speak now of what they meant to the men by whose sides they fought and to the people with whom they mingled with such utter simplicity, as friends who asked only to be of service. They were for all the visible embodiment of America. What they did made America and all that she stood for a living reality in the thoughts not only of the people of France but also of tens of millions of men and women throughout all the toiling nations of a world standing everywhere in peril of its freedom and of the loss of everything it held dear, in deadly fear that its bonds were never to be loosed, its hopes forever to be mocked and disappointed.

And the compulsion of what they stood for was upon us who represented America at the peace table. It was our duty to see to it that every decision we took part in contributed, so far as we were able to influence it, to quiet the fears and realize the hopes of the peoples who had been living in that shadow, the nations that had come by our assistance to their freedom. It was our duty to do everything that it was within our power to do to make the triumph of freedom and of right a lasting triumph in the assurance of which men might everywhere live without fear.

Old entanglements of every kind stood in the way,—promises which Governments had made to one another in the days when might and right were confused and the power of the victor was without restraint. Engagements which contemplated any dispositions of territory, any extensions of sovereignty that might seem to be to the interest of those who had the power to insist upon them, had been entered into without thought of what the peoples concerned might wish or profit by; and these could not always be honorably brushed aside. It was not easy to graft the new order of ideas on the old, and some of the fruits of the grafting may, I fear, for a time be bitter. But, with very few exceptions, the men who sat with us at the peace table desired as sincerely as we did to get away from the bad influences, the illegitimate purposes, the demoralizing ambitions, the international counsels and expedients out of which the sinister designs of Germany had sprung as a natural growth.

It had been our privilege to formulate the principles which were accepted as the basis of the peace, but they had been accepted, not because we had come in to hasten and assure the victory and insisted upon them, but because they were readily acceded to as the principles to which honorable and enlightened minds everywhere had been bred. They spoke the conscience of the world as well as the conscience of America, and I am happy to pay my tribute of respect and gratitude to the able, forward-looking men with whom it was my privilege to coöperate for their unfailing spirit of coöperation, their constant effort to accommodate the interests they represented to the principles we were all agreed upon. The difficulties, which were many, lay in the circumstances, not often in the men. Almost without exception the men who led had caught the true and full vision of the problem of peace as an indivisible whole, a problem, not of mere adjustments of interest, but of justice and right action.

The atmosphere in which the Conference worked seemed created, not by the ambitions of strong governments, but by the hopes and aspirations of small nations and of peoples hitherto under bondage to the power that victory had shattered and destroyed. Two great empires had been forced into political bankruptcy, and we were the receivers. Our task was not only to make peace with the Central Empires and remedy the wrongs their armies had done. The Central Empires had lived in open violation of many of the very rights for which the war had been fought, dominating alien peoples over whom they had no natural right to rule, enforcing, not obedience, but veritable bondage, exploiting those who were weak for the benefit of those who were masters and overlords only by force of arms. There could be no peace until the whole order of Central Europe was set right.

That meant that new nations were to be created,— Poland, Czecho-Slovakia, Hungary itself. No part of ancient Poland had ever in any true sense become a part of Germany, or of Austria, or of Russia. Bohemia was alien in every thought and hope to the monarchy of which she had so long been an artificial part; and the uneasy partnership between Austria and Hungary had been one rather of interest than of kinship or sympathy. The Slavs whom Austria had chosen to force into her empire on the south were kept to their obedience by nothing but fear. Their hearts were with their kinsmen in the Balkans. These were all arrangements of power, not arrangements of natural union or association. It was the imperative task of those who would make peace and make it intelligently to establish a new order which would rest upon the free choice of peoples rather than upon the arbitrary authority of Hapsburgs or Hohenzollerns.

More than that, great populations bound by sympathy and actual kin to Rumania were also linked against their will to the conglomerate Austro-Hungarian monarchy or to other alien sovereignties, and it was part of the task of peace to make a new Rumania as well as a new slavic state clustering about Serbia.

And no natural frontiers could be found to these new fields of adjustment and redemption. It was necessary to look constantly forward to other related tasks. The German colonies were to be disposed of. They had not been governed; they had been exploited merely, without thought of the interest or even the ordinary human rights of their inhabitants.

The Turkish Empire, moreover, had fallen apart, as the Austro-Hungarian had. It had never had any real unity. It had been held together only by pitiless, inhuman force. Its peoples cried aloud for release, for succor from unspeakable distress, for all that the new day of hope seemed at last to bring within its dawn. Peoples hitherto in utter darkness were to be led out into the same light and given at last a helping hand. Undeveloped peoples and peoples ready for recognition but not yet ready to assume the full responsibilities of statehood were to be given adequate guarantees of friendly protection, guidance and assistance.

And out of the execution of these great enterprises of liberty sprang opportunities to attempt what statesmen had never found the way before to do; an opportunity to throw safeguards about the rights of racial, national and religious minorities by solemn international covenant; an opportunity to limit and regulate military establishments where they were most likely to be mischievous; an opportunity to effect a complete and systematic internationalization of waterways and railways which were necessary to the free economic life of more than one nation and to clear many of the normal channels of commerce of unfair obstructions of law or of privilege; and the very welcome opportunity to secure for labor the concerted protection of definite international pledges of principle and practice.

These were not tasks which the Conference looked

about it to find and went out of its way to perform.
They were inseparable from the settlements of peace.
They were thrust upon it by circumstances which could
not be overlooked. The war had created them. In all
quarters of the world old-established relationships had
been disturbed or broken and affairs were at loose ends,
needing to be mended or united again, but could not
be made what they were before. They had to be set
right by applying some uniform principle of justice or
enlightened expediency. And they could not be adjusted by merely prescribing in a treaty what should be
done. New states were to be set up which could not
hope to live through their first period of weakness without assured support by the great nations that had consented to their creation and won for them their independence. Ill-governed colonies could not be put in the
hands of governments which were to act as trustees for
their people and not as their masters if there was to be
no common authority among the nations to which they
were to be responsible in the execution of their trust.
Future international conventions with regard to the control of waterways, with regard to illicit traffic of many
kinds, in arms or in deadly drugs, or with regard to the
adjustment of many varying international administrative arrangements could not be assured if the treaty
were to provide no permanent common international
agency, if its execution in such matters was to be left
to the slow and uncertain processes of coöperation by
ordinary methods of negotiation. If the Peace Conference itself was to be the end of coöperative authority
and common counsel among the governments to which
the world was looking to enforce justice and give pledges
of an enduring settlement, regions like the Saar basin
could not be put under a temporary administrative régime which did not involve a transfer of political sovereignty and which contemplated a final determination
of its political connections by popular vote to be taken
at a distant date; no free city like Danzig could be

created which was, under elaborate international guarantees, to accept exceptional obligations with regard to the use of its port and exceptional relations with a State of which it was not to form a part; properly safeguarded plebiscites could not be provided for where populations were at some future date to make choice what sovereignty they would live under; no certain and uniform method of arbitration could be secured for the settlement of anticipated difficulties of final decision with regard to many matters dealt with in the treaty itself; the long-continued supervision of the task of reparation which Germany was to undertake to complete within the next generation might entirely break down; the reconsideration and revision of administrative arrangements and restrictions which the treaty prescribed but which it was recognized might not prove of lasting advantage or entirely fair if too long enforced would be impracticable. The promises governments were making to one another about the way in which labor was to be dealt with, by law not only but in fact as well, would remain a mere humane thesis if there was to be no common tribunal of opinion and judgment to which liberal statesmen could resort for the influences which alone might secure their redemption. A league of free nations had become a practical necessity. Examine the treaty of peace and you will find that everywhere throughout its manifold provisions its framers have felt obliged to turn to the League of Nations as an indispensable instrumentality for the maintenance of the new order it has been their purpose to set up in the world,—the world of civilized men.

That there should be a League of Nations to steady the counsels and maintain the peaceful understandings of the world, to make, not treaties alone, but the accepted principles of international law as well, the actual rule of conduct among the governments of the world, had been one of the agreements accepted from the first as the basis of peace with the Central Powers. The

statesmen of all the belligerent countries were agreed
that such a league must be created to sustain the settlements that were to be effected. But at first I think there
was a feeling among some of them that, while it must be
attempted, the formation of such a league was perhaps
a counsel of perfection which practical men, long experienced in the world of affairs, must agree to very cau-
tiously and with many misgivings. It was only as the
difficult work of arranging an all but universal adjustment of the world's affairs advanced from day to
day from one stage of conference to another that it became evident to them that what they were seeking would
be little more than something written upon paper, to be
interpreted and applied by such methods as the chances
of politics might make available if they did not provide a means of common counsel which all were obliged
to accept, a common authority whose decisions would be
recognized as decisions which all must respect.

And so the most practical, the most skeptical among
them turned more and more to the League as the authority through which international action was to be secured, the authority without which, as they had come to
see it, it would be difficult to give assured effect either to
this treaty or to any other international understanding
upon which they were to depend for the maintenance of
peace. The fact that the Covenant of the League was
the first substantive part of the treaty to be worked out
and agreed upon, while all else was in solution, helped to
make the formulation of the rest easier. The Conference was, after all, not to be ephemeral. The concert of
nations was to continue, under a definite Covenant which
had been agreed upon and which all were convinced was
workable. They could go forward with confidence to
make arrangements intended to be permanent. The
most practical of the conferees were at last the most
ready to refer to the League of Nations the superintendence of all interests which did not admit of immediate determination, of all administrative problems

which were to require a continuing oversight. What
had seemed a counsel of perfection had come to seem
a plain counsel of necessity. The League of Nations
was the practical statesman's hope of success in many
of the most difficult things he was attempting.

And it had validated itself in the thought of every
member of the Conference as something much bigger,
much greater every way, than a mere instrument for
carrying out the provisions of a particular treaty. It
was universally recognized that all the peoples of the
world demanded of the Conference that it should create
such a continuing concert of free nations as would make
wars of aggression and spoliation such as this that has
just ended forever impossible. A cry had gone out
from every home in every stricken land from which
sons and brothers and fathers had gone forth to the
great sacrifice that such a sacrifice should never again
be exacted. It was manifest why it had been exacted.
It had been exacted because one nation desired
dominion and other nations had known no means of
defense except armaments and alliances. War had lain
at the heart of every arrangement of the Europe,—of
every arrangement of the world,—that preceded the
war. Restive peoples had been told that fleets and
armies, which they toiled to sustain, meant peace; and
they now knew that they had been lied to: that fleets
and armies had been maintained to promote national
ambitions and meant war. They knew that no old
policy meant anything else but force, force,—always
force. And they knew that it was intolerable. Every
true heart in the world, and every enlightened judgment
demanded that, at whatever cost of independent action,
every government that took thought for its people or
for justice or for ordered freedom should lend itself
to a new purpose and utterly destroy the old order of
international politics. Statesmen might see difficulties,
but the people could see none and could brook no denial.
A war in which they had been bled white to beat the

terror that lay concealed in every Balance of Power must not end in a mere victory of arms and a new balance. The monster that had resorted to arms must be put in chains that could not be broken. The united power of free nations must put a stop to aggression, and the world must be given peace. If there was not the will or the intelligence to accomplish that now, there must be another and a final war and the world must be swept clean of every power that could renew the terror. The League of Nations was not merely an instrument to adjust and remedy old wrongs under a new treaty of peace; it was the only hope for mankind. Again and again had the demon of war been cast out of the house of the peoples and the house swept clean by a treaty of peace; only to prepare a time when he would enter in again with spirits worse than himself. The house must now be given a tenant who could hold it against all such. Convenient, indeed indispensable, as statesmen found the newly planned League of Nations to be for the execution of present plans of peace and reparation, they saw it in a new aspect before their work was finished. They saw it as the main object of the peace, as the only thing that could complete it or make it worth while. They saw it as the hope of the world, and that hope they did not dare to disappoint. Shall we or any other free people hesitate to accept this great duty? Dare we reject it and break the heart of the world?

And so the result of the Conference of Peace, so far as Germany is concerned, stands complete. The difficulties encountered were very many. Sometimes they seemed insuperable. It was impossible to accommodate the interests of so great a body of nations,—interests which directly or indirectly affected almost every nation in the world,—without many minor compromises. The treaty, as a result, is not exactly what we would have written. It is probably not what any one of the national delegations would have written. But results were worked out which on the whole bear test. I think that it will be found that the compromises which were accepted as inevitable nowhere cut to the heart of any principle. The work of the Conference squares, as a whole, with the principles agreed upon as the basis of the peace as well as with the practical possibilities of the international situations which had to be faced and dealt with as facts.

I shall presently have occasion to lay before you a special treaty with France, whose object is the temporary protection of France from unprovoked aggression by the Power with whom this treaty of peace has been negotiated. Its terms link it with this treaty. I take the liberty, however, of reserving it for special explication on another occasion.

The rôle which America was to play in the Conference seemed determined, as I have said, before my colleagues and I got to Paris,—determined by the universal expectations of the nations whose representatives, drawn from all quarters of the globe, we were to deal with. It was universally recognized that America had entered the war to promote no private or peculiar interest of her own but only as the champion of rights which she was glad to share with free men and lovers of justice everywhere. We had formulated the principles upon which the settlement was to be made,—the principles upon which the armistice had been agreed to and the parleys of peace undertaken,— and no one doubted that our desire was to see the treaty of peace formulated along the actual lines of those principles,—and desired nothing else. We were welcomed as disinterested friends. We were resorted to as arbiters in many a difficult matter. It was recognized that our material aid would be indispensable in the days to come, when industry and credit would have to be brought back to their normal operation again and communities beaten to the ground assisted to their feet once more, and it was taken for granted, I am proud to say, that we would play the helpful friend in these things as in all others without prejudice or favor. We were generously accepted as the unaffected champions of what was right. It was a very responsible rôle to play; but I am happy to report that the fine group of Americans who helped with their expert advice in each part of the varied settlements sought in every transaction to justify the high confidence reposed in them.

And that confidence, it seems to me, is the measure of our opportunity and of our duty in the days to come, in which the new hope of the peoples of the world is to be fulfilled or disappointed. The fact that America is the friend of the nations, whether they be rivals or associates, is no new fact; it is only the discovery of it by the rest of the world that is new.

America may be said to have just reached her majority as a world power. It was almost exactly twenty-one years ago that the results of the war with Spain put us unexpectedly in possession of rich islands on the other side of the world and brought us into association with other governments in the control of the West Indies. It was regarded as a sinister and ominous thing by the statesmen of more than one European chancellery that we should have extended our power beyond the confines of our continental dominions. They were accustomed to think of new neighbors as a new menace, of rivals as watchful enemies. There were persons amongst us at home who looked with deep disapproval and avowed anxiety on such extensions of our national authority over distant islands and over peoples whom they feared we might exploit, not serve and assist. But we have not exploited them. We have been their friends and have sought to serve them. And our dominion has been a menace to no other nation. We redeemed our honor to the utmost in our dealings with

Cuba. She is weak but absolutely free; and it is her trust in us that makes her free. Weak peoples everywhere stand ready to give us any authority among them that will assure them a like friendly oversight and direction. They know that there is no ground for fear in receiving us as their mentors and guides. Our isolation was ended twenty years ago; and now fear of us is ended also, our counsel and association sought after and desired. There can be no question of our ceasing to be a world power. The only question is whether we can refuse the moral leadership that is offered us, whether we shall accept or reject the confidence of the world.

The war and the Conference of Peace now sitting in Paris seem to me to have answered that question. Our participation in the war established our position among the nations and nothing but our own mistaken action can alter it. It was not an accident or a matter of sudden choice that we are no longer isolated and devoted to a policy which has only our own interest and advantage for its object. It was our duty to go in, if we were indeed the champions of liberty and of right. We answered to the call of duty in a way so spirited, so utterly without thought of what we spent of blood or treasure, so effective, so worthy of the admiration of true men everywhere, so wrought out of the stuff of all that was heroic, that the whole world saw at last, in the flesh, in noble action, a great ideal asserted and vindicated, by a Nation they had deemed material and now found to be compact of the spiritual forces that must free men of every nation from every unworthy bondage. It is thus that a new rôle and a new responsibility have come to this great Nation that we honor and which we would all wish to lift to yet higher levels of service and achievement.

The stage is set, the destiny disclosed. It has come about by no plan of our conceiving, but by the hand of God who led us into this way. We cannot turn back.

We can only go forward, with lifted eyes and freshened spirit, to follow the vision. It was of this that we dreamed at our birth. America shall in truth show the way. The light streams upon the path ahead, and nowhere else.

TO THE CZECHO-SLOVAK ARMY

SPEECH ON REVIEWING A DETACHMENT OF THE CZECHO-SLOVAK ARMY EN ROUTE FROM SIBERIA TO EUROPE, JULY 18, 1919.[1] FROM ORIGINAL IN MR. WILSON'S FILES.

MAJOR VLADIMIR JIRSA, OFFICERS, AND MEN OF THE DETACHMENT OF THE CZECHO-SLOVAK ARMY:

I review with pleasure this detachment of your valiant Army. To you, its officers, and to these brave men I extend a cordial welcome. From afar we have watched your deeds and have been moved to admiration of your actions under the most adverse of circumstances. Having been subjugated to an alien control, you were fired by a love of your former independence and for the institutions of your native land and aligned yourselves with those who fought in opposition to despotism and military autocracy. At the moment when adversity came to the armies with which you were fighting and when darkness and despair cast its gloom upon your cause you declined to accommodate yourselves to circumstances which were of the old order of things and resolutely retained your hope.

Your steadfastness to your purposes, your unshaken

---

[1] The story of this contingent of Czecho-Slovaks is one of the epics of the Great War. Beginning as reluctant soldiers in the Austro-Hungarian Army, they were captured by the Russians and lay for several years in prison camps. When the old Russian Government was overthrown they were released. They organized an army of their own under the Russian provisional Government and fought gallantly in the last advance of the Russian armies in 1917. After the Bolshevik overturn they found themselves ringed around with enemies; they refused amnesty from the Austrian emperor; they broke through the German line at Bachmut in a bloody battle and set straight eastward 5,000 miles to Vladivostok, a contingent finally arriving in Washington, to be reviewed by President Wilson.

belief in high ideals, your valor of mind, of body and
of heart, have evoked the admiration of the world.   In
the midst of disorganization and subject to influences
which worked for ruin you consistently maintained
order within your ranks and by your example helped
those with whom you came in contact to reëstablish some
semblance of order in their affairs.   Too much cannot
be said in praise of the demeanor of your brave Army
under these trying circumstances.   Future generations
will record the influence for good which you had upon
a large part of the world's area and will accord you
the place which you properly deserve.   In the history
of the modern world, and perhaps in all history, there
is no more wonderful nor brilliant record than the withdrawal of your forces in opposition to the armies of
Germany and Austria through a population which developed an hostility, and the march of your armies for
thousands of miles across the great regions of Siberia,
keeping steadfastly in mind the necessity for order and
organization.

You are returning now to your native land, to-day
again a free and independent country.   May you take
back with you that stamina which you so well manifested
all through your trying experiences in Russia and Siberia, and may you keep in mind after your return that
the laws of God, the laws of man, and the laws of nature
require a systematic establishment for their proper
operation, and for the welfare and happiness of the
human race.

PRESENTING A TREATY WITH FRANCE

MESSAGE TO THE SENATE OF THE U. S., JULY 29, 1919.
FROM ORIGINAL IN MR. WILSON'S FILES.

GENTLEMEN OF THE SENATE:

I take pleasure in laying before you a treaty with the Republic of France the object of which is to secure that Republic of the immediate aid of the United States of America in case of any unprovoked movement of aggression against her on the part of Germany. I earnestly hope that this treaty will meet with your cordial approval and will receive an early ratification at your hands, along with the treaty of peace with Germany. Now that you have had an opportunity to examine the great document I presented to you two weeks ago, it seems opportune to lay before you this treaty which is meant to be in effect a part of it.

It was signed on the same day with the treaty of peace and is intended as a temporary supplement to it. It is believed that the treaty of peace with Germany itself provides adequate protection to France against aggression from her recent enemy on the east; but the years immediately ahead of us contain many incalculable possibilities. The Covenant of the League of Nations provides for military action for the protection of its members only upon advice of the Council of the League —advice given, it is to be presumed, only upon deliberation and acted upon by each of the governments of the member States only if its own judgment justifies such action. The object of the special treaty with France which I now submit to you is to provide for immediate military assistance to France by the United States in case of any unprovoked movement of aggression against her by Germany without waiting for the advice of the Council of the League of Nations that such action be taken. It is to be an arrangement, not independent of the League of Nations, but under it.

It is, therefore, expressly provided that this treaty shall be made the subject of consideration at the same time with the treaty of peace with Germany; that this special arrangement shall receive the approval of the Council of the League; and that this special provision for the safety of France shall remain in force only until, upon the application of one of the parties to it, the Council of the League, acting, if necessary, by a majority vote, shall agree that the provisions of the Covenant of the League afford her sufficient protection.

I was moved to sign this treaty by considerations which will, I hope, seem as persuasive and as irresistible to you as they seemed to me. We are bound to France by ties of friendship which we have always regarded, and shall always regard, as peculiarly sacred. She assisted us to win our freedom as a Nation. It is seriously to be doubted whether we could have won it without her gallant and timely aid. We have recently had the privilege of assisting in driving enemies, who were also enemies of the world, from her soil; but that does not pay our debt to her. Nothing can pay such a debt. She now desires that we should promise to lend our great force to keep her safe against the power she has had most reason to fear. Another great nation volunteers the same promise. It is one of the fine reversals of history that that other nation should be the very power from whom France fought to set us free. A new day has dawned. Old antagonisms are forgotten. The common cause of freedom and enlightenment has created new comradeships and a new perception of what it is wise and necessary for great nations to do to free the world of intolerable fear. Two governments who wish to be members of the League of Nations ask leave of the Council of the League to be permitted to go to the assistance of a friend whose situation has been found to be one of peculiar peril, without awaiting the advice of the League to act.

It is by taking such pledges as this that we prove ourselves faithful to the utmost to the high obligations of gratitude and tested friendship. Such an act as this seems to me one of the proofs that we are a people that sees the true heart of duty and prefers honor to its own separate course of peace.

HIGH COST OF LIVING

ADDRESS TO CONGRESS, AUGUST 8, 1919. FROM THE "CONGRESSIONAL RECORD," VOL. 58, PP. 3718-3721.

I HAVE sought this opportunity to address you because it is clearly my duty to call your attention to the present cost of living and to urge upon you with all the persuasive force of which I am capable the legislative measures which would be most effective in controlling it and bringing it down. The prices the people of this country are paying for everything that it is necessary for them to use in order to live are not justified by a shortage in supply, either present or prospective, and are in many cases artificially and deliberately created by vicious practices which ought immediately to be checked by law. They constitute a burden upon us which is the more unbearable because we know that it is willfully imposed by those who have the power and that it can by vigorous public action be greatly lightened and made to square with the actual conditions of supply and demand. Some of the methods by which these prices are produced are already illegal, some of them criminal, and those who employ them will be energetically proceeded against; but others have not yet been brought under the law, and should be dealt with at once by legislation.

I need not recite the particulars of this critical matter: the prices demanded and paid at the sources of supply, at the factory, in the food markets, at the shops, in the restaurants and hotels, alike in the city and in the village. They are familiar to you. They are the talk of every domestic circle and of every group of casual acquaintances even. It is a matter of familiar knowledge, also, that a process has set in which is likely, unless something is done, to push prices and rents and the whole cost of living higher and yet higher, in a vicious cycle to which there is no logical or natural end. With the increase in the prices of the necessaries of life come demands for increases in wages,—demands which are justified if there be no other way of enabling men to live. Upon the increase of wages there follows close an increase in the price of the products whose producers have been accorded the increase,—not a proportionate increase, for the manufacturer does not content himself with that, but an increase considerably greater than the added wage cost and for which the added wage cost is oftentimes hardly more than an excuse. The laborers who do not get an increase in pay when they demand it are likely to strike, and the strike only makes matters worse. It checks production, if it affects the railways it prevents distribution and strips the markets, so that there is presently nothing to buy, and there is another excessive addition to prices resulting from the scarcity.

These are facts and forces with which we have become only too familiar; but we are not justified because of our familiarity with them or because of any hasty and shallow conclusion that they are "natural" and inevitable in sitting inactively by and letting them work their fatal results if there is anything that we can do to check, correct, or reverse them. I have sought this opportunity to inform the Congress what the Executive is doing by way of remedy and control, and to suggest where effective legal remedies are lacking and may be supplied.

We must, I think, frankly admit that there is no complete immediate remedy to be had from legislative and executive action. The free processes of supply and demand will not operate of themselves and no legislative or executive action can force them into full and natural operation until there is peace. There is now neither peace nor war. All the world is waiting,—with what unnerving fears and haunting doubts who can adequately say?—waiting to know when it shall have peace and what kind of peace it will be when it comes,—a peace in which each nation shall make shift for itself as it can, or a peace buttressed and supported by the will and concert of the nations that have the purpose and the power to do and to enforce what is right. Politically, economically, socially the World is on the operating table, and it has not been possible to administer any anesthetic. It is conscious. It even watches the capital operation upon which it knows that its hope of healthful life depends. It cannot think its business out or make plans or give intelligent and provident direction to its affairs while in such a case. Where there is no peace of mind there can be no energy in endeavor. There can be no confidence in industry, no calculable basis for credits, no confident buying or systematic selling, no certain prospect of employment, no normal restoration of business, no hopeful attempt at reconstruction or the proper reassembling of the dislocated elements of enterprise until peace has been established and, so far as may be, guaranteed.

Our national life has no doubt been less radically disturbed and dismembered than the national life of other peoples whom the war more directly affected, with its terrible ravaging and destructive force, but it has been, nevertheless, profoundly affected and disarranged, and our industries, our credits, our productive capacity, our economic processes are inextricably interwoven with those of other nations and peoples,—most intimately of all with the nations and peoples upon whom the chief burden and confusion of the war fell and who are now most dependent upon the coöperative action of the world.

We are just now shipping more goods out of our ports to foreign markets than we ever shipped before, —not food stuffs merely, but stuffs and materials of every sort; but this is no index of what our foreign sales will continue to be or of the effect the volume of our exports will have on supplies and prices. It is impossible yet to predict how far or how long foreign purchasers will be able to find the money or the credit to pay for or sustain such purchases on such a scale; how soon or to what extent foreign manufacturers can resume their former production, foreign farmers get their accustomed crops from their own fields, foreign mines resume their former output, foreign merchants set up again their old machinery of trade with the ends of the earth. All these things must remain uncertain until peace is established and the nations of the world have concerted the methods by which normal life and industry are to be restored and all that we can do, in the meantime, to restrain profiteering and put the life of our people upon a tolerable footing will be makeshift and provisional. There can be no settled conditions here or elsewhere until the treaty of peace is out of the way and the work of liquidating the war has become the chief concern of our Government and of the other Governments of the world. Until then business will inevitably remain speculative and sway now this way and again that, with heavy losses or heavy gains as it may chance, and the consumer must take care of both the gains and the losses. There can be no peace prices so long as our whole financial and economic system is on a war basis.

Europe will not, can not recoup her capital or put her restless, distracted peoples to work until she knows exactly where she stands in respect of peace; and what we will do is for her the chief question upon which her quietude of mind and confidence of purpose depend. While there is any possibility that the peace terms may be changed or may be held long in abeyance or may not be enforced because of divisions of opinion among the Powers associated against Germany, it is idle to look for permanent relief.

But what we can do we should do, and should do at once. And there is a great deal that we can do, provisional though it be. Wheat shipments and credits to facilitate the purchase of our wheat can and will be limited and controlled in such a way as not to raise but rather to lower the price of flour here. The Government has the power, within certain limits, to regulate that. We cannot deny wheat to foreign peoples who are in dire need of it, and we do not wish to do so; but, fortunately, though the wheat crop is not what we hoped it would be, it is abundant if handled with provident care. The price of wheat is lower in the United States than in Europe, and can with proper management be kept so.

By way of immediate relief, surplus stocks of both food and clothing in the hands of the Government will be sold, and of course sold at prices at which there is no profit. And by way of a more permanent correction of prices surplus stocks in private hands will be drawn out of storage and put upon the market. Fortunately, under the terms of the Food Control Act the hoarding of foodstuffs can be checked and prevented; and they will be, with the greatest energy. Foodstuffs can be drawn out of storage and sold by legal action which the Department of Justice will institute wherever necessary; but so soon as the situation is systematically dealt with it is not likely that the courts will often have to be resorted to. Much of the accumulating of stocks has no doubt been due to the sort of speculation which always results from uncertainty. Great surpluses were accumulated because it was impossible to foresee what the market would disclose and dealers were determined to be ready for whatever might happen, as well as eager to reap the full advantage of rising prices. They will now see the disadvantage, as well as the danger, of holding off from the new process of distribution.

Some very interesting and significant facts with regard to stocks on hand and the rise of prices in the face of abundance have been disclosed by the inquiries of the Department of Agriculture, the Department of Labor and the Federal Trade Commission. They seem to justify the statement that in the case of many necessary commodities effective means have been found to prevent the normal operation of the law of supply and demand. Disregarding the surplus stocks in the hands of the Government, there was a greater supply of foodstuffs in this country on June 1 of this year than at the same date last year. In the combined total of a number of the most important foods in dry and cold storage the excess was quite 19 per cent. And yet prices have risen. The supply of fresh eggs on hand in June of this year, for example, was greater by nearly 10 per cent than the supply on hand at the same time last year and yet the wholesale price was forty cents a dozen as against thirty cents a year ago. The stock of frozen fowls had increased more than 298 per cent, and yet the price had risen also, from thirty-four and a half cents per pound to thirty-seven and a half cents. The supply of creamery butter had increased 129 per cent and the price from forty-one to fifty-three cents per pound. The supply of salt beef had been augmented 3 per cent and the price had gone up from thirty-four dollars a barrel to thirty-six dollars a barrel. Canned corn had increased in stock nearly 92 per cent and had remained substantially the same in price. In a few foodstuffs the prices had declined, but in nothing like the proportion in which the supply had increased. For example, the stock of canned tomatoes had increased 102 per cent and yet the price had declined only twenty-five cents per dozen cans. In some cases there had been the usual result of an increase of price following a decrease of supply, but in almost every instance the increase of price had been disproportionate to the decrease in stock.

The Attorney-General has been making a careful study of the situation as a whole and of the laws that can be applied to better it and is convinced that, under the stimulation and temptation of exceptional circumstances, combinations of producers and combinations of traders have been formed for the control of supplies and of prices which are clearly in restraint of trade, and against these prosecutions will be promptly instituted and actively pushed which will in all likelihood have a prompt corrective effect. There is reason to believe that the prices of leather, of coal, of lumber, and of textiles have been materially affected by forms of concert and coöperation among the producers and marketers of these and other universally necessary commodities which it will be possible to redress. No watchful or energetic effort will be spared to accomplish this necessary result. I trust that there will not be many cases in which prosecution will be necessary. Public action will no doubt cause many who have perhaps unwittingly adopted illegal methods to abandon them promptly and of their own motion.

And publicity can accomplish a great deal. The purchaser can often take care of himself if he knows the facts and influences he is dealing with; and purchasers are not disinclined to do anything, either singly or collectively, that may be necessary for their self-protection. The Department of Commerce, the Department of Agriculture, the Department of Labor, and the Federal Trade Commission can do a great deal towards supplying the public, systematically and at short intervals, with information regarding the actual supply of particular commodities that is in existence and available, with regard to supplies which are in existence but not available because of hoarding, and with regard to the methods of price fixing which are being used by dealers in certain foodstuffs and other necessaries. There can be little doubt that retailers are in part,—sometimes in large part,—responsible for exorbitant prices; and it is quite practicable for the Government, through the agencies I have mentioned, to supply the public with full information as to the prices at which retailers buy and as to the costs of transportation they pay, in order that it may be known just what margin of profit they are demanding. Opinion and concerted action on the part of purchasers can probably do the rest.

That is, these agencies may perform this indispensable service provided the Congress will supply them with the necessary funds to prosecute their inquiries and keep their price lists up to date. Hitherto the Appropriation Committees of the Houses have not always, I fear, seen the full value of these inquiries, and the Departments and Commissions have been very much straitened for means to render this service. That adequate funds be provided by appropriation for this purpose, and provided as promptly as possible, is one of the means of greatly ameliorating the present distressing conditions of livelihood that I have come to urge, in this attempt to concert with you the best ways to serve the country in this emergency. It is one of the absolutely necessary means, underlying many others, and can be supplied at once.

There are many other ways. Existing law is inadequate. There are many perfectly legitimate methods by which the Government can exercise restraint and guidance.

Let me urge, in the first place, that the present food control Act should be so extended both as to the period of time during which it shall remain in operation and as to the commodities to which it shall apply. Its provisions against hoarding should be made to apply not only to food but also to feedstuffs, to fuel, to clothing, and to many other commodities which are indisputably necessaries of life. As it stands now it is limited in operation to the period of the war and becomes inoperative upon the formal proclamation of peace. But I should judge that it was clearly within the constitutional power of the Congress to make similar permanent provisions and regulations with regard to all goods destined for interstate commerce, and to exclude them from interstate shipment if the requirements of the law are not complied with. Some such regulation is imperatively necessary. The abuses that have grown up in the manipulation of prices by the withholding of foodstuffs and other necessaries of life cannot otherwise be effectively prevented. There can be no doubt of either the necessity or the legitimacy of such measures. May I not call attention to the fact, also, that, although the present Act prohibits profiteering, the prohibition is accompanied by no penalty. It is clearly in the public interest that a penalty should be provided which will be persuasive.

To the same end, I earnestly recommend, in the second place, that the Congress pass a law regulating cold storage as it is regulated, for example, by the laws of the State of New Jersey, which limit the time during which goods may be kept in storage, prescribe the method of disposing of them if kept beyond the permitted period, and require that goods released from storage shall in all cases bear the date of their receipt. It would materially add to the serviceability of the law, for the purpose we now have in view, if it were also prescribed that all goods released from storage for interstate shipment should have plainly marked upon each package the selling or market price at which they went into storage. By this means the purchaser would always be able to learn what profits stood between him and the producer or the wholesale dealer.

It would serve as a useful example to the other communities of the country, as well as greatly relieve local distress, if the Congress were to regulate all such matters very fully for the District of Columbia, where its legislative authority is without limit.

I would also recommend that it be required that all goods destined for interstate commerce should in every case where their form or package makes it possible be plainly marked with the price at which they left the hands of the producer. Such a requirement would bear a close analogy to certain provisions of the Pure Food

Act, by which it is required that certain detailed information be given on the labels of packages of foods and drugs.

And it does not seem to me that we can confine ourselves to detailed measures of this kind, if it is indeed our purpose to assume national control of the processes of distribution. I take it for granted that that is our purpose and our duty. Nothing less will suffice. We need not hesitate to handle a national question in a national way. We should go beyond the measures I have suggested. We should formulate a law requiring a federal license of all corporations engaged in interstate commerce and embodying in the license, or in the conditions under which it is to be issued, specific regulations designed to secure competitive selling and prevent unconscionable profits in the method of marketing. Such a law would afford a welcome opportunity to effect other such needed reforms in the business of interstate shipment and in the methods of corporations which are engaged in it; but for the moment I confine my recommendations to the object immediately in hand, which is to lower the cost of living.

May I not add that there is a bill now pending before the Congress which, if passed, would do much to stop speculation and to prevent the fraudulent methods of promotion by which our people are annually fleeced of many millions of hard-earned money. I refer to the measure proposed by the Capital Issues Committee for the control of security issues. It is a measure formulated by men who know the actual conditions of business and its adoption would serve a great and beneficent purpose.

We are dealing, Gentlemen of the Congress, I need hardly say, with very critical and very difficult matters. We should go forward with confidence along the road we see, but we should also seek to comprehend the whole of the scene amidst which we act. There is no ground for some of the fearful forecasts I hear uttered about me, but the condition of the world is unquestionably very grave and we should face it comprehendingly. The situation of our own country, as I have said, is exceptionally fortunate. We of all peoples can afford to keep our heads and to determine upon moderate and sensible courses of action which will insure us against the passions and distempers which are working such deep unhappiness for some of the distressed nations on the other side of the sea. But we may be involved in their distresses unless we help, and help with energy and intelligence.

The world must pay for the appalling destruction wrought by the great war, and we are part of the world. We must pay our share. For five years now the industry of all Europe has been slack and disordered. The normal crops have not been produced; the normal quantity of manufactured goods has not been turned out. Not until there are the usual crops and the usual production of manufactured goods on the other side of the Atlantic can Europe return to the former conditions; and it was upon the former conditions, not the present, that our economic relations with Europe were built up. We must face the fact that unless we help Europe to get back to her normal life and production a chaos will ensue there which will inevitably be communicated to this country. For the present, it is manifest, we must quicken, not slacken our own production. We, and we almost alone, now hold the world steady. Upon our steadfastness and self-possession depend the affairs of nations everywhere. It is in this supreme crisis,—this crisis for all mankind,—that America must prove her mettle. In the presence of a world confused, distracted, she must show herself self-possessed, self-contained, capable of sober and effective action. She saved Europe by her action in arms; she must now save it by her action in peace. In saving Europe she will save herself, as she did upon the battlefields of the war. The calmness and capacity with which she deals with and masters the problems of peace will be the final test and proof of her place among the peoples of the world.

And, if only in our own interest, we must help the people over seas. Europe is our best customer. We must keep her going or thousands of our shops and scores of our mines must close. There is no such thing as letting her go to ruin without ourselves sharing in the disaster.

In such circumstances, face to face with such tests, passion must be discarded. Passion and a disregard for the rights of others have no place in the counsels of a free people. We need light, not heat, in these solemn times of self-examination and saving action. There must be no threats. Let there be only intelligent counsel, and let the best reasons win, not the strongest brute force. The world has just destroyed the arbitrary force of a military junta. It will live under no other. All that is arbitrary and coercive is in the discard. Those who seek to employ it will only prepare their own destruction.

We cannot hastily and overnight revolutionize all the processes of our economic life, and we shall not attempt to do so. These are days of deep excitement and extravagant speech; but with us these are of the surface. Everyone who is in real touch with the silent masses of our great people knows that the old strong fiber and steady self-control are still there, firm against violence or any distempered action that would throw their affairs into confusion. I am serenely confident that they will readily find themselves, no matter what the circumstances, and that they will address themselves to the tasks of peace with the same devotion and the same stalwart preference for what is right that they displayed to the admiration of the whole world in the midst of war.

And I entertain another confident hope. I have spoken to-day chiefly of measures of imperative regulation and legal compulsion, of prosecutions and the sharp correction of selfish processes; and these, no doubt, are necessary. But there are other forces that we may count on besides those resident in the Department of Justice. We have just fully awakened to what has been going on and to the influences, many of them very selfish and sinister, that have been producing high prices and imposing an intolerable burden on the mass of our people. To have brought it all into the open will accomplish the greater part of the result we seek. I appeal with entire confidence to our producers, our middlemen, and our merchants to deal fairly with the people. It is their opportunity to show that they comprehend, that they intend to act justly, and that they have the public interest sincerely at heart. And I have no doubt that housekeepers all over the country, and everyone who buys the things he daily stands in need of will presently exercise a greater vigilance, a more thoughtful economy, a more discriminating care as to the market in which he buys or the merchant with whom he trades than he has hitherto exercised.

I believe, too, that the more extreme leaders of organized labor will presently yield to a sober second thought and, like the great mass of their associates, they will think and act like true Americans. They will see that strikes undertaken at this critical time are certain to make matters worse, not better,—worse for them and for everybody else. The worst thing, the most fatal thing that can be done now is to stop or interrupt production or to interfere with the distribution of goods by the railways and the shipping of the country. We are all involved in the distressing results of the high cost of living and we must unite, not divide, to correct it. There are many things that ought to be corrected in the relations between capital and labor, in respect of wages and conditions of labor and other things even more far-reaching, and I, for one, am ready to go into conference about these matters with any group of my fellow countrymen who know what they are talking about and are

willing to remedy existing conditions by frank counsel
rather than by violent contest. No remedy is possible
while men are in a temper, and there can be no settlement which does not have as its motive and standard
the general interest. Threats and undue insistence upon
the interest of a single class make settlement impossible.
I believe, as I have hitherto had occasion to say to the
Congress, that the industry and life of our people and
of the world will suffer irreparable damage if employers
and workmen are to go on in a perpetual contest, as
antagonists. They must, on one plan or another, be
effectively associated. Have we not steadiness and self-
possession and business sense enough to work out that
result? Undoubtedly we have, and we shall work it
out. In the meantime,—now and in the days of readjustment and recuperation that are ahead of us,—let us
resort more and more to frank and intimate counsel
and make ourselves a great and triumphant Nation by
making ourselves a united force in the life of the world.
It will not then have looked to us for leadership in vain.

REPLY TO THE SENATE

MESSAGE TO THE SENATE OF THE UNITED STATES, TRANSMITTING INFORMATION AS REQUESTED, AUGUST 11, 1919. FROM 66TH CONGRESS, 1ST SESSION. SENATE DOCUMENT NO. 72.

TO THE SENATE:

I have received the resolutions of the Senate, dated July 15 and July 17, asking—

First, for a copy of any treaty purporting to have been projected between Germany and Japan, such as was referred to in the press dispatch inclosed, together with any information in regard to it which may be in possession of the State Department, or any information concerning any negotiations between Japan and Germany during the progress of the war. In reply to this resolution, I have the honor to report that I know of no such negotiations. I had heard the rumors that are referred to, but was never able to satisfy myself that there was any substantial foundation for them.

Second, requesting a copy of any letter or written protest by the members of the American Peace Commission or any officials attached thereto against the disposition or adjustment which was made in reference to Shantung, and particularly a copy of a letter written by Gen. Tasker H. Bliss, member of the Peace Commission, on behalf of himself, Hon. Robert Lansing, Secretary of State, and Hon. Henry White, members of the Peace Commission, protesting against the provisions of the treaty with reference to Shantung. In reply to this request, let me say that General Bliss did write me a letter in which he took very strong ground against the proposed Shantung settlement, and that his objections were concurred in by the Secretary of State and Mr. Henry White. But the letter cannot properly be described as a protest against the final Shantung decision, because it was written before that decision had been arrived at, and in response to my request that my colleagues on the Commission apprise me of their judgment in that matter. The final decision was very materially qualified by the policy which Japan undertook to pursue with regard to the return of the Shantung Peninsula in full sovereignty to China.

I would have no hesitation in sending the Senate a copy of General Bliss's letter were it not for the fact that it contains references to other Governments which it was perfectly proper for General Bliss to make in a confidential communication to me, but which I am sure General Bliss would not wish to have repeated outside our personal and intimate exchange of views.

I have received no written protest from any officials connected with or attached to the American Peace Commission with regard to this matter.

I am also asked to send you any memorandum or other information with reference to an attempt of Japan or her peace delegates to intimidate the Chinese peace delegates. I am happy to say that I have no such memorandum or information.

EXPOSITION OF THE LEAGUE TO THE FOREIGN RELATIONS COMMITTEE

STATEMENT TO THE MEMBERS OF THE SENATE COMMIT-
TEE ON FOREIGN RELATIONS, AUGUST 19, 1919.
FROM 66TH CONGRESS, 1ST SESSION. SENATE
DOCUMENT NO. 76.

M R. CHAIRMAN:
I have taken the liberty of writing out a little statement in the hope that it might facilitate discussion by speaking directly on some points that I know have been points of controversy and upon which I thought an expression of opinion would not be unwelcome. I am absolutely glad that the committee should have responded in this way to my intimation that I would like to be of service to it. I welcome the opportunity for a frank and full interchange of views.

I hope, too, that this conference will serve to expedite your consideration of the treaty of peace. I beg that you will pardon and indulge me if I again urge that practically the whole task of bringing the country back to normal conditions of life and industry waits upon the decision of the Senate with regard to the terms of the peace.

I venture thus again to urge my advice that the action of the Senate with regard to the treaty be taken at the earliest practicable moment because the problems with which we are face to face in the readjustment of our national life are of the most pressing and critical character, will require for their proper solution the most intimate and disinterested coöperation of all parties and all interests, and cannot be postponed without manifest peril to our people and to all the national advantages we hold most dear. May I mention a few of the matters which cannot be handled with intelligence until the

574

country knows the character of the peace it is to have? I do so only by a very few samples.

The copper mines of Montana, Arizona and Alaska, for example, are being kept open and in operation only at a great cost and loss, in part upon borrowed money; the zinc mines of Missouri, Tennessee and Wisconsin are being operated at about one-half their capacity; the lead of Idaho, Illinois and Missouri reaches only a portion of its former market; there is an immediate need for cotton belting, and also for lubricating oil, which cannot be met—all because the channels of trade are barred by war when there is no war. The same is true of raw cotton, of which the Central Empires alone formerly purchased nearly 4,000,000 bales. And these are only examples. There is hardly a single raw material, a single important foodstuff, a single class of manufactured goods which is not in the same case. Our full, normal profitable production waits on peace.

Our military plans of course wait upon it. We cannot intelligently or wisely decide how large a naval or military force we shall maintain or what our policy with regard to military training is to be until we have peace not only, but also until we know how peace is to be sustained, whether by the arms of single nations or by the concert of all the great peoples. And there is more than that difficulty involved. The vast surplus properties of the army include not food and clothing merely, whose sale will affect normal production, but great manufacturing establishments also which should be restored to their former uses, great stores of machine tools, and all sorts of merchandise which must lie idle until peace and military policy are definitely determined. By the same token there can be no properly studied national budget until then.

The nations that ratify the treaty, such as Great Britain, Belgium and France, will be in a position to lay their plans for controlling the markets of Central Europe without competition from us if we do not presently act. We have no consular agents, no trade representatives there to look after our interests.

There are large areas of Europe whose future will lie uncertain and questionable until their people know the final settlements of peace and the forces which are to administer and sustain it. Without determinate markets our production cannot proceed with intelligence or confidence. There can be no stabilization of wages because there can be no settled conditions of employment. There can be no easy or normal industrial credits because there can be no confident or permanent revival of business.

But I will not weary you with obvious examples. I will only venture to repeat that every element of normal life amongst us depends upon and awaits the ratification of the treaty of peace; and also that we cannot afford to lose a single summer's day by not doing all that we can to mitigate the winter's suffering, which, unless we find means to prevent it, may prove disastrous to a large portion of the world, and may, at its worst, bring upon Europe conditions even more terrible than those wrought by the war itself.

Nothing, I am led to believe, stands in the way of ratification of the treaty except certain doubts with regard to the meaning and implication of certain articles of the Covenant of the League of Nations; and I must frankly say that I am unable to understand why such doubts should be entertained. You will recall that when I had the pleasure of a conference with your committee and with the committee of the House of Representatives on Foreign Affairs at the White House in March last the questions now most frequently asked about the League of Nations were all canvassed with a view to their immediate clarification. The Covenant of the League was then in its first draft and subject to revision. It was pointed out that no express recognition was given to the Monroe Doctrine; that it was not expressly provided that the League should have no authority to act or to express a judgment on matters of domestic policy; that the right to withdraw from the League was not expressly recognized; and that the constitutional right of the Congress to determine all questions of peace and war was not sufficiently safeguarded. On my return to Paris all these matters were taken up again by the Commission on the League of Nations and every suggestion of the United States was accepted.

The views of the United States with regard to the questions I have mentioned had, in fact, already been accepted by the Commission and there was supposed to be nothing inconsistent with them in the draft of the Covenant first adopted—the draft which was the subject of our discussion in March—but no objection was made to saying explicitly in the text what all had supposed to be implicit in it. There was absolutely no doubt as to the meaning of any one of the resulting provisions of the Covenant in the minds of those who participated in drafting them, and I respectfully submit that there is nothing vague or doubtful in their wording.

The Monroe Doctrine is expressly mentioned as an understanding which is in no way to be impaired or interfered with by anything contained in the Covenant and the expression "regional understandings like the Monroe Doctrine" was used, not because any one of the conferees thought there was any comparable agreement anywhere else in existence or in contemplation, but only because it was thought best to avoid the appearance of dealing in such a document with the policy of a single nation. Absolutely nothing is concealed in the phrase.

With regard to domestic questions Article 16 of the Covenant expressly provides that, if in case of any dispute arising between members of the League the matter involved is claimed by one of the parties "and is found by the council to arise out of a matter which by international law is solely within the domestic jurisdiction of that party, the council shall so report, and shall make no recommendation as to its settlement." The United

States was by no means the only Government interested in the explicit adoption of this provision, and there is no doubt in the mind of any authoritative student of international law that such matters as immigration, tariffs, and naturalization are incontestably domestic questions with which no international body could deal without express authority to do so. No enumeration of domestic questions was undertaken because to undertake it, even by sample, would have involved the danger of seeming to exclude those not mentioned.

The right of any sovereign State to withdraw had been taken for granted, but no objection was made to making it explicit. Indeed, so soon as the views expressed at the White House conference were laid before the commission it was at once conceded that it was best not to leave the answer to so important a question to inference. No proposal was made to set up any tribunal to pass judgment upon the question whether a withdrawing nation had in fact fulfilled "all its international obligations and all its obligations under the Covenant." It was recognized that that question must be left to be resolved by the conscience of the nation proposing to withdraw; and I must say that it did not seem to me worth while to propose that the article be made more explicit, because I knew that the United States would never itself propose to withdraw from the League if its conscience was not entirely clear as to the fulfillment of all its international obligations. It has never failed to fulfill them and never will.

Article X is in no respect of doubtful meaning when read in the light of the Covenant as a whole. The council of the League can only "advise upon" the means by which the obligations of that great article are to be given effect to. Unless the United States is a party to the policy or action in question, her own affirmative vote in the council is necessary before any advice can be given, for a unanimous vote of the council is required. If she is a party, the trouble is hers anyhow. And the unanimous vote of the council is only advice in any case. Each Government is free to reject it if it pleases. Nothing could have been made more clear to the conference than the right of our Congress under our Constitution to exercise its independent judgment in all matters of peace and war. No attempt was made to question or limit that right. The United States will, indeed, undertake under Article X to "respect and preserve as against external aggression the territorial integrity and existing political independence of all members of the League," and that engagement constitutes a very grave and solemn moral obligation. But it is a moral, not a legal, obligation, and leaves our Congress absolutely free to put its own interpretation upon it in all cases that call for action. It is binding in conscience only, not in law.

Article X seems to me to constitute the very backbone of the whole Covenant. Without it the League would be hardly more than an influential debating society.

It has several times been suggested, in public debate and in private conference, that interpretations of the sense in which the United States accepts the engagements of the Covenant should be embodied in the instrument of ratification. There can be no reasonable objection to such interpretations accompanying the act of ratification provided they do not form a part of the formal ratification itself. Most of the interpretations which have been suggested to me embody what seems to me the plain meaning of the instrument itself. But if such interpretations should constitute a part of the formal resolution of ratification, long delays would be the inevitable consequence, inasmuch as all the many Governments concerned would have to accept, in effect, the language of the Senate as the language of the treaty before ratification would be complete. The assent of the German Assembly at Weimar would have to be obtained, among the rest, and I must frankly say that I could only with the greatest reluctance approach that Assembly for permission to read the treaty as we understand it and as those who framed it quite certainly understood it. If the United States were to qualify the document in any way, moreover, I am confident from what I know of the many conferences and debates which accompanied the formulation of the treaty that our example would immediately be followed in many quarters, in some instances with very serious reservations, and that the meaning and operative force of the treaty would presently be clouded from one end of its clauses to the other.

Pardon me, Mr. Chairman, if I have been entirely unreserved and plain-spoken in speaking of the great matters we all have so much at heart. If excuse is needed, I trust that the critical situation of affairs may serve as my justification. The issues that manifestly hang upon the conclusions of the Senate with regard to peace and upon the time of its action are so grave and so clearly insusceptible of being thrust on one side or postponed that I have felt it necessary in the public interest to make this urgent plea, and to make it as simply and as unreservedly as possible.

I thought that the simplest way, Mr. Chairman, to cover the points that I knew to be points of interest.

(Then follows the lengthy discussion between Mr. Wilson and the various members of the Senate Committee on Foreign Relations.)

URGING COÖPERATION UPON RAILWAY EMPLOYEES

REPLY TO REPRESENTATIVES OF THE RAILWAY EM-
PLOYEES' DEPARTMENT OF THE AMERICAN FED-
ERATION OF LABOR, AUGUST 25, 1919. FROM
ORIGINAL SIGNED COPY IN MR. WILSON'S FILES.

I REQUEST that you lay this critical matter before the men in a new light. The vote they have taken was upon the question whether they should insist upon the wage increase they were asking or consent to the submission of their claims to a new tribunal, to be constituted by new legislation. That question no longer has any life in it. Such legislation is not now in contemplation. I request that you ask the men to reconsider the whole matter in view of the following considerations, to which I ask their thoughtful attention as Americans, and which I hope that you will lay before them as I here state them.

We are face to face with a situation which is more likely to affect the happiness and prosperity, and even the life, of our people than the war itself. We have now got to do nothing less than bring our industries and our labor of every kind back to a normal basis after the greatest upheaval known to history, and the winter just ahead of us may bring suffering infinitely greater than the war brought upon us if we blunder or fail in the process. An admirable spirit of self-sacrifice, of patriotic devotion, and of community action guided and inspired us while the fighting was on. We shall need all these now, and need them in a heightened degree, if we are to accomplish the first tasks of peace. They are more difficult than the tasks of war,—more complex, less easily understood,—and require more intelligence, patience, and sobriety. We mobilized our man power for the fighting, let us now mobilize our brain power and our consciences for the reconstruction. If we fail, it will mean national disaster. The primary first step is to increase production and facilitate transportation, so as to make up for the destruction wrought by the war, the terrible scarcities it created, and so as soon as possible relieve our people of the cruel burden of high prices. The railways are at the center of this whole process.

The Government has taken up with all its energy the task of bringing the profiteer to book, making the stocks of necessaries in the country available at lowered prices, stimulating production and facilitating distribution, and very favorable results are already beginning to appear. There is reason to entertain the confident hope that substantial relief will result, and result in increasing measure. A general increase in the levels of wages would check and might defeat all this at its very beginning. Such increases would inevitably raise, not lower, the cost of living. Manufacturers and producers of every sort would have innumerable additional pretexts for increasing profits and all efforts to discover and defeat profiteering would be hopelessly confused. I believe that the present efforts to reduce the costs of living will be successful, if no new elements of difficulty are thrown in the way; and I confidently count upon the men engaged in the service of the railways to assist, not obstruct. It is much more in their interest to do this than to insist upon wage increases which will undo everything the Government attempts. They are good Americans, along with the rest of us, and may, I am sure, be counted on to see the point.

It goes without saying that if our efforts to bring the cost of living down should fail, after we have had time enough to establish either success or failure, it will of course be necessary to accept the higher costs of living as a permanent basis of adjustment, and railway wages should be readjusted along with the rest. All that I am now urging is, that we should not be guilty of the inexcusable inconsistency of making general increases in wages on the assumption that the present cost of living will be permanent at the very time that we are trying with great confidence to reduce the cost of living and are able to say that it is actually beginning to fall.

I am aware that railway employees have a sense of insecurity as to the future of the railroads and have many misgivings as to whether their interests will be properly safeguarded when the present form of federal control has come to an end. No doubt it is in part this sense of uncertainty that prompts them to insist that their wage interests be adjusted now rather than under conditions which they cannot certainly foresee. But I do not think that their uneasiness is well grounded. I anticipate that legislation dealing with the future of the railroads will in explicit terms afford adequate protection for the interests of the employees of the roads; but, quite apart from that, it is clear that no legislation can make the railways other than what they are, a great public interest, and it is not likely that the President of the United States, whether in possession and control of the railroads or not, will lack opportunity or persuasive force to influence the decision of questions arising between the managers of the railroads and the railway employees. The employees may rest assured that, during my term of office, whether I am in actual possession of the railroads or not, I shall not fail to exert the full influence of the Executive to see that justice is done them.

I believe, therefore, that they may be justified in the confidence that hearty coöperation with the Government now in its efforts to reduce the cost of living will by no means be prejudicial to their own interests, but will, on the contrary, prepare the way for more favorable and satisfactory relations in the future.

I confidently count on their coöperation in this time of national test and crisis.

RAILWAY WAGE DIFFICULTIES

STATEMENT TO THE PUBLIC REGARDING RAILWAY WAGE
PROBLEMS AND THE COST OF LIVING, AUGUST 26,
1919. FROM ORIGINAL COPY IN MR. WILSON'S
FILES.

A SITUATION has arisen in connection with the administration of the railways which is of such general significance that I think it my duty to make a public statement concerning it, in order that the whole country may know what is involved.

The railroad shopmen have demanded a large increase in wages. They are now receiving 58, 63, and 68 cents per hour. They demand 85 cents per hour. This demand has been given careful and serious consideration by the Board which was constituted by the Railroad Administration to adjust questions of wages, a Board consisting of an equal number of representatives of employees and of the operating managers of the railroad companies. This Board has been unable to come to an agreement, and it has therefore devolved upon the Director-General of Railroads and myself to act upon the merits of the case.

The shopmen urge that they are entitled to higher wages because of the higher wages for the present received by men doing a similar work in shipyards, navy-yards, and arsenals, as well as in a number of private industries, but I concur with the Director-General in thinking that there is no real basis of comparison between the settled employment afforded mechanics by the railroads under living conditions as various as the location and surroundings of the railway shops themselves and the fluctuating employment afforded in industries exceptionally and temporarily stimulated by the war and located almost without exception in industrial centers where the cost of living is highest.

The substantial argument which the shopmen urge is the very serious increase in the cost of living. This is a very potent argument indeed. But the fact is that the cost of living has certainly reached its peak, and will probably be lowered by the efforts which are now everywhere being concerted and carried out. It will certainly be lowered so soon as there are settled conditions of production and of commerce; that is, so soon as the treaty of peace is ratified and in operation, and merchants, manufacturers, farmers, miners all have a certain basis of calculation as to what their business will be and what the conditions will be under which it must be conducted. The demands of the shopmen, therefore, and all similar demands are in effect this: That we make increases in wages, which are likely to be permanent, in order to meet a temporary situation which will last nobody can certainly tell how long, but in all probability only for a limited time. Increases in wages will, moreover, certainly result in still further increasing the costs of production and, therefore, the cost of living, and we should only have to go through the same process again. Any substantial increase of wages in leading lines of industry at this time would utterly crush the general campaign which the Government is waging, with energy, vigor and substantial hope of success, to reduce the high cost of living. And the increases in the cost of transportation which would necessarily result from increases in the wages of railway employees would more certainly and more immediately have that effect than any other enhanced wage costs. Only by keeping the cost of production on its present level, by increasing production, and by rigid economy and saving on the part of the people can we hope for large decreases in the burdensome cost of living which now weighs us down.

The Director-General of Railroads and I have felt

that a peculiar responsibility rests upon us, because in determining this question we are not studying the balance-sheets of corporations merely, we are in effect determining the burden of taxation which must fall upon the people of the country in general. We are acting, not for private corporations, but in the name of the Government and the public, and must assess our responsibility accordingly. For it is neither wise nor feasible to take care of increases in the wages of railroad employees at this time by increases in freight rates. It is impossible at this time, until peace has come and normal conditions are restored, to estimate what the earning capacity of the railroads will be when ordinary conditions return. There is no certain basis, therefore, for calculating what the increases of freight rates should be, and it is necessary, for the time being at any rate, to take care of all increases in the wages of railway employees through appropriations from the Public Treasury.

In such circumstances it seems clear to me, and I believe will seem clear to every thoughtful American, including the shopmen themselves when they have taken second thought, and to all wage earners of every kind, that we ought to postpone questions of this sort until normal conditions come again and we have the opportunity for certain calculations as to the relation between wages and the cost of living. It is the duty of every citizen of the country to insist upon a truce in such contests until intelligent settlements can be made and made by peaceful and effective common counsel. I appeal to my fellow citizens of every employment to coöperate in insisting upon and maintaining such a truce, and to coöperate also in sustaining the Government in what I conceive to be the only course which conscientious public servants can pursue. Demands unwisely made and passionately insisted upon at this time menace the peace and prosperity of the country as nothing else

could, and thus contribute to bring about the very results which such demands are intended to remedy.

There is, however, one claim made by the railway
shopmen which ought to be met. They claim that they
are not enjoying the same advantages that other railway employees are enjoying because their wages are
calculated upon a different basis. The wages of other
railway employees are based upon the rule that they
are to receive for eight hours' work the same pay they
received for the longer workday that was the usual
standard of the pre-war period. This claim is, I am
told, well founded; and I concur in the conclusion of
the Director-General that the shopmen ought to be
given the additional four cents an hour which the readjustment asked for will justify. There are certain other
adjustments, also, pointed out in the report of the Director-General which ought in fairness to be made, and
which will be made.

Let me add, also, that the position which the Government must in conscience take against general increases in wage levels while the present exceptional and
temporary circumstances exist will of course not pre-
clude the Railroad Administration from giving prompt
and careful consideration to any claims that may be
made by other classes of employees for readjustments
believed to be proper to secure impartial treatment for
all who work in the railway service.

URGING INCREASED PRODUCTION
AND ECONOMY

LABOR DAY MESSAGE TO THE COUNTRY, AUGUST 31,
1919. FROM THE NEW YORK "TIMES," SEPTEM-
BER 1, 1919.

I AM encouraged and gratified by the progress which
is being made in controlling the cost of living. The
support of the movement is widespread and I confidently look for substantial results, although I must
counsel patience as well as vigilance, because such results will not come instantly or without teamwork.

Let me again emphasize my appeal to every citizen
of the country to continue to give his personal support
in this matter, and to make it as active as possible. Let
him not only refrain from doing anything which at the
moment will tend to increase the cost of living, but let
him do all in his power to increase the production; and,
further than that, let him at the same time himself
carefully economize in the matter of consumption. By
common action in this direction we shall overcome a
danger greater than the danger of war. We will hold
steady a situation which is fraught with possibilities of
hardship and suffering to a large part of our population; we will enable the processes of production to over-
take the processes of consumption; and we will speed
the restoration of an adequate purchasing power for
wages.

I am particularly gratified at the support which the
Government's policy has received from the representatives of organized labor, and I earnestly hope that the
workers generally will emphatically indorse the position of their leaders and thereby move with the Government instead of against it in the solution of this greatest
domestic problem.

I am calling for as early a date as practicable a conference in which authoritative representatives of labor and of those who direct labor will discuss fundamental means of bettering the whole relationship of capital and labor and putting the whole question of wages upon another footing.

ADDRESSES

DELIVERED ON WESTERN TOUR SEPTEMBER 4 TO SEPTEM-
BER 25, 1919. FROM 66TH CONGRESS, 1ST SESSION.
SENATE DOCUMENT NO. 120.

AT COLUMBUS, OHIO, SEPTEMBER 4, 1919.

MR. CHAIRMAN, GOVERNOR CAMPBELL, MY FELLOW CITIZENS:

It is with very profound pleasure that I find myself face to face with you. I have for a long time chafed at the confinement of Washington. I have for a long time wished to fulfill the purpose with which my heart was full when I returned to our beloved country, namely, to go out and report to my fellow countrymen concerning those affairs of the world which now need to be settled. The only people I owe any report to are you and the other citizens of the United States.

And it has become increasingly necessary, apparently, that I should report to you. After all the various angles at which you have heard the treaty held up, perhaps you would like to know what is in the treaty. I find it very difficult in reading some of the speeches that I have read to form any conception of that great document. It is a document unique in the history of the world for many reasons, and I think I cannot do you a better service, or the peace of the world a better service, than by pointing out to you just what this treaty contains and what it seeks to do.

In the first place, my fellow countrymen, it seeks to punish one of the greatest wrongs ever done in history, the wrong which Germany sought to do to the world and to civilization; and there ought to be no weak purpose with regard to the application of the punishment. She attempted an intolerable thing, and she must be

590

made to pay for the attempt. The terms of the treaty are severe, but they are not unjust. I can testify that the men associated with me at the Peace Conference in Paris had it in their hearts to do justice and not wrong. But they knew, perhaps, with a more vivid sense of what had happened than we could possibly know on this side of the water, the many solemn covenants which Germany had disregarded, the long preparation she had made to overwhelm her neighbors, and the utter disregard which she had shown for human rights, for the rights of women, of children, of those who were helpless. They had seen their lands devastated by an enemy that devoted himself not only to the effort at victory, but to the effort at terror—seeking to terrify the people whom he fought. And I wish to testify that they exercised restraint in the terms of this treaty. They did not wish to overwhelm any great nation. They acknowledged that Germany was a great nation, and they had no purpose of overwhelming the German people, but they did think that it ought to be burned into the consciousness of men forever that no people ought to permit its government to do what the German Government did.

In the last analysis, my fellow countrymen, as we in America would be the first to claim, a people are responsible for the acts of their Government. If their Government purposes things that are wrong, they ought to take measures to see to it that that purpose is not executed. Germany was self-governed; her rulers had not concealed the purposes that they had in mind, but they had deceived their people as to the character of the methods they were going to use, and I believe from what I can learn that there is an awakened consciousness in Germany itself of the deep iniquity of the thing that was attempted. When the Austrian delegates came before the Peace Conference, they in so many words spoke of the origination of the war as a crime and admitted in our presence that it was a thing intolerable to contemplate. They knew in their hearts that it had done them the deepest conceivable wrong, that it had put their people and the people of Germany at the judgment seat of mankind, and throughout this treaty every term that was applied to Germany was meant, not to humiliate Germany, but to rectify the wrong that she had done.

Look even into the severe terms of reparation—for there was no indemnity. No indemnity of any sort was claimed, merely reparation, merely paying for the destruction done, merely making good the losses so far as such losses could be made good which she had unjustly inflicted, not upon the governments, for the reparation is not to go to the governments, but upon the people whose rights she had trodden upon with absolute absence of everything that even resembled pity. There was no indemnity in this treaty, but there is reparation, and even in the terms of reparation a method is devised by which the reparation shall be adjusted to Germany's ability to pay it.

I am astonished at some of the statements I hear made about this treaty. The truth is that they are made by persons who have not read the treaty or who, if they have read it, have not comprehended its meaning. There is a method of adjustment in that treaty by which the reparation shall not be pressed beyond the point which Germany can pay, but which will be pressed to the utmost point that Germany can pay—which is just, which is righteous. It would have been intolerable if there had been anything else. For, my fellow citizens, this treaty is not meant merely to end this single war. It is meant as a notice to every government which in the future will attempt this thing that mankind will unite to inflict the same punishment. There is no national triumph sought to be recorded in this treaty. There is no glory sought for any particular nation. The thought of the statesmen collected around that table was of their people, of the sufferings that they had gone through, of the losses they had incurred—that great throbbing heart which was so depressed, so forlorn, so sad in every memory that it had had of the five tragical years that have gone. Let us never forget those years, my fellow countrymen. Let us never forget the purpose—the high purpose, the disinterested purpose—with which America lent its strength not for its own glory but for the defense of mankind.

As I said, this treaty was not intended merely to end this war. It was intended to prevent any similar war. I wonder if some of the opponents of the League of Nations have forgotten the promises we made our people before we went to that peace table. We had taken by processes of law the flower of our youth from every household, and we told those mothers and fathers and sisters and wives and sweethearts that we were taking those men to fight a war which would end business of that sort; and if we do not end it, if we do not do the best that human concert of action can do to end it, we are of all men the most unfaithful, the most unfaithful to the loving hearts who suffered in this war, the most unfaithful to those households bowed in grief and yet lifted with the feeling that the lad laid down his life for a great thing and, among other things, in order that other lads might never have to do the same thing. That is what the League of Nations is for, to end this war justly, and then not merely to serve notice on governments which would contemplate the same things that Germany contemplated that they will do it at their peril, but also concerning the combination of power which will prove to them that they will do it at their peril. It is idle to say the world *will* combine against you, because it may not, but it is persuasive to say the world *is* combined against you, and will remain combined against the things that Germany attempted. The League of Nations is the only thing that can prevent the recurrence of this dreadful catastrophe and redeem our promises.

The character of the League is based upon the experience of this very war. I did not meet a single public man who did not admit these things, that Germany would not have gone into this war if she had thought Great Britain was going into it, and that she most certainly would never have gone into this war if she dreamed America was going into it. And they all admitted that a notice beforehand that the greatest powers of the world would combine to prevent this sort of thing would prevent it absolutely. When gentlemen tell you, therefore, that the League of Nations is intended for some other purpose than this, merely reply this to them: If we do not do this thing, we have neglected the central covenant that we made to our people, and there will then be no statesmen of any country who can thereafter promise his people alleviation from the perils of war. The passions of this world are not dead. The rivalries of this world have not cooled. They have been rendered hotter than ever. The harness that is to unite nations is more necessary now than it ever was before, and unless there is this assurance of combined action before wrong is attempted, wrong will be attempted just so soon as the most ambitious nations can recover from the financial stress of this war.

Now, look what else is in the treaty. This treaty is unique in the history of mankind, because the center of it is the redemption of weak nations. There never was a congress of nations before that considered the rights of those who could not enforce their rights. There never was a congress of nations before that did not seek to effect some balance of power brought about by means of serving the strength and interest of the strongest powers concerned; whereas this treaty builds up nations that never could have won their freedom in any other way; builds them up by gift, by largess, not by obligations; builds them up because of the conviction of the men who wrote the treaty that the rights of people transcend the rights of governments, because of the conviction of the men who wrote that treaty that the fer-

tile source of war is wrong. The Austro-Hungarian
Empire, for example, was held together by military
force and consisted of peoples who did not want to live
together, who did not have the spirit of nationality as
towards each other, who were constantly chafing at the
bands that held them. Hungary, though a willing partner of Austria, was willing to be a partner because she
could share Austria's strength to accomplish her own
ambitions, and her own ambitions were to hold under
her the Jugo-Slavic peoples that lay to the south of her;
Bohemia, an unhappy partner, a partner by duress, beating in all her veins the strongest national impulse that
was to be found anywhere in Europe; and north of that,
pitiful Poland, a great nation divided up among the
great powers of Europe, torn asunder, kinship disregarded, natural ties treated with contempt, and an obligatory division among sovereigns imposed upon her—a
part of her given to Russia, a part of her given to Austria, a part of her given to Germany—great bodies of
Polish people never permitted to have the normal intercourse with their kinsmen for fear that that fine instinct
of the heart should assert itself which binds families
together. Poland could never have won her independence. Bohemia never could have broken away from
the Austro-Hungarian combination. The Slavic peoples
to the south, running down into the great Balkan peninsula, had again and again tried to assert their nationality
and independence, and had as often been crushed, not by
the immediate power they were fighting, but by the combined power of Europe. The old alliances, the old balances of power, were meant to see to it that no little
nation asserted its right to the disturbance of the peace
of Europe, and every time an assertion of rights was
attempted they were suppressed by combined influence
and force.

This treaty tears away all that: says these people
have a right to live their own lives under the governments which they themselves choose to set up. That is

the American principle, and I was glad to fight for it. When strategic claims were urged, it was matter of common counsel that such considerations were not in our thought. We were not now arranging for future wars. We were giving people what belonged to them. My fellow citizens, I do not think there is any man alive who has a more tender sympathy for the great people of Italy than I have, and a very stern duty was presented to us when we had to consider some of the claims of Italy on the Adriatic, because strategically, from the point of view of future wars, Italy needed a military foothold on the other side of the Adriatic, but her people did not live there except in little spots. It was a Slavic people, and I had to say to my Italian friends, "Everywhere else in this treaty we have given territory to the people who lived on it, and I do not think that it is for the advantage of Italy, and I am sure it is not for the advantage of the world, to give Italy territory where other people live." I felt the force of the argument for what they wanted, and it was the old argument that had always prevailed, namely, that they needed it from a military point of view, and I have no doubt that if there is no league of nations, they will need it from a military point of view; but if there is a league of nations, they will not need it from a military point of view.

If there is no league of nations, the military point of view will prevail in every instance, and peace will be brought into contempt, but if there is a league of nations, Italy need not fear the fact that the shores on the other side of the Adriatic tower above the lower and sandy shores on her side the sea, because there will be no threatening guns there, and the nations of the world will have concerted, not merely to see that the Slavic peoples have their rights, but that the Italian people have their rights as well. I had rather have everybody on my side than be armed to the teeth. Every settlement that is right, every settlement that is based on the principles I have alluded to, is a safe settlement, because the sympathy of mankind will be behind it.

Some gentlemen have feared with regard to the League of Nations that we will be obliged to do things we do not want to do. If the treaty were wrong, that might be so, but if the treaty is right, we will wish to preserve right. I think I know the heart of this great people whom I, for the time being have the high honor to represent better than some other men that I hear talk. I have been bred, and am proud to have been bred, in the old revolutionary school which set this Government up, when it was set up as the friend of mankind, and I know if they do not that America has never lost that vision or that purpose. But I have not the slightest fear that arms will be necessary if the purpose is there. If I know that my adversary is armed and I am not, I do not press the controversy, and if any nation entertains selfish purposes set against the principles established in this treaty and is told by the rest of the world that it must withdraw its claims, it will not press them.

The heart of this treaty then, my fellow citizens, is not even that it punishes Germany. That is a temporary thing. It is that it rectifies the age-long wrongs which characterized the history of Europe. There were some of us who wished that the scope of the treaty would reach some other age-long wrongs. It was a big job, and I do not say that we wished that it were bigger, but there were other wrongs elsewhere than in Europe and of the same kind which no doubt ought to be righted, and some day will be righted, but which we could not draw into the treaty because we could deal only with the countries whom the war had engulfed and affected. But so far as the scope of our authority went, we rectified the wrongs which have been the fertile source of war in Europe.

Have you ever reflected, my fellow countrymen, on the real source of revolution? Men do not start revo-

lutions in a sudden passion.   Do you remember what
Thomas Carlyle said about the French Revolution?
He was speaking of the so-called Hundred Days Terror
which reigned not only in Paris, but throughout France,
in the days of the French Revolution, and he reminded
his readers that back of that hundred days lay several
hundred years of agony and of wrong.   The French
people had been deeply and consistently wronged by
their Government, robbed, their human rights disregarded, and the slow agony of those hundreds of years
had after awhile gathered into a hot anger that could
not be suppressed.   Revolutions do not spring up overnight.   Revolutions come from the long suppression of
the human spirit.   Revolutions come because men know
that they have rights and that they are disregarded; and
when we think of the future of the world in connection
with this treaty we must remember that one of the chief
efforts of those who made this treaty was to remove
that anger from the heart of great peoples, great peoples who had always been suppressed, who had always
been used, and who had always been the tools in the
hands of governments, generally alien governments, not
their own.   The makers of the treaty knew that if these
wrongs were not removed, there could be no peace in the
world, because, after all, my fellow citizens, war comes
from the seed of wrong and not from the seed of right.
This treaty is an attempt to right the history of Europe,
and, in my humble judgment, it is a measurable success.
I say "measurable," my fellow citizens, because you will
realize the difficulty of this:

Here are two neighboring peoples.   The one people
have not stopped at a sharp line, and the settlements of
the other people or their migrations have not begun at
a sharp line.   They have intermingled.   There are regions
where you cannot draw a national line and say there
are Slavs on this side [illustrating] and Italians on that
[illustrating].   It cannot be done.   You have to approxi-
mate the line.   You have to come as near to it as you

can, and then trust to the processes of history to redistribute, it may be, the people that are on the wrong side of the line. There are many such lines drawn in this treaty and to be drawn in the Austrian treaty, where there are perhaps more lines of that sort than in the German treaty. When we came to draw the line between the Polish people and the German people—not the line between Germany and Poland; there was no Poland, strictly speaking, but the line between the German and the Polish people—we were confronted by such problems as the disposition of districts like the eastern part of Silesia, which is called Upper Silesia because it is mountainous and the other part is not. Upper Silesia is chiefly Polish, and when we came to draw the line of what should be Poland it was necessary to include Upper Silesia if we were really going to play fair and make Poland up of the Polish peoples wherever we found them in sufficiently close neighborhood to one another, but it was not perfectly clear that Upper Silesia wanted to be part of Poland. At any rate, there were Germans in Upper Silesia who said that it did not, and therefore we did there what we did in many other places. We said, "Very well, then, we will let the people that live there decide. We will have a referendum. Within a certain length of time after the war, under the supervision of an international commission which will have a sufficient armed force behind it to preserve order and see that nobody interferes with the elections, we will have an absolutely free vote and Upper Silesia shall go either to Germany or to Poland, as the people in Upper Silesia prefer." That illustrates many other cases where we provided for a referendum, or a plebiscite, as they chose to call it. We are going to leave it to the people themselves, as we should have done, what Government they shall live under. It is none of my prerogative to allot peoples to this Government or the other. It is nobody's right to do that allotting except the people themselves, and I want to testify that this treaty is shot through with the American principle of the choice of the governed.

Of course, at times it went further than we could make a practical policy of, because various peoples were keen upon getting back portions of their population which were separated from them by many miles of territory, and we could not spot the map over with little pieces of separated States. I even reminded my Italian colleagues that if they were going to claim every place where there was a large Italian population, we would have to cede New York to them, because there are more Italians in New York than in any Italian city. But I hope, I believe, that the Italians in New York City are as glad to stay there as we are to have them. But I would not have you suppose that I am intimating that my Italian colleagues entered any claim for New York City.

We of all peoples in the world, my fellow citizens, ought to be able to understand the questions of this treaty without anybody explaining them to us, for we are made up out of all the peoples of the world. I dare say that in this audience there are representatives of practically all the people dealt with in this treaty. You do not have to have me explain national aspirations to you. You have been brought up on them. You have learned of them since you were children, and it is those national aspirations which we sought to release and give an outlet to in this great treaty.

But we did much more than that. This treaty contains among other things a Magna Charta of labor—a thing unheard of until this interesting year of grace. There is a whole section of the treaty devoted to arrangements by which the interests of those who labor with their hands all over the world, whether they be men or women or children, are sought to be safeguarded; and next month there is to meet the first assembly under this section of the League. Let me tell you, it will meet whether the treaty is ratified by that time or not. There is to meet an assembly which represents the interests of laboring men throughout the world. Not their political interests; there is nothing political about it. It is the interests of men concerning the conditions of their labor; concerning the character of labor which women shall engage in, the character of labor which children shall be permitted to engage in; the hours of labor; and, incidentally, of course, the remuneration of labor; that labor shall be remunerated in proportion, of course, to the maintenance of the standard of living, which is proper, for the man who is expected to give his whole brain and intelligence and energy to a particular task. I hear very little said about the Magna Charta of labor which is embodied in this treaty. It forecasts the day, which ought to have come long ago, when statesmen will realize that no nation is fortunate which is not happy and that no nation can be happy whose people are not contented; contented in their lives and fortunate in the circumstances of their lives.

If I were to state what seems to me the central idea of this treaty, it would be this: It is almost a discovery in international conventions that nations do not consist of their governments but consist of their people. That is a rudimentary idea. It seems to us in America to go without saying, but, my fellow citizens, it was never the leading idea in any other international congress that I ever heard of; that is to say, any international congress made up of the representatives of governments. They were always thinking of national policy, of national advantage, of the rivalries of trade, of the advantages of territorial conquest. There is nothing of that in this treaty. You will notice that even the territories which are taken away from Germany, like her colonies, are not given to anybody. There is not a single act of annexation in this treaty. Territories inhabited by people not yet to govern themselves, either because of economical or other circumstances, are put under the care of powers, who are to act as trustees—trustees responsible in the forum of the world at the bar of the League of Nations, and the terms upon which they are to exercise their trusteeship are outlined. They are not to use those people by way of draft to fight their wars for them. They are not to permit any form of slavery among them, or of enforced labor. They are to see to it that there are humane conditions of labor with regard not only to the women and children but to the men also. They are to establish no fortifications. They are to regulate the liquor and the opium traffic. They are to see to it, in other words, that the lives of the people whose care they assume—not sovereignty over whom they assume—are kept clean and safe and wholesome. There again the principle of the treaty comes out, that the object of the arrangement is the welfare of the people who live there, and not the advantage of the trustee.

It goes beyond that. It seeks to gather under the common supervision of the League of Nations the various instrumentalities by which the world has been trying to check the evils that were in some places debasing men, like the opium traffic, like the traffic—for it was a traffic—in women and children, like the traffic in other dangerous drugs, like the traffic in arms among uncivilized people who could use arms only for their own detriment. It provides for sanitation, for the work of the Red Cross. Why, those clauses, my fellow citizens, draw the hearts of the world into league, draw the noble impulses of the world together and make a team of them.

I used to be told that this was an age in which mind was monarch, and my comment was that if that was true, the mind was one of those modern monarchs that reigns and does not govern; that, as a matter of fact, we were governed by a great representative assembly made up of the human passions, and that the best we could manage was that the high and fine passions should be in a majority so that they could control the baser passions, so that they could check the things that were wrong. This treaty seeks something like that. In drawing the humane endeavors of the world together it makes a league of the fine passions of the world, of its philanthropic passions, of its passion of pity, of its passion of human sympathy, of its passion of human friendliness and helpfulness, for there is such a passion. It is the passion which has lifted us along the slow road of civilization. It is the passion which has made ordered government possible. It is the passion which has made justice and established it in the world.

That is the treaty. Did you ever hear of it before? Did you ever know before what was in this treaty? Did anybody before ever tell you what the treaty was intended to do? I beg, my fellow citizens, that you and the rest of those Americans with whom we are happy to be associated all over this broad land will read the treaty yourselves, or, if you will not take the time to do that—for it is a technical document—that you will accept the interpretation of those who made it and know what the intentions were in the making of it. I hear a great deal, my fellow citizens, about the selfishness and the selfish ambitions of other governments, and I would not be doing justice to the gifted men with whom I was associated on the other side of the water if I did not testify that the purposes that I have outlined were their purposes. We differed as to the method very often. We had discussions as to the details, but we never had any serious discussion as to the principle. While we all acknowledged that the principles might perhaps in detail have been better realized, we are all back of those principles. There is a concert of mind and of purpose and of policy in the world that was never in existence before. I am not saying that by way of credit to myself or to those colleagues to whom I have alluded, because what happened to us was that we got messages from our people. We were under instructions, whether they were written down or not, and we did not dare come home without fulfilling those instructions. If I could not have brought back the kind of treaty that I did bring back, I never would have come back, because I would have been an unfaithful servant, and you would have had the right to condemn me in any way that you chose to use. So that I testify that this is an American treaty not only, but it is a treaty that expresses the heart of the great peoples who were associated together in the war against Germany.

I said at the opening of this informal address, my fellow citizens, that I had come to make a report to you. I want to add to that a little bit. I have not come to debate the treaty. It speaks for itself, if you will let it. The arguments directed against it are directed against it with a radical misunderstanding of the instrument itself. Therefore, I am not going anywhere to debate the treaty. I am going to expound it, and I am going, as I do here, now, to-day, to urge you in every vocal method that you can use to assert the spirit of the American people in support of it. Do not let men pull it down. Do not let them misrepresent it. Do not let them lead this Nation away from the high purposes with which this war was inaugurated and fought. As I came through that line of youngsters in khaki a few minutes ago I felt that I could salute them because I had done the job in the way I promised them I would do it, and when this treaty is accepted, men in khaki will not have to cross the seas again. That is the reason I believe in it.

I say "when it is accepted," for it will be accepted. I have never entertained a moment's doubt of that, and the only thing I have been impatient of has been the delay. It is not dangerous delay, except for the temper of the peoples scattered throughout the world who are waiting. Do you realize, my fellow citizens, that the whole world is waiting on America? The only country in the world that is trusted at this moment is the United

States, and the peoples of the world are waiting to see whether their trust is justified or not. That has been the ground of my impatience. I knew their trust was justified, but I begrudged the time that certain gentlemen wish to take in telling them so. We shall tell them so in a voice as authentic as any voice in history, and in the years to come men will be glad to remember that they had some part in the great struggle which brought this incomparable consummation of the hopes of mankind.

From Rear Platform, Richmond, Ind., September 4, 1919

I am trying to tell the people what is in the treaty. You would not know what was in it to read some of the speeches I read, and if you will be generous enough to me to read some of the things I say, I hope it will help to clarify a great many matters which have been very much obscured by some of the things which have been said. Because we have now to make the most critical choice we ever made as a nation, and it ought to be made in all soberness and without the slightest tinge of party feeling in it. I would be ashamed of myself if I discussed this great matter as a Democrat and not as an American. I am sure that every man who looks at it without party prejudice and as an American will find in that treaty more things that are genuinely American than were ever put into any similar document before.

The chief thing to notice about it, my fellow citizens, is that it is the first treaty ever made by great powers that was not made in their own favor. It is made for the protection of the weak peoples of the world and not for the aggrandizement of the strong. That is a noble achievement, and it is largely due to the influence of such great peoples as the people of America, who hold at their heart this principle, that nobody has the right to impose sovereignty upon anybody else; that, in disposing of the affairs of a nation, that nation or people must be its own master and make its own choice. The extraordinary achievement of this treaty is that it gives a free choice to people who never could have won it for themselves. It is for the first time in the history of international transactions an act of systematic justice and not an act of grabbing and seizing.

If you will just regard that as the heart of the treaty —for it is the heart of the treaty—then everything else about it is put in a different light. If we want to stand by that principle, then we can justify the history of America as we can in no other way, for that is the history and principle of America. That is at the heart of it. I beg that, whenever you consider this great matter, you will look at it from this point of view: Shall we or shall we not sustain the first great act of international justice? The thing wears a very big aspect when you look at it that way, and all little matters seem to fall away and one seems ashamed to bring in special interests, particularly party interests. What difference does party make when mankind is involved? Parties are intended, if they are intended for any legitimate purpose, to serve mankind, and they are based upon legitimate differences of opinion, not as to whether mankind shall be served or not, but as to the way in which it shall be served; and, so far as those differences are legitimate differences, party lines are justified.

AT COLISEUM, INDIANAPOLIS, IND., SEPTEMBER 4, 1919

GOVERNOR GOODRICH, MY FELLOW CITIZENS:

So great a company as this tempts me to make a speech, and yet I want to say to you in all seriousness and soberness that I have not come here to make a speech in the ordinary sense of that term. I have come upon a very sober errand indeed. I have come to report to you upon the work which the representatives of the United States attempted to do at the conference of peace on the other side of the sea, because my fellow citizens, I realize that my colleagues and I in the task we attempted over there were your servants. We went there upon a distinct errand, which it was our duty to perform in the spirit which you had displayed in the prosecution of the war and in conserving the purposes and objects of that war.

I was in the city of Columbus this forenoon. I was endeavoring to explain to a body of our fellow citizens there just what it was that the treaty of peace contained, for I must frankly admit that in most of the speeches that I have heard in debate upon the treaty of peace it would be impossible to form a definite conception of what that instrument means. I want to recall to you for the purposes of this evening the circumstances of the war and the purposes for which our men spent their lives on the other side of the sea. You will remember that a prince of the House of Austria was slain in one of the cities of Serbia. Serbia was one of the little kingdoms of Europe. She had no strength which any of the great powers needed to fear, and as we see the war now, Germany and those who conspired with her made a pretext of that assassination in order to make unconscionable demands of the weak and helpless Kingdom of Serbia. Not with a view to bringing about an acquiescence in those demands, but with a view to bringing about a conflict in which other purposes quite separate from the purposes connected with those demands could be achieved. Just so soon as those demands were made on Serbia, the other Governments of Europe sent telegraphic messages to Berlin and Vienna asking that the matter be brought into conference, and the significant circumstance of the beginning of this war is that the Austrian and German Governments did not dare to discuss the demands of Serbia or the purposes which they had in view. It is universally admitted on the other side of the water that if they had ever gone into international conference on the Austrian demands, the war never would have been begun. There was an insistent demand from London, for example, by the British Foreign Minister that the cabinets of Europe should be allowed time to confer with the Governments at Vienna and Berlin, and the Governments at Vienna and Berlin did not dare to admit time for discussion.

I am recalling these circumstances, my fellow citizens, because I want to point out to you what apparently has escaped the attention of some of the critics of the League of Nations, that the heart of the League of Nations Covenant does not lie in any of the portions which have been discussed in public debate. The great bulk of the provisions of that Covenant contain these engagements and promises on the part of the states which undertake to become members of it: That in no circumstances will they go to war without first having done one or other of two things, without first either having submitted the question to arbitration, in which case they agree to abide by the results, or having submitted the question to discussion by the council of the League of Nations, in which case they will allow six months for the discussion and engage not to go to war until three months after the council has announced its opinion upon the subject under dispute. The heart of the Covenant of the League is that the nations solemnly covenant not to go to war for nine months after a controversy becomes acute.

If there had been nine days of discussion, Germany would not have gone to war. If there had been nine days upon which to bring to bear the opinion of the world, the judgment of mankind, upon the purposes of those Governments, they never would have dared to execute those purposes. So that what it is important for us to remember is that when we sent those boys in khaki across the sea we promised them, we promised the world, that we would not conclude this conflict with a mere treaty of peace. We entered into solemn engagements with all the nations with whom we associated ourselves that we would bring about such a kind of settlement and such a concert of the purpose of nations that wars like this could not occur again. If this war has to be fought over again, then all our high ideals and purposes have been disappointed, for we did not go into this war merely to beat Germany. We went into this war to beat all purposes such as Germany entertained.

You will remember how the conscience of mankind was shocked by what Germany did; not merely by the circumstance to which I have already adverted, that unconscionable demands were made upon a little nation which could not resist, but that immediately upon the beginning of the war the solemn engagements of treaty were cast on one side, and the chief representative of the Imperial Government of Germany said that when national purposes were under consideration treaties were mere scraps of paper, and immediately upon that declaration the German armies invaded the territories of Belgium which they had engaged should be inviolate, invaded those territories with the half-avowed purpose that Belgium was to be permanently retained by Germany in order that she should have the proper frontage on the sea and the proper advantage in her contest with the other nations of the world. The act which was characteristic of the beginning of this war was the violation of the territorial integrity of the Kingdom of Belgium.

We are presently, my fellow countrymen, to have the very great pleasure of welcoming on this side of the sea the King and the Queen of the Belgians, and I, for one, am perfectly sure that we are going to make it clear to them that we have not forgotten the violation of Belgium, that we have not forgotten the intolerable wrongs which were put upon that suffering people. I have seen their devastated country. Where it was not actually laid in ruins, every factory was gutted of its contents. All the machinery by which it would be possible for men to go to work again was taken away, and those

parts of the machinery that could not be taken away
were destroyed by experts who knew how to destroy
them. Belgium was a very successful competitor of
Germany in some lines of manufacture, and the German
armies went there to see to it that that competition was
removed. Their purpose was to crush the independent
action of that little kingdom, not merely to use it as a
gateway through which to attack France. And when
they got into France, they not only fought the armies
of France, but they put the coal mines of France out of
commission, so that it will be a decade or more before
France can supply herself with coal from her accustomed sources. You have heard a great deal about
Article X of the Covenant of the League of Nations.
Article X speaks the conscience of the world. Article X
is the article which goes to the heart of this whole bad
business, for that article says that the members of this
League (that is intended to be all the great nations of
the world) engage to respect and to preserve against all
external aggression the territorial integrity and political
independence of the nations concerned. That promise
is necessary in order to prevent this sort of war from
recurring, and we are absolutely discredited if we fought
this war and then neglect the essential safeguard against
it. You have heard it said, my fellow citizens, that we
are robbed of some degree of our sovereign, independent choice by articles of that sort. Every man who
makes a choice to respect the rights of his neighbors
deprives himself of absolute sovereignty, but he does it
by promising never to do wrong, and I cannot for one
see anything that robs me of any inherent right that I
ought to retain when I promise that I will do right,
when I promise that I will respect the thing which,
being disregarded and violated, brought on a war in
which millions of men lost their lives, in which the civilization of mankind was in the balance, in which there
was the most outrageous exhibition ever witnessed in the

history of mankind of the rapacity and disregard for right of a great armed people.

We engage in the first sentence of Article X to respect and preserve from external aggression the territorial integrity and the existing political independence not only of the other member States, but of all States, and if any member of the League of Nations disregards that promise, then what happens? The council of the League advises what should be done to enforce the respect for that Covenant on the part of the nation attempting to violate it, and there is no compulsion upon us to take that advice except the compulsion of our good conscience and judgment. It is perfectly evident that if, in the judgment of the people of the United States the council adjudged wrong and that this was not a case for the use of force, there would be no necessity on the part of the Congress of the United States to vote the use of force. But there could be no advice of the council on any such subject without a unanimous vote, and the unanimous vote includes our own, and if we accepted the advice we would be accepting our own advice. For I need not tell you that the representatives of the Government of the United States would not vote without instructions from their Government at home, and that what we united in advising we could be certain that the American people would desire to do. There is in that Covenant not only not a surrender of the independent judgment of the Government of the United States, but an expression of it, because that independent judgment would have to join with the judgment of the rest.

But when is that judgment going to be expressed, my fellow citizens? Only after it is evident that every other resource has failed, and I want to call your attention to the central machinery of the League of Nations. If any member of that League, or any nation not a member, refuses to submit the question at issue either to arbitration or to discussion by the council, there ensues automatically by the engagements of this Covenant an absolute economic boycott. There will be no trade with that nation by any member of the League. There will be no interchange of communication by post or telegraph. There will be no travel to or from that nation. Its borders will be closed. No citizen of any other State will be allowed to enter it, and no one of its citizens will be allowed to leave it. It will be hermetically sealed by the united action of the most powerful nations in the world. And if this economic boycott bears with unequal weight, the members of the League agree to support one another and to relieve one another in any exceptional disadvantages that may arise out of it.

I want you to realize that this war was won not only by the armies of the world. It was won by economic means as well. Without the economic means the war would have been much longer continued. What happened was that Germany was shut off from the economic resources of the rest of the globe and she could not stand it. A nation that is boycotted is a nation that is in sight of surrender. Apply this economic, peaceful, silent, deadly remedy and there will be no need for force. It is a terrible remedy. It does not cost a life outside the nation boycotted, but it brings a pressure upon that nation which, in my judgment, no modern nation could resist.

I dare say that some of these ideas are new to you, because while it is true, as I said this forenoon in Columbus, that apparently nobody has taken the pains to see what is in this treaty, very few have taken the pains to see what is in the Covenant of the League of Nations. They have discussed, chiefly, three out of twenty-six articles, and the other articles contain this heart of the matter, that instead of war there shall be arbitration, instead of war there shall be discussion, instead of war there shall be the closure of intercourse, instead of war there shall be the irresistible pressure of the opinion of mankind. If I had done wrong, I would a great deal rather have a man shoot at me than stand me up for the judgment of my fellow men. I would a great deal rather see the muzzle of a gun than the look in their eyes. I would a great deal rather be put out of the world than live in the world boycotted and deserted. The most terrible thing is outlawry. The most formidable thing is to be absolutely isolated. And that is the kernel of this engagement. War is on the outskirts. War is a remote and secondary threat. War is a last resort. Nobody in his senses claims for the Covenant of the League of Nations that it is certain to stop war, but I confidently assert that it makes war violently improbable, and even if we cannot guarantee that it will stop war, we are bound in conscience to do our utmost in order to avoid it and prevent it.

I was pointing out, my fellow citizens, this forenoon, that this Covenant is part of a great document. I wish I had brought a copy with me to show you its bulk. It is an enormous volume, and most of the things you hear talked about in that treaty are not the essential things. This is the first treaty in the history of civilization in which great powers have associated themselves together in order to protect the weak. I need not tell you that I speak with knowledge in this matter, knowledge of the purpose of the men with whom the American delegates were associated at the peace table. They came there, every one that I consulted with, with the same idea, that wars had arisen in the past because the strong took advantage of the weak, and that the only way to stop wars was to bind ourselves together to protect the weak; that the example of this war was the example which gave us the finger to point the way of escape: That as Austria and Germany had tried to put upon Serbia, so we must see to it that Serbia and the Slavic peoples associated with her, and the peoples of Rumania, and the people of Bohemia, and the peoples of Hungary and Austria for that matter, should feel assured in the future that the strength of the great powers was behind their liberty and their independence and was not intended to be used, and never should be used, for aggression against them.

So when you read the Covenant, read the treaty with it. I have no doubt that in this audience there are many men which come from that ancient stock of Poland, for example, men in whose blood there is the warmth of old affections connected with that betrayed and ruined country, men whose memories run back to intolerable wrongs suffered by those they love in that country, and I call them to witness that Poland never could have won unity and independence for herself, and those gentlemen sitting at Paris presented Poland with a unity which she could not have won and an independence which she cannot defend unless the world guarantees it to her. There is one of the most noble chapters in the history of the world, that this war was concluded in order to remed the wrongs which had bitten so deep into the experience of the weaker peoples of that great continent. The object of the war was to see to it that there was no more of that sort of wrong done. Now, when you have that picture in your mind, that this treaty was meant to protect those who could not protect themselves, turn the picture and look at it this way:

Those very weak nations are situated through the very tract of country—between Germany and Persia—which Germany had meant to conquer and dominate, and if the nations of the world do not maintain their concert to sustain the independence and freedom of those peoples, Germany will yet have her will upon them, and we shall witness the very interesting spectacle of having spent millions upon millions of American treasure and, what is much more precious, hundreds of thousands of American lives, to do a futile thing, to do a thing which we will then leave to be undone at the leisure of those who are masters of intrigue, at the leisure of those who are masters in combining wrong influences to overcome right influences, of those who are the masters of the very things that we hate and mean always to fight. For, my fellow citizens, if Germany should ever attempt that again, whether we are in the League of Nations or not, we will join to prevent it. We do not stand off and see murder done. We do not profess to be the champions of liberty and then consent to see liberty destroyed. We are not the friends and advocates of free government and then willing to stand by and see free government die before our eyes. If a power such as Germany was, but thank God no longer is, were to do this thing upon the fields of Europe, then America would have to look to it that she did not do it also upon the fields of the Western Hemisphere, and we should at last be face to face with a power which at the outset we could have crushed, and which now it is within our choice to keep within the harness of civilization.

I am discussing this thing with you, my fellow citizens, as if I had a doubt of what the verdict of the American people would be. I have not the slightest doubt. I just wanted to have the pleasure of pointing out to you how absolutely ignorant of the treaty and the Covenant some of the men are who have been opposing them. If they do read the English language, they do not understand the English language as I understand it. If they have really read this treaty and this Covenant they only amaze me by their inability to understand what is plainly expressed. My errand upon this journey is not to argue these matters, but to recall you to the real issues which are involved. And one of the things that I have most at heart in this report to my fellow citizens is that they should forget what party I belong to and what party they belong to. I am making this journey as a democrat, but I am spelling it with a little "d," and I do not want anybody to remember, so far as this errand is concerned, that it is ever spelled with a big D. I am making this journey as an American and as a champion of rights which America believes in; and I need not tell you that as compared with the importance of America the importance of the Democratic party and the importance of the Republican party and the importance of every other party is absolutely negligible. Parties, my fellow citizens, are intended to embody in action different policies of government. They are not, when properly used, intended to traverse the principles which underlie government, and the principles which underlie the Government of the United States have been familiar to us ever since we were children. You have been bred, I have no doubt, as I have been bred, in the revolutionary school of American thought. I mean that school of American thought which takes its inspiration from the days of the American Revolution. There were only three million of us then, but we were ready to stand out against the world for liberty. There are more than a hundred million of us now, and we are ready to insist that everywhere men shall be champions of liberty.

I want you to notice another interesting point that is never dilated upon in connection with the League of Nations. I am treading now upon delicate ground and I must express myself with caution. There were a good many delegations that visited Paris who wanted to be heard by the peace conference who had real causes to present which ought to be presented to the view of the world, but we had to point out to them that they did not happen, unfortunately, to come within the area of settlement, that their questions were not questions which were necessarily drawn into the things that we were deciding. We were sitting there with the pieces of the Austro-Hungarian Empire in our hands. It had fallen apart. It never was naturally cohesive. We were sitting there with various dispersed assets of the German Empire in our hands, and with regard to every one of them we had to determine what we were going to do with them, but we did not have our own dispersed assets in our hands. We did not have the assets of the nations which constituted the body of nations associated against Germany to dispose of, and therefore we had often, with whatever regret, to turn away from questions that ought some day to be discussed and settled and upon which the opinion of the world ought to be brought to bear.

Therefore, I want to call your attention, if you will turn to it when you go home, to Article XI, following Article X, of the Covenant of the League of Nations. That article, let me say, is the favorite article in the treaty, so far as I am concerned. It says that every matter which is likely to affect the peace of the world is everybody's business; that it shall be the friendly right of any nation to call attention in the League to anything that is likely to affect the peace of the world or the good understanding between nations, upon which the peace of the world depends, whether that matter immediately concerns the nation drawing attention to it or not. In other words, at present we have to mind our own business. Under the Covenant of the League of Nations we can mind other peoples' business, and anything that affects the peace of the world, whether we are parties to it or not, can by our delegates be brought to the attention of mankind. We can force a nation on the other side of the globe to bring to that bar of mankind any wrong that is afoot in that part of the world which is likely to affect good understanding between nations, and we can oblige them to show cause why it should not be remedied. There is not an oppressed people in the world which cannot henceforth get a hearing at that forum, and you know, my fellow citizens, what a hearing will mean if the cause of those people is just. The one thing that those who are doing injustice have most reason to dread is publicity and discussion, because if you are challenged to give a reason why you are doing a wrong thing it has to be an exceedingly good reason, and if you give a bad reason you confess judgment and the opinion of mankind goes against you.

At present what is the state of international law and understanding? No nation has the right to call attention to anything that does not directly affect its own affairs. If it does, it can not only be told to mind its own business, but it risks the cordial relationship between itself and the nation whose affairs it draws under discussion; whereas, under Article XI the very sensible provision is made that the peace of the world transcends all the susceptibilities of nations and governments, and that they are obliged to consent to discuss and explain anything which does affect the understanding between nations.

Not only that, but there is another thing in this Covenant which cures one of the principal difficulties we encountered at Paris. I need not tell you that at every turn in those discussions we came across some secret treaty, some understanding that had never been made public before, some understanding which embarrassed the whole settlement. I think it will not be improper for me to refer to one of them. When we came to the settlement of the Shantung matter with regard to China, we found that Great Britain and France were under explicit treaty obligation to Japan that she should get exactly what she got in the treaty with Germany, and the most that the United States could do was to urge upon Japan the promise, which she gave, that she would not take advantage of those portions of the treaty but would return to the Republic of China, without qualification, the sovereignty which Germany had enjoyed in Shantung Province. We have had repeated assurances since then that Japan means to fulfill those promises in absolute good faith. But my present point is that there stood at the very gate of that settlement a secret treaty between Japan and two of the great powers engaged in this war on our side. We could not ask them to disregard those promises. This war had been fought in part because of the refusal to observe the fidelity which is involved in a promise, because of the failure to regard the sacredness of treaties, and this Covenant of the League of Nations provides that no secret treaty shall have any validity. It provides in explicit terms that

every treaty, every international understanding, shall be
registered with the secretary of the League, that it shall
be published as soon as possible after it is there registered, and that no treaty that is not there registered
will be regarded by any of the nations engaged in the
Covenant. So that we not only have the right to discuss
anything, but we make everything open for discussion.
If this Covenant accomplished little more than the abolition of private arrangements between great powers, it
would have gone far towards stabilizing the peace of the
world and securing justice, which it has been so difficult
to secure so long as nations could come to secret understandings with one another.

When you look at the Covenant of the League of
Nations thus, in the large, you wonder why it is a bogey
to anybody. You wonder what influences have made
gentlemen afraid of it. You wonder why it is not obvious to everybody as it is to those who study it with disinterested thought, that this is the central and essential
Covenant of the whole peace. As I was saying this forenoon, I can come through a double row of men in khaki
and acknowledge their salute with a free heart, because
I kept my promise to them. I told them when they went
to this war that it was a war not only to beat Germany
but to prevent any subsequent wars of this kind. I can
look all the mothers of this country in the face and all
the sisters and the wives and the sweethearts and say,
"The boys will not have to do this again."

You would think to hear some of the men who discuss
this Covenant that it is an arrangement for sending our
men abroad again just as soon as possible. It is the only
conceivable arrangement which will prevent our sending
our men abroad again very soon, and if I may use a
very common expression, I would say if it is not to be
this arrangement, what arrangement do you suggest to
secure the peace of the world? It is a case of "put up
or shut up." Opposition is not going to save the world.
Negations are not going to construct the policies of

mankind. A great plan is the only thing that can defeat a great plan. The only triumphant ideas in this world are the ideas that are organized for battle. The only thing that wins against a program is a better program. If this is not the way to secure peace, I beg that the way will be pointed out. If we must reject this way, then I beg that before I am sent to ask Germany to make a new kind of peace with us I should be given specific instructions what kind of peace it is to be. If the gentlemen who do not like what was done at Paris think they can do something better, I beg that they will hold their convention soon and do it now. They cannot in conscience or good faith deprive us of this great work of peace without substituting some other that is better.

So, my fellow citizens, I look forward with profound gratification to the time which I believe will now not much longer be delayed, when the American people can say to their fellows in all parts of the world, "We are the friends of liberty; we have joined with the rest of mankind in securing the guarantees of liberty; we stand here with you the eternal champions of what is right, and may God keep us in the Covenant that we have formed."

AT LUNCHEON AT HOTEL STATLER, ST. LOUIS, MO., SEPTEMBER 5, 1919.

MR. JOHNSON, YOUR HONOR MR. MAYOR, LADIES AND GENTLEMEN:

It is with great pleasure that I find myself in St. Louis again, because I have always found it possible in St. Louis to discuss serious questions in a way that gets mind in contact with mind, instead of that other less desirable thing, passion in contact with passion. I am glad to hear the mayor say, and I believe that it is true, that politics is adjourned. Party politics has no place, my fellow citizens, in the subject we are now obliged to discuss and to decide. Politics in the wider sense has a great deal to do with it. The politics of the world, the policy of mankind, the concert of the methods by which the world is to be bettered, that concert of will and of action which will make every nation a nobler instrument of Divine Providence—that is world politics.

I have sometimes heard gentlemen discussing the questions that are now before us with a distinction drawn between nationalism and internationalism in these matters. It is very difficult for me to follow their distinction. The greatest nationalist is the man who wants his nation to be the greatest nation, and the greatest nation is the nation which penetrates to the heart of its duty and mission among the nations of the world. With every flash of insight into the great politics of mankind, the nation that has that vision is elevated to a place of influence and power which it cannot get by arms, which it cannot get by commercial rivalry, which it can get by no other way than by that spiritual leadership which comes from a profound understanding of the problems of humanity. It is in the light of ideas of this sort that I conceive it a privilege to discuss the matters that I have come away from Washington to discuss.

I have come away from Washington to discuss them because apparently it is difficult to discuss them in Washington. The whole subject is surrounded with a mist which it is difficult to penetrate. I brought home with me from the other side of the water a great document, a great human document, but after you hear it talked about in Washington for awhile you think that it has just about three or four clauses in it. You fancy it has a certain Article X in it, that it has something about Shantung in it, that it has something about the Monroe Doctrine in it, that it has something about quitting, withdrawing from the League, showing that you do not want to play the game. I do not hear about anything else in it. Why, my fellow citizens, those are mere details and incidents of a great human enterprise, and I have sought the privilege of telling you what I conceive that human enterprise to be.

The war that has just been finished was no accident. Any man who had followed the politics of the world up to that critical break must have known that that was the logical outcome of the processes that had preceded it, must have known that the nations of the world were preparing for that very thing and were expecting it. One of the most interesting things that I realized after I got to the other side of the water was that the mental attitude of the French people with regard to the settlement of this war was largely determined by the fact that for nearly fifty years they had expected it, that for nearly fifty years they had dreaded, by the exercise of German force, the very thing that had happened, and their constant theme was, "We must devise means by which this intolerable fear will be lifted from our hearts. We cannot, we will not, live another fifty years under the cloud of that terror." The terror had been there all the time and the war was its flame and consummation. It had been expected, because the politics of Europe were based upon a definite conception. That conception was that the strong had all the rights and that all that the weak could enjoy was what the strong permitted them to enjoy; that no nation had any right that could not be asserted by the exercise of force, and that the real politics of Europe consisted in determining how many of the weak elements in the European combination of families and of nations should be under the influence and control of one set of nations and how many of those elements should be under the influence and control of another set of nations.

One of the centers of all the bad business was in that town of Constantinople. I do not suppose that intrigue was ever anywhere else reduced to such a consummate art or practiced with such ardor and subtlety as in Constantinople. That was because Constantinople was the key to the weak part of Europe. That was where the pawns were, not the kings and the queens and the castles and the bishops and the rest of the chess game of politics, but the little pawns. They made the openings for the heavier pieces. Their maneuvers determined the arrangement of the board, and those who controlled the pawns controlled the outcome of the whole effort to checkmate and to match and to capture and to take advantage. The shrewdest politicians in the diplomatic service of the several nations were put at Constantinople to run the game, which consisted in maneuvering the weak for the advantage of the strong, and every international conference that preceded the conference at Paris, which is still in process, was intended to complete and consummate the arrangements for that game. For the first time in the history of mankind, the recent conference at Paris was convened to destroy that system and substitute another.

I take it, my fellow citizens, that when you look at that volume, for it is a thick volume, that contains the treaty of peace with Germany, in the light of what I have been saying to you, you will read it with greater interest than you have hitherto attached to it. It is the chart and constitution of a new system for the world, and that new system is based upon an absolute reversal of the principles of the old system. The central object of that treaty is to establish the independence and protect the integrity of the weak peoples of the world. I hear some gentlemen, who are themselves incapable of altruistic purposes, say: "Ah, but that is altruistic. It is not our business to take care of the weak nations of the world." No, but it is our business to prevent war, and if we do not take care of the weak nations of the world, there will be war. These gentlemen assume the rôle of being very practical men, and they say, "We do not want to get into war to protect every little nation in the world." Very well then, let them show me how they will keep out of war by not protecting them, and let them show me how they will prove that, having gone into an enterprise, they are not absolute, contemptible quitters if they do not see the game through. They joined with the rest of us in the profession of fine purpose when we went into the war, and what was the fine purpose that they professed? It was not merely to defeat Germany. It is not a handsome enterprise for any great nation to go into a war merely to reduce another nation to obedience. They went in, and they professed to go in, to see to it that nobody after Germany's defeat should repeat the experiment which Germany had tried. And how do they propose to do that? To leave the material that Germany was going to make her dominating empire out of helpless and at her mercy.

What was the old formula of Pan-Germanism? From Bremen to Bagdad, wasn't it? Well, look at the map. What lies between Bremen and Bagdad? After you get past the German territory, there is Poland. There is Bohemia, which we have made into Czecho-Slovakia. There is Hungary, which is divided from Austria and does not share Austria's strength. There is Rumania. There is Jugo-Slavia. There is broken Turkey; and then Persia and Bagdad. The route is open. The route is wide open, and we have undertaken to say, "This route is closed!" If you do not close it, you have no choice but some day or other to enter into exactly the same sort of war that we have just gone through. Those gentlemen are dreaming. They are living in a past age which is gone and all but forgotten when they say that we can mind our own business.

What is our own business? Is there any merchant present here or any manufacturer or any banker who can say that our interests are separate from the interests of the rest of the world, commercially, industrially, financially? There is not a man in any one of those professions who does not admit that our industrial fortunes are tied up with the industrial fortunes of the rest of the world. He knows that, and when he draws a picture to himself, if he is frank, of what some gentlemen propose, this is what he sees: America minding her own business and having no other—despised, suspected, distrusted; and on the other side of the water the treaty and its operation—interrupted? Not at all! We are a great Nation, my fellow citizens, but the treaty is going to be applied just the same whether we take part in it or not, and part of its application, at the center of its application, stands that great problem of the rehabilitation of Germany industrially. I say the problem of her rehabilitation because unless she is rehabilitated she cannot pay the reparation. The reparation commission created by the treaty is created for the purpose of seeing that Germany pays the reparation, and it was admitted in all our conferences that in order to do that steps must be taken to enable Germany to pay the reparation, which means her industrial and commercial rehabilitation. Not only that, but some of you gentlemen know we used to have a trade with Germany. All of that trade is going to be in the hands and under the control of the reparation commission. I humbly asked leave to appoint a member to look after our interests, and I was rebuked for it. I am looking after the industrial interest of the United States. I would like to see the other men who are. They are forgetting the industrial interests of the United States, and they are doing things that will cut us off, and our trade off, from the normal channels, because the reparation commission can determine where Germany buys, what Germany buys, how much Germany buys; the reparation commission can determine in what instruments of credit she temporarily expresses her debt. It can determine how those instruments of credit shall be used for the basis of the credit which must underlie international exchanges. It is going to stand at the center of the financial operations of the world. Now, is it minding our business to keep out of that? On the contrary, it is handing our business over to people who are not particularly interested in seeing that it prospers. These are facts which I can appropriately address to a chamber of commerce because they are facts which nobody can controvert and which yet seem often to be forgotten. The broad aspects of this subject are seldom brought to your attention. It is the little picayune details here and there.

That brings me, my fellow citizens, to the guarantee of this whole thing. We said that we were going to fight this war for the purpose of seeing to it that the mothers and sisters and fathers of this land, and the sweethearts and wives, did not have to send their lads over on the other side of the sea to fight any more, and so we took part in an arrangement by which justice was to be secured throughout the world. The rest of the world, partly at our suggestion, said "Yes" and said it gladly; said "Yes, we will go into the partnership to see that justice is maintained"; and then I come home and hear some gentlemen say, "But will we?" Are we interested in justice? The treaty of peace, as I have just said to you, is based upon the protection of the weak against the strong, and there is only one force that can protect the weak against the strong, and that is the universal concert of the strength of mankind. That is the League of Nations.

But I beg that you will not conceive of the League of Nations as a combination of the world for war, for that is exactly what it is not. It is a combination of the world for arbitration and discussion. I was taking the pains the other day to make a sort of table of contents of the Covenant of the League of Nations, and I found that two-thirds of its provisions were devoted to setting up a system of arbitration and discussion in the world. Why, these are the facts, my fellow citizens: The members of the League agree that no one of them will ever go to war about anything without first doing one or other of two things: without either submitting the question to arbitration, in which case they agree to abide by the decision of the arbitrators absolutely, or submitting it to discussion by the council of the League of Nations, in which case they agree that, no matter what the opinion expressed by the council may be, they will allow six months for the discussion, and, whether they are satisfied with the conclusion or not, will not go to war in less than three months after the rendering of the opinion. I think we can take it for granted that the preliminaries would take two or three months, in which case you have a whole year of discussion even when you do not get arbitration; and I want to call you to witness that in almost every international controversy which has been submitted to thorough canvass by the opinion of the world it has become impossible for the result to be war. War is a process of heat. Exposure is a process of cooling; and what is proposed in this is that every hot thing shall be spread out in the cooling air of the opinion of the world and after it is thoroughly cooled off, then let the nations concerned determine whether they are going to fight about it or not.

And notice the sanction. Any member of the League which breaks these promises with regard to arbitration or discussion is to be deemed thereby to have committed an act of war against the other members of the League; not merely to have done an immoral thing, but by refusing to obey those processes to have committed an act of war and put itself out of court. You know what then happens. You say, "Yes, we form an army and go and fight them." Not at all. We shut their doors and lock them in. We boycott them. Just so soon as that is done they cannot ship cargoes out or receive them shipped in. They cannot send a telegraphic message. They cannot send or receive a letter. Nobody can leave their territory and nobody can enter their territory. They are absolutely boycotted by the rest of mankind. I do not think that after that remedy it will be necessary to do any fighting at all. What brought Germany to her knees was, not only the splendid fighting of the incomparable men who met her armies, but that her doors were locked and she could not get supplies from any part of the world. There were a few doors open, doors to some Swedish ore, for example, that she needed for making munitions, and that kept her going for a time; but the Swedish door would be shut this time. There would not be any door open, and that brings a nation to its senses just as suffocation removes from the individual all inclination to fight.

That is the League of Nations, an agreement to arbitrate or discuss, and an agreement that if you do not arbitrate or discuss, you shall be absolutely boycotted and starved out. There is hardly a European nation, my fellow citizens, that is of a fighting inclination which has enough food to eat without importing food, and it will be a very persuasive argument that it has nothing to eat, because you cannot fight on an empty stomach any more than you can worship God on an empty stomach.

When we add to that some other very interesting particulars, I think the League of Nations becomes a very interesting thing indeed. You have heard of Article X, and I am going to speak about that in a minute, but read Article XI, because, really, there are other articles in the Covenant! Article XI says—I am not quoting its language, but its substance—that anything that is likely to affect the peace of the world or the good understanding upon which the peace of the world depends shall be everybody's business; that any nation, the littlest nation at the table, can stand up and challenge the right of the strongest nation there to keep on in a course of action or policy which is likely to disturb the peace of the world, and that it shall be its "friendly right" to do so. Those are the words. It cannot be regarded as an hostile or unfriendly act. It is its

friendly right to do that, and if you will not give the
secret away, I wrote those words myself. I wanted it to
be our friendly right and everybody's friendly right to
discuss everything that was likely to affect the peace of
the world, because that is everybody's business. It is
everybody's business to see that nothing happens that
does disturb the peace of the world.

And there is added to this particular this very interesting thing: There can hereafter be no secret treaties.
There were nations represented around that board—
I mean the board at which the Commission on the
League of Nations sat, where fourteen nations were
represented— there were nations represented around
that board who had entered into many a secret treaty
and understanding, and they made not the least objection to promising that hereafter no secret treaty should
have any validity whatever. The provision of the Covenant is that every treaty or international understanding
shall be "registered," I believe the word is, with the
general secretary of the League, that the general secretary shall publish it in full just so soon as it is possible
for him to publish it, and that no treaty shall be valid
which is not thus registered. It is like our arrangements with regard to mortgages on real estate, that
until they are registered nobody else need pay any attention to them. So with the treaties: Until they are registered in this office of the League, nobody, not even the
parties themselves, can insist upon their execution. You
have cleared the deck thereby of the most dangerous
thing and the most embarrassing thing that has hitherto
existed in international politics.

It was very embarrassing, my fellow citizens, when
you thought you were approaching an ideal solution of
a particular question to find that some of your principal
colleagues had given the whole thing away. And that
leads me to speak just in passing of what has given a
great many people natural distress. I mean the Shan-

tung settlement, the settlement with regard to a portion of the Province of Shantung in China. Great Britain and, subsequently, France, as everybody now knows, in order to make it more certain that Japan would come into the war and so assist to clear the Pacific of the German fleets, had promised that any rights that Germany had in China should, in the case of the victory of the Allies, pass to Japan. There was no qualification in the promise. She was to get exactly what Germany had, and so the only thing that was possible was to induce Japan to promise—and I want to say in fairness, for it would not be fair if I did not say it, that Japan did very handsomely make the promise which was requested of her—that she would retain in Shantung none of the sovereign rights which Germany had enjoyed there, but would return the sovereignty without qualification to China and retain in Shantung Province only what other nationalities had already had elsewhere, economic rights with regard to the development and administration of the railway and of certain mines which had become attached to the railway. That is her promise, and personally I have not the slightest doubt that she will fulfill that promise. She cannot fulfill it right now because the thing does not go into operation until three months after the treaty is ratified, so that we must not be too impatient about it. But she will fulfill that promise.

Suppose that we said that we would not assent. England and France must assent, and if we are going to get Shantung Province back for China and these gentlemen do not want to engage in foreign wars, how are they going to get it back? Their idea of not getting into trouble seems to be to stand for the largest possible number of unworkable propositions. It is all very well to talk about standing by China, but how are you standing by China when you withdraw from the only arrangement by which China can be assisted. If you are

China's friend, then do not go into the council where you can act as China's friend! If you are China's friend, then put her in a position where even the concessions which have been made need not be carried out! If you are China's friend, scuttle and run! That is not the kind of American I am.

Now, just a word about Article X. Permit me, if you will, to recur to what I said at the opening of these somewhat disjointed remarks. I said that the treaty was intended to destroy one system and substitute another. That other system was based upon the principle that no strong power need respect the territorial integrity or the political independence of any weak power. I need not confine the phraseology to that. It was based upon the principle that no power is obliged to respect the territorial integrity or the political independence of any other power if it has the force necessary to disregard it. So that Article X cuts at the very heart, and is the only instrument that will cut to the very heart, of the old system. Remember that if this Covenant is adopted by the number of nations which it probably will be adopted by, it means that every nation except Germany and Turkey, because we have already said we would let Austria come in (Germany has to undergo a certain period of probation to see whether she has really experienced a change of heart and effected a genuine change of constitutional provision)—it means that all the nations of the world, except one strong and one negligible one, agree that they will respect and preserve against external aggression the territorial integrity and existing political independence of the other nations of the world. You would think from some of the discussions that the emphasis is on the word "preserve."

We are partners with the rest of the world in respecting the territorial integrity and political independence of others. They are all under solemn bonds themselves to respect and to preserve those things, and if they do not preserve them, if they do not respect them or preserve them, what happens? The council of the League then advises the several members of the League what it is necessary to do. I can testify from having sat at the board where the instrument was drawn that advice means advice. I supposed it did before I returned home, but I found some gentlemen doubted it. Advice means advice, and the advice cannot be given without the concurrent vote of the representative of the United States. "Ah," but somebody says, "suppose we are a party to the quarrel!" I cannot suppose that, because I know that the United States is not going to disregard the territorial integrity or the political independence of any other nation, but for the sake of the argument suppose that we are a party. Very well then, the scrap is ours anyway. For what these gentlemen are afraid of is that we are going to get into trouble. If we are a party, we are in trouble already, and if we are not a party, we can control the advice of the council by our vote. To my mind, that is a little like an open and shut game! I am not afraid of advice which we give ourselves; and yet that is the whole of the bugaboo which these gentlemen have been parading before you.

The solemn thing about Article X is the first sentence, not the second sentence. The first sentence says that we will respect and preserve against external aggression the territorial integrity and existing political independence of other nations; and let me stop a moment on the words "external aggression." Why were they put in? Because every man who sat at that board held that the right of revolution was sacred and must not be interfered with. Any kind of a row can happen inside and it is nobody's right to interfere. The only thing that there is any right to object to or interfere with is external aggression, by some outside power undertaking to take a piece of territory or to interfere with the internal political arrangements of the country which is suffering from the aggression; because territorial integrity does not mean that you cannot invade another country; it means that you cannot invade it and stay there. I have not impaired the territorial integrity of your back yard if I walk into it, but I very much impair it if I insist upon staying there and will not get out, and the impairment of integrity contemplated in this article is the kind of impairment as the seizure of territory, as an attempt at annexation, as an attempt at continuing domination either of the territory itself or of the methods of government inside that territory.

When you read Article X, therefore, you will see that it is nothing but the inevitable, logical center of the whole system of the Covenant of the League of Nations, and I stand for it absolutely. If it should ever in any important respect be impaired, I would feel like asking the Secretary of War to get the boys who went across the water to fight together on some field where I could go and see them, and I would stand up before them and say, "Boys, I told you before you went across the seas that this was a war against wars, and I did my best to fulfill the promise, but I am obliged to come to you in mortification and shame and say I have not been able to fulfill the promise. You are betrayed. You fought for something that you did not get." And the glory of the Armies and the Navies of the United States is gone like a dream in the night, and there ensues upon it, in the suitable darkness of the night, the nightmare of dread which lay upon the nations before this war came; and there will come sometime, in the vengeful Providence of God, another struggle in which, not a few hundred thousand fine men from America will have to die, but as many millions as are necessary to accomplish the final freedom of the peoples of the world.

AT COLISEUM, ST. LOUIS, MO., SEPTEMBER 5, 1919.

MR. CHAIRMAN, GOVERNOR GARDNER, MY FELLOW
  COUNTRYMEN:

This is much too solemn an occasion to care how we
look; we ought to care how we think. [The photog-
rapher had just asked the audience to sit still for a
picture.] I have come here to-night to ask permission to discuss with you some of the very curious aberra-
tions of thinking that have taken place in this country
of late. I have sought—I think I have sought without
prejudice—to understand the point of view of the men
who have been opposing the treaty and the Covenant
of the League of Nations. Many of them are men
whose judgment and whose patriotic feeling I have been
accustomed to admire and respect, and yet I must admit
to you, my fellow countrymen, that it is very hard for
me to believe that they have followed their line of
thinking to its logical and necessary conclusion, because
when you reflect upon their position, it is either that
we ought to reject this treaty altogether or that we
ought to change it in such a way as will make it necessary to reopen negotiations with Germany and reconsider the settlements of the peace in many essential
particulars. We cannot do the latter alone, and other
nations will not join us in doing it. The only alternative is to reject the peace and to do what some of our
fellow countrymen have been advising us to do, stand
alone in the world.

I am going to take the liberty to-night of pointing out
to you what this alternative means. I know the course
of reasoning which is either uttered or implicit in this
advice when it is given us by some of the men who propose this course. They believe that the United States is
so strong, so financially strong, so industrially strong,
if necessary so physically strong, that it can impose its
will upon the world if it is necessary for it to stand out

against the world, and they believe that the processes
of peace can be processes of domination and antagonism, instead of processes of coöperation and good feeling, I therefore want to point out to you that only those
who are ignorant of the world can believe that any nation, even so great a nation as the United States, can
stand alone and play a single part in the history of
mankind.

Begin with a single circumstance; for I have not
come here to-night to indulge in any kind of oratory.
I have come here to-night to present to you certain hard
facts which I want you to take home with you and think
about. I suppose that most of you realize that it is
going to be very difficult for the other nations that were
engaged in this war to get financially on their feet
again. I dare say you read the other day the statement
of Mr. Herbert Hoover's opinion, an opinion which I
always greatly respect, that it will be necessary for the
United States immediately to advance four or five billion dollars for the rehabilitation of credit and industry
on the other side of the water, and I must say to you
that I learned nothing in Paris which would lead me to
doubt that conclusion. I think the statement of the
sum is a reasonable and conservative statement. If the
world is going bankrupt, if credit is going to be destroyed, if the industry of the rest of the world is going
to be interrupted, our market is confined to the United
States. Trade will be impossible, except within our
own borders. If we are to save our own markets and
rehabilitate our own industries, we must save the financial situation of the world and rehabilitate the markets
of the world. Very well, what do these gentlemen propose? That we should do that, for we cannot escape
doing it.

Face to face with a situation of this kind, we are not,
let us assume, partners in the execution of this treaty.
What is one of the central features of the execution of
this treaty? It is the application of the reparation

clauses. Germany cannot pay for this war unless her industries are revived, and the treaty of peace sets up a great commission known as the Reparation Commission, in which it was intended that there should be a member from the United States as well as from other countries. The business of this commission will be in part to see that the industries of Germany are revived in order that Germany may pay this great debt which she owes to civilization. That Reparation Commission can determine the currents of trade, the conditions of international credit; it can determine how much Germany is going to buy, where it is going to buy, how it is going to pay for it, and if we must, to save ourselves, contribute to the financial rehabilitation of the world, then without being members of this partnership we must put our money in the hands of those who want to get the markets that belong to us. That is what these gentlemen call playing a lone hand. It is indeed playing a lone hand. It is playing a hand that is frozen out! We must contribute the money which other nations are to use in order to rehabilitate their industry and credit, and we must make them our antagonists and rivals and not our partners! I put that proposition to any business man, young or old, in the United States and ask him how he likes it, and whether he considers that a useful way for the United States to stand alone. We have got to carry this burden of reconstitution whether we will or not or be ruined, and the question is, Shall we carry it and be ruined anyhow? For that is what these gentlemen propose, that at every point we shall be embarrassed by the whole financial affairs of the world being in the hands of other nations.

As I was saying at the luncheon that I had the pleasure of eating with the chamber of commerce to-day, the whole aspect of the matter is an aspect of ignorance. The men who propose these things do not understand the selfish interests of the United States, because here is the rest of the picture: Hot rivalries, burning suspicions, jealousies, arrangements made everywhere if possible to shut us out, because if we will not come in as equals we ought to be shut out. If we are going to keep out of this thing in order to prey upon the rest of the world, then I think we ought to be frozen out of it. That is not the temper of the United States, and it is not like the United States to be ignorant enough to think any such thoughts, because we know that partners profit and enemies lose the game. But that is not all of the picture, my fellow citizens. If every nation is going to be our rival, if every nation is going to dislike and distrust us, and that will be the case, because having trusted us beyond measure the reaction will occur beyond measure (as it stands now they trust us, they look to us, they long that we shall undertake anything for their assistance rather than that any other nation should undertake it)—if we say, "No, we are in this world to live by ourselves, and get what we can out of it by any selfish processes," then the reaction will change the whole heart and attitude of the world towards this great, free, justice-loving people, and after you have changed the attitude of the world, what have you produced? Peace? Why, my fellow citizens, is there any man here or any woman, let me say is there any child here, who does not know that the seed of war in the modern world is industrial and commercial rivalry? The real reason that the war that we have just finished took place was that Germany was afraid her commercial rivals were going to get the better of her, and the reason why some nations went into the war against Germany was that they thought Germany would get the commercial advantage of them. The seed of the jealousy, the seed of the deep-seated hatred was hot, successful commercial and industrial rivalry.

Why, what did the Germans do when they got into Belgium? I have just seen that suffering country. Most of the Belgian factories are standing. You do not witness in Belgium what you witness in France, except upon certain battlefields—factories destroyed, whole towns wiped out. No! the factories are there, the streets are clear, the people are there, but go in the factories. Every piece of machinery that could be taken away has been taken away. If it was too big to take away, experts directed the way in which it should be injured so it could never be used again, and that was because there were textile industries and iron industries in Belgium which the Germans hated Belgium for having, because they were better than the German and outdid them in the markets of the world. This war, in its inception was a commercial and industrial war. It was not a political war.

Very well, then, if we must stand apart and be the hostile rivals of the rest of the world, then we must do something else. We must be physically ready for anything that comes. We must have a great standing army. We must see to it that every man in America is trained to arms. We must see to it that there are munitions and guns enough for an army that means a mobilized nation; that they are not only laid up in store, but that they are kept up to date; that they are ready to use tomorrow; that we are a nation in arms; because you cannot be unfriendly to everybody without being ready that everybody shall be unfriendly to you. And what does that mean? Reduction of taxes? No. Not only the continuation of the present taxes but the increase of the present taxes; and it means something very much more serious than that. We can stand that, so far as the expense is concerned, if we care to keep up the high cost of living and enjoy the other luxuries that we have recently enjoyed, but, what is much more serious than that, we have got to have the sort of organization which is the only kind of organization that can handle arms of that sort. We may say what we please of the German Government that has been destroyed, my fellow citizens, but it was the only sort of government that could handle an armed nation. You cannot handle an armed nation by vote. You cannot handle an armed nation if it is democratic, because democracies do not go to war that way. You have got to have a concentrated, militaristic organization of government to run a nation of that sort. You have got to think of the President of the United States, not as the chief counsellor of the Nation, elected for a little while, but as the man meant constantly and every day to be the Commander in Chief of the Army and Navy of the United States, ready to order them to any part of the world where the threat of war is a menace to his own people. And you cannot do that under free debate. You cannot do that under public counsel. Plans must be kept secret. Knowledge must be accumulated by a system which we have condemned, because we have called it a spying system. The more polite call it a system of intelligence. You cannot watch other nations with your unassisted eye. You have got to watch them by secret agencies planted everywhere. Let me testify to this, my fellow citizens: I not only did not know it until we got into this war, but I did not believe it when I was told that it was true, that Germany was not the only country that maintained a secret service. Every country in Europe maintained it, because they had to be ready for Germany's spring upon them, and the only difference between the German secret service and the other secret services was that the German secret service found out more than the others did, and therefore Germany sprang upon the other nations unawares, and they were not ready for it.

And you know what the effect of a military government is upon social questions. You know how impossible it is to effect social reform if everybody must be under orders from the Government. You know how impossible it is, in short, to have a free nation, if it is a military nation and under military order. You may say, "You have been on the other side of the water and got bad dreams." I have got no dreams at all. I am telling you the things, the evidence of which I have seen with awakened eyes and not with sleeping eyes, and I know that this country, if it wishes to stand alone, must stand alone as part of a world in arms. Because, ladies and gentlemen—I do not say it because I am an American and my heart is full of the same pride that fills yours with regard to the power and spirit of this great Nation, but merely because it is a fact which I think everybody would admit, outside of America, as well as inside of America—the organization contemplated by the League of Nations without the United States would merely be an alliance and not a league of nations. It would be an alliance in which the partnership would be between the more powerful European nations and Japan, and the other party to the world arrangement, the antagonist, the disassociated party, the party standing off to be watched by the alliance, would be the United States of America. There can be no league of nations in the true sense without the partnership of this great people.

Now, let us mix the selfish with the unselfish. If you do not want me to be too altruistic, let me be very practical. If we are partners, let me predict we will be the senior partner. The financial leadership will be ours. The industrial primacy will be ours. The commercial advantage will be ours. The other countries of the world are looking to us for leadership and direction. Very well, then, if I am to compete with the critics of this League and of this treaty as a selfish American, I say I want to get in and get in as quick as I can. I want to be inside and know how the thing is run and help to run it. You have the alternative, armed isolation or peaceful partnership. Can any sane man hesitate as to the choice, and can any sane man ask the question, Which is the way of peace? I have heard some men say with an amazing ignorance that the Covenant of the League of Nations was an arrangement for war. Very well, then, what would the other arrangement be? An arrangement for peace? For kindliness? For coöperation? Would everybody beckon us to their markets? Would everybody say, "Come and tell us how to use your money?" Would everybody come and say, "Tell us how much of your goods you want us to take; tell us how much of what Germany is producing you would like when we want it?" I cannot bring my credulity up to that point. I have reached years of discretion, and I have met some very young men who knew a great deal more than some very old men.

I want you therefore, after seeing this very ugly picture that I have painted—for it is an ugly picture; it is a picture from which one turns away with distaste and disgust and says, "That is not America; it is not like anything that we have ever conceived"—I want you to look at the other side. I wonder if some of the gentlemen who are commenting upon this treaty ever read it! If anybody will tell me which of them has not, I will send him a copy. It is written in two languages. On this side is the English and on that side is the French, and since it is evident that some men do not understand English, I hope that they understand French. There are excellent French dictionaries by which they can dig out the meaning, if they cannot understand English. It is the plainest English that you could desire, particularly the Covenant of the League of Nations. There is not a phrase of doubtful meaning in the whole document.

And what is the meaning? It is that the Covenant of the League of Nations is a covenant of arbitration and discussion. Had anybody ever told you that before? I dare say that everybody you have heard talk about this discusses Article X. Well, there are twenty-five other articles in it, and all of them are about something else. They discuss how soon and how quick we can get out of it. Well, I am not a quitter for one. We can get out just so soon as we want to, but we do not want to get out as soon as we get in. And they talk about the Monroe Doctrine, when it expressly says that nothing in that document shall be construed as affecting in any way the validity of the Monroe Doctrine. It says so in so many words. And there are all the other things they talk about to draw your attention away from the essential matter. The essential matter, my fellow citizens, is this: This League will include all the fighting nations of the world, except Germany. The only nations that will not be admitted into it promptly are Germany and Turkey. All the fighting nations of the world are in it, and what do they promise? This is the center of the document. They promise that they never will go to war without first either submitting the question at issue to arbitration and absolutely abiding by the decision of the arbitrators, or, if they are not willing to submit it to arbitration, submitting it to discussion by the council of the League; that they will give the council of the League six months in which to consider it, and that if they do not like the opinion of the council, they will wait three months after the opinion is rendered before going to war. And I tell you, my fellow citizens, that any nation that is in the wrong and waits nine months before it goes to war never will go to war.

"Ah," but somebody says, "suppose they do not abide by that?" Because all the arguments you hear are based upon the assumption that we are all going to break the Covenant, that bad faith is the accepted rule. There has not been any such bad faith among nations in recent times except the flagrant bad faith of the nation we have just been fighting, and that bad faith is not likely to be repeated in the immediate future. Suppose somebody does not abide by those engagements, then what happens? War? No, not war. Something more terrible than war—absolute boycott of the nation violating the Covenant. The doors are closed upon her, so that she cannot ship anything out or receive anything in. She cannot send a letter out or receive one in. No telegraphic message can cross her borders. No person can cross her borders. She is absolutely closed, and all the fighting nations of the world agree to join in the boycott. My own judgment is that war will not be necessary after that. If it is necessary, then it is perfectly evident that the case is one of a nation that wants to run amuck, and if any nation wants to run amuck in modern civilization, we must all see that the outlaw is captured.

I was saying in one of the first speeches I made upon this little expedition of mine that I was very happy in the circumstance that there were no politics in this business. I meant no party politics, and I invited that audience, as I invite you, to forget all about parties. Forget that I am a Democrat. Forget that some of you are Republicans. Forget all about that. That has nothing to do with it. This afternoon a book I had forgotten all about, one of the campaign books of the last political campaign, was put in my hands, and I found in that book the platforms of the two parties. In both of those platforms they advocate just such an arrangement as the League of Nations. When I was on the other side of the water I did not know that I was obeying orders from both parties, but I was, and I am very happy in that circumstance, because I can testify to you that I did not think anything about parties when I was on the other side of the water. I am just as much, my fellow citizens, in my present office the servant of my Republican fellow citizens as I am the servant of my Democratic fellow citizens. I am trying to be what some gentlemen do not know how to be, just a simple, plain-thinking, plain-speaking, out-and-out American.

I want you to understand, my fellow citizens, that I did not leave Washington and come out on this trip because I doubted what was going to happen. I did not. For one thing, I wanted to have the pleasure of leaving Washington; and for another thing I wanted to have the very much greater pleasure of feeling the inspiration that I would get from you. Things get very lonely in

Washington sometimes. The real voices of the great people of America sometimes sound faint and distant in that strange city! You hear politics until you wish that both parties were smothered in their own gas. I wanted to come out and hear some plain American, hear the kind of talk that I am accustomed to talk, the only kind of talk that I can understand, get the only kind of atmosphere with which I can fill my lungs wholesomely, and, then, incidentally, convey a hint in some quarters that the American people had not forgotten how to think. There are certain places where talk does not count for anything. I am inclined to think that one of those places is the fashionable dinner table. I have never heard so many things that were not so anywhere else. In the little circles of fashion and wealth information circulates the more freely the less true it is. For some reason there is a preference for the things that are incredible. I admit there is a certain intellectual excitement in believing the things that are incredible. It is very much duller to believe only the things that you know are so, but the spicy thing, the unusual thing, the thing that runs athwart the normal and wholesome currents of society is the thing that one can talk about with an unusual vocabulary and have a lot of fun in expounding. But such are not the things that make up the daily substance of thinking on the part of a wholesome nation like this.

This Nation went into this war to see it through to the end, and the end has not come yet. This is the beginning, not of the war but of the processes which are going to render a war like this impossible. There are no other processes than those that are proposed in this great treaty. It is a great treaty, it is a treaty of justice, of rigorous and severe justice, but do not forget that there are many other parties to this treaty than Germany and her opponents. There is rehabilitated Poland. There is rescued Bohemia. There is redeemed Jugo-Slavia. There is the rehabilitated Rumania. All the nations that Germany meant to crush and reduce to the status of tools in her own hands have been redeemed by this war and given the guarantee of the strongest nations of the world that nobody shall invade their liberty again. If you do not want to give them that guarantee, then you make it certain that without your guarantee the attempt will be made again, and if another war starts like this one, are you going to keep out of it? If you keep out of this arrangement, that sort of war will come soon. If you go into it, it never will come. We are in the presence, therefore, of the most solemn choice that this people was ever called upon to make. That choice is nothing less than this: Shall America redeem her pledges to the world? America is made up of the peoples of the world. All the best bloods of the world flow in her veins, all the old affections, all the old and sacred traditions of peoples of every sort throughout the wide world circulate in her veins, and she has said to mankind at her birth: "We have come to redeem the world by giving it liberty and justice." Now we are called upon before the tribunal of mankind to redeem that immortal pledge.

END OF VOL. I

WAR AND PEACE
VOLUME II

CONTENTS

Statement sent October 6, 1919, to Secretary William B. Wilson with request that he read it "at the opening of the labor conference this afternoon." From copy in Mr. Wilson's files.

Letter to the National Industrial Conference, October 22, 1919. From the New York *Times*, October 23, 1919.

Statement issued at Washington, October 25, 1919. From the *Congressional Record*, Vol. 58, p. 7583.

Message to the House of Representatives returning with veto H.R. 6810, October 27, 1919. From copy in Mr. Wilson's files.

Statement to the country, November 11, 1919.

CONTENTS

CONTENTS

WAR AND PEACE

ADDRESSES

DELIVERED ON WESTERN TOUR SEPTEMBER 4 TO
SEPTEMBER 25, 1919; CONTINUED FROM PRECED-
ING VOLUME. FROM 66TH CONGRESS, 1ST SESSION,
SENATE DOCUMENT NO. 120.

AT CONVENTION HALL, KANSAS CITY, MO., SEPTEMBER 6, 1919.

MR. CHAIRMAN, MY FELLOW COUNTRYMEN:

It is very inspiring to me to stand in the presence of
so great a company of my fellow citizens and have the
privilege of performing the duty that I have come to
perform. That duty is to report to my fellow citizens
concerning the work of the peace conference, and every
day it seems to me to become more necessary to report,
because so many people who are talking about it do not
understand what it was.

I came back from Paris bringing one of the greatest
documents of human history, and one of the things that
made it great was that it was penetrated throughout
with the principles to which America has devoted her
life. Let me hasten to say that one of the most delightful circumstances of the work on the other side of the
water was that I discovered that what we called American principles had penetrated to the heart and to the
understanding, not only of the great peoples of Europe,
but of the great men who were leading the peoples of
Europe, and when these principles were written into
this treaty, they were written there by common consent
and common conviction. But it remains true, nevertheless, my fellow citizens, that principles are written into
that treaty which were never written into any great
international understanding before, and that they had

1

their natural birth and origin in this dear country to which we have devoted our life and service.

I have no hesitation in saying that in spirit and essence it is an American document, and if you will bear with me—for this great subject is not a subject for oratory, it is a subject for examination and discussion—— I will remind you of some of the things that we have long desired and which are at last accomplished in this treaty. I think that I can say that one of the things that America has had most at heart throughout her exist- ence has been that there should be substituted for the brutal processes of war the friendly processes of con- sultation and arbitration, and that is done in the Cove- nant of the League of Nations. I am very anxious that my fellow citizens should realize that that is the chief topic of the Covenant of the League of Nations. The whole intent and purpose of the document is expressed in provisions by which all the member States agree that they will never go to war without first having done one or other of two things: Either submitted the mat- ter in controversy to arbitration, in which case they agree to abide by the verdict, or submitted it to discus- sion in the council of the League of Nations, in which case they consent to allow six months for the discus- sion and, whether they like the opinion expressed or not, that they will not go to war for three months after that opinion is expressed. So that you have, whether you get arbitration or not, nine months' discussion, and I want to remind you that that is the central principle of some thirty treaties entered into between the United States of America and some thirty other sovereign na- tions, all of which were confirmed by the Senate of the United States. We have such an agreement with France. We have such an agreement with Great Britain. We have such an agreement with practically every great na- tion except Germany, which refused to enter into any such arrangement, because, my fellow citizens, Germany knew that she intended something that did not bear discussion, and that if she had submitted the purpose which led to this war to so much as one month's discussion, she never would have dared go into the enterprise against mankind which she finally did go into. Therefore, I say that this principle of discussion is the principle already adopted by America.

And what is the compulsion to do this? The compulsion is this, that if any member state violates that promise to submit either to arbitration or to discussion, it is thereby *ipso facto* deemed to have committed an act of war against all the rest. Then, you will ask, "Do we at once take up arms and fight them?" No, we do something very much more terrible than that. We absolutely boycott them. It is provided in that instrument that there shall be no communication even between them and the rest of the world. They shall receive no goods; they shall ship no goods. They shall receive no telegraphic messages; they shall send none. They shall receive no mail; no mail will be received from them. The nationals, the citizens, of the member states will never enter their territory until the matter is adjusted, and their citizens cannot leave their territory. It is the most complete boycott ever conceived in a public document, and I want to say to you with confident prediction that there will be no more fighting after that. Gentlemen talk to you as if the most probable outcome of this great combination of all the fighting peoples of the world was going to be fight; whereas, as a matter of fact, the essence of the document is to the effect that the processes shall be peaceful, and peaceful processes are more deadly than the processes of war. Let any merchant put it to himself, that if he enters into a covenant and then breaks it and the people all around him absolutely desert his establishment and will have nothing to do with him—ask him after that if it will be necessary to send the police. The most terrible thing that can happen to an individual, and the most conclusive thing that can happen to a nation, is to be read out of decent society.

There was another thing that we wished to accomplish which is accomplished in this document. We wanted disarmament, and this document provides in the only possible way for disarmament, by common agreement. Observe, my fellow citizens, that, as I said just now, every great fighting nation in the world is to be a member of this partnership except Germany, and inasmuch as Germany has accepted a limitation of her army to 100,000 men, I do not think for the time being she may be regarded as a great fighting nation. Here in the center of Europe a great nation of more than 60,000,000 that has agreed not to maintain an army of more than 100,000 men, and all around her the rest of the world in concerted partnership to see that no other nation attempts what she attempted, and agreeing among themselves that they will not impose this limitation of armament upon Germany merely, but that they will impose it upon themselves.

You know, my fellow citizens, what armaments mean: Great standing armies and great stores of war material. They do not mean burdensome taxation merely, they do not mean merely compulsory military service which saps the economic strength of the nation, but they mean also the building up of a military class. Again and again, my fellow citizens, in the conference at Paris we were face to face with this circumstance, that in dealing with a particular civil government we found that they would not dare to promise what their general staff was not willing that they should promise; that they were dominated by the military machine which they had created, nominally for their own defense, but really, whether they willed it or not, for the provocation of war. So soon as you have a military class, it does not make any difference what your form of government is, if you are determined to be armed to the teeth, you must obey the orders and directions of the only men who can control the great machinery of war. Elections are of minor importance, because they determine the political policy, and back of that political policy is the constant pressure of the men trained to arms, enormous bodies of disciplined men, wondering if they are never going to be allowed to use their education and their skill and ravage some great people with the force of arms. That is the meaning of armaments. It is not merely the cost of it, though that is overwhelming, but it is the spirit of it, and America has never and I hope, in the providence of God, never will have, that spirit. There is no other way to dispense with great armaments except by the common agreement of the fighting nations of the world. And here is the agreement. They promise disarmament, and promise to agree upon a plan.

There was something else we wanted that is accomplished by this treaty. We wanted to destroy autocratic authority everywhere in the world. We wanted to see to it that there was no place in the world where a small group of men could use their fellow citizens as pawns in a game; that there was no place in the world where a small group of men, without consulting their fellow citizens, could send their fellow citizens to the battlefields and to death in order to accomplish some dynastic ambition, some political plan that had been conceived in private, some object that had been prepared for by universal, world-wide intrigue. That is what we wanted to accomplish. The most startling thing that developed itself at the opening of our participation in this war was, not the military preparation of Germany —we were familiar with that, though we had been dreaming that she would not use it—but her political preparation—to find every community in the civilized world was·penetrated by her intrigue. The German people did not know that, but it was known on Wilhelmstrasse, where the central offices of the German Government were, and Wilhelmstrasse was the master of the German people. And this war, my fellow citizens,

has emancipated the German people as well as the rest
of the world. We do not want to see anything like that
happen again, because we know that democracies will
sooner or later have to destroy that form of Government, and if we do not destroy it now the job is still to
be done. And by a combination of all the great fighting
peoples of the world, to see to it that the aggressive purposes of such governments cannot be realized, you make
it no longer worth while for little groups of men to
contrive the downfall of civilization in private conference.

I want to say something about that that has a different aspect, and perhaps you will regard it as a slight
digression from the discussion which I am asking you
to be patient enough to follow. My fellow citizens, it
does not make any difference what kind of a minority
governs you if it is a minority, and the thing we must
see to is that no minority anywhere masters the majority. That is at the heart, my fellow citizens, of the
tragical things that are happening in that great country
which we long to help and can find no way that is
effective to help. I mean the great realm of Russia.
The men who are now measurably in control of the
affairs of Russia represent nobody but themselves. They
have again and again been challenged to call a constitutional convention. They have again and again been
challenged to prove that they had some kind of a mandate, even from a single class of their fellow citizens,
and they dare not attempt it. They have no mandate
from anybody. There are only thirty-four of them, I
am told, and there were more than thirty-four men who
used to control the destinies of Europe from Wilhelmstrasse. There is a closer monopoly of power in Petro-
grad and Moscow than there ever was in Berlin, and the
thing that is intolerable is, not that the Russian people
are having their way, but that another group of men
more cruel than the Czar himself is controlling the destinies of that great people.

I want to say here and now that I am against the control of any minority anywhere. Search your own economic history and what have you been uneasy about? Now and again you have said there were small groups of capitalists who were controlling the industry and therefore the development of the United States. Very well, my fellow citizens; if that is so, and sometimes I have feared that it was, we must break up that monopoly. I am not now saying that there is any group of our fellow citizens who are consciously doing anything of the kind. I am saying that these allegations must be proved, but if it is proved that any class, any group, anywhere, is, without the suffrage of their fellow citizens, in control of our affairs, then I am with you to destroy the power of that group. We have got to be frank with ourselves, however: If we do not want minority government in Russia, we must see that we do not have it in the United States. If you do not want little groups of selfish men to plot the future of Europe, we must not allow little groups of selfish men to plot the future of America. Any man that speaks for a class must prove that he also speaks for all his fellow citizens and for mankind, and then we will listen to him. The most difficult thing in a democracy, my fellow citizens, is to get classes, where they unfortunately exist, to understand one another and unite, and you have not got a great democracy until they do understand one another and unite. If we are in for seeing that there are no more Czars and no more Kaisers, then let us do a thorough job and see that nothing of that sort occurs anywhere.

Then there was another thing we wanted to do, my fellow citizens, that is done in this document. We wanted to see that helpless peoples were nowhere in the world put at the mercy of unscrupulous enemies and masters. There is one pitiful example which is in the hearts of all of us. I mean the example of Armenia. There a Christian people is helpless, at the mercy of a

Turkish Government which thought it the service of
God to destroy them; and at this moment, my fellow
citizens, it is an open question whether the Armenian
people will not, while we sit here and debate, be absolutely destroyed. When I think of words piled on words,
of debate following debate, while these unspeakable
things that cannot be handled until the debate is over
are happening in this pitiful part of the world, I wonder
that men do not wake up to the moral responsibility of
what they are doing. Great populations are driven out
upon a desert where there is no food and can be none
and there compelled to die, and the men and women
and children thrown into a common grave, so imperfectly covered up that here and there is a pitiful arm
stretched out to heaven and there is no pity in the
world. When shall we wake to the moral responsibility
of this great occasion?

There are other aspects to that matter. Not all the
populations that are having something that is not a
square deal live in Armenia. There are others, and one
of the glories of the great document which I brought
back with me is this, that everywhere within the area
of settlement covered by the political questions involved
in that treaty people of that sort have been given their
freedom and guaranteed their freedom. But the thing
does not end there, because the treaty includes the Covenant of the League of Nations, and what does that say?
That says that it is the privilege of any member state to
call attention to anything, anywhere, that is likely to
disturb the peace of the world or the good understanding between nations upon which the peace of the world
depends, and every people in the world that has not
got what it thinks it ought to have is thereby given a
world forum in which to bring the thing to the bar of
mankind. An incomparable thing, a thing that never
was dreamed of before! A thing that was never conceived as possible before, that it should not be regarded
as an unfriendly act on the part of the representatives

of one nation to call attention to something being done within the confines of another empire which was disturbing the peace of the world and the good understanding between nations. There never before has been provided a world forum in which the legitimate grievances of peoples entitled to consideration can be brought to the common judgment of mankind, and if I were the advocate of any suppressed or oppressed people, I surely could not ask any better forum than to stand up before the world and challenge the other party to make good its excuses for not acting in that case. That compulsion is the most tremendous moral compulsion that could be devised by organized mankind.

I think I can take it for granted, my fellow citizens, that you never realized before what a scope this great treaty has. You have been asked to look at so many little spots in it with a magnifying glass that you did not know how big it is, what a great enterprise of the human spirit it is, and what a thoroughly American document it is from cover to cover. It is the first great international agreement in the history of mankind where the principle adopted has been, not the power of the strong but the right of the weak. To reject that treaty, to alter that treaty, is to impair one of the first charters of mankind. Yet there are men who approach the question with passion, with private passion, with party passion, who think only of some immediate advantage to themselves or to a group of their fellow countrymen, and who look at the thing with the jaundice eyes of those who have some private purpose of their own. When at last in the annals of mankind they are gibbeted, they will regret that the gibbet is so high.

I would not have you think that I am trying to characterize those who conscientiously object to anything in this great document. I take off my hat to any man's genuine conscience, and there are men who are conscientiously opposed, though they will pardon me if I say ignorantly opposed. I have no quarrel with them. It has been a pleasure to confer with some of them and to tell them as frankly as I would have told my most intimate friend the whole inside of my mind and of every other mind that I knew anything about that had been concerned with the conduct of affairs at Paris, in order that they might understand this thing and go with the rest of us in the confirmation of what is necessary for the peace of the world. I have no intolerant spirit in the matter, I assure you, but I also assure you that from the bottom of my feet to the top of my head I have got a fighting spirit about it. If anybody dares to defeat this great experiment, then they must gather together the counsellors of the world and do something better. If there is a better scheme, I for one will subscribe to it, but I want to say now, as I said, the other night, it is a case of "put up or shut up." Negation will not serve the world. Opposition constructs nothing. Opposition is the specialty of those who are Bolshevistically inclined —and again I assure you I am not comparing any of my respected colleagues to Bolshevists; I am merely pointing out that the Bolshevist spirit lacks every element of constructiveness. They have destroyed everything and they propose nothing, and while there is a common abhorrence for political Bolshevism, I hope there will not be such a thing growing up in our country as international Bolshevism, the Bolshevism which destroys the constructive work of men who have conscientiously tried to cement the good feeling of the great peoples of the world.

The majestic thing about the League of Nations is that it is to include the great peoples of the world, all except Germany. Germany is one of the great peoples of the world. I would be ashamed not to say that. Those 60,000,000 industrious and inventive and accomplished people are one of the great peoples of the world. They have been put upon. They have been misled. Their minds have been debased by a false philosophy.

They have been taught things that the human spirit ought to reject, but they will come out of that nightmare, they will come out of that phantasm, and they will again be a great people. And when they are out of it, when they have got over that dream of conquest and of oppression, when they have shown that their Government really is based upon new principles and upon democratic principles, then we, all of us at Paris agreed that they should be admitted to the League of Nations. In the meantime, her one-time partner, Austria, is to be admitted. Hungary, I dare say, will be admitted. The only nations of any consequence outside the League—unless we choose to stay out and go in later with Germany—are Germany and Turkey, and we are just now looking for the pieces of Turkey. She has so thoroughly disintegrated that the process of assembling the parts is becoming increasingly difficult, and the chief controversy now is who shall attempt that very difficult and perilous job?

Is it not a great vision, my fellow citizens, this of the thoughtful world combined for peace, this of all the great peoples of the world associated to see that justice is done, that the strong who intend wrong are restrained and that the weak who cannot defend themselves are made secure? We have a problem ahead of us that ought to interest us in this connection. We have promised the people of the Philippine Islands that we will set them free, and it has been one of our perplexities how we should make them safe after we set them free. Under this arrangement it will be safe from the outset. They will become members of the League of Nations, every great nation in the world will be pledged to respect and preserve against external aggression from any quarter the territorial integrity and political independence of the Philippines. It simplifies one of the most perplexing problems that have faced the American public, but it does not simplify our problems merely, gentlemen. It illustrates the triumph of the American spirit. I do not want to attempt any flight of fancy, but I can fancy those men of the first generation that so thoughtfully set this great Government up, the generation of Washington and Hamilton and Jefferson and the Adamses—I can fancy their looking on with a sort of enraptured amazement that the American spirit should have made conquest of the world.

I wish you could have seen the faces of some of the people that talked to us over there about the arrival of the American troops. At first they did not know that we were going to be able to send so many, but they got something from the first groups that changed the whole aspect of the war. One of the most influential ladies in Paris, the wife of a member of the cabinet, told us that on the Fourth of July of last year she and others had attended the ceremonies with very sad hearts and merely out of courtesy to the United States, because they did not believe that the aid of the United States was going to be effective, but she said, "After we had been there and seen the faces of those men in khaki, seen the spirit of their swing and attitude and seen the vision that was in their eyes, we came away knowing that victory was in sight." What Europe saw in our boys was not merely men under arms, indomitable men under arms, but men with an ideal in their eyes, men who had come a long way from home to defend other peoples, men who had forgotten the convenience of everything that personally affected them and had turned away from the longing love of the people who were dear to them and gone across the broad sea to rescue the nations of the world from an intolerable oppression.

I tell you, my fellow citizens, the war was won by the American spirit. German orders were picked up on the battlefield directing the commanders not to let the Americans get hold of a particular post, because you never could get them out again. You know what one of our

American wits said, that it took only half as long to train an American army as any other, because you had only to train them to go one way. It is true that they never thought of going any other way, and when they were restrained, because they were told it was premature or dangerous, they were impatient, they said, "We didn't come over here to wait, we came over here to fight," and their very audacity, their very indifference to danger, changed the morale of the battlefield. They were not fighting prudently; they were going to get there. And America in this treaty has realized, my fellow countrymen, what those gallant boys we are so proud of fought for. The men who make this impossible or difficult will have a life-long reckoning with the fighting forces of the United States. I have consorted with those boys. I have been proud to call myself their commander in chief. I did not run the business. They did not need anybody to run it. All I had to do was to turn them loose!

And now for a final word, my fellow citizens. If anything that I have said has left the impression on your mind that I have the least doubt of the result, please dismiss the impression. And if you think that I have come out on this errand to fight anybody—any body—please dismiss that from your mind. I have not come to fight or antagonize anybody, or any body of individuals. I have, let me say without the slightest affectation, the greatest respect for the Senate of the United States, but, my fellow citizens, I have come out to fight a cause. That cause is greater than the Senate. It is greater than the Government. It is as great as the cause of mankind, and I intend, in office or out, to fight that battle as long as I live. My ancestors were troublesome Scotchmen, and among them were some of that famous group that were known as the Covenanters. Very well, then, here is the Covenant of the League of Nations. I am a Covenanter!

AT DES MOINES, IOWA, SEPTEMBER 6, 1919.

MR. CHAIRMAN AND FELLOW COUNTRYMEN:

You make my heart very warm with your generous welcome, and I want to express my unaffected gratitude to your chairman for having so truly struck the note of an occasion like this. He has used almost the very words that were in my thought, that the world is inflamed and profoundly disturbed, and we are met to discuss the measures by which its spirit can be quieted and its affairs turned to the right courses of human life. My fellow countrymen, the world is desperately in need of the settled conditions of peace, and it cannot wait much longer. It is waiting upon us. That is the thought, that is the burdensome thought, upon my heart to-night, that the world is waiting for the verdict of the Nation to which it looked for leadership and which it thought would be the last that would ask the world to wait.

My fellow citizens, the world is not at peace. I suppose that it is difficult for one who has not had some touch of the hot passion of the other side of the sea to realize how all the passions that have been slumbering for ages have been uncovered and released by the tragedy of this war. We speak of the tragedy of this war, but the tragedy that lay back of it was greater than the war itself, because back of it lay long ages in which the legitimate freedom of men was suppressed. Back of it lay long ages of recurrent war in which little groups of men, closeted in capitals, determined whether the sons of the land over which they ruled should go out upon the field and shed their blood. For what? For liberty? No; not for liberty, but for the aggrandizement of those who ruled them. And this had been slumbering in the hearts of men. They had felt the suppression of it. They had felt the mastery of those whom they had not chosen as their masters. They had felt the oppression of laws which did not admit them to the equal exercise of human rights. Now, all of this is released and uncovered and men glare at one another and say, "Now we are free and what shall we do with our freedom?"

What happened in Russia was not a sudden and accidental thing. The people of Russia were maddened with the suppression of Czarism. When at last the chance came to throw off those chains, they threw them off, at first with hearts full of confidence and hope, and then they found out that they had been again deceived. There was no assembly chosen to frame a constitution for them, or, rather, there was an assembly chosen to choose a constitution for them and it was suppressed and dispersed, and a little group of men just as selfish, just as ruthless, just as pitiless, as the agents of the Czar himself, assumed control and exercised their power by terror and not by right. And in other parts of Europe the poison spread—the poison of disorder, the poison of revolt, the poison of chaos. And do you honestly think, my fellow citizens, that none of that poison has got in the veins of this free people? Do you not know that the world is all now one single whispering gallery? Those antennæ of the wireless telegraph are the symbols of our age. All the impulses of mankind are thrown out upon the air and reach to the ends of the earth; quietly upon steamships, silently under the cover of the Postal Service, with the tongue of the wireless and the tongue of the telegraph, all the suggestions of disorder are spread through the world. Money coming from nobody knows where is deposited by the millions in capitals like Stockholm, to be used for the propaganda of disorder and discontent and dissolution throughout the world, and men look you calmly in the face in America and say they are for that sort of revolution, when that sort of revolution means government by terror, government by force, not government by vote. It is the negation of everything that is American;

but it is spreading, and so long as disorder continues, so long as the world is kept waiting for the answer to the question, What kind of peace are we going to have and what kind of guarantees are there to be behind that peace? that poison will steadily spread more and more rapidly, spread until it may be that even this beloved land of ours will be distracted and distorted by it.

That is what is concerning me, my fellow countrymen. I know the splendid steadiness of the American people, but, my fellow citizens, the whole world needs that steadiness, and the American people are the makeweight in the fortunes of mankind. How long are we going to debate into which scale we will throw that magnificent equipoise that belongs to us? How long shall we be kept waiting for the answer whether the world may trust us or despise us? They have looked to us for leadership. They have looked to us for example. They have built their peace upon the basis of our suggestions. That great volume that contains the treaty of peace is drawn along the specifications laid down by the American Government, and now the world stands at amaze because an authority in America hesitates whether it will indorse an American document or not.

You know what the necessity of peace is. Political liberty can exist only when there is peace. Social reform can take place only when there is peace. The settlement of every question that concerns our daily life waits for peace. I have been receiving delegations in Washington of men engaged in the service of the Government temporarily in the administration of the railways, and I have had to say to them, "My friends, I cannot tell what the railways can earn until commerce is restored to its normal courses. Until I can tell what the railroads can earn I cannot tell what the wages that the railroads can pay will be. I cannot suggest what the increase of freight and passenger rates will be to meet these increases in wages if the rates must be increased. I cannot tell yet whether it will be necessary to increase the rates or not, and I must ask you to wait." But they are not the only people that have come to see me. There are all sorts of adjustments necessary in this country. I have asked representatives of capital and labor to come to Washington next month and confer—confer about the fundamental thing of our life at present; that is to say, the conditions of labor. Do you realize, my fellow citizens, that all through the world the one central question of civilization is, "What shall be the conditions of labor?" The profound unrest in Europe is due to the doubt prevailing as to what shall be the conditions of labor, and I need not tell you that that unrest is spreading to America.

In the midst of the treaty of peace is a Magna Charta, a great guarantee for labor. It provides that labor shall have the counsels of the world devoted to the discussion of its conditions and of its betterment, and labor all over the world is waiting to know whether America is going to take part in those conferences or not. The confidence of the men who sat at Paris was such that they put it in the document that the first meeting of the labor conference under that part of the treaty should take place in Washington upon the invitation of the President of the United States. I am going to issue that invitation, whether we can attend the conference or not. But think of the mortification! Think of standing by in Washington itself and seeing the world take counsel upon the fundamental matter of civilization without us. The thing is inconceivable, but it is true. The world is waiting, waiting to see, not whether we will take part but whether we will serve and lead, for it has expected us to lead. I want to testify that the most touching and thrilling thing that has ever happened to me was what happened almost every day when I was in Paris. Delegations from all over the world came to me to solicit the friendship of America. They frankly told us that they were not sure they could trust anybody else, but that they did absolutely trust us to do them justice and to see that justice was done them. Why, some of them came from countries which I have, to my shame, to admit that I never heard of before, and I had to ask as privately as possible what language they spoke. Fortunately they always had an interpreter, but I always wanted to know at least what family of languages they were speaking. The touching thing was that from the ends of the earth, from little pocketed valleys, where I did not know that a separate people lived, there came men—men of dignity, men of intellectual parts, men entertaining in their thought and in their memories a great tradition, some of the oldest people of the world—and they came and sat at the feet of the youngest nation of the world and said, "Teach us the way to liberty."

That is the attitude of the world, and reflect, my fellow countrymen, upon the reaction, the reaction of despair, that would come if America said: "We do not want to lead you. You must do without our advice. You must shift without us." Now, are we going to bring about a peace, for which everything waits? We cannot bring it about by doing nothing. I have been very much amazed and very much amused, if I could be amused in such critical circumstances, to see that the statesmanship of some gentlemen consists in the very interesting proposition that we do nothing at all. I had heard of standing pat before, but I never had before heard of standpatism going to the length of saying it is none of our business and we do not care what happens to the rest of the world.

Your chairman made a profoundly true remark just now. The isolation of the United States is at an end, not because we chose to go into the politics of the world, but because by the sheer genius of this people and the growth of our power we have become a determining factor in the history of mankind, and after you have become a determining factor you cannot remain isolated, whether you want to or not. Isolation ended by the processes of history, not by the processes of our independent choice, and the processes of history merely fulfilled the prediction of the men who founded our Republic. Go back and read some of the immortal sentences of the men that assisted to frame this Government and see how they set up a standard to which they intended that the nations of the world should rally. They said to the people of the world, "Come to us; this is the home of liberty; this is the place where mankind can learn how to govern their own affairs and straighten out their own difficulties," and the world did come to us.

Look at your neighbor. Look at the statistics of the people of your State. Look at the statistics of the people of the United States. They have come, their hearts full of hope and confidence, from practically every nation in the world, to constitute a portion of our strength and of our hope and a contribution to our achievement. Sometimes I feel like taking off my hat to some of those immigrants. I was born an American. I could not help it, but they chose to be Americans. They were not born Americans. They saw this star in the west rising over the peoples of the world, and they said, "That is the star of hope and the star of salvation. We will set our footsteps towards the west and join that great body of men whom God has blessed with the vision of liberty." I honor those men. I say, "You made a deliberate choice which showed that you saw what the drift and history of mankind was." I am very grateful, I may say in parentheses, that I did not have to make that choice. I am grateful that ever since I can remember I have breathed this blessed air of freedom. I am grateful that every instinct in me, every drop of blood in me remembers and stands up and shouts at the traditions of the United States. But some gentlemen are not shouting now about that. They are saying, "Yes; we made a great promise to mankind, but it will cost too much to redeem it." My fellow citizens, that is not the spirit of America, and you cannot have peace, you cannot have even your legitimate part in the business of the world unless you are partners with the rest. If you are going to say to the world, "We will stand off and see what we can get out of this," the world will see to it that you do not get anything out of it. If it is your deliberate choice that instead of being friends you will be rivals and antagonists, then you will get exactly what rivals and antagonists always get, just as little as can be grudgingly vouchsafed you.

Yet you must keep the world on its feet. Is there any business man here who would be willing to see the world go bankrupt and the business of the world stop? Is there any man here who does not know that America is the only nation left by the war in a position to see that the world does go on with its business? And is it your idea that if we lend our money, as we must, to men whom we have bitterly disappointed, that money will bring back to us the largess to which we are entitled? I do not like to argue this thing on this basis, but if you want to talk business, I am ready to talk business. If it is a matter of how much you are going to get from your money, I say you will not get half as much as antagonists as you will get as partners. Think that over, if you have none of that thing that is so lightly spoken of, known as altruism. And, believe me, my fellow countrymen, the only people in the world who are going to reap the harvest of the future are the people who can entertain ideals, who can follow ideals to the death.

I was saying to another audience to-day that one of the most beautiful stories I know is the story that we heard in France about the first effect of the American soldiers when they got over there. The French did not believe at first, the British did not believe, that we could finally get 2,000,000 men over there. The most that they hoped at first was that a few American soldiers would restore their morale, for let me say that their morale was gone. The beautiful story to which I re-

ferred is this, the testimony that all of them rendered
that they got their morale back the minute they saw
the eyes of those boys. Here were not only soldiers.
There was no curtain in front of the retina of those
eyes. They were American eyes. They were eyes that
had seen visions. They were eyes the possessors of which
had brought with them a great ardor for a supreme
cause, and the reason those boys never stopped was that
their eyes were lifted to the horizon. They saw a city
not built with hands. They saw a citadel towards which
their steps were bent where dwelt the oracles of God
himself. And on the battlefield were found German orders to commanders here and there to see to it that the
Americans did not get lodgment in particular places,
because if they ever did you never could get them out.
They had gone to Europe to go the whole way towards
the realization of the teaching which their fathers had
handed down to them. There never were crusaders
that went to the Holy Land in the old ages that we read
about that were more truly devoted to a holy cause
than these gallant, incomparable sons of America.

My fellow citizens, you have got to make up your
minds, because, after all, it is you who are going to
make up the minds of this country. I do not owe a report or the slightest responsibility to anybody but you.
I do not mean only you in this hall, though I am free to
admit that this is just as good a sample of America as
you can find anywhere, and the sample looks mighty
good to me. I mean you and the millions besides you,
thoughtful, responsible American men and women all
over this country. They are my bosses, and I am
mighty glad to be their servant. I have come out upon
this journey not to fight anybody but to report to you,
and I am free to predict that if you credit the report
there will be no fighting. It is not only necessary that
we should make peace with Germany and make peace
with Austria, and see that a reasonable peace is made
with Turkey and Bulgaria—that is not only not all of

it, but it is a very dangerous beginning if you do not add something to it. I said just now that the peace with Germany, and the same is true of the pending peace with Austria, was made upon American specifications, not unwillingly. Do not let me leave the impression on your mind that the representatives of America in Paris had to insist and force their principles upon the rest. That is not true. Those principles were accepted before we got over there, and the men I dealt with carried them out in absolute good faith; but they were our principles, and at the heart of them lay this, that there must be a free Poland, for example.

I wonder if you realize what that means. We had to collect the pieces of Poland. For a long time one piece had belonged to Russia, and we cannot get a clear title to that yet. Another part belonged to Austria. We got a title to that. Another part belonged to Germany, and we have settled the title to that. But we found Germany also in possession of other pieces of territory occupied predominately or exclusively by patriotic Poles, and we said to Germany, "You will have to give that up, too; that belongs to Poland." Not because it is ground, but because those people there are Poles and want to be parts of Poland, and it is not our business to force any sovereignty upon anybody who does not want to live under it. When we had determined the boundaries of Poland we set it up and recognized it as an independent Republic. There is a minister, a diplomatic representative, of the United States at Warsaw right now in virtue of our formal recognition of the Republic of Poland.

But upon Poland center some of the dangers of the future. South of Poland is Bohemia, which we cut away from the Austrian combination. Below Bohemia is Hungary, which can no longer rely upon the assistant strength of Austria, and below her is an enlarged Rumania. Alongside of Rumania is the new Slavic Kingdom, that never could have won its own independence, which had chafed under the chains of Austria-Hungary, but never could throw them off. We have said, "The fundamental wrongs of history center in these regions. These people have the right to govern their own Government and control their own fortunes." That is at the heart of the treaty, but, my fellow citizens, this is at the heart of the future: The business men of Germany did not want the war that we have passed through. The bankers and the manufacturers and the merchants knew that it was unspeakable folly. Why? Because Germany by her industrial genius was beginning to dominate the world economically, and all she had to do was to wait for about two more generations when her credit, her merchandise, her enterprise, would have covered all the parts of the world that the great fighting nations did not control. The formula of pan-Germanism, you remember, was Bremen to Bagdad— Bremen on the North Sea to Bagdad in Persia. These countries that we have set up as the new home of liberty lie right along that road. If we leave them there without the guarantee that the combined force of the world will assure their independence and their territorial integrity, we have only to wait a short generation when our recent experience will be repeated. We did not let Germany dominate the world this time. Are we then? If Germany had known then that all the other fighting nations of the world would combine to prevent her action, she never would have dreamed of attempting it. If Germany had known—this is the common verdict of every man familiar with the politics of Europe—if Germany had known that England would go in, she never would have started it. If she had known that America would come in, she never would have dreamed of it. And now the only way to make it certain that there never will be another world war like that is that we should assist in guaranteeing the peace and its settlement.

It is a very interesting circumstance, my fellow countrymen, that the League of Nations will contain all the nations of the world, great and small, except Germany, and Germany is merely put on probation. We have practically said to Germany, "If it turns out that you really have had a change of heart and have gotten nonsense out of your system; if it really does turn out that you have substituted a genuine self-governing Republic for a Kingdom where a few men on Wilhelmstrasse plotted the destiny of the world, then we will let you in as partners, because then you will be respectable." In the meantime, accepting the treaty, Germany's army is reduced to 100,000 men, and she has promised to give up all the war material over and above what is necessary for 100,000 men. For a nation of 60,000,000! She has surrendered to the world. She has said, "Our fate is in your hands. We are ready to do what you tell us to do." The rest of the world is combined, and the interesting circumstance is that the rest of the world, excluding us, will continue combined if we do not go into it. Some gentlemen seem to think they can break up this treaty and prevent this League by not going into it. Not at all.

I can give you an interesting circumstance. There is the settlement, which you have heard so much discussed, about that rich and ancient Province of Shantung in China. I do not like that settlement any better than you do, but these were the circumstances: In order to induce Japan to coöperate in the war and clear the Pacific of the German power England, and subsequently France, bound themselves without any qualification to see to it that Japan got anything in China that Germany had, and that Japan would take it away from her, upon the strength of which promise Japan proceeded to take Kiauchau and occupy the portions of Shantung Province, which had been ceded by China for a term of years to Germany. The most that could be got out of it was that, in view of the fact that America had nothing to do with it, the Japanese were ready to promise that they would give up every item of sovereignty which

Germany would otherwise have enjoyed in Shantung Province and return it without restriction to China, and that they would retain in the Province only the economic concessions such as other nations already had elsewhere in China—though you do not hear anything about that —concessions in the railway and the mines which had become attached to the railway for operative purposes. But suppose that you say that is not enough. Very well, then, stay out of the treaty, and how will that accomplish anything? England and France are bound and cannot escape their obligation. Are you going to institute a war against Japan and France and England to get Shantung back for China? That is an enterprise which does not commend itself to the present generation.

I am putting it in brutal terms, my fellow citizens, but that is the fact. By disagreeing to that provision, we accomplish nothing for China. On the contrary, we stay out of the only combination of the counsels of nations in which we can be of service to China. With China as a member of the League of Nations, and Japan as a member of the League of Nations, and America as a member of the League of Nations, there confronts every one of them that now famous Article X, by which every member of the League agrees to respect and preserve the territorial integrity and existing political independence of all the other member States. Do not let anybody persuade you that you can take that article out and have a peaceful world. That cuts at the root of the German war. That cuts at the root of the outrage against Belgium. That cuts at the root of the outrage against France. That pulls that vile, unwholesome Upas tree of pan-Germanism up by the roots, and it pulls all other "pans" up, too. Every land-grabbing nation is served notice: "Keep on your own territory. Mind your own business. That territory belongs to those people and they can do with it what they please, provided they do not invade other people's rights by the use they make of it." My fellow citizens, the thing is going to be done whether we are in it or not. If we are in it, then we are going to be the determining factor in the development of civilization. If we are out of it, we ourselves are going to watch every other nation with suspicion, and we will be justified, too; and we are going to be watched with suspicion. Every movement of trade, every relationship of manufacture, every question of raw materials, every matter that affects the intercourse of the world, will be impeded by the consciousness that America wants to hold off and get something which she is not willing to share with the rest of mankind. I am painting the picture for you, because I know that it is as intolerable to you as it is to me. But do not go away with the impression, I beg you, that I think there is any doubt about the issue. The only thing that can be accomplished is delay. The ultimate outcome will be the triumphant acceptance of the treaty and the League.

Let me pay the tribute which it is only just that I should pay to some of the men who have been, I believe, misunderstood in this business. It is only a handful of men, my fellow citizens, who are trying to defeat the treaty or to prevent the League. The great majority, in official bodies and out, are scrutinizing it, as it is perfectly legitimate that they should scrutinize it, to see if it is necessary that they should qualify it in any way, and my knowledge of their conscience, my knowledge of their public principle, makes me certain that they will sooner or later see that it is safest, since it is all expressed in the plainest English that the English dictionary affords, not to qualify it—to accept it as it is. I have been a student of the English language all my life and I do not see a single obscure sentence in the whole document. Some gentlemen either have not read it or do not understand the English language; but, fortunately, on the right-hand page it is printed in English and on the left-hand page it is printed in French. Now, if they do not understand English, I hope they will get a French dictionary and dig out the meaning on that side. The French is a very precise language, more precise than the English language, I am told. I am not on a speaking acquaintance with it, but I am told that it is the most precise language in Europe, and that any given phrase in French always means the same thing. That cannot be said of English. In order to satisfy themselves, I hope these gentlemen will master the French version and then be reassured that there are no lurking monsters in that document; that there are no sinister purposes; that everything is said in the frankest way.

For example, they have been very much worried at the phrase that nothing in the document shall be taken as impairing in any way the validity of such regional understandings as the Monroe Doctrine. They say: "Why put in 'such regional understandings as'? What other understandings are there? Have you got something up your sleeve? Is there going to be a Monroe Doctrine in Asia? Is there going to be a Monroe Doctrine in China?" Why, my fellow citizens, the phrase was written in perfect innocence. The men that I was associated with said, "It is not wise to put a specific thing that belongs only to one nation in a document like this. We do not know of any other regional understanding like it; we never heard of any other; we never expect to hear of any other, but there might some day be some other, and so we will say 'such regional understandings as the Monroe Doctrine,'" and their phrase was intended to give right of way to the Monroe Doctrine in the Western Hemisphere. I reminded the Committee on Foreign Relations of the Senate the other day that the conference I held with them was not the first conference I had held about the League of Nations. When I came back to this our own dear country in March last I held a conference at the White House with the Senate Committee on Foreign Relations, and they made various suggestions as to how the Covenant should be al-

tered in phraseology. I carried those suggestions back
to Paris, and every one of them was accepted. I think
that is a sufficient guarantee that no mischief was intended. The whole document is of the same plain,
practical, explicit sort, and it secures peace, my fellow
citizens, in the only way in which peace can be secured.

I remember, if I may illustrate a very great thing
with a very trivial thing, I had two acquaintances who
were very much addicted to profanity. Their friends
were distressed about it. It subordinated a rich vocabulary which they might otherwise have cultivated, and
so we induced them to agree that they never would swear
inside the corporate limits, that if they wanted to swear
they would go out of town. The first time the passion
of anger came upon them they rather sheepishly got in
a street car and went out of town to swear, and by the
time they got out of town they did not want to swear.
That very homely illustration illustrates in my mind the
value of discussion. Let me remind you that every fighting nation in the world is going to belong to this League,
because we are going to belong to it, and they all make
this solemn engagement with each other, that they will
not resort to war in the case of any controversy until
they have done one or other of two things, until they
have either submitted the question at issue to arbitration, in which case they promise to abide by the verdict
whatever it may be, or, if they do not want to submit it
to arbitration, have submitted it to discussion by the
council of the League.

They agree to give the council six months to discuss
the matter, to supply the council with all the pertinent
facts regarding it, and that, after the opinion of the
council is rendered, they will not then go to war if they
are dissatisfied with the opinion until three more months
have elapsed. They give nine months in which to spread
the whole matter before the judgment of mankind, and
if they violate this promise, if any one of them violates
it, the Covenant prescribes that that violation shall in

itself constitute an act of war against the other members of the League. It does not provide that there shall be war. On the contrary, it provides for something very much more effective than war. It provides that that nation, that covenant-breaking nation, shall be absolutely cut off from intercourse of every kind with the other nations of the world; that no merchandise shall be shipped out of it or into it; that no postal messages shall go into it or come out of it; that no telegraphic messages shall cross its borders; and that the citizens of the other member States shall not be permitted to have any intercourse or transactions whatever with its citizens or its citizens with them. There is not a single nation in Europe that can stand that boycott for six months. There is not a single nation in Europe that is self-sufficing in its resources of food or anything else that can stand that for six months. And in those circumstances we are told that this Covenant is a covenant of war. It is the most drastic covenant of peace that was ever conceived, and its processes are the processes of peace. The nation that does not abide by its covenants is sent to coventry, is taboo, is put out of the society of covenant-respecting nations.

This is a covenant of compulsory arbitration or discussion, and just so soon as you discuss matters, my fellow citizens, peace looks in at the window. Did you ever really sit down and discuss matters with your neighbor when you had a difference and come away in the same temper that you went in? One of the difficulties in our labor situation is that there are some employers who will not meet their employees face to face and talk with them. I have never known an instance in which such a meeting and discussion took place that both sides did not come away in a softened temper and with an access of respect for the other side. The processes of frank discussion are the processes of peace not only, but the processes of settlement, and those are the processes which are set up for all the powerful nations of the world.

I want to say that this is an unparalleled achievement of thoughtful civilization. To my dying day I shall esteem it the crowning privilege of my life to have been permitted to put my name to a document like that; and in my judgment, my fellow citizens, when passion is cooled and men take a sober, second thought, they are all going to feel that the supreme thing that America did was to help bring this about and then put her shoulder to the great chariot of justice and of peace which was going to lead men along in that slow and toilsome march, toilsome and full of the kind of agony that brings bloody sweat, but nevertheless going up a slow incline to those distant heights upon which will shine at the last the serene light of justice, suffusing a whole world in blissful peace.

AT AUDITORIUM, OMAHA, NEBR., SEPTEMBER 8, 1919

MR. CHAIRMAN, MY FELLOW CITIZENS:

I never feel more comfortable in facing my fellow citizens than when I can realize that I am not representing a peculiar cause, that I am not speaking for a single group of my fellow citizens, that I am not the representative of a party but the representative of the people of the United States. I went across the water with that happy consciousness, and in all the work that was done on the other side of the sea, where I was associated with distinguished Americans of both political parties, we all of us constantly kept at our heart the feeling that we were expressing the thoughts of America, that we were working for the things that America believed in. I have come here to testify that this treaty contains the things that America believes in.

I brought a copy of the treaty along with me, for I fancy that, in view of the criticisms you have heard of it, you thought it consisted of only four or five clauses.

Only four or five clauses out of this volume are picked out for criticism. Only four or five phrases in it are called to your attention by some of the distinguished orators who oppose its adoption. Why, my fellow citizens, this is one of the great charters of human liberty, and the man who picks flaws in it—or, rather, picks out the flaws that are in it, for there are flaws in it—forgets the magnitude of the thing, forgets the majesty of the thing, forgets that the counsels of more than twenty nations combined and were rendered unanimous in the adoption of this great instrument. Let me remind you of what everybody admits who has read the document. Everybody admits that it is a complete settlement of the matters which led to this war, and that it contains the complete machinery which provides that they shall stay settled.

You know that one of the greatest difficulties in our own domestic affairs is unsettled land titles. Suppose that somebody were mischievously to tamper with the land records of the State of Nebraska, and that there should be a doubt as to the line of every farm. You know what would happen in six months. All the farmers would be sitting on their fences with shotguns. Litigation would penetrate every community, hot feeling would be generated, contests not only of lawyers, but contests of force, would ensue. Very well, one of the interesting things that this treaty does is to settle the land titles of Europe, and to settle them in this way, on the principle that every land belongs to the people that live on it. This is actually the first time in human history that that principle was ever recognized in a similar document, and yet that is the fundamental American principle. The fundamental American principle is the right of the people that live in the country to say what shall be done with that country. We have gone so far in our assertions of popular right that we not only say that the people have a right to have a government that suits them, but that they have a right to change it in any respect at any time. Very well, that principle lies at the heart of this treaty.

There are peoples in Europe who never before could say that the land they lived in was their own, and the choice that they were to make of their lives was their own choice. I know there are men in Nebraska who come from that country of tragical history, the now restored Republic of Poland, and I want to call your attention to the fact that Poland is here given her complete restitution; and not only is she given the land that formerly belonged to the Poles, but she is given the lands which are now occupied by Poles but had been permitted to remain under other sovereignties. She is given those lands on a principle that all our hearts approve of. Take what in Europe they call High Silesia, the mountainous, the upper, portions of the district of Silesia. The very great majority of the people in High Silesia are Poles, but the Germans contested the statement that most of them were Poles. We said: "Very well, then, it is none of our business; we will let them decide. We will put sufficient armed forces into High Silesia to see that nobody tampers with the processes of the election, and then we will hold a referendum there, and those people can belong either to Germany or to Poland, as they prefer, and not as we prefer." And wherever there was a doubtful district we applied the same principle, that the people should decide and not the men sitting around the peace table at Paris. When these referenda are completed the land titles of Europe will be settled, and every country will belong to the people that live on it to do with what they please. You seldom hear of this aspect of this treaty, my fellow citizens.

You have heard of the council that the newspaper men call the "big four." We had a very much bigger name for ourselves than that. We called ourselves the "supreme council of the principal allied and associated powers," but we had no official title, and sometimes

there were five of us instead of four. Those five represented, with the exception of Germany, of course, the
great fighting nations of the world. They could have
done anything with this treaty that they chose to do,
because they had the power to do it, and they chose to
do what had never been chosen before, to renounce
every right of sovereignty in that settlement to which
the people concerned did not assent. That is the great
settlement which is represented in this volume.

And it contains, among other things, a great charter
of liberty for the workingmen of the world. For the
first time in history the counsels of mankind are to be
drawn together and concerted for the purpose of defending the rights and improving the conditions of
working people—men, women, and children—all over
the world. Such a thing as that was never dreamed
of before, and what you are asked to discuss in discussing the League of Nations is the matter of seeing that
this thing is not interfered with. There is no other way
to do it than by a universal league of nations, and what
is proposed is a universal league of nations. Only two
nations are for the time being left out. One of them
is Germany, because we did not think that Germany was
ready to come in, because we felt that she ought to go
through a period of probation. She says that she made
a mistake. We now want her to prove it by not trying
it again. She says that she has abolished all the old
forms of government by which little secret councils of
men, sitting nobody knew exactly where, determined the
fortunes of that great Nation and, incidentally, tried
to determine the fortunes of mankind; but we want her
to prove that her constitution is changed and that it is
going to stay changed; and then who can, after those
proofs are produced, say "No" to a great people 60,-
000,000 strong, if they want to come in on equal terms
with the rest of us and do justice in international affairs?
I want to say that I did not find any of my colleagues
in Paris disinclined to do justice to Germany. But I

hear that this treaty is very hard on Germany. When an individual has committed a criminal act, the punishment is hard, but the punishment is not unjust. This nation permitted itself, through unscrupulous governors, to commit a criminal act against mankind, and it is to undergo the punishment, not more than it can endure, but up to the point where it can pay it must pay for the wrong that it has done.

But the things prescribed in this treaty will not be fully carried out if any one of the great influences that brought that result about is withheld from its consummation. Every great fighting nation in the world is on the list of those who are to constitute the League of Nations. I say every great nation, because America is going to be included among them, and the only choice, my fellow citizens, is whether we will go in now or come in later with Germany; whether we will go in as founders of this covenant of freedom or go in as those who are admitted after they have made a mistake and repented.

I wish I could do what is impossible in a great company like this. I wish I could read that Covenant to you, because I do not believe, if you have not read it yourself and have only listened to certain speeches that I have read, that you know anything that is in it. Why, my fellow citizens, the heart of that Covenant is that there shall be no war. To listen to some of the speeches that you may have listened to or read, you would think that the heart of it was that it was an arrangement for war. On the contrary, this is the heart of that treaty: The bulk of it is concerned with arrangements under which all the members of the League—that means everybody but Germany and dismembered Turkey— agree that they never will go to war without first having done one or other of two things—either submitted the question at issue to arbitration, in which case they agree absolutely to abide by the verdict, or, if they do not care to submit it to arbitration, submitted it to discussion by the council of the League of Nations, in which case they must give six months for the discussion and wait three months after the rendering of the decision, whether they like it or not, before they go to war. They agree to cool off for nine months before they yield to the heat of passion which might otherwise have hurried them into war.

If they do not do that, it is not war that ensues; it is something that will interest them and engage them very much more than war; it is an absolute boycott of the nation that disregards the Covenant. The boycott is automatic, and just as soon as it applies, then this happens: No goods can be shipped out of that country; no goods can be shipped into it. No telegraphic message may pass either way across its borders. No package of postal matter—no letter—can cross its borders either way. No citizen of any member of the League can have any transactions of any kind with any citizen of that nation. It is the most complete isolation and boycott ever conceived, and there is not a nation in Europe that can live for six months without importing goods out of other countries. After they have thought about the matter for six months, I predict that they will have no stomach for war.

All that you are told about in this Covenant, so far as I can learn, is that there is an Article X. I will repeat Article X to you; I think I can repeat it verbatim, the heart of it at any rate. Every member of the League promises to respect and preserve as against external aggression—not as against internal revolution—the territorial integrity and existing political independence of every other member of the League, and if it is necessary to enforce this promise—I mean, for the nations to act in concert with arms in their hands to enforce it—then the council of the League shall advise what action is necessary. Some gentlemen who doubt the meaning of English words have thought that advice did not mean advice, but I do not know anything else that it does mean, and I have studied English most of my life and speak it with reasonable correctness. The point is this: The council cannot give that advice without the vote of the United States, unless it is a party to the dispute; but, my fellow citizens, if you are a party to the dispute you are in the scrap anyhow. If you are a party, then the question is not whether you are going to war or not, but merely whether you are going to war against the rest of the world or with the rest of the world, and the object of war in that case will be to defend that central thing that I began by speaking about. That is the guarantee of the land titles of the world which have been established by this treaty. Poland, Czecho-Slovakia, Rumania, Jugo-Slavia—all those nations which never had a vision of independent liberty until now—have their liberty and independence guaranteed to them. If we do not guarantee them, then we have this interesting choice: I hear gentlemen say that we went into the recent war because we were forced into it, and their preference now is to wait to be forced in again. They do not pretend that we can keep out; they merely pretend that we ought to keep out until we are ashamed not to go in.

This is the Covenant of the League of Nations that you hear objected to, the only possible guarantee against war. I would consider myself recreant to every mother and father, every wife and sweetheart in this country, if I consented to the ending of this war without a guarantee that there would be no other. You say, "Is it an absolute guarantee?" No; there is no absolute guarantee against human passion; but even if it were only 10 per cent of a guarantee, would not you rather have 10 per cent guarantee against war than none? If it only creates a presumption that there will not be war, would you not rather have that presumption than live under the certainty that there will be war? For, I tell you, my fellow citizens, I can predict with absolute certainty that within another generation there will be another world war if the nations of the world do not concert the method by which to prevent it.

But I did not come here this morning, I remind myself, so much to expound the treaty as to talk about these interesting things that we hear about that are called reservations. A reservation is an assent with a big but. We agree—but. Now, I want to call your attention to some of these buts. I will take them, so far as I can remember the order, in the order in which they deal with clauses of the League itself.

In the first article of the Covenant it is provided that a nation can withdraw from the League on two years' notice, provided at the time of its withdrawal, that is to say, at the expiration of the two years, it has fulfilled all its international obligations and all its obligations under the Covenant. Some of our friends are very uneasy about that. They want to sit close to the door with their hands on the knob, and they want to say, "We are in this thing but we are in it with infinite timidity; we are in it only because you overpersuaded us and wanted us to come in, and we are going to try this thing every now and then and see if it is locked, and just as soon as we see anything we don't like, we are going to scuttle." Now, what is the trouble? What are they afraid of? I want you to put this to every man you know who makes this objection, what is he afraid of? Is he afraid that when the United States withdraws it will not have fulfilled its international obligations? Is he willing to bring that indictment against this beloved country? My fellow citizens, we never did fail to fulfill an international obligation and, God guiding and helping us, we never will. I for one am not going to admit in any connection the slightest doubt that, if we ever choose to withdraw, we will then have fulfilled our obligations. If I make reservations, as they are called, about this, what do I do? This Covenant does not set up any tribunal to judge whether we have fulfilled our obligations at that time or not. There is only one thing to restrain us, and that is the opinion of mankind. Are these gentlemen such poor patriots that they are afraid that the United States will cut a poor figure in the opinion of mankind? And do they think that they can bring this great people to withdraw from that League if at that time their withdrawal would be condemned by the opinion of mankind? We have always been at pains to earn the respect of mankind, and we shall always be at pains to retain it. I for one am too proud as an American to say that any doubt will ever hang around our right to withdraw upon the condition of the fulfillment of our international obligations.

I have already adverted to the difficulties under Article X and will not return to it. That difficulty is merely as I repeated it just now, that some gentlemen do not want to go in as partners, they want to go in as late joiners, because they all admit that in a war which imperils the just arrangements of mankind, America, the greatest, richest, freest people in the world must take sides. We could not live without taking sides. We devoted ourselves to justice and to liberty when we were born, and we are not going to get senile and forget it.

They do not like the way in which the Monroe Doctrine is mentioned. Well, I would not stop on a question of style. The Monroe Doctrine is adopted. It is swallowed, hook, line, and sinker, and, being carefully digested into the central organism of the whole instrument, I do not care what language they use about it. The language is entirely satisfactory so far as I understand the English language. That puzzles me, my fellow citizens. The English language seems to have got some new meaning since I studied it that bothers these gentlemen. I do not know what dictionaries they resort to. I do not know what manuals of conscience they can possibly resort to. The Monroe Doctrine is expressly authenticated in this document, for the first time in history, by all the great Nations of the world, and it was put there at our request. When I came back to this dear country in March I brought the first draft, the provisional draft, of the Covenant of the League. I submitted it to the Foreign Relations Committee of the Senate of the United States, and I spent an evening discussing it with them. They made a number of suggestions. I carried every one of those suggestions to Paris, and every one of them was adopted. Now apparently they want me to go back to Paris and say, "We are much obliged to you, but we do not like the language." I suggested the other night that if they do not like that language there is another language in here. That page is English [illustrating]; this page is French [illustrating]—the same thing. If the English does not suit them, let them engage the interest of some French scholar and see if they like the French better. It is the same thing. It is done in perfect good faith. Nobody was trying to fool anybody else. This is the genuine work of honest men.

The fourth matter that they are concerned about is domestic questions, so they want to put in a reservation enumerating certain questions as domestic questions which everybody on both sides of the water admits are domestic questions. That seems to me, to say the least, to be a work of supererogation. It does not seem to me necessary to specify what everybody admits, but they are so careful—I believe the word used to be "meticulous"—that they want to put in what is clearly implied in the whole instrument. "Well," you say, "why not?" Well, why not, my fellow citizens? The conference at Paris will still be sitting when the Senate of the United States has acted upon this treaty. Perhaps I ought not to say that so confidently. No man, even in the secrets of Providence, can tell how long it will take the United States Senate to do anything, but I imagine that in the normal course of human fatigue the Senate will have acted upon this treaty before the conference in Paris gets through with the Austrian treaty and the Bulgarian treaty and the Turkish treaty.

They will still be there on the job. Now—every lawyer will follow me in this—if you take a contract and change the words, even though you do not change the sense, you have to get the other parties to accept those words. Is not that true? Therefore every reservation will have to be taken back to all the signatories of this treaty, and I want you to notice that that includes Germany. We will have to ask Germany's consent to read this treaty the way we understand it. I want to tell you that we did not ask Germany's consent with regard to the meaning of any one of those terms while we were in Paris. We told her what they meant and said, "Sign here." Are there any patriotic Americans who desire the method changed? Do they want me to ask the assembly at Weimar if I may read the treaty the way it means but in words which the United States Senate thinks it ought to have been written in? You see, reservations come down to this, that they want to change the language of the treaty without changing its meaning and involve all the embarrassments. Because, let me say, there are indications—I am judging not from official dispatches but from the newspapers—that people are not in as good a humor over in Paris now as they were when I was there, and it is going to be more difficult to get agreement from now on than it was then. After dealing with some of those gentlemen I found that they were as ingenious as any American in attaching unexpected meanings to plain words, and, having gone through the mill on the existing language, I do not want to go through it again on changed language.

I must not turn away from this great subject without adverting to one particular in the treaty itself, and that is the provision with regard to the transfer of certain German rights in the Province of Shantung, China, to Japan. I have frankly said to my Japanese colleagues in the conference, and therefore I can without impropriety say it here, that I was very deeply dissatisfied with that part of the treaty. But, my fellow citizens,

Japan agreed at that very time, and as part of the understanding upon which those clauses were put into the treaty, that she would relinquish every item of sovereignty that Germany had enjoyed to China, and that she would retain only what other nations have elsewhere in China, certain economic concessions with regard to the railway and the mines, which she was to operate under a corporation and subject to the laws of China. As I say, I wish she could have done more. But suppose, as some have suggested that we dissent from that clause in the treaty. You cannot sign all of the treaty but one part, my fellow citizens. It is like the President's veto. He cannot veto provisions in a bill. He has got either to sign the bill or veto the bill. We cannot sign the treaty with the Shantung provision out of it, and if we could, what sort of service would we be doing to China?

Let us state the facts with brutal frankness. England and France are bound by solemn treaty, entered into before the conference at Paris, before the end of the war, to give Japan what she gets in this treaty in the Province of Shantung. They cannot in honor withdraw from that promise. They cannot consent to a peace treaty which does not contain those provisions with regard to Shantung. England and France, therefore, will stand behind Japan, and if we are not signatories to the treaties and not parties she will get all that Germany had in Shantung, more than she will get under the promises which she made to us, and the only way we can get it away from her is by going to war with Japan and Great Britain and France. Does that look like a workable proposition? Is that doing China a service? Whereas, if we do accept this treaty, we are members of the League of Nations, China is a member of the League, and Japan is a member of the League, and under that much-criticized Article X Japan promises and we guarantee that the territorial integrity and political independence of China will be respected and preserved. That is the way to serve China. That is the only possible way in the circumstances to serve China. Therefore we cannot rewrite this treaty. We must take it or leave it, and gentlemen, after all the rest of the world has signed it, will find it very difficult to make any other kind of treaty. As I took the liberty of saying the other night, it is a case of "put up or shut up." The world cannot breathe in the atmosphere of negations. The world cannot deal with nations who say, "We won't play!" The world cannot have anything to do with an arrangement in which every nation says, "We will take care of ourselves." Is it possible, my fellow citizens—is it possible, for the sinister thing has been suggested to me—that there is a group of individuals in this country who have conceived it as desirable that the United States should exercise its power alone, should arm for the purpose, should be ready for the enterprise, and should dominate the world by arms? There are indications that there are groups of citizens in this country who do not find that an unpalatable program. Are we going to substitute for pan-Germanism a sinister pan-Americanism? The thing is inconceivable. It is hideous. No man dare propose that in plain words to any American audience anywhere. The heart of this people is pure. The heart of this people is true. This great people loves liberty. It loves justice. It would rather have liberty and justice than wealth and power. It is the great idealistic force of history, and the idealism of America is what has made conquest of the spirits of men.

While I was in Paris men of every race, from every quarter of the globe, sought interviews with us in order to tell us how absolutely they believed in America and how all their thoughts, all their pleas for help, all their hope of political salvation, reached out toward America, and my heart melted within me. I said to some of the simpler sort among them: "I pray you that you will not expect the impossible. America cannot do all the things that you are expecting her to do. The most that I can promise is that we will do everything we can." And we are going to redeem that promise, not because I made it, but because when I made it I spoke the purpose and heart of the United States. If I felt that I personally in any way stood in the way of this settlement, I would be glad to die that it might be consummated, because I have a vision, my fellow citizens, that if this thing should by some mishap not be accomplished there would rest forever upon the fair name of this people a stain which could never be effaced, which would be intolerable to every lover of America, inconceivable to any man who knew the duty of America and was ready with stout heart to do it.

I said just now at the opening that I was happy to forget on a campaign like this what party I belonged to, and I hope that you will not think that I am recalling what party I belong to if I say how proud I have been to stand alongside of Senator Hitchcock in this fight. I would be just as glad to stand by Senator Norris if he would let me. I refer to Senator Hitchcock because I know this is his home town and because of my personal regard for him, and because I wanted to make it the preface to say I want to be the brother and comrade and coworker of every man who will work for this great cause. It heartens me when I find, as I found in Des Moines and I find here, that there are more Republicans on the committees that meet me than Democrats. That may be in proportion to the population, but nevertheless I judge from what I see of these gentlemen that they are, at any rate, very favorable specimens and that I can take it for granted, because of what I see in my dealing with them, that they do represent some of the permanence and abiding influences of great communities like this. Why, the heart of America beats in these great prairies and on these hillsides. Sometimes in Washington you seem very far away. The voices that are most audible in Washington are not voices that anybody cares to listen to for very long, and it is refreshing to get out among the great body of one's fellow citizens and feel the touch of hand and the contact of shoulder and the impulse of mass movement which is going to make spiritual conquest of the world.

AT COLISEUM, SIOUX FALLS, S. DAK., SEPTEMBER 8, 1919

GOVERNOR NORBECK, MY FELLOW CITIZENS:

I must admit that every time I face a great audience of my fellow countrymen on this trip I am filled with a feeling of peculiar solemnity, because I believe, my fellow countrymen, that we have come to one of the turning points in the history of the world, and what I as an American covet for this great country is that, as on other great occasions when mankind's fortunes hung in a nice poise and balance, America may have the distinction to lead the way.

In order to enable you to realize some part of what is in my thought to-night, I am going to ask you to turn your thought back to the tragedy through which we have just passed. A little incident as we came along in the train to-day brought very close home to me the things that have been happening. A very quiet lady came up with a little crowd at a way station to shake hands with me, and she had no sooner taken my hand than she turned away and burst into tears. I asked a neighbor what was the matter, and he said she had meant to speak to me of her son who was dead in France, but that the words would not come from her lips. All over this country, my fellow citizens, there are women who have given up their sons, wives who have given up their husbands, young women who have given up their sweethearts, to die on the other side of the sea for a great cause which was not the peculiar cause of America but the cause of mankind and of civilization itself. I love to repeat what the people on the other side of the water said about those boys of ours. They told us that they did not look like any of the other soldiers, that they did not seem to be merely soldiers, that they seemed to be crusaders, that there was something in their eyes that they had never seen in the eyes of any other army, and I was reminded of what I had so often seen on former journeys across the seas: Going over in the steerage, bright-eyed men who had been permeated with the atmosphere of free America; coming back, among the immigrants coming from the old countries, dull-eyed men, tired-looking men, discouraged-looking men. They were all of them going both ways, men who had come from across the sea, but going out they were going with the look of America in their eyes to visit the old people at home; coming back they had the fatigue of Europe in their eyes and had not yet got the feeling that penetrates every American, that there is a great future, that a man can handle his own fortunes, that it is his right to have his place in the world, and that no man that he does not choose is his master. And that is what these people saw in the eyes of the American boys who carried their arms across the sea. There was America in every one of those lively eyes, and America was not looking merely at the fields of France, was not merely seeking to defeat Germany; she was seeking to defeat everything that Germany's action represented, and to see to it that there never happened such a thing again.

I want to remind you, my fellow countrymen, that that war was not an accident. That war did not just happen. There was not some sudden occasion which brought on a conflagration. On the contrary, Germany had been preparing for that war for generations. Germany had been preparing every resource, perfecting every skill, developing every invention, which would enable her to master the European world; and, after mastering the European world, to dominate the rest of the world. Everybody had been looking on. Everybody had known. For example, it was known in every war office in Europe, and in the War Department at Washington, that the Germans not only had a vast supply of great field guns but that they had ammunition enough for every one of those guns to exhaust the gun. Yet we were all living in a fool's paradise. We thought Germany meant what she said—that she was armed for defense; and that she never would use that great store of force against the rest of her fellow men. Why, my friends, it was foreordained the minute Germany conceived these purposes that she should do the thing which she did in 1914. That assassination of the Austrian Crown Prince in Serbia was not what started the war. They were ready to start it and merely made that an occasion and an excuse. Before they started it, Serbia had yielded to practically every demand they made of her, and they would not let the rest of the world know that Serbia had yielded, because they did not want to miss the occasion to start the war. They were afraid that other nations would prepare. They were afraid that they had given too much indication of what they were going to do and they did not want to wait. What immediately happened, when the other foreign offices of Europe learned of what was going on, was that from every other foreign office, so far as I have been able to learn, messages went to Berlin instructing their representatives to suggest to the German Government that the other Governments be informed and that an opportunity be obtained for a discussion, so as to see if war could not be avoided. And Germany did not dare discuss her purpose for twenty-four hours.

I have brought back from Europe with me, my fellow citizens, a treaty in which Germany is disarmed and in which all the other nations of the world agree never to go to war without first of all having done one or other of two things, either having submitted the question in dispute to arbitration, in which case they will abide by the verdict, or, if they do not care to submit it to arbitration, having submitted it to discussion by the League of Nations; that they will allow six months for the discussion; that they will publish all the facts to all the world; and that not until three months after the expiration of the six will they go to war. There is a period of nine months of cooling off, and Germany did not dare cool off for nine days! If Germany had dreamed that anything like the greater part of the world would combine against her, she never would have begun the war, and she did not dare to let the opinion of mankind crystallize against her by the discussion of the purposes which she had in mind. What I want to point out to you to-night is that we are making a fundamental choice. You have either got to have the old system, of which Germany was the perfect flower, or you have got to have a new system. You cannot have a new system unless you provide a substitute, an adequate substitute, for the old, and when certain of our fellow citizens take the position that we do not want to go into any combination at all but want to take care of ourselves, all I have to say to them is that that is exactly the German position.

Germany through the mouth of her Emperor—Germany through the mouths of her orators—Germany through the pens of her writers of all sorts—said: "Here we stand, ready to take care of ourselves. We will not enter into any combination. We are armed for self-defense and no nation dares interfere with our rights." That, it appears, is the American program in the eyes of some gentlemen; and I want to tell you that within the last two weeks the pro-German element in this country has lifted its head again. It is again heartened. It again has air in its lungs. It again says, "Ah, now we see a chance when America and Germany will stand outside this League and take care of themselves." Not take care of themselves as partners, I do not mean to intimate that, but where America will play the same rôle that Germany plays, under that old order which brought us through that agony of bloody sweat, that great agony in which the whole world seemed to be caught in the throes of a crisis, when for a long time we did not know whether civilization itself was going to survive or not. And do not believe, my fellow countrymen, that civilization is saved now. There were passions let loose upon the field of the world by that war which have not grown quiet yet, which will not grow quiet for a long time, and every element of disorder, every element of chaos, is hoping that there may be no steadying hand from a council of nations to hold the order of the world steady until we can make the final arrangements of justice and of peace. The treaty of peace with Germany is very much more than a treaty of peace with Germany. The German part of it takes a good many words, because there are a great many technical details to be arranged, but that is not the heart of the treaty. The heart of the treaty is that it undoes the injustice that Germany did; that it not only undoes the injustice that Germany did but it organizes the world to see that such injustice will in the future be impossible.

And not forgetting, but remembering with intense sympathy the toiling mass of mankind, the conference at Paris wrote into the heart of that treaty a great charter of labor. I think that those of us who live in this happy land can have little conception of the conditions of labor in some of the European countries up to the period of the outbreak of this war, and one of the things that that treaty proposes to do is to organize the opinion of all Nations to assist in the betterment and the release of the great forces of labor throughout the world. It is a laboring man's treaty in the sense that it is the average man's treaty. Why, my fellow citizens, the thing that happened at Paris was absolutely and literally unprecedented. There never was a gathering of the leading statesmen of the world before who did not sit down to divide the spoils, to make the arrangements the most advantageous that they could devise for their own strong and powerful Governments. Yet this gathering of statesmen sat themselves down to do something which a friend of mine the other day very aptly described as establishing the land titles of the world, because the principle underlying the treaty was that every land belonged to the native stock that lived in it, and that nobody had the right to dictate either the form of government or the control of territory to those people who were born and bred and had their lives and happiness to make there. The principle that nobody has the right to impose the sovereignty of any alien government on anybody was for the first time recognized in the counsels of international deliberation. In this League of Nations Covenant, which some men ask you to examine in a spot here and there with a magnifying glass, there lies at the heart of it this great principle, nobody has the right to take any territory any more.

You will see what our situation was: The Austrian Empire, for example, had gone to pieces, and here we were with the pieces on the table. The Austrian treaty is not yet completed, but it is being made on the same principle as the German, and will serve as an illustration. In the old days they would have compacted it between armies. They did not do that this time. They said, "This piece belongs to the Poles and to nobody else. This piece belongs to the Bohemians and to nobody else. This piece belongs to Rumania, though she never could have got it for herself; we are going to turn it over to her, though other people want it. This piece belongs to the Slavs, who live in the northern Balkans—the Jugo-Slavs as we have come to know them to be—and they shall, have what belongs to them." When we turned to the property of Germany, which she had been habitually misgoverning—I mean the German colonies, particularly the colonies in Africa—there were many nations who would like to have had those rich, undeveloped portions of the world; but none

of them got them. We adopted the principle of trusteeship. We said: "We will put you in charge of this,
that, and the other piece of territory, and you will make
an annual report to us. We will deprive you of your
trusteeship whenever you administer it in a way which
is not approved by our judgment, and we will put upon
you this primary limitation, that you shall do nothing
that is to the detriment of the people who live in that
territory. You shall not enforce labor on it, and you
shall apply the same principles of humanity to the work
of their women and children that you apply at home.
You shall not allow the illicit trade in drugs and in
liquors. You shall not allow men who want to make
money out of powder and shot to sell arms and ammunition to those who can use them to their own disadvantage. You shall not make those people fight in your
armies. The country is theirs, and you must remember
that and treat it as theirs." There is no more annexation. There is no more land grabbing. There is no
more extension of sovereignty. It is an absolute reversal of history, an absolute revolution in the way in
which international affairs are treated; and it is all in
the Covenant of the League of Nations.

The old system was, Be ready, and we can be ready.
I have heard gentlemen say, "America can take care
of herself." Yes, she can take care of herself. Every
man would have to train to arms. We would have to
have a great standing army. We would have to have
accumulations of military material such as Germany
used to have. We would enjoy the luxuries of taxes
even higher than we pay now. We could accumulate
our force, and then our force would have to be directed
by some kind of sufficiently vigorous central power. You
would have a military government in spirit if not in
form. No use having a fighting Nation if there is not
somebody to swing it! If you do not want your President to be a representative of the civil purposes of this
country, you can turn him into merely a commander in

choose the seat by the door and keep fumbling with the
knob without creating the impression that you are going
to get out in a minute; that you do not like the company
you are in; that you do not like the job; that you are
by constitution and disposition a scuttler! If America
goes into this thing, she is going to stay in, and she is
going to stay in in order to see that justice is done. She
can see to it, because if you read this Covenant of the
League you will find that, America being one of the
members of the council of the League, nothing material
can be done under that League without a unanimous vote
of the council. America can determine what action is
going to be taken. No action that is against her policy
or against her will can be taken, unless her judgment
is rendered in some case where she is one of the dis-
putants but, my fellow citizens, if she is one of the dis-
putants, she is in trouble anyhow. If the war that they
are trying to avert is her war, then I do not see that
she is any more benefited by being out of the League
than in it. On the contrary, if she is in the League, she
has at least the good offices of other friendly States to
see that some accommodation is reached.

And she is doing exactly what she has done already.
Some gentlemen forget that we already have nearly
thirty treaties with the leading nations of the world.
Yes; and to do the very thing that is in this Covenant,
only we agree to take twelve months to discuss everything, whereas the League gives nine months. The
American choice would be twelve. We promise not to
fight without first talking. I want to call a great many
here witness to this circumstance, for I am sure by looking at you that you know something about it. What is
the certain way to have difficulty between capital and
labor? It is to refuse to sit down in the same room and
talk it over. I cannot understand why one man or set
of men should refuse to discuss claims or grievances
with another set of men, unless they know to begin with
that they are wrong. I am very averse from discussing

anything when I know I have got the wrong end, but when I think I have got either the right end or as good an end as the other fellow, then I am perfectly willing to discuss it.   There is an old saying accredited to ? rather cynical politician of what I hope I may regaī as the older school, who said to his son, "John, do ɔt bother your head about lies; they will take care of thm-selves; but if you ever hear me denying anything, you may be sure it is so."   The only thing we are afraīd of, the only thing we dodge, is the truth.   If we see facts coming our way, it is just as well to get out of the way. Always take this attitude, my friends, towards facts; Always try to see them coming first, so that they will not catch you at unawares.   So with all matters, grading up from the smallest to the greatest.   Human being can get together by discussion, and it is the business civilization to get together by discussion and no fighting.   That is civilization.   The only reas country is civilized is because we do not let tw who have a difference fight one another.   We say : a minute; we have arranged for that.   Just arou corner there you will find a courthouse.   On certain the court is sitting.   Go and state the matter to t men, and neither before nor after the decision s you touch one another."   That is civilization.   Y have got the ordered processes of consultation and dis-cussion.   You have got to act by rule, and justice con-sists in applying the same rule to everybody, not one rule to the rich man and another to the poor; not one rule to the employer and another to the employee, but the same rule to the strong and to the weak.

That is exactly what is attempted in this treaty.   I cannot understand the psychology of men who are re-sisting it.   I cannot understand what they are afraid of, unless it is that they know physical force and do not understand moral force.   Moral force is a great deal more powerful than physical.   Govern the sentiments of mankind and you govern mankind.   Govern their fears, govern their hopes, determine their fortunes, get them together in concerted masses, and the whole thing sways like a team. Once get them suspecting one another, once get them antagonizing one another, and society itself goes to pieces. We are trying to make a society instead of a set of barbarians out of the governments of the world. I sometimes think, when I wake in the night, of all the wakeful nights that anxious fathers and mothers and friends have spent during those weary years of this awful war, and I seem to hear the cry, the inarticulate cry of mothers all over the world, millions of them on the other side of the sea and thousands of them on this side of the sea, "In God's name, give us the sensible and hopeful and peaceful processes of right and of justice!"

America can stay out, but I want to call you to witness that the peace of the world cannot be established without America. America is necessary to the peace of the world. And reverse the proposition: The peace and good will of the world are necessary to America. Disappoint the world, center its suspicion upon you, make it feel that you are hot and jealous rivals of the other nations, and do you think you are going to do as much business with them as you would otherwise do? I do not like to put the thing on that plane, my fellow countrymen, but if you want to talk business, I can talk business. If you want to put it on the low plane of how much money you can make, you can make more money out of friendly traders than out of hostile traders. You can make more money out of men who trust you than out of men who fear you. You can bring about a state of mind where by every device possible foreign markets will be closed to you, and men will say: "No; the wheat of America tastes bitter; we will eat the wheat of Argentina; we will eat the wheat of Australia, for that is the wheat of friendship, and this is the wheat of antagonism. We do not want to wear clothes made out of American cotton; we are going to buy just as much

cotton from India as we can. We are going to develop
new cotton fields. America is up to something; we do
not know just what, and we are going to shut and lock
every door we can against her." You can get the world
in that temper. Do you think that would be profitable?
Do you think there is money in that? But I am not
going to dwell upon that side of it. I am just as sure
of what you are thinking as I am of what I am thinking.
We are not thinking of money. We would rather retain the reputation of America than have all the money
in the world. I am not ready to die for money, and
neither are you, but you are ready and I am ready to
die for America.

A friend of mine made a very poignant remark to me
one day. He said: "Did you ever see a family that hung
its son's yardstick or ledger or spade up over the mantelpiece?" But how many of you have seen the lad's rifle,
his musket, hung up! Well, why? A musket is a barbarous thing. The spade and the yardstick and the
ledger are the symbols of peace and of steady business;
why not hang them up? Because they do not represent
self-sacrifice. They do not glorify you. They do not
dignify you in the same sense that the musket does, because when you took that musket at the call of your
country you risked everything and knew you could not
get anything. The most that you could do was to come
back alive, but after you came back alive there was a
halo about you. That boy was in France! That boy
served his country and served a great cause! That boy
risked everything to see that the weak peoples of the
world were redeemed from intolerable tyranny! Here
comes—ah, how I wish I were going to be in Washington on the 17th—here comes, do you not hear it, the
tread of the First Division; those men, along with their
comrades, to whom the eyes of all Europe turned! All
Europe took heart when they saw that brilliant flag unfurled on French soil.

Did you ever hear that thrilling song that is being

sung so much now of the blind Frenchman wishing to know if the Americans had come, bidding his son watch at the window. "Look, my lad, what are they carrying? What are the colors? Are they red stripes upon a field of white? Is there a piece of heaven in the corner? Is that piece of heaven full of stars? Ah, the Americans have come! Thank God, the Americans have come!" That is what we have at our hearts, my fellow citizens, and we hang the musket up, or the sword, over the mantelpiece. And if the lad is gone and dead, we share the spirit of a noble lady, who said to me, without the glimmer of a tear in her eye: "I have had the honor of losing a son upon the fields of France. I have had the honor, not the pain. I have had the distinction of losing a son of mine upon the field of honor." It is that field of honor that we are going to redeem. We are not going to redeem it with blood any more, but we are going to make out of the counsels of the people of the world counsels of peace and of justice and of honor.

BEFORE STATE LEGISLATURE, ST. PAUL, MINN.,
SEPTEMBER 9, 1919.

MR. SPEAKER, YOUR EXCELLENCY, GENTLEMEN OF THE LEGISLATURE, LADIES AND GENTLEMEN:

I esteem it an unusual privilege to stand in this place to-day and to address the members of this great body, because the errand upon which I have left Washington is so intimate a matter of the life of our own Nation as well as of the life of the world. Yet I am conscious, standing in this presence, that perhaps the most appropriate things I could allude to are those which affect us immediately. I know that you have been called together in special session for special objects. One of those objects you have achieved, and I rejoice with you in the adoption of the suffrage amendment. Another of the objects, I understand, is to consider the high cost of living, and the high cost of living is one of those things which are so complicated; it ramifies in so many directions that it seems to me we cannot do anything in particular without knowing how the particulars affect the whole. It is dangerous to play with a complicated piece of machinery, piece by piece, unless you know how the pieces are related to each other.

The cost of living at present is a world condition. It is due to the fact that the man power of the world has been sacrificed in the agony of the battlefield and that all the processes of industry have been either slackened or diverted. The production of foodstuffs, the production of clothing, the production of all the necessaries of life has either been slackened or it has been turned into channels which are not immediately useful for the general civil population. Great factories, as I need not tell you, in our own country which were devoted to the uses of peace have recently been diverted in such fashion as to serve the purposes of war, and it will take a certain length of time to restore them to their old adjustments, to put their machinery to the old uses again, to redistribute labor so that it will not be concentrated upon the manufacture of munitions and the other stuffs necessary for war, but will be devoted to the general processes of production so necessary for our life.

Back of all that—and I do not say this merely for an argumentative reason, but because it is true—back of that lies the fact that we have not yet learned what the basis of peace is going to be. The world is not going to settle down, my fellow citizens, until it knows what part the United States is going to play in the peace. And that for a very interesting reason. The strain put upon the finances of the other Governments of the world has been all but a breaking strain. I imagine that it will be several generations before foreign Governments can finally adjust themselves to carrying the overwhelming debts which have been accumulated in this war. The United States has accumulated a great debt, but not in proportion to those that other countries have accumulated when you reckon our wealth as compared with theirs. We are the only nation in the world that is likely in the immediate future to have a sufficient body of free capital to put the industrial world, here and elsewhere, on its feet again. Until the industrial world here and elsewhere is put on its feet you cannot finally handle the question of the cost of living, because the cost of living in the last analysis depends upon the things we are always talking about but do not know how to manage—the law of supply and demand. It depends upon manufacture and distribution. It depends upon all the normal processes of the industrial and commercial world. It depends upon international credit. It depends upon shipping. It depends upon the multiplication of transportation facilities domestically. Our railroads at this moment are not adequate to moving the commerce of this country. Every here and there they run through a little neck—for example, the Pennsylvania system at Pittsburgh—where everything is congested and you are squeezing a great commerce through a little aperture. Terminal facilities at the ports are not adequate. The problem grows the more you think of it. What we have to put our minds to is an international problem, first of all—to set the commerce of the world going again and the manufacture of the world going again. And we have got to do that largely. Then we have got to see that our own production and our own methods of finance and our own commerce are quickened in every way that is possible. And then we, sitting in legislatures like this and in the Congress of the United States, have to see to it, if you will permit a vulgar expression, that "nobody monkeys with the process."

I understand that one of the excellent suggestions made by your governor is that you look into the matter of cold storage. Well, there are other kinds of storage besides cold storage. There are all sorts of ways of governing and concentrating the reserve stocks of goods. You do not have to keep everything cold, though you can keep the cold hand of control on it; you can manage by a concert that need not be put on paper to see to it that goods are doled out to the market so that they will not get there so fast as to bring the price down. The communities of the United States are entitled to see that these dams are removed and that the waters that are going to fructify the world flow in their normal courses. It is not easy. It is not always pleasant. You do not like to look censoriously into the affairs of your fellow citizens too much or too often, but it is necessary to look with a very unsympathetic eye at some of the processes which are retarding distribution and the supply which is going to meet the demand.

Not only that, but we have got to realize that we are face to face with a great industrial problem which does not center in the United States. It centers elsewhere, but which we share with the other countries of the world. That is the relation between capital and labor, between those who employ and those who are employed, and we might as well sit up straight and look facts in the face, gentlemen. The laboring men of the world are not satisfied with their relations with their employers. Of course, I do not mean to say that there is universal dissatisfaction, because here, there, and elsewhere, in many cases fortunately, there are very satisfactory relations, but I am now speaking of the general relationship which exists between capital and labor. Everywhere there is dissatisfaction, with it much more acute on the other side of the water than on this side, and one of the things that have to be brought about for mankind can be brought about by what we do in this country, because, as a matter of fact, if I may refer for a moment to the treaty of peace, there is a part of that treaty which sets up an international method of consultation about the conditions of labor. It is a splendid instrument locked up in that great document. I have called it fre-

quently the Magna Charta of labor, for it is that, and
the standards set up, for standards are stated, are the
standards of American labor so far as they could be
adopted in a general conference. The point I wish to
make is that the world is looking to America to set the
standards with regard to the conditions of labor and the
relations between labor and capital, and it is looking to
us because we have been more progressive than other
nations in those matters, though sometimes we have
moved very slowly and with undue caution. As a result
of our progressiveness the ruling influences among our
workingmen are conservative in the sense that they see
that it is not in the interest of labor to break up civilization, and progressive in the sense that they see that a
constructive program has to be adopted. By a progressive I do not mean a man who is ready to move, but a
man who knows where he is going when he moves. A
man who has got a workable program is the only progressive, because if you have not got a workable program you cannot make it good and you cannot progress.
Very well, then, we have got to have a constructive program with regard to labor, and the minute we get it we
will relieve the strain all over the world, because the
world will accept our standards and follow our example.
I am not dogmatic about this matter. I cannot presume
that I know how it ought to be done. I know the principle upon which it ought to be done. The principle is
that the interests of capital and the interests of labor
are not different but the same, and men of business sense
ought to know how to work out an organization which
will express that identity of interest. Where there is
identity of interest there must be community of interest.
You cannot any longer regard labor as a commodity.
You have got to regard it as a means of association, the
association of physical skill and physical vigor with the
enterprise which is managed by those who represent
capital; and when you do, the production of the world
is going to go forward by leaps and bounds.

Why is it that labor organizations jealously limit the amount of work that their men can do? Because they are driving hard bargains with you; they do not feel that they are your partners at all, and so long as labor and capital are antagonistic production is going to be at its minimum. Just so soon as they are sympathetic and coöperative it is going to abound, and that will be one of the means of bringing down the cost of living. In other words, my fellow citizens, we can do something, we can do a great deal, along the lines of your governor's recommendation and along the lines that I took the liberty of recommending to the Congress of the United States, but we must remember that we are only beginning the push, that we are only learning the job, and that its ramifications extend into all the relationships of international credit and international industry. We ought to give our thought to this, gentlemen: America, though we do not like to admit it, has been very provincial in regard to the world's business. When we had to engage in banking transactions outside the United States we generally did it through English bankers or, more often, through German bankers. You did not find American banks in Shanghai and Calcutta and all around the circle of the world. You found every other bank there; you found French banks and English banks and German banks and Swedish banks. You did not find American banks. American bankers have not, as a rule, handled international exchange, and here all of a sudden, as if by the turn of the hand, because of the sweeping winds of this war which have destroyed so many things, we are called upon to handle the bulk of international exchange: We have got to learn it, and we have got to learn it fast. We have got to have American instrumentalities in every part of the world if American money is going to rehabilitate the world, as American money must.

If you say, "Why should we rehabilitate the world?" I will not suggest any altruistic motive; but if you want to trade you have got to have somebody to trade with. If you want to carry your business to the ends of the world, there must be business at the ends of the world to tie in with. And if the business of the world lags your industries lag and your prosperity lags. We have no choice but to be the servants of the world if we would be our own servants. I do not like to put it on that ground because that is not the American ground. America is ready to help the world, whether it benefits her or not. She did not come into the world, she was not created by the great men who set her Government up, in order to make money out of the rest of mankind. She was set up in order to rehabilitate the rest of mankind, and the dollar of American money spent to free those who have been enslaved is worth more than a million dollars put in any American pocket.

It is in this impersonal way that I am trying to illustrate to you how the problem that we are facing in the high cost of living is the end and the beginning and a portion of a world problem, and the great difficulty, just now, my fellow citizens, is in getting some minds adjusted to the world. One of the difficulties that are being encountered about the treaty and the League of Nations, if I may be permitted to say so—and perhaps I can say so the more freely here because I do not think this difficulty exists in the mind of either Senator from this State—the difficulty is, not prejudice so much but that thing which is so common and so inconvenient—just downright ignorance. Ignorance, I mean, of the state of the world and of America's relation to the state of the world. We cannot change that relation. It is a fact. It is a fact bigger than anybody of us, and one of the advantages that the United States has it ought not the advantages that the United States has it ought not to forfeit; it is made up out of all the thinking peoples source; we do not draw our principles from any one nation; we are made up out of all the sturdy stocks of the round world. We have gotten uneasy because some other kinds of stocks tried to come in; but the bulk remains the same; we are made up out of the hard-headed, hard-fisted, practical and yet idealistic, and forward-looking peoples of the world, and we of all people ought to have an international understanding, an ability to comprehend what the problem of the world is and what part we ought to play in that problem. We have got to play a part, and we can play it either as members of the board of directors or as outside speculators. We can play it inside or on the curb, and you know how inconvenient it is to play it on the curb.

There is one thing that I respect more than any other, and that is a fact. I remember, when I was Governor of the State of New Jersey, I was very urgently pressing some measures which a particular member of the Senate of the State, whom I knew and liked very much, was opposed to. His constituents were very much in favor of it, and they sent an influential committee down personally to conduct his vote; and after he had voted for the measure they brought him, looking a little sheepish, into my office to be congratulated. Well, he and I kept as straight faces as we could, and I congratulated him very warmly, and then with a very heavy wink he said to me behind his hand, "Governor, they never get me if I see 'em coming first." Now, that is not a very high political principle, but I commend that principle to you with regards to facts. Never let them get you if you see them coming first; and any man with open eyes can see the facts coming, coming in serried ranks, coming in overwhelming power, not to be resisted by the United States or any other nation. The facts are marching and God is marching with them. You can not resist them. You must either welcome them or subsequently, with humiliation, surrender to them. It is welcome or surrender. It is acceptance of great world conditions and great world duties or scuttle now and come back afterwards.

But I am not arguing this with you, because I do not

believe it is necessary in the State of Minnesota. I am merely telling you. It is like the case of the man who met two of his fellow lawyers and asked them what they were discussing. They said, "We were discussing who is the leading member of the bar of this county," and the other said, "Why, I am." They said, "How do you prove it?" He said, "I don't have to prove it; I admit it." I think that that is the state of mind of the thoughtful persons of our country, and they, thank God, are the chief portions of it, with regard to the great crisis that we are face to face with now.

It has been a privilege, gentlemen, to be permitted in this informal way to disclose to you some part of the thought which I am carrying about with me as really a great burden, because I have seen the disturbed world on the other side of the water. I know the earnest hope and beautiful confidence with which they are looking towards us, and my heart is full of the burden of it. It is a great responsibility for us to carry. We will have to have infinite intelligence and infinite diligence in business to fulfill the expectations of the peoples of the world; and yet that is our duty, our inescapable duty, and we must concert together to perform it.

Everywhere I have been on this trip the majority of the committee that has received me has consisted of Republicans, and nothing has pleased me so much, because I should be ashamed of myself if I permitted any partisan thought to enter into this great matter. If I were a scheming politician and anybody wished to present me with the peace of the world as a campaign issue, it would be very welcome, because there could be no issue easier to win on; but everybody knows that that is not a worthy thought, everybody knows that we are all Americans. Scratch a Democrat or a Republican and underneath it is the same stuff. And the labels rub off upon the slightest effort—not the memories, the recollections; some of them are very stubborn, but it is the principle that matters. The label does not make much

difference. The principle is just the same, and the only
thing we differ about is the way to carry out the principle. Back of all lies that wonderful thing, that thing
which the foreigner was amazed to see in the faces of
our soldiers, that incomparable American spirit which
you do not see the like of anywhere; that universal
brightness of expression, as if every man knew there
was a future and that he had something to do with mold-
ing it, instead of that dull, expressionless face which
means that there is nothing but a past and a burdensome
present. You do not see that in the American face.
The American face mirrors the future, and, my fellow
citizens, the American purpose mirrors the future of
the world.

AT MINNEAPOLIS, MINN., SEPTEMBER 9, 1919.

YOUR HONOR, YOUR EXCELLENCY, MY FELLOW COUN-
    TRYMEN:

I have come here to discuss a very solemn question,
and I shall have to ask your patience while you bear
with me in discussing somewhat in detail the very great
matter which now lies not only before the consideration
of the people of the United States but before the consideration of the people of the world. You have heard
so many little things about the treaty that perhaps you
would like to hear some big things about it. To hear
some gentlemen you would think it was an arrangement
for the inconvenience of the United States, whereas, as
a matter of fact, my fellow citizens, it is a world settlement, the first ever attempted, attempted upon broad
lines which were first laid down in America. For, my
fellow citizens, what does not seem to me realized in
this blessed country of ours is the fact that the world
is in revolution. I do not mean in active revolution. I
do not mean that it is in a state of mind which will bring
about the dissolution of Governments. I mean that it
is in a state of mind which may bring about the dissolu-

tion of Governments if we do not enter into a world settlement which will really in fact and in power establish justice and right.

The old order of things the rest of the world seemed to have got in some sense used to. The old order of things was not to depend upon the general moral judgment of mankind, not to base policies upon international right, but to base policies upon international power. So there were drawn together groups of nations which stood armed, facing one another, which stood drawing their power from the vitality of people who did not wish to be subordinated to them, drawing their vitality from the energy of great peoples who did not wish to devote their energy to force, but wished to devote their energy to peace. The world thought it was inevitable. This group of nations thought that it represented one set of principles; that group of nations thought that it represented another set of principles and that the best that could be accomplished in the world was this that they used to call the balance of power.

Notice the phrase. Not the balance that you try to maintain in a court of justice, not the scales of justice, but the scales of force; one great force balanced against another force. Every bit of the policy of the world, internationally speaking, was made in the interest of some national advantage on the part of the stronger nations of the world. It was either the advantage of Germany or the advantage of Great Britain or the advantage of Italy or the advantage of Japan. I am glad to say that I am not justified in adding that the policy of the world was ever conceived by us upon the basis of the advantage of America. We wished always to be the mediators of justice and of right, but we thought that the cool spaces of the ocean to the east and the west of us would keep us from the infections that came, arising like miasmatic mists out of that arrangement of power and of suspicion and of dread.

I believe, my fellow countrymen, that the only people

in Europe who instinctively realized what was going to happen and what did happen in 1914 was the French people. It has been my privilege to come into somewhat intimate contact with that interesting and delightful people, and I realize now that for nearly fifty years, ever since the settlement which took Alsace-Lorraine away from them in 1871, they have been living under the constant dread of the catastrophe which at last came; and their thought throughout this conference was that they must concert some measure, must draw together some kind of coöperative force, which would take this intolerable dread from their hearts, that they could not live another fifty years, expecting what would come at last. But the other nations took it lightly. There were wise men in Great Britain, there were wise men in the United States, who pointed out to us not only what they suspected, but what we all knew with regard to the preparations for the use of force in Europe. Nobody was ignorant of what Germany was doing. What we shut our eyes against deliberately was the probability that she would make the use of her preparation that she did finally make of it. Her military men published books and told us what they were going to do with it, but we dismissed them. We said: "The thing is a nightmare. The man is a crank. It cannot be that he speaks for a great Government. The thing is inconceivable and cannot happen." Very well, could not it happen? Did not it happen? Are we satisfied now what the balance of power means? It means that the stronger force will sometimes be exercised or an attempt be made to exercise it to crush the other powers.

The great nations of the world have been asleep, but God knows the other nations have not been asleep. I have seen representatives of peoples over there who for generations through, in the dumbness of unutterable suffering, have known what the weight of those armaments and the weight of that power meant. The great Slavic people, the great Rumanian people, the people

who were constantly under the pressure of that power,
the great Polish people—they all knew, but they were
inarticulate; there was no place in the world where they
dared speak out. Now the catastrophe has come.
Blood has been spilled in rivers, the flower of the European nations has been destroyed, and at last the voiceless multitudes of men are awake, and they have made
up their minds that rather than have this happen again,
if the Governments cannot get together, they will destroy the Governments.

I am not speaking revolution, my friends. I believe
that the most disastrous thing that can happen to the
underman, to the man who is suffering, to the man who
has not had his rights, is to destroy public order, for
that makes it certain he never can get his rights. I am
far from intimating that, but I am intimating this, that
the people of the world are tired of every other kind of
experiment except the one we are going to try. I have
called it an experiment; I frankly admit that it is an experiment, but it is a very promising experiment, because
there is not a statesman in the world who does not
know that his people demand it. He is not going to
change his mind. He is not going to change his direction. He is not speaking what he wants, it may be, but
he is speaking what he knows he must speak, and that
there is no turning back; that the world has turned a
corner that it will never turn again. The old order is
gone, and nobody can build it up again.

In the meantime what are men doing? I want you
to reflect upon this, my fellow countrymen, because this
is not a speech-making occasion; this is a conference. I
want you men to reflect upon what I am about to call
your attention to. The object of the war was to destroy autocratic power; that is to say, to make it impossible that there should be anywhere, as there was on
Wilhelmstrasse, in Berlin, a little group of military men
who could brush aside the bankers, brush aside the merchants, brush aside the manufacturers, brush aside the

Emperor himself, and say, "We have perfected a machine with which we can conquer the world; now stand out of the way, we are going to conquer the world." There must not be that possibility any more. There must not be men anywhere in any private place who can plot the mastery of civilization. But in the meantime look at the pitiful things that are happening. There is not a day goes by, my fellow citizens, that my heart is not heavy to think of our fellow beings in that great, pitiful kingdom of Russia, without form, without order, without government. Look what they have done. They have permitted a little handful of men—I am told there are only thirty-four of them constituting the real Bolshevist government—to set up a minority government just as autocratic and just as cruelly unmerciful as the government of the Czar ever was. The danger to the world, my fellow citizens, against which we must absolutely lock the door in this country, is that some Governments of minorities may be set up here as elsewhere. We will brook the control of no minority in the United States. For my own part, I would as leave live under one autocracy as another; I would as leave obey one group as another; I would as leave be the servant of one minority as another, but I do not intend to be the servant of any minority. As I have told you, the mass of men are awake. They are not going to let the world sink back into that old slough of misused authority again.

Very well, then, what are we discussing? What are we debating in the United States? Whether we will take part in guiding and steadying the world or not. And some men hesitate. It is the only country in the world whose leadership and guidance will be accepted. If we do not give it, we may look forward, my fellow citizens, to something like a generation of doubt and of disorder which it will be impossible to pass through without the wreckage of a very considerable part of our slowly constructed civilization. America and her determinations now constitute the balance of moral force in the world, and if we do not use that moral force we will be of all peoples the most derelict. We are in the presence of this great choice, in the presence of this fundamental choice, whether we will stand by the mass of our own people and the mass of mankind. Pick up the great volume of the treaty. It is a great volume. It is as thick as that [illustrating]. You would think it just had three or four articles in it to hear some men talk about it. It is a thick volume, containing the charter of the new order of the world. I took the pains to write down here some of the things that it provides for, and if you will be patient I will read them, because I can make it more brief that way.

It provides for the destruction of autocratic power as an instrument of international control, admitting only self-governing nations to the League of Nations. Had you ever been told that before? No nation is admitted to the League of Nations whose people do not control its Government. That is the reason that we are making Germany wait. She says that henceforth her people are going to control her Government, but we have got to wait and see. If they do control it, she is as welcome to the League as anybody else, because we are not holding nations off. We are holding selfish groups of men off. We are not saying to peoples, "We do not want to be your comrades and serve you along with the rest of our fellow beings," but we are saying, "It depends upon your attitude; if you take charge of your own affairs, then come into the game and welcome." The League of Nations sends autocratic governments to coventry. That is the first point.

It provides for the substitution of publicity, discussion and arbitration for war. That is the supreme thing that it does. I will not go into details now, but every member of the League promises not to go to war until there has been a discussion and a cooling off of nine months, and, as I have frequently said on this tour, if

Germany had submitted to discussion for nine days she never would have dared go to war. Though every foreign office in Europe begged her to do so, she would not grant twenty-four hours for a meeting of the representatives of the Governments of the world to ask what it was all about, because she did not dare tell what it was all about. Nine months' cooling off is a very valuable institution in the affairs of mankind. And you have got to have a very good case if you are willing that all your fellow men should know the whole case, for that is provided for, and talk about it for nine months. Nothing is more valuable, if you think your friend is a fool, than to induce him to hire a hall. If you think he is a fool the only way to prove it is to let him address a mass of his fellow citizens and see how they like his ideas. If they like them and you do not, it may be that you are the fools! The proof is presented at any rate.

Instead of using force after this period of discussion, something very much more effective than force is proposed, namely, an absolute boycott of the nation that does not keep its covenant, and when I say an absolute boycott I mean an absolute boycott. There cannot be any kind of intercourse with that nation. It cannot sell or buy goods. It cannot receive or send messages or letters. It cannot have any transactions with the citizens of any member of the League, and when you consider that the League is going to consist of every considerable nation in the world, except Germany, you can see what that boycott will mean. There is not a nation in the world, except this one, that can live without importing goods for nine months, and it does not make any difference to us whether we can or not, because we always fulfill our obligations, and there will never be a boycott for us.

It provides for placing the peace of the world under constant international oversight, in recognition of the principle that the peace of the world is the legitimate and immediate interest of every nation. Why, as it stands at present, my fellow citizens, if there is likely to be trouble between two nations other than the United States it is considered an unfriendly and hostile act for the United States to intervene. This Covenant makes it the right of the United States, and not the right of the United States merely, but the right of the weakest nation in the world, to bring anything that the most powerful nation in the world is doing that is likely to disturb the peace of the world under the scrutiny of mankind. [Voice in audience, "And that is right!"] My friend in the audience says that is right, and it undoubtedly is, because the peace of the world is everybody's business. Yet this is the first document that ever recognized that principle. We now have the attitude of the Irishman, you know, who went into one of those antique institutions known as a saloon. It was rather a large place, and he saw two men fighting over in the corner. He went up to the bartender and he said, "Is this a private fight, or can everybody get in?" Now, in the true Irish spirit, we are abolishing private fights, and we are making it the law of mankind that it is everybody's business and everybody can get in. The consequence is that there will be no attempt at private fights.

It provides for disarmament on the part of the great fighting nations of the world.

It provides in detail for the rehabilitation of oppressed peoples, and that will remove most of the causes of war.

It provides that there shall be no more annexations of territory anywhere, but that those territories whose people are not ready to govern themselves shall be intrusted to the trusteeship of the nations that can take care of them, the trustee nation to be responsible in annual reports to the League of Nations; that is to say, to mankind in general, subject to removal and restricted in respect to anything that might be done to that population which would be to the detriment of the population itself. So that you cannot go into darkest Africa and

make slaves of those poor people, as some Governments at times have done.

It abolishes enforced labor. It takes the same care
of the women and children of those unschooled races
that we try to take of the women and children of ours.
Why, my fellow citizens, this is the great humane document of all time.

It provides that every secret treaty shall be invalid.
It sweeps the table of all private understandings and
enforces the principle that there shall be no private
understandings of any kind that anybody is bound to
respect. One of the difficulties in framing this treaty
was that after we got over there private—secret—
treaties were springing up on all sides like a noxious
growth. You had to guard your breathing apparatus
against the miasma that arose from some of them.
But they were treaties, and the war had been fought on
the principle of the sacredness of treaties. We could
not propose that solemn obligations, however unwisely
undertaken, should be disregarded, but we could do the
best that was possible in the presence of those understandings and then say, "No more of this; no more
secret understandings." And the representatives of
every great nation in the world assented without demur
—without the slightest difficulty.

I do not think you realize what a change of mind has
come over the world. As we used to say in the old
days, some men that never got it before have got
religion.

It provides for the protection of dependent peoples.

It provides that high standards of labor, such as are
observed in the United States, shall be extended to the
workingman everywhere in the world.

It provides that all the great humane instrumentalities, like the Red Cross, like the conventions against the
opium trade, like the regulation of the liquor traffic
with debased and ignorant people, like the prohibition
of the selling of arms and ammunition to people who

can use them only to their own detriment, shall be under the common direction and control of the League of Nations. Now, did you ever hear of all these things before? That is the treaty, my fellow citizens; and I can only conjecture that some of the men who are fighting the treaty either never read it themselves or are taking it for granted that you will not read it. I say without hesitation that no international agreement has ever before been drawn up along those lines—of the universal consideration of right and the interest of humanity.

Now, it is said that that is all very well, but we need not go in. Well, of course we need not. There is perfect freedom of the will. I am perfectly free to go to the top of this building and jump off, but if I do I will not take very much interest in human affairs. The Nation is at liberty in one sense to do anything it pleases to discredit itself; but this is absolutely as certain as I stand here, that it never will do anything to discredit itself. Our choice in this great enterprise of mankind that I have tried to outline to you is only this: Shall we go in and assist as trusted partners or shall we stay out and act as suspected rivals? We have got to do one or the other. We have got to be either provincials or statesmen. We have got to be either ostriches or eagles. The ostrich act I see being done all around me. I see gentlemen burying their heads in something and thinking that nobody sees that they have submerged their thinking apparatus. That is what I mean by being ostriches. What I mean by being eagles I need not describe to you. I mean leaving the mists that lie close along the ground, getting upon strong wing into those upper spaces of the air where you can see with clear eyes the affairs of mankind, see how the affairs of America are linked with the affairs of men everywhere, see how the whole world turns with outstretched hands to this blessed country of ours and says, "If you will lead, we will follow." God helping us, my fellow country-

men, we will lead when they follow. The march is still
long and toilsome to those heights upon which there
rests nothing but the pure light of the justice of God,
but the whole incline of affairs is towards those distant
heights; and this great Nation, in serried ranks, millions strong—presently hundreds of millions strong—
will march at the fore of the great procession, breasting
those heights with its eyes always lifted to the eternal
goal!

AT AUDITORIUM, ST. PAUL, MINN., SEPTEMBER 9,
1919

MR. CHAIRMAN, MY FELLOW COUNTRYMEN:
I am very happy that the mayor sounded the note
that he has just sounded, because by some sort of divina-
tion he realized what was in my heart to-night. I do
not feel since I have left Washington this time that I
am on an ordinary errand. I do not feel that I am on
a political errand, even in the broad sense of that term.
I feel rather that I am going about to hold counsel with
my fellow countrymen concerning the most honorable
and distinguished course which our great country can
take at this turning point in the history of the world.
And the mayor was quite right when he said that this is
a conference concerning the true interpretation of the
American spirit. I believe, I hope without an undue
touch of national pride, that it is only the American
spirit that can be the true mediator of peace.

The theme that I find uppermost in my thought to-
night is this: We are all actuated, my fellow countrymen, by an intense consciousness and love of America.
I do not think that it is fancy on my part; it is based
upon long experience that in every part of the world I
can recognize an American the minute I see him. Yet
that is not because we are all of one stock. We are of
more varied origins and stocks than any people in the
world. We come from all the great races of the world.

We are made up out of all the nations and peoples who have stood at the center of civilization. In this part of the country it is doubtful whether in some of our great cities 50 per cent of the people come of parents born in America. One of the somewhat serious jests which I allowed myself to indulge on the other side of the water was with my Italian colleagues when they were claiming the city of Fiume upon the Adriatic because of its Italian population, and other cities scattered here and there whose surrounding population was not Italian but in whom an Italian element played an important part. I said, "That is not a sufficient argument for the extension of Italian sovereignty to these people, because there are more Italians in New York City than in any city in Italy, and I doubt if you would feel justified in suggesting that the sovereignty of Italy be extended over the city of New York." I advert to this, my fellow citizens, merely as one illustration, that could be multiplied a hundredfold, of the singular make-up of this great Nation.

I do not know how it happens that we are all Americans; we are so different in origin; we are so different in memories. The memory of America does not go very far back as measured by the distances of history, and great millions of our people carry in their hearts the traditions of other people, the traditions of races never bred in America; yet we are all unmistakably and even in appearance Americans, and nothing else. There is only one possible explanation for that, my fellow citizens, and that is that there is in the practice and in the tradition of this country a set of principles which, however imperfectly, get into the consciousness of every man who lives in this country.

One of the chief elements that make an American is this: In almost every other country there is some class that dominates, or some governmental authority that determines the course of politics, or some ancient system of land laws that limits the freedom of land tenure, or some ancient custom which ties a man into a particular groove in the land in which he lives. There is none of that in America. Every man in America, if he behaves himself, knows that he stands on the same footing as every other man in America, and, thank goodness, we are in sight of the time when every woman will know that she stands upon the same footing. We do not have to ask anybody's leave what we shall think or what we shall do or how we shall vote. We do not have to get the approval of a class as to our behavior. We do not have to square ourselves with standards that have been followed ever since our great-grandfathers. We are very much more interested in being great-grandfathers than in having had great-grandfathers, because our view is to the future. America does not march, as so many other peoples march, looking back over its shoulder. It marches with its eyes not only forward, but with its eyes lifted to the distances of history, to the great events which are slowly culminating, in the Providence of God, in the lifting of civilization to new levels and new achievements. That is what makes us Americans.

And yet I was mistaken a moment ago when I said we are nothing else, because there are a great many hyphens left in America. For my part, I think the most un-American thing in the world is a hyphen. I do not care what it is that comes before the word "American." It may be a German-American, or an Italian-American, a Swedish-American, or an Anglo-American, or an Irish-American. It does not make any difference what comes before the "American," it ought not to be there, and every man who comes to take counsel with me with a hyphen in his conversation I take no interest in whatever. The entrance examination, to use my own parlance, into my confidence is, "Where do you put America in your thoughts? Do you put it first, always first, unquestionably first?" Then we can sit down together and talk, but not otherwise. Now, I want you distinctly to understand that I am not quarreling with the affectionate memories of people who have drawn their origin from other countries. I no more blame a man for dwelling with fond affection upon the traditions of some great race not bred in America than I blame a man for remembering with reverence his mother and his father and his forebears that bred him and that gave him a chance in the world. I am not quarreling with those affections; I am talking about purposes. Every purpose is for the future, and the future for Americans must be for America.

We have got to choose now, my fellow citizens, what kind of future it is going to be for America. I think that what I have said justifies me in adding that this Nation was created to be the mediator of peace, because it draws its blood from every civilized stock in the world and is ready by sympathy and understanding to understand the peoples of the world, their interests, their rights, their hopes, their destiny. America is the only nation in the world that has that equipment. Every other nation is set in the mold of a particular breeding. We are set in no mold at all. Every other nation has certain prepossessions which run back through all the ramifications of an ancient history. We have nothing of the kind. We know what all peoples are thinking, and yet we by a fine alchemy of our own combine that thinking into an American plan and an American purpose. America is the only Nation which can sympathetically lead the world in organizing peace.

Constantly, when I was on the other side of the water, delegations representing this, that, and the other peoples of Europe or of Asia came to visit me to solicit the interest of America in their fortunes, and, without exception, they were able to tell me that they had kinsmen in America. Some of them, I am ashamed to say, came from countries I had never heard of before, and yet even they were able to point, not to a handful, not to a few hundreds, but to several thousand kinsmen in America. I never before knew that they came, but

they are here and they are our interpreters, the interpreters on our behalf of the interests of the people from
whom they sprang.   They came to America as sort of
advanced couriers of those people.   They came in search
of the Golden West.   They came in search of the liberty
that they understood reigned among that free and happy
people.   They were drawn by the lure of justice, by the
lure of freedom, out of lands where they were oppressed, suppressed, where life was made impossible for
them upon the free plane that their hearts had conceived.   They said, "Yonder is our star in the west,"
and then the word went home, "We have found the
land.   They are a free people that are capable of understanding us.   You go to their representatives in Paris
and put your case before them, and they will understand."   What a splendid thing that is, my fellow countrymen!   I want you to keep this in your minds as a
conception of the question that we are now called upon
to decide.

To hear some men talk about the League of Nations
you would suppose that it was a trap set for America;
you would suppose that it was an arrangement by which
we entered into an alliance with other great, powerful
nations to make war some time.   Why, my fellow countrymen, it bears no resemblance to such description.   It
is a great method of common counsel with regard to the
common interests of mankind.   We shall not be drawn
into wars; we shall be drawn into consultation, and we
will be the most trusted adviser in the whole group.
Consultation, discussion, is written all over the whole
face of the Covenant of the League of Nations, for the
heart of it is that the nations promise not to go to war
until they have consulted, until they have discussed, until
all the facts in the controversy have been laid before
the court which represents the common opinion of mankind.

That is the League of Nations.   Nothing can be discussed there that concerns our domestic affairs.   Noth-

ing can be discussed there that concerns the domestic
affairs of any other people, unless something is occurring in some nation which is likely to disturb the peace
of the world, and any time that any question arises
which is likely to disturb the peace of the world, then
the Covenant makes it the right of any member, strong
or weak, big or little, of that universal concert of the
nations to bring that matter up for clarification and discussion. Can you imagine anything more calculated to
put war off, not only to put it off, but to make it violently improbable? When a man wants to fight he does
not go and discuss the matter with the other fellow.
He goes and hits him, and then somebody else has to
come in and either join the fight or break it up. I used
a very homely illustration the other night, which perhaps it may not be amiss for me to use again. I had
two friends who were becoming more and more habitually profane. Their friends did not like it. They not
only had the fundamental scruple that it was wrong,
but they also thought, as I heard a very refined lady say,
"It was not only wrong but, what was worse, it was
vulgar." They did not like to see their friends adjourning all the rest of their vocabulary and using only those
words. So they made them enter into a solemn agreement—I ought to say they lived in a large city—that
they would not swear inside the corporate limits; that
if they got in a state of mind which made it necessary
to explode in profanity they would get out of town and
swear.

The first time the passion came upon them and they
recalled their promise they got sheepishly on a street
car and made for the town limits, and I need hardly
tell you that when they got there they no longer wanted
to swear. They had cooled off. The long spaces of the
town, the people going about their ordinary business,
nobody paying any attention to them, the world seeming to be at peace when they were at war, all brought
them to a realization of the smallness of the whole

business, and they turned around and came into town again. Comparing great things with small, that will suffice as a picture of the advantage of discussion in international matters as well as in individual matters, because it was universally agreed on the other side of the water that if Germany had allowed the other Governments to confer with her twenty-four hours about the recent war, it could not have taken place. We know why. It was an unconscionable war. She did not dare discuss it. You cannot afford to discuss a thing when you are in the wrong, and the minute you feel that the whole judgment of the world is against you, you have a different temper in affairs altogether.

This is a great process of discussion that we are entering into, and my point to-night—it is the point I want to leave with you—is that we are the people of all people in the world intelligently to discuss the difficulties of the Nations which we represent, although we are Americans. We are the predestined mediators of mankind. I am not saying this in any kind of national pride or vanity. I believe that is mere historic truth, and I try to interpret circumstances in some intelligent way. If that is the kind of people we are, it must have been intended that we should make some use of the opportunities and powers that we have, and when I hear gentlemen saying that we must keep out of this thing and take care of ourselves I think to myself, "Take care of ourselves? Where did we come from? Is there nobody else in the world to take care of? Have we no sympathies that do not run out into the great field of human experience everywhere? Is that what America is, with her mixture of bloods?" Why, my fellow citizens, that is a fundamental misconception of what it is to be an American, and these gentlemen are doing a harm which they do not realize. I want to testify to you here to-night, my fellow citizens, because I have the means of information, that since it has seemed to be uncertain whether we are going to play this part of leadership in

the world or not, this part of leadership in accommodation, the old intrigues have stirred up in this country
again. That intrigue which we universally condemn—
that hyphen which looked to us like a snake, the hyphen
between "German" and "American"—has reared its
head again, and you hear the "his-s-s" of its purpose.
What is that purpose? It is to keep America out of
the concert of Nations, in order that America and Germany, being out of that concert, may stand—in their
mistaken dream—united to dominate the world, or, at
any rate, the one assist the other in holding the Nations
of the world off while its ambitions are realized.

There is no conjecture about this, my fellow citizens.
We know the former purposes of German intrigue in
this country, and they are being revived. Why? We
have not reduced very materially the number of the
German people. Germany remains the great power of
central Europe. She has more than 60,000,000 people
now (she had nearly 70,000,000 before Poland and
other Provinces were taken away). You cannot change
the temper and expectations of a people by five years
of war, particularly five years of war in which they are
not yet conscious of the wrong they did or of the wrong
way in which they did it. They are expecting the time
of the revival of their power, and along with the revival of their power goes their extraordinary capacity,
their unparalleled education, their great capacity in
commerce and finance and manufacture. The German
bankers and the German merchants and the German
manufacturers did not want this war. They were making conquest of the world without it, and they knew it
would spoil their plans, not advance them; and it has
spoiled their plans, but they are there yet with their
capacity, with their conception of what it is to serve the
world materially and so subdue the world psycho-
logically. All of that is still there, my fellow countrymen, and if America stays out then the rest of the world
will have to watch Germany and watch America, and

when there are two dissociated powers there is danger that they will have the same purposes.

There can be only one intelligent reason for America staying out of this, and that is that she does not want peace, that she wants war sometimes and the advantage which war will bring her, and I want to say now and here that the men who think that by that thought they are interpreting America are making the sort of mistake upon which it will be useful for them to reflect in obscurity for the rest of their lives. This is a peaceful people. This is a liberty-loving people, and liberty is suffocated by war. Free institutions cannot survive the strain of prolonged military administration. In order to live tolerable lives you must lift the fear of war and the practice of war from the lives of Nations. America is evidence of the fact that no great democracy ever entered upon an aggressive international policy. I want you to know, if you will be kind enough to read the Covenant of the League of Nations—most of the people that are arguing against it are taking it for granted that you have never read it—take the pains to read it, and you will find that no Nation is admitted to the League of Nations that cannot show that it has the institutions which we call free. Nobody is admitted except the self-governing Nations, because it was the instinctive judgment of every man who sat around that board that only a Nation whose government was its servant and not its master could be trusted to preserve the peace of the world. There are not going to be many other kinds of Nations long, my fellow citizens. The people of this world—not merely the people of America, for they did the job long ago—have determined that there shall be no more autocratic governments.

And in their haste to get rid of one of them they set up another. I mean in pitiful Russia. I wish we could learn the lesson of Russia so that it would be burned into the consciousness of every man and woman in

America. That lesson is that nobody can be free where there is not public order and authority. What has happened in Russia is that an old and distinguished and skillful autocracy has had put in its place an amateur autocracy, a little handful of men exercising without the slightest compunction of mercy or pity the bloody terror that characterized the worst days of the Czar. That is what must happen if you knock things to pieces. Liberty is a thing of slow construction. Liberty is a thing of universal coöperation. Liberty is a thing which you must build up by habit. Liberty is a thing which is rooted and grounded in character, and the reason I am so certain that the leadership of the world, in respect of order and progress, belongs to America is that I know that these principles are rooted and grounded in the American character. It is not our intellectual capacity, my fellow-citizens, that has given us our place in the world, though I rate that as high as the intellectual capacity of any other people that ever lived, but it is the heart that lies back of the man that makes America. Ask this question of yourselves. I have no doubt that this room is full of mothers and fathers and wives and sweethearts who sent their beloved young men to France. What did you send them there for? What made you proud that they were going? What made you willing that they should go? Did you think they were seeking to aggrandize America in some way? Did you think they were going to take something for America that had belonged to somebody else? Did you think that they were going in a quarrel which they had provoked and must maintain? The question answers itself. You were proud that they should go because they were going on an errand of self-sacrifice, in the interest of mankind. What a halo and glory surrounds those old men whom we now greet with such reverence, the men who were the soldiers in our Civil War! They saved a Nation. Ah, when these youngsters grow old who have come back from the fields of France, what a

halo will be around their brows! They saved the
world. They are of the same stuff as those old veterans
of the Civil War. Mind you, I was born and bred in the
South, but I can pay that tribute with all my heart to the
men who saved the Union. It ought to have been saved.
It was the greatest thing that men had conceived up to
that time. Now we come to a greater thing—to the
union of great Nations in conference upon the interests
of peace. That is the fruitage, the fine and appropriate
fruitage, of what these men achieved upon the fields of
France.

I saw many fine sights in Paris, many gallant sights,
many sights that quickened the pulse; but my pulse never
beat so fast as when I saw groups of our boys swinging along the street. They looked as if they owned
something, and they did. They owned the finest thing
in the world, the thing that we are going to prove was
theirs. They owned the ideals and conceptions that
will govern the world. And on this errand that I am
going about on I feel that I am doing what I can to
complete what they so gallantly began. I should feel
recreant, my fellow citizens, if I did not do all that is
in my power to do to complete the ideal work which
those youngsters so gallantly began.

This was a war to make similar wars impossible, and
merely to win this war and stop at that is to make it
certain that we shall have to fight another and a final
one. I hear opponents of the League of Nations say,
"But this does not guarantee peace." No; nothing guarantees us against human passion and error, but I would
like to put this business proposition to you: If it increases the probability of peace by, let us say, 10 per
cent, do you not think it is worth while? In my judgment, it increases it about 99 per cent. Henceforth
the genius of the world will be devoted to accommodat-
ing the counsels of mankind and not confusing them; not
supplying heat but supplying light; not putting friction
into the machine, but easing the friction off and com-

bining the parts of the great machinery of civilization
so that they will run in smooth harmony and perfection. My fellow citizens, the tasks of peace that are
ahead of us are the most difficult tasks to which the
human genius has ever been devoted. I will state the
fundamental task, for it is the fundamental task. It is
the relationship between those who toil with their hands
and those who direct that toil. I will not say the relationship between capital and labor; that means something slightly different. I say the relationship between
those who organize enterprise and those who make
enterprise go by the skill and labor of their hands.
There is at present, to say the least, a most unsatisfactory relationship between those two and we must devote
our national genius to working out a method of association between the two which will make this Nation
the Nation to solve triumphantly and for all time the
fundamental problem of peaceful production. You
ask, "What has that got to do with the League of Nations?" I dare say that you do not know because I
have never heard anybody tell you that the great charter,
the new international charter, of labor is in the treaty
of peace and associated with the League of Nations.
A great machinery of consultation is set up there, not
merely about international political affairs, but about
standards of labor, about the relationships between
managers and employees, about the standards of life
and the conditions of labor, about the labor of women
and of children, about the humane side and the business
side of the whole labor problem. And the first conference is going to sit in Washington next month; not
the conference which some of you may have heard of,
which I have just called of our own people, but an international conference to consider the interests of labor
all over the round world. I do not know—nobody
knows—whether the Senate will have stopped debating
by that time or not. I heard a Member of the Senate
say that nobody knew that except God Almighty! But

whether it has finished or not, the conference is going to
sit, and if it has not finished, the only question that will
be left unsettled is whether we are going to sit inside
of it or outside of it. The conference at Paris voted,
in their confidence in the American people, that the first
meeting should be held in Washington and should be
called by the President of the United States. They supposed in their innocence that the President of the United
States represented the people of the United States. And
in calling this conference, as I have called it, I am confident that I am representing the people of the United
States. After I have bidden the delegates welcome,
perhaps I can have a chair just outside the door and
listen.

I am jesting, my fellow citizens, but there is a little
sadness in the jest. Why do we wait to do a great
thing? Why do we wait to fulfill the destiny of America? Why do we make it possible that anybody should
think that we are not coming in now, but are going to
wait later and come in with Germany? I suppose there
is a certain intellectual excitement and pleasure in debate, but I do not experience any when great issues like
this are pending, and I would be very sad, indeed, if
I did not have an absolute, unclouded confidence of the
result. I had the great good fortune to be born an
American, I have saturated myself in the traditions of
our country, I have read all the great literature that
interprets the spirit of our country, and when I read my
own heart with regard to these great purposes, I feel
confident that it is a sample American heart. Therefore I have the most unbounded confidence in the result. All that is needed is that you should be vocal and
audible. I know what you want. Say it and get it. I
am your servant; all the men elected to go to Washington are your servants. It is not our privilege to
follow our private convictions; it is our duty to represent your convictions and execute your purposes, and
therefore all that is needed is a consciousness. Tell me

that you do not want to do what I am urging and I
will go home; but tell me, as your faces and your voices
tell me, that you do want what I want, and I will be
heartened for the rest of my journey, and I will say to
the folks all the way from here to the Pacific, "Minnesota is up and on her tiptoes and behind you. Let's all
of us get in the great team which is to redeem the destinies of mankind."

Our fathers of the revolutionary age had a vision,
my fellow citizens. There were only 3,000,000 Americans then, in a little strip of settlements on the Atlantic
coast. Now the great body of American citizens extends from ocean to ocean, more than a hundred millions strong. These are the people of whom the founders of the Republic were dreaming, those great hosts
of free men and women who should come in the future
and who should say to all the world, "Here are the
testaments of liberty. Here are the principles of freedom. Here are the things which we must do in order
that mankind may be released from the intolerable
things of the past." And there came a day at Paris
when the representatives of all the great governments
of the world accepted the American specifications upon
which the terms of the treaty of peace were drawn.
Shall we have our treaty, or shall we have somebody
else's? Shall we keep the primacy of the world, or
shall we abandon it?

AT BISMARCK, N. DAK., SEPTEMBER 10, 1919.

GOVERNOR FRAZIER, MY FELLOW COUNTRYMEN:
I esteem it a great privilege to stand in your presence
and to continue the discussion that I have been attempting in other parts of the country of the great matter
which is pending for our determination. I say that it
is pending for our determination, because, after all,
it is a question for the thoughtful men and women of the
United States. I believe that the gentlemen at Wash-

ington are trying to assess the opinion of the United States and are trying to embody and express it.

It seems very strange from day to day as I go about that I should be discussing the question of peace. It seems very strange that after six months of conference in Paris, where the minds of more than twenty nations were brought together and where, after the most profound consideration of every question and every angle of every question concerned, an extraordinary agreement should have been reached—that while every other country concerned has stopped debating the peace, America is debating it. It seems very strange to me, my fellow countrymen, because, as a matter of fact, we are debating the question of peace or war. There is only one way to have peace, and that is to have it by the concurrence of the minds of the world. America cannot bring about peace by herself. No other nation can bring about peace by itself. The agreement of a small group of nations cannot bring about peace. The world is not at peace. It is not, except in certain disturbed quarters, actually using military means of war, but the mind of the world is not at peace. The mind of the world is waiting for the verdict, and the verdict they are waiting for is this: Shall we have in the future the same dangers, the same suspicions, the same distractions, and shall we expect that out of those dangers and distractions armed conflict will arise? Or shall we expect that the world will be willing to sit down at the council table to talk the thing over; to delay all use of force until the world has had time to express its judgment upon the matter at issue? If that is not to be the solution, if the world is not to substitute discussion and arbitration for war, then the world is not now in a state of mind to have peace, even for the time being. While victory has been won, my fellow countrymen, it has been won only over the force of a particular group of nations. It has not been won over the passions of those nations, or over the passions of the nations that were set against them. This treaty which I brought back with me is a great world settlement, and it tries to deal with some of the elements of passion which were likely at any time to blaze out in the world and which did blaze out and set the world on fire.

The trouble was at the heart of Europe. At the heart of Europe there were suffering peoples, inarticulate but with hearts on fire against the iniquities practiced against them; held in the grip of military power and submitting to nothing but force; their spirits insurgent; and so long as that continued, there could not be the expectation of continued peace. This great settlement at Paris for the first time in the world considered the cry of the peoples and did not listen to the plea of governments. It did not listen to dynastic claims. It did not read over the whole story of rival territorial ambitions. It said, "The day is closed for that. These lands belong to the stocks, the ancient stocks of people that live upon them, and we are going to give them to those people and say to them, 'The land always should have been yours; it is now yours, and you can govern it as you please.'" That is the principle that is at the heart of this treaty, but if that principle cannot be maintained then there will ensue upon it the passion that dwelt in the hearts of those peoples, a despair which will bring about universal chaos. Men in despair do not construct governments. Men in despair destroy governments. Men whose whole affairs are so upset, whose whole systems of transportation are so disordered that they cannot get food, that they cannot get clothes, that they cannot turn to any authority that can give them anything, run amuck. They do not stop to ask questions. I heard a very thoughtful pastor once preach a sermon which interested me very deeply, on the sequence of the petitions in the Lord's Prayer. He called attention to the fact that the first petition was, "Give us this day our daily bread," and he pointed out that our Saviour probably knew better than anybody else that a man cannot serve God or his fellow men on an empty stomach, that he has got to be physically sustained. When a man has got an empty stomach, most of all when those he loves are starving, he is not going to serve any government; he is going to serve himself by the quickest way he can find.

You say, "What has this got to do with the adoption by the United States Senate of the treaty of peace?" It has this to do with it, my fellow citizens, that the whole world is waiting upon us, and if we stay out of it, if we qualify our assent in any essential way, the world will say, "Then there can be no peace, for that great Nation in the west is the only makeweight which will hold these scales steady." I hear counsels of selfishness uttered. I hear men say, "Very well, let us stay out and take care of ourselves and let the rest of the world take care of itself." I do not agree with that from the point of view of sentiment. I would be ashamed to agree with it from the point of view of sentiment, and I think I have intelligence enough to know that it would not work, even if I wanted it to work. Are we disconnected from the rest of the world? Take a single item. If Europe is disordered, who is going to buy wheat? There is more wheat in this country than we can consume. There is more foodstuff in this country of many sorts than we can consume. There is no foreign market that anybody can count on wherein there is settled peace. Men are not going to buy until they know what is going to happen to-morrow, for the very good reason that they cannot get any money; they cannot earn any money amidst a disordered organization of industry and the absence of those processes of credit which keep business going.

We have managed in the process of civilization, my fellow citizens, to make a world that cannot be taken to pieces. The pieces are dovetailed and intimately fitted with one another, and unless you assemble them as you do the intimate parts of a great machine, civiliza-

tion will not work. I believe that, with the exception
of the United States, there is not a country in the world
that can live without importation. There are only one
or two countries that can live without imported foodstuffs. There are no countries that I know of that can
live in their ordinary way without importing manufactured goods or raw materials, raw materials of many
kinds. Take that great kingdom, for example, for which
I have the most intimately sympathy, the great Kingdom
of Italy. There are no raw materials worth mentioning in Italy. There are great factories there, but they
have to get all the raw materials that they manufacture
from outside Italy. There is no coal in Italy, no fuel.
They have to get all their coal from outside of Italy,
and at the present moment because the world is holding
its breath and waiting the great coal fields of Central
Europe are not being worked except to about 40 per
cent of their capacity. The coal in Silesia, the coal in
Bohemia, is not being shipped out, and industries are
checked and chilled and drawn in, and starvation comes
nearer, unemployment becomes more and more universal. At this moment there is nothing brought to my
attention more often at Washington than the necessity
for shipping out our fuel and our raw materials to start
the world again. If we do not start the world again,
then we check and stop to that extent our own industries
and our exportations, of course. You cannot disentangle the United States from the rest of the world. If
the rest of the world goes bankrupt, the business of the
United States is in a way to be ruined. I do not like
to put the thing upon this basis, my fellow citizens, because this is not the American basis. America was not
founded to make money; it was founded to lead the
world on the way to liberty, and now, while we debate,
all the rest of the world is saying, "Why does America
hesitate? We want to follow her. We shall not know
which way to go unless she leads. We want the direction of her business genius. We want the suggestions

of her principles, and she hesitates. She does not know whether she wants to go or not." Oh, yes, she does, my fellow citizens. Men among us do not know whether we want to go in or not, but we know. There is no more danger of America staying out of this great thing than there is of her reversing all the other processes of her history and forgetting all the principles that she has spilt so much precious blood to maintain. But, in the meantime, the delay is injuring the whole world and ourselves, of course, along with the rest, because we are a very big and, in my opinion, an extremely important part of the world.

I have told many times, but I must tell you again, of the experience that I had in Paris. Almost every day of the week that I was not imperatively engaged otherwise I was receiving delegations. Delegations from where? Not merely groups of men from France and other near-by regions, but groups of men from all over the world—as I have several times admitted, from some parts of the world that I never heard the names of before. I do not think they were in geography when I was at school. If they were, I had forgotten them. Did you ever hear of Adjur-Badjan, for example? A very dignified group of fine-looking men came in from Adjur-Badjan. I did not dare ask them where it was, but I looked it up secretly afterwards and found that it was a very prosperous valley region lying south of the Caucasus and that it had a great and ancient civilization. I knew from what these men said to me that they knew what they were talking about, though I did not know anything about their affairs. They knew, above all things else, what America stood for, and they had come to me, figuratively speaking, with outstretched hands and said, "We want the guidance and the help and the advice of America." And they all said that, until my heart grew fearful, and I said to one group of them, "I beg that you will not expect the impossible. America cannot do the things that you are asking her to do.

We will do the best we can. We will stand as your friends. We will give you every sort of aid that we can give you, but please do not expect the impossible." They believe that America can work miracles merely by being America and asserting the principles of America throughout the globe, and that kind of assertion, my fellow citizens, is the process of peace; and that is the only possible process of peace.

When I say, therefore, that I have come here this morning actually to discuss the question with you whether we shall have peace or war, you may say, "There is no war; the war is over." The fighting is over, but there is not peace, and there cannot be peace without the assistance of America. The assistance of America comes just at the center of the whole thing that was planned in Paris. You have heard some men talk about separating the Covenant of the League of Nations from the treaty. I intended to bring a copy of the treaty with me; it is a volume as thick as that, and the very first thing in it is the League of Nations Covenant. By common consent that was put first, because by common consent that is the only thing that will make the rest of the volume work. That was not the opinion at the beginning of the conference. There were a great many cynics on that side of the water who smiled indulgently when you spoke hopefully of drawing the nations together in a common consent of action, but before we got through there was not a man who had not as a hard, practical judgment, come to the conclusion that we could not do without it, that you could not make a world settlement without setting up an organization that would see that it was carried out, and that you could not compose the mind of the world unless that settlement included an arrangement by which discussion should be substituted for war.

If the war that we have just had had been preceded by discussion, it never would have happened. Every foreign office in Europe urged through its minister at

Berlin that no action should be taken until there should be an international conference and the other governments should learn what if any processes of mediation they might interpose. And Germany did not dare delay it for twenty-four hours. If she had, she never could have begun it. You dare not lay a bad case before mankind. You dare not kill the young men of the world for a dishonest purpose. We have let thousands of our lads go to their death in order to convince, not Germany merely, but any other nation that may have in the back of its thought a similar enterprise, that the world does not mean to permit any iniquity of that sort, and if it had been displayed as an iniquity in open conference for not less than nine months, as the Covenant of the League of Nations provides, it never could have happened.

Your attention is called to certain features of this League—the only features to which your attention ever is called by those who are opposed to it and you are left with the impression that it is an arrangement by which war is just on the hair trigger. You are constantly told about Article X. Now, Article X has no operative force in it unless we vote that it shall operate. I will tell you what Article X is; I think I can repeat it almost verbatim. Under Article X every member of the League undertakes to respect and preserve as against external aggression the territorial integrity and the existing political independence of the other members of the League. So far so good. The second sentence provides that in case of necessity the council of the League shall advise what steps are necessary to carry out the obligations of that promise; that is to say, what force is necessary if any. The council cannot give that advice without a unanimous vote. It cannot give the advice, therefore, without the affirmative vote of the United States, unless the United States is a party to the controversy in question. Let us see what that means. Do you think the United States is likely to seize somebody else's territory? Do you think the United States is likely to disregard the first sentence of the article? And if she is not likely to begin an aggression of that sort, who is likely to begin it against her? Is Mexico going to invade us and appropriate Texas? Is Canada going to come down with her nine or ten millions and overwhelm the hundred millions of the United States? Who is going to grab territory, and, above all things else, who is going to entertain the idea if the rest of the world has said, "No; we are all pledged to see that you do not do that." But suppose that somebody does attempt to grab our territory or that we do attempt to grab somebody else's territory. Then the war is ours anyhow. Then what difference does it make what advice the council gives? Unless it is our war we cannot be dragged into a war without our own consent. If that is not an open and shut security, I do not know of any. Yet that is Article X.

I do not recognize this Covenant when I hear some other men talk about it. I spent hours and hours in the presence of the representatives of thirteen other Governments examining every sentence of it, up and down and crosswise, and trying to keep out of it anything that interfered with the essential sovereignty of any member of the League. I carried over with me in March all the suggestions made by the Foreign Relations Committee of the Senate, and they were all accepted, and yet I come back and find that I do not understand what the document means. I am told that plain sentences which I thought were unmistakable English terms mean something that I never heard of and that nobody else ever intended as a purpose. But whatever you may think of Article X, my fellow citizens, it is the heart of the treaty. You have either got to take it or you have got to throw the world back into that old conquest over land titles, which would upset the State of North Dakota or any other part of the world. Suppose there

were no guarantee of any land title in North Dakota! I
can fancy how every farmer and every man with a city
lot would go armed. He would hire somebody, if he
was too sleepy to sit up all night, to see that nobody
trespassed and took squatter possession of his unsecured
land. We have been trying to do something analagous
to that with the territories of Europe; to fix the land
titles, and then having fixed them, we have got to have
Article X. Under Article X these titles are established,
and we all join to guarantee their maintenance. There
is no other way to quiet the world, and if the world is
not quieted, then America is sooner or later involved
in the *mêlée*. We boast, my fellow citizens—but we
sometimes forget—what a powerful Nation the United
States is. Do you suppose we can ask the other Nations
of the world to forget that we are out of the arrangement? Do you suppose that we can stay out of the
arrangement without being suspected and intrigued
against and hated by all the rest of them? And do you
think that is an advantageous basis for international
transactions? Any way you take this question you are
led straight around to this alternative, either this treaty
with this Covenant or a disturbed world and certain
war. There is no escape from it.

America recalls, I am sure, all the assurances that
she has given to the world in the years past. Some of
the very men who are now opposing this Covenant were
the most eloquent advocates of an international concert
which would be carried to a point where the exercise of
independent sovereignty would be almost estopped.
They put it into measures of Congress. For example,
in one, I believe the last, Navy appropriation bill, by
unanimous vote of the committee, they put in the provision that after the building program had been authorized by Congress the President could cancel it if
in the meantime he had been able to induce the other
Governments of the world to set up an international
tribunal which would settle international difficulties.

They actually had the matter so definitely in mind that they authorized the President not to carry out an act of Congress with regard to the building of great ships if he could get an arrangement similar to the arrangement which I have now laid before them, because their instinctive judgment is, my instinctive judgment and yours is, that we have no choice, if we want to stop war, but to take the steps that are necessary to stop war.

If we do not enter into this Covenant, what is our situation? Our situation is exactly the situation of Germany herself, except that we are not disarmed and Germany is disarmed. We have joined with the rest of the world to defeat the objects that Germany had in mind. We now do not even sign the treaty, let us suppose, that disarms Germany. She is disarmed, nevertheless, because the other nations will enter into the treaty, and there, planted in her heart, planted in the heart of those 60,000,000 people, is this sense of isolation; it may be this sense that some day, by gathering force and change of circumstances, they may have another chance, and the only other Nation that they can look to is the United States. The United States has repudiated the guarantee. The United States has said, "Yes; we sent 2,000,000 men over there to accomplish this, but we do not like it now that we have accomplished it and we will not guarantee the consequences. We are going to stay in such a situation that some day we may send 2,000,000 more over there. We promised the mothers and fathers and the wives and the sweethearts that these men were fighting so that this thing should not happen again, but we are now to arrange it so that it may happen again." So the two nations that will stand and play a lone hand in the world would be Germany and the United States.

I am not pointing this out to you, my fellow citizens, because I think it is going to happen. I know it is not. I am not in the least troubled about that; but I do want you to share fully with me the thought that I have

brought back from Europe. I know what I am talking
about when I say that America is the only nation whose
guarantee will suffice to substitute discussion for war,
and I rejoice in the circumstance. I rejoice that the day
has come when America can fulfill her destiny. Her
destiny was expressed much more in her open doors, for
she said to the oppressed all over the world, "Come
and join us; we will give you freedom; we will give you
opportunity; we have no governments that can act as
your masters. Come and join us to conduct the great
government which is our own." And they came in
thronging millions, and their genius was added to ours,
their sturdy capacity multiplied and increased the capacity of the United States; and now, with the blood of
every great people in our veins, we turn to the rest of
the world and say, "We still stand ready to redeem
you. We still believe in liberty. We still mean to
exercise every force that we have and, if need be, spend
every dollar that is ours to vindicate the standards of
justice and of right."

It is a noble prospect. It is a noble opportunity. My
pulses quicken at the thought of it. I am glad to have
lived in a day when America can redeem her pledges
to the world, when America can prove that her leadership is the leadership that leads out of these age-long
troubles, these age-long miseries into which the world
will not sink back, but which, without our assistance, it
may struggle out of only through a long period of
bloody revolution. The peoples of Europe are in a
revolutionary frame of mind. They do not believe in
the things that have been practiced upon them in the
past, and they mean to have new things practiced. In
the meantime they are, some of them, like pitiful Russia,
in danger of doing a most extraordinary thing, substituting one kind of autocracy for another. Russia repudiated the Czar, who was cruel at times, and set up
her present masters, who are cruel all the time and pity
nobody, who seize everybody's property and feed only

the soldiers that are fighting for them; and now, according to the papers, they are likely to brand every one of those soldiers so that he may not easily, at any rate, escape their clutches and desert. Branding their servants and making slaves of a great and lovable people! There is no people in the world fuller of the naïve sentiments of good will and of fellowship than the people of Russia, and they are in the grip of a cruel autocracy that dares not, though challenged by every friendly Government in Europe, assemble a constituency; they dare not appeal to the people. They know that their mastery would end the minute the people took charge of their own affairs.

Do not let us expose any of the rest of the world to the necessity of going through any such terrible experience as that, my fellow countrymen. We are at present helpless to assist Russia, because there are no responsible channels through which we can assist her. Our heart goes out to her, but the world is disordered, and while it is disordered—we debate!

FROM REAR PLATFORM, MANDAN, N. DAK., SEPTEMBER 10, 1919.

I am glad to get out to see the real folks, to feel the touch of their hand, and know, as I have come to know, how the Nation stands together in the common purpose to complete what the boys did who carried their guns with them over the sea. We may think that they finished that job, but they will tell you they did not; that unless we see to it that peace is made secure, they will have the job to do over again, and we in the meantime will rest under a constant apprehension that we may have to sacrifice the flower of our youth again. The whole country has made up its mind that that shall not happen; and presently, after a reasonable time is allowed for unnecessary debate, we will get out of all this period of doubt and unite the whole force and influence of the United States to steady the world in the lines of peace. It will be the proudest thing and finest thing that America ever did. She was born to do these things, and now she is going to do them.

I am very much obliged to you for coming out.

AT AUDITORIUM, BILLINGS, MONT., SEPTEMBER 11, 1919

MR. MAYOR, JUDGE PIERSON, MY FELLOW COUNTRYMEN:

It is with genuine pleasure that I face this company and realize that I am in the great State of Montana. I have long wanted to visit this great State and come into contact with its free and vigorous population, and I want to thank Judge Pierson for the happy word that he used in speaking of my errand. He said that I had come to consult with you. That is exactly what I have come to do. I have come to consult with you in the light of certain circumstances which I want to explain to you, circumstances which affect not only this great Nation which we love, and of which we try to constitute an honorable part, but also affect the whole world. I wonder when we speak of the whole world whether we have a true conception of the fact that the human heart beats everywhere the same. Nothing impressed me so much on the other side of the water as the sort of longing for sympathy which those people exhibited. The people of France, for example, feeling keenly as they do the terrors that they have suffered at the hands of the enemy, are never so happy as when they realize that we across the sea at a great distance feel with them the keen arrows of sorrow that have penetrated their hearts and are glad that our boys went over there to help rescue them from the terror that lay upon them day and night.

What I have come to say to you to-day, my friends, is this: We are debating the treaty of peace with Ger-

many and we are making the mistake, I take the liberty
of saying, of debating it as if it were an ordinary treaty
with some particular country, a treaty which we could
ourselves modify without complicating the affairs of the
world; whereas, as a matter of fact, this is not merely
a treaty with Germany. Matters were drawn into this
treaty which affected the peace and happiness of the
whole Continent of Europe, and not of the Continent of
Europe merely, but of forlorn populations in Africa, of
peoples that we hardly know about in Asia, in the Far
East and everywhere the influence of German policy
had extended and everywhere that influence had to be
corrected, had to be checked, had to be altered. What
I want to impress upon you to-day is that it is this treaty
or none. It is this treaty because we can have no other.

Consider the circumstances. For the first time in the
world some twenty nations sent their most thoughtful
and responsible men to consult together at the capital
of France to effect a settlement of the affairs of the
world, and I want to render my testimony that these
gentlemen entered upon their deliberations with great
openness of mind. Their discussions were characterized
by the utmost candor, and they realize, my fellow citizens, what as a student of history I venture to say no
similar body ever acknowledged before, that they were
nobody's masters, that they did not have the right to
follow the line of any national advantage in determining what the settlements of the peace should be, but
that they were the servants of their people and the servants of the people of the world. This settlement, my
fellow citizens, is the first international settlement that
was intended for the happiness of the average men and
women throughout the world. This is indeed and in
truth a people's treaty, and it is the first people's treaty,
and I venture to express the opinion that it is not wise
for Parliaments or Congresses to attempt to alter it.
It is a people's treaty, notwithstanding the fact that we
call it a treaty with Germany; and while it is a treaty

with Germany, and in some senses a very severe treaty, indeed, it is not an unjust treaty, as some have characterized it. My fellow citizens, Germany tried to commit a crime against civilization, and this treaty is justified in making Germany pay for that criminal error up to the ability of her payment. Some of the very gentlemen who are now characterizing this treaty as too harsh are the same men who less than a twelvemonth ago were criticizing the administration at Washington in the fear that they would compound with Germany and let her off from the payment of the utmost that she could pay in retribution for what she had done. They were pitiless then; they are pitiful now.

It is very important, my fellow citizens, that we should not forget what this war meant. I am amazed at the indications that we are forgetting what we went through. There are some indications that on the other side of the water they are apt to forget what they went through. I venture to think that there are thousands of mothers and fathers and wives and sisters and sweethearts in this country who are never going to forget. Thousands of our gallant youth lie buried in France, and buried for what? For the redemption of America? America was not directly attacked. For the salvation of America? America was not immediately in danger. No; for the salvation of mankind. It is the noblest errand that troops ever went on. I was saying the other day in the presence of a little handful of men whom I revered, veterans of our Civil War, that it seemed to me that they fought for the greatest thing that there was to fight for in their day, and you know with what reverence we have regarded all the men who fought in the ranks in the Civil War for the Union. I am saying this out of a full heart, though I was born on the other side of the Mason and Dixon line. We revere the men who saved the Union. What are going to be our sentiments with regard to these boys in khaki and the boys who have just been in khaki in this war?

Do you not think that when they are old men a halo will seem to be about them, because they were crusaders for the liberty of the world? One of the hardest things for me to do during this war, as for many another man in this country, was merely to try to direct things and not take a gun and go myself. When I feel the pride that I often have felt in having been the commander in chief of these gallant armies and those splendid boys at sea, I think, "Ah, that is fine, but, oh, to have been one of them and to have accomplished this great thing which has been accomplished!"

The fundamental principle of this treaty is a principle never acknowledged before, a principle which had its birth and has had its growth in this country, that the countries of the world belong to the people who live in them, and that they have a right to determine their own destiny and their own form of government and their own policy, and that no body of statesmen, sitting anywhere, no matter whether they represent the overwhelming physical force of the world or not, has the right to assign any great people to a sovereignty under which it does not care to live. This is the great treaty which is being debated. This is the treaty which is being examined with a microscope. This is the treaty which is being pulled about and about which suggestions are made as to changes of phraseology. Why, my friends, are you going to be so nearsighted as to look that way at a great charter of human liberty? The thing is impossible. You cannot have any other treaty, because you can never get together again the elements that agreed to this treaty. You cannot do it by dealing with separate governments. You cannot assemble the forces again that were back of it. You cannot bring the agreement upon which it rests into force again. It was the laborious work of many, many months of the most intimate conference. It has very, very few compromises in it and is, most of it, laid down in straight lines according to American specifications. The choice is either to accept this treaty or play a lone hand. What does that mean? To play a lone hand means that we must always be ready to play by ourselves. That means that we must always be armed, that we must always be ready to mobilize the man strength and the manufacturing resources of the country; it means that we must continue to live under not diminishing but increasing taxes; it means that we shall devote our thought and the organization of our Government to being strong enough to beat any nation in the world. An absolute reversal of all the ideal of American history. If you are going to play a lone hand, the hand that you play must be upon the handle of the sword. You cannot play a lone hand and do your civil business except with the other hand— one hand incidental for the business of peace, the other hand constantly for the assertion of force. It is either this treaty or a lone hand, and the lone hand must have a weapon in it. The weapon must be all the young men of the country trained to arms, and the business of the country must pay the piper, must pay for the whole armament, the arms and the men. That is the choice. Do you suppose, my fellow citizens, that any nation is going to stand for that? We are not the only people who are sick of war. We are not the only people who have made up our minds that our Government must devote its attention to peace and to justice and to right. The people all over the world have made up their minds as to that. We need peace more than we ever needed it before. We need ordered peace, calm peace, settled peace, assured peace—for what have we to do? We have to re-regulate the fortunes of men. We have to reconstruct the machinery of civilization. I use the words deliberately—we have to reconstruct the machinery of civilization.

The central fact of the modern world is universal unrest, and the unrest is not due merely to the excitement of a recent war. The unrest is not due merely to the fact of recent extraordinary circumstances. It is due to a universal conviction that the conditions under which men live and labor are not satisfactory. It is a conviction all over the world that there is no use talking about political democracy unless you have also industrial democracy. You know what this war interrupted in the United States. We were searching our own hearts; we were looking closely at our own methods of doing business. A great many were convinced that the control of the business of this country was in too few hands. Some were convinced that the credit of the country was controlled by small groups of men, and the great Federal reserve act and the great land-bank act were passed in order to release the resources of the country on a broader and more generous scale. We had not finished dealing with monopolies. We have not finished dealing with monopolies. With monopolies there can be no industrial democracy. With the control of the few, of whatever kind or class, there can be no democracy of any sort. The world is finding that out in some portions of it in blood and terror.

Look what has happened in Russia, my fellow citizens. I find wherever I go in America that my fellow citizens feel as I do, an infinite pity for that great people, an infinite longing to be of some service to them. Everybody who has mixed with the Russian people tells me that they are among the most lovable people in the world, a very gentle people, a very friendly people, a very simple people, and in their local life a very democratic people, people who easily trust you, and who expect you to be trustworthy as they are. Yet this people is delivered into the hands of an intolerable tyranny. It came out of one tyranny to get into a worse. A little group of some thirty or forty men are the masters of that people at present. Nobody elected them. They chose themselves. They maintain their power by the sword, and they maintain the sword by seizing all the food of the country and letting only those who will fight for them eat, the rest of them to go starved; and because they can command no loyalty we are told by the newspapers that they are about to brand the men under arms for them, so that they will be forever marked as their servants and slaves. That is what pitiful Russia has got in for, and there will be many a bloody year, I am afraid, before she finds herself again.

I speak of Russia. Have you seen no symptoms of the spread of that sort of chaotic spirit into other countries? If you had been across the sea with me you would know that the dread in the mind of every thoughtful man in Europe is that that distemper will spread to their countries, that before there will be settled order there will be tragical disorder. Have you heard nothing of the propaganda of that sort of belief in the United States? That poison is running through the veins of the world, and we have made the methods of communication throughout the world such that all the veins of the world are open and the poison can circulate. The wireless throws it out upon the air. The cable whispers it underneath the sea. Men talk about it in little groups, men talk about it openly in great groups not only in Europe but here also in the United States. There are apostles of Lenin in our own midst. I cannot imagine what it means to be an apostle of Lenin. It means to be an apostle of the night, of chaos, of disorder; there can be no creed of disorganization. Our immediate duty, therefore, my fellow countrymen, is to see that no minority, no class, no special interest, no matter how respectable, how rich, how poor, shall get control of the affairs of the United States.

The singular thing about the sort of disorder that prevails in Russia is that while every man is, so to say, invited to take what he can get, he cannot keep it when he gets it, because, even if you had leave to steal, which is the leave very generously given in Russia at present. you have got to get somebody to help you to keep what you steal. Without organization you cannot get any help, so the only thing you can do is to dig a hole and find a cave somewhere. Disordered society is dissolved society. There is no society when there is not settled and calculable order. When you do not know what is going to happen to you to-morrow, you do not much care what is going to happen to you to-day. These are the things that confront us. The world must be satisfied of justice. The conditions of civilized life must be purified and perfected, and if we do not have peace, that is impossible. We must clear the decks of this matter we are now discussing. This is the best treaty that can possibly be got, and, in my judgment, it is a mighty good treaty, for it has justice, the attempt at justice at any rate, at the heart of it.

Suppose that you were feeling that there was a danger of a general conflagration in your part of the country; I mean a literal fire. Which would you rather have, no insurance at all or 10 per cent insurance? Don't you think some insurance is better than none at all? Put the security obtained by this treaty at its minimum, and it is a great deal better than no security at all, and without it there is no security at all, and no man can be sure what his business will be from month to month, or what his life will be from year to year. The leisureliness of some debates creates the impression on my mind that some men think there is leisure. There is no leisure in the world, my fellow citizens, with regard to the reform of the conditions under which men live. There is no time for any talk, but get down to the business of what we are going to do.

I dare say that many of you know that I have called a conference to sit in Washington the first of next month, a conference of men in the habit of managing business and of men engaged in manual labor, what we generally call employers and employees. I have called them together for the sake of getting their minds together, getting their purposes together, getting them to look at the picture of our life at the same time and in the same light and from the same angles, so that they can

see the things that ought to be done. I am trying to
apply there what is applied in the great Covenant of
the League of Nations, that if there is any trouble, the
thing to do is not to fight, but to sit around the table
and talk it over. The League of Nations substitutes
discussion for fight, and without discussion there will be
fight. One of the greatest difficulties that we have been
through in the past is in getting men to understand that
fundamental thing. There is a very interesting story
and a very charming story told of a great English writer
of a past generation. He was a man who stuttered a
little bit, and he stuttered out some very acid comment
on some man who was not present. One of his friends
said, "Why, Charles, I didn't know you knew him."
"Oh, n-n-no," he said, "I-I d-d-don't k-know him;
I-I c-c-can't hate a m-man I-I know." How much truth
there is in that, my fellow countrymen! You cannot
hate a fellow you know. I know some crooks that I
cannot help liking. I can judge them in cool blood and
correctly only when they are not there. They are extremely fetching and attractive fellows; indeed, I suspect that a disagreeable fellow cannot be a successful
crook.

But, to speak seriously, conference is the healing influence of civilization, and the real difficulty between
classes, when a country is unfortunate enough to have
classes, is that they do not understand one another. I
sometimes think that the real barriers in life are the barriers of taste, that some people like one way of doing
things and that other people do not like that way of
doing things; that one sort of people are not comfortable unless the people they are with are dressed the way
they are. I think that goes so much deeper than people
realize. It is the absence of the ability to get at the
point of view and look through the eyes of the persons
with whom you are not accustomed to deal. In order,
therefore, to straighten out the affairs of America, in
order to calm and correct the ways of the world, the first

and immediate requisite is peace, and it is an immediate requisite. We cannot wait. It is not wise to wait, because we ought to devote our best thoughts, the best impulses of our hearts, the clearest thinking of our brain, to correcting the things that are wrong everywhere.

I have been told, my fellow citizens, that this western part of the country is particularly pervaded with what is called radicalism. There is only one way to meet radicalism and that is to deprive it of food, and wherever there is anything wrong there is abundant food for radicalism. The only way to keep men from agitating against grievances is to remove the grievances, and as lon gas things are wrong I do not intend to ask men to stop agitating. I intend to beg that they will agitate in an orderly fashion; I intend to beg that they will use the orderly methods of counsel, and, it may be, the slow processes of correction which can be accomplished in a self-governing people through political means. Otherwise we will have chaos; but as long as there is something to correct, I say Godspeed to the men who are trying to correct it. That is the only way to meet radicalism. Radicalism means cutting up by the roots. Well, remove the noxious growth and there will be no cutting up by the roots. Then there will be the wholesome fruitage of an honest life from one end of this country to the other.

In looking over some papers the other day I was reminded of a very interesting thing. The difficulty which is being found with the League of Nations is that apparently the gentlemen who are discussing it unfavorably are afraid that we will be bound to do something we do not want to do. The only way in which you can have impartial determinations to this world is by consenting to something you do not want to do. Every time you have a case in court one or the other of the parties has to consent to do something he does not want to do. There is not a case in court, and there are hundreds of thousands of them every year, in which one of the parties is not disappointed. Yet we regard that as the foundation of civilization, that we will not fight about these things, and that when we lose in court we will take our medicine. Very well; I say that the two Houses of Congress suggested that there be an international court, and suggested that they were willing to take their medicine. They put it in a place where you would not expect it. They put it in the naval appropriation bill, and, not satisfied with putting it there once, they put it there several times; I mean in successive years. This is the sum of it:

"It is hereby declared to be the policy of the United States to adjust and settle its international disputes through mediation or arbitration (that is, the League of Nations), to the end that war may be honorably avoided. It looks with apprehension and disfavor upon a general increase of armament throughout the world, but it realizes that no single nation can disarm and that without a common agreement upon the subject every considerable power must maintain a relative standing in military strength. In view of the premises, the President is authorized and requested to invite at an appropriate time, not later than the close of the war in Europe (this immediately preceded our entry into the war), all the great Governments of the world to send representatives to a conference which shall be charged with the duty of formulating a plan for a court of arbitration or other tribunal to which disputed questions between nations shall be referred for adjustment and peaceful settlement, and to consider the question of disarmament and submit their recommendations to their respective Governments for approval. The President is hereby authorized to appoint," etc. A provision for an appropriation to pay the expenses is also embodied.

Now that they have got it, they do not like it. They also provided in this legislation that if there could be such an assemblage, if there could be such an agreement, the President was authorized to cancel the naval building program authorized by the bill, or so much of it as he thought was wise in the circumstances. They looked forward to it with such a practical eye that they contemplated the possibility of its coming soon enough to stop the building program of that bill. It came much sooner than they expected, and apparently has taken them so much by surprise as to confuse their minds. I suppose that this would be a very dull world if everybody were consistent, but consistency, my fellow citizens, in the sober, fundamental, underlying principles of civilization is a very serious thing indeed.

If we are, indeed, headed toward peace with the real purpose of our hearts engaged, then we must take the necessary steps to secure it, and we must make the necessary sacrifices to secure it. I repudiate the suggestion which underlies some of the suggestions I have heard that the other nations of the world are acting in bad faith and that only the United States is acting in good faith. It is not true. I can testify that I was coöperating with honorable men on the other side of the water, and I challenge anybody to show where in recent years, while the opinion of mankind has been effective, there has been the repudiation of an international obligation by France or Italy or Great Britain or by Japan. Japan has kept her engagements, and Japan here engages to unite with the rest of the world in maintaining justice and a peace based upon justice. There can be cited no instances where these Governments have been dishonorable, and I need not add that there is, of course, no instance where the United States has not kept faith.

When gentlemen discuss the right to withdraw from the League of Nations and look suspiciously upon the clause which says that we can withdraw upon two years' notice, if at that time we have fulfilled our international obligations, I am inclined to ask, "What are you worried about? Are you afraid that we will not have fulfilled our international obligations?" I am too proud an American to believe anything of the kind. We never have failed to fulfill our international obligations, and we never will, and our international obligations will always look toward the fulfillment of the highest purposes of civilization. When we came into existence as a Nation we promised ourselves and promised the world that we would serve liberty everywhere. We were only 3,000,000 strong then, and shall we, when more than a hundred million strong, fail to fulfill the promise that we made when we were weak? We have served mankind and we shall continue to serve mankind, for I believe, my fellow men, that we are the flower of mankind so far as civilization is concerned.

Please do not let me leave the impression on your mind that I am arguing with you. I am not arguing this case; I am merely expounding it. I am just as sure what the verdict of this Nation is going to be as if it had been already rendered, and what has touched me and convinced me of this, my fellow citizens, is not what big men have told me, not what men of large affairs have said to me—I value their counsel and seek to be guided by it—but by what plain people have said to me, particularly by what women have said to me. When I see a woman plainly dressed, with the marks of labor upon her, and she takes my hand and says, "God bless you, Mr. President; God bless the League of Nations," I know that the League of Nations has gone to the heart of this people. A woman came up to me the other day and grasped my hand and said, "God bless you!" and then turned away in tears. I asked a neighbor, "What is the matter?" and he said, "She intended to say something to you, sir, but she lost a son in France." That woman did not take my hand with a feeling that her son ought not to have been sent to France. I sent her son to France, and she took my hand and blessed me, but she could not say anything more, because the whole well of spirit in her came up into her throat and the thing was unutterable. Down deep in it was the love of her boy, the feeling of what

he had done, the justice and the dignity and the majesty
of it, and then the hope that through such poor instrumentality as men like myself could offer no other
woman's son would ever be called upon to lay his life
down for the same thing. I tell you, my fellow citizens,
the whole world is now in the state where you can fancy
that there are hot tears upon every cheek, and those
hot tears are tears of sorrow. They are also tears of
hope. It is amazing how, through all the sorrows of
mankind and all the unspeakable terrors and injustices
that have been inflicted upon men, hope springs eternal
in the human heart. God knows that men, and governments in particular, have done everything they knew
how to kill hope in the human heart, but it has not died.
It is the one conquering force in the history of mankind.
What I am pleading for, therefore—not with you, for
I anticipate your verdict—but what I am pleading for
with the Senate of the United States is to be done with
debate and release and satisfy the hope of the world.

At Opera House, Helena, Mont., September 11,
1919.

Gov. Stewart and my fellow countrymen:
    I very heartily echo what Gov. Stewart has just said.
I am very glad that an occasion has arisen which has
given me the opportunity and the pleasure of coming
thus face to face with, at any rate, some of the people
of the great State of Montana. I must hasten to say
to you that I am not come from Washington so much
to advise you as to get in touch with you, as to get the
feeling of the purposes which are moving you, because,
my fellow cititzens, I may tell you as a secret that some
people in Washington lose that touch. They do not
know what the purposes are that are running through
the hearts and minds of the people of this great country, and after one stays in Washington too long one is
apt to catch that same remove and numbness which

seems to characterize others that are there. I like to
come out and feel once more the thing that is the only
real thing in public affairs, and that is the great movement of public opinion in the United States.

I want to put the case very simply to you to-night,
for with all its complexity, with all the many aspects
which it wears there is a very simple question at the
heart of it. That question is nothing more nor less
than this: Shall the great sacrifice that we made in this
war be in vain, or shall it not? I want to say to you
very solemnly that, notwithstanding the splendid
achievement of our soldiers on the other side of the
sea, who I do not hesitate to say saved the world, notwithstanding the noble things that they did, their task
is only half done and it remains for us to complete it.
I want to explain that to you. I want to explain to
you why, if we left the thing where it is and did not
carry out the program of the treaty of peace in all
its fullness, men like these would have to die again to
do the work over again and convince provincial statesmen that the world is one and that only by organization
of the world can you save the young men of the world.

As I take up this theme there is a picture very distinct
in my mind. Last Memorial Day I stood in an American cemetery in France just outside Paris, on the slopes
of Suresnes. The hills slope steeply to a little plain,
and when I went out there all the slope of the hill was
covered with men in the American uniform, standing,
but rising tier on tier as if in a great witness stand.
Then below, all over this little level space, were the
simple crosses that marked the resting place of American dead. Just by the stand where I spoke was a group
of French women who had lost their own sons, but, just
because they had lost their own sons and because their
hearts went out in thought and sympathy to the mothers
on this side of the sea, had made themselves, so to say,
mothers of those graves, had every day gone to take
care of them, had every day strewn them with flowers.

They stood there, their cheeks wetted with tears, while I spoke, not of the French dead but of the American boys who had died in the common cause, and there seemed to me to be drawn together on that day and in that little sunny spot the hearts of the world. I took occasion to say on that day that those who stood in the way of completing the task that those men had died for would some day look back upon it as those have looked back upon the days when they tried to divide this Union and prevent it from being a single Nation united in a single form of liberty. For the completion of the work of those men is this, that the thing that they fought to stop shall never be attempted again.

I call you to mind that we did not go into this war willingly. I was in a position to know; in the providence of God, the leadership of this Nation was intrusted to me during those early years of the war when we were not in it. I was aware through many subtle channels of the movements of opinion in this country, and I know that the thing that this country chiefly desired, the thing that you men out here in the West chiefly desired and the thing that of course every loving woman had at her heart, was that we should keep out of the war, and we tried to persuade ourselves that the European business was not our business. We tried to convince ourselves that no matter what happened on the other side of the sea, no obligation of duty rested upon us, and finally we found the currents of humanity too strong for us. We found that a great consciousness was welling up in us that this was not a local cause, that this was not a struggle which was to be confined to Europe, or confined to Asia, to which it had spread, but that it was something that involved the very fate of civilization; and there was one great Nation in the world that could not afford to stay out of it. There are gentlemen opposing the ratification of this treaty who at that time taunted the administration of the United States that it had lost touch with its international conscience. They were eager to go in, and now that they have got in, and are caught in the whole network of human conscience, they want to break out and stay out. We were caught in this thing by the action of a nation utterly unlike ourselves. What I mean to say is that the German nation, the German people, had no choice whatever as to whether it was to go into that war or not, did not know that it was going into it until its men were summoned to the colors. I remember, not once, but often, sitting at the Cabinet table in Washington I asked my colleagues what their impression was of the opinion of the country before we went into the war, and I remember one day one of my colleagues said to me, "Mr. President, I think the people of the country would take your advice and do what you suggested." "Why," I said, "that is not what I am waiting for; that is not enough. If they cannot go in with a whoop, there is no use of their going in at all. I do not want them to wait on me. I am waiting on them. I want to know what the conscience of this country is speaking. I want to know what the purpose is arising in the minds of the people of this country with regard to this world situation." When I thought I heard that voice, it was then that I proposed to the Congress of the United States that we should include ourselves in the challenge that Germany was giving to mankind.

We fought Germany in order that there should be a world fit to live in. The world is not fit to live in, my fellow citizens, if any great government is in a position to do what the German Government did—secretly plot a war and begin it with the whole strength of its people, without so much as consulting its own people. A great war cannot begin with public deliberation. A great war can begin only by private plot, because the peoples of this world are not asleep, as they used to be. The German people is a great educated people. All the thoughtful men in Germany, so far as I have been able to learn, who were following peaceful pursuits—the

bankers and the merchants and the manufacturers—
deemed it folly to go into that war. They said so then
and they have said so since, but they were not consulted.
The masters of Germany were the general military
staff; it was these men who nearly brought a complete
cataclysm upon civilization itself. It stands to reason
that if we permit anything of that sort to happen again
we are recreant to the men we sent across the seas to
fight this war. We are deliberately guilty then of preparing a situation which will inevitably lead to what?
What shall I call it? The final war? Alas, my fellow
citizens, it might be the final arrest, though I pray only
the temporary arrest, of civilization itself; and America
has, if I may take the liberty of saying so, a greater
interest in the prevention of that war than any other
nation. America is less exhausted by the recent war
than the other belligerents; she is not exhausted at all.
America has paid for the war that has gone by less
heavily, in proportion to her wealth, than the other nations. America still has free capital enough for its own
industries and for the industries of the other countries
that have to build their industries anew. The next war
would have to be paid for in American blood and
American money. The nation of all nations that is
most interested to prevent the recurrence of what has
already happened is the nation which would assuredly
have to bear the brunt of that great catastrophe—either
have to bear it or stop where we are. Who is going to
check the growth of this Nation? Who is going to
check the accumulation of physical power by this Nation
—if you choose to put it in that form? Who is going
to reduce the natural resources of this country? Who
is going to change the circumstance that we largely feed
the rest of the world? Who is going to change the circumstance that many of our resources are unique and
indispensable? America is going to grow more and
more powerful; and the more powerful she is the more

inevitable it is that she should be trustee for the peace of the world.

A miracle has happened. I dare say that many of you have in mind the very short course of American history. You know, when this Nation was born and we were just a little group—3,000,000 people on the Atlantic coast—how the nations on the other side of the water and the statesmen of that day watched us with a certain condescension, looked upon us as a sort of group of hopeful children, pleased for the time being with the conception of absolute freedom and political liberty, far in advance of the other peoples of the world because less experienced than they, less aware of the difficulties of the great task that they had accomplished. As the years have gone by they have watched the growth of this Nation with astonishment and for a long time with dismay. They watched it with dismay until a very interesting and significant thing happened. When we fought Cuba's battle for her, then they said, "Ah, it is the beginning of what we predicted. She will seize Cuba and, after Cuba, what she pleases to the south of her. It is the beginning of the history we have gone through ourselves." They ought to have known; they set us the example! When we actually fulfilled to the letter our promise that we would set helpless Cuba up as an independent government and guarantee her independence—when we carried out that great policy we astounded and converted the world. Then began—let me repeat the word again—then began the confidence of the world in America, and I want to testify to you to-night that nothing was more overpowering to me and my colleagues in Paris than the evidences of the absolutely unquestioning confidence of the peoples of the world in the people of America. We were touched by it not only, but I must admit we were frightened by it, because we knew that they were expecting things of us that we could not accomplish; we knew that they were hoping for some miracle of justice which would set

them forward the same hundred years that we have
traveled on the progress toward free government; and
we knew that it was a slow road; we knew that you
could not suddenly transform a people from a people
of subjects into a people of self-governing units. And I
perhaps returned a little bit to my own profession of
teaching and tried to point out to them that some of the
things they were expecting of us could not be done now;
but they refused to be disabused of their absolute confidence that America could and would do anything that
was right for the other peoples of the world. An amazing thing! What was more interesting still, my fellow
citizens, was this: It happened that America laid down
the specifications for the peace. It happened that
America proposed the principles upon which the peace
with Germany should be built. I use the word "happened" because I have found, and everybody who has
looked into the hearts of some of the people on the
other side of the water has found, that the people on
the other side of the water, whatever may be said about
their Governments, had learned their lesson from
America before, and they believed in those principles
before we promulgated them; and their statesmen,
knowing that their people believed in them, accepted
them—accepted them before the American representatives crossed the sea. We found them ready to lay
down the foundations of that peace along the lines that
America had suggested, and all of Europe was aware
that what was being done was building up an American
peace. In such circumstances we were under a peculiar
compulsion to carry the work to the point which had
filled our convictions from the first.

Where did the suggestion first come from? Where
did the idea first spread that there should be a society
of nations? It was first suggested and it first spread
in the United States, and some gentlemen were the chief
proponents of it who are now objecting to the adoption
of the Covenant of the League of Nations. They

went further, some of them, than any principle of that Covenant goes, and now for some reason which I must admit is inscrutable to me they are opposing the very thing into which they put their heart and their genius. All Europe knew that we were doing an American thing when we put the Covenant of the League of Nations at the beginning of the treaty, and one of the most interesting things over there was our dealing with some of the most cynical men I had to deal with, and there were some cynics over there—men who believed in what has come to be known as the old Darwinian idea of the survival of the fittest. They said: "In nature the strong eats up the weak, and in politics the strong overcomes and dominates the weak. It has always been so, and it is always going to be so." When I first got to Paris they talked about the League of Nations indulgently in my presence, politely. I think some of them had the idea, "Oh, well, we must humor Wilson along so that he will not make a public fuss about it," and those very men, before our conferences were over, suggested more often than anybody else that some of the most difficult and delicate tasks in carrying out this peace should be left to the League of Nations, and they all admitted that the League of Nations, which they had deemed an ideal dream, was a demonstrable, practical necessity. This treaty cannot be carried out without the League of Nations, and I will tell you some interesting cases.

I have several times said, and perhaps I may say again, that one of the principal things about this treaty is that it establishes the land titles of the world. It says, for example, that Bohemia shall belong to the Bohemians and not to the Austrians or to the Hungarians; that if the Bohemians do not want to live under a monarchy, dual or single, it is their business and not ours, and they can do what they please with their own country. We have said of the Austrian territories south of Austria and Hungary, occupied by the Jugo-Slavs, "These never did belong to Austria; they always did belong to the Slavs, and the Slavs shall have them for their own, and we will guarantee the title." I have several times asked, "Suppose that the land titles of a State like Montana were clearly enough stated and somewhere recorded, but that there was no way of enforcing them." You know what would happen. Every one of you would enforce his own land title. You used to go armed here long ago, and you would resume the habit, if there was nobody to guarantee your legal title. You would have to resume the habit. If society is not going to guarantee your titles, you have got to see to it yourselves that others respect them. That was the condition of Europe and will be the condition of Europe again if these settled land titles which have been laid out are not guaranteed by organized society, and the only organized society that can guarantee them is a society of nations.

It was not easy to draw the line. It was not a surveyor's task. There were not well-known points from which to start and to which to go, because, for example, we were trying to give the Bohemians the lands where the Bohemians lived, but the Bohemians did not stop at a straight line. If they will pardon the expression, they slopped over. And Germans slopped over into Poland and in some places there was an almost inextricable mixture of the two populations. Everybody said that the statistics lied. They said the German statistics with regard to High Silesia, for example, were not true, because the Germans wanted to make it out that the Germans were in a majority there, and the Poles declared that the Poles were in the majority there. We said, "This is a difficult business. Sitting in Paris we cannot tell by count how many Poles there are in High Silesia, or how many Germans, and if we could count them, we cannot tell from Paris what they want. High Silesia does not belong to us; it does not belong to anybody but the people who live in it. We will do this: We will put that territory under the care of the League of Nations for a little period; we will establish a small armed force there, made up of contingents out of the different allied nations so that no one of them would be in control, and then we will hold a referendum, and High Silesia shall belong either to Germany or to Poland as the people in High Silesia desire." That is only one case out of half a dozen. In regions where the make-up of the population is doubtful or the desire of the population is as yet unascertained, the League of Nations is to be the instrumentality by which the goods are to be delivered to the people to whom they belong. No other international conference ever conceived such a purpose, and no earlier conference of that sort would have been willing to carry out such a purpose. Up to the time of this war, my fellow citizens, it was the firm and fixed conviction of statesmen in Europe that the greater nations ought to dominate and guide and determine the destiny of the weaker nations, and the American principle was rejected. The American principle is that, just as the weak man has the same legal rights that the strong man has, just as the poor man has the same rights as the rich, though I am sorry to say he does not always get them, so as between nations the principle of equality is the only principle of justice, and the weak nations have just as many rights and just the same rights as the strong nations. If you do not establish that principle, then this war is going to come again, because this war came by aggression upon a weak nation.

What happened, my fellow citizens? Don't you remember? The Crown Prince of Austria was assassinated in Serbia. Not assassinated by anybody over whom the Government of Serbia had any control, but assassinated by some man who had at his heart the memory of something that was intolerable to him that had been done to the people that he belonged to, and the Austrian Government, not immediately but by suggestion from Berlin, where it was whispered, "We are ready for the World War, and this is a good chance to begin it; the other nations do not believe we are going to begin it; we will begin it and overwhelm France, first of all, before the others can come to her rescue." The Austrian Government sent an ultimatum to Serbia practically demanding of her that she surrender to them her sovereign rights, and gave her 24 hours to decide. Poor Serbia, in her sudden terror, with memory of things that had happened before and might happen again, practically yielded to every demand, and with regard to a little portion of the ultimatum said she would like to talk it over with them, and they did not dare wait. They knew that if the world ever had the facts of that dispute laid before them the opinion of mankind would overwhelm anybody that took aggression against Serbia in such circumstances. The point is that they chose this little nation. They had always chosen the Balkans as the ground of their intrigue. German princes were planted all through the Balkans, so that when Germany got ready she could use the Balkan situation as pawns in her game.

And what does the treaty of peace do? The treaty of peace sets all those nations up in independence again; gives Serbia back what had been torn away from her, sets up the Jugo-Slavic States and the Bohemian States under the name of Czechoslovakia; and if you leave it at that, you leave those nations just as weak as they were before. By giving them their land titles, you do not make them any stronger. You make them stronger in spirit, it may be, they see a new day, they feel a new enthusiasm, their old love of their country can now express itself in action, but physically they are no stronger than they were before, and that road that we heard so much of—from Bremen to Bagdad—is wide open. The Germans were traveling that road. Their general staff interrupted the game. The merchants and manufacturers and bankers of Germany were making conquest of the world. All they had to do was to wait a little while longer, and long German fingers would have been stretched all through that country which never could have been withdrawn. The war spoiled the game. German intrigue was penetrating all those countries and controlling them. The dirty center of the intrigue, dirty in every respect, was Constantinople, and from there ramified all the threads that made this web, in the center of which was the venomous spider. If you leave that road open, if you leave those nations to take care of themselves, knowing that they cannot take care of themselves, then you have committed the unpardonable sin of undoing the victory which our boys won. You say, "What have we got to do with it?" Let us answer that question, and not from a sentimental point of view at all. Suppose we did not have any hearts under our jackets. Suppose we did not care for these people. Care for them? Why, their kinsmen are everywhere in the communities of the United States, people who love people over there are everywhere in the United States. We are made up out of mankind; we cannot tear our hearts away from them. Our hearts are theirs, but suppose they were not. Suppose we had forgotten everything except the material, commercial, monetary interests of the United States. You cannot get those markets away from Germany if you let her reëstablish her old influence there. The 300,000,000 people between the Rhine and the Ural Mountains will be in such a condition that they cannot buy anything, their industries cannot start, unless they surrender themselves to the bankers of Mittel-Europa, that you used to hear about; and the peoples of Italy and France and Belgium, some 80,000,000 strong, who are your natural customers, cannot buy anything in disturbed and bankrupt Europe. If you are going to trade with them, you have got to go partners with them.

When I hear gentlemen talk about America standing for herself, I wonder where they have been living. Has America disconnected herself from the rest of the world? Her ambition has been to connect herself with all the rest of the world commercially, and she is bankrupt unless she does. Look at the actual situation right now, my fellow citizens. The war was a very great stimulation to some of the greatest of the manufacturing industries of this country, and a very interesting thing has been going on. You remember, some of you perhaps painfully remember, that the Congress of the United States put a very heavy tax on excess profits, and a great many men who were making large excess profits said, "All right, we can manage this. These will not be profits; we will spend these in enlarging our plants, advertising, increasing our facilities, spreading our agencies." They have got ready for a bigger business than they can do unless they have the world to do it in, and if they have not the world to do it in, there will be a recession of prosperity in this country; there will be unemployment; there will be bankruptcy in some cases. The giant is so big that he will burst his jacket. The rest of the world is necessary to us, if you want to put it on that basis. I do not like to put in on that basis. That is not the American basis. America does not want to feed upon the rest of the world. She wants to feed it and serve it. America, if I may say it without offense to great peoples for whom I have a profound admiration on the other side of the water, is the only national idealistic force in the world, and idealism is going to save the world. Selfishness will embroil it. Narrow selfishness will tie things up into ugly knots that you cannot get open except with a sword. All the human passions, if aroused on the wrong side, will do the world an eternal disservice.

I remember somebody said to me one day, using a familiar phrase, that this was an age in which mind was monarch, and my reply was, "Well, if that is true, mind is one of those modern monarchs that reign and do not govern; as a matter of fact, we are governed by a great popular assembly made up of the passions, and the best that we can manage is that the handsome passions shall be in the majority." That is the task of mankind, that the handsome passions, the handsome sentiments, the handsome purposes, shall always have a dominating and working majority, so that they will always be able to outvote the baser passions, to defeat all the cupidities and meannesses and criminalities of the world. That is the program of civilization. The basis of the program of civilization, I want to say with all the emphasis that I am capable of, is Christian and not pagan, and in the presence of this inevitable partnership with the rest of the world, these gentlemen say, "We will not sign the articles of copartnership." Well, why not? You have heard, I dare say, only about four things in the Covenant of the League of Nations. I have not heard them talk about anything else. It is a very wonderful document and you would think there were only four things in it. The things that they talk about are the chance to get out, the dangers of Article X, the Monroe Doctrine, and the risk that other nations may interfere in our domestic affairs. Those are the things that keep them awake at night, and I want very briefly to take those things in their sequence.

I do not like to discuss some of them. If I go to do a thing, I do not say at the beginning, "My chief interest in this thing is how I am going to get out." I will not be a very trusted or revered partner if it is evident that my fear is that I will continue to be a partner. But we will take that risk. We will sit by the door with our hand on the knob, and sit on the edge of our chair. There is nothing in the Covenant to prevent our going out whenever we please, with the single limitation that we give two years' notice. The gentlemen who discuss this thing do not object to the two years' notice; they say, "It says that you can get out after two years' notice if at that time you have fulfilled your international obligations," and they are afraid somebody will have the right to say that they have not. That right

cannot belong to anybody unless you give it to somebody, and the Covenant of the League does not give
it to anybody. It is absolutely left to the conscience of
this Nation, as to the conscience of every other member
of the League, to determine whether at the time of its
withdrawal it has fulfilled its international obligations,
or not; and inasmuch as the United States always has
fulfilled its international obligations I wonder what these
gentlemen are afraid of! There is only one thing to
restrain us from getting out, and that is the opinion of
our fellow men, and that will not restrain us in any
conceivable circumstance if we have followed the honorable course which we always have followed. I would
be ashamed as an American to be afraid that when we
wanted to get out we should not have fulfilled our international obligations.

Then comes Article X, for I am taking the questions
in the order in which they come in the Covenant itself.
Let me repeat to you Article X nearly verbatim; I am
not trying to repeat it exactly as it is written in the
Covenant. Every member of the League agrees to
respect and preserve as against external aggression the
territorial integrity and existing political independence
of the other members of the League. There is the guarantee of the land titles. Without that clause, there is no
guarantee of the land titles. Without that clause the
heart of the recent war is not cut out. The heart of
the recent war was an absolute disregard of the territorial integrity and political independence of the smaller
nations. If you do not cut the heart of the war out,
that heart is going to live and beat and grow stronger,
and we will have the cataclysm again. Then the article
adds that it shall be the duty of the council of the
League to advise the members of the League what steps
may be necessary from time to time to carry out this
agreement; to advise, not to direct. The Congress of
the United States is just as free under that article to
refuse to declare war as it is now; and it is very much

safer than it is now. The opinion of the world and of the United States bade it to declare war in April, 1917. It would have been shamed before all mankind if it had not declared war then. It was not given audible advice by anybody but its own people, but it knew that the whole world was waiting for it to fulfill a manifest moral obligation. This advice cannot be given, my fellow citizens, without the vote of the United States. The advice cannot be given without a unanimous vote of the council of the League. The member of the council representing the United States has to vote aye before the United States or any other country can be advised to go to war under that agreement, unless the United States is herself a party. What does that mean? Unless the United States is going to seize somebody else's territory or somebody else is going to seize the territory of the United States. I do not contemplate it as a likely contingency that we are going to steal somebody else's territory, I dismiss that as not a serious probability, and I do not see anybody within reach who is going to take any of ours. But suppose we should turn highwayman, or that some other nation should turn highwayman, and stretch its hands out for what belongs to us. Then what difference does it make what advice the council gives? We are in the scrap anyhow. In those circumstances Congress is not going to wait to hear what the council of the League says to determine whether it is going to war or not. The war will be its war. So that any way you turn Article X it does not alter in the least degree the freedom and independence of the United States with regard to its action in respect of war. All of that is stated in such plain language that I cannot for the life of me understand how anybody reads it any other way. I know perfectly well that the men who wrote it read it the way I am interpreting it. I know that it is intended to be written that way, and if I am any judge of the English language, they succeeded in writing it that way.

Then they are anxious about the Monroe Doctrine. The Covenant says in so many words that nothing in that document shall be taken as invalidating the Monroe Doctrine. I do not see what more you could say. While the matter was under debate in what was called the commission on the League of Nations, the body that drew the Covenant up, in which were representatives of fourteen nations, I tried to think of some other language that could state it more unqualifiedly and I could not think of any other. Can you? Nothing in that document should be taken as invalidating the Monroe Doctrine—I cannot say it any plainer than that—and yet by a peculiar particularity of anxiety these gentlemen cannot believe their eyes; and from one point of view it is not strange, my fellow citizens. The rest of the world always looked askance on the Monroe Doctrine. It is true, though some people have forgotten it, that President Monroe uttered that doctrine at the suggestion of the British cabinet, and in its initiation, in its birth, it came from Mr. Canning, who was prime minister of England and who wanted the aid of the United States in checking the ambition of some of the European countries to establish their power in South America. Notwithstanding that, Great Britain did not like the Monroe Doctrine as we grew so big. It was one thing to have our assistance and another thing for us not to need her assistance. And the rest of the world had studiously avoided on all sorts of interesting occasions anything that could be interpreted as an acknowledgment of the Monroe Doctrine. So I am not altogether surprised that these gentlemen cannot believe their eyes. Here the nations of Europe say that they are entering into an arrangement no part of which shall be interpreted as invalidating the Monroe Doctrine. I do not have to say anything more about that. To my mind, that is eminently satisfactory, and as long as I am President I shall feel an added freedom in applying, when I think fit, the Monroe Doctrine. I am very much interested in it, and I foresee occasions when it might be appropriately applied.

In the next place they are afraid that other nations will interfere in our domestic questions. There, again, the Covenant of the League distinctly says that if any dispute arises which is found to relate to an exclusively domestic question, the council shall take no action with regard to it and make no report concerning it, and the questions that these gentlemen most often mention, namely the questions of the tariff and of immigration and of naturalization, are acknowledged by every authoritative student of international law without exception to be as, of course, domestic questions. These gentlemen want us to make an obvious thing painfully obvious by making a list of the domestic questions, and I object to making the list for this reason, that if you make a list you may leave something out. I remind all students of law within the sound of my voice of the old principle of the law that the mention of one thing is the exclusion of other things; that if you meant everything, you ought to have said everything; that if you said a few things, you did not have the rest in mind. I object to making a list of domestic questions, because a domestic question may come up which I did not think of. In every such case the United States would be just as secure in her independent handling of the question as she is now.

Then, outside the Covenant is the question of Shantung. Some gentlemen want to make a reservation or something that they clothe with a handsome name with regard to the Shantung provision, which is that the right which Germany illicitly got, for she got it by duress, from China shall pass to Japan. While the war was in progress, Great Britain and France expressly in a written treaty, though a secret treaty, entered into an engagement with Japan that she should have all that Germany had in the Province of Shantung. If we repudiate this treaty in that matter Great Britain and France cannot repudiate the other treaty, and they cannot repudiate this treaty inasmuch as it confirms the other. Therefore, in order to take away from Japan, for she is in physical possession of it now, what Germany had in China, we shall have to fight Japan and Great Britain and France; and at the same time do China no service, because one of the things that is known to everybody is that when the United States consented, because of this promise of Great Britain and France, to putting that provision in the treaty, Japan agreed that she would not take all of what was given to her in the treaty; that, on the contrary, she would, just as soon as possible, after the treaty was carried out return every sovereign right or right resembling a sovereign right that Germany had enjoyed in Shantung to the Government of China, and that she would retain at Shantung only those economic rights with regard to the administration of the railway and the exploitation of certain mines that other countries enjoy elsewhere in China. It is not an exceptional arrangement—a very unfortunate arrangement, I think, elsewhere as there, for China, but not an exceptional arrangement. Under it Japan will enjoy privileges exactly similar and concessions exactly similar to what other nations enjoy elsewhere in China and nothing more. In addition to that, if the treaty is entered into by the United States China will for the first time in her history have a forum to which to bring every wrong that is intended against her or that has been committed against her.

When you are studying Article X, my fellow citizens, I beg of you that you will read Article XI. I do not hear that very often referred to. Article XI—I am not going to quote the words of it—makes it the right of any member of the League to call attention to anything, anywhere, that is likely to disturb the peace of the world or the good understanding between nations upon which the peace of the world depends. Every aspiring people, every oppressed people, every people whose hearts can no longer stand the strain of the tyranny that has been put upon them, can find a champion to speak for it in the forum of the world. Until that Covenant is adopted, what is the international law? International law is that no matter how deeply the United States is interested in something in some other part of the world that she believes is going to set the world on fire or disturb the friendly relations between two great nations, she cannot speak of it unless she can show that her own interests are directly involved. It is a hostile and unfriendly act to call attention to it, and Article XI says, in so many words, that it shall be the friendly right of every nation to call attention to any such matter anywhere; so that if anybody contemplates anything that is an encroachment upon the rights of China he can be summoned to the bar of the world. I do not know when any nation that could not take care of itself, as unfortunately China cannot, ever had such a humane advantage accorded it before. It is not only we, my fellow citizens, who are caught in all the implications of the affairs of the world; everybody is caught in it now, and it is right that anything that affects the world should be made everybody's business.

The heart of the Covenant of the League of Nations is this: Every member of the League promises never to go to war without first having done one or other of two things, either having submitted the matter to arbitration, in which case it agrees absolutely to abide by the award, or having submitted it to discussion by the council of the League of Nations. If it submits it for discussion by the council, it agrees to allow six months for the discussion and to lay all the documents and facts in its possession before the council, which is authorized to publish them; and even if it is not satisfied with the opinion rendered by the council, it agrees that it will not go to war within less than three months after the publication of that judgment. There are nine months in which the whole matter is before the bar of mankind, and, my fellow citizens, I make this confident prediction, that no nation will dare submit a bad case to that jury. I believe that this Covenant is better than 95 per cent insurance against war. Suppose it was only 5 per cent insurance; would not you want it? If you can get any insurance against war, do not you want it? I ask any mother, any father, any brother, anybody with a heart, "Do not you want some insurance against war, no matter how little?" And the experience of mankind, from the conferences between employers and employees, is that if people get together and talk things over, it becomes more and more difficult to fight the longer they talk. There is not any subject that has not two sides to it, and the reason most men will not enter into discussion with antagonists is that they are afraid the other fellows' side will be stronger than theirs. The only thing you are afraid of, my fellow citizens, is the truth.

A cynical old politician once said to his son, "John, do not bother your head about lies; they will take care of themselves, but if you ever hear me denying anything you may make up your mind it is so." The only thing that is formidable is the truth. I learned what I know about Mexico, which is not as much as I should desire, by hearing a large number of liars tell me all about it. At first, I was very much confused, because the narratives did not tally, and then one day, when I had a lucid interval, it occurred to me that that was because what was told me was not true. The truth always matches; it is lies that do not match. I also observed that back of all these confusing contradictions there was a general mass of facts which they all stated, and I knew that that was the region into which their lying capacity did not extend. They had not had time to make up any lies about that, and the correspondences in their narratives constituted the truth. The differences could be forgotten. So I learned a great deal about Mexico by listening to a sufficiently large number of liars. The truth is the regnant and triumphant thing in this world. You may trample it under foot, you may blind its eyes with blood, but you cannot kill it, and sooner or later it rises up and seeks and gets its revenge.

That is what it behooves us to remember, my fellow citizens, in these radical days. The men who want to cure the wrongs of governments by destroying government are going to be destroyed themselves; destroyed, I mean, by the chaos that they have created, because remove the organism of society and, even if you are strong enough to take anything that you want, you are not smart enough to keep it. The next stronger fellow will take it away from you and the most audacious group amongst you will make slaves and tools of you. That is the truth that is going to master society in Russia and in any other place that tries Russia's unhappy example. I hope you will not think it inappropriate if I stop here to express my shame as an American citizen at the race riots that have occurred in some places in this country where men have forgotten humanity and justice and ordered society and have run amuck. That constitutes a man not only the enemy of society but his own enemy and the enemy of justice. I want to say this, too, that a strike of the policemen of a great city, leaving that city at the mercy of an army of thugs, is a crime against civilization. In my judgment, the obligation of a policeman is as sacred and direct as the obligation of a soldier. He is a public servant, not a private employee, and the whole honor and safety of the community is in his hands. He has no right to prefer any private advantage to the public safety. I hope that that lesson will be burned in so that it will never again be forgotten, because the pride of America is that it can exercise self-control. That is what a self-governing nation is, not merely a nation that elects people to do its jobs for it, but a nation that can keep its head, concert its purposes, and find out how its purposes can be executed.

One of the noblest sentences ever uttered was uttered by Mr. Garfield before he became President. He
was a Member of Congress, as I remember it, at the
time of Mr. Lincoln's assassination. He happened to
be in New York City, and Madison Square was filled
with a surging mass of deeply excited people when the
news of the murder came. Mr. Garfield was at the old
Fifth Avenue Hotel, which had a balcony out over the
entrance, and they begged him to go out and say something to the people. He went out and, after he had
attracted their attention, he said this beautiful thing:
"My fellow citizens, the President is dead, but the
Government lives and God Omnipotent reigns." America is the place where you cannot kill your Government
by killing the men who conduct it. The only way you
can kill government in America is by making the men
and women of America forget how to govern, and nobody can do that. They sometimes find the team a little
difficult to drive, but they sooner or later whip it into
harness. And, my fellow citizens, the underlying
thought of what I have tried to say to you to-night is
the organization of the world for order and peace. Our
fortunes are directly involved, and my mind reverts to
that scene that I painted for you at the outset—that
slope at Suresnes, those voiceless graves, those weeping
women—and I say: "My fellow citizens, the pledge
that speaks from those graves is demanded of us. We
must see to it that those boys did not die in vain. We
must fulfill the great mission upon which they crossed
the sea."

At Coeur D'alene, Idaho, September 12, 1919.

Your excellency, my fellow citizens:

It is with the greatest pleasure that I find myself
facing an audience in this great State. I echo the wish
of the governor that it might be our privilege to stay

a long time in Idaho and know something more than
her fame, know her people, come in contact with her
industries, and see the things that we have all so long
read about and admired from a distance; but, unfortunately, it is necessary for us to go back to Washington as soon as we can, though it was a great pleasure
to escape from Washington. Washington is a very interesting place, but it is a very lonely place. The people
of the United States do not live there, and in order to
know what the people of the United States are thinking about and talking about it is necessary to come and
find out for yourself. That really is my errand.

 · I have taken pains since I was a boy so to saturate
myself in the traditions of America that I generally feel
a good deal of confidence that the impulses which I find
in myself are American impulses; but no matter how
thoroughly American a man may be, he needs constantly
to renew his touch with all parts of America and to be
sure that his mind is guided, if he be in public station,
by the thoughts and purposes of his fellow countrymen.
It was, therefore, with the most earnest desire to get in
touch with you and the rest of my fellow countrymen
that I undertook this trip, for, my fellow countrymen,
we are facing a decision now in which we cannot afford
to make a mistake. We must not let ourselves be deceived as to the gravity of that decision or as to the
implications of that decision. It will mean a great deal
now, but it will mean infinitely more in the future. America has to do at this moment nothing less than prove to
the world whether she has meant what she said in the
past.

I must confess that I have been amazed that there are
some men in responsible positions who are opposed
to the ratification of the treaty of peace altogether. It
is natural that so great a document, full of so many particular provisions, should draw criticism upon itself for
this, that, or the other provision. It is natural that a
world settlement, for it is nothing less, should give

occasion for a great many differences of opinion with regard to particular settlements of it, but I must admit that it amazes me that there should be any who should propose that the arrangement be rejected altogether, because, my fellow citizens, this is the issue : We went into this Great War from which we have just issued with certain assurances given ourselves and given the world, and these assurances cannot be fulfilled unless this treaty is adopted. We told the world and we assured ourselves that we went into this war in order to see to it that the kind of purpose represented by Germany in this war should never be permitted to be accomplished by Germany or anybody else. Do not let your thoughts dwell too constantly upon Germany. Germany attempted this outrageous thing, but Germany was not the only country that had ever entertained the purpose of subjecting the peoples of the world to its will, and when we went into this war we said that we sent our soldiers across the seas not because we thought this was an American fight in particular, but because we knew that the purpose of Germany was against liberty, and that where anybody was fighting liberty it was our duty to go into the contest. We set this Nation up with the profession that we wanted to set an example of liberty not only, but to lead the world in the paths of liberty and justice and of right; and at last, after long reflection, after long hesitation, after trying to persuade ourselves that this was a European war and nothing more, we suddenly looked our own consciences in the face and said, "This is not merely a European war. This is a war which imperils the very principles for which this Government was set up, and it is our duty to lend all the force that we have, whether of men or of resources, to the resistance of these designs." And it was America—never let anybody forget this—it was America that saved the world, and those who propose the rejection of the treaty propose that, after having redeemed the world, we should desert the world. It would be nothing less.

The settlements of this treaty cannot be maintained without the concerted action of all the great Governments of the world. I asked you just now not to think exclusively about Germany, but turn your thoughts back to what it was that Germany proposed. Germany did direct her first force against France and against Belgium, but you know that it was not her purpose to remain in France, though it was part of her purpose to remain in Belgium. She was using her arms against these people so that they could not prevent what she intended elsewhere, and what she intended elsewhere was to make an open line of dominion between her and the Far East. The formula that she adopted was Bremen to Bagdad, the North Sea to Persia—to crush not only little Serbia, whom she first started to crush, but all the Balkan States, get Turkey in her grasp, take all the Turkish and Arabian lands beyond, penetrate the wealthy realms of Persia, open the gates of India, and, by dominating the central trade routes of the world, dominate the world itself. That was her plan; and what does the treaty of peace do? For I want you to remember, my fellow countrymen, that this treaty is not going to stand by itself. The treaty with Austria has now been signed; it will presently be sent over, and I shall lay that before the Senate of the United States. It will be laid down along exactly the same lines as the treaty with Germany; and the lines of the treaty with Germany suggest this, that we are setting up the very States which Germany and Austria intended to dominate as independent, self-governing units. We are giving them what they never could have got with their own strength, what they could have got only by the united strength of the armies of the world. But we have not made them strong by making them independent. We have given them what I have called their land titles. We have said, "These lands that others have tried to dominate and exploit for their own uses belong to you, and we assign them to you in fee simple. They never did belong to anybody else. They were loot. It was brigandage to take them. We give them to you in fee simple." But what is the use of setting up the titles if we do not guarantee them? And that guarantee is the only guarantee against the repetition of the war we have gone through just as soon as the German Nation, 60,-000,000 strong, can again recover its strength and its spirit, for east of Germany lies the fertile field of intrigue and power. At this moment the only people who are dealing with the Bolshevist government in Russia are the Germans. They are fraternizing with the few who exercise control in that distracted country. They are making all their plans that the financing of Russia and the commerce of Russia and the development of Russia shall be as soon as possible in the hands of Germans; and just so soon as she can swing that great power, that is also her road to the East and to the domination of the world. If you do not guarantee the titles that you are getting up in these treaties, you leave the whole ground fallow in which again to sow the dragon's teeth with the harvest of armed men.

That, my fellow citizens, is what Article X, that you hear so much talked about in the Covenant of the League of Nations, does. It guarantees the land titles of the world; and if you do not guarantee the land titles of the world, there cannot be the ordered society in which men can live. Off here in this beloved continent, with its great free stretches and its great free people, we have not realized the cloud of dread and terror under which the people of Europe have lived. I have heard men over there say, "It is intolerable. We would rather die now than live another fifty years under the cloud that has hung over us ever since the Franco-Prussian War of 1870-71, because we have known that this force was gathering, we have known what the purpose was ultimately to be, we have known that blood and terror lay ahead of us, and we cannot and will not live under that cloud any more." America, my fellow citizens, is necessary to the peace of the world. America is absolutely necessary to the peace of the world. Germany realizes that; and I want to tell you now and here —I wish I could proclaim it in tones so loud that they would reach the world—Germany wants us to stay out of this treaty. Not under any deception. Not under the deception that we will turn in sympathy toward her. Not under the delusion that we would seek in any direct or conscious way to serve Germany, but with the knowledge that the guarantees will not be sufficient without America, and that, inasmuch as Germany is out of the arrangement, it will be very useful to Germany to have America out of the arrangement. Germany knows that if America is out of the arrangement America will lose the confidence and coöperation of all the other Nations in the world, and, fearing America's strength, she wants to see America alienated from the peoples from whom she has been alienated. It is a perfectly reasonable program. She wants to see America isolated. She is isolated. She wants to see one great nation left out of this combination which she never would again dare face. Evidences are not lacking—nay, evidences are abounding—that the pro-German propaganda has started up in this country coincidently with the opposition to the adoption of this treaty. I want those who have any kind of sympathy with the purposes with which we went into the war now to reflect upon this proposition: Are we going to prove the enemy of the rest of the world just when we have proved their savior? The thing is intolerable. The thing is impossible. America has never been unfaithful and she never will be unfaithful.

Do not let anybody delude you, my fellow citizens, with the pose of being an American. If I am an American I want at least to be an intelligent American. If I am a true American I will study the true interests of

America. If I am a true American I will have the
world vision that America has always had, drawing
her blood, drawing her genius, as she has drawn her
people, out of all the great constructive peoples of the
world. A true American conceives America in the atmosphere and whole setting of her fortune and her destiny. And America needs the confidence of the rest of
the world just as much as other nations do. America
needs the coöperation of the rest of the world to release
her resources, to make her markets, above all things
else to link together the spirits of men who mean to redeem the race from the wrongs that it has suffered. This
western country is *par excellence* the country of progres-
sivism. I am not now using it with a big "P." It does
not make any difference whether you belong to the Progressive Party or not; you belong to the progressive
thought, and I hope every intelligent man belongs to
the progressive thought. It is the only thought that
the world is going to tolerate. If you believe in progress, if you believe in progressive reform, if you believe in making the lot of men better, if you believe in
purifying politics and enlarging the purposes of public
policy, then you have got to have a world in which that
will be possible; and if America does not enter with all
her soul into this new world arrangement, progressives
might as well go out of business, because there is going
to be universal disorder, as there is now universal unrest.

Do not mistake the signs of the times, my fellow
countrymen, and do not think that America is immune.
The poison that has spread all through that pitiful
nation of Russia is spreading all through Europe.
There is not a statesman in Europe who does not dread
the infection of it, and just so certainly as those people
are disconcerted, thrown back upon their own resources,
disheartened, rendered cynical by the withdrawal of
the only people in the world they trust, just so certainly
there will be universal upsetting of order in Europe.

And if the order of Europe is upset, do you think America is going to be quiet? Have you not been reading in the papers of the intolerable thing that has just happened in Boston? When the police of a great city walk out and leave that city to be looted they have committed an intolerable crime against civilization; and if that spirit is going to prevail, where are your programs? How can you carry a program out when every man is taking what he can get? How can you carry a program out when there is no authority upon which to base it? How can you carry a program out when every man is looking out for his own selfish interests and refuses to be bound by any law that regards the interests of the others? There will be no reform in this world for a generation if the conditions of the world are not now brought to settled order, and they cannot be brought to settled order without the coöperation of America.

I am not speaking with conjecture, my fellow citizens. I would be ashamed of myself if upon a theme so great as this I should seek to mislead you by overstatement of any kind. I know what I am talking about. I have spent six months amidst those disturbed peoples on the other side of the water, and I can tell you, now and here, that the only people they depend upon to bring the world to settled conditions are the people of America. A chill will go to their heart, a discouragement will come down upon them, a cynicism will take possession of them, which will make progress impossible, if we do not take part not only, but do not take part with all our might and with all our genius. Everybody who loves justice and who hopes for programs of reform must support the unqualified adoption of this treaty. I send this challenge out to the conscience of every man in America, that if he knows anything of the conditions of the world, if he knows anything of the present state of society throughout the world and really loves justice and purposes just reform, he must support the treaty with Germany. I do not want to say that and have it proved by tragedy, for if this treaty should be refused, if it should be impaired, then amidst the tragedy of the things that would follow every man would be converted to the opinion that I am now uttering, but I do not want to see that sort of conversion. I do not want to see an era of blood and of chaos to convert men to the only practical methods of justice.

My fellow citizens, there are a great many things needing to be reformed in America. We are not exempt from those very subtle influences which lead to all sorts of incidental injustice. We ourselves are in danger at this present moment of minorities trying to control our affairs, and whenever a minority tries to control the affairs of the country it is fighting against the interest of the country just as much as if it were trying to upset the Government. If you think that you can afford to live in a chaotic world, then speak words of encouragement to the men who are opposing this treaty, but if you want to have your own fortunes held steady, realize that the fortunes of the world must be held steady; that if you want to keep your own boys at home after this terrible experience, you will see that boys elsewhere are kept at home. Because America is not going to refuse, when the other catastrophe comes, again to attempt to save the world, and, having given this proof once, I pray God that we may not be given occasion to prove it again! We went into this war promising every loving heart in this country who had parted with a beloved youngster that we were going to fight a war which would make that sacrifice unnecessary again, and we must redeem that promise or be of all men the most unfaithful. If I did not go on this errand through the United States, if I did not do everything that was within my power that is honorable to get this treaty adopted, and adopted without qualification, I never could look another mother in the face upon whose cheeks there were the tears of sorrowful memory with regard to the boy buried across the sea. The moral compulsion laid upon America now is a compelling compulsion, and cannot be escaped. My fellow countrymen, because it is a moral issue, because it is an issue in which is mixed up every sort of interest in America, I am not in the least uneasy about the result.

If you put it on the lowest levels, you cannot trade with a world disordered, and if you do not trade you draw your own industries within a narrower and narrower limit. This great State, with its untold natural resources, with its great undeveloped resources, will have to stand for a long generation stagnant because there are no distant markets calling for these things. All America will have to wait a long, anxious generation through to see the normal courses of her life restored. So, if I were putting it upon the lowest conceivable basis of the amount of money we could make, I would say, "We have got to assist in the restoration of order and the maintenance of order throughout the world by the maintenance of the morale of the world." You will say, "How? By arms?" That, I suspect, is what most of the opponents of the League of Nations, at any rate, try to lead you to believe, that this is a league of arms. Why, my fellow citizens, it is a league to bring about the thing that America has been advocating ever since I was born. It is a league to bring it about that there shall not be war, but that there shall be substituted for it arbitration and the calm settlement of discussion. That is the heart of the League. The heart of the League is this: Every member of the League, and that will mean every fighting nation in the world except Germany, agrees that it will never go to war without first having done one or the other of two things—either having submitted the matter in dispute to arbitration, in which case it agrees absolutely to abide by the result, or having submitted it to consideration by the council of the League of Nations, in which case it promises to lay all the documents, all the facts, in its possession before the council and to give the council six months in which to consider the matter, and, if it does not like the opinion of the council at the end of the six months, still to wait three months more before it resorts to arms. That is what America has been striving for. That is what the Congress of the United States directed me to bring about. Perhaps you do not know where; it was in an unexpected place, in the naval appropriations bill. Congress, authorizing a great building program of ships and the expenditure of vast sums of money to make our Navy one of the strongest in the world, paused a moment and declared in the midst of the appropriation bill that it was the policy of the United States to bring about disarmament and that for that purpose it was the policy of the United States to coöperate in the creation of a great international tribunal to which should be submitted questions of international difference and controversy, and it directed the President of the United States, not later than the close of this war, to call together an international conference for that purpose. It even went so far as to make an appropriation to pay the expenses for the conduct of such a conference in the city of Washington. And that is a continuing provision of the naval appropriations bill. When I came back with this Covenant of the League of Nations, I had fulfilled the mandate of the Congress of the United States; and now they do not like it.

There is only one conceivable reason for not liking it, my fellow citizens, and to me as an American it is not a conceivable reason; that is that we should wish to do some nation some great wrong. If there is any nation in the world that can afford to submit its purposes to discussion, it is the American Nation. If I belonged to some other nations, there are some things that I know that I would not like to see submitted to the discussion of mankind, but I do not know anything in the present purposes of the United States that I would not be perfectly willing to lay upon any table of counsel in the world. In carrying out the mandate of the Congress, I was serving the age-long purpose of this great people, which purpose centers in justice and in peace.

You will say, "Well, why not go in with reservations?" I wonder if you know what that means. If the Senate of the United States passes a resolution of ratification and says that it ratifies on condition that so and so is understood, that will have to be resubmitted to every signatory of the treaty; and what gravels me is that it will have to be submitted to the German Assembly at Weimar. That goes against my digestion. We can not honorably put anything in that treaty, which Germany has signed and ratified, with Germany's consent; whereas it is perfectly feasible, my fellow countrymen, if we put interpretations upon that treaty which its language clearly warrants, to notify the other Governments of the world that we do understand the treaty in that sense. It is perfectly feasible to do that, and perfectly honorable to do that, because, mark you, nothing can be done under this treaty through the instrumentality of the council of the League of Nations except by a unanimous vote. The vote of the United States will always be necessary, and it is perfectly legitimate for the United States to notify the other Governments beforehand that its vote in the council of the League of Nations will be based upon such and such an understanding of the provisions of the treaty.

The treaty is not susceptible of misunderstanding. I do not object to painting the rose or refining fine gold; there is not any phrase in the Covenant of the League of Nations that can legitimately be said to be of doubtful meaning, but if the Congress of the United States wants to state the meaning over again in other words and say to the other nations of the world, "We understand the treaty to mean what it says," I think that is a work of supererogation, but I do not see any moral objection to it. But anything that qualifies the treaty, anything that is a condition to our ratification of it, must be submitted to all the others, and we must go over this process again; this process which took six months of intensive labor, which took six months of very difficult adjustment and arrangement, which quieted jealousies, which allayed suspicions, which set aside controversies, which brought about the most extraordinary union of minds that was ever brought about in so miscellaneous an assembly, divided by so many interests. All that must be gone over again, and in the meantime the world must wait and its unrest grow deeper, and all the pulses of life go slower, waiting to see what is going to happen, all because the United States asks the other governments of the world to accept what they have already accepted in different language. That is all that it amounts to; I mean, all that the reasonable reservations amount to. Some of them amount to staying out altogether, some of them amount to a radical change of the spirit of the instrument, but I am speaking now of those which some men of high conscience and of high public purpose are seriously pressing in order that there may be no misunderstanding. You can avoid a misunderstanding without changing the document. You can avoid a misunderstanding without qualifying the terms of the document, because, as I have said and shall say again and again, America is at liberty as one of the voting members of the partnership to state how she understands the articles of copartnership.

I beg that these things may sink in your thoughts, my fellow countrymen, because we are at a turning point in the fortunes of the world. Out upon these quiet hills and in these great valleys it is difficult sometimes for me to remember the turmoil of the world in which I have been mixing on the other side of the sea; it is difficult for me to remember the surging passions which moved upon the face of the other continents of the world; it is difficult for me to remember the infinite suffering that happened even in this beloved country; it is difficult for me to remember the delegations from weak peoples that came to me in Paris, figuratively speaking, with out-stretched hands, pleading that America should lead the way out of the darkness into the light; it is difficult out here in this great peace for anybody, even, I dare say, for these fine fellows in khaki who were over there and saw something of it, to remember the whole strain and terror of the thing, but we must remember it, my fellow citizens, and we must see to it that that strain and terror never come upon the world again. It is with this solemn thought, that we are at a turning point in the destinies of mankind and that America is the makeweight of mankind, that I, with perfect confidence, leave this great question to your unbiased judgment.

AT SPOKANE, WASH., SEPTEMBER 12, 1919.

MR. MAYOR, MY FELLOW COUNTRYMEN:

I esteem it a real privilege to stand face to face with a representative audience of this great city, because I have come away from Washington, my fellow country-men, not to make speeches but to get into contact with just such bodies of men and women as this, and feel that I have exchanged ideas with them, and with the utmost frankness of which I was capable. I have not come to paint pictures of the fancy. I have come to disclose to you what I understand to be facts, and I want so much as possible to get down to the very essence and marrow of the things that we are now talking about.

I do not think I need tell you, my fellow citizens, that America and the world have come to the point where they must make one of the most critical choices ever made by great bodies of men or by nations. They have now to determine whether they will accept the one chance that has ever been offered to insure the peace of the world. I call it frankly a chance to insure the peace of the world. Nobody can guarantee the world against the ugly passions that sometimes get abroad.

Nobody can engage that the world will not again go mad with blood; but I want to put it frankly to you: Though the chance should be poor, is it not worth taking a chance? Let men discount the proposed arrangements as much as they will; let us regard it as an insurance policy. If you could get 10 per cent insurance of your fortunes in respect of peace, wouldn't you rather take it than no insurance at all? As a matter of fact, I believe, after having sat in conference with men all over the world and found the attitude of their minds, the character of their purposes, that this is a 99 per cent insurance against war. If the nations of the world will indeed and in truth accept this great Covenant of a League of Nations and agree to put arbitration and discussion always first and war always last, I say that we have an immense insurance against war, and that is exactly what this great Covenant does.

I have found it necessary upon this trip, my fellow citizens—I have actually found it necessary—to tell great audiences what the treaty of peace contains. You never could divine it from the discussion of the men who are opposed to it. Let me tell you some of the things that this treaty does, apart from the Covenant of the League of Nations which stands by common consent of those who framed it at the beginning of it. Quite apart from the League of Nations, it is the first attempt ever made by an international congress to substitute justice for national advantage. It is the first attempt ever made to settle the affairs of the world according to the wishes of the people in the parts of the world that were being dealt with. It is a treaty that deals with peoples and nations, and not with dynasties and governments. Every representative of every great Government I met on the other side of the sea acknowledged, as I, of course, acknowledge, that he was master of nobody, that he was the servant of the people whom he represented, and that the people he representd wanted what the people of the United States wanted; they wanted a just and reasonable and permanent settlement, and that is what this treaty tried to give them. It substitutes for the aggression, which always was the beginning of war, a settled title on the part of the weak nations, along with the strong, to their own territories, a settled right to determine their own policies, a settled right to realize the national hopes so long suppressed, to free themselves from the oppression so long endured. Europe was full of people under the iron and relentless hand of military power, and that hand has been removed and crushed. This treaty is the means of doing it.

The guarantee of this treaty is the part of the covenant of nations which you have heard most criticized. I mean the now celebrated Article X. Article X is an engagement of the most extraordinary kind in history. It is an engagement by all the fighting nations of the world never to fight upon the plan upon which they always fought before. They, all of them, agree to respect and preserve against external aggression the territorial integrity and existing political independence of the others, and they agree that if there should be any breach of that covenant, the council of the League shall advise what steps shall be taken to make the promises good. That is the covenant with which you have been frightened. Frightened, my fellow citizens? Why, it is the only possible or conceivable guarantee against the wars that have ravaged the world, because those wars have habitually begun by territorial aggression, by the seizure of territory that did not belong to the power that was effecting the seizure. How did this great war begin? It began by the invasion of Belgium, and it was admitted by all German statesmen that they never meant to get out of Belgium. By guaranteeing the territorial integrity of a country, you do not mean that you guarantee it against invasion. You guarantee it against the invader staying there and keeping the spoils. The integrity is the title, is the ownership. You agree never to take territory away from the people to whom

it belongs, and you agree never to interfere with the
political independence of the people living in these territories whose titles are now made clear by a universal
international guarantee.

I want to discuss with you very frankly, indeed, just
as frankly as I know how, the difficulties that have been
suggested, because I say, not in the spirit of criticism,
but in a spirit of entire intended fairness, that not one
of the qualifications which have been suggested in this
discussion is justified by the language of the instrument.
Let me take them one by one. In the first article of the
Covenant of the League it is provided that any member
State may withdraw from the league upon two years'
notice, provided at the time of withdrawal it has fulfilled its international obligations and its obligations
under the covenant. Gentlemen object that it is not said
who shall determine whether it has fulfilled its international obligations and its obligations under the covenant
or not. Having sat at the table where the instrument
was drawn, I know that that was not by accident, because that is a matter upon which no nation can sit in
judgment upon another. That is left to the conscience
and the independent determination of the nation that is
withdrawing, and there is only one jury that it need fear
and that is the great embodied jury expressing the opinion of mankind. I want to differentiate myself, therefore, from the men who are afraid of that clause,
because I want to record my feeling in the matter that,
as an American, I am never afraid that the United
States will fail to perform its international obligations;
and, being certain that it will never fail in that respect,
I have no fear that an occasion will arise when we need
be sensitive to the opinion of mankind. That is the only
jury set up in the case, and I am ready to go before that
jury at any time. These gentlemen want to say what
the instrument says, that we can withdraw when we
please. The instrument does not say it in those words,
but it says it in effect, and the only limitation upon that

is that we should not please unless we have done our duty. We never will please, God helping us, to neglect our duty.

The second difficulty—taking them in the order in which they have come in the Covenant itself—is the article I was a moment ago discussing, Article X. Article X, as I told you, says that if the promise to respect and preserve as against external aggression the territorial integrity and existing political independence of the member States is broken, then the council shall advise what is to be done. I do not know any but one meaning for the word "advise." I have been very curious and interested to learn how many other meanings have been put into it. I, in my surprise, have looked in the dictionary to be sure I was not mistaken, and so far as I can find out "advise" means "advise." And more interesting than that, the advice cannot be given without the affirmative vote of the United States. There must be unanimous vote of the council before there is advice, and the United States is a member of the council by the constitution of the League itself, a member now and always a member, so that neither the United States nor any other country can be advised to go to war for the redemption of that promise without the concurrent affirmative vote of the United States. Yet I hear gentlemen say that this is an invasion of our sovereignty. My fellow citizens, if it is anything, it is an exaggeration of our sovereignty, because it puts our sovereignty in a way to put a veto on that advice being given to anybody. Our present sovereignty merely extends to making choice whether we will go to war or not, but this extends our sovereignty to saying whether other nations shall go to war or not. If that does not constitute a very considerable insurance against war, I would like somebody to write a provision which would; because, at every point, my fellow citizens, the position of these gentlemen who criticize this instrument is either that they do not understand the Covenant or that they can suggest something better, and I have not heard one of them suggest anything better. In fact, I have never heard one of them suggest anything. If the world is going to be at peace, it must be this or something better, and I want to say again it is a case of "put up or shut up."

Let me make a slight digression here, if I may, to speak about a matter of some delicacy. I have had a great many men say to me, "I am a Republican, but I am in favor of the League of Nations." Why the "but"? I want to tell you, my fellow citizens, that there is one element in this whole discussion which ought not to be in it. There is, though I say it myself, an element of personal bitterness. One would suppose that this Covenant of the League of Nations was first thought of and first invented and first written by a man named Wilson. I wish it were. If I had done that, I would be willing to have it recorded that I had done that and nothing else. But I did not do it. I, along with thousands of my fellow countrymen, got the idea twenty years ago, chiefly from Republican public men. Take men like ex-Senator Burton, of Ohio. He has been preaching a league of nations for twenty years. I do not want to mention names, because I do not want to record gentlemen against themselves, but go through the list and you will find most of the leading, thinking minds on the Republican side in favor of this very kind of thing, and I want to remind every Republican of the criticism that he and his comrades have usually made of the Democratic party, and the boast that they have generally made of their party. They said that the Democratic party was a party of negations and not a party of constructive policies, and that the Republican party was a party of constructive policy. Very well, then, why that "but"? "I am a Republican, but I am in favor of the greatest constructive thing that has ever been suggested!" If I were a Republican, I would say, "I am a Republican and therefore I am in favor of a League of Nations." My present point is to dissociate the League of Nations from the present speaker. I did not originate it. It is not my handiwork. It has originated out of the consciences and thought of men who wanted justice and loved peace for generations, and my relationship to it is just what my relationship ought to be to every public question, the relationship which a man bears to his fellow citizens when he tries to interpret their thought and their conscience. That is what I conceive to be my part in the League of Nations. I did have a part in some of the phraseology, and every time I did it was to carry out the ideas that these gentlemen are fighting for.

For example, there is one part of the Covenant, the principal part of it, where it speaks of arbitration and discussion, where it provides that any member State, failing to keep these particular covenants shall be regarded as thereby *ipso facto* to have committed an act of war against the other members. The way it originally read was, "Shall thereby *ipso facto* be deemed at war with the other members," and I said, "No; I cannot agree to that. That provision would put the United States at war without the consent of the Congress of the United States, and I have no right in this part of the Covenant or any other to assent to a provision which would deprive the Congress of the United States of its free choice whether it makes war or not." There, and at every other point in the Covenant where it was necessary to do so, I insisted upon language which would leave the Congress of the United States free, and yet these gentlemen say that the Congress of the United States is deprived of its liberty. I fought that battle and won it. It is not necessary for them to fight it over again.

You will say, "It is all very well what you say about the vote of the United States being necessary to the advice provided the United States is not one of the parties to the dispute. In that case it cannot vote."

That is very true; but in that case it has got the fight on
its hands anyhow, because if it is one of the parties to
the dispute the war belongs to it.   It does not have to
go into it, and therefore it cannot be forced by the vote
of the United States in the council to go into the war.
The only thing the vote can do is to force it out of the
war.   I want to ask you to think what it means when
it is suggested that the United States may be a party.
A party to what?   A party to seizing somebody else's
territory?   A party to infringing some other country's
political independence?   Is any man willing to stand on
this platform and say that the United States is likely
to do either of those things?   I challenge any man to
stand up before an American audience and say that
that is the danger.   "Ah, but somebody else may seek
to seize our territory or impair our political independence."   Well, who?   Who has an arm long enough,
who has an audacity great enough to try to take a single
inch of American territory or to seek to interfere for
one moment with the political independence of the
United States?   These gentlemen are dreaming of things
that cannot happen, and I cannot bring myself to feel
uneasy in the presence of things that I know are not so.
The great difficulty in this discussion, as in so many
others, is in the number of things that men know that
are not so.

"But the Monroe Doctrine."   I must admit to you,
my fellow citizens, I do not know how the Monroe Doctrine could be any more explicitly accepted than it is in
the Covenant of the League of Nations.   It says that
nothing in the Covenant shall be interpreted as impairing the validity of the Monroe Doctrine.   What more
could you say?   I did try while I was in Paris to define
the Monroe Doctrine and get it written into the document, but I will confide to you in confidence that when
I tried to define it I found that it escaped analysis, that
all that you could say was that it was a principle with
regard to the interference of foreign powers in the poli-

tics of the Western Hemisphere which the United States felt at liberty to apply in any circumstances where it thought it pertinent. That is not a definition. That means that the United States means to play big brother to the Western Hemisphere in any circumstances where it thinks it wise to play big brother. Therefore, inasmuch as you could not or would not define the Monroe Doctrine—at least I would not, because I do not know how much we may want to extend it—what more could you say than that nothing in that instrument shall impair the validity of the Monroe Doctrine? I tell you, my fellow citizens, that is the most extraordinary sentence in that treaty, for this reason: Up to that time there was not a nation in the world that was willing to admit the validity of the Monroe Doctrine. I have made a great many speeches in my life, perhaps too many, but I do not think that I ever put so much of what I hope was the best in me as I put in the speech in the conference on the League of Nations in favor of the Monroe Doctrine, and it was upon that occasion that it was embodied. And we have this extraordinary spectacle, of the world recognizing the validity of the Monroe Doctrine. Yet these gentlemen seem to want something more. What more could you get? Shall we get them to express their belief in the deity of the Monroe Doctrine? They accept it for the first time in the history of the world, and they say that they will do nothing that will interfere with it. I must submit that it is absolutely irrational to ask for anything more.

But there is the question of somebody interfering with the domestic policies of the United States—immigration, naturalization, tariffs; matters of that sort. There, again, I cannot understand or feel the weight of the difficulty because the Covenant says that if any international difficulty is brought under discussion and one of the parties claims and the council finds that it is a matter of domestic jurisdiction, the council shall cease to discuss it and shall make no report about it. The only way you could make the document more clear would be by enumerating the domestic questions you had in mind. Very well. I ask any lawyer here if that would be safe? Might you not be in danger of leaving out something? Might you not be in danger of not mentioning something that would afterwards become important? The danger of making a list is that the mention of the things you do mention constitutes the exclusion of the things you do not mention. Inasmuch as there is no dispute of any authoritative students of international law that these matters that we are most concerned about—immigration, naturalization, tariff, and the rest—are domestic questions, it is inconceivable that the council should ever seek to interfere with or to discuss such questions, unless we had ourselves deliberately made them matters of international agreement, and even the opponents of the League admit they would be suitable and proper subjects for discussion.

Those are the matters upon which they are talking about reservations. The only reservations I can imagine are reservations which say over again what the Covenant itself says in plain language, and make it necessary that we should go back to Paris and discuss new language for things that we all have to admit, if we are frank, are already in the document.

But there is another matter. Somebody has said that this Covenant was an arrangement for the dominance of Great Britain, and he based that upon the fact that in the assembly of the council there are six representatives of the various parts of the British Empire. There are really more than that, because each member of the assembly has three representatives, but six units of the British Empire are represented, whereas the United States is represented as only one unit. Let me be didactic for a moment and tell you how the League is constituted. There is an assembly made up of three members of each of the constituent States, and there is a council. The council is the only part of the organization that can take effective action. No powers of action rest with the assembly at all, and it is only in the assembly that the British Empire is represented as consisting of six units—for brevity's sake I will say as having six votes. There is only one case when the assembly can vote at all, and that is when the council refers a matter in dispute to the assembly, in which case the assembly can decide a matter by a majority, provided all the representatives of the nations represented in the council vote on the side of the majority. So that, alike in the assembly and in the council, the one vote of the United States is an absolute veto. I have said that there was only one case upon which the assembly could vote, and that is literally true. The council of the League is made up of one representative from each of the five principal allied and associated powers; that is to say, the United States, Great Britain, France, Italy, and Japan, and four other nations selected by the assembly of the League. The present members are Spain, Brazil, Belgium, and Greece. In the council are vested all the active powers of the League. Everything that is done by the League is formulated and passed by the council, and a unanimous vote is required. Indeed, my fellow citizens, that is the only thing that seems to me weak about the League; I am afraid that a unanimous vote will sometimes be very difficult to get. The danger is not action, but inaction. The danger is not that they will do something that we do not like, but that upon some critical occasion they will not do anything. If there is any weakness in it, it is the safeguard that has been thrown around the sovereign power of the members of the council. If a matter in controversy arises and one of the parties demands that it shall be taken out of the council and put into the assembly, the council is obliged so to refer it, but in the final vote in the assembly the affirmative action is not valid unless all the States represented in the council shall also in the assembly vote in the affirmative. As we can always veto, always offset with one vote the British six votes, I must say that I look with perfect philosophy upon the difference in number.

The justification for the representation of more than one part of the British Empire was that the British Empire is made up of semi-independent pieces, as no other Empire in the world is. You know how Canada, for example, passes her own tariff law, does what she pleases to inconvenience the trade of the mother country. Canada's voice in the assembly is merely a debating force. The assembly is a great discussing body. It is a body in which some of the most valuable things that the League is going to do can be done, for I want to ask you, after you have read Article X again, to read Article XI. Article XI makes it the right of any member of the League, however weak and small, to call attention to anything, anywhere, that is likely to disturb the peace of the world and to draw it into debate, draw it into the open, draw it where everybody can get the facts and talk about it. It is the only time, my fellow countrymen, in the history of the world when weak and oppressed and restive peoples have been given a hearing before the judgment of mankind. Nothing is going to keep this world fit to live in like exposing in public debate every crooked thing that is going on. If you suspect your friend of being a fool, the best way you can prove it or disprove it is by advising him to hire a hall. Then your judgment will be confirmed or reversed by the popular verdict. If you think a policy is good, you will venture to talk about it. If you think it is bad, you will not consent to talk about it. The League of Nations takes everything into the public. It makes every secret agreement of every kind invalid; it provides that no treaty hereafter shall be valid unless registered with the secretary of the League and published. And after bringing everything into the open, it authorizes the assembly to discuss anything that is likely to affect the peace and happiness of the world. In every direction you look the safeguards of this treaty are thrown around those who are oppressed.

Unless America takes part in this treaty, my fellow citizens, the world is going to lose heart. I cannot too often repeat to you how deep the impression made upon me upon the other side of the water is that this was the Nation upon which the whole world depended to hold the scales of justice even. If we fail them, God help the world! Then despair will ensue. Despair is just at the door on that side of the water now. Men do not hope in Europe as they hope in America. They hope tremblingly. They hope fearfully. They do not hope with confidence and self-reliance as we do on this side of the water. Everywhere in Europe there is that poison of disorder and distrust, and shall we take away from this unsteady world the only thing that reassures it? If we do, then where is the boasted independence of America? Are we indeed independent in our life of the rest of the world? Then why did we go into the war? Germany had not directed her efforts immediately against us. We went in because we were partners with mankind to see that an iniquity was not practiced upon it. You know how we regard the men who fought the Civil War. They did the greatest thing that was to be done in their day. Now, these boys here, and the others like them, have done the greatest thing that it was possible to do in our day. As their fathers saved the Union, they saved the world, and we sit and debate whether we will keep true and finish the job or not! My friends, that debate cannot last one minute longer than the moment when this country realizes what it means. It means that, having sent these men to risk their lives and having sent some, whose mother's hearts can count, to die in France, in order to redeem the world, we, in cool debate, in distant assemblies, say we will not consent that the world should reap the fruit of their victory! Nothing less than that hangs in the balance. I am ready to fight from now until all the fight has been taken out of me by death to redeem the faith and promises of the United States. ·

I leave the verdict with you, and I beg, my Republican fellow citizens, that you will not allow yourselves for one moment, as I do not allow myself for one moment, as God knows my conscience, to think of 1920 when thinking about the redemption of the world. I beg that you will cut that "but" out of your sentences, and that you will stand up, as you are entitled to stand up by the history of your party, and say, "I am a Republican and therefore I am for the League of Nations." I do not admit the indictment which has been brought against the Democratic party, but I do admit the distinguished history of the Republican party; I do admit that it has been the creator of great constructive policies, and I should be very sorry to see it lose the prestige which it has earned by such policies. I should be very sorry to have any man feel that there was any embarrassment in supporting a great world policy because he belonged to a great constructive party, and that party a party of America—the constructive force in the world, the people who have done the most advanced thinking in the world, and the people who, God helping them, will lead and save the world.

At Stadium, Tacoma, Wash., September 13, 1919.

My friends and fellow citizens:

It is very delightful to find myself in this beautiful spot and very thrilling to find myself surrounded by so great a company of my fellow citizens. I cannot in these circumstances make you a speech, but I can say something from my heart. I can say that I am profoundly glad to see you and profoundly touched by a welcome like this. I want to express my particular interest in this charming circle of school children, because one of the thoughts that has been most in my mind recently is that we are making decisions now which will mean more to the children than they mean to us and that as we care for the future generations we will be careful to make the right decisions as to the policy of the United States as one of the factors in the peace of the world. I give you my most cordial greeting and my most profound thanks for this generous welcome.

AT ARMORY, TACOMA, WASH., SEPTEMBER 13, 1919.

MR. MAYOR, MR. CHAIRMAN, YOUR EXCELLENCY, MY FELLOW COUNTRYMEN:

It is with very great pleasure that I find myself in your presence. I have long wantd to get away from Washington and come into contact with the great body of my fellow citizens, because I feel, as I am sure you feel, that we have reached one of the most critical periods in the history of the United States. The shadow of the war is not yet lifted from us, my fellow countrymen, and we have just come out of the depths of the valley of death. I thought that it might be useful if this morning I reminded you of a few things, lest we forget. It is so easy, with the strong tides of our life, to be swept away from one situation into another and to forget the real depths of meaning which lie underneath the things that we are merely touching the surface of. Therefore I thought it would not be impertinent on my part if I asked permission to read you the concluding passage of the address in which I requested the Government of the United States to accept Germany's challenge of war:

"We shall fight," I said, "for the things which we have always carried nearest our hearts, for democracy, for the right of those who submit to authority to have a voice in their own governments, for the rights and liberties of small nations, for a universal dominion of right by such a concert of free peoples as will bring peace and safety to all nations and make the world itself at last free. To such a task we can dedicate our lives and our fortunes, everything that we are and everything that we have, with the pride of those who know that the day has come when America is privileged to spend her blood and her might for the principles that gave her birth and the happiness and the peace which we have treasured. God helping her, she can do no other."

That is the program we started out on. That is the program which all America adopted without respect of party, and shall we now hesitate to carry it out? Shall we now falter at the very critical moment when we are finally to write our name to the standing pledge which we then took? I want to remind you, my fellow citizens, that many other nations were put under a deeper temptation than we. It would have been possible for little Belgium at any time to make terms with the enemy. Belgium was not prepared to resist. Belgium knew that resistance was useless. Belgium knew that she could get any term of advantage from Germany she pleased, if she would only submit, and at the cost of everything that she had Belgium did nothing less than underwrite civilization. I do not know anywhere in history a more inspiring fact than that. I have seen the fields of Belgium. I have seen great spaces swept of cities and towns as clean as if there had never been anything there except piles of stone; and, farther in, in that beautiful country, the factories are standing, the houses there, but everything that could be useful taken out of the factories; the machinery taken out and shipped to Germany, because Germany feared the competition of the skillful Belgians, and where it was too bulky to take away it was destroyed under the direction of experts—not broken to pieces, but the very part that made it impossible to use it without absolutely destroyed. I have been over great plants there that seemed to the eye to have much of the substantial machinery left, but experts showed me that it could never work again. Belgium lies prostrated because she fulfilled her pledge to civilization. Italy could have had her terms with Austria at almost any period of the war, particularly just before she made her final stand at the Piave River, but she would not compound with the enemy. She, too, had underwritten civilization. And, my friends, this passage that I have read you, which the whole country accepted as its pledge, is an underwriting of civilization.

In order to let you remember what the thing cost, just let me read you a few figures. If I did not have them on official authority I would deem them incredible. Here is what the war cost. These figures do not include what the different powers loaned each other; they are direct war costs:

It cost Great Britain and her dominions $38,000,000,-000; France, $26,000,000,000; the United States, $22,000,000,000; Russia, $18,000,000,000; Italy, $13,-000,000,000; a total, including Japan, Belgium, and other countries, of $123,000,000,000. It cost the Central Powers: Germany, $39,000,000,000; Austria-Hungary, $21,000,000,000; Turkey and Bulgaria, $3,000,-000,000; a total of $63,000,000,000. A grand total of direct war costs of $186,000,000,000—an incredible sum—to save civilization. Now, the question is, Are we going to keep it saved? The expenditures of the United States were at the rate of $1,000,000 an hour, including the night time, for two years.

The battle deaths—and this is the cost that touches our hearts—were: Russia, 1,700,000; Germany, 1,600,-000; France, 1,380,000; Great Britain, 900,000; Austria, 800,000; Italy, 364,000; the United States, 50,300 dead. A total for all belligerents of 7,450,200 men dead on the field of battle! Seven and a half million! The totals for the wounded are not obtainable at present, but the number of torn and wounded for the United States Army was 230,000, excluding, of course, those who were killed. The total of all battle deaths in all the wars of the world from the year 1793 to 1914 was something under 6,000,000; in all the wars of the world for more than 100 years fewer men died than have been killed upon the field of battle in the last five years. These are terrible facts, my fellow citizens, and we ought never to forget them. We went into this war to do a thing that was fundamental for the world, and what I have come out upon this journey for is to ascertain whether the country has forgotten it or not. I have found out already. The country has not forgotten, and it never will permit any man who stands in the way of the fulfillment of these great pledges ever to forget the sorrowful day when he made the attempt.

I read you these figures in order to emphasize and set in a higher light, if I may, the substitute which is offered to us, the substitute for war, the substitute for turmoil, the substitute for sorrow and despair. That substitute is offered in the Covenant of the League of Nations. America alone cannot underwrite civilization. All the great free peoples of the world must underwrite it, and only the free peoples of the world can join the League of Nations. The membership is open only to self-governing nations. Germany is for the present excluded, because she must prove that she is self-governing; she must prove that she has changed the processes of her constitution and the purposes of her policy; but when she has proved these things she can become one of the partners in guaranteeing that civilization shall not suffer again the intolerable thing she attempted. It is not only a union of free peoples to guarantee civilization; it is something more than that. It is a League of Nations to advance civilization by substituting something that will make the improvement of civilization possible.

I call you to witness, my fellow citizens, that our present civilization is not satisfactory. It is an industrial civilization, and at the heart of it is an antagonism between those who labor with their hands and those who direct labor. You cannot compose those differences in the midst of war, and you cannot advance civilization unless you have a peace of which you make the peaceful and healing use of bringing these elements of civilization together into a common partnership, in which every man will have the same interest in the work of his community that those have who direct the work of the community. We have got to have leisure and freedom of mind to settle these things. This was a war against autocracy; and if you have disorder, if you have disquieted populations, if you have insurgent elements in your population, you are going to have autocracy, because the strongest is going to seize the power, as it has seized it in Russia. I want to declare that I am an enemy of the rulership of any minority, however constituted. Minorities have often been right and majorities wrong, but minorities cease to be right when they use the wrong means to make their opinions prevail. We must have peaceful means; we must have discussion—we must have frank discussion, we must have friendly discussion—and those are the very things that are offered to us among the nations of the world by the Covenant of the League of Nations.

I cannot too often remind my fellow citizens of what the real heart and center of that Covenant is. It lies in the provisions by which every member of the League —and, mind you, that means every great nation in the world, except, for the time being, Germany—solemnly engages never to go to war without first having either submitted the subject to arbitration—in which case it agrees to abide absolutely by the verdict—or submitted it for discussion to the council of the League of Nations, laying all the documents, all the facts, before that council; consenting that the council shall publish all the facts, so as to take the world into its confidence for the formation of a correct judgment concerning it; it agrees that it will allow six months for the deliberation of the council upon the facts, and that, after those deliberations are concluded, if the advice of the council is not acceptable, it will still not go to war for three months after the rendering of that opinion. In other words, we have the pledge of all the nations of the world that they will sit down and talk everything over that is apt to make trouble amongst them, and that they will talk it over in public, so that the whole illuminating process of public knowledge and public discussion may penetrate every part of the conference. I believe, for my part, that that is a 99 per cent insurance against war. I take it you want some insurance against war rather than none, and if it is not 99 per cent, I dare say you would like 10 per cent. You would like some insurance rather than none at all, and the experience of the world demonstrates that this is an almost complete insurance.

My fellow citizens, imagine what would have happened if there had been a league of nations in 1914. What did happen was this: Some time after the Crown Prince of Austria had been assassinated in Serbia, after the world had begun to forget even so tragical an incident, the Austrian Government was prompted by the Government at Berlin to make that the occasion for war. Their thought was, "We are ready. The others are not. Before they can mobilize, before they can bring this matter even under discussion, we will be at their gates. Belgium cannot resist. We have promised, solemnly promised, not to cross her territories, but promises are scraps of paper. We will get across her territories into France before France can mobilize. We will make that assassination a pretext." They therefore made unconscionable demands of Serbia, and, notwithstanding the fact that Serbia, with her sense of helplessness, practically yielded to all those demands, they would not even tell the world that she had yielded; they went on with the war. In the meantime every foreign office was telegraphing to its representative at Berlin, begging that there might be an international conference to see if a settlement could not be effected, and Germany did not dare sit down in conference. It is the common judgment of every statesman I met on the other side of the water that if this thing had been delayed and discussed, not six months, but six days, it never could have happened.

Here we have all the Governments of the world agreeing to discuss anything that is likely to bring about war, because, after that famous Article X there is an Article XI—there are twenty-six articles altogether, although you are not told about any of them except Article X—and Article XI says that it shall be the friendly right of any member of the League, big or little, to bring to the attention of the League—and, therefore, to the attention of the world—anything, anywhere, which is likely to disturb the peace of the world or to disturb the good understanding between nations upon which the peace of the world depends. Wherever there are oppressed nations, wherever there are suffering populations, wherever there is a smoldering flame, the trouble can be uncovered and brought to the bar of mankind, and the whole influence of public opinion the world over will be brought to bear upon it. It is the greatest process of international conference and of international discussion ever conceived, and that is what we are trying to substitute for war. That is what we must substitute for war.

Then, not in immediate connection with the League of Nations Covenant but in a later part of the treaty, there is what I have ventured to call the Magna Charta of labor. There is the provision for the constant regular international discussion of labor problems, no matter where they arise in the world, for the purpose of lifting the whole level of labor conditions; for the purpose of safeguarding the health of women and of children, for the sake of bringing about those international comities with regard to labor upon which the happiness of mankind so much depends. There is a heart in the midst of the treaty. It is not only made by prudent men but it is made by men with hearts under their jackets. I have seen the light of this thing in the eyes of some men whom the world deemed cynical. I have seen men over there, whose emotions are not often touched, with suffused eyes when they spoke of the purposes of this conference, because they realized that, for the first time in the history of mankind, statesmen had got together, not in order to lay plans for the aggrandizement of governments but in order to lay plans for the liberation of peoples; and what I want everybody in every American audience to understand is this: The first effective impulse toward this sort of thing came from America, and I want to call your attention to the fact that it came from some of the very men who are now opposing its consummation. They dreamed the dream that has now been realized. They saw the vision twenty, twenty-five, thirty years ago which all mankind are now permitted to see. It is of particular importance to remember, my fellow citizens, at this moment when some men have dared to introduce party passion into this question, that some of the leading spirits, perhaps I may say the leading spirits, in the conception of this great idea were the leading figures of the great Republican Party. I do not like to mention parties in this discussion. I hope that there is not a real thoughtful, conscientious person in the United States who will determine his or her opinion about this matter with any thought that there is an election in the year 1920. And, just because I want you to realize how absolutely nonpartisan this thing is, I want you to forget, if you please, that I had anything to do with it. I had the great privilege of being the spokesman of this splendid Nation at this critical period in her history, but I was her spokesman, not my own, and when I advocated the things that are in this League of Nations I had the full and proud consciousness that I was only expressing the best thought and the best conscience of my beloved fellow countrymen. The only things that I have any special personal connection with in the League of Nations Covenant are things that I was careful to have put in there because of the very considerations which are now being urged. I brought the first draft of the Covenant of the League of Nations over to this country in March last. I then held a conference of the frankest sort with the Foreign Relations Committee of the Senate. They made a number of suggestions as to alterations and additions. I then took all of those suggestions back to Paris, and every one of them, without exception, was embodied in the Covenant. I had one or two hard fights to get them in.

You are told, my fellow citizens—it is amazing that anybody should say it—that the Covenant does not satisfactorily recognize the Monroe Doctrine. It says in so many words that nothing in that Covenant shall be construed as impairing the validity of the Monroe Doctrine. The point is that up to that conference there was not a nation in the world that could be induced to give official recognition to the Monroe Doctrine, and here in this great turn of the tides of the world all the great nations of the world are united in recognizing the Monroe Doctrine. It not only is not impaired, but it has the backing of the world. And at every point where suggestions were made they were accepted; and the suggestions came for the most part from the Republican side of the committee. I say that because I am particularly interested, my fellow citizens, to have you realize that there is no politics in this business, except that profoundly important politics, the politics of civilization. I have the honor to-day of speaking under a chairman who, I understand, is a member of the Republican party, and every meeting that I have spoken at on this trip, so far as I remember, has been presided over by a Republican. I am saying these things merely because I want to read the riot act to anybody who tries to introduce politics.

Some very interesting things happened while we were on the other side of the water. One of the most distinguished lawyers in the United States, Mr. Wickersham, of New York, who was the Attorney General in Mr. Taft's Cabinet, came over to Europe, I am told—

I did not see him while he was over there—to oppose the things that he understood the American peace commission was trying to accomplish, and what happened to Mr. Wickersham? He was absolutely converted, above all things else, to the necessity for a league of nations not only, but for this League of Nations. He came back to the United States and has ever since, in season and out of season, been preaching in public advocacy of the adoption of this Covenant. I need not tell you of the conspicuously fine work which his chief, Mr. Taft, has been doing in the same cause. I am very proud, my fellow citizens, to be associated with these gentlemen. I am very proud to forget party lines, because there is one thing that is so much greater than being a Republican or a Democrat that those names ought never to be mentioned in connection with, and that is being an American. There is only one way to be an American, and that is to fulfill the pledges that we gave the world at our birth, that we have given the world at every turn in our history, and that we have just now sealed with the blood of some of our best young men.

Ah, my fellow citizens, do not forget the aching hearts that are behind discussions like this. Do not forget the forlorn homes from which those boys went and to which they never came back. I have it in my heart that if we do not do this great thing now, every woman ought to weep because of the child in her arms. If she has a boy at her breast, she may be sure that when he comes to manhood this terrible task will have to be done once more. Everywhere we go, the train when it stops is surrounded with little children, and I look at them almost with tears in my eyes, because I feel my mission is to save them. These glad youngsters with flags in their hands—I pray God that they may never have to carry that flag upon the battlefield!

There have been, if I may make a slight digression, some very amusing incidents on this journey. At Billings a number of boys were chasing the train as it pulled slowly out with flags and yelling all sorts of pleasant things to their friend "Woody." On this occasion one youngster in his enthusiasm insisted that I should take his flag and he handed it up to me. The boy next to him did not have a flag and he looked a good deal disconcerted for a moment, but then he put his hand in his pocket and said, "Here, I will give you a dime." I would like to believe that that dime has some relation to the widow's mite—others gave something; he gave all that he had. After all, though that is merely a passing incident, it is illustrative of the spirit of this country, my fellow citizens. There is something in this country that is not anywhere else in the world. There is a confident looking forward to better times. There is a confidence that we can work out the most difficult problems. There is none of that heavy leaden discouragement that rests upon some other countries. Have you never crossed the sea in times of peace and noticed the immigrants who were going back to visit their folks, and then, on the return voyage, the immigrants who were coming in for the first time—the extraordinary contrast in the appearance of the two groups? The group going out, having felt the atmosphere of America, their faces bright, a sort of a sense of initiative about it, having been freed to be men and individuals; and those coming back, bearing all sorts of queer bundles, looking a bit anxious, just a little doubtful of the hope with which they are looking forward to the new country. It is the alchemy, the miracle of America, and it is the only country in the world, so far as my observation goes, where that miracle is wrought, and the rest of the world knows that. The rest of the world implores America's aid—not her material aid; they are not looking for our dollars; they are not looking for our guns. They are saying, "Show us the road that led you out of the wilderness and made you great, for we are seeking that road." Now that the great treaty of peace has established the oppressed peoples of the world who were affected by this treaty on their own territory, given them their own freedom, given them command of their own affairs, they are looking to America to show them how to use that new liberty and that new power.

When I was at that wonderful stadium of yours a few minutes ago, a little child, a little girl in white, came and presented me with some kind of a paper—I have not had time to read it yet—from the Poles. I dare say that it is of the sort that I have received a great many of—just an expression of a sort of childlike and pitiful thanks that America assisted to free Poland. Poland never could have freed herself. We not only tore Germany's hands away from where she meant to make ravage of the rights of the others, but we took those old peoples who had been under her power before and said, "You could not free yourselves, but we believe in liberty. Here is your own land to do with as you please." I wish that some of the men who are opposing this treaty could get the vision in their hearts of all it has done. It has liberated great populations. It has set up the standards of right and of liberty for the first time, where they were never unfurled before, and then has placed back of them this splendid power of the nations combined. For without the League of Nations the whole thing is a house of cards. Just a breath of power will blow it down. Whereas with the League of Nations it is as strong as Gibraltar. Let them catch this vision; let them take in this conception; let them take counsel of weeping mothers; let them take counsel of bereaved fathers who used to have their sons at their sides and are now alone; let them take counsel of the lonely farms where there used to be a boy to help the old man and now he cannot even get a hired man to help him, and yet he is trying to feed the world; let them realize that the world is hungry, that the world is naked, that the world is suffering, and that none of these things can be remedied until the minds of men are reassured. That is the fundamental fact, my fellow citizens.

If I wanted to have a joint debate with some man who wanted to put our part in this business down on the lowest possible level of how much money we were going to make out of it, I could silence him by showing that so long as the world is not reassured its industries will not begin again, that unless its industries begin again there will be nothing to pay for anything with, that unless its industries begin again there will be no market for the goods of America, and that we will have to rest content with our domestic markets at the very time when we had enlarged our enterprises in order to make peaceful conquest of the world. The very processes of war have driven our industries to a point of expansion where they will be chilled and ruined if they do not presently get a foreign outlet. Therefore, on the lowest basis, you have got to guarantee and underwrite civilization or you have ruined the United States. But I do not like to talk about that side of it. I believe in my heart that there is hardly a man in America, if you get really back of his superficial thoughts, who is not man enough to be willing to make the sacrifice to underwrite civilization. It is only sacrifice that tells. Don't you remember what we used to cry during the Liberty loans, "Lend until it hurts. Give until it hurts." When I heard, in some Western States, that people drew their savings out of banks that were giving them 4 per cent on the savings and invested them in the first Liberty loan that was to yield them 3½ per cent, I said to myself, "That is America." They were helping the Government at a sacrifice. They were not thinking of dollars. They were thinking of the dignity and might and majesty and destiny of the United States, and it is only that vision, my fellow citizens, that will ever lift us out of the slough in which men now are wading.

It is a pitiful spectacle that the great bodies of our
fellow citizens should be arrayed against each other.
One of the most startling things that I ever realized
was, months and months ago, when I was trying to
moderate and assist in settling some of the difficulties
between the railroads and their employees. I asked the
representatives of the railway brotherhoods to come to
the White House, and I asked the presidents of the
great railway systems to come to the White House,
and I found that each side had a profound suspicion of
the other, that the railway presidents were not willing
to trust what their men said and the men were not willing to trust what the railway presidents said. When I
took over the railroads in the name of the Government,
I said to a group of fine-spirited men, a group of railway presidents, who were trying to unify the administration of the railroads for the purposes of the war—
I said, smilingly, but with a little sadness, "Well, at
any rate, gentlemen, these men will trust me, and they
do not trust you." I did not say it with pride; I said
it with sorrow. I did not know whether I could justify
their trust or not, but I did know that I was willing
to talk things over with them whenever anything was
the matter, and that if we were equally intelligent and
equally conscientious we could get together whenever
anything went wrong. I could not help suspecting that
this distrust, this mutual distrust, was the wedge that
was being driven into society, and society cannot live
with a great wedge at the heart of it. Society cannot
get on industrially or socially with any such wedge
driven into its heart. We must see that the processes
of peace, the processes of discussion, the processes of
fairness, the processes of equity, the processes of sympathy penetrate all our affairs. I have never known
anybody who had a good cause who was unwilling to
discuss it. Whenever I find a man standing out stiffly
against consulting with the other side, I know his case

is bad. The only unconquerable thing in the world is the truth, and a man who has the truth on his side need not be afraid of anybody. You know what witty and eloquent old Dr. Oliver Wendell Holmes once said. He said, "You needn't fear to handle the truth roughly; she is no invalid." The truth is the most robust and indestructible and formidable thing in the world. There is a very amusing story of a distinguished lawyer at Charleston, S. C., of a very much older generation than ours, who was followed out of the court one day after losing a civil suit by his client, who abused him. He called him a thief and a liar and everything that was disagreeable, and Mr. Peddigrew paid not the slightest attention to him, until he called him a Federalist, and then he knocked him down. A friend said to him, "Why, Mr. Peddigrew; why did you knock him down for that? That was the least offensive thing he said." "Yes, damn him," Peddigrew said, "but it was the only true thing he said."

Now, the nations of the world have declared that they are not afraid of the truth; that they are willing to have all their affairs that are likely to lead to international complications brought into the open. One of the things that this treaty incidentally does is absolutely to invalidate all secret treaties. Everything is to be open. Everything is to be upon the table around which sit the representatives of all the world, to be looked at from the point of view of everybody—the Asiatic, the African, the American, the European. That is the promise of the future; that is the security of the future. I hope that no attempts will be made to qualify or embarrass the great process which is inevitable, and I confidently predict that some day we shall look back with surprise upon the fact that men in America, above all places, should ever have hesitated to do this great thing.

It has been a privilege, my fellow citizens, to make

this simple presentation of a great theme to you, and I am happy in carrying away with me recollections of the generous response you have made to a plea which I can only characterize as a plea which has come from the heart of a true American.

AT HIPPODROME, SEATTLE, WASH., SEPTEMBER 13, 1919.

MR. SPANGLER, LADIES AND GENTLEMEN:

It was agreed that I should make no address on this occasion, and I am not going to inflict upon you anything that can bear so dignified a name; but when Mr. Spangler asked me if I would extend a word of greeting to you I at once thought of the wonderful greeting that you and your fellow citizens have extended to me, and it would indeed be ungracious if I did not say how much I have appreciated your welcome and how delightful it is to be associated with you even for a few hours in this great city of Seattle.

I have been in Seattle before, when I attracted less attention. I admired the city then, as I admire it still, and I could see it better then than I have seen it to-day. To-day I had too much of an escort to be really able to see the new features of the city with which I was not familiar. I was reminded of some of our experiences on the other side of the water, when we had to be careful not to let anybody know we were coming to a particular place for fear we would be escorted by so many persons that we would not see the place; and I have found in Washington that I am not to see the interesting things in Washington until my term is over, because all the officials in public buildings feel it necessary to escort me all over the buildings, and I either see the things that I did not care to see, because they insist upon it, or I see nothing.

But, jesting aside, my fellow citizens, it was very delightful to see so many friendly faces on these beautiful streets. What I liked about it was not so much the cheers as the facial expressions that accompanied the cheers. They made me feel really welcome, and I could only fancy and hope that it was the reflection in their faces of the way I felt toward them. I suppose that a man in public life must renew himself constantly by direct contact with his fellow citizens, get the feel of the great power of opinion and of sentiment in this country, and nothing else heartened me so much as I have crossed the continent as to feel the uniformity of impulse and sentiment from one ocean to the other. There is no essential division in the thought or purpose of the American people, and the interesting thing to me is their steadiness. No amount of debate will set them off their balance in their thinking, because their thinking is based upon fundamental impulses of right, and what they want to know is not the difficulties, but the duties ahead of them, and if you point the duties out to them they have a contempt for the difficulties. It is that consciousness which I have so often gained in moving from one part of this beloved country to another that makes me so profoundly proud to be an American. It was not, indeed, my choice to be an American, because I was born here, and I suppose that I cannot ascribe any credit to myself for being an American; but I do claim the profoundest pleasure in sharing the sentiments and in having had the privilege for a few short years of trying to express the sentiments of this free Nation, to which all the world looks for inspiration and leadership.

That is the dominating thought that I have. I will not say the dominating thought; it is the controlling knowledge that I have, for I learned to know on the other side of the water that all the world was looking to us for inspiration and leadership, and we will not deny it to them.

Mr. Chairman, my fellow countrymen:

I esteem it a privilege to have the occasion to stand before this great audience and expound some part of the great question that is now holding the attention of America and the attention of the world. I was led to an unpleasant consciousness to-day of the way in which the debate that is going on in America has attracted the attention of the world. I read in to-day's papers the comments of one of the men who were recently connected with the Imperial Government of Germany. He said that some aspects of this debate seemed to him like the red that precedes a great dawn. He saw in it the rise of a certain renewed sympathy with Germany. He saw in it an opportunity to separate America from the Governments and peoples with whom she had been associated in the war against German aggression. And all over this country, my fellow citizens, it is becoming more and more evident that those who were the partisans of Germany are the ones who are principally pleased by some of the aspects of the debate that is now going on. The world outside of America is asking itself the question, "Is America going to stand by us now, or is it at this moment of final crisis going to draw apart and desert us?" I can answer that question here and now. It is not going to draw apart and it is not going to desert the nations of the world. America responds to nothing so quickly or unanimously as a great moral challenge. It is much more ready to carry through what now lies before it than it was even to carry through what was before it when we took up arms in behalf of the freedom of the world. America is unaccustomed to military tasks, but America is accustomed to fulfilling its pledges and following its visions. The only thing that causes me uneasiness, my fellow countrymen, is not the ultimate outcome, but the impressions that may be created in the meantime by the perplexed delay. The rest of the world believed absolutely in America and was ready to follow it anywhere, and it is now a little chilled. It now asks, "Is America hesitating to lead? We are ready to give ourselves to her leadership. Why will she not accept the gift?"

My fellow citizens, I think that it is my duty, as I go about the country, not to make speeches in the ordinary acceptance of that word, not to appeal either to the imagination or to the emotion of my fellow citizens, but to undertake everywhere what I want to undertake to-night, and I must ask you to be patient while I undertake it. I want to analyze for you what it is that it is proposed we should do. Generalities will not penetrate to the heart of this great question. It is not enough to speak of the general purposes of the peace. I want you to realize just what the Covenant of the League of Nations means. I find that everywhere I go it is desirable that I should dwell upon this great theme, because in so many parts of the country men are drawing attention to little details in a way that destroys the whole perspective of the great plan in a way that concentrates attention upon certain particulars which are incidental and not central. I am going to take the liberty of reading you a list of the things which the nations adhering to the Covenant of the League of Nations undertake. I want to say by way of preface that it seems to me, and I am sure it will seem to you, not only an extraordinarily impressive list, but a list which was never proposed for the counsels of the world before.

In the first place, every nation that joins the League, and that in prospect means every great fighting nation in the world, agrees to submit all controversies which are likely to lead to war either to arbitration or to thorough discussion by an authoritative body, the council of the League of Nations. These great nations,

all the most ambitious nations in the world except
Germany, all the most powerful nations in the world,
as well as the weak ones—all the nations that we have
supposed had imperialistic designs—say that they will
do either one or other of two things in case a controversy arises which cannot be settled by ordinary
diplomatic correspondence: They will either frankly
submit it to arbitration and absolutely abide by the
arbitral verdict or they will submit all the facts, all
the documents, to the council of the League of Nations,
will give the council six months in which to discuss the
whole matter and leave to publish the whole matter,
and at the end of the six months will still refrain for
three months more from going to war, whether they
like the opinion of the council or not. In other words,
they agree to do a thing which would have made the
recent war with Germany absolutely impossible. If
there had been a League of Nations in 1914, whether
Germany belonged to it or not, Germany never would
have dared to attempt the aggression which she did
attempt, because she would have been called to the bar
of the opinion of mankind and would have known that
if she did not satisfy that opinion mankind would
unite against her. You had only to expose the German
case to public discussion and make it certain that the
German case would fall, Germany not dare attempt to
act upon it. It was the universal opinion on the other
side of the water when I was over there that if Germany had thought that England would be added to
France and Russia she never would have gone in,
and if she had dreamed that America would throw
her mighty weight into the scale it would have been
inconceivable. The only thing that reassured the de-
luded German people after we entered the war was the
lying statement of her public men that we could not
get our troops across the sea, because Germany knew if
America got within striking distance the story was done.
Here all the nations of the world, except Germany,

for the time being at any rate, give notice that they will unite against any nation that has a bad case, and they agree that in their own case they will submit to prolonged discussion.

There is nothing so chilling as discussion to a hot temper. If you are fighting mad and yet I can induce you to talk it over for half an hour, you will not be fighting mad at the end of the half hour. I knew a very wise schoolmaster in North Carolina who said that if any boy in that school fought another, except according to the rules, he would be expelled. There would not be any great investigation; the fact that he had fought would be enough; he would go home; but if he was so mad that he had to fight, all he had to do was to come to the head master and tell him that he wanted to fight. The head master would arrange the ring, would see that the fight was conducted according to the Marquis of Queensberry rules, that an umpire and a referee were appointed, and that the thing was fought to a finish. The consequence was that there were no fights in that school. The whole arrangement was too cold-blooded. By the time all the arrangements had been made all the fighting audacity had gone out of the contestants. That little thing illustrates a great thing. Discussion is destructive when wrong is intended; and all the nations of the world agree to put their case before the judgment of mankind. Why, my fellow citizens, that has been the dream of thoughtful reformers for generation after generation. Somebody seems to have conceived the notion that I originated the idea of a league of nations. I wish I had. I would be a very proud man if I had; but I did not. I was expressing the avowed aspirations of the American people, avowed by nobody so loudly, so intelligently, or so constantly as the greater leaders of the Republican party. When Republicans take that road, I take off my hat and follow; I do not care whether I lead or

not. I want the great result which I know is at the
heart of the people that I am trying to serve.

In the second place, all these great nations agree to
boycott any nation that does not submit a perilous question either to arbitration or to discussion, and to support each other in the boycott. There is no "if" or
"but" about that in the Covenant. It is agreed that
just as soon as that member State, or any outside State,
for that matter, refuses to submit its case to the public
opinion of the world its doors will be closed and
locked; that nobody shall trade with it, no telegraphic
message shall leave it or enter it, no letter shall cross
its borders either way; there shall be no transactions
of any kind between the citizens of the members of the
league and the covenant-breaking State. That is the
remedy that thoughtful men have advocated for several
generations. They have thought, and thought truly,
that war was barbarous and that a nation that resorted
to war when its cause was unjust was unworthy of
being consorted with by free people anywhere. The
boycott is an infinitely more terrible instrument of
war. Excepting our own singularly fortunate country,
I cannot think of any other country that can live upon
its own resources. The minute you lock the door, then
the pinch of the thing becomes intolerable; not only
the physical pinch, not only the fact that you cannot
get raw materials and must stop your factories, not
only the fact that you cannot get food and your people
must begin to starve, not only the fact that your credit
is stopped, that your assets are useless, but the still
greater pinch that comes when a nation knows that it
is sent to coventry and despised. To be put in jail
is not the most terrible punishment that happens to
a condemned man; if he knows that he was justly condemned, what penetrates his heart is the look in
other men's eyes. It is the soul that is wounded much
more poignantly than the body, and one of the things
that the German nation has not been able to compre-

hend is that it has lost for the time being the respect of mankind; and as Germans, when the doors of truth were opened to them after the war, have begun to realize that they have begun to look aghast at the probable fortunes of Germany, for if the world does not trust them, if the world does not respect them, if the world does not want Germans to come as immigrants any more, what is Germany to do? Germany's worst punishment, my fellow citizens, is not in the treaty; it is in her relations with the rest of mankind for the next generation. The boycott is what is substituted for war.

In the third place, all the members of this great association pledge themselves to respect and preserve as against external aggression the territorial integrity and existing political independence of the other member States. That is the famous Article X that you hear so much about; and Article X, my fellow citizens, whether you want to assume the responsibility of it or not, is the heart of the pledge that we have made to the other nations of the world. Only by that article can we be said to have underwritten civilization. The wars that threaten mankind begin by that kind of aggression. For every other nation than Germany, in 1914, treaties stood as solemn and respected covenants. For Germany they were scraps of paper, and when her first soldier's foot fell upon the soil of Belgium her honor was forfeited. That act of aggression, that failure to respect the territorial integrity of a nation whose territory she was especially bound to respect, pointed the hand along that road that is strewn with graves since the beginning of history, that road made red and ugly with the strife of men, the strife behind which lies savage cupidity, the strife behind which lies a disregard for the rights of others and a thought concentrated upon what you want and mean to get. That is the heart of war, and unless you accept Article X you do not cut the heart of war out of civilization.

Belgium did not hesitate to underwrite civilization. Belgium could have had safety on her own terms if only she had not resisted the German arms—little Belgium, helpless Belgium, ravaged Belgium. Ah, my fellow citizens, I have seen some of the fields of Belgium. I rode with her fine, democratic king over some of those fields. He would say to me, "This is the village of so and so," and there was no village there, just scattered stones all over the plain, and the plain dug deep every few feet with the holes made by exploding shells. You could not tell whether it was the earth thrown up or the house thrown down that made the débris which covered the desert made by the war. Then we rode farther in, farther to the east, where there had been no fighting, no active campaigning, and there we saw beautiful green slopes and fields that had once been cultivated, and towns with their factories standing, but standing empty; not empty of workers merely, empty of machinery. Every piece of machinery in Belgium that they could put on freight cars the Germans had taken away, and what they could not carry with them they had destroyed, under the devilishly intelligent direction of experts—great bodies of heavy machinery that never could be used again, because somebody had known where the heart of the machine lay and where to put the dynamite. The Belgians are there, their buildings are there, but nothing to work with, nothing to start life with again; and in the face of all that Belgium did not flinch for a moment to underwrite the interests of mankind by saying to Germany, "We will not be bought."

Italy could have had more by compounding with Austria in the later stages of the war than she is going to get out of the peace settlement now, but she would not compound. She also was a trustee for civilization, and she would not sell the birthright of mankind for any sort of material advantage. She underwrote civilization. And Serbia, the first of the helpless nations to be struck down, her armies driven from her own soil, maintained her armies on other soil, and the armies of Serbia were never dispersed. Whether they could be on their own soil or not, they were fighting for their rights and through their rights for the rights of civilized man.

I believe that America is going to be more willing than any other nation in the world, when it gets its voice heard, to do the same thing that these little nations did. Why, my fellow citizens, we have been talking constantly about the rights of little nations. There is only one way to maintain the rights of little nations, and that is by the strength of great nations. Having begun this great task, we are no quitters; we are going to see the thing through. The red that this German counsellor of state saw upon the horizon was not the red of any dawn that will reassure the people who attempted the wrong that Germany did. It was the first red glare of the fire that is going to consume the wrong in the world. As that moral fire comes creeping on, it is going to purify every field of blood upon which free men sacrificed their lives; it is going to redeem France, redeem Belgium, redeem devastated Serbia, redeem the fair lands in the north of Italy, and set men on their feet again, to look fate in the face and have again that hope which is the only thing that leads men forward.

In the next place, every nation agrees to join in advising what shall be done in case any one of the members fails to keep that promise. There is where you have been misled, my fellow citizens. You have been led to believe that the council of the League of Nations could say to the Congress of the United States, "Here is a war, and here is where you come in." Nothing of the sort is true. The council of the League of Nations is to advise what is to be done, and I have not been able to find in the dictionary any meaning of the word "advise," except "to advise." But let us suppose that it means something else; let us suppose that there is some legal compulsion behind the advice. The advice cannot be given except by an unanimous vote of the council and an affirmative vote of the United States. We will be a permanent member of the council of the League of Nations, and no such advice is ever going to be given unless the United States votes "aye," with one exception. If we are parties to the dispute, we cannot vote; but, my fellow citizens, let me remind you that if we are parties to the dispute, we are in the war anyhow, so that we are not forced into war by the vote of the council, we are forced into war by our quarrel with the other party, as we would be in any case. There is no sacrifice in the slightest degree of the independent choice of the Congress of the United States whether it will declare war or not. There is a peculiar impression on the part of some persons in this country that the United States is more jealous of its sovereignty than other countries. That provision was not put in there because it was necessary to safeguard the sovereignty of the United States. All the other nations wanted it, and they were just as keen for their veto as we were keen for our veto. There is not the slightest danger that they will misunderstand that article of the covenant. There is only a danger that some of us who are too credulous will be led to misunderstand it.

All the nations agree to join in devising a plan for general disarmament. You have heard that this Covenant was a plan for bringing on war. Well, it is going to bring on war by means of disarmament and also by establishing a permanent court of international justice. When I voted for that, I was obeying the mandate of the Congress of the United States. In a very unexpected place, namely, in a naval appropriation bill passed in 1915, it was declared to be the policy of the United States to bring about a general disarmament by common agreement, and the President of the United States was requested to call a conference not later than the close of the then present war for the purpose of consulting and agreeing upon a plan for a permanent court of international justice; and he was authorized, in case such an agreement could be reached, to stop the building program provided for by that naval appropriation bill. The Congress of the United States deliberately not only accepted but directed the President to promote an agreement of this sort for disarmament and a permanent court of international justice. You know what a permanent court of international justice implies. You cannot set up a court without respecting its decrees. You cannot make a toy of it. You cannot make a mockery of it. If you, indeed, want a court, then you must abide by the judgments of the court. And we have declared already that we are willing to abide by the judgments of a court of international justice.

All the nations agree to register every treaty, and they agree that no treaty that is not registered and published shall be valid. All private agreements and secret treaties are swept from the table, and thereby one of the most dangerous instruments of international intrigue and disturbance is abolished.

They agree to join in the supervision of the government of helpless and dependent people. They agree that no nation shall hereafter have the right to annex any territory merely because the people that live on it cannot prevent it, and that instead of annexation there shall be trusteeship, under which these territories shall be administered under the supervision of the associated nations of the world. They lay down rules for the protection of dependent peoples of that sort, so that they shall not have enforced labor put upon them, so that their women and children shall be protected from unwholesome and destructive forms of labor, so that they will be kept away from the opium traffic and the traffic in arms. They agree that they will never levy armies there. They agree, in other words, to do what no nation ever agreed to do before, to treat subject nations like human beings.

They agree also to accord and maintain fair and humane conditions of labor for men, women, and children born in their own countries and in all other countries to which their commercial and industrial relations extend, and for that purpose they agree to join in establishing and maintaining the necessary international organization. This great treaty, which we are hesitating to ratify, contains the organization by which the united counsels of mankind shall attempt to lift the levels of labor and see that men who are working with their hands are everywhere treated as they ought to be treated, upon principles of justice and equality. How many laboring men dreamed, when this war began, that four years later it would be possible for all the great nations of the world to enter into a covenant like that? They agree to intrust the League with the general supervision of all international agreements with regard to traffic in women and children and traffic in opium and other dangerous drugs. They agree to intrust the League with the general supervision of the trade in arms and ammunition with the countries in which the control of this traffic is necessary in the common interest. They agree to join in making provision to secure and maintain freedom of communication and of transit and equitable treatment for commerce in respect of all the members of the League. They agree to coöperate in the endeavor to take steps for the prevention and control of disease. They agree to encourage and promote the establishment and coöperation of duly authorized voluntary national Red Cross organizations for the improvement of health, the prevention of disease, and the mitigation of suffering throughout the world.

I ask you, my fellow citizens, is that not a great peace document and a great human document? And is it conceivable that America, the most progressive and humane nation in the world, should refuse to take the same responsibility upon herself that all the other great nations take in supporting this great Covenant? You say, "It is not likely that the treaty will be rejected. It is only likely that there will be certain reservations." Very well, I want very frankly to tell you what I think about that. If the reservations do not change the treaty, then it is not necessary to make them part of the resolution of ratification. If all that you desire is to say what you understand the treaty to mean, no harm can be done by saying it; but if you want to change the treaty, if you want to alter the phraseology so that the meaning is altered, if you want to put in reservations which give the United States a position of special privilege or a special exemption from responsibility among the members of the League, then it will be necessary to take the treaty back to the conference table, and, my fellow citizens, the world is not in a temper to discuss this treaty over again. The world is just now more profoundly disturbed about social and economic conditions than it ever was before, and the world demands that we shall come to some sort of settlement which will let us get down to business and purify and rectify our own affairs. This is not only the best treaty that can be obtained, but I want to say, because I played only a small part in framing it, that it is a sound and good treaty, and America, above all nations, should not be the nation that puts obstacles in the way of the peace of nations and the peace of mind of the world.

The world has not anywhere at this moment, my fellow citizens, peace of mind. Nothing has struck me so much in recent months as the unaccustomed anxiety on the face of people. I am aware that men do not know what is going to happen, and that they know that it is just as important to them what happens in the rest of the world, almost, as what happens in America. America has connections with all the rest of the world not only, but she has necessary dealings

with all the rest of the world, and no man is fatuous
enough to suppose that if the rest of the world is disturbed and disordered, the disturbance and disorder
are not going to extend to the United States. The
center of our anxiety, my fellow citizens, is in that pitiful country to which our hearts go out, that great mass
of mankind whom we call the Russians. I have never
had the good fortune to be in Russia, but I know many
persons who know that lovable people intimately, and
they all tell me that there is not a people in the world
more generous, more simple, more kindly, more
naturally addicted to friendship, more patiently attached to peace than the Russian people. Yet, after
throwing off the grip of terror that an autocratic power
of the Czar had upon them, they have come under a
terror even greater than that; they have come under the
terror of the power of men whom nobody knows how
to find. One or two names everybody knows, but the
rest is intrigue, terror, informing, spying, and military
power, the seizure of all the food obtainable in order
that the fighting men may be fed and the rest go
starved. These men have been appealed to again and
again by the civilized Governments of the world to call
a constituent assembly, let the Russian people say what
sort of government they want to have; and they will
not, they dare not, do it. That picture is before the
eyes of every nation. Shall we get into the clutch of
another sort of minority? My fellow citizens, I am
going to devote every influence I have and all the
authority I have from this time on to see to it that no
minority commands the United States. [Great and
continued applause.] It heartens me, but it does not
surprise me, to know that that is the verdict of every
man and woman here; but, my fellow citizens, there is
no use passing that verdict unless we are going to take
part, and a great part, a leading part, in steadying the
counsels of the world. Not that we are afraid of anything except the spread of moral defection, and moral

defection cannot come except where men have lost faith, lost hope, have lost confidence; and, having seen the attitude of the other peoples of the world toward America, I know that the whole world will lose heart unless America consents to show the way.

It was pitiful, on the other side of the sea, to have delegation after delegation from peoples all over the world come to the house I was living in in Paris and seek conference with me to beg that America would show the way. It was touching. It made me very proud, but it made me very sad; proud that I was the representative of a nation so regarded, but very sad to feel how little of all the things that they had dreamed we could accomplish for them. But we can accomplish this, my fellow citizens: We can, having taken a pledge to be faithful to them, redeem the pledge. We shall redeem the pledge. I look forward to the day when all this debate will seem in our recollection like a strange mist that came over the minds of men here and there in the Nation, like a groping in the fog, having lost the way, the plain way, the beaten way, that America had made for itself for generations together; and we shall then know that of a sudden, upon the assertion of the real spirit of the American people, they came to the edge of the mist, and outside lay the sunny country where every question of duty lay plain and clear and where the great tramp, tramp of the American people sounded in the ears of the whole world, which knew that the armies of God were on their way.

AT LUNCHEON, HOTEL PORTLAND, PORTLAND, OREG., SEPTEMBER 15, 1919.

MR. JACKSON, LADIES AND GENTLEMEN:

As I return to Portland I cannot help remembering that I learned a great deal in Oregon. When I was a teacher I used to prove to my own satisfaction—I do not know whether it was to the satisfaction of my classes or not—that the initiative and referendum would not work. I came to Oregon to find that they did work, and have since been apologizing for my earlier opinion. Because I have always taken this attitude toward facts, that I never let them get me if I see them coming first. There is nothing I respect so much as a fact. There is nothing that is so formidable as a fact, and the real difficulty in all political reform is to know whether you can translate your theories into facts or not, whether you can safely pick out the operative ideas and leave aside the inoperative ideas. For I think you will all agree with me that the whole progress of human affairs is the progress of ideas; not of ideas in the abstract form, but of ideas in the operative form, certain conceptions of justice and of freedom and of right that have got into men's natures and led those natures to insist upon the realization of those ideas in experience and in action.

The whole trouble about our civilization as it looks to me, is that it has grown complex faster than we have adjusted the simpler ideas to the existing conditions. There was a time when men would do in their business what they would not do as individuals. There was a time when they submerged their individual consciences in a corporation and persuaded themselves that it was legitimate for a corporation to do what they individually never would have dreamed of doing. That is what I mean by saying that the organization becomes complex faster than our adjustment of the simpler ideas of justice and right to the developing circumstances of our civilization. I say that because the errand that I am on concerns something that lies at the heart of all progress. I think we are all now convinced that we have not reached the right and final organization of our industrial society; that there are many features of our social life that ought to undergo correction; that while we call ourselves democrats—with a little "d"—while we believe in democratic government, we have not seen

yet the successful way of making our life in fact democratic; that we have allowed classes to disclose themselves; that we have allowed lines of cleavage to be run
through our community, so that there are antagonisms
set up that breed heat, because they breed friction.
The world must have leisure and order in which to see
that these things are set right, and the world cannot
have leisure and order unless it has a guaranteed peace.

For example, if the United States should conceivably
—I think it inconceivable—stay out of the League of
Nations, it would stay out at this cost: We would have
to see, since we were not going to join our force with
other nations, that our force was formidable enough to
be respected by other nations. We would have to maintain a great Army and a great Navy. We would have
to do something more than that: We would have to
concentrate authority sufficiently to be able to use the
physical force of the Nation quickly upon occasion. All
of that is absolutely antidemocratic in its influence. All
of that means that we should not be giving ourselves
the leisure of thought or the release of material resources necessary to work out our own methods of civilization, our own methods of industrial organization
and production and distribution; and our problems are
exactly the problems of the rest of the world. I am
more and more convinced, as I come in contact with the
men who are trying to think for other countries as we
are trying to think for this one, that our problems are
identical, only there is this difference: Peoples of other
countries have lost confidence in their Governments.
Some of them have lost confidence in their form of
government. That point, I hope and believe, has not
been reached in the United States. We have not lost
confidence in our Government. I am not now speaking
of our administration; I am now thinking of our
method of government. We believe that we can manage our own affairs and that we have the machinery
through which we can manage our own affairs, and that

no clique or special interest is powerful enough to run away with it. The other countries of the world also believe that about us. They believe that we are successfully organized for justice, and they therefore want us to take the lead and they want to follow the lead. If we do not take the lead, then we throw them back upon things in which they have no confidence and endanger a universal disorder and discontent in the midst of which it will be impossible to govern our own affairs with success and with constant achievement. Whether you will or not, our fortunes are tied in with the rest of the world, and the choice that we have to make now is whether we will receive the influences of the rest of the world and be affected by them or dominate the influences of the world and lead them. That is a tremendous choice to make, but it is exactly that tremendous choice that we have to make, and I deeply regret the suggestions which are made on some sides that we should take advantage of the present situation in the world but should not shoulder any of the responsibility. Do you know of any business or undertaking in which you can get the advantage without assuming the responsibility? What are you going to be? Boys running around the circus tent and peeping under the canvas? Men declining to pay the admission and sitting on the roof and looking on at the game. Or are you going to play your responsible part in the game, knowing that you are trusted as leader and umpire both?

Nothing has impressed me more, or impressed me more painfully, if I may say so, than the degree in which the rest of the world trusts us and looks to us. I say "painfully" because I am conscious that they are expecting more than we can perform. They are expecting miracles to be wrought by the influence of the American spirit on the affairs of the world, and miracles cannot be wrought. I have again and again recited to my fellow citizens on this journey how deputations from peoples of every kind and every color and every fortune, from all over the world, thronged to the house in which I was living in Paris to ask the guidance and assistance of the United States. They did not send similar delegations to anybody else, and they did not send them to me except because they thought they had heard in what I had been saying the spirit of the American people uttered. Moreover, you must not forget this, that almost all of them had kinsmen in America. You must not forget that America is made up out of all the world and that there is hardly a race of any influence in the world, at any rate hardly a Caucasian race, that has not scores and hundreds, and sometimes millions, of people living in America with whom they are in correspondence, from whom they receive the subtle suggestions of what is going on in American life, and of the ideals of American life. Therefore they feel that they know America from this contact they have had with us, and they want America to be the leading force in the world. Why, I received delegations there speaking tongues that I did not know anything about. I did not know what family of languages they belonged to, but fortunately for me they always brought an interpreter along who could speak Engish, and one of the significant facts was that the interpreter was almost always some young man who had lived in America. He did not talk English to me; he talked American to me. So there always seemed to be a little link of some sort tying them up with us, tying them up with us in fact, in relationship, in blood, as well as in life, and the world will be turned back to cynicism if America goes back on it.

We dare not go back on it. I ask you even as a business proposition whether it is more useful to trade with a cynic or with an optimist. I do not like to trade with a man with a grouch. I do not like to trade with a man who begins by not believing anything I am telling him. I like to trade with a man who is more or less susceptible to the eloquence which I address to him. A salesman has a much longer job if he approaches a grouch than if he approaches a friend. This trivial illustration illustrates, my fellow citizens, our relation to the rest of the world. If we do not do what the rest of the world expects of us, all the rest of the world will have a grouch toward America, and you will find it a hard job to reëstablish your credit in the world. And back of financial credit lies mental credit. There is not a bit of credit that has not got an element of assessment of character. You do not limit your credit to men who can put up the collateral, who have the assets; you extend it also to the men in whose characters and abilities you believe; you think they are going to make good. Your credit is a sort of bet on their capacity, and that is the largest element in the kind of credit that expands enterprise. The credit that merely continues enterprise is based upon asset and past accomplishment, but the credit that expands enterprise is based upon your assessment of character. If you are going to put into the world this germ, I shall call it, of American enterprise and American faith and American vision, then you must be the principal partners in the new partnership which the world is forming.

I take leave to say, without intending the least disrespect to anybody, that, consciously or unconsciously, a man who opposes that proposition either has no imagination or no knowledge, or is a quitter. America has put her hand to this great enterprise already, in the men she sent overseas, and their part was the negative part merely. They were sent over there to see that a malign influence did not interfere with the just fortunes of the world. They stopped that influence, but they did not accomplish anything constructive, and what is the use clearing the table if you are going to put nothing on it? What is the use clearing the ground if you are not going to erect any building? What is the use of going to the pains that we went to, to draw up the specifications of the new building and then saying, "We will have nothing to do with its erection"? For the specifications of this treaty were American specifications, and we have got not only to be the architects, drawing up the specifications, but we have got to be the contractors, too. Isn't it a job worth while? Isn't it worth while, now that the chance has at last come, in the providence of God, that we should demonstrate to the world that America is what she claimed that she was? Every drop of blood that I have in me gets up and shouts when I think of the opportunity that America has.

I come of a race that, being bred on barren hills and unfertile plains in Scotland, being obliged to work where work was hard, somehow has the best zest in what it does when the job is hard, and I was repeating to my friend, Mr. Jackson, what I said the other day about my ancestry and about the implications of it. I come of a certain stock that raised Cain in the northern part of the larger of the British Isles, under the name of the Covenanters. They met in a churchyard—they were church people and they had a convention out of doors—and on the top of a flat tombstone they signed an immortal document called the "solemn league and covenant," which meant that they were going to stand by their religious principles in spite of the Crown of England and the force of England and every other influence, whether of man or the Devil, so long as any of them lived. Now, I have seen men of all nations sit around a table in Paris and sign a solemn league and covenant. The have become Covenanters, and I remain a Covenanter, and I am going to see this job through no matter what influence of evil I must withstand. [Loud applause.] Nothing has heartened me more on this journey than to feel that that really is the judgment of our fellow citizens. America is made up, as I have just said, out of all sorts of elements, but it is a singularly homogeneous people after all; homogeneous in its ideals, not in its blood; homogeneous in the infection which it has caught from a common light; homogeneous in its purpose. Every man has a sort of consciousness that America is put into the world for a purpose that is different in some respects from the purpose conceived by any other national organization.

Throughout America you have got a conducting medium. You do not put forth an American idea and find it halted by this man or that or the other, except he be particularly asleep or cantankerous, but it spreads, it spreads by the natural contact of similar ideas and similar ambitions and similar hopes. For, my fellow citizens, the only thing that lifts the world is hope. The only thing that can save the world is such arrangements as will convince the world that hope is not altogether without foundation. It is the spirit that is in it that is unconquerable. You can kill the bodies of insurgent men who are fighting for liberty, but the more of them you kill the more you seem to strengthen the spirit that springs up out of the bloody ground where they fell. The only thing in the world that is unconquerable is the thought of men. One looks back to that legendary story of the Middle Ages, in which certain men who were fighting under one of the semisavage chiefs of that obscure time refused to obey the order of their chief because they considered it inconsistent with the traditions of their tribe, and he said, "Don't you know that I have the power to kill you?" They said, "Yes; and don't you know that we have the power to die cursing you?" You cannot cut our spirits out. You cannot do anything but lay our bodies low and helpless. If you do, there will spring up, like dragon's teeth out of the earth, armed forces which will overcome you.

This is the field of the spirit here in America. This is the field of the single unconquerable force that there is in the world, and when the world learns, as it will learn, that America has put her whole force into the common harness of civilization, then it will know that the wheels are going to turn, the loads are going to be drawn, and men are going to begin to ascend those difficult heights of hope which have sometimes seemed so inaccessible. I am glad for one to have lived to see this day. I have lived to see a day in which, after saturating myself most of my life in the history and traditions of America, I seem suddenly to see the culmination of American hope and history—all the orators seeing their dreams realized, if their spirits are looking on; all the men who spoke the noblest sentiments of America heartened with the sight of a great Nation responding to and acting upon those dreams, and saying, "At last, the world knows America as the savior of the world!"

AT AUDITORIUM, PORTLAND, OREG., SEPTEMBER 15, 1919.

MR. CHAIRMAN, MR. IRVINE, MY FELLOW COUNTRY-MEN:

Mr. Irvine has very eloquently stated exactly the errand upon which I have come. I have come to confer, face to face, with you on one of the most solemn occasions that have ever confronted this Nation. As I have come along through the country and stopped at station after station, the first to crowd around the train have almost always been little children, bright-eyed little boys, excited little girls, children all seeming sometimes of the same generation, and I have thought as I looked upon them from the car platform that, after all, it was they to whom I had come to report; that I had come to report with regard to the safety and honor of subsequent generations of America, and I felt that if I could not fulfill the task to which I had set my hand, I would have to say to mothers with boy babies at their breast, "You have occasion to weep; you have occasion to fear. The past is only a prediction of the future, and all this terrible thing that your brothers and husbands and sweethearts have been through may have to be gone through with again." Because, as I was saying to some of your fellow citizens to-day, the task, that great and gallant task, which our soldiers performed is only half finished. They prevented a great wrong. They prevented it with a spirit and a courage and with an ability that will always be written on the brightest pages of our record of gallantry and of force. I do not know when I have been as proud, as an American, as when I have seen our boys deploy on the other side of the sea. On Christmas Day last, on an open stretch of country, I saw a great division march past me, with all the arms of the service, walking with that swing which is so familiar to our eyes, with that sense of power and confidence and audacity which is so characteristic of America, and I seemed to see the force that had saved the world. But they merely prevented something. They merely prevented a particular nation from doing a particular, unspeakable wrong to civilization, and their task is not complete unless we see to it that it has not to be done over again, unless we fulfill the promise which we made to them and to ourselves that this was not only a war to defeat Germany, but a war to prevent the recurrence of any such wrong as Germany had attempted; that it was a war to put an end to the wars of aggression forever.

There is only one means of doing that, my fellow citizens. I found quoted in one of your papers the other day a passage so apposite that I do not know that I can do better than read it as the particular thing that it is now necessary to do:

"Nations must unite as men unite in order to preserve peace and order. The great nations must be so united as to be able to say to any single country, 'You must not go to war,' and they can say that effectively when the country desiring war knows that the force which the united nations place behind peace is irresistible. In differences between individuals the decision of a court is final, because in the last resort the entire force of the community is behind the court decision. In differences between nations which go beyond the limited range of arbitral questions, peace can only be maintained by putting behind it the force of united nations determined to uphold it and prevent war."

That is a quotation from an address said to have been delivered at Union College in June, 1915, a year after the war began, by Mr. Henry Cabot Lodge, of Massachusetts. I entirely concur in Senator Lodge's conclusion, and I hope I shall have his coöperation in bringing about the desired result. In other words, the only way we can prevent the unspeakable thing from happening again is that the nations of the world should unite and put an irresistible force behind peace and order. There is only one conceivable way to do that, and that is by means of a league of nations. The very description is a definition of a league of nations, and the only thing that we can debate now is whether the nations of the world, having met in a universal congress and formulated a covenant as the basis for a league of nations, we are going to accept that or insist upon another. I do not find any man anywhere rash or bold enough to say that he does not desire a league of nations. I only find men here and there saying that they do not desire this League of Nations, and I want to ask you to reflect upon what that means. And in order to do that I want to draw a picture for you, if you will be patient with me, of what occurred in Paris.

In Paris were gathered the representatives of nearly thirty nations from all over the civilized globe, and even from some parts of the globe which in our ignorance of them we have not been in the habit of regarding as civilized, and out of that great body were chosen the representatives of fourteen nations, representing all parts of the great stretches of the peoples of the world which the conference as a whole represented. The representatives of those fourteen nations were constituted a commission on the League of Nations. The first resolution passed by the conference of peace in Paris was a resolution in favor of a league of nations, setting up a commission to formulate a league of nations. It was the thought foremost in the mind of every statesman there. He knew that his errand was in vain in Paris if he went away without achieving the formation of a league of nations, and that he dared not go back and face his people unless he could report that the efforts in that direction had been successful. That commission sat day after day, evening after evening. I had the good fortune to be a member of the commission, and I want to testify to the extraordinary good temper in which the discussions were conducted. I want to testify that there was a universal endeavor to subordinate as much as possible international rivalries and conflicting international interests and come out upon a common ground of agreement in the interest of the world. I want to testify that there were many compromises, but no compromises that sacrificed the principle, and that although the instrument as a whole represented certain mutual concessions, it is a constructive instrument and not a negative instrument. I shall never lose so long as I live the impression of generous, high-minded, states-manlike coöperation which was manifested in that interesting body. It included representatives of all the most powerful nations, as well as representatives of some of those that were less powerful.

I could not help thinking as I sat there that the representatives of Italy spoke as it were in the tones of the long tradition of Rome; that we heard the great Latin people who had fought, fought, fought through generation after generation of strife down to this critical moment, speaking now in the counsels of peace. And there sat the prime minister of Greece—the ancient Greek people—lending his singular intelligence, his singularly high-minded and comprehensive counsel, to the general result. There were the representatives also of France, our ancient comrade in the strife for liberty. And there were the representatives of Great Britain supposed to be the most ambitious, the most desirous of ruling the world of any of the nations of the world, coöperating with a peculiar interest in the result, with a constant and manifestly sincere profession that they wanted to subordinate the interests of the British Empire, which extended all over the world, to the common interests of mankind and of peace. The representatives of Great Britain I may stop to speak of for a moment. There were two of them. One of them was Lord Robert Cecil, who belongs to an ancient family in Great Britain, some of the members of which—particularly Lord Salisbury of a past generation—had always been reputed as most particularly keen to seek and maintain the advantage of the British Empire; and yet I never heard a man speak whose heart was evidently more in the task of the humane redemption of the world than Lord Robert Cecil. And alongside of him sat General Smuts, the South African Boer, the man who had fought Great Britain so successfully that, after the war was over and the Boers nominally defeated, Great Britain saw that the wisest thing she could do was to hand the government of the country over to the Boers themselves. General Botha and General Smuts were both members of the peace conference; both had been successful generals in fighting the British arms. Nobody in the conference was more outspoken in criticizing some aspects of British policy than General Botha and General Smuts, and General Smuts was of the same mind with Sir Robert Cecil. They were both serving the common interests of free people everywhere. You seem to see a sort of epitome of the history of the world in that conference. There were nations that had long been subordinated and suffering. There were nations that had been indomitably free but, nevertheless, not so free that they could really accomplish the objects that they had always held dear. I want you to realize that this conference was made up of many minds and of many nations and of many traditions, keen to the same conclusion, with a unanimity, an enthusiasm, a spirit which speaks volumes for the future hopes of mankind.

When this Covenant was drawn up in its first form I had the occasion—for me the very happy occasion—to return for a week or so to this country in March last. I brought the Covenant in its first draft. I submitted it to the Foreign Relations Committee of the Senate and the Committee on Foreign Affairs in the House. We discussed all parts of the document. Many suggestions were made. I took all of those suggestions with me back to Paris, and the conference on the League of Nations adopted every one of the suggestions made. No counsels were listened to more carefully or yielded to more willingly in that conference than the counsels of the United States. Some things were put into the Covenant which, personally, I did not think necessary, which seemed to me to go without saying, but which they had no objection to putting in there explicitly.

For example, take the Monroe Doctrine. As a matter of fact, the Covenant sets up for the world a Monroe Doctrine. What is the Monroe Doctrine? The Monroe Doctrine is that no nation shall come to the Western Hemisphere and try to establish its power or interfere with the self-government of the peoples in this hemisphere; that no power shall extend its governing and controlling influence in any form to either of the Americas. Very well; that is the doctrine of the Covenant. No nation shall anywhere extend its power or seek to interfere with the political independence of the peoples of the world; and inasmuch as the Monroe Doctrine had been made the universal doctrine, I did not think that it was necessary to mention it particularly, but when I suggested that it was the desire of the United States that it should be explicitly recognized, it was explicitly recognized, for it is written in there that nothing in the Covenant shall be interpreted as affecting the validity of the Monroe Doctrine. The Monroe

Doctrine is left intact, and the United States is left free to enforce it.

That is only a sample. The members of the Foreign Relations Committee and of the Committee on Foreign Affairs did not see it anywhere explicitly stated in the Covenant that a member of the League could withdraw. I told them that the matter had been discussed in the commission on the League and that it had been the universal opinion that, since it was a combination of sovereigns, any sovereign had the right to withdraw from it; but when I suggested that that should be explicitly put in, no objection was made whatever, and at the suggestion of the United States it was explicitly provided that any member of the League could withdraw. Provision was made that two years' notice should be given, which I think everybody will recognize as perfectly fair, so that no nation is at liberty suddenly to break down this thing upon which the hope of mankind rests; but with that limitation and with the provision that when they withdraw they shall have fulfilled all their international obligations they are perfectly free to withdraw. When gentlemen dwell upon that provision, that we must have fulfilled all our international obligations, I answer all their anxieties by asking them another question, "When did America ever fail to fulfill her international obligations?" There is no judge in the matter set up in the Covenant, except the conscience of the withdrawing nation and the opinion of mankind, and I for one am a proud enough American to dismiss from my mind all fear of at any time going before the judgment of mankind on the conduct of the United States, knowing that we will go with clean hands and righteous purpose.

I am merely illustrating now the provisions that were put in at the suggestion of the United States. Without exception, the suggestions of the United States were adopted, and I want to say, because it may interest you, that most of these suggestions came from Re-

publican sources. I say that, my fellow citizens, not
because it seems to me to make the least difference
among Americans in a great matter like this which
party such things came from, but because I want to
emphasize in every discussion of this matter the absolutely nonpartisan character of the Covenant and of
the treaty. I am not in favor of the ratification of this
treaty, including the Covenant of the League of Nations,
because I am a Democrat. I am in favor of it because
I am an American and a lover of humanity. If it will
relieve anybody's mind, let me add that it is not my
work, that practically every portion of the Covenant
of the League of Nations emanates from counsels running back ten, twenty, thirty years, among the most
thoughtful men in America, and that it is the fulfillment
of a dream which five years ago, when the war began,
would have been deemed unattainable. What we are
discussing ought not to be disfigured, ought not to be
tainted, with the least thought of domestic politics.
If anybody in this audience allows himself when thinking of this matter to think of the elections of 1920 I
want to declare that I separate myself from him.

I draw all this picture of the care with which the
Covenant was drawn up, every phrase scrutinized, every
interest considered, the other nations at the board just
as jealous of their sovereignty as we could possibly be
of ours, and yet willing to harness all of these sovereignties in a single great enterprise of peace, and how
the whole thing was not the original idea of any man
in the conference, but had grown out of the counsels of
hopeful and thoughtful and righteous men all over the
world; because just as there was in America a league to
enforce peace, which even formulated a constitution
for the league of peace before the conference met, before the conference was thought of, before the war
began, so there were in Great Britain and in France
and in Italy and, I believe, even in Germany similar
associations of equally influential men, whose ideal was

that some time there might come an occasion when men would be sane enough and right enough to get together to do a thing of this great sort. I draw that picture in order to show you the other side of what is going on, and I want to preface this part by saying that I hope you will not construe anything that I say as indicating the least lack of respect for the men who are criticizing any portion of this treaty. For most of them, I have reason to have respect, for I have come into close contact and consultation with them. They are just as good Americans as I claim to be; they are just as thoughtful of the interests of America as I try to be; they are just as intelligent as anybody who could address his mind to this thing; and my contest with them is a contest of interpretation, not a contest of intention. All I have to urge with those men is that they are looking at this thing with too critical an eye as to the mere phraseology, without remembering the purpose that everybody knows to have been in the minds of those who framed it, and that if they go very far in attempting to interpret it by resolutions of the Senate they may, in appearance at any rate, sufficiently alter the meaning of the document to make it necessary to take it back to the council board. Taking it back to the council board means, among other things, taking it back to Germany; and I frankly tell you, my fellow citizens, it would sit very ill upon my stomach to take it back to Germany. Germany, at our request—I may say almost at our dictation—signed the treaty and has ratified it. It is a contract, so far as her part in it is concerned. I can testify that we tried to be just to Germany, and that when we had heard her arguments and examined every portion of the counterproposals that she made, we wrote the treaty in its final form and then said, "Sign here." What else did our boys die for? Did they die in order that we might ask Germany's leave to complete our victory? They died in order that we might say to Germany what the terms of victory were in the interest of justice and of peace, and we were entitled to take the course that we did take. I can only beg these gentlemen in their criticism of the treaty and in their action in the Senate not to go so far as to make it necessary to ask the consent of the other nations to the interpretations which they are putting upon the treaty. I have said in all frankness that I do not see a single phrase in the Covenant of the League of Nations which is of doubtful meaning, but if they want to say what that undoubted meaning is, in other words that do not change the undoubted meaning, I have no objection. If they change the meaning of it, then all the other signatories have to consent; and what has been evident in the last week or two is that on the part of some men, I believe a very few, the desire is to change the treaty, and particularly the Covenant, in a way to give America an exceptional footing.

My fellow citizens, the principle that America went into this war for was the principle of the equality of sovereign nations. I am just as much opposed to class legislation in international matters as in domestic matters. I do not, I tell you plainly, believe that any one nation should be allowed to dominate, even this beloved Nation of our own, and it does not desire to dominate. I said in a speech the other night in another connection that so far as my influence and power as President of the United States went, I was going to fight every attempt to set up a minority government. I was asked afterwards whom I was hitting at, what minority I was thinking of. I said, "Never mind what minority I may have been thinking of at the moment; it does not make any difference with me which minority it is; whether it is capital or labor. No sort of privilege will ever be permitted in this country." It is a partnership or it is a mockery. It is a democracy, where the majority are the masters, or all the hopes and purposes of the men who founded this Government have been defeated and forgotten. And I am of the same principle in international affairs. One of the things that gave the world a new and bounding hope was that the great United States had said that it was fighting for the little nation as well as the great nation; that it regarded the rights of the little nation as equal to its own rights; that it would make no distinction between free men anywhere; that it was not fighting for a special advantage for the United States but for an equal advantage for all free men everywhere. Let gentlemen beware, therefore, how they disappoint the world. Let gentlemen beware how they betray the immemorial principles of the United States. Let men not make the mistake of claiming a position of privilege for the United States which gives it all the advantages of the League of Nations and none of the risks and responsibilities. The principle of equity everywhere is that along with a right goes a duty; that if you claim a right for yourself you must be ready to support that right for somebody else; that if you claim to be a member in a society of any sort you must not claim the right to dodge the responsibilities and avoid the burden, but you must carry the weight of the enterprise along with the hope of the enterprise. That is the spirit of free men everywhere, and that I know to be the spirit of the United States.

Our decision, therefore, my fellow citizens, rests upon this: If we want a league of nations, we must take this League of Nations, because there is no conceivable way in which any other league of nations is obtainable. We must leave it or take it. I should be very sorry to have the United States indirectly defeat this great enterprise by asking for something, some position of privilege, which other nations in their pride cannot grant. I would a great deal rather say flatly, "She will not go into the enterprise at all." And that, my fellow citizens, is exactly what Germany is hoping and beginning to dare to expect. I am not uttering a conjecture; I am speaking of knowledge, knowledge of the things that are said in the German newspapers and by German public men. They are taking heart because the United States, they hope, is not going to stand with the other free nations of the world to guarantee the peace that has been forced upon them. They see the hope that there will be two nations standing outside the League— Germany and the United States. Germany because she must; the United States because she will. She knows that that will turn the hostility and enmity of all the other nations of the world against the United States, as their hostility is already directed against her. They do not expect that now the United States will in any way align themselves with Germany. They do not expect the sympathy of the United States to go out to them now, but they do expect the isolation of the United States to bring about an alienation between the United States and the other free nations of the world, which will make it impossible for the world ever to combine again against such enterprises as she was defeated in attempting. All over this country pro-German propaganda is beginning to be active again, beginning to try to add to the force of the arguments against the League in particular and against the treaty and the several items of the treaty. And the poison of failure is being injected into the whole fine body politic of the united world, a sort of paralysis, a sort of fear. Germany desires that we should say, "What have we created? A great power which will bring peace, but will that power be amiable to us? Can we control that power?" We cannot control it for any but its proper purpose—the purpose of righteousness and peace—but for that purpose we are invited to control it by the opinion of mankind, for all over the world peoples are looking to us with confidence, our rivals along with the weaker nations. They believe in the honesty of purpose and the indomitable rectitude of purpose of the United States, and they are willing to have us lead.

I pray God that the gentlemen who are delaying this thing may presently see it in a different light. I fain

would appeal to their hearts. I wonder if they have
forgotten what this war meant. I wonder if they have
had mothers who lost their sons take them by the hand,
as they have taken my own, and looked things that their
hearts were too full to speak, praying me to do all in
my power to save the sons of other mothers from this
terrible thing again. I had one fine woman come to me
and say as steadily as if she were saying a commonplace,
"I had the honor to lose a son in the war." How fine
that is—"I had the honor to sacrifice a son for the redemption of mankind!" And yet there is a sob back
of the statement, there is a tear brushed hastily away
from the cheek. A woman came up to the train the
other day and seized my hand and was about to say
something when she turned away in a flood of tears.
I asked a standerby what was the matter, and he said,
"Why, sir, she lost a son in France." Mind you, she
did not turn away from me. I ordered her son overseas. I advised the Congress of the United States to
sacrifice that son. She came to me as a friend. She
had nothing in her heart except the hope that I could
save other sons, though she had given hers gladly, and,
God helping me, I will save other sons. Through evil
report and good report, through resistance and mis-
representation and every other vile thing, I shall fight
my way to that goal. I call upon the men to whom I
have referred—the honest, patriotic, intelligent men,
who have been too particularly concerned in criticizing
the details of that treaty—to forget the details, to remember the great enterprise, to stand with me, and fulfill the hopes and traditions of the United States.

My fellow citizens, there is only one conquering force
in the world. There is only one thing you can not kill,
and that is the spirit of free men. I was telling some
friends to-day of a legendary story of the Middle Ages,
of a chieftain of one of the half-civilized peoples that
overran Europe commanding some of his men to do a
certain thing which they believed to be against the tradi-

tions of their tribe. They refused, and he blazed out upon them, "Don't you know that I can put you to death?" "Yes," they said, "and don't you know that we can die cursing you?" He could not kill their spirits; and they knew perfectly well that if he unjustly slew them the whole spirit of their tribe would curse him; they knew that, if he did an unjust thing, out of the blood that they spilled would spring up, as it were, armed men, like dragons' teeth, to overwhelm him. The thing that is vindicated in the long run is the right, and the only thing that is unconquerable is the truth. America is believed in throughout the world, because she has put spirit before material ambition. She has said that she is willing to sacrifice everything that she is and everything that she has not only that her people may be free but that freedom may reign throughout the world.

I hear men say—how often I heard it said on the other side of the water!—how amazing it was that America went into this war. I tell you, my fellow citizens—I tell it with sorrow—it was universally believed on the other side of the water that we would not go into the war because we were making money out of it, and loved the money better than we loved justice. They all believed that. When we went over there they greeted us with amazement. They said, "These men did not have to come. Their territories are not invaded. Their independence is not directly threatened. Their interests were not immediately attacked, only indirectly. They were getting a great prosperity out of this calamity of ours, and we were told that they worshipped the almighty dollar; but here come, tramping, tramping, tramping, these gallant fellows with something in their faces we never saw before—eyes lifted to the horizon, a dash that knows no discouragement, a knowledge only of how to go forward, no thought of how to go backward—3,000 miles from home. What are they fighting for? Look at their faces and you will see the answer. They see a vision. They see a cause. They see mankind redeemed. They see a great force which would recall civilization. They love something they have never touched. They love the things that emanate from the throne of justice, and they have come here to fight with us and for us, and they are our comrades."

We were told by certain people in France that they went to the Fourth of July celebration last calendar year in Paris with sinking hearts. Our men had just begun to come over in numbers. They did not expect they would come soon enough or fast enough to save them. They went out of courtesy; and before the day was over, having been in the presence of those boys, they knew that Europe was saved, because they had seen what that blind man saw in the song. You have heard that spirited song of the blind Frenchman, his boy at the window, music in the streets, the marching of troops, and he says to the lad, "See what that is. What do you see, lad? What are the colors? What are the men? Is there a banner with red and white stripes upon it? Is there a bit of heaven in the corner? Are there stars in that piece of the firmament? Ah, thank God, the Americans have come!" It was the revelation to Europe of the heart of a great Nation, and they believe in that heart now. You never hear the old sneers. You never hear the old intimation that we will seek our interest and not our honor. You never hear the old fear that we shall not stand by free men elsewhere who make common cause with us for justice to mankind. You hear, on the contrary, confident prediction, confident expectation, a confident hope that the whole world will be steadied by the magnificent purpose and force of the United States. If I was proud as an American before I went over there—and I hope my pride had just foundation—I was infinitely more proud when I came back to feel that I could bring you this message.

My fellow citizens, let us—every one of us—bind ourselves in a solemn league and covenant of our own that we will redeem this expectation of the world, that we will not allow any man to stand in the way of it, that the world shall hereafter bless and not curse us, that the world hereafter shall follow us and not turn aside from us, and that in leading we will not lead along the paths of private advantage, we will not lead along the paths of national ambition, but we will be proud and happy to lead along the paths of right so that men shall always say that American soldiers saved Europe and American citizens saved the world.

AT LUNCHEON, PALACE HOTEL, SAN FRANCISCO, CALIF., SEPTEMBER 17, 1919.

MRS. MOTT AND MY FELLOW CITIZENS:

Mrs. Mott has very happily interpreted the feeling with which I face this great audience. I have come to get a consciousness of your support and of your sentiment, at a time in the history of the world, I take leave to say, more critical than has ever been known during the history of the United States. I have felt a certain burden of responsibility as I have mixed with my fellow countrymen across the continent, because I have feared at times that there were those amongst us who did not realize just what the heart of this question is. I have been afraid that their thoughts were lingering in a past day when the calculation was always of national advantage, and that it had not come to see the light of the new day in which men are thinking of the common advantage and safety of mankind. The issue is nothing else. Either we must stand apart, and in the phrase of some gentlemen, "take care of ourselves," which means antagonize others, or we must join hands with the other great nations of the world and with the weak nations of the world, in seeing that justice is everywhere maintained.

Quite apart from the merits of any particular question that may be raised about the treaty itself, I think we are under a certain moral compulsion to accept this treaty. In the first place, my fellow citizens, it was laid down according to American specifications. The initial suggestions upon which this treaty is based emanated from America. I would not have you understanding me as meaning that they were ideas confined to America, because the promptness with which they were accepted, the joy with which they were hailed in some parts of the world, the readiness of the leaders of nations that had been supposed to be seeking chiefly their own interest in adopting these principles as the principles of the peace, show that they were listening to the counsels of their own people, that they were listening to those who knew the critical character of the new age and the necessity we were under to take new measures for the peace of the world. Because the thing that had happened was intolerable. The thing that Germany attempted, if it had succeeded, would have set the civilization of the world back a hundred years. We have prevented it, but prevention is not enough. We have shown Germany—and not Germany only, but the world —that upon occasion the great peoples of the world will combine to prevent an iniquity, but we have not shown how that is going to be done in the future with a certainty that will make every other nation know that a similar enterprise must not be attempted.

Again and again, as I have crossed the continent, generous women, women I did not know, have taken me by the hand and said, "God bless you, Mr. President." Some of them, like many of you, had lost sons and husbands and brothers in the war. Why should they bless me? I advised Congress to declare war. I advised Congress to send their sons to their death. As Commander in Chief of the Army, I sent them over the seas, and they were killed. Why should they bless me? Because in the generosity of their hearts they want the sons of other women saved henceforth, and they believe that the methods proposed at any rate create a

very hopeful expectation that similar wars will be prevented, and that other armies will not have to go from
the United States to die upon distant fields of battle.
The moral compulsion upon us, upon us who at the critical stage of the world saved the world and who threw
in our fortunes with all the forward-looking peoples of
the world—the moral compulsion upon us to stand by
and see it through is overwhelming. We cannot now
turn back. We made the choice in April, 1917. We
cannot with honor reverse it now.

Not only is there the compulsion of honor, but there
is the compulsion of interest. I never like to speak of
that, because, notwithstanding the reputation that we
had throughout the world before we made the great
sacrifice of this war, this Nation does love its honor
better than it loves its interest. It does yield to moral
compulsion more readily than to material compulsion.
That is the glory of America. That is the spirit in
which she was conceived and born. That is the mission
that she has in the world. She always has lived up to
it, and, God helping her, she always will live up to it.
But if you want, as some of our fellow countrymen insist, to dwell upon the material side of it and our interest in the matter, our commercial interest, draw the
picture for yourselves. The other nations of the world
are drawing together. We who suggested that they
should draw together in this new partnership stand
aside. We at once draw their suspicion upon us. We
at once draw their intense hostility upon us. We at
once renew the thing that had begun to be done before
we went into the war. There was a conference in Paris
not many months before we went into the war in which
the nations then engaged against Germany attempted to
draw together in an exclusive economic combination
where they should serve one another's interest and exclude those who had not participated in the war from
sharing in that interest, and just so certainly as we stay
out, every market that can possibly be closed against

us will be closed. If you merely look at it from the point of view of the material prosperity of the United States, we are under compulsion to stay in the partnership. I was asking some gentlemen the other day who were engaged in commerce of various sorts, "Can you sell more easily to a man who trusts you or to a man who distrusts you?" There can be but one answer to that question. Can you sell more easily to a man who takes your goods because he cannot do without them or to a man who wants them and believes them the best? The thing demonstrates itself. You make all the lines of trade lines of resistance unless you prove true to the things that you have attempted and undertaken.

Then, there is a deeper compulsion even than those, the compulsion of humanity. If there is one thing that America ought to have learned more promptly than any other country it is that, being made up out of all the ranks of humanity, in serving itself it must serve the human race. I suppose I could not command the words which would exaggerate the present expectations of the world with regard to the United States. Nothing more thrilling, nothing more touching, happened to me on the other side of the water than the daily evidences that, not the weak peoples merely, not the peoples of countries that had been allowed to shift for themselves and had always borne the chief burden of the world's sufferings, but the great peoples as well, the people of France as well as the people of Serbia, the people of all the nations that had looked this terror in the face, were turning to the United States and saying, "We depend upon you to take the lead, to direct us how to go out of this wilderness of doubt and fear and terror." We cannot desert humanity. We are the trustees of humanity, and we must see that we redeem the pledges which are always implicit in so great a trusteeship.

So, feeling these compulsions, the compulsion of honor, the compulsion of interest, and the compulsion

of humanity, I wonder what it is that is holding some
minds back from acquiescence in this great enterprise
of peace. I must admit to you, my fellow citizens, that
I have been very much puzzled. I cannot conceive a
motive adequate to hold men off from this thing, and
when I examine the objections which they make to the
treaty I can but wonder if they are really thinking, or
if, on the other hand, there is some emotion coming
from fountains that I do not know of which are obliging
them to take this course.

Let me take the point in which my initial sympathy
is most with them, the matter of the cession to Japan
of the interests of Germany in Shantung, in China. I
said to my Japanese colleagues on the other side of the
sea, and therefore I am at liberty to say in public, I
am not satisfied with that settlement, I think it ought
to have been different, but when gentlemen propose to
cure it by striking that clause out of the treaty or by
ourselves withholding our adherence to the treaty, they
propose an irrational thing. Let me remind you of
some of the history of this business. It was in 1898
that China ceded these rights and concessions to Germany. The pretext was that some German missionaries
had been killed. My heart aches, I must say, when I
think how we have made an excuse of religion sometimes to work a deep wrong. The central Government
of China had done all that they could to protect those
German missionaries; their death was due to local disturbances, to local passion, to local antipathy against
the foreigner. There was nothing that the Chinese
Government as a whole could justly be held responsible
for; but suppose there had been. Two Christian missionaries are killed, and therefore one great nation robs
another nation and does a thing which is fundamentally
un-Christian and heathen! For there was no adequate
excuse for what Germany exacted of China. I read
again only the other day the phrases in which poor
China was made to make the concessions. She was

made to make them in words dictated by Germany, in view of her gratitude to Germany for certain services rendered—the deepest hypocrisy conceivable! She was obliged to do so by force.

Then, what happened, my fellow citizens? Then Russia came in and obliged China to cede to her Port Arthur and Talien Wan, not for quite so long a period, but upon substantially the same terms. Then England must needs have Wei-Hai-Wai as an equivalent concession to that which had been made to Germany; and presently certain ports, with the territory back of them, were ceded upon similar principles to France. Everybody got in, except the United States, and said, "If Germany is going to get something, we will get something." Why? None of them had any business in there on such terms.

Then when the Japanese-Russian War came, Japan did what she has done in this war. She attacked Port Arthur and captured Port Arthur, and Port Arthur was ceded to her as a consequence of the war. Not one official voice was raised in the United States against that cession. No protest was made. No protest was made by the Government of the United States against the original cession of this Shantung territory to Germany. One of the highest minded men of our history was President at that time—I mean Mr. McKinley. One of the ablest men that we have had as Secretary of State, Mr. John Hay, occupied that great office. In the message of Mr. McKinley about this transaction, he says—I am quoting his language—that inasmuch as the powers that had taken these territories had agreed to keep the door open there for our commerce, there was no reason why we should object. Just so we could trade with these stolen territories we were willing to let them be stolen. Which of these gentlemen who are now objecting to the cession of the German rights in Shantung to Japan were prominent in protesting against the original cession or any one of those original cessions? It makes my heart burn when some men are so late in doing justice.

In the meantime, before we got into this war, but after the war had begun, because they deemed the assistance of Japan in the Pacific absolutely indispensable, Great Britain and France both agreed that if Japan would enter and coöperate in the war she could do the same thing with regard to Shantung that she had done with regard to Port Arthur; that is if she would take what Germany had in China she could keep it. She took it. She has it now. Her troops are there. She has it as spoils of war. Observe, my fellow citizens, we are not taking this thing away from China; we are taking it from Germany. China had ceded it for ninety-nine years, and there are seventy-eight of those ninety-nine to run yet. They were Germany's rights in Shantung, not China's, that were ceded by the treaty to Japan, but with a difference—a difference which never occurred in any of these other cases—a difference which was not insisted upon at the cession of Port Arthur—upon a condition that no other nation in doing similar things in China has ever yielded to. Japan is under solemn promise to forego all sovereign rights in the Province of Shantung and to retain only what private corporations have elsewhere in China, the right of concessionaires with regard to the operation of the railway and the exploitation of the mines. Scores of foreign corporations have that right in other parts of China.

But it does not stop there. Coupled with this arrangement is the League of Nations, under which Japan solemnly undertakes, with the rest of us, to protect the territorial integrity of China, along with the territorial integrity of other countries, and back of her promise lies the similar promise of every other nation, that nowhere will they countenance a disregard for the territorial integrity or the political independence of that great helpless people, lying there hitherto as an object of prey in the great Orient. It is the first time in the history of the world that anything has been done for China, and sitting around our council board in Paris I put this question: "May I expect that this will be the beginning of the retrocession to China of the exceptional rights which other Governments have enjoyed there?" The responsible representatives of the other great Governments said, "Yes; you may expect it." Expect it?

Your attention is constantly drawn to Article X, and that is the article—the heart of the Covenant—which guarantees the territorial integrity and political independence not only of China, but of other countries more helpless even than China; but besides Article X, there is Article XI, which makes it the right of every member of the League, big or little, influential or not influential, to draw attention to anything, anywhere, that is likely to disturb the peace of the world or the good understanding between nations upon which the peace of the world depends. Whenever formerly anything was done in detriment of the interests of China, we had to approach the Government that did it with apologies. We had, as it were, to say, "This is none of our business, but we would like to suggest that this is not in the interest of China." I am repeating, not the words but the purport of notes that I have signed myself to Japan, in which I was obliged to use all the genuflections of apology and say, "The United States believes that this is wrong in principle and suggests to the Japanese Government that the matter be reconsidered." Now, when you have the League of Nations the representative of the United States has the right to stand up and say, "This is against the covenants of peace; it cannot be done," and if occasion arises we can add, "It shall not be done." The weak and oppressed and wronged peoples of the world have never before had a forum made for them in which they can summon their enemies into the presence of the judgment of mankind, and if there is one tribunal that the wrongdoer ought to dread more than another it is that tribunal of the opinion of mankind. Some nations keep their international promises only because they wish to obtain the respect of mankind. You remember those immortal words in the opening part of the Declaration of Independence. I wish I could quote them literally, but they run this way, that out of respect for the opinion of mankind the leaders of the American Revolution now state the causes which have led them to separate themselves from Great Britain. America was the first to set that example, the first to admit that right and justice and even the basis of revolution was a matter upon which mankind was entitled to form a judgment.

If we do not take part in this thing, what happens? France and England are absolutely bound to this thing without any qualifications. The alternative is to defend China in the future with important concessions to begin with, or else let the world go back to its old methods of rapacity; or else take up arms against France and England and Japan, and begin the shedding of blood over again, almost fratricidal blood. Does that sound like a practical program? Does that sound like doing China a service? Does that sound like anything that is rational?

Go to other matters with which I have less patience, other objections to the League. I have spoken of Article X. Those who object to Article X object to entering the League with any responsibilities whatever. They want to make it a matter of opinion merely and not a matter of action. They know just as well as I know that there is nothing in Article X that can oblige the Congress of the United States to declare war if it does not deem it wise to declare war. We engage with the other nations of the world to preserve as against external aggression—not as against internal revolution—the territorial integrity and existing political independence of the other members of the League; and then, in the next sentence, it is said that the council of the League of

Nations shall advise with regard to the measures which may be necessary to carry out this promise on the part of the members. As I have said several times in my speeches, I have in vain searched the dictionary to find any other meaning for the word "advise" than "advise." These gentlemen would have you believe that our armies can be ordered abroad by some other power or by a combination of powers. They are thinking in an air-tight compartment. America is not the only proud nation in the world. I can testify from my share in the counsels on the other side of the sea that the other nations are just as jealous of their sovereignty as we are of ours. They would no more have dreamed of giving us the right of ordering out their armies than we would have dreamed of giving them the right to order out our armies. The advice can come from the United States only after the United States representative votes in the affirmative.

We have got an absolute veto on the thing, unless we are parties to the dispute, and I want again to call attention to what that means. That means unless we want to seize somebody's territory or invade somebody's political independence, or unless somebody else wants to seize our territory and invade our political independence. I regard either of those contingencies as so remote that they are not troubling me in the least. I know the people of this country well enough to know that we will not be the aggressors in trying to execute a wrong, and in looking about me I do not see anybody else that would think it wise to try it on us. But suppose we are parties. Then is it the council of the League that is forcing war upon us? The war is ours anyhow. We are in circumstances where it is necessary for Congress, if it wants to steal somebody's territory or prevent somebody from stealing our territory, to go to war. It is not the council of the League that brings us into war at that time, in such circumstances; it is the unfortunate circumstances which have arisen in some matter of aggression. I want to say again that Article X is the very heart of the Covenant of the League, because all the great wrongs of the world have had their root in the seizure of territory or the control of the political independence of other peoples. I believe that I speak the feeling of the people of the United States when I say that, having seen one great wrong like that attempted and having prevented it, we are ready to prevent it again.

Those are the two principal criticisms, that we did not do the impossible with regard to Shantung and that we may be advised to go to war. That is all there is in either of those. But they say, "We want the Monroe Doctrine more distinctly acknowledged." Well, if I could have found language that was more distinct than that used, I should have been very happy to suggest it, but it says in so many words that nothing in that document shall be construed as affecting the validity of the Monroe Doctrine. I do not see what more it could say, but, as I say, if the clear can be clarified, I have no objection to its being clarified. The meaning is too obvious to admit of discussion, and I want you to realize how extraordinary that provision is. Every nation in the world had been jealous of the Monroe Doctrine, had studiously avoided doing or saying anything that would admit its validity, and here all the great nations of the world sign a document which admits its validity. That constitutes nothing less than a moral revolution in the attitude of the rest of the world toward America.

What does the Monroe Doctrine mean in that Covenant? It means that with regard to aggressions upon the Western Hemisphere we are at liberty to act without waiting for other nations to act. That is the Monroe Doctrine. The Monroe Doctrine says that if anybody tries to interfere with affairs in the Western Hemisphere it will be regarded as an unfriendly act to the United States—not to the rest of the world—and that means that the United States will look after it, and will not ask anybody's permission to look after it. The document says that nothing in this document must be construed as interfering with that. I dismiss the objections to the Monroe Doctrine all the more because this is what happened: I brought the first draft of the Covenant to this country in March last. I then invited the Foreign Affairs Committee of the House and the Foreign Relations Committee of the Senate to the White House to dinner, and after dinner we had the frankest possible conference with regard to this draft. When I went back to Paris I carried every suggestion that was made in that conference to the commission on the League of Nations, which consisted of representatives of fourteen nations, and every one of the suggestions of those committees was embodied in the document. I suppose it is a pride of style. I suppose that, although the substance was embodied, they would rather write it differently, but, after all, that is a literary matter. After all, that is a question of pride in the command of the English language, and I must say that there were a great many men on that commission on the League of Nations who seemed perfectly to understand the English language and who wished to express, not only in the English text but in its French equivalent, exactly what we wanted to say.

One of the suggestions I carried over was that we should have the right to withdraw. I must say that I did not want to say, "We are going into this if you promise we can scuttle whenever we want to." That did not seem to me a very handsome thing to propose, and I told the men in the conference at the White House, when they raised the question, that it had been raised in the commission on the League of Nations and that it was the unanimous opinion of the international lawyers of that body that, inasmuch as this was an association of sovereigns, they had the right to withdraw. But I conceded that if that right was admitted there could be no harm in stating it, and so in the present draft of the Covenant it is stated that any member may withdraw upon two years' notice, which, I think, is not an unreasonable length of time, provided that at the end of the two years all the international obligations of that power under the Covenant shall have been fulfilled. Would you wish any other condition? Would you wish the United States allowed to withdraw without fulfilling its obligations? Is that the kind of people we are? Moreover, have we ever failed to fulfill our international obligations? It is a point of pride with me, my fellow citizens, not to debate this question. I will not debate with anybody whether the United States is likely to withdraw without fulfilling its obligations or not, and if other gentlemen entertain that possibility and expectation, I separate myself from them.

But there is another matter. They say that the British Empire has six votes and we have only one. It happens that our one is as big as the six, and that satisfies me entirely. Let me explain what I mean. It is only in the assembly that the British Empire has six votes—not in the council—and there is only one thing that the assembly votes on in which it can decide a matter without the concurrence of all the States represented on the council, and that is the admission of new members to the League of Nations. With regard to every other matter, for example, amendments to the Covenant, with regard to cases referred out of the council to the assembly, it is provided that if a majority of the assembly and the representatives of all the States represented on the council concur, the vote shall be valid and conclusive, which means that the affirmative vote of the United States is in every instance just as powerful as the six votes of the British Empire. I took the pains yesterday, I believe it was, on the train, to go through the Covenant almost sentence by sentence again, to find if there was any case other than the one I have mentioned in which that was not true, and there is no other case in which that is not true. Of course, you will

understand that wherever the United States is a party
to a quarrel and that quarrel is carried to the assembly,
we cannot vote; but, similarly, if the British Empire
is a party her six representatives cannot vote. It is an
even break any way you take it, and I would rather
count six as one person than six as six persons. So far
as I can see, it makes me a bigger man. The point to
remember is that the energy of the League of Nations
resides in the council, not in the assembly, and that in
the council there is a perfect equality of votes. That
settles that matter, and even some of my fellow countrymen who insist upon keeping a hyphen in the middle
of their names ought to be satisfied with that. Though
I must admit that I do not care to argue anything with
a hyphen. A man that puts anything else before the
word "American" is no comrade of mine, and yet I am
willing even to discomfit him with a statement of fact.

Those are the objections to yielding to these compulsions of honor, interest, and humanity, and it is because
of the nature of these objections, their flimsiness, the
impossibility of supporting them with conclusive argument that I am profoundly puzzled to know what is
back of the opposition to the League of Nations. I
know one of the results, and that is to raise the hope
in the minds of the German people that, after all, they
can separate us from those who were our associates in
the war. I know that the pro-German propaganda
which had theretofore not dared to raise its head again
has now boldly raised its head and is active all over the
United States. These are disturbing and illuminating
circumstances. Pray understand me; I am not accusing
some of the honorable men whose objections I am trying to answer with trying to draw near to Germany.
That is not my point; but I am saying that what they
are attempting to do is exactly what Germany desires,
and that it would touch the honor of the United States
very near if at the end of this great struggle we should

seek to take the position which our enemies desire and our friends deplore.

I am arguing the matter only because I am a very patient man. I have not the slightest doubt as to what the result is going to be. I have felt the temper and high purpose of this great people as I have crossed this wonderful land of ours, and one of the things that make it most delightful to stand here is to remember that the people of the Pacific coast were the first to see the new duty in its entirety. It is a remarkable circumstance that you people, who were farthest from the field of conflict, most remote from that contact of interests which stirred so many peoples, yet outdid the rest of the country in volunteering for service and volunteering your money. As I came through that wonderful country to the north of us it occurred to me one day that the aspiring lines of those wonderful mountains must lead people's eyes to be drawn upward and to look into the blue serene and see things apart from the confusions of affairs, to see the real, pure vision of the interests of humanity; and that, after all, the spirit of America was best expressed where people withdrew their thoughts from the entangling interests of everyday life, purified their motives from all that was selfish and groveling and based upon the desire to seize and get and turned their thoughts to those things that are worth living for.

The only thing that makes the world inhabitable is that it is sometimes ruled by its purest spirits. I want to leave this illustration, which I have often used, in your minds of what I mean. Some years ago someone said to me that the modern world was a world in which the mind was monarch, and my reply was that if that was true it must be one of those modern monarchs that reigned and did not govern; that, as a matter of fact, the world was governed by a great popular assembly made up of the passions and that the constant struggle of civilization was to see that the handsome passions had a working majority. That is the problem of civilization, that the things that engage the best impulses of the human spirit should be the prevailing things, the conquering things, the things that one can die comfortably after achieving. How do men ever go to sleep that have conceived wrong? How do men ever get their own consent to laugh who have not looked the right in the face and extended their hand to it? If America can in the future look the rest of the world in the face, it will be because she has been the champion of justice and of right.

AT AUDITORIUM, SAN FRANCISCO, CALIF., SEPTEMBER 17, 1919.

MR. CHAIRMAN, MR. ROLPH, MY FELLOW COUNTRYMEN:

You have given me a very royal welcome, and I am profoundly appreciative of the greeting that you have extended me. It is a matter of gratification to me to be permitted to speak to this great audience representing as it does one of the most forward-looking States of the Union, representing as it does a great body of people who are accustomed to look and plan to the future. As I picture to myself the history of this great country which we love, I remember the surging tides of humanity moving always westward, over the eastern mountains and the plains, deploying upon the great further slopes of the Rockies, then overflowing into these fertile and beautiful valleys by the Pacific; and that is a picture to me of the constant forward, confident, hopeful movement of the American people. I feel that it is not without significance that this was the portion of the country which responded with the most extraordinary spirit to the call to arms, responded with the utmost spontaneity and generosity to the call for the money of the people to be loaned to the Government for the conduct of the Great War, responded to all those impulses of purpose and of freedom which underlay the great struggle we have just passed through.

As I have passed through your streets to-day, and through others in the many generous communities north of you and east of you, you have made me feel how the spirit of the American people is coming to a single vision, how the thought of the American people is back of a single purpose. I have come before you, my fellow citizens, to discuss a very serious theme. I want to analyze for you the very important issue with which this Nation is now face to face. It is by far the most important question that has ever come before this people for decision, and the reason I have come out upon this long journey is that I am conscious that it is the people, their purpose, their wish, that is to decide this thing, and not the thought of those who are planning any private purpose of their own.

What I first want to call your attention to, my fellow citizens, is this: You know that the debate in which we are engaged centers first of all upon the League of Nations, and there seems to have arisen an idea in some quarters that the League of Nations is an idea recently conceived, conceived by a small number of persons, somehow originated by the American representatives at the council table in Paris. Nothing could be further from the truth than that. I would not feel the confidence that I feel in the League of Nations if I felt that it was so recent and novel a growth and birth as that. On the contrary, it is the fruit of many generations of thoughtful, forward-looking men, not only in this country but in the other countries of the world, who have been able to look forward to the combined fortunes of mankind. The men who have conceived this great purpose are not men who through these generations, when they were concerting counsel in this great matter, thought of the fortunes of parties, thought of the fortunes of individuals. I would be ashamed of myself, as I am frankly ashamed of any fellow

countryman of mine who does it, if I discussed this
great question with any portion of my thought devoted
to the contest of parties and the elections of next year.

Some of the greatest spirits, some of the most instructed minds of both parties have been devoted to
this great idea for more than a generation. It has
come before the Paris conference out of the stage of
ideal conception. It had long before that begun to
assume the shape of a definite program and plan for
the concert and coöperation of the nations in the interest of the peace of the world, and when I went to Paris
I was conscious that I was carrying there no plan
which was novel either to America or to Europe, but a
plan which all statesmen who realized the real interests
of their people had long ago hoped might be carried out
in some day when the world would realize what the
peace of the world meant and what were its necessary
foundations. When I got to Paris I was not conscious
of presenting anything that they had not long considered, and I felt that I was merely the spokesman of
thoughtful minds and hopeful spirits in America. I
was not putting forward any purpose of my own. So
that I beg you will dismiss any personal appearance or
personal relationship which this great plan may bear.
I would indeed be a very proud man if I had personally
conceived this great idea, but I can claim no such honor.
I can only claim the privilege of having been the obedi-
ent servant of the great ideals and purposes of beloved
America.

I want you to realize, my fellow countrymen, that
those Americans who are opposing this plan of the
League of Nations offer no substitute. They offer
nothing that they pretend will accomplish the same
object. On the contrary, they are apparently willing
to go back to that old and evil order which prevailed
before this war began and which furnished a ready
and fertile soil for those seeds of envy which sprung
up like dragon's teeth out of the bloody soil of Europe.

They are ready to go back to that old and ugly plan of armed nations, of alliances, of watchful jealousies, of rabid antagonisms, of purposes concealed, running by the subtle channels of intrigue through the veins of people who do not dream what poison is being injected into their systems. They are willing to have the United States stand alone, withdraw from the concert of nations; and what does that mean, my fellow citizens? It means that we shall arm as Germany was armed, that we shall submit our young men to the kind of constant military service that the young men of Germany were subjected to. It means that we shall pay not lighter but heavier taxes. It means that we shall trade in a world in which we are suspected and watched and disliked, instead of in a world which is now ready to trust us, ready to follow our leadership, ready to receive our traders, along with our political representatives as friends, as men who are welcome, as men who bring goods and ideas for which the world is ready and for which the world has been waiting. That is the alternative which they offer.

It is my purpose, fellow citizens, to analyze the objections which are made to this great League, and I shall be very brief. In the first place, you know that one of the difficulties which have been experienced by those who are objecting to this League is that they do not think that there is a wide enough door open for us to get out. For my own part, I am not one of those who, when they go into a generous enterprise, think first of all how they are going to turn away from those with whom they are associated. I am not one of those who, when they go into a concert for the peace of the world, want to sit close to the door with their hand on the knob and constantly trying the door to be sure that it is not locked. If we want to go into this thing—and we do want to go into it—we will go in it with our whole hearts and settled purpose to stand by the great enterprise to the end. Nevertheless, you will remember

—some of you, I dare say—that when I came home in March for an all too brief visit to this country, which seems to me the fairest and dearest in the world, I brought back with me the first draft of the Covenant of the League of Nations. I called into consultation the Committees on Foreign Affairs and on Foreign Relations of the House and Senate of the United States, and I laid the draft of the Covenant before them. One of the things that they proposed was that it should be explicitly stated that any member of the League should have the right to withdraw. I carried that suggestion back to Paris, and without the slightest hesitation it was accepted and acted upon; and every suggestion which was made in that conference at the White House was accepted by the conference of peace in Paris. There is not a feature of the Covenant, except one, now under debate upon which suggestions were not made at that time, and there is not one of those suggestions that was not adopted by the conference of peace.

The gentlemen say, "You have laid a limitation upon the right to withdraw. You have said that we can withdraw upon two years' notice, if at that time we shall have fulfilled all our international obligations and all our obligations under the Covenant." "Yes," I reply; "is it characteristic of the United States not to fulfill her international obligations? Is there any fear that we shall wish to withdraw dishonorably? Are gentlemen willing to stand up and say that they want to get out whether they have the moral right to get out or not?" I for one am too proud as an American to debate that subject on that basis. The United States has always fulfilled its international obligations, and, God helping her, she always will. There is nothing in the Covenant to prevent her acting upon her own judgment with regard to that matter. The only thing she has to fear, the only thing she has to regard, is the public opinion of mankind, and inasmuch as we have always scrupulously satisfied the public opinion of mankind with regard to justice and right, I for my part am not afraid at any time to go before that jury. It is a jury that might condemn us if we did wrong, but it is not a jury that could oblige us to stay in the League, so that there is absolutely no limitation upon our right to withdraw.

One of the other suggestions I carried to Paris was that the committees of the two Houses did not find the Monroe Doctrine safeguarded in the Covenant of the League of Nations. I suggested that to the conference in Paris, and they at once inserted the provision which is now there that nothing in that Covenant shall be construed as affecting the validity of the Monroe Doctrine. What is the validity of the Monroe Doctrine? The Monroe Doctrine means that if any outside power, any power outside this hemisphere, tries to impose its will upon any portion of the Western Hemisphere the United States is at liberty to act independently and alone in repelling the aggression; that it does not have to wait for the action of the League of Nations; that it does not have to wait for anything but the action of its own administration and its own Congress. This is the first time in the history of international diplomacy that any great government has acknowledged the validity of the Monroe Doctrine. Now for the first time all the great fighting powers of the world except Germany, which for the time being has ceased to be a great fighting power, acknowledge the validity of the Monroe Doctrine and acknowledge it as part of the international practice of the world.

They are nervous about domestic questions. They say, "It is intolerable to think that the League of Nations should interfere with domestic questions," and whenever they begin to specify they speak of the question of immigration, of the question of naturalization, of the question of the tariff. My fellow citizens, no competent or authoritative student of international law would dream of maintaining that these were anything but exclusively domestic questions, and the Covenant of the League expressly provides that the League can take no action whatever about matters which are in the practice of international law regarded as domestic questions. We did not undertake to enumerate samples of domestic questions for the very good reason, which will occur to any lawyer, that if you made a list it would be inferred that what you left out was not included. Nobody with a thoughtful knowledge of international practice has the least doubt as to what are domestic questions, and there is no obscurity whatever in this Covenant with regard to the safeguarding of the United States, along with other sovereign countries, in the control of domestic questions. I beg that you will not fancy, my fellow citizens, that the United States is the only country that is jealous of its sovereignty. Throughout these conferences it was necessary at every turn to safeguard the sovereign independence of the several governments who were taking part in the conference, and they were just as keen to protect themselves against outside intervention in domestic matters as we were. Therefore the whole heartiness of their concurrent opinion runs with this safeguarding of domestic questions.

It is objected that the British Empire has six votes and we have one. The answer to that is that it is most carefully arranged that our one vote equals the six votes of the British Empire. Anybody who will take the pains to read the Covenant of the League of Nations will find out that the assembly—and it is only in the assembly that the British Empire has six votes—is not a voting body. There is a very limited number of subjects upon which it can act at all, and I have taken the pains to write them down here, after again and again going through the Covenant for the purpose of making sure that I had not omitted anything, in order that I might give you an explicit account of the thing. There are two things which a majority of the assembly

may do without the concurrent vote of the United
States. A majority of the assembly can admit a new
member to the League of Nations. A majority of the
assembly can recommend to any nation a member of the
League a reconsideration of such treaties as are apparently in conflict with the provisions of the Covenant
itself; it can advise any member of the League to seek
a reconsideration of any international obligation which
seems to conflict with the Covenant itself, but it has
no means whatever of obliging it to reconsider even
so important a matter as that, which is obviously a moral
duty on the part of any member of the League. All
the action, all the energy, all the initiative, of the
League of Nations is resident in the council, and in the
council a unanimous vote is necessary for action, and
no action is possible without the concurrent vote of the
United States. I would rather, personally, as one man
count for six than be six men and count only one. The
United States can offset six votes. Here are the cases:
When a matter in dispute is referred by the council to
the assembly its action must be taken by a majority
vote of the assembly, concurred in by the representatives of all the governments represented in the council,
so that the concurrence of the vote of the United States
is absolutely necessary to an affirmative vote of the
assembly itself. In the case of an amendment to the
Covenant it is necessary that there should be a unanimous vote of the representatives of the nations
which are represented in the council in addition to a
majority vote of the assembly itself. And there is all
the voting that the assembly does.

Not a single affirmative act or negative decision upon
a matter of action taken by the League of Nations
can be validated without the vote of the United States
of America. We can dismiss from our dreams the six
votes of the British Empire, for the real underlying
conception of the assembly of the League of Nations
is that it is the forum of opinion, not of action. It

is the debating body; it is the body where the thought
of the little nation along with the thought of the big
nation is brought to bear upon those matters which
affect the peace of the world, is brought to bear upon
those matters which affect the good understanding between nations upon which the peace of the world depends; where this stifled voice of humanity is at last
to be heard, where nations that have borne the unspeakable sufferings of the ages that must have seemed
to them like æons will find voice and expression, where
the moral judgment of mankind can sway the opinion
of the world. That is the function of the assembly.
The assembly is the voice of mankind. The council,
where unanimous action is necessary, is the only means
through which that voice can accomplish action.

You say, "We have heard a great deal about Article
X." I just now said that the only substitute for the
League of Nations which is offered by the opponents is
a return to the old system. What was the old system?
That the strong had all the rights and need pay no
attention to the rights of the weak; that if a great
powerful nation saw what it wanted, it had the right
to go and take it; that the weak nations could cry out
and cry out as they pleased and there would be no
hearkening ear anywhere to their rights. I want to
bring in another subject connected with this treaty, but
not with the League of Nations, to illustrate what I
am talking about. You have heard a great deal about
the cession to Japan of the rights which Germany
had acquired in Shantung Province in China. What
happened under the old order of things, my fellow
citizens? The story begins in 1898. Two German
missionaries were killed in China by parties over whom
the Central Government of China was unable to exercise control. It was one of those outbreaks, like the
pitiful Boxer rebellion, where a sudden hatred of
foreigners wells up in the heart of a nation uninformed,
aware of danger, aware of wrong, but not knowing

just how to remedy it, not knowing just what was the instrumentality of right. And, my fellow citizens, why should not the Chinaman hate the foreigner? The foreigner has always taken from him everything that he could get. When by irresponsible persons these German missionaries were murdered, the German Government insisted that a great part of the fair Province of Shantung should be turned over to them for exploitation. They insisted that the accessible part of Kiaochow Bay, the part where trade entered and left, should be delivered over to them for sovereign control for ninety-nine years, and that they should be given a concession for a railway into the interior and for the right to exploit mines in that rich mineral country for thirty miles on either side of the railway.

This was not unprecedented, my fellow countrymen. Other civilized nations had done the same thing to China, and at that time what did the Government of the United States do? I want to speak with the utmost respect for the administration of that time, and the respect is unaffected. That very lovable and honest gentleman, William McKinley, was President of the United States. His Secretary of State was one of the most honorable and able of the long series of our Secretaries of State, the Hon. John Hay. I believe Mr. Hay, if he had seen any way to accomplish more than he did accomplish, would have attempted to accomplish it, but this is all that the administration of Mr. McKinley attempted: They did not even protest against this compulsory granting to Germany of the best part of a rich Province of a helpless country, but only stipulated that the Germans should keep it open to the trade of the United States. They did not make the least effort to save the rights of China; they only tried to save the commercial advantages of the United States. There immediately followed upon that cession to Germany a cession to Russia of Port Arthur and the region called Talien-Wan for 25 years, with the privilege of renewing it for a similar period. When, soon afterwards, Japan and Russia came to blows, you remember what happened. Russia was obliged to turn over to Japan Port Arthur and Talien-Wan, just exactly as Japan is now allowed to take over the German rights in Shantung. This Government, though the conference which determined these things was held on our own soil, did not, so far as I have been able to learn, make the slightest intimation of objecting. At the time Germany got Kiaochow Bay, England came in and said that since Germany was getting a piece of Shantung and Russia was getting Port Arthur and Talien-Wan, she would insist upon having her slice of China, too, and the region of Wei-Hai-Wei was ceded to her. Immediately upon that France got into the unhandsome game, and there was ceded to France for ninety-nine years one of the ports of China with the region lying behind it. In all of those transactions there was not a single attempt made by the government of the United States to do anything except to keep those regions open to our traders.

You now have the historic setting of the settlement about Shantung. What I want to call your attention to is that the treaty of peace does not take Shantung from China; it takes it from Germany. There are seventy-eight years of the ninety-nine of that lease still to run, and not only do we not take it from China, but Japan promises in an agreement which is formally recorded, which is acknowledged by the Japanese Government, to return all the sovereign rights which Germany enjoyed in Shantung without qualification to China, and to retain nothing except what foreign corporations have throughout China, the right to run that railroad and exploit those mines. There is not a great commercial and industrial nation in Europe that does not enjoy privileges of that sort in China, and some of them enjoy them at the expense of the sovereignty of China. Japan has promised to release everything that savors of sovereignty and return it to China itself. She will have no right to put armed men anywhere into that portion of China. She will have no right to interfere with the civil administration of that portion of China. She will have no rights but economic and commercial rights. Now, if we choose to say that we will not assent to the Shantung provision, what do we do for China? Absolutely nothing. Japan has what Germany had in China in her military possession now. She has the promise of Great Britain and France that so far as they are concerned she can have it without qualification, and the only way we can take it away from Japan is by going to war with Japan and Great Britain and France.

The League of Nations for the first time provides a tribunal in which not only the sovereign rights of Germany and of Japan in China, but the sovereign rights of other nations can be curtailed, because every member of the League solemnly covenants to respect and preserve the territorial integrity and existing political independence of the other members, and China is to be a member. Never before, my fellow citizens, has there been a tribunal to which people like China could carry the intolerable grievances to which they have been subjected. Now a great tribunal has been set up in which the pressure of the whole judgment of the world will be exercised in her behalf.

That is the significance of Article X. Article X is the heart of the whole promise of peace, because it cuts out of the transactions of nations all attempts to impair the territorial integrity or invade the political independence of the weak as well as of the strong. Why did not Mr. Hay protest the acquisition of those rights in Shantung by Germany? Why did he not protest what England got, and what France got, and what Russia got? Because under international law, as it then stood, that would have been a hostile act toward those governments. The law of the world was actually such that if you mentioned anybody else's wrong but your own, you spoke as an enemy. After you have read Article X, read Article XI. Article XI says that it shall be the friendly right of any member of the League, strong or weak, to call the attention of the League to any matter, anywhere, that affects the peace of the world or the good understanding between nations upon which the peace of the world depends; so that for the first time it affords fine spirits like Mr. McKinley and Mr. John Hay the right to stand up before mankind and protest, and to say, "The rights of China shall be as sacred as the rights of those nations that are able to take care of themselves by arms." It is the most hopeful change in the law of the world that has even been suggested or adopted.

But there is another subject upon which some of our fellow citizens are particularly sensitive. They say, "What does the League of Nations do for the right of self-determination?" I think I can answer that question; if not satisfactorily, at any rate very specifically. It was not within the privilege of the conference of peace to act upon the right of self-determination of any peoples except those which had been included in the territories of the defeated empires—that is to say, it was not then within their power—but the moment the Covenant of the League of Nations is adopted it becomes their right. If the desire for self-determination of any people in the world is likely to affect the peace of the world or the good understanding between nations, it becomes the business of the League; it becomes the right of any member of the League to call attention to it; it becomes the function of the League to bring the whole process of the opinion of the world to bear upon that very matter. Where before, and when before, may I ask some of my fellow countrymen who want a forum upon which to conduct a hopeful agitation, were they ever offered the opportunity to bring their case to the judgment of mankind? If they are not satisfied with that, their case is not good. The only case that you ought to bring with diffidence before the great jury of men throughout the world is the case that you can not establish. The only thing I shall ever be afraid to see the League of Nations discuss, if the United States is concerned, is a case which I can hardly imagine, where the United States is wrong, because I have the hopeful and confident expectation that whenever a case in which the United States is affected is brought to the consideration of that great body we need have no nervousness as to the elements of the argument so far as we are concerned. The glory of the United States is that it never claimed anything to which it was not justly entitled.

I look forward with a quickened pulse to the days that lie ahead of us as a member of the League of Nations, for we shall be a member of the League of Nations—I look forward with confidence and with exalted hope to the time when we can indeed legitimately and constantly be the champions and friends of those who are struggling for right anywhere in the world, and no nation is likely to forget, my fellow citizens, that behind the moral judgment of the United States resides the overwhelming force of the United States. We were respected in those old Revolutionary days when there were three millions of us. We are, it happens, very much more respected, now that there are more than a hundred millions of us. Now that we command some of the most important resources of the world, back of the majesty of the United States lies the strength of the United States. If Germany had ever dreamed, when she conceived her ungodly enterprise, that the United States would have come into the war, she never would have dared to attempt it.

But now, my fellow citizens, the hope of Germany has revived. The hope of Germany has revived, because in the debates now taking place in the United States she sees a hope of at last doing what her arms could not do—dividing the United States from the great nations with which it was associated in the war. Here is a quotation from a recent utterance of one of her counsellors of state:

"All humanity, Germany particularly, is tensely awaiting the decision of the American Senate on the peace treaty," ex-Minister of State von Scheller-Steinwartz said to-day. "Apparently"—out of respect for him I will not mention the name that that ex-Minister Steinwartz mentions—"apparently Senator Blank is the soul of the opposition. The Senator is no German hater. He hates all non-Americans equally, and he is absolutely a just man of almost Quaker-like moral strength." How delightful to receive such praise from such a source! "When he and other important Senators fight the peace treaty, their course means that the treaty displeases them because in the excessive enslavement of Germany, for which America would be forever responsible, they see grave danger of future complications. That course is thus to be hailed like the morning red of a new dawn." A new dawn for the world? Oh, no; a new dawn for Germany. "There is promise of a still better realization of conditions in the prospect that America, in all seriousness, may express the wish for a separate peace with the Central Powers."

A separate peace with the Central Empires could accomplish nothing but our eternal disgrace, and I would like, if my voice could reach him, to let this German counsellor know that the red he sees upon the horizon is not the red of a new dawn, but the red of a consuming fire which will consume everything like the recent purposes of the Central Empires. It is not without significance, my fellow citizens, that coincidentally with this debate with regard to the ratification of this treaty the whole pro-German propaganda has shown its head all over the United States. I would not have you understand me to mean that the men who are opposing the ratification of the treaty are consciously en-

couraging the pro-German propaganda. I have no
right to say that or to think it, but I do say that what
they are doing is encouraging the pro-German propaganda, and that it is bringing about a hope in the minds
of those whom we have just spent our precious blood
to defeat that they may separate us from the rest of
the world and produce this interesting spectacle, only
two nations standing aside from the great concert and
guarantee of peace—beaten Germany and triumphant
America.

See what can be accomplished by that. By that the
attitude of the rest of the world toward America will
be exactly what its recent attitude was toward Germany, and we will be in the position absolutely alien
to every American conception of playing a lone hand
in the world for our selfish advantage and aggrandizement. The thing is inconceivable. The thing is intolerable. The thing can and will never happen.

I speak of these things in order that you may realize,
my fellow citizens, the solemnity and the significance of
this debate in which we are engaged; its solemnity because it involves the honor of the United States and
the peace of humanity, its significance because whether
gentlemen plan it or not, not only refusal on our part,
but long hesitation on our part to cast our fortunes
permanently in with the fortunes of those who love
right and liberty will be to bring mankind again into
the shadow of that valley of death from which we have
just emerged. I was saying to some of your fellow
citizens to-day how touching it had been to me as I came
across the continent to have women who I subsequently learned had lost their sons or their husbands
come and take my hand and say, "God bless you, Mr.
President." Why should they say "God bless" me? I
advised the Congress of the United States to take the
action which sent their sons to their death. As Commander in Chief of the Army and Navy, I ordered
their sons to their death. Why should they take my

hand and with tears upon their cheeks say, "God bless you"? Because they understood, as I understood, as their sons who are dead upon the fields of France understood, that they had gone there to fight for a great cause, and, above all else, they had gone there to see that in subsequent generations women should not have to mourn their dead. And as little children have gathered at every station in playful lightheartedness about the train upon which I was traveling, I have felt as if I were trustee for them. I have felt that this errand that I am going about upon was to save them the infinite sorrows through which the world has just passed, and that if by any evil counsel or unhappy mischance this great enterprise for which we fought should fail, then women with boys at their breasts ought now to weep, because when those lads come to maturity the great battle will have to be fought over again.

And, my fellow citizens, there is another battle of which we are now upon the eve. That is the battle for the right organization of industrial society. I do not need to tell an audience in this great progressive State what I mean by that. We cannot work out justice in our communities if the world is to continue under arms and ready for war. We must have peace, we must have leisure of mind and detachment of purpose, if we are going to work out the great reforms for which mankind is everywhere waiting. I pray God that normal times may not much longer be withheld from us. The world is profoundly stirred. The masses of men are stirred by thoughts which never moved them before. We must not again go into the camp. We must sit down at the council table and, like men and brethren, lovers of liberty and justice, see that the right is done, see that the right is done to those who bear the heat and burden of the day, as well as to those who direct the labor of mankind. I am not a partisan of any party to any of these contests, and I am not an enemy of anybody except the minority that tries to control. I do not care where the minority is drawn from, I do not care how influential or how insignificant, I do not care which side of the labor question it has been on, if the power of the United States under my direction can prevent the domination of a minority, it will be prevented. I am a champion of that sort of peace, that sort of order, that sort of calm counsel out of which, and out of which alone, can come the satisfactory solutions of the problems of society. You cannot solve the problems of society amidst chaos, disorder, and strife. You can only solve them when men have agreed to be calm, agreed to be just, agreed to be conciliatory, agreed that the right of the weak is as majestic as the right of the strong; and when we have come to that mind in the counsels of nations we can then more readily come to that mind in our domestic counsels, upon which the happiness and prosperity of our own beloved people so intimately and directly depend.

I beg, my fellow citizens, that you will carry this question home with you, not in little pieces, not with this, that, and the other detail at the front in your mind, but as a great picture including the whole of the Nation and the whole of humanity, and know that now is the golden hour when America can at last prove that all she has promised in the day of her birth was no dream but a thing which she saw in its concrete reality, the rights of men, the prosperity of nations, the majesty of justice, and the sacredness of peace.

AT LUNCHEON, PALACE HOTEL, SAN FRANCISCO, CALIF., SEPTEMBER 18, 1919.

MR. TOASTMASTER, MY FELLOW COUNTRYMEN:
I stood here yesterday, but before a very different audience, an audience that it was very delightful to address, and it is no less delightful to find myself face to face with this thoughtful group of citizens of one of the most progressive States in the Union. Because,

after all, my fellow citizens, our thought must be of the present and the future. The men who do not look forward now are of no further service to the Nation. The immediate need of this country and of the world is peace not only, but settled peace, peace upon a definite and well-understood foundation, supported by such covenants as men can depend upon, supported by such purposes as will permit of a concert of action throughout all the free peoples of the world. The very interesting remarks of your toastmaster have afforded me the opportunity to pay the tribute which they earn to the gentlemen with whom I was associated on the other side of the water. I do not believe that we often enough stop to consider how remarkable the peace conference in Paris has been. It is the first great international conference which did not meet to consider the interests and advantages of the strong nations. It is the first international conference that did not convene in order to make the arrangements which would establish the control of the strong. I want to testify that the whole spirit of the conference was the spirit of men who do not regard themselves as the masters of anybody, but as the servants of the people whom they represent. I found them quick with sympathy for the peoples who had been through all these dolorous ages imposed upon, upon whom the whole yoke of civilization seemed to have been fastened so that it never could be taken off again.

The heart of this treaty, my fellow citizens, is that it gives liberty and independence to people who never could have got it for themselves, because the men who constituted that conference realized that the basis of war was the imposition of the will of strong nations upon those who could not resist them. You have only to take the formula of the recent war in order to see what was the matter. The formula of pan-Germanism was Bremen to Bagdad. What is the line from Bremen to Bagdad? It leads through partitioned

Poland, through prostrated Rumania, through subjugated Slavia, down through disordered Turkey, and
on into distressed Persia, and every foot of the line is
a line of political weakness. Germany was looking
for the line of least resistance to establish her power,
and unless the world makes that a line of absolute resistance this war will have to be fought over again.
You must settle the difficulties which gave occasion to
the war or you must expect war again. You know
what had happened all through that territory. Almost
everywhere there were German princes planted on
thrones where they did not belong, where they were
alien, where they were of a different tradition and a
different people, mere agents of a political plan, the
seething center of which was that unhappy city of Constantinople, where, I dare say, there was more intrigue
to the square inch than there has ever been anywhere
else in the world, and where not the most honest minds
always but generally the most adroit minds were sent
to play upon the cupidity of the Turkish authorities
and upon the helplessness of the Balkan States, in order
to make a field for European aggression. I am not now
saying that Germany was the only intriguer. I am not
now saying that hers were the only plans of advantage,
but I am saying that there was the field where lay the
danger of the world in regard to peace. Every statesman in Europe knew it, and at last it dawned upon
them that the remedy was not balances of power but
liberty and right.

An illumination of profound understanding of human
affairs shines upon the deliberations of that conference
that never shone upon the deliberations of any other
international conference in history, and therefore it is
a happy circumstance to me to be afforded the opportunity to say how delightful it was to find that
these gentlemen had not accepted the American specifications for the peace—for you remember they were
the American specifications—because America had come

in and assisted them and because America was powerful and they desired her influence and assistance, but because they already believed in them. When we uttered our principles, the principles for which we were fighting, they had only to examine the thoughts of their own people to find that those were also the principles for which their people were fighting as well as the people of the United States; and the delightful enthusiasm which showed itself in accomplishing some of the most disinterested tasks of the peace was a notable circumstance of the whole conference. I was glad after I inaugurated it that I drew together the little body which was called the big four. We did not call it the big four; we called it something very much bigger than that. We called it the supreme council of the principal allied and associated Powers. We had to have some name, and the more dramatic it was the better; but it was a very simple council of friends. The intimacies of that little room were the center of the whole peace conference, and they were the intimacies of men who believed in the same things and sought the same objects. The hearts of men like Clemenceau and Lloyd-George and Orlando beat with the people of the world as well as with the people of their own countries. They have the same fundamental sympathies that we have, and they know that there is only one way to work out peace and that is to work out right.

The peace of the world is absolutely indispensable to us, and immediately indispensable to us. There is not a single domestic problem that can be worked out in the right temper or opportunely and in time unless we have conditions that we can count on. I do not need to tell business men that they cannot conduct their business if they do not know what is going to happen tomorrow. You cannot make plans unless you have certain elements in the future upon which you can depend. You cannot seek markets unless you know whether you are going to seek them among people who suspect you or people who believe in you. If the United States is going to stand off and play truant in this great enterprise of justice and right then you must expect to be looked upon with suspicion and hostile rivalry everywhere in the world. They will say, "These men are not intending to assist; they are intending to exploit us." You know what happened just a few months before we went into the war. There was a conference at Paris consisting of representatives of the principal allied Powers for the purpose of concerting a sort of economic league in which they would manage their purchasing as well as their selling in a way which would redound to their advantage and make use of the rest of the world. That was because they then thought what they will be obliged to think again if we do not continue our partnership with them—that we were standing off to get what we could out of it, and they were making a defensive economic arrangement. Very well; they will do that again. Almost of instinct they will do it again, not out of a deliberate hostility to the United States but by the general instinctive impulse of their own business interest and their own business men. Therefore we cannot arrange a single element of our business until we have settled peace and know whether we are going to deal with a friendly world or an unfriendly world.

We cannot determine our own internal economic reforms until then, and there must be some very fundamental economic reforms in this country. There must be a reconsideration of the structure of our economic society. Whether we will or no, the majority of mankind demand it, in America as well as elsewhere, and we have got to sit down in the best temper possible, in times of quiet, in times permitting conciliation and not hostility, and determine what we are going to do. We cannot do it until we have peace. We cannot release the great industrial and economic power of America and let it run free until there are channels that are free in which it can run. And the channels of business are mental channels as well as physical channels. In an open market men's minds must be open. It has been said so often that it is a very trite saying, but it remains nevertheless true, that a financial panic is a mere state of mind. There are no fewer resources in a country at the time of a panic than there were the day before it broke. There is no less money, there is no less energy, there is no less individual capacity and initiative, but something has frightened everybody and credits are drawn in and everybody builds a fence around himself and is careful to keep behind the fence and wait and see what is going to happen. That is a panic. It is a waiting, a fearful expecting of something to happen. Generally it does not happen. Generally men slowly get their breath again and say, "Well, the world looks just the same as it did; we had better get to work again." Even when business is absolutely prostrate they are at least in the condition that a friend of mine described. He was asked at the time of one of our greatest panics, some 25 years ago, if business was not looking up. He said, "Yes; it is so flat on its back that it cannot look any other way." Even if it is flat on its back, it can see the world; it is not lying on its face, and it will presently sit up and begin to take a little nourishment and take notice, and the panic is over. But while the whole world is in doubt what to expect, the whole world is under the partial paralysis that is characteristic of a panic. You do not know what it is safe to do with your money now. You do not know what plans it is safe to make for your business now. You have got to know what the world of to-morrow is going to be, and you will not know until we have settled the great matter of peace.

I want to remind you how the permanency of peace is at the heart of this treaty. This is not merely a treaty of peace with Germany. It is a world settlement; not affecting those parts of the world, of course, which were not involved in the war, because the conference had no jurisdiction over them, but the war did extend to most parts of the world, and the scattered, dismembered assets of the Central Empires and of Turkey gave us plenty to do and covered the greater part of the distressed populations of the world. It is nothing less than a world settlement, and at the center of that stands this covenant for the future which we call the Covenant of the League of Nations. Without it the treaty cannot be worked, and without it it is a mere temporary arrangement with Germany. The Covenant of the League of Nations is the instrumentality for the maintenance of peace.

How does it propose to maintain it? By the means that all forward-looking and thoughtful men have desired for generations together, by substituting arbitration and discussion for war. To hear some gentlemen talk you would think that the council of the League of Nations is to spend its time considering when to advise other people to fight. That is what comes of a constant concentration of attention upon Article X. Article X ought to have been somewhere further down in the Covenant, because it is in the background; it is not in the foreground. I am going to take the liberty of expounding this to you, though I assume that you have all read the Covenant. At the heart of that Covenant are these tremendous arrangements: Every member of the League solemnly agrees—and let me pause to say that that means every fighting nation in the world, because for the present, limited to an army of 100,000, Germany is not a fighting nation—that it will never go to war without first having done one or another of two things, without either submitting the matter in dispute to arbitration, in which case it promises absolutely to abide by the verdict, or, if it does not care to submit it to arbitration, without submitting it to discussion by the council of the League of Nations, in which case it promises to lay all the documents and all the pertinent facts before that council; it consents that that council shall publish all the documents and all the pertinent facts, so that all the world shall know them; that it shall be allowed six months in which to consider the matter; and that even at the end of the six months, if the decision of the council is not acceptable, it will still not go to war for three months following the rendering of the decision. So that, even allowing no time for the preliminaries, there are nine months of cooling off, nine months of discussion, nine months not of private discussion, not of discussion between those who are heated, but of discussion between those who are disinterested except in the maintenance of the peace of the world, when the purifying and rectifying influence of the public opinion of mankind is brought to bear upon the contest. If anything approaching that had been the arrangement of the world in 1914, the war would have been impossible; and I confidently predict that there is not an aggressive people in the world who would dare bring a wrongful purpose to that jury. It is the most formidable jury in the world. Personally, I have never, so far as I know, been in danger of going to jail, but I would a great deal rather go to jail than do wrong and be punished merely by the look in the eyes of the men amongst whom I circulated. I would rather go to jail than be sent to Coventry. I would rather go to jail than be conscious every day that I was despised and distrusted. After all, the only over-whelming force in the world is the force of opinion.

If any member of the League ignores these promises with regard to arbitration and discussion, what happens? War? No; not war, but something more tremendous, I take leave to say, than war. An absolute isolation, a boycott. It is provided in the Covenant that any nation that disregards these solemn promises with regard to arbitration and discussion shall be thereby deemed *ipso facto* to have committed an act of war against the other members of the League, and that there shall thereupon follow an absolute exclusion of that nation from communication of any kind with the members of the League. No goods can be shipped in or out; no telegraphic messages can be exchanged, except through the elusive wireless perhaps; there shall be no communication of any kind between the people of the other nations and the people of that nation. There is not a nation in Europe that can stand that for six months. Germany could have faced the armies of the world more readily than she faced the boycott of the world. Germany felt the pinch of the blockade more than she felt the stress of the blow; and there is not, so far as I know, a single European country—I say European because I think our own country is an exception—which is not dependent upon some other part of the world for some of the necessaries of its life. Some of them are absolutely dependent, some of them are without raw materials practically of any kind, some of them are absolutely without fuel of any kind, either coal or oil; almost all of them are without that variety of supply of ores which are necessary to modern industry and necessary to the manufacture of munitions of war. When you apply that boycott, you have got your hand upon the throat of the offending nation, and it is a proper punishment. It is an exclusion from civilized society.

Inasmuch as I have sometimes been said to have been very disregardful of the constitutional rights of Congress, may I not stop to speak just for a moment of a small matter that I was punctilious to attend to in regard to that article? You will notice the language that any member of the League that makes breach of its covenants shall be regarded thereby *"ipso facto* to have committed an act of war." In the original draft it read, "Shall thereby be *ipso facto* regarded as at war with the other nations of the world." I said, "No; I cannot subscribe to that, because I am bound to safeguard the right of Congress to determine whether it is at war or not. I consent to its being an act of war by the party committing it, but whether Congress takes up the gage thus thrown down or not is another matter which I cannot participate in determining in a document of this sort." Germany committed several acts of war against us before we accepted the inevitable and took up her challenge, and it was only because of a sort of accumulation of evidence that Germany's design was not merely to sink American ships and injure American citizens, that was incidental to her design, but that her design was to destroy free political society. I remember saying to Congress before we went into the war that if Germany committed some act of war against us that was intolerable, I might have to give them different advice, and I remember a newspaper correspondent asked me what I thought would constitute such an act. I said, "I don't know, but I am perfectly certain I will know it when I see it. I cannot hypothetically define it, but it will be perfectly obvious when it occurs." And if Congress regards this act by some other member of the League as such an act of war against it as necessitates the maintenance of the honor of the United States, then it may in those circumstances declare war, but it is not bound to declare war under the engagement of the Covenant. What I am emphasizing, my fellow citizens, is this: That the heart of this Covenant is arbitration and discussion, and that is the only possible basis for peace in the future.

It is a basis for something better than peace. Civilization proceeds on the principle of understanding one another. You know peace between those who employ labor and those who labor depends upon conference and mutual understanding. If you do not get together with the other side, it will be hostility to the end; and after you have heard the case of the other fellow it sometimes becomes a little awkward for you to insist upon the whole of your case, because the human mind does have this fine quality—that it finds it embarrassing to face the truth and deny it. Moreover, the basis of friendship is intercourse. I know—I am very fond of— a very large number of men whom I know to be crooks. They are very engaging fellows, and when I form a judgment against them I have to be in another room. I cannot, because of my personal attitude toward them, form a harsh judgment; indeed, I suppose the very thing that gives some men the chance to be crooks is their fascinating personality. They put it over on you. You remember that very charming remark of Charles Lamb. One night, in company with some friends who were speaking of some person not present, Lamb, in his stuttering fashion, said, "I—I—I h—hate that fellow." Some one said, "Why, Charles, I didn't know you knew him." "Oh, I—I d—d—don't," he said, "I—I c—cant h—h—hate a m—man I—I know." That is one of the most genial utterances of the human spirit I have ever read, and one of the truest. It is mighty hard to hate a fellow you know, and it is mighty hard to hate a nation you know. If you had mixed, as I have had the good fortune to mix, with scores of people of other nations in recent months, you would have the same feeling that I do if, after you got over superficial matters like differences of language and some differences of manner, they were the same kind of folks.

As I have said to a number of audiences on this trip, the most thrilling thing that happened to me over there was the constant intercourse I was having with delegations of people representing nations from all over the globe, some of which, I had shamefacedly to admit, I had never heard of before. Do you know where Azerbaijan is? Well, one day there came in a very dignified and interesting group of gentlemen from Azerbaijan. I did not have time until they were gone to find out where they came from, but I did find this out immediately, that I was talking to men who talked the same language that I did in respect of ideas, in respect of conceptions of liberty, in respect of conceptions of right and justice, and I did find this out, that they were, with all the other delegations that came to see me, metaphorically speaking, holding their hands out to America and saying, "You are the disciples and leaders of the free peoples of the world; can't you come and help us?" Until we went into this war, my fellow citizens, it was the almost universal impression of the world that our idealism was a mere matter of words; that what we were interested in was getting on in the world and making as much as we could out of it. That was the sum and substance of the usual opinion of us outside of America; and in the short space that we were in this war that opinion was absolutely reversed.

Consider what they saw: The flower of our youth sent three and four thousand miles away from their home, a home which could not be directly touched by the flames of that war, sent to foreign fields to mix with foreign and alien armies to fight for a cause which they recognized as the common cause of mankind, and not the peculiar cause of America. It caused a revulsion of feeling, a revulsion of attitude which, I dare say, has never been paralleled in the world; and at this moment, unless the cynical counsels of some of our acquaintances should prevail—which God forbid—they are expecting and inviting us to lead the civilized world, because they trust us—they really and truly trust us. They would not believe, no matter where we sent an army to be of assistance to them, that we would ever use that army for any purpose but to assist them. They know that when we say, as we said when we sent men to Siberia, that we are sending them to assist in the distribution of food and clothing and shoes so that brigands will not seize them, and that for the rest we are ready to render any assistance which they want us to render, and will interfere in absolutely nothing that concerns their own affairs, we mean it, and they believe us. There is not a place in this world now, unless we wait a little while longer, where America's political ambitions are looked upon with suspicion. That was frankly admitted in this little conference that I have spoken of. Not one of those gentlemen thought that America had any ulterior designs whatever. They were, therefore, in all our conferences, in consulting our economical experts, in consulting our geographical experts, constantly turning to America to act as umpire; and in nine cases out of ten, just because America was disinterested and could look at the thing without any other purpose than reaching a practicable solution, it was the American solution that was accepted.

In order that we may not forget, I brought with me the figures as to what this war meant to the world. This is a body of business men, and you will understand these figures. They are too big for the imagination of men who do not handle big things. Here is the cost of the war in money, exclusive of what we loaned one another: Great Britain and her dominions, $38,000,000,000; France, $26,000,000,000; the United States, $22,000,000,000 (this is the direct cost of our operations); Russia, $18,000,000,000; Italy, $13,-000,000,000; and the total, including Belgium, Japan, and other countries, $123,000,000,000. This is what it cost the Central Powers: Germany, $39,000,000,-000, the biggest single item; Austria-Hungary, $21,-000,000,000; Turkey and Bulgaria, $3,000,000,000; a total of $63,000,000,000, and a grand total of direct war costs of $186,000,000,000—almost the capital of the world. The expenditures of the United States were at the rate of $1,000,000 an hour for two years, including night time with day time. The battle deaths during the war were as follows: Russia lost in dead 1,700,000 men, poor Russia, that got nothing but terror and despair out of it all; Germany, 1,600,000; France, 1,385,-

000; Great Britain, 900,000; Austria, 800,000; Italy, 364,000; the United States, 50,300 dead. The total for all the belligerents, 7,450,200 men—just about seven and a half million killed because we could not have arbitration and discussion, because the world had never had the courage to propose the conciliatory methods which some of us are now doubting whether we ought to accept or not. The totals for wounded are not obtainable except our own. Our own wounded were 230,000, excluding those who were killed. The total of all battle deaths in all the wars of the world from the year 1793 to 1914 was something under 6,000,000 men, so that about a million and a half more men were killed in this war than in all the wars of something more than 100 preceding years. We really cannot realize that. Those of us who lost sons or brothers can realize it. We know what it meant. The women who have little children crowding about their knees know what it means; they know that the world has hitherto been devoted to brutal methods of settlement, and that every time a war occurs it is the flower of the manhood that is destroyed; that it is not so much the present generation as the next generation that goes maimed off the stage or is laid away in obscure graves upon some battle field; and that great nations are impaired in their vitality for two generations together and all their life embittered by a method of settlement for which we could find, and have now found, a substitute.

My fellow citizens, I believe in Divine Providence. If I did not, I would go crazy. If I thought the direction of the disordered affairs of this world depended upon our finite intelligence, I should not know how to reason my way to sanity, and I do not believe that there is any body of men, however they concert their power or their influence, that can defeat this great enterprise, which is the enterprise of divine mercy and peace and good will.

AT BERKELEY, CALIF., SEPTEMBER 18, 1919.

DEAN JONES, MR. MAYOR, LADIES AND GENTLEMEN:
I feel an old feeling come over me as I stand in this presence, and my great danger and temptation is to revert to type and talk to you as college men and women from a college man. I was reminded as I received your very generous welcome of a story told of Mr. Oliver Herford, a very delightful wit and artist. He was one day sitting in his club, and a man came by who did not know him very well, but who took many liberties. He slapped him on the back and said, "Hello, Ollie, old boy, how are you?" Herford writhed a little under the blow, looked at him a little coldly, and said: "I don't know your name; I don't know your face; but your manners are very familiar." I can say to you young ladies and gentlemen, I do not know your names or your faces, but your manners are very familiar, and very delightfully familiar. I think also of a rebuke I used often to address to my classes. I used to say that the trouble about the college youth of America was that it refused to grow up; that the men and women alike continued to be schoolboys and schoolgirls. I used to remind them that on the continent of Europe revolutions often began in the universities, and statesmen were nervous of nothing so much as of the concerted movements of opinion at the centers of learning; and I asked them what Cabinet at Washington ever cared a peppercorn what they were thinking about. It is your refusal, my fellow students, to grow up. One reason I am glad to see that the boys who have been at the front come back is that they have grown up; they have seen the world; seen it at its worst, but nevertheless seen it in action; seen it with its passions in action; seen it with its savage and its liberal passions in action. They have come back to know what they are preparing for, to know the kind of world that they are going to go out in, not to do physi-

cal fighting, but to do the kind of thinking that is better than fighting, the kind of thinking that makes men conscious of their duties, the kind of thinking that purifies the impulses of the world and leads it on to better things.

The burden that is upon my heart as I go about on this errand is that men are hesitating to give us the chance. We cannot do any effective thinking for the world until we know that there is settled peace. We cannot make any long plans for the betterment of mankind until these initial plans are made, and we know that there is going to be a field and an opportunity to make the plans that will last and that will become effective. That is the ground of my impatience with the debate. I admit that there are debatable things, but I do not admit that they need be debated so long. Not only that, but I do insist that they should be debated more fairly. A remark was repeated to me that was made after the address I made in San Francisco last night. Some man said that after hearing an exposition of what was really in the treaty he was puzzled; he wondered what the debate was about; it all seemed so simple. That was not, I need not assure you, because I was misleading anybody or telling what was not in the treaty, but because the men he had heard debate it, some of the newspapers he had heard debate it, had not told him what was in the treaty.. This great document of human rights, this great settlement of the world, had been represented to him as containing little traps for the United States. Men had been going about dwelling upon this, that, and the other feature and distorting the main features and saying that that was the peace proposed. They are responsible for some of the most serious mistakes that have ever been made in the history of this country; they are responsible for misleading the opinion of the United States. It is a very distressing circumstance to me to find that when I recite the mere facts they are, novel to some of my fellow citizens. Young gentlemen and young ladies, what we have got to do is to see that that sort of thing cannot happen. We have got to know what the truth is and insist that everybody shall know what the truth is, and, above all things else, we must see that the United States is not defeated of its destiny, for its destiny is to lead the world in freedom and in truth.

.

AT AUDITORIUM, OAKLAND, CALIF., SEPTEMBER 18, 1919.

DR. RINEHART, MY FELLOW CITIZENS:

You have indeed warmed my heart with your splendid welcome and I esteem it a great privilege to stand here, before you, to-night to look at some of the serious aspects of the great turning point in the history of this Nation and the history of the world which affairs have brought us to. Dr. Rinehart expressed my own feeling when she said that in my own consciousness those great ranks of little children seemed to me my real clients, seemed to be that part of my fellow citizens for whom I am pleading. It is not likely, my fellow citizens, that with the depleted resources of the great fighting nations of Europe, there will be another war soon, but unless we concert measures to prevent it, there will be another and a final war, at just about the time these children come to maturity; and it is our duty to look in the face the real circumstances of the world in order that we may not be unfaithful to the great duty which America undertook in the hour and day of her birth.

One thing has been impressed upon me more than another as I have crossed the continent, and that is that the people of the United States have been singularly and, I some times fear deliberately, misled as to the character and contents of the treaty of peace. Some one told me that after an address I delivered in San Francisco last night one of the men who had been present, a very thoughtful man I was told, said that after listening to what I had said he wondered what the debate was about, it all seemed so simple, so obvious, so natural. I was at once led to reflect that that was not because of any gift of exposition that I have, but because I had told that audience what the real character and purpose of the covenant of nations is. They had been led to look at certain incidental features of it, either on the assumption that they had not read the document or in the hope that they would not read it and would not realize what the real contents of it were. I have not come out from Washington, my fellow citizens, on a speech-making tour. I do not see how anybody could get his own consent to think of the way in which he was saying the things that it is necessary for me to say. I should think that every man's consciousness would be fixed, as my own is, upon the critical destiny of the world which hangs upon the decision of America. I am confident what that decision is going to be because I can see the tide of sentiment and the tide of conviction rising in this country in such a manner that any man who tries to withstand it will be overwhelmed. But we are an intelligent and thoughtful people; we want to know just what it is that we are about, and if you will be patient with me I am going to try to point out some of the things I did not dwell upon last night that are the salient and outstanding characteristics of this treaty.

I am not going to speak to-night particularly of the Covenant of the League of Nations. I am going to point out to you what the treaty as a whole is. In the first place, of course, that treaty imposes upon Germany the proper penalty for the crime she attempted to commit. It is a just treaty in spite of its severity. It is a treaty made by men who had no intention of crushing the German people, but who did mean to have it burnt into the consciousness of the German people, and through their consciousness into the apprehension of the world, that no people could afford to live under a

Government which was not controlled by their purpose and will and which was at liberty to impose secret ambitions upon the civilization of the world. It was intended as notice to all mankind that any Government that attempted what Germany attempted would meet with the same concerted opposition of mankind and would have meted out to it the same just retribution. All that this treaty amounts to, so far as Germany is concerned, is that she shall be obliged to pay every dollar that she can afford to pay to repair the damage that she did; except for the territorial arrangements which it includes, that is practically the whole of the treaty so far as it concerns Germany. What has not been borne in upon the consciousness of some of our people is that, although most of the words of the treaty are devoted to the settlement with Germany, the greater part of the meaning of its provisions is devoted to the settlement of the world.

The treaty begins with the Covenant of the League of Nations, which is intended to operate as a partnership, a permanent partnership, of the great and free self-governing peoples of the world to stand sponsor for the right and for civilization. Notice is given in the very first articles of the treaty that hereafter it will not be a matter of conjecture whether the other great nations of the world will combine against a wrongdoer, but a matter of certainty that hereafter nations contemplating what the Government of Germany contemplated will not have to conjecture whether Great Britain and France and Italy and the great United States will join hands against them, but will know that mankind, in serried ranks, will defend to the last the rights of human beings wherever they are. This is the first treaty ever framed by such an international convention, whose object was not to serve and defend governments but to serve and defend peoples. This is the first people's treaty in the history of intentional dealings. Every member of that great convention of peace

was poignantly aware that at last the people of the
world were awake, that at last the people of the world
were aware of what wrong had been wrought by irresponsible and autocratic governments, that at last all
the peoples of the world had seen the vision of liberty,
had seen the majesty of justice, had seen the doors
thrown open to the aspirations of men and women and
the fortunes of children everywhere, and they did not
dare assume that they were the masters of the fortunes
of any people, but knew that in every settlement they
must act as the servants not only of their own people
but of the people who were waiting to be liberated, the
people who could not win their own liberty, the people
who had suffered for centuries together the intolerable
wrongs of misgovernment. This is a treaty not merely
for the peoples who were represented at the peace table
but for the people who were the subjects of the governments whose wrongs were forever ended by the victory
on the fields of France.

My fellow citizens, you know and you hear it said
every day, you read it in the newspapers, you hear it in
the conversation of your friends, that there is unrest
all over the world. You hear that in every part of the
world, not excluding our own beloved country, there
are men who feel that society has been shaken to its
foundations, and that it ought to have been shaken to
its foundations, in order that men might be awakened
to the wrongs that had been done and were continuing to be done. When you look into the history, not of
our own free and fortunate continent, happily, but of
the rest of the world, you will find that the hand of
pitiless power has been upon the shoulders of the great
mass of mankind since time began, and that only with
that glimmer of light which came at Calvary that first
dawn which came with the Christian era, did men begin
to wake to the dignity and right of the human soul,
and that in spite of professions of Christianity, in spite
of purposes of reform, in spite of theories of right

and of justice, the great body of our fellow beings have been kept under the will of men who exploited them and did not give them the full right to live and realize the purposes that God had meant them to realize. There is little for the great part of the history of the world except the bitter tears of pity and the hot tears of wrath, and when you look, as we were permitted to look in Paris, into some of the particular wrongs which the peoples of Central Europe, the peoples upon whom the first foundations of the new German power were to be built, had suffered for generations together, you wonder why they lay so long quiet, you wonder why men, statesmen, men who pretended to have an outlook upon the world, waited so long to deliver them. The characteristic of this treaty is that it gives liberty to peoples who never could have won it for themselves. By giving that liberty, it limits the ambitions and defeats the hopes of all the imperialistic governments in the world. Governments which had theretofore been considered to desire dominion, here in this document forswore dominion, renounced it, said, "The fundamental principle upon which we are going to act is this, that every great territory of the world belongs to the people who live in it and that it is their right and not our right to determine the sovereignty they shall live under and the form of government they shall maintain." It is astonishing that this great document did not come as a shock upon the world. If the world had not already been rent by the great struggle which preceded this settlement, men would have stood at amaze at such a document as this; but there is a subtle consciousness throughout the world now that this is an end of governing people who do not desire the government that is over them.

And, going further than that, the makers of the treaty proceeded to arrange, upon a coöperative basis, those things which had always been arranged before upon a competitive basis. I want to mention a very practical thing, which most of you, I dare say, never

thought about. Most of the rivers of Europe traverse
the territory of several nations, and up to the time of
this peace conference there had been certain historic
rights and certain treaty rights over certain parts of the
courses of those rivers which had embarrassed the people who lived higher up upon the streams; just as if the
great Mississippi, for example, passed through half a
dozen States and the people down at New Orleans lived
under a government which could control the navigation
of the lower part of the Mississippi and so hamper the
commerce of the States above them to the north which
wished to pass to the sea by the courses of the Mississippi. There were abundant instances of that sort in
Europe, and this treaty undertakes to internationalize
all the great waterways of that continent, to see to it
that their several portions are taken out of national
control and put under international control, so that the
stream that passes through one nation shall be just as
free in all its length to the sea as if that nation owned
the whole of it, and nobody shall have the right to put
a restriction upon their passage to the sea. I mention
this in order to illustrate the heart of this treaty, which
is to cut out national privilege and give to every people
the full right attaching to the territory in which they
live.

Then the treaty did something more than that. You
have heard of the Covenant of the League of Nations
until, I dare say, you suppose that is the only thing in
the treaty. On the contrary, there is a document almost
as extensive in the latter part of the treaty which is
nothing less than a great charter of liberty for the
working men and women of the world. One of the
most striking and useful provisions of the treaty is
that every member of the League of Nations undertakes to advance the humane conditions of labor for
men, women, and children, to consider the interests of
labor under its own jurisdiction, and to try to extend to
every nation with which it has any dealings the stand-

ards of labor upon which it itself insists; so that America, which has by no means yet reached the standards in those matters which we must and shall reach, but which, nevertheless, is the most advanced in the world in respect of the conditions of labor, undertakes to bring all the influence it can legitimately bear upon every nation with which it has any dealings to see that labor there is put upon as good a footing as labor in America. Perhaps some of you have not kept in mind the seamen's act which was passed in a recent session of Congress. Under the law before that act, seamen could be bound to the service of their ship in such fashion that when they came to the ports of the United States, if they tried to leave their ship, the Government of the United States was bound to arrest them and send them back to their ship. The seamen's act abrogates that law and practically makes it necessary for every ship that would take away from the United States the crew that it brings to it shall pay American wages to get it. Before this treaty was entered into the United States had entered upon the business of trying to extend to laboring men elsewhere the advantages which laboring men in the United States enjoy, and supplementing that promise in the Covenant of the League there is an elaborate arrangement for a periodic international conference in the interest of labor. It provides that that conference shall be called next month in the city of Washington by the President of the United States, and the President of the United States has already called it. We are awaiting to learn from the Senate of the United States whether we can attend it or not. We can at least sit and listen and wonder how long we are going to be kept out of membership of this great humane endeavor to see that working men and women and children everywhere in the world are regarded as human beings and taken care of as they ought to be taken care of.

This treaty does not stop there. It attempts to coördinate all the great humane endeavors of the world.

It tries to bring under international coöperation every effort to check international crime. I mean like that unspeakable traffic in women, like that almost equally unspeakable traffic in children. It undertakes to control the dealing in deadly drugs like opium. It organizes a new method of coöperation among all the great Red Cross societies of the world. I tell you, my fellow citizens, that simple red cross has come to mean to the world more than it ever meant before. Everywhere— in the remotest recesses of the world—there are people who wear that symbol, and every time I look at it I feel like taking off my hat, as if I had seen a symbol of the world's heart. This treaty is nothing less than an organization of liberty and mercy for the world. I wish you would get a copy of it and read it. A good deal of it is technical and you could skip that part, but read all of it that you do not need an expert to advise you with regard to the meaning of. The economic and financial clauses which particularly affect the settlements with Germany are, I dare say, almost unintelligible to most people, but you do not have to understand them; they are going to be worked out by experts. The rest of it is going to be worked out by the experience of free self-governed peoples.

One of the interesting provisions of the Covenant of the League of Nations is that no nation can be a member of that League which is not a self-governing nation. No autocratic government can come into its membership; no government which is not controlled by the will and vote of its people. It is a league of free, independent peoples, all over the world, and when that great arrangement is consummated there is not going to be a ruler in the world that does not take his advice from his people. Germany is for the present excluded, but she is excluded only in order that she may undergo a period of probation, during which she shall prove two things—first, that she has really changed her constitution permanently, and, second, that she intends to administer that constitution in the spirit of its terms. You read in the newspapers that there are intrigues going on in Germany for the restoration of something like the old government, perhaps for the restoration of the throne and placing upon it some member of the family of Hohenzollern. Very well, if that should be accomplished Germany is forever excluded from the League of Nations. It is not our business to say to the German people what sort of government they shall have; it is our fundamental principle that that is their business and not ours, but it is our business to say whom we will keep company with, and if Germany wishes to live in respectable society she will never have another Hohenzollern. The other day, you will notice, Hungary for a little while put one of the Austrian princes upon her throne, and the peace conference, still sitting in Paris, sent word that they could not deal with a government which had one of the Hapsburgs at its head. The Hapsburgs and the Hohenzollerns are permanently out of business. I dare say that they personally, from what I can learn, feel antiquated and out of date. They are out of date because, my fellow citizens, this Great War, with its triumphant issue, marks a new day in the history of the world. There can no more be any such attempts as Germany made if the great leading free people of the world lends its countenance and leadership to the enterprise. I say if, but it is a mere rhetorical if. There is not the least danger that America, after a treaty has been drawn up exactly along the specifications stipulated by America, will desert its associates. We are a people that redeems its honor. We are not, and never will be quitters.

You notice that one of the grounds of anxiety of a small group of our fellow citizens is whether they can get out of the League if they ever get in, and so they want to have the key put in their pockets; they want to be assigned a seat right by the door; they want to sit on the edge of their chairs and say, "If anything happens in this meeting to which I am in the least sensitive, I leave." That, my fellow citizens, is not the spirit of America. What is going to happen is this: We are not going to sit by the door; we are going to sit in the high seats, and if the present attitude of the peoples of the world toward America is any index of what it will continue to be, the counsels of the United States will be the prevailing counsels of the League. If we were humbly at the outset to sit by the door, we would be invited to go up and take the chair. I, for one, do not want to be put in the attitude of children who, when the game goes against them, will not play, because I have such an unbounded confidence in the rectitude of the purpose of the United States that I am not afraid she will ever be caught proposing something which the other nations will defeat. She did not propose anything in Paris which the other nations defeated. The only obstacles, the only insuperable obstacles, met there were obstacles which were contained in treaties of which she had no notice, in secret treaties which certain great nations were bound in honor to respect, and the Covenant of the League of Nations abolishes secret treaties. From this time forth all the world is going to know what all the agreements between nations are. It is going to know, not their general character merely, but their exact language and contents, because the provision of the League is that no treaty shall be valid which is not registered with the general secretary of the League, and the general secretary of the League is instructed to publish it in all its details at the earliest possible moment. Just as you can go to the courthouse and see all the mortgages on all the real estate in your county, you can go to the general secretariat of the League of Nations and find all the mortgages on all the nations. This treaty, in short, is a great clearance house. It is very little short of a canceling of the past and an insurance of the future.

Men have asked me, "Do you think that the League

of Nations is an absolute guarantee against war?" Of course it is not; no human arrangement can give you an absolute guarantee against human passion, but I answer that question with another, "If you thought you had fifty per cent insurance against war, would not you jump at it? If you thought you had thirty per cent insurance against war, would not you take it? If you thought you had ten per cent insurance against war, would not you think it better than nothing?" Whereas, in my judgment, this is ninety-nine per cent insurance, because the one thing that a wrong cause cannot stand is exposure. If you think that you have a friend who is a fool, encourage him to hire a hall. The particular thing that this treaty provides in the Covenant of the League of Nations is that every cause shall be deliberately exposed to the judgment of mankind. It substitutes what the whole world has long been for, namely, arbitration and discussion for war. In other words, all the great fighting nations of the world—for Germany for the time being, at any rate, is not a great fighting nation—promise to lay their case, whatever it may be, before the whole jury of humanity. If there had been any arrangement comparable with this in 1914, the calamitous war which we have just passed through would have been inconceivable.

Look what happened. The Austrian crown prince was assassinated inside the Austrian dominions, in Bosnia, which was under the Empire of Austria-Hungary, though it did not belong to it, and Austria had no business to have it; and because it was suspected that the assassination was connected with certain groups of agitators and certain revolutionary societies in Serbia war was made on Serbia, because the Austrian crown prince was assassinated in Austria! Just as if some great personage were to be assassinated, let us say, in Great Britain, and because the assassin was found to have society connections—I mean certain connections with a society that had an active membership—in the United

States, Great Britain should declare war on the United States. That is a violently improbable supposition, but I am merely using it as an illustration. Every foreign office in Europe, when it got sudden news of what was afoot, sent messages to its representative in Berlin asking the German Government to hold an international conference to see if the matter could not be adjusted, and the German Government would not wait twenty-four hours. Under the treaty of the League of Nations every fighting nation is bound to wait at least nine months, and to lay all the facts pertinent to the case before the whole world. There is nothing so overpowering and irresistible, my fellow citizens, as the opinion of mankind. One of the most interesting and, I think, in one way, one of the most moving sentences in the great Declaration of Independence, is one of the opening sentences—"that out of respect to the opinion of mankind the causes which have led the people of the American Colonies to declare their independence are here set forth." America was the first country in the world which laid before all mankind the reason why it went to war, and this treaty is the exaltation and permanent establishment of the American principle of warfare and of right. Why, therefore, do we hesitate to redeem the destiny of America? Why do we hesitate to support the most American thing that has ever been attempted? Why do we debate details when the heart of the thing is sound? And the beauty of it, my fellow citizens, is that the heart of America is sound.

We sent our boys across the sea to beat Germany, but that was only the beginning. We sent them across the sea to assure the world that nothing such as Germany attempted should ever happen again. That is the halo that is going to be about the brows of these fine boys that have come back from overseas. That is the light that is going to rest upon the graves oversea of the boys we could not bring back. That is the glory that is going to attach to the memories of that great

American Army, that it made conquest of the armies of Germany not only, but made conquest of peace for the world. Greater armies than sought the Holy Grail, greater armies than sought to redeem the Holy Sepulchre, greater armies than fought under that visionary and wonderful girl, Joan of Arc, greater than the armies of the American Revolution that sought to redeem us from the unjust rule of Britain, greater even than the armies of our Civil War which saved the Union, will be this noble army of Americans who saved the world!

At Stadium, San Diego, Calif., September 19, 1919.

Mr. Mayor, my fellow countrymen:

As you know, I have come from Washington on a very serious errand, indeed, and I need not tell you with what a thrill the sight of this great body of my fellow citizens fills my heart, because I believe that one of the most important verdicts of history has now to be rendered by the great people of the United States. I believe that this is a choice from which we cannot turn back. Whether it be the choice of honor or of dishonor, it will be a final choice that we shall make in this great hour of our history.

One of the most unexpected things that I have found on my journey is that the people of the United States have not been informed as to the real character and scope and contents of the great treaty of peace with Germany. Whether by omission or by intention, they have been directed in all of the speeches that I have read to certain points of the treaty which are incidental, and not central, and their attention has been drawn away from the real meaning of this great human document. For that, my fellow citizens, is just what it is. It not only concludes a peace with Germany and imposes upon Germany the proper penalties for the outrage she attempted upon mankind, but it also concludes the peace in the spirit in which the war was undertaken by the nations opposed to Germany. The challenge of war was accepted by them not with the purpose of crushing the German people but with the purpose of putting an end once and for all to such plots against the free governments of the world as had been conceived on Wilhelmstrasse, in Berlin, unknown to the people of Germany, unconceived by them, advised by little groups of men who had the military power to carry out private ambitions.

We went into this war not only to see that autocratic power of that sort never threatened the world again but we went into it for even larger purposes than that. Other autocratic powers may spring up, but there is only one soil in which they can spring up, and that is the wrongs done to free peoples of the world. The heart and center of this treaty is that it sets at liberty people all over Europe and in Asia who had hitherto been enslaved by powers which were not their rightful sovereigns and masters. So long as wrongs like that exist in the world, you cannot bring permanent peace to the world. I go further than that. So long as wrongs of that sort exist, you ought not to bring permanent peace to the world, because those wrongs ought to be righted, and enslaved peoples ought to be free to right them. For my part, I will not take any part in composing difficulties that ought not to be composed, and a difficulty between an enslaved people and its autocratic rulers ought not to be composed. We in America have stood from the day of our birth for the emancipation of people throughout the world who were living unwillingly under governments which were not of their own choice. The thing which we have held more sacred than any other is that all just government rests upon the consent of the governed, and all over the world that principle has been disregarded, that principle has been flouted by the strong, and only the weak have suffered.

The heart and center of this treaty is the principle adopted not only in this treaty but put into effect also in the treaty with Austria, in the treaty with Hungary, in the treaty with Bulgaria, in the treaty with Turkey, that every great territory in the world belongs to the people who are living on it, and that it is not the privilege of any authority anywhere—certainly not the privilege of the peace conference at Paris—to impose upon those peoples any government which they accept unwillingly and not of their own choice.

Nations that never before saw the gleam of hope have been liberated by this great document. Pitiful Poland, divided up as spoils among half a dozen nations, is by this document united and set free. Similarly, in the treaty with Austria, the Austrian power is taken off of every people over whom it had no right to reign. You know that the great populations of Bosnia and Herzegovina, which lay between Austria and the Balkan Peninsula, were unjustly under the power of the Austro-Hungarian Empire, and it was in a city of Bosnia that the Crown Prince of Austria was assassinated—Bosnia which was under the power of Austria. Though Bosnia was part of Austrian territory, Austria had the audacity to hold Serbia, an outside neighbor, responsible for an act of assassination on Austrian territory, the Austrian Government choosing to believe that certain societies with which it connected the assassin, societies active in Serbia, had planned and executed the assassination. So the world was deluged in blood, and 7,400,000 men lie dead—not to speak of the pitiful wounded, not to speak of the blinded, not to speak of those with distracted brain, not to speak of all the pitiful, shattered nerves of millions of men all over the world—because of an insurgent feeling in a great population which was ruled over by rulers not of their own choice. The peace conference at Paris knew that it would not go to the root of this matter unless it destroyed power of that kind. This treaty sets those great peoples free.

But it does not stop with that. In the heart of the treaty you will find a new charter for those who labor—men, women, and children all over the world. The heart of the world is depressed, my fellow citizens, the heart of the world is uneasy. The heart of the world is a little despairful of its future, because the economic arrangements of the world have not been just, and the people who are having unjust conditions imposed upon them are, of course, not content to live under them. When the whole world is at unrest you may be sure that there is some real cause for the unrest. It is not whimsical. Men do not disturb the foundations of their lives just to satisfy a sudden impulse. All these troubles, whatever shape they may take, whether the action taken is just or unjust, have their root in age-long wrongs which ought to be, must be, and will be righted, and this great treaty makes a beginning in that great enterprise of humanity. It provides an arrangement for recurrent and periodic international conferences, the main and sole object of which will be to improve the conditions of labor, to safeguard the lives and the health of women and children who work and whose lives would otherwise be impaired or whose health rendered subject to all the inroads of disease. The heart of humanity beats in this document. It is not a statesman's arrangement. It is a liberation of the peoples and of the humane forces of the world, and yet I never hear the slightest intimation of any of these great features in the speeches of the gentlemen who are opposing this treaty. They never tell you what is really in this treaty. If they did your enthusiasm would sweep them off their feet. If they did they would know that it was an audacity which they had better not risk to impair the peace and the humane conditions of mankind.

At the very front and heart of the treaty is the part which is most criticized, namely, the great Covenant for a League of Nations. This treaty could not be executed without such a powerful instrumentality. Unless all the right-thinking nations of the world are going to concert their purpose and their power, this treaty is not worth the paper that it is written on, because it is a treaty where peace rests upon the right of the weak, and only the power of the strong can maintain the right of the weak. If we as a nation indeed mean what we have always said, that we are the champions of human right, now is the time when we shall be brought to the test, the acid test, as to whether we mean what we said or not. I am not saying that because I have the least doubt as to the verdict. I am just as sure of it as if it had been rendered already. I know this great people among whom I was born and bred and whom I have had the signal honor to serve, whose mouthpiece it has been my privilege to be on both sides of the water, and I know that I am speaking their conscience, when I speak in the name of my own conscience that that is the duty of America and that it will be assumed and performed.

You have been led to believe that the Covenant of the League of Nations is in some sense a private invention. It is not always said of whom, and I need not mention who is suspected. It is supposed that out of some sort of personal ambition or party intention an authorship, an origination is sought. My fellow countrymen, I wish that I could claim the great distinction of having invented this great idea, but it is a great idea which has been growing in the minds of all generous men for several generations. Several generations? Why, it has been the dream of the friends of humanity through all the ages, and now for the first time a great body of practical statesmen, immersed in the business of individual nations, gets together and realizes the dream of honest men. I wish that I could claim some originative part in so great an enterprise, but I cannot. I was the spokesman in this matter, so far as I was influential at all, of all sorts and kinds of Americans and of all parties and factions in America. I would be ashamed, my fellow countrymen, if I treated a matter of this sort with a single thought of so small a matter as the national elections of 1920. If anybody discusses this question on the basis of party advantage, I repudiate him as a fellow American. And in order to validate what I have said, I want to make one or two quotations from representatives of a party to which I do not belong. The first I shall make from a man who has for a long time been a member of the United States Senate. In May, 1916, just about two years after the Great War began, this Senator, at a banquet at which I was myself present, uttered the following sentences:

"I know, and no one I think can know better than one who has served long in the Senate, which is charged with an important share of the ratification and confirmation of all treaties, no one can, I think, feel more deeply than I do the difficulties which confront us in the work which this League"—(that is, the great association extending throughout the country known as the League to Enforce Peace)—"undertakes. But the difficulties cannot be overcome unless we try to overcome them. I believe much can be done. Probably it will be impossible to stop all wars, but it certainly will be possible to stop some wars, and thus diminish their number. The way in which this problem is to be worked out must be left to this League and to those who are giving this great question the study which it deserves. I know the obstacles. I know how quickly we shall be met with the statement that this is a dangerous question which you are putting into your agreement, that no nation can submit to the judgment of other nations, and we must be careful at the beginning not to attempt too much. I know the difficulties which arise when we speak of anything which seems to involve an alliance. But I do not believe that when Washington warned us against entangling alliances he meant for one moment that we should not join with the other civilized nations of the world if a method could be found to diminish war and encourage peace.

"It was a year ago," he continues, "that in delivering the chancellor's address at Union College I made an argument on this theory: that if we were to promote international peace at the close of the present terrible war, if we were to restore international law as it must be restored, we must find some way in which the united forces of the nations could be put behind the cause of peace and law. I said then that my hearers might think that I was picturing a Utopia, but it is in the search for Utopias that great discoveries have been made. Not failure, but low aim, is the crime.

"This League certainly has the highest of all aims for the benefit of humanity, and because the pathway is sown with difficulties is no reason that we should turn from it."

The quotation is from the Hon. Henry Cabot Lodge.[1] I read another quotation from one of the most energetic, practical, and distinguished leaders of the Republican party, uttered in an article published in the New York "Times" in October, 1914:[2]

"The one permanent move for obtaining peace which has yet been suggested with any reasonable chance of attaining its object is by an agreement among the great powers, in which each should pledge itself not only to abide by the decisions of a common tribunal, but to back with force the decision of that common tribunal. The great civilized nations of the world which do possess force, actual or immediately potential, should combine by solemn agreement in a great world league for the peace of righteousness." A very worthy utterance by Theodore Roosevelt. I am glad to align myself with such utterances as those. I subscribe to every word of them. And here in concrete form is the fulfillment of

[1] Excerpt from speech by Senator Lodge at a meeting of the League to Enforce Peace, in Washington, May 16, 1916.

[2] Excerpt from article by Theodore Roosevelt, published in the New York "Times," October 18, 1914.

the plan which they advocate. We cannot in reason, we cannot as lovers of liberty, we cannot as supporters of right turn away from it.

What are those who advise us to turn away from it afraid of? In the first place, they are afraid that it impairs in some way that long traditional policy of the United States which was embodied in the Monroe Doctrine, but how they can fear that I cannot conceive, for the document expressly says in words which I am now quoting that nothing in this Covenant shall be held to affect the validity of the Monroe Doctrine. The phrase was inserted under my own eye, at the suggestion—not of the phrase but the principle—of the Foreign Relations Committees of both Houses of Congress. I think I am justified in dismissing all fear that the Monroe Doctrine is in the least impaired. And what is the Monroe Doctrine? It is that no outside power shall attempt to impose its will in any form upon the Western Hemisphere, and that if it does the United States, acting upon its own initiative and alone, if it chooses, can resist and will resist the attempt. Could anything leave the United States freer as a champion of the independence of the Western Hemisphere than this world acknowledgment of the validity and potency of the Monroe Doctrine?

They are afraid that the League will in some way deal with our domestic affairs. The Covenant expressly says that it will have no right to deal with the domestic affairs of any member of the League, and I cannot imagine anything more definite or satisfactory than that. There is no ambiguity about any part of this Covenant, for the matter of that, but there is certainly no ambiguity about the statement concerning domestic affairs, for it is provided that if any matter brought before the council is found to be a matter which, under international law, lies within the exclusive jurisdiction of the State making the claim, the council shall dismiss consideration of it and shall not even make a report about it. And the subjects which are giving these gentlemen the most concern are agreed by all students of international law to be domestic questions; for example, immigration, naturalization, the tariff—these are the subjects most frequently spoken of. No one of those can be dealt with by the League of Nations, so far as the sovereignty of the United States is concerned. We have a perfectly clear field there, as we have in regard to the Monroe Doctrine.

It is feared that our delegates will be outvoted, because I am constantly hearing it said that the British Empire has six votes and we have one. I am perfectly content to have only one when the one counts six, and that is exactly the arrangement under the League. Let us examine that matter a little more particularly. Besides the vote of Great Britain herself, the other five votes are the votes of Canada, of South Africa, of Australia, of New Zealand, and of India. We ourselves were champions and advocates of giving a vote to Panama, of giving a vote to Cuba—both of them under the direction and protectorate of the United States—and if a vote was given to Panama and to Cuba, could it reasonably be denied to the great Dominion of Canada? Could it be denied to that stout Republic in South Africa, that is now living under a nation which did, indeed, overcome it at one time, but which did not dare retain its government in its hands, but turned it over to the very men whom it had fought? Could we deny it to Australia, that independent little Republic in the Pacific, which has led the world in so many liberal reforms? Could it be denied New Zealand? Could we deny it to the hundreds of millions who live in India? But, having given these six votes, what are the facts? For you have been misled with regard to them. The League can take no active steps without the unanimous vote of all the nations represented on the council, added to a vote of the majority in the assembly itself. These six votes are in the assembly, not in the council. The assembly is not a voting body, except upon a limited number of questions, and whenever those questions are questions of action, the affirmative vote of every nation represented on the council is indispensable, and the United States is represented on the council. The six votes that you hear about can do nothing in the way of action without the consent of the United States. There are two matters in which the assembly can act, but I do not think we will be jealous of those. A majority of the assembly can admit new members into the League. A majority of the assembly can advise a member of the League to reconsider any treaty which in the opinion of the assembly of the League is apt to conflict with the operation of the League itself, but that is advice which can be disregarded, which has no validity of action in it, which has no compulsion of law in it. With the single exception of admitting new members to the League, there is no energy in the six votes which is not offset by the energy in the one vote of the United States, and I am more satisfied to be one and count six than to be six and count only one. This thing that has been talked about is a delusion. The United States is not easily frightened, and I dare say it is least easily frightened by things that are not true.

It is also feared that causes in which we are interested will be defeated. Well, the United States is interested in a great many causes, for the very interesting and compelling reason that the United States is made up out of all the civilized peoples of the world. There is not a national cause, my fellow citizens, which has not quickened the heartbeat of men in America. There is not a national cause which men in America do not understand, because they come of the same blood, they come of the same traditions, they recollect through long tradition the wrongs of their peoples, the hopes of their peoples, the passions of their peoples, and everywhere in America there are kinsmen to stand up and speak words of sympathy for great causes. For the first time in the history of the world, the League of Nations presents a forum, a world forum, where any one of these ambitions or aspirations can be brought to the consideration of mankind. Never before has this been possible. Never before has there been a jury of mankind to which nations could take their causes, whether they were weak or strong. You have heard a great deal about Article X of the Covenant. Very well, after you have read it suppose you read Article XI. Article XI provides that it shall be the friendly right of any member of the League, big or little, strong or weak, to call attention to anything, anywhere, which is likely to disturb the peace of the world or the good understanding between nations upon which the peace of the world depends. When anybody of kin to us in America is done wrong by any foreign government, it is likely to disturb the good understanding between nations upon which the peace of the world depends, and thus any one of the causes represented in the hearts of the American people can be brought to the attention of the whole world. One of the most effective means of winning a good cause is to bring it before that great jury. A bad cause will fare ill, but a good cause is bound to be triumphant in such a forum. Until this, international law made it an unfriendly act for any nation to call attention to any matter which did not immediately affect its own fortunes and its own right. I am amazed that so many men do not see the extraordinary change which this will bring in the transaction of human affairs. I am amazed that they do not see that now, for the first time, not selfish national policy but the general judgment of the world as to right is going to determine the fortunes of peoples, whether they be weak or whether they be strong, and I myself glory in the provisions of Article XI more than I glory in any other part of the Covenant, for it draws all men together in a single friendly court, where they may discuss their own affairs and determine the issues of justice—just exactly what was desired in the hearts of the men from whom I have read extracts of opinion.

But what disturbs me, perhaps the only thing that disturbs me, my fellow countrymen, about the form which the opposition to the League is taking is this: Certain reservations, as they are called, are proposed which in effect—I am not now stopping to form an opinion as to whether that is the intention or not; I have no right to judge the intention of a man who has not stated what his intention is—which in effect amount to this, that the United States is unwilling to assume the same obligations under the Covenant of the League that are assumed by the other members of the League; that the United States wants to disclaim any part in the responsibility which the other members of the League are assuming. I want to say with all the emphasis of which I am capable that that is unworthy of the honor of the United States. The principle of justice, the principle of right, the principle of international amity is this, that there is not only an imaginary but a real equality of standing and right among all the sovereign peoples of the world. I do not care to defend the rights of a people if I must regard them as my inferiors, if I must do so with condescension, if I must do so because I am strong and they are weak. You know the men, and the women, too, I dare say, who are respectful only to those whom they regard as their social equals or their industrial equals and of whom they are more or less afraid, who will not exercise the same amenities and the same consideration for those whom they deem beneath them. Such people do not belong in democratic society, for one thing, and, for another, their whole point of view is perverted; they are incapable of justice, because the foundation of justice is that the weakest has the same rights as the strongest. I must admit, my fellow citizens, and you cannot deny—and I admit it with a certain profound regret not only but with a touch of shame—that while that is the theory of democratic institutions it is not always the practice. The weak do not always fare as well as the strong, the poor do not always get the same advantage of justice that the rich get; but that is due to the passions and imperfections of human nature. The foundation of the law, the glory of the law, is that the weakest is equal to the strongest in matter of right and privilege, and the goal to which we are constantly though stumblingly and with mistakes striving to go toward is the goal of actual equality, of actual justice, upon the basis of equality of rights, and unless you are going to establish the society of nations upon the actual foundation of equality, unless the United States is going to assume the same responsibility and just as much responsibility as the other nations of the world we ought not to commit the mockery of going into the arrangement at all.

I will not join in claiming under the name of justice an unjust position of privilege for the country I love and honor. Neither am I afraid of responsibility. Neither will I scuttle. Neither will I be a little American. America, in her make-up, in her purposes, in her principles, is the biggest thing in the world, and she must measure up to the measure of the world. I will be no party in belittling her. I will be no party in saying that America is afraid of responsibilities which I know she can carry and in which in carrying I am sure she shall lead the world. Why, if we were to decline to go into this humane arrangement we would be declining the invitation which all the world extends to us to lead them in the enterprise of liberty and of justice. I, for one, will not decline that invitation. I, for one, believe more profoundly than in anything else human in the destiny of the United States. I believe that she has a spiritual energy in her which no other nation can contribute to the liberation of mankind, and I know that the heart of America is stronger than her business calculations. That is what the world found out when we went into the war. When we went into the war there was not a nation in the world that did not believe we were more interested in making money out of it than in serving the cause of liberty. And when we went in, in those few months the whole world stood at amaze and ended with an enthusiastic conversion. They now believe that America will stand by anybody that is fighting for justice and for right, and we shall not disappoint them.

The age is opening, my fellow citizens, upon a new scene. We are substituting in this Covenant—and this is the main purpose of it—arbitration and discussion for war. Senator Lodge says if we can stop some wars it is worth while. If you want insurance against war, I take it you would rather have ten per cent insurance than none; I take it that you would be delighted with fifty per cent insurance; and here I verily believe is ninety-nine per cent insurance against war. Here are all the great fighting nations of the world, with the exception of Germany—because for the time being Germany is not a great fighting nation—solemnly covenanting with one another that they will never go to war without first having either submitted the matter in dispute to arbitration and bound themselves to abide by the verdict, or, having submitted it to discussion by the council of the League of Nations in which case they will lay all the facts and documents by publication before the world, wait six months for the opinion of the council, and if they are dissatisfied with that opinion—for they are not bound by it —they will wait another three months before they go to war. There is a period of nine months of the process which is absolutely destructive of unrighteous causes— exposure to public opinion. When I find a man who in a public matter will not state his side of the case, and state it fully, I know that his side of the case is the losing side, that he dare not state it.

At the heart of most of our industrial difficulties, my fellow citizens, and most of you are witness to this, lies the unwillingness of men to get together and talk it over. Half of the temper which now exists between those who perform labor and those who direct labor is due to the fact that those who direct labor will not talk differences over with the men whom they employ, and I am in every such instance convinced that they are wrong and dare not talk it over. Not only that, but every time the two sides do get together and talk it over they come out of the conference in a different temper from that with which they went in. There is nothing that softens the attitude of men like really, frankly laying their minds alongside of each other and their characters alongside of each other and making a fair and manly and open comparison. That is what all the great fighting nations of the world agree to with every matter of difference between them. They put it either before a jury by whom they are bound or before a jury which will publish all the facts to mankind and express a frank opinion regarding it.

You have here what the world must have, what America went into this war to obtain. You have here an estoppel of the brutal, sudden impulse of war. You have here a restraint upon the passions of ambitious nations. You here have a safeguard of the liberty of weak nations, and the world is at last ready to stand up and in calm counsel discuss the fortunes of men and women and children everywhere. Why, my fellow citizens, nothing brings a lump into my throat quicker on this journey I am taking than to see the thronging children that are everywhere the first, just out of childish curiosity and glee, no doubt, to crowd up to the train when it stops, because I know that if by any chance we should not win this great fight for the League of Nations it would be their death warrant. They belong to the generation which would then have to fight the final war, and in that final war there would not be merely seven and a half million men slain. The very existence of civilization would be in the balance, and I for one dare not face the responsibility of defeating the very purpose for which we sent our gallant men over-seas. Every mother knows that her pride in the son that she lost is due to the fact, not that he helped to beat Germany, but that he helped to save the world. It was that light the other people saw in the eyes of the boys that went over there, that light as of men who see a distant horizon, that light as of men who have caught the gleam and inspiration of a great cause, and the armies of the United States seemed to those people on the other side of the sea like bodies of crusaders come out of a free nation to give freedom to their fellows, ready to sacrifice their lives for an idea, for an ideal, for the only thing that is worth living for, the spiritual purpose of redemption that rests in the hearts of mankind.

AT SAN DIEGO, CALIF., SEPTEMBER 19, 1919.

MR. MAYOR, LADIES, AND GENTLEMEN:

It is very agreeable to have been indirectly intro-duced by my friend Mr. Gage, for whom I have so affectionate a regard. I know he will not mind my saying that I first met him when we were both "lame ducks." I had just come out of the hospital after an operation and he had one arm out of commission from neuritis, and we met sitting, rather helplessly and per-haps hopelessly, on one of the broad piazzas of one of the hotels at Palm Beach. Being fellow sufferers and comrades in misery, we were drawn toward each other and drawn into confidences which I greatly enjoyed, and which I now recall with peculiar pleasure in seeing Mr. Gage without his hand bound up and in the sort of health I would wish to see him in. What he has said has reminded me of one of the thoughts which has been prominent in my mind of late. He has spoken of our dealings with the Philippine Islands. One of the perplexities under which we have suffered is that, although we are leading the Philippine Islands toward independence, we were in doubt of what would happen to them when they obtained their independence. Before this conference at Paris, the only thing that could be suggested was that we should get a common guarantee from all the nations of the world that the Philippines should be regarded as neutral, just as Belgium was once regarded as neutral, and that they should guarantee her inviolability, because it was certainly to be expected that she would not be powerful enough to take care of herself against those who might wish to commit aggression against her. That serves as a very useful illustration of one of the purposes for which the League of Nations has been established, for do you not observe that the moment we are ready to give independence to the Philippines her independence is already guaranteed, because all the great nations of the world are under engagement of the most solemn sort to respect and preserve her territorial integrity and her existing political independence as against external aggression? Those words "external aggression" are sometimes left out of the exposition of Article X. There was not a member of that peace conference with whom I conferred who did not hold the same opinion that I hold as to the sacred right of self-determination and did not hold the principle which all Americans hold, that it was not the right of any nation to dictate to another nation what sort of government it should have or under what sort of sovereignty it would live.

For us the problem of the future of the Philippines is solved by the League of Nations. It is the first time that the world has come to this mind about matters of that sort, and what brought it to that mind? The breakdown of the neutrality of Belgium. You know you cannot establish civil society if anybody is going to be a neutral with regard to the maintenance of the law. We are all bound in conscience, and all public officers are bound in oath, not to remain neutral with regard to the maintenance of the law and the vindication of the right, and one of the things that occurred in this conference, as a sort of practical joke on myself, was this: One of the principles that I went to Paris most insisting on was the freedom of the seas. Now, the freedom of the seas means the definition of the right of neutrals to use the seas when other nations are at war, but under the League of Nations there are no neutrals, and, therefore, what I have called the practical joke on myself was that by the very thing that I was advocating it became unnecessary to define the freedom of the seas. All nations are engaged to maintain the right, and in that sense no nation can be neutral when the right is invaded, and, all being comrades and partners in a common cause, we all have an equal right to use the seas. To my mind it is a much better solution than had occurred to me, or than had occurred to anyone else with regard to that single definition of right.

We have no choice, my fellow citizens, in this matter except between these alternatives: We must go forward with this concert of nations or we must go back to the old arrangement, because the guarantees of peace will not be sufficient without the United States, and those who oppose this Covenant are driven to the necessity of advocating the old order of balances of power. If you do not have this universal concert, you have what we have always avoided, necessary alignment of this or that nation with one other nation or with some other group of nations. What is disturbing me most about the present debate—not because I doubt its issue, but because I regret its length—is that it is heartening the representatives of Germany to believe that at last they are going to do in this way what they were not able to do by arms, separate us in interest and purpose from our associates in the war. I am not suggesting, I have no right to suggest, that the men who are opposing this Covenant have any thought of assisting Germany in their minds, but my point is that by doing what they are doing they are assisting Germany, whether they want to do so or not. And it is not without significance, my fellow countrymen, that coincidentally with this debate there has been a revival of the pro-German propaganda all over the United States, for this is Germany's calculation that, inasmuch as she is obliged to stand apart and be for the time suspected and have other nations come slowly to accommodation with her, if we hold off other nations will be similarly alienated from us, as they will be, and that there will be, whether we design it or not, a community of interest between the two isolated nations. It is an inevitable psychological result. We must join this arrangement to complete the psychology of this war.

The psychology of this war is this, that any nation that attempts to do what Germany did will certainly have the world combined against it. Germany not only did not know she would have the world combined against her, but she never dreamed she would. Germany confidently expected that Great Britain would not go into the war; she never dreamed that America would go into the war, and in order not absolutely to dishearten her people she had continuously to lie to them and tell them that the submarine warfare was so effective that American troops could not be sent to Europe. Friends of mine who, before we went into the war, conversed with Germans on the other side and told them that they had come over since the submarine warfare began were not believed. The Germans said, "Why, you cannot cross the sea." The body of the German people actually thought that the sea was closed, and that we could send 2,000,000 men over there without losing any of them, except on a single transport, was incredible to them. If they had ever dreamed that that would happen they never would have ventured upon so foolish an attack upon the liberties of mankind.

What is impressed upon my mind by my stay on the other side of the water more than any one thing is that, while old rivalries and old jealousies and many of the intricate threads of history woven in unhappy patterns have made the other nations of the world suspect one another, nobody doubts or suspects America. That is the amazing and delightful discovery that I made on the other side of the water. If there was any place in our discussions where they wanted troops sent, they always begged that American troops might be sent, because they said none of the other associated powers would suspect them of any ulterior designs, and that the people of the country itself would know that they had not gone there to keep anything that they took, that they had not gone there to interfere with their internal affairs; that they had gone not as exploiters but as friends. That is the reputation of American soldiers throughout Europe, and it is their reputation because it is true. That is the beautiful background of it. That is the temper in which they go; that is the principle upon which they act and upon which the Government back of them acts, and the great people whom that Government represents. There is something more than the choosing between peace and armed isolation, for that is one aspect of the choice. We are choosing between a doubtful peace and an assured peace, guided and led by the United States of America.

I was very much interested to scan the names on a very beautifully engrossed communication that was put in my hands to-day by Mr. Gage, a communication from the representatives of the League to Enforce Peace. I found upon it the names of many of the principal and most representative citizens and professional men of San Diego, and it happened, I believe, unless I am misinformed, that practically all the signers were Republicans. There is one thing against which I wish to enter a protest. I have had, I do not know how many, men come to me and say, "Mr. President, I am a Republican, but I am for the League of Nations." Why but? For as a Democrat you will permit me to remind you who are Republicans that you have always boasted that your party was the party of constructive programs. Here is the most constructive, the greatest constructive, program ever proposed. Why should you say but? If I were in your place and had in my heart the pride which you very properly entertain because of the accomplishments of your party, I would say, "I am a Republican, and for that reason I am in favor of the League of Nations." But I am not going to say that I am a Democrat, and therefore in favor of the League of Nations, because I am not in favor of it because I am a Democrat. I am in favor of it because I am an American and a believer in humanity, and I believe in my heart that if the people of this country, as I am going about now, were to suspect that I had political designs they would give me evident indication that they wanted me to go back to Washington right away. They would not give me the splendid and delightful welcomes they are giving me. Men and women would not come up to me as they are doing now and take my hand in theirs and say, "Mr. President, God bless you!" I wonder if you realize, as I have tried to realize, what that gracious prayer means. I have had women who had lost their dearest in the war come up to me with tears upon their cheeks and say, "God bless you!" Why did they bless me? I advised the Congress to go into the war and to send their sons to their death. As Commander in Chief of the Army and Navy, I sent their sons to their death, and they died, and their mothers come and say "God bless you!" There can be only one explanation. They are proud of the cause in which their sons died; and, my friends, since we all have to die, the way those fellows died is the best way after all. There was nothing in it for them, no possible personal gain, nothing except the noble performance of a disinterested duty, and that is the highest distinction that any man can achieve.

I remember years ago reading an essay that left a permanent impression on my mind. It was entitled "Christmas: Its Unfinished Business." It was a dis-

course upon what was then a very common occurrence—
the meeting of assemblies to promote peace. You know,
we used to be always having conventions to promote
peace, and most of the men who sat on the platform
were men who were doing everything they could to
bring on war by unjustly exploiting other countries and
taking advantages that they should not take, that were
sure to exasperate the feeling of people elsewhere. But
they did not realize that they were really bringing on
wars; they, in their minds, were trying to bring on
peace, and the writer of the essay called attention to
this. His thesis was, "There will be peace when peace
is as handsome as war." He hurried to explain that
what he meant was this: That leaving aside the men
who may have unjustly and iniquitously plotted war—
like the general staff in Germany—the men in the ranks
gave everything that they had, their lives included, for
their country, and that while you would always hang the
boy's musket or the boy's sword up over the mantelpiece, you never would hang up his ledger or his yardstick or his spade; not that civil employments meant to
support yourself are dishonorable, but that they are centered upon yourself, whereas the sword and the gun
mean that you had forgotten yourself and remembered
only the call of your country. Therefore, there was a
certain sacredness about that implement that could not
attach to any implement of civil life. "Now," said my
essayist, "when men are devoted to the purposes of
peace with the same self-forgetfulness and the same
thought for the interest of their country and the cause
that they are devoted to that they display under arms in
war, then there will be no more war. When the motives of peace are as disinterested and as handsome as
the motives of war for the common soldier, then we will
all be soldiers in an army of peace and there will be no
more wars." Now, that comes about when there is a
common conception of peace, and the heart of this
covenant of peace is to bring nations together into con-

sultation so that they will see which of their objects are common, so that they will discuss how they can accommodate their interests, so that their chief objective will be conciliation and not alienation; and when they understand one another, they will coöperate with one another in promoting the general interest and the common peace. It is the parliament of nations at last, where everyone is under covenant himself to do right, to respect and preserve the territorial integrity and existing political independence of the others, and where everyone engages never to go to war without first trying to settle the matter by the slow-cooling, disinterested processes of discussion. It is what we have been striving for for generation after generation, and now some men hesitate to accept it when the golden thing is placed in their hand. It would be incredible to me if I did not understand some of them, but it is not permitted to one occupying my present office to make personal remarks. After all, personal remarks are neither here nor there. What does any one of us matter in so great a thing as this? What difference does it make whether one man rises and another falls, or we all go down or go up together? We have got to serve humanity. We have got to redeem the honor of the United States. We have got to see this thing through to its great end of justice and peace.

At Hotel Alexandria, Los Angeles, Calif., September 20, 1919.

MR. TOASTMASTER AND LADIES AND GENTLEMEN:

May I not first thank you, Mr. Toastmaster, for your very generous introduction? It spoke in the same delightful tone of welcome that I have heard in the voices on the street to-day, and, although I do not accept for myself the praise that you have so generously bestowed upon me, I nevertheless do recognize in it that you have set just the right note for the discussion which I wanted for a few moments to attempt.

There is only one thing, my fellow citizens, that has daunted me on this trip. My good father used to teach me that you cannot reason out of a man what reason did not put in him, and, suspecting—may I not say knowing—that much of the argument directed against the League of Nations is not based upon reason, I must say I have sometimes been puzzled how to combat it, because it is true, as your toastmaster has said, that there is a great constructive plan presented, and no man in the presence of the present critical situation of mankind has the right to oppose any constructive plan except by a better constructive plan. I will say now that I am ready to take ship again and carry back to Paris any constructive proposals which appear a suitable and better substitute for those which have been made.

There is a peculiarity about this constructive plan which ought, I think, to facilitate our acceptance of it. It is laid out in every part upon American principles. Everybody knows that the principles of peace proposed by America were adopted, were adopted as the basis of the armistice and have been acted upon as the basis of the peace, and there is a circumstance about those American principles which gives me absolute confidence in them. They were not principles which I originated. They would have none of the strength in them that they have if they had been of individual origination. I remember how anxiously I watched the movements of opinion in this country during the months immediately preceding our entrance into the war. Again and again I put this question to the men who sat around the board at which the Cabinet meets. They represented different parts of the country, they were in touch with the opinion in different parts of the United States, and I would frequently say to them, "How do you think the people feel with regard to our relation to this war?" And I remember, one day, one of them said, "Mr. President, I think that they are ready to do anything you suggest." I said, "That is not what I am waiting for. That is not enough. If they do not go in of their own impulse, no impulse that I can supply will suffice, and I must wait until I know that I am their spokesman. I must wait until I know that I am interpreting their purpose. Then I will know that I have got an irresistible power behind me." And that is exactly what happened.

That is what is now appreciated as it was not at first appreciated on the other side of the sea. They wondered and wondered why we did not come in. They had come to the cynical conclusion that we did not come in because we were making money out of the war and did not want to spoil the profitable game; and then at last they saw what we were waiting for, in order that the whole plot of the German purpose should develop, in order that we might see how the intrigue of that plot had penetrated our own life, how the poison was spreading, and how it was nothing less than a design against the freedom of the world. They knew that when America once saw that she would throw her power in with those who were going to redeem the world. And at every point of the discussion I was attempting to be the mouthpiece of what I understood right-thinking and forward-thinking and just-thinking men without regard to party or section in the United States to be purposing and conceiving, and it was the consciousness in Europe that that was the case that made it possible to construct the peace upon American principles. The American principles were not only accepted. They were acted upon, and when I came back to this country with that plan I think you will bear me out that the Nation was prepared to accept it. I have no doubt, and I have not met anybody who had any well-reasoned doubt, that if immediate action could have been secured upon the treaty at that time only a negligible percentage of our people would have objected to its acceptance, without a single change in either the wording or the punctuation. But then something intervened, and, my fellow citizens, I am not only not going to try to analyze what that was, I am not going to allow my own judgment to be formed as regards what it was. I do not understand it, but there is a certain part of it that I do understand. It is to the immediate interest of Germany to separate us from our associates in the war, and I know that the opposition to the treaty is most acceptable in those quarters of the country where pro-German sentiment was strongest. I know that all over the country German propaganda has lifted its hideous head again, and I hear the hiss of it on every side.

When gentlemen speak of isolation, they forget we would have a companion. There would be another isolated nation, and that is Germany. They forget that we would be in the judgment of the world in the same class and at the same disadvantage as Germany. I mean sentimental disadvantage. We would be regarded as having withdrawn our coöperation from that concerted purpose of mankind which was recently conceived and exercised for the liberation of mankind, and Germany would be the only nation in the world to profit by it. I have no doubt there are scores of business men present. Do you think we would profit materially by isolating ourselves and centering upon ourselves the hostility and suspicion and resistance of all the liberal minds in the world? Do you think that if, after having won the absolute confidence of the world and excited the hope of the world, we would lead if we should turn away from them and say, "No; we do not care to be associated with you any longer; we are going to play a lone hand; we are going to play it for our single advantage"? Do you think after that there is a very good psychology for business, there is a very good psychology for credit? Do you think that throws foreign markets open to you? Do you remember what happened just before we went into the war? There was a conference in Paris, the object of which was to unite the peoples fighting against Germany in an economic combination which would be exclusively for their own benefit. It is possible now for those powers to organize and combine in respect of the purchase of raw materials, and if the foreign market for our raw materials is united, we will have to sell at the price that they are willing to pay or not sell at all. Unless you go into the great economic partnership with the world, you have the rest of the world economically combined against you. So that if you bring the thing down to this lowest of all bases, the basis of material self-interest, you lose in the game, and, for my part, I am free to say that you ought to lose.

We are told that we are strong and they are weak; that we still have economic or financial independence and they have not. Why, my fellow citizens, what does that mean? That means that they went into the redemption of the freedom of the world sooner than we did and gave everything that they had to redeem it. And now we, because we did not go in so soon or lose so much, want to make profit of the redeemers! The thing is hideous. The thing is unworthy of every tradition of America. I speak of it not because I think that sort of thing takes the least hold upon the consciousness or the purpose of America but because it is a pleasure to condemn so ugly a thing.

When we look at the objections which these gentlemen make, I have found in going about the country that the result has been that in the greater part of the United States the people do not know what is in the treaty. To my great surprise, I have had to stand up and expound the treaty—tell the people what is in it—and I have had man after man say, "Why, we never dreamed that those things were in the treaty. We never heard anything about that." No; you never heard anything about the greater part of the enterprise; you only

heard about some of the alleged aspects of the method
in which the enterprise was to be carried out. That
is all you have heard about. I remember saying—and I
believe it was the thought of America—that this was a
people's war and the treaty must be a people's peace.
That is exactly what this peace treaty proposes. For
the first time in the history of civilized society, a great
international convention, made up of the leading statesmen of the world, has proposed a settlement which is
for the benefit of the weak and not for the benefit of
the strong. It is for the benefit of peoples who could
not have liberated themselves, whose weakness was
profitable to the ambitious and imperialistic nations,
whose weakness had been traded in by every cabinet in
Europe; and yet these very cabinets represented at the
table in Paris were unanimous in the conviction that
the people's day had come and that it was not their
right to dispose of the fortunes of people without the
consent of those people themselves.

At the front of this great settlement they put the
only thing that will preserve it. You cannot set weak
peoples up in independence and then leave them to
be preyed upon. You cannot give a false gift. You
cannot give to people rights which they never enjoyed
before and say, "Now, keep them if you can." That
is an Indian gift. That is a gift which cannot be kept.
If you have a really humane purpose and a real knowledge of the conditions of peace in the world, you will
have to say, "This is the settlement and we guarantee its
continuance." There is only one honorable course when
you have won a cause, to see that it stays won and nobody interferes with or disturbs the results. That is
the purpose of the much-discussed Article X in the
Covenant of the League of Nations. It is the Monroe
Doctrine applied to the world. Ever since Mr. Monroe
uttered his famous doctrine we have said to the world,
"We will respect and preserve as against external aggression the territorial integrity and the political in-

dependence of every State in the Western Hemisphere,"
and those are practically the words of Article X.
Under Article X all the members of the League engage
to respect and preserve as against external aggression
the territorial integrity and existing political independence of the other member States, and if that guarantee
is not forthcoming the whole structure of peace will
crumble, because you cannot point out a great war that
has not begun by a violation of that principle; that
has not begun by the intention to impair the territorial
integrity or to interfere with the political independence
of some body of people of some nation. It was the
heart of the Pan-German plan. It is the heart of every
imperialistic plan, because imperialism is the design to
control the destinies of people who did not choose
you to control them. It is the principle of domination.
It is at the opposite extreme from the principle of self-
determination and self-government, and in that same
Covenant of the League of Nations is the provision that
only self-governing States shall be admitted to the
membership of the League. No influence shall be injected there which is not sympathetic with the fundamental principle, namely, that ancient and noble principle
that underlies our institutions, that all just government
depends upon the consent of the governed.

You have no choice, my fellow citizens, because the
peoples of the world, even those that slept, are awake.
There is not a country in the world where the great
mass of mankind is not now aware of its rights and
determined to have them at any cost, and the present
universal unrest in the world, which renders return to
normal conditions impossible so long as it continues,
will not stop until men are assured by some arrangement they can believe in that their rights will be protected and that they can go about the normal production of the necessaries of life and begin to enjoy the
ordinary pleasures and privileges of life without the
constant shadow of some cloud of terror over them,

some threat of injustice, some tyranny of control. Men
are not going to stand it. If you want to quiet the
world, you have got to reassure the world, and the
only way in which you can reassure it is to let it know
that all the great fighting powers of the world are
going to maintain that quiet, that the fighting power
is no longer to be directed toward aggression, but is
to be directed toward protection. And every great
fighting nation in the world will be in the League—
because Germany for the time being is not a great
fighting power. That great nation of over 60,000,000
people has consented in the treaty to reduce its standing
armed force to 100,000 men and to give up all the
war material over and above what is necessary to
maintain an army of 100,000 men; so that for the time
being we may exclude Germany from the list of the
fighting nations of the world. The whole power of the
world is now offered to mankind for the maintenance of
peace, and for the maintenance of peace by the very
processes we have all professed to believe in, by substituting arbitration and discussion for war, by substituting the judgment of mankind for the force of arms.
I say without qualification that every nation that
is not afraid of the judgment of mankind will go
into this arrangement. There is nothing for any nation
to lose whose purposes are right and whose cause is
just. The only nations that need fear to go into it are
those that have designs which are illegitimate, those
which have designs that are inconsistent with justice
and are the opposite of peace.

The whole freedom of the world not only, but
the whole peace of mind of the world, depends upon
the choice of America, because without America in this
arrangement the world will not be reassured. I can
testify to that. I can testify that no impression was
borne in deeper upon me on the other side of the water
than that no great free peoples suspected the United
States of ulterior designs, and that every nation, the

weakest among them, felt that its fortunes would be safe if intrusted to the guidance of America; that America would not impose upon it. At the peace table one of the reasons why American advice constantly prevailed, as it did, was that our experts—our financial experts, our economic experts, and all the rest of us, for you must remember that the work of the conference was not done exclusively by the men whose names you all read about every day; it was done in the most intensive labor of experts of every sort who sat down together and got down to the hardpan of every subject that they had to deal with—were known to be disinterested, and in nine cases out of ten, after a long series of debates and interchanges of views and counterproposals, it was usually the American proposal that was adopted. That was because the American experts came at last into this position of advantage, they had convinced everybody that they were not trying to work anything, that they were not thinking of something that they did not disclose, that they wanted all the cards on the table, and that they wanted to deal with nothing but facts. They were not dealing with national ambitions, they were not trying to disappoint anybody, and they were not trying to stack the cards for anybody. It was that conviction, and that only, which led to the success of American counsel in Paris.

Is not that a worthy heritage for people who set up a great free Nation on this continent in order to lead men in the ways of justice and of liberty? My heart was filled with a profound pride when I realized how America was regarded, and my only fear was that we who were over there would not have wisdom enough to play the part. Delegations from literally all parts of the world came to seek interviews with me as the spokesman of America, and there was always a plea that America should lead; that America should suggest. I remember saying to one of the delegations, which seemed to me more childlike in its confidence than the rest, "I beg that you gentlemen will not expect the impossible. America will do everything that she can, but she cannot do some of the things that you are expecting of her. My chief fear is to disappoint, because you are expecting what cannot be realized." My fear was not that America would not prove true to herself, but that the things expected of her were so ideal that in this practical world, full of obstacles, it would be impossible to realize the expectation. There was in the back-ground the infinite gratification at the reputation and confidence that this country had won.

The world is in that situation industrially, economically, politically. The world will be absolutely in despair if America deserts it. But the thing is inconceivable. America is not going to desert it. The people of America are not going to desert it. The job is to get that into the consciousness of men who do not understand it. The job is to restore some of our fellow citizens to that large sort of sanity which makes a man bigger than himself. We have had a great many successful men in America, my fellow citizens, but we have seldom erected a statue to a man who was merely successful in a business way. Almost all the statues in America, almost all the memorials, are erected to men who forgot themselves and worked for other people. They may not have been rich, they may not have been successful in the worldly sense, they may have been deemed in their generation dreamers and idealists, but when they were dead America remembered that they loved mankind, America remembered that they embodied in those dreamy ideals of theirs the visions that America had had, America remembered that they had a great surplus of character that they spent not upon themselves but upon the enterprises of humanity. A man who has not got that surplus capital of character that he spends upon the great enterprises of communities and of nations will sink into a deserved oblivion, and the only danger is that in his concentration upon his own ambitions, in his centering of everything that he spends upon himself, he will lead others astray and work a disservice to great communities which he ought to have served. It is now an enterprise of infection ahead of us—shall I call it? We have got to infect those men with the spirit of the Nation itself. We have got to make them aware that we will not be led; that we will not be controlled; that we will not be restrained by those who are not like ourselves; and that America now is in the presence of the realization of the destiny for which she has been waiting.

You know, you have been told, that Washington advised us against entangling alliances, and gentlemen have used that as an argument against the League of Nations. What Washington had in mind was exactly what these gentlemen want to lead us back to. The day we have left behind us was a day of alliances. It was a day of balances of power. It was a day of "every nation take care of itself or make a partnership with some other nation or group of nations to hold the peace of the world steady or to dominate the weaker portions of the world." Those were the days of alliances. This project of the League of Nations is a great process of disentanglement. I was reading only this morning what a friend of mine reminded me of, a speech that President McKinley made the day before he was assassinated, and in several passages of that speech you see the dawn of this expectation in his humane mind. His whole thought was against isolation. His whole thought was that we had by process of circumstance, as well as of interest, become partners with the rest of the world. His thought was that the world had grown little by quickened methods of intercommunication. His whole thought was that the better we knew each other and the closer we drew together, the more certain it would be that the processes of arbitration would be adopted; that men would not fight but would talk things over; that they would realize their community of interest; and shot all through that speech you see the morning light of just such a day as this. It would look as if the man had been given a vision just before he died—one of the sweetest and most humane souls that have been prominent in our affairs, a man who thought with his head and with his heart. This new day was dawning upon his heart, and his intelligence was beginning to draw the lines of the new picture which has been completed and sketched in a constructive document that we shall adopt and that, having adopted it, we shall find to reflect a new glory upon the things that we did. Then what significance will attach to the boy's sword or the boy's musket over the mantelpiece—not merely that he beat Germany, but that he redeemed the world.

AT AUDITORIUM, LOS ANGELES, CALIF., SEPTEMBER 20, 1919.

MR. MAYOR, MRS. COWLES, MY FELLOW COUNTRYMEN:

I esteem it a great privilege to stand before this audience, and I esteem it one of the most interesting occasions that I have had to expound a theme so great that I am always afraid that I am inadequate to its exposition. I esteem it a privilege to be in the presence that I find myself in, on the stage with this committee of gentlemen representing the nations with whom we have been associated in the war, with these men who saved the Union and with these men who saved the world.

I feel that there is a certain sense in which I am rendering my account to the soldiers and sailors whose Commander in Chief I have been, for I sent them across the sea believing that their errand was not only to defeat Germany, but also to redeem the world from the danger to which Germany had exposed it, to make the world a place in which arbitration, discussion, the processes of peace, the processes of justice should supplant the brutal processes of war. I came back from the other side proud that I was bringing with me a document which contained a great constructive plan to accomplish that very thing. It is a matter of unaffected amazement on my part, my fellow citizens, that there should be men in high station who oppose its adoption. It is a matter of amazement that they should devote their scrutiny to certain details and forget the majesty of the plan, that they should actually have made it necessary that I should go throughout the country telling the people of the United States what is in the treaty of peace. For they have not told you. They have given you no conception of its scope. They have not expounded its objects. They have not shown you how it is a people's and not a statesmen's peace. They have not shown you how at its heart lies the liberation of nations. They have not shown you that in it is the redemption of our promise that we were fighting for the right of the weak and not for the power of the strong. These promises are redeemed in that great document, these hopes are realized, and the only buttress for that great structure is the League of Nations. If that should fail, there is no guarantee that any part of the settlement will stand. If that should fail, nations will once more sink back into that slough of despond in which they formerly struggled, suspecting one another, rivaling one another in preparation for war, intriguing against one another, plotting against the weak in order to supplement the power of the strong.

And they did more than that, because mankind is now aware that the rights of the greater portion of mankind have not been safeguarded and regarded. Do not for a moment suppose that the universal unrest in the world at the present time, my fellow citizens, is due to any whim, to any newborn passion, to any newly discovered ambition. It is due to the fact, the sad, the tragic fact, that great bodies of men have throughout the ages been denied the mere rights of humanity. The peoples of the world are tired of a time with governments that exploit their people, and they are determined to have, by one process or another, that concerted order of conciliation and debate and conference which is set up in the great document that we know as the Covenant of the League of Nations. The heart of that document is not in the mere details that you have heard about. The heart of that document is that every great fighting nation in the world—for Germany at present is not a great fighting nation—solemnly engages that it will never resort to war without first having done one or other of two things, either submitted the matter in dispute to arbitration, in which case it agrees to abide by the verdict, or, if it does not choose to submit it to arbitration, submit it to the discussion and examination of the council of the League of Nations, before whom it promises to lay all the documents, to whom it promises to disclose all the pertinent facts, by whom it agrees all the documents and facts shall be published and laid before the opinion of the world. It agrees that six months shall be allowed for the examination of those documents and facts by the council of the League and that, even if it is dissatisfied with the opinion finally uttered, it will still not resort to war until three months after the opinion has been rendered. All agree that there shall be nine months of deliberate discussion and frank weighing of the merits of the case before the whole jury of mankind before they will go to war.

If any one of them disregards that promise and refuses to submit the question in dispute either to arbitration or to discussion, or goes to war within less than the nine months, then there is an automatic penalty that is applied, more effective, I take leave to say, than war itself, namely, the application of an absolute boycott. The nation that disregards that promise, we all agree, shall be isolated; shall be denied the right to ship out goods or to ship them in, to exchange telegraphic messages or messages by mail, to have any dealings of any kind with the citizens of the other members of the League. First, the pressure of opinion and then the compelling pressure of economic necessity—those are the great bulwarks of peace. Do you say they are not sufficient? I put this proposition to you: You want insurance against war. Wouldn't you rather have ten per cent insurance than none? If you could get twenty per cent insurance, wouldn't you be delighted? If you got fifty per cent insurance, wouldn't you think it Utopian? Why, my fellow citizens, if you examine the provisions of this League of Nations, I think you will agree with me that you have got ninety-nine per cent insurance. That is what we promised the mothers and wives and sweethearts of these men that they should have—insurance against the terrible danger of losing those who were dear to them, slain upon the battlefield because of the unhallowed plots of autocratic governments. Autocratic governments are excluded henceforth from respectable society. It is provided in the Covenant of the League of Nations that only self-governing peoples shall be admitted to its membership, and the reason that Germany is for the time being excluded is that we want to wait and see whether she really has changed permanently her form of constitution and her habit of government. If she has changed her mind in reality, if her great people have taken charge of their own affairs and will prove it to us, they are entitled to come into respectable society and join the League of Nations. Until then they are on probation, and to hear some of them talk now you would think the probation had to be rather long, because they do not seem to have repented of their essential purpose.

Now, offset against this, my fellow citizens, some of the things that are being said about the Covenant of the League and about the treaty. I want to begin with one of the central objections which are made to the treaty, for I have come here disposed to business. I do not want to indulge in generalities. I do not want to dwell more than it is proper to dwell upon the great ideal purposes that lie behind this peace and this Covenant. I want to contrast some things that have been said with the real facts. There is nothing that is formidable in this world in public affairs except facts. Talk does not matter. As I was saying the other night, if you suspect any acquaintance of yours of being a fool, encourage him to hire a hall. Your fellow citizens will then know whether your judgment of him was right or wrong, and it will not be you that convinced them; it will be he who does the convincing. The best way to dissipate nonsense is to expose it to the open air. It is a volatile thing, whereas fact and truth are concrete things and you cannot dissipate them that way. Perhaps I may tell a rather trivial story. When I was governor of New Jersey I got rather reluctant support for a certain measure of reform that I was very much interested in from a particular member of the senate of the State who, I think, if he had been left to his own devices, would probably have not voted for the measure, but to whom an influential committee of his fellow townsmen came and, so to say, personally conducted his vote. After they had successfully conducted it in the way that they wished, they solemnly brought him into my office to be congratulated. It was a great strain upon my gravity, but I pulled as straight a face as I could and thanked him and congratulated him. Then, tipping a very heavy wink indeed, he said, "Governor, they never get me if I see them coming first." Now, I have adopted that as my motto with regard to facts. I never let them get me if I see them coming first. The danger for some of the gentlemen we are thinking about to-night, but not mentioning, is that the facts are coming and they do not see them. My prediction is that the facts are going to get them and make a very comfortable meal off of them.

Let us take up some of these things, to grow serious

again. In the first place, there is that very complex question of the cession of the rights which Germany formerly enjoyed in Shantung Province, in China, and which the treaty transfers to Japan. The only way in which to clear this matter up is to know what lies back of it. Let me recall some circumstances which probably most of you have forgotten. I have to go back to the year 1898, for it was in March of that year that these cessions which formerly belonged to Germany were transferred to her by the Government of China. What had happened was that two German missionaries in China had been murdered. The central Government at Peking had done everything that was in its power to do to quiet the local disturbances, to allay the local prejudice against foreigners which led to the murders, but had been unable to do so, and the German Government held them responsible, nevertheless, for the murder of the missionaries. It was not the missionaries that the German Government was interested in. That was a pretext. Ah, my fellow citizens, how often we have made Christianity an excuse for wrong! How often in the name of protecting what was sacred we have done what was tragically wrong! That was what Germany did. She insisted that, because this thing had happened for which the Peking Government could not really with justice be held responsible, a very large and important part of one of the richest Provinces of China should be ceded to her for sovereign control, for a period of ninety-nine years, that she should have the right to penetrate the interior of that Province with a railway, and that she should have the right to exploit any ores that lay within thirty miles either side of that railway. She forced the Peking Government to say that they did it in gratitude to the German Government for certain services which she was supposed to have rendered but never did render. That was the beginning. I do not know whether any of the gentlemen who are criticizing the present Shantung settlement were in public affairs at that time or not, but I will tell you what happened, so far as this Government was concerned.

One of the most enlightened and humane Presidents we have ever had was at the head of the Government— William McKinley, a man who loved his fellow men and believed in justice—and associated with him was one of our ablest Secretaries of State—Mr. John Hay. The state of international law was such then that they did not feel at liberty to make even a protest against these concessions to Germany. Neither did they make any protest when, immediately following that, similar concessions were made to Russia, to Great Britain, and to France. It was almost immediately after that that China granted to Russia the right of the possession and control of Port Arthur and a portion of the region of Talien-Wan. Then England, not wishing to be out-done, although she had similar rights elsewhere in China, insisted upon a similar concession and got Wei-Hai-Wai. Then France insisted that she must have a port, and got it for ninety-nine years. Not against one of those did the Government of the United States make any protest whatever. They only insisted that the door should not be shut in any of these regions against the trade of the United States. You have heard of Mr. Hay's policy of the open door. That was his policy of the open door—not the open door to the rights of China, but the open door to the goods of America. I want you to understand, my fellow country-men, I am not criticizing this because, until we adopt the Covenant of the League of Nations, it is an un-friendly act for any government to interfere in the affairs of any other unless its own interests are imme-diately concerned. The only thing Mr. McKinley and Mr. Hay were at liberty to do was to call attention to the fact that the trade of the United States might be un-favorably affected and insist that in no circumstances it should be. They got from all of these powers the promise that it should not be—a promise which was more or less kept. Following that came the war between Russia and Japan, and at the close of that war Japan got Port Arthur and all the rights which Russia enjoyed in China, just as she is now getting Shantung and the rights her recently defeated enemy had in China—an exactly similar operation. That peace that gave her Port Arthur was concluded, as you know, on the territory of the United States—at Portsmouth, N. H. Nobody dreamed of protesting against that. Japan had beaten Russia. Port Arthur did not at that time belong to China; it belonged for the period of the lease to Russia, and Japan was ceded what Japan had taken by the well-recognized processes of war.

Very well, at the opening of this war, Japan went and took Kiauchau and supplanted Germany in Shantung Province. The whole process is repeated, but repeated with a new sanction. In the meantime, after this present war began, England and France, not at the same time, but successively, feeling that it was essential that they should have the assistance of Japan on the Pacific, agreed that if Japan would go into this war and take whatever Germany had in the Pacific she should retain everything north of the equator which had belonged to Germany. That treaty now stands. That treaty absolutely binds Great Britain and France. Great Britain and France cannot in honor, having offered Japan this inducement to enter the war and to continue her operations, consent to an elimination of the Shantung provision from the present treaty. Very well, let us put these gentlemen who are objecting to the Shantung settlement to the test. Are they ready to fight Great Britain and France and Japan, who will have to stand together, in order to get this Province back for China? I know they are not, and their interest in China is not the interest of assisting China, but of defeating the treaty. They know beforehand that a modification of the treaty in that respect cannot be obtained, and they are insisting upon what they know is impossible; but if they ratify the treaty and accept the Covenant of the League of Nations they do put themselves in a position to assist China. They put themselves in that position for the very first time in the history of international engagements. They change the whole faith of international affairs, because after you have read the much debated Article X of the Covenant I advise you to read Article XI. Article XI says that it shall be the friendly right of any member of the League to call attention at any time to anything, anywhere, that threatens to disturb the peace of the world or the good understanding between nations upon which the peace of the world depends. That in itself constitutes a revolution in international relationships. Anything that affects the peace of any part of the world is the business of every nation. It does not have simply to insist that its trade shall not be interfered with; it has the right to insist that the rights of mankind shall not be interfered with. Not only that, but back of this provision with regard to Shantung lies, as everybody knows or ought to know, a very honorable promise which was made by the Government of Japan in my presence in Paris, namely, that just as soon as possible after the ratification of this treaty they will return to China all sovereign rights in the Province of Shantung. Great Britain has not promised to return Wei-Hai-Wai; France has not promised to return her part. Japan has promised to relinquish all the sovereign rights which were acquired by Germany for the remaining seventy-eight of the ninety-nine years of the lease, and to retain only what other Governments have in many other parts of China, namely, the right to build and operate the railway under a corporation and to exploit the mines in the immediate neighborhood of that railway. In other words, she retains only the rights of economic concessionaires. Personally, I am frank to say that I think all of these nations have invaded some of the essential rights of China by going too far in the concessions which they have demanded, but that is an old story now, and we are beginning a new story. In the new story we all have the right to talk about what they have been doing and to convince them, by the pressure of the public opinion of the world, that a different course of action would be just and right. I am for helping China and not turning away from the only way in which I can help her. Those are the facts about Shantung. Doesn't the thing look a little different?

Another thing that is giving some of our fellow countrymen pangs of some sort—pangs of jealousy, perhaps—is that, as they put it, Great Britain has six votes in the League and we have only one. Well, our one vote, it happens, counts just as heavily as if every one of our States were represented and we had forty-eight because it happens, though these gentlemen have overlooked it, that the assembly is not an independent voting body. Great Britain has only one representative and one vote in the council of the League of Nations, which originates all action, and its six votes are in the assembly, which is a debating and not an executive body. In every matter in which the assembly can vote along with the council it is necessary that all the nations represented on the council should concur in the affirmative vote to make it valid, so that in every vote, no matter how many concur in it in the assembly, in order for it to become valid, it is necessary that the United States should vote aye.

Inasmuch as the assembly is a debating body, that is the place where this exposure that I have talked about to the open air is to occur. It would not be wise for anybody to go into the assembly with purposes that will not bear exposure, because that is the great cooling process of the world; that is the great place where gases are to be burned off. I ask you, in debating the affairs of mankind, would it have been fair to give

Panama a vote, as she will have, Cuba a vote, both of them very much under the influence of the United States, and not give a vote to the Dominion of Canada, to that great energetic Republic in South Africa, to that place from which so many liberal ideas and liberal actions have come, that stout little Commonwealth of Australia? When I was in Paris the men I could not tell apart, except by their hats, were the Americans and the Australians. They both had the swing of fellows who say, "The gang is all here, what do we care?" Could we deny a vote to that other little self-governing nation, for it practically is such in everything but its foreign affairs, New Zealand, or to those toiling—I was about to say uncounted—millions in India? Would you want to deprive these great communities of a voice in the debate? My fellow citizens, it is a proposition which has never been stated, because to state it answers it. But they cannot outvote us. If we, as I said a minute ago, had forty-eight votes in the assembly, they would not count any more than our one, because they would have to be combined, and it is easier to combine one than to combine forty-eight. The vote of the United States is potential to prevent anything that the United States does not care to approve. All this nonsense about six votes and one vote can be dismissed and you can sleep with perfect quiet. In order that I may not be said to have misled you, I must say that there is one matter upon which the assembly can vote, and which it can decide by a two-thirds majority without the concurrence of all the States represented in the council, and that is the admission of new members to the League.

Then, there is that passion that some gentlemen have conceived, that we should never live with anybody else. You can call it the policy of isolation or the policy of taking care of yourself, or you can give any name you choose to what is thoroughly impossible and selfish. I say it is impossible, my fellow citizens. When men tell you that we are, by going into the League of Nations, reversing the policy of the United States, they have not thought the thing out. The statement is not true. The facts of the world have changed. It is impossible for the United States to be isolated. It is impossible for the United States to play a lone hand, because it has gone partners with all the rest of the world with regard to every great interest that it is connected with. What are you going to do? Give up your foreign markets? Give up your influence in the affairs of other nations and arm yourselves to the teeth and double your taxes and be ready to spring instead of ready to coöperate? We are tied into the rest of the world by kinship, by sympathy, by interest in every great enterprise of human affairs. The United States has become the economic center of the world, the financial center. Our economic engagements run everywhere, into every part of the globe. Our assistance is essential to the establishment of normal conditions throughout the world. Our advice is constantly sought. Our standards of labor are being extended to all parts of the world just so fast as they can be extended. America is the breeding center for all the ideas that are now going to fecundate the great future. You can no more separate yourselves from the rest of the world than you can take all the tender roots of a great tree out of the earth and expect the tree to live. All the tendrils of our life, economic and social and every other, are interlaced in a way that is inextricable with the similar tendrils of the rest of mankind. The only question which these gentlemen can ask us to decide is this: Shall we exercise our influence in the world, which can henceforth be a profound and controlling influence, at a great advantage or at an insuperable disadvantage? That is the only question that you can ask. As I put it the other night, you have got this choice: You have got to be either provincials, little Americans, or big Americans, statesmen. You have got to be either ostriches with your heads in the sand or eagles. I doubt if the comparison, with the head in the sands, is a good one, because I think even an ostrich can think in the sand. What he does not know is that people are looking at the rest of him. Our choice is in the bird kingdom, and I have in my mind's eye a future in which it will seem that the eagle has been misused. You know that it was a double-headed eagle that represented the power of Austria-Hungary, you have heard of the eagles of Germany, but the only proper symbol of the eagle is the symbol for which we use it—as the bird of liberty and justice and peace.

I want to put it as a business proposition, if I am obliged to come down as low as that, for I do not like in debating the great traditions of a free people to bring the debate down to the basis of dollars and cents; but if you want to bring it down to that, if anybody wants to bring it down to that, reason it out on that line. Is it easier to trade with a man who suspects and dislikes you or with one who trusts you? Is it easier to deal with a man with a grouch or with a man who opens his mind and his opportunities to you and treats you like a partner and a friend? There is nothing which can more certainly put a drop of acid into every relationship we have in the world than if we now desert our former associates in this war. That is exactly what we should be doing if we rejected this treaty, and that is exactly what, speaking unwisely and too soon, the German leaders have apprised us that they want us to do. No part of the world has been so pleased by our present hesitation as the leaders of Germany, because their hope from the first has been that sooner or later we would fall out with our associates. Their hope was to divide us before the fighting stopped, and now their hope is to divide us after the fighting. You read how a former German privy councillor, I believe he was, said in an interview the other day that these debates in the Senate looked to him like the dawn of a new day.

A new day for the world? No; a new day for the hopes of Germany, because he saw what anybody can see who lifts his eyes and looks in the future—two isolated nations; one isolated nation on probation, and then two, the other a nation infinitely trusted, infinitely believed in, that had given magnificent purpose of its mettle and of its trustworthiness, now drawing selfishly and suspiciously apart and saying, "You may deceive us, you may draw us into broils, you may get us into trouble; we will take care of ourselves, we will trade with you and we will trade on you." The thing is inconceivable. America is no quitter, and least of all is she a quitter in a great moral enterprise where her conscience is involved. The only immortal thing about America is her conscience. America is not going to be immortal because she has immense wealth. Other great nations had immense wealth and went down in decay and disgrace, because they had nothing else. America is great because of the ideas she has conceived. America is great because of the purposes she has set herself to achieve. America is great because she has seen visions that other nations have not seen, and the one enterprise that does engage the steadfast loyalty and support of the United States is an enterprise for the liberty of mankind.

How can we make the purpose evident? I was saying in one place to-night that my dear father had once taught me that there was no use trying to reason out of a man what reason did not put in him, and yet here to-night I am trying to apply the remedy of reason. We must look about and find some other remedy, because in matters of this sort remedies are always homeopathic—like must cure like. Men must be made to see the great impulses of the Nation in such a fashion that they will not dare to resist them. I do not mean by any threat of political disaster. Why, my fellow citizens, may I indulge in a confidence? I have had men politically disposed say to me, as a Democrat,

"This is all to the good. These leaders of the Republican Party in Washington are going to ruin the party." They seem to think that I will be pleased. I do not want to see the great Republican Party misrepresented and misled. I do not want to see any advantage reaped by the party I am a member of because another great party has been misrepresented, because I believe in the loyalty and Americanism and high ideals of my fellow citizens who are Republicans just as much as I believe in those things in Democrats. It seems almost absurd to say that; of course I do. When we get to the borders of the United States we are neither Republicans nor Democrats. It is our privilege to scrap inside the family just as much as we please, but it is our duty as a Nation in those great matters of international concern which distinguish us to subordinate all such differences and to be a united family and all speak with one voice what we all know to be the high conceptions of American manhood and womanhood.

There is a tender side to this great subject. Have these gentlemen no hearts? Do they forget the sons that are dead in France? Do they forget the great sacrifice that this Nation has made? My friends, we did not go to France to fight for anything special for America. We did not send men 3,000 miles away to defend our own territory. We did not take up the gage that Germany had thrown down to us because America was being specially injured. America was not being specially injured. We sent those men over there because free people everywhere were in danger and we had always been, and will always be, the champion of right and of liberty. That is the glory of these men that sit here. The hardest thing that I had to do, and the hardest thing that a lot of you had to do, was to continue to wear civilian clothes during the war, not to don a uniform, not to risk something besides reputation —risk life and everything. We knew that an altar had been erected upon which that sacrifice could be made more gloriously than upon any other altar that had ever been lifted among mankind, and we desired to offer ourselves as a sacrifice for humanity. And that is what we shall do, my fellow citizens. All the mists will pass away. A number of halls are being hired. All the gases are being burned off; and when you come down, as the gases have passed away, to the solid metal of which this Nation is made, it will shine as lustrously and bright as it has ever shone throughout the history of the Nation we love and the Nation we will always consecrate ourselves to redeem.

FROM REAR PLATFORM, SACRAMENTO, CALIF.,
SEPTEMBER 22, 1919.

MY FELLOW COUNTRYMEN:

It is impossible in these circumstances for me to attempt a speech, but I cannot let the occasion go by without telling you how strong it makes my heart that you should have given me so extraordinary and delightful a welcome as this. It is the more delightful to me because I believe that it is not only a desire to welcome me, but a desire to show your interest and your support of the great cause I have come out to advocate. The happy circumstance of this journey is that I have not come out to advocate anything personal to myself; that I have not come out to seek the fortunes of any man or group of men, but to seek the safety and guaranteed peace of mankind. We undertook a great war for a definite purpose. That definite purpose is carried out in a great treaty. I have brought the treaty back, and we must not much longer hesitate to ratify it, because that treaty is the guarantee of peace; it is the guarantee of permanent peace, for all the great fighting nations of the world are combined in it to maintain a just settlement. Without this treaty, without the Covenant of the League of Nations which it contains, we would simply sink back into that slough of despond in which man-

kind was before this war began, with the threat of war
and of terror constantly over them. We cannot go back.
We will not go back.

It is more than a guarantee of peace. It is a guarantee
of justice. For example, it affords the only hope that
China can get of the restoration to herself not only of
the sovereignty of Shantung, but of the sovereignty
which other nations as well have taken away from her.
It affords the only expectation in similar cases elsewhere, that by the pressure, the terrible, irresistible
pressure of public opinion throughout the world, ancient wrongs will be righted and men will get the chance
to live that they never had before. It is the first combination of the power of the world to see that justice
shall reign everywhere. We cannot turn away from
such an arrangement, and I am sure, my fellow citizens,
not only from this great outpouring here, but from the
great outpourings I have seen everywhere in this country, that the heart of America is right and her purpose
is irresistible.

AT RENO, NEV., SEPTEMBER 22, 1919.

GOVERNOR BOYLE, MR. CHAIRMAN, MY FELLOW
    COUNTRYMEN:

The governor and your chairman have both alluded
to the fact that it does not often happen that the President comes to Nevada. Speaking for this President, I
can say that it was not because he did not want to come
to Nevada more than once, because from the first, when
I have studied the movements of the history of this
great country, nothing has fascinated me so much or
seemed so characteristic of that history as the movement to the frontier, the constant spirit of adventure,
the constant action forward. A wit in the East recently
said, explaining the fact that we were able to train a
great army so rapidly, that it was so much easier to
train an American army than any other because you had

to train them to go only one way. That has been true
of America and of the movement of population. It
has always been one way. They have never been returning tides. They have always been advancing tides,
and at the front of the advancing tide have always been
the most adventurous spirits, the most originative spirits, the men who were ready to go anywhere and to take
up any fortune to advance the things that they believed
in and desired. Therefore, it is with a sense of exhilaration that I find myself in this community, which your
governor has described as still a frontier community.
You are a characteristic part of this great country which
we all love.

And it is the more delightful to look at your individual aspect, because the subject that I have come to
speak about is a forward-looking subject. Some of the
critics of the League of Nations have their eyes over
their shoulders; they are looking backward. I think
that is the reason they are stumbling all the time; they
are always striking their feet against obstacles which
everybody sees and avoids and which do not lie in the
real path of the progress of civilization. Their power
to divert, or to pervert, the view of this whole thing
has made it necessary for me repeatedly on this journey
to take the liberty that I am going to take with you
to-night, of telling you just what kind of a treaty this is.
Very few of them have been at pains to do that. Very
few of them have given their audiences or the country
at large any conception of what this great document
contains or of what its origin and purpose are. Therefore, I want, if you will be patient with me, to set the
stage for the treaty, to let you see just what it was that
was meant to be accomplished and just what it was
that was accomplished.

Perhaps I can illustrate best by recalling some history. Something over a hundred years ago the last
so-called peace conference sat in Vienna—back in the
far year 1815, if I remember correctly. It was made

up, as the recent conference in Paris was, of the leading statesmen of Europe. America was not then drawn into that general family and was not represented at that conference, and practically every Government represented at Vienna at that time, except the Government of Great Britain, was a Government like the recent Government of Germany, where a small coterie of autocrats were able to determine the fortunes of their people without consulting them, were able to use their people as puppets and pawns in the game of ambition which was being played all over the stage of Europe. But just before that conference there had been many signs that there was a breaking up of that old order, there had been some very ominous signs, indeed. It was not then so long ago that, though there were but 3,000,000 people subject to the Crown of Great Britain in America, they had thrown off allegiance to that Crown successfully and defied the power of the British Empire on the ground that nobody at a distance had a right to govern them and that nobody had a right to govern them whom they did not choose to be their government; founding their government upon the principle that all just government rests upon the consent of the governed. And there had followed, as you remember, that whirlwind of passion that we know as the French Revolution, when all the foundations of French government not only, but of French society, had been shaken and disturbed—a great rebellion of a great suffering population against an intolerable authority that had laid all the taxes on the poor and none of them on the rich, that had used the people as servants, that had made the boys and men of France play upon the battlefield as if they were chessmen upon a board. France revolted and then the spirit spread, and the conference of Vienna was intended to check the revolutionary spirit of the time. Those men met in order to concert methods by which they could make monarchs and monarchies safe, not only in Europe but throughout the world.

The British representatives at that conference were alarmed because they heard it whispered that European governments, European monarchies, particularly those of the center of Europe, those of Austria and Germany—for Austria was then stronger than Germany—were purposing to extend their power to the Western Hemisphere, to the Americas, and the prime minister of Great Britain suggested to Mr. Rush, the minister of the United States at the Court of Great Britain, that he put it in the ear of Mr. Monroe, who was then President, that this thing was afoot and it might be profitable to say something about it. Thereupon, Mr. Monroe uttered his famous Monroe Doctrine, saying that any European power that sought either to colonize this Western Hemisphere or to interfere with its political institutions, or to extend monarchical institutions to it, would be regarded as having done an unfriendly act to the United States, and since then no power has dared interfere with the self-determination of the Americas. That is the famous Monroe Doctrine. We love it, because it was the first effective dam built up against the tide of autocratic power. The men who constituted the Congress of Vienna, while they thought they were building of adamant, were building of cardboard. What they threw up looked like battlements, but presently were blown down by the very breath of insurgent people, for all over Europe during the middle of the last century there spread, spread irresistibly, the spirit of revolution. Government after government was changed in its character; people said, "It is not only in America that men want to govern themselves, it is not only in France that men mean to throw off this intolerable yoke. All men are of the same temper and of the same make and same rights." So the time of revolution could not be stopped by the conclusions of the Congress of Vienna; until it came about, my fellow citizens, that there was only one stronghold left for that sort of power, and that was at Berlin.

In the year 1914 that power sought to make reconquest of Europe and the world. It was nothing less than the reassertion of that old, ugly thing which the hearts of men everywhere always revolt against, the claim of a few men to determine the fortunes of all men, the ambition of little groups of rulers to dominate the world, the plots and intrigues of military staffs and men who did not confide in their fellow citizens what it was that was their ultimate purpose. So the fire burned in Europe, until it spread and spread like a great forest conflagration, and every free nation was at last aroused; saw the danger, saw the fearful sparks blowing over, carried by the winds of passion and likely to lodge in their own dear countries and destroy their own fair homes; and at last the chief champion and spokesman of liberty, beloved America, got into the war, and said, "We see the dark plot now. We promised at our birth to be the champions of humanity and we have never made a promise yet that we will not redeem." I know how the tides of war were going when our men began to get over there in force, and I think it is nothing less than true to say that America saved the world.

Then a new congress of peace met to complete the work that the Congress of Vienna tried to stop and resist. At the very front of this treaty of peace, my fellow citizens, is the Covenant of the League of Nations, and at the heart of that lies this principle, that no nation shall be a member of that League which is not a self-governing and free nation; that no autocratic power may have any part in the partnership; that no power like Germany—such as Germany was—shall ever take part in its counsels. Germany has changed her constitution, as you know—has made it a democratic constitution, at any rate in form—and she is excluded for the time being from the League of Nations only in order that she may go through a period of probation to show that she means what she professes; to demonstrate that she actually does intend permanently to alter

the character of her constitution and put into the hands
of her people what was once concentrated as authority
in Wilhelmstrasse in Berlin. If she can prove her change
of heart and the permanency of her change of institutions, then she can come into respectable society; but
if she cannot, she is excluded forever. At last the
cycle is completed, and the free peoples who were resisted at Vienna have come into their own. There was
not a single statesman at Paris who did not know that
he was the servant, and not the master, of his people.
There was not one of them who did not know that the
whole spirit of the times had changed and that they
were there to see that people were liberated, not dominated; that people were put in charge of their own territories and their own affairs. The chief business of
the Congress was to carry out that great purpose, and
at last, in the Covenant of the League of Nations, the
Monroe Doctrine became the doctrine of the world.
Not only may no European power impair the territorial
integrity or interfere with the political independence of
any State in the Americas but no power anywhere may
impair the territorial integrity or invade the political
independence of another power. The principle that Mr.
Canning suggested to Mr. Monroe has now been vindicated by its adoption by the representatives of mankind.

When I hear gentlemen ask the question, "Is the
Monroe Doctrine sufficiently safeguarded in the Covenant of the League of Nations?" I can only say that
it is, if I understand the English language. It says in
plain English that nothing in that Covenant shall be
interpreted as affecting the validity of the Monroe Doctrine. Could anything be plainer than that? And when
you add to that that the principle of the Monroe Doctrine is applied to the whole world, then surely I am
at liberty to say that the heart of the document is the
Monroe Doctrine itself. We have at last vindicated the
policy of America, because all through that treaty, and
you will presently see all through the Austrian treaty,

all through the Bulgarian treaty, all through the Turkish treaty, all through the separate treaty we must make with Hungary, because she is separated from Austria, runs the same principle, not only that no Government can impose its sovereignty on unwilling people, but that Governments which have imposed their sovereignty upon unwilling people must withdraw it. All the regions that were unwillingly subject to Germany, subject to Austria-Hungary, and subject to Turkey are now released from that sovereignty, and the principle is everywhere adopted that territories belong to the people that live on them, and that they can set up any sort of government they please, and that nobody dare interfere with their self-determination and autonomy. I conceive this to be the greatest charter—nay, it is the first charter—ever adopted of human liberty. It sets the world free everywhere from autocracy, from imposed authority, from authority not chosen and accepted by the people who obey it.

By the same token it removes the grounds of ambition. My fellow citizens, we never undertake anything that we do not see through. This treaty was not written, essentially speaking, at Paris. It was written at Chateau-Thierry and in Belleau Wood and in the Argonne. Our men did not fight over there for the purpose of coming back and letting the same thing happen again. They did not come back with any fear in their heart that their public men would go back on them and not see the thing through. They went over there expecting that the business would be finished, and it shall be finished. Nothing of that sort shall happen again, because America is going to see it through, and what she is going to see through is this, what is contained in Article X of the Covenant of the League. Article X is the heart of the enterprise. Article X is the test of the honor and courage and endurance of the world. Article X says that every member of the League, and that means every great fighting power in the world,

Germany for the time being not being a great fighting power, solemnly engages to respect and preserve as against external aggression the territorial integrity and existing political independence of the other members of the League. If you do that, you have absolutely stopped ambitious and aggressive war. There is one thing you have not stopped, and that I for my part do not desire to stop, and I think I am authorized to speak for a great many of my colleagues, if not all of my colleagues at Paris, that they do not wish to stop it. It does not stop the right of revolution. It does not stop the choice of self-determination. No nation promises to protect any Government against the wishes and actions of its own people or of any portion of its own people. Why, how could America join in a promise like that? She threw off the yoke of a Government. Shall we prevent any other people from throwing off the yoke that they are unwilling to bear? She never will, and no other Government ever will, under this Covenant. But as against external aggression, as against ambition, as against the desire to dominate from without, we all stand together in a common pledge, and that pledge is essential to the peace of the world.

I said that our people were trained to go only one way, that our soldiers were trained to go only one way, and that America will never turn about upon the path of emancipation upon which she has set out. Not once, but several times, German orders were picked up, or discovered during the fighting, the purport of which was to certain commanders, "Do not let the Americans capture such and such a post, because if they ever get there you can never get them out." They had got other troops out, temporarily at any rate, but they could not get the Americans out. The Americans were under the impression that they had come there to stay, and I am under that impression about American political purposes. I am under the impression that we have come to the place where we have got in order to stay, and that some gentlemen are going to find that no matter how anxious they are to know that the door is open and that they can get out any time they want to they will be allowed to get out by themselves. We are going to stay in. We are going to see this thing finished, because, my fellow citizens, that is the only possibility of peace; and the world not only desires peace but it must have it. Are our affairs entirely in order? Isn't the rest of the world aflame? Have you any conception of the recklessness, of the insubordinate recklessness, of the great population of Europe and of great portions of Asia? Do you suppose that these people are going to resume any sort of normal life unless their rulers can give them adequate and ample guarantee of the future? And do you realize —I wonder if America does realize—that the rest of the world deems America indispensable to the guarantee? For a reason of which we ought to be very proud. They see that America has no designs on any other country in the world. They keep in mind—they keep in mind more than you realize—what happened at the end of the Spanish-American War. There were many cynical smiles on the other side of the water when we said that we were going to liberate Cuba and then let her have charge of her own affairs. They said, "Ah, that is a very common subterfuge. Just watch. America is not going to let that rich island, with its great sugar plantations and its undeveloped agricultural wealth, get out of its grip again." And all Europe stood at amaze when, without delay or hesitation, we redeemed our promise and gave Cuba the liberty we had won for her. They know that we have not imperialistic purposes.

They know that we do not desire to profit at the expense of other peoples. And they know our power, they know our wealth, they know our indomitable spirit; and when we put our names to the bond then Europe will begin to be quiet, then men will begin to seek the peaceful solutions of days of normal industry and nor-

mal life, then men will take hope again, then men will
cease to think of the revolutionary things they can do
and begin to think of the constructive things they can
do, will realize that disorder profits nobody and that
order can at last be had upon terms of liberty and peace
and justice. Then the reaction will come on our own
people, because, do you think, my fellow citizens, does
any body of Americans think, that none of this restlessness, this unhappy feeling, has reached America? Do
you find everybody about you content with our present
industrial order? Do you hear no intimations of radical change? Do you learn of no organizations the
object of which is nothing less than to overturn the Government itself? We are a self-possessed Nation. We
know the value of order. We mean to maintain it.
We will not permit any minority of any sort to dominate it. But it is rather important for America as well
as for the rest of the world, that this infection should
not be everywhere in the air, and that men everywhere
should begin to look life and its facts in the face and
come to calm counsels and purposes that will bring order
and happiness and prosperity again. If you could see
the stopped, the arrested factories over there, the un-
tilled fields, the restless crowds in the cities with nothing
to do, some of them, you would realize that they are
waiting for something. They are waiting for peace, and
not only for peace but for the assurance that peace will
last, and they cannot get that assurance if America
withholds her might and her power and all the freshness
of her strength from the assurance. There is a deep
sense in which what your chairman said just now is profoundly true. We are the hope of humanity, and I for
one have not the slightest doubt that we shall fulfill that
hope.

Yet, in order to reassure you about some of the things
about which you have been diligently misinformed, I
want to speak of one or two details. I have set the
stage now, and I have not half described the treaty. It

not only fulfills the hopes of mankind by giving territories to the people that belong to them and assuring them that nobody shall take it from them, but it goes into many details. It rearranges, for example, the great waterways of Europe, so that no one nation can control them, so that the currents of European life through the currents of its commerce may run free and unhampered and undominated. It embodies a great charter for labor by setting up a permanent international organization in connection with the League of Nations which shall periodically bring the best counsels of the world to bear upon the problem of raising the levels and conditions of labor for men, women, and children. It goes further than that. We did not give Germany back her colonies, but we did not give them to anybody else. We put them in trust in the League of Nations, said that we would assign their government to certain powers by assigning the powers as trustees, responsible to the League, making annual report to the League and holding the power under mandates which prescribe the methods by which they should administer those territories for the benefit of the people living in them, whether they were developed or undeveloped people. We have put the same safeguards, and as adequate safeguards, around the poor, naked fellows in the jungles of Africa that we have around those peoples almost ready to assume the rights of self-government in some parts of the Turkish Empire, as, for example, in Armenia. It is a great charter of liberty and of safety, but let me come to one or two details.

It sticks in the craw of a great many persons that in the constitution of the League of Nations, as it is said, Great Britain has been given six votes and the United States only one. That would be very interesting if true, but it does not happen to be true; that is to say, it is not true in this sense, that the one American vote counts as much as the British six. In the first place, they have not got six votes in the council of the League, which is the only body that originates action, but in the assembly of the League, which is the debating and not the voting body. Every time the assembly participates in any active resolution of the League that resolution must be concurred in by all the nations represented on the council, which makes the affirmative vote of the United States in every instance necessary. The six votes of the British Empire cannot do anything to which the United States does not consent. Now—I am mistaken—there is one thing they can do. By a two-thirds vote they can admit new members to the League, but I do not think that is a formidable privilege since almost everybody is going to be in the League to begin with, and since the only large power that is not in the League enjoys, if I may use that word, a universal prejudice against it, which makes its early admission, at least, unlikely. But aside from admission of any members, which requires a two thirds vote—in which the six British votes will not count a very large figure—every affirmative vote that leads to action requires the assent of the United States, and, as I have frequently said, I think it is very much more important to be one and count six than to be six and count one. So much for this bugaboo, for it is nothing else but a bugaboo. Bugaboos have been very much in fashion in the debates of those who have been opposing this League. The whole energy of that body is in the council of the League, for whose every action in the way of formulating policy or directing energetic measures a unanimous vote is necessary. That may sometimes, I am afraid, impede the action of the League; but, at any rate, it makes the sovereignty and the sovereign choice of every nation that is a member of that League absolutely safe. And pray do not deceive yourselves. The United States is not the only Government that is jealous of its sovereignty. Every other Government, big or little or middle sized, that had to be dealt with in Paris, was just as jealous of its sovereignty as the United States. The only difference between some of them and us is that we could take care of our sovereignty and they could not take care of theirs, but it has been a matter of principle with the United States to maintain that in respect of rights there was and should be no difference between a weak State and a strong State. Our contention has always been, in international affairs, that we should deal with them upon the principle of the absolute equality of independent sovereignty, and that is the basis of the organization of the League. Human society has not moved fast enough yet or far enough yet, my fellow citizens, for any part of that principle of sovereignty to be relinquished, by any one of the chief participants at any rate.

Then there is another matter, that lies outside the League of Nations, that I find my fellow citizens, in this part of the continent particularly, are deeply interested in. That is the matter of the cession of certain German rights in Shantung Province in China to Japan. I think that it is worth while to make that matter pretty clear, and I will have to ask you to be patient while I make a brief historical review in order to make it clear. In the first place, remember that it does not take anything from China, it takes it from Germany, and I do not find that there is any very great jealousy about taking things from Germany. In 1898 China granted to Germany for a period of ninety-nine years certain very important rights around Kiauchau Bay, in the rich and ancient Province of Shantung, together with the right to penetrate the interior with a railway and exploit such ores as might be found in that Province for thirty miles on either side of the railway. We are thinking so much about that concession to Germany that we have forgotten that practically all of the great European powers had exacted similar concessions of China previously; they already had their foothold of control in China; they already had their control of railways; they already had their exclusive concessions over mines. Germany was doing an outrageous thing, I take the liberty of saying, as the others had done outrageous things, but it was not the first; at least it had been done before. China lay rich and undeveloped and the rest of the world was covetous and it had made bargains with China, generally to China's disadvantage, which enabled the world to go in and exploit her riches. I am not now going to discuss the merits of that question, because it has no merits. The whole thing was bad, but it was not unprecedented. Germany obliged China to give her what China had given others previously. Immediately thereafter China was obliged, because she had done this thing, to make fresh concessions to Great Britain of a similar sort, to make fresh concessions to France, to make concessions of a similar kind to Russia. It was then that she gave Russia Port Arthur and Talien-Wan.

Now, remember what followed. The Government of the United States did not make any kind of protest against any of those cessions. We had at that time one of the most public-spirited and humane men in the Executive Chair at Washington that have ever graced that chair—I mean William McKinley—and his Secretary of State was a man whom we have all always delighted to praise, Mr. John Hay. But they made no protest against the cession to Germany, or to Russia, or to Great Britain, or to France. The only thing they insisted on was that none of those powers should close the door of commerce to the goods of the United States in those territories which they were taking from China. They took no interest, I mean so far as what they did was concerned, in the liberties and rights of China. They were interested only in the rights of the merchants of the United States. I want to hasten to add that I do not say this even to imply criticism on those gentlemen, because as international law stood then it would have been an unfriendly act for them to protest in any one of these cases. Until this treaty was written in Paris it was not even proposed that it should be the privilege of anybody to protest in any such case if his own rights were not directly affected. Then, some time after that, followed the war between Russia and Japan. You remember where that war was brought to a close— by delegates of the two powers sitting at Portsmouth, N. H., at the invitation of Mr. Roosevelt, who was then President. In that treaty, Port Arthur—China's Port Arthur, ceded to Russia—was ceded to Japan, and the Government of the United States, though the discussions were occurring on its own territory, made no suggestion even to the contrary. Now, the treaty in Paris does the same thing with regard to the German rights in China. It cedes them to the victorious power, I mean to the power that took them by force of arms, the power which was in the Pacific victorious in this war, namely, to Japan, and there is no precedent which would warrant our making a protest. Not only that, but, in the meantime, since this war began, Great Britain and France entered into solemn covenants of treaty with Japan that if she would come into the war and continue her operations against Germany in the Pacific they would lend their whole influence and power to the cession to Japan of everything that Germany had in the Pacific, whether on the mainland or in the islands, north of the Equator, so that if we were to reject this provision in the treaty Great Britain and France would not in honor be at liberty to reject it, and we would have to devise means to do what, let me say with all solemnity only war could do, force them to break their promise to Japan.

Well, you say, "Then, is it just all an ugly, hopeless business?" It is not, if we adopt the League of Nations. The Government of the United States was not bound by these treaties. The Government of the United States was at liberty to get anything out of the bad business that it could get by persuasion and argument, and it was upon the instance of the Government of the United States that Japan promised to return to China what none of these other powers has yet promised to return—all rights of sovereignty that China had granted Germany over any portion of the Province of Shantung—the greatest concession in that matter that has ever been made by any power that has interested itself in the exploits of China—and to retain only what corporations out of many countries have long enjoyed in China, the right to run the railroad and extend its line to certain points and to continue to work the mines that have already been opened. Not only that, but I said a minute ago that Mr. Hay and Mr. McKinley were not at liberty to protest. Turn to the League of Nations and see what will be the situation then. Japan is a member of the League of Nations, all these other powers that have exploited China are members, and they solemnly promise to respect and preserve the territorial integrity and existing political independence of China. Not only that, but in the next article the international law of the world is revolutionized. It is there provided that it is the friendly right of any member of the League at any time to call attention to anything anywhere that is likely to disturb the peace of the world or the good understanding between nations upon which the peace of the world depends. If we had had the Covenant at that time, Mr. McKinley could, and I venture to say would, have said to Germany, "This is directly none of our business, for we are seeking no competitive enterprise of that sort in China, but this is an invasion of the territorial integrity of China. We have promised, and you have promised, to preserve and respect that integrity, and if you do not keep that promise it will destroy the good understanding which exists between the peaceful nations of the world. It will be an invasion, a violation of the essential principle of peace and of justice." Do you suppose for one moment that if the matter had been put in that aspect, with the attention of the world called to it by the great power of the United States, Germany would have persisted in that enterprise?

How had she begun it? She had made the excuse of the death of two German missionaries at the hands of irresponsible mobs in certain Provinces of China an excuse for taking this valuable part of China's territory. Ah, my fellow citizens, it makes anybody who regards himself as a Christian blush to think what Christian nations have done in the name of protecting Christianity! But it cannot be done any more under the League of Nations. It cannot be done without being cited to the bar of mankind, and if Germany had been cited to the bar of mankind before she began her recent tragical enterprise she never would have undertaken it. You cannot expose such matters to the cool discussion of the world without disclosing all their ugliness, their illegitimacy, their brutality. This treaty sets up, puts in operation, so to say, puts into commission the moral force of the world. Our choice with regard to Shantung, therefore, is to keep out of the treaty, for we cannot change it in that respect, or go in and be an effective friend of China. I for one am ready to do anything or to coöperate in anything in my power to be a friend, and a helpful friend, to that great, thoughtful, ancient, interesting, helpless people—in capacity, in imagination, in industry, in numbers one of the greatest peoples in the world and entitled to the wealth that lies underneath their feet and all about them in that land which they have not as yet known how to bring to its development.

There are other things that have troubled the opponents of the League. One thing is they want to be sure they can get out. That does not interest me very much. If I go into a thing, my first thought is not how I can get out. My first thought is not how I can scuttle, but how I can help, how I can be effective in the game, how I can make the influence of America tell for the guidance and salvation of the world—not how I can keep out of trouble. I want to get into any kind of trouble that will help liberate mankind. I do not want always to be thinking about my skin or my pocketbook or my friendships. Is it just as comfortable to die quietly in your bed, never having done anything worth anything, as to die as some of those fellows that we shall always love when we remember them died upon the field of freedom? Is there any choice? Do you think anybody outside the family is going to be interested in any souvenir of you after you are dead? They are going to be interested in souvenirs of the boys in khaki, whether they are of their family or not. They are going to touch with reverence any sword or musket or rapid-fire gun or cannon that was fired for liberty upon the fields of France. I am not thinking of sitting by the door and keeping my hand on the knob, but if you want to do that you can get out any time you want to. There is absolutely nothing in the Covenant to prevent you. I was present at its formulation, and I know what I am talking about, besides being able to understand the English language. It not only meant this, but said it, that any nation can, upon two years' notice, withdraw at any time, provided that at the time it withdraws it has fulfilled its international obligations and its obligations under the Covenant, but it does not make anybody judge as to whether it has fulfilled those obligations, except the nation that withdraws.

The only thing that can ever keep you in the League is being ashamed to get out. You can get out whenever you want to after two years' notice, and the only risk you run is having the rest of the world think you ought not to have got out. I, for my part, am not very sensitive about that, because I have a memory. I have read the history of the United States. We are in the habit of keeping our international obligations, and I do not believe that there will ever come a time when any just question can be raised as to whether we have fulfilled them or not. Therefore, I am not afraid to go before the jury of mankind at any time on the record of the United States with regard to the fulfillment of its international obligations; and when these gentlemen who are criticizing it once feel, if they ever should feel, the impulse of courage instead of the impulse of coward, ice, they will realize how much better it feels. Your blood is at least warm and comfortable, and the red corpuscles are in command, when you have got some spunk in you; but when you have not, when you are afraid somebody is going to put something over on you, you are furtive and go about looking out for things, and your blood is cold and you shiver when you turn a dark corner. That is not a picture of the United States. When I think of these great frontier communities, I fancy I can hear the confident tread, tread, tread of the great hosts that crossed this continent. They were not afraid of what they were going to find in the next canyon. There were not looking over their shoulders to see if the trail was clear behind them. They were making a trail in front of them and they had not the least notion of going back.

What I have come to suggest to you, my fellow citizens, is that you do what I am sure all the rest of our fellow countrymen are doing—clear the deck of these criticisms, that really have nothing in them, and look at the thing in its large aspect, in its majesty. Particularly, look at it as a fulfillment of the destiny of the United States, for it is nothing less. At last, after this long century and more of blood and terror, the world has come to the vision that that little body of 3,000,000 people, strung along the Atlantic coast of this continent, had in that far year 1776. Men in Europe laughed at them, at this little handful of dreamers, this little body of men who talked dogmatically about liberty, and since then that fire which they started on that little coast has consumed every autocratic government in the world, every civilized autocratic government, and now at last the flame has leaped to Berlin, and there is the funeral pyre of the German Empire.

FROM REAR PLATFORM, OGDEN, UTAH,
SEPTEMBER 23, 1919.

I cannot make a real speech in the circumstances, but it would be ungracious of me if I did not say how delightful I have felt the welcome of Ogden to be and how refreshing it is to me to come into contact with you, my fellow citizens, in this part of the world which I wish I knew much better. You will understand that the theme that I have most at heart needs a lot of sea room to turn in, and I would despair of making any adequate remarks about so great a matter as the treaty of peace or the League of Nations; but I do find this, my fellow countrymen, that the thing is very near the heart of the people. There are some men in public life who do not seem to be in touch with the heart of the people, but those who are know how that heart throbs deep and strong for this great enterprise of humanity, for it is nothing less than that. We must set our purposes in a very definite way to assist the judgment of public men. I do not mean in any way to coerce the judgment of public men, but to enlighten and assist that judgment, for I am convinced, after crossing the continent, that there is no sort of doubt that eighty per cent of the people of the United States are for the League of Nations, and that the chief opposition outside legislative halls comes from the very disquieting element that we had to deal with before and during the war. All the elements that tended toward disloyalty are against the League, and for a very good reason. If this League is not adopted we will serve Germany's purpose, because we will be dissociated from the nations, and I am afraid permanently dissociated from the nations with whom we coöperated in defeating Germany. Nothing is so gratifying, we now learn by cable, to public opinion in Germany as the possibility of their doing now what they could not do by arms, separating us in feeling when they could not separate us in fact. I for my part am in to see this thing through, because these men who fought the battles on the fields of France are not now going to be betrayed by the rest of us; we are going to see that the thing they fought for is accomplished, and it does not make any difference how long the fight or how difficult the fight, it is going to be won, and triumphantly won.

AT TABERNACLE, SALT LAKE CITY, UTAH, SEPTEMBER 23, 1919.

GOVERNOR BAMBERGER, PRESIDENT GRANT, MY FELLOW COUNTRYMEN:

It is indeed inspiring to stand before this great audience, and yet I feel that I have come to present a theme which deserves the greatest of all audiences. I must admit to a very considerable degree of unaffected diffidence in presenting this theme, because the theme is so much bigger than any man's capacity to present it adequately. It is a theme which must engage the enthusiastic support of every lover of humanity and every man who professes Christian conviction, because we are now as a nation to make what I cannot help characterizing as the most critical decision we have ever made in the history of America. We sent our boys across the sea to defeat the purposes of Germany, but we engaged that after we had defeated the purposes of Germany we would complete what they had begun and effect such arrangements of international concert as would make it impossible for any such attempt ever to be made again. The question therefore is, Shall we see it through or shall we now at this most critical juncture of the whole transaction turn away from our associates in the war and decline to complete and fulfill our sacred promise to mankind?

I have now crossed the continent, my fellow countrymen, and am on my way East again, and I feel qualified to render testimony as to the attitude of this great Nation toward the Covenant of the League. I say without the slightest hesitation that an overwhelming majority of our fellow countrymen purpose that this Covenant shall be adopted. One by one the objections to it have melted away. One by one it has become evident that the objections urged against it were without sufficient foundation. One by one it has become impossible to support them as objections, and at last we come to the point of critical choice as to the very heart of the whole matter.

You know it troubled some of our public men because they were afraid it was not perfectly clear that we could withdraw from this arrangement whenever we wanted to. There is no justification for doubt in any part of the language of the Covenant on that point. The United States is at liberty to withdraw at any time upon two years' notice, the only restriction being that when it withdraws it shall have fulfilled its international obligations and its obligations under the Covenant of the League, but it is left to its own conscience and to no other tribunal whatever to determine whether those obligations have been fulfilled or not. I, for one, am not afraid of the judgment of mankind with regard to matters of this sort. The United States never has failed to fulfill its international obligations. It never will fail, and I am ready to go to the great jury of humanity upon that matter at any time that within our judgment we should withdraw from this arrangement. But I am not one of those who when they go into a great enterprise think first of how they are going to get out of it. I think first of how I am going to stay in it and how, with the power and influence I can command, I am going to promote the objects of the great concert and association which is being formed. And that is the temper of America.

I was quoting the other night the jest of an American wit who, commenting upon the extraordinary rapidity with which we had trained an army, said that it was easier to train an army in America than anywhere else; it took less time, because you had to train them to go only one way. They showed the effects of the training. They went only one way, and the issues that we are now debating were really decided at Chateau-Thierry and Belleau Wood and in the Argonne. We are now put to the test by these men who fought, as they were put to the test by those of us who ordered them to the field of battle. And the people of the United States have the same training as their Army; they do not look back, they go only one way.

The doubt as to whether some superior authority to our own Congress could intervene in matters of domestic policy is also removed. The language of the Covenant expressly excludes the authorities of the League from taking any action or expressing any judgment with regard to domestic policies like immigration, like naturalization, like the tariff, like all of those things which have lain at the center so often of our political action and of our choice of policy.

Nobody doubts any longer that the Covenant gives explicit, unqualified recognition to the Monroe Doctrine. Indeed, it does more than that. It adopts the principle of the Monroe Doctrine as the principle of the world. The principle of the Monroe Doctrine is that no nation has the right to interfere with the affairs or to impose its own will in any way upon another nation in the Western Hemisphere, and President Monroe said to the Governments of Europe, "Any attempt of that sort on the part of any Government of Europe will be regarded as an act unfriendly to the United States." The Covenant of the League indorses that. The Covenant of the League says that nothing in that document shall be construed as affecting the validity of the Monroe Doctrine, which means that if any power seeks to impose its will upon any American State in North America, Central America, or South America, the world now acknowledges the right of the Government of the United States to take the initiative and check that action.

The forces of objection being driven out of one position after another are now centering upon the heart of the League itself. I have come here to-night, my fellow countrymen, to discuss that critical matter that you constantly see in the newspapers, which we call "reservations." I want you to have a very clear idea of what is meant by reservations. Reservations are to all intents and purposes equivalent to amendments. I can say, I believe with confidence, that it is the judgment of the people of the United States that neither the treaty nor the Covenant should be amended. Very well, then; look at the character of the reservations. What does a reservation mean? It means a stipulation that this particular Government insists upon interpreting its duty under that Covenant in a special way, insists upon interpreting it in a way in which other Governments, it may be, do not interpret it. This thing, when we ratify it, is a contract. You can not alter so much as the words of a contract without the consent of the other parties. Any reservation will have to be carried to all the other signatories, Germany included, and we shall have to get the consent of Germany, among the rest, to read this Covenant in some special way in which we prefer to read it in the interest of the safety of America. That, to my mind, is one of the most unacceptable things that could happen. To my mind, to reopen the question of the meaning of this clearly written treaty is to reopen negotiations with Germany, and I do not believe that any part of the world is in the temper to do that. In order to put this matter in such a shape as will lend itself to concrete illustration, let me read you what I understand is a proposed form of reservation:

The United States assumes no obligation under the provisions of Article X to preserve the territorial integrity or political independence of any other country or to interfere in controversies between other nations, whether members of the League or not, or to employ the military and naval forces of the United States under any article of the treaty for any purpose, unless in any particular case the Congress, which under the Constitution has the sole power to declare war or authorize the employment of the military and naval forces of the United States, shall by act or joint resolution so declare.

That is a rejection of the Covenant. That is an absolute refusal to carry any part of the same responsibility that the other members of the League carry. Does the United States want to be in on that special footing? Does the United States want to say to the nations with whom it stood in this great struggle, "We have seen you through on the battle field, but now we are done. We are not going to stand by you"? Article X is an engagement on the part of all the great fighting nations of the world, because all the great fighting nations are going to be members of the League, that they will respect and preserve as against external aggression the territorial integrity and the existing political independence of the other members of the League. That is cutting at the heart of all wars. Every war of any consequence that you can cite originated in an attempt to seize the territory or interfere with the political independence of some other nation. We went into this war with the sacred promise that we regarded all nations as having the same rights, whether they were weak or strong, and unless we engage to sustain the weak we have guaranteed that the strong will prevail, we have guaranteed that imperialistic enterprise may revive, we have guaranteed that there is no barrier to the ambition of nations that have the power to dominate, we have abdicated the whole position of right and substituted the principle of might. This is the heart of the Covenant, and what are these gentlemen afraid of? Nothing can be done under that article of the treaty without the consent of the United States. I challenge them to draw any other deduction from the provisions of the Covenant itself. In every case where the League

takes action the unanimous vote of the council of the
League is necessary; the United States is a permanent
member of the council of the League, and its affirmative
vote is in every case necessary for every affirmative, or
for that matter every negative, action.

Let us go into particulars. These gentlemen say,
"We do not want the United States drawn into every
little European squabble." Of course, we do not, and
under the League of Nations it is entirely within our
choice whether we will be or not. The normal processes
of the action of the League are certainly to be this:
When trouble arises in the Balkans, when somebody sets
up a fire somewhere in central Europe among those
little nations, which are for the time being looking upon
one another with a good deal of jealousy and suspicion,
because the passions of the world have not cooled—
whenever that happens, the council of the League will
confer as to the best methods of putting out the fire.
If you want to put out a fire in Utah, you do not send
to Oklahoma for the fire engine. If you want to put
out a fire in the Balkans, if you want to stamp out the
smoldering flame in some part of central Europe, you
do not send to the United States for troops. The
council of the League selects the powers which are most
ready, most available, most suitable, and selects them
only at their own consent, so that the United States
would in no such circumstances conceivably be drawn in
unless the flame spread to the world. And would they
then be left out, even if they were not members of the
League? You have seen the fire spread to the world
once, and did not you go in? If you saw it spread
again, if you saw human liberty again imperiled, would
you wait to be a member of the League to go in?

My fellow citizens, the whole thing goes directly to
the conscience of the Nation. If the fight is big enough
to draw the United States in, I predict that they will
be drawn in anyhow, and if it is not big enough to bring
them in inevitably, they can go in or stay out according

to their own decision. Why are these gentlemen afraid? There is no force to oblige the United States to do anything except moral force. Is any man, any proud American, afraid that the United States will resist the duress of duty? I am intensely conscious of the great conscience of this Nation. I see the inevitableness, as well as the dignity and the greatness, of such declarations as President Grant has made aligning all the great organized moral forces of the world on the same side. It is inconceivable they should be on different sides.

There is no necessity for the last part of this reservation. Every public man, every statesman, in the world knows, and I say that advisedly, that in order that the United States should go to war it is necessary for the Congress to act. They do not have to be told that, but that is not what this resolution says. This resolution says the United States assumes no obligation under the provisions of Article X to preserve the territorial integrity or political independence of any other country —washes its hands of the whole business; says, "We do not want even to create the presumption that we will do the right thing. We do not want to be committed even to a great principle, but we want to say that every time a case arises the Congress will independently take it up as if there were no Covenant and determine whether there is any moral obligation; and after determining that, determining whether it will act upon that moral obligation or not, it will act." In other words, that is an absolute withdrawal from the obligations of Article X. That is why I say that it would be a rejection of the Covenant and thereby a rejection of the treaty, for the treaty cannot be executed without the Covenant.

I appeal, and I appeal with confidence, my fellow countrymen, to the men whose judgment I am told has approved of reservations of this sort. I appeal to them to look into the matter again. I know some of the gentlemen who are quoted as approving a reservation of that sort; I know them to be high-minded and patriotic Americans, and I know them to be men whose character and judgment I entirely respect, and whose motives I respect as much as I respect the motives of any man, but they have not looked into the matter. Are they willing to ask the rest of the world to go into this Covenant and to let the United States assume none of its obligations? Let us have all the advantages of it and none of the responsibilities? Are they willing that proud America should ask for special exemptions, should show a special timidity, should ask to go into an arrangement depending upon a judgment when its own judgment is a different judgment? I confidently believe, my fellow citizens, that they will do no such thing. This is not an interpretation of the Covenant. I have been trying to interpret it to you. This is a rejection of the Covenant, and if this is adopted, the whole treaty falls to the ground, for, my fellow citizens, we must realize that a great and final choice is between this people. Either we are going to guarantee civilization or we are going to abandon it. I use the word with perhaps the admission that it may carry a slight exaggeration, but nevertheless advisedly, when I say abandon civilization, for what is the present condition of civilization? Everywhere, even in the United States, there is an attitude of antagonism toward the ordered processes of government. We feel the evil influence on this side of the Atlantic, and on the other side of the Atlantic every public man knows that it is knocking at the door of his government.

While this unrest is assuming this menacing form of rebellion against authority, of determination to cut roads of force through the regular processes of government, the world is waiting on America, for—I say it with entire respect for the representatives of other governments, but I say it with knowledge—the Government of the United States is the only government in the world that the rest of the world trusts. It knows that the Government of the United States speaks for the people of the United States, that it is not anybody's master, but the servant of a great people. It knows that that people can always oblige its governors to be its servants. It knows that nobody has ever dared defy the public judgment of the people of the United States, and it knows that that public judgment is on the side of right and justice and of peace. It has seen the United States do what no other nation ever did. When we fought the war with Spain there was many a cynical smile on the other side of the water when we said that we were going to win freedom for Cuba and then present it to her. They said, "Ah, yes; under the control of the United States. They will never let go of that rich island which they can exploit so much to their own advantage!" When we kept that promise and proved our absolute disinterestedness, and, notwithstanding the fact that we had beaten Spain until she had to accept anything that we dictated, paid her $20,-000,000 for something that we could have taken, namely, the Philippine Islands, all the world stood at amaze and said, "Is it true, after all, that this people believes and means what it says? Is it true, after all, that this is a great altruistic force in the world?"

And now look what has happened, my fellow citizens. Poland, Bohemia, the released parts of Rumania, Jugo-Slavia—there are kinsmen, I dare say, of these people in this audience—these could, none of them, have won their own independence any more than Cuba could have won hers, and they were under an authority just as reckless in the exercise of its force, just as regardless of the people and of humanity, as the Spanish Government ever was in Cuba and the Philippines; and by the force of the world these people have been liberated. Now the world is waiting to hear whether the United States will join in doing for them what it sanely did for Cuba, guaranteeing their freedom and saying to them, "What we have given to you no man shall take away." It is our final heroic test of character, and I for one have not the slightest doubt as to what the result of the test is going to be, because I know that at heart this people loves freedom and right and justice more than it loves money and material prosperity or any of the things that anybody can get but nobody can keep unless they have elevation of spirit enough to see the horizons of the destiny of man.

Instead of wishing to ask to stand aside, get the benefits of the League, but share none of its burdens or responsibilities, I for my part want to go in and accept what is offered to us, the leadership of the world. A leadership of what sort, my fellow citizens? Not a leadership that leads men along the lines by which great nations can profit out of weak nations, not an exploiting power, but a liberating power, a power to show the world that when America was born it was indeed a finger pointed toward those lands into which men could deploy some of these days and live in happy freedom, look each other in the eyes as equals, see that no man was put upon, that no people were forced to accept authority which was not of their own choice, and that out of the general generous impulse of the human genius and the human spirit we were lifted along the levels of civilization to days when there should be wars no more, but men should govern themselves in peace and amity and quiet. That is the leadership we said we wanted, and now the world offers it to us. It is inconceivable that we should reject it. It is inconceivable that men should put any conditions upon accepting it, particularly—for I speak this with a certain hurt pride, my fellow citizens, as an American—particularly when we are so safeguarded that the world under the Covenant cannot do a thing that we do not consent to being done. Other nations, other governments, were just as jealous of their sovereignty as we have been, and this guarantees the sovereignty of all the equal members

of this great union of nations. There is only one nation
for the time being excluded. That is Germany, and
Germany is excluded only in order that she may go
through a period of probation, only in order that she
may prove to the world that she has made a real and
permanent change in her constitution, and that hereafter, not Wilhelmstrasse but the votes of the German
people will determine the policy of the German
Government.

If I may say so without even by implication involving
great public men whom I entirely respect, I want to
say that the only popular forces back of serious reservations, the only popular forces back of the impulse to
reject any part of this treaty, proceed from exactly the
same sources that the pro-German propaganda proceeded from. I ask the honorable and enlightened men
who I believe thoughtlessly favor reservations such as
I have read to reflect upon that and examine into the
truth of it, and to reflect upon this proposition: We,
by holding off from this League, serve the purposes of
Germany, for what Germany has sought throughout the
war was, first to prevent our going in, and, then, to
separate us in interest and purpose from the other
Governments with which we were associated. Now,
shall we by the vote of the United States Senate do for
Germany what she could not do with her arms? We
shall be doing it, whether we intend it or not. I ex-
culpate the men I am thinking of entirely from the
purpose of doing it; it would be unworthy of me to
suggest such a purpose, but I do suggest, I do state with
confidence, that that is the only end that would be
gained, because Germany is isolated from the other
nations, and she desires nothing so much as that we
should be isolated, because she knows that then the same
kind of suspicion, the same kind of hostility, the same
kind of unfriendliness—that subtle poison that brings
every trouble that comes between nations—will center
on the United States as well as upon Germany. Her

isolation will be broken; she will have a comrade, whether that nation wants to be her comrade or not, and what the lads did on the fields of France will be undone. We will allow Germany to do in 1919 what she failed to do in 1918!

It would be unworthy of me, my fellow citizens, in the responsible position into which you have put me, if I were to overstate any of these things. I have searched my conscience with regard to them. I believe I am telling you the sober truth, and I am telling you what I get, not by intuition, but through those many voices that inevitably reach the Government and do not always reach you from over sea. We know what the leading men of Germany are thinking and saying, and they are praying that the United States may stand off from the League. I call upon you, therefore, my fellow citizens, to look at this thing in a new aspect, to look upon it not with calculations of interest, not with fear of responsibility, but with a consciousness of the great moral issue which the United States must now decide and which, having decided, it cannot reverse. If we keep out of this League now, we can never enter it except alongside of Germany. We can either go in now or come in later with our recent enemies, and to adopt a reservation such as I have read, which explicitly renounces responsibility under the central engagement of the Covenant, is to do nothing less than that.

I hope that in order to strengthen this impression on your minds you will take pains to read the treaty of peace. You need not read all of it; a lot of it is technical and you can skip that; but I want you to get a picture of what is in this great document. It is much too narrow a view of it to think of it as a treaty of peace with Germany. It is that, but it is very much more than a treaty of peace with Germany; it is a treaty in which an attempt is made to set up the rights of peoples everywhere, for exactly the lines of this treaty are going to be projected—have been projected—into the treaty with Austria, into the treaty with Bulgaria, into the treaty with Hungary, into the treaty with Turkey. Everywhere the same principle is adopted, that the men who wrote the treaties at Versailles were not at liberty to give anybody's property to anybody else. It is the first great international agreement in the history of civilization that was not based on the opposite principle. Every other great international arrangement has been a division of spoils, and this is an absolute renunciation of spoils, even with regard to the helpless parts of the world, even with regard to those poor benighted people in Africa, over whom Germany had exercised a selfish authority which exploited them and did not help them. Even they are not handed over to anybody else. The principle of annexation, the principle of extending sovereignty to territories that are not occupied by your own people, is rejected in this treaty. All of those regions are put under the trust of the League of Nations, to be administered for the benefit of their inhabitants—the greatest humane arrangement that has ever been attempted—and the rules are laid down in the Covenant itself which forbid any form of selfish exploitation of these helpless people by the agents of the League who will exercise authority over them during the period of their development.

Then see how free course is given to our sympathies. I believe that there is no region of the world toward which the sympathies of the United States have gone out so abundantly as to the poor people of Armenia, those people infinitely terrified and infinitely persecuted. We have poured out money, we have sent agents of all sorts to relieve their distress, and at every turn we have known that every dollar we spent upon them might be rendered useless by the cruel power which had authority over them, that under pretense of not being able to control its own forces in those parts of the empire, the Turkish Government might say that it was unable to restrain the horrible massacres which have made that

country a graveyard. Armenia is one of the regions
that are to be under trust of the League of Nations.
Armenia is to be redeemed. The Turk is to be for-
bidden to exercise his authority there, and Christian
people are not only to be allowed to aid Armenia but
they are to be allowed to protect Armenia. At last
this great people, struggling through night after night
of terror, knowing not what day would see their land
stained with blood, are now given a promise of safety,
a promise of justice, a possibility that they may come
out into a time when they can enjoy their own rights
as free people, as they never dreamed they would be
able to exercise them before. All of the great humane
impulses of the human heart are expressed in this treaty,
and we would be recreant to every humane obligation
if we did not lend our whole force and, if necessary,
make our utmost sacrifice to maintain its provisions.
We are approaching the time in the discussions of the
Senate when it will be determined what we are going to
say about it, and I am here making this public appeal
to you and, through you, to gentlemen who have
favored such utterances as I have read to you to-night,
to take a second thought upon the matter, to realize
that what they are after is already accomplished. The
United States cannot be drawn into anything it does not
wish to be drawn into, but the United States ought not
to be itself in the position of saying, "You need not expect of us that we assume the same moral obligations
that you assume. You need not expect of us that we
will respect and preserve the territorial integrity and
political independence of other nations."

Let me remove another misapprehension about the
clause, my fellow citizens. Almost every time it is
quoted the words "external aggression" are left out of
it. There was not a member of that conference with
whom I conferred who wanted to put the least restraint
upon the right of self-determination by any portion of
the human family, who wished to put the slightest ob-

stacle in the way of throwing off the yoke of any Government if that yoke should become intolerable. This does not guarantee any country, any Government, against an attempt on the part of its own subjects to throw off its authority. The United States could not keep its countenance and make a promise like that, because it began by doing that very thing. The glory of the United States is that when we were a little body of 3,000,000 people strung along the Atlantic coast we threw off the power of a great empire because it was not a power chosen by or consented to by ourselves. We hold that principle. We never will guarantee any Government against the exercise of that right, and no suggestion was made in the conference that we should. We merely ourselves promised to respect the territorial integrity and existing political independence of the other members of the League and to assist in preserving them against external aggression.

And if we do not do that the taproot of war is still sunk deep into the fertile soil of human passion. I am for cutting the taproot of war. I am for making an insurance against war, and I am prudent enough to take ten per cent insurance if I cannot get any more. I would be very pleased to get twenty-five per cent. I would be delighted to get fifty per cent, and here, in conscience, I believe we are getting ninety-nine per cent. No man, no body of men, can give you absolute one hundred per cent insurance against war any more than they can give you one hundred per cent insurance against losing your temper. You cannot insure men against human passion, but notice what this Covenant does: It provides nine months as a minimum for the cooling off of human passion. It is pretty hard to be crazy mad for nine months. If you stay crazy mad, or crazy anything else, for nine months, it will be wise to segregate you from your fellow citizens. The heart of this Covenant, to which very few opponents ever draw attention, is this, that every great fighting nation in the world engages never to go to war without first having done one or the other of two things, without having either submitted the point in controversy to arbitration, in which case it promises absolutely to abide by the verdict or submit it to the council of the League of Nations, not for decision but for discussion; it agrees to lay all the documents and all the pertinent facts before the council and agrees that the council shall publish the documents and the facts to mankind, that it will give six months to the council for the consideration of the matter, and that, even if it does not accept the result, it will not go to war for three months after the opinion is rendered. You have nine months in which to accomplish all the gentle work of mediation, all the same work of discussion, all the quieting work of a full comprehension of what the result of bringing the matter to the issue of war would be upon the nations immediately concerned and upon the nations of the world. And in Article XI, which follows Article X, it is made the right of any member of the League to call attention to anything, anywhere, which is likely to affect the peace of the world or the good understanding between nations upon which the peace of the world depends. So that, after the storm begins to gather, you can call the attention of the world to it, and the cleansing, purifying, cooling processes of public opinion will at once begin to operate.

When a very important part of Shantung Province was ceded by China to Germany in March, 1898, the Government of the United States uttered not a single protest. One of the most enlightened and humane men that have ever sat in the executive chair was President of the United States William McKinley. One of the ablest Secretaries of State in the long list of distinguished men who have occupied that office was associated with him as Secretary of State, the Hon. John Hay. They made not a single intimation of protest. Why? Because under international law as it was, and as it is until this Covenant is adopted, it would have been a hostile act for them to do any such thing unless they could show that the material or political interest of the United States was directly affected. The only ground which they insisted upon was that Germany should not close Shantung Province to the trade of the United States. They could not lift a little finger to help China. They could only try to help the trade of the United States. Immediately after that cession China made similar cessions to England, to Russia, to France, and again no protest, only an insistence that the door should be kept open to our goods—not to our moral ideas, not to our sympathy with China, not to our sense of right violated, but to our merchandise. You do not hear anything about the cessions in that year to Great Britain or to France, because, unhappily, they were not unprecedented, as the cession to Germany was not unprecedented. Poor China had done the like not once but many times before. What happened afterwards? In the treaty between Japan and Russia, after the Japanese-Russian war, a treaty signed on our own territory—in Portsmouth, N. H.—Port Arthur, the Chinese territory ceded to Russia, was transferred to Japan. Here were our own people sitting about, here was our own Government that had invited these gentlemen to sit at Portsmouth—did they object to Port Arthur being not handed back to China but handed to Japan?

I am not going to stop, my fellow citizens, to discuss the Shantung provision in all its aspects, but what I want to call your attention to is that just as soon as this Covenant is ratified every nation in the world will have the right to speak out for China. And I want to say very frankly, and I ought to add that the representatives of those great nations themselves admit, that Great Britain and France and the other powers which have insisted upon similar concessions in China will be put in a position where they will have to reconsider them. This is the only way to serve and redeem China, unless, indeed, you want to start a war for the purpose. At the beginning of the war and during the war Great Britain and France engaged by solemn treaty with Japan that if she would come into the war and continue in the war, she could have, provided she in the meantime took it by force of arms, what Germany had in China. Those are treaties already in force. They are not waiting for ratification. France and England cannot withdraw from those obligations, and it will serve China not one iota if we should dissent from the Shantung arrangement; but by being parties to that arrangement we can insist upon the promise of Japan—the promise which the other governments have not matched —that she will return to China immediately all sovereign rights within the Province to Shantung. We have got that for her now, and under the operations of Article XI and of Article X it will be impossible for any nation to make any further inroads either upon the territorial integrity or upon the political independence of China. I for one want to say that my heart goes out to that great people, that learned people, that accomplished people, that honest people, hundreds of millions strong but never adequately organized for the exercise of force, therefore always at the mercy of anyone who has effective armies or navies, always subject to be commanded, and never in a position unassisted by the world to insist upon its own rights.

It is a test—an acid test: Are you willing to go into the great adventure of liberating hundreds of millions of human beings from the threat of foreign power? If you are timid, I can assure you you can do it without shedding a drop of human blood. If you are squeamish about fighting, I will tell you you will not have to fight. The only force that outlasts all others and is finally triumphant is the moral judgment of mankind. Why is it that when a man tells a lie about you you do not wince, but when he tells the truth about you, if it is not creditable, then you wince? The only thing you are afraid of is the truth. The only thing you dare not face is the truth. The only thing that will get you sooner or later, no matter how you sneak or dodge, is the truth; and the only thing that will conquer nations is the truth. No nation is going to look the calm judgment of mankind in the face for nine months and then go to war. You can illustrate the great by the little. I dare say you have taken time to cool off sometimes. I know I have. It is very useful for a person, particularly with a Scotch disposition like mine, to withdraw from human society when he is mad all through and just think about the situation and reflect upon the consequences of making a conspicuous ass of himself. It is for that reason that I have always said that if you have an acquaintance whom you suspect of being a fool, encourage him to hire a hall. There is nothing that tests a man's good sense like exposure to the air. We are applying this great, healing, sanitary influence to the affairs of nations and of men, and we can apply it only by the processes of peace which are offered to us after a conference, which I can testify was taken part in in the knowledge and in the spirit that never obtained before in any such conference; that we were not at liberty to work out the policy and ambition of any nation, but that our single duty and our single opportunity was to put the peoples of the world in possession of their own affairs.

So, as much of the case, my fellow citizens, as I can lay before you on a single occasion—as much of this varied and diversified theme—is laid before you, and I ask your assistance to redeem the reputation of the United States. I ask you to make felt everywhere that it is useful to make it felt, not by way of threat, not by way of menace of any sort, but by way of compelling judgment, that the thing for us to do is to redeem the promises of America made in solemn presence of mankind when we entered this war, for I see a happy vision before the world, my fellow countrymen. Every previ-

ous international conference was based upon the authority of governments. This, for the first time, was based
upon the authority of peoples. It is, therefore, the
triumphant establishment of the principle of democracy
throughout the world, but only the establishment of
the principle of political democracy. What the world
now insists upon—order and peace in order to consider
and in order to achieve—is the establishment of industrial democracy, is the establishment of such relationships between those who direct labor and those who
perform labor as shall make a real community of interest, as shall make a real community of purpose, as shall
lift the whole level of industrial achievement above bargain and sale, into a great method of coöperation by
which men, purposing the same thing and justly organizing the same thing, may bring about a state of happiness and of prosperity such as the world has never
known before. We want to be friends of each other as
well as friends of mankind. We want America to be
united in spirit as well as the world. We want America
to be a body of brethren, and if America is a body of
brethren, then you may be sure that its leadership will
bring the same sort of comradeship and intimacy of
spirit and purity of purpose to the counsels and
achievements of mankind.

AT CHEYENNE, WYO., SEPTEMBER 24, 1919.

GOVERNOR CAREY, MY FELLOW COUNTRYMEN:

It is with genuine satisfaction that I find myself in
this great State, which I have only too seldom visited,
and I appreciate this close contact with a body of its
citizens in order that I may make clear some of the
matters which have emerged in the discussion in the
midst of which we now find ourselves. Governor Carey
is quite right in saying that no document ever drew upon
it more widespread discussion than the great treaty
of peace with which your representatives returned from

Paris. It is not to be wondered at, my fellow citizens, because that treaty is a unique document. It is the most remarkable document, I venture to say, in human history, because in it is recorded a complete reversal of the processes of government which had gone on throughout practically the whole history of mankind. The example that we set in 1776, which some statesmen in Europe affected to disregard and others presumed to ridicule, nevertheless set fires going in the hearts of men which no influence was able to quench, and one after another the Governments of the world have yielded to the influences of democracy. No man has been able to stay the tide, and there came a day when there was only one bulwark standing against it. That was in Berlin and Vienna—standing in the only territory which had not been conquered by the liberal forces of the opinion of the world, continued to stand fast where there was planted a pair of Governments that could use their people as they pleased, as pawns and instruments in a game of ambition, send them to the battle field without condescending to explain to them why they were sent, send them to the battle field to work out a dominion over free peoples on the part of a Government that had never been liberalized and made free.

The world did not realize in 1914 that it had come to the final grapple of principle. It was only by slow degrees that we realized that we had any part in the war. We started the forces in 1776, as I have said, that made this war inevitable, but we were a long time realizing that, after all, that was what was at issue. We had been accustomed to regarding Europe as a field of intriguing, of rival ambitions, and of attempts to establish empire, and at first we merely got the impression that this was one of the usual European wars, to which, unhappily, mankind had become only too accustomed. You know how unwilling we were to go into it. I can speak for myself. I made every effort to keep this country out of the war, until it came to my conscience, as it came to yours, that after all it was our war as well as Europe's war, that the ambition of these central empires was directed against nothing less than the liberty of the world, and that if we were indeed, what we had always professed to be, champions of the liberty of the world, it was not within our choice to keep out of the great enterprise. We went in just in time. I can testify, my fellow countrymen, that the hope of Europe had sunk very low when the American troops began to throng overseas. I can testify that they had begun to fear that the terror would be realized and that the German power would be established. At first they were incredulous that our men could come in force enough to assist them. At first they thought that it was only a moral encouragement they would get from seeing that gallant emblem of the Stars and Stripes upon their fields. Presently they realized that the tide was real, that here came men by the thousands, by the hundreds of thousands, by the millions; that there was no end to the force which would now be asserted to rescue the free peoples of the world from the terror of autocracy; and America had the infinite privilege of fulfilling her destiny and saving the world. I do not hesitate to say, as a sober interpretation of history, that American soldiers saved the liberties of the world.

I want to remind you of all this, my fellow citizens, because it is pertinent to the discussion that is now going on. We saved the liberties of the world, and we must stand by the liberties of the world. We cannot draw back. You remember what happened in that fateful battle in which our men first took part. You remember how the French lines had been beaten and separated and broken at Chateau-Thierry, and you remember how the gates seemed open for the advancement of the Germans upon Paris. Then a body of men, a little body of men—American soldiers and American marines—

against the protests of French officers, against the command of the remote commanders, nevertheless dared to fill that breach, stopped that advance, turned the Germans back, and never allowed them to turn their faces forward again. They were advised to go back, and they asked the naïve American question, "What did we come over here for? We did not come over here to go back; we came over here to go forward." And they never went in any other direction. The men who went to Chateau-Thierry, the men who went into Belleau Wood, the men who did what no other troops had been able to do in the Argonne, never thought of turning back, not only, but they never thought of making any reservations on their service. They never thought of saying, "We are going to do this much of the job and then scuttle and leave you to do the rest." I am here, I am on this journey, to help this Nation, if I can by my counsel, to fulfill and complete the task which the men who died upon the battle fields of France began, and I am not going to turn back any more than they did. I am going to keep my face just as they kept their face—forward toward the enemy.

My friends—I use the words advisedly—the only organized forces in this country, outside of Congressional Halls, against this treaty are the forces of hyphenated Americans. I beg you to observe that I say the only organized forces, because I would not include many individuals whom I know in any such characterization, but I do repeat that it is the pro-German forces and the other forces that showed their hyphen during the war that are now organized against this treaty. We can please nobody in America except these people by rejecting it or qualifying it in our acceptance of it. I want you to recall the circumstances of this Great War lest we forget. We must not forget to redeem absolutely and without qualification the promises of America in this great enterprise. I have crossed the continent now, my friends, and am a part of my way back. I can testify to the sentiment of the American people. It is unmistakable. The overwhelming majority of them demand the ratification of this treaty, and they demand it because, whether they have analyzed it or not, they have a consciousness of what it is that we are fighting for. We said that this was a people's war—I have explained to you that it was, though you did not need the explanation—and we said that it must be a people's peace. It is a people's peace. I challenge any man to find a contradiction to that statement in the terms of the great document with which I returned from Paris. It is so much of a people's peace that in every portion of its settlement every thought of aggrandizement, of territorial or political aggrandizement, on the part of the great powers was brushed aside, brushed aside by their own representatives. They declined to take the colonies of Germany in sovereignty, and said they would consent and demand that they be administered in trust by a concert of the nations through the instrumentality of a league of nations. They did not claim a single piece of territory. On the contrary, every territory that had been under the dominion of the Central Powers, unjustly and against its own consent, is by that treaty and the treaties which accompany it absolutely turned over in fee simple to the people who live in it. The principle is adopted without qualification upon which America was founded, that all just government proceeds from the consent of the governed. No nation that could be reached by the conclusions of this conference was obliged to accept the authority of a government by which it did not wish to be controlled. It is a peace of liberation. It is a peace in which the rights of peoples are realized, and when objection is made to the treaty, is any objection made to the substance of the treaty? There is only one thing in the substance of the treaty that has been debated seriously, and that is the arrangement by which Japan gets the rights that Germany had in Shantung Province

in China. I wish I had time to go through the story of
that fully. It was an unavoidable settlement, and nothing can be done for China without the League of
Nations.

Perhaps you will bear with me if I take time to tell
you what I am talking about. You know that China
has been the common prey of the great European
powers. Perhaps I should apologize to the representatives of those powers for using such a word, but I think
they would admit that the word is justified. Nation
after nation has demanded rights, semisovereign rights,
and concessions with regard to mines and railways and
every other resource that China could put at their disposition, and China has never been able to say "No"—
a great learned, patient, diligent people, numbering
hundreds of millions; has had no organized force with
which to resist, and has yielded again and again and
again to unjust demands. One of these demands was
made upon her in March, 1898, by Germany—unjustly
made. I will not go into the particulars, but I could
justify that word "unjustly." A concession was demanded of her of the control of the whole district
around Kiauchau Bay, one of the open doors to the
trade and resources of China. She was obliged to yield
to Germany practically sovereign control over that
great region by the sea, and into the interior of the
Province Germany was privileged to extend a railway
and to exploit all the deposits of ore that might be
found for thirty miles on either side of the railway
which she was to build. The Government of the United
States at that time, presided over by one of the most
enlightened and beloved of our Presidents—I mean
William McKinley—and the Department of State,
guided by that able and high-minded man, John Hay,
did not make the slightest protest. Why? Not because they would not if they could have aided China,
but because under international law as it then stood no
nation had the right to protest against anything that

other nations did that did not directly affect its own rights. Mr. McKinley and Mr. Hay did insist that if Germany took control of Kiauchau Bay, she should not close those approaches to China against the trade of the United States. How pitiful, when you go into the court of right, you cannot protect China, you can only protect your own merchandise! You cannot say, "You have done a great wrong to these people." You have got to say, "We yield to the wrong, but we insist that you should admit our goods to be sold in those markets!" Pitiful, but nevertheless it was international law. All nations acted in that way at that time. Immediately following these concessions to Germany, Russia insisted upon concessions and got Port Arthur and other territories. England insisted, though she had had similar concessions in the past, upon an additional concession and got Wei-Hai-Wai. France came into the game and got a port and its territory lying behind it for the same period of time that Germany had got her concession, namely, ninety-nine years.

Then came the war between Russia and Japan, and what happened? In a treaty signed on our own sacred territory, at Portsmouth in New Hampshire, Japan was allowed to take from Russia what had belonged to China, the concession of Port Arthur and of Talien-wan, the territory in that neighborhood. The treaty was written here; it was written under the auspices, so to say, of our own public opinion, but the Government of the United States was not at liberty to protest and did not protest; it acquiesced in the very thing which is being done in this treaty. What is being done in this treaty is not that Shantung is being taken from China. China did not have it. It is being taken from Germany, just as Port Arthur was not taken from China but taken from Russia and transferred to Japan. Before we got into the war, Great Britain and France had entered into solemn covenant by treaty with Japan that if she would take what Germany had in Shantung

by force of arms, and also the islands lying north of the
Equator which had been under German dominion in the
Pacific, she could keep them when the peace came and
its settlements were made.   They were bound by a
treaty of which we knew nothing, but which, notwithstanding our ignorance of it, bound them as much as
any treaty binds.   This war was fought to maintain
the sacredness of treaties.   Great Britain and France,
therefore, cannot consent to a change of the treaty in
respect of the cession of Shantung, and we have no
precedent in our history which permits us even to protest against it until we become members of the League
of Nations.

I want this point to sink in, my fellow countrymen:
The League of Nations changes the international law
of the world with regard to matters of this sort.   You
have heard a great deal about Article X of the Covenant of the League, and I will speak of it presently,
but read Article XI in conjunction with Article X.
Every member of the League, in Article X, agrees
never to impair the territorial integrity of any other
member of the League or to interfere with its existing
political independence.   Both of those things were done
in all these concessions.   There was a very serious impairment of the territorial integrity of China in every
one of them, and a very serious interference with the
political independence of that great but helpless Kingdom.   Article X stops that for good and all.   Then,
in Article XI, it is provided that it shall be the
friendly right of any member of the League at any time
to call attention to anything anywhere that is likely to
disturb the peace of the world or the good understanding between nations upon which the peace of the world
depends, so that the ban would have been lifted from
Mr. McKinley and Mr. Roosevelt in the matter of
these things if we had the Covenant of the League;
they could have gone in and said, "Here is your promise to preserve the territorial integrity and political

independence of this great people. We have the friendly right to protest. We have the right to call your attention to the fact that this will breed wars and not peace, and that you have not the right to do this thing." Henceforth, for the first time, we shall have the opportunity to play effective friends to the great people of China, and I for one feel my pulses quicken and my heart rejoice at such a prospect. We, a free people, have hitherto been dumb in the presence of the invasion of the freedom of other free peoples, and now restraint is taken away. I say it is taken away, for we will be members of the Covenant. Restraint is taken away, and, like the men that we profess to be, we can speak out in the interest of free people everywhere.

But that is not all. America, as I have said, was not bound by the agreements of Great Britain and France, on the one hand, and Japan on the other. We were free to insist upon a prospect of a different settlement, and at the instance of the United States Japan has already promised that she will relinquish to China immediately after the ratification of this treaty all the sovereign rights that Germany had in Shantung Province—the only promise of that kind ever made, the only relinquishment of that sort ever achieved—and that she will retain only what foreign corporations have all over China—unfortunately but as a matter of fact— the right to run the railroad and the right to work the mines under the usual conditions of Chinese sovereignty and as economic concessionaires, with no political rights or military power of any kind. It is really an emancipation of China, so far as that Province is concerned, from what is imposed upon her by other nations in other Provinces equally rich and equally important to the independence of China herself. So that inside the League of Nations we now have a foothold by which we can play the friend to China.

And the alternative? If you insist upon cutting out the Shantung arrangement, that merely severs us from the treaty. It does not give Shantung back to China. The only way you can give Shantung back to China is by arms in your hands, armed ships and armed men, sent against Japan and France and Great Britain. A fratricidal strife, in view of what we have gone through! We have just redeemed France. We cannot with arms in our hands insist that France break a covenant, however ill judged, however unjust; we cannot as her brothers in arms commit any such atrocious act against the fraternity of free people. So much for Shantung. Nobody can get that provision out of that treaty and do China any service whatever, and all such professions of friendship for China are empty noise, for the gentlemen who make those professions must know that what they propose will be not of the slightest service to her.

That is the only point of serious criticism with regard to the substance of the treaty. All the rest refers to the Covenant of the League of Nations. With regard to that, my fellow citizens, I have this to say: Without the Covenant of the League of Nations that treaty cannot be executed. Without the adherence of the United States to that Covenant, the Covenant cannot be made effective. To state it another way, the maintenance of the peace of the world and the execution of the treaty depend upon the whole-hearted participation of the people of the United States. I am not stating it as a matter of power. I am not stating it with the thought that the United States has greater material wealth and greater physical power than any other nation. The point that I want you to get is a very profound point; the point is that the United States is the only nation of the world that has sufficient moral force with the rest of the world. It is the only nation which has proved its disinterestedness. It is the only nation which is not suspected by the other nations of the world of ulterior purposes. There is not a Province in Europe in which American troops would not at this moment be welcomed with open arms, because the population would know that they had come as friends and would go so soon as their errand was fulfilled. I have had delegations come to me, delegations from countries where disorder made the presence of troops necessary, and beg me to order American troops there. They said, "We trust them; we want them. They are our friends." And all the world, provided we do not betray them by rejecting this treaty, will continue to regard us as their friends and follow us as their friends and serve us as their friends. It is the noblest opportunity ever offered to a great people, and we will not turn away from it.

We are coming now to the grapple, because one question at a time is being cleared away. We are presently going to have a show-down, a show-down on a very definite issue, and I want to bring your minds to that definite issue. A number of objections have been made to the Covenant of the League of Nations, but they have been disposed of in candid minds. The first was the question whether we could withdraw when we pleased. That is no longer a question in the mind of anybody who has studied the language and real meaning of the Covenant. We can withdraw, upon two years' notice, when we please. I state that with absolutely no qualification. Then there was the question as to whether it interfered with self-determination; that is to say, whether there was anything in the guarantee of Article X about territorial integrity and political independence which would interfere with the assertion of the right of great populations anywhere to change their governments, to throw off the yoke of sovereignties which they did not desire to live under. There is absolutely no such restraint. I was present and can testify that when Article X was debated the most significant words in it were the words "against external aggression." We do not guarantee any government against anything that may happen within its own borders or within its own sovereignty. We merely say that we will not impair its territorial integrity or interfere with its political independence, and we will not countenance other nations outside of it making prey of it in the one way or the other. Every man who sat around that table, and at the table where the conference on the League of Nations sat there were fourteen free peoples represented, believed in the sacred right of self-determination, would not have dared to go back and face his own people if he had done or said anything that stood in the way of it. That is out of the way. There was some doubt as to whether the Monroe Doctrine was properly recognized, though I do not see how anybody who could read the English language could have raised the doubt. The Covenant says that nothing contained in it shall be construed as affecting the validity of the Monroe Doctrine, so that by a sudden turn in the whole judgment of the world the Monroe Doctrine was accepted by all the great powers of the world. I know what their first impressions were about it. I know the history of their change of mind, and I know the heartiness and unanimity of the conclusion. Nothing can henceforth embarrass the policy of the United States in applying the Monroe Doctrine according to her own judgment. But there was apprehension that some kind of a supergovernment had been set up which could some day interfere in our domestic affairs, say that our immigration laws were too rigorous and wrong; that our laws of naturalization were too strict and severe; that our tariff policy did not suit the rest of the world. The Covenant expressly excludes interference with domestic questions, expressly states that it shall not be the right of any authority of the League to interfere in matters of that sort. That matter is cleared away by everybody who can understand the clauses in question.

There is another matter in that connection I want to speak of. The constitution of the League of Nations is not often enough explained. It is made up of two bodies. One body, which is a comparatively large body, is called the assembly. The assembly is not an originative body. The assembly is, so to say, the court of the public opinion of the world. It is where you can broach questions, but not decide them. It is where you can debate anything that affects the peace of the world, but not determine upon a course of action upon anything that affects the peace of the world. The whole direction of the action of the League is vested in another body known as the council, and nothing in the form of an active measure, no policy, no recommendation with regard to the action of the governments composing the League can proceed except upon a unanimous vote of the council. Mark you, a unanimous vote of the council. In brief, inasmuch as the United States of America is to be a permanent member of the council of the League, the League can take no step whatever without the consent of the United States of America. My fellow citizens, think of the significance of that in view of the debates you have been listening to. There is not a single active step that the League can take unless we vote aye. The whole matter is, in that negative sense, in the ability to stop any action, in our hands. I am sometimes inclined to think that that weakens the League, that it has not freedom of action enough, notwithstanding that I share with all of my fellow countrymen a very great jealousy with regard to setting up any power that could tell us to do anything, but no such power is set up. Whenever a question of any kind with regard to active policy—and there are only three or four of them—is referred to the assembly for its vote, its vote in the affirmative must include the representatives of all the nations which are represented on the council. In the assembly, as in the council, any single nation that is a member of the council has a veto upon active conclusions. That is my comment upon what you have been told about Great Britain having six votes and our having one. I am perfectly content with the arrangement, since our one offsets the British six. I do not want to be a repeater; if my one vote goes, I do not want to repeat it five times.

And is it not just that in this debating body, from which without the unanimous concurrence of the council no active proceeding can originate, that these votes should have been given to the self-governing powers of the British Empire? I am ready to maintain that position. Is it not just that those stout little Republics out in the Pacific, of New Zealand and Australia, should be able to stand up in the councils of the world and say something? Do you not know how Australia has led the free peoples of the world in many matters that have led to social and industrial reform? It is one of the most enlightened communities in the world and absolutely free to choose its own way of life independent of the British authority, except in matters of foreign relationship. Do you not think that it is natural that that stout little body of men whom we so long watched with admiration in their contest with the British Crown in South Africa should have the right to stand up and talk before the world? They talked once with their arms, and, if I may judge by my contact with them, they can talk with their minds. They know what the interests of South Africa are, and they are independent in their control of the interests of South Africa. Two of the most impressive and influential men I met in Paris were representatives of South Africa, both of them members of the British peace delegation in Paris, and yet both of them generals who had made British generals take notice through many months of their power to fight— the men whom Great Britain had fought and beaten and felt obliged to hand over their own government to, and say, "It is yours and not ours." They were men who spoke counsel, who spoke frank counsel. And take our neighbor on the north—do you not think Canada is entitled to a speaking part? I have pointed out to you that her voting part is offset, but do you not think

she is entitled to a speaking part? Do you not think
that that fine dominion has been a very good neighbor?
Do you not think she is a good deal more like the
United States than she is like Great Britain? Do you
not feel that probably you think alike? The only other
vote given to the British Empire is given to that
hitherto voiceless mass of humanity that lives in that
region of romance and pity that we know as India. I
am willing that India should stand up in the councils of
the world and say something. I am willing that speaking parts should be assigned to these self-governing,
self-respecting, energetic portions of the great body
of humanity.

I take leave to say that the deck is cleared of these
bugaboos. We can get out if we want to. I am not
interested in getting out. I am interested in getting in.
But we can get out. The door is not locked. You can
sit on the edge of your chair and scuttle any time you
want to. There are so many who are interested first of
all in knowing that they are not in for anything that
can possibly impose anything on them. Well, we
are not in for anything that we do not want to continue
to carry. We can help in the matters of self-determination, as we never helped before. The six votes of the
British Empire are offset by our own, if we choose to
offset them. I dare say we shall often agree with them;
but if we do not, they cannot do anything that we do
not consent to. The Monroe Doctrine is taken care of.
There is no danger of interference with domestic
questions.

Well, what remains? Nothing except Article X,
and that is the heart of the whole Covenant. Anybody
who proposes to cut out Article X proposes to cut all
the supports from under the peace and security of the
world, and we must face the question in that light; we
must draw the issue as sharply as that; we must see it
through as distinctly as that. Let me repeat Article X.
I do not know that I can do it literally, but I can come

very near. Under Article X every member of the League engages to respect and preserve as against external aggression the territorial integrity and existing political independence of the other members of the League. That cuts at the taproot of war. The wars of the past have been leveled against the liberties of peoples and territories of those who could not defend them, and if you do not cut at that taproot that upas tree is going to grow again; and I tell you my fellow countrymen, that if you do not cut it up now it will be harder to cut it up next time. The next time will come; it will come while this generation is living, and the children that crowd about our car as we move from station to station will be sacrificed upon the altar of that war. It will be the last war. Humanity will never suffer another, if humanity survives. My fellow countrymen, do you realize that at the end of the war that has just closed new instruments of destruction had been invented and were about to be used that exceeded in terrible force and destructive power any that had been used before in this war? You have heard with wonder of those great cannon from which the Germans sent shells seventy miles into Paris. Just before the war closed shells had been invented that could be made to steer themselves and carry immense bodies of explosives a hundred miles into the interior of countries, no matter how great the serried ranks of their soldiers were at the border. This war will be child's play as compared with another war. You have got to cut the root of that upas tree now or betray all future generations.

And we cannot without our vote in the council, even in support of Article X, be drawn into wars that we do not wish to be drawn into. The second sentence of Article X is that the council shall advise as to the method of fulfilling this guarantee, that the council which must vote by unanimous vote, must advise—cannot direct—what is to be done for the maintenance of the honor of its members and for the maintenance of the peace of the world. Is there anything that can frighten a man or a woman or a child, with just thought or red blood, in those provisions? And yet listen. I understand that this reservation is under consideration. I ask your very attentive ear.

The United States assumes no obligation under the provisions of Article X to preserve the territorial integrity or political independence of any other country or to interfere in controversies between other nations, whether members of the League or not, or to employ the military and naval forces of the United States under any article of the treaty for any purpose, unless in any particular case the Congress, which under the Constitution has the sole power to declare war or authorize the employment of the military and naval forces of the United States, shall by act or joint resolution so declare.

In other words, my fellow citizens, what this proposes is this: That we should make no general promise, but leave the nations associated with us to guess in each instance what we were going to consider ourselves bound to do and what we were not going to consider ourselves bound to do. It is as if you said, "We will not join the League definitely, but we will join it occasionally. We will not promise anything, but from time to time we may coöperate. We will not assume any obligations." Observe, my fellow citizens, as I have repeatedly said to you and cannot say too often, the council of the League cannot oblige us to take military action without the consent of Congress. There is no possibility of that. But this reservation proposes that we should not acknowledge any moral obligation in the matter; that we should stand off and say, "We will see, from time to time; consult us when you get into trouble, and then we will have a debate, and after two or three months we will tell you what we are going to do." The thing is unworthy and ridiculous, and I want to say distinctly that, as I read this, it would change the entire meaning of the treaty and exempt the United States from all responsibility for the preservation of peace. It means the rejection of the treaty, my fellow countrymen, nothing less. It means that the United States would take from under the structure its very foundations and support.

I happen to know that there are some men in favor of that reservation who do not in the least degree realize its meaning, men whom I greatly respect, men who have just as much ardor to carry out the promises of the United States as I have, and I am not indicting their purpose, but I am calling their attention to the fact that if any such reservation as that should be adopted I would be obliged as the Executive of the United States to regard it as a rejection of the treaty. I ask them, therefore, to consider this matter very carefully, for I want you to realize, and I hope they realize, what the rejection of the treaty means—two isolated and suspected people, the people of Germany and the people of the United States. Germany is not admitted to respectable company yet. She is not permitted to enter the League until such time as she shall have proved to the satisfaction of the world that her change of government and change of heart is real and permanent. Then she can be admitted. Now, her dearest desire, feeling her isolation, knowing all the consequences that would result, economic and social, is to see the United States also cut off its association with the gallant peoples with whom side by side we fought this war. I am not making this statement by conjecture. We get it directly from the mouths of authoritative persons in Germany that their dearest hope is that America will now accomplish by the rejection of the treaty what Germany was not able to accomplish by her arms. She tried to separate us from the rest of the world. She tried to antagonize the rest of the world against the United States, and she failed so long as American armies were in the field. Shall she succeed now, when only American voters are in the field? The issue is final. We cannot avoid it. We have got to make it now, and, once made, there can be no turning back. We either go in with the other free peoples of the world to guarantee the peace of the world now, or we stay out and on some dark and disastrous day we seek admission to the League of Nations along with Germany. The rejection of this treaty, my fellow citizens, means the necessity of negotiating a separate treaty with Germany. That separate treaty between Germany and the United States could not alter any sentence of this treaty. It could not affect the validity of any sentence of this treaty. It would simply be the Government of the United States going, hat in hand, to the assembly at Weimar and saying, "May it please you, we have dissociated ourselves from those who were your enemies; we have come to you asking if you will consent to terms of amity and peace which will dissociate us, both of us, from the comradeship of arms and liberty." There is no other interpretation. There is no other issue. That is the issue, and every American must face it.

But I talk, my fellow citizens, as if I doubted what the decision would be. I happen to have been born and bred in America. There is not anything in me that is not American. I dare say that I inherit a certain stubbornness from an ancient stock from which I am remotely derived; but, then, all of you are derived, more or less remotely, from other stocks. You remember the exclamation of the Irishman who said, when he was called a foreigner, "You say we are furriners; I'd like to know who sittled this kintry but furriners!" We were all foreigners once, but we have undergone a climatic change, and the marvel of America is its solidarity, is its homogeneity, in the midst of its variety. The marvel about America is that, no matter what a man's stock and origin, you can always tell that he is an American the minute he begins to express an opinion. He may look sometimes like a foreigner, but tap him and you will find that the contents is American. Having been bred in that way myself, I do not have to conjecture what the judgments of America are going to be about a great question like this. I know beforehand, and I am only sorry for the men who do not know. If I did not know the law of custom and of honor against betting on a certainty, I would like to bet with them. But it would not be fair; I would be taking advantage of them.

If I may close with a word, not of jest, but of solemnity, I want to say, my fellow citizens, that there can be no exaggerating the importance of this peace and the importance of its immediate ratification, because the world will not and cannot settle down to normal conditions, either in America or anywhere else, until it knows what the future is going to be. If it must know that the future is going to be one of disorder and of rivalry and of the old contests of power, let it know it at once, so it can make its arrangements and its calculations and lay its taxes and recruit its armies and build its ships for the next great fight; but if, on the other hand, it can be told that it will have an insurance against war, that a great body of powerful nations has entered into a solemn Covenant to substitute arbitration and discussion for war, for that is the heart of the Covenant, that all the great fighting peoples of the world have engaged to forego war and substitute arbitration and discussion—if it can know that the minds will be quieted, the disorders will presently cease; then men will know that we have the opportunity to do that great, that transcendent duty that lies ahead of us, sit quietly down in council chambers and work out the proper reforms of our own industrial and economic life. They have got to be worked out. If this treaty is not ratified, they will be worked out in disorder throughout the world. I am not now intimating, for I do not think, that disorder will shake the foundations of our own affairs, but it will shake the foundations of the world, and these inevitable, indispensable reforms will be worked out amongst disorder and suspicion and hatred and violence, whereas if we can have the healing influences of assured peace they will be worked out in amity and quiet and by the judgment of men rather than by the passions of men. God send that day may come, and come soon! Above all, may God grant that it may come under the leadership of America!

AT AUDITORIUM, DENVER, COLO.,
SEPTEMBER 25, 1919.

MR. CHAIRMAN, MY FELLOW COUNTRYMEN:

I always feel a thrill of pride in standing before a great company of my fellow citizens to speak for this great document which we shall always know as the treaty of Versailles. I am proud to speak for it, because for the first time in the history of international consultation men have turned away from the ambitions of governments and have sought to advance the fortunes of peoples. They have turned away from all those older plans of domination and sought to lay anew the foundations for the liberty of mankind. I say without hesitation that this is a great document of liberation. It is a new charter for the liberty of men.

As we have advanced from week to week and from month to month in the debate of this great document, I think a great many things that we talked about at first have cleared away. A great many difficulties which were at first discovered, or which some fancied that they had discovered, have been removed. The center and heart of this document is that great instrument which is placed at the beginning of it, the Covenant of the League of Nations. I think everybody now understands that you cannot work this treaty without that Covenant. Everybody certainly understands that you have no insurance for the continuance of this settlement without the Covenant of the League of Nations, and you will notice that, with the single exception of the provision with regard to the transfer of the German rights in Shantung in China to Japan, practically nothing in the body of the treaty has seemed to constitute any great obstacle to its adoption. All the controversy, all the talk, has centered on the League of Nations, and I am glad to see the issue center; I am glad to see the issue clearly drawn, for now we have to decide, Shall we stand by the settlements of liberty, or shall we not?

I want, just by way of introduction and clarification, to point out what is not often enough explained to audiences in this country, the actual constitution of the League of Nations. It is very simply constituted. It consists of two bodies, a council and an assembly. The assembly is the numerous body. In it every self-governing State that is a member of the League is represented, and not only the self-governing independent States, but the self-governing colonies and dominions, such as Canada, New Zealand, Australia, India, and South Africa, are all represented in the assembly. It is in the assembly that the combined representation of the several parts of the British Empire are assigned six votes, and you are constantly being told that Great Britain has six votes and we have one. I want you to appreciate the full significance of that. They have six votes in the assembly, and the assembly does not vote. That bubble is exploded. There are several matters in which the vote of the assembly must coöperate with the vote of the council, but in every such case an unanimous vote of the council is necessary, and, inasmuch as the United States is a permanent member of the council, her vote is necessary to every active policy of the League. Therefore the single vote of the United States always counts six, so far as the votes of the British Empire are concerned, and if it is a mere question of pride, I would rather be one and count six than six and count one.

That affords emphasis to the point I wish you to keep

distinctly in mind with regard to reservations and all
the qualifications of ratification which are being discussed. No active policy can be undertaken by the
League without the assenting vote of the United States.
I cannot understand the anxiety of some gentlemen for
fear something is going to be put over on them. I cannot understand why, having read the Covenant of the
League and examined its constitution, they are not satisfied with the fact that every active policy of the League
must be concurred in by a unanimous vote of the council, which means that the affirmative vote of the United
States is in every instance necessary. That being the
case, it becomes sheer nonsense, my fellow citizens, to
talk about a supergovernment being set up over the
United States; it becomes sheer nonsense to say that
any authority is constituted which can order our armies
to other parts of the world, which can interfere with
our domestic questions, which can direct our international policy even in any matter in which we do not consent to be directed. We would be under our own direction just as much under the Covenant of the League of
Nations as we are now. Of course, I do not mean to
say that we do not, so to say, pool our moral issues.
We do that. In acquiescing in the Covenant of the
League we do adopt, and we should adopt, certain fundamental moral principles of right and justice, which,
I dare say, we do not need to promise to live up to, but
which we are certainly proud to promise to live up to.
We are not turning any corner. We always have lived
up to them, and we do not intend to change our course
of action or our standards of action. And it is American standards of action that are set up in the Covenant
of the League of Nations.

What is the Covenant for? To hear most of the
debate, you would think that it was an ingenious con-
trivance for a subtle interference with the affairs of the
United States. On the contrary, it is one of the most
solemn covenants ever entered into by all the great fight-

ing powers of the world that they never will resort to war again without first having either submitted the question at issue to arbitration and undertaken to abide by the verdict of the arbitrators or submitted it to discussion by the Council of the League of Nations, laying all the documents, all the facts, before that council, consenting that that council should lay all those documents and all those facts before the world; they agree to allow six months for that discussion, and, even if they are not satisfied with the opinion, for it is only an opinion in that case, rendered by the council, they agree not to go to war for three months after the opinion has been rendered. There you have nine months' submission to the moral judgment of the world. In my judgment, that is an almost complete assurance against war. If any such covenant as that had existed in 1914, Germany never would have gone to war. The one thing that Germany could not afford to do, and knew that she could not afford to do, was to submit her case to the public opinion of the world. We have now abundant proof of what would have happened, because it was the moral judgment of the world that combined the world against Germany. We were a long time, my fellow citizens, seeing that we belonged in the war, but just so soon as the real issues of it became apparent we knew that we belonged there. And we did an unprecedented thing. We threw the whole power of a great nation into a quarrel with the origination of which it had nothing to do. I think there is nothing that appeals to the imagination more in the history of men than those convoyed fleets crossing the ocean with millions of American soldiers aboard—those crusaders, those men who loved liberty enough to leave their homes and fight for it upon distant fields of battle, those men who swung out into the open as if in fulfillment of the long prophecy of American history. There is nothing finer in the records of public action than the united spirit of the American people behind this great enterprise.

I ask your close observation to current events, my fellow countrymen. Out of doors, that is to say, out of legislative halls, there is no organized opposition to this treaty except among the people who tried to defeat the purpose of this Government in the war. Hyphens are the knives that are being stuck into this document. The issue is clearly drawn. Inasmuch as we are masters of our own participation in the action of the League of Nations, why do we need reservations? If we cannot be obliged to do anything that we do not ourselves vote to do, why qualify our acceptance of a perfectly safe agreement? There can be only one object, my fellow citizens, and that is to give the United States a standing of exceptional advantage in the League, to exempt it from obligations which the other members assume, or to put a special interpretation upon the duties of the United States under the Covenant which interpretation is not applied to the duties of other members of the League under the Covenant. I, for my part, say that it is unworthy of the United States to ask any special privilege of that kind. I am for going into a body of equals or staying out. That is the very principle we have been fighting for and have been proud to fight for, that the rights of a weak nation were just as sacred as the rights of a great nation. That is what this treaty was drawn to establish. You must not think of this treaty alone. The lines of it are being run out into the Austrian treaty and the Hungarian treaty and the Bulgarian treaty and the Turkish treaty, and in every one of them the principle is this, to deliver peoples who have been living under sovereignties that were alien and unwelcome from the bondage under which they have lived, to turn over to them their own territory, to adopt the American principle that all just government is derived from the consent of the governed. All down through the center of Europe and into the heart of Asia has gone this process of liberation, taking alien yokes off the necks of such peoples and vindicating the American principle that you cannot impose upon anybody a sovereignty that is not of its own choice. And if the results of this great liberation are not guaranteed, then they will fall down like a house of cards. What was the program of Pan Germanism? You know the formula—from Bremen to Bagdad. Very well; that is the very stretch of country over which these people have been liberated. New States, one after another, have been set up by the action of the conference at Paris all along the route that was intended to be the route of German dominion, and if we now merely set them up and leave them in their weakness to take care of themselves, then Germans can at their leisure, by intriguing, by every subtle process of which they are master, accomplish what they could not accomplish by arms, and we will have abandoned the people whom we redeemed. The thing is inconceivable. The thing is impossible.

We therefore have come to the straight-cut line—adoption or rejection. Qualified adoption is not adoption. It is perfectly legitimate, I admit, to say in what sense we understand certain articles. They are all perfectly obvious in meaning, so far as I can see, but if you want to make the obvious more obvious I do not see any objection to that; if by the multiplication of words you can make simple words speak their meaning more distinctly, I think that that is an interesting rhetorical exercise, but nothing more. Qualification means asking special exemptions and privileges for the United States. We cannot ask that. We must either go in or stay out. Now, if we go in what do we get? I am not now confining my view to ourselves. America has shown the world that she does not stop to calculate the lower sort of advantage and disadvantage; that she goes in upon a high plane of principle, and is willing to serve mankind while she is serving herself. What we gain in this treaty is, first of all, the substitution of arbitration and discussion for war. If you got nothing else, it is worth the whole game to get that. My fellow citizens, we fought this war in order that there should not be another like it. I am under bonds, I am under bonds to my fellow citizens of every sort, and I am particularly under bonds to the mothers of this country and to the wives of this country and to the sweethearts that I will do everything in my power to see to it that their sons and husbands and sweethearts never have to make that supreme sacrifice again. And when I passed your beautiful Capitol Square just now and saw thousands of children there to greet me, I felt a lump in my throat. These are the little people that I am arguing for. These are my clients, these lads coming on and these girls that, staying at home, would suffer more than the lads who died on the battlefield, for it is the tears at home that are more bitter than the agony upon the field. I dare not turn away from the straight path I have set myself to redeem this promise that I have made.

If you say, "What is there? An absolute insurance against war?" I say, "Certainly not." Nobody can give you an insurance against human passion, but if you can get a little insurance against an infinite catastrophe, is it not better than getting none at all? Let us assume that it is only twenty-five per cent insurance against war. Can any humane man reject that insurance? Let us suppose that it is fifty per cent insurance against war. Why, my friends, my calm judgment is that it is ninety-nine per cent insurance against war. That is what I went over to Europe to get, and that is what I got, and that is what I have brought back.

Stop for a moment to think about the next war, if there should be one. I do not hesitate to say that the war we have just been through, though it was shot through with terror of every kind, is not to be compared with the war we would have to face next time. There were destructive gases, there were methods of explosive destruction unheard of even during this war, which were just ready for use when the war ended—great projectiles that guided themselves and shot into the heavens, went for a hundred miles and more and then burst tons of explosives upon helpless cities, something to which the guns with which the Germans bombarded Paris from a distance were not comparable. What the Germans used were toys as compared with what would be used in the next war. Ask any soldier if he wants to go through a hell like that again. The soldiers know what the next war would be. They know what the inventions were that were just about to be used for the absolute destruction of mankind. I am for any kind of insurance against a barbaric reversal of civilization.

And by consequence, the adoption of the treaty means disarmament. Think of the economic burden and the restraint of liberty in the development of professional and mechanic life that resulted from the maintenance of great armies, not only in Germany but in France and in Italy and, to some extent, in Great Britain. If the United States should stand off from this thing we would have to have the biggest army in the world. There would be nobody else that cared for our fortunes. We would have to look out for ourselves, and when I hear gentlemen say, "Yes; that is what we want to do, we want to be independent and look out for ourselves," I say, "Well, then, consult your fellow citizens. There will have to be universal conscription. There will have to be taxes such as even yet we have not seen. There will have to be a concentration of authority in the Government capable of using this terrible instrument. You cannot conduct a war or command an army by a debating society. You cannot determine in community centers what the command of the Commander in Chief is going to be; you will have to have a staff like the German staff, and you will have to center in the Commander in Chief of the Army and Navy the right to take instant action for the protection of the Nation." America will never consent to any such thing.

Then, if we have this great treaty, we have what the world never had before—a court of public opinion of the world. I do not think that you can exaggerate the significance of that, my fellow countrymen. International law up to this time has been the most singular code of manners. You could not mention to any other Government anything that concerned it unless you could prove that your own interests were immediately involved. Unless you could prove that it was your own material interest that was involved, it was impolite to speak of it. There might be something brooding that threatened the peace of the world, and you could not speak of it unless the interests of the United States were involved. I am going to allude for a moment to a matter so interesting that I wish I could develop it. This cession in Shantung Province in China, which China gave to Germany in 1898, was an iniquitous thing at the outset; but our great President, William McKinley, and our great Secretary of State, John Hay, did not protest against it. It was an outrageous invasion of the rights of China. They not only did not protest, but all they asked was that Germany, after she got what did not belong to her, would please not close the doors against the trade of the United States. I am not saying this by way of criticism. That is all that under international manners they had a right to ask. International law has been the principle of minding your own business, particularly when something outrageous was up; and Article XI of the League of Nations makes matters of that sort everybody's business. Under Article XI any member of the League can at any time call attention to anything, anywhere, which is likely to affect the peace of the world or the good understanding between nations upon which the peace of the world depends. The littlest nation, along with the biggest—Panama, to take one of our own near neighbors—can stand up and challenge the right of any nation in the world to do a thing which threatens the peace of the world. It does not have to be a big nation to do it.

The voice of the world is at last released. The conscience of the world is at last given a forum, and the rights of men not liberated under this treaty are given a place where they can be heard. If there are nations which wish to exercise the power of self-determination but are not liberated by this treaty, they can come into that great forum, they can point out how their demands affect the peace and quiet of the world, they can point out how their demands affect the good understanding between nations. There is a forum here for the rights of mankind which was never before dreamed of, and in that forum any representative has the right to speak his full mind. If that is not a wholesome moral clearing house, I wish somebody would suggest a better. It is just a moral clearing house that the world needs. There have been a great many things unspoken that ought to have been spoken. There have been voiceless multitudes all over the world who had nobody to speak for them in any court of conscience anywhere, and now they are given spokesmen. All forward-looking men may now see their way to the method in which they may help forward the real processes of civilization.

There is another matter which I am sure will interest a great many in sound of my voice. If we do not have this treaty of peace, labor will continue to be regarded, not as it ought to be regarded, a human function, but as a purchasable commodity throughout the world. There is inserted in this great treaty a Magna Charta of labor. There is set up here a means of periodic examination of the conditions of labor all over the world, particularly the labor of women and children and those who have not the physical force to handle some of the burdens that are put upon them, and it is made the duty of the nations of the world constantly to study the methods of raising the levels of human labor. You know what that means. We have not done our full duty with regard to the amelioration and betterment of the conditions of labor in America, but the conditions here are better than they are anywhere else. We now have an opportunity to exercise our full influence to raise the levels everywhere to the levels which we have tried to maintain in this country, and then to take them higher into the fields of that sort of association between those who employ labor and those who execute it as will make it a real human relationship and not a mere commercial relationship. The heart of the world has never got into this business yet. The conscience of the world has never been released along lines of action in regard to the improvement of the conditions of labor. And more than that, until we find such methods as I have been alluding to, we are never releasing the real energies of this people. Men are not going to work and produce what they would produce if they feel that they are not justly treated. If you want to realize the real wealth of this country, then bring about the human relationship between employers and employees which will make them co-laborers and partners and fellow workers. All of that is open to us through the instrumentality of the League of Nations under this great treaty, and still we debate whether we should ratify it or not.

There is a great deal of pleasure in talking, I admit; and some men, even some men I do not agree with, I admit, talk very well, indeed. It is a pleasure to hear them when they are honest; it is a pleasure to be instructed by them when they know what they are talking about. But we have reached the stage now when all the things that needed to be debated have been debated and all the doubts are cleared up. They are cleared up just as thoroughly as the English language can clear them. The people of the United States are no longer susceptible to being misled as to what is in this Covenant, and they now have an exceedingly interesting choice to make. I have said it a great many times, my fellow countrymen, but I must say it again, because it is a pleasant thing to testify about, the fundamental thing that I discovered on the other side of the water was that all the great peoples of the world are looking to America for leadership. There can be no mistaking that. The evidences were too overwhelming, the evidences were too profoundly significant, because what underlay them was this: We are the only Nation which so far has not laid itself open to suspicion of ulterior motives. We are the only Nation which has not made it evident that when we go to anybody's assistance we mean to stay there longer than we are welcome. Day after day I received delegations in Paris asking—what? Credits from the United States? No. Merchandise from the United States? Yes, if possible; but that was not the chief point. They were asking that I send American troops to take the place of other troops, because they said, "Our people will welcome them with open arms as friends who have come for their sakes and not for anything that America can possibly in the future have in mind." What an extraordinary tribute to the principles of the United States! What an extraordinary tribute to the sincerity of the people of the United States! I never was so proud in my life as when these evidences began to accumulate. I had been proud always of being an American, but I never before realized fully what it meant. It meant to stand at the front of the moral forces of the world.

My fellow citizens, I think we must come to sober and immediate conclusions. There is no turning aside from the straight line. We must now either accept this arrangement or reject it. If we accept it, there is no danger either to our safety or to our honor. If we reject it, we will meet with suspicion, with distrust, with dislike, with disillusionment everywhere in the world. This treaty has to be carried out. In order to carry this treaty out, it is necessary to reconstruct Europe economically and industrially. If we do not take part in that reconstruction, we will be shut out from it, and by consequence the markets of Europe will be shut to us. The combinations of European Governments can be formed to exclude us wherever it is possible to exclude us; and if you want to come to the hard and ugly basis of material interest, the United States will everywhere trade at an overwhelming disadvantage just so soon as we have forfeited, and deserve to forfeit, the confidence of the world. I ask merchants, "Who are good customers, friends or enemies? Who are good customers, those who open their doors to you, or those who have made some private arrangement elsewhere which makes it impossible for them to trade with you?" I have heard Europe spoken of as bankrupt. There may be great difficulties in paying the public debts, but there are going to be no insuperable difficulties to rebeginning the economic and industrial life of Europe. The men are there, the materials are there, the energy is there, and the hope is there. The nations are not crushed. They are ready for the great enterprises of the future, and it is for us to choose whether we will enter those great enterprises upon a footing of advantage and of honor or upon a footing of disadvantage and distrust.

Therefore, from every point of view, I challenge the opponents of this treaty to show cause why it should not be ratified. I challenge them to show cause why there should be any hesitation in ratifying it. I do not understand delays. I do not understand covert processes of opposition. It is time that we knew where we shall stand, for observe, my fellow citizens, the negotiation of treaties rests with the Executive of the United States. When the Senate has acted, it will be for me to determine whether its action constitutes an adoption or a rejection, and I beg the gentlemen who are responsible for the action of the United States Senate to make it perfectly clear whether it is an adoption or a rejection. I do not wish to draw doubtful conclusions. I do not wish to do injustice to the process of any honest mind. But when that treaty is acted upon

I must know whether it means that we have ratified it or rejected it, and I feel confident that I am speaking for the people of the United States.

When it is around election time, my fellow citizens, a man ought to be doubtful of what the meaning of his intercourse with his fellow citizens is, because it is easy for applause to go to the head; it is easy for applause to seem to men more than it does; it is easy for the assurances of individual support to be given a wider implication than can properly be given to them. I thank God that on this occasion the whole issue has nothing to do with me. I did not carry any purpose of my own to Paris. I did not carry any purpose that I did not know from the action of public opinion in the United States was the purpose of the United States. It was not the purpose of a party. It was not the purpose of any section of our fellow citizens. It was a purpose subscribed to by American public opinion and formally adopted by the Governments with which we had to deal on the other side, and I came back with a document embodying the principles insisted upon at the outset and carried by the American delegation to Paris. Therefore I think that I have the right to say that I have the support of the people of the United States. The issue is so big that it transcends all party and personal things. I was a spokesman; I was an instrument. I did not speak any privately conceived idea of my own. I had merely tried to absorb the influences of public opinion in the United States, and that, my fellow citizens, is the function of all of us. We ought not in a great crisis like this to follow any private opinion; we ought not to follow any private purpose; we ought, above all things, to forget that we are ever divided into parties when we vote. We are all democrats—I will not insist upon the large "D"—we are all democrats because we believe in a people's government, and what I am pleading for is nothing less than a people's peace.

At Pueblo, Colo., September 25, 1919.

Mr. Chairman and Fellow Countrymen:

It is with a great deal of genuine pleasure that I find myself in Pueblo, and I feel it a compliment that I should be permitted to be the first speaker in this beautiful hall. One of the advantages of this hall, as I look about, is that you are not too far away from me, because there is nothing so reassuring to men who are trying to express the public sentiment as getting into real personal contact with their fellow citizens. I have gained a renewed impression as I have crossed the continent this time of the homogeneity of this great people to whom we belong. They come from many stocks, but they are all of one kind. They come from many origins, but they are all shot through with the same principles and desire the same righteous and honest things. I have received a more inspiring impression this time of the public opinion of the United States than it was ever my privilege to receive before.

The chief pleasure of my trip has been that it has nothing to do with my personal fortunes, that it has nothing to do with my personal reputation, that it has nothing to do with anything except great principles uttered by Americans of all sorts and of all parties which we are now trying to realize at this crisis of the affairs of the world. But there have been unpleasant impressions as well as pleasant impressions, my fellow citizens, as I have crossed the continent. I have perceived more and more that men have been busy creating an absolutely false impression of what the treaty of peace and the Covenant of the League of Nations contain and mean. I find, moreover, that there is an organized propaganda against the League of Nations and against the treaty proceeding from exactly the same sources that the organized propaganda proceeded from which threatened this country here and there with

disloyalty, and I want to say—I cannot say too often—
any man who carries a hyphen about with him carries a
dagger that he is ready to plunge into the vitals of this
Republic whenever he gets ready. If I can catch any
man with a hyphen in this great contest I will know
that I have got an enemy of the Republic. My fellow
citizens, it is only certain bodies of foreign sympathies,
certain bodies of sympathy with foreign nations that
are organized against this great document which the
American representatives have brought back from
Paris. Therefore, in order to clear away the mists, in
order to remove the impressions, in order to check
the falsehoods that have clustered around this great
subject, I want to tell you a few very simple things about
the treaty and the Covenant.

Do not think of this treaty of peace as merely a settlement with Germany. It is that. It is a very severe
settlement with Germany, but there is not anything in
it that she did not earn. Indeed, she earned more than
she can ever be able to pay for, and the punishment
exacted of her is not a punishment greater than she can
bear, and it is absolutely necessary in order that no
other nation may ever plot such a thing against humanity and civilization. But the treaty is so much more
than that. It is not merely a settlement with Germany;
it is a readjustment of those great injustices which
underlie the whole structure of European and Asiatic
society. This is only the first of several treaties. They
are all constructed upon the same plan. The Austrian
treaty follows the same lines. The treaty with Hungary
follows the same lines. The treaty with Bulgaria follows the same lines. The treaty with Turkey, when it
is formulated, will follow the same lines. What are
those lines? They are based upon the purpose to see
that every government dealt with in this great settlement is put in the hands of the people and taken out of
the hands of coteries and of sovereigns who had no
right to rule over the people. It is a people's treaty,

that accomplishes by a great sweep of practical justice the liberation of men who never could have liberated themselves, and the power of the most powerful nations has been devoted not to their aggrandizement but to the liberation of people whom they could have put under their control if they had chosen to do so. Not one foot of territory is demanded by the conquerors, not one single item of submission to their authority is demanded by them. The men who sat around that table in Paris knew that the time had come when the people were no longer going to consent to live under masters, but were going to live the lives that they chose themselves, to live under such governments as they chose themselves to erect. That is the fundamental principle of this great settlement.

And we did not stop with that. We added a great international charter for the rights of labor. Reject this treaty, impair it, and this is the consequence to the laboring men of the world, that there is no international tribunal which can bring the moral judgments of the world to bear upon the great labor questions of the day. What we need to do with regard to the labor questions of the day, my fellow countrymen, is to lift them into the light, is to lift them out of the haze and distraction of passion, of hostility, not into the calm spaces where men look at things without passion. The more men you get into a great discussion the more you exclude passion. Just so soon as the calm judgment of the world is directed upon the question of justice to labor, labor is going to have a forum such as it never was supplied with before, and men everywhere are going to see that the problem of labor is nothing more nor less than the problem of the elevation of humanity. We must see that all the questions which have disturbed the world, all the questions which have eaten into the confidence of men toward their governments, all the questions which have disturbed the processes of industry, shall be brought out where men of all points of view, men of all attitudes of mind, men of all kinds of experience, may contribute their part to the settlement of the great questions which we must settle and cannot ignore.

At the front of this great treaty is put the Covenant of the League of Nations. It will also be at the front of the Austrian treaty and the Hungarian treaty and the Bulgarian treaty and the treaty with Turkey. Every one of them will contain the Covenant of the League of Nations, because you cannot work any of them without the Covenant of the League of Nations. Unless you get the united, concerted purpose and power of the great Governments of the world behind this settlement, it will fall down like a house of cards. There is only one power to put behind the liberation of mankind, and that is the power of mankind. It is the power of the united moral forces of the world, and in the Covenant of the League of Nations the moral forces of the world are mobilized. For what purpose? Reflect, my fellow citizens, that the membership of this great League is going to include all the great fighting nations of the world, as well as the weak ones. It is not for the present going to include Germany, but for the time being Germany is not a great fighting country. All the nations that have power that can be mobilized are going to be members of this League, including the United States. And what do they unite for? They enter into a solemn promise to one another that they will never use their power against one another for aggression; that they never will impair the territorial integrity of a neighbor; that they never will interfere with the political independence of a neighbor; that they will abide by the principle that great populations are entitled to determine their own destiny and that they will not interfere with that destiny; and that no matter what differences arise amongst them they will never resort to war without first having done one or other of two things—either submitted the matter of controversy to arbitration, in

which case they agree to abide by the result without
question, or submitted it to the consideration of the
council of the League of Nations, laying before that
council all the documents, all the facts, agreeing that
the council can publish the documents and the facts to
the whole world, agreeing that there shall be six months
allowed for the mature consideration of those facts
by the council, and agreeing that at the expiration of
the six months, even if they are not then ready to accept
the advice of the council with regard to the settlement
of the dispute, they will still not go to war for another
three months. In other words, they consent, no matter
what happens, to submit every matter of difference
between them to the judgment of mankind, and just
so certainly as they do that, my fellow citizens, war
will be in the far background, war will be pushed out
of that foreground of terror in which it has kept the
world for generation after generation, and men will
know that there will be a calm time of deliberate
counsel. The most dangerous thing for a bad cause
is to expose it to the opinion of the world. The most
certain way that you can prove that a man is mistaken
is by letting all his neighbors know what he thinks, by
letting all his neighbors discuss what he thinks, and if
he is in the wrong you will notice that he will stay at
home, he will not walk on the street. He will be afraid
of the eyes of his neighbors. He will be afraid of their
judgment of his character. He will know that his cause
is lost unless he can sustain it by the arguments of right
and of justice. The same law that applies to individuals
applies to nations.

But, you say, "We have heard that we might be at
a disadvantage in the League of Nations." Well, who-
ever told you that either was deliberately falsifying or
he had not read the Covenant of the League of Nations.
I leave him the choice. I want to give you a very simple
account of the organization of the League of Nations
and let you judge for yourselves. It is a very simple

organization. The power of the League, or rather the
activities of the League, lie in two bodies. There is the
council, which consists of one representative from each
of the principal allied and associated powers—that is
to say, the United States, Great Britain, France, Italy,
and Japan, along with four other representatives of
smaller powers chosen out of the general body of the
membership of the League. The council is the source
of every active policy of the League, and no active
policy of the League can be adopted without a unanimous vote of the council. That is explicitly stated
in the Covenant itself. Does it not evidently follow
that the League of Nations can adopt no policy whatever without the consent of the United States? The
affirmative vote of the representative of the United
States is necessary in every case. Now, you have heard
of six votes belonging to the British Empire. Those
six votes are not in the council. They are in the assembly, and the interesting thing is that the assembly
does not vote. I must qualify that statement a little,
but essentially it is absolutely true. In every matter in
which the assembly is given a voice, and there are only
four or five, its vote does not count unless concurred in
by the representatives of all the nations represented on
the council, so that there is no validity to any vote of
the assembly unless in that vote also the representative
of the United States concurs. That one vote of the
United States is as big as the six votes of the British
Empire. I am not jealous for advantage, my fellow
citizens, but I think that is a perfectly safe situation.
There is no validity in a vote, either by the council or
the assembly, in which we do not concur. So much for
the statements about the six votes of the British Empire.

Look at it in another aspect. The assembly is the
talking body. The assembly was created in order that
anybody that purposed anything wrong should be subjected to the awkward circumstance that everybody
could talk about it. This is the great assembly in which

all the things that are likely to disturb the peace of the world or the good understanding between nations are to be exposed to the general view, and I want to ask you if you think it was unjust, unjust to the United States, that speaking parts should be assigned to the several portions of the British Empire? Do you think it unjust that there should be some spokesman in debate for that fine little stout Republic down in the Pacific, New Zealand? Do you think it was unjust that Australia should be allowed to stand up and take part in the debate—Australia, from which we have learned some of the most useful progressive policies of modern time, a little nation only five million in a great continent, but counting for several times five in its activities and in its interest in liberal reform? Do you think it unjust that that little Republic down in South Africa, whose gallant resistance to being subjected to any outside authority at all we admired for so many months and whose fortunes we followed with such interest, should have a speaking part? Great Britain obliged South Africa to submit to her sovereignty, but she immediately after that felt that it was convenient and right to hand the whole self-government of that colony over to the very men whom she had beaten. The representatives of South Africa in Paris were two of the most distinguished generals of the Boer Army, two of the realest men I ever met, two men that could talk sober counsel and wise advice, along with the best statesmen in Europe. To exclude General Botha and General Smuts from the right to stand up in the parliament of the world and say something concerning the affairs of mankind would be absurd. And what about Canada? Is not Canada a good neighbor? I ask you, Is not Canada more likely to agree with the United States than with Great Britain? Canada has a speaking part. And then, for the first time in the history of the world, that great voiceless multitude, that throng hundreds of millions strong in India, has a voice, and I want to testify that some of the wisest and most dignified figures in the peace conference at Paris came from India, men who seemed to carry in their minds an older wisdom than the rest of us had, whose traditions ran back into so many of the unhappy fortunes of mankind that they seemed very useful counselors as to how some ray of hope and some prospect of happiness could be opened to its people. I for my part have no jealousy whatever of those five speaking parts in the assembly. Those speaking parts cannot translate themselves into five votes that can in any matter override the voice and purpose of the United States.

Let us sweep aside all this language of jealousy. Let us be big enough to know the facts and to welcome the facts, because the facts are based upon the principle that America has always fought for, namely, the equality of self-governing peoples, whether they were big or little—not counting men, but counting rights, not counting representation, but counting the purpose of that representation. When you hear an opinion quoted you do not count the number of persons who hold it; you ask, "Who said that?" You weigh opinions, you do not count them, and the beauty of all democracies is that every voice can be heard, every voice can have its effect, every voice can contribute to the general judgment that is finally arrived at. That is the object of democracy. Let us accept what America has always fought for, and accept it with pride that America showed the way and made the proposal. I do not mean that America made the proposal in this particular instance; I mean that the principle was an American principle, proposed by America.

When you come to the heart of the Covenant, my fellow citizens, you will find it in Article X, and I am very much interested to know that the other things have been blown away like bubbles. There is nothing in the other contentions with regard to the League of Nations, but there is something in Article X that you ought to realize and ought to accept or reject. Article X is the heart of the whole matter. What is Article X? I never am certain that I can from memory give a literal repetition of its language, but I am sure that I can give an exact interpretation of its meaning. Article X provides that every member of the League covenants to respect and preserve the territorial integrity and existing political independence of every other member of the League as against external aggression. Not against internal disturbance. There was not a man at that table who did not admit the sacredness of the right of self-determination, the sacredness of the right of any body of people to say that they would not continue to live under the Government they were then living under, and under Article XI of the Covenant they are given a place to say whether they will live under it or not. For following Article X is Article XI, which makes it the right of any member of the League at any time to call attention to anything, anywhere, that is likely to disturb the peace of the world or the good understanding between nations upon which the peace of the world depends. I want to give you an illustration of what that would mean.

You have heard a great deal—something that was true and a great deal that was false—about that provision of the treaty which hands over to Japan the rights which Germany enjoyed in the Province of Shantung in China. In the first place, Germany did not enjoy any rights there that other nations had not already claimed. For my part, my judgment, my moral judgment, is against the whole set of concessions. They were all of them unjust to China, they ought never to have been exacted, they were all exacted by duress, from a great body of thoughtful and ancient and helpless people. There never was any right in any of them. Thank God, America never asked for any, never dreamed of asking for any. But when Germany got this concession in 1898, the Government of the United States made no protest whatever. That was not because the Government of the United States was not in the hands of high-minded and conscientious men. It was. William McKinley was President and John Hay was Secretary of State—as safe hands to leave the honor of the United States in as any that you can cite. They made no protest because the state of international law at that time was that it was none of their business unless they could show that the interests of the United States were affected, and the only thing that they could show with regard to the interests of the United States was that Germany might close the doors of Shantung Province against the trade of the United States. They, therefore, demanded and obtained promises that we could continue to sell merchandise in Shantung. Immediately following that concession to Germany there was a concession to Russia of the same sort, of Port Arthur, and Port Arthur was handed over subsequently to Japan on the very territory of the United States. Don't you remember that when Russia and Japan got into war with one another the war was brought to a conclusion by a treaty written at Portsmouth, N. H., and in that treaty without the slightest intimation from any authoritative sources in America that the Government of the United States had any objection, Port Arthur, Chinese territory, was turned over to Japan? I want you distinctly to understand that there is no thought of criticism in my mind. I am expounding to you a state of international law. Now, read Articles X and XI. You will see that international law is revolutionized by putting morals into it. Article X says that no member of the League, and that includes all these nations that have demanded these things unjustly of China, shall impair the territorial integrity or the political independence of any other member of the League. China is going to be a member of the League. Article XI says that any member of the League can call attention to anything that is likely to disturb the peace of the world or the good understanding between nations, and China is for the first time in the history of mankind afforded a standing before the jury of the world. I, for my part, have a profound sympathy for China, and I am proud to have taken part in an arrangement which promises the protection of the world to the rights of China. The whole atmosphere of the world is changed by a thing like that, my fellow citizens. The whole international practice of the world is revolutionized.

But you will say, "What is the second sentence of Article X? That is what gives very disturbing thoughts." The second sentence is that the council of the League shall advise what steps, if any, are necessary to carry out the guarantee of the first sentence, namely, that the members will respect and preserve the territorial integrity and political independence of the other members. I do not know any other meaning for the word "advise" except "advise." The council advises, and it cannot advise without the vote of the United States. Why gentlemen should fear that the Congress of the United States would be advised to do something that it did not want to do I frankly cannot imagine, because they cannot even be advised to do anything unless their own representative has participated in the advice. It may be that that will impair somewhat the vigor of the League, but, nevertheless, the fact is so, that we are not obliged to take any advice except our own, which to any man who wants to go his own course is a very satisfactory state of affairs. Every man regards his own advice as best, and I dare say every man mixes his own advice with some thought of his own interest. Whether we use it wisely or unwisely, we can use the vote of the United States to make impossible drawing the United States into any enterprise that she does not care to be drawn into.

Yet Article X strikes at the taproot of war. Article X is a statement that the very things that have always been sought in imperialistic wars are henceforth forgone by every ambitious nation in the world. I would have felt very lonely, my fellow countrymen, and I would have felt very much disturbed if, sitting at the peace table in Paris, I had supposed that I was expounding my own ideas. Whether you believe it or not, I know the relative size of my own ideas; I know how they stand related in bulk and proportion to the moral judgments of my fellow countrymen, and I proposed nothing whatever at the peace table at Paris that I had not sufficiently certain knowledge embodied the moral judgment of the citizens of the United States. I had gone over there with, so to say, explicit instructions. Don't you remember that we laid down fourteen points which should contain the principles of the settlement? They were not my points. In every one of them I was conscientiously trying to read the thought of the people of the United States, and after I uttered those points I had every assurance given me that could be given me that they did speak the moral judgment of the United States and not my single judgment. Then when it came to that critical period just a little less than a year ago, when it was evident that the war was coming to its critical end, all the nations engaged in the war accepted those fourteen principles explicitly as the basis of the armistice and the basis of the peace. In those circumstances I crossed the ocean under bond to my own people and to the other governments with which I was dealing. The whole specification of the method of settlement was written down and accepted beforehand, and we were architects building on those specifications. It reassures me and fortifies my position to find how before I went over men whose judgment the United States has often trusted were of exactly the same opinion that I went abroad to express. Here is something I want to read from Theodore Roosevelt:

"The one effective move for obtaining peace is by an agreement among all the great powers in which each should pledge itself not only to abide by the decisions of a common tribunal but to back its decisions by force. The great civilized nations should combine by solemn agreement in a great world league for the peace of righteousness; a court should be established. A changed and amplified Hague court would meet the requirements, composed of representatives from each nation, whose representatives are sworn to act as judges in each case and not in a representative capacity." Now there is Article X. He goes on and says this: "The nations should agree on certain rights that should not be questioned, such as territorial integrity, their right to deal with their domestic affairs, and with such matters as whom they should admit to citizenship. All such guarantee each of their number in possession of these rights."

Now, the other specification is in the Covenant. The Covenant in another portion guarantees to the members the independent control of their domestic questions. There is not a leg for these gentlemen to stand on when they say that the interests of the United States are not safeguarded in the very points where we are most sensitive. You do not need to be told again that the Covenant expressly says that nothing in this Covenant shall be construed as affecting the validity of the Monroe Doctrine, for example. You could not be more explicit than that. And every point of interest is covered, partly for one very interesting reason. This is not the first time that the Foreign Relations Committee of the Senate of the United States has read and considered this Covenant. I brought it to this country in March last in a tentative, provisional form, in practically the form that it now has, with the exception of certain additions which I shall mention immediately. I asked the Foreign Relations Committees of both Houses to come to the White House and we spent a long evening in the frankest discussion of every portion that they wished to discuss. They made certain specific suggestions as to what should be contained in this document when it was to be revised. I carried those suggestions to Paris, and every one of them was adopted. What more could I have done? What more could have been obtained? The very matters upon which these gentlemen were most concerned were, the right of withdrawal, which is now expressly stated; the safeguarding of the Monroe Doctrine, which is now accomplished; the exclusion from action by the League of domestic questions, which is now accomplished. All along the line, every suggestion of the United States was adopted after the Covenant had been drawn up in its first form and had been published for the criticism of the world. There is a very true sense in which I can say this is a tested American document.

I am dwelling upon these points, my fellow citizens, in spite of the fact that I dare say to most of you they are perfectly well known, because in order to meet the present situation we have got to know what we are dealing with. We are not dealing with the kind of document which this is represented by some gentlemen to be; and inasmuch as we are dealing with a document simon-pure in respect of the very principles we have professed and lived up to, we have got to do one or other of two things—we have got to adopt it or reject it. There is no middle course. You cannot go in on a special-privilege basis of your own. I take it that you are too proud to ask to be exempted from responsibilities which the other members of the League will carry. We go in upon equal terms or we do not go in at all; and if we do not go in, my fellow citizens, think of the tragedy of that result—the only sufficient guarantee to the peace of the world withheld! Ourselves drawn apart with that dangerous pride which means that we shall be ready to take care of ourselves, and that means that we shall maintain great standing armies and an irresistible navy; that means we shall have the organization of a military nation; that means we shall have a general staff, with the kind of power that the general staff of Germany had; to mobilize this great manhood of the Nation when it pleases, all the energy of our young men drawn into the thought and preparation for war. What of our pledges to the men that lie dead in France? We said that they went over there not to prove the prowess of America or her readiness for another war but to see to it that there never was such a war again. It always seems to make it difficult for me to say anything, my fellow citizens, when I think of my clients in this case. My clients are the children; my clients are the next generation. They do not know what promises and bonds I undertook when I ordered the armies of the United States to the soil of France, but I know, and I intend to redeem my pledges to the children; they shall not be sent upon a similar errand.

Again and again, my fellow citizens, mothers who lost their sons in France have come to me and, taking my hand, have shed tears upon it not only, but they have added, "God bless you, Mr. President!" Why, my fellow citizens, should they pray God to bless me? I advised the Congress of the United States to create the situation that led to the death of their sons. I ordered their sons oversea. I consented to their sons being put in the most difficult parts of the battle line, where death was certain, as in the impenetrable difficulties of the forest of Argonne. Why should they weep upon my hand and call down the blessings of God upon me? Because they believe that their boys died for something that vastly transcends any of the immediate and palpable objects of the war. They believe, and they rightly believe, that their sons saved the liberty of the world. They believe that wrapped up with the liberty of the world is the continuous protection of that liberty by the concerted powers of all civilized people. They believe that this sacrifice was made in order that other sons should not be called upon for

a similar gift—the gift of life, the gift of all that died—
and if we did not see this thing through, if we fulfilled
the dearest present wish of Germany and now dissociated ourselves from those alongside whom we
fought in the war, would not something of the halo go
away from the gun over the mantelpiece, or the sword?
Would not the old uniform lose something of its significance? These men were crusaders. They were not
going forth to prove the might of the United States.
They were going forth to prove the might of justice and
right, and all the world accepted them as crusaders,
and their transcendent achievement has made all the
world believe in America as it believes in no other nation organized in the modern world. There seems to
me to stand between us and the rejection or qualification
of this treaty the serried ranks of those boys in khaki,
not only these boys who came home, but those dear
ghosts that still deploy upon the fields of France.

My friends, on last Decoration Day I went to a
beautiful hillside near Paris, where was located the
cemetery of Suresnes, a cemetery given over to the
burial of the American dead. Behind me on the slopes
was rank upon rank of living American soldiers, and
lying before me upon the levels of the plain was rank
upon rank of departed American soldiers. Right by
the side of the stand where I spoke there was a little
group of French women who had adopted those graves,
had made themselves mothers of those dear ghosts by
putting flowers every day upon those graves, taking
them as their own sons, their own beloved, because they
had died in the same cause—France was free and the
world was free because America had come! I wish
some men in public life who are now opposing the settlement for which these men died could visit such a
spot as that. I wish that the thought that comes out
of those graves could penetrate their consciousness. I
wish that they could feel the moral obligation that rests
upon us not to go back on those boys, but to see the

thing through, to see it through to the end and make good their redemption of the world. For nothing less depends upon this decision, nothing less than the liberation and salvation of the world.

You will say, "Is the League an absolute guarantee against war?" No; I do not know any absolute guarantee against the errors of human judgment or the violence of human passion, but I tell you this: With a cooling space of nine months for human passion, not much of it will keep hot. I had a couple of friends who were in the habit of losing their tempers, and when they lost their tempers they were in the habit of using very unparliamentary language. Some of their friends induced them to make a promise that they never would swear inside the town limits. When the impulse next came upon them, they took a street car to go out of town to swear, and by the time they got out of town they did not want to swear. They came back convinced that they were just what they were, a couple of unspeakable fools, and the habit of getting angry and of swearing suffered great inroads upon it by that experience. Now, illustrating the great by the small, that is true of the passions of nations. It is true of the passions of men however you combine them. Give them space to cool off. I ask you this: If it is not an absolute insurance against war, do you want no insurance at all? Do you want nothing? Do you want not only no probability that war will not recur, but the probability that it will recur? The arrangements of justice do not stand of themselves, my fellow citizens. The arrangements of this treaty are just, but they need the support of the combined power of the great nations of the world. And they will have that support. Now that the mists of this great question have cleared away, I believe that men will see the truth, eye to eye and face to face. There is one thing that the American people always rise to and extend their hand to, and that is the truth of justice and of liberty and of peace. We have accepted that truth and we are going to be led by it, and it is going to lead us, and through us the world, out into pastures of quietness and peace such as the world never dreamed of before.

GREETING AT OPENING OF LABOR CONFERENCE

STATEMENT SENT OCTOBER 6, 1919 TO SECRETARY WILLIAM B. WILSON WITH REQUEST THAT HE READ IT "AT THE OPENING OF THE LABOR CONFERENCE THIS AFTERNOON." FROM COPY IN MR. WILSON'S FILES.

IT IS a matter of the deepest regret that I cannot meet with you at the opening of your conference from which I expect so much of hope will come to the country. I venture to suggest that it is the expectation of the people that you will make a searching investigation into those ways and means by which peace and harmony have been secured in a large number of our industries, that these methods may be extended more universally. This work must be carried on in the confidence that there is a way by which thinking, reasonable men may be brought to an agreement so that every party may know that it is given that consideration which it deserves because of the service which it renders to the public. For we are all parts of a larger system. The nation's interests are paramount at all times and if we look for that policy which will carry us forward upon lines of fair dealing, this conference cannot fail and the value of democracy will again be made manifest.

INDUSTRIAL PEACE

LETTER TO THE NATIONAL INDUSTRIAL CONFERENCE,
OCTOBER 22, 1919. FROM THE NEW YORK "TIMES,"
OCTOBER 23, 1919.

I AM advised by your chairman that you have come to a situation which appears to threaten the life of your conference, and because of that I am presuming to address a word of very solemn appeal to you as Americans. It is not for me to assess the blame for the present condition.

I do not speak in a spirit of criticism of any individual or of any group. But having called this conference, I feel that my temporary indisposition should not bar the way to a frank expression of the seriousness of the position in which this country will be placed should you adjourn without having convinced the American people that you had exhausted your resourcefulness and your patience in an effort to come to some common agreement.

At a time when the nations of the world are endeavoring to find a way to avoid international war, are we to confess that there is no method to be found for carrying on industry except in the spirit and with the very method of war? Must suspicion and hatred and force rule us in civil life? Are our industrial leaders and our industrial workers to live together without faith in each other, constantly struggling for advantage over each other, doing naught but what is compelled?

My friends, this would be an intolerable outlook, a prospect unworthy of the large things done by this people in the mastering of this continent—indeed, it would be an invitation to national disaster. From such a possibility my mind turns away, for my confidence is abiding that in this land we have learned how to accept the general judgment upon matters that affect the public weal. And this is the very heart and soul of democracy.

It is my understanding that you have divided upon one portion only of a possible large program which has not fully been developed. Before a severance is effected, based upon present differences, I believe you should stand together for the development of that full program touching the many questions within the broad scope of your investigations.

It was in my mind when this conference was called that you would concern yourselves with the discovery of those methods by which a measurable coöperation within industry may have been secured and if new machinery needs to be designed by which a minimum of conflict between employers and employees may reasonably be hoped for, that we should make an effort to secure its adoption.

It cannot be expected that at every step all parties will agree upon each proposition or method suggested. It is to be expected, however, that as a whole a plan or program can be agreed upon which will advance further the productive capacity of America through the establishment of a surer and heartier coöperation between all the elements engaged in industry. The public expects not less than that you shall have that one end in view and stay together until the way is found leading to that end or until it is revealed that the men who work and the men who manage American industry are so set upon divergent paths that all effort at coöperation is doomed to failure.

I renew my appeal with full comprehension of the almost incomparable importance of your tasks to this and to other people, and with full faith in the high patriotism and good faith of each other that you push your task to a happy conclusion.

WARNING TO COAL STRIKERS

STATEMENT ISSUED AT WASHINGTON, OCTOBER 25, 1919. FROM THE "CONGRESSIONAL RECORD," VOL. 58, P. 7583.

ON SEPTEMBER 23, 1919, the convention of the United Mine Workers of America at Cleveland, Ohio, adopted a proposal declaring that all contracts in the bituminous field shall be declared as having automatically expired November 1, 1919, and making various demands, including a 60-per-cent increase in wages and the adoption of a six-hour workday and a five-day week, and providing, that in the event a satisfactory wage agreement should not be secured for the central competitive field before November 1, 1919, the national officials should be authorized and instructed to call a general strike of all bituminous miners and mine workers throughout the United States, effective November 1, 1919.

Pursuant to these instructions, the officers of the organization have issued a call to make the strike effective November 1.

This is one of the gravest steps ever proposed in this country, affecting the economic welfare and the domestic comfort and health of the people.

It is proposed to abrogate an agreement as to wages which was made with the sanction of the United States Fuel Administration, and which was to run during the continuance of the war, but not beyond April 1, 1920. This strike is proposed at a time when the government is making the most earnest effort to reduce the cost of living and has appealed with success to other classes of workers to postpone similar disputes until a reasonable opportunity has been afforded for dealing with the cost of living.

It is recognized that the strike would practically shut off the country's supply of its principal fuel at a time when interference with that supply is calculated to create a disastrous fuel famine. All interests would be affected alike by a strike of this character, and its victims would be not the rich only, but the poor and the needy as well—those least able to provide in advance a fuel supply for domestic use.

It would involve the shutting down of countless industries and the throwing out of employment of a large number of the workers of the country. It would involve stopping the operation of railroads, electric light and gas plants, street railway lines, and other public utilities, and the shipping to and from this country, thus preventing our giving aid to the allied countries with supplies which they so seriously need.

The country is confronted with this prospect at a time when the war itself is still a fact, when the world is still in suspense as to negotiations for peace, when our troops are still being transported, and when their means of transport is in urgent need of fuel.

From whatever angle the subject may be viewed, it is apparent that such a strike in such circumstances would be the most far-reaching plan ever presented in this country to limit the facilities of production and distribution of a necessity of life and thus indirectly to restrict the production and distribution of all the necessaries of life. A strike under these circumstances is not only unjustifiable; it is unlawful.

The action proposed has apparently been taken without any vote upon the specific proposition by the individual members of the United Mine Workers of America throughout the United States, an almost unprecedented proceeding. I cannot believe that any right of any American worker needs for its protection the taking of this extraordinary step, and I am convinced that when the time and money are considered it constitutes a fundamental attack, which is wrong, both morally and legally, upon the rights of society and upon the welfare of our country.

I feel convinced that individual members of the United Mine Workers would not vote, upon full consideration, in favor of such a strike under these conditions.

When a movement reaches a point where it appears to involve practically the entire productive capacity of the country with respect to one of the most vital necessities of daily domestic and industrial life, and when the movement is asserted in the circumstance I have stated, and at a time and in a manner calculated to involve the maximum of dangers in the public welfare in this critical hour of our country's life, the public interest becomes the paramount consideration.

In these circumstances I solemnly request both the national and the local officers and also the individual members of the United Mine Workers of America to recall all orders looking to a strike on November 1, and to take whatever step may be necessary to prevent any stoppage of work.

It is time for plain speaking. These matters with which we now deal touch not only the welfare of a class but vitally concern the well-being, the comfort, and the very life of all the people.

I feel it is my duty in the public interest to declare that any attempt to carry out the purpose of this strike and thus to paralyze the industry of the country, with the consequent suffering and distress of all our people, must be considered a grave moral and legal wrong against the government and the people of the United States.

I can do nothing else than to say that the law will be enforced, and the means will be found to protect the interests of the Nation in any emergency that may arise out of this unhappy business.

I express no opinion on the merits of the controversy. I have already suggested a plan by which a settlement may be reached, and I hold myself in readiness at the request of either or both sides to appoint at once a tribunal to investigate all the facts with a view to aiding in the earliest possible orderly settlement of the questions at issue between the coal operators and the coal miners, to the end that the just rights, not only of those interests but also of the general public may be fully protected.

AGAINST CONTINUANCE OF WAR TIME PROHIBITION

MESSAGE TO THE HOUSE OF REPRESENTATIVES, RETURNING WITH VETO, H.R. 6810, OCTOBER 27, 1919. FROM COPY IN MR. WILSON'S FILES.

I AM returning, without my signature, H.R. 6810, "An act to prohibit intoxicating beverages, and to regulate the manufacture, production, use, and sale of high-proof spirits for other than beverage purposes, and to insure an ample supply of alcohol and promote its use in scientific research and in the development of fuel, dye, and other lawful industries."

The subject matter treated in this measure deals with two distinct phases of the prohibition legislation. One part of the act under consideration seeks to enforce war-time prohibition. The other provides for the enforcement which was made necessary by the adoption of the Constitutional Amendment. I object to and cannot approve that part of this legislation with reference to war-time prohibition. It has to do with the enforcement of an act which was passed by reason of the emergencies of the war and whose objects have been satisfied in the demobilization of the Army and Navy, and whose repeal I have already sought at the hands of Congress. Where the purposes of particular legislation arising out of war emergency have been satisfied, sound public policy makes clear the reason and necessity for repeal.

It will not be difficult for Congress in considering this important matter to separate these two questions and effectively to legislate regarding them, making the proper distinction between temporary causes which arose out of war-time emergencies and those like the Constitutional Amendment of prohibition which is now part of the fundamental law of the country. In all matters having to do with the personal habits and customs of large numbers of our people we must be certain that the established processes of legal change are followed. In no other way can the salutary object sought to be accomplished by great reforms of this character be made satisfactory and permanent.

ON THE FIRST ANNIVERSARY OF ARMISTICE DAY

STATEMENT TO THE COUNTRY, NOVEMBER 11, 1919.

A YEAR ago to-day our enemies laid down their arms in accordance with an armistice which rendered them impotent to renew hostilities, and gave to the world an assured opportunity to reconstruct its shattered order and to work out in peace a new and juster set of international relations.

The soldiers and people of the European allies had fought and endured for more than four years to uphold the barrier of civilization against the aggressions of armed force. We ourselves had been in the conflict something more than a year and a half.

With splendid forgetfulness of mere personal concerns, we remodeled our industries, concentrated our financial resources, increased our agricultural output and assembled a great army, so that at the last our power was a decisive factor in the victory. We were able to bring the vast resources, material and moral, of a great and free people to the assistance of our associates in Europe who had suffered and sacrificed without limit in the cause for which we fought.

Out of this victory there arose new possibilities of political freedom and economic concert. The war showed us the strength of great nations acting together for high purposes, and the victory of arms foretells the enduring conquests which can be made in peace when nations act justly, and in furtherance of the common interests of men.

To us in America the reflections of Armistice Day will be filled with solemn pride in the heroism of those who died in the country's service, and with gratitude for the victory, both because of the thing from which it has freed us and because of the opportunity it has given America to show her sympathy with peace and justice in the councils of nations.

ANNUAL MESSAGE

MESSAGE COMMUNICATED TO THE TWO HOUSES OF CONGRESS, AT THE BEGINNING OF THE SECOND SESSION OF THE SIXTY-SIXTH CONGRESS, DECEMBER 2, 1919. FROM 66TH CONGRESS 2D SESSION HOUSE DOCUMENT NO. 399.

TO THE SENATE AND HOUSE OF REPRE-SENTATIVES:

I sincerely regret that I cannot be present at the opening of this session of the Congress. I am thus prevented from presenting in as direct a way as I could wish the many questions that are pressing for solution at this time. Happily, I have had the advantage of the advice of the heads of the several executive departments who have kept in close touch with affairs in their detail and whose thoughtful recommendations I earnestly second.

In the matter of the railroads and the readjustment of their affairs growing out of federal control, I shall take the liberty at a later date of addressing you.

I hope that Congress will bring to a conclusion at this session legislation looking to the establishment of a budget system. That there should be one single authority responsible for the making of all appropriations and that appropriations should be made not independently of each other, but with reference to one single comprehensive plan of expenditure properly related to the Nation's income, there can be no doubt. I believe the burden of preparing the budget must, in the nature of the case, if the work is to be properly done and responsibility concentrated instead of divided, rest upon the executive. The budget so prepared should be submitted to and approved or amended by a single committee of each House of Congress and no single appropriation should be made by the Congress, except such as may have been included in the budget prepared by the executive or added by the particular committee of Congress charged with the budget legislation.

Another and not less important aspect of the problem is the ascertainment of the economy and efficiency with which the moneys appropriated are expended. Under existing law the only audit is for the purpose of ascertaining whether expenditures have been lawfully made within the appropriations. No one is authorized or equipped to ascertain whether the money has been spent wisely, economically and effectively. The auditors should be highly trained' officials with permanent tenure in the Treasury Department, free of obligations to or motives of consideration for this or any subsequent administration, and authorized and empowered to examine into and make report upon the methods employed and the results obtained by the executive departments of the Government. Their reports should be made to the Congress and to the Secretary of the Treasury.

I trust that the Congress will give its immediate consideration to the problem of future taxation. Simplification of the income and profits taxes has become an immediate necessity. These taxes performed indispensable service during the war. They must, however, be simplified, not only to save the taxpayer inconvenience and expense, but in order that his liability may be made certain and definite.

With reference to the details of the Revenue Law, the Secretary of the Treasury and the Commissioner of Internal Revenue will lay before you for your consideration certain amendments necessary or desirable in connection with the administration of the law—recommendations which have my approval and support. It is of the utmost importance that in dealing with this matter the present law should not be disturbed so far as regards taxes for the calendar year 1920, payable in the calendar year 1921. The Congress might well consider whether the higher rates of income and profits taxes can in peace times be effectively productive of revenue, and whether they may not, on the contrary, be destructive of business activity and productive of waste and inefficiency. There is a point at which in peace times high rates of income and profits taxes discourage energy, remove the incentive to new enterprise, encourage extravagant expenditures and produce industrial stagnation with consequent unemployment and other attendant evils.

The problem is not an easy one. A fundamental change has taken place with reference to the position of America in the world's affairs. The prejudice and passions engendered by decades of controversy between two schools of political and economic thought,—the one believers in protection of American industries, the other believers in tariff for revenue only,—must be subordinated to the single consideration of the public interest in the light of utterly changed conditions. Before the war America was heavily the debtor of the rest of the world and the interest payments she had to make to foreign countries on American securities held abroad, the expenditures of American travelers abroad and the ocean freight charges she had to pay to others, about balanced the value of her pre-war favorable balance of trade. During the war America's exports have been greatly stimulated, and increased prices have increased their value. On the other hand, she has purchased a large proportion of the American securities previously held abroad, has loaned some $9,000,000,000 to foreign governments, and has built her own ships. Our favorable balance of trade has thus been greatly increased and Europe has been deprived of the means of meeting it heretofore existing. Europe can have only three ways of meeting the favorable balance of trade in peace times: by imports into this country of gold or of goods, or by establishing new credits. Europe is in no position at the present time to ship gold to us nor could we contemplate large further imports of gold into this country without concern. The time has nearly passed for international governmental loans and it will take time to develop in this country a market for foreign securities. Anything, therefore, which would tend to prevent foreign countries from settling for our exports by shipments of goods into this country could only have the effect of preventing them from paying for our exports and therefore of preventing the exports from being made. The productivity of the country greatly stimulated by the war must find an outlet by exports to foreign countries and any measures taken to prevent imports will inevitably curtail exports, force curtailment of production, load the banking machinery of the country with credits to carry unsold products and produce industrial stagnation and unemployment. If we want to sell, we must be prepared to buy. Whatever, therefore, may have been our views during the period of growth of American business concerning tariff legislation, we must now adjust our own economic life to a changed condition growing out of the fact that American business is full grown and that America is the greatest capitalist in the world.

No policy of isolation will satisfy the growing needs and opportunities of America. The provincial standards and policies of the past, which have held American business as if in a strait-jacket, must yield and give way to the needs and exigencies of the new day in which we live, a day full of hope and promise for American busi. ness, if we will but take advantage of the opportunities that are ours for the asking. The recent war has ended our isolation and thrown upon us a great duty and responsibility. The United States must share the expanding world market. The United States desires for itself only equal opportunity with the other nations of the world, and that through the process of friendly coöperation and fair competition the legitimate interests of the nations concerned may be successfully and equitably adjusted.

There are other matters of importance upon which I urged action at the last session of Congress which are still pressing for solution. I am sure it is not necessary for me again to remind you that there is one immediate and very practicable question resulting from the war which we should meet in the most liberal spirit. It is a matter of recognition and relief to our soldiers. I can do no better than to quote from my last message urging this very action:

"We must see to it that our returning soldiers are assisted in every practicable way to find the places for which they are fitted in the daily work of the country. This can be done by developing and maintaining upon an adequate scale the admirable organization created by the Department of Labor for placing men seeking work; and it can also be done, in at least one very great field, by creating new opportunities for individual enterprise. The Secretary of the Interior has pointed out the way by which returning soldiers may be helped to find and take up land in the hitherto undeveloped regions of the country which the Federal Government has already prepared or can readily prepare for cultivation and also on many of the cutover or neglected areas which lie within the limits of the older states; and I once more take the liberty of recommending very urgently that his plans shall receive the immediate and substantial support of the Congress."

In the matter of tariff legislation, I beg to call your attention to the statements contained in my last message urging legislation with reference to the establishment of the chemical and dyestuffs industry in America:

"Among the industries to which special consideration should be given is that of the manufacture of dyestuffs and related chemicals. Our complete dependence upon German supplies before the war made the interruption of trade a cause of exceptional economic disturbance.

The close relation between the manufacture of dye-stuffs, on the one hand, and of explosives and poisonous gases, on the other, moreover, has given the industry an exceptional significance and value. Although the United States will gladly and unhesitatingly join in the program of international disarmament, it will, nevertheless, be a policy of obvious prudence to make certain of the successful maintenance of many strong and well-equipped chemical plants. The German chemical industry, with which we will be brought into competition, was and may well be again, a thoroughly knit monopoly capable of exercising a competition of a peculiarly insidious and dangerous kind."

During the war the farmer performed a vital and willing service to the nation. By materially increasing the production of his land, he supplied America and the Allies with the increased amounts of food necessary to keep their immense armies in the field. He indispensably helped to win the war. But there is now scarcely less need of increasing the production in food and the necessaries of life. I ask the Congress to consider means of encouraging effort along these lines. The importance of doing everything possible to promote production along economical lines, to improve marketing, and to make rural life more attractive and healthful, is obvious. I would urge approval of the plans already proposed to the Congress by the Secretary of Agriculture, to secure the essential facts required for the proper study of this question, through the proposed enlarged programs for farm management studies and crop estimates. I would urge, also, the continuance of federal participation in the building of good roads, under the terms of existing law and under the direction of present agencies; the need of further action on the part of the States and the Federal Government to preserve and develop our forest resources, especially through the practice of better forestry methods on private holdings and the extension of the publicly owned

forests; better support for country schools and the more
definite direction of their courses of study along lines
related to rural problems; and fuller provision for sanitation in rural districts and the building up of needed
hospital and medical facilities in these localities.   Perhaps the way might be cleared for many of these desirable reforms by a fresh, comprehensive survey made
of rural conditions by a conference composed of representatives of the farmers and of the agricultural
agencies responsible for leadership.

I would call your attention to the widespread condition of political restlessness in our body politic.   The
causes of this unrest, while various and complicated,
are superficial rather than deep seated.   Broadly, they
arise from or are connected with the failure on the part
of our Government to arrive speedily at a just and permanent peace permitting return to normal conditions,
from the transfusion of radical theories from seething
European centers pending such delay, from heartless
profiteering resulting in the increase of the cost of living, and lastly from the machinations of passionate and
malevolent agitators.   With the return to normal conditions, this unrest will rapidly disappear.   In the meantime, it does much evil.   It seems to me that in dealing
with this situation Congress should not be impatient or
drastic but should seek rather to remove the causes.   It
should endeavor to bring our country back speedily to
a peace basis, with ameliorated living conditions under
the minimum of restrictions upon personal liberty that
is consistent with our reconstruction problems.   And it
should arm the Federal Government with power to deal
in its criminal courts with those persons who by violent
methods would abrogate our time-tested institutions.
With the free expression of opinion and with the advocacy of orderly political change, however fundamental, there must be no interference, but towards
passion and malevolence tending to incite crime and in-
surrection under guise of political evolution there

should be no leniency. Legislation to this end has been recommended by the Attorney General and should be enacted. In this direct connection, I would call your attention to my recommendations on August 8, pointing out legislative measures which would be effective in controlling and bringing down the present cost of living, which contributes so largely to this unrest. On only one of these recommendations has the Congress acted. If the Government's campaign is to be effective, it is necessary that the other steps suggested should be acted on at once.

I renew and strongly urge the necessity of the extension of the present Food Control Act as to the period of time in which it shall remain in operation. The Attorney General has submitted a bill providing for an extension of this Act for a period of six months. As it now stands it is limited in operation to the period of the war and becomes inoperative upon the formal proclamation of peace. It is imperative that it should be extended at once. The Department of Justice has built up extensive machinery for the purpose of enforcing its provisions; all of which must be abandoned upon the conclusion of peace unless the provisions of this Act are extended.

During this period the Congress will have an opportunity to make similar, permanent provisions and regulations with regard to all goods destined for interstate commerce and to exclude them from interstate shipment, if the requirements of the law are not complied with. Some such regulation is imperatively necessary. The abuses that have grown up in the manipulation of prices by the withholding of foodstuffs and other necessaries of life cannot otherwise be effectively prevented. There can be no doubt of either the necessity or the legitimacy of such measures.

As I pointed out in my last message, publicity can accomplish a great deal in this campaign. The aims of the Government must be clearly brought to the attention of the consuming public, civic organizations and state officials, who are in a position to lend their assistance to our efforts. You have made available funds with which to carry on this campaign, but there is no provision in the law authorizing their expenditure for the purpose of making the public fully informed about the efforts of the Government. Specific recommendation has been made by the Attorney General in this regard. I would strongly urge upon you its immediate adoption, as it constitutes one of the preliminary steps to this campaign.

I also renew my recommendation that the Congress pass a law regulating cold storage as it is regulated, for example, by the laws of the State of New Jersey, which limit the time during which goods may be kept in storage, prescribe the method of disposing of them if kept beyond the permitted period, and require that goods released from storage shall in all cases bear the date of their receipt. It would materially add to the serviceability of the law, for the purpose we now have in view, if it were also prescribed that all goods released from storage for interstate shipment should have plainly marked upon each package the selling or market price at which they went into storage. By this means the purchaser would always be able to learn what profits stood between him and the producer or the wholesale dealer.

I would also renew my recommendation that all goods destined for interstate commerce should in every case, where their form or package makes it possible, be plainly marked with the price at which they left the hands of the producer.

We should formulate a law requiring a federal license of all corporations engaged in interstate commerce and embodying in the license, or in the conditions under which it is to be issued, specific regulations designed to secure competitive selling and prevent unconscionable profits in the method of marketing. Such a law would afford a welcome opportunity to effect other much needed reforms in the business of interstate shipment and in the methods of corporations which are engaged in it; but for the moment I confine my recommendations to the object immediately in hand, which is to lower the cost of living.

No one who has observed the march of events in the last year can fail to note the absolute need of a definite program to bring about an improvement in the conditions of labor. There can be no settled conditions leading to increased production and a reduction in the cost of living if labor and capital are to be antagonists instead of partners. Sound thinking and an honest desire to serve the interests of the whole Nation, as distinguished from the interests of a class, must be applied to the solution of this great and pressing problem. The failure of other nations to consider this matter in a vigorous way has produced bitterness and jealousies and antagonisms, the food of radicalism. The only way to keep men from agitating against grievances is to remove the grievances. An unwillingness even to discuss these matters produces only dissatisfaction and gives comfort to the extreme elements in our country which endeavor to stir up disturbances in order to provoke Governments to embark upon a course of retaliation and repression. The seed of revolution is repression. The remedy for these things must not be negative in character. It must be constructive. It must comprehend the general interest. The real antidote for the unrest which manifests itself is not suppression, but a deep consideration of the wrongs that beset our national life and the application of a remedy.

Congress has already shown its willingness to deal with these industrial wrongs by establishing the eight-hour day as the standard in every field of labor. It has sought to find a way to prevent child labor. It has served the whole country by leading the way in developing the means of preserving and safeguarding lives and health in dangerous industries. It must now help in the difficult task of finding a method that will bring about a genuine democratization of industry based upon the full recognition of the right of those who work, in whatever rank, to participate in some organic way in every decision which directly affects their welfare. It is with this purpose in mind that I called a conference to meet in Washington on December 1, to consider these problems in all their broad aspects, with the idea of bringing about a better understanding between these two interests.

The great unrest throughout the world, out of which has emerged a demand for an immediate consideration of the difficulties between capital and labor, bids us put our own house in order. Frankly, there can be no permanent and lasting settlements between capital and labor which do not recognize the fundamental concepts for which labor has been struggling through the years. The whole world gave its recognition and endorsement to these fundamental purposes in the League of Nations. The statesmen gathered at Versailles recognized the fact that world stability could not be had by reverting to industrial standards and conditions against which the average workman of the world had revolted. It is, therefore, the task of the statesmen of this new day of change and readjustment to recognize world conditions and to seek to bring about, through legislation, conditions that will mean the ending of age-long antagonisms between capital and labor and that will hopefully lead to the building up of a comradeship which will result not only in greater contentment among the mass of workmen but also bring about a greater production and a greater prosperity to business itself.

To analyze the particulars in the demands of labor is to admit the justice of their complaint in many matters that lie at their basis. The workman demands an adequate wage, sufficient to permit him to live in comfort, unhampered by the fear of poverty and want in his old age. He demands the right to live and the right to work amidst sanitary surroundings, both in home and in workshop, surroundings that develop and do not retard his own health and well-being; and the right to provide for his children's wants in the matter of health and education. In other words, it is his desire to make the conditions of his life and the lives of those dear to him tolerable and easy to bear.

The establishment of the principles regarding labor laid down in the Covenant of the League of Nations offers us the way to industrial peace and conciliation. No other road lies open to us. Not to pursue this one is longer to invite enmities, bitterness, and antagonisms which in the end only lead to industrial and social disaster. The unwilling workman is not a profitable servant. An employee whose industrial life is hedged about by hard and unjust conditions, which he did not create and over which he has no control, lacks that fine spirit of enthusiasm and volunteer effort which are the necessary ingredients of a great producing entity. Let us be frank about this solemn matter. The evidences of world-wide unrest which manifest themselves in violence throughout the world bid us pause and consider the means to be found to stop the spread of this contagious thing before it saps the very vitality of the nation itself. Do we gain strength by withholding the remedy? Or is it not the business of statesmen to treat these manifestations of unrest which meet us on every hand as evidences of an economic disorder and to apply constructive remedies wherever necessary, being sure that in the application of the remedy we touch not the vital tissues of our industrial and economic life? There can be no recession of the tide of unrest until constructive instrumentalities are set up to stem that tide.

Governments must recognize the right of men collectively to bargain for humane objects that have at their base the mutual protection and welfare of those engaged in all industries. Labor must not be longer treated as a commodity. It must be regarded as the activity of human beings, possessed of deep yearnings and desires. The business man gives his best thought to the repair and replenishment of his machinery, so that its usefulness will not be impaired and its power to produce may always be at its height and kept in full vigor and motion. No less regard ought to be paid to the human machine, which after all propels the machinery of the world and is the great dynamic force that lies back of all industry and progress. Return to the old standards of wage and industry in employment is unthinkable. The terrible tragedy of war which has just ended and which has brought the world to the verge of chaos and disaster would be in vain if there should ensue a return to the conditions of the past. Europe itself, whence has come the unrest which now holds the world at bay, is an example of standpatism in these vital human matters which America might well accept as an example, not to be followed but studiously to be avoided. Europe made labor the differential, and the price of it all is enmity and antagonism and prostrated industry. The right of labor to live in peace and comfort must be recognized by governments and America should be the first to lay the foundation stones upon which industrial peace shall be built.

Labor not only is entitled to an adequate wage, but capital should receive a reasonable return upon its investment and is entitled to protection at the hands of the government in every emergency. No government worthy of the name can "play" these elements against each other, for there is a mutuality of interest between them which the government must seek to express and to safeguard at all cost.

The right of individuals to strike is inviolate and ought not to be interfered with by any process of government, but there is a predominant right and that is the right of the Government to protect all of its people and to assert its power and majesty against the challenge of any class. The Government, when it asserts that right, seeks not to antagonize a class but simply to defend the right of the whole people as against the irreparable harm and injury that might be done by the attempt by any class to usurp a power that only government itself has a right to exercise as a protection to all.

In the matter of international disputes which have led to war, statesmen have sought to set up as a remedy arbitration for war. Does this not point the way for the settlement of industrial disputes, by the establishment of a tribunal, fair and just alike to all, which will settle industrial disputes which in the past have led to war and disaster? America, witnessing the evil consequences which have followed out of such disputes between these contending forces, must not admit itself impotent to deal with these matters by means of peaceful processes. Surely, there must be some method of bringing together in a council of peace and amity these two great interests, out of which will come a happier day of peace and coöperation, a day that will make men more hopeful and enthusiastic in their various tasks, that will make for more comfort and happiness in living and a more tolerable condition among all classes of men. Certainly human intelligence can devise some acceptable tribunal for adjusting the differences between capital and labor.

This is the hour of test and trial for America. By her prowess and strength, and the indomitable courage of her soldiers, she demonstrated her power to vindicate on foreign battlefields her conceptions of liberty and justice. Let not her influence as a mediator between capital and labor be weakened and her own failure to settle matters of purely domestic concern be proclaimed to the world. There are those in this country who threaten direct action to force their will upon a majority. Russia to-day, with its blood and terror, is a painful object lesson of the power of minorities. It makes little difference what minority it is; whether capital or labor, or any other class; no sort of privilege will ever be permitted to dominate this country. We are a partnership or nothing that is worth while. We are a democracy, where the majority are the masters, or all the hopes and purposes of the men who founded this government have been defeated and forgotten. In America there is but one way by which great reforms can be accomplished and the relief sought by classes obtained, and that is through the orderly processes of representative government. Those who would propose any other method of reform are enemies of this country. America will not be daunted by threats nor lose her composure or calmness in these distressing times. We can afford, in the midst of this day of passion and unrest, to be self-contained and sure. The instrument of all reform in America is the ballot. The road to economic and social reform in America is the straight road of justice to all classes and conditions of men. Men have but to follow this road to realize the full fruition of their objects and purposes. Let those beware who would take the shorter road of disorder and revolution. The right road is the road of justice and orderly process.

URGING MINERS TO RESUME WORK

TEXT OF PROPOSAL TO THE MINERS IN CONFERENCE AT
INDIANAPOLIS, DECEMBER 9, 1919. FROM THE
NEW YORK "TIMES," DECEMBER 10, 1919.

I HAVE watched with deep concern the developments in the bituminous coal strike and am convinced there is much confusion in the minds of the people generally and possibly of both parties to this unfortunate controversy as to the attitude and purposes of the Government in its handling of the situation.

The mine owners offered a wage increase of twenty per cent, conditioned, however, upon the price of coal being raised to an amount sufficient to cover this proposed increase of wages, which would have added at least $150,000,000 to the annual coal bill of the people. The Fuel Administrator, in the light of present information, has taken the position, and I think with entire justification, that the public is now paying as high prices for coal as it ought to be requested to pay, and that any wage increase made at this time ought to come out of the profits of the coal operators.

In reaching this conclusion, the Fuel Administrator expressed the personal opinion that the fourteen-per-cent increase in all mine wages is reasonable because it would equalize the miners' wages on the average with the cost of living, but he made it perfectly clear that the operators and the miners are at liberty to agree upon a large increase provided the operators will pay it out of their profits so that the price of coal would remain the same.

The Secretary of Labor, in an effort at conciliation between the parties, expressed his personal opinion in favor of a larger increase. His effort at conciliation failed, however, because the coal operators were unwilling to pay the scale he proposed unless the Government

443

would advance the price of coal to the public, and this the Government was unwilling to do.

The Fuel Administrator had also suggested that a tribunal be created in which the miners and operators would be equally represented to consider further questions of wages and working conditions, as well as profits of operators and proper prices for coal. I shall, of course, be glad to aid in the formation of such a tribunal.

I understand the operators have generally agreed to absorb an increase of fourteen per cent in wages, so that the public would pay not to exceed the present price fixed by the Fuel Administrator, and thus a way is opened to secure the coal of which the people stand in need, if the miners will resume work on these terms pending a thorough investigation by an impartial commission which may readjust both wages and prices.

By the acceptance of such a plan, the miners are assured immediate steady employment at a substantial increase in wages and are further assured prompt investigation and action upon questions which are not now settled to their satisfaction. I must believe that with a clear understanding of these points they will promptly return to work. If, nevertheless, they persist in remaining on strike they will put themselves in an attitude of striking in order to force the Government to increase the price of coal to the public, so as to give a still further increase in wages at this time rather than allow the question of a further increase in wages to be dealt with in an orderly manner by a fairly constituted tribunal representing all parties interested.

No group of our people can justify such a position, and the miners owe it to themselves, their families, their fellow workmen in other industries, and to their country to return to work.

Immediately upon a general resumption of mining, I shall be glad to aid in the prompt formation of such a tribunal as I have indicated to make further inquiries into this whole matter and to review not only the reasonableness of the wages at which the miners start to work, but also the reasonableness of the Government prices for coal. Such a tribunal should within sixty days make its report which could be used as a basis for negotiation, for a wage agreement. I must make it clear, however, that the Government cannot give its aid to any such further investigation until there is a general resumption of work.

I ask every individual miner to give his personal thought to what I say. I hope he understands fully that he will be hurting his own interest and the interest of his family and will be throwing countless other laboring men out of employment if he shall continue the present strike, and, further that he will create an unnecessary and unfortunate prejudice against organized labor which will be injurious to the best interests of workingmen everywhere.

COMMISSION TO INVESTIGATE THE BITU-
MINOUS COAL INDUSTRY[1]

LETTER TO MR. HENRY M. ROBINSON, REPRESENTATIVE
OF THE PUBLIC, DECEMBER 19, 1919. FROM ORIGI-
NAL IN MR. WILSON'S FILES.

MY DEAR MR. ROBINSON:
On October 6, 1917, with the official approval
and sanction of the United States Fuel Administration,
an agreement (since known as the "Washington Wage
Agreement") was entered into between the operators
and the union miners and mine workers of the so-called
"Central Competitive Bituminous Coal Fields," composed of Western Pennsylvania, Ohio, Indiana, and Illinois, which provided for an increase in the production
of bituminous coal and an increase in wages to the
miners and mine workers from the then existing scale
of compensation. The agreement contained the following clause:

"Subject to the next biennial convention of the
United Mine Workers of America, the mine workers'
representatives agree that the present contract be extended during the continuation of the war and not to
exceed two years from April 1, 1918."

Subsequently, on January 19, 1918, this agreement
was approved by the convention of the International
Union United Mine Workers of America.

At the fourth biennial convention of the International Union United Mine Workers of America, held
in Cleveland, Ohio, from September 9 to September 23,
1919, the so-called Scale Committee submitted a report
recommending, among other things, that the convention

---

[1] The report of this Commission, dated March 10, 1920, recommended a twenty-seven per cent increase in wages with no change in
hours or working conditions.

demand a sixty per cent increase applicable to all classifications of day labor and to all tonnage, yardage and
dead work rates throughout the central competitive
field; that all new wage agreements replacing existing
agreements should be based on a six-hour workday from
bank to bank, five days per week; the abolition of all
automatic penalty clauses; that all contracts in the bituminous field should be declared to expire on November
1, 1919; and that "in the event a satisfactory wage
agreement is not secured for the central competitive
field before November 1, 1919, to replace the one now
in effect, the international officers be authorized to and
are hereby instructed to call a general strike of all bituminous miners and mine workers throughout the United
States, the same to become effective November 1,
1919."

Subsequently conferences were held between representatives of the operators and of the miners, at which
the miners' demands were submitted and declined on
the part of the operators. The officers of the International Union United Mine Workers of America then
issued so-called strike orders to all of their local unions
and members, requiring them to cease work in the mining of bituminous coal at midnight on Friday, October
31.

On October 15, 1919, the Secretary of Labor called
a conference between the operators and miners of the
bituminous mines in the central competitive field, which
conference also resulted in failure to reach an agreement. In a letter to Secretary Wilson, which was submitted to the conference, I said:

"If for any reason the miners and operators fail to
come to a mutual understanding, the interests of the
public are of such vital importance in connection with
the production of coal, that it is incumbent upon them
to refer the matters in dispute to a board of arbitration for determination and to continue the operation
of the mines pending the decision of the board." Subse-

quently, on October 25, 1919, I issued a statement in which I said that a strike in the circumstances therein described "is not only unjustifiable; it is unlawful," and added:

"I express no opinion on the merits of the controversy. I have already suggested a plan by which a settlement may be reached, and I hold myself in readiness, at the request of either or both sides, to appoint at once a tribunal to investigate all the facts with a view to aiding in the earliest possible orderly settlement of the questions at issue between the coal operators and the coal miners, to the end that the just rights, not only of those interests but also of the general public, may be fully protected."

Despite my earnest appeals that the men remain at work, the officers of the United Mine Workers of America rejected all the proposals for a peaceful and orderly adjustment and declared that the strike would go on. Accordingly, at my direction, the Attorney General filed a bill in equity in the United States District Court at Indianapolis, praying for an injunction to restrain the officers of the United Mine Workers of America from doing any act in furtherance of the strike. A restraining order was issued by the Court, followed by a writ of temporary injunction on November 8, 1919, in which the defendants were commanded to cancel and revoke the strike orders theretofore issued. These strike orders were accordingly revoked in a form approved by the Court, but the men did not return to work in sufficiently large number to bring about a production of coal anywhere approaching normal.

On December 6, 1919, I issued a statement in which I restated the Government's position, appealed to the miners to return to work and renewed my suggestion that upon the general resumption of mining operations a suitable tribunal would be erected for the purpose of investigating and adjusting the matters in controversy between the operators and the miners. This statement was submitted to a meeting of the officers of the International Union United Mine Workers of America, having authority to take action, which meeting adopted as its act a memorandum prepared by the Attorney General and approved by me, embodying the suggestions contained in my statement of December 6. I am informed also that the operators have generally agreed to the plan therein outlined. I enclose for your information a copy of my statement of December 6, 1919, and the memorandum just referred to.

There has now been a general resumption of operation in all parts of the bituminous coal fields sufficient to warrant the appointment of a commission such as is referred to in the memorandum of the Attorney General, and I have accordingly appointed you; Mr. Rembrandt Peale, a mine owner and operator in active business; and Mr. John P. White, a practical miner, as a commission with the powers and duties as set forth in the memorandum agreed to and adopted by the miners and operators, who conducted all the prior negotiations. If a readjustment of the prices of coal shall be found necessary, I shall be pleased to transfer to the commission, subject to its unanimous action, the powers heretofore vested in the Fuel Administrator for that purpose.

I am sure it is not necessary for me to call your attention to the tremendous importance of the work of this commission or the great opportunity which it presents for lasting service to the coal industry and to the country. If the facts covering all the phases of the coal industry necessary to a proper adjustment of the matters submitted to you shall be investigated and reported to the public, I am sure that your report, in addition to being accepted as the basis for a new wage agreement for the bituminous coal miners, will promote the public welfare and make for a settled condition of the industry. No settlement can be had in this matter, permanent and lasting in its benefits, as affecting either the miners, the coal operators, or the general public, unless the findings of this body are comprehensive in their character and embrace and guard at every point the public interest. To this end, I deem it important that your conclusion should be reached by unanimous action. Upon your acceptance of this appointment, I shall be pleased to call an early meeting of the commission in Washington so that you may promptly lay out plans for your work.

Sincerely yours,

WOODROW WILSON.

RELINQUISHING FEDERAL CONTROL OF RAILROADS

PROCLAMATION ISSUED DECEMBER 24, 1919. FROM "UNITED STATES STATUTES AT LARGE," VOL. 41, PT. 2, PP. 1782-1783.

WHEREAS, in the exercise of authority committed to me by law, I have heretofore, through the Secretary of War, taken possession of and have, through the Director General of Railroads, exercised control over certain railroads, systems of transportation and property appurtenant thereto or connected therewith; including systems of coastwise and inland transportation engaged in general transportation and owned or controlled by said railroads or systems of transportation; including also terminals, terminal companies and terminal associations, sleeping and parlor cars, private cars and private car lines, elevators, warehouses, telegraph and telephone lines, and all other equipment and appurtenances commonly used upon or operated as a part of such railroads and systems of transportation; and

Whereas, I now deem it needful and desirable that all railroads, systems of transportation and property now under such Federal control be relinquished therefrom;

Now, therefore, under authority of Section 14 of the Federal Control Act approved March 21, 1918, and of all other powers and provisions of law thereto me enabling, I, Woodrow Wilson, President of the United States, do hereby relinquish from Federal control, effective the first day of March, 1920, at 12:01 o'clock A.M. all railroads, systems of transportation and property, of whatever kind, taken or held under such Federal control and not heretofore relinquished, and restore the same to the possession and control of their respective owners.

Walker D. Hines, Director General of Railroads, or his successor in office, is hereby authorized and directed, through such agents and agencies as he may determine, in any manner not inconsistent with the provisions of said Act of March 21, 1918, to adjust, settle and close all matters, including the making of agreements for compensation, and all questions and disputes of whatsoever nature arising out of or incident to Federal control, until otherwise provided by proclamation of the President or by act of Congress; and generally to do and perform, as fully in all respects as the President is authorized to do, all and singular the acts and things necessary or proper, in order to carry into effect this proclamation and the relinquishment of said railroads, systems of transportation and property.

For the purposes of accounting and for all other purposes, this proclamation shall become effective on the first day of March 1920, at 12:01 o'clock A. M.

"GREAT AND SOLEMN REFERENDUM"

MESSAGE FOR JACKSON DAY CELEBRATION, ADDRESSED
TO THE CHAIRMAN, THE HON. HOMER S. CUM-
MINGS, OF CONNECTICUT, JANUARY 8, 1920. FROM
THE "CONGRESSIONAL RECORD," VOL. 59, P. 1249.

MY DEAR MR. CHAIRMAN:
It is with the keenest regret that I find that I am to be deprived of the pleasure and privilege of joining you and the other loyal Democrats who are to assemble to-night to celebrate Jackson Day and renew their vows of fidelity to the great principles of our party, the principles which must now fulfill the hopes not only of our own people but of the world.

The United States enjoyed the spiritual leadership of the world until the Senate of the United States failed to ratify the treaty by which the belligerent nations sought to effect the settlements for which they had fought throughout the war.

It is inconceivable that at this supreme crisis and final turning point in the international relations of the whole world, when the results of the Great War are by no means determined and are still questionable and dependent upon events which no man can foresee or count upon, the United States should withdraw from the concert of progressive and enlightened nations by which Germany was defeated, and all similar Governments (if the world be so unhappy as to contain any) warned of the consequences of any attempt at a like iniquity, and yet that is the effect of the course which the United States has taken with regard to the Treaty of Versailles.

Germany is beaten, but we are still at war with her, and the old stage is reset for a repetition of the old plot. It is now ready for a resumption of the old offensive and defensive alliances which made settled peace impossible. It is now open again to every sort of intrigue.

The old spies are free to resume their former abominable activities. They are again at liberty to make it impossible for Governments to be sure what mischief is being worked among their own people, what internal disorders are being fomented.

Without the Covenant of the League of Nations there may be as many secret treaties as ever, to destroy the confidence of Governments in each other, and their validity cannot be questioned.

None of the objects we professed to be fighting for has been secured, or can be made certain of, without this Nation's ratification of the treaty and its entry into the Covenant. This Nation entered the Great War to vindicate its own rights and to protect and preserve free government. It went into the war to see it through to the end, and the end has not yet come. It went into the war to make an end of militarism, to furnish guarantees to weak nations, and to make a just and lasting peace. It entered it with noble enthusiasm. Five of the leading belligerents have accepted the treaty and formal ratifications soon will be exchanged. The question is whether this country will enter and enter whole-heartedly. If it does not do so, the United States and Germany will play a lone hand in the world.

The maintenance of the peace of the world and the effective execution of the treaty depend upon the whole-hearted participation of the United States. I am not stating it as a matter of power. The point is that the United States is the only Nation which has sufficient moral force with the rest of the world to guarantee the substitution of discussion for war. If we keep out of this agreement, if we do not give our guarantees, then another attempt will be made to crush the new nations of Europe.

I do not believe that this is what the people of this

country wish or will be satisfied with. Personally, I do not accept the action of the Senate of the United States as the decision of the Nation.

I have asserted from the first that the overwhelming majority of the people of this country desire the ratification of the treaty, and my impression to that effect has recently been confirmed by the unmistakable evidences of public opinion given during my visit to seventeen of the States.

I have endeavored to make it plain that if the Senate wishes to say what the undoubted meaning of the League is I shall have no objection. There can be no reasonable objection to interpretations accompanying the act of ratification itself. But when the treaty is acted upon, I must know whether it means that we have ratified or rejected it.

We cannot rewrite this treaty. We must take it without changes which alter its meaning, or leave it, and then, after the rest of the world has signed it, we must face the unthinkable task of making another and separate treaty with Germany.

But no mere assertions with regard to the wish and opinion of the country are credited. If there is any doubt as to what the people of the country think on this vital matter, the clear and single way out is to submit it for determination at the next election to the voters of the Nation, to give the next election the form of a great and solemn referendum, a referendum as to the part the United States is to play in completing the settlements of the war and in the prevention in the future of such outrages as Germany attempted to perpetrate.

We have no more moral right to refuse now to take part in the execution and administration of these settlements than we had to refuse to take part in the fighting of the last few weeks of the war which brought victory and made it possible to dictate to Germany what the settlements should be. Our fidelity to our associates in the war is in question and the whole future of mankind. It will be heartening to the whole world to know the attitude and purpose of the people of the United States.

I spoke just now of the spiritual leadership of the United States, thinking of international affairs. But there is another spiritual leadership which is open to us and which we can assume.

The world has been made safe for democracy, but democracy has not been finally vindicated. All sorts of crimes are being committed in its name, all sorts of preposterous perversions of its doctrines and practices are being attempted.

This, in my judgment, is to be the great privilege of the democracy of the United States, to show that it can lead the way in the solution of the great social and industrial problems of our time, and lead the way to a happy, settled order of life as well as to political liberty. The program for this achievement we must attempt to formulate, and in carrying it out we shall do more than can be done in any other way to sweep out of existence the tyrannous and arbitrary forms of power which are now masquerading under the name of popular government.

Whenever we look back to Andrew Jackson we should draw fresh inspiration from his character and example. His mind grasped with such a splendid definiteness and firmness the principles of national authority and national action. He was so indomitable in his purpose to give reality to the principles of the Government, that this is a very fortunate time to recall his career and to renew our vows of faithfulness to the principles and the pure practices of democracy.

I rejoice to join you in this renewal of faith and purpose. I hope that the whole evening may be of the happiest results as regards the fortunes of our party and the Nation. With cordial regard,

Sincerely yours,

WOODROW WILSON.

CALLING FIRST MEETING OF LEAGUE OF NATIONS

CABLEGRAM ADDRESSED TO THE GOVERNMENT OF GREAT BRITAIN,[1] JANUARY 13, 1920. FROM THE NEW YORK "TIMES," JANUARY 14, 1920.

IN COMPLIANCE with Article V of the Covenant of the League of Nations, which went into effect at the same time as the Treaty of Versailles of June 28, 1919, of which it is a part, the President of the United States, acting on behalf of those nations which have deposited their instruments of ratifications in Paris as certified in a *procès verbal* drawn up by the French Government, dated January 10, 1920, has the honor to inform the Government of Great Britain that the first meeting of the council of the League of Nations will be held in Paris at the Ministry of Foreign Affairs on Friday, January 16, at 10:30 A. M.

The President ventures to hope that the Government of Great Britain will be in a position to send a representative to this first meeting. He feels that it is unnecessary for him to point out the deep significance attached to this meeting, or the importance which it must assume in the eyes of the world.

It will mark the beginning of a new era in international coöperation and the first great step toward the ideal concert of nations. It will bring the League of Nations into being as a living force devoted to the task of assisting the peoples of all countries in their desire for peace, prosperity, and happiness. The President is convinced that its progress will accord with the noble purposes to which it is dedicated.

---

[1] The same cablegram was sent to the Governments of the other nations which had deposited "instruments of ratification" in Paris: France, Italy, Japan, Belgium, Brazil, and Spain.

WELCOME TO PAN-AMERICAN FINANCIAL CONFERENCE

MESSAGE READ AT THE OPENING SESSION OF THE SECOND PAN-AMERICAN FINANCIAL CONFERENCE, IN THE PAN-AMERICAN UNION BUILDING, WASHINGTON, JANUARY 19, 1920. FROM ORIGINAL COPY SUPPLIED BY THE PAN-AMERICAN UNION.

GENTLEMEN OF THE AMERICAS:

I regret more deeply than I can well express that the condition of my health deprives me of the pleasure and privilege of meeting with you and personally expressing the gratification which every officer of this Government feels because of your presence at the National Capital, and particularly because of the friendly and significant mission which brings you to us. I rejoice with you that in these troubled times of world reconstruction the Republics of the American Continent should seek no selfish purpose, but should be guided by a desire to serve one another and to serve the world to the utmost of their capacity. The great privileges that have been showered upon us, both by reason of our geographical position and because of the high political and social ideals that have determined the national development of every country of the American Continent, carry with them obligations, the fulfillment of which must be regarded as a real privilege of every true American. It is no small achievement that the Americas are to-day able to say to the world, "Here is an important section of the globe which has to-day eliminated the idea of conquest from its national thought and from its international policy." The spirit of mutual helpfulness which animates this Conference supplements and strengthens this important achievement of international policy. I rejoice with you that we are privileged to assemble with the sole purpose of ascertaining how we can serve one another, for in so doing we best serve the world.

WOODROW WILSON.

ACCEPTING HITCHCOCK RESERVATIONS

LETTER TO SENATOR G. M. HITCHCOCK OF NEBRASKA ACCEPTING CERTAIN RESERVATIONS PROPOSED AS SUBSTITUTES FOR THE LODGE RESERVATIONS, JANUARY 26, 1920. FROM ORIGINAL COPY IN MR. WILSON'S FILES.

MY DEAR SENATOR HITCHCOCK:
I have greatly appreciated your thoughtful kindness in keeping me informed concerning the conferences you and some of your colleagues have had with spokesmen of the Republican Party concerning the possibility of ratification of the treaty of peace, and send this line in special appreciative acknowledgment of your letter of the twenty-second. I return the clipping you were kind enough to enclose.

To the substance of it I, of course, adhere. I am bound to. Like yourself I am solemnly sworn to obey and maintain the Constitution of the United States. But I think the form of it very unfortunate. Any reservation or resolution stating that "The United States assumes no obligation under such and such an Article unless or except" would, I am sure, chill our relationship with the nations with which we expect to be associated in the great enterprise of maintaining the world's peace.

That association must in any case, my dear Senator, involve very serious and far-reaching implications of honor and duty which I am sure we shall never in fact be desirous of ignoring. It is the more important not to create the impression that we are trying to escape obligations.

But I realize that negative criticism is not all that is called for in so serious a matter. I am happy to be able to add, therefore, that I have once more gone over the reservations proposed by yourself, the copy of which I return herewith, and am glad to say that I can accept them as they stand.

I have never seen the slightest reason to doubt the good faith of our associates in the war, nor ever had the slightest reason to fear that any nation would seek to enlarge our obligations under the Covenant of the League of Nations, or seek to commit us to lines of action which, under our Constitution, only the Congress of the United States can in the last analysis decide.

May I suggest that with regard to the possible withdrawal of the United States it would be wise to give to the President the right to act upon a resolution of Congress in the matter of withdrawal? In other words, it would seem to be permissible and advisable that any resolution giving notice of withdrawal should be a joint rather than a concurrent resolution.

I doubt whether the President can be deprived of his veto power under the Constitution, even with his own consent. The use of a joint resolution would permit the President, who is, of course, charged by the Constitution with the conduct of foreign policy, to merely exercise a voice in saying whether so important a step as withdrawal from the League of Nations should be accomplished by a majority or by a two-thirds vote.

The Constitution itself providing that the legislative body was to be consulted in treaty-making and having prescribed a two-thirds vote in such cases, it seems to me that there should be no unnecessary departure from the method there indicated.

I see no objection to a frank statement that the United States can accept a mandate with regard to any territory under Article XIII, Part 1, or any other provision of the treaty of peace, only by the direct authority and action of the Congress of the United States.

I hope, my dear Senator, that you will never hesitate to call upon me for any assistance that I can render in this or any other public matter.

Cordially and sincerely yours,

WOODROW WILSON.

THREE CABLEGRAMS ON THE ADRIATIC QUESTION

FROM THE NEW YORK "TIMES," FEBRUARY 27, 1920, AND MARCH 8, 1920.

I

CABLEGRAM TO THE AMERICAN AMBASSADOR AT PARIS, SIGNED BY SECRETARY LANSING, REFUSING THE BRITISH AND FRENCH PROPOSAL WITH REGARD TO THE ADRIATIC QUESTION, FEBRUARY 9, 1920.

THE President has carefully considered the joint telegram addressed to this Government by the French and British Prime Ministers and communicated by the American Ambassador in Paris, in regard to the negotiations on the Adriatic question. The President notes with satisfaction that the French, British, and Japanese Governments have never had the intention of proceeding to a definite settlement of this question except in consultation with the American Government. The President was particularly happy to receive this assurance as he understood that Monsieur Clemenceau and Mr. Lloyd George, in agreement with Signor Nitti, had decided upon a solution of the Adriatic question which included provisions previously rejected by the American Government, and had called upon the Jugoslav representatives to accept this solution, on pain of having the Treaty of London enforced in case of rejection. The President is glad to feel that the associates of this Government would not consent to embarrass it by placing it in the necessity of refusing adhesion to a settlement which in form would be an agreement by both parties to the controversy, but which in fact would not have that great merit if one party was forced to submit to material injustice by threats of still greater calamities in default of submission.

The President fully shares the view of the French and British Governments that the future of the world largely depends upon the right solution of this question, but he cannot believe that a solution containing provisions which have already received the well-merited condemnation of the French and British Governments can in any sense be regarded as right. Neither can he share the opinion of the French and British Governments that the proposals contained in their memorandum delivered to the Jugoslav representatives on January 14 leave untouched practically every important point of the joint memorandum of the French, British, and American Governments of December 9, 1919, and that "only two features undergo alterations, and both these alterations are to the positive advantage of Jugoslavia." On the contrary, the President is of the opinion that the proposal of December 9 has been profoundly altered to the advantage of improper Italian objectives, to the serious injury of the Jugoslav people, and to the peril of world peace. The view that very positive advantages have been conceded to Italy would appear to be borne out by the fact that the Italian Government rejected the proposal of December 9 and accepted that of January 14.

The memorandum of December 9 rejected the device of connecting Fiume with Italy by a narrow strip of coast territory as quite unworkable in practice and as involving extraordinary complexities as regards customs control, coast-guard services, and cognate matters in a territory of such unusual configuration. The French and British Governments, in association with the American Government, expressed the opinion that "the plan appears to run counter to every consideration of geography, economics, and territorial convenience." The American Government notes that this annexation of

Jugoslav territory by Italy is nevertheless agreed to by the memorandum of January 14.

The memorandum of December 9 rejected Italy's demand for the annexation of all of Istria, on the solid ground that neither strategic nor economic considerations could justify such annexation, and that there remained nothing in defense of the proposition save Italy's desire for more territory admittedly inhabited by Jugoslavs. The French and British Governments then expressed their cordial approval of the way in which the President had met every successive Italian demand for the absorption in Italy of territories inhabited by peoples not Italian and not in favor of being absorbed, and joined in the opinion that, "it is neither just nor expedient to annex as the spoils of war territories inhabited by an alien race." Yet this unjust and inexpedient annexation of all of Istria is provided for in the memorandum of January 14.

The memorandum of December 9 carefully excluded every form of Italian sovereignty over Fiume. The American Government cannot avoid the conclusion that the memorandum of January 14 opens the way for Italian control of Fiume's foreign affairs, thus introducing a measure of Italian sovereignty over, and Italian intervention in, the only practicable port of a neighboring people; and, taken in conjunction with the extension of Italian territory to the gates of Fiume, paves the way for possible future annexation of the port by Italy, in contradiction of compelling considerations of equity and right.

The memorandum of December 9 afforded proper protection to the vital railway connecting Fiume northward with the interior. The memorandum of January 14 establishes Italy in dominating military positions close to the railway at a number of critical points.

The memorandum of December 9 maintained in large measure the unity of the Albanian State. That of

January 14 partitions the Albanian people, against their vehement protests, among three different alien powers.

These and other provisions of the memorandum of January 14, negotiated without the knowledge or approval of the American Government, change the whole face of the Adriatic settlement and, in the eyes of this Government, render it unworkable and rob it of the measure of justice which is essential if this Government is to coöperate in maintaining its terms. The fact that the Jugoslav representatives might feel forced to accept, in the face of the alternative of the Treaty of London, a solution which appears to this Government so unfair in principle and so unworkable in practice, would not in any degree alter the conviction of this Government that it cannot give its assent to a settlement which both in the terms of its provisions and in the methods of its enforcement constitutes a positive denial of the principles for which America entered the war.

The matter would wear a very different aspect if there were any real divergence of opinion as to what constitutes a just settlement of the Adriatic issue. Happily no such divergence exists. The opinions of the French, British, and Americans as to a just and equitable territorial arrangement at the head of the Adriatic Sea were strikingly harmonious. Italy's unjust demands had been condemned by the French and British Governments in terms no less severe than those employed by the American Government. Certainly the French and British Governments will yield nothing to their American associate as regards the earnestness with which they have sought to convince the Italian Government that fulfillment of its demands would be contrary to Italy's own best interests, opposed to the spirit of justice in international dealings and fraught with danger to the peace of Europe. In particular, the French and British Governments have opposed Italy's demands for specific advantages which it is now proposed to yield to her by the memorandum of January

14, and have joined in informing the Italian Government that the concessions previously made "afford to Italy full satisfaction of her historic national aspirations based on the desire to unite the Italian race, give her the absolute strategic control of the Adriatic and offer her complete guarantees against whatever aggressions she might fear in the future from her Jugoslav neighbors."

While there is thus substantial agreement as to the injustice and inexpediency of Italy's claims, there is a difference of opinion as to how firmly Italy's friends should resist her importunate demands for alien territories to which she can present no valid title. It has seemed to the President that the French and British associates of the American Government, in order to prevent the development of possibly dangerous complications in the Adriatic region, have felt constrained to go very far in yielding to demands which they have long opposed as unjust. The American Government, while no less generous in its desire to accord to Italy every advantage to which she could offer any proper claims, feels that it cannot sacrifice the principles for which it entered the war to gratify the improper ambitions of one of its associates, or to purchase a temporary appearance of calm in the Adriatic at the price of a future world conflagration. It is unwilling to recognize either an unjust settlement based on a secret treaty the terms of which are inconsistent with the New World conditions, or an unjust settlement arrived at by employing that secret treaty as an instrument of coercion. It would welcome any solution of the problem based on a free and unprejudiced consideration of the merits of the controversy, or of terms which the disinterested great Powers agreed to be just and equable. Italy, however, has repeatedly rejected such solutions. This Government cannot accept a settlement the terms of which have been admitted to be unwise and unjust, but which it is proposed to grant to Italy in view of her persistent refusal to accept any wise and just solution.

It is a time to speak with the utmost frankness. The Adriatic issue as it now presents itself raises the fundamental question as to whether the American Government can on any terms coöperate with its European associates in the great work of maintaining the peace of the world by removing the primary causes of war. This Government does not doubt its ability to reach amicable understandings with the Associated Governments as to what constitutes equity and justice in international dealings, for differences of opinion as to the best methods of applying just principles have never obscured the vital fact that in the main the several Governments have entertained the same fundamental conception of what those principles are. But if substantial agreement on what is just and reasonable is not to determine international issues; if the country possessing the most endurance in pressing its demands rather than the country armed with a just cause, is to gain the support of the powers; if forcible seizure of coveted areas is to be permitted and condoned, and is to receive ultimate justification by creating a situation so difficult that decision favorable to the aggressor is deemed a practical necessity; if deliberately incited ambition is, under the name of national sentiment, to be rewarded at the expense of the small and the weak; if, in a word, the old order of things which brought so many evils on the world is still to prevail, then the time is not yet come when this Government can enter a concert of powers the very existence of which must depend upon a new spirit and a new order. The American people are willing to share in such high enterprise, but many among them are fearful lest they become entangled in international policies and committed to international obligations foreign alike to their ideals and their traditions. To commit them to such a policy as that embodied in the latest Adriatic proposals, and to obligate them to maintain injustice as against the claims of justice, would be to provide the most solid ground for such fears. This Government can undertake no such grave responsibility.

The President desires to say that if it does not appear feasible to secure acceptance of the just and generous concessions offered by the British, French, and American Governments to Italy in the joint memorandum of those powers of December 9, 1919, which the President has already clearly stated to be the maximum concession that the Government of the United States can offer, the President desires to say that he must take under serious consideration the withdrawal of the treaty with Germany and the agreement between the United States and France of June 28, 1919, which are now before the Senate and permitting the terms of the European settlement to be independently established and enforced by the Associated Governments.

II

CABLEGRAM TO THE AMERICAN AMBASSADOR AT
PARIS, SIGNED BY ACTING SECRETARY OF STATE
FRANK L. POLK, REGARDING THE ADRIATIC
SETTLEMENT, FEBRUARY 24, 1920.

THE joint memorandum of February 17 of the
Prime Ministers of France and Great Britain has
received the careful and earnest consideration of the
President. He has no desire whatever to criticize the
attitude of the Governments of France and Great Britain concerning the Adriatic settlement, but feels that
in the present circumstances he has no choice but to
maintain the position he has all along taken as regards
that settlement. He believes it to be the central principle
fought for in the war that no Government or group of
Governments has the right to dispose of the territory or
to determine the political allegiance of any free people.
The five great Powers, though the Government of the
United States constitutes one of them, have in his conviction no more right than had the Austrian Government
to dispose of the free Jugoslavic peoples without the
free consent and coöperation of those peoples. The
President's position is that the Powers associated against
Germany gave final and irrefutable proof of their sincerity in the war by writing into the Treaty of Versailles Article X of the Covenant of the League of
Nations, which constitutes an assurance that all the
great Powers have done what they have compelled Germany to do—have foregone all territorial aggression
and all interference with the free political self-determination of the peoples of the world. With this principle lived up to, permanent peace is secured and the
supreme object of the recent conflict has been achieved.
Justice and self-determination have been substituted for

aggression and political dictation. Without it, there is no security for any nation that conscientiously adheres to a non-militaristic policy. The object of the war, as the government of the United States understands it, was to free Europe from that cloud of anxiety which had hung over it for generations because of the constant threat of the use of military force by one of the most powerful Governments of the Continent, and the President feels it important to say again, that in the opinion of the American Government terms of the peace settlement must continue to be formulated upon the basis of the principles for which America entered the war. It is in a spirit of coöperation, therefore, and of desire for mutual understanding, that the President reviews the various considerations which the French and British Prime Ministers have emphasized in their memorandum of February 17. He is confident that they will not mistake his motives in undertaking to make plain what he feels to be the necessary conclusions from their statements.

The President notes that the objections of the Italians and Jugoslavs were made the basis for discarding the project of the Free State of Fiume. It would seem to follow, therefore, that the joint consent of these two Powers should have been required for the substitute project. The consent of Italy has been obtained. He does not find, however, that the Jugoslavs have also expressed a willingness to accept the substitute plan. Are they to be required now to accept a proposal which is more unsatisfactory because they have raised objections to the solution proposed by the British, French and American Governments in the memorandum of December 9? The President would, of course, make no objection to a settlement mutually agreeable to Italy and Jugoslavia regarding their common frontier in the Fiume region, provided that such an agreement is not made on the basis of compensations elsewhere at the expense of nationals of a third Power.

His willingness to accept such proposed joint agreement of Italy and Jugoslavia is based on the fact that only their own nationals are involved. In consequence the results of direct negotiations of the two interested Powers would fall within the scope of the principle of self-determination. Failing in this, both parties should be willing to accept a decision of the Governments of Great Britain, France, and the United States.

The British and French Governments appear to find in the President's suggestion that the latest proposals would pave the way for the annexation of the City of Fiume, an implication that the guarantee of the League of Nations is worthless, and that the Italian Government does not intend to abide by a treaty into which it has entered. The President cannot but regard this implication as without basis and as contrary to his thought. In his view the proposal, to connect Fiume with Italy by a narrow strip of coast territory is quite impracticable. As he has already said, it involves extraordinary complexities in customs control, coast-guard services, and other related matters, and he is unable to detach himself from the previous views of the British and French Governments, as expressed jointly with the American Government in the memorandum of December 9, that "the plan appears to run counter to every consideration of geography, economics, and territorial convenience."

He further believes that to have Italian territory join Fiume would be to invite strife, out of which annexation might issue. Therefore, in undertaking to shape the solution so as to prevent this, he is acting on the principle that each part of the final settlement should be based upon the essential justice of that particular case. This was one of the principles adopted by the allied and associated Powers as a basis for treaty-making. To it have been added the provisions of the League of Nations, but it has never been the policy of either this Government or its associates to invoke the

League of Nations as a guarantee that a bad settlement shall not become worse. The sum of such actions would of necessity destroy faith in the League and eventually the League itself.

The President notes with satisfaction that the Governments of Great Britain and France will not lose sight of the future interests and well-being of the Albanian peoples. The American Government quite understands that the three-fold division of Albania in the British-French agreement might be most acceptable to the Jugoslav Government, but it is just as vigorously opposed to injuring the Albanian people for the benefit of Jugoslavia as it is opposed to injuring the Jugoslav people for the benefit of Italy. It believes that the differences between the Christian and Mohammedan populations will be increased by putting the two sections under the control of nations of unlike language, government, and economic strength. Moreover, one part would be administered by the Italian Government, which is represented on the council of the League, the other part by the Jugoslav Government, which has no such representation. Therefore, to alter or withdraw the mandate at some future time would be well-nigh impossible.

Regarding the Treaty of London, the French and British Prime Ministers will appreciate that the American Government must hesitate to speak with assurance, since it is a matter in which the French and British Governments can alone judge their obligations and determine their policies. But the President feels that it is not improper to recall a few of the arguments which have already been advanced against this treaty, namely, the dissolution of Austria-Hungary, the secret character of the treaty, and its opposition to the principles unanimously accepted as the basis for making peace.

In addition he desires to submit certain further considerations. In the northern Italian frontier agreements have already been reached which depart from the Treaty of London line and which were made with the understanding that negotiations were proceeding on quite a new basis. It has been no secret that the parties to the treaty did not themselves now desire it and that they have thus far refrained from putting its provisions into effect. In mutually disregarding their secret treaty commitments the parties to the treaty have recognized the change in circumstances that has taken place in the interval between the signing of the secret treaty and its proposed execution at the present time. For nearly eight months discussion of the Adriatic problem has proceeded on the assumption that a better basis for an understanding could be found than those provided by the Treaty of London. The greater part of the resulting proposals have already received Italy's assent. These proposals in some cases affected territory beyond the Treaty of London line, as in the Tarvis and Sexton Valleys. In others, the territory fell short of the Treaty of London line, as in the case of the islands of Lussin, Unie, Lissa, and Pelagosa, to mention only a few of the many proposals upon which tentative agreements have long been reached and which would be upset by an application of the treaty at this late day.

The coupling of the Treaty of London as an obligatory alternative to the Adriatic settlement proposed on January 14 came as a surprise to the American Government, because this Government had already by the agreement of December 9 entered into a distinct understanding with the British and French Governments regarding the basis of a settlement of the question. By their action of January 14 the Government of the United States was confronted with a definite solution, to which was added on January 20 a threat to fall back upon the terms of the Treaty of London. This course was followed without any attempt to seek the views of this Government or to provide such opportunity of discussion as was easily arranged in many other matters dealt with in the same period.

The President notes that the memorandum of February 17 refers to the difficulty of reconciling ethnographic with other considerations in making territorial adjustments, and cites the inclusion of 3,000,000 Germans in Czechoslovakia and more than 3,000,000 Ruthenes in Poland, as examples of necessary modifications of ethnographic frontiers. He feels compelled to observe that this is a line of reasoning which the Italian representatives have advanced during the course of negotiations, but which the British and French have hitherto found themselves unable to accept. There were cases where for sufficient geographical and economic reasons slight deflections of the ethnographical frontier were sanctioned by the conference, and the American Government believes that if Italy would consent to apply the same principles in Istria and Dalmatia the Adriatic question would not exist.

The American Government heartily subscribes to the sentiments expressed by the Governments of Great Britain and France regarding Italy's participation in the war. It fully appreciates the vital consequences of her participation and is profoundly grateful for her heroic sacrifices. These sentiments have been repeatedly expressed by the American Government. But such considerations cannot be made the reason for unjust settlements which will be provocative of future wars. A course thus determined would be short-sighted and not in accord with the terrible sacrifices of the entire world, which can be justified and ennobled only by leading finally to settlements in keeping with the principles for which the war was fought.

The President asks that the Prime Ministers of France, Great Britain and Italy will read his determination in the Adriatic matter in the light of these principles and settlements, and will realize that, standing upon such a foundation of principle, he must of necessity maintain the position which he arrived at after months

of earnest consideration. He confidently counts upon
their coöperation in this effort on his part to maintain
for the allied and associated powers that direction of
affairs which was initiated by the victory over Germany
and the Peace Conference at Paris.

III

CABLEGRAM TO THE AMERICAN AMBASSADOR AT PARIS, SIGNED BY ACTING SECRETARY OF STATE FRANK L. POLK, REGARDING THE ADRIATIC SETTLEMENT, MARCH 4, 1920.

THE President desires to express his sincere and cordial interest in the response of the French and British Prime Ministers received on February 27. He notes with satisfaction their unaltered desire to reach "an equitable solution, in conformity alike with the principles of the Peace Conference and of the legitimate, though conflicting, aspirations of the Italian and Jugoslav peoples." He further welcomes their expressed intention, regarding certain essential points, "to urge upon the Governments interested that they should bring their desires into line with the American point of view."

The President is surprised, however, that they should find in the statement of his own willingness to leave to the joint agreement of Italy and Jugoslavia the settlement of "their common frontiers in the Fiume region" any ground for suggesting the withdrawal of the joint memorandum of December 9. In this he could not possibly join. The memorandum represents deliberate and disinterested judgment after months of earnest discussion. It constituted more than a mere exchange of views; it was a statement of principles and a recapitulation of the chief points upon which agreement had been reached. There was thus afforded a summary review of these points of agreement of the French, British, and American Governments, and the memorandum should remain, as it was intended to be, the basis of reference representing the combined opinion of these Governments.

In referring to the "common frontier in the Fiume

region," the President had in mind the express desire of the two interested Governments to abandon the project of the Free State of Fiume as defined in the memorandum of December 9. If, as he understands, the Government of Italy and the Government of the Serb-Croat-Slovene State prefer to abandon the so-called buffer State, containing an overwhelming majority of Jugoslavs, and desire to limit the proposed free State to the *corpus separatum* of Fiume, placing the sovereignty in the League of Nations, without either Italian or Jugoslav control, then the Government of the United States is prepared to accept this proposal and is willing, under such circumstances, to leave the determination of the common frontier to Italy and Jugoslavia.

In this connection the President desires to reiterate that he would gladly approve a mutual agreement between the Italian and Jugoslav Governments reached without prejudice to the territorial or other interests of any third nation. But Albanian questions should not be included in the proposed joint discussion of Italy and Jugoslavia, and the President must reaffirm that he cannot possibly approve any plan which assigns to Jugoslavia in the northern districts of Albania territorial compensation for what she is deprived of elsewhere. Concerning the economic outlets for Jugoslavia in the region of Scutari suggested in the note under reply, the President desires to refer to the memorandum of December 9 as making adequate provisions to meet the needs of Jugoslavia.

Regarding the character and applicability of the Treaty of London, the President is led to speak with less reserve on account of the frank observations of the French and British Prime Ministers. He is unable to find in the "exigencies of military strategy" sufficient warrant for exercising secrecy with a Government which was intimately associated with the signatories of the Treaty of London in the gigantic task of defending hu-

man freedom and which was being called upon for
unlimited assistance and for untold treasure. The
definite and well-accepted policy of the American Government throughout its participation in the deliberations
of the Peace Conference was that it did not consider
itself bound by secret treaties of which it had previously not known the existence. Where the provisions
of such treaties were just and reasonable, the United
States was willing to respect them. But the French and
British Prime Ministers will of course not expect the
Government of the United States to approve the execution of the terms of the Treaty of London, except in so
far as that Government may be convinced that those
terms are intrinsically just and are consistent with the
maintenance of peace and settled order in southeastern
Europe.

The absence of an American representative with
plenary power is to be regretted and may have been
a source of inconvenience, but the President can recall
several instances where decisions in the Supreme Council were delayed while the British and French representatives sought the views of their Governments, and he
is convinced that time would have been saved and many
misunderstandings avoided if, before actual decisions
had been reached and communicated to the Italian and
Jugoslav delegations, this Government had been given
sufficient indication of the fact that the British and
French Governments intended radically to depart from
the memorandum of December 9.

In conclusion the President desires to express his concurrence in the view of the British and French Prime
Ministers that a speedy settlement of the Adriatic question is of urgent importance. But he cannot accept as
just the implied suggestion of his responsibility for the
failure to reach a solution. He has merely adhered to
the provisions of a settlement which the French and
British Governments recognized as equitable in the joint
memorandum of December 9, and has declined to ap-

prove a new settlement negotiated without the knowledge or approval of the American Government, which was unacceptable to one of the interested Governments and which, in his opinion, was in direct contradiction of the principles for the defense of which America entered the war.

These views he has fully explained in his note of February 10, and he ventures to express the earnest hope that the allied Governments will not find it necessary to decide on a course which the American Government in accordance with its reiterated statement will be unable to follow.

STATUS OF AMERICAN FORCES IN GERMAN TERRITORY

MESSAGE TO THE HOUSE OF REPRESENTATIVES, MARCH 29, 1920. FROM THE "CONGRESSIONAL RECORD," VOL. 59, P. 5101.

TO THE SPEAKER OF THE HOUSE OF REP-
RESENTATIVES:

SIR:

I am in receipt of H. Res. 500, adopted March 25, 1920, which reads as follows:

> Resolved, That the President be, and he is hereby, requested, if not incompatible with the public interest, to inform the House of the exact status of the American military forces now stationed in German territory; the scope to which their operations are confined under the terms of the armistice between the allied nations, the Government of the United States, and Germany; the extent of the authority exercised over them by Field Marshal Ferdinand Foch, commander in chief of the allied forces in the occupied Rhine Provinces, and how far their activities may be directed without express orders from the President of the United States.

The American forces in Germany on March 26 were reported to comprise 726 officers and 16,756 enlisted men. These forces are stationed principally in the Coblenz area, the exact location of the units being set forth on the accompanying map. They are occupying that territory under the armistice agreements, which, with its annexes and conventions, was transmitted by me to the Senate and published as Senate Document 147, Sixty-sixth Congress, first session. The paragraph specifically covering this occupation is Paragraph V of the clauses relating to the western front.

The original armistice, signed on November 11, 1918, provided that its duration should be 36 days, with option to extend. On December 13, the armistice was extended until 5 A.M. on the 17th day of January, 1919; on January 16, 1919, it was still further extended until the 17th day of February, 1919, at 5 A.M.; on February 16, 1919, it was still further extended to a date not fixed: "the allied Powers and those associated with them reserving to themselves the right to terminate the period at three days' notice."

The American forces in Germany are at present operating under the terms of the original armistice and the subsequent conventions prolonging the armistice. The instructions proposed to be issued to the commanding general American forces in Germany, at the time of their occupying the Coblenz area, were submitted to the War Department by Gen. Pershing, and contained the following statement of policy:

The American forces will, however, undertake no action beyond the occupied regions, nor beyond that in strict accordance with the terms of the treaty. Any use of the American forces beyond that mentioned above must be specifically authorized in each case by the Government of the United States.

In reply, it was directed that—

It should be stated in the orders issued to the commanding general American forces in Germany that the function of the American forces in Germany at present is to enforce the conditions of the armistice, and that when a peace treaty shall have been ratified by the United States the function of the American forces will be as outlined.

Upon the ratification of the treaty of peace by the allied Powers, an Interallied Rhineland High Commission was organized in the manner set forth in the message from the President of the United States to the Senate, containing the agreement between the allied and associated Powers and Germany with regard to the military occupation of the territories of the Rhine. This document is published as Senate Document No. 81, Sixty-sixth Congress, first session.

This commission having been organized and having formulated ordinances for the zone of occupation, the question arose as to whether these ordinances should govern in the American sector, and the representatives of the State Department and the commanding general of the American forces in Germany were instructed as follows:

This Government cannot admit jurisdiction of that commission over portion of Rhinish Provinces occupied by the American forces. Consequently, neither you (representative of State Department) nor General Allen should issue any ordinances which conflict with or exceed the terms of the armistice, which the Department (of State) regards as continuing in force as to the United States. You should, however, maintain the closest touch with the high commission and endeavor in so far as possible to conform administrative régime within territory occupied by American forces to régime adopted by high commission for other portions of occupied territory. There is no objection to your sitting informally with high commission provided you are requested to do so, nor of continuing your activities, as well as those of your staff, in connection with special committees to handle distribution of coal, etc. Ordinances, orders, regulations, etc., relating to financial and economic matters, including those similar to ones adopted by high commission, which it is desired to put into force in territory occupied by American forces should be issued by General Allen as commanding general of American forces in Germany, but only after having first been approved by you. In general, endeavor to coöperate fully with high commission and avoid all friction with that body, while at the same time make it perfectly clear that you are still operating under the armistice as before January 10, and are in no way bound by the terms of the Rhineland agreement or the memorandum of June 13, 1919, defining the relations between the military authorities and the high commission.

Replying specifically to the remaining questions in the resolution of the House of Representatives, I will state that Field Marshal Ferdinand Foch has no authority over the United States troops in German territory, nor can anyone direct their activities without express orders from the President of the United States.

It should be stated further that under his general police powers, under the terms of the armistice, General Allen has full authority to utilize his troops for the police of the occupied district, the preservation of order, and to repel any attack which may be made upon him.

WOODROW WILSON.

LEAGUE OF NATIONS AS A CAMPAIGN ISSUE

TELEGRAM TO G. E. HAMAKER, CHAIRMAN OF THE MULTNOMAH COUNTY, OREGON, DEMOCRATIC CENTRAL COMMITTEE, MAY 9, 1920. FROM COPY SUPPLIED BY MR. HAMAKER.

I THINK it imperative that the party should at once proclaim itself the uncompromising champion of the Nation's honor and the advocate of everything that the United States can do in the service of humanity; that it should therefore endorse and support the Versailles Treaty and condemn the Lodge reservations as utterly inconsistent with the Nation's honor and destructive of the world's leadership which it had established and which all the free peoples of the world, including the great Powers themselves, had shown themselves ready to welcome. It is time that the party should proudly avow that it means to try, without flinching or turning at any time away from the path for reasons of expediency, to apply moral and Christian principles to the problems of the world. It is trying to accomplish social, political and internaitional reforms and is not daunted by any of the difficulties it has to contend with. Let us prove to our late associates in the war that at any rate the great majority party of the Nation, the party which expresses the true hope and purpose of the people of the country, intends to keep faith with them in peace as well as in war. They gave their treasures, their best blood, and everything that they valued in order not merely to beat Germany, but to effect a settlement and bring about arrangements of peace which they have now tried to formulate in the Treaty of Versailles. They are entitled to our support in this settlement and in the arrangement for which they have striven.

The League of Nations is the hope of the world. As a basis for the armistice I was authorized by all the great fighting nations to say to the enemy that it was our object in proposing peace to establish a general association of nations under specific covenants for the purpose of affording mutual guarantees of political independence and territorial integrity to great and small States alike, and the Covenant of the League of Nations is the deliberate embodiment of that purpose of the treaty of peace.

The chief motives which led us to enter the war will be defeated unless that Covenant is ratified and acted upon with vigor. We cannot in honor whittle it down or weaken it as the Republican leaders of the Senate have proposed to do. If we are to exercise the kind of leadership to which the founders of the Republic looked forward and which they depended upon their successors to establish, we must do this with courage and unalterable determination. They expected the United States to be always the leader in the defense of liberty and ordered peace throughout the world, and we are unworthy to call ourselves their successors unless we fulfill the great purpose they entertained and proclaimed.

The true Americanism, the only true Americanism, is that which puts America at the front of free nations and redeems the great promises which we made the world when we entered the war, which was fought, not for the advantage of any single nation or group of nations, but for the salvation of all. It is in this way we shall redeem the sacred blood that was shed and make America the force she should be in the counsels of mankind. She cannot afford to sink into the place that nations have usually occupied and become merely one of those who scramble and look about for selfish advantage. The Democratic party has a great opportunity, to which it must measure up. The honor of the Nation is in its hands.

WOODROW WILSON.

PROTEST AGAINST ANTHRACITE COAL STRIKE

Message to Representatives of Anthracite Coal
Operators and Miners,[1] May 21, 1920. From
Copy in Mr. Wilson's Files.

GENTLEMEN:

I have watched with more than passing interest
your efforts to negotiate a new wage scale for the
anthracite coal fields. The arrangement to continue
work at the mines after April 1, pending the adoption
of a new agreement, which you entered into when the
previous wage scale was about to expire, was highly
commendable and filled us all with hope that a new contract would be mutually worked out and the supply of
anthracite coal continued without interruption. I
sincerely trust that the hope will be fully realized.

I have, however, been advised that there is a possibility you may not come to an agreement. I am sure
I need not remind you that we have not yet recovered
from the economic losses incident to the war. We need
the fullest productivity of our people to restore and
maintain their own economic standards and to assist in
the rehabilitation of Europe. A strike at any time in a
great basic industry like anthracite coal mining would
be a very disturbing factor in our lives and industries.
To have one take place now while we are actively engaged in the problems of reconstruction would be a
serious disaster. Anthracite coal is used principally in
domestic consumption. Any shortage in the supply
would affect a multitude of homes that have been
specially equipped for the use of this kind of fuel. It

[1] The wage agreement between the anthracite coal miners and
operators had expired on April 1, 1920, and the representatives who
had met to consider the renewal of the agreement had been unable to
come to an understanding.

would have to be supplemented by the use of substitutes such as bituminous coal or oil, diverting these commodities from transportation and manufacturing industries which they now supply, using more cars because of the longer hauls and thereby reducing the efficiency of our transportation systems that are already burdened beyond their capacity. Such a condition must not occur if there is any way of avoiding it.

I am not familiar with the technical problems affecting the making of your wage scale. You are. You should therefore be able to effect an agreement. If for any reason you are unable to do so, I shall insist that the matters in dispute be submitted to the determination of a commission to be appointed by me, the award of the commission to be retroactive to the first of April in accordance with the arrangement you have already entered into, and that work be continued at the mines pending the decision of the commission. I shall hold myself in readiness to appoint a commission similarly constituted to the one which I recently appointed in connection with the bituminous coal mining industry as soon as I learn that both sides have signified their willingness to continue at work and abide by its decision.

Respectfully yours,

WOODROW WILSON

MANDATE OVER ARMENIA [1]

MESSAGE TO CONGRESS, MAY 24, 1920. FROM THE "CONGRESSIONAL RECORD," VOL. 59, PP. 7533-7534.

ON the 14th of May an official communication was received at the Executive Office from the Secretary of the Senate of the United States conveying the following preambles and resolutions: ..

Whereas the testimony adduced at the hearings conducted by the sub-committee of the Senate Committee on Foreign Relations has clearly established the truth of the reported massacres and other atrocities from which the Armenian people have suffered; and

Whereas the people of the United States are deeply impressed by the deplorable conditions of insecurity, starvation, and misery now prevalent in Armenia; and

Whereas the independence of the Republic of Armenia has been duly recognized by the Supreme Council of the Peace Conference and by the Government of the United States of America; therefore be it

Resolved, That the sincere congratulations of the Senate of the United States are hereby extended to the people of Armenia on the recognition of the independence of the Republic of Armenia, without prejudice respecting the territorial boundaries involved; and be it further

Resolved, That the Senate of the United States hereby expresses the hope that stable government, proper protection of individual liberties and rights, and the full realization of nationalistic aspirations may soon be attained by the Armenian people; and be it further

Resolved, That in order to afford necessary protection for the lives and property of citizens of the United States at the port of Batum and along the line of the railroad leading to Baku, the President is hereby requested, if not incompatible with the public interest, to cause a United States warship and a force of marines to be dispatched to such port with instructions to such marines to disembark and to protect American lives and property.

I received and read this document with great interest and with genuine gratification, not only because it em-

[1] On June 1, 1920, the Senate refused to grant the power requested.

487

bodied my own convictions and feelings with regard to Armenia and its people, but also, and more particularly, because it seemed to me the voice of the American people expressing their genuine convictions and deep Christian sympathies and intimating the line of duty which seemed to them to lie clearly before us.

I cannot but regard it as providential, and not as a mere casual coincidence that almost at the same time I received information that the conference of statesmen now sitting at San Remo for the purpose of working out the details of peace with the Central Powers which it was not feasible to work out in the conference at Paris, had formally resolved to address a definite appeal to this Government to accept a mandate for Armenia. They were at pains to add that they did this, "not from the smallest desire to evade any obligations which they might be expected to undertake but because the re-sponsibilities which they are already obliged to bear in connection with the disposition of the former Ottoman Empire will strain their capacities to the uttermost, and because they believe that the appearance on the scene of a power emancipated from the prepossessions of the Old World will inspire a wider confidence and afford a firmer guarantee for stability in the future than would the selection of any European power."

Early in the conferences at Paris it was agreed that to those colonies and territories which as a consequence of the late war have ceased to be under the sovereignty of the States which formerly governed them and which are inhabited by peoples not yet able to stand by them-selves under the strenuous conditions of the modern world there should be applied the principle that the well-being and development of such peoples form a sacred trust of civilization, and that securities for the performance of this trust should be afforded.

It was recognized that certain communities formerly belonging to the Turkish Empire have reached a stage of development where their existence as independent

nations can be provisionally recognized, subject to the
rendering of administrative advice and assistance by a
mandatory until such time as they are able to stand
alone.

It is in pursuance of this principle and with a desire
of affording Armenia such advice and assistance that the
statesmen conferring at San Remo have formally requested this Government to assume the duties of
mandatory in Armenia. I may add, for the information of the Congress, that at the same sitting it was resolved to request the President of the United States
to undertake to arbitrate the difficult question of the
boundary between Turkey and Armenia in the Vilayets
of Erzerum, Trebizond, Van, and Bitlis, and it was
agreed to accept his decision thereupon, as well as any
stipulation he may prescribe as to access to the sea
for the independent state of Armenia. In pursuance of
this action, it was resolved to embody in the treaty with
Turkey, now under final consideration, a provision that
"Turkey and Armenia and the other high contracting
parties agree to refer to the arbitration of the President
of the United States of America the question of the
boundary between Turkey and Armenia in the Vilayets
of Erzerum, Trebizond, Van, and Bitlis, and to accept
his decision thereupon as well as any stipulations he
may prescribe as to access to the sea for the independent
State of Armenia;" pending that decision the boundaries
of Turkey and Armenia to remain as at present. I
have thought it my duty to accept this difficult and
delicate task.

In response to the invitation of the Council at San
Remo, I urgently advise and request that the Congress
grant the Executive power to accept for the United
States a mandate over Armenia. I make this suggestion in the earnest belief that it will be the wish of the
people of the United States that this should be done.
The sympathy with Armenia has proceeded from no
single portion of our people, but has come with extra-

ordinary spontaneity and sincerity from the whole of the great body of Christian men and women in this country by whose free-will offerings Armenia has practically been saved at the most critical juncture of its existence. At their hearts this great and generous people have made the cause of Armenia their own. It is to this people and to their government that the hopes and earnest expectations of the struggling people of Armenia turn as they now emerge from a period of indescribable suffering and peril, and I hope that the Congress will think it wise to meet this hope and expectation with the utmost liberality. I know from unmistakable evidences given by responsible representatives of many peoples struggling towards independence and peaceful life again that the Government of the United States is looked to with extraordinary trust and confidence, and I believe that it would do nothing less than arrest the hopeful processes of civilization if we were to refuse the request to become the helpful friends and advisers of such of these people as we may be authoritatively and formally requested to guide and assist.

I am conscious that I am urging upon the Congress a very critical choice, but I make the suggestion in the confidence that I am speaking in the spirit and in accordance with the wishes of the greatest of the Christian peoples. The sympathy for Armenia among our people has sprung from untainted consciences, pure Christian faith, and an earnest desire to see Christian people everywhere succored in their time of suffering, and lifted from their abject subjection and distress and enabled to stand upon their feet and take their place among the free nations of the world. Our recognition of the independence of Armenia will mean genuine liberty and assured happiness for her people, if we fearlessly undertake the duties of guidance and assistance involved in the functions of a mandatory.

It is, therefore, with the most earnest hopefulness

and with the feeling that I am giving advice from which the Congress will not willingly turn away that I urge the acceptance of the invitation now formally and solemnly extended to us by the Council at San Remo, into whose hands has passed the difficult task of composing the many complexities and difficulties of government in the one-time Ottoman Empire and the maintenance of order and tolerable conditions of life in those portions of that Empire which it is no longer possible in the interest of civilization to leave under the government of the Turkish authorities themselves.

VETOING RESOLUTION FOR PEACE WITH CENTRAL EMPIRES

MESSAGE TO THE HOUSE OF REPRESENTATIVES, MAY 27, 1920. FROM 66TH CONGRESS, 2ND SESSION, HOUSE DOCUMENT 799.

I HEREWITH return, without my signature, House joint resolution 327, intended to repeal the joint resolution of April 6, 1917, declaring a state of war to exist between the United States and Germany, and the joint resolution of December 7, 1917, declaring a state of war to exist between the United States and the Austro-Hungarian Government, and to declare a state of peace. I have not felt at liberty to sign this joint resolution because I cannot bring myself to become party to an action which would place ineffaceable stain upon the gallantry and honor of the United States. The resolution seeks to establish peace with the German Empire without exacting from the German Government any action by way of setting right the infinite wrongs which it did to the peoples whom it attacked and whom we professed it our purpose to assist when we entered the war. Have we sacrificed the lives of more than 100,000 Americans and ruined the lives of thousands of others and brought upon thousands of American families an unhappiness that can never end for purposes which we do not now care to state or take further steps to attain? The attainment of these purposes is provided for in the Treaty of Versailles by terms deemed adequate by the leading statesmen and experts of all the great peoples who were associated in the war against Germany. Do we now not care to join in the effort to secure them?

We entered the war most reluctantly. Our people were profoundly disinclined to take part in a European

war, and at last did so only because they became convinced that it could not in truth be regarded as only a
European war, but must be regarded as a war in which
civilization itself was involved and human rights of
every kind as against a belligerent Government. Moreover, when we entered the war we set forth very definitely the purposes for which we entered, partly because
we did not wish to be considered as merely taking part
in a European contest. This joint resolution which I
return does not seek to accomplish any of these objects,
but in effect makes a complete surrender of the rights
of the United States so far as the German Government
is concerned. A treaty of peace was signed at Versailles
on the twenty-eighth of June last which did seek to
accomplish the objects which we had declared to be in
our minds, because all the great Governments and peoples which united against Germany had adopted our
declarations of purpose as their own and had in solemn
form embodied them in communications to the German
Government preliminary to the armistice of November 11, 1918. But the treaty as signed at Versailles
has been rejected by the Senate of the United States,
though it has been ratified by Germany. By that rejection and by its methods we have in effect declared that
we wish to draw apart and pursue objects and interests of our own, unhampered by any connections of
interest or of purpose with other Governments and
peoples.

Notwithstanding the fact that upon our entrance into
the war we professed to be seeking to assist in the maintenance of common interests, nothing is said in this resolution about the freedom of navigation upon the seas,
or the reduction of armaments, or the vindication of
the rights of Belgium, or the rectification of wrongs
done to France, or the release of the Christian populations of the Ottoman Empire from the intolerable subjugation which they have had for so many generations
to endure, or the establishment of an independent Polish

State, or the continued maintenance of any kind of understanding among the great powers of the world which would be calculated to prevent in the future such outrages as Germany attempted, and in part consummated. We have now in effect declared that we do not care to take any further risks or to assume any further responsibilities with regard to the freedom of nations or the sacredness of international obligation or the safety of independent peoples. Such a peace with Germany—a peace in which none of the essential interests which we had at heart when we entered the war is safeguarded—is, or ought to be, inconceivable, is inconsistent with the dignity of the United States, with the rights and liberties of her citizens, and with the very fundamental conditions of civilization.

I hope that in these statements I have sufficiently set forth the reasons why I have felt it incumbent upon me to withhold my signature.

CONDEMNING CONGRESS AS ACTUATED BY POLITICAL EXPEDIENCY

TELEGRAM TO RAILROAD UNION OFFICIALS,[1] JUNE 5, 1920. FROM THE NEW YORK "TIMES," JUNE 6, 1920.

I RECEIVED your telegram of June 3. You call my attention to matters that I presented to the present Congress in a special message delivered at a joint session of the two houses on August 8, 1919. In nine months this Congress has, however, taken no important remedial action with respect to the problem of the cost of living on the lines indicated in that address or on any other line. Not only has the present Congress failed to deal directly with the cost of living, but it has failed even to give serious consideration to the urgent appeal, oft repeated by me and by the Secretary of the Treasury, to revise the tax laws which in their present form are indirectly responsible in part for the high cost of living.

The protracted delay in dealing with the problem of the railroads, the problem of the Government-owned merchant marine and other similar urgent matters has resulted in unnecessary burdens upon the public treasury, and ultimately in legislation so unsatisfactory that I could accept it, if at all, only because I despaired of anything better.

The present Congress has not only prevented the conclusion of peace in Europe, but has failed to prevent any constructive plan for dealing with the deplorable conditions there, the continuance of which can only reflect upon us.

[1] This message was in answer to a telegram received from the heads of sixteen railroad unions, protesting against the adjournment of the 66th Congress without legislation for reducing the cost of living.

In the light of the record of the present Congress, I have no reason whatever to hope that its continuance in session would result in constructive measures for the relief of the economic conditions to which you call attention. It must be evident to all that the dominating motive which has actuated this Congress is political expediency rather than lofty purpose to serve the public welfare.

URGING TENNESSEE TO ACT ON WOMAN SUFFRAGE

TELEGRAM TO GOVERNOR A. H. ROBERTS OF TENNESSEE,[1] JUNE 23, 1920. FROM ORIGINAL COPY IN MR. WILSON'S FILES.

IT WOULD be a real service to the party and to the Nation if it is possible for you under the peculiar provisions of your State Constitution, having in mind the recent decision of the Supreme Court in the Ohio case, to call a special session of the Legislature of Tennessee to consider the suffrage amendment. Allow me to urge this very earnestly.

WOODROW WILSON.

[1] Prompt action was especially desired in this case, since thirty-five state legislatures had already ratified the suffrage amendment, and only one more was needed to enable women to vote in the coming presidential election. The legislature of Tennessee ratified the amendment on August 18.

INSISTING THAT STRIKING MINERS
RETURN TO WORK

STATEMENT TO THE MEMBERS OF THE UNITED MINE
WORKERS OF AMERICA,[1] JULY 30, 1920. FROM
ORIGINAL IN MR. WILSON'S FILES.

IT IS with a feeling of profound regret and sorrow
that I have learned that many of the members of
your organization, particularly in the State of Illinois,
have engaged in a strike in violation of the terms of
the award of the Bituminous Coal Commission and your
agreement with the Government that the findings of
the Commission would be accepted by you as final and
binding. I am distressed not only because your action
in refusing to mine coal upon the terms which you had
accepted may result in great suffering in many households during the coming winter and interfere with the
continuation of industrial and agricultural activity,
which is the basis of the prosperity which you in common with the balance of our people have been enjoying,
but also, and what is of far more importance to you,
because the violation of the terms of your solemn obligation impairs your own good name, destroys the confidence which is the basis of all mutual agreements, and
threatens the very foundation of fair industrial relations. No government, no employer, no person having
any reputation to protect can afford to enter into con-
tractual relations with any organization that repeatedly
or systematically violates its contracts.

The United Mine Workers of America is the largest
single labor organization in the United States, if not in
the world, but no organization can long endure that sets

[1] Bituminous coal miners in Illinois and Indiana. As a result of
this statement the men were instructed by their president to return to
work and soon afterward Mr. Wilson called a conference of operators
and miners to adjust the award of the Coal Commission.

up its own strength as being superior to its plighted faith or its duty to society at large. It has in the past built up an enviable reputation for abiding by its contracts, which has been one of its most valuable assets in making wage agreements. It may now make temporary gains by taking advantage of the dire necessities of the balance of the people through the violation of these contracts, but what of the future? How can it expect wage contracts with the employers to be continued, in the face of such violations, when normal conditions have been restored and the country is free from the fear of immediate shortage of coal? How will it be able to resist the claims of the operators in the future who take advantage of the precedent which the miners have established and decrease wage rates in the middle of a wage contract under the plea that they are unable to sell the coal at the then existing cost of production? A mere statement of these questions ought to be sufficient to awaken the mine workers to the dangerous course they are pursuing and the injuries they are inflicting upon themselves and the country at large by the adoption of these unwarranted strike policies.

In the consideration of the nation-wide wage scale involving many different classes of labor by the Bituminous Coal Commission in the limited time at its disposal some inequalities may have developed in the award that ought to be corrected. I cannot, however, recommend any consideration of such inequalities as long as the mine workers continue on strike in violation of the terms of the award which they had accepted as their wage agreement for a definite length of time. I must therefore insist that the striking mine workers return to work, thereby demonstrating their good faith in keeping their contract. When I have learned that they have thus returned to work, I will invite the scale committees of the operators and miners to reconvene for the purpose of adjusting any such inequalities as they may mutually agree should be adjusted.

INSISTING UPON ACCEPTANCE OF THE ANTHRACITE WAGE COMMISSION AWARD

TELEGRAM TO ANTHRACITE COAL MINERS, AUGUST 30, 1920. FROM ORIGINAL COPY IN MR. WILSON'S FILES.

REPLYING to your telegram of August 29, your attention is particularly directed to the following language contained in the minority report of Mr. Ferry of the Anthracite Coal Commission:

"In conclusion, Mr. President, we wish to say, as we did in the beginning, that the majority report shall have the full practical acceptance of the officers of the United Mine Workers of America, and we shall devote ourselves to its application, as we obligated ourselves to do when we submitted our cause to this commission."

That was the manly and honest thing for Mr. Ferry to do. He courageously sets forth his views in the minority report and then just as courageously declares he will abide by the decision of the majority, as the miners had obligated themselves to do.

It should be understood that there was no agreement between the operators and miners to have me decide the questions at issue. With the many other important duties devolving upon me, I could not have devoted the time necessary to hear and digest all of the evidence presented. I therefore proposed the creation of a commission whose findings would be binding upon both parties. The representatives of the miners on the Scale Committee declined to accepted the suggestion until it had been submitted to a convention of the United Mine Workers of Districts One, Seven, and Nine. In that convention, by a vote of the men direct from the mines, a resolution was adopted accepting the proposition and solemnly obligating the mine workers to abide by the award.

By all the laws of honor upon which civilization rests that pledge should be fulfilled. Any intimation that the anthracite mine workers will refuse to work under the award because it does not grant them all that they expected is a reflection upon the sincerity of the men who constitute the backbone of the community in which they live. Collective bargaining would soon cease to exist in industrial affairs if contracts solemnly entered into can be set aside by either party whenever it wills to do so. I am sure that the miners themselves would vigorously protest against the injustice of the act if the President attempted to set aside the award of the commission because the operators had protested against it.

May I add that I am personally and officially interested in promoting the welfare of every man who has to work for a living. Every influence my Administration has been able to exert has been exercised to improve the standards of living of the Nation's working men and women without doing any injustice to other portions of our people.

A large part of the domestic fuel supply of the eastern States is dependent upon the continued operation of the anthracite coal mines. Any prolonged stoppage of production will mean hardship and suffering to many people including millions of wage workers and their families.

Yet if your communication, declaring your intention to refrain from working unless I set aside the award of the Anthracite Coal Commission on or before September 1, 1920, is intended as a threat you can rest assured that your challenge will be accepted and that the people of the United States will find some substitute fuel to tide them over until the real sentiment of the anthracite mine workers can find expression and they are ready to abide by the obligations they have entered into.

You are therefore advised that I cannot and will not set aside the judgment of the Commission, and I shall expect the anthracite mine workers to accept the award and carry it into effect in good faith.

WOODROW WILSON.

NATIONAL REFERENDUM ON THE LEAGUE OF NATIONS

AN APPEAL TO THE COUNTRY TO MAKE THE PRESIDEN-
TIAL ELECTION AN EXPRESSION OF THE NATION'S
OPINION ON THE LEAGUE OF NATIONS, OCTOBER
3, 1920. FROM THE NEW YORK "TIMES," OCTOBER
4, 1920.

THE issues of the present campaign are of such tremendous importance, of such far-reaching significance for the influence of the country and the development of its future relations, and I have necessarily had
so much to do with their development, that I am sure
you will think it natural and proper that I should address
to you a few words concerning them.

Every one who sincerely believes in government by
the people must rejoice at the turn affairs have taken
in regard to this campaign. This election is to be a
genuine national referendum. The determination of a
great policy upon which the influence and authority of
the United States in the world must depend is not to
be left to groups of politicians of either party, but is to
be referred to the people themselves for a sovereign
mandate to their representatives. They are to instruct
their own Government what they wish done.

The chief question that is put to you is, of course:
Do you want your country's honor vindicated and the
Treaty of Versailles ratified? Do you in particular
approve of the League of Nations as organized and
empowered in that treaty? And do you wish to see the
United States play its responsible part in it?

You have been grossly misled with regard to the
treaty, and particularly with regard to the proposed
character of the League of Nations, by those who have
assumed the serious responsibility of opposing it. They

have gone so far that those who have spent their lives, as I have spent my life, in familiarizing themselves with the history and traditions and policies of the Nation, must stand amazed at the gross ignorance and impudent audacity which have led them to attempt to invent an "Americanism" of their own, which has no foundation whatever in any of the authentic traditions of the Government.

Americanism, as they conceive it, reverses the whole process of the last few tragical years. It would substitute America for Prussia in the policy of isolation and defiant segregation. Their conception of the dignity of the Nation and its interest is that we should stand apart and watch for opportunities to advance our own interests, involve ourselves in no responsibility for the maintenance of the right in the world or for the continued vindication of any of the things for which we entered the war to fight.

The conception of the great creators of the Government was absolutely opposite to this. They thought of America as the light of the world as created to lead the world in the assertion of the rights of peoples and the rights of free nations; as destined to set a responsible example to all the world of what free Government is and can do for the maintenance of right standards, both national and international.

This light the opponents of the League would quench. They would relegate the United States to a subordinate rôle in the affairs of the world.

Why should we be afraid of responsibilities which we are qualified to sustain and which the whole of our history has constituted a promise to the world we would sustain!

This is the most momentous issue that has ever been presented to the people of the United States, and I do not doubt that the hope of the whole world will be verified by an absolute assertion by the voters of the country of the determination of the United States to live up to all the great expectations which they created by entering the war and enabling the other great nations of the world to bring it to a victorious conclusion, to the confusion of Prussianism and everything that arises out of Prussianism. Surely we shall not fail to keep the promise sealed in the death and sacrifice of our incomparable soldiers, sailors and marines who await our verdict beneath the sod of France.

Those who do not care to tell you the truth about the League of Nations tell you that Article X of the Covenant of the League would make it possible for other nations to lead us into war, whether we will it by our own independent judgment or not. This is absolutely false. There is nothing in the Covenant which in the least interferes with or impairs the rights of Congress to declare war or not declare war, according to its own independent judgment, as our Constitution provides.

Those who drew the Covenant of the League were careful that it should contain nothing which interfered with or impaired the constitutional arrangements of any of the great nations which are to constitute its members. They would have been amazed and indignant at the things that are now being ignorantly said about this great and sincere document.

The whole world will wait for your verdict in November as it would wait for an intimation of what its future is to be.

TO PRO-LEAGUE REPUBLICANS

ADDRESS TO FIFTEEN PRO-LEAGUE REPUBLICANS AT THE
WHITE HOUSE,[1] OCTOBER 27, 1920. FROM THE
NEW YORK "TIMES," OCTOBER 28, 1920.

IT IS to be feared that the supreme issue presented for
your consideration in the present campaign is growing more obscure rather than clearer by reason of the
many arbitrary turns the discussion of it has taken.
The editors and publishers of the country would render
a great service if they would publish the full text of the
Covenant of the League of Nations, because, having
read that text, you would be able to judge for yourselves a great many things in which you are now in
danger of being misled. I hope sincerely that it will be
very widely and generally published entire. It is with
a desire to reclarify the issue and to assist your judgment that I take the liberty of stating again the case
submitted to you in as simple terms as possible.

Three years ago it was my duty to summon you to
the concert of war, to join the free nations of the world
in meeting and ending the most sinister peril that had
ever been developed in the irresponsible politics of the
Old World. Your response to that call really settled
the fortunes of war. You will remember that the
morale of the German people broke down long before
the strength of the German armies was broken. That
was obviously because they felt that a great moral force,
which they could not look in the face, had come into the
contest, and that thenceforth all their professions of
right were discredited and they were unable to pretend
that their continuation of the war was not the support

---

[1] This was the first formal address made by the President for over
a year. He received this small group of Republican men and women
while sitting in his invalid chair.

of a Government that had violated every principle of right and every consideration of humanity.

It is my privilege to summon you now to the concert of peace and the completion of the great moral achievement on your part which the war represented, and in the presence of which the world found a reassurance and a recovery of force which it could have experienced in no other way.

We entered the war, as you remember, not merely to beat Germany, but to end the possibility of the renewal of such iniquitous schemes as Germany entertained. The war will have been fought in vain and our immense sacrifices thrown away unless we complete the work we then began, and I ask you to consider that there is only one way to assure the world of peace; that is by making it so dangerous to break the peace that no other nation will have the audacity to attempt it.

We should not be deceived into supposing that imperialistic schemes ended with the defeat of Germany, or that Germany is the only nation that entertained such schemes or was moved by sinister ambitions and long-standing jealousies to attack the very structure of civilization. There are other nations, which are likely to be powerfully moved or are already moved by commercial jealousy, by the desire to dominate and to have their own way in politics and in enterprise, and it is necessary to check them and to apprise them that the world will be united against them as it was against Germany if they attempt any similar thing.

The mothers and sisters and wives of the country know the sacrifice of war. They will feel that we have misled them and compelled them to make an entirely unnecessary sacrifice of their beloved ones if we do not make it as certain as it can be made that no similar sacrifice will be demanded of mothers and sisters and wives in the future. This duty is so plain that it seems to me to constitute a primary demand upon the conscience of every one of us.

It is inconceivable to most of us that any men should have been so false or so heartless as to declare that the women of the country would again have to suffer the intolerable burden and privation of war if the League of Nations were adopted.

The League of Nations is the well-considered effort of the whole group of nations who were opposed to Germany to secure themselves and the rest of mankind against the repetition of the war. It will have back of it the watchfulness and material force of all these nations and is such a guarantee of a peaceful future as no well-informed man can question who does not doubt the whole spirit with which the war was conducted against Germany.

The great moral influence of the United States will be absolutely thrown away if we do not complete the task which our soldiers and sailors so heroically undertook to execute.

One thing ought to be said and said very clearly, about Article X of the Covenant of the League of Nations. It is the specific pledge of the members of the League that they will unite to resist exactly the things which Germany attempted, no matter who attempts them in the future. It is as exact a definition as could be given in general terms of the outrage which Germany would have committed if it could.

Germany violated the territorial integrity of her neighbors and flouted their political independence in order to aggrandize herself, and almost every war of history has originated in such designs. It is significant that the nations of the world should have at last combined to define the general cause of war and to exercise such concert as may be necessary to prevent such methods.

Article X, therefore, is the specific redemption of the pledge which the free Governments of the world gave to their people when they entered the war. They promised their people not only that Germany would be prevented from carrying out her plot, but that the world would be safeguarded in the future from similar designs.

We have now to choose whether we will make good or quit. We have joined issue, and the issue is between the spirit and purpose of the United States and the spirit and purpose of imperialism, no matter where it shows itself. The spirit of imperialism is absolutely opposed to free government, to the safe life of free nations, to the development of peaceful industry, and to the completion of the righteous processes of civilization. It seems to me, and I think it will seem to you, that it is our duty to show the indomitable will and irresistible majesty of the high purpose of the United States, so that the part we played in the war as soldiers and sailors may be crowned with the achievement of lasting peace.

No one who opposes the ratification of the Treaty of Versailles and the adoption of the Covenant of the League of Nations has proposed any other adequate means of bringing about settled peace. There is no other available or possible means, and this means is ready to hand. They have, on the contrary, tried to persuade you that the very pledge contained in Article X, which is the essential pledge of the whole plan of security, is itself a threat of war. It is, on the contrary, an assurance of the concert of all the free peoples of the world in the future, as in the recent past, to see justice done and humanity protected and vindicated.

·This is the true, the real Americanism. This is the rôle of leadership and championship of the right which the leaders of the Republic intended that it should play. The so-called Americanism which we hear so much prating about now is spurious and invented for party purposes only.

This choice is the supreme choice of the present campaign. It is regrettable that this choice should be associated with a party contest. As compared with the choice of a course of action that now underlies every other, the fate of parties is a matter of indifference. Parties are significant now in this contest only because the voters must make up their minds which of the two parties is most likely to secure the indispensable result.

The Nation was never called upon to make a more solemn determination than it must now make. The whole future moral force of right in the world depends upon the United States rather than upon any other nation, and it would be pitiful, indeed, if, after so many great free peoples had entered the great League, we should hold aloof.

I suggest that the candidacy of every candidate for whatever office be tested by this question: Shall we, or shall we not, redeem the great moral obligations of the United States?

MEDIATION IN ARMENIA

CABLEGRAM TO M. PAUL HYMANS, PRESIDENT OF THE
COUNCIL OF THE LEAGUE OF NATIONS, NOVEMBER
30, 1920. FROM COPY IN MR. WILSON'S FILES.

I HAVE the honor to acknowledge the receipt of your cabled message setting forth the resolution adopted by the assembly of the League of Nations requesting the council of the League to arrive at an understanding with the Governments with a view to intrusting a power with the task of taking necessary measures to stop the hostilities in Armenia.

You offered to the United States the opportunity of undertaking the humanitarian task of using its good offices to end the present tragedy being enacted in Armenia, and you assure me that your proposal involves no repetition of the invitation to accept a mandate for Armenia.

While the invitation to accept a mandate for Armenia has been rejected by the Senate of the United States, this country has repeatedly declared its solicitude for the fate and welfare of the Armenian people in a manner and to an extent that justifies you in saying that the fate of Armenia has always been of special interest to the American people.

I am without authorization to offer or employ military forces of the United States in any project for the relief of Armenia, and any material contributions would require the authorization of the Congress, which is not now in session, and whose action I could not forecast.

I am willing, however, upon assurances of the moral and diplomatic support of the principal powers and in a spirit of sympathetic response to the request of the council of the League of Nations to use my good offices and to proffer my personal mediation through a representative whom I may designate to end the hostilities now being waged against the Armenian people and to bring peace and accord to the contending parties, relying upon the council of the League of Nations to suggest to me the avenues through which my proffer should be conveyed and the parties to whom it should be addressed.

WOODROW WILSON.

ANNUAL MESSAGE

MESSAGE TO THE TWO HOUSES OF CONGRESS AT THE BE-
GINNING OF THE THIRD SESSION OF THE SIXTY-
SIXTH CONGRESS, DECEMBER 7, 1920. FROM OFFI-
CIAL GOVERNMENT PUBLICATION IN MR. WILSON'S
FILES.

WHEN I addressed myself to performing the duty laid upon the President by the Constitution to present to you an annual report on the state of the Union, I found my thought dominated by an immortal sentence of Abraham Lincoln's,

Let us have faith that right makes might, and in that faith let us dare to do our duty as we understand it,—

a sentence immortal because it embodies in a form of utter simplicity and purity the essential faith of the Nation, the faith in which it was conceived and the faith in which it has grown to glory and power. With that faith and the birth of a nation founded upon it came the hope into the world that a new order would prevail throughout the affairs of mankind, an order in which reason and right would take precedence of covetousness and force, and I believe that I express the wish and purpose of every thoughtful American when I say that this sentence marks for us in the plainest manner the part we should play alike in the arrangement of our domestic affairs and in our exercise of influence upon the affairs of the world. By this faith, and by this faith alone, can the world be lifted out of its present confusion and despair. It was this faith which prevailed over the wicked force of Germany. You will remember that the beginning of the end of the war came when the German people found themselves face to face with the conscience of the world and realized that right was everywhere arrayed against the wrong that their gov-

ernment was attempting to perpetrate. I think, therefore, that it is true to say that this was the faith which
won the war. Certainly this is the faith with which our
gallant men went into the field and out upon the seas
to make sure of victory.

This is the mission upon which democracy came into
the world. Democracy is an assertion of the right of
the individual to live and to be treated justly as against
any attempt on the part of any combination of individuals to make laws which will overburden him or which
will destroy his equality among his fellows in the matter
of right or privilege, and I think we all realize that the
day has come when democracy is being put upon its
final test. The old world is just now suffering from a
wanton rejection of the principle of democracy and a
substitution of the principle of autocracy as asserted in
the name but without the authority and sanction of the
multitude. This is the time of all others when democracy should prove its purity and its spiritual power to
prevail. It is surely the manifest destiny of the United
States to lead in the attempt to make this spirit prevail.

There are two ways in which the United States can
assist to accomplish this great object: First, by offering
the example within her own borders of the will and
power of democracy to make and enforce laws which
are unquestionably just and which are equal in their
administration,—laws which secure its full right to
labor and yet at the same time safeguard the integrity of
property, and particularly of that property which is devoted to the development of industry and the increase
of the necessary wealth of the world. Second, by standing for right and justice as towards individual nations.
The law of democracy is for the protection of the weak,
and the influence of every democracy in the world should
be for the protection of the weak nation, the nation
which is struggling towards its right and towards its
proper recognition and privilege in the family of nations.
The United States cannot refuse this rôle of champion

without putting the stigma of rejection upon the great and devoted men who brought its government into existence and established it in the face of almost universal opposition and intrigue, even in the face of wanton force, as, for example, against the Orders in Council of Great Britain and the arbitrary Napoleonic Decrees which involved us in what we know as the War of 1812. I urge you to consider that the display of an immediate disposition on the part of the Congress to remedy any injustices or evils that may have shown themselves in our own national life will afford the most effectual offset to the forces of chaos and tyranny which are playing so disastrous a part in the fortunes of the free peoples of more than one part of the world. The United States is of necessity the sample democracy of the world, and the triumph of democracy depends upon its success.

Recovery from the disturbing and sometimes disastrous effects of the late war has been exceedingly slow on the other side of the water and has given promise, I venture to say, of early completion only in our own fortunate country; but even with us the recovery halts and is impeded at times and there are immediately serviceable acts of legislation which it seems to me we ought to attempt, to assist that recovery and prove the indestructible recuperative force of a great government of the people. One of these is to prove that a great democracy can keep house as successfully and in as business-like a fashion as any other government. It seems to me that the first step towards proving this is to supply ourselves with a systematic method of handling our estimates and expenditures and bringing them to the point where they will not be an unnecessary strain upon our income or necessitate unreasonable taxation, in other words, a workable budget system, and I respectfully suggest that two elements are essential to such a system; namely, not only that the proposal of appropriations should be in the hands of a single body, such as a single appropriations committee in each house of the Congress, but also that this body should be brought into such coöperation with the departments of the Government and with the Treasury of the United States as would enable it to act upon a complete conspectus of the needs of the Government and the resources from which it must draw its income. I reluctantly vetoed the Budget Bill passed by the last session of the Congress because of a Constitutional objection. The house of Representatives subsequently modified the Bill in order to meet this objection. In the revised form I believe that the Bill, coupled with action already taken by the Congress to revise its rules and procedure, furnishes the foundations for an effective national budget system. I earnestly hope, therefore, that one of the first steps taken by the present session of the Congress will be to pass the Budget Bill.

The nation's finances have shown marked improvement during the past year. The total ordinary receipts of $6,694,000,000 for the fiscal year 1920 exceeded those for 1919 by $1,542,000,000, while the total net ordinary expenditures decreased from $18,514,000,000 to $6,403,000,000. The gross public debt, which reached its highest point on August 31, 1919, when it was $26,596,000,000, had dropped on November 30, 1920, to $24,175,000,000. There has also been a marked decrease in holdings of Government war securities by the banking institutions of the country, as well as in the amount of bills held by the Federal Reserve Banks secured by Government war obligations. This fortunate result has relieved the banks and left them freer to finance the needs of agriculture, industry, and commerce. It has been due in large part to the reduction of the public debt, especially of the floating debt, but more particularly to the improved distribution of government securities among permanent investors. The cessation of the Government's borrowings except through short-term certificates of indebtedness has been a matter of great consequence to the people of the country at large, as well as to the holders of Liberty bonds and Victory notes, and has had an important bearing on the matter of effective credit control. The year has been characterized by the progressive withdrawal of the Treasury from the domestic credit market and from a position of dominant influence in that market. The future course will necessarily depend upon the extent to which economies are practiced and upon the burdens placed upon the Treasury, as well as upon industrial developments and the maintenance of tax receipts at a sufficiently high level.

The fundamental fact which at present dominates the Government's financial situation is that seven and a half billions of its war indebtedness mature within the next two and a half years. Of this amount, two and a half billions are floating debt and five billions Victory notes and War Savings certificates. The fiscal program of the Government must be determined with reference to these maturities. Sound policy demands that Government expenditures be reduced to the lowest amount which will permit the various services to operate efficiently and that Government receipts from taxes and salvage be maintained sufficiently high to provide for current requirements, including interest and sinking fund charges on the public debt, and at the same time retire the floating debt and part of the Victory Loan before maturity. With rigid economy, vigorous salvage operations and adequate revenues from taxation, a surplus of current receipts over current expenditures can be realized and should be applied to the floating debt. All branches of the Government should coöperate to see that this program is realized.

I cannot overemphasize the necessity of economy in Government appropriations and expenditures and the avoidance by the Congress of practices which take money from the Treasury by indefinite or revolving fund appropriations. The estimates for the present year show that over a billion dollars of expenditures were authorized by the last Congress in addition to the amounts shown in the usual compiled statements of appropriations. This strikingly illustrates the importance of making direct and specific appropriations. The relation between the current receipts and current expenditures of the Government during the present fiscal year, as well as during the last half of the last fiscal year, has been disturbed by the extraordinary burdens thrown upon the Treasury by the Transportation Act, in connection with the return of the railroads to private control. Over $600,000,000 has already been paid to the railroads under this Act,—$350,000,000 during the present fiscal year; and it is estimated that further payments aggregating possibly $650,000,000 must still be made to the railroads during the current year. It is obvious that these large payments have already seriously limited the Government's progress in retiring the floating debt.

Closely connected with this, it seems to me, is the necessity for an immediate consideration of the revision of our tax laws. Simplification of the income and profits taxes has become an immediate necessity. These taxes performed an indispensable service during the war. The need for their simplification, however, is very great, in order to save the taxpayer inconvenience and expense and in order to make his liability more certain and definite. Other and more detailed recommendations with regard to taxes will no doubt be laid before you by the Secretary of the Treasury and the Commissioner of Internal Revenue.

It is my privilege to draw to the attention of Congress for very sympathetic consideration the problem of providing adequate facilities for the care and treatment of former members of the military and naval forces who are sick or disabled as the result of their participation in the war. These heroic men can never be paid in money for the service they patriotically rendered the nation. Their reward will lie rather in realization of the fact that they vindicated the rights of their country and aided in safeguarding civilization. The nation's gratitude must be effectively revealed to them by the most ample provision for their medical care and treatment as well as for their vocational training and placement. The time has come when a more complete program can be formulated and more satisfactorily administered for their treatment and training, and I earnestly urge that the Congress give the matter its early consideration. The Secretary of the Treasury and the Board for Vocational Education will outline in their annual reports proposals covering medical care and rehabilitation which I am sure will engage your earnest study and command your most generous support.

Permit me to emphasize once more the need for action upon certain matters upon which I dwelt at some length in my message to the second session of the Sixty-sixth Congress: the necessity, for example, of encouraging the manufacture of dyestuffs and related chemicals; the importance of doing everything possible to promote agricultural production along economic lines, to improve agricultural marketing and to make rural life more attractive and healthful; the need for a law regulating cold storage in such a way as to limit the time during which goods may be kept in storage, prescribing the method of disposing of them if kept beyond the permitted period, and requiring goods released from storage in all cases to bear the date of their receipt. It would also be most serviceable if it were provided that all goods released from cold storage for interstate shipment should have plainly marked upon each package the selling or market price at which they went into storage, in order that the purchaser might be able to learn what profits stood between him and the producer or the wholesale dealer. Indeed, it would be very serviceable to the public if all goods destined for interstate commerce were made to carry upon every packing case whose form made it possible a plain statement of the price at which they left the hands of the producer. I respectfully call your attention, also, to the recommendations of the message referred to with regard to a federal license for all corporations engaged in interstate commerce.

In brief, the immediate legislative need of the time is the removal of all obstacles to the realization of the best ambitions of our people in their several classes of employment and the strengthening of all instrumentalities by which difficulties are to be met and removed and justice dealt out, whether by law or by some form of mediation and conciliation. I do not feel it to be my privilege at present to suggest the detailed and particular methods by which these objects may be attained, but I have faith that the inquiries of your several committees will discover the way and the method.

In response to what I believe to be the impulse of sympathy and opinion throughout the United States, I earnestly suggest that the Congress authorize the Treasury of the United States to make to the struggling Government of Armenia such a loan as was made to several of the Allied Governments during the war; and I would also suggest that it would be desirable to provide in the legislation itself that the expenditure of the money thus loaned should be under the supervision of a commission, or at least a commissioner, from the United States, in order that revolutionary tendencies within Armenia itself might not be afforded by the loan a further tempting opportunity.

Allow me to call your attention to the fact that the people of the Philippine Islands have succeeded in maintaining a stable government since the last action of the Congress in their behalf, and have thus fulfilled the condition set by the Congress as precedent to a consideration of granting independence to the Islands. I respectfully submit that this condition precedent having been fulfilled, it is now our liberty and our duty to keep our promise to the people of those Islands by granting them the independence which they so honorably covet.

I have not so much laid before you a series of recommendations, gentlemen, as sought to utter a confession of faith, of the faith in which I was bred and which it is my solemn purpose to stand by until my last fighting day. I believe this to be the faith of America, the faith of the future, and of all the victories which await national action in the days to come, whether in America or elsewhere.

VETO OF CHANGES IN CLAYTON ACT

VETO MESSAGE ACCOMPANYING SENATE BILL 4526, DECEMBER 30, 1920. FROM ORIGINAL COPY IN MR. WILSON'S FILES.

I RETURN herewith without my signature Senate bill No. 4526, amending Section 501 of the Transportation Act, by extending the effective date of Section 10 of the Clayton Act.

The Clayton Anti-Trust Act was responsive to recommendations which I made to the Congress on December 2, 1913, and January 20, 1914, on the subject of legislation regarding the very difficult and intricate matter of trusts and monopolies. In speaking of the changes which opinion deliberately sanctions and for which business waits I observed:

"It waits with acquiescence, in the first place, for laws which will effectually prohibit and prevent such interlockings of the *personnel* of the directorates of great corporations—banks and railroads, industrial, commercial and public service bodies—as in effect result in making those who borrow and those who lend practically one and the same, those who sell and those who buy but the same persons trading with one another under different names and in different combinations, and those who affect to compete in fact partners and masters of some whole field of business. Sufficient time should be allowed, of course, in which to effect these changes of organization, without inconvenience or confusion."

This particular recommendation is reflected in Section 10 of the Clayton Anti-Trust Act. That Act became law on October 15, 1914, and it was provided that Section 10 should not become effective until two years after that date, in order that the carriers and others affected might be able to adjust their affairs so that no inconvenience or confusion might result from the enforcement of its provisions. Further extensions of time, amounting in all to more than four years and two months, have since been made. These were in part due to the intervention of Federal control, but ten months have now elapsed since the resumption of private operation. In all, over six years have elapsed since this enactment was put upon the statute book, so that all interests concerned have had long and ample notice of the obligations it imposes.

The Interstate Commerce Commission has adopted rules responsive to the requirements of Section 10. In deferring the effective date of Section 10, the Congress has excepted corporations organized after January 12, 1918, and as to such corporations the commission's rules are now in effect. Therefore, it appears that the necessary preliminary steps have long since been taken to put Section 10 into effect, and the practical question now to be decided is whether the partial application of those rules shall be continued until January 1, 1922, or whether their application shall now become general, thus bringing under them all common carriers engaged in commerce and at last giving full effect to this important feature of the Act of October 15, 1914.

The grounds upon which further extension of time is asked, in addition to the six years and more that have already elapsed, have been stated as follows:

"That the carrying into effect of the existing provisions of Section 10 will result in needless expenditures on the part of carriers in many instances; that some of its provisions are unworkable, and that the changed status of the carriers and the enactment of the Transportation Act require a revision of Section 10, in order to make it consistent with provisions of the Transportation Act."

When it is considered that the Congress is now in session and can readily adopt suitable amendments if they shall be found to be necessary, such reasons for further delay appear to me to be inadequate. The soundness of the principle embodied in Section 10 appears to be generally admitted. The wholesome effects which its application was intended to produce should no longer be withheld from the public and from the common carriers immediately concerned, for whose protection it was particularly designed.

REFUSING TO SUBMIT RAILWAY LABOR PROBLEMS TO CONGRESS

TELEGRAM TO THE CHAIRMAN OF THE ASSOCIATION OF RAILWAY EXECUTIVES AND TO THE OFFICERS OF TWO RAILWAY UNIONS, FEBRUARY 6, 1921. FROM ORIGINAL COPY IN MR. WILSON'S FILES.

I HAVE carefully considered the several telegrams addressed to me dealing with the labor questions and railroad management now under consideration by the Railroad Labor Board in Chicago.

The Transportation Act approved February 28, 1920, to a greater extent than any previous legislation places all questions dealing with finances and railroad management and necessary rates under the jurisdiction of the Interstate Commerce Commission; hence all questions involving the expense of operation, the necessities of the railroads and the amount of money necessary to secure the successful operation thereof are now under the jurisdiction of the commission.

At the same time the act placed all questions of dispute between carriers and their employees and subordinate officials under the jurisdiction of the Railroad Labor Board, now sitting in Chicago. This board is composed of three members constituting the labor group, representing the employees and subordinate officials of the carriers; three members constituting the management group, representing the carriers; and three members constituting the public group, representing the public. So far as I am advised, the board may be relied on to give careful and intelligent consideration to all questions within its jurisdiction. To seek to influence either of these bodies upon anything which has been placed within their jurisdiction by Congress would be unwise and open to grave objection.

It would be manifestly unwise for me, therefore, to take any action which would interfere with the orderly procedure of the Interstate Commerce Commission or of the Railroad Labor Board; and all the matters mentioned in your telegrams are within the jurisdiction of one or the other of these bodies; and in their action I think we may repose entire confidence.

In view of the foregoing, it does not seem wise to comply with your suggestion that the matter be submitted to the Congress, and the only action deemed necessary is to submit copies of the telegrams received from you and from the representatives of the railroad executives to the Interstate Commerce Commission and to the Railroad Labor Board for such action as these bodies may deem wise in the premises. This will be done.

WOODROW WILSON.

THE BELGIAN DEBT

MESSAGE TO CONGRESS, FEBRUARY 22, 1921. FROM THE "CONGRESSIONAL RECORD," VOL. 60, P. 3598.

I HEREWITH call your attention to an agreement with Belgium made by the British and French premiers and myself, which is embodied in the following letter:

June 16, 1919.

M. HYMANS,
  Ministre des Affaires Etrangeres, Hotel Lotti, Paris.

SIR: The Reparation Clauses of the draft Treaty of Peace with Germany obligate Germany to make reimbursement of all sums which Belgium has borrowed from the Allied and Associated Governments up to November 11, 1918, on account of the violation by Germany of the Treaty of 1839. As evidence of such an obligation Germany is to make a special issue of bonds to be delivered to the Reparation Commission.

Each of the undersigned will recommend to the appropriate governmental agency of his Government that upon the delivery to the Reparation Commission of such bonds his Government accept an amount thereof corresponding to the sums which Belgium has borrowed from his Government since the war and up to November 11, 1918, together with interest at 5 per cent unless already included in such sums, in satisfaction of Belgium's obligation on account of such loans, which obligation of Belgium's shall thereupon be canceled.

We are, dear Mr. Minister,

Very truly yours,
G. CLEMENCEAU.
WOODROW WILSON.
D. LLOYD-GEORGE.

In recommending to you that Congress take appropriate action with regard to this agreement, certain facts should be brought to your attention.

The neutrality of Belgium was guaranteed by the Treaty of London of 1839. In considering the reparation to be made by Germany it was agreed that the action of Germany in grossly violating this treaty by an attack on Belgium, obligated the German Government under international law to repay to Belgium the costs of war. On this principle the Treaty of Versailles (Art. 232) provided that in accordance with Germany's pledges already given as to the complete restoration for Belgium, Germany should undertake, in addition to the compensation for material damage, to make reimbursement of all sums which Belgium had borrowed from the Allied and Associated Governments up to November 11, 1918, together with interest at five per cent per annum on such sums. This obligation was to be discharged by a special issue of bearer bonds to an equivalent amount payable in gold marks on May 1, 1926, or at the option of the German Government on the 1st of May in any year up to 1926.

For various reasons the undertaking defined in the above letter was not embodied in the treaty. Belgium's obligations to the United States for advances made up to the date of the armistice amounted to approximately $171,000,000, and to England and France they amounted, I am informed, to about £164,700,000. In view of the special circumstances in which Belgium became involved in the war and the attitude of this country towards Belgium, it was felt that the United States might well agree to make the same agreement respecting pre-armistice loans to Belgium as England and France offered to do.

Advances made by the Treasury to the Belgian Government from the beginning of the war to the armistice amounted to $171,780,000. This principal sum, however, includes advances of $499,400 made to enable the Belgians to pay the interest due November 15, 1917, and $1,571,468.42 to enable the payment of the interest due May 15, 1918. The interest on the advances has been paid up to April 15, 1919, the interest due from May 15, 1918, to that date having been paid out of the Treasury loans for which the United States holds Belgian obligations, which, how-

ever, were made after November 11, 1918, the date
of the armistice. This latter advance would not come
within the terms of the agreement above mentioned.
If, therefore, the United States accepts payment of
Belgian obligations given before the armistice by receiving a corresponding amount of German obligations, it
would seem that it should receive German obligations
amounting to $171,780,000 with interest from April
15, 1919.

Although it is understood that England and France
will take their share of the German bonds when
received by Belgium, I am informed that the Reparation Commission has not as yet finally determined the
details of the issuance of the necessary bonds by the
German Government. A recommendation at this time
that suitable legislative action should be taken may
appear somewhat premature, but in view of the
aproaching termination of my administration I have
brought this matter to your attention, hoping that suitable action may be taken at the appropriate time.

VETO OF EMERGENCY TARIFF BILL

MESSAGE TO THE HOUSE OF REPRESENTATIVES, MARCH 3, 1921. FROM THE "CONGRESSIONAL RECORD," VOL. 60, PPS. 4498-4499.

I RETURN herewith without my approval H. R. 15,275, an act imposing temporary duties upon certain agricultural products to meet present emergencies to provide revenue and for other purposes.

The title of this measure indicates that it has several purposes. The report of the Committee on Ways and Means reveals that its principal object is to furnish relief to certain producers in the nation who have been unable to discover satisfactory markets in foreign countries for their products and whose prices have fallen.

Very little reflection would lead any one to conclude that the measure would not furnish in any substantial degree the relief sought by the producers of most of the staple commodities which it covers. This Nation has been for very many years a large exporter of agricultural products. For nearly a generation before it entered the European war its exports exceeded its imports of agricultural commodities by from approximately $200,000,000 to more than $500,000,000. In recent years this excess has greatly increased, and in 1919 reached the huge total of $1,904,292,000. The excess of exports of staple products is especially marked. In 1913 the nation imported 783,481 bushels of wheat, valued at $670,931, and in 1920, 35,848,648 bushels, worth $75,398,834; while it exported in 1913, 99,508,968 bushels, worth $95,098,838, and in 1920, 218,280,231 bushels, valued at $596,957,796.

In the year 1913 it imported 85,183 barrels of wheat flour valued at $347,877, and in 1920, 800,788 barrels valued at $8,669,300; while it exported in the first year 12,278,206 barrels valued at $56,865,444, and in 1920, 19,853,952, barrels valued at $224,472,448. In 1913 it imported $3,888,604 worth of corn, and in 1920, $9,257,377 worth, while its exports in the first year were valued at $26,515,146 and in 1920 at $26,453,-681. Of unmanufactured cotton in 1920 it imported approximately 300,000,000 pounds valued at $138,-743,000, while it exported more than 3,179,000,000 pounds worth over $1,136,000,000. Of preserved milk, in the same year, it imported $3,331,812 worth and exported $65,239,020 worth. Its imports in the same year of sugar and wool of course greatly exceeded its exports.

It is obvious that for the commodities, except sugar and wool, mentioned in the measure, which make up the greater part of our agricultural international trade, the imports can have little or no effect on the prices of the domestic products. This is strikingly true of such commodities as wheat and corn. The imports of wheat have come mainly from Canada and Argentina and have not competed with the domestic crop. Rather they have supplemented it. The domestic demand has been for specific classes and qualities of foreign wheat to meet particular milling and planting needs. They are a small fraction of our total production and of our wheat exports. The price of wheat is a world price; and it is a matter of little moment whether the Canadian wheat goes directly into the markets of the other countries of the world or indirectly through this country. The relatively small quantity of corn imported into this country has a specialized use and does not come into competition with the domestic commodity.

The situation in which many of the farmers of the country find themselves cannot be remedied by a measure of this sort. This is doubtless generally understood. There is no short way out of existing conditions, and measures of this sort can only have the effect of deceiving the farmers and of raising false hopes among them. Actual relief can come only from the adoption of constructive measures of a broader scope, from the restoration of peace everywhere in the world, the resumption of normal industrial pursuits, the recovery particularly of Europe, and the discovery there of additional credit foundations on the basis of which her people may arrange to take from farmers and other producers of this Nation a greater part of their surplus production.

One does not pay a compliment to the American farmer who attempts to alarm him by dangers from foreign competition. The American farmers are the most effective agricultural producers in the world. Their production is several times as great for each worker as that of their principal foreign rivals. This grows out of the intelligence of the American farmer, the nature of his agricultural practices and economy, and the fact that he has the assistance of scientific and practical agencies, which in respect to variety of activity, of personnel, and of financial support exceed those of any other two or three nations in the world combined. There is little doubt that the farmers of this Nation will not only continue mainly to supply the home demand, but will be increasingly called upon to supply a large part of the needs of the rest of the world.

What the farmer now needs is not only a better system of domestic marketing and credit, but especially larger foreign markets for his surplus products.

Clearly, measures of this sort will not conduce to an expansion of the foreign market. It is not a little singular that a measure which strikes a blow at our foreign trade should follow so closely upon the action of Congress directing the resumption of certain activities of the War Finance Corporation, especially at the urgent insistence of representatives of the farming interests, who believed that its resumption would improve foreign marketing. Indeed, when one surveys recent activities in the foreign field, and measures enacted affecting the foreign trade, one cannot fail to be impressed with the fact that there is consistency only in their contradictions and inconsistencies.

We have been vigorously building up a great merchant marine and providing for improvement of marketing in foreign countries by the passage of an export trade law and of measures for the promotion of banking agencies in foreign countries. Now it appears that we propose to render these measures abortive in whole or in part.

I imagine there is little doubt that while this measure is temporary, it is intended as a foundation for action of a similar nature of a very general and permanent character. It would seem to be designed to pave the way for such action. If there ever was a time when America had anything to fear from foreign competition, that time has passed. I cannot believe that American producers who in most respects are the most effective in the world can have any dread of competition when they view the fact that their country has come through the great struggle of the last few years, relatively speaking, untouched, while their principal competitors are in varying degrees sadly stricken and laboring under adverse conditions from which they will not recover for many years.

Changes of a very radical character have taken place. The United States has become a great creditor Nation. She has lent certain Governments of Europe more than $9,000,000,000, and as a result of the enormous excess of our exports there is an additional commercial indebtedness of foreign nations to our own of perhaps not less than $4,000,000,000. There are only three ways in which Europe can meet her part of her indebtedness, namely, by the establishment of private credits, by the shipment of gold, or of commodities. It is difficult for Europe to discover the requisite securities as a basis for the necessary credits. Europe is not in a position at the present time to send us the amount of gold which would be needed, and we could not view further large imports of gold into this country without concern. The result, to say the least, would be a larger disarrangement of international exchange and disturbance of international trade.

If we wish to have Europe settle her debts, governmental or commercial, we must be prepared to buy from her, and if we wish to assist Europe and ourselves by the export either of food, of raw materials, or finished products, we must be prepared to welcome commodities which we need and which Europe will be prepared, with no little pain, to send us.

Clearly, this is no time for the erection here of high trade barriers. It would strike a blow at the large and successful efforts which have been made by many of our great industries to place themselves on an export basis. It would stand in the way of the normal readjustment of business conditions throughout the world, which is as vital to the welfare of this country as to that of all the other nations. The United States has a duty to itself as well as to the world, and it can discharge this duty by widening, not by contracting, its world markets.

This measure has only slight interest so far as its prospective revenue yields are concerned. It is estimated that the aggregate addition to the Nation's income from its operation for ten months would be less than $72,000,000, and of this more than half would arise from the proposed duty on sugar. Obviously this and much more can be secured in ways known to the Congress, which would be vastly less burdensome to the American consumer and American industry.

The rates, however, have a peculiar interest. In practically every case they either equal or exceed those established under the Payne-Aldrich Act, in which the principle of protection reached its high-water mark, and the enactment of which was followed by an effective exhibition of protest on the part of the majority of the American people. I do not believe that the sober judgment of the masses of the people of the Nation, or even of the special class whose interests are immediately affected by this measure, will sanction a return, especially in view of conditions which lend even less justification for such action, to a policy of legislation for selfish interests which will foster monopoly and increase the disposition to look upon the Government as an instrument for private gain instead of an instrument for the promotion of the general well-being.

Such a policy is antagonistic to the fundamental principle of equal and exact justice to all, and can only serve to revive the feeling of irritation on the part of the great masses of the people and of lack of confidence in the motives of rulers and the results of government.

"THE ROAD AWAY FROM REVOLUTION"

FROM THE "ATLANTIC MONTHLY," AUGUST, 1923.

IN THESE doubtful and anxious days, when all the world is at unrest and, look which way you will, the road ahead seems darkened by shadows which portend dangers of many kinds, it is only common prudence that we should look about us and attempt to assess the causes of distress and the most likely means of removing them.

There must be some real ground for the universal unrest and perturbation. It is not to be found in superficial politics or in mere economic blunders. It probably lies deep at the sources of the spiritual life of our time. It leads to revolution; and perhaps if we take the case of the Russian Revolution, the outstanding event of its kind in our age, we may find a good deal of instruction for our judgment of present critical situations and circumstances.

What gave rise to the Russian Revolution? The answer can only be that it was the product of a whole social system. It was not in fact a sudden thing. It had been gathering head for several generations. It was due to the systematic denial to the great body of Russians of the rights and privileges which all normal men desire and must have if they are to be contented and within reach of happiness. The lives of the great mass of the Russian people contained no opportunities, but were hemmed in by barriers against which they were constantly flinging their spirits, only to fall back bruised and dispirited. Only the powerful were suffered to secure their rights or even to gain access to the means of material success.

It is to be noted as a leading fact of our time that it was against 'capitalism' that the Russian leaders directed their attack. It was capitalism that made them see red; and it is against capitalism under one name or another that the discontented classes everywhere draw their indictment.

There are thoughtful and well-informed men all over the world who believe, with much apparently sound reason, that the abstract thing, the system, which we call capitalism, is indispensable to the industrial support and development of modern civilization. And yet everyone who has an intelligent knowledge of social forces must know that great and widespread reactions like that which is now unquestionably manifesting itself against capitalism do not occur without cause or provocation; and before we commit ourselves irreconcilably to an attitude of hostility to this movement of the time, we ought frankly to put to ourselves the question, Is the capitalistic system unimpeachable? which is another way of asking, Have capitalists generally used their power for the benefit of the countries in which their capital is employed and for the benefit of their fellow men?

Is it not, on the contrary, too true that capitalists have often seemed to regard the men whom they used as mere instruments of profit, whose physical and mental powers it was legitimate to exploit with as slight cost to themselves as possible, either of money or of sympathy? Have not many fine men who were actuated by the highest principles in every other relationship of life seemed to hold that generosity and humane feeling were not among the imperative mandates of conscience in the conduct of a banking business, or in the development of an industrial or commercial enterprise?

And, if these offenses against high morality and true citizenship have been frequently observable, are we to say that the blame for the present discontent and turbulence is wholly on the side of those who are in revolt against them? Ought we not, rather, to seek a way to remove such offenses and make life itself clean for those who will share honorably and cleanly in it?

The world has been made safe for democracy. There need now be no fear that any such mad design as that entertained by the insolent and ignorant Hohenzollerns and their counselors may prevail against it. But democracy has not yet made the world safe against irrational revolution. That supreme task, which is nothing less than the salvation of civilization, now faces democracy, insistent, imperative. There is no escaping it, unless everything we have built up is presently to fall in ruin about us; and the United States, as the greatest of democracies, must undertake it.

The road that leads away from revolution is clearly marked, for it is defined by the nature of men and of organized society. It therefore behooves us to study very carefully and very candidly the exact nature of the task and the means of its accomplishment.

The nature of men and of organized society dictates the maintenance in every field of action of the highest and purest standards of justice and of right dealing; and it is essential to efficacious thinking in this critical matter that we should not entertain a narrow or technical conception of justice. By justice the lawyer generally means the prompt, fair, and open application of impartial rules; but we call ours a Christian civilization, and a Christian conception of justice must be much higher. It must include sympathy and helpfulness and a willingness to forego self-interest in order to promote the welfare, happiness, and contentment of others and of the community as a whole. This is what our age is blindly feeling after in its reaction against what it deems the too great selfishness of the capitalistic system.

The sum of the whole matter is this, that our civilization cannot survive materially unless it be redeemed spiritually. It can be saved only by becoming permeated with the spirit of Christ and being made free and happy by the practices which spring out of that spirit. Only thus can discontent be driven out and all the shadows lifted from the road ahead.

Here is the final challenge to our churches, to our political organizations, and to our capitalists—to everyone who fears God or loves his country. Shall we not all earnestly coöperate to bring in the new day?

"HIGH SIGNIFICANCE OF ARMISTICE DAY"

LAST PUBLIC ADDRESS, DELIVERED OVER THE RADIO NOVEMBER 10, 1923. FROM THE NEW YORK "TIMES" WHICH REPORTED THE SPEECH AS ACTUALLY DELIVERED, NOT AS WRITTEN BY MR. WILSON.

THE anniversary of Armistice Day should stir us to great exaltation of spirit because of the proud recollection that it was our day, a day above those early days of that never-to-be-forgotten November which lifted the world to the high levels of vision and achievement upon which the great war for democracy and right was fought and won, although the stimulating memories of that happy triumph are forever marred and embittered for us by the shameful fact that when the victory was won—won, be it remembered, chiefly by the indomitable spirit and ungrudging sacrifices of our own incomparable soldiers—we turned our backs upon our associates and refused to bear any responsible part in the administration of peace, or the firm and permanent establishment of the results of the war—won at so terrible a cost of life and treasure—and withdrew into a sullen and selfish isolation, which is deeply ignoble because manifestly cowardly and dishonorable.

This must always be a source of deep mortification to us and we shall inevitably be forced by the moral obligations of freedom and honor to retrieve that fatal error and assume once more the rôle of courage, self-respect, and helpfulness which every true American must wish to regard as our natural part in the affairs of the world.

That we should have thus done a great wrong to civilization at one of the most critical turning points in the history of the world is the more to be deplored because every anxious year that has followed has made the exceeding need for such service as we might have rendered more and more pressing as demoralizing circumstances which we might have controlled have gone from bad to worse.

And now, as if to furnish a sort of sinister climax, France and Italy between them have made waste paper of the Treaty of Versailles, and the whole field of international relationship is in perilous confusion.

The affairs of the world can be set straight only by the firmest and most determined exhibition of the will to lead and make right prevail.

Happily, the present situation in the world of affairs affords us the opportunity to retrieve the past and to render to mankind the inestimable service of proving that there is at least one great and powerful nation which can turn away from programs of self-interest and devote itself to practicing and establishing the highest ideals of disinterested service and the consistent standards of conscience and of right.

The only way in which we can worthily give proof of our appreciation of the high significance of Armistice Day is by resolving to put self-interest away and once more formulate and act upon the highest ideals and purposes of international policy.

Thus, and only thus, can we return to the true traditions of America.

LAST PUBLIC STATEMENT

TELEGRAM TO MR. JOSEPH F. GUFFEY CONVEYING JACKSON DAY GREETINGS TO THE DEMOCRATS OF PITTSBURGH, JANUARY 6, 1924. FROM ORIGINAL COPY IN MR. WILSON'S FILES.

PLEASE give my warmest salutations and greetings to those who will assemble for the Jackson Day dinner. They are to be congratulated on representing the party to which must be entrusted the redemption of the nation from the degradation of purpose into which it has in recent days been drawn. An aggressive fight for the establishment of high principles and just action will restore the prestige of our nation as nothing else could, and I shall be glad to take part.

Pray accept my warm personal regard.

WOODROW WILSON.

(Woodrow Wilson died February 3, 1924.)

BIBLIOGRAPHY

OF THE PUBLISHED WRITINGS AND ADDRESSES OF WOODROW
WILSON, MARCH 5, 1917, TO 1927. COMPILED BY HOWARD
SEAVOY LEACH, LIBRARIAN OF LEHIGH UNIVERSITY.

This bibliography is a continuation of that published in volumes 2
and 4 of the Public Papers of Woodrow Wilson. It is founded
upon the Princeton bibliography compiled by me and published in
1922. There are 666 additional citations.

Our thanks are extended to the Library of Princeton University
for permission to reprint the edition of 1922.

Note should be made here that the Library of Congress has an
analytical subject index on cards to the speeches and addresses of
President Wilson practically complete from January 1, 1913, to
June 30, 1920.

H. S. L.

BIBLIOGRAPHY OF WOODROW WILSON

Inaugural Address of President Woodrow Wilson, March 5,
1917. Washington, 1917.
Also in:—(65th Cong., special sess. Senate Doc. 2.)
Also in:—America and freedom. . . . London [1917],
pp. 38-44.
Also in:—America por la libertad, Valencia, 1918, pp.
37-42.
Also in:—Discursos y mensajes de estado, N. Y., 1919,
pp. 156-165.
Also in:—Independent, vol. 89, p. 432.
Also in:—In our first year of war, N. Y., 1918, pp. 1-8.
Also in:—Mensagens, Allocuções e discursos, Rio de
Janeiro, 1918, pp. 73-77.
Also in:—Messages, Discours. . . . Paris, 1919, vol. 1,
pp. 129-136.
Also in:—President Wilson; his problems and his policy,
an English view, by H. Wilson Harris, N. Y., 1917,
pp. 267-272.
Also in:—Le President Wilson, La Guerre: La Paix,
Paris, 1918, pp. 31-36.
Also in:—President Wilson's addresses, ed. by George
McLean Harper, N. Y., 1918, pp. 236-240.
Also in:—President Wilson's foreign policy, messages

addresses, papers, ed. by J. B. Scott, N. Y., 1918, pp. 268-273.

Also in:—President Wilson's great speeches and other history-making documents, N. Y., c1917, pp. 166-170.

Also in:—President Wilson's state papers and addresses, ed. by Albert Shaw, N. Y., 1917, pp. 368-372. 1918, pp. 368-372. 1924, vol. 1, pp. 368-372.

Also in:—Public papers; War and Peace (1917-1924), vol. 1, pp. 1-5.

Also in:—Second Inauguration, Washington, 1918 (65th Cong., 1st sess. Senate Doc. 116, pp. 43-46.)

Also in:—Selected addresses and public papers, ed. by Albert Bushnell Hart, N. Y., 1918, pp. 184-188.

Also in:—Wilson; Das staatsmännische werk. . . . Berlin, 1919, pp. 163-166.

Also in:—Woodrow Wilson; Udvalg af taler, Köbenhavn, 1918, pp. 84-89.

Also in:—Woodrow Wilson's worte. . . . Heilbronn, a.N., 1924, pp. 56-61.

Letter to Col. R. N. Harper, March 22, 1917. In:—Second inauguration. . . . Washington, 1918. (65th Cong., 1st sess. Senate Doc. 116, p. 8.)

Statement (Recalling American officials from Belgium). March 24, 1917. In:—New York Times, March 25, 1917.

Also in:—President Wilson's great speeches and other history-making documents, Chicago, c1917, pp. 300-301.

Telegram to Julius Rosenwald (Jewish Fund), March 29, 1917. In:—New York Times, March 30, 1917.

Address delivered at a joint session of the two houses of Congress, April 2, 1917, Washington, 1917.

(Great war message, "The world must be made safe for democracy.")

Also in:—(65th Cong., 1st sess. House Doc. 1.)

Also in:—(65th Cong., 1st sess. Senate Doc. 5.)

Also in:—America and freedom, being the statements of President Wilson on the war. . . . London [1917], pp. 45-59.

Also in:—America por la libertad, Valencia, 1918, pp. 43-55.

Also in:—America joins the world, N. Y., [c1919], pp. 41-53.

Also in:—Americanism, Chicago [c1918], pp. 36-44.

Also in:—Calodikes, C. S. The golden book, N. Y., 1917, pp. 8-41. (English and Greek on opposite pages.)

Also in:—Carnegie endowment for international peace. Division of international law. Two ideals of government, Washington, 1917, Pamphlet 29.

Also in:—Cong. Rec., vol. 55, pp. 102-104, also 118-120.

Also in:—Diplomatic correspondence between the United States and Germany, ed. by J. B. Scott, August 1, 1914–April 6, 1917, N. Y., 1918, pp. 317-325.

Also in:—Discursos y mensajes de estado, N. Y., 1919, pp. 166-185.

Also in:—Gauss, Democracy today, N. Y., 1919, pp. 126-140.

Also in:—In our first year of war, N. Y., 1918, pp. 9-25.

Also in:—Independent, vol. 90, pp. 56-57.

Also in:—International Conciliation, no. 114.

Also in:—Messages, Discours. . . . Paris, 1919, vol. 1, pp. 137-153.

Also in:—Mensagens, Allocuções e discursos, Rio de Janeiro, 1918, pp. 79-90.

Also in:—New York Times Current History Magazine, vol. 6, pp. 191-198.

Also in:—Le President Wilson, La Guerre: La Paix, Paris, 1918, pp. 37-49.

Also in:—President Wilson's addresses, ed. by George McLean Harper, N. Y., 1918, pp. 241-252.

Also in:—President Wilson's foreign policy, messages, addresses, papers, ed. by J. B. Scott, N. Y., 1918, pp. 274-287.

Also in:—President Wilson's great speeches and other history-making documents, N. Y., c1917, pp. 11-22.

Also in:—President Wilson's state papers and addresses, ed. by Albert Shaw, N. Y., 1917, pp. 372-383. 1918, pp. 372-383. 1924, vol. 1, pp. 372-383.

Also in:—Public papers; War and Peace (1917-1924), vol. 1, pp. 6-16.

Also in:—Die Reden, Englisch und Deutsch, Bern, 1919, pp. 19-41.

Also in:—Selected addresses and public papers, ed. by Albert Bushnell Hart, N. Y., 1918, pp. 188-197.

Also in:—Selection from war addresses, Philadelphia, 1918, pp. 7-10.

Also in:—Sürktokansan Kalenteri, Ely, Minnesota, 1919, pp. 78-91.

Also in:—Survey, vol. 38, pp. 16-17.

Also in:—A survey of international relations between

the United States and Germany, ed. by J. B. Scott, N. Y., 1917, pp. xiii-xxi.

Also in:—Visscher, William Lightfoot, The stars of our country, Philadelphia, c1917.

Also in:—White, Wm. Allen, Woodrow Wilson; the man, his times and his task, Boston, 1924, pp. 491-500.

Also in:—Why we are at war, N. Y., [1917] pp. 39-59.

Also in:—Wilson; Das staatsmännische werk. . . . Berlin, 1919, pp. 167-175.

Also in:—Woodrow Wilson; udvalg af taler, Köbenhavn, 1918, pp. 89-101.

Also in:—Woodrow Wilson's worte. . . . Heilbronn a.N., 1924, pp. 61-71.

Also as:—Address of the President of the United States, delivered at a joint session of the two houses of Congress, April 2, 1917, N. Y., Edward J. Clode, 1917.

Also as:—Address of the President of the United States, delivered at a joint session of the two houses of Congress, April 2, 1917, Garden City, N. Y., Doubleday, Page & Company, 1917.

Also as:—Address of the President of the United States. . . . Patriotic Publishing Company, Boston, 1917.

Also as:—Address of the President of the United States, delivered at a joint session of the two houses of Congress, April 2, 1917.
[Privately printed, The Riverside Press, Cambridge, Mass., U. S. A.] 1918.

Also as:—The challenge accepted: President Wilson's address to Congress, April 2, 1917, London, T. F. Unwin, Ltd., 1917.

Also as:—Mensaje de guerra y Proclama del presidente Wilson; discurso historico pronunciado el Congreso de los Estados Unidos por Woodrow Wilson, 2 de Avril de 1917, pub. para el Chronicle de San Francisco, por Paulo Elder Y Giá. San Francisco, Cal., Guatemala, Tipografiá nacional, 1917.

Also as:—President Wilson's new declaration of freedom: a charter for humanity and world peace, London, The St. Catherine Press, 1917.

Also as:—President Wilson's war address to Congress and proclamation, together with joint resolution of House and Senate, giving names of those voting for and against the measure. [n. p.] 1917.

Also as:—President Wilson's war address to Congress

April 2, 1917, I. & M. Ottenheimer, Baltimore, Md., 1917.

Also as:—President Wilson's address to Congress, April 2, 1917, N. Y., G. Willmann, 1917.

Also as:—President Wilson's address to Congress, April 2, 1917, President Wilson's toespraak tot het Congres, 2 April, 1917, Origneele tekst met Hollandsche vertaling, Amsterdam, Vennootschap: "Letteren en kunst" [1917].

Also as:—The War administration; an illustrated presentation of President Wilson's memorable war address, Boston, P. Walton, 1917.

Also as:—The War message and facts behind it; annotated text of President Wilson's message, April 2, 1917. (War Information Series no. 1, June, 1917.) Washington, 1917.

Also as:—The War message of President Woodrow Wilson, delivered to the Congress of the United States, April 2, 1917; also the proclamation of war signed by the President, April 6, 1917, with cablegrams from the President of France and the Premier of Great Britain, A. M. Robertson, San Francisco, California, 1917.

Also as:—The War message, with annotations giving the leading facts on which the rupture with Germany was developed, the issues in international law and contrasting the spirit of Prussianism with the spirit of Americanism, Pub. by the superintendent of public instruction, Lansing, 1917. (Bulletin No. 14, reprint 1917.)

Proclamation (State of war with Germany), April 6, 1917. Washington, 1917.

Also in:—Diplomatic correspondence between the United States and Germany, N. Y., 1918, pp. 339-342.

Also in:—In our first year of war, N. Y., 1918, pp. 26-31.

Also in:—International conciliation, no. 114.

Also in:—Messages, Discours. . . . Paris, 1919, vol. 1, pp. 154-161.

Also in:—New York Times Current History Magazine, vol. 6, pp. 198-200.

Also in:—President Wilson's great speeches and other history-making documents, N. Y., c1917, p. 23.

Also in:—President Wilson's state papers and addresses; ed. by Albert Shaw, N. Y., 1917, pp. 383-387. 1918, pp. 383-387. 1924, vol. 1, 383-387.

Also in:—Public papers; War and Peace (1917-1924), vol. 1, pp. 17-21.

Also in:—The War message, San Francisco, 1917, pp. 20-26.

Also in:—Why we are at war, N. Y., 1917, pp. 61-68.

Message transmitting report of the Board of Directors of the Panama Railroad Company, April 11, 1917, Cong. Rec., vol. 55, p. 570, also 609.

Letter to Hon. Charles A. Culberson on bill to control exports, April 14, 1917, Cong. Rec., vol. 55, p. 1788.

President Wilson's address to his fellow countrymen, April 16, 1917, Washington, 1917. (A plea to all to serve the nation.)

Also in:—Americanism, Chicago (c1918), pp. 46-50.

Also in:—Cong. Rec., vol. 55, pp. 743-746. Also Appendix 71-72.

Also in:—In our first year of war, N. Y., 1918, pp. 32-39.

Also in:—Independent, vol. 90, p. 155.

Also in:—International Conciliation, no. 114.

Also in:—Mensagens, Allocuções e discursos, Rio de Janeiro, 1918, pp. 91-96.

Also in:—Messages, Discours. . . . Paris, 1919, vol. 1, pp. 162-169.

Also in:—National Geographic Magazine, vol. 31, pp. 289-293.

Also in:—New York Times Current History Magazine, vol. 6, pp. 200-202.

Also in:—Our flag and its message, by J. A. Moss, Philadelphia, 1917, pp. 3-15.

Also in:—Outlook, vol. 115, pp. 728-729.

Also in:—President Wilson's addresses; ed. by George McLean Harper, N. Y., 1918, pp. 253-258.

Also in:—President Wilson's foreign policy, messages, addresses, papers; ed. by J. B. Scott, N. Y., 1918, pp. 288-294.

Also in:—President Wilson's great speeches and other history-making documents, N. Y., c1917, pp. 24-29.

Also in:—President Wilson's state papers and addresses; ed. by Albert Shaw, N. Y., 1917, pp. 387-392. 1918, pp. 387-392. 1924, vol. 1, pp. 387-392.

Also in:—Public papers; War and Peace (1917-1924), vol. 1, pp. 22-27.

Also in:—Selected addresses and public papers; ed. by Albert Bushnell Hart, N. Y., 1918, pp. 197-201.

Also in:—Selection of war addresses, Philadelphia, 1918, pp. 10-12.

Also in:—U. S. Committee on public information. Loyalty leaflets, no. 6.

Also in:—Why we are at war, N. Y., 1917, pp. 69-79.

Also in:—Wilson; Das staatsmännische werk . . . Berlin, 1919, pp. 176-179.

Treason and misprision of treason. By the President of the United States of America. A proclamation no. 1368, April 16, 1917.

Also in:—Official Bulletin, no. 2, May 11, 1917.

Address before the Daughters of the American Revolution, Continental Hall, Washington, D. C., April 17, 1917. In:—Home and country, Daughters of the American Revolution Magazine, vol. 48, pp. 388-389.

Letter to Mr. Arthur Brisbane regarding the proposed Espionage law, April 25, 1917, Cong. Rec., vol. 55, pp. 1700-1701.

Letter transmitting claims of the crew of the Norwegian ship *Ingrid,* April 28, 1917, Cong. Rec., vol. 55, p. 1557, also 1563.

Letter to the House presenting credentials of Resident Commissioners of the Philippine Legislature, April 28, 1917, Cong. Rec., vol. 55, p. 1659.

Letter to Hon. Thomas R. Marshall transmitting recommendations from the Secretary of the Navy for ammunition depot at St. Juliens Creek, Va., May 1, 1917. Cong. Rec., vol. 55, p. 1661.

Address to governors and representatives of state councils of national defense, May 2, 1917. Official Bulletin, no. 1, May 10, 1917.

Also in:—Public papers; War and Peace (1917-1924), vol. 1, pp. 28-29.

Letter to Mr. Eliot Wadsworth, May 10, 1917. Official Bulletin, no. 2, May 11, 1917.

Also in:—Public papers; War and Peace (1917-1924), vol. 1, p. 30.

Letter to Mr. Henry P. Davison, May 10, 1917. Official Bulletin, no. 2, May 11, 1917.

Also in:—Public papers; War and Peace (1917-1924), vol. 1, p. 31.

Letter to Hon. S. Hubert Dent, Jr., regarding the army bill, May 11, 1917, Cong. Rec., vol. 55, p. 2215.

Address at the dedication of the Red Cross building, D. A. R. Hall, May 12, 1917. Official Bulletin, no. 4, May 14, 1917.

Also in:—Cong. Rec., vol. 55, p. 2500.

Also in:—President Wilson's foreign policy, messages, addresses, papers; ed. by J. B. Scott, N. Y., 1918, pp. 295-299.

Also in:—President Wilson's state papers and addresses; ed. by Albert Shaw, N. Y., 1917, pp. 392-395. 1918, pp. 392-395. 1924, vol. 1, 392-395.

Also in:—Public papers; War and Peace (1917-1924), vol. 1, pp. 32-35.

Also in:—Selected addresses and public papers; ed. by Albert Bushnell Hart, N. Y., 1918, pp. 202-204.

Also in:—Wilson; Das staatsmännische werk. . . . Berlin, 1919, pp. 180-182.

Address to the Labor Committee of the Council of National Defense, May 15, 1917. Official Bulletin, no. 5, May 15, 1917.

Also in:—Public papers; War and Peace (1917-1924), vol. 1, pp. 36-37.

Proclamation (Registration day), May 18, 1917, no. 1370. Washington, 1917.

Also in:—In our first year of war, N. Y., 1918, pp. 40-48.

Also in:—New York Times Current History Magazine, vol. 6, pp. 381-384.

Also in:—Official Bulletin, no. 9, May 19, 1917.

Also in:—President Wilson's great speeches and other history-making documents, N. Y., c1917, pp. 33-36.

Also in:—President Wilson's state papers and addresses; ed. by Albert Shaw, N. Y., 1917, pp. 395-399. 1918, pp. 395-399. 1924, vol. 1, pp. 385-399.

Also in:—Public papers; War and Peace (1917-1924), vol. 1, pp. 38-39.

Statement declining Col. Roosevelt's offer for "Immediate service in France," May 18, 1917. In:—President Wilson's great speeches and other history-making documents, c1917, pp. 36-38.

Also in:—Official Bulletin, no. 9, May 19, 1919.

Also in:—Public papers; War and Peace (1917-1924), vol. 1, pp. 40-41.

Statement on the food law, May 19, 1917. In:—President Wilson's great speeches and other history-making documents, c1917, pp. 39-42.

Also in:—In our first year of war, N. Y., 1918, pp. 49-53.

Also in:—Official Bulletin, no. 10, May 21, 1917.

Also in:—President Wilson's state papers and addresses;

ed. by Albert Shaw, N. Y., 1917, pp. 399-402. 1918, pp. 399-402. 1924, vol. 1, pp. 399-402.

Also in:—Public papers; War and Peace (1917-1924), vol. 1, pp. 42-44.

Letter to Mr. Lawrence Perry, May 21, 1917. Official Bulletin, no. 12, May 23, 1917. (Continuance of College athletics.)

Also in:—Public papers; War and Peace (1917-1924), vol. 1, p. 45.

Letter to Hon. Edwin Y. Webb, May 22, 1917. Official Bulletin, no. 12, May 23, 1917 (censorship).

Also in:—Cong. Rec., vol. 55, p. 3144.

Also in:—Public papers; War and Peace (1917-1924), vol. 1, p. 46.

Also in:—Selected addresses and public papers; ed. by Albert Bushnell Hart, N. Y., 1918, pp. 205-206.

Letter to Hon. J. Thomas Heflin, May 22, 1917. Official Bulletin, no. 12, May 23, 1917 (War).

Also in:—Cong. Rec., vol. 55, p. 2761.

Also in:—In our first year of war, N. Y., 1918, pp. 54-55.

Also in:—President Wilson's great speeches and other history-making documents, c1917, p. 153.

Also in:—Public papers; War and Peace (1917-1924), vol. 1, pp. 47-48.

Also in:—Selected addresses and public papers; ed. by Albert Bushnell Hart, N. Y., 1918, pp. 204-205.

Proclamation (making the week ending June 25, 1917, Red Cross Week), May 1917. Official Bulletin, no. 14, May 25, 1917.

Communication to the provisional government of Russia, May 26, 1917, Official Bulletin, no. 26, June 9, 1917.

Also in:—Americanism, Chicago (c1918), pp. 52-54.

Also in:—Cong. Rec., vol. 55, p. 5723.

Also in:—Discursos y mensajes de estado, N. Y., 1919, pp. 186-191.

Also in:—In our first year of war, N. Y., 1918, pp. 59-63.

Also in:—Independent, vol. 90, p. 483.

Also in:—Messages, Discours. . . . Paris, 1919, vol. 1, pp. 170-174.

Also in:—New York Times Current History Magazine, vol. 6, pt. 2, pp. 49-50.

Also in:—President Wilson's foreign policy, messages, addresses, papers; ed. by J. B. Scott, N. Y., 1918, pp. 318-321.

Also in:—President Wilson's great speeches and other history-making documents, c1917, pp. 309-312.

Also in:—President Wilson's state papers and addresses; ed. by Albert Shaw, N. Y., 1917, pp. 405-408. 1918, pp. 405-408. 1924, vol. 1, pp. 405-408.

Also in:—Public papers; War and Peace (1917-1924), vol. 1, pp. 49-51.

Also in:—Selected addresses and public papers; ed. by Albert Bushnell Hart, N. Y., 1918, pp. 206-208.

Also in:—Wilson; Das staatsmännische werk. . . . Berlin, 1919, pp. 188-190.

Message transmitting a communication from the Secretary of State covering topics of a note from the British Ambassador relative to our entry into the war, May 26, 1917. Cong. Rec., vol. 55, pp. 2930 and 2961.

Message transmitting copies of acts and resolutions enacted by the Eighth Legislature of Porto Rico, May 28, 1917. Cong. Rec., vol. 55, p. 2965.

Message transmitting Report No. 4 of the Commission on Navy Yards and Naval Stations, May 28, 1917. Cong. Rec., vol. 55, p. 2965; also 3025.

Letter to Senator Owen on Federal Reserve Act amendment, May 29, 1917. Cong. Rec., vol. 55, p. 3761.

Memorial Day address at Arlington National Cemetery, May 30, 1917. Official Bulletin, no. 18, May 31, 1917.

Also in:—In our first year of war, N. Y., 1918, pp. 56-58.

Also in:—President Wilson's foreign policy, messages, addresses, papers; ed. by J. B. Scott, N. Y., 1918, pp. 300-302.

Also in:—Public papers; War and Peace (1917-1924), vol. 1, pp. 52-53.

Also in:—Selected addresses and public papers; ed. by Albert Bushnell Hart, N. Y., 1918, pp. 209-210.

Also in:—Wilson; Das staatsmännische werk. . . . Berlin, 1919, pp. 183-184.

Letter to Hon. M. G. Brumbaugh, June 4, 1917. Official Bulletin, no. 23, June 6, 1917.

Address to Confederate veterans at Washington, June 5, 1917. Official Bulletin, no. 22, June 5, 1917.

Also in:—America joins the world, N. Y. [c1919], pp. 54-64.

Also in:—Cong. Rec., vol. 55, appendix p. 271.

Also in.—President Wilson's foreign policy, messages,

addresses, papers; ed. by J. B. Scott, N. Y., 1918, pp. 303-307.

Also in:—President Wilson's state papers and addresses; ed. by Albert Shaw, N. Y., 1917, pp. 408-411. 1918, pp. 408-411. 1924, vol. 1, pp. 408-411.

Also in.—Public papers; War and Peace (1917-1924), vol. 1, pp. 54-57.

Also in:—Wilson; Das staatsmännische werk. . . . Berlin, 1919, pp. 185-187.

Letter to Hon. Lemuel P. Padgett, urging the establishment of a naval base at Hampton Roads, June 12, 1917. Cong. Rec., vol. 55, p. 3539.

Letter to Mr. Herbert Hoover (to begin mobilization of food economy forces), June 12, 1917. Official Bulletin, no. 33, June 18, 1917.

Also in:—Public papers; War and Peace (1917-1924), vol. 1, pp. 58-59.

Telegram to the President of Salvador, June 1917. Official Bulletin, no. 28, June 12, 1917.

Address of President Wilson delivered at Washington, D. C., Flag Day, June 14, 1917. Washington, 1917.

Also in:—America and freedom, London [1917], pp. 63-70.

Also in:—America por la libertad, Valencia, 1918, pp. 57-62.

Also in:—Americanism, Chicago [c1918], pp. 55-61.

Also in:—Cong. Rec., vol. 55, appendix pp. 332-334.

Also in:—Discursos y mensajes de estado, N. Y., 1919, pp. 192-206.

Also in:—Gauss, Democracy today, N. Y., 1919, pp. 141-150.

Also in:—In our first year of war, N. Y., 1918, pp. 64-75.

Also in:—Independent, vol. 90, pp. 530-531.

Also in:—Mensagens, Allocuções e discursos, Rio de Janeiro, 1918, pp. 97-102.

Also in:—Messages, Discours. . . . Paris, 1919, vol. 1, pp. 175-185.

Also in:—New York Times Current History Magazine, vol. 6, pt. 2, pp. 1-5.

Also in:—Official Bulletin, no. 30, June 14, 1917.

Also in:—Le President Wilson, La Guerre: La Paix, Paris, 1918, pp. 50-56.

Also in:—President Wilson's addresses; ed. by George McLean Harper, N. Y., 1918, pp. 259-264.

Also in:—President Wilson's foreign policy, messages,

addresses, papers; ed. by J. B. Scott, N. Y., 1918, pp. 308-317.

Also in:—President Wilson's state papers and addresses; ed. by Albert Shaw, N. Y., 1917, pp. 411-418. 1918, pp. 411-418. 1924, vol. 1, pp. 411-418.

Also in:—Public papers; War and Peace (1917-1924), vol. 1, pp. 60-67.

Also in:—Die Reden, Englisch und Deutsch. Bern, 1919, pp. 43-59.

Also in:—Selected addresses and public papers; ed. by Albert Bushnell Hart, N. Y., 1918, pp. 210-217.

Also in:—Selection of war addresses, Philadelphia, 1918, pp. 12-14.

Also in:—What are we fighting for. Hartford, Conn., 1917.

Also in:—Wilson; Das staatsmännische werk. . . . Berlin, 1919, pp. 191-197.

Also in:—Woodrow Wilson; udvalg af taler, Köbenhavn, 1918, pp. 101-109.

Also in:—Woodrow Wilson's worte. . . . Heilbronn a.N., 1924, pp. 71-78.

Also as:—The Great faith, President Wilson's speech on American Flag day, London, Hodder and Stoughton, 1917.

Also in:—The President's Flag Day address, with evidence of Germany's plan. Issued by the committee on public information, June 14, 1917. (U. S. Committee on Public Information. Red, White and Blue series, no. 4.)

Proclamation (Recruiting week, June 23 to June 30), June 15, 1917. Official Bulletin, no. 36, June 21, 1917.

Letter to Hon. William C. Redfield, June 18, 1917. Official Bulletin, no. 36, June 21, 1917.

Letter to Hon. William P. Borland, June 18, 1917. Official Bulletin, no. 33, June 18, 1917.

Also in:—Cong. Rec., vol. 55, p. 3910, also p. 3950 and p. 4467.

Letter to Mr. E. P. V. Ritter, June 16, 1917. Official Bulletin, no. 33, June 18, 1917.

Letter to Mrs. Louis Meyer, June 16, 1917. Official Bulletin, no. 36, June 21, 1917.

Reply to address of Baron Moncheur delivering message of King Albert to President Wilson, June 18, 1917. Official Bulletin, no. 34, June 19, 1917.

Also in:—Public papers; War and Peace (1917-1924), vol. 1, p. 68.

Letter to Mr. Bent Wilson, June 19, 1917. Cong. Rec., vol. 55, p. 4504.

Letter to Hon. Newton D. Baker, June 1917. Official Bulletin, no. 38, June 23, 1917.

Statement regarding the policy of export control, June 1917, Official Bulletin, no. 40, June 26, 1917.

Also in:—Public papers; War and Peace (1917-1924), vol. 1, pp. 69-70.

Proclamation [July 5, Registration day for Alaska, Porto Rico and Hawaii], June 27, 1917. Official Bulletin, no. 42, June 28, 1917.

Letter to Mr. William A. Brady, June 28, 1917. Official Bulletin, no. 45, July 2, 1917.

Letter to Rev. James Cannon, Jr., regarding the food-administration legislation, June 29, 1917. Cong. Rec., vol. 55, p. 4585; also p. 4744, pp. 4748-9, p. 4749, p. 5081.

Also in:—Official Bulletin, no. 44, June 30, 1917.

Message to Congress transmitting a request that Mr. Brand Whitlock be allowed to accept a Belgian decoration, June 29, 1917. Cong. Rec., vol. 55, p. 4451, also p. 4494.

Proclamation [Allowing Alaska two months for registration], June 30, 1917. Official Bulletin, no. 46, July 3, 1917.

Statement issued with the announcement of the rules and regulations governing the Selective Service law, July 1917. Official Bulletin, no. 45, July 2, 1917.

Proclamation [Naming July 31, 1917, Registration day for Hawaii], July 2, 1917. Official Bulletin, no. 47, July 5, 1917.

Foreword July 3, 1917. Through darkness to dawn, by William North Rice, with a foreword by Woodrow Wilson, N. Y., Beattys & Co., 1917.

Proclamation [Federalization of National Guard], July 3, 1917. Official Bulletin, no. 51, July 10, 1917.

Reply to the Russian Ambassador, Mr. Boris Bakhmeteff, on presenting his credentials, July 5, 1917. Official Bulletin, no. 48, July 6, 1917.

Also in:—Public papers; War and Peace (1917-1924), vol. 1, pp. 71-72.

Statement regarding amelioration of food conditions in the United States, July 9, 1917. Official Bulletin, no. 50, July 9, 1917.

Also in:—President Wilson's state papers; ed. by Albert Shaw, 1918, pp. 403-404. 1924, vol. 1, pp. 403-404.

Also in:—Public papers; War and Peace (1917-1924), vol. 1, p. 73.

Appeal against profiteering, July 12, 1917, New York Times Current History Magazine, vol. 6, pt. 2, pp. 257-258.

Also in:—Americanism, Chicago [c1918], pp. 62-65.

Also in:—Cong. Rec., vol. 55, pp. 4995-4996, also pp. 5059-5060.

Also in:—In our first year of war, N. Y., 1918, pp. 76-82.

Also in:—Independent, vol. 91, p. 112.

Also in:—Official Bulletin, no. 53, July 12, 1917.

Also in:—Public papers; War and Peace (1917-1924), vol. 1, pp. 74-78.

Cablegram to the French government (Bastile Day), July 16, 1917. In:—Selected addresses and public papers; ed. by Albert Bushnell Hart, N. Y., 1918, p. 217.

Also in:—Official Bulletin, no. 56, July 16, 1917.

Also in:—President Wilson's state papers and addresses; ed. by Albert Shaw, N. Y., 1917, p. 419. 1918, p. 419. 1924, vol. 1, p. 419.

Also in:—Public papers; War and Peace (1917-1924), vol. 1, p. 79.

Letter to Hon. Franklin K. Lane, July 20, 1917. Official Bulletin, no. 62, July 23, 1917 (urging colleges and technical schools to maintain their courses as usual).

Message to Congress transmitting a request to allow Mr. Aurelio Collazo, of Cuba, to study at West Point, July 20, 1917. Cong. Rec., vol. 55, p. 5329, also p. 5376.

Message to Dr. J. Vicente Concha, July 20, 1917. Official Bulletin, no. 68, July 30, 1917.

Telegram to the Prince of Udine, July 21, 1917. Official Bulletin, no. 65, July 30, 1917.

Letter to Hon. Asbury F. Lever, July 23, 1917. Official Bulletin, no. 63, July 24, 1917.

Letter recommending the reading of the Bible, July 23, 1917. In:—Woodrow Wilson on the Bible and the American Bible Society, N. Y., n.d. p. [33].

Letter to Gen. George W. Goethals, July 24, 1917. Official Bulletin, no. 63, July 24, 1917.

Letter to Hon. John B. White, July 24, 1917. Official Bulletin, no. 63, July 24, 1917.

Letter to Mr. Denman, July 24, 1917. Official Bulletin, no. 63, July 24, 1917.

Letter to Sec. D. F. Houston, July 28, 1917. Official Bulletin, no. 68, July 30, 1917. (Food conservation.)

Also in:—Public papers; War and Peace (1917-1924), vol. 1, pp. 80-81.

Message to the President of Peru, August 2, 1917. Official Bulletin, no. 71, August 2, 1917.

Letter to Hon. William G. McAdoo, August 7, 1917, Washington, 1917. (War family allowance. Insurance, etc.) (65th Cong., 1st sess., Senate Doc. 75.)

Also in:—Cong. Rec., vol. 55, p. 6902.

Also in:—Official Bulletin, no. 78, August 10, 1917.

Letter to Hon. J. W. Alexander, August 9, 1917. Cong. Rec., vol. 55, p. 7474.

Address of President Wilson to the officers of the Atlantic fleet, August 11, 1917, Washington, 1920.

Also in:—Public papers; War and Peace (1917-1924), vol. 1, pp. 82-88.

Also in:—Woodrow Wilson's worte. . . . Heilbronn a.N., 1924, pp. 78-81.

Letter to the soldiers and sailors of the United States. (The Bible and the soldier.) Cong. Rec., vol. 55, p. 6041.

Also in:—Selected addresses and public papers; ed. by Albert Bushnell Hart, N. Y., 1918, pp. 217-218.

Also in:—Public papers; War and Peace (1917-1924), vol. 1, p. 89.

Letter to school officers of the United States, August 23, 1917. In:—In our first year of war, N. Y., 1918, pp. 89-91. Also in:—Official Bulletin, no. 121, October 1, 1917.

Also in:—Public papers; War and Peace (1917-1924), vol. 1, pp. 90-91.

Also in:—School and Society, vol. 6, p. 404.

Also in:—Selected addresses and public papers; ed. by Albert Bushnell Hart, N. Y., 1918, pp. 218-219.

Reply to remarks of Viscount Ishii, August 23, 1917. Official Bulletin, no. 90, August 24, 1917.

Also in:—President Wilson's state papers and addresses; ed. by Albert Shaw, N. Y., 1917, pp. 419-420. 1918, pp. 419-420. 1924, vol. 1, pp. 419-420.

Also in:—Public papers; War and Peace (1917-1924), vol. 1, p. 92.

Letter to Hon. Jouett Shouse, August 27, 1917. In:—Cong. Rec., vol. 55, appendix 704.

Reply of the United States to the communication of the Pope to the belligerent governments, August 27, 1917, Washington, 1917.

Also in:—America and freedom, London [1917], pp. 71-76

Also in:—America por la libertad, Valencia, 1918, pp. 63-66.

Also in:—Americanism, Chicago [c1918], pp. 67-69.

Also in:—Cong. Rec., vol. 55, pp. 6407-6408.

Also in:—Discursos y mensajes de estado, N. Y., 1919, pp. 207-214.

Also in:—Gauss, Democracy today, N. Y., 1919, pp. 151-155.

Also in:—In our first year of war, N. Y., 1918, pp. 83-88.

Also in:—Independent, vol. 91, p. 378.

Also in:—International conciliation, no. 119.

Also in:—Mensagens, Allocuções e discursos, Rio de Janeiro, 1918, pp. 102-107.

Also in:—Messages, Discours. . . . Paris, 1919, vol. 1, pp. 190-195.

Also in:—New York Times Current History Magazine, vol. 7, pt. 1, pp. 81-82.

Also in:—Official Bulletin, no. 94, August 29, 1917.

Also in:—Outlook, vol. 117, pp. 13-14.

Also in:—Le President Wilson, La Guerre: La Paix, Paris, 1918, pp. 57-61.

Also in:—President Wilson's addresses; ed. by George McLean Harper, N. Y., 1918, pp. 265-268.

Also in:—President Wilson's foreign policy, messages, addresses, papers; ed. by J. B. Scott, N. Y., 1918, pp. 322-325.

Also in:—President Wilson's state papers and addresses; ed. by Albert Shaw, N. Y., 1917, pp. 421-424. 1918, pp. 421-424. 1924, vol. 1, pp. 421-424.

Also in:—Public papers; War and Peace (1917-1924), vol. 1, pp. 93-96.

Also in:—Die Reden, Englisch und Deutsch. Bern, 1919, pp. 61-69.

Also in:—Selected addresses and public papers; ed. by Albert Bushnell Hart, N. Y., 1918, pp. 219-222.

Also in:—Survey, vol. 38, p. 506.

Also in:—A Survey of international relations between the United States and Germany; ed. by J. B. Scott, N. Y., 1917, pp. 361-363.

Also in:—Wilson; Das staatsmännische werk. . . . Berlin, 1919, pp. 198-200.

Also in:—Woodrow Wilson; udvalg af taler, København, 1918, pp. 109-113.

Also in:—Woodrow Wilson's worte. . . . Heilbronn a.N., 1924, pp. 81-84.

Also as:—America's terms of peace; President Wilson's reply to the Pope's letter, August 28, 1917, St. Paul. Printed for the Minnesota commission of public safety by Louis F. Dow Co., 1917.

Statement [Explaining exports control list proclamation], August 27, 1917. Official Bulletin, no. 93, August 28, 1917.

Also in:—President Wilson's state papers and addresses; ed. by Albert Shaw, N. Y., 1917, pp. 404-405. 1918, pp. 404-405. 1924, vol. 1, pp. 404-405.

Also in:—Public papers; War and Peace (1917-1924), vol. 1, p. 97.

Telegram to President of the National Council Assembly, Moscow, August 1917. Official Bulletin, no. 92, August 27, 1917.

Also in:—President Wilson's state papers and addresses; ed. by Albert Shaw, N. Y., 1917, p. 420. 1918, p. 420. 1924, vol. 1, p. 420.

Also in:—Public papers; War and Peace (1917-1924), vol. 1, p. 98.

Statement announcing the price of wheat, August 30, 1917. In:—President Wilson's State papers and addresses; ed. by Albert Shaw, N. Y., pp. 425-426. 1918, pp. 425-426. 1924, vol. 1, pp. 425-426.

Also in:—Public papers; War and Peace (1917-1924), vol. 1, pp. 99-100.

Letter to Mr. Thomas L. Chadbourne, Jr., August 30, 1917. Official Bulletin, no. 98, September 4, 1917.

Letter to Samuel Gompers, August 31, 1917. Official Bulletin, no. 98, September 4, 1917.

Also in:—Cong. Rec., vol. 55, pp. 6738-6739.

Letter to Hon. W. C. Adamson, September 1, 1917. Official Bulletin, no. 98, September 4, 1917.

Letter endorsing the work of the American Bible Society in distributing Bibles among the Army and Navy personnel, September 1, 1917. In:—Woodrow Wilson on the Bible and the American Bible Society, N. Y., n.d. p. 4.

Message to the Soldiers of the National Army, September 4, 1917. Official Bulletin, no. 98, September 4, 1917.

Also in:—Americanism, Chicago [c1918], p. 71.

Also in:—President Wilson's state papers and addresses; ed. by Albert Shaw, N. Y., 1917, p. 426. 1918, p. 426. 1924, vol. 1, p. 426.

Also in:—Public papers; War and Peace (1917-1924), vol. 1, p. 101.

Also in:—Selected addresses and public papers; ed. by Albert Bushnell Hart, N. Y., 1918, pp. 222-223.

Also in:—Woodrow Wilson on the Bible and the American Bible Society, N. Y., n.d. p. 8.

Proclamation [To the school children to enroll in Red Cross service], dated September 5, 1917, issued September 15, 1917. Official Bulletin, no. 111, September 19, 1917.

Also in:—President Wilson's state papers and addresses, ed. by Albert Shaw, N. Y., 1917, p. 427. 1918, p. 427. 1924, vol. 1, p. 427.

Also in—Public papers; War and Peace (1917-1924), vol. 1, pp. 102-103.

Also in:—Selected addresses and public papers; ed. by Albert Bushnell Hart, N. Y., pp. 223-224.

Letter to Mr. Conlin H. Livingstone, September 17, 1917. Official Bulletin, no. 116, September 25, 1917. (Boy Scouts and Second Liberty Loan.)

Memorandum naming commission to end coast labor disputes, September 19, 1917. Official Bulletin, no. 113, September 21, 1917.

Also in:—President Wilson's state papers and addresses; ed. by Albert Shaw, N. Y., 1917, pp. 428-429. 1918, pp. 428-429. 1924, vol. 1, pp. 428-429.

Letter to Dr. H. N. MacCracken, September, 1917. Official Bulletin, no. 112, September 20, 1917. (Junior Red Cross.)

Reply to remarks of the Greek minister made upon the occasion of the presentation of his letters of credence, September 21, 1917. Official Bulletin, no. 116, September 25, 1917.

Letter to Mr. George Creel, September 25, 1917. Official Bulletin, no. 117, September 26, 1917.

Statement commending the work of the 65th Congress, October 6, 1917. Official Bulletin, no. 126, October 6, 1917.

Also in:—Cong. Rec., vol. 55, p. 7913.

Also in:—President Wilson's state papers and addresses; ed. by Albert Shaw, N. Y., 1918, pp. 429-430. 1924, vol. 1, pp. 429-430.

Also in:—Public papers; War and Peace (1917-1924), vol. 1, p. 104.

Letter to His Eminence James, Cardinal Gibbons, October 9, 1917. Official Bulletin, no. 131, October 12, 1917.

Letter to Mr. Herbert Hoover, October 10, 1917. Official Bulletin, no. 132, October 13, 1917.

Proclamation [Liberty Loan day, October 24, 1917], October 12, 1917. [Folder advertising "United America."] Philadelphia, 1917.
    Also in:—Official Bulletin, no. 133, October 15, 1917.
    Also in:—President Wilson's state papers and addresses; ed. by Albert Shaw, N. Y., 1918, p. 431. 1924, vol. 1, p. 431.
    Also in:—Public papers; War and Peace (1917-1924), vol. 1, pp. 105-106.

Statement urging all banks to join the Reserve system in mobilizing the nation's finances, October 13, 1917. Official Bulletin, no. 134, October 16, 1917.

Telegram to Mme. Catherine Bressovsky, October 1917. Official Bulletin, no. 136, October 18, 1917.
    Also in:—Public papers; War and Peace (1917-1924), vol. 1, p. 107.

Telegram to Mr. and Mrs. J. P. Husting, October 1917. Official Bulletin, no. 141, October 24, 1917.

Reply to a delegation from the New York State Women's Suffrage Party at the White House, October 25, 1917.
    In:—Selected addresses and public papers; ed. by Albert Bushnell Hart, N. Y., 1918, pp. 224-226.
    Also in:—In our first year of war, N. Y., 1918, pp. 92-95.
    Also in:—Public papers; War and Peace (1917-1924), vol. 1, pp. 108-110.

Letter to H. A. Garfield, October 1917. Official Bulletin, no. 144, October 27, 1917.

Statement regarding economy in use of food, October 28, 1917, Official Bulletin, no. 145, October 29, 1917.

An appeal to the American people, October 29, 1917. Official Bulletin, no. 145, October 29, 1917. (Armenian and Syrian Relief.)

Message to Dr. Wenceslao Braz, President of Brazil, welcoming Brazil as a warring nation against Germany, October 30, 1917. In:—President Wilson's state papers and addresses, N. Y., ed. by Albert Shaw, 1918, p. 432. 1924, vol. 1, p. 432.
    Also in:—Discursos y mensajes de estado, N. Y., 1919, pp. 77-78.
    Also in:—Official Bulletin, no. 148, November 1, 1917.

Letter to J. R. Potts, November 6, 1917. Official Bulletin, no. 155, November 9, 1917.

Proclamation [Thanksgiving day], November 7, 1917. Official Bulletin, no. 154, November 8, 1917.
    Also in:—Americanism, Chicago [c1918], pp. 73-74.

Also in:—In our first year of war, N. Y., 1918, pp. 96-98.

Also in:—Messages, Discours. . . . Paris, 1919, vol. 1, pp. 196-198.

Also in:—President Wilson's state papers and addresses; ed. by Albert Shaw, N. Y., 1918, pp. 433-434. 1924, vol. 1, pp. 433-434.

Also in:—Public papers; War and Peace (1917-1924), vol. 1, pp. 111-112.

Foreword to the Selective Service Regulations, November 8, 1917. Official Bulletin, no. 156, November 10, 1917.

Also in:—Public papers; War and Peace (1917-1924), vol. 1, pp. 113-115.

Address of President Wilson to the American Federation of Labor Convention, Buffalo, N. Y., November 12, 1917, Washington, 1917.

Also in:—Americanism, Chicago [c1918], pp. 75-81.

Also in:—Gauss, Democracy today, N. Y., 1919, pp. 182-193.

Also in:—In our first year of war, N. Y., 1918, pp. 99-111.

Also in:—Messages, Discours. . . . Paris, 1919, vol. 1, pp. 199-212.

Also in:—New York Times Current History Magazine, vol. 7, pt. 1, pp. 441-444.

Also in:—Official Bulletin, no. 157, November 13, 1917.

Also in:—President Wilson's addresses; ed. by George McLean Harper, N. Y., 1918, pp. 269-278.

Also in:—President Wilson's foreign policy, messages, addresses, papers; ed by J. B. Scott, N. Y., 1918, pp. 326-336.

Also in:—President Wilson's state papers and addresses; ed. by Albert Shaw, N. Y., 1918, pp. 434-443. 1924, vol. 1, pp. 434-443.

Also in:—Public papers; War and Peace (1917-1924), vol. 1, pp. 116-124.

Also in:—Die Reden, Englisch und Deutsch. Bern, 1919, pp. 71-88.

Also in:—Wilson; Das staatsmännische werk. . . . Berlin, 1919, pp. 201-207.

Also in:—Woodrow Wilson's worte. . . . Heilbronn a.N., 1924, pp. 84-92.

Also in:—Selected addresses and public papers; ed. by Albert Bushnell Hart, N. Y., 1918, pp. 226-230. 1924, vol. 1, pp. 226-230. (Incomplete text.)

Also in:—U. S. Committee on Public Information. Loyalty leaflets, no. 3.

Letter to Mr. William L. Chambers, November 1917. Ofcial Bulletin, no. 160, November 16, 1917. (Interruption of traffic on railways.)

Telegram to His Excellency the President of Brazil on Anniversary of Independence, November 15, 1917. Ofcial Bulletin, no. 162, November 17, 1917.

Also in:—Discursos y mensajes de estado, N. Y., 1919, pp. 78-79.

Also in:—President Wilson's state papers and addresses; ed. by Albert Shaw, N. Y., 1918, p. 432. 1924, vol. 1, p. 432.

Also in:—Public papers; War and Peace (1917-1924), vol. 1, p. 125.

Cablegram to King Albert of Belgium, November 16, 1917. Official Bulletin, no. 162, November 17, 1917.

Also in:—President Wilson's foreign policy, messages, addresses, papers; ed. by J. B. Scott, N. Y., 1918, p. 338.

Also in:—Public papers; War and Peace (1917-1924), vol. 1, p. 126.

Also in:—Selected addresses and public papers; ed. by Albert Bushnell Hart, N. Y., 1918, pp. 231-232.

Proclamation [Enemy Aliens], November 16, 1917. Official Bulletin, no. 163, November 19, 1917.

Remarks to District Directors of the War Savings Campaign, November 16, 1917. Official Bulletin, no. 162, November 17, 1917.

Telegram to Northwest Loyalty meetings, St. Paul, Minn. R. W. Hargadine, November 16, 1917. Official Bulletin, no. 162, November 17, 1917.

Also in:—President Wilson's foreign policy, messages, addresses, papers; ed. by J. B. Scott, N. Y., 1918, p. 337.

Also in:—Public papers; War and Peace (1917-1924), vol. 1, p. 127.

Also in:—Selected addresses and public papers; ed. by Albert Bushnell Hart, N. Y., 1918, p. 231.

Letter to the fifteen thousand Four-minute Men of the United States, November 1917. Official Bulletin, no. 163, November 19, 1917.

Letter to Rear Admiral W. L. Capps, November 23, 1917. Official Bulletin, no. 168, November 24, 1917.

Message to His Imperial Majesty Yoshito, Emperor of

Japan, December 1917. Official Bulletin, no. 174, December 3, 1917.

Message to King of Rumania, December 1917. Official Bulletin, no. 174, December 3, 1917.

Address of the President of the United States delivered at a joint session of the two houses of Congress, December 4, 1917. Washington, 1917, reprinted, 1919. (War with Austria-Hungary.) (65th Cong., 2d sess. House Doc. 468.)

Also in:—Americanism, Chicago [c1918], pp. 83-91.

Also in:—Cong. Rec., vol. 56, pp. 18-21, also pp. 21-23.

Also in:—Discursos y mensajes de estado, N. Y., 1919, pp. 109-130.

Also in:—Gauss, Democracy today, N. Y., 1919, pp. 194-208.

Also in:—In our first year of war, N. Y., 1918, pp. 112-129.

Also in:—Independent, vol. 92, pp. 508-509, 532-533.

Also in:—International conciliation, no. 122.

Also in:—Mensagens, Allocuções e discursos, Rio de Janeiro, 1918, pp. 109-118.

Also in:—Messages, Discours. . . . Paris, 1919, vol. 1, pp. 213-229.

Also in:—New York Times Current History Magazine, vol. 7, pt. 2, pp. 63-68.

Also in:—Official Bulletin, no. 175, December 4, 1917.

Also in:—Le President Wilson, La Guerre: La Paix, Paris, 1918, pp. 62-74.

Also in:—President Wilson's addresses; ed. by George McLean Harper, N. Y., 1918, pp. 279-291.

Also in:—President Wilson's foreign policy, messages, addresses, papers; ed. by J. B. Scott, N. Y., 1918, pp. 339-353.

Also in:—President Wilson's state papers and addresses; ed. by Albert Shaw, N. Y., 1918, pp. 443-454. 1924, vol. 1, pp. 443-454.

Also in:—Public papers; War and Peace (1917-1924), vol. 1, pp. 128-139.

Also in:—Die Reden, Englisch und Deutsch. Bern, 1919, pp. 89-111.

Also in:—Selected addresses and public papers; ed. by Albert Bushnell Hart, N. Y., 1918, pp. 232-238. (Incomplete text.)

Also in:—A survey of international relations between the United States and Germany; ed. by J. B. Scott, N. Y., 1917, pp. 364-372.

Also in:—Wilson; Das staatsmännische werk. . . . Berlin, 1919, pp. 208-218.

Also in:—Woodrow Wilson's worte. . . . Heilbronn a.N., 1924, pp. 92-103.

Letter to Mr. Gutzon Borglum, December 5, 1917. Official Bulletin, no. 303, May 7, 1918.

Letter to Hon. William B. Wilson, December 8, 1917. Official Bulletin, no. 184, December 14, 1917.

Message of sympathy to Canada over the Halifax disaster, December, 1917. Official Bulletin, no. 179, December 8, 1917.

Proclamation [Limiting alcoholic content of malt liquor], December 8, 1917. Official Bulletin, no. 181, December 11, 1917.

Proclamation [State of War between U. S. and Austria-Hungary], December 11, 1917. Official Bulletin, no. 183, December 13, 1917.

Also in:—In our first year of war, N. Y., 1918, pp. 130-133.

Also in:—Public papers; War and Peace (1917-1924), vol. 1, pp. 140-142.

Proclamation [Red Cross], December 1917. Official Bulletin, no. 181, December 11, 1917.

Letter to Mr. Montaville Flowers, December 14, 1917. Official Bulletin, no. 190, December 21, 1917.

Letter to Hon. W. J. Bryan, December 17, 1917. Official Bulletin, no. 187, December 18, 1917.

Letter to Dr. A. J. McKelway, December 20, 1917. Official Bulletin, no. 197, January 2, 1918.

Proclamation [Taking over the railroads for the duration of the war], December 26, 1917. Official Bulletin, no. 193, December 27, 1917.

Also in:—(65th Cong., 2d sess. Senate Doc. 159).

Also in:—In our first year of war, N. Y., 1918, pp. 137-142.

Also in:—President Wilson's state papers and addresses; ed. by Albert Shaw, N. Y., 1918, pp. 455-459. 1924, vol. 1, pp. 455-459.

Also in:—Public papers; War and Peace (1917-1924), vol. 1, pp. 143-146.

Also as:—Government control of railroads. A proclamation, December 26, 1917. Washington, 1918.

Statement to Congress on government control of railroads, December 26, 1917. In:—Selected addresses and public papers; ed. by Albert Bushnell Hart, N. Y., 1918, pp. 238-240.

Also in:—In our first year of war, N. Y., 1918, pp. 134-137.

Also in:—Official Bulletin, no. 193, December 27, 1917.

Also in:—Public papers; War and Peace (1917-1924), vol. 1, pp. 147-149.

Telegram to His Excellency Estrada Cabrera, President of Guatemala, December 28, 1917. Official Bulletin, no. 196, December 31, 1917.

BOOKS, 1918

America and freedom. América por la libertad por el Presidente Wilson con un prólogo del Vizconde Grey; traducción directa del inglés por V. E. Oliver con un epilogo de D. Lloyd George. Valencia, Cervantes, 1918.

Americanism, Woodrow Wilson's speeches on the war—why he made them—and what they have done; the President's principal utterances in the first year of war; with notes, comments and war dates, giving them their historical setting, significance and consequences, and with brief quotations from earlier speeches and papers. Comp., ed. and annotated by Oliver Marble Gate, Chicago, The Baldwin Syndicate [c1918].

The Bases of durable peace as voiced by President Wilson, Chicago, The Union League Club, 1918 (contains 5 addresses, January 8–September 27, 1918).

The Bases of lasting peace as voiced by President Wilson, Chicago, The Union League Club, 1918 (contains 5 addresses, January 8–September 27, 1918).

Division and reunion, New York, Longmans, Green & Co., 1918, other printings 1920 and 1921; first printed March 1893.

France, Amérique, 1776-1789-1917. Déclaration d'indépendence; Déclaration des droits de l'homme et du citoyen; Message de guerre du Président Woodrow Wilson; Response de M. Alexandre Ribot; traduction française de P. H. Loyson et anglaise de J. H. Woods, dessins de Bernard Naudin, Paris, R. Helleu, 1918 (text and translation on opposite pages).

Der Friedensgedanke in Reden und staatsakten des Präsidenten Wilson, Berlin, Reimar Hobbing, 1918. (Selections from addresses, etc., 1916-1918.)

Histoire du Peuple Américain traduit par Désiré Roustan. Préface de M. Emile Boutroux, Paris, Bossard, 1918-1919, 2 vols.

A History of the American people by Woodrow Wilson, Ph.D., Litt.D., LL.D., President of the United States. Enlarged by the addition of original sources and leading documents of American history, including narratives of early explorers, grants, charters, concessions, treaties, revolutionary documents, state papers, proclamations and enactments. Illustrated with contemporary views, portraits, facsimiles and maps selected from rare books and prints in ten volumes. N. Y., Harper & Brothers, Publishers, 1918.

In our first year of war, messages and addresses to the Congress and the people, March 5, 1917, to April 6, 1918. New and enlarged edition. New York and London, Harper & Brothers, 1918.

Mensagens, Allocuções e discursos do presidente Wilson concernentes á querra actual com um prologo de José Carlos Rodrigues. Rio de Janeiro, J. Ribeiro dos Santos, 1918 (contains selected addresses from December 8, 1914, to September 27, 1918).

Le Président Wilson, La Guerre: La Paix, Recueil des déclarations du Président des Etats-Unis d'Amérique sur la Guerre et la paix, 20 Décembre, 1916—6 Avril, 1918. Librairie Berger-Levrault, Paris, 1918.

Präsident Wilson; Der krieg—Der friede. Zürich, 1918. (Contains addresses from December 20, 1916, to September 27, 1918) not annalized.

President Wilson's addresses; ed. by George McLean Harper, N. Y., H. Holt and Co. [c1918], (contains addresses from March 4, 1913, to April 6, 1918).

President Wilson's foreign policy, messages, addresses, papers; edited with introduction and notes by James Brown Scott, N. Y., Oxford University Press, 1918 (contains addresses, etc., from August 27, 1913, to April 6, 1918).

President Wilson's great speeches and other history-making documents, Chicago, Stanton and Van Vliet Co., 1918 (contains addresses, etc., from March 4, 1913, to May 22, 1917).

President Wilson's state papers and addresses, introduction by Albert Shaw . . . with editorial notes, a biographical sketch and an analytical index, N. Y., George H. Doran Co. [c1918]. First issued by the Review of Reviews Co., 1918 (contains addresses, etc., from March 4, 1913, to April 6, 1918).

Proclamations by the President of the United States, January 1, 1918—December 23, 1918. U. S. Laws, Statutes, etc. The statutes at large, vol. 40, pt. 2, pp. 1736-1919.

Proclamations and executive orders by the President under and by the virtue of the food control act of August 10, 1917, November 25, 1918, Washington, 1918.

Réception du Président Wilson à l'Université de Paris le 21 Décembre, 1918. Extrait de la Revue Internationale de l'Enseignement 15 Janvier et Février, 1919. Imprimé par Philippe Renouard, Paris [1919].

Selected addresses and public papers of Woodrow Wilson, edited with an introduction by Albert Bushnell Hart (the Modern Library of the World's best books). N. Y., Boni and Liveright, 1918 (contains addresses, letters, etc., 1913-1918).

A Selection from President Wilson's war addresses, 1917-1918, Philadelphia, McKinley Publishing Company, 1918 (historical outlook, war reprint, no. 6).

Also in:—Collected materials for the study of the war; comp. by Albert E. McKinley, 1918 (pp. 9-26).

The State; elements of historical and practical politics, by Woodrow Wilson. Special edition, revised to December, 1918, by Edward Elliott, Boston, D. C. Heath & Co., [c1918].

War addresses with an introduction and notes by Arthur Roy Leonard. Boston, Ginn and Company [c1918] (contains addresses, etc., from January 22, 1917, to February 11, 1918).

War, labor and peace. Some recent addresses and writings of President Wilson. Issued by the Committee on Public Information. Washington, D. C., 1918 (U. S. Committee on Public Information, Red, White and Blue series, no. 9, March 1918).

Woodrow Wilson; udvalg af taler og noter under verdenskrigen . . . ved Arthur Christensen. Köbenhavn, G. E. C. Gads. 1918.

MESSAGES AND ADDRESSES, 1918

Letter to Mr. Gutzon Borglum, January 2, 1918 (Investigation of Aircraft Service). Official Bulletin, no. 303, May 7, 1918.

Address of the President of the United States delivered at a joint session of the two houses of Congress, January 4, 1918, Washington, 1918 (government operation of railroads).

Also in:—(65th Cong., 2d sess. House Doc. 764.)

Also in:—Con. Rec., vol. 56, pp. 559-560; also pp. 586-587.

Also in:—In our first year of war, N. Y., 1918, pp. 143-149.

Also in:—Official Bulletin, no. 199, January 4, 1918.

Also in:—President Wilson's addresses; ed. by George McLean Harper, N. Y., 1918, pp. 292-296.

Also in:—President Wilson's state papers and addresses, ed. by Albert Shaw, 1918, pp. 459-463, 1924, vol. 1, pp. 459-463.

Also in:—Public Papers; War and Peace (1917-1924), vol. 1, pp. 150-154.

Also in:—Selected addresses and public papers; ed. by Albert Bushnell Hart, N. Y., 1918, pp. 241-244. (Incomplete text.)

Address of the President of the United States delivered at a joint session of the two houses of Congress, January 8, 1918. Washington, 1918. (Fourteen conditions of peace.) (65th Cong. 2d sess. House Doc. 765.)

Also in:—America joins the World, N. Y. [c1919], pp. 70-79.

Also in:—América por la libertad, Valencia, 1918, pp. 67-76.

Also in:—Americanism, Chicago [c1918], pp. 95-100.

Also in:—Bases of durable peace, Chicago, 1918, pp. 11-18.

Also in:—Cong. Rec., vol. 56, pp. 680-681; also pp. 690-691.

Also in:—Discursos y mensajes de estado, N. Y., 1919, pp. 215-229.

Also in:—Gauss, Democracy today, N. Y., 1919, pp. 209-218.

Also in:—In our first year of war, N. Y., 1918, pp. 150-161.

Also in:—Independent, vol. 93, pp. 99-100, 119-120.

Also in:—International conciliation, no. 123.

Also in:—Knight, Lucian Lamar. Woodrow Wilson; The Dreamer and the Dream. The Johnson-Dallis Co., Atlanta, Ga. [c1914], pp. 129-131.

Also in:—Mensagens, Allouções e discursos, Rio de Janeiro, 1918, pp. 119-124.

Also in:—Messages, Discours. . . . Paris, 1919, vol. 1, pp. 231-242.

Also in:—New York Times Current History Magazine, vol. 7, pt. 2, pp. 273-276.

Also in:—Official Bulletin, no. 202, January 8, 1918.

Also in:—Le Président Wilson, La Guerre: La Paix, Paris, 1918, pp. 75-84.

Also in:—President Wilson's addresses; ed. by George McLean Harper, N. Y., 1918, pp. 297-305.

Also in:—President Wilson's foreign policy, messages, addresses, papers; ed. by J. B. Scott, N. Y., 1918, pp. 354-363.

Also in:—President Wilson's state papers and addresses; ed. by Albert Shaw, N. Y., 1918, pp. 464-472, 1924, vol. 1, pp. 464-472.

Also in:—Public papers; War and Peace (1917-1924), vol. 1, pp. 155-162.

Also in:—Die Reden, Englisch und Deutsch. Bern, 1919, pp. 113-128.

Also in:—Selected addresses and public papers; ed. by Albert Bushnell Hart, 1918, pp. 244-251.

Also in:—Selection of war addresses, Philadelphia, 1918, pp. 14-16.

Also in:—White, Wm. Allen. Woodrow Wilson; the man, his times and his task, Boston, 1924, pp. 501-503 (in part).

Also in:—Wilson; Das staatsmännische werk . . . Berlin, 1919, pp. 219-226. (Gives also English text of 14 points.)

Also in:—Woodrow Wilson, udvalg af taler. Köbenhavn, 1918, pp. 114-123.

Also in:—Woodrow Wilson's worte. . . . Heilbronn, a.N., 1924, pp. 104-111.

Also in:—Missatge del President Wilson, endreçat al Congrés dels Estats Units el 8 de janer 1918. Traduccio catalana. Barcelona, 1918.

Letter to George Creel, January 14, 1918, commending him on work of Committee on Public Information, Official Bulletin, no. 225, February 4, 1918.

Reply to Rumanian Minister upon the presentation of his credentials, January 15, 1918, Official Bulletin, no. 211, January 18, 1918.

Also in:—Public papers; War and Peace (1917-1924), vol. 1, pp. 163-164.

Telegram to Edward L. Hines, January 16, 1918, Official Bulletin, no. 210, January 17 1918. (State Councils of Defense.)

Statement upholding fuel curtailment order, January, 1918, Official Bulletin, no. 212, January 19, 1918.

Also in:—Public papers; War and Peace (1917-1924), vol. 1, p. 165.

Letter to Senator George E. Chamberlain regarding his New York statement of inefficiency in government bureaus, January 20, 1918. Cong. Rec., vol. 56, p. 1195.

Message to Army and Navy, January 20, 1918, Official Bulletin, no. 214, January 22, 1918. (Observance of Sunday.)
    Also in:—Public papers; War and Peace (1917-1924), vol. 1, p. 166.

Letter to Colin H. Livingstone, January, 1918 (Boy Scouts), Official Bulletin, no. 213, January 21, 1918.

Statement answering Senator Chamberlain's criticism of Departmental management of the war, January, 1918. Official Bulletin, no. 214, January 22, 1918.
    Also in:—Public papers; War and Peace (1917-1924), vol. 1, pp. 167-168.

Letter to William D. Stephens urging postponement of execution of the sentence in the Mooney case, January 22, 1918. Cong. Rec., vol. 56, p. 5470.

Letter to Chauncey M. Depew about his address to the Pilgrims Society, January 26, 1918. In:—Depew. Speeches and literary contributions at Fourscore and four, N. Y., 1918, p. 404.

Message sent by the President to the Farmers' Conference at Urbana, Ill., January 31, 1918, Washington, 1918.
    Also in:—Cong. Rec., vol. 56, appendix pp. 68-69.
    Also in:—Guarantees of peace, N. Y., 1919, pp. 1-8.
    Also in:—Official Bulletin, no. 222, January 31, 1918.
    Also in:—Public papers; War and Peace (1917-1924), vol. 1, pp. 169-174.
    Also in:—Selected addresses and public papers; ed. by Albert Bushnell Hart, N. Y., 1918, pp. 251-255.
    Also in:—U. S. Committee on public information, Loyalty leaflets, no. 4.

Letter to Newton D. Baker, February 1, 1918 (Borglum's criticism of aircraft service). Official Bulletin, no. 303, May 7, 1918.

Proclamation (Enemy Aliens interned), February 5, 1918. Official Bulletin, no. 227, February 6, 1918.

Remarks to delegation from the Farmers' Co-operative and Educational Union, February 8, 1918. Official Bulletin, no. 230, February 9, 1918.
    Also in:—Public papers; War and Peace (1917-1924), vol. 1, pp. 175-176.

Address of the President of the United States delivered at a joint session of the two houses of Congress, February 11, 1918. Washington, 1918. (Addresses of the German and Austro-Hungarian governments.)

Also in:—América por la libertad, Valencia, 1918, pp. 77-86.

Also in:—Americanism, Chicago [c1918], pp. 103-109.

Also in:—Bases of durable peace, Chicago, 1918, pp. 19-25.

Also in:—Cong. Rec., vol. 56, pp. 1936-1938. Also pp. 1951-1953.

Also in:—Discursos y mensajes de estado, N. Y., 1919, pp. 230-244.

Also in:—Gauss, Democracy today, N. Y., 1919, pp. 219-228.

Also in:—Guarantees of peace, N. Y., 1919, pp. 9-20.

Also in:—In our first year of war, N. Y., 1918, pp. 162-173.

Also in:—Messages, Discours. . . . Paris, 1919, vol. 2, pp. 244-255.

Also in:—New York Times Current History Magazine, vol. 7, pt. 2, pp. 400-403.

Also in:—Official Bulletin, no. 231, February 11, 1918.

Also in:—Le Président Wilson, La Guerre: La Paix, Paris, 1918, pp. 85-94.

Also in:—President Wilson's foreign policy, messages, addresses, papers; ed. by J. B. Scott, N. Y., 1918, pp. 364-373.

Also in:—President Wilson's state papers and addresses; ed. by Albert Shaw, N. Y., 1918, pp. 472-479, 1924, vol. 1, pp. 472-479.

Also in:—Public papers; War and Peace (1917-1924), vol. 1, pp. 177-184.

Also in:—Die Reden, Englisch und Deutsch, Bern, 1919, pp. 129-144.

Also in:—Selection of war addresses, Philadelphia, 1918, pp. 16-19.

Also in:—Wilson; Das Staatsmännische werk. . . . Berlin, 1919, pp. 227-233.

Also in:—Woodrow Wilson, udvalg af taler. Köbenhavn, 1918, pp. 123-131.

Also in:—Woodrow Wilson's worte. . . . Heilbronn, a.N., 1924, pp. 111-118.

Letter to T. W. Gregory, February 13, 1918 (Hog Island), Official Bulletin, no. 235, February 15, 1918.

Reply to the remarks of the Ambassador of Great Britain, February 13, 1918. Official Bulletin, no. 234, February 14, 1918.

Message to striking carpenters in eastern shipyards, February 17, 1918. In:—Guarantees of peace, N. Y., 1919, pp. 21-22.

Also in:—Official Bulletin, no. 237, February 18, 1918.

Also in:—President Wilson's state papers and addresses, ed. by Albert Shaw, N. Y., 1918, pp. 485-486, 1924, vol. 1, pp. 485-486.

Also in:—Public papers; War and Peace (1917-1924), vol. 1, pp. 185-186.

Letter to Herbert Hoover regarding coöperation of packing trade, February 19, 1918. Cong. Rec., vol. 57, pp. 1909-1910.

Letter to William G. McAdoo, February 19, 1918 (Public Service Utilities). Official Bulletin, no. 241, February 23, 1918.

Telegram to Roy C. Vandercook, February 19, 1918 (State War Conferences). Official Bulletin, no. 240, February 21, 1918.

Letter to William McCormick Blair, thanking moving picture theater owners for aid to Four-minute Men [February 20, 1918]. Official Bulletin, no. 266, March 25, 1918.

Statement regarding guaranteed wheat prices for 1918, Official Bulletin, no. 242, February 25, 1918.

Also in:—Public papers; War and Peace (1917-1924), vol. 1, pp. 187-190.

Letter to Newton D. Baker, February 22, 1918 (His visit to France), Official Bulletin, no. 256, March 13, 1918.

Letter to Franklin K. Lane, February 25, 1918 (Home gardens), Official Bulletin, no. 253, March 9, 1918.

Letter to Bernard M. Baruch, March 4, 1918, Official Bulletin, no. 250, March 6, 1918. (Reorganization of War Industries Board.)

Also in:—Cong. Rec., vol. 56, pp. 10554-10555.

Letter to the Acting Secretary of War, March 4, 1918. Protesting against prejudice against "foreign-born and especially Jews," expressed in draft instructions to medical advisory boards. Official Bulletin, no. 250, March 6, 1918.

Message to Russia, March 11, 1918. In:—Guarantees of peace, N. Y., 1919, pp. 23-24. (Meeting of the Soviet.)

Also in:—Messages, Discours. . . . Paris, 1919, vol. 2, pp. 256-257.

Also in:—Official Bulletin, no. 255, March 12, 1918, and no. 262, March 20, 1918.

Also in:—Public papers; War and Peace (1917-1924), vol. 1, p. 191.

Telegram to California Farmers, March 11, 1918 (Emergency food production conference), Official Bulletin, no. 259, March 16, 1918.

Letter to Robert Lansing regarding open diplomacy, March 12, 1918. Cong. Rec., vol. 56, p. 7653; also vol. 57, p. 734.

Also in:—Public papers; War and Peace (1917-1924), vol. 1, p. 192.

Letter to Colin H. Livingstone, March 13, 1918 (Boy Scouts), Official Bulletin, no. 263, March 21, 1918.

Letter to Gutzon Borglum, March 15, 1918 (His criticism of aircraft service), Official Bulletin, no. 303, May 7, 1918.

Letter to Democrats of New Jersey urging them to forget party lines and work for humanity, March 20, 1918. Cong. Rec., vol. 56, pp. 5491-5492.

Also in:—Public papers; War and Peace (1917-1924), vol. 1, pp. 193-195.

Statement regarding the taking over of the Dutch vessels, March 20, 1918, Official Bulletin, no. 263, March 21, 1918.

Message of confidence to Field Marshal Haig, March 25, 1918, Official Bulletin, no. 266, March 25, 1918.

Also in:—Public papers; War and Peace (1917-1924), vol. 1, p. 196.

Letter to Gutzon Borglum, March 29, 1918 (criticism of aircraft service), Official Bulletin, no. 303, May 7, 1918.

Letter to Secretary of Labor Wilson, March 29, 1918 (Protecting American children), Official Bulletin, no. 274, April 3, 1918.

Telegram of congratulation to General Foch, March 29, 1918, Official Bulletin, no. 271, March 30, 1918.

Also in:—Public papers; War and Peace (1917-1924), vol. 1, p. 197.

Letter to Gutzon Borglum, April 4, 1918 (Aircraft Service), Official Bulletin, no. 303, May 7, 1918.

Address of President Wilson, Baltimore, April 6, 1918, Washington, 1918. (Opening Third Liberty Loan Campaign.)

Also in:—Americanism, Chicago [c1918], pp. 111-115.

Also in:—Bases of durable peace, Chicago, 1918, pp. 26-30.

Also in:—Cong. Rec., vol. 56, pp. 4747-4758.

Also in:—Discursos y mensajes de estado, N. Y., 1919, pp. 245-254.

Also in:—Gauss, Democracy today, N. Y., 1919, pp. 229-234.

Also in:—Guarantees of peace, N. Y., 1919, pp. 25-32.

Also in:—In our first year of war, N. Y., 1918, pp. 174-181.

Also in:—Independent, vol. 94, p. 113.

Also in:—International Conciliation, no. 126.

Also in:—Mensagens, Allocuções e discursos, Rio de Janeiro, 1918, pp. 125-130.

Also in:—Messages, Discours. . . . Paris, 1919, vol. 2, pp. 259-266.

Also in:—New York Times Current History Magazine, vol. 8, pt. 1, pp. 275-277.

Also in:—Official Bulletin, no. 277, April 6, 1918.

Also in:—Le Président Wilson, La Guerre: La Paix, Paris, 1918, pp. 95-101.

Also in:—President Wilson's addresses; ed. by George McLean Harper, N. Y., 1918, pp. 306-311.

Also in:—President Wilson's foreign policy, messages, addresses, papers; ed. by J. B. Scott, N. Y., 1918, pp. 374-380.

Also in:—President Wilson's state papers and addresses; ed. by Albert Shaw, N. Y., 1918, pp. 480-484, 1924, vol. 1, pp. 480-484.

Also in:—Public papers; War and Peace (1917-1924), vol. 1, pp. 198-202.

Also in:—Selection of war addresses, Philadelphia, 1918, pp. 19-20.

Also in:—Wilson; Das staatsmännische werk. . . . Berlin, 1919, pp. 234-238.

Also in:—Woodrow Wilson, udvalg af taler. Köbenhavn, 1918, pp. 132-137.

Also in:—Woodrow Wilson's worte. . . . Heilbronn, a.N., 1924, pp. 118-122.

Message to King George V, April 6, 1918 (Acknowledgment of message of congratulation upon anniversary of the decision of the United States to enter the war). Official Bulletin, no. 280, April 10, 1918.

Proclamation (National War Labor Board), April 8, 1918, Official Bulletin, no. 280, April 10, 1918.

Address to correspondents of foreign newspapers, April 8, 1918. In:—Woodrow Wilson's worte. . . . Heilbronn, a.N., 1924, pp. 123-127.

Message to His Majesty, Victor Emmanuel III, King of

Italy, April, 1918 (Acknowledgment of messages of congratulation upon anniversary of the entrance of the United States into the war). Official Bulletin, no. 282, April 12, 1918.

Letter to Gutzon Borglum, April 15, 1918 (Aircraft Service), Official Bulletin, no. 303, May 7, 1918.

Message from the President of the United States returning without approval Senate bill 2917. (National defense Army Chaplains.) April 18, 1918, Washington, 1918. (65th Cong., 2d sess. Senate Doc. 216.)

Proclamation (Liberty Day, April 26, 1918), April 18, 1918, Official Bulletin, no. 288, April 19, 1918.

Also in:—Public papers; War and Peace (1917-1924), vol. 1, pp. 203-204.

Special statement, April 19, 1918, for "Keeping our fighters fit for war and after," by Edward Frank Allen, N. Y., The Century Company, 1918.

Letter to Senator Overman, April 20, 1918, opposing court-martial bill. Official Bulletin, no. 291, April 23, 1918.

Reply to the Japanese Ambassador upon the presentation of his credentials, April 30, 1918, Official Bulletin, no. 298, May 1, 1918.

Letter to the Workmen and Executive staff of the New York Shipbuilding Company, Camden, New Jersey, congratulating them on record in work on steamship *Tuckahoe*, May 3, 1918, Official Bulletin, no. 302, May 6, 1918.

Proclamation (Red Cross week), May 4, 1918, Official Bulletin, no. 304, May 8, 1918.

Letter to Charles S. Thomas, May 6, 1918 (Aircraft inquiry), Official Bulletin, no. 303, May 7, 1918.

Also in:—Cong. Rec., vol. 55, p. 6145.

Telegram to Howard Coffin, May 6, 1918 (Aircraft inquiry), Official Bulletin, no. 303, May 7, 1918.

Letter to S. Hubert Dent, Jr., May 7, 1918 (Draft credits), Official Bulletin, no. 307, May 11, 1918.

Letter to the Directors of the Division of Advertising Committee on Public Information, May 7, 1918 (Congratulations on their record of achievement), Official Bulletin, no. 307, May 11, 1918.

Telegram to Delegates of Trenton War Conference (Appreciation of their public spirit), May, 1918, Official Bulletin, no. 303, May 7, 1918.

Message (Mothers' Day, May 12), May 11, 1918, Official Bulletin, no. 307, May 11, 1918.

Proclamation (day of fasting and prayer, May 30), May 11, 1918, Official Bulletin, no. 308, May 13, 1918.

    Also in:—Americanism, Chicago [c1918], pp. 116-117.

    Also in:—New York Times Current History Magazine, vol. 8, pt. 2, pp. 141-142.

Letter to Charles E. Hughes, May 13, 1918, requesting him to investigate aircraft charges. Official Bulletin, no. 311, May 16, 1918.

Letter to Mr. Busch expressing appreciation for offered support of Spanish War Veterans, May 14, 1918. Cong. Rec., vol. 56, appendix p. 529.

Letter to Senator Martin, protesting against usurpation by Senate Committee. Official Bulletin, no. 311, May 16, 1918.

Address of President Wilson opening the campaign in New York for the second Red Cross Fund, Saturday, May 18, 1918, Washington, 1918.

    Also in:—Cong. Rec., vol. 56, pp. 6751-6762.

    Also in:—Discursos y mensajes de estado, N. Y., 1919, pp. 255-265.

    Also in:—Messages, Discours. . . . Paris, 1919, vol. 2, pp. 267-275.

    Also in:—New York Times Current History Magazine, vol. 8, pt. 2, pp. 137-139.

    Also in:—Official Bulletin, no. 314, May 20, 1918.

    Also in:—President Wilson's state papers and addresses, ed. by Albert Shaw, N. Y., 1918, pp. 486-491, 1924, vol. 1, pp. 486-491.

    Also in:—Public papers; War and Peace (1917-1924), vol. 1, pp. 205-210.

    Also in:—Die Reden, Englisch und Deutsch. Bern, 1919, pp. 145-157.

    Also in:—Selected addresses and public papers; ed. by Albert Bushnell Hart, N. Y., 1918, pp. 256-260.

    Also in:—Wilson; Das staatsmännische werk. . . . Berlin, 1919, pp. 239-243.

    Also in:—Woodrow Wilson, udvalg af taler. Köbenhavn, 1918, pp. 137-139.

    Also in:—Woodrow Wilson's worte. . . . Heilbronn, a.N., 1924, pp. 128-133.

Proclamation (June 5, date for registering young men who have reached the age of 21 during past year), May 20, 1918, Official Bulletin, no. 315, May 21, 1918.

Message to the French people through James Kerney, Paris representative of the Committee on Public Information. Official Bulletin, no. 316, May 22, 1918.

Letter to Dr. Anna Howard Shaw, May 22, 1918 (War mourning), Official Bulletin, no. 319, May 25, 1918.

Message of greeting to the Italian people, May 23, 1918. Official Bulletin, no. 318, May 24, 1918.

 Also in:—President Wilson's state papers and addresses; ed. by Albert Shaw, N. Y., 1918, pp. 491-492, 1924, vol. 1, pp. 491-492.

 Also in:—Public papers; War and Peace (1917-1924), vol. 1, p. 211.

Letter to Congressman Sherley, May 24, 1918 (Expenditure of special President's Fund). In:—Official Bulletin, no. 338, June 12, 1912.

 Also in:—Public papers; War and Peace (1917-1924), vol. 1, pp. 212-215.

Reply to our citizens of foreign extraction, Official Bulletin, no. 319, May 25, 1918.

Reply to message of His Majesty Albert, King of Belgium, May 25, 1918 (Red Cross service in Belgium), Official Bulletin, no. 320, May 27, 1918.

Address of the President of the United States delivered at a joint session of the two houses of Congress, May 27, 1918, Washington, 1918. (The finances.)

 Also in:—(65th Cong., 2d sess. House Doc. 1141.)

 Also in:—Cong. Rec., vol. 56, pp. 7114-7115; also pp. 7137-7138.

 Also in:—Guarantees of peace, N. Y., 1919, pp. 33-41.

 Also in:—New York Times Current History Magazine, vol. 8, pt. 2, pp. 139-141.

 Also in:—Official Bulletin, no. 320, May 27, 1918.

 Also in:—President Wilson's state papers and addresses, ed. by Albert Shaw, N. Y., 1918, pp. 492-497, 1924, vol. 1, pp. 492-497.

 Also in:—Public papers; War and Peace (1917-1924), vol. 1, pp. 216-220.

 Also in:—Woodrow Wilson's worte. . . . Heilbronn, a.N., 1924, pp. 133-138.

Letter to Senator Sheppard, May 28, 1918. (War-time prohibition.) In:—Selected addresses and public papers; ed. by Albert Bushnell Hart, N. Y., 1918, pp. 260-261.

 Also in:—Cong. Rec., vol. 56, pp. 56-7421.

Statement urging the buying of government securities and war savings stamps, Official Bulletin, no. 323, May 31, 1918.

 Also in:—New York Times Current History Magazine, vol. 8, pt. 2, p. 141.

BIBLIOGRAPHY

Also in:—Public papers; War and Peace (1917-1924), vol. 1, pp. 221-222.

Letter to Maurice Francis Egan, accepting his resignation, May 31, 1918, Official Bulletin, no. 327, June 5, 1918.

Telegram of condolence to His Excellency, Ciro Luis Urriola, Acting President of Panama, upon the death of President Valdes. Official Bulletin, no. 328, June 6, 1918.

Attitude of the United States toward Mexico. Address delivered before a party of editors from the Republic of Mexico at the White House, June 7, 1918, Washington, 1918. (65th Cong., 2d sess. Senate Doc. 264.)

Also in:—Americanism, Chicago [c1918], pp. 120-123.

Also in:—Discursos y mensajes de estado, N. Y., 1919, pp. 66-76.

Also in:—Gauss, Democracy today, N. Y., 1919, pp. 250-256.

Also in:—Official Bulletin, no. 332, June 11, 1918.

Also in:—Messages, Discours. . . . Paris, 1919, vol. 2, pp. 278-285.

Also in:—New York Times Current History Magazine, vol. 8, pt. 2, pp. 142-144.

Also in:—Public papers; War and Peace (1917-1924), vol. 1, pp. 223-228.

Also in:—Selected addresses and public papers; ed. by Albert Bushnell Hart, N. Y., 1918, pp. 261-266.

Also in:—The World Court, July, 1918, pp. 445-447.

Letter to Robert Maisel, June 10, 1918 (greetings to convention of American Alliance for Labor and Democracy), Official Bulletin, no. 332, June 11, 1918.

Letter to Samuel Gompers, June 10, 1918 (greetings to convention of American Federation of Labor), Official Bulletin, no. 332, June 11, 1918.

Letter to Clarence H. Mackay, President of the Postal Telegraph Company, June 11, 1918, insisting upon acceptance of the decision of the National War Labor Board, Official Bulletin, no. 336, June 15, 1918.

Letter to Mrs. Carrie Chapman Catt transmitting a reply to the memorial of the Union Française pour le Suffrage des Dames, June 13, 1918, Official Bulletin, no. 335, June 14, 1918.

Also in:—Americanism, Chicago [c1918], pp. 124-125.

Also in:—Cong. Rec., vol. 56, pp. 7795 and 7815.

Also in:—Public papers; War and Peace (1917-1924), vol. 1, pp. 229-230.

Message to President Poincaré, June 14, 1918, Official Bulletin, no. 336, June 15, 1918.

Statement asking all patriotic employers to recruit labor only through U. S. agency, June 17, 1918, Official Bulletin, no. 338, June 18, 1918.

Letter to Dr. Van H. Manning, June 26, 1918 (War gas service), Official Bulletin, no. 351, July 3, 1918.

Letter to Edward H. Hurley, June 26, 1918 (Congratulations to shipyard workers). Official Bulletin, no. 352, July 5, 1918.

Message to General Diaz, June 26, 1918 (Congratulations on Success of Italian Armies), Official Bulletin, no. 346, June 27, 1918.

Letter to Thetus W. Sims, June 29, 1918, on taking over telegraph and telephone lines, Official Bulletin, no. 350, July 2, 1918.

Message vetoing H. R. 7237 (Appropriations for the Post Office Department), June 29, 1918, Washington, 1918. (65th Cong., 2d sess. House Doc. 1206.)

Message to the House of Representatives, July 1, 1918, Official Bulletin, no. 350, July 2, 1918. (Veto H. R. 10358.)

Also in:—(65th Cong., 2d sess. House Doc. 1207.)

Statement making public correspondence with Secretary Baker (July 1, 1918, July 2, 1918) regarding the forwarding of troops to France. July 2, 1918. Official Bulletin, no. 351, July 3, 1918.

Address of President Wilson delivered at Mount Vernon, July 4, 1918, Washington, 1918. (65th Cong., 2d sess. Senate Doc. 258.) (Four factors of world peace.)

Also in:—America joins the world, N. Y. [c1919], pp. 80-84.

Also in:—Americanism, Chicago [c1918], pp. 125-128.

Also in:—Bases of durable peace, Chicago, 1918, pp. 31-34.

Also in:—Cong. Rec., vol. 56, p. 8671.

Also in:—Discursos y mensajes de estado, N. Y., 1919, pp. 266-273.

Also in:—Gauss, Democracy today, N. Y., 1919, pp. 235-239.

Also in:—Guarantees of peace, N. Y., 1919, pp. 42-48.

Also in:—Knight, Lucian Lamar. Woodrow Wilson; The Dreamer and the dream. The Johnson-Dallis Co., Atlanta, Ga. [c1924], pp. 131-132.

Also in:—Mensagens, Allocuções e discursos, Rio de Janeiro, 1918, pp. 135-139.

Also in:—Messages, Discours. . . . Paris, 1919, vol. 2, pp. 286-292.

Also in:—New York Times Current History Magazine, vol. 8, pt. 2, pp. 191-193.

Also in:—Official Bulletin, no. 352, July 5, 1918.

Also in:—Outlook, vol. 119, pp. 446-447.

Also in:—Pan-American Union Bulletin, vol. 47, pp. 1-7.

Also in:—Woodrow Wilson, udvalg af taler. Köbenhavn, 1918, pp. 139-143.

Also in:—President Wilson's state papers and addresses, ed. by Albert Shaw, N. Y., 1918, pp. 497-501, 1924, vol. 1, pp. 497-501.

Also in:—Public papers; War and Peace (1917-1924), vol. 1, pp. 231-235.

Also in:—Die Reden, Englisch und Deutsch. Bern, 1919, pp. 159-168.

Also in:—Selected addresses and public papers; ed. by Albert Bushnell Hart, N. Y., 1918, pp. 266-269.

Also in:—Wilson; Das Staatsmännische werk. . . . Berlin, 1919, pp. 244-247.

Also in:—Woodrow Wilson's worte. . . . Heilbronn, a.N., 1924, pp. 139-143.

The first Independence Day for all people. (Four-minute Independence Day address by the President read in 5,300 communities), July 4, 1918, Official Bulletin, no. 352, July 5, 1918.

Also in:—President Wilson's state papers and addresses, ed. by Albert Shaw, N. Y., 1918, pp. 502-503, 1924, vol. 1, pp. 502-503.

Also in:—Public papers; War and Peace (1917-1924), vol. 1, pp. 236-237.

Greeting to American citizens beyond the seas, on Independence Day, July 4, 1918, Official Bulletin, no. 354, July 8, 1918.

Letter to His Excellency, the Earl of Reading, acknowledging congratulations from the Prime Minister of Great Britain on the launching of 100 ships in the United States. July 5, 1918. Official Bulletin, no. 353, July 6, 1918.

Letters to His Excellency, the Earl of Reading, July 5, 1918 (Independence Day greetings from Australia), Official Bulletin, no. 353, July 6, 1918. (Two letters.)

Telegram to the American Ambassador at Rome, July 5, 1918, accepting citizenship of Florence, Official Bulletin, no. 353, July 6, 1918.

Telegram to the Governor of the Virgin Islands, July 5,

1918 (Independence Day), Official Bulletin, no. 353, July 6, 1918.

Reply to the message of His Excellency, Eleutarios Venizelos, Premier of Greece, July 6, 1918 (Independence Day), Official Bulletin, no. 355, July 9, 1918.

Reply to the message of His Excellency, M. G. Menocal, President of Cuba, July 6, 1918 (Independence Day), Official Bulletin, no. 355, July 9, 1918.

Reply to the message of His Majesty, Albert, King of the Belgians, July 6, 1918 (Independence Day), Official Bulletin, no. 335, July 9, 1918.

Reply to the message of His Majesty, Alexander, King of Greece, July 6, 1918 (Independence Day), Official Bulletin, no. 355, July 9, 1918.

Reply to the message of His Majesty, Victor Emmanuel III, King of Italy, July 6, 1918 (Independence Day), Official Bulletin, no. 355, July 9, 1918.

Reply to the message of Son Excellence, Raymond Poincaré, July 6, 1918 (Independence Day), Official Bulletin, no. 355, July 9, 1918.

Reply to message from His Excellency, Sidonio Paes, President of Portugal, July 8, 1918 (Independence Day), Official Bulletin, no. 358, July 12, 1918.

Reply to message from His Excellency, President Dartiguenave, Haiti, July 9, 1918 (Independence Day), Official Bulletin, no. 358, July 12, 1918.

Reply to message from His Majesty, Ahmed Kadjar, Sultan of Persia, July 9, 1918 (Independence Day), Official Bulletin, no. 358, July 12, 1918.

Reply to message from His Majesty, Nicholas, King of Montenegro, July 9, 1918 (Independence Day), Official Bulletin, no. 358, July 12, 1918.

Reply to message from His Royal Highness, The Prince of Monaco, July 9, 1918 (Independence Day), Official Bulletin, no. 358, July 12, 1918.

Reply to message from His Excellency, José Pardo, President of Peru, July 10, 1918 (Independence Day), Official Bulletin, no. 358, July 12, 1918.

Reply to the message of His Excellency, The President of Honduras, July 10, 1918 (Independence Day), Official Bulletin, no. 358, July 12, 1918.

Letter to Henry P. Davison, July 11, 1918. (Work of the Territorial, Insular, and Foreign Division of the Red Cross.) Official Bulletin, no. 367, July 23, 1918.

Message sent to Congress (veto of resolution on relinquishing certain railroads under federal control), July 11, 1918, Official Bulletin, no. 358, July 12, 1918.

Also in:—(65th Cong., 2d sess. Senate Doc. 267.)

Message from the President of the United States vetoing H. R. 9054, An act making appropriations for the Department of Agriculture for the fiscal year ending June 30, 1919. July 13, 1918, Washington, 1918. (65th Cong., 2d sess. House Doc. 1229.)

Also in:—Official Bulletin, no. 359, July 13, 1918.

Message to the French people (Bastille Day), July 14, 1918, Official Bulletin, no. 360, July 15, 1918.

Also in:—Messages, Discours. . . . Paris, 1919, vol. 2, p. 292.

Message to His Excellency, José Vicente Concha, President of Colombia, July 20, 1918 (Anniversary of the Independence Day of Colombia), Official Bulletin no. 366, July 22, 1918.

Message of greeting to His Majesty, Albert, King of the Belgians, July 21, 1918, Official Bulletin, no. 366, July 22, 1918.

Proclamation (Control of Telegraph, Telephone and Cable lines), July 22, 1918, Official Bulletin, no. 368, July 24, 1918.

Also in:—President Wilson's state papers and addresses, ed. by Albert Shaw, N. Y., 1918, pp. 504-506, 1924, vol. 1, pp. 504-506.

Reply to message from King George V on his visit to one of our naval vessels, July 24, 1918, Official Bulletin, no. 387, August 15, 1918.

Statement denouncing mob violence and appealing to his fellow countrymen to keep the nation's fame untarnished, Washington, 1918.

Also in:—Guarantees of peace, N. Y., 1919, pp. 49-52.

Also in:—Independent, vol. 95, p. 177.

Also in:—Official Bulletin, no. 370, July 26, 1918.

Also in:—Pan-American Magazine, vol. 27, pp. 271-272.

Also in:—President Wilson's state papers and addresses, ed. by Albert Shaw, N. Y., 1918, pp. 506-508, 1924, vol. 1, pp. 506-508.

Also in:—Public papers; War and Peace (1917-1924), vol. 1, pp. 238-240.

Also in:—Selected addresses and public papers; ed. by Albert Bushnell Hart, N. Y., 1918, pp. 270-271.

Also in:—Survey, vol. 40, p. 512.

Also in:—Woodrow Wilson's worte. . . . Heilbronn, a.N., 1924, pp. 143-145.

Letter to N. D. Baker on state councils of defense, July 30, 1918, Official Bulletin, no. 384, August 12, 1918.

Message to the Swiss Republic on the National holiday, July 31, 1918, Official Bulletin, no. 376, August 2, 1918.

Message to Liberia on war anniversary, August 3, 1918, Official Bulletin, no. 383, August 10, 1918.

Message to the King of England on war anniversary, August 4, 1918, Official Bulletin, no. 378, August 5, 1918.

Reply to message from the President of San Salvador, August 5, 1918, Official Bulletin, no. 379, August 6, 1918.

Appeal to persons engaged in coal mining to increase output, August 11, 1918, Official Bulletin, no. 384, August 12, 1918.

Also in:—President Wilson's state papers and addresses, ed. by Albert Shaw, N. Y., 1918, pp. 508-510, 1924, vol. 1, pp. 508-510.

Also in:—Public papers; War and Peace (1917-1924), vol. 1, pp. 241-242.

Letter to Henry P. Davison on the draft and Red Cross workers, August 14, 1918, Official Bulletin, no. 389, August 17, 1918.

Message to His Excellency, the President of Uruguay, August, 1918, Official Bulletin, no. 397, August 27, 1918.

Decision in the action of court-martial in cases growing out of riot by soldiers at Houston, August 31, 1918, Official U. S. Bulletin, no. 404, September 5, 1918.

Letter to Rabbi Wise on rebuilding of Palestine, August 31, 1918. In:—Selected addresses and public papers; ed. by Albert Bushnell Hart, N. Y., 1918, p. 272.

Also in:—Official U. S. Bulletin, no. 404, September 5, 1918.

Also in:—Public papers; War and Peace (1917-1924), vol. 1, p. 243.

Proclamation (second conscription), August 31, 1918. In:—Guarantees of peace, N. Y., 1919, pp. 53-56.

Also in:—President Wilson's state papers and addresses, ed. by Albert Shaw, N. Y., 1918, pp. 510-512, 1924, vol. 1, pp. 510-512.

Also in:—Public papers; War and Peace (1917-1924), vol. 1, pp. 244-245.

Public message to labor on Labor Day, September 2, 1918. (German war against labor.) In:—Selected addresses and public papers; ed. by Albert Bushnell Hart, N. Y., 1918, pp. 272-274.

Also in:—Messages, Discours. . . . Paris, 1919, vol. 2, pp. 294-298.

Also in:—New York Times Current History Magazine, vol. 9, pt. 1, pp. 57-58.

Also in:—Official U. S. Bulletin, no. 402, September 3, 1918.

Also in:—President Wilson's state papers and addresses, ed. by Albert Shaw, N. Y., 1918, pp. 512-515, 1924, vol. 1, pp. 512-515. (Here dated September 2, 1918.)

Also in:—Public papers; War and Peace (1917-1924), vol. 1, pp. 246-248.

Also in:—Wilson; Das Staatsmännische werk. . . . Berlin, 1919, pp. 248-250.

Also in:—Woodrow Wilson, udvalg af taler. Köbenhavn, 1918, pp. 143-146. (In part.)

Also in:—Woodrow Wilson's worte. . . . Heilbronn, a.N., 1924, pp. 145-147.

Also in:—St. Nicholas, vol. 45, p. 1077.

Letter to William G. McAdoo, September 4, 1918. (On report of Director-General of railroads.) Official U. S. Bulletin, no. 416, September 19, 1918.

Message transmitting text of treaty between France and the United States providing for reciprocal military service of citizens, September 6, 1918, Official U. S. Bulletin, no. 418, September 21, 1918.

Message transmitting text of treaty between the United States and Greece providing for reciprocal military service of citizens, September 6, 1918, Official U. S. Bulletin, no. 418, September 21, 1918.

Statement to public regretting war questions confine him to Washington during 4th Liberty Loan campaign, September, 1918, Official U. S. Bulletin, no. 408, September 10, 1918.

Letters to District Lodge, no. 55, International Association of Machinists and other striking workmen of Bridgeport, Conn., September 13, 1918, Official U. S. Bulletin, no. 412, September 14, 1918.

Also in:—President Wilson's state papers and addresses, ed. by Albert Shaw, N. Y., 1918, pp. 515-516, 1924, vol. 1, pp. 515-516.

Also in:—Woodrow Wilson's worte. . . . Heilbronn, a.N., 1924, pp. 147-149.

Message of congratulations to General Pershing on the success at St. Mihiel, September 14, 1918, Official U. S. Bulletin, no. 413, September 16, 1918.

Proclamation (Forbidding the use of foodstuffs in the pro-

duction of malt liquors) September 16, 1918. In:—
President Wilson's state papers and addresses, ed. by
Albert Shaw, N. Y., 1918, pp. 517-518, 1924, vol. 1,
pp. 517-518.

Also in:—Public papers; War and Peace (1917-1924),
vol. 1, pp. 249-250.

Dispatch to the Austrian Government through Secretary
Lansing, September 17, 1918. In:—Selected addresses
and public papers; ed. by Albert Bushnell Hart, N. Y.,
1918, p. 275.

Also in:—Americanism, Chicago [c1918], p. 129.

Also in:—Guarantees of peace, N. Y., 1919, p. 57.

Also in:—Messages and addresses, ed. by Albert Shaw,
N. Y., 1924, vol. 1, pp. 534-535.

Also in:—Official U. S. Bulletin, no. 414, September
17, 1918.

Also in:—Public papers; War and Peace (1917-1924),
vol. 1, p. 251.

Letter to the Remington Arms, U. M. C. Plant, Liberty
Ordnance Company and others, Bridgeport, Conn.,
demanding reinstatement of striking workmen, September 17, 1918, Official U. S. Bulletin, no. 415, September 18, 1918.

Also in:—Public papers; War and Peace (1917-1924),
vol. 1, p. 252.

Proclamation (October 12, Columbus Day, 1918), September 20, 1918. In:—Woodrow Wilson's worte. . . .
Heilbronn, a.N., 1924, pp. 150-151.

Letter to Thetus W. Sims urging the passage of the Emergency power bill, September 21, 1918. Cong. Rec.,
vol. 56, p. 10603.

Statement commending the work of Congress, September 23,
1918, Cong. Rec., vol. 56, p. 10667.

Opening campaign for Fourth Liberty Loan, address of
President Wilson delivered in New York City, September 27, 1918, Washington, 1918. (65th Cong.
2d sess. Senate Doc. 283.)

Also in:—Americanism, Chicago [c1918], pp. 130-136.

Also in:—Bases of durable peace, Chicago, 1918, pp.
3-10.

Also in:—Cong. Rec., vol. 56, pp. 10886-10888.

Also in:—Discursos y mensajes de estado, N. Y., 1919,
pp. 274-289.

Also in:—Gauss, Democracy today, N. Y., 1919, pp.
240-249.

Also in:—Guarantees of peace, N. Y., 1919, pp. 58-70.

Also in:—International conciliation, no. 131.

Also in:—Mensagens, Allocuções e discursos, Rio de Janeiro, 1918, pp. 141-149.

Also in:—Messages, Discours. . . . Paris, 1919, vol. 2, pp. 302-304.

Also in:—New York Times Current History Magazine, vol. 9, pt. 1, pp. 251-254.

Also in:—Official U. S. Bulletin, no. 424, September 28, 1918.

Also in:—President Wilson's state papers and addresses, ed. by Albert Shaw, 1924, vol. 1, pp. 520-528.

Also in:—Public papers; War and Peace (1917-1924), vol. 1, pp. 253-261.

Also in:—Die Reden, Englisch und Deutsch. Bern, 1919, pp. 169-185.

Also in:—Selected addresses and public papers; ed. by Albert Bushnell Hart, N. Y., 1918, pp. 275-282.

Also in:—Wilson; Das Staatsmännische werk. . . . Berlin, 1919, pp. 251-258.

Also in:—Woodrow Wilson, udvalg af taler. Köbenhavn, 1918, pp. 146-156.

Also in:—Woodrow Wilson's worte. . . . Heilbronn, a.N., 1924, pp. 151-159.

Also in:—Principles for which America, China and the Allies are fighting. Reprinted from Millard's review of October 5, 1918, Shanghai, China. (English and Chinese texts.)

Endorsement of the 4th Liberty loan, September 28, 1918. In:—Public papers; War and Peace (1917-1924), vol. 1, p. 262.

Also in:—Official U. S. Bulletin, no. 424, September 28, 1918.

Address of the President of the United States delivered in the Senate of the United States, September 30, 1918, Washington, 1918. (Woman Suffrage.) (65th Cong., 2d sess. Senate Doc. 284.)

Also in:—Cong. Rec., vol. 56, pp. 10928-10929.

Also in:—Discursos y mensajes de estado, N. Y., 1919, pp. 290-298.

Also in:—Guarantees of peace, N. Y., 1919, pp. 71-72.

Also in:—The messages and papers; ed. by Albert Shaw, N. Y., 1924, vol. 1, pp. 528-532.

Also in:—Official U. S. Bulletin, no. 425, September 30, 1918.

Also in:—Public papers; War and Peace (1917-1924), vol. 1, pp. 263-267.

Also in:—Wilson; Das Staatsmännische werk. . . . Berlin, 1919, pp. 259-262.

Also in:—Woodrow Wilson's worte. . . . Heilbronn, a.N., 1924, pp. 159-163.

Wilson's first draft of the Covenant of the League of Nations, completed during September, 1918. In:—Ray Stannard Baker, Woodrow Wilson and world settlement, N. Y., 1922, vol. 3, pp. 88-93.

Public message to the Student Corps, October 1, 1918. In:— Selected addresses and public papers; ed. by Albert Bushnell Hart, N. Y., 1918, pp. 282-283.

Also in:—Official U. S. Bulletin, no. 426, October 1, 1918.

Also in:—Public papers; War and Peace (1917-1924), vol. 1, p. 268.

Also in:—Woodrow Wilson's worte. . . . Heilbronn, a.N., 1924, pp. 163-164.

Statement urging all seafaring men to rally to call of the merchant marine, October, 1918, Official U. S. Bulletin, no. 426, October 1, 1918.

Also in:—Public papers; War and Peace (1917-1924), vol. 1, pp. 269-271.

Address on woman suffrage at the White House, October 3, 1918. In:—Public papers; War and peace (1917-1924), vol. 1, pp. 272-273.

Dispatch to the German Government through Secretary Lansing, October 8, 1918. (Question of an Armistice.) In:—Selected addresses and public papers; ed. by Albert Bushnell Hart, N. Y., 1918, pp. 283-284.

Also in:—Americanism, Chicago [c1918], p. 141.

Also in:—Discursos y mensajes de estado, N. Y., 1919, pp. 301-303.

Also in:—Guarantees of peace, N. Y., 1919, pp. 78-79.

Also in:—International conciliation, no. 133.

Also in:—Messages and addresses, ed. by Albert Shaw, N. Y., 1924, vol. 1, pp. 536-537.

Also in:—Messages, Discours. . . . Paris, 1919, vol. 2, pp. 316-317.

Also in:—Official U. S. Bulletin, no. 433, October 9, 1918.

Also in:—Preliminary history of the Armistice. Carnegie Endowment for International Peace. Division of International Law, N. Y., Oxford University Press, 1924, p. 52.

Also in:—Public papers; War and Peace (1917-1924), vol. 1, pp. 274-275.

Also in:—Woodrow Wilson, udvalg af taler. Köbenhavn, 1918, pp. 156-157.

Also in:—Woodrow Wilson's worte. . . . Heilbronn, a.N., 1924, pp. 164-165.

Letter to Lloyd England concerning the "give-a-bushel war fund," October 9, 1918. Cong. Rec., vol. 56, p. 11524.

Statement on Fourth Liberty Loan Campaign, October 11, 1918, Official U. S. Bulletin, no. 435, October 11, 1918.

Also in:—President Wilson's state papers and addresses, ed. by Albert Shaw, N. Y., 1924, vol. 1, p. 519.

Also in:—Public papers; War and Peace (1917-1924), vol. 1, p. 276.

Dispatch to the German Government through Secretary Lansing, October 14, 1918. (No negotiated peace with Germany.) In:—Selected addresses and public papers; ed. by Albert Bushnell Hart, N. Y., 1918, pp. 284-286.

Also in:—Americanism, Chicago [c1918], pp. 141-142.

Also in:—Cong. Rec., vol. 56, p. 11241.

Also in:—Discursos y mensajes de estado, N. Y., 1919, pp. 304-308.

Also in:—Guarantees of peace, N. Y., 1919, pp. 80-83.

Also in:—Independent, vol. 96, p. 113.

Also in:—International conciliation, no. 133.

Also in:—Messages and addresses, ed. by Albert Shaw, N. Y., 1924, vol. 1, pp. 538-540.

Also in:—Messages, Discours. . . . Paris, 1919, vol. 2, pp. 319-322.

Also in:—Official U. S. Bulletin, no. 437, October 15, 1918.

Also in:—Preliminary history of the Armistice. Carnegie Endowment for International Peace. Division of International Law, N. Y., Oxford Univ. Press, 1924, pp. 67-68.

Also in:—Public papers; War and Peace (1917-1924), vol. 1, pp. 277-279.

Also in:—Woodrow Wilson, udvalg af taler. Köbenhavn, 1918, pp. 157-160.

Also in:—Woodrow Wilson's worte. . . . Heilbronn, a.N., 1924, pp. 166-168.

Message transmitting to the Senate the text of a treaty between the United States and Italy providing for

reciprocal military service, October 14, 1918, Official
U. S. Bulletin, no. 446, October 25, 1918.

Statement on Fourth Liberty Loan, October 14, 1918, Official
U. S. Bulletin, no. 437, October 15, 1918.

Also in:—Public papers; War and Peace (1917-1924),
vol. 1, p. 280.

Message to Austria-Hungary through Secretary Lansing,
October 18, 1918. In:—Guarantees of peace, N. Y.,
1919, pp. 84-86.

Also in:—Cong. Rec., vol. 56, p. 11402.

Also in:—Discursos y mensajes de estado, N. Y., 1919,
pp. 309-311.

Also in:—Messages and addresses, ed. by Albert Shaw,
N. Y., 1924, vol. 1, pp. 540-541.

Also in:—Messages, Discours. . . . Paris, 1919, vol. 2,
pp. 333-334.

Also in:—Official U. S. Bulletin, no. 441, October 19,
1918.

Also in:—Woodrow Wilson, udvalg af taler. Köbenhavn, 1918, pp. 163-164.

Also in:—Public papers; War and Peace (1917-1924),
vol. 1, pp. 281-282.

Also in:—Woodrow Wilson's worte. . . . Heilbronn,
a.N., 1924, pp. 168-169.

Letter replying to Newton D. Baker, regarding 2,000,000
men overseas, October 22, 1918, Official U. S. Bulletin, no. 445, October 24, 1918.

Letter to Senator G. W. Hitchcock regarding article 3 of
peace terms in the address of January 8th, October
22, 1918, Cong. Rec., vol. 56, p. 11489.

Also in:—Ray Stannard Baker, Woodrow Wilson and
world settlement, N. Y., 1922, vol. 2, p. 413.

Message to Frederick Oederlin, Chargé d'Affaires of Switzerland through the Secretary of State, October 23,
1918. In:—Guarantees of peace, N. Y., 1919, pp.
86-90.

Also in:—Americanism, Chicago [c1918], pp. 143-144.

Also in:—Discursos y mensajes de estado, N. Y., 1919,
pp. 312-316.

Also in:—International conciliation, no. 133.

Also in:—Messages and addresses, ed. by Albert Shaw,
N. Y., 1924, vol. 1, pp. 543-546.

Also in:—Messages, Discours. . . . Paris, 1919, vol. 2,
pp. 325-328.

Also in:—Official U. S. Bulletin, no. 445, October 24,
1918.

Also in:—Preliminary history of the Armistice. Carnegie Endowment for International Peace. Division of International Law, N. Y., Oxford Univ. Press, 1924, pp. 113-115.

Also in:—Public papers; War and Peace (1917-1924), vol. 1, pp. 283-285.

Also in:—Woodrow Wilson, udvalg af taler. København, 1918, pp. 160-163.

Also in:—Woodrow Wilson's worte. . . . Heilbronn, a.N., 1924, pp. 169-172.

An appeal to the Electorate for political support, October 25, 1918. In:—Guarantees of peace, N. Y., 1919, pp. 91-94.

Also in:—Cong. Rec., vol. 56, p. 11494, also appendix p. 732.

Also in:—Messages and addresses, ed. by Albert Shaw, N. Y., 1924, vol. 1, pp. 557-559. (Here dated September 24, 1918.)

Also in:—Public papers; War and Peace (1917-1924), vol. 1, pp. 286-288.

Also in:—Woodrow Wilson's worte. . . . Heilbronn, a.N., 1924, pp. 172-174.

Letter of support to Charles O'Connor Hennessy, October 26, 1918, Cong. Rec., vol. 56, p. 11497.

Letter replying to Senator Simmons about speech of January 8, October 28, 1918, Official U. S. Bulletin, no. 449, October 29, 1918.

Also in:—Cong. Rec., vol. 56, p. 11490.

Also in:—Messages, Discours. . . . Paris, 1919, vol. 2, pp. 336-337.

Also in:—Public papers; War and Peace (1917-1924), vol. 1, pp. 289-290.

Telegram to W. P. Metcalf telling of non-support of the administration by Senator Fall, October 28, 1918. Cong. Rec., vol. 56, p. 11525.

Letter to Franklin K. Lane, November 4, 1918. (Council of National Defense.) Official U. S. Bulletin, no. 454, November 4, 1918.

Message of congratulation to His Majesty, Victor Emmanuel III, of Italy, November, 1918, Official U. S. Bulletin, no. 455, November 5, 1918.

Reply to Germany, November 5, 1918. In:—Americanism, Chicago [c1918], p. 144.

Also in:—International conciliation, no. 133.

Also in:—Messages and addresses, ed. by Albert Shaw, N. Y., 1924, vol. 1, pp. 546-547.

Also in:—Messages, Discours. . . . Paris, 1919, vol. 2, pp. 329-331.

Also in:—Official U. S. Bulletin, no. 456, November 6, 1918.

Also in:—Preliminary history of the Armistice. Carnegie Endowment for International Peace. Division of International Law, N. Y., Oxford Univ. Press, 1924, pp. 143-144.

Also in:—Public papers; War and Peace (1917-1924), vol. 1, pp. 291-292.

Announcement of the signing of the Armistice with Germany, November 11, 1918, Official U. S. Bulletin, no. 460, November 11, 1918.

Also in:—Public papers; War and Peace (1917-1924), vol. 1, p. 293.

Address of the President of the United States delivered at a joint session of the two houses of Congress, November 11, 1918, Washington, 1918. (Armistice with Germany.) (65th Cong. 2d sess. House Doc. 139.)

Also in:—Americanism, Chicago [c1918], pp. 138-140.

Also in:—Cong. Rec., vol. 56, pp. 11537-11539; also pp. 11541-11543.

Also in:—Discursos y mensajes de estado, N. Y., 1919, pp. 317-323.

Also in:—Gauss, Democracy today, N. Y., 1919, pp. 257-261.

Also in:—Guarantees of peace, N. Y., 1919, pp. 95-110.

Also in:—International conciliation, no. 133.

Also in:—Messages and addresses, ed. by Albert Shaw, N. Y., 1924, vol. 1, pp. 548-556. (Text of the terms are here corrected.)

Also in:—Messages, Discours. . . . Paris, 1919, vol. 2, pp. 338-343.

Also in:—New York Times Current History Magazine, vol. 9, pt. 1, pp. 363-364.

Also in:—Official U. S. Bulletin, no. 460, November 11, 1918.

Also in:—Public papers; War and Peace (1917-1924), vol. 1, pp. 294-302.

Also in:—Die Reden, Englisch und Deutsch. Bern, 1919, pp. 187-194.

Also in:—Selected addresses and public papers; ed. by Albert Bushnell Hart, N. Y., 1918, pp. 286-289. (Incomplete text.)

Also in:—Wilson; Das staatsmännische werk. . . . Berlin, 1919, pp. 263-265.

Also in:—Woodrow Wilson, udvalg af taler. Köbenhavn, 1918, pp. 165-168.

Also in:—Woodrow Wilson's worte. . . . Heilbronn,
a.N., 1924, pp. 175-178.

Birthday greetings to His Majesty, Victor Emmanuel III,
King of Italy, November 11, 1918, Official U. S. Bulletin, no. 460, November 11, 1918, and no. 469, November 21, 1918.

Statement urging former teachers to return to the teaching
profession, November 12, 1918, Official U. S. Bulletin,
no. 465, November 16, 1918.

Reply to congratulations from Belisario Porras, Panama,
November 13, 1918, Official U. S. Bulletin, no. 469,
November 21, 1918.

Messages of felicitation to His Majesty, Albert, King of the
Belgians, November 15, 1918, Official U. S. Bulletin,
no. 465, November 16, 1918.

Reply to congratulations from His Majesty, Yoshihito,
Japan, November 15, 1918, Official U. S. Bulletin,
no. 469, November 21, 1918.

Reply to message from His Excellency, Hon. Shihchang,
China, November 15, 1918, Official U. S. Bulletin, no.
469, November 21, 1918.

Proclamation (Thanksgiving for Victory), November 16,
1918. In:—Guarantees of peace, N. Y., 1919, pp.
111-112.

Also in:—Official U. S. Bulletin, no. 466, November 18,
1918.

Also in:—Public papers; War and Peace (1917-1924),
vol. 1, pp. 303-304.

Also in:—Woodrow Wilson's worte. . . . Heilbronn,
a.N., 1924, pp. 179-180.

Statement announcing his intention to visit Europe, November 18, 1918. In:—America and the League of Nations, N. Y., 1919, p. 61.

Also in:—Public papers; War and Peace (1917-1924),
vol. 1, p. 305.

Reply to message of congratulation on the ending of the war
from His Majesty, Victor Emmanuel III, November
20, 1918, Official U. S. Bulletin, no. 469, November
21, 1918.

Letter to William G. McAdoo, accepting his resignation as
Secretary of the Treasury, November 21, 1918, Official U. S. Bulletin, no. 471, November 23, 1918.

Message felicitating King Albert on his re-entry into Brus-

sels, November 21, 1918, Official U. S. Bulletin, no.
471, November 23, 1918.

Telegram to Herr Bodholt, 22 Novbr. (Slesvigs). In:—
Woodrow Wilson; udvalg af taler, Köbenhavn, 1918,
pp. 168-169.

Letter to Frank P. Walsh (accepting his resignation as chairman of War Labor Board), November 27, 1918, Official U. S. Bulletin, no. 479, December 4, 1918.

Address to B'Nai B'rith, Washington, November 28, 1918.
In:—Public papers; War and Peace (1917-1924), vol.
1, pp. 306-307.

Announcement of the membership of the delegation of the
United States to the Peace Conference, November 29,
1918. In:—America and the League of Nations,
N. Y., 1919, p. 61.

Letter to Dr. C. A. Prosser on healing the wounded, November 29, 1918, Official U. S. Bulletin, no. 508, January
10, 1919.

Letter to Bernard M. Baruch (resignation), November 30,
1918, Official U. S. Bulletin, no. 480, December 5,
1918.

Address of the President of the United States delivered at a
joint session of the two houses of Congress, December
2, 1918, Washington, 1918. (Address before going
abroad.) (65th Cong., 3d sess. House Doc. 1668.)
(Also as Bureau edition.)

Also in:—America and the League of Nations, N. Y.,
1919, pp. 62-64. (In part.)

Also in:—Cong. Rec., vol. 57, pp. 5-8; also pp 12-15.

Also in:—Guarantees of peace, N. Y., 1919, pp. 113-137.

Also in:—Messages and addresses, ed. by Albert Shaw,
N. Y., 1924, vol. 1, pp. 559-575.

Also in:—Messages, Discours. . . . Paris, 1919, vol. 2,
pp. 344-349. (In part.)

Also in:—New York Times Current History Magazine, vol. 9, pt. 2, pp. 106-110.

Also in:—Official U. S. Bulletin, no. 477, December 2,
1918.

Also in:—Public papers; War and Peace (1917-1924),
vol. 1, pp. 308-323.

Also in:—Selected addresses and public papers; ed. by
Albert Bushnell Hart, N. Y., 1918, pp. 289-303.

Also in:—Wilson; Das staatsmännische werk. . . . Berlin, 1919, pp. 266-279.

Also in:—Woodrow Wilson's worte. . . . Heilbronn,
a.N., 1924, pp. 180-195.

Wireless message from U. S. S. *George Washington* to Charles M. Schwab (resignation), December 9, 1918, Official U. S. Bulletin, no. 483, December 9, 1918.

Wireless message of welcome to editors of Norway, Sweden and Denmark in Washington, December 10, 1918, Official U. S. Bulletin, no. 484, December 10, 1918.

Note to Chile and Peru urging them to compose their differences, Official U. S. Bulletin, no. 486, December 12, 1918.

Response to President Poincaré's address of welcome, Paris, December 14, 1918. In:—International ideals, N. Y., 1919, pp. 1-4.

    Also in:—Messages, Discours. . . . Paris, 1919, vol. 2, pp. 350-354.

    Also in:—Public papers; War and Peace (1917-1924), vol. 1, pp. 324-325.

    Also in:—Woodrow Wilson's worte. . . . Heilbronn, a.N., 1924, pp. 196-198.

Reply to the greeting of a Socialist delegation, Paris, December 16, 1918. In:—International ideals, N. Y., 1919, pp. 5-6.

    Also in:—Public papers; War and Peace (1917-1924), vol. 1, p. 326.

    Also in:—Woodrow Wilson's worte. . . . Heilbronn, a.N., 1924, pp. 198-199.

Reply to greetings of the Prefect of the Seine and of the President of the Municipal Council, Paris, December 16, 1918. In:—International ideals, N. Y., 1919, pp. 7-9.

    Also in:—Messages, Discours. . . . Paris, 1919, vol. 2, pp. 355-357.

    Also in:—Public papers; War and Peace (1917-1924), vol. 1, pp. 327-328.

    Also in:—Woodrow Wilson's worte. . . . Heilbronn, a.N., 1924, pp. 199-200.

Address acknowledging the honor bestowed upon him by the University of Paris in the form of a Doctor's degree, December 21, 1918. In:—International ideals, N. Y., 1919, pp. 16-19.

    Also in:—Addresses on first trip to Europe, Washington, 1919, pp. 5-6.

    Also in:—Chicago Daily News Almanac, 1920, p. 268.

    Also in:—Messages and addresses, ed. by Albert Shaw, N. Y., 1924, vol. 1, pp. 576-578.

    Also in:—Messages, Discours. . . . Paris, 1919, vol. 2, pp. 358-361.

Also in:—Public papers; War and Peace (1917-1924), vol. 1, pp. 329-331.

Also in:—Réception du Président Wilson à l'Université de Paris, le 21 Decembre 1918, Paris [1919], pp. 15-16.

Also in:—School and Society, vol. 9, pp. 23-24.

Also in:—Wilson; Das staatsmännische werk. . . . Berlin, 1919, pp. 280-281.

Also in:—Woodrow Wilson's worte. . . . Heilbronn, a.N., 1924, pp. 201-203.

Letter accepting the resignation of Ambassador Wm. G. Sharp, December 21, 1918, Official U. S. Bulletin, no. 540, February 17, 1919.

Message to America, December 24, 1918. In:—Woodrow Wilson's worte. . . . Heilbronn, a.N., 1924, pp. 203-204.

Address to the American troops at Humes, December 25, 1918. In:—International ideals, N. Y., 1919, pp. 12-15.

Also in:—Addresses on first trip to Europe, Washington, 1919, pp. 6-8.

Also in:—Chicago Daily News Almanac, 1920, pp. 268-269.

Also in:—Cong. Rec., vol. 57, p. 844.

Also in:—Messages and addresses, ed. by Albert Shaw, N. Y., 1924, vol. 1, pp. 578-581.

Also in:—Official U. S. Bulletin, no. 497, December 27, 1918.

Also in:—Public papers; War and Peace (1917-1924), vol. 1, pp. 332-334.

Also in:—Woodrow Wilson's worte. . . . Heilbronn, a.N., 1924, pp. 204-206.

Response to an address of welcome by the Mayor of Chaumont, December 25, 1918. In:—International ideals, N. Y., 1919, pp. 10-11.

Also in:—Addresses on first trip to Europe, Washington, 1919, pp. 8-9.

Also in:—Chicago Daily News Almanac, 1920, p. 269.

Also in:—Public papers; War and Peace (1917-1924), vol. 1, p. 335.

Reply to the address of welcome from the Mayor of Dover, December 26, 1918. In:—International ideals, N. Y., 1919, pp. 20-21.

Also in:—Addresses on first trip to Europe, Washington, 1919, p. 10.

Also in:—Chicago Daily News Almanac, 1920, p. 270.

Also in:—Official U. S. Bulletin, no. 497, December 27, 1918.

Also in:—Public papers; War and Peace (1917-1924), vol. 1, p. 336.

Reply to King George's speech of welcome at Buckingham Palace, December 27, 1918. In:—International ideals, N. Y., 1919, pp. 22-25.

Also in:—Addresses on first trip to Europe, Washington, 1919, pp. 10-11.

Also in:—Chicago Daily News Almanac, 1920, p. 272.

Also in:—Messages and addresses, ed. by Albert Shaw, N. Y., 1924, vol. 1, pp. 581-582.

Also in:—Messages, Discours. . . . Paris, 1919, vol. 2, pp. 362-366.

Also in:—Official U. S. Bulletin, no. 499, December 30, 1918.

Also in:—Public papers; War and Peace (1917-1924), vol. 1, pp. 337-338.

Also in:—Woodrow Wilson's worte. . . . Heilbronn, a.N., 1924, pp. 207-208.

Reply to Committee of National Council of the Evangelical Free Churches, London, December 28, 1918. In:— Addresses on first trip to Europe, Washington, 1919, p. 12.

Also in:—Public papers; War and Peace (1917-1924), vol. 1, p. 339.

Reply to League of Nations Union, American Embassy, London, December 28, 1918. In:—Addresses on first trip to Europe, Washington, 1919, p. 12.

Also in:—Public papers; War and Peace (1917-1924), vol. 1, p. 340.

Reply to an address by the Lord Mayor at the Guildhall, on behalf of the Corporation of the city of London, December 28, 1918. In:—International ideals, N. Y., 1919, pp. 26-31.

Also in:—Addresses on first trip to Europe, Washington, 1919, pp. 12-14.

Also in:—Chicago Daily News Almanac, 1920, pp. 272-273.

Also in:—Cong. Rec., vol. 57, p. 980.

Also in:—Messages and addresses, ed. by Albert Shaw, N. Y., 1924, vol. 1, pp. 583-586.

Also in:—Official U. S. Bulletin, no. 499, December 30, 1918.

Also in:—Public papers; War and Peace (1917-1924), vol. 1, pp. 341-344.

Also in:—Wilson; Das staatsmännische werk. . . . Berlin, 1919, pp. 282-284.

Also in:—Woodrow Wilson's worte. . . . Heilbronn, a.N., 1924, pp. 209-211.

Address at the luncheon given by the Lord Mayor at the Mansion House, December 28, 1918. In:—International ideals, N. Y., 1919, pp. 32-34.

Also in:—Addresses on first trip to Europe, Washington, 1919, pp. 15-16.

Also in:—Chicago Daily News Almanac, 1920, pp. 273-274.

Also in:—Messages and addresses, ed. by Albert Shaw, N. Y., 1924, vol. 1, pp. 586-587.

Also in:—Messages, Discours. . . . Paris, 1919, vol. 2, pp. 367-372.

Also in:—Public papers; War and Peace (1917-1924), vol. 1, pp. 345-346.

Also in:—Woodrow Wilson's worte. . . . Heilbronn, a.N., 1924, pp. 212-214.

Speech to the congregation of the Lowther Street Congregational Church, Carlisle, England, December 29, 1918. In:—International ideals, N. Y., 1919, pp. 35-37.

Also in:—Public papers; War and Peace (1917-1924), vol. 1, pp. 347-348.

Also in:—Woodrow Wilson's worte. . . . Heilbronn, a.N., 1924, pp. 214-215.

Address at Free Trade Hall, Manchester, December 30, 1918. In:—Addresses on first trip to Europe, Washington, 1919, pp. 17-20.

Also in:—Chicago Daily News Almanac, 1920, pp. 274-275.

Also in:—Messages and addresses, ed. by Albert Shaw, N. Y., 1924, vol. 1, pp. 590-594.

Also in:—Public papers; War and Peace (1917-1924), vol. 1, pp. 352-356.

Also in:—Wilson's; Das staatsmännische werk. . . . Berlin, 1919, pp. 285-288.

Also in:—Woodrow Wilson's worte. . . . Heilbronn, a.N., 1924, pp. 216-221.

Address at luncheon, Midland Hotel, Manchester, December 30, 1918. In:—Addresses on first trip to Europe, Washington, 1919, pp. 16-17.

Also in:—Chicago Daily News Almanac, 1920, p. 276.

Also in:—Messages and addresses, ed. by Albert Shaw, N. Y., 1924, vol. 1, pp. 587-590.

Also in:—Messages, Discours. . . . Paris, 1919, vol. 2, pp. 373-377. (In part.)

Also in:—Public papers; War and Peace (1917-1924), vol. 1, pp. 349-351.

Also in:—Woodrow Wilson's worte. . . . Heilbronn, a.N., 1924, pp. 221-223.

BOOKS, 1919

Addresses of President Wilson. Addresses delivered by President Wilson on his Western tour, September 4 to September 25, 1919, on The League of Nations, Treaty of Peace With Germany, Industrial Conditions, High Cost of Living, Race Riots, etc., Washington, 1919. (66th Cong., 1st sess. Senate Doc. 120.)

Addresses of President Wilson, Boston, Mass., February 24, 1919, N. Y., March 4, 1919, Washington, 1919.

Addresses of President Wilson on first trip to Europe, December 3, 1918, to February 24, 1919, Washington, 1919.

America and the League of Nations addresses in Europe, compiled by Lyman P. Powell and Fred B. Hodgins, N. Y., Rand McNally and Company [c1919]. (Contains addresses, etc., from November 18, 1918, to March 4, 1919.)

America joins the world; selections from the speeches and state papers of President Wilson, 1914-1918; with an introduction [A. O. Lovejoy], N. Y., Association Press [c1919].

Betrachtungen e Amerikaners. obers. v. Hans Winand. München, 1919.

Chile. Ministerio de relaciones exteriores. El mensaje del presidente Wilson. Discurso pronunciados en la Camara de diputados por el ministro de relaciones exteriores, Don Luis Barros Borgono, en las sesiones 12 y 13 de Decembre 1918. Santiago de Chile. Imprenta universitaria. 1919. (La cuestión chileno-peruana. no. 5.)

Discursos y mensajes de estado del Presidente Wilson, recopilados y ed. por F. Eugenio Ackerman, tr. de Juan F. Urquidi, introduccion por Dr. Roberto Brenes Mesen. New York, D. Appleton y compania. 1919. (Contains addresses, etc., from October 27, 1913, to November 11, 1918.)

Guarantees of peace; messages and addresses to the Congress and the people, January 31, 1918, to December 2,

1918, together with the peace notes to Germany and Austria. New York, Harper & Brothers, 1919.

International ideals; speeches and addresses made during the President's European visit, December 14, 1918, to February 14, 1919. New York, Harper & Brothers, 1919.

League of Nations. Comparison of the plan for the League of Nations, showing the original draft as presented to the commission constituted by the preliminary Peace Conference in session at Versailles, France, together with the covenant as finally reported and adopted at the plenary session of the Peace conference, also the presentation speeches of the President of the United States relating thereto. Washington, 1919. (66th Cong., 1st sess. Senate Doc. 7.)

Mémoire sur la delimitation des droits de l'Etat et de la nation d'aprés la doctrine du President Wilson, par André Mandelstam, Paris, 1919. (Contains many quotations from addresses and state papers.)

Messages, discours, documents, diplomatiques relatifs à la guerre mondiale. tr. par Désiré Roustan. Paris, Bossard. 1919, 2 vols. (Contains addresses, etc., from August 18, 1914, to March 4, 1919.)

Die neue freiheit, ein aufruf zur berfreiung der edlen kräfte eines volkes. Mit einer einleitung von Hans Winand. München, G. Müller, 1919.

The new freedom; a call for the emancipation of the generous energies of a people, N. Y., Doubleday, Page & Co., 1919. (First published in 1913.)

La Nuova libertà; invito di liberazione alle generose forze di un popolo, 2 ed. Milano, Facchi, 1919.

La Nueva libertad. . . . Valencia, Prometeo, n.d.

President Wilson's great speeches and other history-making documents, Chicago, Stanton and Van Vliet Co., 1919. (Contains selected addresses, papers, etc., from April 2, 1917, to February 24, 1919.)

Proclamations by the President of the United States, January 7, 1919 to March 4, 1919. U. S. Laws, Statutes, etc. The statutes at large, vol. 40, pt. 2, pp. 1919-1938. Also March 19, 1919 to December 27, 1919, id. vol. 41, pt. 2, pp. 1741-1784.

Die Reden Woodrow Wilson, Englisch und Deutsch. hrsg. vom Committee on Public Information of the United States of America. Bern. 1919. (Addresses, etc., from January, 1917, to November, 1918.)

The triumph of ideals; speeches, messages and addresses made by the President between February 24, 1919, and

July 8, 1919, covering the active period of the Peace
Conference at Paris, New York, Harper & Brothers
[1919].
Wilson; Das staatsmännische werk des Präsidenten in seinen
reden hrsg., von Georg Ahrens und Carl Brinkmann.
Berlin, Dietrich Reimer, 1919. (Contains addresses,
etc., from October, 1913, to February, 1919.)
The wisdom of Woodrow Wilson; being selections from his
thoughts and comments on political, social and moral
questions compiled and with an introduction by
Charles J. Herold, New York, Brentano's, 1919.
Woodrow Wilson's friedensplan mit augsgewahlten briefen,
schriften und reden aus der zeit vom 12 März, 1913,
bis zum 14. Februar 1919. Hrsg. Heinrich Laun-
nasch, Leipzig, E. P. Tal & Co., 1919.

MESSAGES AND ADDRESSES, 1919

Address at the Quirinal, Rome, Italy, January 3, 1919.
In:—Addresses on first trip to Europe, Washington,
1919, pp. 21-22.
Also in:—Messages and addresses, ed. by Albert Shaw,
N. Y., 1924, vol. 1, pp. 598-600.
Also in:—Messages, Discours. . . . Paris, 1919, vol. 2,
pp. 385-388.
Also in:—Public papers; War and Peace (1917-1924),
vol. 1, pp. 357-359.
Also in:—Wilson; Das staatsmännische werk. . . . Ber-
lin, 1919, p. 291.
Also in:—Woodrow Wilson's worte. . . . Heilbronn,
a.N., pp. 228-229.
Address, The Capitol, Rome, January 3, 1919. In:—Ad-
dresses on first trip to Europe, Washington, 1919, pp.
22-23.
Also in:—Chicago Daily News Almanac, 1920, p. 279.
Also in:—Messages and addresses, ed. by Albert Shaw,
N. Y., 1924, vol. 1, pp. 594-595.
Also in:—Messages, Discours. . . . Paris, 1919, vol. 2,
pp. 389-391.
Also in:—Official U. S. Bulletin, no. 504, January 6,
1919.
Also in:—Public papers; War and Peace (1917-1924),
vol. 1, pp. 360-361.
Also in:—Woodrow Wilson's worte. . . . Heilbronn,
a.N., 1924, pp. 229-231.
Address before Italian Parliament, Rome, January 3, 1919.

In:—Addresses on first trip to Europe, Washington, 1919, pp. 23-25.

Also in:—Chicago Daily News Almanac, 1920, p. 277.

Also in:—Messages and addresses, ed. by Albert Shaw, N. Y., 1924, vol. 1, pp. 596-598.

Also in:—Messages, Discours. . . . Paris, 1919, vol. 2, pp. 381-384.

Also in:—Public papers; War and Peace (1917-1924), vol. 1, pp. 362-364.

Also in:—Wilson: Das staatsmännische werk. . . . Berlin, 1919, pp. 289-290.

Also in:—Woodrow Wilson's worte. . . . Heilbronn, a.N., 1924, pp. 225-227.

Address in the Academy of the Lencei, Rome, January 4, 1919. In:—Addresses on first trip to Europe, Washington, 1919, pp. 25-26.

Also in:—Chicago Daily News Almanac, 1920, p. 279.

Also in:—Messages and addresses, ed. by Albert Shaw, N. Y., 1924, vol. 1, pp. 600-602.

Also in:—Public papers; War and Peace (1917-1924), vol. 1, pp. 367-368.

Also in:—Woodrow Wilson's worte. . . . Heilbronn, a.N., 1924, pp. 231-233.

Cablegram to the Secretary of the Treasury, requesting the appropriation of $100,000,000 for the relief of European peoples outside Germany, January 4, 1919. (65th Cong., 3d sess. House Doc. 1640.)

Also in:—Official U. S. Bulletin, no. 504, January 6, 1919.

Also in:—Public papers; War and Peace (1917-1924), vol. 1, pp. 365-366.

Also in:—Woodrow Wilson's worte. . . . Heilbronn, a.N., 1924, pp. 224-225.   (Dated January 2, 1919.)

Reply to the press representatives at Rome, January 4, 1919. In:—Addresses on first trip to Europe, Washington, 1919, pp. 26-27.

Also in:—Public papers; War and Peace (1917-1924), vol. 1, pp. 369-370.

Speeches at Genoa, January 5, 1919. In:—Addresses on first trip to Europe, Washington, 1919, pp. 27-28.

Also in:—Chicago Daily News Almanac, 1920, p. 280.

Also in:—Messages and addresses, ed. by Albert Shaw, N. Y., 1924, vol. 1, pp. 602-603.

Also in:—Public papers; War and Peace (1917-1924), vol. 1, pp. 371-373.

Also in:—Woodrow Wilson's worte. . . . Heilbronn, a.N., 1924, pp. 233-234.

Speeches at Milan, January 5, 1919. In:—Addresses on first trip to Europe, Washington, 1919, pp. 28-32.

Also in:—Chicago Daily News Almanac, 1920, pp. 280-282.

Also in:—Messages and addresses, ed. by Albert Shaw, N. Y., 1924, vol. 1, pp. 604-608.

Also in:—Messages, Discours. . . . Paris, 1919, vol. 2, pp. 392-394.

Also in:—Public papers; War and Peace (1917-1924), vol. 1, pp. 374-379.

Also in:—Woodrow Wilson's worte. . . . Heilbronn, a.N., 1924, pp. 235-239.

Addresses, The Municipalité, Turin January 6, 1919. In:— Addresses on first trip to Europe, Washington, 1919, pp. 32-33.

Also in:—Chicago Daily News Almanac, 1920, pp. 282-283.

Also in:—Messages and addresses, ed. by Albert Shaw, N. Y., 1924, vol. 1, pp. 608-609.

Also in:—Official U. S. Bulletin, no. 506, January 8, 1919.

Also in:—Public papers; War and Peace (1917-1924), vol. 1, pp. 380-381.

Addresses at the Philharmonic Club, Turin, January 6, 1919. In:—Addresses on first trip to Europe, Washington, 1919, pp. 33-35.

Also in:—Messages and addresses, ed. by Albert Shaw, N. Y., 1924, vol. 1, pp. 609-612.

Also in:—Public papers; War and Peace (1917-1924), vol. 1, pp. 381-384.

Also in:—Wilson; Das staatsmännische werk. . . . Berlin, 1919, pp. 292-293.

Address at the University, Turin, January 6, 1919. In:— Addresses on first trip to Europe, Washington, 1919, pp. 35-36.

Also in:—Chicago Daily News Almanac, 1920, p. 283.

Also in:—Messages and addresses, ed. by Albert Shaw, N. Y., 1924, vol. 1, pp. 612-613.

Also in:—Public papers; War and Peace (1917-1924), vol. 1, pp. 384-386.

Proclamation (Death of Theodore Roosevelt), January 7, 1919, Official U. S. Bulletin, no. 506, January 8, 1919.

Also in:—Public papers; War and Peace (1917-1924), vol. 1, pp. 387-388.

Letter accepting the resignation of Attorney-General T. W.
Gregory, January 10, 1919, Official U. S. Bulletin,
no. 511, January 14, 1919.

Wilson's second draft of the Covenant of the League of
Nations. (Distributed in printed form, January 10,
1919.) In:—Ray Stannard Baker, Woodrow Wilson
and world settlement, N. Y., 1922, vol. 3, pp. 100-110.

Cablegram through J. P. Tumulty to Messrs. Taft and
Manly, National War Labor Board, January, 1919,
Official U. S. Bulletin, no. 510, January 13, 1919.

Also in:—Woodrow Wilson's worte. . . . Heilbronn,
a.N., 1924, pp. 245-246.

Cablegram to Congressman Swagar Sherley ($100,000,000
for food for Europe), January, 1919, Official U. S.
Bulletin, no. 511, January 15, 1919.

Also in:—Public papers; War and Peace (1917-1924),
vol. 1, p. 389.

Letter to Robert S. Brookings accepting the resignation of
the members of the price-fixing committee, January
13, 1919, Official U. S. Bulletin, no. 531, February
6, 1919.

Wilson's third draft of the Covenant of the League of Nations. In:—Ray Stannard Baker, Woodrow Wilson
and world settlement, N. Y., 1922, vol. 3, pp. 117-129.

Address opening the Peace Conference, Paris, January 18,
1919. In:—Addresses on first trip to Europe, Washington, 1919, p. 37.

Also in:—Cong. Rec., vol. 57, pp. 1731-1732.

Also in:—International Conciliation, no. 139.

Also in:—Messages and papers, ed. by Albert Shaw,
N. Y., 1924, vol. 2, pp. 614-615.

Also in:—Messages, Discours. . . . Paris, 1919, vol. 2,
pp. 395-397.

Also in:—Public papers; War and Peace (1917-1924),
vol. 1, pp. 390-391.

Also in:—Woodrow Wilson's worte. . . . Heilbronn,
a.N., 1924, pp. 246-247.

Response to an address of welcome at a dinner in the Luxembourg palace, Paris, January 20, 1919. In:—Chicago
Daily News Almanac, 1920, p. 284.

Also in:—Messages and papers; ed. by Albert Shaw,
N. Y., 1924, vol. 2, pp. 615-617.

Also in:—Messages, Discours. . . . Paris, 1919, vol. 2,
pp. 398-402.

Also in:—Public papers; War and Peace (1917-1924),
vol. 1, pp. 392-394.

Also in:—Woodrow Wilson's worte. . . . Heilbronn a.N., 1924, pp. 247-249.

Proposition of Wilson relating to Russia, approved by the Peace Conference, January 22, 1919. In:—Messages Discours. . . . Paris, 1919, vol. 2, pp. 403-406.

Also in:—Russian-American Relations, Documents and Papers, compiled by C. K. Cumming and W. W. Pettit, N. Y., 1920, pp. 297-298.

Address before the Peace Conference, January 25, 1919. In:—Addresses on first trip to Europe, Washington, 1919, pp. 39-43.

Also in:—Independent, vol. 97, p. 174, 203.

Also in:—International Conciliation, no. 139.

Also in:—Messages and papers, ed. by Albert Shaw, N. Y., 1924, vol. 2, pp. 618-623.

Also in:—Messages, Discours. . . . Paris, 1919, vol. 2, pp. 407-415.

Also in:—New York Times Current History Magazine, vol. 9, pt. 2, pp. 383-385.

Also in:—Official U. S. Bulletin, no. 522, January 27, 1919.

Also in:—Public papers; War and Peace (1917-1924), vol. 1, pp. 395-400.

Also in:—Wilson; Das staatsmännische werk. . . . Berlin, 1919, pp. 294-297.

Also in:—Woodrow Wilson's case for the League of Nations, Princeton, 1923, pp. 211-219.

Also in:—Woodrow Wilson's worte. . . . Heilbronn, a.N., 1924, pp. 249-254.

Reply to address of working women of France, Paris, January 25, 1919. In:—Addresses on first trip to Europe, Washington, 1919, pp. 43-44.

Also in:—Chicago Daily News Almanac, 1920, pp. 284-285.

Also in:—Official U. S. Bulletin, no. 522, January 27, 1919.

Also in:—Public papers; War and Peace (1917-1924), vol. 1, pp. 401-403.

Reply to the League for the Rights of Man, Paris, January 28, 1919. In:—Addresses on first trip to Europe, Washington, 1919, p. 45.

Also in:—Public papers; War and Peace (1917-1924), vol. 1, p. 404.

Message through Secretary Lansing to Ignace Paderewski, extending full recognition to the provisional Polish

Government, January 1919, Official U. S. Bulletin, no. 525, January 30, 1919.

Address before the French Chamber of Deputies, Paris, February 3, 1919. In:—Chicago Daily News Almanac, 1920, pp. 285-286.

Also in:—Cong. Rec., vol. 57, pp. 2826-2827.

Also in:—Messages, Discours. . . . Paris, 1919, vol. 2, pp. 421-427.

Also in:—Official U. S. Bulletin, no. 530, February 5, 1919.

Also in:—Public papers; War and Peace (1917-1924), vol. 1, pp. 405-409.

Reply to delegation from French Society of Nations, Paris, February 12, 1919. In:—Addresses on first trip to Europe, Washington, 1919, pp. 45-46.

Also in:—Chicago Daily News Almanac, 1920, p. 286.

Also in:—Messages, Discours. . . . Paris, 1919, vol. 2, pp. 428-430. (Here dated February 4, 1919.)

Also in:—Public papers; War and Peace (1917-1924), vol. 1, pp. 410-411.

Also in:—Woodrow Wilson's worte. . . . Heilbronn, a.N., 1924, pp. 255-256.

Cablegram from Paris through Secretary Tumulty to members of the Foreign Relations Committee of the U. S. Senate and the Foreign Affairs Committee of the House. (League of Nations) February 14, 1919, Official U. S. Bulletin, no. 540, February 17, 1919.

Also in:—Cong. Rec., vol. 57, p. 3689.

Also in:—Public papers; War and Peace (1917-1924), vol. 1, p. 412.

Also in:—Woodrow Wilson's worte. . . . Heilbronn, a.N., 1924, p. 256.

Address before the Third Plenary Session of the Peace Conference upon presenting the draft for the League of Nations, February 14, 1919, Washington, 1919. (66th Cong., 1st sess. Senate Doc. 7.) (66th Cong., 1st sess. Senate Doc. 46.)

Also in:—Addresses on first trip to Europe, Washington, 1919, pp. 47-58.

Also in:—Cong. Rec., vol. 57, pp. 3408-3411.

Also in:—Independent, vol. 97, pp. 288-290, p. 307.

Also in:—Messages and papers; ed. by Albert Shaw, N. Y., 1924, vol. 2, pp. 623-638.

Also in:—Messages, Discours. . . . Paris, 1919, vol. 2, pp. 431-456.

Also in:—New York Times Current History Magazine, vol. 9, pt. 2, pp. 398-401.

Also in:—Official U. S. Bulletin, no. 541, February 18, 1919. (Text of League covenant given in no. 538, February 14, 1919.)

Also in:—Public papers; War and Peace (1917-1924), vol. 1, pp. 413-429.

Also in:—Woodrow Wilson's case for the League of Nations, Princeton, 1923, pp. 220-233.

Also in:—Woodrow Wilson's worte. . . . Heilbronn, a.N., 1924, pp. 257-264.

Farewell message to the French people, February 14, 1919. In:—Chicago Daily News Almanac, 1920, p. 286.

Also in:—Public papers; War and Peace (1917-1924), vol. 1, p. 430.

Wireless message from the U. S. S. *George Washington* to M. Clemenceau expressing sympathy over his injury caused by an attempt at his assassination, February 20, 1919. In:—Public papers; War and Peace (1917-1924), vol. 1, 431.

The League of Nations. Address delivered by the President of the United States at Boston, Mass., on February 24, 1919, on the plan for the League of Nations, Washington, 1919. (65th Cong., 3d sess. Senate Doc. 431.)

Also in:—Chicago Daily News Almanac, 1920, pp. 287-289.

Also in:—Cong. Rec., vol. 57, pp. 4201-4203.

Also in:—Independent, vol. 97, pp. 321-322.

Also in:—International Conciliation, Special Bulletin, March, 1919.

Also in:—Messages and papers, ed. by Albert Shaw, N. Y., 1924, vol. 2, pp. 638-647.

Also in:—Messages, Discours. . . . Paris, 1919, vol. 2, pp. 456-470.

Also in:—New York Times Current History Magazine, vol. 10, pt. 1, pp. 87-90.

Also in:—Official U. S. Bulletin, no. 546, February 25, 1919.

Also in:—Public papers; War and Peace (1917-1924), vol. 1, pp. 432-440.

Also in:—Triumph of ideals, N. Y., 1919, pp. 1-16.

Also in:—Wilson; Das staatsmännische werk. . . . Berlin, 1919, pp. 298-305.

Also in:—Woodrow Wilson's worte. . . . Heilbronn, a.N., 1924, pp. 264-275.

Message submitting information regarding the designation of Bar Harbor, Me., as a port of entry, February 26, 1919, Washington, 1919. (65th Cong., 3d sess. House Doc. 1831.)

Letter to Dr. Anna Howard Shaw accepting the resignation of the Woman's Committee, Council of National Defense, February 27, 1919, Official U. S. Bulletin, no. 571, March 26, 1919.

Letter to William B. Bankhead urging passage of the Americanization bill, February 28, 1919. Cong. Rec., vol. 57, p. 4565.

Letter to Robert S. Brookings (Price-fixing Committee), February 28, 1919, Official U. S. Bulletin no. 558, March 11, 1919.

Address before Governors and Mayors called to discuss the labor situation, March 3, 1919. In:—Triumph of ideals, N. Y., 1919, pp. 17-21.

Also in:—Chicago Daily News Almanac, 1920, pp. 289-290.

Also in:—Official U. S. Bulletin, no. 551, March 3, 1919.

Also in:—Public papers; War and Peace (1917-1924), vol. 1, pp. 441-443.

Also in:—Woodrow Wilson's worte. . . . Heilbronn, a.N., pp. 276-278.

Letter to the Commission of the Philippine Legislature through Secretary of War Baker, March 3, 1919. In:—United States Bulletin, no. 577, April 7, 1919.

Message transmitting information in detail of the administration of the provisions of the so-called Overman act, authorizing the President to co-ordinate or consolidate executive bureaus, agencies, and offices, etc., March 3, 1919, Washington, 1919. (65th Cong., 3d sess. House Doc. 1841.)

Message transmitting statement from the Acting Secretary of State, with accompanying papers, of appropriations, expenditures, and balances of appropriations under the Department of State for the fiscal year ending June 30, 1918, March 3, 1919, Washington, 1919. (65th Cong., 3d sess. House Doc. 1842.)

Address at New York, March 4, 1919. In:—Addresses of President Wilson, Boston, Mass., February 24, 1919, N. Y., March 4, 1919, Washington, 1919.

Also in:—Chicago Daily News Almanac, 1920, pp. 290-293.

Also in:—International Conciliation, Special Bulletin, March 1919.

Also in:—Messages and papers, ed. by Albert Shaw, N. Y., 1924, vol. 2, pp. 647-658.

Also in:—Messages, Discours. . . . Paris, 1919, vol. 2, pp. 471-488.

Also in:—New York Times Current History Magazine, vol. 10, pt. 1, pp. 104-108.

Also in:—Official U. S. Bulletin, no. 554, March 6, 1919.

Also in:—Public papers; War and Peace (1917-1924), vol. 1, pp. 444-455.

Also in:—Triumph of ideals, N. Y., 1919, pp. 22-40. (Dated here March 5.)

Also in:—Woodrow Wilson's worte. . . . Heilbronn, a.N., pp. 279-289.

Statement regarding the deliberate attempt to embarrass the administration by Congress, March 4, 1919, Official U. S. Bulletin, no. 552, March 4, 1919.

Also in:—Public papers; War and Peace (1917-1924), vol. 1, p. 456.

Also in:—Woodrow Wilson's worte. . . . Heilbronn, a.N., 1924, pp. 278-279.

Statement in Paris regarding the League covenant as an integral part of the treaty of peace, March 15, 1919, Official U. S. Bulletin, no. 563, March 17, 1919.

Also in:—Public papers; War and Peace (1917-1924), vol. 1, p. 457.

Also in:—Ray Stannard Baker, Woodrow Wilson and world settlement, N. Y., 1922, vol. 1, p. 311.

Joint letter asking Mr. Lloyd George to remain in Paris, signed with M. Clemenceau and M. Orlando, March 17, 1919, Official U. S. Bulletin, no. 566, March 20, 1919.

Also in:—Public papers; War and Peace (1917-1924), vol. 1, p. 458.

Cablegram to Secretary Tumulty, March 18, 1919, expressing appreciation of suggestions offered by Mr. Taft. In:—Woodrow Wilson's case for the League of Nations, Princeton, 1923, p. 240.

Statement issued in Paris, March 27, 1919. (League of Nations.) In:—Triumph of ideals, N. Y., 1919, pp. 41-42.

Also in:—United States Bulletin, no. 576, April 3, 1919.

Also in:—Public papers; War and Peace (1917-1924), vol. 1, p. 459.

Also in:—Woodrow Wilson's worte. . . . Heilbronn, a.N., 1924, pp. 289-290.

Also in:—Ray Stannard Baker, Woodrow Wilson and world settlement, N. Y., 1922, vol. 2, pp. 36-37.

Memorandum sent to the Italian delegation to the Peace Conference, April 14, 1919. Made public April 30, 1919. In:—Public papers; War and Peace (1917-1924), vol. 1, pp. 460-463.

Also in:—Triumph of ideals, N. Y., 1919, pp. 59-65.

Also in:—United States Bulletin, no. 588, May 19, 1919.

Also in:—Ray Stannard Baker, Woodrow Wilson and world settlement, N. Y., 1922, vol. 3, pp. 274-277.

Statement in behalf of the Council of Four, April 14, 1919. In:—Triumph of ideals, N. Y., 1919, pp. 43-44.

Also in:—Woodrow Wilson's worte. . . . Heilbronn, a.N., 1924, pp. 290-291.

Also in:—Public papers; War and Peace (1917-1924), vol. 1, p. 464.

Also in:—Ray Stannard Baker, Woodrow Wilson and world settlement, N. Y., 1922, vol. 2, p. 77.

Letter to Dr. Isaiah Bowman, regarding the Italian claims on the Adriatic, April 18, 1919. In:—Ray Stannard Baker, Woodrow Wilson and world settlement, N. Y., 1922, vol. 2, pp. 153-154.

Letter to M. Clemenceau, April 22, 1919. In:—Woodrow Wilson's worte. . . . Heilbronn, a.N., 1924, pp. 291-292.

Also in:—Ray Stannard Baker, Woodrow Wilson and world settlement, N. Y., 1922, vol. 2, p. 88.

Statement on the controversy with Italy over the Adriatic question, April 23, 1919. In:—Triumph of ideals, N. Y., 1919, pp. 45-51.

Also in:—Ray Stannard Baker, Woodrow Wilson and world settlement, N. Y., 1922, vol. 3, pp. 287-290.

Also in:—Messages and papers; ed. by Albert Shaw, N. Y., 1924, vol. 2, pp. 659-662.

Also in:—Public papers; War and Peace (1917-1924), vol. 1, pp. 465-468.

Also in:—United States Bulletin, no. 583, April 28, 1919.

Also in:—Woodrow Wilson's worte. . . . Heilbronn, a.N., 1924, pp. 292-295.

Appeal for Victory Liberty Loan, April 24, 1919. In:—United States Bulletin, no. 582, April 24, 1919.

Speech delivered before the fifth plenary session of the Peace Conference, April 28, 1919. In:—International Conciliation, no. 139.

Also in:—Messages and papers; ed. by Albert Shaw, N. Y., 1924, vol. 2, pp. 663-667.

Also in:—Public papers; War and Peace (1917-1924), vol. 1, pp. 469-473.

Also in:—Triumph of ideals, N. Y., 1919, pp. 52-58.

Statement on the Shantung settlement cabled to Secretary Tumulty April 30, 1919. In:—Ray Stannard Baker, Woodrow Wilson and world settlement, N. Y., 1922, vol. 3, pp. 315-316.

Also in:—Public papers; War and Peace (1917-1924), vol. 1, pp. 474-475.

Proclamation (Boy Scouts). Paris, May 1, 1919. In:— Triumph of ideals, N. Y., 1919, pp. 66-69.

Also in:—Public papers; War and Peace (1917-1924), vol. 1, pp. 476-477.

Cablegram to Secretary Tumulty, May 2, 1919. In:— Woodrow Wilson's worte. . . . Heilbronn, a.N., 1924, p. 295.

Letter to David Lloyd George criticizing the Keynes financial scheme, May 5, 1919. In:—Ray Stannard Baker, Woodrow Wilson and world settlement, N. Y., 1922, vol. 3, pp. 344-346.

Address before the International Law Society, Paris, May 9, 1919. In:—Messages and papers, ed. by Albert Shaw, N. Y., 1924, vol. 2, pp. 667-670.

Also in:—Public papers; War and Peace (1917-1924), vol. 1, pp. 478-481.

Cablegram to Washington, May 9, 1919. In:—Woodrow Wilson's worte. . . . Heilbronn, a.N., 1924, p. 296.

Address at the session of the Academy of moral and political science, Paris, May 10, 1919. In:—Triumph of ideals, N. Y., 1919, pp. 70-78.

Also in:—Public papers; War and Peace (1917-1924), vol. 1, pp. 482-484.

Cablegram to Jane Addams. In:—Woodrow Wilson's worte. . . . Heilbronn, a.N., 1924, p. 296.

Message communicated to the two houses of Congress at the beginning of the first session of the Sixty-sixth Congress, Washington, 1919. (Transmitted by cable May 20, 1919.)

Also in:—(66th Cong., 1st sess. House Doc. 20.)

Also in:—Chicago Daily News Almanac, 1920, pp. 378-381.

Also in:—Cong. Rec., vol. 58, pp. 40-42, also pp. 67-70.

Also in:—Messages and papers, ed. by Albert Shaw, N. Y., 1924, vol. 2, pp. 671-682.

Also in:—Public papers; War and Peace (1917-1924), vol. 1, pp. 485-496.

Also in—Triumph of ideals, N. Y., 1919, pp. 79-96.

Also in:—United States Bulletin, no. 589, May 26, 1919.

Also in:—Woodrow Wilson's worte. . . . Heilbronn, a.N., 1924, pp. 296-307.

Cablegram to Secretary Tumulty, May 24, 1919. In:— Woodrow Wilson's worte. . . . Heilbronn, a.N., 1924, p. 307.

Cablegram to Secretary Tumulty, May 25, 1919. In:— Woodrow Wilson's worte. . . . Heilbronn, a.N., 1924, pp. 307-308.

Speech at dinner given by the Pan-American peace delegation in honor of Dr. Epitacio Pessoa, President-elect of Brazil, Paris, May 27, 1919. In:—Triumph of ideals, N. Y., 1919, pp. 97-103.

Also in:—Chicago Daily News Almanac, 1920, pp. 294-295.

Also in:—Messages and papers, ed. by Albert Shaw, N. Y., 1924, vol. 2, pp. 682-686.

Also in:—Public papers; War and Peace (1917-1924), vol. 1, pp. 497-500.

Also in:—Woodrow Wilson's worte. . . . Heilbronn, a.N., 1924, pp. 308-311.

Memorial Day message to the American people, Paris, May 30, 1919. In:—Triumph of ideals, N. Y., 1919, pp. 104-105.

Also in:—Chicago Daily News Almanac, 1920, p. 295.

Also in:—Cong. Rec., vol. 58, p. 446.

Also in:—Public papers; War and Peace (1917-1924), vol. 1, p. 501.

Also in:—Woodrow Wilson's worte. . . . Heilbronn, a.N., 1924, pp. 311-312.

Address of President Woodrow Wilson delivered at the memorial exercises held at Suresnes cemetery, near Paris, France, on May 30, 1919, Washington, 1919. (66th Cong., 1st sess. Senate Doc. 20.)

Also in:—Chicago Daily News Almanac, 1920, pp. 295-297.

Also in:—Cong. Rec., vol. 58, pp. 494-495, also appendix pp. 8837-8838; also vol. 59, appendix p. 9200.

Also in:—Public papers; War and Peace (1917-1924), vol. 1, pp. 502-507.

Also in:—Triumph of ideals, N. Y., 1919, pp. 106-115.

Also in:—Woodrow Wilson's worte. . . . Heilbronn, a.N., 1924, pp. 312-318.

Stenographic report of meeting between President Wilson, the Peace Commissioners and technical advisers,

Paris, June 3, 1919. In:—Ray Stannard Baker, Woodrow Wilson and world settlement, N. Y., 1922, vol. 3, pp. 468-504.

Also in:—Woodrow Wilson's worte. . . . Heilbronn, a.N., 1924, pp. 318-333.

Cablegram to Senator Hitchcock through Mr. Tumulty regarding the possession of copies of the treaty by unauthorized persons, June 7, 1919. Cong. Rec., vol. 58, p. 781; also p. 783.

Also in:—Public papers; War and Peace (1917-1924), vol. 1, p. 508.

Addresses at Brussels, June 19, 1919. In:—Triumph of ideals, N. Y., 1919, pp. 116-125.

Also in:—Chicago Daily News Almanac, 1920, pp. 297-298.

Also in:—Cong. Rec., vol. 58, pp. 1428-1429.

Also in:—Messages and papers, ed. by Albert Shaw, N. Y., 1924, vol. 2, pp. 686-692.

Also in:—Public papers; War and Peace (1917-1924), vol. 1, pp. 509-519.

Also in:—Woodrow Wilson's worte. . . . Heilbronn, a.N., 1924, pp. 335-340.

Speech at dinner given by President Poincaré in honor of President Wilson and the delegates to the Peace Conference, Paris, June 26, 1919. In:—Triumph of ideals, N. Y., 1919, pp. 127-131.

Also in:—Chicago Daily News Almanac, 1920, pp. 298-299.

Also in:—Public papers; War and Peace (1917-1924), vol. 1, pp. 520-521.

Also in:—Woodrow Wilson's worte. . . . Heilbronn, a.N., 1924, pp. 341-343.

Cablegram to Mr. Tumulty (Irish question), June 27, 1919. In:—Woodrow Wilson's worte. . . . Heilbronn, a.N., 1924, p. 343.

Statement on the eve of his departure from France, June 28, 1919. In:—Triumph of ideals, N. Y., 1919, pp. 135-136.

Also in:—Chicago Daily News Almanac, 1920, p. 299.

Also in:—Public papers; War and Peace (1917-1924), vol. 1, p. 522.

Message to the American people given out by Secretary Tumulty, June 28, 1919. In:—Triumph of ideals, N. Y., 1919, pp. 132-134.

Also in:—Chicago Daily News Almanac, 1920, p. 299.

Also in:—Cong. Rec., vol. 58, pp. 1952-1953; also p. 2016.

Also in:—Messages and papers, ed. by Albert Shaw, N. Y., 1924, vol. 2, pp. 692-693.

Also in:—Public papers; War and Peace (1917-1924), vol. 1, pp. 523-524.

Also in:—United States Bulletin, vol. 1, no. 16, July 7, 1919.

Also in:—Woodrow Wilson's worte. . . . Heilbronn, a.N., 1924, pp. 343-344.

Peace message to Great Britain, June 30, 1919. In:— Triumph of ideals, N. Y., 1919, pp. 137-138.

Also in:—Public papers; War and Peace (1917-1924), vol. 1, p. 525.

Address given to the soldiers and sailors on the after-hatch of the U. S. S. *George Washington,* July 4, 1919. In:—*The Hatchet,* published on the high seas, 1919, series 2, vol. 6, no. 5.

Also in:—Chicago Daily News Almanac, 1920, pp. 299-301.

Also in:—Public papers; War and Peace (1917-1924), vol. 1, pp. 526-531.

Also in:—Triumph of ideals, N. Y., 1919, pp. 139-148.

Also in:—Woodrow Wilson's worte. . . . Heilbronn, a.N., 1924, pp. 345-349.

Address in Carnegie Hall, July 8, 1919. In:—Triumph of ideals, N. Y., 1919, pp. 149-156.

Also in:—Chicago Daily News Almanac, 1920, pp. 301-302.

Also in:—Messages and papers, ed. by Albert Shaw, N. Y., 1924, vol. 2, pp. 694-697.

Also in:—Public papers; War and Peace (1917-1924), vol. 1, pp. 532-535.

Also in:—Woodrow Wilson's worte. . . . Heilbronn, a.N., 1924, pp. 349-352.

Reply to greeting of citizens in Washington upon his arrival, July 8, 1919. In:—Chicago Daily News Almanac, 1920, p. 302.

Also in:—Public papers; War and Peace (1917-1924), vol. 1, p. 536.

Address of the President of the United States to the Senate of the United States relative to the treaty of peace with Germany, July 10, 1919, Washington, 1919. (66th Cong., 1st sess. Senate Doc. 50.)

Also in:—Cong. Rec., vol. 58, pp. 2336-2339.

Also in:—Hope of the world, N. Y., 1920, pp. 1-23.

Also in:—Messages and papers, ed. by Albert Shaw, N. Y., 1924, vol. 2, pp. 698-712.

Also in:—Public papers; War and Peace (1917-1924), vol. 1, pp. 537-552.

Also in:—Woodrow Wilson's worte. . . . Heilbronn, a.N., 1924, pp. 353-366.

Message recommending granting to John J. Pershing and Peyton C. March the permanent rank of General, and to William S. Benson and William S. Sims the permanent rank of Admiral, July 18, 1919, Washington, 1919. (66th Cong., 1st sess. House Doc. 153.)

Also in:—Cong. Rec., vol. 58, p. 2811, also p. 2852.

Address to a detachment of the Czecho-Slovak army, July 18, 1919. In:—Public papers; War and Peace (1917-1924), vol. 1, pp. 553-554.

Message transmitting an agreement between the U. S., and France which was signed at Versailles, June 28, 1919, to secure the Republic of France the immediate aid of the U. S. in case of unprovoked movement of aggression against her on the part of Germany, July 29, 1919, Washington, 1919. (66th Cong., 1st sess. Senate Doc. 63.)

Also in:—International conciliation, no. 145.

Also in:—Public papers; War and Peace (1917-1924), vol. 1, pp. 555-557.

American troops in Siberia. Message in response to a resolution of the Senate agreed to, June 23, 1919, informing the Senate of the reasons for sending United States soldiers to and maintaining them in Siberia, Washington, 1919. (66th Cong., 1st sess. Senate Doc. 60.)

Protocol to the treaty of peace with Germany; message July 31, 1919, transmitting a letter of the Secretary of State submitting a certified copy of the protocol to the treaty of peace with Germany, signed at Versailles on June 28, 1919, Washington, 1919. (66th Cong., 1st sess. Senate Doc. 66.)

Letter to Frederick H. Gillett regarding the postponement of recess of Congress, August 1, 1919. Cong. Rec., vol. 58, p. 3543; also p. 4637.

Also in:—United States Bulletin, vol. 1, no. 21, August 11, 1919.

Letter to John J. Esch regarding railroad legislation, August 1, 1919. Cong. Rec., vol. 58, p. 3543. This letter was also addressed to Hon. Albert B. Cummins, August 1, 1919. Cong. Rec., vol. 58, p. 3626.

Also in:—United States Bulletin, vol. 1, no. 21, August 11, 1919.

Cablegram to President Pessoa giving greetings upon his inaugural as President of Brazil, August 2, 1919. In:—United States Bulletin, vol. 1, no. 20, August 4, 1919.

The cost of living. Address of the President of the United States delivered at a joint session of the two Houses of Congress, August 8, 1919, Washington, 1919.

Also in:—Chicago Daily News Almanac, 1920, pp. 143-146.

Also in:—Cong. Rec., vol. 58, pp. 3718-3721; also pp. 3728-3730.

Also in:—Hope of the world, N. Y., 1920, pp. 24-47. (Dated August 6, here.)

Also in:—Messages and papers, ed. by Albert Shaw, N. Y., 1924, vol. 2, pp. 713-726.

Also in:—Public papers; War and Peace (1917-1924), vol. 1, pp. 558-571.

Also in:—Woodrow Wilson's worte. . . . Heilbronn, a.N., pp. 367-379.

Letter to Director General of Railroads Hines regarding railway wages, August, 1919. In:—United States Bulletin, vol. 1, no. 21, August 11, 1919.

Message transmitting, in response to Senate resolutions of July 15 and 17, information concerning the purported German-Japanese treaty, the adjustment in reference to Shantung, and the intimidation of Chinese peace delegates by Japan, August 11, 1919, Washington, 1919. (66th Cong., 1st sess. Senate Doc. 72.)

Also in:—Hope of the world, N. Y., 1920, pp. 45-47.

Also in:—Public papers; War and Peace (1917-1924), vol. 1, pp. 572-573.

Letter to Pope Benedict XV, August 15, 1919. In:—Woodrow Wilson's worte. . . . Heilbronn, a.N., 1924, pp. 379-380.

Reply to questions on the Treaty of Peace submitted to the President by Senator Fall, August 19, 1919. Cong. Rec., vol. 58, pp. 4177-4178.

Treaty of Peace with Germany. Report of the Conference between members of the Senate Committee on Foreign Relations and the President of the United States at the White House, Tuesday, August 19, 1919,

Washington, 1919. (66th Cong., 1st sess. Senate
Doc. 76.)

Also in:—Public papers; War and Peace (1917-1924),
vol. 1, pp. 574-580.

Also in:—Woodrow Wilson's worte. . . . Heilbronn,
a.N., 1924, pp. 380-407.

Message transmitting an agreement between the U. S.,
Belgium, the British Empire, and France of the one
part, and Germany of the other part, which was
signed at Versailles, June 28, 1919, with regard to the
military occupation of the territories of the Rhine,
August 23, 1919, Washington, 1919. (66th Cong.,
1st sess. Senate Doc. 81.)

Message transmitting an agreement between the U. S., the
British Empire, France, Italy and Japan on the one
hand and Poland on the other hand, which was signed
at Versailles, June 28, 1919. August 23, 1919, Washington, 1919. (66th Cong., 1st sess. Senate Doc. 82.)

Message transmitting a communication from the Secretary of
State suggesting that the passport-control act of May
22, 1918, be extended for one year after peace shall
have been concluded between the U. S. and the Cen-
'ral Powers of Europe, August 25, 1919, Washington, 1919. (66th Cong., 1st sess. Senate Doc. 79.)

Also in:—United States Bulletin, vol. 1, no. 24, September 1, 1919.

Statement to representatives of the Railway employees' department, American federation of labor, and report
of Walter D. Hines, August 25, 1919, Washington,
1919.

Also in:—Cong. Rec., vol. 58, pp. 4344-4345.

Also in:—The hope of the world, N. Y., 1920, pp.
54-58.

Also in:—Public papers; War and Peace (1917-1924),
vol. 1, pp. 581-583.

Statement to the public on railway labor and the high cost
of living, August 26, 1919. In:—Hope of the world,
N. Y., 1920, pp. 48-53.

Also in:—Cong. Rec., vol. 58, pp. 4343-4344.

Also in:—Public papers; War and Peace (1917-1924),
vol. 1, pp. 584-587.

Labor Day message, August 31, 1919. In:—Hope of the
world, N. Y., 1920, pp. 59-60.

Also in:—Public papers; War and Peace (1917-1924),
vol. 1, pp. 588-589.

Also in:—Woodrow Wilson's worte. . . . Heilbronn, a.N., 1924, pp. 407-408.

Address at Columbus, Ohio, September 4, 1919. (League of Nations.) In:—Addresses delivered on his Western tour, Washington, 1919, pp. 5-15.

Also in:—Chicago Daily News Almanac, 1920, pp. 698-702.

Also in:—Cong. Rec., vol. 58, pp. 4997-5000.

Also in:—Hope of the world, N. Y., 1920, pp. 61-84.

Also in:—Messages and papers, ed. by Albert Shaw, N. Y., 1924, vol. 2, pp. 727-743.

Also in:—Public papers; War and Peace (1917-1924), vol. 1, pp. 590-605.

Address from rear platform, Richmond, Indiana, September 4, 1919. In:—Addresses delivered on his Western tour, Washington, 1919, pp. 17-18.

Also in:—Cong. Rec., vol. 58, p. 5000.

Also in:—Public papers; War and Peace (1917-1924), vol. 1, pp. 605-606.

Address at Coliseum, Indianapolis, Indiana, September 4, 1919. (Peace Treaty.) In:—Addresses delivered on his Western tour, Washington, 1919, pp. 19-28.

Also in:—Cong. Rec., vol. 58, pp. 5000-5003.

Also in:—Hope of the world, N. Y., 1920, pp. 85-91.

Also in:—Messages and papers, ed. by Albert Shaw, N. Y., 1924, vol. 2, pp. 743-754.

Also in:—Public papers; War and Peace (1917-1924), vol. 1, pp. 606-620.

Address at Luncheon at Hotel Statler, St. Louis, Missouri, September 5, 1919. (League of Nations.) In:—Addresses delivered on his Western tour, Washington, 1919, pp. 29-38.

Also in:—Cong. Rec., vol. 58, pp. 5003-5005.

Also in:—Hope of the world, N. Y., 1920, pp. 92-97.

Also in:—Messages and papers, ed. by Albert Shaw, N. Y., 1924, vol. 2, pp. 754-767.

Also in:—Public papers; War and Peace (1917-1924), vol. 1, pp. 620-633.

Address at Coliseum, St. Louis, Mo., September 5, 1919. (Peace Treaty and League of Nations.) In:—Addresses delivered on his Western tour, Washington, 1919, pp. 39-47.

Also in:—Cong. Rec., vol. 58, pp. 5005-5008.

Also in:—Hope of the world, N. Y., 1920, pp. 98-103.

Also in:—Messages and papers, ed. by Albert Shaw, N. Y., 1924, vol. 2, pp. 767-777.

Also in:—Public papers; War and Peace (1917-1924), vol. 1, pp. 634-645.

Address at Convention Hall, Kansas City, Mo., September 6, 1919. (Treaty of Peace.) In:—Addresses delivered on his Western tour, Washington, 1919, pp. 49-57.

Also in:—Cong. Rec., vol. 58, pp. 5008-5010.

Also in:—Hope of the world, N. Y., 1920, pp. 104-110.

Also in:—Messages and papers, ed. by Albert Shaw, N. Y., 1924, vol. 2, pp. 777-787.

Also in:—Public papers; War and Peace (1917-1924), vol. 2, pp. 1-13.

Address at Des Moines, Iowa, September 6, 1919. (Peace Treaty.) In:—Addresses delivered on his Western tour, Washington, 1919, pp. 59-70.

Also in:—Cong. Rec., vol. 58, pp. 5585-5588.

Also in:—Hope of the world, N. Y., 1920, pp. 111-116.

Also in:—Messages and papers, ed. by Albert Shaw, N. Y., 1924, vol. 2, pp. 788-803.

Also in:—Public papers; War and Peace (1917-1924), vol. 2, pp. 14-30.

Address at Auditorium, Omaha, Neb., September 8, 1919. (Peace Treaty). In:—Addresses delivered on his Western tour, Washington, 1919, pp. 71-80.

Also in:—Cong. Rec., vol. 58, pp. 5588-5591.

Also in:—Hope of the world, N. Y., 1920, pp. 117-120.

Also in:—Messages and papers, ed. by Albert Shaw, N. Y., 1924, vol. 2, pp. 803-816.

Also in:—Public papers; War and Peace (1917-1924), vol. 2, pp. 30-44.

Address at Coliseum, Sioux Falls, S. Dak., September 8, 1919. (Peace Treaty.) In:—Addresses delivered on his Western tour, Washington, 1919, pp. 81-90.

Also in:—Cong. Rec., vol. 58, pp. 5591-5593.

Also in:—Hope of the world, N. Y., 1920, pp. 121-124. (In part.)

Also in:—Messages and papers, ed. by Albert Shaw, N. Y., 1924, vol. 2, pp. 816-828.

Also in:—Public papers; War and Peace (1917-1924), vol. 2, pp. 44-57.

Address before State Legislature, St. Paul, Minn., September 9, 1919. (High cost of living.) In:—Addresses delivered on his Western tour, Washington, 1919, pp. 91-97.

Also in:—Cong. Rec., vol. 58, pp. 5593-5595.

Also in:—Messages and papers, ed. by Albert Shaw, N. Y., 1924, vol. 2, pp. 828-835.

Also in:—Public papers; War and Peace (1917-1924), vol. 2, pp. 57-66.

Address at Minneapolis, Minn., September 9, 1919. (League of Nations.) In:—Addresses delivered on his Western tour, Washington, 1919, pp. 99-105.

Also in:—Cong. Rec., vol. 58, pp. 5937-5939.

Also in:—Messages and papers, ed. by Albert Shaw, N. Y., 1924, vol. 2, pp. 835-844.

Also in:—Public papers; War and Peace (1917-1924), vol. 2, pp. 66-76.

Address at Auditorium, St. Paul, Minn., September 9, 1919. (League of Nations.) In:—Addresses delivered on his Western tour, Washington, 1919, pp. 107-116.

Also in:—Cong. Rec., vol. 58, pp. 5939-5942.

Also in:—Messages and papers, ed. by Albert Shaw, N. Y., 1924, vol. 2, pp. 844-856.

Also in:—Public papers; War and Peace (1917-1924), vol. 2, pp. 76-89.

Address at Bismarck, N. Dak., September 10, 1919. (Peace Treaty.) In:—Addresses delivered on his Western tour, Washington, 1919, pp. 117-125.

Also in:—Cong. Rec., vol. 58, pp. 5942-5944.

Also in:—Messages and papers, ed. by Albert Shaw, N. Y., 1924, vol. 2, pp. 856-866.

Also in:—Public papers; War and Peace (1917-1924), vol. 2, pp. 89-101.

Address from rear platform, Mandan, N. Dak., September 10, 1919. (Peace Treaty.) In:—Addresses delivered on his Western tour, Washington, 1919, p. 127.

Also in:—Cong. Rec., vol. 58, p. 5944.

Also in:—Messages and papers, ed. by Albert Shaw, N. Y., 1924, vol. 2, pp. 866-867.

Also in:—Public papers; War and Peace (1917-1924), vol. 2, pp. 101-102.

Address at Auditorium, Billings, Mont., September 11, 1919. (Peace Treaty.) In:—Addresses delivered on his Western tour, Washington, 1919, pp. 129-138.

Also in:—Cong. Rec., vol. 58, pp. 5944-5947.

Also in:—Hope of the world, N. Y., 1920, pp. 125-131. (In part.)

Also in:—Messages and papers, ed. by Albert Shaw, N. Y., 1924, vol. 2, pp. 867-878.

Also in:—Public papers; War and Peace (1917-1924), vol. 2, pp. 102-115.

Address at Opera House, Helena, Mont., September 11, 1919. (League of Nations.) In:—Addresses de-

livered on his Western tour, Washington, 1919, pp.
139-154.

Also in:—Cong. Rec., vol. 58, pp. 5947-5951.

Also in:—Hope of the world, N. Y., 1920, pp. 132-135.

Also in:—Messages and papers, ed. by Albert Shaw,
N. Y., 1924, vol. 2, pp. 878-900.

Also in:—Public papers; War and Peace (1917-1924),
vol. 2, pp. 115-137.

Address at Cœur D'Alene, Idaho, September 12, 1919.
(League of Nations.) In:—Addresses delivered on
his Western tour, Washington, 1919, pp. 155-163.

Also in:—Cong. Rec., vol. 58, pp. 6175-6177.

Also in:—Messages and papers, ed. by Albert Shaw,
N. Y., 1924, vol. 2, pp. 900-911.

Also in:—Public papers; War and Peace (1917-1924),
vol. 2, pp. 137-150.

Address at Spokane, Wash., September 12, 1919. (League
of Nations.) In:—Addresses delivered on his Western tour, Washington, 1919, pp. 165-174.

Also in:—Cong. Rec., vol. 58, pp. 6177-6180.

Also in:—Hope of the world, N. Y., 1920, pp. 136-139.
(In part.)

Also in:—Messages and papers, ed. by Albert Shaw,
N. Y., 1924, vol. 2, pp. 911-924.

Also in:—Public papers; War and Peace (1917-1924),
vol. 2, pp. 150-163.

Address at Stadium, Tacoma, Wash., September 13, 1919.
(Reply to greeting.) In:—Addresses delivered on his
Western tour, Washington, 1919, p. 175.

Also in:—Cong. Rec., vol. 58, p. 6180.

Also in:—Public papers; War and Peace (1917-1924),
vol. 2, pp. 163-164.

Address at Armory, Tacoma, Wash., September 13, 1919.
(Peace Treaty.) In:—Addresses delivered on his
Western tour, Washington, 1919, pp. 177-187.

Also in:—Cong. Rec., vol. 58, pp. 6180-6183.

Also in:—Hope of the world, N. Y., 1920, pp. 140-145.
(In part.)

Also in:—Messages and papers, ed. by Albert Shaw,
N. Y., 1924, vol. 2, pp. 924-936.

Also in:—Public papers; War and Peace (1917-1924),
vol. 2, pp. 164-179.

Address at Hippodrome, Seattle, Wash., September 13, 1919.
(Peace Treaty.) In:—Addresses delivered on his
Western tour, Washington, 1919, pp. 189-190.

Also in:—Cong. Rec., vol. 58, p. 6183.

Also in:—Public papers; War and Peace (1917-1924), vol. 2, pp. 179-180.

Address at Arena, Seattle, Wash., September 13, 1919. (Peace Treaty.) In:—Addresses delivered on his Western tour, Washington, 1919, pp. 191-200.

Also in:—Cong. Rec., vol. 58, pp. 6234-6236.

Also in:—Messages and papers, ed. by Albert Shaw, N. Y., 1924, vol. 2, pp. 936-949.

Also in:—Public papers; War and Peace (1917-1924), vol. 2, pp. 181-194.

Address at luncheon, Hotel Portland, Portland, Ore., September 15, 1919. (League of Nations.) In:—Addresses delivered on his Western tour, Washington, 1919, pp. 201-206.

Also in:—Cong. Rec., vol. 58, pp. 6236-6238.

Also in:—Messages and papers, ed. by Albert Shaw, N. Y., 1924, vol. 2, pp. 949-954.

Also in:—Public papers; War and Peace (1917-1924), vol. 2, pp. 194-202.

Address at Auditorium, Portland, Ore., September 15, 1919. (League of Nations.) In:—Addresses delivered on his Western tour, Washington, 1919, pp. 207-217.

Also in:—Cong. Rec., vol. 58, pp. 6238-6241.

Also in:—Hope of the world, N. Y., 1920, pp. 146-149. (In part.)

Also in:—Messages and papers, ed. by Albert Shaw, N. Y., 1924, vol. 2, pp. 955-966.

Also in:—Public papers; War and Peace (1917-1924), vol. 2, pp. 202-217.

Address at luncheon, Palace Hotel, San Francisco, Cal., September 17, 1919. (Peace Treaty.) In:—Addresses delivered on his Western tour, Washington, 1919, pp. 219-229.

Also in:—Cong. Rec., vol. 58, pp. 6241-6243.

Also in:—Hope of the world, N. Y., 1920, pp. 150-155. (In part.)

Also in:—Messages and papers, ed. by Albert Shaw, N. Y., 1924, vol. 2, pp. 966-979.

Also in:—Public papers; War and Peace (1917-1924), vol. 2, pp. 217-232.

Address at Auditorium, San Francisco, Cal., September 17, 1919. (League of Nations.) In:—Addresses delivered on his Western tour, Washington, 1919, pp. 231-242.

Also in:—Cong. Rec., vol. 58, pp. 6244-6247.

Also in:—Messages and papers, ed. by Albert Shaw, N. Y., 1924, vol. 2, pp. 979-992.

Also in:—Public papers; War and Peace (1917-1924), vol. 2, pp. 232-249.

Call for a National Industrial Conference, September 17, 1919. In:—Messages and papers, ed. by Albert Shaw, N. Y., 1924, vol. 2, p. 1131.

Address at luncheon, Palace Hotel, San Francisco, Cal., September 18, 1919. (Peace Treaty.) In:—Addresses delivered on his Western tour, Washington, 1919, pp. 243-252.

Also in:—Cong. Rec., vol. 58, pp. 6247-6249.

Also in:—Hope of the world, N. Y., 1920, pp. 156-159.

Also in:—Messages and papers, ed. by Albert Shaw, N. Y., 1924, vol. 2, pp. 993-1005.

Also in:—Public papers; War and Peace (1917-1924), vol. 2, pp. 249-262.

Address at Berkeley, Cal., September 18, 1919. In:—Addresses delivered on his Western tour, Washington, 1919, pp. 253-254.

Also in:—Cong. Rec., vol. 58, pp. 6249-6250.

Also in:—Public papers; War and Peace (1917-1924), vol. 2, pp. 263-265.

Address at Auditorium, Oakland, Cal., September 18, 1919. (Peace Treaty.) In:—Addresses delivered on his Western tour, Washington, 1919, pp. 255-263.

Also in:—Cong. Rec., vol. 58, pp. 6250-6252.

Also in:—Messages and papers, ed. by Albert Shaw, N. Y., 1924, vol. 2, pp. 1005-1013.

Also in:—Public papers; War and Peace (1917-1924), vol. 2, pp. 265-277.

Address at Stadium, San Diego, Cal., September 19, 1919. (Peace Treaty.) In:—Addresses delivered on his Western tour, Washington, 1919, pp. 265-275.

Also in:—Cong. Rec., vol. 58, pp. 6252-6255.

Also in:—Messages and papers, ed. by Albert Shaw, N. Y., 1924, vol. 2, pp. 1014-1027.

Also in:—Public papers; War and Peace (1917-1924), vol. 2, pp. 277-292.

Address at San Diego, Cal., September 19, 1919. (League of Nations.) In:—Addresses delivered on his Western tour, Washington, 1919, pp. 277-282.

Also in:—Cong. Rec., vol. 58, pp. 6403-6404.

Also in:—Public papers; War and Peace (1917-1924), vol. 2, pp. 292-299.

Address at Hotel Alexandria, Los Angeles, Cal., September

20, 1919. (League of Nations.) In:—Addresses delivered on his Western tour, Washington, 1919, pp. 283-290.

Also in:—Cong. Rec., vol. 58, pp. 6404-6406.

Also in:—Messages and papers, ed. by Albert Shaw, N. Y., 1924, vol. 2, pp. 1027-1037.

Also in:—Public papers; War and Peace (1917-1924), vol. 2, pp. 299-310.

Address at Auditorium, Los Angeles, Cal., September 20, 1919. (Peace Treaty.) In:—Addresses delivered on his Western tour, Washington, 1919, pp. 291-301.

Also in:—Cong. Rec., vol. 58, pp. 6406-6409.

Also in:—Messages and papers, ed. by Albert Shaw, N. Y., 1924, vol. 2, pp. 1037-1050.

Also in:—Public papers; War and Peace (1917-1924), vol. 2, pp. 310-325.

Telegram to American diplomatic corps in allied and neutral countries. In:—Woodrow Wilson's worte. . . . Heilbronn, a.N., 1924, pp. 408-409.

Address from rear platform, Sacramento, Cal., September 22, 1919. In:—Addresses delivered on his Western tour, Washington, 1919, p. 303.

Also in:—Public papers; War and Peace (1917-1924), vol. 2, pp. 325-326.

Address at Reno, Neb., September 22, 1919. (Peace Treaty and League of Nations.) In:—Addresses delivered on his Western tour, Washington, 1919, pp. 307-319.

Also in:—Cong. Rec., vol. 58, pp. 6410-6413.

Also in:—Messages and papers, ed. by Albert Shaw, N. Y., 1924, vol. 2, pp. 1050-1067.

Also in:—Public papers; War and Peace (1917-1924), vol. 2, pp. 326-344.

Address from rear platform at Ogden, Utah, September 23, 1919. (Peace Treaty.) In:—Addresses delivered on his Western tour, Washington, 1919, p. 305.

Also in:—Cong. Rec., vol. 58, pp. 6409-6410.

Also in:—Public papers; War and Peace (1917-1924), vol. 2, pp. 345-346.

Address at Tabernacle, Salt Lake City, Utah, September 23, 1919. (League of Nations.) In:—Addresses delivered on his Western tour, Washington, 1919, pp. 321-324.

Also in:—Cong. Rec., vol. 58, pp. 6413-6417.

Also in:—Messages and papers, ed. by Albert Shaw, N. Y., 1924, vol. 2, pp. 1067-1084.

Also in:—Public papers; War and Peace (1917-1924), vol. 2, pp. 346-365.

Address at Cheyenne, Wyo., September 24, 1919. (Peace Treaty.) In:—Addresses delivered on his Western tour, Washington, 1919, pp. 335-348.

Also in:—Cong. Rec., vol. 58, pp. 6417-6421.

Also in:—Messages and papers, ed. by Albert Shaw, N. Y., 1924, vol. 2, pp. 1084-1101.

Also in:—Public papers; War and Peace (1917-1924), vol. 2, pp. 365-385.

Address at Auditorium, Denver, Colo., September 25, 1919. (League of Nations.) In:—Addresses delivered on his Western tour, Washington, 1919, pp. 349-358.

Also in:—Cong. Rec., vol. 58, pp. 6421-6424.

Also in:—Messages and papers, ed. by Albert Shaw, N. Y., 1924, vol. 2, pp. 1101-1112.

Also in:—Public papers; War and Peace (1917-1924), vol. 2, pp. 385-398.

Address at Pueblo, Colo., September 25, 1919. (League of Nations.) In:—Addresses delivered on his Western tour, Washington, 1919, pp. 359-370.

Also in:—Cong. Rec., vol. 58, pp. 6424-6427.

Also in:—Hope of the world, N. Y., 1920, pp. 163-169.

Also in:—Messages and papers, ed. by Albert Shaw, N. Y., 1924, vol. 2, pp. 1113-1130.

Also in:—Public papers; War and Peace (1917-1924), vol. 2, pp. 399-416.

Message transmitting in response to a Senate resolution of September 11, 1919, certain information as to a copy of the report made by Mr. Paul Whitham on "Neutralization of transportation in China," September 29, 1919, Washington, 1919. (66th Cong., 1st sess. Senate Doc. 115.)

Statement to Labor Conference, October 6, 1919. In:—Public papers; War and Peace (1917-1924), vol. 2, p. 417.

Letter to National Industrial Conference, October 22, 1919. In:—Hope of the world, N. Y., 1920, pp. 170-172.

Also in:—Messages and papers, ed. by Albert Shaw, N. Y., 1924, vol. 2, pp. 1131-1133.

Also in:—Public papers; War and Peace (1917-1924), vol. 2, pp. 418-419.

Also in:—Woodrow Wilson's worte. . . . Heilbronn, a.N., 1924, pp. 429-430.

Statement warning coal strikers of Federal action, October 25, 1919. Cong. Rec., vol. 58, p. 7583.

Also in:—Hope of the world, N. Y., 1920, pp. 173-177.

Also in:—Messages and papers, ed. by Albert Shaw, N. Y., 1924, vol. 2, pp. 1133-1136.

Also in:—Public papers; War and Peace (1917-1924), vol. 2, pp. 420-423.

Also in:—Woodrow Wilson's worte. . . . Heilbronn, a.N., 1924, pp. 432-435.

Message returning to the House of Representatives without approval House bill 6810, "An act to prohibit intoxicating beverages," etc., and stating certain objections thereto, October 27, 1919, Washington, 1919. (66th Cong., 1st sess. House Doc. 282.)

Also in:—Public papers; War and Peace (1917-1924), vol. 2, pp. 424-425.

Letter to the people of the country about the Red Cross Roll Call, November 2-11, 1919. In:—Hope of the world, N. Y., 1920, pp. 178-180.

Message returning without approval H. R. 8272, "An act to restore Harry Graham, Captain of Infantry, to his former position on lineal list of Captains of Infantry," November 5, 1919, Washington, 1919. (66th Cong., 1st sess. House Doc. 291.)

Message to his fellow countrymen on Armistice Day, November 11, 1919. In:—Hope of the world, N. Y., 1920, pp. 181-182.

Also in:—Messages and papers, ed. by Albert Shaw, N. Y., 1924, vol. 2, pp. 1136-1137.

Also in:—Public papers; War and Peace (1917-1924), vol. 2, pp. 426-427.

Telegraph, telephone and cable properties. Message transmitting a report of the Postmaster-General, Washington, 1919. (66th Cong., 1st sess. Senate Doc. 152.)

Message returning without approval the bill (S. 641) to amend section 10 of an act entitled "An act to provide for the operation of transportation systems while under federal control, for the just compensation of their owners, and for other purposes," approved March 21, 1918, November 19, 1919, Washington, 1919. (66th Cong., 1st sess. Senate Doc. 155.)

Message communicated to the two houses of Congress at the beginning of the second session of the sixty-sixth Congress, December 2, 1919, Washington, 1919. (66th Cong., 2d sess. House Doc. 399.)

Also in:—Chicago Daily News Almanac, 1920, pp. 737-741.

Also in:—Cong. Rec., vol. 59, pp. 29-31; also pp. 53-56.

Also in:—Hope of the world, N. Y., 1920, pp. 183-204.

Also in:—Messages and papers, ed. by Albert Shaw, N. Y., 1924, vol. 2, pp. 1138-1152.

Also in:—Public papers; War and Peace (1917-1924), vol. 2, pp. 428-442.

Also in:—Woodrow Wilson's worte. . . . Heilbronn, a.N., 1924, pp. 435-448.

Text of proposal to the miners at Indianapolis, December 9, 1919. In:—Hope of the world, N. Y., 1920, pp. 205-208.

Also in:—Messages and papers, ed. by Albert Shaw, N. Y., 1924, vol. 2, pp. 1152-1155.

Also in:—Public papers; War and Peace (1917-1924), vol. 2, pp. 443-445.

Letter sent to Henry M. Robinson, Rembrandt Peale and John P. White regarding the Bituminous coal industry and the basis of a new wage agreement, December 20, 1919. In:—Messages and papers, ed. by Albert Shaw, N. Y., 1924, vol. 2, pp. 1155-1159.

Also in:—Public papers; War and Peace (1917-1924), vol. 2, pp. 446-450.

Proclamation (Relinquishing government control of Railroads) December 24, 1919. In:—Messages and papers, ed. by Albert Shaw, N. Y., 1924, vol. 2, pp. 1159-1161.

Also in:—Public papers; War and Peace (1917-1924), vol. 2, pp. 451-452.

BOOKS, 1920

The Hope of the world, messages and addresses delivered between July 10, 1919, and December 9, 1919, including selections from his country-wide speeches in behalf of the Treaty and Covenant, N. Y., Harper & Brothers [1920].

President Wilson's Great speeches and other history-making documents, Chicago, Stanton and Van Vliet Co., [c1920]. (Contains addresses, etc., from March 4, 1913, to April 6, 1918.)

Proclamations by the President of the United States, January 16, 1920, December 9, 1920. U. S. Laws, Statutes, etc. The statutes at large, vol. 41, pt. 2, pp. 1784-1812.

MESSAGES AND ADDRESSES, 1920.

Letter to Homer S. Cummings defining his treaty stand,
January 8, 1920 (Jackson Day message). Cong. Rec.,
vol. 59, p. 1249.

Also in:—Messages and papers, ed. by Albert Shaw,
N. Y., 1924, vol. 2, pp. 1161-1164.

Also in:—Public papers; War and Peace (1917-1924),
vol. 2, pp. 453-456.

Also in:—Woodrow Wilson's worte. . . . Heilbronn,
a.N., 1924, pp. 449-452.

Conditions in the Ukraine respecting treatment of Jews.
Message, January 12, 1920, Washington, 1920. (66th
Cong., 2d sess. Senate Doc. 176.)

Cablegram to Great Britain calling meeting of League of
Nations, January 13, 1920. In:—Public papers; War
and Peace (1917-1924), vol. 2, p. 457.

Also in:—Messages and papers, ed. by Albert Shaw,
N. Y., 1924, vol. 2, p. 1165.

Mission of the United States to Poland. A message, January 15, 1920, Washington, 1920. (66th Cong., 2d
sess. Senate Doc. 177.)

Welcome to Pan-American Financial Congress, Washington,
D. C., January 19, 1920. In:—Public papers; War
and Peace (1917-1924), vol. 2, pp. 458-459.

Letter to Senator Hitchcock accepting his peace treaty reservations, January 26, 1920. In:—Messages and
papers; ed. by Albert Shaw, N. Y., 1924, vol. 2, pp.
1166-1168.

Also in:—Public papers; War and Peace (1917-1924),
vol. 2, pp. 460-461.

Also in:—Woodrow Wilson's worte. . . . Heilbronn,
a.N., 1924, pp. 452-454.

Letter to Robert Lansing regarding meetings of the Cabinet held during his illness, February 7, 1920. Cong.
Rec., vol. 59, p. 2882.

Cablegram sent to France and Great Britain regarding
Fiume, February 9, 1920. In:—Messages and
papers, ed. by Albert Shaw, N. Y., 1924, vol. 2, pp.
1168-1174.

Also in:—Public papers; War and Peace (1917-1924),
vol. 2, pp. 462-468.

Letter replying to Robert Lansing regarding his resignation
as Secretary of State, February 11, 1920. Cong. Rec.,
vol. 59, p. 2882.

Letter to Robert Lansing accepting his resignation, February 13, 1920. Cong. Rec., vol. 59, p. 2883.

Letter to Railway strikers, February 13, 1920. In:—Woodrow Wilson's worte. . . . Heilbronn, a.N., 1924, pp. 460-464.

Telegram to Mr. Barker (Railway strike) February 14, 1920. In:—Woodrow Wilson's worte. . . . Heilbronn, a.N., 1924, pp. 464-465.

Message transmitting in response to a Senate resolution of February 14, 1920, information with respect to the disposition of the ex-German vessels in possession of the U. S. and transmitting a draft of a proposed undertaking in regard to ex-enemy merchant tonnage, February 18, 1920. (66th Cong., 2d sess. Senate Doc. 231.)

Also in:—Cong. Rec., vol. 59, p. 3221.

Second cablegram to France and Great Britain regarding Fiume, February 24, 1920. In:—Messages and papers, ed. by Albert Shaw, N. Y., 1924, vol. 2, pp. 1174-1180. (Signed Polk.)

Also in:—Public papers; War and Peace (1917-1924), vol. 2, pp. 469-475.

Also in:—Woodrow Wilson's worte. . . . Heilbronn, a.N., 1924, pp. 466-471.

Letter to the heads of rail unions on wage issue, February 28, 1920. Cong. Rec., vol. 59, p. 3667.

Amnesty to prisoners since the armistice, message, March 1, 1920, Washington, 1920. (66th Cong., 2d sess. Senate Doc. 241.) (66th Cong., 2d sess. Senate Doc. 249.)

Cablegram regarding the Adriatic settlement, March 4, 1920. In:—Messages and papers, ed. by Albert Shaw, N. Y., 1924, vol. 2, pp. 1180-1183. (Signed Polk.)

Also in:—Public papers; War and Peace (1917-1924), vol. 2, pp. 476-479.

Letter to Senator Hitchcock, March 8, 1920. In:—Woodrow Wilson's worte. . . . Heilbronn, a.N., 1924, pp. 474-479.

Note to French Ambassador regarding peace terms for Turkey and the future of Constantinople, March 24, 1920. In:—Messages and papers, ed. by Albert Shaw, N. Y., 1924, vol. 2, pp. 1183-1187. (Signed Colby.)

Message transmitting in response to House Resolution 500, information regarding the status of the American military forces now stationed in German territory, March 29, 1920. (66th Cong., 2d sess. House Doc. 709.)

Letter to Mr. Shouse, April 22, 1920. In:—Woodrow Wilson's worte. . . . Heilbronn, a.N., 1924, pp. 479-481.

Also in:—Cong. Rec., vol. 59, p. 5101.

Also in:—Public papers; War and Peace (1917-1924), vol. 2, pp. 480-482.

Telegram to G. E. Hamaker (League of Nations as a campaign issue) May 9, 1920. In:—Messages and papers, ed. by Albert Shaw, N. Y., 1924,, vol. 2, pp. 1187-1189.

Also in:—Public papers; War and Peace (1917-1924), vol. 2, pp. 483-484.

Also in:—Woodrow Wilson's worte. . . . Heilbronn, a.N., 1924, pp. 481-483.

Message returning without approval H. B. 12610, "An act making appropriations for the legislative, executive and judicial expenses of the government for the fiscal year ending June 30, 1921, and for other purposes," May 13, 1920, Washington, 1920. (66th Cong., 2d sess. House Doc. 764.)

Message transmitting report regarding the sixth international sanitary conference, May 15, 1920, Washington, 1920. (66th Cong., 2d sess. House Doc. 765.)

Restriction on American petroleum prospectors in certain foreign countries. Message transmitting a report of the Secretary of State, May 17, 1920, Washington, 1920. (66th Cong., 2d sess. Senate Doc. 272.)

United States Railroad administration. Message transmitting statements of receipts and expenditures for the years ending December 31, 1918, and December 31, 1919, May 20, 1920, Washington, 1920. (66th Cong., 2d sess. Senate Doc. 275.)

Letter to operators and miners regarding anthracite coal strike, May 21, 1920. In:—Messages and papers, ed. by Albert Shaw, N. Y., 1924, vol. 2, pp. 1189-1191.

Also in:—Public papers; War and Peace (1917-1924), vol. 2, pp. 485-486.

Message from the President of the United States, requesting that the Congress grant the executive power to accept for the United States a mandate for Armenia, Washington, 1920. (66th Cong., 2d sess. House Doc. 791.

Also in:—Cong. Rec., vol. 59, pp. 7533-7534; also 7549.

Also in:—International conciliation, no. 151.

Also in:—Messages and papers, ed. by Albert Shaw, N. Y., 1924, vol. 2, pp. 1191-1195.

Also in:—Public papers; War and Peace (1917-1924), vol. 2, pp. 487-491.

Letter to Felix M. Warburg, May 27, 1920. In:—Woodrow Wilson's worte. . . . Heilbronn, a.N., 1924, pp. 485-486.

Message returning without approval House joint resolution declaring a state of peace to exist between the U. S. and the German and Austro-Hungarian Governments, May 27, 1920, Washington, 1920. (66th Cong., 2d sess. House Doc. 799.)

Also in:—Messages and papers, ed. by Albert Shaw, N. Y., 1924, vol. 2, pp. 1195-1198.

Also in:—Public papers; War and Peace (1917-1924), vol. 2, pp. 492-494.

Also in:—Woodrow Wilson's worte. . . . Heilbronn, a.N., pp. 483-485.

Message returning without approval H. R. 7629, "An act to amend the penal laws of the U. S.," and suggesting certain changes therein, June 2, 1920. (66th Cong., 2d sess. House Doc. 802.)

Message returning without approval H. B. 4927, "An act for the relief of Nancy A. Parsons, etc.," and stating certain objections thereto, June 4, 1920. (66th Cong., 2d sess. House Doc. 808.)

Message returning without approval H. B. 9783, "An act to provide a national budget system, an independent audit of government accounts, and for other purposes," and stating certain objections thereto, June 4, 1920. (66th Cong., 2d sess. House Doc. 805.)

Telegram to Railroad Union Officials (condemning Congress for inaction) June 5, 1920. In:—Messages and papers, ed. by Albert Shaw, N. Y., 1924, vol. 2, pp. 1198-1199.

Also in:—Public papers; War and Peace (1917-1924), vol. 1, pp, 495-496.

Telegram to the Governor of Tennessee (Woman Suffrage Amendment) June 23, 1920. In:—Messages and papers, ed. by Albert Shaw, N. Y., 1924, vol. 2, p. 1199.

Also in:—Public papers; War and Peace (1917-1924), vol. 2, p. 497.

Letter to Homer S. Cummings, July 2, 1920. In:—Woodrow Wilson's worte. . . . Heilbronn, a.N., 1924, pp. 486-487.

Message to Bituminous coal miners urging them to abide by their agreement, July 30, 1920. In:—Messages and papers, ed. by Albert Shaw, N. Y., 1924, vol. 2, pp. 1200-1201.

Also in:—Public papers; War and Peace (1917-1924), vol. 2, pp. 498-499.

Message to Anthracite coal miners (Acceptance of arbitrator's award) August 30, 1920. In:—Messages and papers, ed. by Albert Shaw, N. Y., 1924, vol. 2, pp. 1202-1204.

Also in:—Public papers; War and Peace (1917-1924), vol. 2, pp. 500-502.

Appeal to his Fellow-countrymen (To make the election a referendum on the League of Nations) October 3, 1920. In:—Messages and papers, ed. by Albert Shaw, N. Y., 1924, vol. 2, pp. 1204-1206.

Also in:—Public papers; War and Peace (1917-1924), vol. 2, pp. 503-505.

An address to Pro-League Republicans, October 27, 1920. In:—Messages and papers, ed. by Albert Shaw, N. Y., 1924, vol. 2, pp. 1207-1211.

Also in:—Public papers; War and Peace (1917-1924), vol. 2, pp. 506-510.

Statement to his Secretary, November 3, 1920. In:—Woodrow Wilson's worte. . . . Heilbronn, a.N., 1924, pp. 487-488.

Cablegram to M. Paul Hymans (End hostilities in Armenia) November 30, 1920. In:—Messages and papers, ed. by Albert Shaw, N. Y., 1924, vol. 2, pp. 1211-1212.

Also in:—Public papers; War and Peace (1917-1924), vol. 2, pp. 511-512.

Message communicated to the two houses of Congress at the beginning of the third session of the Sixty-sixth Congress, December 7, 1920, Washington, 1920. (66th Cong., 3d sess. House Doc. 903.)

Also in:—Cong. Rec., vol. 60, pp. 24-26; also pp. 32-33.

Also in:—Messages and papers, ed. by Albert Shaw, N. Y., 1924, vol. 2, pp. 1212-1220.

Also in:—Public papers; War and Peace (1917-1924), vol. 2, pp. 513-521.

Also in:—Woodrow Wilson's worte. . . . Heilbronn, a.N., 1924, pp. 488-496.

Nobel peace prize, December 10, 1920. In:—Woodrow Wilson's worte. . . . Heilbronn, a.N., 1924, pp. 496-497.

Veto changes in Clayton act, December 30, 1920. In:—Public papers; War and Peace (1917-1924), vol. 2, pp. 522-524.

BOOKS, 1921

Division and reunion, with additional chapters bringing the narrative down to the end of 1918, by Edward S. Cowin, N. Y., Longmans, Green & Co., 1921. First printed in May, 1893.

Proclamations by the President of the United States, February 3, 1921, to March 3, 1921. U. S. Laws, Statutes, etc. The statutes at large, vol. 41, pt. 2, pp. 1813-1819.

MESSAGES AND ADDRESSES, 1921

Reviving the War Finance Corporation; message returning to the Senate without approval resolution 212, January 3, 1921, Washington, 1921. (66th Cong., 3d sess. Senate Doc. 350.)

Telegram to Railway Union Officials. (New Railway wage demands) February 6, 1921. In:—Messages and papers, ed. by Albert Shaw, N. Y., 1924, vol. 2, pp. 1220-1221.

Also in:—Public papers; War and Peace (1917-1924), vol. 2, pp. 525-526.

Message to Congress requesting fulfillment of a pledge to Belgium, February 22, 1921. In:—Messages and papers, ed. by Albert Shaw, N. Y., 1924, vol. 2, pp. 1222-1224.

Also in:—Cong. Rec., vol. 60, p. 3598.

Also in:—Public papers; War and Peace (1917-1924), vol. 2, pp. 527-529.

Telegraph, telephone and cable properties. Message transmitting the report of the Postmaster-General and a supplementary financial report, February 25, 1921, Washington, 1921. (66th Cong., 3d sess. Senate Doc. 415.)

Letter to Finis Garrett regarding the fixing of the price of copper by Mr. Baruch during the war, March 1, 1921. Cong. Rec., vol. 60, p. 4200.

Veto of Emergency Tariff Bill, March 3, 1921. In:—Messages and papers, ed. by Albert Shaw, N. Y., 1924, vol. 2, pp. 1224-1229.

Also in:—Cong. Rec., vol. 60, pp. 4498-4499.

Also in:—Public papers; War and Peace (1917-1924), vol. 2, pp. 530-535.

BOOKS, 1922

Être Humain suive de quand un homme se trouve lui-même,
traduit par P. Chavannes, Paris, Payot & Cie, 1922.

MESSAGES AND ADDRESSES, 1922

Letter to James Kerney, January 13, 1922 (Moral leadership of the U. S.). In:—Saturday Evening Post,
March 29, 1924, p. 77. [Printed and in facsimile.]
(Edition recalled from circulation after a few copies
were sold.)

Note to Samuel Gompers, January 15, 1922. In:—Woodrow Wilson's worte. . . . Heilbronn, a.N., 1924, p.
497.

Letter to the New York Times, April 12, 1922 (Message to
Cox dinner). In:—New York Times, April 13, 1922.

Letter to Wade Safford, September 19, 1922, accepting
honorary membership in "Order of Merrymen" in
Nature Magazine, vol. 3, p. 113, 1924.

BOOKS, 1923

The Road away from Revolution. . . . Boston, The Atlantic
Monthly Press, 1923.

Woodrow Wilson's Case for the League of Nations. Compiled with his approval by Hamilton Foley, Princeton, Princeton University Press, 1923.

Woodrow Wilson Memoriem und dokumente über den Ver-
trag zu Versailles anno, 1919, hrsg. von R. St. Baker
in autorisierter übersetzung von Curt Thesing, Leipzig, Paul List, 1923, 3 vols. (Contains many papers
of Mr. Wilson while at the peace conference.)

MESSAGES AND ADDRESSES, 1923

Letter to Hamilton Foley, April 26, 1923, expressing his approval of the publication of Woodrow Wilson's Case
for the League of Nations. In:—Woodrow Wilson's
Case for the League of Nations, Princeton, 1923.

The Road away from Revolution. Aug., 1923. In:—The
Atlantic Monthly, vol. 132, pp. 145-146, Boston, 1923.
Also in:—The English Review, vol. 37, pp. 173-175.

INDEX

A

Aborigines, treatment of, *i,* 471

"Academy of the Lencei, Rome, At the," *i,* 367-368

"Accepting Hitchcock Reservations," *ii,* 460-461

Act of November, 21, 1918, *i,* 495

Adams, John, *ii,* 12

Adams, John Quincy, *ii,* 12

"A Day of Noble Memories, a Day of Dedication," *i,* 54-57

Addresses, *i,* 590-645; *ii,* 1-416

Adjur-Badjan, *ii,* 94, 259

"Adriatic, Italian Claims on the," *i,* 460-463

Adriatic question, *i,* 461-463, 464, 465-468, 596; *ii,* 76

"Adriatic Question, Three Cablegrams on the," *ii,* 462-479

Advertising agencies, appeal to, *i,* 26

Africa, German colonies in, *ii,* 49

"Against Continuance of War-Time Prohibition," *ii,* 424-425

"Aggression, external," *ii,* 293, 350, 359

Agitators, *i,* 264; *ii,* 434, 437

Agriculture, Department of, *i,* 42, 81, 171, 172, 189, 190, 562, 564

Albania, *ii,* 464, 465, 472, 477

Alien enemies, *i,* 17, 18-20, 136, 141, 213

Allen, General, *ii,* 482

Alliance, offensive and defensive, *ii,* 454

Alliances, entangling, *ii,* 282, 309

Allied and Associated Governments, *ii,* 527, 528

Allied war aims, *i,* 177

Allies, *i,* 22-23, 40, 58, 99, 135, 187, 190, 225, 243, 277-278, 280, 287, 291, 292, 294, 295, 296, 297, 298, 322, 325, 333, 365; *ii,* 433, 481, 520, 527— *See also* Belgium; France; Great Britain; Italy; Japan; Serbia

Allocation of labor, *i,* 212

Alps, *i,* 467

Alsace-Lorraine, *i,* 118, 160, 294, 295; *ii,* 68

Amateur nation, America the prize, *i,* 86

Amateurs, no war for, *i,* 34

Amateurs, war for, *i,* 83

"Amelioration of Food Conditions," *i,* 73

America. *See* United States

"America Was Born to Serve Mankind," *i,* 52-53

American Expeditionary Force, *i,* 532

American Federation of Labor, *i,* 116, 581

"American Forces in German Territory, Status of," *ii,* 480-482

American Mission (Paris), *i,* 431

American Mission to Russia, *i,* 49-51

American National Red Cross, *i,* 30, 31, 32-35, 102-103, 205-210, 225, 471, 476, 630; *ii,* 74

American Peace Commission, *i,* 572, 573

American people, *i,* 246-248, 337, 453, 501, 523-524, 620, 643; *ii,* 16, 151, 194, 265, 277, 308, 311, 345, 354, 388, 395, 398, 418, 455, 456, 467, 489, 501, 535

637

F

R